Aspects of Perception

Perception is the gateway to understanding our world. This book describes the perceptions you experience and what researchers have discovered about the mechanisms that create these perceptions. These pictures indicate a few of the aspects of perception described in this book.

We can take in a substantial amount of information through the sense of touch, especially when we are able to actively explore an object with our fingers *(Chapter 13, The Cutaneous Senses).*

Any scene contains a wealth of information for perception. This scene illustrates how information for depth is provided by the relative sizes of objects, the way they overlap, and our ability to perceive details in the foreground and background *(Chapter 7, Perceiving Depth and Size).*

Our perception of this figure skater's motion depends on a number of physiological and cognitive mechanisms *(Chapter 8, Perceiving Motion).* The skater's ability to execute her complex routines depends on an interaction between her perceptions and her actions *(Chapter 9, Perception and Action).*

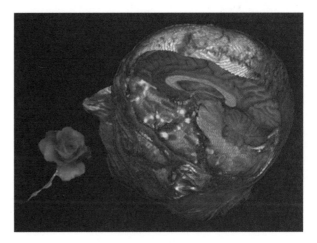

Advances in brain imaging techniques have enabled researchers to determine the connection between perception and activation of specific areas of the brain in humans. The yellow areas in this picture indicate brain areas being activated by smell, as measured by functional magnetic resonance imaging *(Chapter 14, The Chemical Senses). (Picture courtesy of Noam Sobel.)*

SENSATION AND PERCEPTION

SIXTH EDITION

E. BRUCE GOLDSTEIN

University of Pittsburgh

WADSWORTH

™

THOMSON LEARNING

Australia • Canada • Mexico • Singapore • Spain • United Kingdom • United States

Sponsoring Editor: *Marianne Taflinger*
Developmental Editor: *Penelope Sky*
Marketing Manager: *Joanne Terhaar*
Marketing Assistant: *Justine Ferguson*
Editorial Assistant: *Stacy Green*
Production Editor: *Kirk Bomont*
Production Service: *Heckman & Pinette*
Manuscript Editor: *Margaret Pinette*
Permissions Editor: *Joohee Lee*

Interior Design: *John Edeen*
Cover Design: *Roy R. Neuhaus*
Cover Art: *Judith Larzelere*
Interior Illustration: *Lisa Torri and Suffolk Graphics*
Photo Researcher: *Kathleen Olson*
Print Buyer: *Vena Dyer*
Typesetting: *Argosy Publishing*
Printing and Binding: *R. R. Donnelley, Crawfordsville*

For more information about this or any other Wadsworth products, contact:
WADSWORTH
511 Forest Lodge Road
Pacific Grove, CA 93950
USA
www.wadsworth.com
1-800-423-0563 (Thomson Learning Academic Resource Center)

For permission to use material from this work, contact us by:
Web: www.thomsonrights.com
Fax: 1-800-730-2215
Phone: 1-800-730-2214

Printed in the United States of America

10   9   8   7   6   5

Library of Congress Cataloging-in-Publication Data
Goldstein, E. Bruce, [date]
    Sensation and perception / E. Bruce Goldstein.—6th ed.
        p.   cm.
    Includes bibliographical references and index.
    ISBN 0-534-63991-7
    1. Senses and sensation. 2. Perception. I. Title.

QP431 .G64 2002
152.1—dc21
                                            2001026542

TO MY STUDENTS
AND
TO MY WIFE BARBARA

ABOUT THE AUTHOR

E. Bruce Goldstein is Associate Professor of Psychology and Director of Undergraduate Programs in Psychology at the University of Pittsburgh. He recently received the Chancellor's Distinguished Teaching Award for his classroom teaching and textbook writing. He received his bachelor's degree in chemical engineering from Tufts University and his Ph.D. in experimental psychology from Brown University, and he was a postdoctoral fellow in the biology department at Harvard University. Bruce has published numerous papers on visual physiology and visual perception and is the editor of the *Blackwell Handbook of Perception* (2001). He teaches sensation and perception, cognitive psychology, introductory psychology, and the psychology of art.

BRIEF CONTENTS

CONTENTS

8

PERCEIVING MOVEMENT   269

Contents

DEMONSTRATIONS

WEBTUTOR ADVANTAGE CONTENTS

WebTutor Advantage, available to students whose instructors ordered it, consists of study material for every chapter in the text and WebTutor Exercises for Chapters 1–14. Go to http://webtutor.thomsonlearning.com for sample chapters.

KEY FEATURES

- **Introduction.** Sets the context for what the chapter discusses.

- **Preview.** Lists the core ideas presented in the chapter.

- **Outline.** Reviews the major headings in the chapter.

- **Concept Checks.** Help students to identify the major ideas in the chapter and organizes and keys them according to the Study Questions in the book.

- **Key Terms.** Organized by major headings and give the full definitions for the boldfaced terms in the book; flashcards are provided for each.

- **Multiple-Choice Questions.** Approximately 25 to 30 per chapter provide feedback for every correct and incorrect answer.

- **Annotated Web Pages.** Provide three to five strong Web sites with demonstrations of various phenomena such as point light walkers, motion aftereffects, and the like.

- **WebTutor Exercises.** Interactive modules, demonstrations, experiments, and examples of stimuli used in experiments discussed in the text. These exercises, and their page numbers, are listed below. An asterisk (*) indicates that the phenomenon is not specifically described in the text.

WEBTUTOR EXERCISES

Chapter 1: Introduction to Perception

The Psychophysical Approach: Linking Stimulation and Perception

- *Method of limits* — Demonstration: Trial-by-trial method of limits (14)

- *Measurement fluctuation and error* — Experiment: How accurately can you match size? (13)

- *Adjustment and PSE* — Experiment: Length matching (13)*

- *DL by method of limits* — Experiment: Judging differences in size (14)*

PREFACE

This is an exciting time to be doing research in perception or to be reading about it. It is exciting because so many impressive advances in our knowledge have occurred in recent years. Just a few examples of these advances are the development of brain imaging techniques, which make it possible to identify brain areas involved in perception; discovery of the large effects of experience on the structure and functioning of the brain; demonstration of the close links between perception and action; and an increased appreciation of cognitive and inferential processes in perception. One of my goals in this edition of this book has been to describe these exciting new advances. To this end, I have added over 360 new references, most from the last five years; over 110 new key terms; and over 150 new illustrations. Of course, these new results didn't come out of nowhere—they were built upon the foundation created by over 100 years of previous research and theory, and these foundations of perception are the major topic of this book.

In describing both the foundations of perception and recent advances in our knowledge, I have made numerous changes in both content and presentation, while keeping the characteristics that so many people have appreciated in the previous editions. The following summarizes some of the features of the 6th edition of *Sensation and Perception*.

Increased Clarity

In every new edition of this book I strive to increase the clarity of the presentation. I do this by listening to feedback from my students and from instructors who have used previous editions. I have used this feedback as my guide in revising sections that students found difficult and in reorganizing sections of the book to enhance the logical flow from one topic to the next.

Organization of the Whole Book and Within Chapters

As I began this revision I asked myself how I could organize the book to make sensation and perception easier to teach. I achieved this by changing the order of a few of the chapters (object perception now directly follows higher-order visual processing), moving some material formerly in its own chapter into others (the material on color and size constancy is now in the chapters on color and depth, respectively), and carefully scrutinizing every chapter to be sure one topic followed logically from the other.

Overall Organization

The book begins with five chapters that progress in a logical sequence that takes students step-by-step from the beginning principles of psychophysics and physiology in Chapter 1; to higher order cortical processing, with an emphasis on object perception, in Chapter 4; and then to the psychophysical approach to object perception in Chapter 5. With the basic principles established in these initial chapters, the book then applies the psychophysical and physiological levels of analysis to the perception of color (Chapter 6), depth and size (Chapter 7), movement perception (Chapter 8), and the visual control of action (Chapter 9). This new chapter on perception and action consolidates the classic work of Gibson with modern research on invariant information for perception and cutting-edge physiological research on the connection between perception and action.

Chapter 10 introduces three chapters on auditory perception, with Chapters 10 and 11 being reorganized to create a clearer progression from the basic physiology and psychophysics of pitch perception in Chapter 10 to the perception of sound quality and auditory scene analysis in Chapter 11. Chapter 12, on speech perception, which was reorganized for the fifth edition, remains the same; and the organization of Chapter 13, on the cutaneous senses, remains essentially the same, but additional sections on plasticity and phantom limbs have been added.

In Chapter 14, the chemical senses, an updated discussion of flavor perception has been moved to the end of the chapter, so students first learn about the basic principles of olfaction and taste and then learn about how these two qualities are combined to create flavor. Chapters 15, perceptual development, and 16, clinical aspects of vision and hearing, have been updated but are largely unchanged. The net result of all of these changes is a book that retains the same basic outline as the fifth edition but explains perception even more clearly.

New Feature: Brain Scan

A new feature called **Brain Scan** has been added to highlight the rapidly developing body of research that has applied neuroimaging techniques to the study the human brain as it is operating. This boxed feature, which appears once in each of Chapters 2 through 14, focuses on functional magnetic resonance imaging (fMRI) experiments. Some examples: face area in the human cortex (Chapter 4); stereopsis in the human brain (Chapter 7); activation of the auditory cortex during silent lipreading (Chapter 12); sniff responses in the human brain (Chapter 14).

New Feature: The Plasticity of Perception

A section titled **The Plasticity of Perception** at the end of each chapter describes how the structure and operation of the brain can be changed by experience. Some examples: selective rearing for orientation

(Chapter 3); how vision can affect hearing (Chapter 11); differences between Japanese and American listeners (Chapter 12); plasticity after amputation of a limb (Chapter 13); learning taste–smell associations (Chapter 14).

More Pedagogy!

Summary Tables that recap the main points in each chapter appear at the middle and end of each chapter. These tables are designed to give students a broad perspective on what they have just read. In addition, the new WebTutor option provides access to Web-based learning that supports and supplements the material in the text. This feature is described in more detail below.

Features from Past Editions

The following features from past editions have been continued in this one:

- **Demonstrations.** The Demonstrations have been a popular feature of previous editions, because they provide perceptual experiences that illustrate principles discussed in the text. The demonstrations are simple enough so that students can easily do them and they are integrated into the flow of the text so that they become part of the ongoing story. The demonstrations are listed on page xix.

- **Across the Senses.** This is a one- to two-page section at the end of each chapter that describes parallels between the topic of the chapter and a similar phenomenon in another sense, sometimes comparing or contrasting the senses and sometimes showing how the senses interact. Some examples: neurons that respond to vision and touch (Chapter 4); visual and auditory space (Chapter 7); Tadoma: "hearing" with touch (Chapter 13); intermodal perception in infants (Chapter 15).

- **Study Questions.** These questions at the end of each chapter, which are keyed to page numbers in the book, are designed to help students master the detailed information in the chapter.

Complete Technology Integration through WebTutor

This edition includes the WebTutor option, available in WebCT and Blackboard formats, which provide the following valuable Web-based study aids:

- Glossary items in a flashcard format.

- Study questions with rejoinders.

- Over 100 interactive modules that include animations allowing students to explore perceptual principles in a way not possible in the book alone.

- Animated examples of actual stimuli used in experiments described in the text.

- Two dozen auditory demonstrations that enable students to hear auditory phenomena described in the text.

When the WebTutor icon WebTUTOR occurs immediately following a major heading, this indicates that there are WebTutor interactions related to material in that section. See pages xxi–xxvi, following the regular Table of Contents, for a listing of all of the WebTutor demonstrations and interactions.

A Message to the Student

Although most of this preface has been directed to instructors, I want to close by addressing a few words to the students who will be using this book. As you read this book you will see that it is a story about experiences that may initially seem simple, such as seeing a face or smelling a rose, but that turn out to be extremely complex. I hope that reading this book helps you appreciate both the complexity and the beauty of the mechanisms responsible for these experiences. I hope that as you gain an appreciation for the impressive advances that researchers have made toward understanding perception, you will also appreciate how much is still left to be discovered. But most important of all, I hope that reading this book will make you more aware of how perception affects you personally. After all, perception is something you experience all the time, and the study of perception can enhance this experience. I've found that studying perception has made me more observant of my environment and more appreciative of the miraculous process that transforms energy falling on receptors into the richness of experience. I hope reading this book has the same effect on you. If you have questions, comments, or other feedback about this book, I invite you to communicate with me via email at bruceg@pitt.edu. In fact, if you alert me to mistakes in the text or to parts of the text that are unclear, and I can use this information to make corrections to this edition or improve future editions, I would be glad to cite your name and university in the acknowledgment section that will appear in the 7th edition or in later printings of this edition.

E. Bruce Goldstein

ACKNOWLEDGMENTS

Creating a textbook like this one is a group effort, and I would like to thank a number of people at Wadsworth for their extraordinary efforts in support of this book.

- Marianne Taflinger, my editor, for her overall commitment to this book, for supporting the continual upgrading of the illustration program, and for making the creation of WebTutor possible. Most important of all I thank you, Marianne, for your faith in me as an author, for supporting me personally throughout the writing of this book, and for your sense of humor.

- Vicki Knight, psychology guru, for her leadership of the psychology list and for her friendship.

- Kirk Bomont, production editor, for his calm demeanor and obvious commitment to publishing a quality book. It is always a pleasure to work with Kirk, and I consider myself lucky to have him on the team.

- Margaret Pinette, editor and production service, who brought together all of the various components that make up a book with humor and grace. This is the first book I've done with Margaret, but I hope it's not the last.

- Stacy Green, for all of her efforts in so many areas, including obtaining reviews, finding photographs for the illustration program, compiling lists for the glossary and WebTutor, and many other things that I'm probably not even aware of.

- Lisa Torri, for her shepherding of the art program and good humor in dealing with my sometimes less-than-clear instructions and my tendency to sometimes change my mind about a figure in midstream. One of the joys of the production process is working with Lisa on yet another book.

- Leslie Krongold, for her dedication to pulling together all of the components of the WebTutor project. I particularly appreciate her commitment to keeping the project on course, her ability to get the job done when working under a tight schedule, and her humor during the lighter moments on this project.

- Colin Ryan, for creating the pioneering *Exploring Perception* CD, which was developed in conjunction with the 5th edition of *Sensation & Perception*. This CD brought a new level of professionalism and pedagogy to the teaching of perception through animated visual demonstrations and interactions, and we are fortunate to be able to include many of the components of *Exploring Perception* in WebTutor.

- Laddie Odom for his skill in creating the computer programs that integrated the *Exploring Perception* and auditory demonstrations into WebTutor and for creating the new interactions that were designed especially for this edition.

- Billa Reiss, for creating the instructors manual/test bank and for alertness in spotting a number of errors in the text.

- Janet Proctor, for writing the study guide material that is part of WebTutor.

- Joohee Lee, for obtaining permissions; Roy Nehaus, for his elegant cover design; and Joanne Terhan, for creating clear and informative marketing materials.

In addition to the help I received from all of the above people on the editorial and production side, I also received a great deal of help from teachers and reviewers who have given me feedback on what I have written, made suggestions regarding new work in the field, and provided illustrations for the text and video and audio material for WebTutor. I thank the following people for their help in these areas:

Reviewers for the 6th edition

Deborah Aks,
University of Wisconson, Whitewater

Eric Amazeen, Arizona State University

Jeffrey Andre, James Madision University

Chris Ball, College of William and Mary

Michael Biderman, University of Tennessee

Greg Bohemier, Culver-Stockton College

Sandy Bolanowski, Syracuse University

Frederick Bonato, St. Peter's College

Hugo Critchley, University College, London

James Cutting, Cornell University

Stuart Derbyshire, University of Pittsburgh

Patricia Duchamp-Viret, University of Lyon

Rhea T. Eskew, Northeastern University

Charles Fox

Isabel Gauthier, Vanderbilt University

Alan Gilchrist, Rutgers University

Troy Hackett, Vanderbilt University

Michael Hall, University of Nevada, Las Vegas

Phillip Kellman,
University of California at Los Angeles

Timothy Klitz,
Washington and Jefferson College

Peter Lennie, New York University

Jack Loomis,
University of California, Santa Barbara

Arien Mack, New School for Social Research

B. C. J. Moore, Cambridge University

Kensaku Mori, University of Tokyo

John C. Middlebrooks,
University of Michigan

Jay Neitz, Medical College of Wisconsin

William Newsome, Stanford University

Bruno Olshausen,
University of California, Davis

Catherine Palmer, University of Pittsburgh

Richard Pastore, Binghamton University

Sheena Rogers, James Madison University

Lawrence Rosenblum,
University of California at Riverside

Beverly Roskos-Ewoldsen,
University of Alabama

Maggie Shiffrar, Rutgers University

Michael Silverman,
New School for Social Research

Noam Sobel,
University of California at Berkeley

William H. Warren, Brown University

Peter Wenderoth, Macquarie University

Jack Yellott, University of California, Irvine

William Yost, Loyola University

Acknowledgments

Reviewers for the 5th edition

Frank M. Bagrash,
California State University, Fullerton

William P. Banks, Pomona College

Michael Biderman,
University of Tennessee, Chattanooga

Bruce Bridgeman,
University of California, Santa Cruz

Patrick Cavanagh, Harvard University

James C. Craig, Indiana University

W. Jay Dowling, University of Texas at Dallas

Susan E. Dutch, Westfield State College

Bradley Gibson, University of Notre Dame

Norma Graham, Columbia University

Donald Greenfield, Eye Institute of New Jersey

Timothy S. Klitz,
University of Minesota, Twin Cities

Harry Lawless, Cornell University

W. Trammell Neill, SUNY, Albany

Catherine Palmer,
University of Pittsburgh

David B. Pisoni, Indiana University

Dennis Proffitt, University of Virginia

Lawrence D. Rosenblum,
University of California at Riverside

Colin Ryan, James Cook University

H. A. Sedgwick,
State University of New York

Kenneth R. Short, Creighton University

Steven M. Specht,
Lebanon Valley College

Leslie Tolbert, University of Arizona

Robert G. Vautin, Wheaton College

William Yost, Loyola University of Chicago

I would also like to thank the following people who were kind enough to alert me to errors in the previous printing of this book.

Carissa Engemann, Westmont College

Felix Eschenburg,
University of Marburg (Germany)

Zili Liu, University of California at Los Angeles

Karsten Loepelmann, University of Alberta

Marianne Mann,
California State University, San Marcos

Robert O'Shea,
University of Otago (New Zealand)

Derek Pontin, University of Calgary

Jon Prince, University of Rochester

John Waschin, University of Minnesota

SENSATION AND PERCEPTION

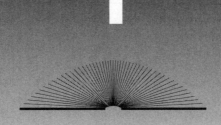

INTRODUCTION
TO PERCEPTION

SOME QUESTIONS WE WILL CONSIDER

- What is the difference between perceiving something and recognizing it? (6)

- How can we measure perception? (11)

- How are physiological processes involved in perception? (18)

- How can the physiological response to perceptual stimuli be studied in the human brain? (26)

We begin by asking you to imagine that you have been given the following hypothetical science project.

Science project:
 Design a device that can locate, describe, and identify all objects in the environment, including their distance from the device and their relationships to each other.

Extra credit:
 Transform the information obtained by the device into conscious experience in a person.

Warning:
 This project, should you decide to accept it, is extremely difficult. It has not yet been solved by the best computer scientists even though they are equipped with the world's most powerful computers.

Hint:
 Humans and animals have solved this problem in a particularly elegant way. They use two spherical sensors, which contain a light-sensitive chemical, to sense light; two

detectors on the sides of the head, which are fitted with tiny vibrating hairs to sense pressure changes in the air; small pressure detectors of various shapes imbedded under the skin to sense stimuli on the skin; and two types of chemical detectors to detect gases that are inhaled and solids and liquids that are ingested.

Additional note:

Designing the detectors is just the first step in designing the system. An information processing system is also needed. In the case of the human, this information processing is a computer with 100 billion active units and interconnections so complex that they have still not been completely deciphered. Although the detectors are an important part of the project, the design of the computer is crucial, because the information that is picked up by the detectors needs to be analyzed. Note that operation of the human system is still not completely understood and that the best scientific minds in the world have made little progress in dealing with the extra credit part of the problem. Focus on the main problem first, and leave conscious experience until later.

The "science project" above is what this book is about. Our goal is to understand the human model, starting with the detectors—the eyes, ears, skin receptors, and receptors in the nose and mouth—and then to move on to the computer—the brain. Our goal is to understand how we sense things in the environment and interact with them. The paradox we face in searching for this understanding is that although we still don't understand perception, perceiving is something that is easy for us to do. In most situations, we simply open our eyes and see what is around us, or listen and hear sounds, without expending any particular effort.

Because of the ease with which we perceive, many people don't see the feats achieved by our senses as complex or amazing. "After all," the skeptic might say, "for vision, a picture of the environment is focused on the back of my eye, and that picture provides all the information my brain needs to duplicate the environment in my consciousness." But the idea that perception is not that complex is exactly what

misled computer scientists in the 1950s and 1960s to propose that it would only take about a decade or so to create "perceiving machines" that could negotiate the environment with humanlike ease. That prediction, made over 40 years ago, has yet to come true, even though a computer defeated the world chess champion in 1997. From a computer's point of view, perceiving a scene is more difficult than playing world championship chess.

One of the goals of this book is to make you aware of the hidden perceptual processes that occur "behind the scenes" to create our perceptions. We can draw an analogy between these hidden perceptual processes and what happens as we watch a play in the theater. As we sit comfortably in our seats watching a play, our attention is focused on the unfolding drama created by the characters in the play. But backstage, something entirely different is happening: An actress is rushing to complete her costume change; an actor is pacing back and forth to calm his nerves just before he goes on; the stage manager is checking to be sure the next scene change is ready to go; and behind the glass window above the last row of the audience, the lighting director is getting ready to make the next lighting change.

Just as the audience sees only a small part of what is actually happening during a play, your effortless perception of the world around you is also just a small part of what is happening as you perceive. This book is about both the perceptions of which you are aware and the backstage activity that is hidden from your view. One of the messages of this book is that perception does not just happen but is the end result of complex processes, many of which are not available to your awareness. After reading this book you will appreciate the complexity of the mechanisms underlying perception.

The Importance of Perception

One purpose of perception is to inform us about properties of the environment that are important for our survival. Whatever we are doing, be it hiking along a woodland trail, getting ready to cross a busy city street, or taking notes in a classroom, we need to be able to see what is there and hear what is happening. Our perceptual system accomplishes this by creating a likeness of the environment in our minds. Another purpose of perception is to help us act in relation to the environment. Perception helps us stay on the hiking trail, safely cross the street, and transcribe the professor's words and blackboard writings into our notes. So perception both creates an experience of the environment and enables us to act within it.

This ability to perceive is something that most of us take for granted, but consider what life would be like without the senses. What would it be like to be without vision? Or without hearing? Or without touch? Most people who are missing just one of these senses learn to cope with their loss. But what if you were born lacking all three of these senses plus lacking the ability to taste and smell? The effect would be shattering because you would be isolated from everything in your environment. Consider for a moment what this would mean. If you survived infancy, would you ever become conscious of your isolation? Would you ever be able to develop language or the capacity

to think? We can only speculate on the answers to these questions, but one thing is certain: Your experience would be barren, and your very survival would depend on others.

Thus, one reason to study perception is to satisfy our intellectual curiosity about something that is of great importance in our lives. But there are also practical reasons to study it. Precise measurements of perceptual capacities have enabled us to describe normal perception and, more important, have enabled us to describe the perceptual losses that occur because of aging, disease, or injury.

Understanding perception is an important step in designing devices to restore perception to those who have lost some or all of their vision or hearing and also to devise treatments for other perceptual problems, such as the inability to recognize objects, chronic pain, and problems in thinking such as dyslexia (difficulty in perceiving and understanding words and numbers), which are related to perception. Understanding perception is also important for understanding the perceptual demands encountered when driving cars, piloting airplanes, and making observations from inside space vehicles (Figure 1.1).

Figure 1.1
Flying this airplane depends on a number of perceptual abilities to perceive form, depth, and motion (George Hall/Corbis).

Introduction to Perception

THE PERCEPTUAL PROCESS

To describe how perception works, we will now introduce the **perceptual process**, which is diagrammed in Figure 1.2 as a sequence of steps leading from the environment to perception of a particular stimulus, recognition of the stimulus, and action with regard to the stimulus. We will consider each of the steps in Figure 1.2, beginning with the stimuli in the environment.

The Environmental Stimulus and the Attended Stimulus

The environmental stimulus is all of the things in our environment that we can potentially perceive. Consider, for example, the potential stimuli that are presented to Ellen, who has just arrived at the circus. As she takes her seat on the bleachers, she observes an animal act in the center ring, a number of clowns to the right, trapezes hanging from above, and the band, over on the right (Figure 1.3a). The amount of stimulation presented in the circus is so overwhelming that it isn't possible for Ellen to perceive every-

thing in the scene. Thus, she focuses her attention on something that she finds particularly interesting—the tiger performing in the center ring (Figure 1.3b).

The Stimulus on the Receptors

When Ellen focuses her attention on the tiger she looks directly at it, and this creates an image of the tiger on the receptors of her retina, a 0.4-mm thick network of light-sensitive receptors and other neurons that line the back of Ellen's eye (Figure 1.4a).

Before considering what happens next, let's consider an idea many people have about the image on the retina. Figure 1.4a indicates a basic fact of optics—the image formed on the retina is inverted. My students often refer to this fact and tell me that the visual system has to correct for this upside-down image, so that our perception will be right-side-up. I respond to this idea by pointing out two things: (1) We don't perceive the image on the retina. It is just an early step in the perceptual process; and (2) the "upside-down-ness" of the image is such a

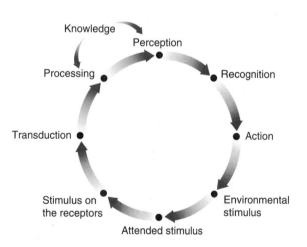

Figure 1.2
The perceptual process. The various steps in this process are arranged in a circle to emphasize that the process is dynamic and continually changing.

Figure 1.3
(a) We take the circus as the starting point for our description of the perceptual process and call it the environmental stimulus. (b) There is so much going on in the environment that Ellen selects one thing to concentrate on. The tiger is the attended stimulus.

small transformation compared to what happens next that it isn't worth worrying about. What happens next is transduction. The pattern of light on the retina is transformed into electrical signals in the receptors.

Transduction

Transduction is the transformation of one form of energy into another form of energy. An example of transduction is the sequence of events that occurs when you touch the "withdrawal" button on the screen of the automated teller machine at the bank. The pressure exerted by your finger is transduced into electrical energy, which is then transduced into mechanical energy to push your money out of the machine. In the nervous system, transduction occurs when environmental energy is transformed into electrical energy. In our example, the pattern of light created by the tiger on Ellen's retina is transformed into electrical signals in tens or hundreds of thousands of her visual receptors (Figure 1.4b).

Neural Processing

After the tiger's image has been transformed into electrical signals in Ellen's receptors, these signals in the receptors generate new signals in cells called neu-rons that we will describe shortly. These neurons create a series of interconnected pathways far more complex than the map that would be created if we could shrink the entire U.S. highway system down to the size of this page. It is along these pathways that electrical signals travel, first from the eye to the brain (with some stops in between) and then within the brain itself. During their travels through this network of neurons, the electrical signals undergo neural processing (Figure 1.4c).

Neural processing refers to the operations that change the electrical responses of neurons in various ways. In Chapter 2 we will describe exactly how these electrical responses are processed, but we can understand processing on a simple level by returning to our analogy of the road map. Imagine that you are hovering above the city in a traffic helicopter looking down on the traffic patterns on a network of busy city streets at rush hour. You see one place where traffic from three or four other streets is flowing into a single street that has become totally clogged and almost looks like a parking lot; another street has stop-and-go traffic because there are traffic lights at each intersection; and a third is a limited-access highway that is flowing smoothly. It is apparent, from this scene, that the way different streets are laid out and the number of traffic signals are affecting the flow of cars through the city.

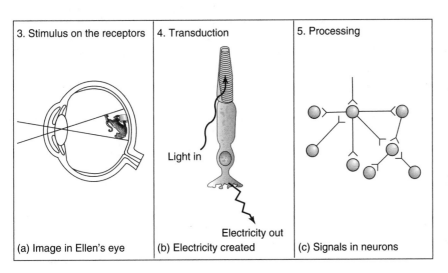

3. Stimulus on the receptors	4. Transduction	5. Processing
(a) Image in Ellen's eye	Light in / Electricity out / (b) Electricity created	(c) Signals in neurons

Figure 1.4
(a) When Ellen looks at the tiger, an image of the tiger is formed on her retina. (b) Transduction occurs when light stimulates the receptors and the receptors create electrical energy. (c) This electrical energy is processed through networks of neurons.

Introduction to Perception

In Chapter 2 we will see that a similar situation occurs for the nervous system. The way the pathways of the nervous system are laid out and the nature of the interconnections between the various pathways can affect the flow of electrical signals. This is extremely important because it is this flow of signals that creates the next step in the perceptual process—perception.

Perception

Perception is conscious sensory experience. It occurs when the electrical signals that represent the tiger are somehow transformed by Ellen's brain into her experience of seeing the tiger (Figure 1.5a).

In the past, some accounts of the perceptual process have stopped at this stage. After all, once Ellen sees the tiger, hasn't she perceived it? The answer to this question is yes, she has perceived it, but other things may have happened as well—she probably recognized the form as an "animal" and specifically, a "tiger," and she has taken action based on her perception, as when she turned her head to get a better view of the tiger. These two additional steps—recognition and action—are perceptual behaviors that are important outcomes of the perceptual process.

Recognition

Recognition is our ability to place an object in a category, such as "tiger," that gives it meaning (Figure 1.5b). Although we might be tempted to group perception and recognition together, researchers have shown that they are separate processes. For example, consider the case of Dr. P., a patient who is described by neurologist Oliver Sacks (1985) in the title story of his book *The Man Who Mistook His Wife for a Hat*.

Dr. P., a well-known musician and music teacher, first noticed a problem when he began having trouble recognizing his students visually, although he could immediately identify them by the sound of their voices. But when Dr. P. began misperceiving common objects, for example addressing a parking meter as if it were a person or expecting a carved knob on a piece of furniture to engage him in conversation, it became clear that his problem was more serious than

just a little forgetfulness. Was he blind, or perhaps crazy? It was clear from an eye examination that he could see well, so poor vision wasn't his problem. Also, by many other criteria, it was obvious that he was not crazy.

Dr. P.'s problem was eventually diagnosed as **visual form agnosia**—the inability to recognize objects—that was caused by a brain tumor. He perceived the parts of objects but couldn't identify the whole object, so when Sacks showed him a glove, Dr. P. described it as "a continuous surface unfolded on itself. It appears to have five outpouchings, if this is the word." When Sacks asked him what it was, Dr. P. hypothesized that it was "a container of some sort. It could be a change purse, for example, for coins of five sizes." The normally easy process of object recognition had, for Dr. P., been derailed by his brain tumor. He could perceive the object, and recognize parts of it, but couldn't perceptually assemble the parts in a way that would enable him to recognize the object as a whole. Cases such as this show that perception and recognition are not the same.

Action

Action includes motor activities such as moving the head or eyes and locomoting through the environment. In our example, Ellen turns her head as she is observing the tiger (Figure 1.5c). Some researchers see action as being an important outcome of the perceptual process because of its importance for survival. David Milner and Melvyn Goodale (1995) propose that early in the evolution of animals the major goal of visual processing was not to create a conscious perception or "picture" of the environment but to help the animal control navigation, catch prey, avoid obstacles, and detect predators—all crucial functions for the animal's survival.

The fact that perception often leads to action, whether it be an animal's increasing its vigilance when it hears a twig snapping in the forest or Ellen turning her head to get a better view at the circus, means that perception is a continuously changing process. This change occurs because of the observer's movements, as well as shifts in attention from one place to another, which is how our description of the

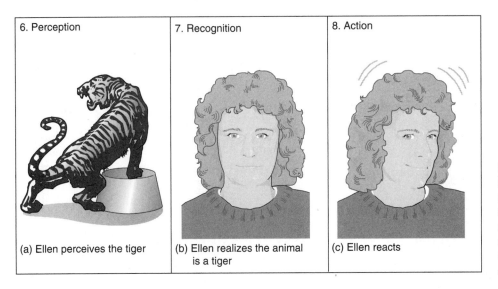

6. Perception	7. Recognition	8. Action

(a) Ellen perceives the tiger

(b) Ellen realizes the animal is a tiger

(c) Ellen reacts

Figure 1.5
(a) Ellen has conscious perception of the tiger. (b) She recognizes the tiger and (c) takes action by moving her head to get a better view.

perceptual process began, when Ellen first focused her attention on the tiger in the center ring. Of course, the scene that Ellen is observing is also changing, with the circus being a particularly dramatic example of a continually changing environmental stimulus.

When we consider the changes that are occurring as people perceive you can appreciate why the steps of the perceptual process in Figure 1.2 are arranged in a circle. Although we can describe the perceptual process as a series of steps that begin with the environmental stimulus, the overall process is a dynamic one that doesn't really have a beginning point or an ending point.

Knowledge

Feats such as Ellen's ability to recognize different animals would not be possible without the knowledge about different animals stored in her memory. To recognize a tiger, she has to compare the animal she sees with the conception of "tiger" stored in her memory and then retrieve the name "tiger" that goes with the animal. We will see, as we study perception, that the information a person brings to a situation plays an important role in determining both recognition and perception.

This information that the person brings to the perceptual situation is indicated by the label "knowledge" in Figure 1.2. We use the term "knowledge" rather broadly to stand for any information the perceiver brings to the perceptual situation. This information can consist of things you learned years ago, such as the names of different animals, or knowledge you have obtained from events that have just happened. An example of how perception can be influenced by knowledge that you have just acquired is provided by the following demonstration.

D E M O N S T R A T I O N

Perceiving a Picture

After looking at the drawing in Figure 1.6, close your eyes, turn to page 10, and open and shut your eyes rapidly to briefly expose the picture in Figure 1.8. Decide what the picture is, and then open your eyes and read the explanation below it.
○ STOP ○ Do this now, before reading further.   ●

Did you identify Figure 1.8 as a rat (or a mouse)? If you did, you were influenced by the clearly rat- or mouselike figure you observed initially. But people

Figure 1.6

Look at this drawing first, then close your eyes and turn the page, so you are looking at the same place on the page directly under this one. Then open and shut your eyes rapidly. (Adapted from Bugelski & Alampay, 1961.)

who first observe Figure 1.10 (page 12) instead of Figure 1.6 usually identify Figure 1.8 as a man. (Try this demonstration on someone else.) This demonstration, which is called the **rat–man demonstration**, shows how recently acquired knowledge ("that pattern is a rat") can influence perception. In this case, your recently acquired knowledge has set up an expectation that a pattern like Figure 1.6 will be a rat.

Top-Down and Bottom-Up Processing

The addition of "knowledge" to the perceptual process enables us to make a distinction between two types of perceptual processing. Processing that begins with the information received by the receptors is called **bottom-up processing**. Thus, when we followed the perceptual process from stimulation of the receptors to transduction, to neural processing, we were describing bottom-up processing.

But the presence of knowledge in the perceptual process acknowledges that the brain is not an empty computer waiting to receive and process information. It is packed full of knowledge, which includes not only the facts we know about but also memories and the expectations that we bring to a particular situation. Processing that begins by considering the effect of the knowledge a person brings to the perceptual situation is called **top-down processing**. In this book we will see that perception often involves both bottom-up and top-down processing, working together.

Bottom-up processing is essential for perception, because the perceptual process usually begins with stimulation of the receptors.[1] Thus, when a pharmacist reads what to you might look like an unreadable scribble on your doctor's prescription, she starts with bottom-up processing, which is based on the pattern that the doctor's handwriting creates on her retina, but she also uses top-down processing, which makes use of her knowledge of the names of drugs and perhaps past experience with this particular doctor's writing, to help her decipher the prescription.

STUDYING THE PERCEPTUAL PROCESS

The goal of perceptual research is to understand each of the steps in the perceptual process. Thus, our goal is to understand the mechanisms responsible for perception, recognition, and action. (For simplicity, we will use the term *perception* to stand for all of these in the discussion that follows.)

Levels of Analysis

The first step in studying mechanisms is to decide on our **level of analysis**. The idea behind level of analysis is that we can observe processes at different scales. We can illustrate this idea of different scales by returning to the traffic situation we described when we considered neural processing. High above the traffic, in our helicopter, we were observing the "big picture." This vantage point enabled us to see how the flow of automobiles is affected by the way the streets are laid out, the locations of traffic lights, and other factors.

But if we want to understand the operation of an individual automobile we would need to zoom in on an individual car and perhaps take it out for a road

---

[1] Occasionally perception can occur without stimulation of the receptors. For example, being hit on the head might cause you to "see stars," or closing your eyes and imagining something may cause an experience called "imagery," which shares many characteristics of perception (Kosslyn, 1994).

test that might include determining performance measures like acceleration, braking, and handling. We could also zoom in even further by looking under the hood to gain an understanding of the inner workings of the automobile's engine. The point is that studying the automobile at each of these levels gives us a much deeper understanding of automobiles than we would get from studying them at only one level.

The same reasoning applies to our study of perception. In this book we will study perception at two different levels of analysis. We will consider how a person's perception is related to stimulation in the environment. This is called the **psychophysical level of analysis**, and it focuses on the relationship between the stimulus and perception, which is indicated by arrow A in the diagram of the perceptual process in Figure 1.7.

As you will see shortly, when we describe some of the methods used to study perception at the psychophysical level, the term *psychophysics* was introduced by Gustav Fechner in 1860, to refer to quantitative methods for precisely measuring relationships between the stimulus (*physics*) and perception (*psycho*). But since there are also a number of

other, nonquantitative, methods to measure the relationship between the stimulus and perception, we will use the term **psychophysics** more broadly in this book to refer to any measurement of the relationship between the stimulus and perception. An example of a study at the psychophysical level would be one that we will describe in Chapter 2, which determined the smallest amount of light energy that a person can just detect (Figure 1.9a).

We will also consider how a person's perception is related to physiological processes that are occurring within the person. This is called the **physiological level of analysis**, and it focuses on the relationship between the stimulus and physiology, which is indicated by arrow B in Figure 1.7, and the relationship between physiology and perception, which is indicated by arrow C in Figure 1.7.

An example of measuring the stimulus–physiology relationship would be an experiment we will describe in Chapter 3, in which the electrical activity generated by neurons in a cat's cortex was measured in response to the presentation of bars of light with different orientations (Figure 1.9b).[2] An example of measuring the physiology–perception relationship is a study we will describe in Chapter 2 in which a person's brain activity is measured as the person describes an object they are seeing (Figure 1.9c). (See Tables 1.1 and 1.2.)

Cognitive Influences on Perception

As we study perception at both the psychophysical and physiological levels, we will also be concerned with how the knowledge, memories, and expectations

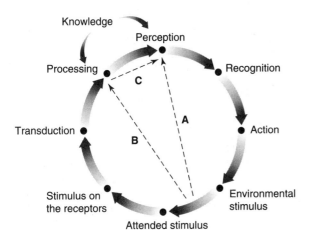

Figure 1.7
The perceptual process, from Figure 1.2, with arrows added to indicate important relationships: A: Stimulus–perception relationship; B: Stimulus–physiology relationship; C: Physiology–perception relationship.

[2] Because a great deal of physiological research has been done on cats and monkeys, students often express concerns about how these animals are treated. All animal research in the United States follows strict guidelines for the care of animals established by organizations such as the American Psychological Association and the Society for Neuroscience. The central tenet of these guidelines is that every effort should be made to ensure that animals are not subjected to pain or distress. Research on animals has provided essential information for developing aids to help people with sensory disabilities such as blindness and deafness and for helping develop techniques to ease severe pain.

Introduction to Perception

Figure 1.8

Did you see a rat or a man? Looking at the more ratlike picture in Figure 1.6 increased the chances that you would see this one as a rat. But if you had first seen the man version (Figure 1.10), you would have been more likely to perceive this figure as a man. (From Bugelski & Alampay, 1961.)

Table 1.1

Levels of analysis in the study of perception

Level of Analysis	Type of Information	Relationships
Psychophysical level	Stimuli in the environment	Stimulus → perception
Physiological level	Physiological processes in the body	Stimulus → physiology
		Physiology → perception

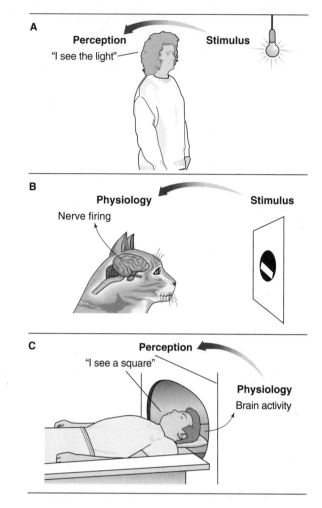

Figure 1.9

Examples of experiments measuring the relationships indicated by the arrows in Figure 1.7: (a) Relationship A: The relationship between the intensity of the stimulus (the light) and perception (seeing the light); (b) Relationship B: The relationship between the stimulus (the moving bar) and physiology (the response of neurons in the cat's cortex); (c) Relationship C: The relationship between physiology (activation of specific brain areas) and perception (recognizing a picture).

that a person brings to the situation influence their perception. These factors, which we have described as being the starting place for top-down processing, are called **cognitive influences**. Researchers study cognitive influences by measuring how knowledge and other factors, such as memories and expectations, affect each of the three relationships in Figure 1.7. For example, consider the rat–man demonstration. If we were to measure the stimulus–perception relationship by showing just Figure 1.8 to a number of people, we would probably find that some people see a rat and some people see a man. But by adding some "knowledge" by first presenting the more ratlike picture in Figure 1.6, most of the people say "rat" when we present Figure 1.8. Thus, in this example,

knowledge has affected the stimulus–perception relationship. Notice in Figure 1.7 that the arrows from the knowledge box in the perceptual process point both to perception and to physiological aspects of the

Table 1.2

Methods for studying relationships in the perceptual process

Relationship	How Studied?
A. Stimulus → perception	Psychophysically. Present a stimulus and determine the person's response.
B. Stimulus → physiology	Physiologically. Present a stimulus and measure the electrical response in the nervous system; also look for connections between anatomy and perception.
C. Physiology → perception	Physiologically and psychophysically. Measure physiological and perceptual responses to the same stimuli.

perceptual process. We will see, later in the book, that a person's knowledge can also affect physiological responding.

Cross-Talk Between the Levels of Analysis

One of the things that becomes apparent when we step back and look at the psychophysical and physiological levels of analysis is that each one provides information about different aspects of the perceptual process. Thus, to truly understand perception, we have to study it at both levels. It is important, however, to realize that even though we are distinguishing between these two levels, there is a great deal of "cross-talk" between them. That is, they are intimately related to one another. Just as the mechanical characteristics of a car's engine affect the car's performance, the physiological characteristics of a person's perceptual system affect his or her perceptions.

One consequence of the close relationship between the psychophysical and physiological levels of analysis is that we can learn about one level by studying the other one (Goldstein, 2001a). For example, consider a patient who has suffered a stroke caused by blockage of one of the arteries serving his brain. When we test the patient's vision, we find that he has trouble seeing objects that are located in an area off to his left.

This measurement of the relationship between stimulus (an object on the left) and perception (the ability to see the object) suggests that there is a problem in a particular area in the right hemisphere of the patient's brain (since the right hemisphere is responsible for vision in the left visual field), a guess that we can then check by doing a brain scan that creates a picture of the brain's physiological operation. Thus, even without looking inside the person, we can use psychophysical measurements to obtain clues regarding the person's inner workings. Later in the book, we will have a number of opportunities to show how researchers have used perceptual information to provide important clues about what is going on physiologically, "under the hood," both for abnormal perception, as in our patient with brain damage, and for normal perception as well.

To begin to understand how we study perception at the two levels of analysis, we need to know something about the procedures we use to measure the relationships in Figure 1.7. We begin with the psychophysical level. See Summary Table 1.1 on page 13 for an overview of the material we have covered so far.

THE PSYCHOPHYSICAL APPROACH: LINKING STIMULATION AND PERCEPTION

webTUTOR [3]   We have seen that the psychophysical approach to perception focuses on Relationship A in Figure 1.7, the relationship between the physical properties of stimuli and the perceptual responses to these stimuli. We will describe how we measure this relationship by considering the following ways that a person could respond to a stimulus:

1. *Description:* "It's red and about 15 feet long."

2. *Recognition:* "It's a car."

3. *Detection:* "It's just barely moving."

---

[3] This icon appears when there is material at the WebTutor site related to material in the following section.

Figure 1.10
Man version of the rat–man stimulus. (Adapted from Bugelski & Alampay, 1961.)

(a) Flash line on left   (b) 50 ms of darkness   (c) Flash line on right   (d) Perception: movement from left to right

Figure 1.11
(a) Flashing a light in one position and then, (b) after a brief pause, (c) flashing it in another position, creates (d) an illusion called "apparent movement." Research on apparent movement uses the phenomenological method because it requires that the subject describe what he or she is perceiving.

4. *Magnitude:* "Your car's horn sounds twice as loud as mine."

5. *Search:* "There it is, over in the corner of the parking lot."

Description: The Phenomenological Method

The first step in studying perception is just describing what we perceive. This description can be at a very basic level, such as when we notice that we can perceive some objects as being farther away than others, or that there is a perceptual quality we call "color," or that there are different qualities of taste, such as bitter, sweet, and sour. These are such common observations that we might take them for granted, but this is where the study of perception begins, because it is these very basic properties that we are seeking to explain.

When we describe our experience in this way we are using the **phenomenological method**. This method has been applied to describing not only basic perceptions such as those mentioned above but less obvious perceptions as well. For example, it has been observed that if we flash a light with the right timing, first at one position and then at another, as in Figure 1.11, the light can appear to move from one position to the other, just as if it were really moving, rather than just flashing. Describing this phenomenon, which is called *apparent movement*, raises questions for perception researchers to answer, such as "why do we see movement when no movement is actually occurring?" (We will consider movement perception in detail in Chapter 8.)

Recognition: Categorizing a Stimulus

The procedure for measuring recognition is simple: A stimulus is presented, and the subject indicates what it is. Your response to the rat–man demonstration involved recognition since you were asked to name what you saw. This procedure is widely used in testing patients with brain damage, such as the musician, Dr. P., with visual agnosia, whom we described earlier. Often the stimuli in these experiments are pictures of objects rather than the actual object (thereby avoiding having to bring elephants and other large objects into the laboratory!).

Describing perceptions phenomenologically and measuring their recognition by asking people to name objects provides information about what a person is perceiving. Often, however, it is useful to be able to establish a quantitative relationship between the stimulus and perception. To achieve this we look at some methods that were developed in the 19th century to measure the amount of stimulus energy that is necessary for detecting a stimulus.

Detection

In 1860 the physiologist Gustav Fechner (1801–1887) published a book called *Elements of Psychophysics* in which he described a number of quantitative meth-

The Science Project

Designing detectors that can locate, describe, and identify objects in the environment is extremely difficult, as evidenced by the fact that computers are still unable to accomplish this. However, humans and animals accomplish this task with relative ease.

The Perceptual Process

The perceptual process is a sequence of the following steps: (1) environmental stimulus; (2) attended stimulus; (3) transduction; (4) neural processing; (5) perception; (6) recognition; (7) action, and also includes (8) the effects of knowledge.

Perception, Recognition and Action

Perception, recognition and action are all outcomes of the perceptual process. Perception and recognition are not the same, as shown by cases such as Dr. P. with visual form agnosia. Action is important for survival.

Top-Down and Bottom-Up Processing

Processing that begins with information received by the receptors is called bottom-up processing. Processing that begins by considering the effect of the knowledge a person brings to the perceptual situation is called top-down processing. Both types of processing work together to achieve perception and recognition.

Levels of Analysis

The psychophysical level of analysis is based on studying the relationship between stimuli in the environment and perception. The physiological level of analysis, which is based on studying physiological processes in the body, is studied by focusing on the stimulus–physiology relationship and the physiology–perception relationship.

Cognitive Influences on Perception

Cognitive influences on perception, which are the basis of top-down processing, can influence a person's response as studied at both the psychophysical and physiological levels of analysis.

Cross-Talk Between Levels

The psychophysical and physiological levels of analysis provide information about different parts of the perceptual process, and there is a great deal of cross-talk between them. Thus, sometimes we can draw conclusions about one level by studying the other. For example, observing behavior can lead to physiological hypotheses.

---

ods to measure the relationship between stimuli and perception. The methods Fechner described are called the **classical psychophysical methods** because they were the original methods that were used to measure the stimulus–perception relationship. He described three methods to measure the **absolute threshold**, which is the smallest amount of stimulus energy necessary to detect a stimulus. These methods were called the method of limits, the method of adjustment, and the method of constant stimuli.

The Absolute Threshold   To measure the threshold by using the **method of limits**, the experimenter presents stimuli in either ascending or descending order, as shown in Figure 1.12, which indicates the results of an experiment that measures a person's threshold for seeing a light.

On the first series of trials, the experimenter presents a light with an intensity of 105, and the observer indicates by a "yes" response that he sees the light. This response is indicated by a Y at an intensity of 105 on the table. The experimenter then decreases the intensity, and the observer makes a judgment at each intensity until he responds "no," that he did not see the light. This change from "yes" to "no" is the crossover point, and the threshold for this series is taken as the mean between 99 and 98, or 98.5. By repeating this procedure a number of times, starting above the threshold half the time and starting below the threshold half the time, the threshold can be determined by calculating the average of all of the crossover points.

In the **method of adjustment**, the observer or the experimenter adjusts the stimulus intensity in a continuous manner (as opposed to the stepwise presentation for the method of limits) until the observer can just barely detect the stimulus. This just barely detectable intensity is then taken as the absolute

	1 ↓	2 ↑	3 ↓	4 ↑	5 ↓	6 ↑	7 ↓	8 ↑
Intensity								
105	Y						Y	
104	Y		Y		Y		Y	
103	Y		Y		Y		Y	
102	Y		Y		Y		Y	
101	Y		Y		Y		Y	Y
100	Y	Y	Y	Y	Y		Y	Y
99	Y	N	Y	N	Y	Y	Y	Y
98	N	N	Y	N	N	N	N	Y
97		N	N	N		N		N
96		N		N		N		N
95		N		N		N		N

Crossover → 98.5 99.5 97.5 99.5 98.5 98.5 98.5 97.5
values

Threshold = Mean of crossovers = 98.5

Figure 1.12
The results of an experiment to determine the threshold using the method of limits. There are eight series of trials in this experiment, the descending trials alternating with the ascending trials. In the first series, the observer indicates by an answer of "no" that he or she no longer sees the light. This change from "yes" at 99 to "no" at 98 is the crossover point, and the threshold value for this run is taken as the mean between 99 and 98, or 98.5. The procedure is then repeated in reverse, starting below the threshold and increasing the intensity until the subject says "yes." Both the descending and the ascending presentations are repeated a number of times, and the threshold is calculated as the mean of the crossover values for each run. The threshold is therefore 98.5 in this experiment.

threshold. This procedure can be repeated several times and the threshold determined by taking the average setting.

In the **method of constant stimuli**, the experimenter presents five to nine stimuli in random order. The results of a hypothetical determination of the threshold for seeing a light are shown in Figure 1.13. The data points in this graph were determined by presenting six light intensities ten times each and determining the percentage of times that the subject perceives each intensity. The results indicate that the light with an intensity of 150 is never detected, the light with an intensity of 200 is always detected, and lights with intensities in between are sometimes detected and sometimes not detected. The threshold is usually taken as the intensity that results in detection on 50 percent of the trials, so in this case the threshold is an intensity of 180.

The choice among the methods of limits, adjustment, and constant stimuli is usually determined by the accuracy that is needed and the amount of time available. The method of constant stimuli is the most accurate method but takes the longest time, whereas the method of adjustment is the least accurate but the fastest.

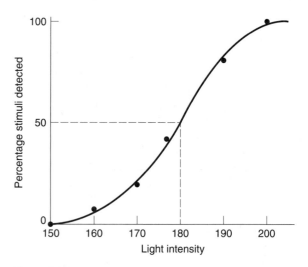

Figure 1.13
Results of a hypothetical experiment in which the threshold for seeing a light is measured by the method of constant stimuli. The threshold, the intensity at which the light is seen on half of its presentations (as indicated by the dashed line), is 180 in this experiment.

When Fechner published *Elements of Psychophysics*, he not only described his methods for measuring the absolute threshold but also described the work of Ernst Weber (1795–1878), a physiologist, who, a few years before the publication of Fechner's book, measured another type of threshold, the difference threshold.

The Difference Threshold   The **difference threshold** (called DL from the German *Differenze Limen*, which is translated as "difference threshold") is the smallest difference between two stimuli that a person can detect. To measure the difference threshold, Weber had subjects lift a small "standard" weight and then lift a slightly heavier "comparison" weight and judge which was heavier (Figure 1.14). When the difference between the standard and comparison weights was small, subjects found it difficult to detect the difference in the weights, but they easily detected larger differences. That much is not surprising, but Weber went further. He found that the size of the DL depended on the size of the standard weight. For example, the DL for a 100-gram weight is 5 grams (a subject could tell the difference between a 100- and 105-gram weight, but could not detect smaller differences), and the DL for a 200-gram weight is 10 grams. Thus, as the magnitude of the stimulus increases, so does the size of the DL.

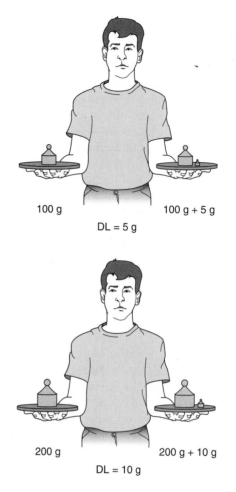

100 g   100 g + 5 g

DL = 5 g

200 g   200 g + 10 g

DL = 10 g

Figure 1.14

The difference threshold (DL). The person can detect the difference between a 100-gram weight and a 105-gram comparison weight but cannot detect a smaller difference, so the DL is 5 grams. With a 200-gram weight, the comparison weight must be 210 grams before the person can detect the difference, so the DL is 10 grams. Note that for both the 100- and 200-gram weights, the ratio of DL to weight is the same. This ratio is the Weber fraction.

 D E M O N S T R A T I O N

Measuring the Difference Threshold

By doing a simple experiment with two boxes of wooden matches, you can show that the DL gets larger as the standard stimulus gets larger. Have a friend place 10 matches in one box (the standard) and 11 in the other (the comparison). Comparing the weights of the two boxes with your eyes closed, try to decide which box is heavier. After making this judgment, repeat this procedure; if you can't correctly judge which is heavier on three out of three trials, have your friend place another match in the comparison box, and try again. Continue this procedure until you can consistently judge which box is heavier. If, for example, you can consistently tell that the comparison box is heavier when it contains 12 matches, then the DL equals 2 matches. Now repeat the above procedures, but start with 20 matches in the standard box and 21 in the comparison. Since the DL gets larger as the weight of the standard gets larger, you should find that the

Introduction to Perception

DL for the 20-match standard is larger than the DL for the 10-match standard. ●

Research on a number of senses has shown that over a fairly large range of intensities, the ratio of the DL to the standard stimulus is constant. This relationship, which is based on Weber's research, was stated mathematically by Fechner as $DL/S=K$ and was called **Weber's law**. K is a constant called the **Weber fraction**, and S is the value of the standard stimulus. Applying this equation to our example of lifted weights, we find that, for the 100-gram standard, $K = 5/100 = 0.05$, and that, for the 200-gram standard, $K = 10/200 = 0.05$. Thus, in this example, the Weber fraction (K) is constant. In fact, numerous modern investigators have found that Weber's law is true for most senses, as long as the stimulus intensity is not too close to the threshold (Engen, 1972; Gescheider, 1976).

Fechner's proposal of three psychophysical methods for measuring the absolute threshold and his statement of Weber's law for the difference threshold were extremely important events in the history of scientific psychology because they demonstrated that mental activity could be measured quantitatively. This was a notable achievement, because in the 1800s many people thought that it was impossible to measure mental activity. But perhaps the most notable thing about these methods is that even though they were proposed in the 1800s, they are still used today. In addition to being used to determine thresholds in research laboratories, simplified versions of the classical psychophysical methods have been used to measure people's detail vision when determining prescriptions for glasses or measuring people's hearing when testing for possible hearing loss.

The classical psychophysical methods were developed to measure absolute and difference thresholds. But what about perceptions that occur above threshold? Most of our everyday experience consists of perceptions that are far above threshold, when we can easily see and hear what is happening around us. In order to measure these above-threshold perceptions, S. S. Stevens developed a technique called *magnitude estimation*.

Perceiving Magnitude: Magnitude Estimation

If we double the intensity of a tone, does it sound twice as loud? If we double the intensity of a light, does it look twice as bright? Although a number of researchers, including Fechner, proposed equations that related perceived magnitude and stimulus intensity, it wasn't until 1957 that S. S. Stevens developed a technique called scaling or **magnitude estimation** that accurately measured this relationship (Stevens, 1957, 1961, 1962).

Magnitude estimation is relatively simple: The experimenter first presents a "standard" stimulus to the observer (let's say a light of moderate intensity) and assigns it a value of, say, 10; he or she then presents lights of different intensities, and the observer is asked to assign a number to each of these lights that is proportional to the brightness of the light. If the light appears twice as bright as the standard, it gets a rating of 20; half as bright, a 5; and so on. Thus, each light intensity has a brightness assigned to it by the observer.

The results of a magnitude estimation experiment on brightness are plotted in Figure 1.15. This

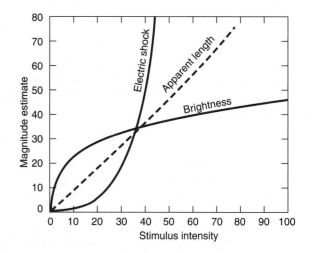

Figure 1.15
Curves showing the relationship between perceived magnitude and stimulus intensity for electric shock, line length, and brightness. (Adapted from Stevens, 1962.)

graph plots the means, for a number of observers, of the magnitude estimates of the brightness of a light versus the intensity of the light. You can see from the way this curve bends down that doubling the intensity does not necessarily double the perceived brightness. Doubling the intensity causes only a small change in perceived brightness, particularly at higher intensities. This result is called **response compression**. As intensity is increased, the responses increase, but not as rapidly as the intensity. To double the brightness, it is necessary to multiply the intensity by about 9.

Figure 1.15 also shows the results of magnitude estimation experiments for the sensation caused by an electric shock presented to the finger and for the length of a line. The electric shock curve bends up, indicating that doubling the strength of a shock more than doubles the sensation of being shocked. This is called **response expansion**. As intensity is increased, perceptual magnitude increases more than intensity. The curve for estimating length is straight, with a slope of close to 1.0, so the magnitude of the response almost exactly matches increases in the stimulus (i.e., doubling the line length doubles the observer's estimate of the length of the line).

The beauty of the relationships derived from magnitude estimation is that the relationship between the intensity of a stimulus and our perception of its magnitude follows the same general equation for each sense. This is illustrated by the fact that plotting the logarithm of the magnitude estimates versus the logarithm of the stimulus intensity causes all three curves to become straight lines (Figure 1.16). These functions are called **power functions** and are described by the equation $P = KS^n$. Perceived magnitude, P, equals a constant, K, times the stimulus intensity, S, raised to a power, n. This relationship is called **Stevens's power law**.

The power n, the exponent of the power law, indicates the slope of the lines in Figure 1.16. Remembering our discussion of the three types of curves in Figure 1.15, we can see that the curve that shows response compression has a slope of less than 1.0, the straight line has a slope of about 1.0, and the curve that shows response expansion has a slope of greater than 1.0. Thus, the relationship between response magnitude and stimulus intensity is de-

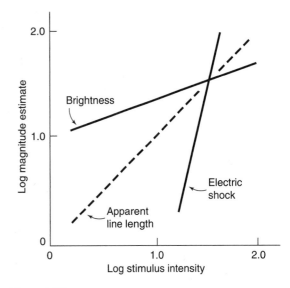

Figure 1.16

The three curves from Figure 1.15 plotted on log–log coordinates. Taking the logarithm of the magnitude estimates and the logarithm of the stimulus intensity turns the curves into straight lines. (Adapted from Stevens, 1962.)

scribed by a power law for all senses, and the exponent of the power law indicates whether doubling the stimulus intensity causes more or less than a doubling of the response.

These exponents not only illustrate that all senses follow the same basic relationship, they also illustrate how the operation of each sense is adapted to how organisms function in their environment. Consider, for example, our experience of brightness. On a bright sunny day sunlight on a white sidewalk or on the white sand of a beach can appear extremely bright. But from Figure 1.15 we can see that the curve for brightness bends over (exponent = 0.6), so increasing intensity causes only a small change in brightness, especially at high intensities. Consider, however, how bright the sunlight would appear if the brightness was rising rapidly at high intensities. The brightness of the sidewalk would increase greatly, perhaps causing bright glare that would impair your ability to see.

The opposite situation occurs for electric shock, which has an exponent of 3.5 so that just small increases in shock intensity cause large increases in pain. This rapid increase in pain even to small increases in shock intensity serves to warn us of impending danger, and we therefore tend to withdraw even from weak shocks.

Searching

If you have ever had the experience of searching for a friend's face in a crowd you know that sometimes it is easy (if you know your friend is wearing a bright red hat and no one else is) and sometimes it is difficult (if there are lots of people and your friend doesn't stand out). The process of searching for information, be it a person's face in a crowd or a "target stimulus" in a laboratory experiment, can tell us important things about perceptual mechanisms. When we consider object perception in Chapter 5, we will describe visual search experiments in which the subjects' task is to find a target letter that is hidden among a number of other letters. We will see how measuring "reaction time"—how long it takes the subject to find the target—has provided information about events that occur very early in the perceptual process.

Other Methods

Numerous other methods in addition to those described above have also been used to measure the stimulus–perception relationship. For example, in some experiments, subjects are asked to decide whether two stimuli are the same or different, or to adjust the brightness or the colors of two lights so they appear the same, or to close their eyes and walk, as accurately as possible, to a distant target stimulus in a field. We will encounter methods such as these, and others as well, as we describe perceptual research in the chapters that follow.

We will now describe some of the methods that are used to study perception at the physiological level. In order to describe these methods we also need to introduce some of the basic principles of

physiology that will form the basis for understanding the physiological material in the chapters that follow.

THE PHYSIOLOGICAL APPROACH: LINKING STIMULATION AND NEURAL FIRING

WebTUTOR Modern research designed to determine the physiological mechanisms of perception has focused on determining the relationship between the stimulus and electrical signals called nerve impulses and on determining the relationship between these nerve impulses and perception. We begin by looking at some of the early history of this physiological approach to perception.

The Physiological Approach: Early History

Our modern ideas about the physiological basis of perception are descended from a long line of speculation and research regarding the physiological workings of the mind. Early thinking about the physiology of perception focused on determining the anatomical structures involved in the operation of the mind. In the 4th century B.C. the philosopher Aristotle (384–322 B.C.) stated that the heart, not the brain, was the seat of the mind and the soul. Most of those following Aristotle did not repeat his error and correctly identified the brain as the seat of the mind.

It is interesting to note how speculations about how the brain works have been influenced by the technology of the day (Bloom, Lazerson, & Hofstadter, 1985; Nelson & Bower, 1990). For example, the Greek physician Galen (ca. 130–200 A.D.) likened the functioning of the brain to the aqueducts and sewer systems of ancient Rome. Galen saw human health, thoughts, and emotions as being determined by four different fluids flowing from the cavities in the center of the brain, an idea that remained popular for 1,500 years.

Later ideas were also influenced by technology. The philosopher René Descartes (1596–1650) pic-

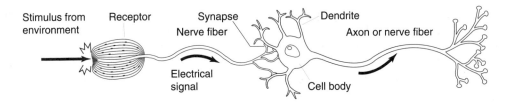

Figure 1.17

The neuron shown on the right consists of a cell body, dendrites, and an axon, or nerve fiber. A neuron that receives stimuli from the environment, shown on the left, has a receptor in place of the cell body.

tured the human body as operating like a machine that resembled the mechanical devices popular in the 17th century. His contemporary, the "father of astronomy" Johannes Kepler (1571–1630), thought the eye operated like an ordinary optical instrument that projected images onto the sensory nerves of the retina. This idea was partially true but did not explain the physiological processes that occur after the image is formed. Understanding these physiological processes had to await a better understanding of the nature of both electricity and the electrical signals that are conducted by these nerves.

Neurons and Electrical Signals

By the end of the 19th century, researchers had shown that a wave of electricity is transmitted down the nerve. To explain how these electrical signals result in different perceptions, Johannes Mueller in 1842 proposed the **doctrine of specific nerve energies**, which stated that our perceptions depend on "nerve energies" reaching the brain and that the specific quality we experience depends on which nerves are stimulated. Thus he proposed that stimulating the eye results in seeing, stimulating the ear results in hearing, and so on. By the end of the 1800s, this idea had expanded to conclude that nerves from each of these senses reach different areas of the brain.

Another important development during the 19th century was the realization that **nerves**, such as the optic nerve that conducts signals from the eye, are composed of smaller structures called **neurons** that consist of (1) a **cell body**, which contains a nucleus and other structures whose metabolic mechanisms are needed to keep the cell alive; (2) **dendrites**, which branch out from the cell body to receive electrical signals from other neurons; and (3) an **axon**, or **nerve fiber**, a tube filled with fluid that conducts electrical signals (Figure 1.17).

When many neurons combine to create a nerve it is the axons of the neurons that form the individual components of the nerve, just as many individual wires travel within a telephone cable (Figure 1.18). For example, the optic nerve contains about one million axons or nerve fibers.

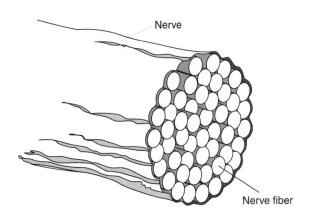

Figure 1.18

Nerves are made up of many nerve fibers. Most nerves contain many more fibers than are shown here. For example, the optic nerve, which conducts signals from the eye, contains about one million nerve fibers.

Introduction to Perception

There are variations on this basic neuron structure: Some neurons have long axons; others have short axons or none at all. Especially important for perception are a type of neuron called **receptors**, which are specialized to respond to environmental stimuli such as light or sound waves.

By the beginning of the 20th century, researchers understood that these receptors transduce environmental energy into electrical signals and that these signals are transmitted along neurons to different areas of the brain for different senses. But an understanding of the nature of the electrical signals that are transmitted to the brain had to await the development of electronic amplifiers that were powerful enough to make visible the extremely small electrical signals generated by the neuron. When this equipment became available in the 1920s, researchers began recording these electrical signals, called nerve impulses, and began to understand the chemical basis of nerve signals (Adrian, 1928, 1932). Since nerve impulses are crucial for our understanding of the physiology of perception, we will look at some basic facts about these signals.

Recording Electrical Signals in Neurons

What kinds of electrical signals are transmitted by neurons? When most people think of electrical signals, they imagine signals conducted along electrical power lines or along the wires used for household appliances. Unlike the electrical wires of your television set, however, neurons are bathed in liquid. Some people find this fact disconcerting because we are taught that we should keep electricity and water separated. However, as we shall see, the body has devised ways to create electrical signals within a liquid environment.

The key to understanding the "wet" electrical signals transmitted by neurons is to understand the components of the neuron's liquid environment. Neurons are immersed in a solution rich in **ions**, molecules that carry an electrical charge. Ions are created when molecules gain or lose electrons, as happens when compounds are dissolved in water. For example, adding table salt (sodium chloride, NaCl) to water creates positively charged sodium ions (Na^+) and negatively charged chlorine ions (Cl^-). The solution outside the axon of a neuron is rich in positively charged sodium (Na^+) ions, while the solution inside the axon is rich in positively charged potassium (K^+) ions (Figure 1.19).

These and other ions create electrical signals in the neuron when they flow across the cell membrane of the axon. We can see how this works by observing the ion flow as electrical signals are conducted down the axon. To measure the electrical signals, we use two **microelectrodes**, small shafts of glass or metal with tips small enough to record the electrical signals from a single neuron.

Figure 1.20a shows a pressure-sensitive receptor and its nerve fiber with two microelectrodes positioned to record signals from the axon. The tip of the recording electrode is positioned inside the fiber, and the tip of the null electrode is positioned outside the axon. The recording device that measures the difference in charge between these two electrodes indicates that the inside of the neurons has a charge that is 70 millivolts (mV; 1 mV = 1/1,000 volt) more negative than the outside of the neuron. This negative charge inside the neuron is called the neuron's **resting potential**, because it is the neuron's charge when it is at rest (Figure 1.20a).

Now that we have measured the resting potential, we are ready to push on the axon's pressure receptor. If we push hard enough, we measure the rapid

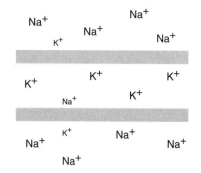

Figure 1.19
Cross section of a nerve fiber, showing the high concentration of sodium outside the fiber and potassium inside the fiber. Other ions that are present, such as negatively charged chlorine, are not shown.

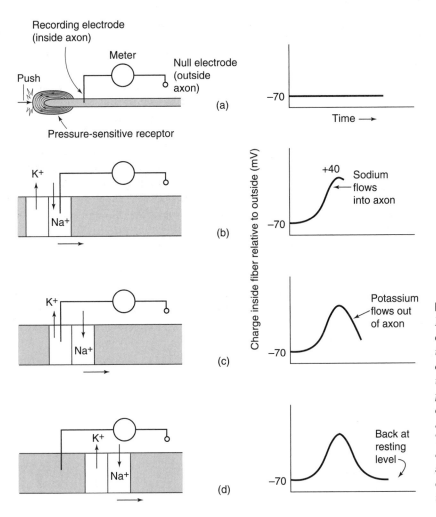

Charge inside fiber relative to outside (mV)

(a)
Recording electrode
(inside axon)
Meter
Null electrode
(outside axon)
Push
Pressure-sensitive receptor

−70
Time →

(b)
K+
Na+

+40
Sodium
flows
into axon
−70

(c)
K+
Na+

Potassium
flows out
of axon
−70

(d)
K+
Na+

Back at
resting
level
−70

Figure 1.20
Effect of a nerve impulse as it travels down a nerve fiber. As long as the fiber is at rest, there is a difference in charge of −70 mV between the inside and the outside of the fiber, as shown in (a). Events that occur once a nerve impulse is generated are shown in (b), (c), and (d). The flow of sodium into the fiber and potassium out of the fiber is shown on the left, and the resulting change in the charge measured by the electrodes is shown on the right.

change in charge shown in Figure 1.20b. The charge inside the fiber rapidly increases from −70 mV to +40 mV compared to the outside and then returns back to the resting potential, all within about 1 ms (1/1,000 s). This rapid increase in positive charge is called the nerve impulse or **action potential**.[4]

If we observe the Na^+ and K^+ ions in the vicinity of the recording electrode, we see that positively charged sodium ions (Na^+) rush into the fiber at the

beginning of the action potential. This Na^+ inflow is what causes the inside of the fiber to become more positive and creates the rising phase of the action potential (Figure 1.20b) This inflow of Na^+ is followed by an outflow of positively charged potassium (K^+). This K^+ outflow is what causes the inside of the fiber to become more negative and creates the downward phase of the action potential that brings the charge back to its original level (Figure 1.20c and d).

These rapid changes in sodium and potassium flow that create the action potential are caused by changes in the fiber's permeability to sodium and potassium. **Permeability** is a property of the cell

[4] There are also slower electrical potentials in nerve fibers. See Kalat (2001) for a description of these potentials.

membrane that refers to the ease with which a molecule can pass through the membrane. Before the action potential occurs, the membrane's permeability to sodium and potassium is low, so there is little flow of these molecules across the membrane. Stimulation of the receptor triggers a process that causes the membrane to become permeable to sodium. Sodium pours across the membrane to the inside of the axon for about 1/2,000 second, and then the membrane's permeability to sodium decreases and its permeability to potassium increases, causing potassium to flow out of the axon for 1/2,000 of a second.[5]

This process creates the rapid increase and then decrease in positive charge inside the axon which lasts about 1/1,000 second at our electrode. The signal that is picked up by the electrode is the change in charge caused by the action potential as it passes by the electrode on its way down the axon. The fact that the action potential travels down the axon reflects the fact that it is a **propagated response**—once it is triggered it travels all the way down the axon. This is an extremely important property of the action potential, because it enables neurons to transmit signals over long distances. Let's now consider some additional properties of action potentials.

Basic Properties of Action Potentials

As an action potential propagates down the axon, it remains the same size no matter how far it has traveled and no matter how intense the stimulus is. We can show that the size of the action potential remains the same, even when stimulus intensity changes, by determining how the neuron fires at different stimulus intensities. Figure 1.21 shows what happens when

we do this. Each action potential appears as a sharp spike in these records because we have compressed the time scale so that we can display a number of action potentials.

The three records in Figure 1.21 represent the axon's response to three intensities of stimulation. Figure 1.21a shows how the axon responds to gentle stimulation applied to the skin, while Figures 1.21b and 1.21c show how the response changes as the stimulation is increased. Comparing these three records leads to an important conclusion: Changing the stimulus intensity does not affect the size of the action potentials but does affect the rate of firing.

Although increasing the stimulus intensity can increase the rate of firing, there is an upper limit to the number of nerve impulses per second that can be conducted down an axon. This limit occurs because a neuron takes about 1 millisecond (1 ms = 1/1,000s) to recover from conducting an action potential before it can conduct another one. This interval is

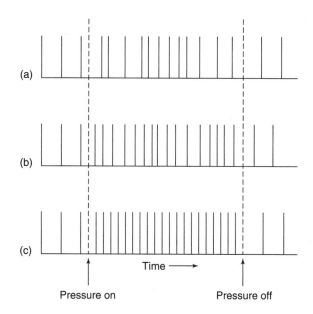

Figure 1.21
Response of a nerve fiber to (a) soft, (b) medium, and (c) strong stimulation. Increasing the stimulus strength increases both the rate and the regularity of nerve firing in this fiber.

---

[5] After hearing this description of how Na+ flows into the axon and K+ flows out, students often wonder whether sodium would accumulate inside the axon and if potassium would accumulate outside the axon. This accumulating is prevented by a mechanism called the **sodium–potassium pump**, which continuously returns sodium to the outside of the axon and potassium to the inside, thereby maintaining sodium and potassium concentrations at their original levels so the axon can continue to generate nerve impulses.

called the **refractory period**, and it sets the upper limit of the firing rate at about 500 to 800 impulses per second.

Another important property of action potentials is illustrated by the beginning of each of the records in Figure 1.21. Some action potentials occur even before the pressure stimulus is applied. In fact, many axons fire without any stimuli from the environment, and this firing is called **spontaneous activity**. Although you may wonder why an axon would be designed to fire in the absence of outside stimulation, you will see later that this spontaneous activity plays an important role in determining our perceptions.

What do these properties of the action potential mean in terms of their function for perceiving? The action potential's function is to communicate information. We have seen that pushing harder on a pressure receptor increases the rate of nerve firing. Thus, these increased rates of nerve firing carry information about the intensity of the stimulus. But if this information remains within a single neuron, it serves no function. In order to be meaningful, this information must be transmitted to other neurons and eventually to the brain or other organs that can react to this information.

The idea that the action potential in one neuron must be transmitted to other neurons poses the following problem: Once an action potential reaches the end of the axon, how is the message that the action potential carries transmitted to other neurons? One idea, put forth by the Italian anatomist Camillo Golgi (1844–1926), was that neurons make direct contact with each other, so that a signal reaching the end of one neuron passes directly to the next neuron. But the Spanish anatomist Santiago Ramon y Cajal (1852–1934) showed that there is a very small space between the neurons, which is known as a **synapse** (Figure 1.22). Ramon y Cajal's discovery earned him the Nobel Prize in 1906. (He shared the prize with Golgi, who was recognized for his research on the structure of the neuron.)

The discovery of the synapse raised the question of how the electrical signals generated by one neuron are transmitted across the space separating the neurons. As we will see, the answer lies in a remarkable chemical process that takes place at the synapse.

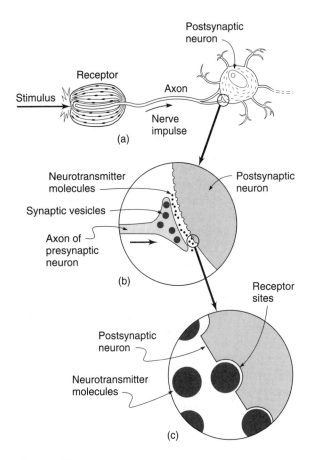

Figure 1.22

Synaptic transmission from one neuron to another. (a) A signal traveling down the axon of a neuron reaches the synapse at the end of the axon. (b) Close-up of the synapse showing the presynaptic neuron on the left and the postsynaptic neuron on the right. The nerve impulse reaching the synapse causes the release of neurotransmitter molecules from the synaptic vesicles of the presynaptic neuron. (c) The neurotransmitters fit into receptor sites and cause a voltage change in the postsynaptic neuron.

Chemical and Electrical Events at the Synapse

Early in the 1900s, it was discovered that the action potentials themselves do not travel across the synapse. Instead, they trigger a chemical process that bridges the gap between the sending neuron (which is called

Introduction to Perception

the *presynaptic neuron*) and the receiving neuron (which is called the *postsynaptic neuron*). When the action potential reaches the end of the presynaptic neuron, it causes the release of chemicals called **neurotransmitters** that are stored in **synaptic vesicles** in the presynaptic neuron. As the name implies, neurotransmitters transmit neural information.

When the action potential reaches the synaptic vesicles at the end of the axon, the vesicles release their packets of neurotransmitters. The neurotransmitter molecules flow into the synapse to small areas called **receptor sites** on the postsynaptic neuron that are sensitive to specific neurotransmitters. These receptor sites exist in a variety of shapes that match the shapes of particular neurotransmitter molecules. When a neurotransmitter makes contact with a receptor site matching its shape, it activates the receptor site and triggers a voltage change in the postsynaptic neuron. Thus, a neurotransmitter is like a key that fits a specific lock. It has an effect on the postsynaptic neuron only if its shape matches that of the receptor site.

At the synapse, then, an electrical signal generates a chemical process that, in turn, triggers a change in voltage in the postsynaptic neuron. The neurotransmitter's action at the receptor site does not, however, automatically generate a new action potential in the postsynaptic neuron. Instead, when a neurotransmitter molecule makes contact with a receptor site that matches its shape, it has one of two effects, depending on the type of transmitter and the nature of the cell body of the postsynaptic neuron. It can cause **excitation**, which increases the rate of nerve firing, or it can cause **inhibition**, which decreases the rate of nerve firing.

Why does inhibition exist? If one of the purposes of the neuron is to transmit its information to other neurons, why would the action potential trigger a process that decreases the rate of nerve firing or stops further action potentials from being generated? The answer to these questions is that the function of the neuron is to transmit information *and* to process it, and both excitation and inhibition are necessary for this processing.

You will understand how both excitation and inhibition help create this processing after we describe neural processing in Chapter 2, but one way

to look at processing is to consider the synapse as being a control center, which controls the flow of information carried by action potentials. We will see in Chapter 2 that the flow of information through this synaptic "control center" is achieved by the interplay of excitation and inhibition.

The basic nature of this interplay is shown in Figure 1.23, which shows one excitatory synapse (E) and one inhibitory synapse (I) on the same neuron. When the neuron receives excitatory input, the rate of firing increases above the spontaneous level, as shown in Figure 1.23a, but, as the amount of inhibition relative to excitation increases (Figure 1.23b through Figure 1.23e), the firing rate decreases. In Figure 1.23d and Figure 1.23e, the inhibition is so strong that the rate of nerve firing is decreased to below the level of spontaneous activity.

These facts about how neurons operate—especially the characteristics of their action potentials and the interplay between excitation and inhibition that occurs at the synapse—provide the basis for much of the discussion of neurons and perception in the rest of this book. However, to complete our presentation of background information about the physiological approach to perception, we need to consider how these neurons work together in the brain.

Basic Structure of the Brain

One of the major concerns of this book is the human brain, a structure that, with its 100 billion neurons, has been called the most complex structure in the universe. This complexity comes not just from the number of neurons, but from the vast number of interconnections between them, numbering in the thousands for many neurons.

Although we are far from understanding the vast complexity of how the brain operates, we have learned a tremendous amount in the last few decades about the connection between operations of the brain and our perceptions. Much of the research on this connection has focused on activity in the **cerebral cortex**, the 2-mm-thick layer that covers the surface of the brain and contains the brain's machinery for creating perception, as well as for other functions, such as language, memory, and thinking. A basic principle of

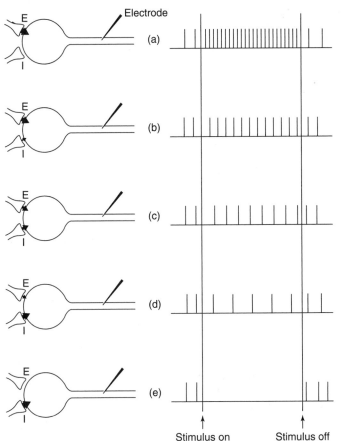

Figure 1.23
Effect of excitatory (E) and inhibitory (I) input on the firing rate of a neuron. The amount of excitatory and inhibitory input to the neuron is indicated by the size of the arrows at the synapse. The responses recorded by the electrode are indicated by the records on the right. The firing that occurs before the onset of the stimulus is spontaneous activity.

cortical function is **modular organization**—specific functions are served by specific areas of the cortex.

One example of modular organization is how the senses are organized into **primary receiving areas**, the first areas in the cerebral cortex to receive the signals initiated by that sense's receptors (Figure 1.24). The primary receiving area for vision occupies most of the **occipital lobe**; the area for hearing is located in part of the **temporal lobe**; and the area for the skin senses—touch, temperature, and pain—is located in an area in the **parietal lobe**. As we study each sense in detail, we will see that other areas in addition to the primary receiving areas are also associated with each sense. For example, in Chapter 4 we will see that there are areas outside of the primary visual receiving area that are specialized for processing

information about specific visual qualities. For example, there is an area high in the temporal lobe concerned mainly with the perception of visual movement, and an area lower in the temporal lobe concerned with the perception of form.

Most of the research that has determined the organization and function of various areas of the brain has involved microelectrode recording from neurons in the cat and monkey. Until recently, studying human brain function has focused primarily on **neuropsychology**—studying the effects of brain damage on behavior, as in the case of Dr. P., which we described earlier. But recent technological advances that have occurred over just the past few decades have begun to change this situation, so it is now possible to study brain activity in awake, behaving humans.

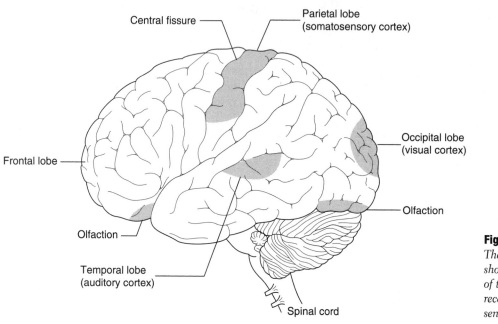

Central fissure

Parietal lobe
(somatosensory cortex)

Frontal lobe

Occipital lobe
(visual cortex)

Olfaction

Olfaction

Temporal lobe
(auditory cortex)

Spinal cord

Figure 1.24
*The human brain,
showing the location
of the primary
receiving areas for the
senses.*

Studying Brain Activity in Humans

One way brain activity has been measured in humans has been to measure **evoked potentials**. These potentials are recorded with disc electrodes that are placed on the person's scalp and record activity from thousands of neurons that are located under the electrodes (Figure 1.25). However, most research on human brain activity and perception has focused on **neuroimaging** techniques, which have enabled researchers to visualize activity in the human brain in response to sensory stimulation.

One of these techniques, **positron emission tomography (PET)**, was introduced in 1976 (Hoffman et al., 1976; ter-Pogossian et al., 1975). In the PET procedure a person is injected with a low dose of a radioactive tracer that is not harmful to the person. The tracer enters the bloodstream and indicates the volume of blood flow. The basic principle behind the PET scan is that changes in the activity of the brain are accompanied by changes in blood flow, and monitoring the radioactivity of the injected tracer provides a measure of this blood flow (Figure 1.26).

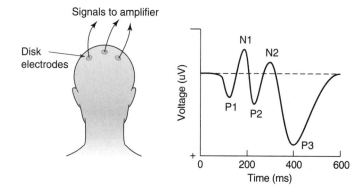

Signals to amplifier

Disk
electrodes

N1
N2
P1
P2
P3

Voltage (uV)

0   200   400   600
Time (ms)

Figure 1.25
*The evoked potential response is recorded with
small disc electrodes on the person's scalp. The
record on the right shows that the response consists of a number of positive and negative waves,
each of which is associated with specific events
that are occurring during perceptual processing.*

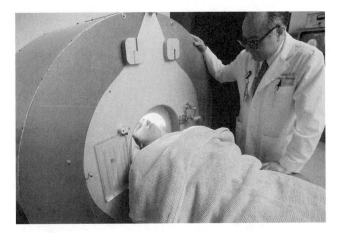

Figure 1.26
A person in a functional magnetic resonance imaging (fMRI) apparatus.

PET provided a tool that enabled researchers to determine which brain areas were being activated. To use this tool, researchers developed the **subtraction technique**. Brain activity is first measured in a "control state" before stimulation is presented and is then measured while the stimulus is presented. The activity during stimulation minus the activity in the control state indicates the site of activity due to stimulation (Figure 1.27).

Recently, another neuroimaging technique called **functional magnetic resonance imaging (fMRI)** has been introduced. Like PET, fMRI is based on the measurement of blood flow. An advantage of fMRI is

that blood flow can be measured without radioactive tracers. fMRI takes advantage of the fact that hemoglobin, which carries oxygen in the blood, contains a ferrous molecule and therefore has magnetic properties. Thus, if a magnetic field is presented to the brain, the hemoglobin molecules line up, like tiny magnets.

fMRI indicates the presence of brain activity because the hemoglobin molecules in areas of high brain activity lose some of the oxygen they are transporting. This makes the hemoglobin more magnetic, so these molecules respond more strongly to the magnetic field. The fMRI apparatus determines the relative activity of various areas of the brain by detecting

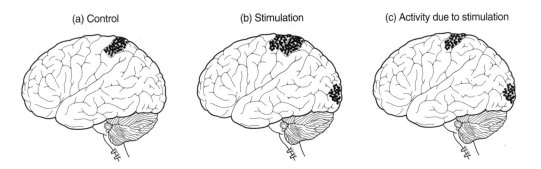

(a) Control   (b) Stimulation   (c) Activity due to stimulation

Figure 1.27
The subtraction technique for determining the relationship between a particular function and brain activity. In this hypothetical example, dark areas indicate activity in the brain. (a) In the control condition, an object is placed in a subject's hand. (b) In the stimulation condition, in which the subject actively manipulates the object with her hand, additional brain areas are activated. (c) The activity that remains after subtracting the response measured in the control condition from the response measured in the stimulation condition indicates the brain areas activated by manipulation of the object.

Introduction to Perception

changes in the magnetic response of the hemoglobin. The subtraction technique described above for PET is also used for the fMRI and, because fMRI doesn't require radioactive tracers and because it is more accurate, this technique has become the main method for localizing brain activity in humans. The "Brain Scan" feature in each chapter provides examples of how brain imaging has been used to identify which areas of the brain are activated by different types of perceptual stimuli.

The Approach in this Book

By looking in detail at the processes that underlie our perceptions, this book describes how perception researchers have gone about answering the questions posed in the instructions for the science project at the beginning of the chapter. We now describe some of the ways we will accomplish this.

Studying Perception at the Psychophysical and Physiological Levels

In this book we will be studying perception at both the psychophysical and physiological levels of analysis. To do this we will be approaching the study of perception by measuring all three relationships, A, B, and C, in Figure 1.7 and will also consider cognitive influences on perception. Using all of these approaches together gives us a more complete picture of the perceptual processes than using any of them alone.

Going Beyond Perception to Study Recognition and Action

The study of perception used to be almost exclusively about how we attain a consciousness of the world around us. But recently the study of perception has expanded to include a great deal of research on recognition and on studying the actions that result from perception and recognition. This book reflects this expansion of the field of perception by including a number of studies of people whose recognition ability

has been impaired by brain damage and by adding a new chapter (Chapter 9, "Visual Control of Action") devoted exclusively to the relationship between perception and action.

Considering Perception Across the Senses

This book is also based on the idea that all of the senses—vision, hearing, the skin senses, taste, and smell—share many mechanisms. This is reasonable, because all of the senses are served by the same nervous system. Thus, although we focus on vision at the beginning of the book, most of the basic principles we will describe will hold for the other senses as well. One way we illustrate the similarities between the senses and also how they interact is through a section called "Across the Senses." This feature, which appears at the end of each chapter beginning in Chapter 2, includes information showing how a sense different from the one we are considering in the chapter shares properties with the sense we have been discussing. For example, the "Across the Senses" section for the chapter on visual space perception compares how we locate objects in space based on vision to how we can also locate objects based on hearing.

Focusing on Cutting-Edge Research on Plasticity and Brain Imaging

This edition of *Sensation and Perception* includes the following features, which highlight particularly significant current research.

1. *"Plasticity of Perception"*   Each chapter ends with a section showing that our perceptual systems are "plastic." That is, they are molded and changed by the stimulation they receive. What this means is that the way our perceptual systems operate is shaped by the environment, so they can operate efficiently within the environment. This exciting new research, which has important theoretical and practical implications, is first introduced at the end of Chapter 3.

2. *"Brain Scan"*   This feature highlights research using the brain imaging techniques that, over just

the past decade, have made it possible to identify the brain activity that accompanies perception in humans in ways that were never available before. There is one of these "Brain Scan" features in each chapter, and additional research on brain imaging is included within the chapters as well.

How to Get the Most Out of This Book

The topic of this book is fascinating, since it is about how we make contact with the world. But along with the fascinating part comes many facts and principles that you will probably be asked to commit to memory. The Summary Tables in each chapter and the Study Questions at the end of each chapter are designed to help you focus on the important facts and principles in your studying. Although some students are able to read the book and then answer the study questions without much effort, this doesn't work for most students.

A method which works for many students is to read the chapter and then go through the study questions and write down the answers to each one. If you do this, however, I strongly advise you against just copying the answers from the book. The key is to create an answer *in your own words*. This is important because the very act of creating your own wording for the answer involves you in an *active process* that increases the chances you will remember the answer later. In contrast, copying the answer from the book is a *passive process*, which won't help you commit the material to memory.

Once you have created answers for your questions, you still need to learn the answers. Many students make the mistake of simply reading over their answers. This is a start, but it should not be the end of the process, because often reading over an answer does not mean that you actually understand it or will remember it later. Just reading over the answers can, in fact, create the illusion that you know the material when in reality you don't. To be sure you actually know the answers, repeat them without referring back to the text or your notes. You can say the answer to yourself, write it down again, or, best of all, explain it to someone else. My experience as a teacher has taught me that the ultimate test of whether I understand something is whether I can explain it to someone else.

The Psychophysical Approach

The psychophysical approach to perception focuses on the relationship between physical properties of stimuli and the perceptual responses to the stimuli. A number of methods have been used to measure this relationship.

The Psychophysical Methods

The following methods are used to study perception at the psychophysical level:

1. Phenomenological method—A person describes what he or she is perceiving.
2. Recognition—Placing a stimulus in a category by naming it.
3. Detection—Measuring thresholds using one of the following classical psychophysical methods: limits, adjustment, or constant stimuli.
4. Magnitude estimation—Assigning numbers to stimuli to indicate their perceived magnitude for qualities such as brightness and loudness.
5. Searching—Measuring the reaction time for finding a stimulus among other stimuli.

Thresholds

Thresholds, which are typically measured by one of the classical psychophysical methods, are very important because they specify basic properties of perceptual systems. The absolute threshold is the minimum amount of energy needed to detect a stimulus. The difference threshold is the smallest difference between two stimuli that are just detected. According to Weber's law, the difference threshold divided by the stimulus intensity is constant.

Magnitudes

Measuring the relationship between stimulus intensity and perceived magnitude yields power functions for all of the senses. The magnitude of some qualities, such as brightness, increases slowly as intensity increases (response compression). Others, like pain, increase rapidly (response expansion).

The Physiological Approach

The physiological approach to perception focuses on determining the relationship between the stimulus and electrical signals in the nervous system and between these electrical signals and perception.

Basic Components of the Nervous System

The nervous system is made up of basic units called neurons, which consist of a number of components, including the axon, a fluid-filled tube that conducts electrical signals. Axons of many neurons traveling together form a nerve.

Electrical Signals in Neurons

Electrical signals in neurons occur when charged molecules called ions flow across the cell membrane. Recording these potentials with microelectrodes reveals the resting potential, a difference in charge between the inside and outside of the fiber that occurs when the fiber is at rest, and the action potential, a rapid increase in positive charge that, once it is triggered, travels all the way down the axon without decreasing in size.

Properties of the Action Potential

The action potential of a particular neuron is always the same size, but the rate of firing can increase in response to increases in stimulation. Spontaneous activity is the firing of neurons in the absence of outside stimulation.

Events at the Synapse

The synapse is a small space between the end of the sending neuron and the cell body of the receiving neuron. Signals jump across this space by the action of neurotransmitters. These neurotransmitters can have either an excitatory or inhibitory influence on the receiving neuron. The interaction between excitation and inhibition is a major mechanism of information processing in the nervous system.

The Brain

Much of the research on the connection between brain activity and perception focuses on the cerebral cortex, a layer of neurons that covers the brain and contains the basic mechanisms of perception and other higher-order processes, such as memory and thinking. The brain contains a number of lobes and areas that receive information from the different senses. The relationship between the activity of different areas of the brain and perception has been studied in humans using brain imaging techniques such as PET scans and fMRI scans.

Study Questions

1. What is the paradox we face while searching for ways to understand human perception? (2)

2. How are perception and a play at the theater similar? (2)

The Importance of Perception

3. What are two purposes of perception? (3)

4. What might your experience be like if you could not perceive? (3)

5. What are some reasons to study perception? (3)

The Perceptual Process

6. What is the perceptual process? (4)

The Environmental Stimulus

7. What is the environmental stimulus? (4)

The Stimulus on the Receptors

8. On what structure in the visual system is the image of the environment formed? (4)

9. Why is it not that important to account for the fact that the retinal image is inverted? (4)

Transduction

10. What is transduction? What form of energy is involved in transduction in the nervous system? (5)

Neural Processing

11. How does the complexity of the neural pathways compare to the U.S. highway system? (5)

12. What is neural processing? (5)

Perception

13. What is perception? Is it the end point in the perceptual process? (6)

Recognition

14. What is recognition? How does the case of Dr. P. lead to the conclusion that recognition is a separate process from perception? (6)

Action

15. What activities does the action step of the perceptual process include? (6)

16. What is the major goal of visual processing, according to Milner and Goodale? (6)

17. Why can we say that the process of perception doesn't have a beginning or an ending point? (7)

Knowledge

18. How does recognition depend on knowledge? (8)

19. What is the rat–man demonstration? What does it illustrate about the role of knowledge in perception? (7)

Top-Down and Bottom-Up Processing

20. What is bottom-up processing? Top-down processing? How would you apply these two types of processing to explain how a pharmacist can read the writing on your doctor's prescription? (8)

Studying the Perceptual Process

Levels of Analysis

21. What is the idea behind levels of analysis? How would it apply to studying (a) automobiles and (b) perception? (8)

22. What relationship does the psychophysical level of analysis focus on? (9)

23. What kinds of measurement did *psychophysics* originally refer to? (9)

24. How will the term *psychophysics* be used in this text? (9)

25. What relationships does the physiological level of analysis focus on? (9)

Cognitive Influences on Perception

26. What factors are associated with cognitive influences on perception? What kinds of processing are associated with cognitive influences? (9)

27. What relationships involving stimuli, perception, and physiology are affected by a person's knowledge? (10)

Cross-Talk Between the Levels of Analysis

28. Why is it important to study perception at both levels of analysis? (11)

29. How does the example of the person with brain damage from a stroke illustrate how studying at the psychophysical level can provide information about the physiological level? (11)

The Psychophysical Approach: Linking Stimulation and Perception

30. What relationship is the major concern of the psychophysical approach to perception? (11)

Description: The Phenomenological Method

31. What is the first step in studying perception? (12)

32. What is the phenomenological method? Cite an example of a perceptual phenomenon in which the phenomenological method has been used. (12)

Recognition: Categorizing a Stimulus

33. What is the procedure for measuring recognition? How has it been applied to studying the effects of brain damage? (12)

Detection

34. Who was the pioneer in developing the classical psychophysical methods? (12)

35. Define absolute threshold. Describe the three major psychophysical methods for measuring the absolute threshold. (13)

36. What is the difference threshold, and who was the first to measure it? (15)

37. What is Weber's law, and why was it especially important? (16)

Perceiving Magnitude: Magnitude Estimation

38. Describe the magnitude estimation technique. When would you want to use it? (16)

39. What is response compression? response expansion? (17)

40. What is a power function? What is Stevens's power law? (17)

41. What does the exponent of the power function tell us? What is the functional significance of exponents of less than 1.0 and of more than 1.0? (17)

Searching

42. What response measure is usually used in a search experiment? The results of search experiments provide information about what part of the perceptual process? (18)

Other Methods

43. What are some other methods of measuring perception? (18)

The Physiological Approach: Linking Stimulation and Neural Firing

44. What relationships are the concern of the physiological approach to perception? (18)

The Physiological Approach: Early History

45. Where did Aristotle place the location of the mind? (18)

46. What did the following people think about the operation of the mind or the brain: Galen, Descartes, Kepler? (18)

Neurons and Electrical Signals

47. What is the doctrine of specific nerve energies? Who is associated with it? (19)

48. Describe the parts of a neuron. (19)

49. What is special about receptors? (20)

Recording Electrical Signals in Neurons

50. Define: ion, microelectrode, resting potential, action potential. What chemicals are found inside and outside the nerve fiber? (20)

51. How are electrical signals in neurons recorded? (20)

52. Describe the chemical events that occur in conjunction with the changes in charge that occur during the action potential. (21)

53. Why do we say that the action potential is a propagated response? (22)

Basic Properties of Action Potentials

54. How does the size of the action potential change as it travels down the axon? (22)

55. What property of the action potential changes as stimulus intensity is increased? (22)

56. What is the refractory period? spontaneous activity? (23)

57. In order to be meaningful, the information caused by neural firing must be transmitted _____. (23)

58. What problem occurs when an action potential reaches the end of a neuron? (23)

59. What is a synapse? (23)

Chemical and Electrical Events at the Synapse

60. What happens at the synapse when the action potential gets there? (24)

61. What is excitation? inhibition? Describe how excitation and inhibition can interact at the synapse and how this interaction influences nerve firing. (24)

62. Why does inhibition exist? (24)

Basic Structure of the Brain

63. Where is the cerebral cortex? What is modular organization? What are the primary receiving areas, and where are they located for each sense? (24)

64. What is neuropsychology? (25)

Studying Brain Activity in Humans

65. What is the evoked potential? How is it recorded? What does it indicate about neural activity? (26)

66. What is neuroimaging? (26)

67. What is positron emission tomography (PET)? How does it work? (26)

68. What is the subtraction technique? (27)

69. What is functional magnetic resonance imaging? How does it work? Why is it the dominant imaging technique? (27)

The Approach in This Book

Studying Perception at the Psychophysical and Physiological Levels

70. Which levels of analysis will be considered in this book? Which relationships in Figure 1.7 will be covered? (28)

Going Beyond Perception to Study Recognition and Action

71. What three outcomes of the perceptual process will be studied in this book? (28)

Considering Principles Across the Senses

72. Why does it make sense that the different senses share many mechanisms? (28)

Focusing On Cutting-Edge Research on Plasticity and Brain Imaging

73. What does it mean to say that the nervous system is "plastic"? (28)

How to Get the Most Out of This Book

74. What technique does the author suggest for being sure that you know the answers to the study questions? (29)

2

RECEPTORS AND
NEURAL PROCESSING

CHAPTER CONTENTS

SOME QUESTIONS WE WILL CONSIDER

- How is light transformed into electricity in the eye? (46)

- Why is it so difficult to pick one person's face out of a crowd? (57)

- How does neural processing determine what we see? (64)

- What do we mean when we say that perception is indirect? (72)

Imagine that you are standing in a room. You can see everything clearly, especially the colored bindings of the books lining the shelves on your right. When you turn out the lights, only the moonlight coming in through the window illuminates the room, and you can see only large forms, like the outline of the bookcase. But, after some time in the dark, it becomes easier to see, and eventually you can make out the books on the shelves and some of the other objects in the room, although they are not very clear and you can't see any color. Everything is in shades of gray.

You may not be surprised at the above description because you've probably experienced something similar before. But let's look a little more closely at what happens when the lights go out. You wouldn't expect to see things very well, since there is much less light. But why does the color go away, and why don't you see sharp details any more? Where did all the colors and the details go?

The answer to these questions is both simple and profound. The simple answer is that you have two types of visual receptors: cones, which control vision under high illuminations, and rods, which control vision under low illuminations. The cones are able to resolve fine details and extract information that enables you to see colors. The rods are poor at resolving details and are not able to extract information for color. In the light, you are using your cones to see details and colors. But, under dim illuminations, you are using your rods, and although they slowly become more sensitive so you can begin to see things better as you stay in the dark, they are unable to pick up details or create colors. Thus, the simple answer to the question "Where did all the colors and details go?" is that you use different detectors in the light and the dark.

The more profound answer to our questions is that our perception of the environment depends not only on the properties of objects in the environment, but on the properties of our visual system as well. One of the main messages of this chapter is that we do not just perceive what is out there. We perceive what is out there *as filtered through the properties of the visual system.*[1] This message is an important one because it holds not only for seeing but also for hearing, feeling with the skin, tasting, and smelling.

The idea that what we see depends on the properties of the visual system isn't really surprising when we consider the perceptual process, which we introduced in Figure 1.2, and which is repeated here in Figure 2.1, in a way that indicates some of the specific processes and structures in the visual system that are involved in perceptual processing. Remember from our discussion in Chapter 1 that, after an image is formed on the retina, light is transduced into electrical signals and these electrical signals must be processed by other neurons in the visual system before perception can occur. We will see in this chap-

ter and the ones that follow that your perception of the books on the shelves is the end result of many transformations. Those transformations begin when light reflected from the books falls on the receptors and is transformed into electricity and continues as this electricity finds its way to many different areas of the cortex.

This idea that perception is the result of many transformations is one of the themes of this book. This chapter is the starting point of a journey through the visual system, which will continue in Chapters 3 and 4. In the first half of this chapter, we will describe how light is focused on the receptors and how the properties of the receptors influence perception. In the second half of the chapter, we will introduce some basic principles of neural processing and will consider how this neural processing might affect perception. In Chapter 3, we will follow the electrical signals from the retina to a structure called the thalamus and then to the visual receiving area in the cortex. In Chapter 4, we follow these signals into higher-level areas of the cortex. Thus, the story that we begin here, in the receptors, eventually reaches higher centers in the cortex.

Figure 2.1 indicates the structures that we will be considering in each chapter and also indicates a theme that we will emphasize in each chapter. The theme for this chapter is "transformation," because we describe transformation from environmental stimuli to the image on the retina to electrical signals in neurons. In Chapter 3 the theme is "organization," because we describe how neurons are organized in the visual system, based on where they come from and what they do. Chapter 4 has two closely related themes, "modularity" and "parallel streams," because we describe how processing occurs in modules (groups of neurons that serve particular perceptual functions) and in parallel streams (neural pathways that send signals to different destinations and that serve different perceptual functions).

In each of these chapters, we will be focusing predominately on the physiological level of analysis, but we will never lose sight of the fact that our goal is not just to describe physiological processes but to describe how these physiological processes lead to perception, recognition, and action.

---

[1] We could make the same statements about hearing, touch, smell, or taste as well, but we will use mainly visual examples in these initial chapters of the book.

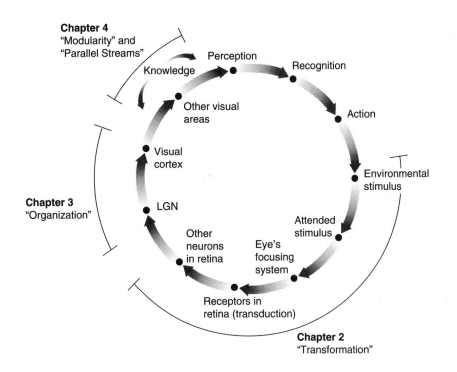

Figure 2.1

The perceptual process from Figure 1.2 has been expanded here to show specific structures that are involved in focusing the image, transduction, and neural processing. The parts of the cycle that will be covered in this chapter and Chapters 3 and 4 are indicated along with the theme of each chapter.

THE STIMULUS FOR VISION AND THE STRUCTURE OF THE VISUAL SYSTEM

WebTUTOR   We begin by describing the stimulus for vision and the structure of the visual system. We then focus on our main concern in this chapter: what happens after the light entering the eye is transformed by the receptors into the electrical information that enables us to perceive.

Light: The Stimulus for Vision

Seeing involves a stimulus—light—and a mechanism—the visual system—that reacts to this light. Vision is based on visible light, which is a band of energy within the electromagnetic spectrum. The **electro-** **magnetic spectrum** is a continuum of electromagnetic energy, which is energy produced by electric charges that is radiated as waves (Figure 2.2). The energy in this spectrum can be described by its **wavelength**—the distance between the peaks of the electromagnetic waves. The wavelengths in the electromagnetic spectrum range from extremely short-wavelength gamma rays (wavelength about 10^{-12} meters) to long-wavelength radio waves (about 10^{+4} meters).[2]

Visible light, the energy within the electromagnetic spectrum that humans can perceive, has wavelengths ranging from about 400 to 700 nanometers (nm), where 1 nanometer = 10^{-9} meters. For humans

---

[2] 10^{-12} meters is 0.00000000001 meters, or one ten-billionth of a meter; 10^4 meters is 10,000 meters.

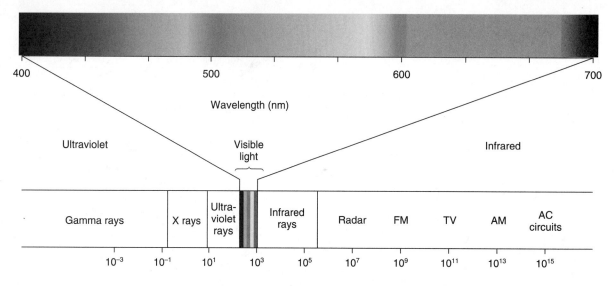

400   500   600   700

Wavelength (nm)

Ultraviolet			Visible light		Infrared				

Gamma rays	X rays	Ultra-violet rays	Infrared rays	Radar	FM	TV	AM	AC circuits

10^{-3} 10^{-1} 10^{1} 10^{3} 10^{5} 10^{7} 10^{9} 10^{11} 10^{13} 10^{15}

Wavelength (nm)

Figure 2.2

The electromagnetic spectrum, showing the wide range of electrical energy in the environment and the small range within this spectrum, called visible light, that we can see.

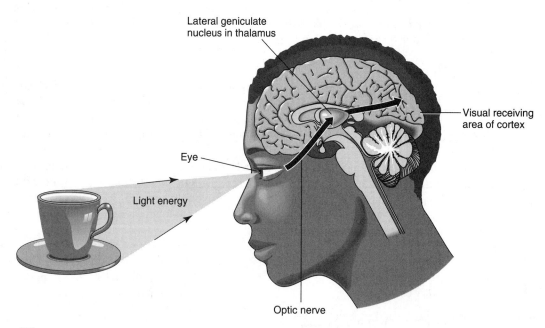

Lateral geniculate nucleus in thalamus

Visual receiving area of cortex

Eye

Light energy

Optic nerve

Figure 2.3

A side view of the visual system, showing the three major sites along the primary visual pathway where processing takes place: the retina, the lateral geniculate nucleus, and the visual receiving area of the cortex. Source: Adapted from Linsay & Norman, 1977.

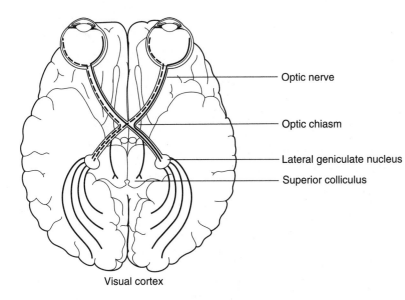

- Optic nerve
- Optic chiasm
- Lateral geniculate nucleus
- Superior colliculus

Visual cortex

Figure 2.4
The visual system seen from underneath the brain showing how some of the nerve fibers from the retina cross over to the opposite side of the brain at the optic chiasm. A small proportion of optic nerve fibers goes to the superior colliculus. Most go to the lateral geniculate nucleus and then to the visual receiving area in the occipital lobe of the cortex.

and some other animals, the wavelength of visible light is associated with the different colors of the spectrum (Color Plate 1.1).

Although we will usually specify light in terms of its wavelength, light can also be described as consisting of small packets of energy called photons, with one photon being the smallest possible packet of light energy. We will use this way of describing light energy when we consider the process of visual transduction later in this chapter.

The Visual System

The three major divisions of the visual system are the **eye**, the **lateral geniculate nucleus** in the thalamus, and the **visual receiving area** in the occipital lobe (Figures 2.3 and 2.4). The visual receiving area is also called the **striate cortex**, because of the presence of white stripes (striate = striped) created by nerve fibers that run through it (Glickstein, 1988). In addition, there are also higher processing areas for vision, which are outside the striate cortex. These higher-level processing areas, which are called the **extrastriate cortex**, include areas in the temporal, parietal, and frontal lobes (Figure 2.5).

These pictures of the overall visual system in Figures 2.3, 2.4, and 2.5 are really "previews of coming events," because, as we indicated in Figure 2.1, we are going to start at the beginning of the visual

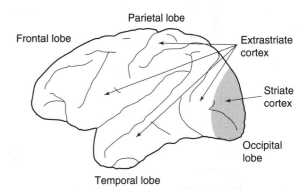

Parietal lobe

Frontal lobe

Extrastriate cortex

Striate cortex

Occipital lobe

Temporal lobe

Figure 2.5
The monkey cortex, showing the primary visual receiving area, or striate cortex, in the occipital lobe. The term extrastriate cortex is used to refer to a number of areas that lie outside the striate cortex, which are activated by visual stimuli.

Receptors and Neural Processing

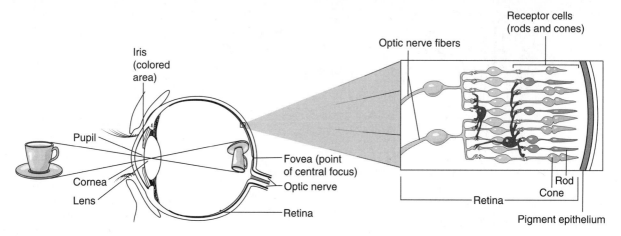

Figure 2.6

A cross section of the human eye. Structures we will be referring to in this chapter are the focusing elements (the lens and the cornea); the retina, which contains the receptors for vision as well as other neurons; the pigment epithelium, a layer containing nutrients and enzymes, upon which the retina rests; and the optic nerve, which contains the optic nerve fibers that transmit electrical energy out of the retina. The small depression in the retina, which is called the fovea, contains only cone receptors. The rest of the retina, which is called the peripheral retina, contains both rod and cone receptors.

system in this chapter by focusing our attention on the eye and on the complex network of neurons called the retina, which lines the back of the eye.

We can appreciate the function of various structures of the eye by following a ray of light that has been reflected from an object (Figure 2.6 and Color Plate 1.2). As light enters the eye, it passes through the transparent cornea and lens, which are the eye's focusing elements. The cornea and lens create a focused image on the retina, and the light in this image stimulates the receptors.

There are two kinds of visual receptors, **rods** and **cones**, which have different properties. These receptors contain light-sensitive chemicals called visual pigments, which react to light and trigger electrical signals. These signals flow through a network of neurons, which consists of four types of cells—**amacrine cells, bipolar cells, horizontal cells**, and **ganglion cells** (Figure 2.7 and Color Plate 1.3). The axons of the ganglion cells leave the eye to form the **optic nerve**, which conducts signals to the lateral geniculate nucleus. The elements of the eye—the cornea and lens and the receptors and various other neurons—all

play important roles in shaping what we see. As you will see in this chapter, they all contribute to the transformations that occur at the beginning of the perceptual process.

THE FIRST TRANSFORMATIONS: LIGHT, RECEPTORS, AND ELECTRICITY

WebTUTOR   Our story of transformation begins as light is reflected from an object into the eye.

Light Is Reflected into the Eye and Focused on the Retina

We see objects because light is reflected from them into our eyes (Figure 2.8). The **cornea**, the transparent covering of the front of the eye, accounts for about 80 percent of the eye's focusing power, but it is fixed in place, so can't change its focus. The lens,

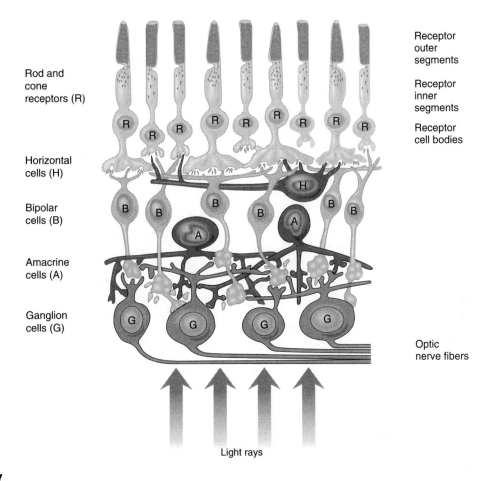

Figure 2.7
Cross section of the primate retina showing the five major cell types and their interconnections. Notice that the receptors are divided into inner segments and outer segments. The outer segments contain light-sensitive chemicals that trigger a signal in response to light. (Adapted from Dowling & Boycott, 1966.)

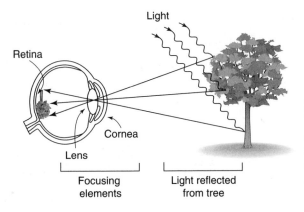

Figure 2.8
We see the tree because light is reflected from the tree into our eyes. This light is focused to create an image of the tree on the retina. The focusing elements that accomplish this are the cornea and the lens. The cornea has the most focusing power, but the lens can change its shape to focus for different distances, a process called accommodation.

Receptors and Neural Processing

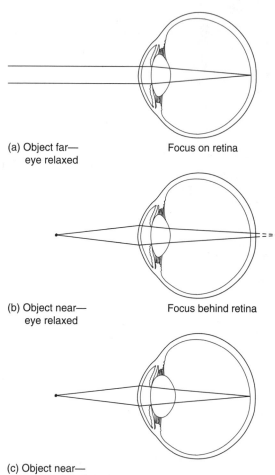

(a) Object far—
eye relaxed   Focus on retina

(b) Object near—
eye relaxed   Focus behind retina

(c) Object near—
accommodation

Figure 2.9
Focusing of light rays by the normal eye. (a) Parallel rays, from a spot of light farther away than 20 feet, are focused onto the retina. (b) When the spot of light is moved closer to the eye, the rays are no longer parallel, and the focus point of the light is pushed back behind the retina. (c) Accommodation, indicated by the fatter lens in this picture, pushes the focus point forward onto the retina.

which supplies the remaining 20 percent of the eye's focusing power, changes its shape to adjust the eye's focus for stimuli located at different distances.

We can understand how the lens works by first considering what happens when we look at an object

that is located more than 20 feet away. Light rays that reach the eye from this distance are essentially parallel (Figure 2.9a), and these parallel rays are brought to a focus on the retina. If, however, we move the object closer to the eye, the rays that enter the eye are no longer parallel and the focus point is pushed back, to a point behind the retina (Figure 2.9b). Of course, the light never comes to a focus in this situation because it is stopped by the retina, and if things remain in this state, both the object's image on the retina and our perception of the object will be out of focus.

To bring the image into focus, the eye increases its **focusing power** by a process called **accommodation**, in which tightening muscles at the front of the eye increases the curvature of the lens so that it gets thicker (Figure 2.9c). This increased curvature bends the light rays passing through the lens more sharply so the focus point moves forward and creates a sharp image on the retina. The beauty of the process of accommodation is that we don't have to think about it; the lens' focusing power is constantly being adjusted to keep the image of the object we are looking at in focus.

 D E M O N S T R A T I O N

Becoming Aware of What Is in Focus

Accommodation occurs unconsciously, so you are usually unaware that the lens is constantly changing its focusing power so that you can see clearly at different distances. This unconscious focusing process works so efficiently that most people assume that everything, near and far, is always in focus. You can demonstrate that this is not so by holding a pencil point up, at arm's length, and looking at an object that is at least 20 feet away. As you look at the faraway object, move the pencil point toward you without actually looking at it (stay focused on the far object). It will probably appear blurred.

Then move the pencil closer, while still looking at the far object, and notice that the point becomes more blurred and appears double. When the pencil is about 12 inches away, focus on the pencil point. You now see the point sharply, but the faraway object you were focusing on before has become blurred. Now, bring the pencil even closer until you can't see the point sharply no matter how hard you try. Notice the strain in your eyes as you try unsuccessfully to bring the point into focus. ●

When you changed focus during this demonstration, you were changing your accommodation. You saw that accommodation enables you to bring both near and far objects into focus but that objects at different distances are not in focus at the same time. You also saw that accommodation has its limits. When the pencil was too close, you couldn't see it clearly, even though you were straining to accommodate. The distance at which your lens can no longer adjust to bring close objects into focus is called the **near point**. We will see in Chapter 16 that the distance of the near point increases as a person gets older, a condition called **presbyopia** (for "old eye") that occurs because aging causes a loss in the ability to accommodate.

Once an image is focused on the retina, the next step in the visual process is stimulation of two kinds of visual receptors, the rods and the cones.

Light Stimulates the Rod and Cone Receptors

Before considering how the visual receptors react to light, we will describe the rods and cones. As we will see, these two types of receptors have different properties, and these properties affect our perceptions.

The structural differences between the rods and cones that gives them their names was first noticed by Max Schultze, who in 1865 looked through his microscope and saw large rod-shaped receptors and smaller cone-shaped receptors. Figure 2.10 shows modern drawings of the rods and cones, and Figure 2.11 is a picture created by a scanning electron microscope.

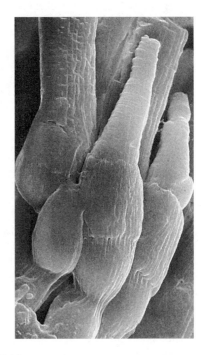

Figure 2.11
Scanning electron micrograph showing the rod and cone outer segments. The rod outer segment on the left is so large that it extends out of the picture, but the cylindrical shape of the rods and the tapered shape of the cones can be clearly seen in this picture (Lewis, Zeevi, & Werblin, 1969).

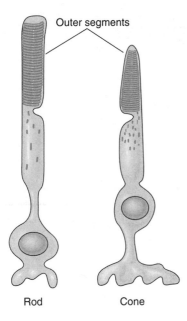

Figure 2.10
A drawing of the rod and cone receptors. The rod- and cone-shaped parts of the receptors are the outer segments, which contain light-sensitive visual pigments.

Receptors and Neural Processing

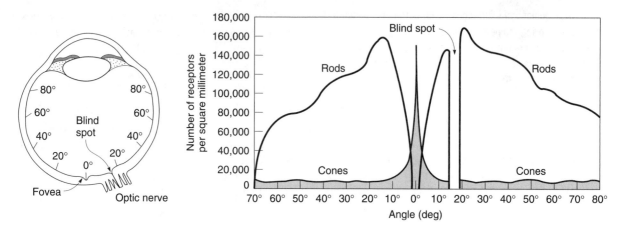

Figure 2.12

The distribution of rods and cones in the retina. The eye on the left indicates locations in degrees relative to the fovea, which are repeated along the bottom of the chart on the right. Notice in the distribution on the right that there are no receptors at all at the blind spot, the place where the ganglion cells leave the eye in the optic nerve. (Adapted from Lindsay & Norman, 1977.)

Distribution of the Rods and Cones on the Retina

The rods and the cones differ not only in their shapes but also in the way they are distributed on the retina (Figure 2.12). There is one small area in the retina, the **fovea** (see Figure 2.6), that contains only cones. The fovea is located directly on the line of sight, so any time we look directly at an object, the center of its image falls on the fovea.

There are about 5 million cones in each retina, but since the fovea is so small, about the size of this "o," it contains only about 50,000 cones—1 percent of the total number of cones in the retina (Tyler, 1997a, 1997b). Most of the cones are in the **peripheral retina**, the area surrounding the fovea that contains both rods and cones. However, in the peripheral retina the rods outnumber the cones by about a 20-to-1 ratio, since all 120 million rods in the retina are in the periphery. See Color Plate 1.4 for pictures of the "mosaic" of receptors created by the rods and cones.

The cross section of the retina in Figure 2.7 shows that the rods and cones are facing away from the light, so the light passes through the other neurons in the retina before it reaches the receptors. One reason the receptors face away from the light is so

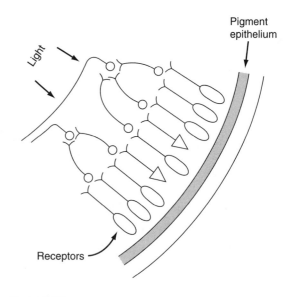

Figure 2.13

Close-up of the retina showing how the receptors face away from the light so the light must pass through other retinal neurons before reaching the receptors. Since these neurons are transparent, they do not prevent the light from reaching the receptors.

they can be in contact with a layer of cells called the **pigment epithelium** (Figure 2.13), which contains nutrients and chemicals called enzymes that are vital to the receptors' functioning in ways we will describe later in this chapter. Backward-facing receptors pose little problem for vision, however, since the light easily passes through the transparent ganglion, amacrine, bipolar, and horizontal cells on its way to the receptors.

The backward-facing receptors do, however, create a problem for the ganglion cells: If the receptors lined the entire back of the eye, they would block the ganglion cells from leaving the eye in the optic nerve. Figure 2.14 shows how the eye solves this problem. There is a small area with no receptors, where the eye's 1 million ganglion cell fibers stream out of the eye to form the optic nerve. Since there are no receptors in the place where the optic nerve leaves the eye, this area is called the **blind spot**. Although you are not normally aware of the blind spot, you can become aware of it by doing the following demonstration.

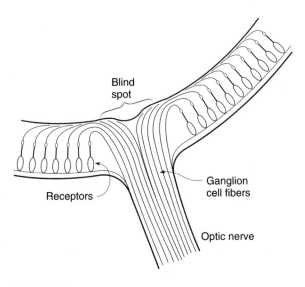

Figure 2.14
There are no receptors at the place where the optic nerve leaves the eye. This enables the receptor's ganglion cell fibers to flow into the optic nerve. The absence of receptors in this area creates the blind spot.

D E M O N S T R A T I O N

"Seeing" the Blind Spot

You can demonstrate the existence of the blind spot perceptually by closing your right eye and, with the cross in Figure 2.15 aligned with your left eye, looking at the cross while moving the book (or yourself) slowly back and forth. When the book is 6 to 12 inches from your eye, the circle disappears. This is the point at which the image of the circle is falling on the blind spot.

Why aren't we usually aware of the blind spot? One reason is that the blind spot is located off to the side of our visual field, where objects are not in sharp focus. Because of this and because we don't know exactly where to look for it (as opposed to the demonstration, in which we are focusing our attention on the circle), the blind spot is hard to detect.

But the most important reason that we don't see the blind spot is that some mechanism in the brain "fills in" the place where the image disappears (Churchland & Ramachandran, 1996). Think about what happened when the spot in the demonstration disappeared. The place where the spot used to be wasn't replaced by a hole or by nothingness—it was filled in by the white page.

D E M O N S T R A T I O N

Filling in the Blind Spot

To experience the blind spot's filling-in process in another way, close your right eye and, with the cross in Figure 2.16 lined up with your left eye, move the "wheel" toward you. When the center of the wheel falls on your blind spot, notice how the spokes of the wheel fill in the hole (Ramachandran, 1992).

Figure 2.15

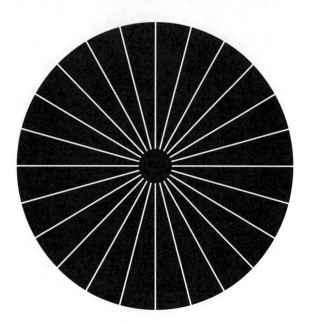

Figure 2.16
View this pattern as described in the text, and observe what happens when the center of the wheel falls on your blind spot (Ramachandran, 1992).

Transduction of Light into Electricity The part of the receptors called the **outer segments** are the center of action for the visual receptors, because it is here that the light acts to create electricity. These outer segments contain stacks of discs (Figure 2.17a) which contain visual pigment molecules (Figure 2.17b). These molecules, which loop back and forth across the disc membrane seven times (Figure 2.17c), have two components: (1) a large protein called **opsin** with a molecular weight of about 40,000, and (2) a small light-sensitive molecule called **retinal** (molecular weight = 268).

Retinal, which is attached to the opsin at the point shown, reacts to light and is therefore responsible for **visual transduction**—the transformation of light energy into electrical energy. The transduction process begins when the light-sensitive retinal absorbs one photon of light. (Remember that a photon is the smallest possible packet of light energy.) When the retinal absorbs this photon it changes its shape (Figure 2.18), a process called **isomerization**.

How does this isomerization result in an electrical signal? This question has been approached in two ways: Psychophysical experiments have shown that only one visual pigment molecule needs to be iso-

merized to excite a receptor, and physiological and biochemical experiments have uncovered the molecular mechanisms that make this excitation possible. We will describe the psychophysical experiment and the reasoning behind it in some detail, since it is an excellent example of how research at the psychophysical level of analysis can lead to physiological conclusions.

The psychophysical experiment that showed that only one visual pigment molecule needs to be activated to excite a rod receptor was done in 1942 by Selig Hecht, Simon Shlaer, and Maurice Pirenne (1942). They did this by using a precisely calibrated light source to measure the absolute threshold for detecting a light. They determined that this threshold is 100 photons, and that of these 100 photons, 50 bounce off the surface of the cornea before entering the eye or are reflected or absorbed by the lens, just inside the eye, or by the jellylike vitreous humor that fills the inside of the eye. Of the remaining 50 photons, only about 7 are actually absorbed by visual pigment molecules. The rest either slip between the receptors or pass through a receptor without hitting the light-sensitive part of a visual pigment molecule. Thus, Hecht determined that 7 visual pigment

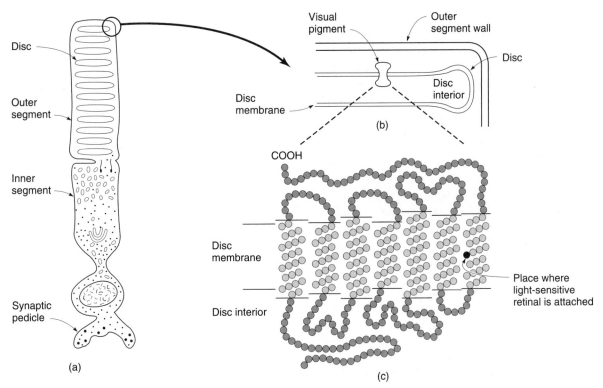

Figure 2.17

(a) Rod receptor showing discs in the outer segment. (b) Close-up of one disc showing one visual pigment molecule in the membrane. Notice how the molecule straddles the disc membrane. (c) Close-up showing how the protein opsin in one visual pigment molecule crosses the disc membrane seven times. The light-sensitive retinal molecule is attached at the place indicated.

Figure 2.18

Model of a visual pigment molecule. The horizontal part of the model shows a tiny portion of the huge opsin molecule near where the retinal is attached. The smaller molecule on top of the opsin is the light-sensitive retinal. The model on the left shows the retinal molecule's shape before it absorbs light. The model on the right shows the retinal molecule's shape after it absorbs light. This change in shape is one of the steps that accompanies the generation of an electrical response in the receptor.

Receptors and Neural Processing

molecules need to be activated for the subject to see a light. (See also Sackett, 1972.)

But Hecht wasn't satisfied just to show that 7 visual pigment molecules need to be activated for perception to occur. He reasoned that since the flash of light seen by the subject covered about 500 receptors, it is highly unlikely that more than one of the 7 activated visual pigment molecules would be in the same receptor. Look at it this way: You are in a helicopter flying over an array of 500 small cylinders. When you are directly above the cylinders, you release 7 Ping-Pong balls. What is the probability that 2 of these balls would fall into the same cylinder? The answer is "very small." Similarly, it is equally unlikely that of the 7 visual pigment molecules that absorb light, 2 of them would be in the same receptor. Hecht therefore concluded that only one visual pigment molecule needs to be isomerized in order to *excite a rod receptor* and that we *see the light* when 7 receptors are activated simultaneously. Notice that although Hecht's measurements were psychophysical, his results led to a conclusion about the physiology of the visual receptors (see Goldstein, 2001).

About 30 years after Hecht, Shlaer, and Pirenne concluded that a rod can be excited by the isomerization of only one visual pigment molecule, physiologists began uncovering the physiological mechanisms that make this amazing feat possible. What the physiologists found was that isomerizing a single visual pigment molecule triggers thousands of chemical reactions, which, in turn, trigger thousands more (Figure 2.19).

A biological chemical that in small amounts facilitates chemical reactions in this way is called an enzyme, and the sequence of reactions triggered by the activated visual pigment molecule is therefore called the **enzyme cascade**. Just as pulling the plug covering the drain in your bathtub can empty the entire tub, isomerizing one visual pigment molecule can cause a chemical effect that is large enough to activate the entire rod receptor. For more specific details as to how this is accomplished see Baylor (1992), Ranganathan, Harris, and Zuker (1991), Stryer (1986), and Tessier-Lavigne (1991).

The visual pigments play an essential role in vision by triggering the electrical response in the

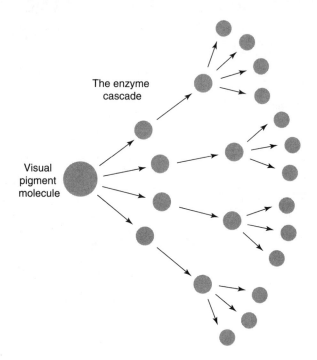

Figure 2.19

This sequence symbolizes the enzyme cascade that occurs when a single visual pigment molecule is activated by absorption of a quantum of light. In the actual sequence of events, each visual pigment molecule activates hundreds more molecules, which, in turn, each activates about a thousand more molecules. The net result is that isomerization of one visual pigment molecule activates about a million other molecules. This massive activation leads to generation of an electrical signal in the receptor.

receptors. As we will see in the next sections, the properties of the visual pigments determine a number of the basic properties of vision.

VISUAL PIGMENTS AND PERCEPTION

WebTUTOR   At the beginning of the chapter we noted that when you turn off the lights you can't see well at first but that you can begin to make out things as you spend more time in the dark. This increase in the eye's sensitivity in the dark is a process called **dark adaptation**. We will now describe how this process illustrates a difference between rod visual pigments and cone visual pigments.

Dark Adaptation of the Rods and Cones

You can experience the gradual increase in the eye's sensitivity in the dark by doing the following demonstration.

D E M O N S T R A T I O N

Spending Some Time in Your Closet

Find a dark place where you will make some observations as you adapt to the dark. A closet is a good place to do this, because it is possible to regulate the intensity of light inside the closet by opening or closing the door. The idea is to create an environment in which there is dim light (no light at all, as in a darkroom with the safelight out, is too dark).

Take this book into the closet. Have the book opened to this page. Close the closet door all the way so it is very dark, and then open the door slowly until you can just barely make out the white circle on the far left of Figure 2.20 but can't see the others or can see them only as being very dim.

Your task is simple. Just sit in the dark and become aware that your sensitivity is increasing by noting how the circles to the right in Figure 2.20 slowly become visible over a period of about 20 minutes. Also note that once a circle becomes visible, it gets easier to see as time passes. If you stare directly at the circles, they may fade, so move your eyes around every so often. Also, the circles will be easier to see if you look slightly above them.

This demonstration demands patience, but remember that to become a Buddhist monk you would have to sit motionless in front of the temple door for two days! Sitting in a closet for 20 minutes is easy compared to that. As you sit there, also notice that other objects in the closet slowly become visible, but be careful not to look directly at the light coming through the door, because that will slow the process of dark adaptation.   ●

Although it is easy to demonstrate that your sensitivity to light increases as you spend time in the dark, it is not obvious that this increase takes place in two distinct stages: an initial rapid stage and a later, slower stage. We will now describe three ways of measuring the dark adaptation curve that show that the initial rapid stage is due to adaptation of the cone receptors and that the second slower stage is due to adaptation of the rod receptors. We will first describe how to measure a **dark-adaptation curve**, a plot of sensitivity versus the time in the dark, which shows the two-stage process of dark adaptation. We will then measure the dark adaptation of the cones alone and of the rods alone. Once we have done this we will show how the different adaptation rates of the rods and the cones can be explained by differences in their visual pigments.

Determining a Two-Stage Dark-Adaptation Curve
In all of our dark-adaptation experiments, we ask our observer to adjust the intensity of a small, flashing test light so he or she can just barely see it. This is similar to the psychophysical *method of adjustment* that we described in Chapter 1 (see p. 13). In the first experiment, our observer looks at a small fixation point while paying attention to a flashing test light that is off to the side. Since the observer is looking directly at

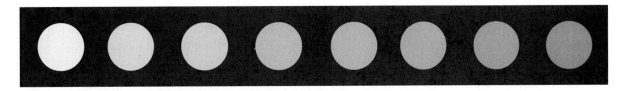

Figure 2.20

the fixation point, its image falls on the fovea, and the image of the test light falls in the periphery (Figure 2.21). Thus, the test light stimulates both rods and cones, and any adaptation measured with this test light should reflect the activity of both the rod and the cone receptors. The procedure for measuring the dark-adaptation curve is as follows:

- Light adapt the observer by exposure to an intense light.

- Measure the **light-adapted sensitivity** by having the observer adjust the intensity of the test light so he or she can just barely see it (Figure 2.22).

- Turn off the light. This begins the process of dark adaptation.

- Measure the course of dark adaptation by having the observer keep adjusting the intensity of the test light so it remains just barely detectable.

The solid line of Figure 2.22 shows the dark-adaptation curve measured during 28 minutes in the dark. As dark adaptation proceeds, the observer slowly turns down the intensity of the test light. Since decreases in test light intensity correspond to increases in sensitivity (a person is more sensitive if he

or she can detect less intense lights), we can describe dark adaptation as an increase in sensitivity over time.

The dark-adaptation curve indicates that the observer's sensitivity increases in two phases. It increases rapidly for the first 3 to 4 minutes after the light is extinguished and then levels off; then, after about 7 to 10 minutes, sensitivity begins to increase further and continues to do so for another 20 to 30 minutes. The sensitivity at the end of dark adaptation, labeled **dark-adapted sensitivity**, is about 100,000 times greater than the light-adapted sensitivity measured before dark adaptation began.

Measuring Cone Adaptation   To measure the adaptation of the cones, we repeat the first experiment but have the observer look directly at a test light so small that its entire image falls within the all-cone fovea. Since the test light is stimulating only cones, the resulting dark-adaptation curve, indicated by the dashed curve in Figure 2.22, reflects only the activity of the cones. This curve matches the initial phase of our original dark-adaptation curve but does not include the second phase. Does this mean that the second part of the curve is due to the rods? We can show that the answer to this question is "yes" by doing another experiment.

Measuring Rod Adaptation   We know that the dashed curve of Figure 2.22 is due only to cone adaptation because our test light was focused on the all-cone fovea. To determine a pure rod dark-adaptation curve, we use a **rod monochromat**—a person who has a retina that, because of a rare genetic defect, contains only rods. (Students sometimes wonder why we can't simply place the test flash in the periphery, which contains mostly rods. The answer is that the few cones in the periphery will influence the beginning of the dark-adaptation curve.)

Because the rod monochromat has no cones, we can measure the light-adapted sensitivity of the rods just before we turn off the lights. (Normally, the cones control vision when the lights are on, so they cover up any rod activity that might be there.) The point we determine, which is the "rod light-adapted sensitivity," is much lower than that of the cones. Once dark adaptation begins, the rods increase their

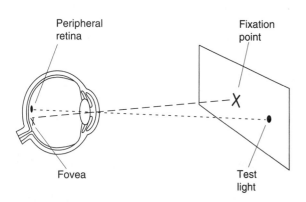

Figure 2.21
Viewing conditions for a dark-adaptation experiment. The image of the fixation point falls on the fovea, and the image of the test light falls in the peripheral retina.

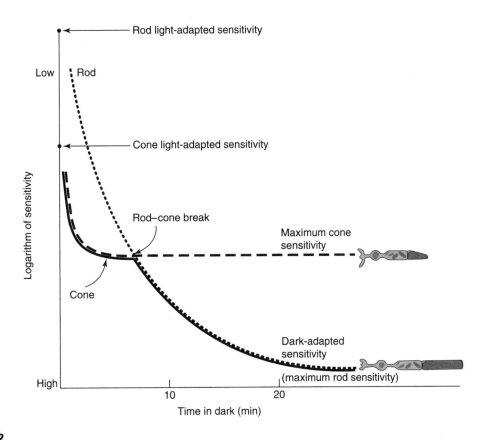

Figure 2.22

Dark-adaptation curves. Actually, three curves are shown in this figure. The solid line shows the two-stage dark-adaptation curve measured in experiment 1, with a cone branch at the beginning and a rod branch at the end. The dashed line shows the cone adaptation curve measured in experiment 2. The curves actually begin at the point marked "cone light-adapted sensitivity," but there is a slight delay between the time the lights are turned off and the time the measurement of the curves begins. The dotted line shows the rod adaptation curve measured in experiment 3. The point marked "rod light-adapted sensitivity" is where the curve actually begins. Note that moving downward indicates an increase in sensitivity.

sensitivity and reach their final dark-adapted level in about 25 minutes (Rushton, 1961). The fact that the rods begin adapting to the dark immediately after the light is extinguished means that they are also adapting during the cone phase of a normal person's dark-adaptation curve; however, we aren't aware of this early rod adaptation because cones are more sensitive at the beginning of dark adaptation.

We can summarize the process of dark adaptation in a normal observer as follows: Both the rods and cones begin gaining in sensitivity as soon as the lights are extinguished, but since the cones are more sensitive at the beginning of dark adaptation, they determine the early part of the dark-adaptation curve. After about 3 to 5 minutes, the cones finish their adaptation, and the curve levels off. However, by about 7 minutes after the beginning of dark adaptation, the rods (which have been increasing in sensitivity all along) finally catch up to the cones and then become more sensitive. When this occurs, the curve starts down again, creating the **rod–cone break**—the place where the sensitivity of the rods begins to determine the dark-adaptation curve (Figure 2.22). As the rods continue their adaptation, the dark-adaptation curve continues downward for about 15 more minutes.

The rods reach their maximum sensitivity by about 20 to 30 minutes from the beginning of dark adaptation, compared to only 3 to 4 minutes for the cones. We will now show that these differences in the rate of adaptation can be traced to a process called visual pigment regeneration that occurs with different speeds in the rods and the cones.

Visual Pigment Regeneration   When the visual pigment absorbs light, the light-sensitive retinal molecule changes shape and triggers the transduction process. It then separates from the larger opsin molecule, and this separation causes the retina to become lighter in color, a process called **pigment bleaching** (Color Plate 1.6). Before the visual pigment can again change light energy into electrical energy, the retinal and the opsin must be rejoined. This process, which is called **pigment regeneration**, occurs in the dark with the aid of enzymes supplied to the visual pigments by the nearby pigment epithelium (refer to Figure 2.13).

As the retinal and opsin components of the visual pigment recombine in the dark, the pigment begins to become darker again. William Rushton (1961) devised a procedure to measure the regeneration of visual pigment in humans by measuring the darkening of the visual pigment during dark adaptation. Rushton's measurements showed that cone pigment takes 6 minutes to regenerate completely, while rod pigment takes over 30 minutes. When he compared the course of pigment regeneration to the rate of psychophysical dark adaptation, he found that the rate of cone dark adaptation matched the rate of cone pigment regeneration and the rate of rod dark adaptation matched the rate of rod pigment regeneration.

Rushton's result demonstrated two important connections between perception and physiology:

1. The increase in sensitivity of both rods and cones that occurs during dark adaptation is related to visual pigment regeneration.

2. The slow adaptation of the rods compared to the cones occurs because rod pigment regenerates more slowly than cone pigment.

The next time you enter a darkened room, remember that both the rod and the cone visual pigments begin regenerating immediately and that the regenerating pigments are what enable you, after 10 or 15 minutes in the dark, to see dimly illuminated objects that you couldn't see just after you turned out the light.

Spectral Sensitivity of the Rods and Cones

Another way to show that perception is determined by the properties of the visual pigments is to compare rod and cone **spectral sensitivity**—an observer's sensitivity to light at each wavelength across the visible spectrum.

Rod and Cone Spectral Sensitivity Curves   In our dark-adaptation experiments, we used a white test light, which contains all wavelengths in the visible spectrum. To determine spectral sensitivity, we use flashes of **monochromatic light**, light that contains only a single wavelength. We determine the threshold for seeing these monochromatic lights for wavelengths across the visible spectrum. For example, we might first determine the threshold for seeing a 420-nm light, then a 440-nm light, and so on, using one of the psychophysical methods for measuring threshold described in Chapter 1. The result is the curve in Figure 2.23a, which shows that the threshold for seeing light is lowest in the middle of the spectrum; that is, less light is needed to see wavelengths in the middle of the spectrum than to see wavelengths at either the short- or long-wavelength ends of the spectrum.

We can change threshold to **sensitivity** by the formula, sensitivity = 1/threshold, and when we do this, our threshold curve of Figure 2.23a becomes the sensitivity curve of Figure 2.23b, which is called a **spectral sensitivity curve**. We measure the cone spectral sensitivity curve by having people look directly at the test light, so that it stimulates only the cones in the fovea. We measure the rod spectral sensitivity curve by measuring sensitivity after the eye is dark adapted (so the rods are the most sensitive receptors) and presenting test flashes off to the side of the fixation point.

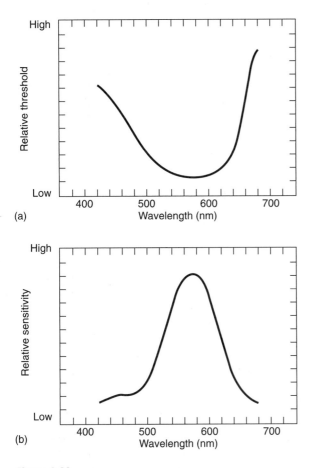

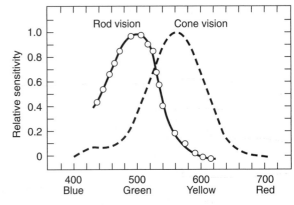

Figure 2.24

Spectral sensitivity curves for rod vision and cone vision. The maximum sensitivities of these two curves have been set equal to 1.0. However, as we saw in Figure 2.22, the relative sensitivities of the rods and the cones depend on the conditions of adaptation: The cones are more sensitive in the light, and the rods are more sensitive in the dark. The circles plotted on top of the rod curve represent the absorption spectrum of the rod visual pigment. (From Wald, 1964; Wald & Brown, 1958.)

Figure 2.23

(a) The threshold for seeing a light versus wavelength.
(b) If we take the reciprocal of the thresholds of the curve in (a) (reciprocal = 1/threshold), the curve turns over and becomes a plot of sensitivity versus wavelength, commonly known as a spectral sensitivity curve. *(Adapted from Wald, 1964.)*

The cone and rod spectral sensitivity curves, shown in Figure 2.24, show that the rods are more sensitive to short-wavelength light than are the cones, with the rods being most sensitive to light of 500 nm and the cones being most sensitive to light of 560 nm. This difference in the sensitivity of the rods and the cones to different wavelengths means that, as vision shifts from the cones to the rods during dark adaptation, we become relatively more sensitive to short-

wavelength light, that is, light nearer the blue and green end of the spectrum.

You may have noticed an effect of this shift to short-wavelength sensitivity if you have observed how green foliage seems to stand out more near dusk. This shift from cone vision to rod vision that causes this enhanced perception of short wavelengths during dark adaptation is called the **Purkinje** (Pur-kin-jee) **shift**, after Johann Purkinje, who described this effect in 1825. You can experience this shift in color sensitivity that occurs during dark adaptation by dark adapting one of your eyes, by closing it for about 10 minutes, and then switching back and forth between your eyes and noticing how the blue flower in Color Plate 1.5 is brighter compared to the red flower in your dark-adapted eye.

Pigment Absorption Spectra The difference between the rod and cone spectral sensitivity curves is caused by differences in the absorption spectra of the rod and cone visual pigments. An **absorption spectrum** is a plot of the amount of light absorbed by a substance versus the wavelength of the light. The absorption spectra of the rod and cone pigments are shown in Figure 2.25. The rod pigment absorbs best at 500 nm, the blue-green area of the spectrum.

There are three absorption spectra for the cones because there are three different cone pigments, each contained in its own receptor. The **short-wavelength pigment** absorbs light best at about 419 nm; the **medium-wavelength pigment** absorbs light best at about 531 nm; and the **long-wavelength pigment** absorbs light best at about 558 nm.

The absorption of the rod visual pigment closely matches the rod spectral sensitivity curve (Figure 2.24), and the short-, medium-, and long-wavelength cone pigments that absorb best at 419, 531, and 558 nm, respectively, add together to result in a psychophysical spectral sensitivity curve that peaks at 560 nm. Since there are fewer short-wavelength receptors and therefore much less of the short-wavelength pigment, the spectral sensitivity curve is determined mainly by the medium- and long-wavelength pigments (Bowmaker and Dartnall, 1980; Stiles, 1953). (See Color Plate 1.4b.)

It is clear that the rates of rod and cone dark adaptation and the shapes of the rod and cone spectral sensitivity curves are determined by the properties of the rod and cone visual pigments. The idea that our perceptions are determined by physiological properties, such as the characteristics of the visual pigments, is a theme that continues throughout this book. Next, we will describe what happens as the electrical signals generated by the rods and cones are transmitted to the other neurons in the retina. See Summary Table 2.1 for an overview of the material we have covered so far.

NEURAL PROCESSING BY CONVERGENCE

WebTUTOR   The transformation of electrical signals that occurs as the signals generated by the rods and cones travel through the retina is accomplished by neural processing, which we introduced in Chapter 1 (see page 5). One way neural processing occurs is through arrangements of neural connections. We will describe how these connections differ in the rods and the cones and how these differences affect perception.

The Convergence of Rod and Cone Signals

When we look at how the rods and cones connect to other neurons in the retina we see that they differ in the amount of convergence. **Convergence** occurs when more than one neuron synapses on another neuron. Figure 2.26 illustrates different amounts of convergence. In 2.26a there is no convergence, since our target neuron receives signals from just one other neuron. In 2.26b some convergence occurs, with two neurons converging onto one, and in 2.26c more convergence occurs, with six neurons converging onto one.

There is more convergence of signals from the rods than there is for signals from the cones. We can appreciate this difference by considering that the 126 million receptors in each retina converge on 1 million ganglion cells. Since there are 120 million rods in the retina but only 6 million cones, the rods must converge much more than the cones. On the average, about 120 rods pool their signals to one ganglion cell (Figure 2.27), but only about six cones send signals to a single ganglion cell.

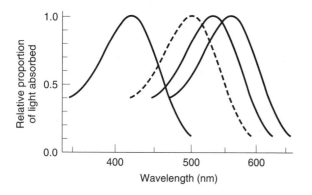

Figure 2.25

Absorption spectra of the human rod pigment (dashed curve) and the three human cone pigments. All curves have been scaled so their maximum absorption equals 1.0. (From Wald & Brown, 1958; Dartnall, Bowmaker, & Mollon, 1983.)

Perception and the Nervous System

We do not simply perceive what is out there in the environment. We perceive what is out there as filtered through the properties of our nervous system.

Light and the Visual System

Visible light, the narrow band of electromagnetic energy that we can see, is the stimulus for vision. The three major divisions of the visual system are the eye, the lateral geniculate nucleus in the thalamus, and the visual receiving area in the occipital cortex. There are also cortical areas outside the visual receiving area, called extrastriate cortex, that are responsible for higher-level processing.

The Beginning of the Visual Process

The visual process begins when light reflected from objects enters the eye and is focused by the cornea and lens to form a sharp image on the retina. The process of accommodation, in which the lens changes shape, enables the eye to adjust focus for different distances.

The Visual Receptors

There are two different types of receptors, rods and cones, which have different properties. They are distributed differently on the retina, with a small area called the fovea containing only cones. When we look directly at an object, its image is formed on the fovea. The place where the optic nerve leaves the eye contains no receptors and is therefore called the blind spot.

Transduction

When a light-sensitive visual pigment molecule in a receptor absorbs light, it isomerizes and starts a chain reaction that leads to activation of the receptor. Psychophysical experiments have shown that a rod receptor can be activated by the isomerization of one molecule, and activation of seven rod receptors can result in perception.

Visual Pigments and Perception

Dark-adaptation experiments indicate that a person's sensitivity increases in the dark in two phases: a fast phase, which is controlled by the cones; and a slower phase, which is controlled by the rods. The difference in the rate of cone and rod adaptation is caused largely by differences in the rates at which the cone and rod visual pigments regenerate after bleaching. The rods and cones also differ in their spectral sensitivity, the sensitivity to light at different wavelengths across the spectrum, and these differences have been linked to the different absorption properties of the rod and cone visual pigments.

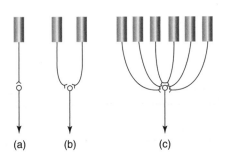

(a)   (b)   (c)

Figure 2.26

Different degrees of convergence. (a) No convergence; (b) a little convergence, since two receptors synapse on the other neuron; (c) more convergence, with six receptors synapsing on the other neuron.

This difference between rod and cone convergence becomes even greater when we consider that many of the foveal cones have "private lines" to ganglion cells. In these situations, with each ganglion cell receiving signals from only one cone, there is no convergence. The greater convergence of the rods compared to the cones translates into two differences in perception: (1) the rods are more sensitive in the dark than the cones, and (2) the cones result in better detail vision than the rods.

The Rods Are More Sensitive in the Dark than the Cones

One reason rod vision is more sensitive than cone vision is that it takes less light to generate a response from an individual rod receptor than from an individ-

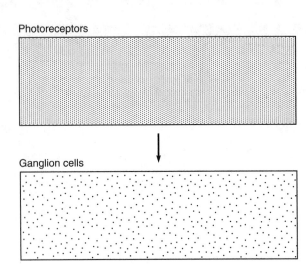

Photoreceptors

Ganglion cells

Figure 2.27

Convergence of receptors onto ganglion cells in the periphery of the rabbit retina. Each dot in the top panel represents three receptors, and each dot in the bottom panel represents one ganglion cell. The large difference between the number of receptors and the number of ganglion cells means that signals from many receptors converge onto each ganglion cell. (From Masland, 1988.)

ual cone receptor (Barlow & Mollon, 1982; Baylor, 1992), but there is another reason as well: The rods have greater convergence than the cones.

How does the difference in rod and cone convergence translate into differences in the maximum sensitivities of the cones and the rods? We can answer this question by considering the two circuits in Figure 2.28, in which five rod receptors converge onto one ganglion cell and five cone receptors each synapse onto their own ganglion cells. We have left out the bipolar, horizontal, and amacrine cells in these circuits for simplicity, but our conclusions will not be affected by these omissions.

For the purposes of our discussion, we will assume that we can present small spots of light to individual rods and cones. We will also make the following additional assumptions:

1. One unit of light intensity causes one unit of response in a receptor.

2. A ganglion cell must receive ten "response units" to fire.

3. The ganglion cell must fire before perception of the light can occur.

When we present spots of light with an intensity of 1.0 to each receptor, the rod ganglion cell receives 5 response units, 1 from each of the 5 receptors, and each of the cone ganglion cells receives 1.0 response units, 1 from each receptor. Thus, when intensity = 1.0, neither the rod nor the cone ganglion cells fire. If, however, we increase the intensity to 2.0, the rod ganglion cell receives 2.0 response units from each of its five receptors, for a total of 10 response units. This total reaches the threshold for the rods' ganglion cell, it fires, and we see the light. Meanwhile, at the same intensity, the cones' ganglion cells are still below threshold, each receiving only 2 response units. For the cones' ganglion cells to fire, we must increase the intensity to 10.0.

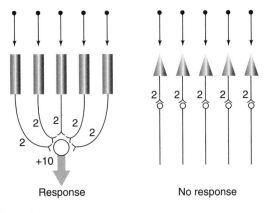

Response   No response

Figure 2.28

The wiring of the rods (left) and the cones (right). The dot and arrow above each receptor represent "spots" of light that stimulate the receptor. The numbers represent the number of response units generated by the rods and the cones in response to a spot intensity of 2.0. At this intensity, the rod ganglion cell receives ten units of excitation and fires, but each cone ganglion cell receives only two units and therefore does not fire. Thus, the rods' greater spatial summation enables them to cause ganglion cell firing at lower stimulus intensities than the cones'.

These results demonstrate that one reason for the rods' high sensitivity compared to the cones' is that of the rods' greater convergence, which creates greater **spatial summation** in the rods than in the cones. That is, many rods summate their responses by feeding into the same ganglion cell, but cones summate less, because only one or a few cones feed into a single ganglion cell.

The Cones Result in Better Detail Vision than the Rods

Have you ever found it difficult to locate a friend's face in a crowd? Unless your friend attracted your attention by wearing a distinctive color of clothing or by shouting your name, you probably found it necessary to scan the crowd, looking at one face after another, until you finally came upon your friend's face.

The reason you needed to scan the crowd was that to see enough detail to recognize a face you need to focus the image of the face on your fovea, which contains only cones. Only all-cone foveal vision has good **visual acuity**—the ability to see details. The high acuity of foveal vision means that the particular face at which you are looking is seen in enough detail to be recognized, while the rest of the faces in the crowd fall on the rod-rich peripheral retina and can't be recognized.

Visual acuity can be measured in a number of ways, one of which is to determine how far apart two dots have to be before a space can be seen between them. We make this measurement by presenting a pair of closely spaced dots and asking whether there are one or two dots. We can also measure acuity by determining how large the elements of a checkerboard or a pattern of alternating black and white bars must be for the pattern to be detected. The letters of the Snellen chart (left) and the Landolt rings (right) in Figure 2.29 are perhaps the most familiar ways of measuring acuity. The observer's task is to identify the Snellen letters or to indicate the location of the gaps in the Landolt rings.

In the demonstration above, we showed that acuity is better in the fovea than in the periphery. Since you were light adapted, the comparison in this demonstration was between the foveal cones, which are tightly packed, and the peripheral cones, which are more widely spaced. Comparing the foveal cones to the rods results in even greater differences in acuity. We can make this comparison by measuring how acuity changes during dark adaptation. When we do this, we find that visual acuity drops (that is, details must be larger in order to be seen) as vision changes from cone function to rod function during dark adaptation. This poor acuity of the rods is why the sharp

 D E M O N S T R A T I O N

Foveal versus Peripheral Acuity

D I H C N R L A Z I F W N S M Q P Z K D **X**

You can demonstrate that foveal vision is superior to peripheral vision for seeing details by looking at the X in the line of letters and, without moving your eyes, seeing how many letters you can identify to the left. If you do this without cheating (no fair moving your eyes!), you will find that although you can read the letters right next to the X, you can read only a few of the letters that are off to the side and therefore fall on the peripheral retina.   ●

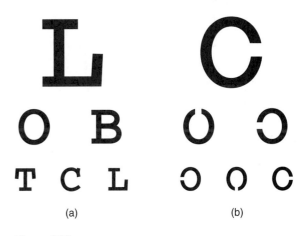

(a)   (b)

Figure 2.29
Snellen letters (a) and Landolt rings (b) used to test visual acuity. (From Riggs, 1965.)

details vanished when you turned out the lights in the example at the beginning of the chapter and is also why it is difficult to read in dim illuminations.

We can understand how differences in rod and cone wiring explain the cones' greater acuity by returning to our rod and cone neural circuits. As we stimulate the receptors in the circuits in Figure 2.30 with two spots of light, each with an intensity of 10, we will ask the following question: Under what conditions can we tell that there are two separate spots of light? We begin by presenting the two spots next to each other, as in Figure 2.30a. When we do this, the rod ganglion cell fires, and the two adjacent cone ganglion cells fire. The firing of the single rod ganglion cell provides no hint that two separate spots were presented, and the firing of the two adjacent cone ganglion cells could have been caused by a sin-

gle large spot. However, when we spread the two spots apart, as in Figure 2.30b, the output of the cones signals two separate spots, because there is a silent ganglion cell between the two that are firing, but the output of the rods still provides no information that would enable us to say that there are two spots. Thus, the rods' convergence decreases their ability to resolve details (Teller, 1990).

We have seen that convergence is one of the ways that neurons process information. We will now show how excitation and inhibition provide another way for neurons to process information.

NEURAL PROCESSING BY EXCITATION AND INHIBITION

WebTUTOR All sensory systems consist of networks of neurons that we will call **neural circuits**. A neural circuit is nothing more than a number of interconnected neurons. Neural circuits can be very simple, consisting of a few neurons connected by excitatory synapses, like the ones we used to illustrate convergence in Figure 2.30, or extremely complex, consisting of hundreds or thousands of neurons that are interconnected in complex ways and contain both excitatory and inhibitory synapses. To illustrate how neural circuits can process electrical signals, we will compare how three different neural circuits affect a neuron's response to a bar-shaped light stimulus of different lengths.

Introduction to Neural Circuits

We begin with a simple neural circuit and then increase the complexity of this circuit in two stages, noting how this increased complexity affects the circuit's response to the stimulus. In these circuits we represent receptors by ellipses ($\bigcirc$), cell bodies by circles (o), nerve fibers by straight lines (—), excitatory synapses by Y's ($\prec$) and inhibitory synapses by T's (—|). For this example, we will assume that the receptors respond to light, although the principles we will establish hold for any form of stimulation.

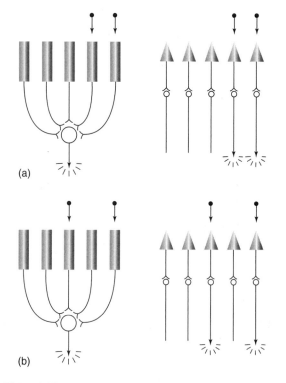

Figure 2.30
Neural circuits for the rods (left) and the cones (right). The receptors are being stimulated by two spots of light.

First, let's consider the circuit in Figure 2.31. We call this circuit a **linear circuit** because there is no convergence—the signal generated by each receptor travels straight to the next neuron, and no other neurons are involved. Also, all six of the synapses in this circuit are excitatory. We stimulate the circuit by first illuminating receptor 4 with a spot of light. We then change this spot into a bar of light by adding light to illuminate receptors 3, 4, and 5 (3 through 5), then receptors 2 through 6, and finally receptors 1 through 7. When we measure the response of neuron B and indicate this response in the graph to the right of the circuit, we find that neuron B fires when we stimulate receptor 4 but that stimulating the other receptors has no effect on neuron B, since it is still receiving exactly the same input from receptor 4. For the linear circuit, therefore, the firing of neuron B simply indicates that its receptor has been stimulated and doesn't

provide any information about the length of the bar of light.

We now increase the complexity of the circuit by adding convergence, as shown in the circuit in Figure 2.32. In this circuit, receptors 1 and 2 converge onto neuron A; 6 and 7 converge onto C; and 3, 4, and 5 and A and C converge onto B. As in the previous circuit, all of the synapses are excitatory; but, with the addition of convergence, cell B now collects information from all of the receptors. When we monitor the firing rate of neuron B, we find that each time we increase the length of the stimulus, neuron B's firing rate increases, as shown in the graph in Figure 2.32. This occurs because stimulating more receptors increases the amount of excitatory transmitter released onto neuron B. Thus, in this circuit, neuron B's response provides information about the length of the stimulus.

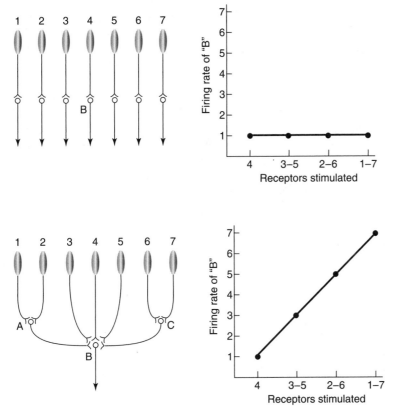

Figure 2.31
A linear circuit (left) and the responses of neuron B generated as we increase the number of receptors stimulated (right). Stimulating receptor 4 causes neuron B to fire, but stimulating the other neurons has no effect because they are not connected with neuron B.

Figure 2.32
When we add convergence to the circuit, so that B receives inputs from all of the receptors, increasing the size of the stimulus increases the size of neuron B's response.

Receptors and Neural Processing

We now increase the circuit's complexity further by adding two inhibitory synapses to create the circuit in Figure 2.33, in which neurons A and C inhibit neuron B (review Figure 1.23 on inhibition, if necessary). Now consider what happens as we increase the number of receptors stimulated. The spot of light stimulates receptor 4, which, through its excitatory connection, increases the firing rate of neuron B. Extending the illumination to include receptors 3 through 5 adds the output of two more excitatory synapses to B and increases its firing. So far, this circuit is behaving similarly to the circuit in Figure 2.32. However, when we extend the illumination further to also include receptors 2 through 6, something different happens: Receptors 2 and 6 stimulate neurons A and C, which, in turn, inhibit neuron B, decreasing its firing rate. Increasing the size of the stimulus again to illuminate receptors 1 through 7 increases the inhibition and further decreases the response of neuron B.

In this circuit, neuron B fires weakly to small stimuli (a spot illuminating only receptor 4) or longer stimuli (illuminating receptors 1 through 7) and fires best to a stimulus of medium length (illuminating receptors 3 through 5). The combination of convergence and inhibition has therefore caused neuron B to respond best to a light stimulus of a specific size. The neurons that synapse with neuron B are therefore doing much more than simply transmitting electrical signals; they are acting as part of a neural circuit that processes the signals in a way that enables the fir-

ing of neuron B to indicate the size of the stimulus falling on the receptors. We will now see how the kind of neural processing shown in Figure 2.33 actually occurs in the retina.

Introduction to Receptive Fields

We have already seen, from Figure 2.7, that signals generated in the receptors travel through bipolar, horizontal, and amacrine cells to finally reach the ganglion cells, which then transmit these signals out of the back of the eye in the optic nerve. An important property of this network of retinal neurons is that signals from many receptors converge onto each ganglion cell (Figure 2.27). This convergence, combined with inhibition, which is mostly transmitted across the retina by the horizontal and amacrine cells, gives the retina properties like the circuit of Figure 2.33.

To measure the results of the retina's convergence and inhibition we record from a ganglion cell axon and determine how that axon responds to stimulation of the receptors. Many experiments like this have been done on cats and monkeys, using a setup like the one shown in Figure 2.34, in which stimuli are presented on a screen at which the animal (a cat, in this case) is looking. Since the cat's eye is kept stationary, presenting stimuli on the screen is equivalent to shining lights on different places on the retina, because for each point on the screen, there is a corresponding point on the cat's retina (Figure 2.35).

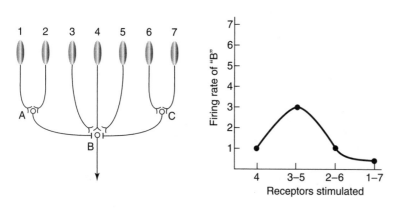

Figure 2.33

When we add inhibition to the circuit, so that stimulation of receptors 1, 2, 6, and 7 now inhibits B, neuron B responds best to stimulation of receptors 3 through 5.

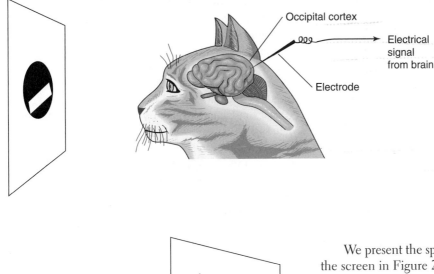

Figure 2.34
Recording electrical signals from the visual cortex of an anesthetized cat. The bar-shaped stimulus on the screen causes nerve cells in the cortex to fire, and a recording electrode picks up the signals generated by these nerve cells. In an actual experiment, the cat is anesthetized, and its head is held in place for accurate positioning.

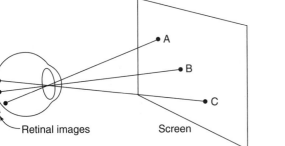

Figure 2.35
For every point on the screen on which we present the stimuli, there is a corresponding point on the retina.

We present the spot of light at different places on the screen in Figure 2.36 and note how the ganglion cell responds. Our goal is to determine the **receptive field** of the ganglion cell—*the area of the retina that, when stimulated, influences the firing rate of the ganglion cell.*

We find that stimulating anywhere in area A causes no change in the activity of our neuron (Figure 2.36a). Eventually, however, we discover that stimulating in area B causes an **excitatory** or **on response**, an increase in the neuron's firing rate when the light is turned on (Figure 2.36b). We mark this area with + signs to indicate that the response to

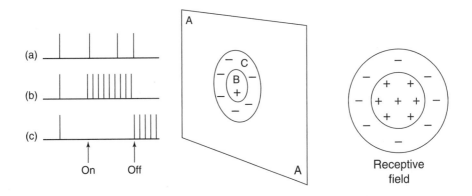

On   Off

Figure 2.36
Response of a ganglion cell in the cat's retina to stimulation (a) outside the cell's receptive field (area A on the screen to the right); (b) inside the excitatory area of the cell's receptive field (area B); and (c) inside the inhibitory area of the cell's receptive field (area C). The excitatory-center-inhibitory-surround receptive field is shown on the far right without the screen.

Receptors and Neural Processing

stimulation from this area is excitatory. We also find that stimulating in area C causes an **inhibitory response**, a decrease in nerve firing when the stimulus is turned on, plus an **off response**, a burst of firing when the stimulus is turned off (Figure 2.36c) (Kuffler, 1953; Schiller, 1992). We mark this area with − signs to indicate that responses to stimuli from this area are inhibitory. Areas B and C, taken together, are the neuron's receptive field.

The receptive field in Figure 2.36 is called a **center-surround receptive field** because the excitatory and inhibitory areas are arranged in a center region that responds one way and is surrounded by a region that responds in the opposite way. This particular receptive field is an **excitatory-center-inhibitory-surround** receptive field, but there are also **inhibitory-center-excitatory-surround** receptive fields.

The fact that the center and the surround of the receptive field respond in opposite ways causes an effect called **center-surround antagonism**. This effect is illustrated in Figure 2.37, which shows what happens as we increase the size of a spot of light presented to the ganglion cell's receptive field. A small spot that is presented to the excitatory center of the receptive field causes a small increase in the rate of nerve firing (a), and increasing the light's size so that it covers the entire center of the receptive field increases the cell's response, as shown in (b). (Notice that we have used the term *cell* in place of *neuron* here. Since neurons are a type of cell, the word *cell* is often substituted for *neuron* in the research literature. In this book, we will often use these terms interchangeably.)

Center-surround antagonism comes into play when the spot of light becomes large enough so that it begins to cover the inhibitory area, as in (c) and (d). Stimulation of the inhibitory surround counteracts the center's excitatory response, causing a decrease in the neuron's firing rate. Thus, this neuron responds best to a spot of light that is the size of the excitatory center of the receptive field.

The circuit in Figure 2.38 is a simplified picture of how neurons are connected in the retina to create the effects shown in Figure 2.37. From this circuit, we can see that stimulating neurons in the surround sends signals across the retina that inhibit our neuron. This sending of inhibitory signals across the

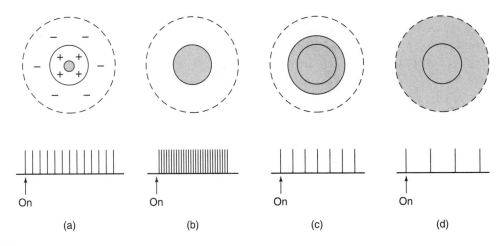

Figure 2.37

Response of an excitatory-center-inhibitory-surround receptive field. The area stimulated with light is indicated by the shading, and the response to the stimulus is indicated by the records below each receptive field. As the stimulus size increases inside the excitatory region of the receptive field in (a) and (b), the response increases. As the stimulus increases further, so that it covers the inhibitory region of the receptive field in (c) and (d), the response decreases. This cell responds best to stimulation that is the size of the receptive field center. (Adapted from Hubel & Wiesel, 1961.)

THE VISUAL PROCESS

The stimulus for vision is visible light, a small band of energy contained within the electromagnetic spectrum. The electromagnetic spectrum stretches from X-rays, which have wavelengths as short as 10^{-12} meters, to radio waves, which have wavelengths as long as 10^{+4} meters (Plate 1.1). Visible light is located between these extremes, with wavelengths on the order of 10^{-6} meters. Expanding this visible part of the electromagnetic spectrum reveals the familiar array of colors seen by humans with normal color vision (see text pages 39 and 187).

The visual process begins when visible light enters the eye and forms images on the retina, a thin layer of neurons lining the back of the eye (Plate 1.2). The magnified view of the retina shown to the right in Plate 1.2 reveals that the retina consists of a number of different types of neurons, including the rod and cone receptors, which transform light energy into electrical energy, and fibers that transmit electrical energy out of the retina in the optic nerve. (See Figure 2.7

on page 41 for a more detailed picture of the different retinal neurons.)

The cross section of the rhesus monkey retina in Plate 1.3 illustrates the layered nature of the retina. In this picture, light is coming from the top, and the receptors are facing the dark-colored pigment epithelium (shown in the lower-right corner) that lines the back of the retina. We can clearly see the layering by looking at the cell bodies of the retinal neurons. The red circles near the bottom of the picture are the cell bodies of the receptors (labeled R in Figure 2.7), the circles in the next layer are the cell bodies of the bipolar cells (labeled B in Figure 2.7), and the circles in the top, bluish layer are the cell bodies of the ganglion cells (labeled G in Figure 2.7) (page 41)

Looking down on the receptors reveals the "mosaic" of rods and cones in Plate 1.4a. In this picture of the periphery of a monkey's retina, the rods are the small circles and the cones are the larger circles (DeMonasterio, et al., 1981). The

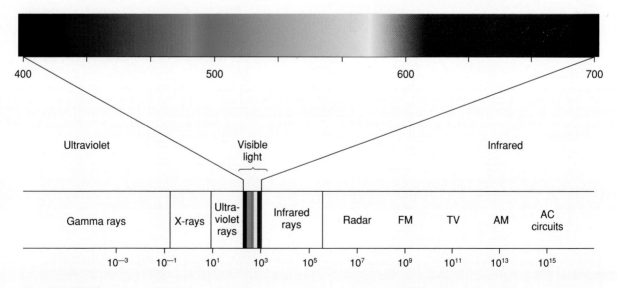

Wavelength (nm)

Plate 1.1

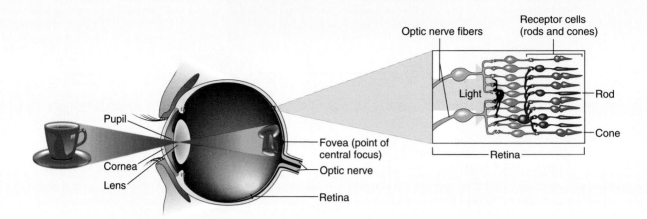

Plate 1.2

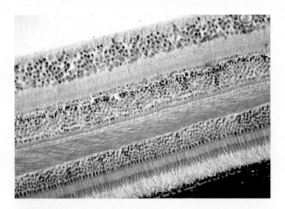

Plate 1.3

cones appear larger because the retina has been sliced across the receptors' inner segments which are fatter in the cones than in the rods. Since this is the peripheral retina, there are many more rods than cones (page 41). A special dye, which affects only the cones that absorb light at the short-wavelength end of the spectrum, has stained them yellow.

Plate 1.4b shows the human cones, measured in an area near the fovea of a living human (Roorda & Williams, 1999). The imaging of cones in the intact human is an impressive technological feat that was accomplished using a technique called adaptive optics to compensate for distortions caused when light passes through the eye's optical system. This technique was originally developed to overcome the blur in

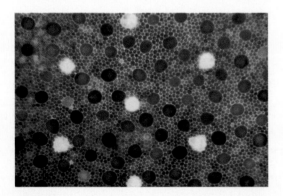

Plate 1.4a

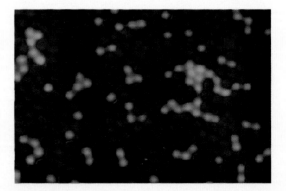

Plate 1.4b

Plate 1.5

ground-based telescopes. The different types of cones have been given different colors to distinguish them: Blue = short-wavelength cones; Green = medium-wavelength; Red = long-wavelength. Notice that there are many more long-wavelength and fewer short-wavelength cones and that in the fovea the cones are not distributed in the orderly pattern seen in the peripheral monkey retina.

The rods and cones have different properties, with the rod system being more sensitive to short wavelengths than the cone system. To demonstrate this perceptually close one eye for about 10 minutes, and then, within the darkness of a closet (see page 49), observe Plate 1.5 with the door almost all the way closed, so you can just barely see the flowers with your opened eye. Then switch to the dark adapted eye and notice that the flowers become visible, and that the blue

flower appears brighter compared to the red one. Viewed in the light, with the light adapted eye, the flowers have about the same brightness. This shift in perception is caused by the shift from cone to rod vision that occurs during dark adaptation (page 53).

Both the rod and cone receptors contain light-sensitive visual pigments that react to light by changing shape and generating an electrical signal. This change in shape is accompanied by a change in the color of the pigment, which is called bleaching. In Plate 1.6, the left photograph shows a frog retina taken immediately after a light was turned on, so little bleaching has occurred and the retina appears red. When the retina is placed on a flat surface, as shown here, its edges bend over, causing a double layer of retina and a deeper red color around the edges. The black spots are small

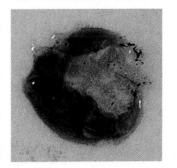 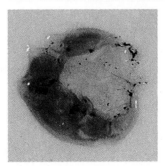 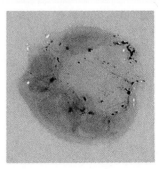

Plate 1.6

pieces of the pigment epithelium, the cell layer on which the retina rests when in the eye. The middle photograph was taken after some bleaching, so the retina is lighter red; in the right photograph, further bleaching has resulted in a light orange appearance. When bleaching is complete, the orange fades and the retina becomes transparent. If this retina were still in the frog's eye, the transparent retina would regain its red color as the pigment regenerated in the dark; however, little regeneration occurs when the retina is dissected from the eye, as in these photographs (page 52).

The signals generated in the receptors trigger electrical signals in the next layer of the retina, the bipolar cells, and these signals are transmitted through the various neurons in the retina, until eventually they are transmitted out of the eye by ganglion cell fibers. These ganglion cell fibers flow out of the back of the eye and become fibers in the optic nerve. Most of these optic nerve fibers reach the lateral geniculate nucleus (LGN), the first major way station on the way to the brain. The LGN is a bilateral nucleus, which means that there is an LGN on the left side of the brain, and also one on the right side.

Shown in cross section in Plate 1.7, the LGN has been colored to indicate two types of organization: (1) *Organization by eye*. Layers 2, 3, and 5 (red) receive inputs from the ipsilateral eye, the eye on the same side of the body as the LGN, and layers 1, 4, and 6 (blue) receive inputs from the contralateral eye, the eye on the opposite side of the body; (2) *Organization by type of ganglion cell*. Layers 1 and 2 (dots), called the magno layer, receive inputs from the large M-ganglion cells; layers 3, 4, 5, and 6 (solid), called the parvo layer, receive inputs from the smaller P-ganglion cells (page 80).

Fibers from the LGN stream to the primary visual receiving area, the striate cortex or V1, in the occipital lobe. Plate 1.8 shows the location of this area as well as a number of the major extrastriate areas that are involved in processing visual information. IT = inferior temporal cortex; P = parietal cortex. Area V3 is located between V2 and V4, but isn't visible because it is hidden by a fold in the cortex. Area MT (middle temporal cortex) is indicated by a dashed border because it also isn't visible on the surface of the cortex. Another hidden area that is involved in vision is STP (superior temporal polysensory area), which contains neurons that serve vision, and other senses as well. See Figure 9.21 on page 317 for the locations of additional areas that are involved in vision, in the interaction between vision and the other senses, and in the visual control of action.

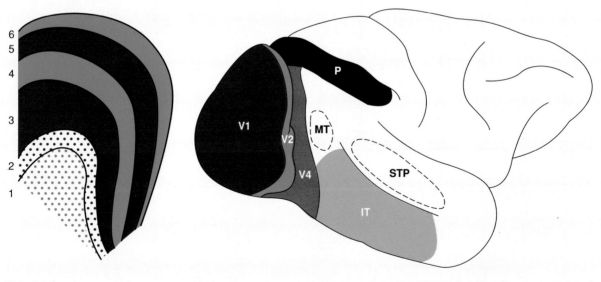

Plate 1.7   **Plate 1.8**

retina is called **lateral inhibition**. This lateral inhibition has been studied extensively in the simple organism called the *Limulus*, shown in Figure 2.39.

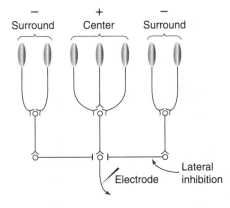

Figure 2.38

A neural circuit that would result in a center-surround receptive field. Signals from the surround receptors reach the cell from which we are recording via inhibitory synapses, while signals from the center receptors reach the cell via an excitatory synapse. Thus, stimulation of the center receptors increases the firing rate recorded by our electrode, and stimulation of the surround receptors decreases the firing rate. In the retina these inhibitory signals are carried by horizontal and amacrine cells.

Lateral Inhibition

In an experiment that is now considered a classic, Keffer Hartline, Henry Wagner, and Floyd Ratliff (1956) used the *Limulus* to demonstrate lateral inhibition. They chose the *Limulus* because of the structure of its eye. The *Limulus* eye is made up of hundreds of tiny structures called **ommatidia**, and each ommatidium has a small lens on the eye's surface that is located directly over a single receptor. Since each lens and receptor is roughly the diameter of a pencil point (very large compared to human receptors), it is possible to illuminate and record from a single receptor without illuminating its neighboring receptors.

When Hartline et al. recorded from the nerve fiber of receptor A, as shown in Figure 2.40, they found that illumination of that receptor caused a large response. But when they added illumination to the three nearby receptors at B, the response of receptor A decreased (Figure 2.40b). They also found that increasing the illumination of B further decreased A's response (Figure 2.40c). Thus, illumination of the neighboring receptors inhibited the firing of receptor A. This inhibition is called lateral inhibition because it is transmitted laterally, across the retina. This lateral inhibition is transmitted in a structure called the lateral plexus in the *Limulus* eye and in the horizontal and amacrine cells in the human retina (Figure 2.7).

Figure 2.39

A Limulus, or horseshoe crab. Its large eyes are made up of hundreds of ommatidia, each containing a single receptor.

Receptors and Neural Processing

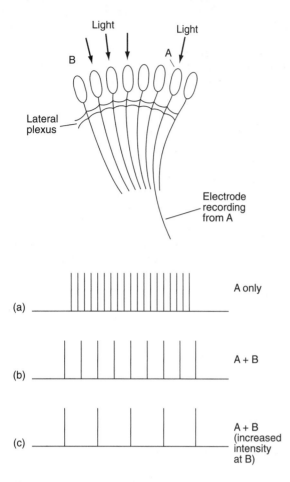

Figure 2.40
A demonstration of lateral inhibition in the limulus. The records below show the response recorded by the electrode recording from the nerve fiber of receptor A when receptor A is stimulated and (a) no other receptors are stimulated, (b) the receptors at B are stimulated simultaneously, and (c) the receptors at B are stimulated at an increased intensity. (Adapted from Ratliff, 1965.)

NEURAL PROCESSING AND PERCEPTION

WebTUTOR What does neural processing have to do with perception? We have already seen how the convergence of signals from many rods can increase rod

dark adapted sensitivity and how the small amount of convergence of cones is responsible for the cone's high acuity. But what about the kind of neural processing we described in the last section that involves lateral inhibition? One example which demonstrates an effect of inhibition on perception is shown in Figure 2.41, which is called the **Hermann grid**.

Lateral Inhibition and the Hermann Grid

Notice the ghostlike gray image at the intersection of the white "corridors" in Figure 2.41. You can prove that this grayness is not physically present by noticing that it is reduced or it vanishes when you look directly at an intersection. Apparently, lateral inhibition in the peripheral retina is creating the ghost images.

Figure 2.42 shows how this works. Figure 2.42a shows the four squares of the grid and five receptors. Receptor A is at the intersection of two of the white corridors, where the gray spot is perceived, and the surrounding receptors are located in the corridors. Figure 2.42b shows another view of the grid and the receptors, which indicates that each receptor sends its signals to a bipolar cell and that each of the bipolar cells sends lateral inhibition, indicated by the arrows,

Figure 2.41
The Hermann grid. Notice the gray "ghost images" at the intersections of the white areas, which decrease or vanish when you look directly at the intersection.

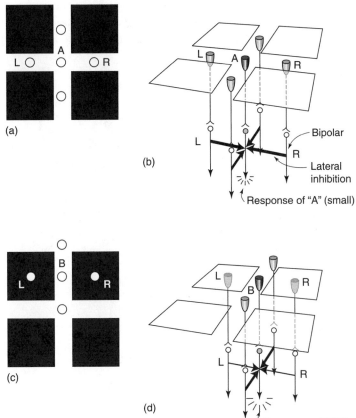

(a)

(b)

Bipolar

Lateral inhibition

Response of "A" (small)

(c)

(d)

Response of "B" (larger)

Figure 2.42

How lateral inhibition can explain the dark spots at the intersections of the Hermann grid. (a) Top view of four squares of the grid showing the position of receptor A, at the intersection, and the surrounding receptors in the "corridors." (b) Perspective view of the squares and receptors in (a), showing that each receptor connects to a bipolar cell, and that the bipolar cells that surround A all send a large amount of lateral inhibition to A's bipolar cell (indicated by the thick arrows). (c) Same as (a) above but focusing on receptor B, which is located in the corridor of the grid. In this situation, receptors L and R are located under the black squares and so receive less illumination. This results in less lateral inhibition being sent to B's bipolar cell, as shown in (d).

to receptor A's bipolar cell. The thickness of the arrows indicates the strength of the inhibition.

Figure 2.42c shows another array of five receptors. In this example, receptor B is in the corridor between two black squares, and the other receptors surround it. The key difference between this group of receptors and the ones in Figure 2.42a is that in this group the receptors to the left and right, L and R, receive reduced illumination because they are under the black squares.

Our goal is to compare the responses of the bipolar cells for receptors A and B, because we are assuming, for the purposes of this example, that our perception of the lightness at A and at B is determined by the responses of these bipolar cells. (It would be more accurate to use ganglion cells, because they are the neurons that send signals out of

the retina; but, to simplify things for the purposes of this example, we will focus on the bipolar cells.)

The size of the bipolar cell responses depends on how much stimulation each one receives from its receptor and on the amount that this response is decreased by the lateral inhibition it receives from its neighboring cells. Since receptors A and B are both illuminated by white areas of the grid, they send the same amount of stimulation to their bipolar cells. However, the bipolar cells of A and B receive different amounts of lateral inhibition, as indicated by the thickness of the horizontal arrows coming from the neighboring bipolar cells. A's bipolar cell receives a large amount of lateral inhibition from each of its neighboring cells, because all four of the neighboring receptors are strongly illuminated by the white corridors. However, B's bipolar cell receives less inhibition

Receptors and Neural Processing

from the cells associated with receptors L and R, because these receptors are under the black squares and so are only weakly illuminated.

Since A's bipolar cell receives more lateral inhibition than B's bipolar cell, it will fire less than B, and this lower rate of firing is translated into the gray spots we see at the intersections. These gray spots provide a good example of the principle we stated at the beginning of the chapter: *We do not just perceive what is out there. We perceive what is out there as filtered through the properties of our visual system.*

Lateral Inhibition and Mach Bands

Lateral inhibition also creates another illusion, called **Mach bands**, an effect described by Ernst Mach in the 1880s based on displays like the one in Figure 2.43a. If we measure the intensity across the stripes in Figure 2.43a with a light meter by starting at A and measuring the amount of light reflected as we move along the line between A and D, we obtain the result shown in Figure 2.43b. This shows that the intensity distribution across each stripe is flat. Thus, the same amount of light is reflected across the entire distance between A and B. Then the intensity drops sharply to a lower level at C and stays the same between C and D.

Although our light meter tells us that the intensities remain constant across the two stripes, we actually perceive something different. We perceive a small light band at B and a small dark band at C. These are the Mach bands. They are represented graphically in Figure 2.43c, which indicates what we actually perceive across the two stripes. It is important to remember that the bands you see in Figure 2.43a, which are indicated graphically in Figure 2.43c, are illusions that, just like the gray "ghosts" in the Hermann grid, are created by lateral inhibition.

DEMONSTRATION

Creating Mach Bands in Shadows

In Figure 2.43 we created Mach bands with gray stripes. You can also create Mach bands by casting a shadow, as shown in Figure 2.44. When you do this, you will see a dark Mach band near the border of the shadow and a light Mach band on the other side of the border. The light Mach band is often harder to see than the dark band. ●

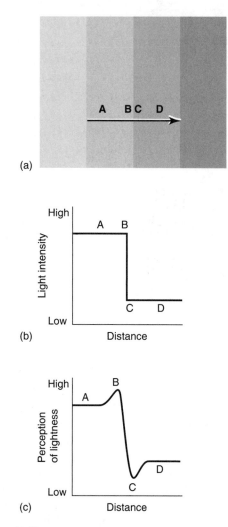

(a)

(b)

(c)

Figure 2.43
(a) Mach bands at a contour. Just to the left of the contour, near B, a faint light band can be perceived, and just to the right, at C, a faint dark band can be perceived. (b) A plot showing the physical intensity distribution of the light, as measured with a light meter. (c) A plot showing the perceptual effect described in (a). The bump in the curve at B indicates the light Mach band, and the dip in the curve at C indicates the dark Mach band. Note that the bumps are not present in the physical intensity distribution (b).

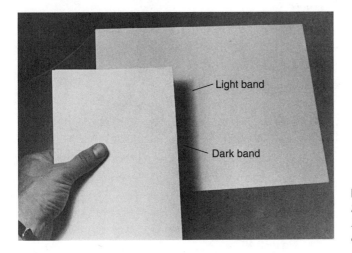

Figure 2.44
Shadow-casting technique for observing Mach bands. Illuminate a sheet of white paper with your desk lamp and then cast a shadow with another piece of paper.

The hypothetical circuit in Figure 2.45 shows how these illusory Mach bands can be explained by lateral inhibition. We use the same reasoning we did for the Hermann grid. Each of the six receptors in this circuit sends signals to bipolar cells, and each bipolar cell sends lateral inhibition to its neighbors on both sides. Receptors A, B, and C receive intense illumination, and D, E, and F receive dim illumination. This is what would occur if we illuminated all six receptors equally and then cast a shadow on receptors D, E, and F.

Let's assume that receptors A, B, and C generate responses of 100, whereas D, E, and F generate responses of 20, as shown in Figure 2.45. Thus, without inhibition, A, B, and C send the same responses to their bipolar cells, and D, E, and F send the same

responses to their bipolar cells. If perception were determined only by these responses we would see a bright bar with equal intensity across its width in the area served by receptors A, B, and C and a dim bar with equal intensity across its width in the area served by D, E, and F. The following calculation shows how lateral inhibition would modify these initial responses to produce a physiological effect that would result in the perception of Mach bands:

1. Start with the response received by each bipolar cell: 100 for A, B, and C and 20 for D, E, and F.

2. Determine the amount of inhibition that each bipolar cell receives from its neighbor on each

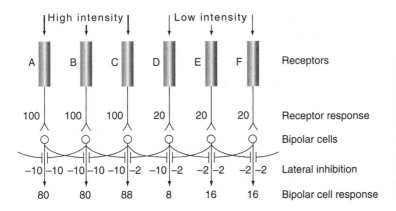

Figure 2.45
Circuit to explain the Mach band effect based on lateral inhibition. The circuit works like the one for the Hermann grid in Figure 2.42, with each bipolar cell sending inhibition to its neighbors. If we know the initial output of each receptor and the amount of lateral inhibition, we can calculate the final output of the receptors. (See text for a description of the calculation.)

Receptors and Neural Processing

side. For the purposes of our calculation, we will assume that each cell sends inhibition to its neighbor equal to one-tenth of that cell's initial output. Thus, cells A, B, and C will send $100 \times 0.1 = 10$ units of inhibition to their neighbors, and cells D, E, and F will send $20 \times 0.1 = 2$ units of inhibition to their neighbors.

3. Determine the final response of each cell by subtracting the amount of inhibition from the initial response. Remember that each cell receives inhibition from its neighbor on either side. (We assume here that cell A receives 10 units of inhibition from an unseen cell on its left and that F receives 2 units of inhibition from an unseen cell on its right.) Here is the calculation for each cell:

Cell A: Final response = $100 - 10 - 10 = 80$

Cell B: Final response = $100 - 10 - 10 = 80$

Cell C: Final response = $100 - 10 - 2 = 88$

Cell D: Final response = $20 - 10 - 2 = 8$

Cell E: Final response = $20 - 2 - 2 = 16$

Cell F: Final response = $20 - 2 - 2 = 16$

The graph of these neural responses in Figure 2.46 looks similar to Figure 2.43c, where there is an increase in brightness on the light side of the border at C and a decrease in brightness on the dark side at D. The lateral inhibition in our circuit has therefore created a neural pattern that looks like the Mach bands we perceive. A circuit similar to this one, but of much greater complexity, is probably responsible for the Mach bands that we see.

We have shown how lateral inhibition may be involved in determining our perception of the gray ghosts of the Hermann grid and of the light and dark Mach bands. However, lateral inhibition cannot explain all of our perceptions of lightness and darkness. We can appreciate the difficulty in using lateral inhibition to explain some perceptions that involve light and dark, by considering a phenomenon called simultaneous contrast, which at one time was explained in terms of lateral inhibition.

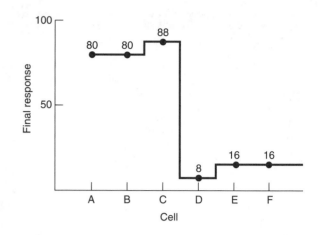

Figure 2.46
A plot showing the final receptor output calculated for the circuit of Figure 2.45. The bump at C and the dip at D correspond to the light and dark Mach bands, respectively.

Lateral Inhibition and Simultaneous Contrast

Simultaneous contrast occurs when our perception of the brightness or color of one area is affected by the presence of an adjacent or surrounding area.

 **D E M O N S T R A T I O N**

Simultaneous Contrast

When you look at the two center squares in Figure 2.47, the one on the left appears much darker than the one on the right. Now, punch two holes 2 inches apart in a card or a piece of paper, place the two holes over the squares, and compare your perception of the squares, as seen through the holes. ●

You may have been surprised to see that the two squares look the same when you viewed them through the holes, even though they look different when the whole pattern is visible. This effect is called **simultaneous lightness contrast**—surrounding one area by

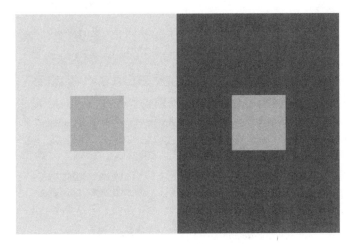

Figure 2.47
Simultaneous contrast. The two center squares reflect the same amount of light into your eyes but, because of the simultaneous contrast effect, look different.

another area that is either lighter or darker changes the appearance of the surrounded area. Based on the results of the above demonstration, we can say that simultaneous lightness contrast is caused by the backgrounds surrounding the central squares. But what is the physiological mechanism behind this effect?

An explanation for simultaneous contrast that is based on lateral inhibition is diagrammed in Figure 2.48, which indicates, by the size of the arrows, how much lateral inhibition would be sent from the cells under the surround areas to the cells under the central squares. Since the cells receiving signals from the receptors under the left surround are intensely stimulated, they send a large amount of inhibition toward the cells in the center (large arrows). Since the cells receiving signals from the receptors under the right surround are less intensely stimulated, they send only a small amount of inhibition to the cells in the center (small arrows). Since the cells under the left square receive more inhibition than the cells under the right square, their response is decreased more, they fire less than the cells under the right square, and the left square therefore looks darker. This explanation based on lateral inhibition makes sense and is still accepted by some researchers. However, there are some problems with it (Albright, 1994).

One problem with explaining simultaneous contrast in terms of lateral inhibition is that we would expect the inhibition to be strongest at the edges of the center squares and to become weaker toward the

centers of the squares. But the center squares look about the same from the edge into the center.

But the biggest problem for the lateral inhibition explanation of simultaneous contrast is posed by displays like the ones in Figures 2.49 and 2.50. Figure 2.49 is called the **Benary cross** (Benary, 1924). Triangle B looks slightly lighter than triangle A, even though both reflect the same amount of light and are surrounded by the same amount of dark and light. Both triangles should receive the same amount of lateral inhibition, but they look different.

Figure 2.50 illustrates an even stronger effect, called **White's illusion** (White, 1981). This looks like

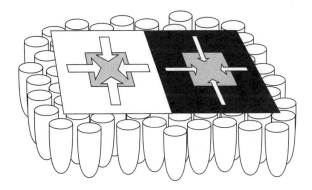

Figure 2.48
How lateral inhibition has been used to explain the simultaneous contrast effect. See text for explanation.

Receptors and Neural Processing

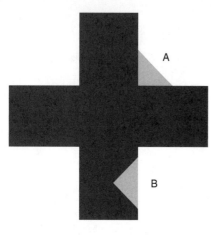

Figure 2.49
The Benary cross. See text for explanation.

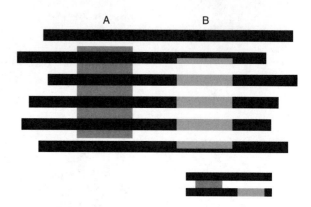

Figure 2.50
White's illusion. See text for explanation. (From White, 1981.)

a light gray rectangle (rectangle B) and a dark gray rectangle (rectangle A), but in reality the bars that create each rectangle reflect exactly the same amount of light. You can demonstrate this to yourself by masking off everything but one of the horizontal bars in each rectangle. When you do this, you will see that they look the same.

Let's look at this display in terms of what lateral inhibition would predict. The cells stimulated by the bars of rectangle B receive a lot of lateral inhibition from the bordering white areas, which would make them appear darker. The cells stimulated by the bars of rectangle A receive less inhibition because of the bordering black areas, so they should appear lighter. However, as you can see, the opposite happens. The areas receiving the most inhibition look the lightest! Clearly, lateral inhibition can't explain the White illusion.

What's happening here, according to Alan Gilchrist and coworkers (1999) is that our perception of lightness operates according to the principle of **belongingness**, which states that an area's appearance is influenced by which part of the surroundings to which the area appears to belong. For example, in the Benary cross triangle B "belongs" to the dark cross, because it is located within it, but triangle A "belongs" to the white area outside the cross. Thus, the dark cross makes triangle B appear lighter, and

the light background makes triangle A appear darker. White's illusion works the same way since rectangle B "belongs" to the dark bars and rectangle A "belongs" to the white background.

Whether or not this idea of belongingness holds up for other types of displays, there is no question that some mechanism other than lateral inhibition is involved in the Benary cross, White's illusion, and many other displays (see Adelson, 1993; Knill and Kersten, 1991; Williams, McCoy, & Purues, 1998). Contrary to what perception researchers once thought, the mechanism behind many contrast effects appears to be based not in the retina, but farther upstream, probably in the cortex, although at this point we don't know what the physiological mechanism is.

So it appears that the neural processing that occurs in the retina helps determine some of the properties of rod and cone vision and probably perception of lightness at edges, as in the Mach band effect. Although inhibition plays a very important role in perception, it isn't surprising that there are perceptions we can't explain based just on what is happening in the retina. There is still much more processing to be done before perception occurs, and, as we will see in Chapters 3 and 4, this processing happens later in the visual system, in the visual receiving area of the cortex and beyond.

What are the pictures in the accompanying Figures A and B? After you have pondered this question for a while, go to the figure on page 73 for some hints.

Did you find that your perception changed based on the added information in the figure on page 73? Many people find it difficult to perceive Figure A as a cow or to see B as a three-dimensional object. However, the additional information provided by the pictures in the figure on page 73 not only causes people to change their perceptions but often makes it difficult for them to switch back to their original perceptions.

The effect you observed when the black-and-white object in Figure B became a three-dimensional object after you saw the second version has been studied physiologically using functional magnetic resonance imaging (fMRI) by C. Moore and S. A. Engel (1999). They studied two areas in the occipital lobe of the cortex that they knew responded well to three-dimensional forms. They first measured the fMRI response in these areas to black-and-white forms such as the one in Figure B that appeared like flat shapes. They then showed their subjects shaded versions of these forms (as on page 73), which changed their interpretation of the black-and-white forms so they saw them as three-dimensional volumes.

When the fMRI response to the forms in Figures A and B was measured again, the brain's response was larger than when the forms were interpreted as being flat. Thus, even though the retinal image remained exactly the same, the responses to these patterns was changed because processing triggered by the observer's experience had changed how the forms were interpreted. This experiment, therefore, shows that the pattern of stimulation on the retina is just the starting point for perception and that later processing can influence both our perceptions and physiological responding.

Another way to describe this result is in terms of the role of "knowledge" in the perceptual process (Figure 1.2). The knowledge provided by viewing the three-dimensional representations on page 73 provides information for top-down processing that modifies both our perception of the forms in Figures A and B and the way the brain responds to these forms.

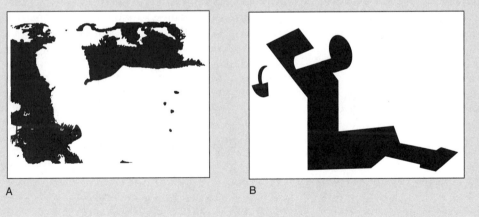

A

B

What are these two figures?

Receptors and Neural Processing

THE INDIRECTNESS
OF PERCEPTION

Remember the question we posed at the beginning of Chapter 1, asking what your experience might be like if you lost all of your senses? Our answer was that you might not have much experience at all, because perception is what links us to our environment. But perception doesn't just link us to our environment. It gives us the feeling that we are in *direct contact* with the environment. I look up from my writing, and I can tell that there is a cardboard coffee cup sitting on the table directly in front of me. I know where the cup is, so I can easily reach for it, and as I pick it up I feel the texture of the cardboard beneath my fingers. As I drink the coffee, I also sense heat, the taste and smell of coffee, and liquid on my tongue.

But as much as I feel that all of these experiences are due to my direct contact with the coffee cup and the liquid in it, I know that this feeling of directness is largely an illusion. Perception, as we will see throughout this text, is an indirect process.

We have already seen this in considering vision. I see the cup not because of any direct contact with it, but because of the light it reflects into my eyes. And when this light is changed into electricity, my visual experience of the cup becomes dependent on how this electricity is processed by neurons in the visual system.

"Well, vision may be indirect," you might say, "but how about the perceptions of heat and texture that occur from picking up the cup? Weren't your fingers in direct contact with the cup?" The answer to this question is, yes, it is true that my fingers were in direct physical contact with the cup, but my perception of the heat of the coffee and the texture of the cardboard was due to the stimulation of temperature- and pressure-sensitive receptors in my fingers, which translated the temperature and pressure into electrical impulses, just as the light energy that causes vision is translated into electrical impulses.

Smell and taste also involve more physical contact than vision, because these experiences are triggered when chemicals in the coffee make direct contact with receptor sites in the nose and tongue. But physical contact of molecules with receptor sites aside, experiences of taste and smell are still the result of the processing of electrical signals in the nervous system.

Hearing is the same. Air pressure waves transmitted through the air cause vibrations of receptors inside the ear, and these vibrations generate the electrical signals our auditory system uses to create the experience of sound.

The amazing thing about perception is that despite this indirectness, it seems so real. And it is real, in the sense that our perceptions usually provide us with accurate information about what's out there in the distance or what's up close under our noses or beneath our fingers. But in all of these cases, this information is created through the actions of receptors that change environmental stimulation into electrical signals that eventually, somewhere in the brain, create our sensory impressions of the environment.

Neural Processing by Convergence

Convergence occurs when a number of neurons synapse on a single neuron. In general, the rods converge far more than the cones, and this difference in convergence has perceptual consequences. The high convergence of the rods results in greater spatial summation, which leads to greater sensitivity in the dark for rod vision compared to cone vision. The low convergence of the cones is partially responsible for the cones' higher visual acuity compared to the rods.

Neural Processing by Excitation and Inhibition

Neural circuits are formed by a number of interconnected neurons. By combining convergence, excitation, and inhibition, circuits can process information in a way that causes individual neurons to respond best to specific properties of a stimulus, such as a line of a specific length.

Receptive Fields

A receptive field of a neuron in the visual system is the area of retina which, when stimulated, influences the firing rate of that neuron. Ganglion cells have center-surround receptive fields, causing an excitatory response when the center is stimulated and an inhibitory response when the surround is stimulated. In other cells, the center can be inhibitory, and the surround can be excitatory.

Lateral Inhibition

Lateral inhibition, the sending of inhibition of signals across the retina, has been studied in classic experiments in the *Limulus*. These experiments show how stimulation of receptors at one place on the retina can influence the response of neurons at another place on the retina. Lateral inhibition can explain perceptual effects such as the darkening that occurs at the intersections of the Hermann grid and the illusory Mach bands that occur at borders between light and dark areas. Lateral inhibition cannot, however, explain some other perceptual phenomena, such as simultaneous contrast, which involves the perception of light and dark. These properties involve higher-order processing.

The Indirectness of Perception

Although we have the feeling that we are in direct contact with the environment, this feeling is an illusion, because everything we perceive is determined indirectly, through transformation of environmental stimuli into electrical signals and the transformation of these signals into conscious experience.

A

B

These go with the two figures in the "Brain Scan" box.

STUDY QUESTIONS

1. What are two answers to the problem posed by the fact that in dim illumination we don't see in color and see details less clearly? (36)

2. Why do we say that perception is the result of transformations? (36)

The Stimulus for Vision and the Structure of the Visual System

Light: The Stimulus for Vision

3. What is the electromagnetic spectrum? (37)

4. What part of the electromagnetic spectrum is the stimulus for vision? (37)

5. What are two different ways that we can describe light? (39)

The Visual System

6. What are the major divisions of the visual system? (39)

7. Where is the primary visual receiving area, and what is it called? (39)

8. What are visual cortical areas outside of the primary visual receiving area called? (39)

9. What are the two kinds of visual receptors? (40)

10. What are the four types of cells in the retina in addition to the receptors? (40)

11. The axons of which kinds of neurons leave the eye? What nerve do they form? (40)

The First Transformations: Light, Receptors, and Electricity

Light Is Reflected into the Eye and Focused on the Retina

12. What are the eye's two focusing elements? (40)

13. Which focusing element accounts for most of the eye's focusing power? (40)

14. Which focusing element can change its shape? (42)

15. How is light that is reflected from a faraway object focused onto the retina? What happens when we move the object closer? (42)

16. How does the eye bring the image of a nearby object into focus? (42)

17. What is focusing power? Accommodation? When you accommodate, what happens to the shape of the lens? What is the near point? Presbyopia? (42)

Light Stimulates the Rod and Cone Receptors

18. How do the rods and cones differ in shape and distribution on the retina? (44)

19. What is the fovea? The peripheral retina? Which area of the retina contains only cones? What percentage of the retina's cones are in this area? Where are most of the cones? (44)

20. Why do the rods and cones face away from the light? What "problem" do the backward-facing receptors create and how does the eye solve this problem? (45)

21. What is the blind spot? (45)

22. What are three reasons that we are usually not aware of the blind spot? (45)

23. Where are the visual pigments located in the visual receptors? (46)

24. Describe the structure of the visual pigment molecule. Which part of the molecule is sensitive to light? What happens when this part of the molecule absorbs light? (46)

25. Describe the Hecht, Shlaer, and Pirenne psychophysical experiment. What did they show about the sensitivity of the eye to light? Based on what they found, what can we conclude about the effect of isomerizing one visual pigment molecule? (46)

26. Describe the enzyme cascade and its role in transduction. (48)

Visual Pigments and Perception

27. What is dark adaptation? (49)

Dark Adaptation of the Rods and Cones

28. Describe the dark-adaptation curve. How many stages does it have? (49)

29. Describe how to measure the dark-adaptation curve and how this procedure can be used to show (a) that the curve has two phases; (b) that the first part of the curve is due to adaptation of the cones; and (c) that the second part of the curve is due to adaptation of the rods. (49)

30. During the process of dark adaptation, when do the rods begin adapting? When do the cones begin adapting? (51)

31. When does the sensitivity of the rods surpass the sensitivity of the cones? What is the rod–cone break? (51)

32. What is visual pigment bleaching? Visual pigment regeneration? What structure in the eye is needed for visual pigment regeneration to occur? (52)

33. Compare the rates of rod and cone visual pigment regeneration. How is this related to the dark-adaptation curve? (52)

Spectral Sensitivity of the Rods and Cones

34. What is spectral sensitivity? (52)

35. How is spectral sensitivity determined using monochromatic lights? (52)

36. What is the relationship between sensitivity and threshold? (52)

37. How do we measure the cone spectral sensitivity curve? The rod spectral sensitivity curve? (52)

38. What is the Purkinje shift? Which wavelengths become more sensitive relative to the others when the Purkinje shift occurs as dusk approaches? (53)

39. What is plotted in an absorption spectrum? (53)

40. How does the absorption spectrum for rod visual pigment compare to the rod spectral sensitivity curve? (53)

41. What are the three types of cone pigments? (54)

Neural Processing by Convergence

42. What is one way that neural processing occurs? (54)

The Convergence of Rod and Cone Signals

43. What is convergence? (54)

44. Compare rod convergence and cone convergence. (54)

45. What two differences in perception are associated with differences in rod and cone convergence? (55)

The Rods Are More Sensitive in the Dark than the Cones

46. Describe how the differences in rod and cone convergence shown in Figure 2.28 can explain the rod's greater sensitivity. (55)

47. What is spatial summation? How do rod and cone spatial summation compare? (57)

The Cones Result in Better Detail Vision than the Rods

48. Why is it necessary to scan the faces in a crowd in order to recognize a particular face? (57)

49. What is visual acuity? Which receptor system results in the best visual acuity, the rods or the cones? (57)

50. Describe how the differences in rod and cone visual acuity can be explained in terms of differences in rod and cone wiring. (58)

Neural Processing by Excitation and Inhibition

51. What is a neural circuit? (58)

Introduction to Neural Circuits

52. Compare how the following three types of circuits respond to a spot of light that is increased in length so it becomes a bar of light: (a) linear circuit; (b) circuit with convergence; (c) circuit with convergence and inhibition. (59)

53. What kind of information does circuit (c) above, with convergence and inhibition, provide about the properties of the stimulus? (60)

Introduction to Receptive Fields

54. Presenting stimuli on a screen in front of a cat or monkey is equivalent to presenting the stimuli to _____. (60)

55. What is the receptive field of a neuron? Where is the receptive field of a retinal ganglion cell located, and how are excitatory and inhibitory areas arranged? (61)

56. What is a center-surround receptive field? (62)

57. What is center-surround antagonism, and how does it affect the firing of a cat's ganglion cell? (62)

58. Be able to draw a neural circuit that would result in a center-surround receptive field. (62)

Lateral Inhibition

59. Why did Hartline and coworkers choose the *Limulus* for their experiments? (63)

60. Describe the Hartline experiment. How does lateral inhibition affect neural firing? (63)

Neural Processing and Perception

Lateral Inhibition and the Hermann Grid

61. What illusion occurs in the Hermann grid? (64)

62. How can this illusion be explained by lateral inhibition? (64)

Lateral Inhibition and Mach Bands

63. What is the Mach band effect? Why do we say it is an illusion? (Be sure you understand the difference between the intensity distribution across the Mach band display and the observer's perception of the display.) (66)

64. Be able to calculate the output of the circuit in Figure 2.45 if you are given the initial output of the receptors and the amount of inhibition each receptor sends to its neighbors. (67)

Lateral Inhibition and Simultaneous Contrast

65. What is simultaneous contrast? Simultaneous lightness contrast? (68)

66. How has lateral inhibition been used to explain simultaneous contrast? (69)

67. What are two problems with the lateral inhibition explanation of simultaneous contrast? (69)

68. What is the Benary cross? Why is it difficult to explain the lightness of the triangles in terms of lateral inhibition? (69)

69. What is White's illusion? Why is it difficult to explain the lightness of the rectangles in terms of lateral inhibition? (69)

70. What is the principle of belongingness, and how has it been applied to the Benary and White illusions? (70)

71. What can we conclude about the role of lateral inhibition in determining contrast? (70)

Brain Scan: Going Beyond the Information on the Retina

72. Under what conditions does the fMRI change for pictures like the ones on page 71? (71)

73. What do the fMRI results tell us about the roles of the retinal image and higher-order processes in perception? (71)

Across the Senses: The Indirectness of Perception

74. Perception gives us the feeling that we are in _____ contact with the environment. (72)

75. Why do we say that perception is largely an indirect process? (72)

76. Why is perception indirect even for senses like touch in which we make direct physical contact with the stimulus? (72)

3

THE LATERAL GENICULATE NUCLEUS AND STRIATE CORTEX

SOME QUESTIONS WE WILL CONSIDER

- How do electrical signals in neurons represent objects in the environment? (78)

- Is there an electrical "picture" of an object in the brain that looks like the object's image on the retina? (99)

- What happens to an animal's visual system if it is raised in an abnormal environment, such as being exposed only to horizontals or only to verticals? (100)

In Chapter 2, we described how the perceptual process begins in the retina. We can summarize this process as follows: An image is formed on the retina. Light, in a pattern that illuminates some receptors intensely and some dimly, is absorbed by the visual pigment molecules that pack the rod and cone outer segments. Chemical reactions in the outer segments transduce the light into electrical signals. As these electrical signals travel through the retina, they inter- act, excite, and inhibit, eventually reaching the ganglion cells, which because of this processing have center-surround receptive fields on the retina. The axons of the ganglion cells leave the back of the eye, each becoming a fiber in the optic nerve.

Our goal in this chapter is to see what happens to the signals in these fibers as they travel first to the lateral geniculate nucleus (LGN) in the thalamus, and then to the visual receiving area in the cortex (see

Figures 2.3 and 2.4). But before we start moving up the visual pathways toward the LGN, let's consider Figure 3.1, which shows a tree that has been transformed into electrical signals in the ganglion cell fibers in the optic nerve.

In this chapter we begin to answer the question, "How is the tree, or any other object, represented by neural signals?" Although we know that there is information in the optic nerve that represents the tree, this information is in a crude form. We can appreciate how crude this information is by remembering that the fibers in the optic nerve have center-surround receptive fields, so they respond best to small spots of light. It's hard to tell how the tree is represented by this activity, but the information has to be in there somewhere, otherwise we wouldn't be able to perceive the tree.

To solve this problem of finding the tree in the electrical signals in the optic nerve, the visual system processes these signals in the lateral geniculate nucleus, the visual cortex, and additional areas in the cortex. As we move to the LGN and visual cortex in this chapter, we will begin to appreciate how the visual system goes about achieving this processing. We begin as signals from the optic nerve are arriving at the LGN.

INFORMATION FLOW AND ORGANIZATION IN THE LATERAL GENICULATE NUCLEUS

What happens to the information that arrives at the lateral geniculate nucleus? One way to answer this question is to record from neurons in the LGN and determine what their receptive fields look like. When we do this, we find that LGN neurons have the same center-surround configuration as retinal ganglion cells (see Figure 2.36). The major function of the LGN is apparently not to create new receptive field properties but to regulate neural information as it flows from the retina to the visual cortex (Casagrande & Norton, 1991; Humphrey & Saul, 1994).

Information Flow in the Lateral Geniculate Nucleus

The LGN does not simply receive signals from the retina and then transmit them to the cortex. Figure 3.2 shows that it is much more complex than that.

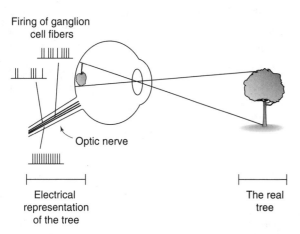

Figure 3.1
This tree is transformed into electrical signals by the receptors, and then these signals are transmitted out of the eye in the fibers of the optic nerve. Somewhere in the signals in the optic nerve is information that represents the tree.

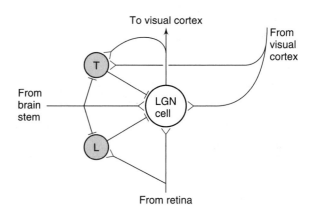

Figure 3.2
Inputs and outputs of an LGN neuron. In addition to the incoming signals carried in optic nerve fibers from the retina, this neuron is also receiving signals from the cortex, from a nucleus elsewhere in the thalamus (T), from another LGN neuron (L), and from the brain stem. Excitatory synapses are indicated by Y's and inhibitory ones by T's. (Adapted from Kaplan, Mukherjee, & Shapley, 1993.)

Ninety percent of the fibers in the optic nerve arrive at the LGN. (The other 10 percent travel to the superior colliculus, a structure involved in controlling eye movements.) But these signals are not the only ones that arrive at the LGN. The LGN also receives signals from the cortex, from the brain stem, from other neurons in the thalamus (T), and from other neurons in the LGN (L). Thus, the LGN receives information from many sources, including back from the cortex, and then sends its output to the cortex.

Figure 3.3 indicates the amount of flow between the retina, LGN, and cortex. Notice that (1) the LGN receives more input back from the cortex than it receives from the retina (Sherman and Koch, 1986; Sitito, 1994; Wilson, Friedlander, and Sherman, 1984); and (2) the smallest signal of all is from the LGN to the cortex. For every ten nerve impulses the LGN receives from the retina, it sends only four to the cortex. This decrease in firing that occurs at the LGN is one reason for the suggestion that one of the purposes of the LGN is to regulate neural information as it flows from the retina to the cortex.

But the LGN not only regulates information flowing through it, it also organizes the information that flows into it. Organizing information is important. It is the basis of finding a document in a filing system, or locating a book in the library, and, as we will see in this chapter, of filing information in different structures in the visual system. The LGN is a good place to begin discussing the idea of organization, because although this organization begins in the retina, it becomes more obvious in the LGN. We will see that the signals arriving at the LGN are sorted and organized based on the eye they came from, the receptors that generated them, and the type of environmental information that is represented in them.

Organization by Left and Right Eyes

The lateral geniculate nucleus (LGN) is a bilateral structure, which means there is one LGN in the left hemisphere and one in the right hemisphere. Viewing one of these nuclei in cross section reveals six layers (Figure 3.4 and Color Plate 1.7). Each layer receives signals from only one eye. The **ipsilateral eye** (the eye on the same side of the body as the LGN) sends neurons to layers 2, 3, and 5 of the LGN. The **contralateral eye** (the eye on the opposite side of the body from the LGN) sends neurons to layers 1, 4, and 6. Thus, each eye sends half of its neurons to the LGN in the

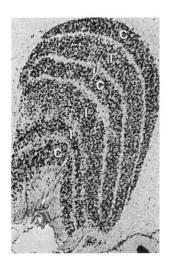

Figure 3.4
Cross section of the lateral geniculate nucleus. This is what the LGN looks like when treated with stain that darkens the cell bodies of the LGN neurons. This darkening shows that there are six layers of cell bodies, each separated by a light band. Layers 1, 4, and 6, marked C, receive input from the contralateral eye; and layers 2, 3, and 5, marked I, receive input from the ipsilateral eye. See the text for details. (From Livingstone & Hubel, 1988.)

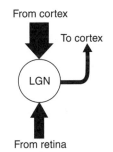

Figure 3.3
Information flow into and out of the LGN. The size of the arrow indicates the size of the signals.

LGN and Striate Cortex

left hemisphere of the brain and half to the LGN in the right hemisphere, and the signals from each eye are sorted into different layers, so the information from the left and right eyes is kept separated.

Organization as a Retinotopic Map

Fibers entering the LGN are arranged so fibers carrying signals from the same area of the retina end up in the same area of the LGN. This creates a map of the retina on the LGN called a **retinotopic map**. Retinotopic means that each location on the LGN corresponds to a location on the retina, and neighboring locations on the LGN correspond to neighboring locations on the retina. Thus, the receptive fields of neurons that are near to each other in the LGN, such as neurons A, B, C, and D in layer 6 (Figure 3.5), are adjacent to each other at A′, B′, C′, and D′ on the retina.

Retinotopic maps occur not only in layer 6 but in each of the other layers as well, and the maps of each of the layers are lined up with one another. Thus, all of the neurons along the electrode track, indicated by the dashed line in Figure 3.5, have receptive fields in the same location on the retina.

These aligned retinotopic maps prompted the anatomist Gordon Walls (1953) to compare the LGN to a club sandwich, because a toothpick piercing the LGN's "sandwich" layers would encounter neurons that all receive information from the same place on the retina (Mollon, 1990). This is an amazing feat of organization: One million ganglion cell fibers travel to each LGN, and, on arriving there, each fiber goes to the correct LGN layer (remember that fibers from each eye go to different layers) and finds its way to a location next to other fibers that left from the same place on the retina. Meanwhile, all of the other fibers are doing the same thing in the other layers of the club sandwich!

Organization by Types of Ganglion Cells Arriving at the LGN

Three kinds of ganglion cells transmit signals from the retina to the LGN. **P-cells** (for *parvocellular*), which have small or medium-sized cell bodies and respond to sustained stimuli with sustained firing, synapse in layers 3, 4, 5, and 6. **M-cells** (for *magnocellular*),which have larger cell bodies and respond with brief bursts of firing, synapse in layers 1 and 2

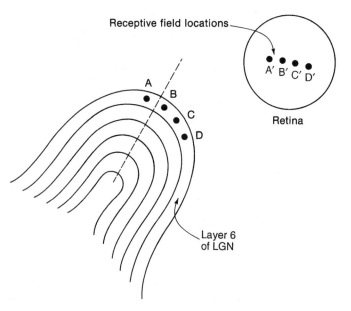

Figure 3.5
Retinotopic mapping of neurons in the LGN. The neurons at A, B, C, and D in layer 6 of the LGN have receptive fields located at positions A′, B′, C′, and D′ on the retina. The receptive fields of neurons encountered along an electrode track perpendicular to the surface of the LGN (dashed line) all have approximately the same location on the retina.

(Table 3.1 and Color Plate 1.7). There is also a third kind of ganglion cell, called the **K-cell** (for *kinocellular*), but its function is unclear (see Casagrande, 1994).

Layers 1 and 2, which receive input from the M-cells, are called the **magnocellular** (or **magno**) layers. Layers 3, 4, 5, and 6, which receive input from the P-cells, are called the **parvocellular** (or **parvo**) layers (Color Plate 1.7). The reason it is important to distinguish between these layers is that they process different kinds of information from the environment. This has been demonstrated in an experiment by Peter Schiller and his coworkers (1990), who determined the behavioral effects of destroying either the magno or the parvo layers.

Schiller and his coworkers first tested rhesus monkeys behaviorally to determine their ability to perceive movement, pattern, shape, color, and depth. They then anesthetized the monkeys and injected a neurotoxin called ibotenic acid so part of the magno layers was destroyed in some monkeys and part of the parvo layers was destroyed in other monkeys (Figure 3.6). After recovering from the operation, the monkeys with lesions in the magnocellular layer had lost their ability to detect movement, and the monkeys with lesions in the parvocellular layer had lost their ability to detect color, fine textures and patterns, and the depth of small or finely detailed objects. Schiller and coworkers therefore concluded that neurons in the magno and parvo layers represent two channels: The magno channel sends information about motion to the cortex, and the parvo channel sends information about color, texture, shape, and depth to the cortex (Table 3.2). We will see in the next section that

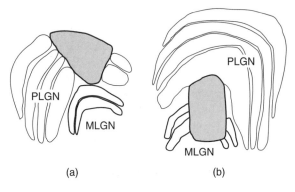

(a)   (b)

Figure 3.6
The areas of the LGN destroyed by Schiller and his coworkers are indicated by the shaded areas: (a) destruction of neurons in the parvocellular layers (PLGN); (b) destruction of neurons in the magnocellular layers (MLGN). (From Schiller, Logothetis, and Charles, 1990.)

Table 3.2
Layers of the LGN

LGN Layer	Function
Magnocellular (1 and 2)	Movement
Parvocellular (3, 4, 5, and 6)	Color Fine texture and pattern Depth

once this information reaches the cortex, it is processed further in separate pathways.

INFORMATION PROCESSING IN THE STRIATE CORTEX (V1)

WebTUTOR One and a half million axons travel from each LGN to the visual receiving area of the brain, which is called the striate cortex because of the presence of white stripes (striate = striped) created by nerve fibers that run through it (Glickstein, 1988). The striate cortex (area V1), is vastly more complex than the LGN, containing over 250 million neurons, compared to one million in the LGN (Connolly &

Table 3.1
Two types of retinal ganglion cells

Type of Ganglion Cell	Characteristics	Destination in LGN
M ganglion cell	Large cell body Fires in bursts	Magnocellular layers (1 and 2)
P ganglion cell	Small cell body Sustained firing	Parvocellular layers (3, 4, 5, and 6)

Van Essen, 1984; Spear et al., 1996). Like the LGN, the striate cortex is organized into layers (Figure 3.7).

The signals in the fibers of the LGN contain information that represents features of the visual scene, ranging from simple changes in light intensity to complex patterns such as people's faces or the visual clutter of a city street. The task of the striate cortex is to process this incoming information so these aspects of the visual scene become more clearly represented in the firing of individual neurons or groups of neurons. This process begins in the striate cortex and continues in the extrastriate cortex, which we will describe in the next chapter.

The story we have to tell about the striate cortex is an important one, because it establishes a number of principles regarding how the nervous system responds to stimuli and how it is organized. What you will see in the sections that follow is that (1) neurons in the striate cortex are specialized to respond best to specific aspects of stimuli, such as orientation, movement, and size; and (2) we can demonstrate this specialization physiologically, by recording from neurons, and psychophysically, by using a technique called selective adaptation. We will first describe how recording from neurons has shown that cortical neurons are tuned to respond best to specific orientations, to movement, and to length.

The Physiology of Neurons That Respond to Orientation, Length, and Movement

David Hubel and Torsten Wiesel began research on the visual system in the late 1950s. Their research, which focused on describing the responding and organization of neurons in the lateral geniculate nucleus and the visual cortex, culminated in their winning the Nobel Prize in Physiology and Medicine in 1981.

When Hubel and Wiesel began their research on the cortex, it was known that retinal ganglion cells had center-surround receptive fields and responded

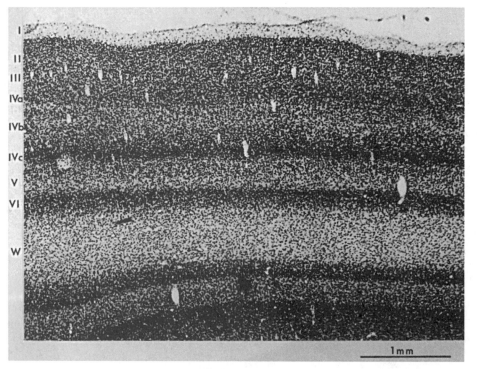

Figure 3.7
The layers of the visual cortex. Fibers from the LGN enter from the bottom, through the white matter (W) below layer VI, and synapse in layer IV. (From Hubel & Wiesel, 1977.)

well to spots of light. But as they recorded from cortical neurons and stimulated different areas of a cat's visual field with spots of light that would have caused large responses in ganglion cells, they were met with silence. The cortical neurons wouldn't respond.

After attempting to elicit cortical responses for a number of hours, Hubel and Wiesel experienced something startling: As they inserted a glass slide containing a spot stimulus into their slide projector, a cortical neuron "went off like a machine gun" (Hubel, 1982). The neuron, as it turned out, was responding not to the spot at the center of the slide, but to the image of the slide's edge moving downward on the screen as the slide dropped into the projector (Figure 3.8). Upon realizing this, Hubel and Wiesel changed their stimuli from small spots to moving lines and were then able to elicit responses from neurons in the cortex.

Once Hubel and Wiesel began stimulating the retina with moving lines while recording from neurons in the cortex, they discovered that most cortical neurons respond best to barlike stimuli with specific orientations. They distinguished three types of neurons based on the type of stimuli to which the neurons responded best (Hubel, 1982).

Simple Cortical Cells **Simple cells** have receptive fields that, like center-surround receptive fields, have excitatory and inhibitory areas. However, these areas are arranged side-by-side rather than in the center-surround configuration (Figure 3.9). This side-by-side arrangement means that a simple cell responds best to a bar of light with a particular orientation. The cell responds best when the bar is oriented along the length of the receptive field, as in Figure 3.9a, and responds less and less as the bar is tilted away from this best orientation (Figure 3.9b and c) (Hubel & Wiesel, 1959).

This preference of simple cortical cells for bars with particular orientations is shown in the **orientation tuning curve** of Figure 3.10. This curve, which is determined by measuring the responses of a simple cortical cell to bars with different orientations, shows that the cell responds with 25 nerve impulses per second to a vertically oriented bar and that the cell's response decreases as the bar is tilted away from the vertical, until a bar tilted 20 degrees from the vertical elicits only a small response. (We can appreciate the narrowness of this tuning by noting that when a clock indicates that the time is 12:04, the angle between the hour hand and the minute hand is 24 degrees.) While this particular simple cell responds best to a bar with a vertical orientation, there are other simple cells that respond to other orientations, so there are

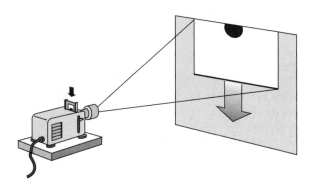

Figure 3.8
When Hubel and Wiesel dropped a slide into their slide projector, the image of the edge of the slide moving down unexpectedly triggered activity in a cortical neuron.

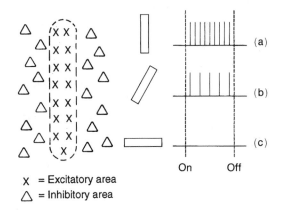

X = Excitatory area
△ = Inhibitory area

Figure 3.9
The receptive field of a simple cortical cell. This cell responds best to a vertical bar of light that covers the excitatory area of the receptive field (a) and responds less well as the bar is tilted so that it covers the inhibitory area (b and c). (Adapted from Hubel & Wiesel, 1959.)

LGN and Striate Cortex

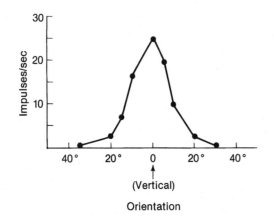

Figure 3.10

An orientation tuning curve of a simple cortical cell. This cell responds best to a vertical bar (orientation = 0) and responds less well as the bar is tilted in either direction.

types of neurons we have described so far, makes clear an important fact about neurons in the visual system: As we travel farther from the retina, neurons fire to more complex stimuli. Retinal ganglion cells respond best to spots of light, whereas end-stopped cells respond best to bars of a certain length that are moving in a particular direction. Later, we will see that this responding to more complex stimuli increases even further as we move into other visual areas of the cortex.

neurons that respond to all of the orientations that exist in the environment.

Complex Cortical Cells **Complex cells**, like simple cells, respond best to bars of a particular orientation. However, while simple cells will respond to small spots of light or to stationary stimuli, most complex cells respond only when a correctly oriented bar of light moves across the entire receptive field. Further, many complex cells respond best to a particular direction of movement (Figure 3.11).

End-Stopped Cells **End-stopped cells** fire to moving lines of a specific length or to moving corners or angles. The cell in Figure 3.12 responds best to a corner that is moving upward across the receptive field, as shown in Figure 3.12c. End-stopped cells will not fire if the stimulus is too long, so if we extend the length of this stimulus, as in Figure 3.12e, the cell no longer fires (Hubel & Wiesel, 1965a).

From our vantage point in the striate cortex, we can see that the processing that occurs in the cortex has created cortical neurons that fire in response to specific features of the stimulus, such as orientation or direction of movement. For this reason, these neurons are sometimes called **feature detectors**. Table 3.3, which summarizes the properties of the four

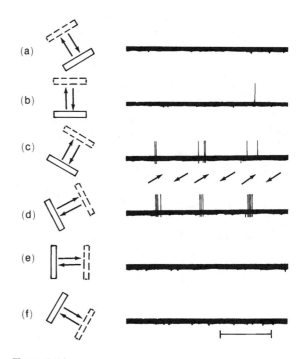

Figure 3.11

Response of a complex cell recorded from the visual cortex of the cat. The stimulus bar is moved back and forth across the receptive field. The records on the right indicate that the cell fires only when the bar is moved at a specific angle. The cell does not respond when the bar is oriented as in (a), (b), (e), and (f). A slight response occurs in (c). The best response occurs in (d); but, even when the bar is at this optimal orientation, a response occurs only when the bar is moved from left to right, as indicated by the arrows above the records. No response occurs when the bar moves from right to left. The horizontal bar at the lower right represents 1 second. (From Hubel & Wiesel, 1959.)

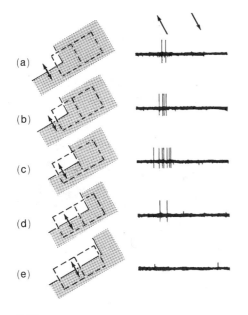

Figure 3.12
Response of an end-stopped cell recorded from the visual cortex of the cat. The stimulus is indicated by the light area on the left. This cell responds best to a light corner moving up (see the arrows above the records); there is no response when the corner moves down. Note that, as the corner is made longer as we progress from (a) to (b) to (c), the cell's firing rate increases, but that, when the length is increased further, as in (d) and (e), the firing rate decreases. (From Hubel & Wiesel, 1965a.)

Table 3.3
Properties of neurons in optic nerve, LGN, and cortex

Type of Cell	Characteristics of Receptive Field
Optic nerve fiber (ganglion cell)	Center-surround receptive field. Responds best to small spots but will also respond to other stimuli.
Lateral geniculate	Center-surround receptive fields very similar to the receptive field of a ganglion cell.
Simple cortical	Excitatory and inhibitory areas arranged side by side. Responds best to bars of a particular orientation.
Complex cortical	Responds best to movement of a correctly oriented bar across the receptive field. Many cells respond best to a particular direction of movement.
End-stopped cortical	Responds to corners, angles, or bars of a particular length moving in a particular direction.

The Psychophysics of Orientation Detectors

Selective adaptation is a psychophysical technique that has been used to demonstrate connections between neural activity and perception.

The Rationale Behind Selective Adaptation The idea behind selective adaptation is that when we view a stimulus with a specific property, neurons tuned to that property fire, and that, if viewing continues for long enough, these neurons adapt. What this adaptation means is that (1) the neuron's firing rate decreases, and (2) it will fire less when that stimulus is presented again. According to this idea, presenting a vertical line will cause neurons that respond to vertical lines to respond, and eventually these neurons will fire less to vertical lines.

The basic assumption behind a psychophysical selective adaptation experiment is that if these adapted neurons have anything to do with perception, then adaptation of neurons that respond to verticals should cause us to become less sensitive to verticals. The following general procedure for psychophysical selective adaptation experiments is used to determine whether this decrease in sensitivity does,

Hubel and Wiesel's demonstration of the existence of specialized orientation-selective neurons was a major advance in our understanding of visual physiology, because it provided a way to link the visual stimulus and neural activity. The fact that an object such as a table or a chair would cause numerous detectors with different orientations to fire provides what might be the first step toward neural representation of the object.

But is there any evidence that these orientation detectors actually have any impact on perception? We can answer this question by looking at the results of psychophysical experiments that make use of a technique called selective adaptation.

in fact, occur. We will use orientation as an example, but this same procedure is used for other stimulus properties as well.

1. Measure sensitivity to a range of orientations.

2. Adapt to one orientation.

3. Remeasure sensitivity to the range of orientations.

Now that we know the general procedure for a selective adaptation experiment, let's get down to specifics. For orientation, these specifics begin with determining the stimulus that we use to present different orientations to our observer.

The Stimulus for Measuring Selective Adaptation to Orientation How can we adapt our subject to a particular orientation? One way is to use an adapting stimulus with alternating bars, like the ones in Figure 3.13. This type of stimulus is called a **grating**. Gratings have a number of properties, including the thickness of the grating's bars, the orientation of the bars, the sharpness of the borders between the bars, and the contrast between the bars. For the purposes

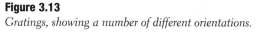

Figure 3.13
Gratings, showing a number of different orientations.

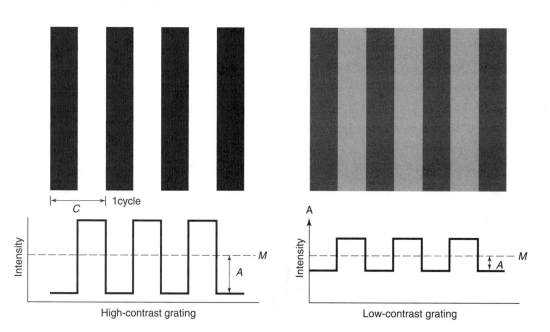

Figure 3.14
A high-contrast grating (left) and a low-contrast grating (right), with the intensity distributions for the bars indicated under each grating. Both gratings have the same mean intensity, M, indicated by the dashed line on the intensity distributions, but the grating on the left has a larger amplitude, A. The contrast of the gratings can be determined by dividing the amplitude of the grating by the mean intensity. The distance marked C on the grating on the left indicates the size of one cycle. Each of these gratings contains 3 ¹/₂ cycles. These gratings are called square-wave gratings because of the abrupt intensity changes at the borders of the bars. Sine-wave gratings, which have more gradual intensity changes, are described in Appendix B.

of our orientation experiment, we will focus on the two properties of orientation and contrast:

- *Orientation:* The **orientation** of a grating is its angle relative to vertical. Gratings may be oriented vertically or may be tilted at various angles (Figure 3.13).

- *Contrast:* The **contrast** of a grating is equal to its amplitude, A, divided by its mean intensity, M, which is indicated by the dashed line in Figure 3.14. This figure shows two gratings with different contrasts. In Figure 3.14a, the contrast is high, whereas in Figure 3.14b, the contrast is lower.

Remember that the basic idea behind adaptation is to present the adapting stimulus and then determine how this adaptation affects perception. The measure of perception that we use for our gratings is called contrast sensitivity. The **contrast sensitivity** of a grating is a measure of how sensitive people are to the differences between the light and dark bars. To measure contrast sensitivity, we first measure the **contrast threshold** by decreasing the intensity difference between the dark and light bars until the observer can just barely tell the difference between the dark and light bars. The intensity difference between the bars that can just barely be seen is the contrast threshold, and we can calculate the contrast sensitivity by the formula, sensitivity = 1/threshold. Thus, a low contrast threshold results in high contrast sensitivity, which means that the subject can detect a grating in which there is only a small intensity difference between the light and dark bars.

A Selective Adaptation Experiment   We are now ready to describe our selective adaptation experiment. The first step is to measure the observer's contrast sensitivity to gratings of a number of different orientations, like the ones in Figure 3.13. We then adapt the observer to a high-contrast grating with a particular orientation. In our example, we have our subject view a vertical grating, like the one that is indicated by the arrow in Figure 3.13, for about one minute.

Once the observer has been adapted to this grating, we then remeasure the observer's contrast sensi-

tivity to all of the orientations that we measured before the adaptation. Figure 3.15 shows how the contrast sensitivity has changed due to the adaptation. Our subject's contrast sensitivity has decreased to vertical gratings and to some nearly vertical orientations but not to orientations far from vertical. This is what we would predict if adapting with the vertical grating decreased the response of neurons that respond best to verticals and also some that respond best to orientations near vertical.

The important result of this experiment is that our psychophysical curve shows that adaptation selectively affects only some orientations, just as neurons selectively respond to only some orientations. The results of this experiment therefore support the idea that orientation detectors play a role in perception. We will now consider how the visual system responds to an aspect of the environment called spatial frequency. We will do this by first describing neurons that respond to this property and then by looking at the results of another selective adaptation experiment.

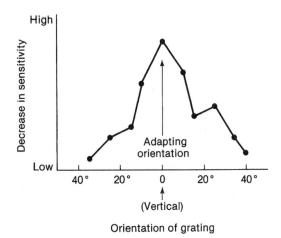

Figure 3.15
Results of a selective adaptation experiment. This graph shows that the subject's adaptation to the vertical grating causes a large decrease in her ability to detect the vertical grating when it is presented again but that this adaptation has less effect on gratings that are tilted to either side of the vertical. Gratings tilted more than about 35 degrees from the vertical are essentially unaffected by adaptation to the vertical grating.

Figure 3.16
A scene that contains many spatial frequencies. See text for details.

The Physiology of Neurons That Respond to Spatial Frequency

One of the most obvious aspects of the environment is that it often contains things that range from small to large. For example, consider the rooftops in Figure 3.16. Some things, such as the tiles on the rooftops, are such small details that they are difficult to see. The individual chimneys and the windows in the turrets are clearly visible, but are small details compared to the overall shapes of the buildings. One way to describe this range of object sizes would be to say that the scene has various levels of "grain," ranging from extremely small (the tiles on the roof) to very coarse (the overall shape of the buildings). A technical way to describe this grain is by using a measure called spatial frequency.

What Is Spatial Frequency? **Spatial frequency** is how rapidly a stimulus changes across space. For example, the grating on the right in Figure 3.17 has a higher spatial frequency than the one on the left, because it has more bars per unit distance. As we will see, there are neurons in the cortex that are tuned to respond best to specific spatial frequencies. But before we describe these neurons, we will describe how we measure spatial frequency.

From our grating example, we can see that spatial frequency is related to size, with smaller bars being associated with higher spatial frequencies. Thus, one way to specify spatial frequency could be in terms of size. But rather than doing this by measuring the actual size of an object, perception researchers specify spatial frequency in terms of size on the retina, using a measure called visual angle.

Visual Angle and Spatial Frequency **Visual angle** is the angle of an object relative to the observer's eye. For example, Figure 3.18a shows how we determine

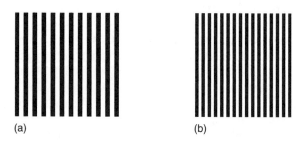

(a)   (b)

Figure 3.17
Two gratings. The one on the right has a higher spatial frequency than the one on the left. (From Blakemore & Sutton, 1969.)

Humans are more sensitive to horizontally or vertically oriented gratings than to other, oblique, orientations. This enhanced sensitivity for vertical and horizontal gratings is called the **oblique effect** (Campbell et al., 1966; Orban et al., 1984). The oblique effect appears to be linked to the activity of orientation-selective neurons, because recordings from these neurons in animals reveals that there are more neurons that respond to horizontals and verticals (DeValois et al., 1982) and that these neurons are allotted proportionally more space in the visual cortex (Coppola et al., 1998).

Christopher Furmanski and Stephen Engel (2000) have demonstrated an oblique effect in the striate cortex in humans by measuring the behavioral sensitivity and fMRI response to gratings with different orientations. The accompanying figure shows their results. The graph at (a), which plots the behavioral results, shows that subjects were more sensitive to vertical (0 degrees) and horizontal (90 degrees) gratings. The graph at (b) indicates the size of the fMRI response to the same gratings. The remarkable match between the behavioral and physiological result and the failure to see this effect in cortical areas outside of V1 supports the idea that responding of neurons in the striate cortex is responsible for the oblique effect.

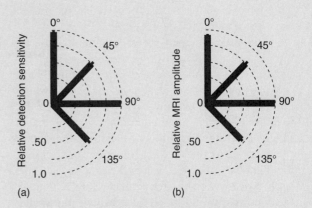

(a)   (b)

Results of the experiment by Furmanski and Engel. (a) Sensitivity to gratings oriented at 0, 45, 90, and 135 degrees measured behaviorally; longer bars indicate higher sensitivity. (b) fMRI response from area V1 of the cortex to the same orientations. (From Furmanski & Engel, 2000.)

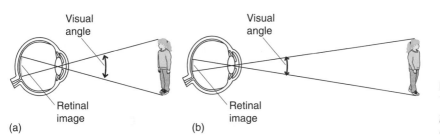

(a)   (b)

Figure 3.18
When the person moves farther from the observer's eye, the visual angle decreases.

the visual angle of a stimulus (a person in this example) by extending lines from the person to the lens of the observer's eye. The angle between the lines is the visual angle. Notice that the visual angle depends on both the size of the stimulus and on its distance from the observer, so when the person moves to a greater distance, as in Figure 3.18b, her visual angle becomes smaller.

LGN and Striate Cortex

Basically, what visual angle tells us is how large the object will be on the back of the eye. Since there are 360 degrees around the entire circumference of the eyeball, an object with a visual angle of 1 degree would take up 1/360 of this circumference, which is about 0.3 mm on an average-sized adult eye. One way to get a feel for visual angle is to fully extend your arm and look at your thumb, as the woman in Figure 3.19 is doing. The approximate visual angle of the thumb at arms length is 2 degrees (O'Shea, 1991). Thus, any object that is exactly covered by the thumb has a visual angle of 2 degrees.

The usual method for specifying spatial frequency of a grating is in terms of "cycles per degree"—the number of cycles in the grating that fit within an angle of one degree on the retina, where one cycle is a dark bar and a light bar. In Figure 3.19, the woman is using her thumb to measure the spatial frequency of a grating. Since the width of her thumb just covers two cycles of the grating (two pairs of dark and light bars), this means that these two cycles take up two degrees on the retina. Therefore, the angle for one cycle would be one degree, and the spatial frequency of this grating would be one cycle per degree.

Spatial Frequency and Fourier Analysis Spatial frequency is a useful measure of the grain of visual stimuli, because we can determine the spatial frequencies not just of gratings but also of objects in scenes like the one in Figure 3.16. This is accomplished by analyzing the intensities in the scene using a mathematical technique called **Fourier analysis,** which takes into account the sizes of objects and also things such as intensity changes that occur at edges, such as the change in intensity between the dark tiles on the roof and the white end of the house or between the tiles and the light-colored chimneys. (Remember that spatial frequency is a measure of how rapidly the stimulus changes across space. Thus, high spatial frequencies are associated with small objects and also with the rapid changes that often occur at borders.) For a more detailed explanation of how spatial frequencies can be determined by Fourier analysis, see Appendix B.

Figure 3.20 shows a picture that has been analyzed into its low spatial frequency and high spatial frequency components. Figure 3.20b, which shows the low spatial frequency components, indicates that low spatial frequencies are what you would see when viewing an object or scene through frosted glass, so

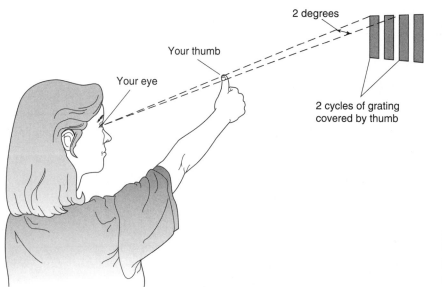

Figure 3.19
"Thumb method" for measuring visual angle. See text for explanation.

Figure 3.20
(a) Picture of Groucho Marx. (b) The low spatial frequencies in the picture. Details are lost, and larger components, such as the hair and the overall shape of the face, are emphasized, as would occur when viewing through frosted glass. (c) High spatial frequencies in the picture. Details such as the eyes and glasses and places where there are abrupt changes in contrast are emphasized. (From Frisby, 1979).

you can see just large forms and overall shapes. Figure 3.20c, which shows the high spatial frequency components, indicates that high spatial frequencies provide information about small details and places in the image where there are abrupt changes in contrast.

The Physiology of Spatial Frequency Analyzers
The different spatial frequency components of objects or scenes are important because there are neurons in the striate cortex that are tuned to respond best to specific spatial frequencies. These neurons, which are called **spatial frequency analyzers**, have been determined in two ways: (1) physiologically, by determining how cortical neurons respond to gratings with different spatial frequencies; and (2) psychophysically, by determining the effects of selective adaptation to specific frequencies.

Figure 3.21 shows the results of the physiological experiments—tuning curves for three simple cortical cells that each respond to a narrow range of frequencies (Maffei & Fiorentini, 1973; cf. Albrecht, DeValois, & Thorell, 1980; DeValois, DeValois, & Yund, 1979; Robson et al., 1988). Cell A responds best to low spatial frequencies, and C to high spatial frequencies.

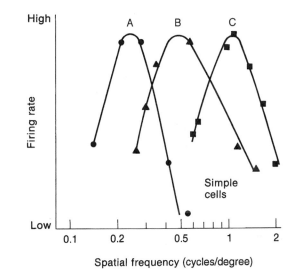

Figure 3.21
Tuning curves for three simple cortical cells to gratings moved across their receptive fields. Each cell requires gratings with a narrow range of frequencies. (Adapted from Maffei and Fiorentini, 1973.)

The Psychophysics of Spatial Frequency Analyzers

The psychophysical evidence for spatial frequency analyzers comes from using a selective adaptation procedure like the one we used for orientation detectors. We first measure the contrast sensitivity for gratings with a range of spatial frequencies, like the ones in Figure 3.17. These measurements result in a plot of contrast sensitivity vs. spatial frequency, which is called a **contrast sensitivity function** (Figure 3.22) (Campbell & Robson, 1968).

This CSF in Figure 3.22 tells us that the visual system is most sensitive to gratings with frequencies between about four and six cycles per degree (observers can see these gratings even if the contrast between the bars is very low) and that sensitivity drops off at lower and higher frequencies. Thus, at very low and very high spatial frequencies, the contrast must be much higher in order for an observer to see these gratings.

Once we have determined the contrast sensitivity function, we adapt the observer for 1 to 2 minutes to a grating with a particular spatial frequency—in this example, 7.1 cycles per degree—and we then remeasure the CSF. The CSF measured after adaptation shows a decreased contrast sensitivity in the frequency range around the adapting frequency of 7.1 cycles/degree, as indicated by the dotted line in Figure 3.22. This decrease indicates that we have adapted neurons sensitive to spatial frequencies around 7.1 cycles per degree. Results such as these, combined with the physiological results in Figure 3.21, have led researchers to conclude that the CSF is actually the sum of a number of separate channels, each of which is sensitive to a narrow range of spatial frequencies (Figure 3.23). You can experience the effect of adapting spatial frequency channels by doing the following demonstration.

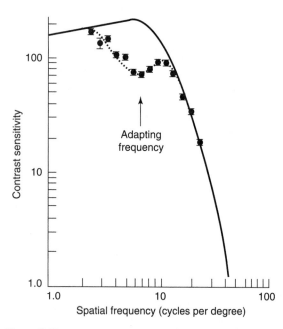

Figure 3.22
Squares and solid curve: contrast sensitivity function for a sine-wave grating. (From Campbell & Robinson, 1968.) Dotted curve: contrast sensitivity measured after adaptation to a 7.1 cycles/degree grating.

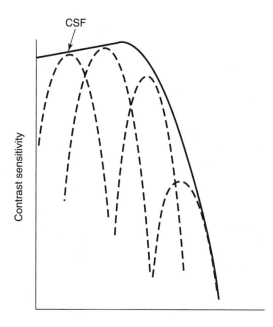

Figure 3.23
The contrast sensitivity function (solid line) and some of its underlying channels (dashed lines). These channels, each of which is sensitive to a narrow range of frequencies, add together to create the CSF.

Adaptation to Spatial Frequency

Look at Figure 3.24 by moving your eyes back and forth along the horizontal line between the two gratings on the left for about 60 seconds. This adapts you to the wide (low-frequency) bars above the line and to the narrow (high-frequency) bars below the line. After this adaptation, shift your gaze to the dot between the two gratings on the right and compare the spacing between the lines of the top and bottom gratings. ●

After adapting to the gratings on the left, the lines of the top right grating may appear more closely spaced than those of the bottom right grating, even though the sizes of the bars are actually the same for both gratings. We can relate this perception back to the adaptation of neurons that respond to spatial frequencies by first considering the neural response generated by the two gratings on the right before the

adaptation. Both of these gratings generate a large response in neurons that are sensitive to the gratings' frequency, indicated by bar M in Figure 3.25a and b. These gratings also generate some response in neurons that respond best to lower (L) and higher (H) frequencies than the gratings.

We can appreciate what happens as you were adapting to the gratings on the left by looking at Figure 3.25c and d. Adapting to the low-frequency grating decreases the responding of neurons that respond best to low frequencies. Thus, when we shift our eyes to the grating on the top right, we get the response shown in Figure 3.25c, in which the neu-

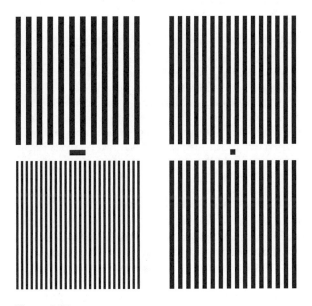

Figure 3.24
Stimuli for selective adaptation to spatial frequencies. See text for instructions.

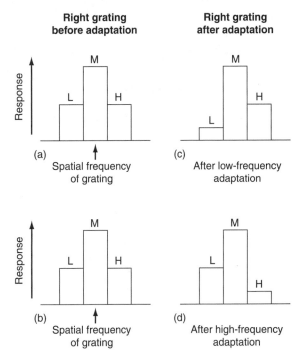

Figure 3.25
How neurons that respond best to low (L), medium (M), and high (H) spatial frequencies respond to the gratings on the right of Figure 3.24: (a) and (b) before adaptation; (c) after adaptation to the low-frequency grating at the top left; and (d) after adaptation to the high-frequency grating on the bottom left. These changes in the pattern of firing caused by adaptation are accompanied by changes in our perception of the grating.

rons tuned to low frequencies respond less than before they were adapted. This pattern of firing, which is weighted toward high spatial frequencies, explains why we perceive the top right bars as narrower. In contrast, adapting to the high-frequency grating decreases the responding of neurons that respond best to high frequencies. Thus, when we shift our eyes to the grating on the bottom right, we get the

response shown in Figure 3.25d, in which the neurons tuned to high frequencies respond less than before they were adapted. This pattern of firing, which is weighted toward low frequencies, explains why we perceive the bottom right bars as wider.

We have seen that there are cortical neurons that are tuned to respond to orientation, movement, length, and spatial frequency. We now consider how cortical

SUMMARY TABLE 3.1

Information Flow in the Lateral Geniculate Nucleus

The lateral geniculate nucleus (LGN) in the thalamus is the first place that most of the signals in the optic nerve arrive after they leave the eye. LGN neurons have center-surround receptive fields similar to those of ganglion cells. The LGN receives information from many sources, including information flowing back from the cortex. It appears to be important for regulating the flow of information between the retina and the cortex.

Organization in the Lateral Geniculate Nucleus

Information reaching the LGN from the retina is organized based on the left and right eyes, which reach layers 2, 3, and 5 and layers 1, 4, and 6, respectively. It is also organized as a retinotopic map so each location on the LGN corresponds to a location on the retina, and neighboring locations on the LGN correspond to neighboring locations on the retina. The LGN is also organized in terms of the types of ganglion cells arriving from the retina, with the M-cells arriving at layers 1 and 2 and the P-cells arriving at layers 3, 4, 5, and 6.

Receptive Fields of Neurons in the Striate Cortex

Hubel and Wiesel conducted a series of classic experiments in which they identified three types of neurons: simple cortical cells, which respond best to lines with specific orientations; complex cortical cells, which respond best to oriented lines that are moving in a specific direction; and end-stopped cells, which respond best to oriented lines of a specific length that are moving in a specific direction. Since these neurons respond to specific features of stimuli, they are called feature detectors.

Selective Adaptation for Orientation

Selective adaptation is a technique that has been used psychophysically to demonstrate connections between neural activity and perception. The basis of this technique is that prolonged exposure to a specific stimulus property, such as orientation, reduces the activity of neurons that respond to this property and that this reduction in physiological activity will show up in reductions in sensitivity to this property measured psychophysically. Experiments in which human subjects are adapted to gratings with a specific orientation provide evidence that orientation detectors are involved in perception.

The Oblique Effect

The oblique effect refers to the observation that people tend to be more sensitive to vertical and horizontal orientations. Recent fMRI studies on humans show that there is a good match between this effect measured psychophysically and the response of neurons in area V1.

Neurons That Respond to Spatial Frequency

Spatial frequency is how rapidly a stimulus changes across space, with high spatial frequencies corresponding to small details in the environment and low spatial frequencies corresponding to larger forms. Spatial frequency is measured in terms of cycles per degree of visual angle. A mathematical technique called Fourier analysis has made it possible to analyze spatial frequencies contained in environmental scenes. Electrophysiological studies indicate that some neurons in the striate cortex respond best to specific ranges of spatial frequency.

Psychophysics of Spatial Frequency

Psychophysical selective adaptation experiments indicate that adaptation to a specific spatial frequency causes decreases in sensitivity to narrow bands of spatial frequencies. This provides evidence for the existence of spatial frequency channels in the visual system. This indicates that the contrast sensitivity function, a plot of contrast sensitivity versus spatial frequency, may represent the sum of a number of these channels.

neurons that receive signals from different places on the retina and that respond to different properties are organized in the cortex. See Summary Table 3.1 for an overview of the material we have covered so far.

ORGANIZATION OF THE STRIATE CORTEX

The first step in describing the organization of the cortex is to describe how the retina is mapped on the cortex.

The Retinotopic Map on the Cortex

Just as in the LGN, there is a retinotopic map of the retina in the visual cortex, so each point on the cortex corresponds to a point on the retina. An important feature of this map is that the area on the cortex that represents the fovea is much larger than would be expected based only on the small size of the fovea. Even though the fovea is only a small dot on the retina, accounting for only 0.01 percent of the retina's area, signals from the fovea reach 8 to 10 percent of the visual cortex (Van Essen & Anderson, 1995). The fact that the small fovea is allotted a large area on the cortex is called the **cortical magnification factor**.

We can understand why the area allotted to the fovea is magnified by comparing how neurons are packed in the retina to how they are packed in the cortex. The foveal receptors are packed very closely together in the retina, whereas the peripheral receptors are much more widely spaced (Figure 3.26a). This packing of the receptors also occurs for the ganglion cells that receive signals from these receptors: There are about 50,000 ganglion cells per square millimeter of retina near the fovea but fewer than 1,000 cells per square millimeter in the peripheral retina (Figure 3.26b) (Stone, 1965; Wassle et al., 1990).

But when we move to the visual cortex, we find that the neurons that receive signals from the fovea are packed with the same density as the neurons that receive signals from the peripheral retina (Figure 3.26c). What this means is that the signals from the 50,000 ganglion cells coming from 1 mm of retina near the fovea will need more space on the cortex than the signals from the 1,000 ganglion cells coming from 1 mm of retina in the periphery.

The result is the cortical magnification factor: More cortical space is allotted to parts of the retina that send more ganglion cell signals to the cortex. In fact, recent research shows that the magnification factor occurs both because the fovea sends more ganglion cell signals per unit area to the cortex than does the peripheral retina, and also because each foveal

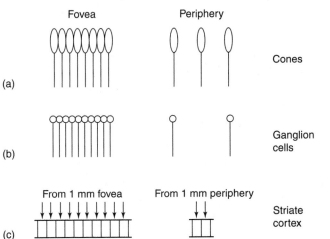

(a)

(b)

(c)

Figure 3.26
Packing densities in: (a) the retina, where foveal cones are packed much more closely in the fovea than in the periphery; (b) the ganglion cells, where those receiving signals from foveal cones are packed more densely than ganglion cells receiving signals from the periphery; and (c) the cortex, where cells are distributed evenly no matter where they came from, so the larger number of signals from the fovea, indicated by the arrows, take up more space in the cortex than do the smaller number of signals from the peripheral retina.

input is allotted extra cortical neurons, so a ganglion cell from near the fovea is allotted three to six times more cortical tissue than a ganglion cell from the periphery (Azzopardi & Cowey, 1993).

This magnified representation of the fovea in the cortex is related to the high acuity of the foveal cones. The foveal cones have high acuity both because of the way the cones are wired within the retina, with many having "private lines" to the ganglion cells, and also because the cones are allotted a large amount of space on the cortex. This extra cortical space is available for the extra neural processing needed to accomplish high-acuity tasks such as reading or identifying your friend's face in a crowd (Azzopardi & Cowey, 1993).

Location Columns

The retinotopic map on the surface of the cortex also extends below the surface in columns called **location columns**, which contain neurons that all have their receptive fields on about the same place on the retina. Hubel and Wiesel demonstrated this by penetrating the cortex with an electrode oriented perpendicularly to the cortical surface, as in Figure 3.27a. As they moved their electrode through the cortex, they stopped at closely spaced intervals and recorded from neurons

along the electrode track. When they did this they found that all of the neurons had receptive fields either on top of each other or very close together on the retina (Figure 3.27b). They concluded from this result that the cortex is organized into location columns that are perpendicular to the surface of the cortex, and that the neurons within a location column have their receptive fields at the same location on the retina.

When Hubel and Wiesel penetrated the cortex obliquely (at an angle to the surface), as in Figure 3.27c, and recorded from neurons separated by 1 mm along the electrode track, they found that the receptive fields were systematically displaced and that neurons close to each other along the electrode track corresponded to receptive fields close to each other on the retina (Figure 3.27d). This result shouldn't surprise us, because it reflects the retinotopic map on the cortex we described earlier. What the results in Figure 3.27 mean is that stimuli that fall on a particular area of the retina are processed by neurons in the location columns for that area of retina.

Orientation Columns

As Hubel and Wiesel lowered their electrodes perpendicular to the surface of the cortex they noted not

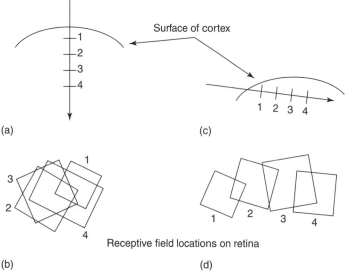

(a)

(b)

Surface of cortex

(c)

Receptive field locations on retina

(d)

Figure 3.27
(a) When an electrode penetrates the cortex perpendicularly, (b) the receptive fields of the neurons encountered along this track overlap. The receptive field recorded at each numbered position along the electrode track is indicated by a correspondingly numbered square. (c) When the electrode penetrates obliquely, (d) the receptive fields of neurons recorded from the numbered positions along the track are displaced, as indicated by the numbered receptive fields; neurons near each other in the cortex have receptive fields near each other on the retina.

only that the neurons along this track had receptive fields with the same location on the retina but that these neurons all preferred stimuli with the same orientations. Thus, all cells encountered along the electrode track at A in Figure 3.28 respond best to horizontal lines, whereas all those along electrode track B respond best to lines oriented at about 45 degrees. Based on this result, Hubel and Wiesel concluded that the cortex is organized into **orientation columns**, with each column containing cells that respond best to a particular orientation.

Hubel and Wiesel's discovery of orientation columns was based solely on electrophysiological responding. Looking at the cortex provides no clue that these columns exist because they are not normally visible. But a technique called the **2-deoxyglucose (2-DG) technique** has made it possible to see these orientation columns. The 2-DG technique is based on the following facts:

1. Brain cells depend on glucose as a source of metabolic energy.

2. Cells that are more active use more glucose.

3. 2-Deoxyglucose (2-DG), a specialized form of glucose, can masquerade as glucose, so it is taken up by active cells as glucose is.

4. After 2-DG is taken up by the cell, it begins to be metabolized, but since the resultant metabolite can't cross the cell's wall, it accumulates inside the cell.

These properties of 2-DG enabled Hubel, Wiesel, and Stryker (1978) to do the following experiment: After injecting a monkey with radioactively labeled 2-DG, they stimulated the monkey's visual system by moving a black-and-white vertical grating back and forth in front of the animal for 45 minutes. This movement of the grating's vertical stripes increased activity in the cells that prefer vertical orientations, causing them to increase their uptake of radioactive 2-DG. After this stimulation, the monkey was sacrificed, and when a slice of its visual cortex was placed in contact with a special photographic emulsion, the radioactive areas showed up as the dark stripes in Figure 3.29. These dark stripes correspond to the orientation columns that Hubel and Wiesel measured by recording from neurons. Thus, orientation columns have been demonstrated both by observing how neurons respond electrically to different orientations and how neurons take up glucose to different orientations.

In addition to demonstrating that the visual cortex consists of columns of cells with the same preferred orientation, Hubel and Wiesel showed that adjacent columns have cells with slightly different preferred orientations. They showed this by moving an electrode through the cortex obliquely, as in Figure 3.27c, so that the electrode cut across orientation columns. When they did this, they found that the neurons' preferred orientations changed in an orderly fashion, so a column of cells that respond best to 45 degrees is right next to the column of cells that respond best to 40 degrees. Hubel and Wiesel also found that as they moved their electrode one millimeter across the cortex, their electrode passed through orientation columns that represented the entire range of orientations.

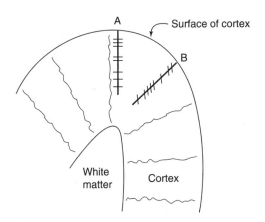

Figure 3.28
Electrophysiological evidence of orientation columns in the visual cortex. The microelectrode tracks (A and B), which are both perpendicular to the surface of the cortex, encounter simple, complex, and end-stopped cells along their paths, but all of these cells have the same preferred stimulus orientation (indicated by the lines cutting across each electrode track).

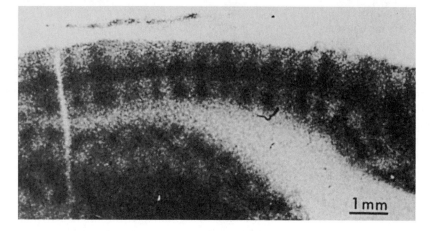

Figure 3.29
Magnified picture of a slice of visual cortex that has taken up radioactive 2-DG, as described in the text. The dark vertical bands, produced by the radioactive 2-DG, are orientation columns. The dark horizontal band is layer 4 of the cortex. Neurons in this layer receive inputs from the LGN and respond to all orientations. (From Hubel, Wiesel, & Stryker, 1978.)

Ocular Dominance Columns

Neurons in the cortex are also organized with respect to the eye to which they respond best. About 80 percent of the neurons in the cortex respond to stimulation of both the left and the right eyes. However, most cells respond better to one eye than to the other. This preferential response to one eye is called **ocular dominance**, and cells with the same ocular dominance are organized into **ocular dominance columns** in the cortex.

Hubel and Wiesel observed these columns during their oblique penetrations of the cortex. They found that a given area of cortex usually contains cells that all respond best to one of the eyes, but when the electrode was moved about 0.25 to 0.50 mm across the cortex, the dominance pattern changes to the other eye. Thus, the cortex consists of a series of columns that alternate in ocular dominance in a left-right-left-right pattern.

Hypercolumns

Hubel and Wiesel proposed that all three types of columns could be combined into one larger unit called a **hypercolumn**. Figure 3.30 is a schematic diagram showing two side-by-side hypercolumns. Each hypercolumn contains a single location column (since it represents a particular place on the retina), right and left ocular dominance columns, and a complete set of orientation columns that cover all possible stimulus orientations from 0 to 180 degrees.

The most important thing about a hypercolumn is that all of the neurons in a hypercolumn fire to stimulation of one specific location on the retina (remember that there is one location column in a hypercolumn). This means that we can think of a hypercolumn as a processing module that processes

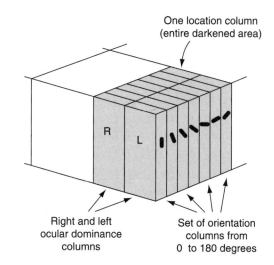

Figure 3.30
Schematic diagram of a hypercolumn. The light area on the left is one hypercolumn, and the darkened area on the right is another hypercolumn. The darkened area is labeled to show that it consists of one location column, right and left ocular dominance columns, and a complete set of orientation columns.

information about any stimulus that falls within the area served by the location column. With this property of hypercolumns in mind, we are now in a position to consider how an object in the environment might be represented by the firing of neurons in the cortex.

Representation of an Object in the Striate Cortex

To describe how objects are represented in the striate cortex we will consider the situation in which an observer views a tree. Figure 3.31a and b show that looking at the tree creates an image of the tree on the retina. To keep things simple, we are just going to focus on the trunk of the tree. The connection between three areas on the retina that correspond to parts of the tree trunk and hypercolumns in the cortex is indicated in Figure 3.32. The tree's image is large enough so it stimulates the areas served by three hypercolumns, so the tree will cause neurons within each of the hypercolumns to fire.

But the tree trunk doesn't cause every neuron in each of the hypercolumns' columns to fire. The only neurons that fire are those that are tuned to respond to the tree's orientation on the retina, which in our example is 0 degrees, since the tree is oriented vertically. Since neurons are organized into orientation columns, the tree will cause neurons in the 0 degree orientation column in each hypercolumn to fire, as

indicated by the dark lines in Figure 3.32. In other words, the tree trunk is translated into a pattern of cortical stimulation in three separate hypercolumns, and this cortical stimulation bears little resemblance to the actual shape of the tree.

Although the fact that the tree is represented in a number of separate columns in the cortex may be surprising, it simply confirms a basic property of our perceptual system: The cortical representation of a stimulus does not have to resemble the stimulus; it just has to contain information that *represents* the stimulus. The representation of a tree in the visual cortex is contained in the firings of neurons in different cortical columns. Of course, our perception of the tree may not be based on this particular representation, because, as we will see in the next chapter, signals from area V1 travel to a number of other places in the cortex for further processing.

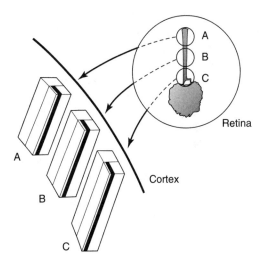

Figure 3.32
The image of the tree trunk stretches across an area of retina served by a number of hypercolumns. The places on the retina served by three hypercolumns are shown here, along with the corresponding hypercolumns in the cortex. The darkened columns in each hypercolumn indicates the orientation columns that correspond to the tree's orientation. The tree therefore causes firing of neurons in these orientation columns.

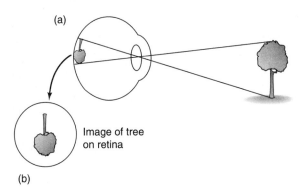

Figure 3.31
(a) Looking at a tree creates an image of the tree that (b) covers an area on the retina.

In this chapter we begin a feature called "The Plasticity of Perception," which will appear at the end of most of the chapters in the book. **Plasticity** refers to the way our perceptual system is molded and changed by the stimulation it receives. In other words, plasticity is the idea that the structure and functioning of the visual system, or any other sensory system, can be shaped by an animal's or person's perceptual experience.

The basic physiological principle behind changes in the nervous system caused by experience was proposed by Donald Hebb (1949). Hebb proposed that repeated experiences, such as those that occur during the process of learning, causes the same groups of neurons to fire and that this repeated firing strengthens the synaptic connections between these neurons. Learning creates groups of neurons called **cell assemblies** that are more likely to fire when a learned stimulus is seen or a memory is retrieved. According to this idea, seeing a familiar face activates a particular group of neurons that is associated with that face, and this firing causes us to recognize the face. Although Hebb's proposal was theoretical, later research has generally confirmed it.

Research on the plasticity in the visual system has focused on how an animal's perceptual experience affects neural firing. Early research in plasticity used a technique called **selective rearing** in which cats or monkeys were reared in environments that consisted of only one type of stimulus.

Selective Rearing
for Orientation in Kittens

The kitten's visual system is well developed early in life. Neurons that respond best to specific orientations are present within the first six weeks

(Hubel & Wiesel, 1963; Mitchell & Timney, 1984; Sherk & Stryker, 1976). But even though kittens have orientation-selective neurons that respond to the full range of orientations, the properties of these neurons can be changed if the kittens are exposed to a special environment as they are developing.

In one selective rearing experiment, Colin Blakemore and Grahame Cooper (1970) placed kittens in striped tubes like the one in Figure 3.33 so each kitten was exposed to only one orientation, either vertical or horizontal. The kittens were kept in the dark from birth to two weeks of age, at which time they were placed in the tube for five hours a day; the rest of the time they remained in the dark. Since the kittens sat on a Plexiglas platform and the tube extended both above and below them, there were no visible corners or edges in their environment other than the stripes on the sides of the tube. The kittens wore neck ruffs to prevent them from turning vertical stripes into oblique or horizontal stripes by turning their heads; however, according to Blakemore and Cooper, "The kittens did not seem upset by the monotony of their surroundings and they sat for long periods inspecting the walls of the tube" (p. 477).

When the kittens' behavior was tested after five months of selective rearing, they seemed blind to the orientations that they hadn't seen in the tube. For example, a kitten that was reared in an environment of vertical stripes would pay attention to a vertical rod but ignored a horizontal rod. Following behavioral testing, Blakemore and Cooper recorded from cells in the visual cortex and determined the stimulus orientation that caused the largest response from each cell. Their

(continued)

The Plasticity of Perception (*continued*)

results indicate that many of the cells of the horizontally reared cats respond best to horizontal stimuli, but none respond to vertical stimuli (Figure 3.34).

"Selective Rearing" for Orientation in Humans

The perceptual plasticity that changes the characteristics of neurons in the rearing experiments with kittens may also be affecting the characteristics of neurons in humans. This appears to have occurred in some people with a condition called **astigmatism**, which is caused by a distortion in the shape of the cornea, resulting in an image that is out of focus either in the horizontal or vertical (Figure 3.35). Thus, a person who has an astigmatism at an early age is essentially exposed to an environment in which lines in one orientation are imaged sharply on the retina, but lines 90 degrees from this orientation are out of focus.

Ralph Freeman and John Pettigrew (1973) showed that cats reared with an artificial astigmatism, created by wearing a mask containing astigmatic lenses, develop cortical cells that favor whatever orientation is in sharp focus during rearing. This result in cats resembles a condition known as **meridional amblyopia** in humans. People with this condition often had an astigmatism at a young age that was not corrected by

(*continued*)

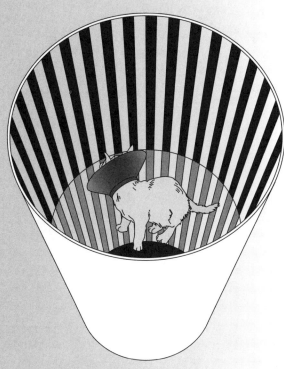

Figure 3.33
Blakemore and Cooper's (1970) striped tube. The kitten wore a black ruff to mask its body from its eyes and stood on a glass platform in the middle of the cylinder. A spotlight (not shown) illuminated the walls from above.

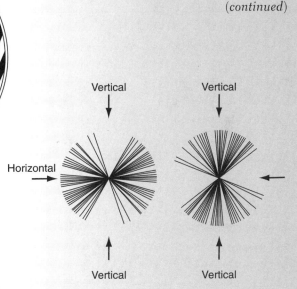

Figure 3.34
Distribution of optimal orientations for 52 cells from a horizontally experienced cat, on the left, and for 72 cells from a vertically experienced cat, on the right. (Blakemore & Cooper, 1970.)

LGN and Striate Cortex

The Plasticity of Perception (*continued*)

glasses and now, as adults, have astigmatisms that cannot be optically corrected. That is, even if these people wear glasses that compensate for their distorted corneas so that all orientations are sharply imaged on the retina, they still have impaired acuity for objects with orientations that were originally blurred by their astigmatism (see Mitchell and Wilkinson, 1974).

Apparently, just as the cortical neurons of Freeman and Pettigrew's astigmatic cats respond less well to orientations blurred by the astigmatism, so the cortical neurons of people with meridional amblyopia may be responding less well to orientations that were blurred when they were children. The smaller response causes their vision to be impaired for those orientations, even if the image on the retina is sharp.

Figure 3.35
Left: An astigmatic fan chart is used to test for astigmatism. Right: An astigmatic patient will perceive the lines in one orientation (in this case vertical) as sharp and the lines in the other orientations as blurred. (From Trevor-Roper, 1970.)

MAPS AND COLUMNS

The retinotopic maps on the LGN and striate cortex organize neural information in these structures along an important dimension—the location of the image on the retina. Similar mapping also occurs in other senses. For the sense of touch, there is a map of the body on the brain, so touching a particular place on the body activates a particular place on the somatosensory cortex in the parietal lobe (Figure 3.36). This map, which is arranged so that adjacent parts of the body are located adjacent to each other on the brain, is called a **somatotopic map**.

The maps for vision and touch are both distorted. Just as there is a magnification factor in vision in which the fovea is represented by a large area in the cortex, there is also a magnification factor in touch, so that parts of the body, such as the tips of the fingers, that are very sensitive to details and fine tex-

tures are allotted an area on the cortex that is far out of proportion to their area on the skin.

Mapping also occurs in the auditory system so that sound frequencies, which correspond to differently pitched tones, are arranged in an orderly way on the auditory cortex, with low frequencies represented by neurons at one end and high frequencies

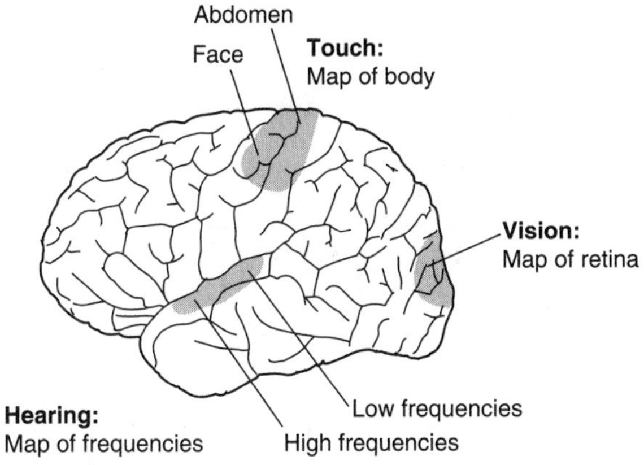

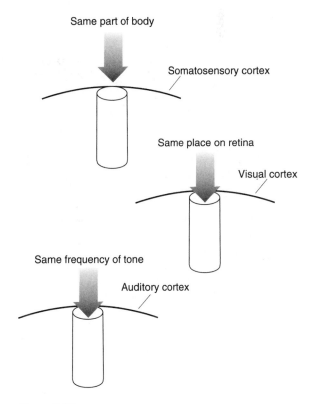

Figure 3.36
Each of the cortical receiving areas for hearing, vision, and touch (shaded areas) contain maps—neurons arranged in an orderly way that represents sound frequency, location on the retina, and places on the body.

Figure 3.37
The cortical areas for touch, vision, and hearing all contain columns that process information about a specific location or property of the stimulus.

by neurons at the other end. This auditory map is called a **tonotopic map**.

In addition to having mapping in common, the visual, auditory, and somatosensory (touch) systems are also organized in columns (Figure 3.37). An electrode lowered perpendicularly to the cortical surface will encounter neurons that respond to the same location or orientation in the visual cortex, to the same location on the body in the somatosensory cortex, and to the same frequency of sound in the auditory cortex.

This organization of these senses into maps and columns is probably an aid to further neural processing. For example, the fact that visual neurons with the same orientation preference are organized into columns might make it easier to construct complex cells from inputs from a number of simple cells with the same preferred orientation and end-stopped cells from a number of complex cells with the same preferred orientation. It is not unreasonable to suspect that columnar organization may serve similar functions in the somatosensory and auditory systems.

SUMMARY TABLE 3.2

Retinotopic Organization of the Striate Cortex

The striate cortex is organized in a number of ways. There is a retinotopic map in the cortex. This map indicates that signals reaching the cortex from the fovea take up a larger area of cortex than would be expected based just on the small area of the fovea on the retina. This is called the cortical magnification factor.

Columnar Organization of the Striate Cortex

The cortex is organized into location columns in which all neurons in a column that is perpendicular to the surface of the cortex have receptive fields in about the same place on the retina. The striate cortex is also organized into orientation columns, in which all neurons in a column are tuned to respond best to the same orientation, and ocular dominance columns, in which neurons in the column all respond best to stimulation of one of the eyes. Finally, all of these columns can be thought of as being organized into hypercolumns, which form a module for processing information that is imaged on a particular place on the retina.

Representing an Object in the Striate Cortex

An object that has an image on the retina large enough to stimulate a number of different location columns will be represented in the cortex by the firing of neurons in a number of separate hypercolumns that are tuned to the object's orientation. Thus, a single object, such as the trunk of a tree, can be represented by activity in a number of separated areas of striate cortex.

Plasticity: Selective Rearing for Orientation

Plasticity refers to the fact that our experience with specific stimuli can shape the functioning of the visual system. Selective rearing experiments, in which cats are raised in environments consisting of just one orientation, support the idea of plasticity, since the cat's cortex becomes dominated by neurons that are tuned to that orientation. There is also evidence that similar effects occur in the brains of people who have had a condition called astigmatism in which some orientations are blurred.

Across the Senses: Maps and Columns

The maps and columns observed in the visual system can also be demonstrated in other senses as well. There are somatotopic maps of the body on the somatosensory cortex, which serves the sense of touch, and tonotopic maps of frequencies in the auditory cortex. There is also evidence that neurons in the somatosensory and auditory systems are organized into columns.

STUDY QUESTIONS

1. What do we mean when we say that a tree is "transformed" by the visual system? (78)

2. What do we mean when we say that a tree is "represented" by electrical signals? (78)

Information Flow and Organization in the Lateral Geniculate Nucleus

3. How do the receptive fields of neurons in the LGN compare to the receptive fields of retinal ganglion cells? (78)

4. What is a major function of the LGN? (78)

Information Flow in the Lateral Geniculate Nucleus

5. Which structures send inputs to the LGN? (78)

6. Which are more numerous, signals traveling from the cortex to the LGN or those traveling from the retina to the LGN? Signals traveling from the cortex or those traveling from the LGN to the cortex? (79)

7. For every 10 nerve impulses the LGN receives from the retina, it sends _____ back to the cortex. (79)

Organization by Left and Right Eyes

8. What does it mean to say that the LGN is a bilateral structure? What is the ipsilateral eye? The contralateral eye? (79)

9. Describe how signals from each eye send signals to the six layers of the LGN. (79)

Organization as a Retinotopic Map

10. What is a retinotopic map? What does the existence of a retinotopic map say about the correspondence between neurons in the LGN and the retina? (80)

11. Why has the LGN been compared to a club sandwich? (80)

Organization by Types of Ganglion Cells Arriving at the LGN

12. Describe the M- and P-ganglion cells in the retina and the magnocellular and parvocellular layers that send their fibers to the LGN. (80)

13. Describe Schiller's experiment in which the magno and parvo layers of the LGN were selectively destroyed. What did Schiller conclude from the results of this experiment about the functions of the magno and parvo layers? (81)

Information Processing in the Striate Cortex (V1)

14. How many neurons reach the striate cortex from the LGN, and how many neurons does the striate cortex contain? (81)

15. What is the task of the striate cortex? (82)

The Physiology of Neurons That Respond to Orientation, Length, and Movement

16. How did Hubel and Wiesel discover that neurons in the striate cortex fire to moving lines? (82)

17. Describe the properties of a simple cortical cell. What is an orientation tuning curve, and what does it tell us about the response of a neuron? (83)

18. Describe the properties of complex cells and end-stopped cells. Why are these neurons sometimes called feature detectors? (84)

19. As we travel farther from the retina, do neurons require more complex or less complex stimuli in order to fire? (84)

The Psychophysics of Orientation Detectors

20. What is selective adaptation? What is the basic rationale behind selective adaptation? (85)

21. What is the basic assumption behind a selective adaptation experiment? (85)

22. What is the procedure for a selective adaptation experiment? (86)

23. What is a grating? What is a grating's orientation? Contrast? (86)

24. What is contrast sensitivity, and how is it measured? (87)

25. What is the typical result that occurs after selective adaptation to orientation? What is the neural explanation of that result and what conclusion does that explanation support? (87)

Brain Scan:
The Oblique Effect in the Striate Cortex

26. What is the oblique effect? (89)

27. What is the evidence that links the oblique effect to the activity of orientation-selective neurons? (89)

28. How were psychophysical measurements and fMRI used to study the oblique effect? What did these experiments indicate about the possible cortical site for determining the oblique effect? (89)

The Physiology of Neurons That Respond to Spatial Frequency

29. What is spatial frequency? How is it related to the "grain" of the environment? (88)

30. What is visual angle? What does it tell us about the size of the retinal image? (88)

31. What is the "thumb method" for determining the visual angle? (90)

32. How can the thumb method be applied to determining the spatial frequency of a grating in cycles per degree? (90)

33. What is Fourier analysis, and what does it tell us about the spatial frequencies in a scene? (90)

34. Describe the kinds of objects in a scene that would have low spatial frequencies and the kinds that would have high spatial frequencies. (90)

35. What is the physiological evidence for spatial frequency analyzers? (90)

The Psychophysics of Spatial Frequency Analyzers

36. What is the contrast sensitivity function (CSF)? What does it tell us about how sensitive people are to different spatial frequencies? (92)

37. What are the steps in the procedure for selectively adapting to spatial frequency? (92)

38. What are the results of selective adaptation to spatial frequency? What do these results tell us about neural spatial frequency analyzers? (92)

39. What have researchers concluded about the CSF based on the results of selective adaptation to spatial frequency? (92)

40. Describe the result of the demonstration involving the gratings in Figure 3.24 and explain how the result of that demonstration could occur based on adaptation of neurons that respond to specific ranges of spatial frequencies. (93)

Organization of the Striate Cortex

The Retinotopic Map on the Cortex

41. Why do we say that there is a retinotopic map of the retina on the cortex? (95)

42. What is the cortical magnification factor? (95)

43. Explain how the magnification factor occurs based on the relative densities of ganglion cell neurons in the fovea and the periphery and the way the neurons that receive signals from the fovea and periphery are packed in the striate cortex. (95)

44. What is another cause of the cortical magnification factor? (96)

45. How is the magnified representation of the fovea in the cortex related to perception? (96)

Location Columns

46. How did Hubel and Wiesel show that the cortex is organized into location columns? (96)

47. What are location columns? If two neurons are in the same location column, what does that mean? (96)

Orientation Columns

48. How did Hubel and Wiesel determine that there are orientation columns in the striate cortex? What does it mean to say that two neurons are in the same orientation column? (96)

49. What is the 2-deoxyglucose technique, and what does it demonstrate? (97)

Ocular Dominance Columns

50. What is ocular dominance? What are ocular dominance columns? (98)

Hypercolumns

51. What is a hypercolumn, and what do we mean when we say it is a processing module? (98)

52. Describe how neurons in a hypercolumn respond to the image of a trunk of a tree on the retina. (98)

53. What do we mean when we say that the pattern of cortical stimulation does not resemble the stimulus but contains information that represents the stimulus? (99)

The Plasticity of Perception: Selective Rearing for Orientation

54. What does "plasticity" refer to? (100)

55. What is the basic physiological principle behind plasticity, as proposed by Hebb? (100)

Selective Rearing for Orientation in Kittens

56. How well developed is the kitten's visual system? Are orientation-selective neurons present at an early age? (100)

57. Describe Blakemore and Cooper's selective rearing experiment in which they used a striped tube. (100)

58. What was the behavioral result of Blakemore and Cooper's experiment? The neural result? (100)

"Selective Rearing" for Orientation in Humans

59. What is astigmatism? (101)

60. What happens to the cortical cells of kittens raised with an artificial astigmatism? (101)

61. What is meridional amblyopia? (101)

62. What is the acuity of a person with meridional amblyopia after the retinal image is corrected so it is sharp? What does this result mean? (102)

Across the Senses: Maps and Columns

63. Describe the maps on the somatosensory cortex and on the auditory cortex. How are these maps similar to maps on the visual cortex? (103)

64. Describe the columnar arrangement of neurons in the somatosensory cortex and the auditory cortex. (103)

65. How might the organization of the senses into maps and columns be an aid to neural processing? (104)

4

HIGHER-LEVEL
VISUAL PROCESSING

SOME QUESTIONS WE WILL CONSIDER

- What can happen to a person's perception when he or she suffers brain damage? (115)

- Are there separate brain areas that determine our perception of different qualities, such as form and movement? (117)

- How is the operation of our visual system shaped by evolution and by our day-to-day experiences? (127)

- How does the brain combine information about all of the qualities of an object into our perception of a whole object? (134)

As we left our description of the visual system at the end of Chapter 3, signals had reached the striate cortex (V1) and had been processed so neurons in V1 responded to oriented, moving lines—Hubel and Wiesel's simple, complex, and end-stopped neurons.

Hubel and Wiesel's research on how neurons in V1 respond and how they are organized helped them win the Nobel Prize in 1981. But, as important as their contribution to our understanding of vision was, Hubel and Wiesel's description of simple, complex and end-stopped neurons was only a first step in explaining perception, because these neurons provide only a crude explanation of how objects might be represented in the visual system.

An example of how Hubel and Wiesel's feature detectors were used to explain perception is shown in Figure 4.1. The table, according to what we knew about feature detectors in the 1960s, was represented by the firing of orientation detectors that fired to various features of the table. However, many aspects of perception are difficult to explain based on simple feature detectors, including how the responding of the different orientation detectors is combined into the perception of a table and how we are still able to recognize the table when it is located at different places in our visual field and when we view it from different angles (Figure 4.2).

But even as Hubel and Wiesel were describing the properties of simple, complex, and end-stopped neurons in V1, it was beginning to become apparent that there were cells in the visual system that re-

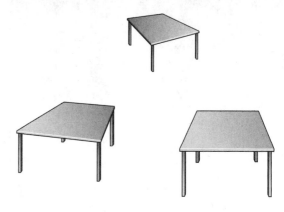

Figure 4.2
Any physiological explanation of object perception has to be able to deal with the fact that we see objects like the table from different viewpoints and from different distances.

sponded to stimuli far more complex than oriented lines (Gross et al., 1969, 1972). By the late 1970s a new era in the study of the physiology of perception was about to begin, with research showing that the processing of visual information extends into the **extrastriate cortex**, where extrastriate means, literally, everything in the cerebral cortex that is *not* the striate cortex (Figure 2.5 and Color Plate 1.8). We will see that large areas of the temporal and parietal lobes are involved in visual perception and that parts of the frontal lobe are involved as well. Today we know that over half of the cerebral cortex can be activated by visual stimuli (Mishkin, 1986).

This chapter is mainly about how neural processing in the extrastriate cortex is related to perception. But before moving on to the extrastriate cortex, we are going to spend a little more time in V1, to describe some recent research that has shown that some neurons in V1 respond to stimuli that are more complex than Hubel and Wiesel's oriented lines.

HIGHER-LEVEL PROCESSING IN THE STRIATE CORTEX

According to the picture we have painted so far, area V1 contains some neurons tuned to orientations, some to spatial frequencies, and some to length, and

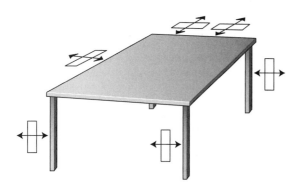

Figure 4.1
How a table might be represented by the firing of orientation detectors in the cortex. Each of the bars with arrows stands for the firing of an orientation detector. The table legs stimulate orientation detectors sensitive to verticals, and the edges of the table stimulate orientation detectors sensitive to horizontals. Although the table is stationary, these features of the table move on the retina because the eyes are always jiggling slightly.

when stimuli with these properties fall within a neuron's receptive field, the neuron fires.

But recent research has shown that there are neurons in area V1 of the monkey that have a property called **contextual modulation**, which means that their response to a stimulus can be modulated, or influenced, by the context which surrounds the stimulus. For example, Figure 4.3a shows a vertical bar in the middle of a neuron's receptive field (indicated by the square). The neuron responds well to the bar as shown in Figure 4.3d. But when the vertical bar is surrounded with randomly oriented bars, as in Figure 4.3b, the neuron's response decreases. This is not the same thing as the center-surround antagonism we described in Chapter 2 (Figure 2.37), in which stimulation of the inhibitory surround of a receptive field can decrease responding caused by stimulation of the

excitatory center. The difference is that in the present example, the additional bars fall outside of the neuron's receptive field and have no effect on responding when presented by themselves (also see Lamme & Spekreijse, 2000).

But Figure 4.3c shows how we can restore the neuron's responding by adding vertical bars that are positioned so they create a group that includes the center bar. From results such as these, it has been suggested that the neuron's response to the bar appears to depend on the bar's **salience**, where salience is the degree to which the line stands out. Thus, when the context hides the bar, as in Figure 4.3b, the bar's salience is low and firing decreases. When a different context includes the bar, as in Figure 4.3c, the bar's salience becomes higher and firing increases.

What causes this contextual modulation to occur? Figure 4.4, from an experiment by Karl Zipser and coworkers (1996), suggests an answer to this question by showing that the contextual modulation effect in V1 neurons takes some time to develop. Figure 4.4a shows how a monkey V1 neuron responds when its receptive field and surrounding areas are covered by a pattern of slanted lines. The record on the right follows the firing rate for 300 ms after the onset of this stimulus. Notice that there is a burst of firing at the beginning and that firing then decreases to a lower level and continues.

But observe what happens when we change part of the background so the center square now stands out, as in Figure 4.4b. The initial burst of firing is the same as before, but the firing after this burst stays at a higher level than before, as indicated by the shading in the firing record. Thus, increasing the salience of the stimulus (now the square stands out, whereas before it didn't) increases the neuron's response, beginning at about 80 ms after the start of firing. What this delay means is that taking context into account probably involves additional processing by some extra synapses. This processing could occur within area V1 or perhaps occurs in areas outside of V1, which then send signals back to V1 (Shapley and Ringach, 2000).

Now that we have seen that signals from beyond V1 might be sent back to signal the effects of context, we are ready to move to these areas beyond V1 and

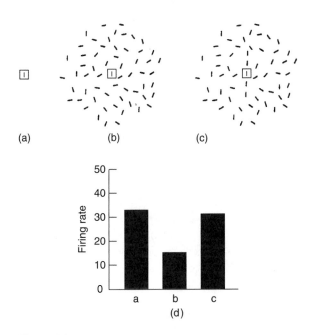

(a)   (b)   (c)

(d)

Figure 4.3

How context affects responding of a cell in V1: (a) a vertical bar by itself in the receptive field (indicated by the square); (b) the same bar surrounded by bars with many orientations; (c) the same bar with other bars that are lined up to create a group; (d) responses to conditions a, b, and c. (Adapted from Zapadia et al., 1995.)

Higher-Level Visual Processing

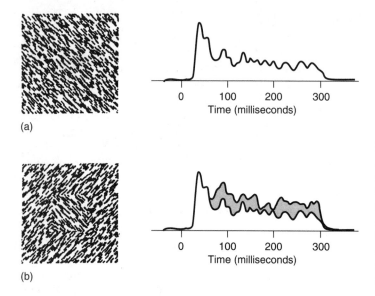

(a)

(b)

Figure 4.4

Effect of context on the response of a monkey V1 neuron, showing the stimulus on the left and the response on the right. (a) The elements that make up the "background" and center of the stimulus both have the same orientation; (b) the orientation of the elements that make up the background are changed so the center square stands out. This increases the response, as indicated by the shading. (From Zipser et al., 1996.)

look at what is happening further "upstream," in the extrastriate cortex. Our story of research on the extrastriate cortex begins in the early 1980s, when it was found that there are pathways, or "streams," that extend from V1 in the occipital lobe into extrastriate areas in the temporal lobe and the parietal lobe.

PROCESSING STREAMS IN THE EXTRASTRIATE CORTEX

WebTUTOR The idea that there are pathways or "streams" that transmit information from the striate cortex to other areas was introduced by a paper published by Leslie Ungerleider and Mortimer Mishkin in 1982. In this paper, Ungerleider and Mishkin distinguished two processing streams and showed that they served different functions.

Streams for Information About "What" and "Where"

Figure 4.5 shows the two streams that Ungerleider and Mishkin described. The stream reaching the parietal lobe is called the **dorsal pathway**, and the stream reaching the temporal lobe is called the **ven-**

tral pathway. (Dorsal corresponds to the back or the upper surface of an organism. Thus, the dorsal fin of a shark or dolphin is the fin on the back that sticks out of the water. Figure 4.6 shows that for upright

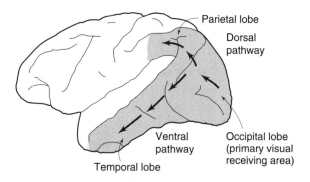

Figure 4.5

The monkey cortex, showing pathways from the primary visual receiving area, in the occipital lobe, to the parietal and temporal lobes. The pathway to the parietal lobe is called the dorsal pathway, because its destination is the dorsal (top) surface of the brain. The pathway to the temporal lobe is called the ventral pathway, because its destination is the ventral (bottom) surface of the brain (see Figure 4.6). The sequences of arrows indicate that there are a number of synapses along these pathways. (From Mishkin et al., 1983.)

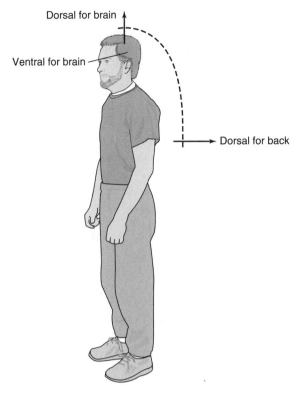

Figure 4.6
As described in the text, dorsal refers to the back surface of an organism. In upright standing animals such as humans, dorsal refers to the back of the body and to the top of the head, as indicated by the arrows and the curved dashed line. Ventral is the opposite of dorsal.

walking animals such as humans, the dorsal part of the brain is the top of the brain. Ventral is the opposite of dorsal, so would be on the lower part of the brain.)

Ungerleider and Mishkin (1982) determined that these two streams have different functions, based on the results of experiments in which they presented monkeys with two tasks: (1) an object discrimination problem and (2) a landmark discrimination problem. In the object discrimination problem, a monkey was shown one object, such as a rectangular solid, and was then presented with a two-choice task like the one shown in Figure 4.7a, which included the "target" object (the rectangular solid) and another stimulus,

such as the triangular shape. If the monkey pushed aside the target object, it received the food reward that was hidden in a well under the object. Normal monkeys and monkeys with their parietal lobes removed could easily identify the target. However, monkeys with their temporal lobes removed found this task to

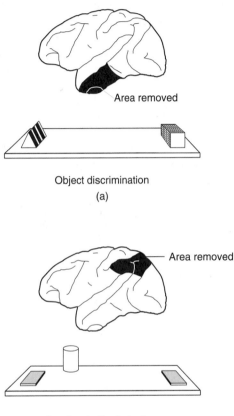

Object discrimination
(a)

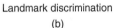

Landmark discrimination
(b)

Figure 4.7
The two types of discrimination tasks used by Ungerleider and Mishkin. (a) In the object discrimination task the monkey had to pick the correct object. Monkeys with an area of their temporal lobes removed (shaded area of brain) had difficulty with this task.(b) For the landmark discrimination, the monkey had to pick the food well closer to the cylinder. Monkeys with an area of their parietal lobes removed found this task difficult. (From Mishkin, Ungerleider, & Macko, 1983.)

Higher-Level Visual Processing

be extremely difficult. This result indicates that the ventral pathway, which reaches the temporal lobes, is responsible for determining an object's identity. Ungerleider and Mishkin therefore called the ventral pathway the **what pathway**.

The landmark discrimination problem is shown in Figure 4.7b. Here, the monkey's task is to remove the food well cover that is marked by the location of the tall cylinder. This task was accomplished by normal monkeys or monkeys with their temporal lobes removed, but was difficult for monkeys lacking part of their parietal lobe. This result indicates that the dorsal pathway, which leads to the parietal lobe, is responsible for determining an object's location. Ungerleider and Mishkin therefore called the dorsal pathway the **where pathway**.

Research on the dorsal and ventral pathways and the structures associated with them has generally confirmed the idea that there are parallel pathways that serve different functions. Figure 4.8 is a simplified diagram that shows some of the main structures in the two pathways (also see Color Plate 1.8). Notice that the ventral (what) pathway begins with the retinal P-ganglion cells and the LGN parvo layers and the

dorsal (where) pathway begins with the retinal M-ganglion cells and the LGN magno layers. Most of the research on the idea of parallel pathways has been done on monkeys, but fMRI research has confirmed the idea that parallel pathways also exist in humans (Haxby et al., 1995).

Although there is good evidence that the ventral and dorsal pathways serve different functions, the two pathways are not as separated as they may seem from Figure 4.8. There are many anatomical connections that create "cross-talk" between the pathways (Boussourd, Ungerleider, & Desimone, 1990; Nakamura et al., 1993; Ungerleider & Haxby, 1994). For example, signals from both the magno and parvo layers of the LGN reach area V4 in the ventral pathway (Maunsell, Nealey, & DePriest, 1990; Merigan & Maunsell, 1993). Thus, the picture of channels that serve specific functions is generally correct, but the idea of totally separate and independent channels for different qualities is an oversimplification. We should also note that these pathways do not travel in just one direction. We've already seen that area V1 may receive signals back from higher areas, and this is generally true for all of the structures in Figure 4.8.

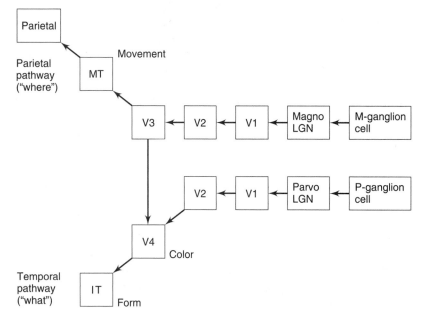

Figure 4.8

Simplified diagram of the visual pathways. Signals flow from right to left, starting with the M- and P-ganglion cells on the far right, which feed into the parietal and temporal pathways, respectively. V1 is the striate cortex, and V2, V3, and V4 are extrastriate visual areas; other extrastriate areas are IT, inferotemporal cortex; MT, medial temporal cortex; and parietal, which refers to other areas in the parietal lobe. The visual qualities most strongly associated with areas MT, V4, and IT are indicated. Note that information also flows back in the other direction.

As information flows from the striate cortex toward the parietal and temporal lobes, some information is also flowing back in the other direction.

Streams for Information About "What" and "How"

While the idea of ventral and dorsal streams has been generally accepted, David Milner and Melvyn Goodale (1995; see also Goodale and Humphrey, 2001) have suggested that rather than being called the *what* and *where* streams, they should be called the *what* and *how* streams. The ventral stream to the temporal cortex, they argue, is for perceiving objects, an idea that fits with the idea of "what." However, they propose that the dorsal stream to the parietal cortex is for taking action, such as picking up an object. Taking this action would involve knowing the location of the object, consistent with the idea of "where," but it also involves a physical interaction with the object. Thus, reaching to pick up a coffee cup involves information about the cup's location *plus* movement of the hand toward the cup. According to this idea, the dorsal stream provides information about *how* to direct action with regard to a stimulus.

Evidence supporting the idea that the dorsal stream is involved in how to direct action is provided by neurons in the parietal cortex that respond (1) when a monkey looks at an object and (2) when it reaches toward the object (Sakata et al., 1992; also see Taira et al., 1990). But the most dramatic evidence supporting the idea of a dorsal "action" or "how" stream comes from the behavior of a human patient with cortical damage.

Introduction to Neuropsychology   Understanding the behavior of patients with cortical damage is the goal of a field called **neuropsychology**, which has taught us a great deal about the mechanisms underlying memory, thinking, language, and perception. The basic idea behind neuropsychology is that we can understand how a system operates by studying **dissociations**—situations in which one function is absent while another is present.

To help us understand what dissociations tell us, we will consider the example of a broken television set (Parkin, 1996). One observation about broken television sets is that they can lose their color but still have a picture. This situation, when one function (color) is absent and the other (picture) is present, is called a **single dissociation**. The existence of a single dissociation indicates that the two functions involve different mechanisms, although they may not operate totally independently of one another.

Demonstrating a single dissociation involves just one TV set, like the one we just described with a picture but no color. Now let's consider a situation in which we have two TV sets. Set A has no sound but has a picture. Set B does have sound but has no picture. A **double dissociation** occurs when we can demonstrate that one function is absent and the other is present in one TV set (Set A: no sound, but the picture is OK) and that the opposite can also occur in another set (Set B: sound OK, but there is no picture) (top of Table 4.1). When a double dissociation occurs this means that the two functions—sound and picture, in this example—involve different mechanisms and that these mechanisms operate independently of one another. This makes sense for our television example because the television picture is created by the picture tube and the sound is created by the amplifier and speakers.

The Behavior of Patient D.F.   Neuropsychological research applies the reasoning used in this television example to observations of what happens to people's abilities when they suffer brain damage. An example of how this approach has been applied to studying visual processing is provided by D.F., a 34-year-old woman studied by Milner and Goodale, who suffered damage to her ventral pathway from carbon monoxide poisoning caused by a gas leak in her home.

The accident left her with good color and detail vision, but, just like Dr. P., the musician we described in Chapter 1, she had **visual form agnosia**. She was unable to recognize simple geometric forms and was unable to identify pictures of objects. For example, she identified a picture of a screwdriver as "long, black, thin" even though she knew what a screwdriver was, as indicated by the fact that she could easily identify a real screwdriver by feeling it with her hand.

Two TV Sets

	Function 1 Sound	Function 2 Picture
Broken TV set #1	OK	No
Broken TV set #2	No	OK

Two People

	Function 1 Visual-Motor Orientation	Function 2 Judging Visual Orientation
Ventral stream damage	OK	No
Dorsal stream damage	No	OK

Table 4.1
Double dissociations for TV sets (top) and people with brain damage (bottom). In both cases function 1 is present and function 2 is missing in one example, and the opposite occurs for the other example.

Another example of D.F.'s inability to recognize objects is shown by her response to the drawings in Figure 4.9. She was unable to recognize the apple or the book and was unable to copy these drawings. The drawings on the right, which she produced when she was asked to draw an apple and an open book from memory, indicate that her inability to recognize or copy pictures wasn't due to a problem with her general knowledge about apples and books or a lack of drawing ability. Interestingly, however, when she was later shown the drawings she had produced, she had no idea what they were (Milner & Goodale, 1995). D.F. also had difficulty perceiving orientations, so she could not accurately match the orientation of a card held in her hand to different orientations of a slot (Figure 4.10a).

Model Copy Memory

Figure 4.9
Patient D.F. could not recognize the apple or book drawings on the left or copy the drawings, as shown by her attempts in the middle column. The drawings on the right are ones she produced from memory. (From Milner & Goodale, 1995.)

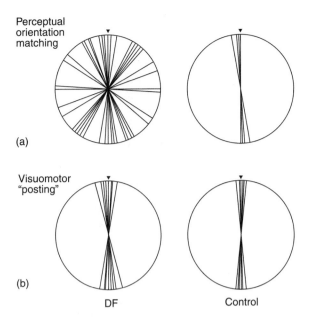

Perceptual orientation matching

(a)

Visuomotor "posting"

(b)

DF   Control

Figure 4.10

These plots indicate the orientation of a hand-held card in two tasks involving orientation. The top left plot shows patient D.F.'s attempts to match the orientation of the card to different orientations of a slot placed in front of her. Since correct performance for all orientations is indicated by a vertical line, this plot shows that D.F. was unable to accurately match the orientation of the card to the orientation of the slot. The bottom left plot show's patient D.F.'s performance when she was asked to place the card into the slot, as in mailing a letter. The nearly vertical lines in this plot indicate that she was able to accomplish this task. The plots on the right are for a normal control. (Adapted from Goodale et al., 1991.)

Since D.F. had trouble orienting a card to match the orientation of the slot, it would seem reasonable that she would also have trouble placing the card through the slot, since to do this she would have to turn the card so it was lined up with the slot. But when D.F. was asked to "mail" the card through the slot, she could do it! Even though D.F. could not turn the card to match the slot's orientation, as she started moving the card toward the slot, she rotated it to match the orientation of the slot (Figure 4.10b). Thus, D.F. performed poorly in the static orientation-matching task but did well as soon as *action* was involved (Murphy,

Racicot, & Goodale, 1996). Milner and Goodale interpreted D.F.'s behavior as showing that there is one mechanism for judging orientation and another for coordinating vision and action.

These results for D.F. demonstrate a single dissociation, which indicates that judging orientation and the coordination of vision and action involve different mechanisms. To show that these two functions are not only served by different mechanisms but are also independent from one another, we have to demonstrate a double dissociation. As we saw in our TV example, this involves finding a person whose symptoms are the opposite of D.F.'s, and such patients do, in fact, exist. These patients can judge visual orientation, but they can't accomplish the task that combines vision and action. As we would expect, whereas D.F.'s damage was to her ventral stream, the damage in these patients was to their dorsal streams.

These results, combined with the results from D.F., establish a double dissociation and suggest that perception and action operate independently in the brain (bottom of Table 4.1). Based on these results, Milner and Goodale suggested that the ventral pathway should still be called the what pathway, as Ungerleider and Mishkin suggested, but that a better description of the dorsal pathway would be the **how pathway** or the **action pathway**, because it determines how a person carries out an action.

While there is some disagreement as to exactly what functions to emphasize for the dorsal pathway, researchers agree that there are structures along the dorsal and ventral pathways that are specialized to serve different functions. We will now consider the evidence for these specialized structures, by describing the evidence for a property called modularity in the extrastriate cortex.

MODULARITY IN THE EXTRASTRIATE CORTEX

WebTUTOR   One of the primary results of research on the extrastriate cortex has been the demonstration that certain cortical areas process information about specific visual qualities. This specialization is called

modularity. If a particular structure contains a large proportion of neurons that respond selectively to a particular quality, we say that that structure is a **module** for that quality.[1]

An example of specialized modules is provided by a comparison of how the neurons of the middle temporal (MT) area and area V4 respond to movement. Figure 4.11 shows that about 90 percent of neurons in area MT respond selectively to an object's direction of movement, while less than 5 percent of the neurons in area V4 are directionally selective (Merigan & Maunsell, 1993). We will now look more closely at research on area MT, in the dorsal stream, and will also describe research on the inferotemporal cortex (IT), in the ventral stream, which contains neurons that respond to complex forms.

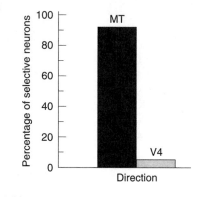

Figure 4.11
Most of the neurons in area MT (black bar) are directionally selective, whereas few in area V4 (shaded bar) are. (Adapted from Felleman & Van Essen, 1991.)

Middle Temporal Cortex (MT): A Module for Movement

William Newsome and Edward Paré (1988) developed an ingenious technique for determining a monkey's threshold for detecting the direction of movement. They used a stimulus that consisted of a random pattern of moving dots created by a computer, which varied the degree to which the dots moved in the same direction. For example, Figure 4.12a represents zero correlation in the direction of the dots' movement, so that all dots moved randomly, much like the "snow" you see when your TV set is tuned between channels. Figure 4.12b represents 50 percent correlation, so that at any point in time half of the dots were moving in the same direction. Figure 4.12c represents 100 percent correlation, so that all of the dots were moving in the same direction.

On each trial there was a particular direction in which the correlated dots were moving. Monkeys

trained to indicate this direction could detect the direction in patterns with correlations as low as 1 to 2 percent. However, if area MT was lesioned, the monkeys could detect the direction of movement only for patterns with correlations of 10 to 20 percent, so more of the dots were moving in the same direction. Thus, lesioning MT decreases the monkey's ability to detect the direction of movement (also see Movshon & Newsome, 1992; Pasternak & Merigan, 1994). This study, and other research by Newsome that we will describe when we consider motion perception in Chapter 8 and in the section on perceptual plasticity at the end of this chapter, is important not just because MT neurons respond to movement but because it links the response of MT neurons with the monkeys' *perception* of movement. This result therefore is an example of research on the physiology—perception relationship (relationship C in Figure 1.7).

Inferotemporal Cortex (IT): A Module for Form

In Chapter 3 we saw that neurons in the striate cortex respond to simple forms like bars or corners. We will now see that there are neurons in the extrastriate cortex that respond best to more complex stimuli. We will focus specifically on the inferotemporal (IT) cor-

---

[1] See Fodor's (1984) book, *The Modularity of Mind* for a detailed discourse on modularity, the properties of modules, and criteria for determining what a module is. Our definition of a module, which is somewhat different than Fodor's, is that a module is a structure that is specialized to process information about a specific perceptual quality.

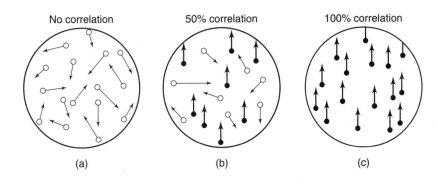

Figure 4.12
Stimuli used by Newsome and Paré. The dots on the left (a) moved randomly, with no connection to one another. The ones in the center (b) were partially correlated, half (the black dots) always moving in the same direction. The ones on the right (c) were fully correlated, all moving in the same direction. (From Newsome & Paré, 1988.)

tex, in the ventral pathway, because it is here that we find neurons that respond to complex forms and to faces.

Neurons That Respond to Complex Forms   Keiji Tanaka and his coworkers (Ito et al., 1995; Kobatake & Tanaka, 1994; Tanaka, 1993; Tanaka et al., 1991) recorded from cells in IT cortex that responded best to fairly simple stimuli like slits, spots, ellipses, and squares. They called these cells **primary cells**. They also recorded from neurons that responded to more complex stimuli such as specific shapes or shapes

combined with a color or a texture. They called these cells **elaborate cells**.

Figure 4.13 shows an example of how one of these elaborate cells responds to a number of similar stimuli. As they began testing this cell, Tanaka and his coworkers noticed that it responded well to a model of an apple, but that if they removed the apple's stem, the cell stopped responding. The way this cell responds to other shapes fits with this observation. The cell responds best to a circular disc with a thin bar (A), but it responds poorly to the bar alone (B), the disc alone (C), the disc and a short bar (D),

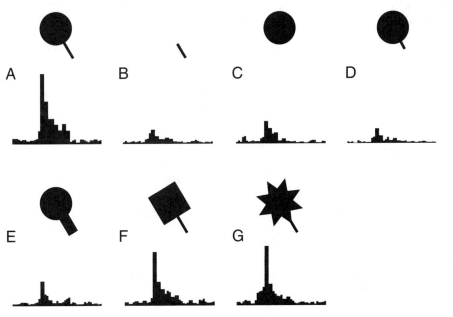

Figure 4.13
Responses of an elaborate cell to various stimuli. This cell responds best to a circular disc with a thin bar protruding from it. See text for details. (Tanaka et al., 1991.)

Higher-Level Visual Processing

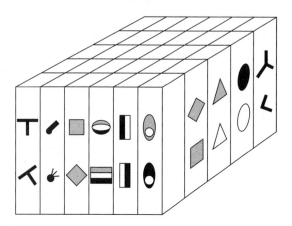

Figure 4.14
Neurons in the same column of IT cortex tend to respond to similar stimuli. This schematic diagram shows a number of columns in IT cortex and the kinds of shapes that cause neurons in each column to respond. (Young, 1995.)

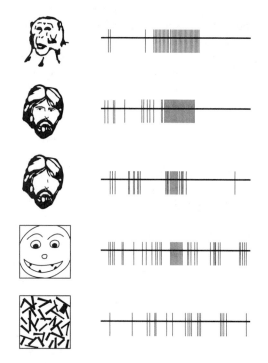

Figure 4.15
Responses of a neuron in a monkey's area IT to various stimuli. This neuron responds best to a full face, as shown by its response to monkey and human faces in the top two records. Removing the eyes or presenting a caricature of a face reduces the response. This neuron does not respond to a random arrangement of lines. (From Bruce, Desimone, & Gross, 1981.)

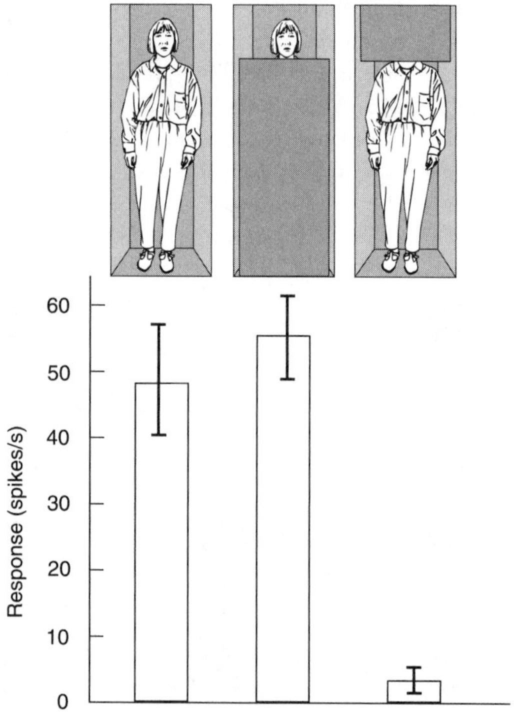

Figure 4.16
Response of a neuron in IT cortex for which the person's head is the important part of the stimulus, because firing stops when the head is covered. See text for details. (From Wachsmuth, Oram, & Perrett, 1994.)

or the disc and a fat bar (E). The cell does respond to a square shape and the bar (F) or a star shape and the bar (G), but not as well as to the best stimulus—the circular disc and the bar.

Figure 4.14 shows some of the other shapes that elicited good responses from IT neurons and also shows that these cells are arranged in columns with cells responding to similar shapes in the same columns (see also Fujita et al., 1992). Tanaka proposed that a complex form stimulates a number of these neurons and that we perceive a particular form when the information from all of these neurons is combined.

Neurons That Respond to Faces IT cells, such as the one that responds as shown in Figure 4.15, respond best to pictures of faces (Gross, 1992, 1994; Rolls, 1992). Figure 4.16 shows the responses of a neuron that responds only to the head. Notice that it responds well to a photograph of a whole person and to just the person's head but stops responding when the head is covered up (Wachsmuth, Oram, & Perrett, 1994).

To determine the degree to which some IT neurons are specialized for faces, Edmund Rolls and Martin Tovee (1995) measured the response of neurons to a number of face and nonface stimuli. Figure 4.17 shows how one of these neurons responded to stuimuli like the ones shown in Figure 4.18. Rolls and Martin used a total of 68 different stimuli, 23 pictures of faces, and 45 pictures of nonface stimuli, mostly landscapes and food.

The height of each bar in Figure 4.17 represents the neuron's response to a different stimulus. The face stumuli, which are indicated by F's, caused large responses, with the tall bars on the left indicating the faces that resulted in the largest responses. This neuron also responded to many of the other faces but responded poorly to the nonface stimuli.

The research that we have been describing on neurons that respond best to faces has involved recording from single neurons in the monkey's cortex. But recently, fMRI research on humans has also identified an area in the human IT cortex called the **fusiform face area (FFA),** which is specialized to respond to faces (See "Brain Scan").

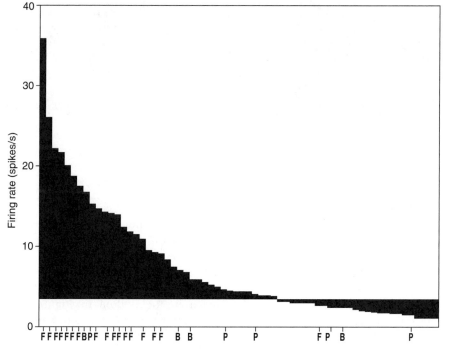

Figure 4.17
Firing rates of a single neuron to all 68 stimuli presented by Rolls and Tovee (1995). The bars marked F are the rates for pictures of faces. The bars marked P are the rates for pictures of faces in profile; the bars marked B were pictures of scenes that also contained a face; and the unmarked bars are the responses to the nonface stimuli. Bars that are below the line represent firing rates that are below the level of spontaneous activity.

Higher-Level Visual Processing

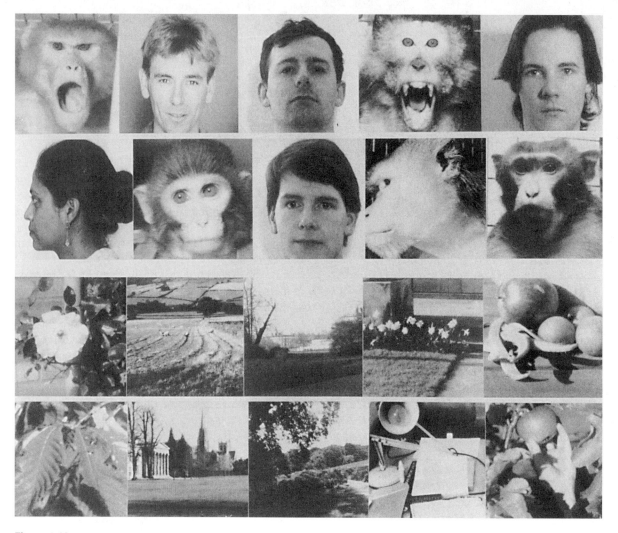

Figure 4.18
Some of the stimuli used in Rolls and Tovee (1995).

What does the fact that the IT cortex contains neurons that are specialized to respond to specific forms mean about how objects in the environment are represented in the brain? Does the fact that there are neurons that fire specifically to complex shapes and to faces mean that you can identify your car in the parking lot or your best friend's face because of neurons that are specialized to respond well to the shape of your car or to your friend's face?

The results in Figure 4.17 give us a hint at the answer to this question. These results show that this neuron responds well to faces and poorly to other types of objects. This neuron might respond well to the monkey face in the top left corner of Figure 4.18, and poorly to pictures of other types of objects, like the ones shown in the bottom of Figure 4.18. However, in addition to firing to the rather threatening monkey face in the upper left corner, this neuron

Neurophysiological and neuropsychological research indicates that there is an area in the brain that is specialized to respond to faces. The neurophysiological evidence comes mainly from results like those illustrated in Figures 4.15 through 4.17, which show that there are neurons in the monkey's IT cortex that respond selectively to faces.

The neuropsychological evidence comes from studies of people with brain damage. These studies show that damage to the temporal lobe can cause a condition called **prosopagnosia**, in which the person has difficulty recognizing the faces of familiar people. Even very familiar faces are affected, so a person with prosopagnosia might not be able to recognize close friends, family members, and even the reflection of his or her own face in the a mirror (Burton et al., 1991; Hecaen & Angelerques, 1962; Parkin, 1996).

A number of recent fMRI studies have shown that pictures of faces activate the fusiform gyrus in the temporal lobe (Clark et al., 1996; Puce et al., 1995, 1996). An experiment by Nancy Kanwisher and coworkers (1997) illustrates the basic procedure used to determine that neurons in this area respond selectively to faces. They first determined that pictures of faces caused brain activity in the fusiform gyrus and some other structures, as well. They then determined the areas activated by other objects, such as pictures of scrambled faces, household objects, houses, and hands. When she subtracted the response to the other objects from the response to the faces, Kanwisher found that activity remained in an area in the fusiform gyrus. She interpreted this result to mean that this area, which in humans is called the fusiform face area, is specialized to respond to faces.

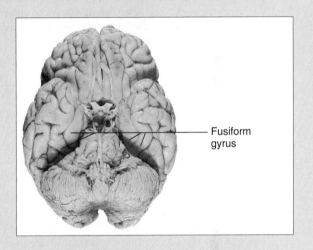

Fusiform gyrus

The fusiform face area (FFA) is located in the fusiform gyrus.

might also respond to the more peaceful monkey faces in the second row, and perhaps even to the human faces as well. Thus, just because a neuron is specialized to respond to faces doesn't necessarily mean that its firing signals the presence of a specific face. In the next section, following Summary Table 4.1, we will consider how neurons like the one in Figure 4.17 might be involved in helping you recognize your friend. See Summary Table 4.1 for an overview of the material we have covered so far.

THE SENSORY CODE: HOW OBJECTS ARE REPRESENTED IN THE VISUAL SYSTEM

One of the questions we set out to answer in Chapter 3 was *How is a tree or other object represented by neural signals?* We will now consider how this representation actually occurs by introducing the idea of the sensory code. The **sensory code** is the information

Higher-level Processing in the Striate Cortex

Recent research has shown that the response of some neurons in striate cortex (V1) is affected by the context that surrounds a stimulus. This effect, which is called contextual modulation, takes some time to develop and so could be due to signals that are sent back to V1 from higher levels of the cortex.

Processing Streams in the Extrastriate Cortex

There are two processing streams that conduct information from striate cortex into the extrastriate cortex. The dorsal stream travels to the parietal lobe, and the ventral stream travels to the temporal lobe. The dorsal stream has been called the "where" pathway by some researchers and the "how" or "action" pathway by other researchers. The ventral stream has been called the "what" pathway.

Neuropsychology

Research studying the dissociations that occur in brain-damaged patients has yielded information about the functions of the normal brain. Studies of subject D.F., who had damage to her ventral processing stream, have shown that two separate functions, judging orientation and coordinating vision and action, involve different mechanisms that probably operate largely independently of one another.

Modules for Movement and Form

Electrophysiological research on the monkey has provided evidence that the middle temporal area (MT) is a module that is specialized for processing information about movement, and the inferior temporal area (IT) is specialized for processing information about form. There are neurons in IT cortex that respond best to faces. This area, which has also been demonstrated in humans, is called the fusiform face area (FFA).

---

contained in the firing of neurons that represents what we perceive.

How might the sensory code work? To answer this question, we will consider two ideas about sensory coding, *specificity coding*, which states that specific perceptions are signaled by activity in specific neurons, and *distributed coding*, which states that specific perceptions are signaled by the pattern of activity that is distributed across many neurons.

Specificity Coding

Specificity coding is the representing of specific stimuli by the firing of neurons that are specialized to respond just to these stimuli. According to the idea of specificity coding, our perception of the faces in Figure 4.19 would be signaled by the firing of a neuron that is tuned to respond to each specific face. Neuron 1 responds to Bill, neuron 2 to Samantha, and neuron 3 to Roger. Notice that the responses of these neurons are *specific*—neuron 1 fires only to Bill, and neurons 2 and 3 do not fire at all to Bill. It is unlikely, however, that this extreme form of specificity coding could work, because although there are

neurons that are specialized to respond to faces, even these face neurons respond to more than one face.

Another reason that specificity coding won't work is that there are just too many different faces and other objects in the environment to assign a specific neuron to each one. This is symbolized by the fact that if there are just three specifically tuned neurons it is not possible to code for the other two faces in Figure 4.19. There are also other problems, such as how do we perceive objects we've never seen before, and how do we perceive objects when we view them from different angles or if they move to different places in our visual field? We will see that these problems can be handled by distributed coding.

Distributed Coding

Distributed coding is the representation of specific stimuli by the pattern of firing of many neurons. We can appreciate how this would work for faces by considering how the five faces in Figure 4.19 would be represented by the pattern of firing of just three neurons. In this case, all three neurons fire to each face, but the pattern of firing is different for each one.

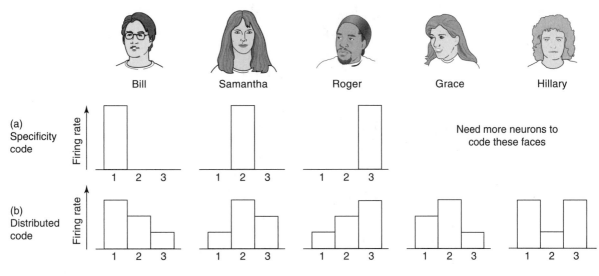

Figure 4.19

How faces could be coded according to (a) specificity coding and (b) distributed coding. The height of the bars indicates the response of neurons 1, 2, and 3 to each stimulus face. See text for explanation.

Thus, Bill's face causes a high firing rate in neuron 1, less in neuron 2, and even less in neuron 3, whereas Samantha's face causes high firing in neuron 2 and less in 1 and 3. Notice that two faces that look similar, like Samantha's and Grace's, have similar patterns but differ slightly, since the faces are not identical.

One of the advantages of distributed coding is that a large number of stimuli can be signaled by just a few neurons. In our example, the firing of three neurons signals five faces, but these three neurons could signal more than five faces, because many different patterns can be created from just three neurons. How many neurons are actually involved in coding for an object like a face or a perceptual quality like the direction of movement? The answer to this question appears to depend on the specific object or property. For example, we will see in Chapter 8 that there are neurons in MT cortex that are tuned so precisely for the direction of movement that the firing of just a few neurons contains enough information to accurately signal the direction in which an object is moving (Newsome et al., 1989). In contrast, more neurons are required to provide enough information to identify complex stimuli such as faces or other

environmental objects (Abbott, Rolls, & Tovee, 1996; Rolls & Tovee, 1995).

Another thing we need to consider when asking how objects are represented by neural firing is the fact that we are able to identify objects even when we see them at different distances, or at different places in our visual field, or when we view them from different angles. The following three types of neurons that are found in the IT cortex help us accomplish these feats:

- **Size-invariant neurons**: Neurons that respond to an object no matter what its size on the retina. Size-invariant neurons continue to fire to an object even when the object is at different distances, which would cause the size of the object's image to change on the retina.

- **Location-invariant neurons**: Neurons that respond to an object no matter where it is in the visual field. Location-invariant neurons continue to fire when an object moves from one place to another.

- **View-invariant neurons**: Neurons that respond to an object no matter what viewpoint we see it from.

View-invariant neurons respond even when an object is seen from different angles, as shown in Figure 4.20.

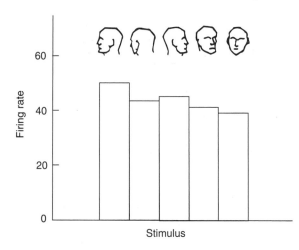

Figure 4.20

Response of a view-invariant neuron that responds with about the same firing rate to different views of a face. (From Perrett & Oram, 1993.)

Table 4.2

Types of neurons that respond to faces in the IT cortex

Type of Cortical Neuron	What They Fire to
Size-specific	A small number of faces of a particular size
Location-specific	A small number of faces in a particular location
View-specific	A small number of faces shown in a particular view (see Figure 4.21)
Size-invariant	Many different sizes of a small group of faces
Location-invariant	A small group of faces located in many different places in the visual field. These neurons have very large receptive fields.
View-invariant	A small number of faces seen in many different views (see Figure 4.20)

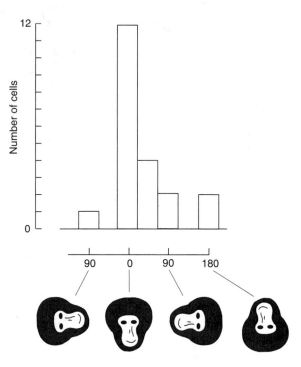

Figure 4.21

There are cells in IT cortex that respond best to a specific view a face. This graph shows how many cells out of a group of 21 responded best to each of the four orientations of the monkey face shown. (From Tanaka et al., 1991.)

We can contrast these invariant neurons with **size-specific**, **location-specific**, and **view-specific neurons**, which respond only to specific sizes, locations, or views of an object. Figure 4.21 shows that there are neurons in the monkey's IT cortex that respond best to different views of a face. The properties of these different types of neurons are summarized in Table 4.2.

What all of this means is that our ability to identify and recognize the huge number of different objects in our environment is the end result of a distributed cooperation between many neurons. This occurs even for stimuli like faces that are served by specialized neurons that respond just to faces. It may not take many neurons to let you know that you are seeing a face, but a number of neurons work together to signal the presence of one particular face.

How Do Neurons Become Specialized?

The fact that there are neurons that are specialized to fire to specific stimuli such as faces raises an interesting and important question: How come faces have their own neurons, which are located in their own module in the cortex? Let's consider two possible answers to this question: (1) Neural selectivity is shaped by evolution, so people are born with face neurons; (2) Neural selectivity is shaped by experience, so face neurons are shaped by all of the experience that people have in looking at and identifying faces.

Is Neural Selectivity Shaped by Evolution?

One answer to the question of why neurons become selective is that the nervous system may have evolved to respond best to situations and stimuli that are commonly found in the environment. According to the theory of natural selection, genetically based characteristics that enhance an animal's ability to survive, and therefore reproduce, will be passed on to future generations. Thus, a person whose visual system contains neurons that fire to important things in the environment (like faces) will be more likely to survive and pass on his or her characteristics than will a person whose visual system does not contain these specialized neurons. Through this evolutionary process, the visual system may have been shaped to contain neurons that respond to faces and other important perceptual information. In fact, there are neurons in the visual cortex of the newborn monkey that signal infor-

mation about the direction objects are moving and the relative depths of objects, two qualities that are important for the monkey's survival (Chino et al., 1997).

The problem with the evolutionary explanation is that although there is no question that the basic layout and functioning of all of the senses is the result of evolution, it is difficult to prove whether a particular capacity is, in fact, "built in" by evolution or if it is caused by learning. In the case of face neurons, there is recent evidence that learning is involved. We will first describe some single-neuron recording experiments that show that neurons in the monkey IT cortex can become tuned by experience with complex objects or geometrical shapes, and we will then describe a study which specifically considers neural activity in the human cortex.

Evidence That Neural Selectivity Is Shaped by Experience

The idea that neural selectivity can be shaped by experience is suggested by recent experiments on both monkeys and humans. The monkey experiments show that when a monkey is trained to recognize pictures of complex three-dimensional objects, neurons in its IT cortex fire selectively to those particular objects.

The Effect of Experience on Neural Responding in Monkeys   Nikos Logothetis and Jon Pauls (1995; also see Logothetis, Pauls, & Poggio, 1995; Logothetis et al., 1994) trained monkeys to recognize a specific view of an unfamiliar object, like the one in Figure 4.22. After training, the monkey was tested psychophysically to see how well it recognized this view of the object,

Figure 4.22
A number of different views of one of the stimuli used by Logothetis and Pauls (1995). Monkeys were trained to recognize one of these views and were then tested to see how well they recognized the training view and others as well.

other views of the same object rotated to different orientations, and some completely different objects. The results, shown in Figure 4.23a, show that the monkey recognized the view that it had been trained to recognize, and that recognition declined gradually as the object was rotated from this preferred view.

When Logothetis and Pauls repeated the same procedure, recording from neurons in IT cortex instead of testing psychophysically, they found neurons that responded to objects that the monkey had been trained to recognize but found no neurons that responded to objects that the monkey had not been trained to recognize. The tuning curve for a neuron that responded to one of the training stimuli, shown in Figure 4.23b, is very similar to the psychophysically determined recognition curve.

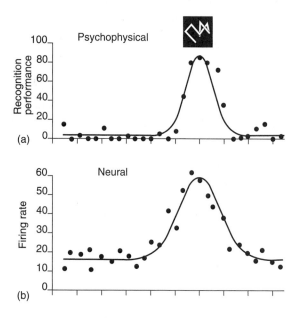

Figure 4.23

(a) A monkey's ability to recognize different views of an object. The monkey was trained on the view shown (0-degree orientation) and was then tested to see how well it recognized the object when it was shown in a number of different views. (b) Neural response of a neuron in a monkey's IT cortex to different views of the same object. The key result of this experiment is that the neural curve is similar to the curve for recognition performance. (From Logothetis & Pauls, 1995.)

Logothetis and Pauls's experiment is an example of one that measures both the stimulus–perception relationship (relationship A in Figure 1.7) (Figure 4.23a) and the stimulus–physiology relationship (relationship B in Figure 1.7) (Figure 4.23b) in the same animal. Experiments such as this are particularly useful for studying the relationship between physiology and perception, and, based on their results, Logothetis and Pauls concluded that these neurons are involved in perceiving the shapes and that they must have become "tuned" to the shape that was seen during training. Thus, some cells in IT cortex can apparently "learn from experience" to fire to unusual objects like Logothetis and Pauls's stimuli. (See also Kobatake et al., 1998, for another example of learning by neurons.)

The Effect of Experience on Neural Responding in Humans By using fMRI, Isabel Gauthier and coworkers (1999) have been able to show that practice in recognizing a specific kind of object can increase the activity of neurons in the human fusiform face area (FFA), which we have seen is an area that is specialized for faces. Gauthier first determined the level of activity in the FFA in response to faces and to objects called Greebles—families of computer-generated "beings" that all have the same basic configuration but that differ in the shapes of their parts (Figure 4.24). The results for this part of the experiment, shown in Figure 4.25a, indicate that the FFA neurons responded poorly to the Greebles but well to the faces.

The subjects were then trained in "Greeble recognition" for seven hours over a four-day period. After the training sessions, subjects had become "Greeble experts," as indicated by their ability to rapidly identify many different Greebles by the names they learned during the training.

Figure 4.25b shows how becoming a Greeble expert affected the responding of neurons in the subject's FFA. After the training, the FFA neurons responded about as well to Greebles as to faces. Apparently, the FFA area of the cortex is an area that responds not just to faces but to other complex objects as well. The objects that the neurons respond to are established by experience with the object. In

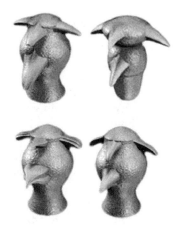

Figure 4.24
Greeble stimuli used by Gauthier. Subjects were trained to be able to name each different Greeble.

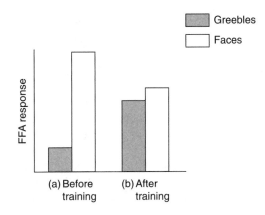

Legend:
■ Greebles
□ Faces

FFA response (vertical axis)

(a) Before training
(b) After training

Figure 4.25
(a) Response to Greebles and faces before Greeble training; (b) response after Greeble training.

fact, Gauthier has also shown that neurons in the FFA of people who are experts in recognizing cars and birds respond well not only to human faces but to cars (for the car experts) and to birds (for the bird experts) (Gauthier et al., 2000).

So the answer to the question, "How do neurons become specialized?" seems to be that specialized tuning is at least partially the result of neural plasticity, which makes it possible for neurons to adapt their

tuning to objects that are seen often and that are behaviorally important. Thus, evolution has apparently achieved exactly what it is supposed to achieve—it has created an area that is able to adapt to the specific environment in which an animal or human lives. According to this idea, if we moved to a new planet inhabited by Greebles or other strange-looking creatures, and that contained landscapes and objects quite different from Earth's, our neurons that previously responded well to Earth creatures and objects would eventually change to respond best to the creatures and environment of this new, and previously strange, environment (Gauthier, 1999).

CONNECTING PHYSIOLOGY AND PERCEPTION

We have seen that neural responding is related to various kinds of stimuli—a face stimulus causes neurons in IT cortex to fire; dots moving in a particular direction cause neurons in MT cortex to fire. But showing that a neuron fires to a particular stimulus does not prove that this firing is actually related to perception of the stimulus. One way to demonstrate a connection between neural activity and perception is to show that destroying neurons in a particular structure affects perception, as when lesioning neurons in MT cortex decreased a monkey's ability to perceive the direction of movement (Figure 4.12). Another way to demonstrate the connection between neural activity and perception is to simultaneously measure neural firing and perception (relationship C in Figure 1.7).

D. L. Sheinberg and Nikos Logothetis (1997) did an experiment that accomplished this. They used stimuli like the ones in Figure 4.26 in which the sunburst pattern was presented to a monkey's left eye, and a picture such as the butterfly or other animal or object was presented to the right eye. This situation, when two very different images are presented to the same places on the left and right eyes, causes **binocular rivalry**—the monkey's perception alternates back and forth between the two images, so it first sees the sunburst pattern and then, a few seconds later, it sees the butterfly.

Higher-Level Visual Processing

| Left eye | Right eye |
| (Ineffective stimulus) | (Effective stimulus) |

Figure 4.26
Stimuli used by Sheinberg and Logothetis. The "sunburst" stimulus was presented to the monkey's left eye and the butterfly to the right eye. Since two different stimuli are presented to the left and right eyes, binocular rivalry occurs, and the monkey sees either the sunburst or the butterfly but not both at the same time.

Sheinberg and Logothetis trained a monkey to pull the left lever when it perceived the sunburst pattern and the right lever when it perceived the butterfly. As the monkey was reporting what it was perceiving in this way, they recorded the activity of a neuron in area IT that had previously been shown to respond to the butterfly (so they called this the *effective stimulus*), but which did not respond to the sunburst (so they called this the *ineffective stimulus*). The result of this experiment was straightforward: The cell fired vigorously when the monkey was perceiving the effective stimulus and ceased firing when the monkey was perceiving the ineffective stimulus.

This demonstration of a connection between neural firing and perception is particularly interesting because, even though the monkey's perception was changing, the stimulus remained the same on the retina. The image of the sunburst remained steady on the left retina and the image of the butterfly or other picture remained steady on the right retina. However, when the monkey's perception changed, the firing of the neurons changed as well.

This demonstration of a close relationship between neural firing and perception supports the idea of a connection between the firing of these IT neurons and the monkey's perception. Similar results have recently been obtained in humans using fMRI (Lumer, Friston, & Rees, 1998; Lumer & Rees, 1999).

VISUAL ATTENTION: VISUAL AND NEURAL SELECTIVITY

WebTUTOR The assumption behind our discussion so far has been that when a stimulus is imaged on the retina, it is processed by neurons in a number of structures, and, if our visual system isn't damaged, at the end of this processing we perceive the stimulus. But this way of thinking about neural processing and perception doesn't tell the whole story, because people usually don't sit passively as stimuli are presented. They usually take an active role in their perception by seeking out interesting or important stimuli. The process of seeking out stimuli and then focusing on them is called **attention**.

The Selectivity of Attention

Attention is important both because it directs our receptors to stimuli we want to perceive and also because it influences the way information is processed once the receptors are stimulated (Wallace, 1994). Attention can enhance perception of the stimuli to which we are paying attention and decrease our awareness of stimuli we are ignoring. Thus, when we focus our attention on something that interests us, we become both more aware of what we are looking at and less aware of other objects or parts of the scene. This selective property of attention is what William James (1890/1981) was referring to when he said that

> Millions of items . . . are present to my senses which never properly enter my experience. Why? Because they have no interest for me. My experience is what I agree to attend to . . . Everyone knows what attention is. It is the taking possession by the mind, in clear and vivid form, of one out of what seem several simultaneously possible objects of trains of thought . . . It implies withdrawal from some things in order to deal effectively with others.

Thus, normal attention, according to James, causes the things to which we attend to become clearer and more vivid and causes things to which we don't attend to never enter our experience. This idea that

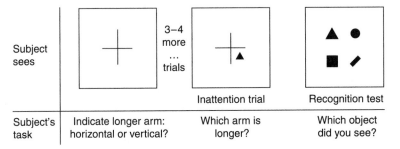

Subject sees			
Subject's task	Indicate longer arm: horizontal or vertical?	Which arm is longer?	Which object did you see?

Figure 4.27

Inattentional blindness experiment. (a) Subjects judge whether the horizontal or vertical arm is larger on each trial; (b) after a few trials a geometrical object is flashed, along with the arms; then (c) the subject is asked to pick which geometrical stimulus was presented.

things to which we don't attend never enter our experience may seem like a rather strong statement, but there is a good deal of evidence to support that claim. We will consider three illustrations of situations in which a lack of attention results in a lack of awareness.

Can We See Without Attention?

There are a number of demonstrations that support the idea that we must pay attention to something in order to see it.

Inattentional Blindness   **Inattentional blindness** is a situation in which a stimulus that is not attended is not perceived, even though a person is looking directly at it. Arien Mack and Irvin Rock (1998) demonstrated this effect using the procedure shown in Figure 4.27. For the first few trials, subjects have to indicate which arm of the cross is longer, the horizontal or the vertical. Then, on the inattention trial, a small test object is added to the display. When subjects are then given a recognition test in which they are asked to pick the object that was presented, they can't pick out the shape that was presented, because they were not paying attention to it.

The Attentional Blink   The **attentional blink** is the inability to see a second target stimulus that is presented as one of a string of briefly presented stimuli within about half a second after the first target stimulus. The attentional blink is demonstrated using a procedure called **rapid serial visual presentation (RSVP)** (Shapiro, Arnell, & Raymond, 1997). In the RSVP procedure a string of 10 to 20 stimuli, which could be letters, numbers, words, or pictures, depending on the experiment, are presented one after the other for about 100 ms (1/10 second) each. In a typical experiment using this procedure, all of the stimuli are letters, except the two target stimuli, which are numbers (Figure 4.28). When subjects attempt to identify the target numbers, they can do so easily for the first number in the series but are not able to identify the second number if it follows the first within about 500 ms.

Why is the second number difficult or impossible to identify? One idea is that focusing attention on the first target number uses up the subject's attention for about 500 ms afterward. Without the availability of attention, the second target number is not seen. This phenomenon is called the attentional blink, because it is similar to the brief loss of vision that occurs when we blink our eyes.

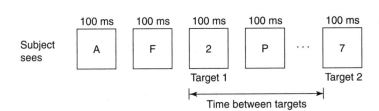

Figure 4.28

Attentional blink experiment. A series of letters are presented for 100 ms each. The first target is the number. A number of additional letters are presented between the first target and the second target. If the time between the two targets is less than 500 ms, the subject cannot detect the second target.

Higher-Level Visual Processing

Change Blindness   In inattentional blindness and the attentional blink, the stimuli are presented very rapidly, usually just for a fraction of a second. But what about attention in more realistic settings in which we have more time to look at various objects in a scene? There is evidence that people are not very good at seeing unattended objects, even when presentations are slow enough so that everything in a scene can be perceived easily.

The inability to detect unattended changes that are occurring in changing environments is called **change blindness**. Change blindness was demonstrated by Daniel Levin and Daniel Simons (1997) by having subjects view a video of a brief conversation between two women. Four frames from this video, shown in Figure 4.29, show the changes that take place when the camera angle changes. In Shot B, the woman's scarf has disappeared; in Shot C, the other woman's hand is on her chin, although moments later, in Shot D, her arms are on the table. Also, the plates change color from red in the initial views to white in Shot D.

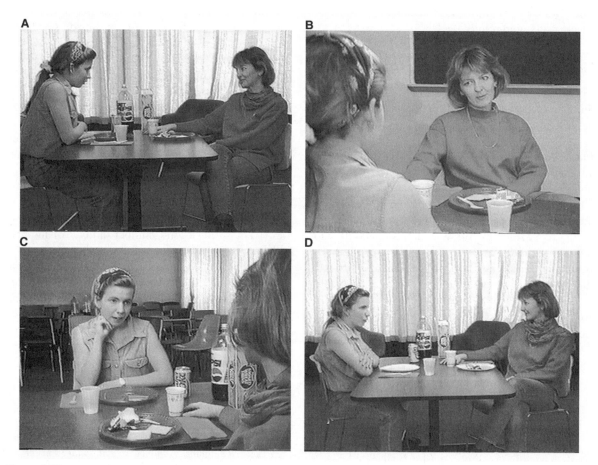

Figure 4.29
Stills from the video shown in the Levin and Simons (1997) experiment. Note that the woman on the right is wearing a scarf around her neck in Shots A, C, and D, but not in Shot B. Also, the color of the plates changes from red in the first three frames to white in frame D, and the hand position of the woman on the left changes between Shots C and D.

Even though subjects were told to "pay close attention" to the film, only one of ten subjects claimed to notice any changes. Even when the subjects were shown the video again and were warned that there would be changes in "objects, body position, or clothing," they noticed fewer than a quarter of the changes that occurred.

Although this may seem like a counterintuitive result, it has been duplicated in a number of other experiments (Grimes, 1996; Rensink, O'Regan, & Clark, 1996; Wolfe, 1997). Apparently, we have a general awareness of our surroundings and the objects in it, but we are less aware of many of the details than we might think.

The examples of inattentional blindness, the attentional blink, and change blindness all illustrate how important attention is for seeing. As it turns out, we can take in some information about the world without attention (for example, in the inattentional blindness experiment of Figure 4.27, subjects can detect the color or location of the test stimulus, even though they can't identify its shape). However, it is accurate to say that our awareness of much of our world depends on attention. This perceptual conclusion has been studied physiologically in experiments that show that there is a connection between paying attention and neural responding.

Attention Affects Neural Responding

In one of the early experiments demonstrating how attention affects neural responding, Jeffry Moran and Robert Desimone (1985) trained monkeys to keep their eyes fixated on a dot such as the one shown in Figure 4.30 and, while recording from a neuron in area V4 in the ventral stream (see Figure 4.8), simultaneously presented two stimuli that fell within the neuron's receptive field. One of these stimuli, the preferred stimulus, was a color that caused the V4 neuron to fire vigorously, and the other, the nonpreferred stimulus, was a color that caused little or no response in the neuron.

While recording from this V4 neuron, Moran and Desimone signaled the monkey to pay attention to either the preferred or the nonpreferred stimulus on different trials. The results show that the stimulus

to which the monkey attended had a large effect on the neuron's response (Figure 4.30): Attention to the preferred stimulus caused a strong response, and attention to the nonpreferred stimulus caused a weaker response. The important thing to remember about this experiment is that the monkey never moved its eyes, so the stimulus always remained on the same place on the retina. The larger response in the left record was therefore due solely to the monkey's attentional state. Moran and Desimone also obtained similar results for neurons in IT cortex.

Another attention experiment, by Carol Colby and coworkers (1995), shows that attention also affects the firing of neurons in the dorsal stream. The monkey keeps its eyes fixated on the dot marked "Fix" in the display in Figure 4.31a, and a light is presented off to the right of the receptive field of a neuron in the parietal cortex. In the "fixation" condition, the

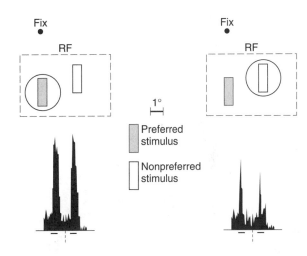

Figure 4.30

The effect of selective attention on the response of a neuron in area V4; the receptive field (RF) is indicated by the dashed line. The monkey kept its eyes fixed on the dot. When the monkey paid attention to the neuron's preferred stimulus, as indicated by the "spotlight" on the left display, the neuron fired (see record at the lower left). When the monkey paid attention to the nonpreferred stimulus, as indicated by the spotlight on the right display, the neuron fired less vigorously (see the record at the lower right). (Adapted from Moran & Desimone, 1985.)

Higher-Level Visual Processing

monkey doesn't have to pay attention to the light, but in the "fixation and attention" condition the monkey has to pay attention to the light since it has to signal

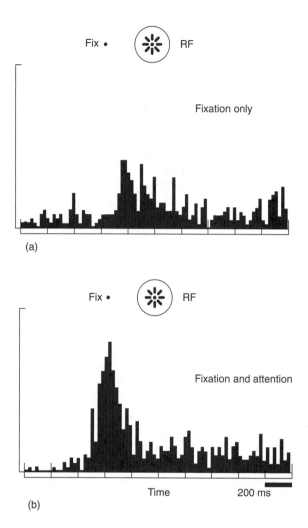

(a)

(b)

Time   200 ms

Figure 4.31

The results of Colby et al.'s. (1995) experiment showing how attention affects the responding of a neuron in a monkey's parietal cortex. In (a) the monkey fixates on the fixation dot (Fix) while a light is flashed in the neuron's receptive field (RF) off to the right. In (b) the monkey fixates on the fixation dot and simultaneously pays attention to the light in the neuron's receptive field. The records below indicate that the neuron fired more when the monkey was paying attention.

any time the light dims in intensity—an event that occurs every so often when the light is on.

The response of the parietal cortex neuron is shown for both conditions in Figures 4.31a and b. The difference is striking, because even though the monkey is always looking at the fixation point and the stimuli flashed to the receptive field to the right are exactly the same for both conditions, the neuron's response is larger when the monkey is paying attention (see also Maunsell & McAdams, 2000).

The results of these experiments, and many others, show that attention affects the processing of the stimulus by creating a greater neural response to the attended stimulus compared to the unattended stimulus.

THE BINDING PROBLEM: COMBINING INFORMATION FROM DIFFERENT AREAS

We have seen that perceiving something causes activity in many different areas of the brain (Lamme & Roelfesma, 2000). Consider, for example, what is happening in your cortex as you see a blue Corvette drive by: Cells sensitive to complex forms fire in IT cortex; cells sensitive to movement fire in MT cortex; and cells sensitive to color are also firing in other areas as well. But even though the Corvette's shape, movement, and color cause firing in different areas of the cortex, you don't perceive the car as separated shape, movement, and color perceptions. You experience an integrated perception of a car, with all of these components occurring together.

This raises an important question: How are the Corvette's qualities combined, so that you perceive a unified perception of it rather than separate, independent qualities? This problem of combining information that is being signaled in physically separated areas of the visual system is called the **binding problem**.

To begin dealing with the binding problem, we return to our discussion from Chapter 3 of how neurons in the striate cortex respond to a tree trunk. We saw that the tree's image on the retina causes activity in a number of location columns, so the electrical picture of a vertically oriented tree trunk might look like Figure 3.32. Three different location columns are activated and within each of these columns there is activity in the 0-degree orientation columns.

The way the representation of the tree trunk is split up into electrical activity in separated places in the cortex raises an important question: How is the information in each of these areas combined to result in a perception of the whole tree? This is the binding problem for the tree, because it asks how the separated areas of electrical signals generated by the tree are related to one another and combined (or bound together) to create a signal that stands for the tree.

One approach to solving the binding problem starts with evidence that columns in the cortex are connected with each other by a network of neurons (Gilbert & Wiesel, 1989). This communication between different columns is a first step toward solving the problem, because it enables them to share information, but we need to go a step further, by asking what kinds of information might be shared between columns.

A description of the possible nature of the column-to-column messages has been proposed in a hypothesis by a number of German researchers (Engel et al., 1991; Engel, Konig, & Singer, 1991; Engel et al., 1992; Gray & Singer, 1989; Singer et al.,

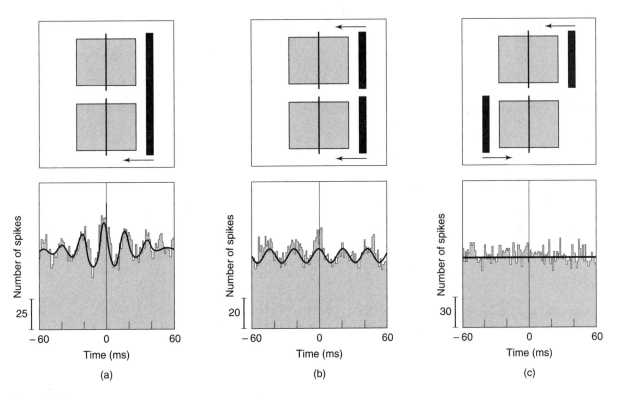

Figure 4.32
The top diagrams show the following three ways that a bar was swept across the receptive fields of two neurons in the cat's striate cortex: (a) the whole bar; (b) the bar split in two; and (c) the bar split and the parts moved in opposite directions. Each neuron responded with an oscillatory response (one that alternates between bursts of high and low firing). The bottom diagrams are cross-correlograms for each stimulus condition. Larger peaks and troughs, as in (a), indicate that the firing patterns generated by the two neurons were synchronized with each other. (Adapted from Engel et al., 1992.)

Higher-Level Visual Processing

1993). They suggest that when an object is represented by activity in different places in the cortex, the firing of the neurons in these different places is synchronized with each other. Evidence for this idea is provided by the results of an experiment described by Andreas Engel and his coworkers (1992).

Engel used two electrodes to simultaneously record activity from two neurons, separated by 7 mm in the striate cortex, that both responded best to vertically oriented bars. Figure 4.32 shows three different ways that stimuli were presented to the neurons' receptive fields (top records) and shows plots called **cross-correlograms** (bottom graphs) that indicate whether the neurons were firing in synchrony with each other.

Figure 4.32a shows the cross-correlogram when a single long bar was swept across the two receptive fields. The wavy record means that the neurons both fired in bursts separated by quieter periods and that the two neurons' bursts were synchronized. When two smaller bars were swept across the receptive fields, as in Figure 4.32b, the synchronization between the two neurons' responses became weaker, and, when the two bars were moved in opposite directions, as in Figure 4.32c, the flatness of the cross-correlogram indicates that there was no synchronization at all. In other words, the bursting pattern of the firing of these two neurons was synchronized when a whole bar moved across their receptive fields, but the bursts were less synchronized if the bar was split, and not synchronized at all if the two halves were moving in opposite directions.

The results of Engel's experiment support the idea that responses that are synchronized in two or more neurons signal the presence of a whole object. Another way to describe this result is to say that this synchrony is the glue that binds together responses that are generated by the same object, but that occur in different places in the cortex. Carrying this idea one step further, it has been proposed that synchrony may occur between neurons representing different qualities of an object. According to this idea, when the blue Corvette drives by, it will cause neurons in different parts of the cortex that respond to color, movement, and shape to fire in synchrony with each other, and this synchronized firing will indicate that these three qualities all belong to the Corvette (Stryker, 1989).

This idea that synchrony is a "binding" agent is a controversial one that is not accepted by all researchers, and while it is supported by a number of experiments (see also Brosch, Bauer, & Eckhorn, 1997; Neuenschwander & Singer, 1996; Roskies, 1999; Treisman, 1999), the final explanation of the binding problem may be quite different from this one. The important point is that any object causes activity in many places in the brain, so before we can say we understand the connection between neural responses and perception, we need to discover how all of these many separated signals somehow combine their information to create our perception of meaningful objects.

Improved Neural Response Leads to Improved Perception

We have seen that there is a connection between experience with shapes, faces, and Greebles and the tuning of neurons. Plasticity has also been demonstrated to accompany improvement in the perceptual ability to judge the direction of movement in dot patterns. Ehud Zohary and coworkers (1994) used monkeys that had been trained to discriminate the direction of movement in patterns like the ones in Figure 4.12.

In these displays only a small percentage of the dots are moving in the same direction, with the rest moving randomly. The monkey's task on each trial was to indicate in which of two directions the dots were moving. A different value of dot coherence (the percentage of dots that were moving in the same direction) was presented on each trial, and, from the data collected in about 200 trials, it was possible to calculate the threshold for perceiving the direction of movement. The thresholds were based on the coherence needed to achieve 75 percent correct (50 percent would be chance, since the monkey is choosing between two directions).

The bars on the left of Figure 4.33 show the psychophysical threshold calculated from the results from the first block of 200 trials and from the second block. It is clear from these data that the monkey's performance improved on the second block of trials.

What is special about this experiment is that on the same trials on which the monkeys were making their psychophysical judgments, Zohary was simultaneously measuring the neural response of directionally selective neurons in areas MT and MST (which both contain large proportions of directionally selective neurons). The bars on the right in Figure 4.33 show that the thresholds calcu-lated from these physiological data also improve on the second block of trials. This is an impressive demonstration of a match between psychophysics and neural firing. This experiment is another example of one in which both the stimulus–perception relationship and the stimulus–physiology relationship are measured in the same animal. (Remember that the Logothetis and Pauls experiment also did this; see Figure 4.24.)

The similarity of the psychophysical and neural results led Zohary to suggest that the improvement in psychophysical threshold may be caused by the improvement in neural sensitivity. This is therefore a demonstration of how a short-term change in neural responding caused by learning is translated into a change in perception.

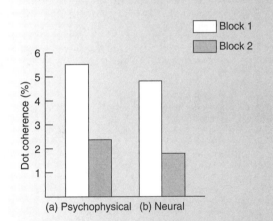

Figure 4.33
Results of Zohary's (1994) experiment. (a) The monkey's psychophysical threshold for detecting motion, for the first block of trials and for the second block. The threshold is smaller for the second block. (b) Thresholds for detecting motion calculated from the physiological results.

NEURONS THAT RESPOND TO VISION AND TOUCH

WebTUTOR   In this chapter we have focused on neurons that respond to visual stimuli. Neurons have also been discovered that respond both to visual stimuli and to energy that stimulates other senses as well. These neurons are called **bimodal** (two senses) neurons or **multimodal** (many senses) **neurons**.

An example of bimodal neurons that respond to both visual and tactile stimuli is provided by an experiment in which Michael Graziano and Charles Gross (1995) recorded from neurons in an area of a monkey's parietal lobe that responds to tactile stimulation. They found a neuron that responded when they covered the animal's eyes and lightly stroked its face with a cotton swab (Figure 4.34). But Graziano and Gross discovered that this same neuron also responded to visual stimulation, when they uncovered the monkey's eyes and found that the neuron began responding as they moved the swab toward the face, beginning when the swab was about 10 cm

away. Further study showed that this neuron responded when the swab was moving anywhere within an area attached to the tactile receptive field.

Graziano and Gross also found bimodal neurons that responded to touching the hand (shaded area in Figure 4.35) and to visual stimuli presented near the hand (circle in Figure 4.35). The fact that this neuron responds any time a visual stimulus appears in the circle around the hand challenges the definition of a neuron's receptive field that we presented in Chapter 2. Remember that we defined a neuron's visual receptive field as the "area of retina which, when stimulated, influences the neuron's firing." But this definition doesn't work for our bimodal cell, because when the monkey moves its hand, the circle around the hand moves with it, and so the visual stimulus that causes a response falls on a different area of the retina (Figure 4.36). It therefore makes more sense to define the visual receptive field of this

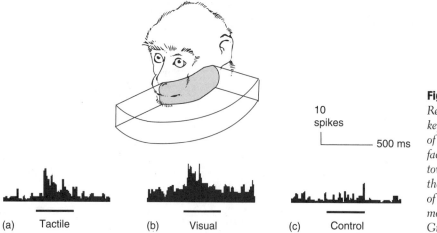

Figure 4.34
Responses of a neuron in the monkey's parietal cortex to (a) stroking of the shaded area of the monkey's face, (b) movement of an object toward the monkey's face within the area shown, and (c) movement of the object as in b, but with the monkey's eyes covered. (From Graziano & Gross, 1995.)

(a) Tactile   (b) Visual   (c) Control

10 spikes — 500 ms

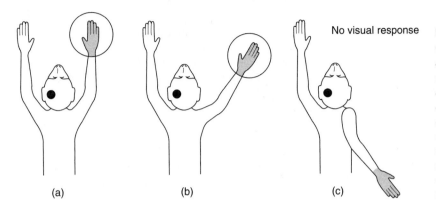

No visual response

Figure 4.35
Graziano and Gross (1995) found a bimodal cell that responded both to tactile stimulation of the hand and visual stimulation of the area around the hand (indicated by the circle). If the hand was visible as in (a) and (b), the neuron responded to both tactile and visual stimulation. However, when the hand was not visible, the cell responded only to tactile stimulation.

(a)   (b)   (c)

neuron not in terms of the area of retina that causes a response in the neuron but in terms of the part of the body that the visual stimuli are associated with. Since we define this neuron's visual receptive field with relation to the body (the area surrounding the hand), we call this neuron a **body-centered neuron**.

What do body-centered neurons do? Graziano and Gross suggest that since the visual receptive fields move as the body moves, these cells could indicate the location of stimuli with respect to the body surface. These kinds of neurons would, therefore, provide useful information to a monkey interacting with the environment, with neurons like the hand neuron being particularly useful for coordinating vision and touch as an animal reaches for an object. Later in this book, in Chapter 9 on "Vision and Action," we will describe some other neurons that are involved in reaching for objects.

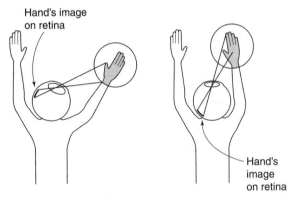

Hand's image on retina

Hand's image on retina

Figure 4.36
When the monkey moves its hand, the visual stimulus that causes a response moves to different places on the retina. Thus, we don't define this neuron's receptive field in terms of the area on the retina that influences the cells firing.

The Sensory Code

The sensory code is the information contained in the firing of neurons that represents what we perceive. There are two major ideas about sensory coding. Specificity coding is the representation of specific stimuli by the firing of neurons that are specialized to respond to these stimuli. Distributed coding is the representation of specific stimuli by the pattern of firing of many neurons.

Specificity vs. Distributed Coding

It is likely that most sensory coding in the visual system is distributed coding, since even neurons such as "face neurons" that are specialized to respond to a specific category of stimuli (faces) respond to a number of stimuli within that category. In addition, distributed coding is more efficient than specificity coding since the activity of only a small number of neurons can represent a large number of different objects.

How Do Neurons Become Specialized?

Although it is clear that evolution plays an important role in determining the properties of the visual system, there is evidence from both animal and human studies that the tuning of neurons to respond to specific stimuli can be shaped by experience. That is, neurons can "learn," based on the stimuli to which they are exposed.

Connecting Physiology and Perception

Binocular rivalry experiments, in which an animal's perception is measured while recording electrical activity from its cortex, have demonstrated a close connection between neural firing and perception.

Visual Attention

Attention is the process of seeking out stimuli and then focusing on them. Psychophysical experiments studying phenomena like inattentional blindness, the attentional blink, and change blindness have shown that without attention we often fail to take in information, even if it is imaged on our receptors. Physiological research has demonstrated heightened neural responding to attended stimuli and less responding to unattended stimuli.

The Binding Problem

The binding problem refers to the problem of combining information that is occurring in separated areas of the cortex, in order to achieve a coherent perception of an object. It has been hypothesized that binding may be based on the synchronization of neural responding that occurs in different areas of the cortex, in response to a particular object.

Plasticity:
Improved Neural Responding and Perception

Experiments that have compared neural and psychophysical responding to a movement detection task indicate that the improvement in neural responding that occurs with practice is mirrored by a similar improvement in psychophysical responding.

Across the Senses:
Neurons That Respond to Vision and Touch

There are neurons in the monkey visual system that respond both to touching a particular place on the body and to visual stimuli presented near that place on the body. These neurons are called bimodal neurons since they respond to more than one sense. They are called body-centered neurons since their response to visual stimuli is best described with reference to the place on the body that causes a response rather than to the place stimulated on the retina.

STUDY QUESTIONS

1. What is the extrastriate cortex? (110)

2. What percentage of the cortex can be activated by visual stimuli? (110)

Higher-Level Processing in the Striate Cortex

3. What is contextual modulation? (111)

4. Describe the Kapadia experiment, which showed how the response to a bar stimulus is affected by its context. (111)

5. What did Kapadia conclude about the relationship of nerve firing to the salience of the bar? (111)

6. Describe the Zipser experiment, which demonstrates contextual modulation. What about that experiment suggests that the response to context is the result of additional processing in either V1 or higher areas? (111)

Processing Streams in the Extrastriate Cortex

Streams for Information About "What" and "Where"

7. What were the two streams that Ungerleider and Mishkin described? (112)

8. What parts of the body and the brain are designated as "dorsal" and "ventral"? (112)

9. Describe the two kinds of behavioral tasks that Ungerleider and Mishkin used to identify the two streams. Be sure you know which of these streams is ventral and which is dorsal. (113)

10. What are the main structures in the dorsal and ventral pathways, beginning in the retina? (114)

11. Is there any evidence for ventral and dorsal pathways in humans? (114)

12. Are there any connections between the dorsal and ventral pathways? (114)

Streams for Information About "What" and "How"

13. Describe Milner and Goodale's proposal that the two streams in the extrastriate cortex should be called the "what" and "how" streams. (115)

14. What is neuropsychology? (115)

15. What is a single dissociation? A double dissociation? What does the existence of each one tell us about the relationship between two functions? (115)

16. Describe the case of patient D.F. What was her condition called? What could she do perceptually? What was she unable to do perceptually? (115)

17. Describe the double dissociation that involves judgment of visual orientation and the coordination between vision and action. (117)

18. What did Milner and Goodale conclude from this double dissociation? (117)

19. What are the "what" and "how" pathways? (117)

Modularity in the Extrastriate Cortex

20. What is modularity? (118)

21. What is some evidence that area MT is a module for movement? (118)

Medial Temporal Cortex (MT): A Module for Movement

22. Describe the Newsome and Paré research on motion perception in monkeys. What was their procedure, and what did they conclude from their results? (118)

Inferotemporal Cortex (IT): A Module for Form

23. Describe the evidence that there are neurons in IT cortex that respond to complex shapes. What are primary cells? What are elaborate cells? (119)

24. What do we mean when we say that neurons in IT cortex are arranged in columns? (121)

25. Describe the monkey neurons that respond to faces. (121)

26. What is the area in the human IT cortex that is specialized to respond to faces? (122)

Brain Scan: The Human Face Area

27. What is the neurophysiological evidence for a special area for faces? (123)

28. What is the neuropsychological evidence for a special area for faces? (123)

29. What is prosopagnosia? (123)

30. Describe the fMRI evidence that led Kanwisher to conclude that there is an area for faces in the fusiform gyrus. (123)

The Sensory Code: How Objects Are Represented in the Visual System

31. What is the sensory code? (123)

Specificity Coding

32. What is specificity coding? (124)

33. Why is it unlikely that specificity coding would work? (124)

Distributed Coding

34. What is distributed coding? (124)

35. How many neurons are needed to code an object like a face or a perceptual quality like the direction of movement? (125)

36. What are size-, location-, and view-invariant neurons? What function do they serve for perception? (125)

37. What are size-, location-, and view-specific neurons? (126)

How Do Neurons Become Specialized?

38. What are two possible answers to the question, "How come faces have their own neurons?" (127)

Is Neural Selectivity Shaped by Evolution?

39. How would the theory of natural selection explain the selectivity of face neurons? (127)

Evidence That Neural Selectivity Is Shaped by Experience

40. Describe Logothetis and Pauls's experiment, which provided evidence that cells can gain the ability to respond to specific stimuli through experience. What two relationships did they measure? (127)

41. Describe Gauthier's Greeble experiments. (128)

42. Describe Gauthier's experiment in which she tested car experts and bird experts. (129)

43. What is the conclusion of the results in 40 through 42 above regarding the role of experience in making a neuron specialized? (129)

44. What might happen to neurons in your FFA if you moved to an environment that is very different visually than the one you live in now? (129)

Connecting Physiology and Perception

45. If a neuron responds best to a particular stimulus such as a face, does that mean that the neuron's firing is related to an animal's perception of that stimulus? (129)

46. What is binocular rivalry? How was it used by Sheinberg and Logothetis to demonstrate a connection between neural responding and perception? (129)

Visual Attention: Visual and Neural Selectivity

47. What is attention? (130)

The Selectivity of Attention

48. What are the functions of attention? (130)

49. What happens to things we attend to, according to William James? (130)

Can We See Without Attention?

50. What is inattentional blindness? Describe Mack and Rock's experiment that illustrates this effect. (131)

51. What is the attentional blink? Describe the RSVP procedure that illustrates this effect. (131)

52. What is change blindness? (132)

53. Describe Levin and Simons' experiment that demonstrated change blindness. (132)

Attention Affects Neural Responding

54. Describe the Moran and Desimone and the Colby et al. experiments on the effects of attention on neural firing. Understand their procedures and what their results mean. (133)

The Binding Problem:
Combining Information from Different Areas

55. What is the binding problem? (134)

56. Describe the solution to the binding problem involving synchronized firing of neurons that has been proposed by Engel and coworkers. (135)

57. What is the evidence for Engel's proposal? (136)

The Plasticity of Perception:
Improved Neural Response Leads
to Improved Perception

58. Describe Zohary's experiment, in which he showed that practice improved a monkey's perception of the direction of movement. (137)

59. What did Zohary conclude about the connection between perception and neural responding? How is this related to plasticity? (137)

Across the Senses:
Neurons That Respond to Vision and Touch

60. What is a bimodal neuron? (138)

61. Describe the properties of the neurons that respond to both touch and vision that were studied by Graziano and Gross. (138)

62. What happens to the visual receptive field in Graziano and Gross's bimodal neurons, when the monkey moves different parts of its body? (138)

63. What property of these neurons leads to them being called body-centered neurons? (139)

64. What is a possible function of the monkey's body-centered neurons? (139)

5

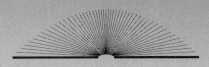

PERCEIVING OBJECTS

SOME QUESTIONS WE WILL CONSIDER

- Why do some perceptual psychologists say "the whole is different than the sum of its parts"? (148)

- How do we use "rules-of-thumb" to aid us in arriving at a perception of the environment? (153)

- What makes it possible to distinguish an object from its background? (156)

- Why haven't we been able to program a computer to see objects as well as people can? (172)

W e began this book in Chapter 1 by stating some goals. One goal was to understand how we sense things in our environment and interact with them. Another goal was to explain hidden perceptual processes that occur behind the scenes to create our perceptions. In Chapters 2 through 4 we looked closely at the behind-the-scenes processes from a physiological point of view, by considering things like nerve impulses and modules in the brain and espe-

cially focusing our attention, in Chapter 4, on the physiology behind how we perceive faces and other objects.

In this chapter we continue looking at behind-the-scenes processes, but at the psychophysical level of analysis. This means that we will be describing research that has looked at the relationship between stimuli and perception. We will see that we can learn a lot about perception without using electrodes or brain scans and also that there are a number of different kinds of information that we can get about perception by working at the psychophysical level.

We can understand this idea that there are a number of different kinds of information within a particular level of analysis by looking at Figure 5.1. Figure 5.1a reviews the kinds of information we considered when we were working at the physiological level of analysis in Chapters 2 through 4. We began at the molecular level, considering how ions flowing across membranes create nerve impulses and how perception can be triggered by the action of photons of light on visual pigment molecules. We then looked at how information in the nervous system is represented by the firing of single neurons and how specific objects can be represented by the firing of groups of these neurons. We then saw how larger groups of neurons became brain areas or modules that specialize in the perception of specific perceptual qualities, and we saw that perception depends on the coordination of information between modules across the brain as a whole. Thus, we investigated perception at the physiological level by considering scales ranging from molecules to the whole brain.

Figure 5.1b shows that a similar situation occurs when we study perception at the psychophysical level. At the smallest scale we can look at elementary features of perception such as lines, colors, or orientations. We can then consider how these features can be combined and how we perceive individual objects and groups of objects, and, finally, we can consider characteristics of scenes that contain many objects.

In this chapter we are going to describe how perception researchers working at the psychophysical level have studied object perception at these different scales. We will begin at the large end of the scale in Figure 5.1b by considering an approach to how we perceive objects called Gestalt psychology, which was proposed early in the 20th century. We will do this by starting with some psychological history that takes us back to Wilhelm Wundt's psychology laboratory late in the 19th century.

THE GESTALT APPROACH TO PERCEPTUAL ORGANIZATION: HOW ELEMENTS ARE GROUPED

webTUTOR Wilhelm Wundt is credited with founding the first laboratory of scientific psychology at the University of Leipzig in 1879. Wundt, and others who followed him, established an approach to psychology called structuralism. This approach, which dominated psychology until the 1920s, is important because it stimulated the founding of Gestalt psychology, which has made important contributions to our understanding of object perception.

The Beginnings of Gestalt Psychology

The basic idea behind **structuralism** was that behavior is created by adding elementary elements. When applied to perception, structuralism stated that perceptions were created by combining elements called **sensations**, just as each of the dots in the face in Figure 5.2 add together to create our perception of a face.

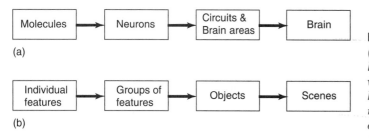

(a)

(b)

Figure 5.1

(a) Perception can be studied at the physiological level at scales ranging from molecules to the whole brain or nervous system. (b) Perception can be studied at the psychophysical level at scales ranging from individual features that make up objects to whole scenes.

Figure 5.2

According to structuralism, a number of sensations (represented by the dots) add up to create our perception of the face.

The dominance of structuralism as an explanation for perception set the stage for the founding of Gestalt psychology. In 1911 the psychologist Max Wertheimer was on a train ride through Germany. He got off the train at Frankfurt and bought a toy stroboscope on the train platform (Boring, 1942). The stroboscope, a mechanical device that created an illusion of movement by rapidly alternating two slightly different pictures, caused Wertheimer to wonder how Wundt's idea that experience is created from sensations could explain the illusion of movement he observed. We can understand why this question arose by looking at Figure 5.3, which diagrams the principle behind the illusion of movement created by the stroboscope.

If two stimuli that are in slightly different positions are flashed, with the correct timing, one after the other, movement is perceived between the two. This is an illusion called **apparent movement** because there is actually no movement in the display, just two stationary stimuli flashing on and off. How, wondered Wertheimer, can the movement that appears to occur between the two flashing stimuli be caused by sensations? After all, there is no stimulation in the space between the two stimuli, and therefore there are no sensations to provide an explanation for the movement.

With this question as his inspiration, Wertheimer and two colleagues, Kurt Koffka and Ivo Kohler, set up a laboratory at the University of Frankfurt, called themselves the Gestalt psychologists, and proceeded to do research and publish papers that posed serious problems for the structuralist idea that perceptions are created from sensations (Wertheimer, 1912). The following demonstration illustrates another phenomenon that is difficult to explain on the basis of sensations.

D E M O N S T R A T I O N

Making Illusory Contours Vanish

Consider the picture in Figure 5.4. If you see this as a cube floating in space in front of black circles, you probably perceive faint **illusory contours** that represent the edges of the cube (Bradley & Petry, 1977). These contours are called illusory because they aren't actually present in the physical stimulus. You can prove this to yourself by (1) placing your

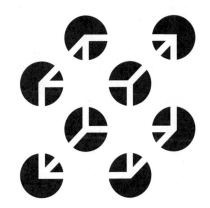

Figure 5.4

This figure can be seen as a cube floating in front of eight disks or as a cube seen through eight holes. In the first case, the edges of the cube appear as illusory contours. (From Bradley & Petry, 1977.)

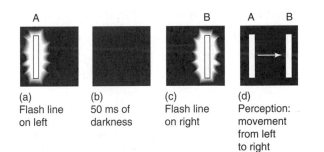

(a)
Flash line on left

(b)
50 ms of darkness

(c)
Flash line on right

(d)
Perception: movement from left to right

Figure 5.3

The principle behind the illusion of movement created by rapidly presenting two stimuli.

147

Perceiving Objects

finger over one of the black circles or (2) imagining that the black circles are holes and that you are looking at the cube through these holes. Notice how the illusory contours vanish in both situations. ●

When you made the contours vanish by placing your finger over the black circle, you showed that the contour was illusory and that our perception of one part of the display (the contours) is affected by the presence of another part (the black circle). The structuralists would have a hard time explaining illusory contours because, just as in the apparent movement example, they would not be able to identify any sensations along the contours that could lead to our perception of the contour.

Making the contours vanish by imagining that you are looking through black holes poses a similar problem for the structuralists. It is difficult to explain a perception that is present one moment and gone the next in terms of sensations, especially since the stimulus on the page and the image it creates on your retina are exactly the same when the contours are visible and when they are not.

Examples such as these led the Gestalt psychologists to state one of the basic principles of Gestalt psychology: _The whole is different than the sum of its parts_. This principle is illustrated by apparent movement and illusory contours and also by pictures such as the one in Figure 5.5. Our interpretation of whether the horse is rearing back or moving forward depends on the whole display, not just the horse. Thus, the horse in Figure 5.5a appears to be rearing back, but the identical horse in Figure 5.5b appears to be moving forward. The presence of the rider in one case and of the lead horse in the other changes our interpretation of the horse's movement.

This emphasis on "wholes" led the Gestalt psychologists to focus on determining principles to explain **perceptual organization**—how small elements become grouped into larger objects, as when some of the dark areas in Figure 5.6 group to form a Dalmation, and others are seen as shadows in the background. The Gestalt approach to perceptual organization was to propose a number of rules that they called the "laws of perceptual organization."

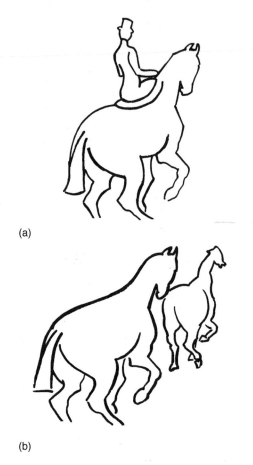

(a)

(b)

Figure 5.5
(a) A rearing horse. (b) One horse following another. (From Arnheim, 1974.)

The Gestalt Laws of Perceptual Organization

The **laws of perceptual organization** are a series of rules that specify how we organize small parts into wholes. Let's look at six of the Gestalt laws.

**Pragnanz**   Pragnanz, roughly translated from the German, means "good figure." The **law of Pragnanz,** the central law of Gestalt psychology, which is also called the **law of good figure** or the **law of simplicity,** states: _Every stimulus pattern is seen in such a way that the resulting structure is as simple as possible._ The familiar Olympic symbol in Figure 5.7a is an

Figure 5.6
Some black and white shapes that can become perceptually organized into a Dalmatian (look for the Dalmation head in the center of the picture). (Photograph by R. C. James.)

example of the law of simplicity at work. We see this display as five circles, and not as other, more complicated, shapes such as the ones in Figure 5.7b.

Similarity Most people perceive Figure 5.8a as either horizontal rows of circles, vertical columns of circles, or both. But when we change some of the

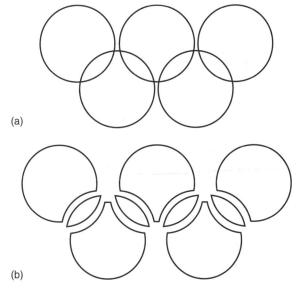

(a)

(b)

Figure 5.7
(a) This is usually perceived as five circles, and not as the nine shapes in (b).

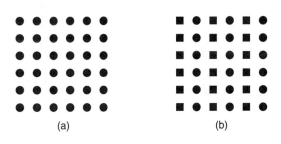

(a)   (b)

Figure 5.8
(a) Perceived as horizontal rows or vertical columns or both.
(b) Perceived as vertical columns.

Perceiving Objects

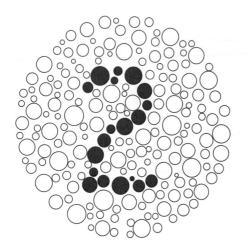

Figure 5.9
Grouping due to similarity of lightness. The light objects form one group, and the dark objects form another group.

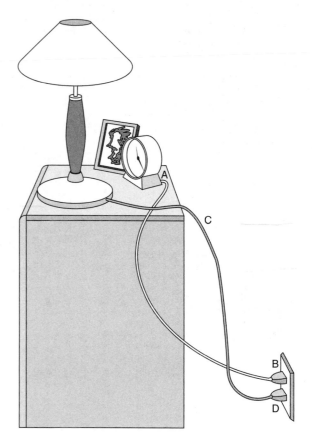

Figure 5.11
Good continuation: Both electric cords follow a smooth path to the electrical outlet.

Figure 5.10
Grouping due to similarity of orientation. In this scene from Swan Lake, the perceptual unity of these two dancers is greatly enhanced by the similar orientations of their arms and bodies.

circles to squares, as in Figure 5.8b, most people perceive vertical columns of squares and circles. This perception illustrates the **law of similarity**: *Similar things appear to be grouped together*. This law causes the circles to be grouped with other circles and the squares to be grouped with other squares. Grouping can also occur because of similarity of lightness (Figure 5.9), hue, size, or orientation (Figure 5.10).

Grouping also occurs for auditory stimuli. For example, notes that have similar pitches and that follow each other closely in time can become perceptually grouped to form a melody. We will consider this and other auditory grouping effects when we describe organizational processes in hearing in Chapter 11.

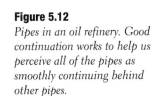

Figure 5.12
Pipes in an oil refinery. Good continuation works to help us perceive all of the pipes as smoothly continuing behind other pipes.

Good Continuation We see the electric cord starting at A in Figure 5.11 as flowing smoothly to B. It does not go to C or D, because that path would involve making sharp turns and would violate the **law of good continuation**: *Points that, when connected, result in straight or smoothly curving lines are seen as belonging together, and the lines tend to be seen in such a way as to follow the smoothest path.* Thus, even though the pipes in Figure 5.12 cross in front of other pipes, we do not see some of the pipes as being broken into many pieces. Because of good continuation, we see each pipe in this oil refinery as continuing smoothly behind the pipes in front. Good continuation also helped us to perceive the smoothly curving circles in Figure 5.7a.

Proximity or Nearness Our perception of Figure 5.13a as horizontal rows of circles illustrates the **law of proximity** or **nearness**: *Things that are near to each other appear to be grouped together.* And although every other circle is changed to a square in Figure 5.13b, we still perceive horizontal rows (in this case the law of proximity overpowers the law of similarity.)

Common Fate The dancers in Figure 5.14 form a group by virtue of their nearness and similar orientation, but perhaps most important is their common fate—the fact that they are moving in the same direction. The **law of common fate** states: *Things that are moving in the same direction appear to be grouped together.* Although dance choreographers may not be familiar with the Gestalt laws, they are well aware that one way to create perceptual grouping is to choreograph groups of dancers moving together.

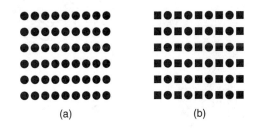

(a)   (b)

Figure 5.13
Two examples of the law of nearness. (a) Perceived as horizontal rows of circles. (b) Still perceived as horizontal rows, even though half of the circles have been changed to squares.

Perceiving Objects

Figure 5.14
Grouping due to common fate. The perceptual grouping of these dancers is enhanced both by their similarity of orientation and by their common fate, that is, the fact that they are both moving in the same direction at the same speed.

Meaningfulness or Familiarity According to the **law of familiarity**, *things are more likely to form groups if the groups appear familiar or meaningful* (Helson, 1933; Hochberg, 1971). You can appreciate how meaningfulness determines perceptual organization by doing the following demonstration.

 **D E M O N S T R A T I O N**

Finding Faces in a Landscape

Consider the picture in Figure 5.15. At first glance, this scene appears to contain mainly trees, rocks, and water. But on closer inspection you can see some faces in the trees in the background; and, if you look more closely, you can see that a number of faces are formed by various groups of rocks. There are, in fact, 12 hidden faces in this picture. ●

Figure 5.15
The Forest Has Eyes *by Bev Doolittle (1985). Can you find 12 faces in this picture?*

In this demonstration some people find it difficult to perceive the faces at first, but then suddenly they succeed. The change in perception from "rocks in a stream" or "trees in a forest" into "faces" is a change in the perceptual organization of the rocks and the trees. The two shapes that you at first perceive as two separate rocks in the stream become perceptually grouped together when they become the left and right eyes of a face. In fact, once you perceive a particular grouping of rocks as a face, it is often difficult not to perceive them in this way—they have become permanently organized into a face.

Meaningfulness also helps us separate the horses from their background in Figure 5.16. But there are other Gestalt laws at work here as well. Good contin-

uation (the contours of the horses' backs and legs) and similarity (the similar shading of the horses' legs and bodies) also help us perceive the horses as separate from their background. (Look back at the picture in Figure 5.6. Which laws of organization help to group the black shapes into a Dalmation?)

The Gestalt "Laws" Are Really Heuristics

Although the Gestalt psychologists called the principles we have just described "laws," most perceptual psychologists call them the Gestalt "principles." The reason for rejecting the term *laws* is that the rules proposed by the Gestalt psychologists don't make strong enough predictions to qualify as laws. In fact the

Figure 5.16
Pintos *by Bev Doolittle (1979).*

Perceiving Objects

Gestalt principles are most accurately described as being "heuristics." **Heuristics** are rules of thumb that provide a best-guess solution to a problem. We can understand what heuristics are by comparing them to another way of solving a problem, called algorithms.

Comparing Heuristics and Algorithms An **algorithm** is a procedure that is guaranteed to solve a problem. An example of an algorithm is the procedures we learn for addition, subtraction, and long division. If we apply these procedures correctly, we get the right answer every time. In contrast, a heuristic may not result in a correct solution every time. For example, suppose that you want to find a cat that is hiding somewhere in the house. An algorithm for doing this would be to systematically search every room in the house (being careful not to let the cat sneak past you!). If you do this, you will eventually find the cat, although it may take a while. A heuristic for finding the cat would be to first look in the places where the cat likes to hide. So you check under the bed and in the hall closet. This may not always lead to finding the cat, but, if it does, it has the advantage of being faster than the algorithm.

The Gestalt Principles as Heuristics We say the Gestalt principles are heuristics, because, like heuristics, they are best-guess rules that do not work every time. Consider, for example, the situation depicted in Figure 5.17a. Coming upon this in the woods, we would be most likely to perceive it as a single branch partially hidden by a tree. This perception would follow the principle of good continuation, since the branch appears to continue smoothly from one side of the tree to the other. However, in this case, good continuation doesn't work, because the real situation, shown in Figure 5.17b, is that there are actually two branches. Although good continuation doesn't work in this case, in most cases it does, because, as we will see below, the Gestalt laws are based on the way things usually occur in the environment.

The algorithm for solving this particular perceptual problem would involve looking at the branches from a number of different angles that are not obscured by the tree. This would provide a more accurate solution to our problem but takes longer. We often need to know rapidly what is going on in the environment, so perception needs to be fast, and heuristics like the Gestalt principles provide this speed.

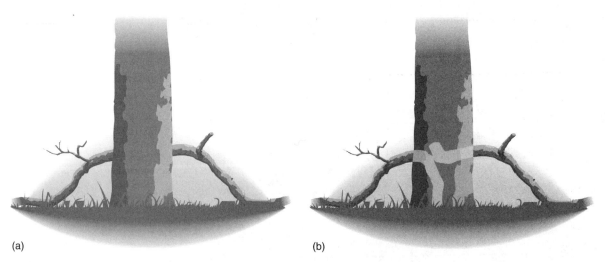

(a) (b)

Figure 5.17

(a) Is this a single branch behind the tree? It's most likely that it is, and this is what the law of good continuation would predict. However, it is also possible that two different branches could create this perception, as shown in (b).

Where Do the Heuristics Come From? In the last chapter we wondered what caused some neurons to respond selectively to faces. We decided that one possibility is that the properties of face neurons might have been determined by evolution, and another possibility is that they could be determined by our experience in perceiving faces. We can pose the same two possibilities for the question, "Where do the Gestalt principles come from?" Evolution could certainly play a role, but it also seems likely that learning would be important as well. After all, we have been practicing "perceptual problem solving" since infancy and have encountered many different perceptual situations. It is likely that we have learned, during these many perceptual encounters, that there are certain regularities in the environment, such as the way tree branches usually appear in the woods (Figure 5.17).

Whether the Gestalt principles are built in by evolution, or are determined by learning that occurs as we develop, or by some combination of the two, it is clear that the Gestalt principles reflect common regularities that we often see in our environment. Things generally tend to follow smooth paths, rather than changing abruptly, and things that are similar tend to be part of the same object. These regularities in the environment are also the basis of some principles of perceptual organization that have been proposed recently.

More Principles of Perceptual Organization

Stephen Palmer (1992, 1999) and Palmer and Irvin Rock (1994) have proposed three new grouping principles: the principle of common region, the principle of element connectedness, and the principle of synchrony.

Common Region Figure 5.18a illustrates the **principle of common region**: *Elements that are within the same region of space are grouped together.* Even though the dots inside the ellipses are farther apart than the dots that are next to each other in neighboring ellipses, we see the dots inside the ellipses as belonging together. This occurs because each ellipse is seen as a separate region of space.

Element Connectedness In Figure 5.18b we perceive a series of dumbbells rather than pairs of dots, even though the dots separated by the spaces are closer together than the ones connected by the lines. This is the **principle of element connectedness**: *Things that are physically connected are perceived as a unit.*

Synchrony The **principle of synchrony** states that *visual events that occur at the same time will be perceived as going together.* For example, in the display in Figure 5.18c, the lights that blink together are seen as belonging together. Notice that synchrony is like common fate because they are both dynamic, but synchrony can occur without movement, and the elements don't have to change in the same direction. Thus, one light can go on, and another can go off, but if they change together, they will be perceived as belonging together.

Quantitative Measurement of the Grouping Effects

The Gestalt psychologists' main method for studying perception was phenomenological. They created displays and described how the elements appear to be grouped. Recently, Palmer and Jacob Beck (2000) have devised a way to quantitatively measure the

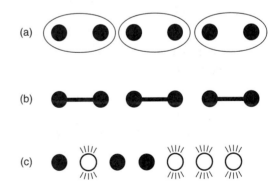

Figure 5.18
Grouping by (a) common region; (b) connectedness; and (c) synchrony. The lights indicated by the open circles blink on and off together.

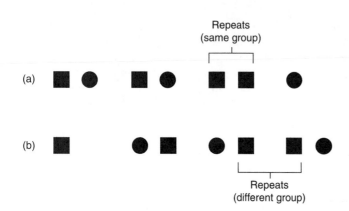

Figure 5.19

Repetition discrimination task. The repeating squares are (a) in the same group, and (b) in different groups. Subjects identify the repetition faster in (a).

strength of grouping. Their technique, which is called the **repetition discrimination task**, has subjects look at a series of objects like the ones in Figure 5.19a.

The subject's task is to find two identical shapes that are next to each other in the series and then to press one key if they are squares and another key if they are circles. For example, squares are the repeated objects in both (a) and (b). However, in (a) the squares are in the same group, by the principle of proximity, and in (b) they are in different groups. Palmer and Beck found that the grouping in (a) resulted in a reaction time of 719 milliseconds (ms), compared to 1144 ms for the grouping in (b). Grouping, therefore, not only affects the way a display looks, it also affects our ability to extract information from the display.

In our consideration of perceptual organization, we have focused on how small elements become perceptually grouped to form larger objects. But when we perceive things in the environment, we usually perceive not just a single object but many different objects. Our ability to perceptually separate objects from one another is called **perceptual segregation**. Thus, in Figure 5.6 we perceptually organize a number of black elements into a perception of a Dalmation (perceptual organization), but we also see the Dalmation as separated from its background (perceptual segregation). Both the Gestalt psychologists and modern researchers have been concerned with how this segregation occurs.

PERCEPTUAL SEGREGATION: HOW OBJECTS ARE SEPARATED

WebTUTOR The problem of what causes perceptual segregation is often referred to as the problem of **figure–ground segregation**, to indicate that when we see a separate object, it is usually seen as a **figure** that stands out from its background, which is called the **ground**. For example, you would probably see a book or papers on your desk as figure and the surface of your desk as ground. We will consider the topic of perceptual segregation in the same way we approached perceptual organization. We consider first the pioneering work of the Gestalt psychologists and then some modern ideas.

The Gestalt Approach to Figure–Ground Segregation

The Gestalt psychologists were interested in determining the properties of the figure and the ground and in determining what makes one area be perceived as figure and the other as ground.

What Are the Properties of Figure and Ground?
One way the Gestalt psychologists studied the properties of figure and ground was by considering patterns like the one in Figure 5.20, which was introduced by Danish psychologist Edgar Rubin in 1915. This pattern is an example of **reversible**

Figure 5.20
A version of Rubin's reversible face–vase figure.

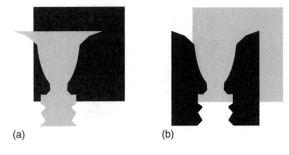

Figure 5.21
(a) When the vase is perceived as figure, it is perceived in front of a homogeneous dark background; (b) When the faces are seen as figure, they are seen in front of a homogeneous light background.

figure–ground, because it can be perceived alternately either as two black faces looking at each other, in front of a white background, or as a white vase on a black background. Some of the properties of the figure and ground are that: (1) The figure is more "thinglike" and more memorable than the ground; (2) the figure is seen as being in front of the ground; (3) the ground is seen as unformed material and seems to extend behind the figure; and (4) the contour separating the figure from the ground appears to belong to the figure.

You can demonstrate these four properties of figure and ground to yourself by noting that when the vase is seen as figure, it appears to be in front of the black background (Figure 5.21a), and when the faces are seen as figure, they are on top of the light background (Figure 5.21b). Also notice that, when you are perceiving the one pattern as figure, it is difficult, if not impossible, to simultaneously perceive the other one. Remember that the ground is seen as "unformed material," so as soon as you perceive the light area as figure, the vase is seen in front and the black area can't be two faces because it has become "unformed material" that extends behind the vase. Similarly, when the black area is seen as figure, the faces are seen in front, and the light area is seen as unformed material.

What Factors Determine Which Area Is Figure and Which Is Ground? In addition to describing the properties of the figure and the ground, the Gestalt psychologists proposed a number of factors that determine which part of a display will be seen as figure. To get a feel for these factors, do the following demonstration.

 **D E M O N S T R A T I O N**

Determinants of Figure and Ground

Look at the following displays and decide, as quickly as possible, which areas you see as the figure and which as ground:

- Figure 5.22: The white areas or the black areas? (look on both the left and right)
- Figure 5.23: The wide-blade propeller shape of the cross figure or the narrow-blade propeller shape of the plus figure?
- Figure 5.24: The upright propeller shape or the tilted propeller shape?
- Figure 5.25: The black areas or the white areas? ●

There are no "correct" perceptions of these displays, but experiments have shown that certain properties of the stimulus influence which areas are seen as figure and which are seen as ground. Symmetrical

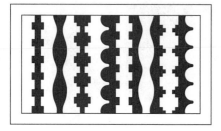

Figure 5.22
Symmetry and figure ground. Look to the left and to the right and observe which colors become figure and which become ground. (Adapted from Hochberg, 1971.)

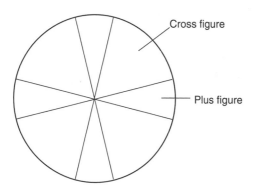

Cross figure

Plus figure

Figure 5.23
The effect of area on figure–ground perception. Which is more likely to be seen as figure, the wide-blade propeller shape of the cross figure or the narrow-blade propeller shape of the plus figure?

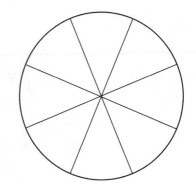

Figure 5.24
The effect of orientation on figure–ground perception. Which is easier to see as a figure, the vertical-horizontal propeller shape or the tilted propeller shape? What is your initial perception? Allow your perception to flip back and forth between the two alternatives. Which perception is present the longest?

areas tend to be seen as figure, so in Figure 5.22 the symmetrical black areas on the left and the symmetrical white areas on the right are seen as figure.

The Gestalt psychologists also found that stimuli with comparatively smaller areas are more likely to be seen as figure, so the plus figure in Figure 5.23 is more likely to be seen as figure than is the cross figure (Kunnapas, 1957; see also Oyama, 1960). Vertical or horizontal orientations are more likely to be seen as figure than are other orientations. Thus, the vertical-horizontal propeller shape in Figure 5.24 is more likely to be seen as figure than is the tilted propeller shape. Finally, as we saw in looking at Figures 5.15 and 5.16, meaningful objects are more likely to be seen as figure. Thus, the black areas in Figure 5.25, which include three arrows, tend to be seen as figure (the smaller size of the black areas compared to the white areas also helps make the black into figures). However, adding two more black areas on either side, as in Figure 5.27, makes it easier to see that the white areas spell a word, so these white areas dominate our perception. We will return to the idea that meaningful objects are likely to be seen as figure in a moment, because this property of figure–ground has been used to investigate the mechanisms that underlie figure–ground perception.

Modern Ideas About Figure–Ground Segregation

Modern psychologists have extended the Gestalt psychologists' work by looking more closely at the mechanisms underlying figure–ground perception. Two important concerns are (1) the role of contours on figure–ground perception, and (2) where in the perceptual process figure–ground segregation occurs.

Contours and Figure–Ground Segregation One approach to studying figure–ground segregation has been to focus on the contour that divides the two

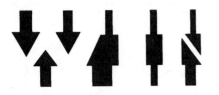

Figure 5.25
Which do you see as figure, the black area or the white area? After deciding, turn to Figure 5.27 on page 160.

areas in reversible figure–ground displays. For example, we can understand why we tend to see just one area at a time as figure in a reversible figure–ground display by considering how likely it would be that a vase and two faces would have exactly the same contours, as in Figure 5.26a, and that they would also just happen to be viewed so their contours exactly coincided, as in Figure 5.26b. The answer is that although it is not impossible that this could happen, it is a highly unlikely occurrence.

The unlikeliness that two contours would be identical and then would line up perfectly brings us back to our discussion of the basis of the Gestalt principles. Remember that the Gestalt principles provide a best guess as to what a particular stimulus display is. Since it is so unlikely for two meaningful contours to exactly line up, as would have to occur if Figure 5.26b represented both a vase and two faces, the visual system assumes the most likely occurrence—

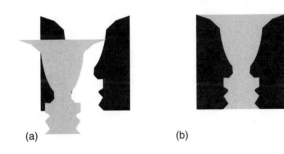

(a)   (b)

Figure 5.26
(a) It is unlikely that two objects in the world as shown here would have identical contours or (b) that these two objects would be viewed so their contours would exactly coincide. (Adapted from Bayliss & Driver, 1995.)

that the contour separating the two regions belongs to only one object. The area that belongs to that contour then becomes figure, and the other one ground (Bayliss and Driver, 1995).

When in the Perceptual Process Does Figure–Ground Segregation Occur? We've seen that meaningfulness can help determine which area we see as figure. But exactly when in the perceptual process does meaning come into play? One idea that has been very popular among perception researchers is that the process proceeds in the following order: First the figure is segregated from ground, and then the meaning of the figure is recognized. But Mary Peterson (1994) has done an experiment that indicates that meaningfulness may occur before or at the same time as figure–ground segregation.

Peterson presented a display like the one in Figure 5.28, which can be perceived in two ways: (1) a standing woman (the black part of the display) or (2) a less meaningful shape (the white part of the display). When Peterson presented stimuli such as this for a fraction of a second and asked subjects which region seemed to be the figure, she found that her subjects were more likely to say that the meaningful part of the display (the woman in this example) was the figure.

Why were the subjects more likely to perceive the woman? One possibility is that they must have recognized that the black area was a familiar object. In fact, when Peterson turned the display upside down, so that it was more difficult to recognize the black area as a woman, subjects were less likely to see that area as being the figure. Thus, figure–ground segregation may not always occur before recognition. Perhaps some recognition occurs before the figure is perceived, or perhaps perception of the figure and recognition of its meaning are occurring at about the same time (see also Vecera & O'Reilly, 2000, for another idea about how this might work).

This idea that perception isn't a simple straight-line process, like our diagram of the perceptual process in Figure 1.2, makes sense when we remember the following facts about physiology from Chapters 3 and 4: (1) There is a great deal of feedback of information from higher centers to lower ones (Figure 3.2); and (2) there is cross-talk between

Perceiving Objects

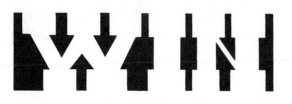

Figure 5.27
In this version of Figure 5.25, which area is figure, white or black? Look for a three-letter word starting with W.

Figure 5.28
Stimulus for Peterson's (1994) experiment.

different areas in the extrastriate cortex (Figure 4.8). Even though Peterson's experiment was looking at the relationship between the stimulus and perception, the results may be telling us something about the underlying physiology, as well. See Summary Table 5.1 for an overview of the material we have covered so far.

HOW OBJECTS ARE CONSTRUCTED

WebTUTOR So far, we've looked at how the Gestalt psychologists and modern psychologists have studied how small elements are grouped together to form larger objects and how figure is separated from ground. Other researchers have approached object perception in another way, by starting at the very beginning of the diagram in Figure 5.1b.

We are going to consider a number of approaches to object perception that are based on the idea that at the beginning of the process of object perception an object is broken down, or analyzed, into elementary features. We will consider three different variations on this theme, beginning with the approach of David Marr, a vision researcher who, at the age of 32, discovered that he had leukemia and spent the last two years of his life writing a book titled *Vision* (1982), which, along with a number of papers (Marr, 1976; Marr & Hildreth, 1980; Marr & Nishihara, 1978), had a large influence on much of the research and theorizing on object perception that followed.

Marr's Computational Approach to Object Perception

David Marr's approach to object perception is called a **computational approach**, because it treats the visual system as if it were a computer that has been programmed to perceive objects. We will describe how this human "computer" is programmed by referring to the stages in the computational approach shown in Figure 5.29.

The starting point for object perception, according to Marr's proposal, is the image of the object or scene on the retina. This image is analyzed to determine areas of light and dark and where intensity

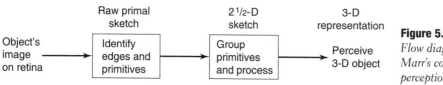

Figure 5.29
Flow diagram indicating the stages in Marr's computational approach to perception.

The Beginnings of the Gestalt Approach

An early approach to perception, called structuralism, hypothesized that perception is determined by the addition of tiny elements called sensations. Based initially on observations of apparent movement, Wertheimer questioned this approach and stated instead that the whole is different than the sum of its parts. This was the beginning of Gestalt psychology.

The Gestalt Laws of Perceptual Organization

The Gestalt laws of organization are a series of rules that specify how we organize small stimulus elements into wholes. Six of the most important laws are good figure, similarity, good continuation, proximity, common fate, and meaningfulness. Since the Gestalt laws don't make strong enough predictions to qualify as laws, it is more common to call them "principles." The Gestalt principles are heuristics that provide "best-guess" rules that work most, but not all, of the time. This property of Gestalt principles enables them to work rapidly. The principles may be determined by evolution, or learning, or a combination of the two. However they are determined, they reflect regularities in the environment.

More Principles of Perceptual Organization

Modern psychologists have proposed additional principles of organization that include common region, element connectedness, and synchrony. The results of experiments using a quantitative measure of the strength of grouping, called the repetition discrimination task, indicate that perceptual grouping determines not only the way a display looks but also how well we can extract information from the display.

The Gestalt Approach to Figure–Ground Segregation

Perceptual segregation is our ability to perceptually separate objects from one another. The Gestalt psychologists studied perceptual segregation by determining stimulus factors that are responsible for figure–ground segregation—how one area becomes the figure and the other becomes the ground. Among the factors that the Gestalt psychologists identified as being associated with figures are symmetry, small area, orientation, and meaningfulness.

Modern Ideas about Figure–Ground Segregation

Modern work on figure–ground segregation has proposed that the reason that we don't see two adjacent areas as figure simultaneously is because it is highly unlikely that the objects would have identical contours that line up. This idea is a reflection of the way perception reflects regularities in the environment. Other research provides evidence that recognition of an area's meaning could occur before figure–ground segregation has occurred.

---

changes occur. This analysis determines a collection of basic features called the **raw primal sketch**, which includes closed areas such as circles and ellipses and also segments of lines, the ends of lines, and lines that define the object's edges.

According to Marr, the visual system's major problem at this early stage of perception is to identify the object's edges and the object's features. We can appreciate the difficulty in determining an object's edges by looking at Figure 5.30. In this figure, intensity changes are caused by the edges of the object and by changes in illumination caused by the lighting conditions. To determine the shape of an object, the visual system must ignore shadows and other changes in illumination and locate the object's true edges.

According to Marr, the visual system accomplishes this by (1) mathematically analyzing how intensities change in the image; and (2) taking into account what he calls natural constraints in the world. **Natural constraints** are basic properties of the environment, like the "regularities" we discussed when we described the Gestalt approach. Examples of natural constraints that Marr considered important are the fact that intensity usually changes gradually at borders created by shadows and highlights but changes more abruptly at borders created by an object's edges. According to Marr, the visual system takes these facts about the world into account and labels gradual borders as shadows and sharper intensity changes as borders between objects.

The primal sketch is the result of this initial stage of computations. We do not, however, see the primal sketch. For conscious perception to occur, the information contained in the primal sketch must be

Perceiving Objects

Figure 5.30
Intensity changes occur both at the edges of this object and at the border created by the shadows and highlights on the surface of the object. To identify the object's shape, the visual system must identify the object's true edges.

processed further. First, features that are similar in size and orientation are grouped, following Gestalt principles. These groups of features are then processed, by procedures we will not describe here (see Marr, 1982, for details), to yield a representation of the object's surfaces and their layouts that Marr called the **2½-D sketch**. The information in the 2½-D sketch is then transformed into a three-dimensional representation that we actually see.

One way to look at Marr's system is to think of it as a computer that is programmed to take into account certain physical properties of the world (for example, the fact that shadows often have fuzzy borders). The data fed into this computer are the characteristics of the retinal image, particularly the pattern of light and dark areas in the image. The computer calculates the existence of edges and other features of objects based on these data and by also taking into account what it knows about the properties of images in the world. Our description of the way these calculations are carried out has been vague, because of the complexity of the calculations and also because Marr did not have time to work out many of the specific details of his system.

Marr's theory is important because it illustrates a theoretical approach to the problem of object perception. That is, Marr's approach is a proposal of how the system *might* work. It is based on some experimental data, such as Marr's knowledge of physiological detectors like Hubel and Wiesel's simple, complex, and end-stopped neurons that respond to elementary features in an image. But ideas such as how the system mathematically analyzes the image or how the system takes natural constraints into account were proposals that remained to be tested through future research.

It is important to remember that when Marr proposed his theory, it was an incomplete work-in-progress, which undoubtedly would look different today if he had been able to continue working on it. But his ideas influenced other researchers, many of whom were working on the same problems Marr was concerned with. One particularly important theory of object perception that was being developed at about the same time as Marr's theory is called feature integration theory. This theory differs in a number of ways from Marr's theory but shares an important characteristic: It proposes that we perceive an object by breaking it into basic features and then recombining these features into our perception of the object.

Feature Integration Theory

Feature integration theory, which we will call **FIT** for short, proposes that object perception occurs according to the sequence of stages shown in Figure 5.31 (Treisman, 1987, 1993, 1998). In the first stage, called the **preattentive stage**, the visual system analyzes the image and determines the existence of the features that are the basic units of perception. Some examples of these features are curvature, orientation, ends of lines, color, and movement (Figure 5.32).

In the second stage, called the **focused attention stage**, the features are combined to result in perception of the object. Then, after the object is perceived, it is recognized by comparing this perception to information stored in memory. We will first consider how Treisman identified the basic features and will then describe the preattentive and focused attention stages in more detail.

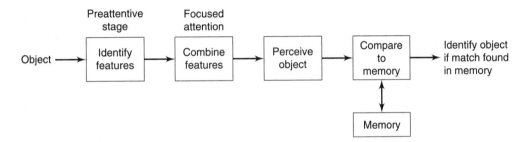

Figure 5.31
Flow diagram showing steps in Treisman's (1986, 1987, 1993) feature integration theory of object perception.

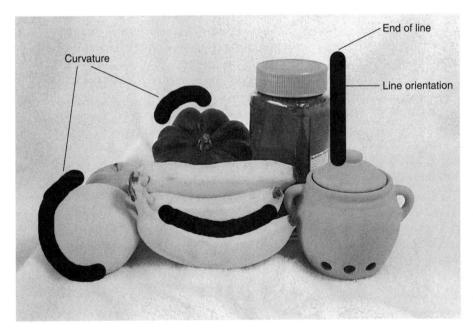

Figure 5.32
Some of the features in this scene, indicated by the markings, are curvature, line orientation, and the ends of lines. In addition, the different colors of the objects are also features. According to feature integration theory, the first thing the visual system does upon being exposed to this scene is to break it down into its features.

Perceiving Objects

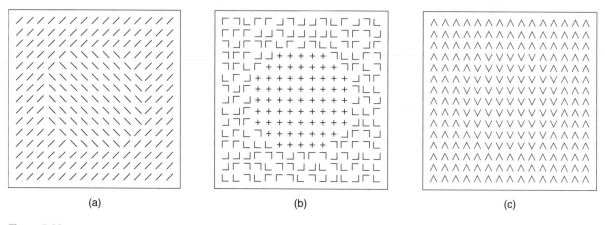

Figure 5.33
Texture segmentation based on differences in features: (a) difference in orientation; (b) difference in line crossings. In (c) there is no difference in features, so texture segregation doesn't occur. (From Nothdurft, 1990.)

Determining the Basic Features FIT's features were determined in two ways: (1) by determining pop-out boundaries between areas made up of different elements, and (2) by a visual search procedure (Julesz, 1981; Treisman, 1987).

For the **pop-out boundary** method, two sets of elements are displayed next to each other to create textured fields, as in Figure 5.33. If the two areas either contain different features or have different values of the same feature, then an immediately obvious boundary "pops out" between the two areas. For example, in Figure 5.33a the boundaries occur because the com-

ponents have different orientations (different values of the same feature). In Figure 5.33b, the boundary occurs because one component (the pluses) has "line crossings," two lines that cross each other, and the other (the L's) does not (there is a feature in one of the fields but not in the other). However, no pop-out boundary occurs in Figure 5.33c, so no features can be identified.

In the **visual search** procedure for determining features, subjects are presented with a display that contains a number of elements and are told to find one particular element. You can appreciate how this works by doing the following demonstration.

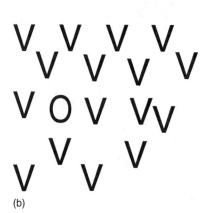

(a)

(b)

Figure 5.34
Visual search stimuli. Subjects tend to find the target (O) rapidly when (a) there are few distractors and (b) when there are many distractors.

Visual Search

- In Figure 5.34 on the previous page, find the letter O in the display on the left and then in the display on the right.
- As you look at the figure the bottom of this page (Figure 5.35), find the letter R in the display on the left and then in the display on the right. ●

The usual result for these visual search tasks is that the "O's" on the left and right in Figure 5.34 both exhibit an effect called **pop-out**—we see the O's almost instantaneously. This happens for both the left and the right displays, so even though there are more distractor items (the V's) in the display on the right, we see the O's equally rapidly in the left and right displays. However, the usual result for the R's in Figure 5.35 is different. The R's don't pop out, and it usually takes longer to find the R in the right than on the left.

When Treisman did experiments similar to these demonstrations, she found that for targets that pop out (like in Figure 5.34), the reaction time was fast no matter how many distractors were present in the display. This result is plotted as line a in Figure 5.36. However, for targets that did not pop out (like Figure 5.35), increasing the number of distractors increased

the reaction time. This result is plotted as line b in Figure 5.36b.

Why are the results different for the O and the R? We can answer this question by comparing the features of the target letter and the distractor letters. In Figure 5.34, the O's feature of *curvature* differs from the V's feature of *straight lines*. If the target's features are different than the distractor's features, the target pops out, and the number of distractors doesn't affect the time it takes to find the target.

However, in Figure 5.35, the R has features in common with the distractors. The R has straight lines like the P, slanted lines like the Q, and a curved line like both the P and the Q. These shared features prevent pop-out, and so you need to scan each letter to find the target, just as you would have to scan the faces in a crowd to locate one particular person. Since scanning is necessary, adding more distractors increases the time it takes to find the target.

By determining which features lead to the pop-out effect in search tasks, Treisman and other researchers have identified curvature, tilt, line ends, movement, color, brightness, and direction of illumination as basic features (Beck, 1982; Julesz, 1984; Treisman, 1986, 1998). These features are detected at the beginning of processing, during the preattentive stage, and, according to feature integration theory, are not yet combined to form objects at this early stage of processing. We can understand what this means by considering the following experiment,

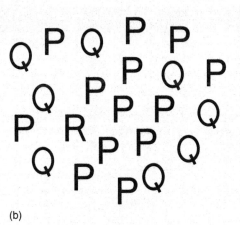

(a)   (b)

Figure 5.35
Visual search stimuli. Subjects tend to find the target (R) faster in (a), when there are few distractors, than in (b), when there are many distractors.

Perceiving Objects

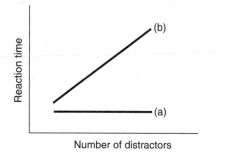

Figure 5.36
Typical results of a visual search experiment: (a) the result when pop-out occurs, as in Figure 5.34; (b) the result when there is no pop-out, as in Figure 5.35.

which shows that at the very beginning of the perceptual process, features exist independently of each other.

The Preattentive Stage: Independent Features
The following example illustrates Treisman's experiment (Figure 5.37): A display consisting of a red X, a blue S, and a green T is flashed onto a screen for one fifth of a second, followed by a random dot masking field designed to eliminate any residual image that may remain after the stimuli are turned off. When the subjects report what they have seen, they sometimes report seeing **illusory conjunctions**—incorrect combinations of two features. An example of an illusory conjunction for the display in Figure 5.37 would be a "red S" or "green X." This happens on about a third of the trials and occurs even if the stimuli differ greatly in shape and size. For example, a small blue circle and a large green square might be seen as a large blue square and a small green circle.

According to Treisman, the fact that features can be incorrectly combined in laboratory situations when briefly flashed stimuli are followed by a masking field shows that at the beginning of the perceptual process each feature exists independently of the others. That is, features such as "redness," "curvature," or "tilted line" have not yet been combined to create our perception of an object.

Although the fact that these qualities can exist independently of each other at an early stage of processing may at first seem surprising, this situation is

actually what we might expect from what we know about visual physiology. Remember that properties such as form and movement are processed in separate physiological structures, or modules, and that neurons that respond to different orientations and shapes are located in different columns in the cortex. Eventually all of these properties are combined to create a unified perception of an object, but, before that happens, they exist independently of one another. It is possible that Treisman's psychophysical result reflects this aspect of physiological processing (Tarr, 1994).

One way to think about Treisman's features is that they are components of an alphabet of vision. At the very beginning of the perceptual process, these components of perception exist independently of one another, just as the individual letter tiles in a game of Scrabble exist as individual units when the tiles are scattered at the beginning of the game. Eventually, however, just as the individual Scrabble tiles are combined to form words, the individual features for vision

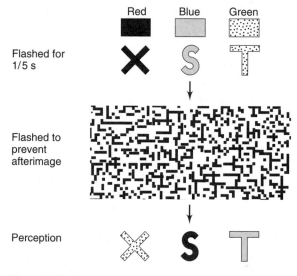

Figure 5.37
Treisman's experiment that illustrates illusory conjunctions. The X, S, and T are briefly flashed, followed by a random dot pattern flashed in the same location as the letters. On some trials observers report letters with colors different from the letter's actual color when it was presented. These changes in color are illusory conjunctions.

combine to form perceptions of whole objects. This combining occurs during the focused attention stage of perception.

The Focused Attention Stage: Combining the Features

Before we can see an object, the various features that make up the object must be combined. This occurs in the focused attention stage, and, according to Treisman, attention plays an important role combining these features. Let's look at an experiment that supports the idea that attention is important during this "combining" stage.

A display consisting of many red O's, many blue X's and, on some of the trials, a single target (a green X) is briefly flashed and is immediately followed by a random dot pattern designed to eliminate any afterimage that may remain after the stimulus is turned off (Figure 5.38a). The subject's task is to indicate if the target (green X) is in the display and, if it is, to specify its location. Subjects easily detect the green X, because it is the only green object in the display, but they have difficulty specifying its location. The reason for this difficulty, according to Treisman, is that only one feature is involved (the color green) so the X pops out and focused attention is not required; the subject, therefore, does not need to pay attention to the object's location.

Consider, however, what happens when the target is changed to a blue O (Figure 5.38b). This task requires focused attention because the blue O doesn't pop out, since it shares the color blue with the X's and its shape with the O's; so the subject must scan the display to find it. Doing this requires attention, and this enables the subject to indicate the target's location. According to Treisman, a similar process takes place when we perceive everyday objects. Before we perceive the object, it is broken down into features, and then, with the aid of attention, the features that are at a particular location are combined.

The idea that attention is necessary for object perception is something that we usually aren't aware of, because we usually direct our attention automatically as we focus on things that interest us in the environment. But remember from our discussion in Chapter 4 of inattentional blindness, the attentional blink, and change blindness (pages 131–132) that there is a great deal of evidence that supports the idea that attention is an essential component of the perceptual process.

We can deal with the question of why attention is a necessary part of the perceptual process physiologically by remembering that visual information is processed in two separated streams—the ventral stream, which flows toward the temporal cortex and processes information about "what" an object is; and the dorsal stream, which flows toward the parietal cortex and processes information about "where" the object is or "how" we interact with it. Eventually the information from these two pathways must be combined, and according to Treisman (1993), attention is the mechanism that accomplishes this combination.

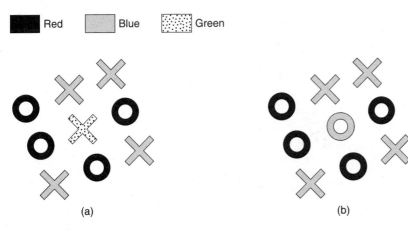

Figure 5.38
Two of Treisman's search patterns. In (a) the task is to find a green X; in (b) it is to find a blue O. See the text for details.

Perceiving Objects

Attention is the "glue" that binds together the features at a location. (See Treisman, 1992, for a more detailed description of how attention operates in feature integration theory.)

The Recognition-by-Components Approach

Another approach to object perception that proposes an "alphabet" of basic features is Irving Biederman's **recognition-by-components (RBC)** approach. A difference between Biederman's features and those of Treisman and Marr is that Biederman's features are **volumetric primitives**—three-dimensional shapes that correspond to an object's parts. Biederman calls these volumetric primitives **geons**, for geometric ions.

Figure 5.39a shows some geons. According to RBC theory, an object or scene is analyzed into these features, which are three-dimensional shapes such as cylinders, rectangular solids, and pyramids. There are 36 different geons in Biederman's system, and by combining these geons it is possible to construct many thousands of objects. A few of these objects are shown in Figure 5.39b. According to Biederman, geons have the following basic properties:

- **View invariance**. View invariance means that geons can be identified even when viewed from different angles. This view invariance occurs because geons contain view invariant properties, properties such as the three parallel edges of the rectangular solid in Figure 5.39a that remain visible over a wide range of viewpoints.

  You can test the view invariant properties of a rectangular solid yourself by picking up a book and moving it around so you are viewing it from many different angles. As you do this, notice what

(a) Geons   **(b) Objects**

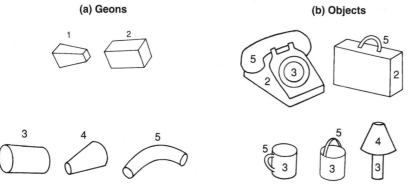

Figure 5.39
Left: Some geons. Right: Some objects created from the geons on the left. The numbers on the objects indicate which geons are present. Note that recognizable objects can be formed by combining just two or three geons. Also note that the relations between the geons matter, as illustrated by the cup and the pail. (From Biederman, 1987.)

Figure 5.40
(a) A teapot. (b) The same teapot seen from a viewpoint that obscures most of its geons and therefore makes it difficult to recognize.

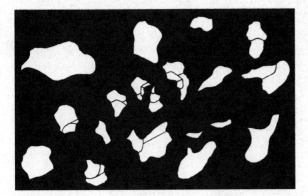

Figure 5.41
What is the object behind the mask? See the legend of Figure 5.42 for the answer. (From Biederman, 1987.)

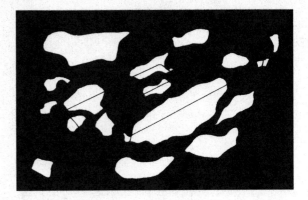

Figure 5.42
The same object as in Figure 5.41 (a flashlight) with the geons obscured. (From Biederman, 1987.)

percentage of the time you can see the three parallel edges. Also notice that occasionally you view the book from an angle so you can't see all three edges. This happens, for example, when you look at the book end-on. However, these situations occur only rarely, and when they do occur it becomes more difficult to recognize the object. For example, when we view the object in Figure 5.40a from the unusual perspective in Figure 5.40b, we can't see its basic geons and, therefore, have difficulty identifying it.

- **Discriminability**. Discriminability means that each of the geons can be distinguished from each of the others from almost all viewpoints.

- **Resistance to visual noise**. A geon is resistant to visual noise if it can be perceived even under "noisy" conditions. For example, look at Figure 5.41. The reason you can identify this object (what is it?), even though over half of its contour is obscured, is because you can still identify its geons.

The ability to identify an object if we can identify its geons is called the **principle of componential recovery**. This principle is what is behind our ability to identify objects in the natural environment even when parts of the objects are hidden by other objects. Figure 5.42 shows a situation in which componential

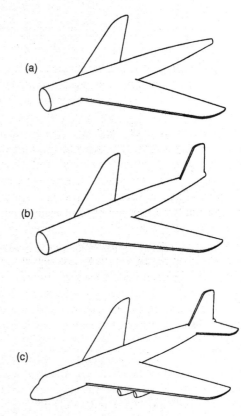

Figure 5.43
An airplane, as represented (a) by three geons, (b) by four geons, and (c) by nine geons. (From Biederman, 1987.)

Perceiving Objects

BRAIN SCAN
Representation of Global Three-Dimensional Structure

Where is the three-dimensional structure of objects represented in the brain? Daniel Schacter and coworkers (1995) investigated this question by measuring the PET response that occurs when subjects made judgments as to whether a drawing represented a possible three-dimensional object (see accompanying figure, left) or an impossible object (accompanying figure, right). The PET measurements showed that there was increased activity in the IT cortex for the possible objects but not for the impossible objects. Schacter and his coworkers therefore concluded that this area of cortex is involved in constructing representations of three-dimensional structure. Although the impossible drawings did not cause activity in the IT cortex, they did cause an increase in activity in the hippocampus, a subcortical structure that has been shown to respond to novel or unexpected stimuli.

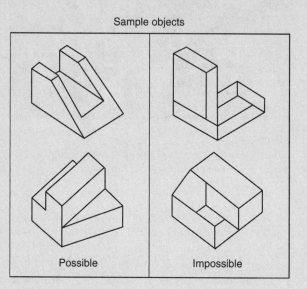

Sample objects

Possible   Impossible

Possible objects (left) and impossible objects (right) used by Schacter and coworkers (1995) in their brain imaging experiments.

recovery can't occur because the visual noise is arranged so the geons cannot be identified. Luckily, parts of objects are rarely obscured in this way in the natural environment, so we can usually identify geons and, therefore, the object.

The basic message of RBC theory is that, if enough information is available to enable us to identify an object's basic geons, we will be able to identify the object (see also Biederman & Cooper, 1991; Biederman et al., 1993). A strength of Biederman's theory is that it shows that we can recognize objects based on a relatively small number of basic shapes. For example, it isn't hard to recognize Figure 5.43a as an airplane, even though it contains only three geons. However, some researchers have criticized RBC theory on the grounds that, while geons may enable us to distinguish between classes of objects (airplanes vs.

toasters, for example), they do not always provide enough information to enable us to distinguish between different objects that have the same basic components.

For example, many birds have tapered beaks, which would be described by the same geon, but there are differences in the rate of the beaks' taper in different birds. Thus, based on geons, we might not be able to distinguish between two finches with slightly different beaks (Perrett & Oram, 1993).

Also, if we consider the physiology of neurons such as the elaborate cells (Figure 4.13), we find that these neurons are tuned to respond to much smaller differences between shapes than exist between Biederman's geons. Thus, the RBC model describes how we recognize broad classes of objects, but it may need to be refined in order to explain how we can dif-

Chapter 5

ferentiate between objects that differ in detail, such as birds, human faces, or automobiles, which are constructed from the same basic components.

Why Are There So Many Approaches to Object Perception?

We have seen that the question of how we perceive objects has been answered in a number of different ways, ranging from the Gestalt principles to approaches such as Marr's, FIT, and RBC that involve elementary features. Also relevant here is our consideration of the neural mechanisms of object perception in Chapter 4. Table 5.1, which summarizes these approaches, shows that there are similarities across some of the approaches (FIT,

computational, RBC, and the neural approach all involve basic units, or features). It also shows that the different approaches describe different facets of object perception, and each therefore contributes something different to our knowledge of object perception.

For example, the FIT and computational approaches describe rapid initial processes that involve features, whereas the Gestalt approach describes the grouping and perceptual segmentation that occurs after this rapid process is over. RBC theory also hypothesizes features but is more concerned with explaining how we recognize three-dimensional objects at different angles than with the rapid processing that combines the features.

We can also compare the approach taken in this chapter, which looks at object perception at the psychophysical level, with the approach in Chapter 4,

Table 5.1

Summary of Approaches to Object Perception

Approach	Main Proponents	Main Concerns	Basic Principles
Gestalt	Max Wertheimer	Perceptual organization Figure–ground segregation	• Laws of organization • Wholes and parts • Figure–ground
Computational	David Marr	Perceiving objects in real-world setting	• Basic features • Taking into account natural constraints in the environment • Primal sketch • 2 1/2-D sketch
Feature integration theory	Anne Treisman	Early feature extraction and processing	• Basic features • Preattentive processing • Focused attention
Recognition by components	Irving Biederman	Recognizing 3D objects	• Geons • Invariant properties • Principle of componential recovery
Neural feature detectors (see Chapters 3 and 4)	David Hubel, Torsten Wiesel, and many others	Physiology of object perception	• Feature detectors • Columnar organization • Distributed coding • Neural specificity • Neural tuning determined by experience • Contextual modulation of V1 neurons

Perceiving Objects

which looks at object perception at the physiological level. We have mentioned a number of physiological mechanisms that may be involved in some of the phenomena we have described in this chapter. For example, when we discussed how features are combined in the focused attention stage of FIT theory, we suggested that perhaps this involves combining information from the dorsal and ventral streams in the extrastriate cortex.

When we discussed the Gestalt principles we didn't mention physiology, but at the beginning of Chapter 4 we described some neurons that might provide a physiological way of looking at the Gestalt principles. For example, we saw that there is a neuron in V1 that responds well to the display in Figure 5.44a, in which the five bars are grouped together because of similarity of orientation and good continuation. However, this neuron responds poorly when this perceptual grouping is absent, as in Figure 5.44b. The approach in this chapter describes some of the properties of stimuli that are associated with perceptual grouping, The approach in Chapter 4 describes what might be happening physiologically. Both approaches together provide a more complete understanding of how we perceive objects than either one alone.

Although Table 5.1 describes a number of approaches, an important part of object perception is

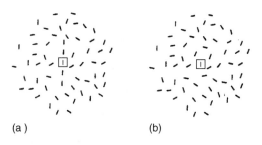

(a)   **(b)**

Figure 5.44

There are neurons in area V1 that respond well when a bar that is located in the neurons' receptive field (the square) (a) is part of a group of lines. These neurons do not respond well, however, (b) when the bar is not part of a group, because it is surrounded by bars with many orientations. See Figure 4.3, page 111, for more details on these neurons. (Adapted from Zapadia et al., 1995.)

missing. That "something" is how a person's knowledge and past experiences affect object perception. As we will see in the next section, these factors can have a large effect on our ability to perceive objects.

THE INTELLIGENCE OF OBJECT PERCEPTION

When we introduced our diagram of the perceptual process in Figure 1.2 we included "knowledge" to indicate that perception involves more than just analyzing the pattern of light and dark on the retina. It also involves a taking into account cognitive factors such as the meanings of objects and our knowledge of characteristics of the environment.

Since we do take the characteristics of the environment into account and also bring additional information in the form of knowledge, memories, and expectations to perceptual situations, it is correct to say that perception is "intelligent." The fact that this intelligence is necessary for perception becomes obvious when we return to the observation we made at the beginning of Chapter 1, that although a computer has defeated the human world chess champion, it has proven difficult to program a computer to perceive even simple scenes. The computer's difficulty stems from a lack of the perceptual intelligence that humans take for granted. Let's consider a few of the things about perception that make perceiving particularly difficult for computers.

Why Computers Have Trouble Perceiving Objects

We can understand why it has been difficult to program computers to perceive, by considering a few of the problems that the computer must deal with in order to accurately perceive a scene.

The Stimulus on the Receptors Is Ambiguous. Objects seen from just one viewpoint result in ambiguous information on the receptors. For example, you might think that the scene in Figure 5.45a is a circle of rocks, but viewing it from another angle

Figure 5.45

An environmental sculpture by Thomas Macaulay. (a) When viewed from exactly the right vantage point (the second-floor balcony of the Blackhawk Mountain School of Art, Black Hawk, Colorado), the stones appear to be arranged in a circle. (b) Viewing the stones from the ground floor reveals a truer picture of their configuration.

reveals its true configuration (Figure 5.45b). This ambiguity occurs because a particular image on the retina can be caused by an infinite number of different objects. This fact, which is called the **inverse projection problem**, is illustrated by Figure 5.46. This figure shows a square stimulus (solid lines) that is cre-

ating a square image on the retina. It also shows, however, that there are a number of other stimuli (dashed lines) that could create exactly the same image on the retina. A larger square that is further away, a trapezoid that is tilted, as well as an infinite number of other objects, can create the same retinal image as the

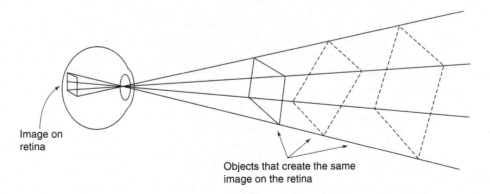

Image on retina

Objects that create the same image on the retina

Figure 5.46

The principle behind the inverse projection problem. The small square stimulus (solid lines) creates a square image on the retina. However, this image could also have been created by the larger, more distant, square, by the tilted trapezoid (dashed lines) and many other stimuli. This is why we say that the image on the retina is ambiguous.

Perceiving Objects

square. Thus, any image on the retina can be created by an infinite number of objects. This creates serious problems for a computer, but humans usually perceive the correct object and not any of the other potential objects that could cast the same image on the retina.

Objects Need to Be Separated. It is often difficult to determine where one object ends and another begins. This is part of the problem of object segregation we discussed earlier. For example, in Figure 5.47, how do we know that the intersection at (a) is the corner of object 1, but the intersection at (b) is created by objects 1 and 2 together? Although computers have been programmed successfully to answer this kind of question for problems involving blocks, it is still difficult for a computer to answer it for more complex natural objects.

Parts of Objects Can Be Hidden. It is difficult to determine the shapes of objects that are partially hidden. Imagine, for example, how difficult it would be to program a computer to be able to identify the hidden object in Figure 5.48, something we can do with little effort.

The Reasons for Changes in Lightness and Darkness Can Be Unclear. In a scene such as the one in Figure 5.49, it is necessary to determine which changes in lightness and darkness are due to properties of

Figure 5.48
A computer would have a difficult time determining what this object is. Humans can easily tell that it is an animal hiding, probably a member of the cat family.

objects in the scene and which are due to changes in the illumination. Changes in lightness and darkness are caused by how much light objects reflect. For example, the tree trunk and roof tiles reflect less light than the white walls. Changes in lightness and darkness are also caused by sunlight and shadows. It is difficult for a computer to determine which changes are due to differences in the objects and which are due to uneven illumination.

These are only a few of the problems facing computer vision. Things become even more complex when we consider the many varied shapes we see in the real world. (For more detailed discussions of the problems involved in computer vision, see Barrow & Tannenbaum, 1986; Beck, Hope, & Resenfeld, 1983;

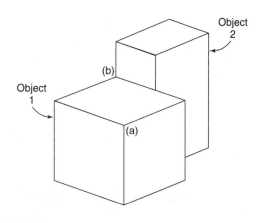

Figure 5.47

Figure 5.49
For this scene, it would be difficult for a computer to sort out which changes are due to properties of the objects in the scene and which are due to changes in illumination. It would be particularly difficult for a computer to determine what is happening in the shaded area just above the tile roof.

Brown, 1984; McArthur, 1982; Poggio, 1984; and Srinivasan & Ventatesh, 1997.)

The reason for this brief foray into computer vision is to make the point that humans are presented with the same information as the computer, in the form of a two-dimensional image of the scene on our retina, yet we are able to solve the problems above and translate this image into a correct perception of the scene much more easily than even the most powerful computer. Although we are some-

times fooled (perhaps Object 1 in Figure 5.47 is not really a rectangular solid), most of the time we are able to deal effortlessly with the complexities of object perception and to arrive at a correct perception of objects and the scenes in which these objects exist.

One thing that helps us perceive objects much more easily than computers is our ability to use what we have learned about the environment through past experience. One example of this learning is provided by the heuristics that the visual system uses to interpret what's happening in the environment. Examples of heuristics that we have already considered are the Gestalt principles of organization and the rule that only one side of a contour can be part of a figure. Let's consider a few more examples of how heuristics shape our perceptions.

Heuristics: "Best Guesses" for Perception

What do you see when you look at Figure 5.50a? Most people see a bunch of meaningless fragments. However, when you look at 5.50b you may see five B's, even though the fragments are identical to the ones in (a). The addition of the inkblot in (b) activates a perceptual heuristic that we will call the **occlusion heuristic**, which states that when a large object is occluded by a smaller one, we see the larger one as continuing behind the occluder. This rule, like the Gestalt principle of good continuation, prevents us from seeing things in our environment as

(a)

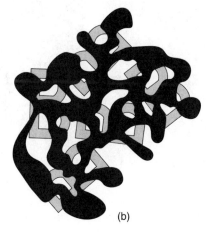

(b)

Figure 5.50
The gray areas are the same in (a) and (b), but they become perceptually organized into five B's when an occluding blob fills in the missing parts of the letters. (From Bregman, 1981.)

Perceiving Objects

being chopped into pieces when they are partially obscured by other objects.

The following demonstration illustrates another perceptual heuristic.

 D E M O N S T R A T I O N

Shape from Shading

Look at Figure 5.51. Notice that the nine discs look like spheres and form a square pattern, and the other discs, like the one just below the dot, look like indentations. After observing this, turn the book over so the dot is on the bottom of the display and notice what happens to your perception of the discs. ●

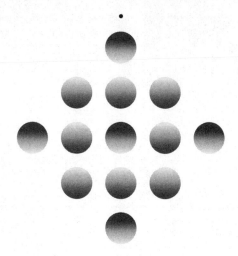

Figure 5.51
Your perception of some of these discs as spheres and some as indentations is governed by the assumption that light is coming from above. See text for viewing instructions.

If the discs forming the square pattern changed from spheres to indentations when you viewed Figure 5.51 upside down, your perception is being influenced by the **light-from-above heuristic,** the assumption that light is coming from above (Kleffner & Ramachandran, 1992). This assumption influences the way you perceive the pattern in Figure 5.51 and also how you perceive the two pictures in Figure 5.52.

You may perceive the picture in Figure 5.52a as a series of rounded ridges in the sand, separated by flat "valleys," and the picture in Figure 5.52b as "steps," with the sun shining on the part you would step on if you were to climb them. [Note that the picture in (b) is sometimes also perceived as ridges in the

(a) (b)

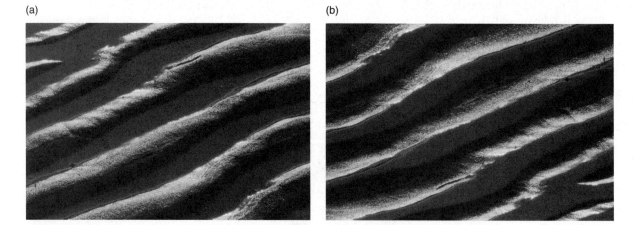

Figure 5.52
These may appear to be two different photographs, but (b) is simply (a) printed upside down. If (a) looks like ridges in the sand and (b) looks like steps, it is because the light-from-above heuristic is influencing your perception.

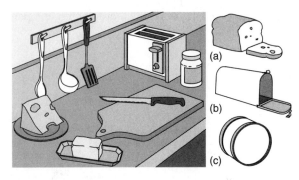

Figure 5.53
Stimuli used in Palmer's (1975) experiment. The scene at the left is presented first, and the observer is then asked to identify one of the objects on the right.

sand separated by valleys, as in (a).] But if you turn the book upside down, your perception of (a) and (b) will switch, in accordance with the assumption that light is coming from above, because (b) is simply (a) printed upside down.

The heuristics we have been describing are closely related to top-down processing, which we described in Chapter 1. We will now consider some examples of how top-down processing can influence object perception.

Top-Down Processing and Object Perception

An experiment that illustrates top-down processing is one by Steven Palmer (1975), which used the stimuli in Figure 5.53. Palmer first presented a context scene such as the one on the left and then briefly flashed one of the target pictures on the right. When Palmer asked subjects to identify the object in the target picture, they correctly identified an object like the loaf of bread (which is appropriate to the kitchen scene) 80 percent of the time, but correctly identified the mailbox or the drum (two objects that don't fit into the scene) only 40 percent of the time. This experiment shows how top-down processing that depends on a person's knowledge of the context provided by a particular scene can influence perception.

Top-down processing is also included in some of the theories of object perception we have described previously. When Treisman (FIT theory) presented the elements of Figure 5.54 and asked subjects to identify the objects in the center, the usual illusory conjunctions occurred, so the orange triangle would, for example, sometimes be perceived as being black. However, when she told subjects that they were being shown a carrot, a lake, and a tire, illusory conjunctions were less likely to occur, so subjects were more likely to perceive the triangular "carrot" as being orange. Thus, the subjects' knowledge of the usual colors of objects influenced their perception.

Top-down processing again comes into play in FIT theory once we have perceived a stimulus and want to name it. As indicated by the FIT flow diagram

Figure 5.54
An orange triangle, a blue ellipse, and a black O used to demonstrate the effect of top-down processing in an illusory conjunction experiment.

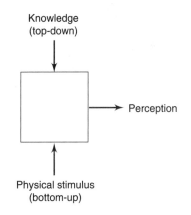

Figure 5.55
Top-down processing, which is based on the knowledge and expectations that an observer brings to a situation, and bottom-up processing, which is based on the physical stimulus on the receptors, combine to create perception.

of Figure 5.31, our ability to name the object involves comparing our perception of it to knowledge stored in memory. Thus, in many situations, bottom-up and top-down processing work together to determine perception (Figure 5.55).

THE PLASTICITY OF PERCEPTION
The Co-Occurrence Effect

In Chapter 4 we saw how experience can shape the firing of neurons so that they become selective for objects that are common and that we recognize often. Although we haven't been directly concerned with neural responding in this chapter, we have mentioned a number of situations in which it is likely that neural mechanisms would be shaped by our experiences in perceiving "regularities" in our environment.

This idea that neural firing can be shaped by frequent experiences is supported by an experiment by Thad Polk and Martha Farah (1998), who measured the fMRI of people while they read letters (A, B, C) and digits (1, 2, 3). They found that viewing the letters caused more activation in IT cortex than viewing the digits.

Why would letters cause a larger response than digits? One possible explanation is that we are constantly seeing letters together, as we read, but we are have less practice in seeing numbers together (unless you happen to be an accountant or a mathematician!). Based on this fact that we often see letters together, Polk and Farah interpreted their result in terms of the **co-occurrence hypothesis**, which states that stimuli that occur together will tend to be represented by activity in the same, or nearby, areas of the cortex. According to this idea, since we often perceive letters and, when we do, they occur together, letters as a group activate a specific area of the cortex.

This difference between the way we process letters and digits has been demonstrated psychophysically by the **alphanumeric category effect**, in which letters pop out when seen with digits, so are identified faster when surrounded with digits than when surrounded by other letters. The idea that it is our experience in seeing letters together that separates them from digits is supported by comparing U.S. and Canadian postal workers' performance on this task. Since the Canadian postal workers have a great deal of experience in dealing with mixed letter-digit zip codes (like VA5 1S6), we would expect the Canadians to show a reduced alphanumeric category effect, and this is, in fact, what happens. Although the experiment has not yet been done, we would also expect that perhaps Canadian postal workers would not show the different patterns of brain responding to letters and digits that Polk and Farah observed in their American subjects.

OBJECT PERCEPTION ACROSS THE SENSES

When we think about perceiving objects, we usually assume that vision is involved. To identify something, we look at it. But when we consider that blind people can identify objects by touch, we realize that there are more ways to identify objects than just by looking at them. When we consider the cutaneous senses in Chapter 13 we will mention how blind people use the raised dots of braille to read and how the biologist Geerat Vermeij can identify different kinds of shells by touch alone, often surpassing his sighted colleagues in his ability to detect subtle features of these shells.

You can experience object identification by touch yourself if you have someone select a few objects for you to identify. Close your eyes and have the person place an object in your hand. Identify it, relying on touch alone, and then open your eyes and look at it. You might be surprised at how easily you can identify familiar objects, although unfamiliar objects may take longer. Based on this experience, how would you compare the experience of perceiving objects through these two different senses? One thing that stands out when perceiving objects by touch is the quality of being in direct contact with the object, rather than sensing the object from a distance, as occurs in vision.

A system that experimented with the possibility of using touch to sense the properties of objects at a distance was developed by Paul Bach-y-Rita (1972; Bach-y-Rita et al., 1969, 1970). This system, which was called a **sensory substitution system**, consisted of an array of 400 small vibrators that created patterns of vibration on a person's back corresponding to the pattern of light and dark in an image picked up by a television camera, with vibration being more intense for light areas and less intense for dark areas. Some highly trained subjects were able to use these vibrations to "see" remarkable details, as indicated by one

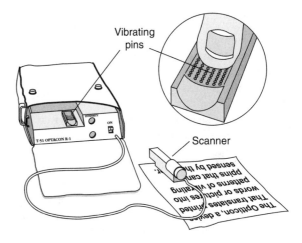

Figure 5.56

The Optacon, a device that translates printed words or pictures into patterns of vibrating pins that can be sensed by the finger. The user moves the scanner over the text and senses the vibrations by placing a finger on the pins.

subject's description: "That is Betty; she is wearing her hair down today and does not have her glasses on. Her mouth is open, and she is moving her right hand from her left side to the back of her head."

A portable sensory substitution system, based on some of the principles studied by Bach-y-Rita, has been developed to enable blind people to read text or perceive graphic displays. This device, called the Optacon, transforms printed letters or graphic images into patterns of vibration that can be sensed through the fingers (Figure 5.56). (With the development of computer technology, the Optacon has now been replaced by computer systems that can translate printed text into voice output.)

Although vision and touch might be the most obvious ways to perceive objects, hearing and the chemical senses can provide information about objects as well. For example, you might see a sculpture that appears to be carved from stone, but feeling it may reveal that it is actually plastic; and, if you aren't sure, listening to the sound it makes as you run your fingers over its surface or as you tap on it will often reveal what it is made of. Another example of how sound can be used for object perception is familiar to anyone who has tried to locate a wooden stud behind a wall by tapping on the wall. Although the stud is not visible, its presence can be detected based on sound.

Smell is also useful for identifying objects, but only those that have the property of volatility, so they release molecules into the air. Think of it this way: If you couldn't see, what would be the best way to detect a rose, by touch or by smell?

Sensing objects visually is clearly of great importance, especially when we need to perceive objects rapidly and at a distance and if we need to know how they are arranged in a scene. But there are other ways to perceive objects as well, some of which may reveal information that adds to what is visible to the eye.

Marr's Approach to Object Perception

David Marr proposed a computational approach to object perception that treats the visual system as if it is programmed to analyze the features of the stimulus. It does this by first determining a collection of features called the raw primal sketch, which takes into account both the pattern of light and dark in the stimulus and natural constraints of the environment. After the raw primal sketch, the visual system determines the $2^1/_2$-D sketch and finally the three-dimensional representation that we see.

Feature Integration Theory (FIT)

Anne Treisman proposed feature integration theory, which states that the first stage of object perception is a preattentive stage, in which the visual system breaks a stimulus into individual features. The next stage is the focused attention stage, in which the features are combined through a process of focusing attention on specific locations.

Determining the Features of FIT

The features of FIT have been determined using the pop-out boundary method and the visual search method. Pop-out boundaries occur if different areas contain different features. In the visual search procedure, reaction times to identify stimuli are determined. When pop-out occurs, indicating the presence of a specific feature, then reaction time does not increase with an increased number of distractors.

Preattentive and Focused Attention Stages

Evidence that the features exist independently in the preattentive stage is indicated by the presence of illusory conjunctions. The necessity of attention for perception is indicated by search experiments that show that the subject can't determine the location of a stimulus if focused attention is not needed to find the stimulus.

The Recognition by Components (RBC) Theory

Irving Biederman proposed the RBC theory, which is based on the idea that objects are perceptually constructed from volumetric primitives called geons. These geons have the properties of view invariance, discriminability, and resistance to visual noise. The principle of computational recovery states that we can identify an object if we can identify its geons.

Brain Scan: Representation of Global Three-Dimensional Structure

Brain imaging studies indicate that three-dimensional objects activate an area in IT cortex. Impossible objects do not activate this area, but do activate the hippocampus, which is involved in processing novel stimuli.

Why So Many Approaches?

The reason there are a number of different approaches to object perception is that the approaches describe different facets of object perception.

Why Do Computers Have Trouble Perceiving Objects?

It has been difficult to program computers to perceive objects because (1) the stimulus on the receptors is ambiguous, as indicated by the inverse projection problem; (2) objects need to be separated; (3) parts of objects can be hidden; and (4) the reasons for changes in lightness and darkness can be unclear. Humans, however, solve these problems with relative ease.

Heuristics and Top-Down Processing

The visual system uses heuristics such as the occlusion heuristic and the light-from-above heuristic to help determine object perception in certain situations. Top-down processing, which involves a subject's knowledge, also contributes to object perception.

Plasticity: The Co-Occurrence Effect

Brain imaging studies indicate that letters activate a specific area of the cortex, but that the effect isn't as strong for numbers. This may be related to the co-occurrence hypothesis and the alphanumeric category effect.

Object Perception Across the Senses

Object perception can be achieved not only by vision, but by touch, hearing, and smell. A system called sensory substitution shows that subjects can perceive objects based on touch.

Perceiving Objects

Study Questions

1. What level of analysis is this chapter concerned with? (145)

2. What does it mean to say that different kinds of information are available within a particular level of analysis? (146)

The Gestalt Approach to Perceptual Organization: How Elements Are Grouped

The Beginnings of Gestalt Psychology

3. What is structuralism? Who was associated with it? (146)

4. How was structuralism applied to perception? (147)

5. How did Max Wertheimer use the phenomenon of apparent motion to question the idea behind structuralism? (147)

6. What is an illusory contour? How does the existence of illusory contours in Figure 5.4 argue against structuralism? (147)

7. What did the Gestalt psychologists say about the relation between "wholes" and "parts?" (148)

8. What is perceptual organization? (148)

The Gestalt Laws of Perceptual Organization

9. What do the laws of perceptual organization specify? (148)

10. Describe each of the following laws: Pragnanz, similarity, good continuation, proximity, common fate, meaningfulness. (148)

11. Give an example of how a change in an object's meaning can cause a change in perceptual organization. (152)

The Gestalt "Laws" Are Really Heuristics

12. What do modern researchers call the Gestalt laws? (153)

13. What is a heuristic? An algorithm? Given an example of using each one of these strategies to find a cat. (154)

14. Why can we call the Gestalt principles heuristics? (154)

15. What are two possible mechanisms that could have established the heuristics for perception? (155)

16. What aspects of the environment are reflected by the Gestalt principles? (155)

More Principles of Perceptual Organization

17. Describe the principles of common region, element connectedness, and synchrony. How does synchrony differ from common fate? (155)

Quantitative Measurement of Grouping Effects

18. Describe the repetition discrimination task. What does it demonstrate about grouping? (155)

Perceptual Segregation: How Objects Are Separated

19. What is figure–ground segregation? (156)

The Gestalt Approach to Figure–Ground Segregation

20. What is reversible figure–ground? (156)

21. What are four properties of figure and ground? (157)

22. What are four factors that help determine which area we see as figure? (157)

Modern Ideas About Figure–Ground Segregation

23. How could considerations about how contours occur and line up in the real world lead the visual system to the conclusion that only one area in a reversible figure–ground display can be seen as figure at a time? (158)

24. Describe Peterson's experiment. What does her result say about when figure–ground segregation and when recognition occurs in the perceptual process? (159)

How Objects Are Constructed

Marr's Computational Approach to Object Perception

25. How does the computational approach conceive of the visual system? Who is the person most closely associated with the computational approach? (160)

26. What are the steps in the computational approach? (160)

27. What is the starting point for object perception, according to Marr? (160)

28. What is the raw primal sketch? (161)

29. How does the visual system determine the raw primal sketch? (161)

30. What are natural constraints, and how are they involved in determining the raw primal sketch? (161)

31. What must occur before conscious perception can occur, according to the computational approach to perception? What is the $2^{1}/_{2}$-D sketch? (162)

32. What kind of approach to object perception does Marr's approach illustrate? (162)

Feature Integration Theory

33. What sequence of stages is proposed by feature integration theory? (163)

34. What two methods have been used to determine the features of FIT? (164)

35. Describe the pop-out boundary and the visual search procedures for determining features. (164)

36. During what stage of processing are the features detected? (166)

37. Describe the experiment that demonstrated the existence of illusory conjunctions. What does the existence of illusory conjunctions mean? (166)

38. How does the idea that features can exist independently of one another at an early stage of processing fit with what we know about visual physiology? (166)

39. During what stage of processing are individual features for vision combined to form perceptions? (167)

40. Focused attention is needed for what kinds of search tasks? (167)

41. How are inattentional blindness, the attentional blink, and change blindness, from Chapter 4, relevant to the focused attention stage of object perception? (167)

42. What is a possible physiological reason that attention is a necessary part of the perceptual process? (167)

The Recognition-by-Components Approach

43. Who is the person most closely associated with this approach to object recognition? (168)

44. What are volumetric primitives? What are the three basic properties of geons? (168)

45. What is the principle of componential recovery? (169)

46. What is a strength of Biederman's theory? How has it been criticized? (170)

Brain Scan: Representation of Global Three-Dimensional Structure

47. Describe Schacter's PET experiment. What is the function of the area in the brain that he located? (170)

48. What is an impossible object? What area of the cortex does the perception of impossible objects activate? (170)

Why Are There So Many Approaches to Object Perception?

49. What do the approaches to object perception we have discussed (including the neural approach from Chapter 4) have in common? (171)

50. Which aspect of object perception does each approach describe? (171)

The Intelligence of Object Perception

51. Why is it correct to say that perception is intelligent? (172)

Why Computers Have Trouble Perceiving Objects

52. Describe the four problems a computer must deal with to perceive a scene. (172)

53. What is the inverse projection problem? (173)

54. What information do humans have that computers don't have that enables humans to get around the problems that cause trouble for computers? (175)

Heuristics: Best Guesses for Perception

55. What is the occlusion heuristic? Describe the example of the operation of this heuristic described in the book. (175)

56. What is the light-from-above heuristic? Describe the example of the operation of this heuristic described in the book. (176)

Top-Down Processing and Object Perception

57. Describe Palmer's kitchen experiment. What does his result indicate about the role of top-down processing in perception? (177)

58. How is top-down processing relevant to the FIT theory of object perception? (177)

The Plasticity of Perception: The Co-Occurrence Effect

59. Describe Polk and Farah's experiment in which they used fMRI as people read letters and digits. (178)

60. What is the co-occurrence hypothesis, and how is it relevant to Polk and Farah's result? (178)

61. What is the alphanumeric category effect? (178)

62. How is the alphanumeric category effect different in U.S. and Canadian postal workers? How come these two groups give different results? What does this say about their possible brain organization? (178)

Across the Senses: Object Perception Across the Senses

63. Give examples of how object perception can be achieved by touch, hearing, and smell. (179)

64. What is sensory substitution? How was it used by Bach-y-Rita? How was it used in the Optacon system? (179)

6

PERCEIVING COLOR

SOME QUESTIONS WE WILL CONSIDER

- Why do blue dots appear after a flashbulb goes off? (195)

- What does someone who is color-blind see? (203)

- What colors does a honeybee perceive? (206)

Color is one of the most obvious and pervasive qualities in our environment. We interact with it every time we note the color of a traffic light, choose clothes that are color coordinated, or appreciate the colors of a painting. We pick favorite colors (blue being the most favored; Terwogt & Hoeksma, 1994). We react emotionally to colors (so, not coincidentally, colors are part of our emotional discourse, as in purple with rage, green with envy, or feeling blue; Terwogt & Hoeksma, 1994; Valdez & Mehribian, 1994), and we imbue colors with special meanings (for example, red meaning danger; purple, royalty; green, ecology). But for all of our involvement with color, we sometimes take it for granted, and, just as with our other perceptual abilities, we may not fully appreciate color until we lose our ability to experience it. The depth of this loss for one person is illustrated by the case of Mr. I, a painter who became color blind at the age of 65 after suffering a concussion in an automobile accident:

> In March of 1986, the neurologist Oliver Sacks[1] received an anguished letter from Mr. I, who, identifying himself as a "rather successful artist," described how ever since he had been involved in an automobile accident, he had lost his ability to experience colors, and he exclaimed with some anguish, that "My dog is gray. Tomato juice is black. Color TV is a hodge-podge . . ."
>
> In the days following his accident, Mr. I had became more and more depressed. His studio, normally awash with the brilliant colors of his abstract paintings, appeared drab to him, and his paintings, meaningless. Food, now gray, became difficult for him to look at while eating; and sunsets, once seen as rays of red, had become streaks of black against the sky.

Mr. I's color blindness was caused by cortical injury experienced after a lifetime of experiencing color, whereas most cases of total color blindness or of color deficiency (partial color blindness) occur at birth because of the genetic absence of one or more types of cone receptors. Most people who are born color-blind are not disturbed by their lack of color perception, since they have never known the perception of color, but some of their reports, such as the darkening of reds, are similar to Mr. I's. People with total color blindness often echo Mr. I's complaint that it is sometimes difficult to distinguish one object from another, as when his brown dog, which he could easily see silhouetted against a light-colored road, became very difficult to perceive when seen against irregular foliage.

Eventually, Mr. I overcame his strong psychological reaction and began creating striking black-and-

[1] Dr. Sacks, well known for his elegant writings describing interesting neurological cases, came to public attention when he was played by Robin Williams in the 1995 film *Awakenings*.

white pictures. But his account of his experiences upon losing his ability to perceive color provides an impressive testament to the central place of color in his life. (See Heywood, Cowey, & Newcombe, 1991; Nordby, 1990; Young, Fishman, & Chen, 1980; and Zeki, 1990, for additional descriptions of cases of complete color blindness.)

FOUR QUESTIONS ABOUT COLOR

What do we want to know about color vision? We begin by posing the following four questions:

- What are some functions of color vision?
- What physical attributes are associated with color?
- How can we describe color experience?
- What is the neural code for color?

What Are Some Functions of Color Vision?

Color adds beauty to our lives, but it is more than that. Color serves important signaling functions, both natural and contrived by humans. The natural world has provided many signals that help us identify and classify things. I know the rock on my desk contains copper by the rich vein of blue that runs through it. I know a banana is ripe when it has turned yellow, and I know to stop when the traffic light turns red.

In addition to its signaling function, color helps facilitate perceptual organization, the process we discussed in Chapter 5 by which the world is organized into separated areas. The ability to tell one object from another and especially to see objects against a varied background, such as flowers in a field or individual people in a crowd, is greatly facilitated by the ability to see in color. In fact, this ability is crucial to the survival of many species. Consider, for example, a monkey foraging for fruit in the forest. A monkey with good color vision easily detects red fruit against a green background (Color Plate 2.1a), but a color-blind monkey would find it more difficult to find the fruit (Color Plate 2.1b).

Some researchers have even proposed that monkey and human color vision evolved for the express purpose of detecting fruit in the forest (Mollon, 1989, 2000; Walls, 1942). This suggestion sounds reasonable when we consider the difficulty color-blind human observers have when confronted with the seemingly simple task of picking berries. Knut Nordby (1990), a totally color-blind visual scientist who sees the world in shades of gray, described his experience as follows: "Picking berries has always been a big problem. I often have to grope around among the leaves with my fingers, feeling for the berries by their shape" (p. 308). If Nordby's experience, which is similar to Mr. I's difficulty in seeing his dog against foliage, is any indication, a color-blind monkey would have difficulty finding berries or fruit and might be less likely to survive than monkeys with color vision.

What Physical Attributes Are Associated with Color?

What is it about objects that gives them their color? One way to answer this question is to consider an object that changes color, such as leaves that change from green to yellow or red in the fall. We know that this change occurs as the chlorophyll that gives the leaves their green color is degraded or replaced by other substances.

To understand why these different compounds cause different colors, we need to remember that we see objects because of the light that has reflected from them and that light in the visible spectrum has wavelengths that are associated with different colors. Wavelengths from about 400 to 450 nm appear violet; 450 to 490 nm, blue; 500 to 575 nm, green; 575 to 590 nm, yellow; 590 to 620, orange; and 620 to 700, red (Color Plate 1.1).

With this knowledge in hand, we can measure how the wavelengths reflected from the leaf change in the fall by determining the leaf's **reflectance curve** —a plot of **reflectance**—the percentage of light reflected versus wavelength. Curve (a) in Figure 6.1 shows the reflectance curve for the green leaf. Notice that the leaf reflects light in the middle part of the spectrum. Curve (b) shows the reflectance curve for

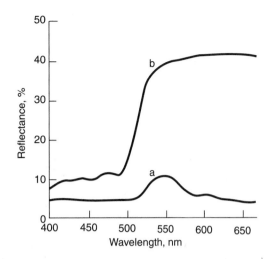

Figure 6.1

Reflectance of a maple leaf before and after it changes color in the fall. Curve (a) is the curve for the dark green leaf before it has changed. Notice that it reflects light best at about 550 nm. Curve (b) is the curve for the leaf after it has changed to yellow. Notice the large increase in reflectance at long wavelengths. The shift to long wavelengths causes us to perceive the leaf as yellow, and the high reflectance causes it to appear bright. (Adapted from Merzlyak et al., 1999.)

the same kind of leaf after it has changed color. New compounds that have formed in the leaf reflect longer wavelengths, and so the leaf now appears yellow.

Figure 6.2 shows reflectance curves for some other objects. Notice that black paper and white paper both reflect all wavelengths equally across the spectrum, but blue pigment, green pigments, and a tomato reflect some wavelengths and not others. When light reflection is flat across the spectrum, such as white, black, or gray, we call these colors **achromatic colors**. When some wavelengths are reflected more than others, as for our leaf and the foods, we call the colors **chromatic colors**.[2] This

---

[2] Another term for chromatic color is **hue**, but this term is rarely used in everyday language. We usually say, "The color of the fire engine is red" rather than "The hue (or chromatic color) of the fire engine is red." Therefore, throughout the rest of this book, we will use the word color to mean "chromatic color" or "hue," and we will use the term achromatic color to refer to white, gray, or black.

Perceiving Color

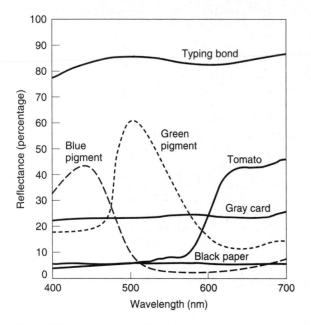

Figure 6.2
Reflectance curves for surfaces that appear white, gray, and black; for blue and green pigments; and for a tomato. (Adapted from Clulow, 1972.)

some of the wavelengths in the spectrum. For example, cranberry juice selectively transmits long-wavelength light and appears red, while limeade selectively transmits medium-wavelength light and appears green.

Table 6.1
Relationship between predominant wavelengths reflected and color perceived

Wavelengths Reflected	Perceived Color
Short	Blue
Medium	Green
Long	Red
Long and medium	Yellow
Long and a little medium	Orange
Long and short	Purple
Long, medium, and short	White

property of reflecting some wavelengths more than others, which is a characteristic of chromatic colors, is called **selective reflection**. Table 6.1 indicates the relationship between the wavelengths reflected and the color perceived.

An excellent example of the difference between achromatic and chromatic color is provided by the colors of some glaciers (Color Plate 3.3). The snow on top of glaciers appears white because it reflects all wavelengths equally. But inside the glacier, where ice has been subjected to extreme pressure, a crystalline structure is formed that does not reflect all wavelengths equally. This ice selectively reflects the short wavelengths, which causes the ice to appear deep blue (Figure 6.3).

So far we have described how colors are created by the way objects selectively reflect some wavelengths. But color is also created by the way some objects selectively *transmit* some wavelengths. Examples are things such as liquids, plastics, and glass, which appear colored if they selectively transmit only

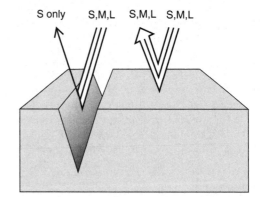

Figure 6.3
How light is reflected from two different areas of a glacier. On the right, short-, medium-, and long-wavelength light from the sun reaches the glacier, and, since all wavelengths are reflected equally, that area appears white. On the left, inside the crevice, the crystal structure of the tightly packed ice absorbs the medium and short wavelengths, leaving only the short wavelengths to be reflected. This area, therefore, appears blue. See Color Plate 3.3.

As we will see later, there are other things that influence color perception, in addition to wavelength. For example, our perception of an object's color can be influenced by the object's background. We will consider this effect later on, but for now we will focus on how the wavelengths reflected from objects influence color experience.

How Can We Describe Color Experience?

We can describe all the colors we can discriminate by using the terms red, yellow, green, blue, and their combinations (Abramov & Gordon, 1994; Hurvich, 1981). When people are presented with many different colors and are asked to describe them, they can describe all of them if they are allowed to use all four terms, but they can't if one of these terms is omitted. Furthermore, other colors, such as orange, violet, purple, and brown, are not needed to achieve these descriptions (Fuld, Wooten, & Whalen, 1981; Quinn, Rosano, & Wooten, 1988). Red, yellow, green, and blue are therefore considered to be basic colors by color researchers (Buckhaus, 1998).

Figure 6.4 and Color Plate 2.3 show the four basic colors arranged in a circle, so that each is perceptually similar to the one next to it. The order of the four basic colors in the color circle—blue, green, yellow, and red—matches the order of the colors in the visible spectrum, in which the short-wavelength end of the spectrum is blue, green is in the middle of the spectrum and yellow and red are at the long-wavelength end of the spectrum.

Although the color circle is based on four colors, there are more than four colors in the circle. In fact, people can discriminate about 200 different colors across the length of the visible spectrum (Color Plate 1.1) (Gouras, 1991a), and we can create even more colors by changing the intensity to make colors brighter or dimmer or by adding white, which is equal amounts of all wavelengths across the spectrum, to change a color's **saturation**. Adding more white decreases a color's saturation. For example, adding white to the deep red at the top of the color circle makes it become pink, which is a less saturated (or **desaturated**) form of red.

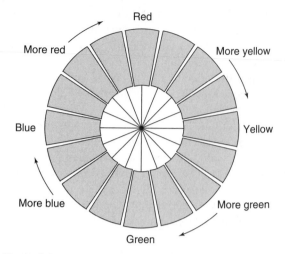

Figure 6.4

The color circle. In this circle, also shown in Color Plate 2.3, we arrange colors by placing perceptually similar colors next to each other. When we do this, we find that the colors can be arranged in a circle with the four basic colors at 12, 3, 6, and 9 o'clock on the circle. (From Hurvich, 1981.)

By changing the wavelength, the intensity, and the saturation, we can create about a million or more different discriminable colors (Backhaus, 1998; Gouras, 1991a). Of course, the differences between some of these colors are extremely small, as you can demonstrate by changing the color palette of your computer from "hundreds of colors" to "thousands of colors" to "millions of colors." When you do this, you will notice that the screen doesn't look that much different for "hundreds of colors" and "millions of colors." Although we may be able to discriminate millions of colors, in everyday experience the gamut of colors we encounter when we look at the paint chips at the paint store numbers less than a thousand, and the *Munsell Book of Colors*, once the color "bible" for designers, contained 1,225 color samples (Wysecki and Stiles, 1965). The Pantone Matching System in current use by graphic artists has about 1,200 color choices.

What Is the Neural Code for Color?

How is the experience of color we have been describing above represented by signals in the nervous

system? This is the question of neural coding. Researchers working on this question have used the connection between color experience and wavelength that we have described above to restate the question "What is the neural code for color?" as "What is the neural code for wavelength?" In other words, to determine the neural code for color, researchers have set out to determine how different wavelengths are represented by signals in the visual system.

Historically, this problem has been approached in two different ways that have led to two different theories of color vision. Both of these theories were proposed in the 1800s based on psychophysical data, long before we knew enough about physiology to be able to determine how neurons respond to different wavelengths. So the beginnings of our understanding of color vision were strictly at the psychophysical level of analysis, and it is remarkable that the two theories that were proposed based on psychophysical observations were basically correct, even through the physiological evidence to support them didn't become available until over 70 years after they were originally proposed.

We will consider each of the theories in turn by first describing the psychophysical evidence on which the theory was based and then describing the physiological evidence that became available later.

TRICHROMATIC THEORY OF COLOR VISION

WebTUTOR   The **trichromatic theory of color vision,** which stated that color vision depends on the activity of three different receptor mechanisms, was proposed by two eminent 19th-century researchers, Thomas Young (1773–1829) and Hermann von Helmholtz (1821–1894; Figure 6.5) based on the results of a psychophysical procedure called color matching.

Color-Matching Experiments

In Helmholtz's **color-matching experiments,** observers were asked to adjust the amounts of three different wavelengths of light mixed together in a "comparison field," until the color of this mixture matched the color of a single wavelength in a "test field." For example, the observer might be asked to mix together 420-nm, 560-nm, and 640-nm lights in a comparison field until the field matched the color of a 500-nm light presented in the test field (Figure 6.6). The key findings of these color-matching experiments were that:

1. By correctly adjusting the proportions of three wavelengths, it was possible to make the comparison and test fields match.

2. A person with normal color vision needed to use at least three wavelengths in order to match all wavelengths in the spectrum. (Any three wavelengths can be used in the comparison field, as long as any one of them can't be matched by mixing the other two.) People with normal color vision could not, however, match all wavelengths in the spectrum with only two wavelengths. For example, if they were given only the 420-nm and 640-nm lights to mix, they would be unable to match certain colors. As we will see later, people who are color deficient, and therefore can't perceive all colors in the spectrum, can match the colors of all wavelengths in the spectrum by mixing only two other wavelengths.

Trichromatic Theory

Based on the finding that people with normal color vision need at least three wavelengths to match any

Figure 6.5
Hermann von Helmholtz (1821–1894), who championed the trichromatic theory of color vision.

COLOR PERCEPTION AND COLOR MECHANISMS

The world of color is a world of yellow Miatas, brightly painted window shutters, orange-red sunsets, and multicolored football jerseys. But what does color do for us in addition to creating aesthetic experiences, moods, and easier identification of opposing teams? For a monkey searching for food in the forest, color vision makes yellow or orange fruit easily visible against the green of the foliage (Plate 2.1a). In black and white this fruit becomes more difficult to detect

(Plate 2.1b), so a monkey without color vision would find food gathering difficult, a result which would have negative consequences for the monkey's survival. (Page 187)

Plate 2.2 shows the change in color perception that occurs as illumination changes from dawn to daylight. The view in (a) shows the scene as it would be perceived under the dim illumination of early dawn. The scene lacks color because the rods are responsible for vision under dim

Plate 2.1a

Plate 2.1b

Plate 2.2a

Plate 2.2b

Plate 2.3

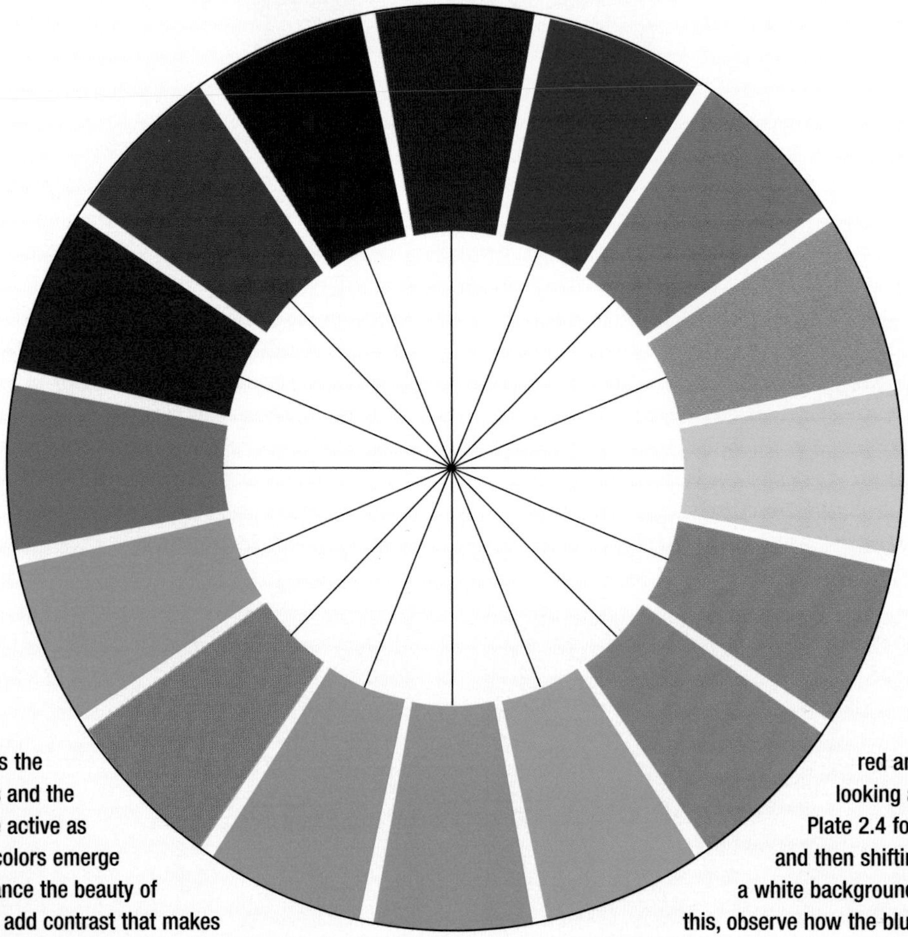

illumination. As the scene lightens and the cones become active as shown in (b), colors emerge that both enhance the beauty of the scene and add contrast that makes it easier to make out the scene's components. One of the many functions of color is to enhance the contrast between objects. (Page 189)

The experience we call color is closely linked to the spectral characteristics of light, as illustrated by the visible spectrum in Color Essay 1 (Plate 1.1). Another way to organize the perceptual experience of color is by using the color circle, which places colors in the same order as they appear in the spectrum, but arranges them in a circle (Plate 2.3). This arrangement helps show that all colors consist of various proportions of red, yellow, green and blue—the colors that appear at 12, 3, 6, and 9 o'clock on the circle. (Page 189)

We can study some of the mechanisms of color vision by noting how our perception of color changes under different viewing conditions. For example, the cones synapse with other neurons in the retina to form opponent cells that fire in opposite ways to blue and yellow or red and green. You can experience the opponent responses of blue and yellow and

red and green by looking at the center of Plate 2.4 for 30 seconds and then shifting your gaze to a white background. When you do this, observe how the blue and yellow and red and green panels reverse positions in the resulting afterimage (see "Opposing Afterimages" Demonstration, page 195)

Another way to demonstrate the opponent nature of the visual system is to place a small square of white paper within one of the squares in Plate 2.4, and follow the viewing instructions in the Demonstration "Afterimages and Simultaneous Contrast" on page 195. You will observe an effect called simultaneous contrast, in which a surrounding field induces a color into the smaller, surrounded area. The simultaneous contrast effect is also illustrated in Plate 2.5, which is a composition by Josef Albers, an artist who often used simultaneous contrast in his paintings (Courtesy of Yale University Press). Although one X looks yellow and the other looks gray, they are actually physically the same, as you can see by looking at the place where they are connected.

Color is by no means universally experienced. Many animals experience no colors and others perceive fewer than

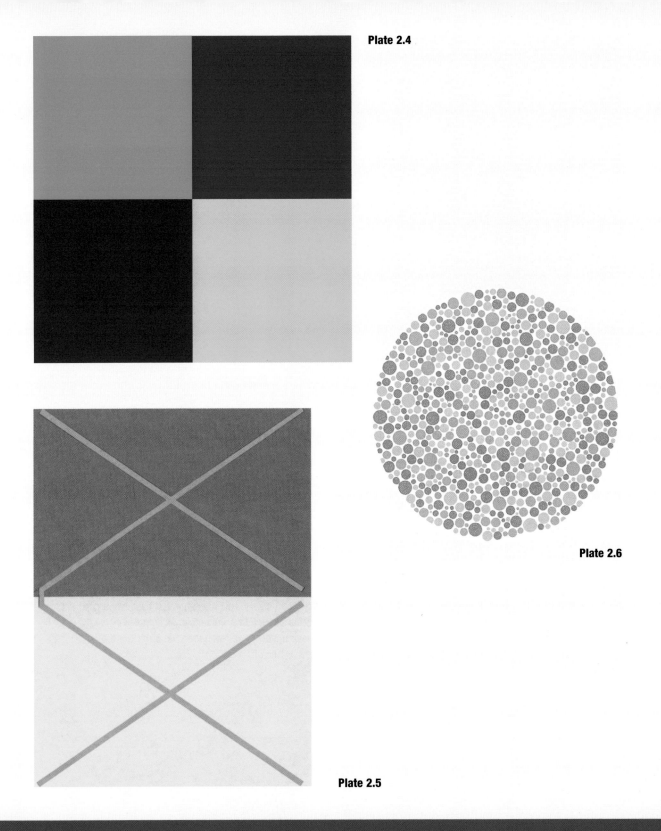

Plate 2.4

Plate 2.5

Plate 2.6

Plate 2.7

Plate 2.8

humans. Cats, dogs, and squirrels have color vision that is similar to the vision of color deficient humans (see page 200). Among humans, about 4 percent of males and a much smaller percentage of females are color deficient and there-fore perceive a reduced palate of colors. One way to diagnose color deficiency is through a display such as the one in Plate 2.6, which is called an Ishihara plate. People with normal color vision see a 74, which is not seen by people with a form of red-green color deficiency. You can induce a mild (and temporary) form of color deficiency in yourself, by doing the following demonstration: Illuminate Plate 2.7 with bright sun-light or a desk lamp and view it with one eye open and the other closed for about one minute. Then blink back and forth and you will notice that reds viewed with the eye that was opened appear more washed out than reds viewed with the

eye that was closed. The reason for this is that viewing the red field selectively bleached cone pigments sensitive to long wavelengths, making them less sensitive. People with red-green color deficiency are missing either their medium- or long-wave cone pigment. (Page xx)

Adapting the eye to one color, as you did when you looked at the red field, is called chromatic adaptation. For an explanation of how chromatic adaptation can partially explain color constancy, see the "Adapting to Red" demonstration on page 207. Research has also shown that color constancy words best if an object is surrounded by objects with many different colors. This research, that has investigated how color perception is influenced by complex visual displays, has used multicolored "Mondrian" displays like the one in Plate 2.8 as stimuli. (Page 209).

CREATING COLOR BY SUBTRACTION OR ADDITION

In his room at Cambridge University, Isaac Newton placed a prism so that sunlight shining through a hole in the shutter of his window entered a prism. He observed that the prism split the sunlight into a spectrum of colors like the one in Color Plate 1.1. When Newton then recombined these spectral colors with a lens, he recreated the white sunlight with which he had started. This result contains an important message regarding our perception of chromatic colors: We see white when we are stimulated by equal intensities of all wavelengths in the spectrum and we see chromatic colors when we are stimulated by only a portion of the spectrum.

CHROMATIC COLOR CREATED BY SUBTRACTION FROM WHITE

One way to interpret Newton's result is that the perception of chromatic color occurs when some wavelengths are subtracted from white light. There are a number of ways that this subtraction can occur. One way, which we can observe in our natural environment, is by the scattering of light by the atmosphere.

This is illustrated by the way light from the sun is scattered by particles in the air to create perceptions of the blue sky and yellow sun during the day, and of the red sun at sunset.

Sunlight entering the atmosphere encounters many small particles, which scatter the light. When these particles are small in relation to the wavelength of the light, a condition known as **Rayleigh scattering** occurs, in which short wavelengths are scattered more than long wavelengths. As shown on the left side of Plate 3.1, this causes short wavelengths to be separated from the light entering the atmosphere, and it is these short wavelengths that cause us to see the sky as blue. The scattered light also causes objects in the distance to appear blue, since we must look through scattered short-wavelength light to see the object (Plate 3.2).

With short wavelengths scattered in the sky, the remaining light, which passes directly through the atmosphere, is rich in long wavelengths, so the sun appears yellow. This effect is exaggerated at sunset (Plate 3.1, right), when the light from the setting sun travels a greater distance through the atmosphere than it does at noon, thereby increasing the amount of short and medium wavelengths scattered and leaving only the longest wavelengths, which we perceive as the red setting sun.

Another way chromatic color is created by subtraction is illustrated by objects that appear colored because the substances they are made of subtract some wavelengths by a

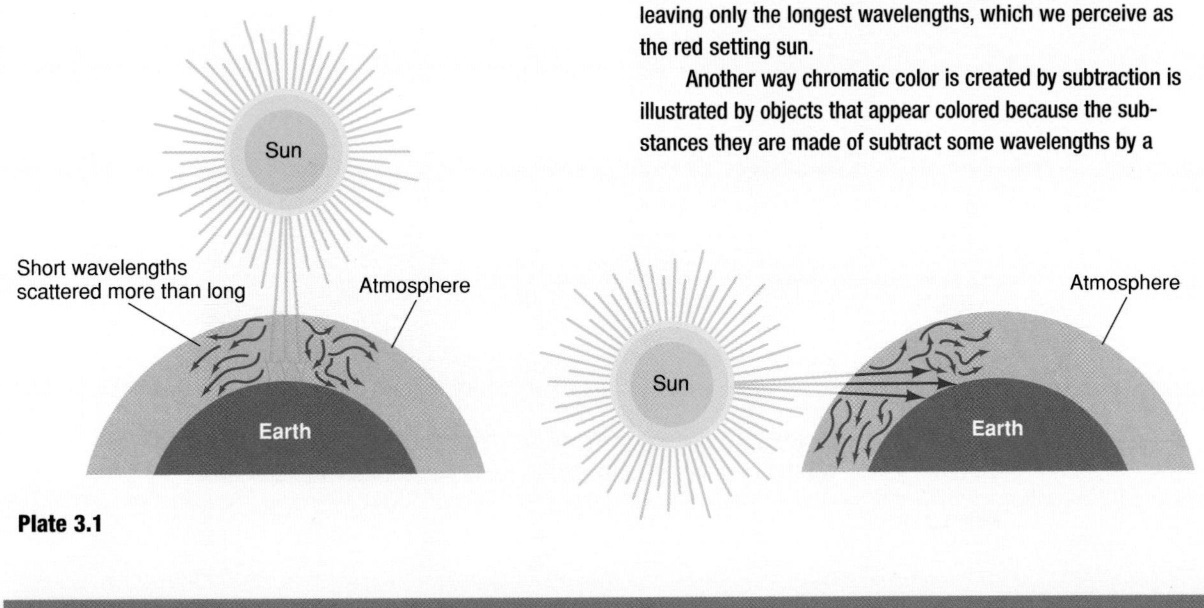

Short wavelengths
scattered more than long

Atmosphere

Sun

Earth

Atmosphere

Sun

Earth

Plate 3.1

process called absorption, and reflect others by selective reflection (described on page 188). Thus, a ripe tomato appears red because the tomato absorbs short and medium wavelengths and reflects long wavelengths (Figure 6.2, page 188).

Plate 3.3 illustrates a situation in which complete reflection and selective reflection exist side-by-side. The white ice

Plate 3.2

Plate 3.3

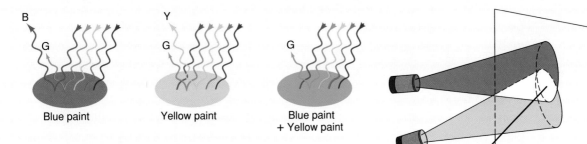

Blue paint

Yellow paint

Blue paint
+ Yellow paint

Plate 3.4

B + Y = W

Plate 3.5

and snow in this close-up of an Alaskan glacier appears white because it reflects all wavelengths equally. Further inside the glacier, however, the ice has been subjected to intense pressure that has changed its properties. This highly compacted ice absorbs medium and long wavelengths and selectively reflects short wavelengths, thereby causing it to appear blue (see Figure 6.3, page 188).

The process of absorption also explains the colors we see when we mix paints—a process called **subtractive color mixture.** For example, many people have had the experience of mixing blue and yellow paints to create green (see page 192). We can understand how subtraction causes blue and yellow together to make green by first considering the wavelengths that are subtracted from white by the blue paint and the yellow paint separately (Plate 3.4 and Table 1).

Blue paint absorbs wavelengths associated with yellow, orange, red, and some of the green, and reflects blue and a little green. Yellow paint absorbs blue, orange, red, and some of the green, and reflects yellow and a little green. When we mix the two paints together, both paints still absorb the same colors they absorbed when alone. From Table 1 we can see that the mixture of blue and yellow will therefore absorb all of the blue, yellow, orange, and red. What we perceive is the color that is reflected by both paints in common. From Table

1 we can see that green is the only color reflected by both paints. Therefore, blue plus yellow paints appears green.

The reason that our blue and yellow mixture resulted in green was that both paints reflected a little green. If our blue paint had reflected only blue and our yellow paint had reflected only yellow, these paints would reflect no color in common, so mixing them would result in little or no reflection across the spectrum, and the mixture would appear black. It is rare, however, for paints to reflect light in only one region of the spectrum. Most paints reflect a broad band of wavelengths. If paints didn't reflect a range of wavelengths, then many of the color mixing effects that painters take for granted would not occur.

CHROMATIC COLOR CREATED BY ADDITION OF OTHER CHROMATIC COLORS

Chromatic colors can also be created by adding together two or more other chromatic colors. This process occurs when we superimpose two or more colored lights (Plate 3.5). Mixing

Table 1
Parts of the spectrum that are absorbed and reflected by blue and yellow paint. The colors that are totally absorbed are indicated by shaded squares for each paint. Light that is usually seen as green is the only light that is reflected in common by both paints.

Wavelengths associated with . . .					
	Blue	**Green**	**Yellow**	**Orange**	**Red**
BLUE PAINT	Reflects all	Reflects some Absorbs some	Absorbs all	Absorbs all	Absorbs all
YELLOW PAINT	Absorbs all	Reflects some Absorbs some	Reflects all	Absorbs all	Absorbs all

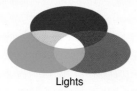
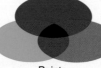

Lights   Paints

Plate 3.6

Plate 3.7

lights is called **additive color mixture,** because all of the wavelengths contained in each light still reach the eye when the lights are superimposed. Consider what happens when we look at blue and yellow lights that have been superimposed on a white projection screen. The short wavelengths of the blue light are reflected from the screen into our eyes, and the medium and long wavelengths of the yellow light are also reflected from the screen into our eyes. The result is that short, medium, and long wavelengths reach our eyes and we perceive white.

We can appreciate the difference between creating chromatic colors by addition (mixing lights) and by subtraction (mixing paints) by noting that every time we superimpose a light onto another light, we add to the amount of light reflected from the screen into the observer's eye. However, every time we add an additional glob of paint into a mixture of paints, we subtract from the amount of light reflected. The opposite nature of additive and subtractive color mixture is perhaps best illustrated by comparing the color that results from mixing blue, green, and red *lights* to the color that results from mixing blue, green, and red paints. Mixing the lights results in white, while mixing the paints results in brown or black (Plate 3.6).

Finally, there is another way that chromatic colors can be created by addition. This is a process called **optical color mixing,** in which colors add in the eye when small spots with different colors are viewed from a distance. You can experience this effect by propping up your book and slowly walking back from Plate 3.7. As you increase your distance, you are eventually unable to resolve the green and rod dots, which add in your eye just as if they were lights projected on top of one another to create a perception of yellow. This technique, which in painting is called

pointillism, was used by French painters such as George Seurat and Paul Signac to create optical color mixing effects and to create shimmering effects often associated with natural light. An example of pointillism is illustrated by Signac's painting in Plate 3.8, in which the foreground is made up of tiny blue and orange dots. Move back from this picture and notice how the appearance of the foreground changes as it becomes more difficult to see the individual dots.

Plate 3.8

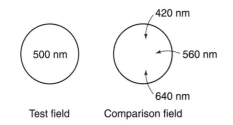

500 nm

420 nm

560 nm

640 nm

Test field · Comparison field

Figure 6.6

The basic idea behind a color-matching experiment is that the observer adjusts the amount of three wavelengths in the comparison field on the right so the field matches the color of the single wavelength in the test field on the left.

wavelength in the test field, Thomas Young (1802) proposed the trichromatic theory of color vision. This theory, which was later championed by Helmholtz (1852) and is therefore also called the **Young-Helmholtz theory of color vision**, proposes that color vision depends on three receptor mechanisms, each with different spectral sensitivities. (Remember from Chapter 2 that spectral sensitivity indicates the sensitivity to wavelengths across the visible spectrum, as shown in curves like the ones in Figure 2.24.)

According to this theory, light of a particular wavelength stimulates the three receptor mechanisms to different degrees, and the pattern of activity in the three mechanisms results in the perception of a color. Each wavelength is therefore coded in the nervous system by its own pattern of activity in the three receptor mechanisms.

Physiology of Trichromatic Theory

Over 70 years after the trichromatic theory was first proposed, physiological research identified the three receptor mechanisms proposed by the theory.

Cone Pigments Physiological researchers who were working to identify the receptor mechanisms proposed by trichromatic theory asked the following question: Are there three mechanisms, and, if so, what are their physiological properties? This question was answered in the 1960s, when researchers were

able to measure the absorption spectra of three different cone visual pigments, with maximum absorption in the short- (419-nm), middle- (531-nm), and long-wavelength (558-nm) regions of the spectrum (S, M, and L in Figure 6.7) (Brown & Wald, 1964; Dartnall et al., 1983; Schnapf, Kraft, & Baylor, 1987).

Another important advance in our understanding of the physiology of color vision came in the 1980s, when Nathans, Thomas, and Hogness (1986) isolated and sequenced the genes encoding the protein parts of the three different cone pigments (called opsins, see Figure 2.17). This enabled Nathans and coworkers to show that different types of pigments have different sequences of the small molecular groups called amino acids that make up the opsin molecule (see Mollon, 1989; 1993).

These differences in the opsin's amino acids are what cause different pigments to have different absorption spectra. Thus, the short- and middle-wavelength cones, which have only 44 percent of their amino acid sequences in common, have peak absorptions that are separated by 112 nm. In contrast, the middle- and long-wavelength cones, which have about 96 percent identical amino acid sequences, have peak absorptions that are separated by only 27 nm.

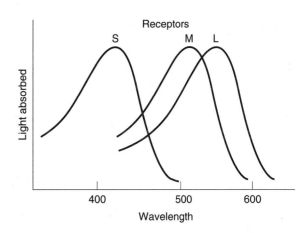

Figure 6.7

Absorption spectra of the three cone pigments. (From Dartnall et al., 1983.)

Perceiving Color

Cone Responding and Color Perception If color perception is based on the pattern of activity of these three receptor mechanisms, we should be able to determine which colors will be perceived if we know the response of each of the receptor mechanisms. Figure 6.8 shows the relationship between the responses of the three kinds of receptors and our perception of color. In this figure, the responses in the S, M, and L receptors are indicated by the size of the receptors. For example, blue is signaled by a large response in the S receptor, a smaller response in the M receptor, and an even smaller response in the L receptor. Yellow is signaled by a very small response in the S receptor and large, approximately equal responses in the M and L receptors.

Thinking of wavelengths as causing certain patterns of receptor responding helps us to predict which colors should result when we combine lights of different colors. For example, what color should result if we project a spot of blue light onto a spot of yellow light? The patterns of receptor activity in Figure 6.8 show that blue light causes high activity in the S receptors and that yellow light causes high activity in the M and L receptors. Thus, combining both lights should stimulate all three receptors equally, and we should perceive white, since white light contains an equal distribution of wavelengths across the spectrum. This is exactly the result we achieve if we mix

blue and yellow lights. (This result surprises some people, because mixing blue and yellow *paints* results in green. The reason we achieve different results from lights and paints is explained in Color Essay 3.)

Now that we know that our perception of colors is determined by the pattern of activity in different kinds of receptors, we can explain the physiological basis behind the color-matching experiments that led to the proposal of trichromatic theory. Remember that in a color-matching experiment, a wavelength in one field is matched by adjusting the proportions of three different wavelengths in another field (Figure 6.6). This result is interesting because the two fields are physically different (they contain different wavelengths) but they are perceptually identical (they match). This situation, in which two physically different stimuli are perceptually identical, is called **metamerism**, and the two identical fields in a color matching experiment are called **metamers**.

The reason metamers look alike is that they both result in the same pattern of response in the three cone receptors. For example, when the proportions of a 620-nm red light and a 530-nm green light are

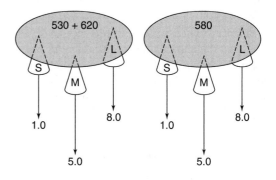

Figure 6.9
The proportions of 530- and 620-nm lights in the field on the left have been adjusted so that the mixed lights appear to be identical to the 580-nm light in the field on the right. The numbers, which indicate the responses of the short-, medium-, and long-wavelength receptors, show that there is no difference in the responses of the two sets of receptors. The identical neural responding causes the two fields to be perceptually indistinguishable.

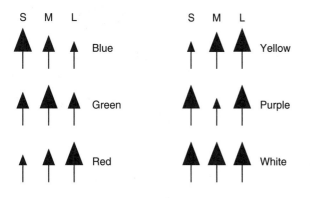

Figure 6.8
Patterns of firing of the three types of cones to different colors. The size of the cone symbolizes the size of the receptor's response.

adjusted so the mixture matches the color of a 580-nm light, which looks yellow, the two mixed wavelengths create the same pattern of activity in the cone receptors as the single 580-nm light (Figure 6.9). The 530-nm green light causes a large response in the M receptor, and the 620-nm red light causes a large response in the L receptor. Together, they result in a large response in the M and L receptors and a much smaller response in the S receptor. This is the pattern for yellow and is the same as the pattern generated by the 580-nm light. Thus, as far as the visual system is concerned, these lights are identical.

Are Three Receptor Mechanisms Necessary for Color Vision?

According to trichromatic theory, a light's wavelength is signaled by the pattern of activity of three receptor mechanisms. But do we need three different mechanisms to see colors? The answer to this question is that color vision is possible with two receptor types but not with one. Let's first consider why color vision cannot occur with just one receptor type.

The key to understanding why just one receptor type won't work is that the absorption of a quantum (or photon) of light by a pigment molecule always isomerizes one pigment molecule no matter what the wavelength of the light. The fact that absorption of a photon causes the same effect no matter what the wavelength is called the **principle of univariance**.

Figure 6.10a indicates what the principle of univariance means if a person has only one visual pigment, which we will call pigment 1. Presenting 1,000 photons of a 550-nm light to this person's eye will isomerize 100 molecules of pigment 1, since the pigment absorbs 10 percent of the light at 550 nm. Presenting 1,000 photons of 590-nm light isomerizes 50 pigment molecules, since the pigment absorbs 5 percent of the light at 590 nm. The response to the 590-nm light will, therefore, be smaller than the response to the 550-nm light.

You might think that this difference between the response to 550 and 590 nm would signal two different wavelengths and therefore two different colors. However, this difference in response does not enable us to tell the difference between the two wavelengths, because we can adjust the intensity of the 590-nm light so it causes exactly the same response as the 550-nm light. As you can see from Figure 6.10b, doubling the intensity of the 590-nm light to 2,000 photons causes this wavelength to isomerize 100 pigment molecules, just like the 550-nm light. Thus, if there is just one visual pigment, we can make any two wavelengths cause the same response by adjusting the intensity of one of them.

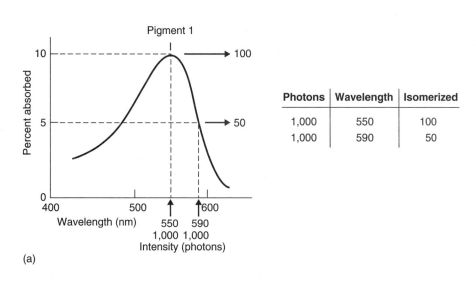

Figure 6.10

(a) Absorption spectrum for pigment 1, showing how to determine the number of molecules isomerized by 1,000 photons of 550- and 590-nm light. The number on the left axis is the percentage of light absorbed. The numbers indicated by the arrows on the right are this percentage applied to the intensity of each wavelength. The result, shown in the table, is the number of pigment molecules isomerized by each wavelength.

Perceiving Color

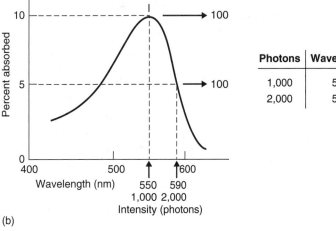

Photons	Wavelength	Isomerized
1,000	550	100
2,000	590	100

Figure 6.10 *(continued)*
(b) Same as (a), but the intensity of the 590-nm light has been increased to 2,000 photons. The result is that both wavelengths isomerize 100 pigment molecules.

(b)

Since we can make any two wavelengths look identical by adjusting their intensities, one pigment does not provide the information needed to tell one wavelength from another and can't serve as the basis for color vision. This is why we see in shades of gray when the single rod pigment controls our vision under dim illuminations (see page 36).

Adding a second pigment solves the problem created by the principle of univariance, because although we can still adjust the intensity of two wavelengths to cause the same response in one of the pigments, it is not possible to adjust them to cause the same responses in both pigments simultaneously. An example is shown in Figure 6.11. We saw from Figure 6.10b that 1,000 photons of 550-nm light and 2,000 photons of 590-nm light both isomerize 100 molecules of pigment 1. But from Figure 6.11 we can see the 1,000-photon 550-nm light isomerizes 50 molecules of pigment 2 and the 2,000-photon 590-nm light isomerizes 20 molecules of pigment 2.

We could present other intensities of these wavelengths, but we would always find that, when there are two pigments, the responses to different wavelengths are always different. Since this gives the visual system

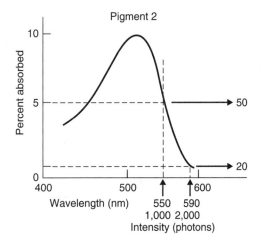

Photons	Wavelength	Isomerized
1,000	550	50
2,000	590	20

Figure 6.11
Same as 6.10b but for pigment 2. The table shows that the same intensities and wavelengths that had identical effects for pigment 1 have different effects for pigment 2.

a way to tell the difference between different wavelengths, no matter what the intensities, color vision becomes possible. As we will see when we consider color deficiency later in this chapter, there are people with just two types of cone pigment. These people, who are called dichromats, see colors, just as our calculations predict, but they see fewer colors than people with three visual pigments, who are called trichromats. The addition of a third pigment, although not necessary for creating color vision, increases the number of colors that can be seen across the visual spectrum.

OPPONENT-PROCESS THEORY OF COLOR VISION

webTUTOR   Although trichromatic theory explains a number of color vision phenomena, including color matching and color mixing, there are some color perceptions that it cannot explain. These color perceptions were demonstrated by Ewald Hering (1834–1918; Figure 6.12), another eminent physiologist who was working at about the same time as Helmholtz. Hering used the results of phenomenological observations, in which stimuli were presented and observers described what they perceived, to propose the **opponent-process theory of color vision**, which stated that color vision was caused by opposing responses generated by blue and yellow and by red and green.

Figure 6.12
Ewald Hering (1834–1918), who proposed the opponent-process theory of color vision.

The Phenomenological Observations

You can make some phenomenological observations similar to those made by Hering by doing the following demonstrations.

 D E M O N S T R A T I O N

"Opposing" Afterimages

Cover the blue and yellow squares in Color Plate 2.4 with a piece of white paper and illuminate the red and green squares with your desk lamp. Pick a spot on the border between the two squares and look at it for about 30 seconds. If you then look at a piece of white paper and blink, the image you see, which is called an *afterimage*, is colored. Notice the position of the red and green areas in the afterimage. Then repeat this procedure for the blue and yellow squares.   ●

Hering's observation that viewing a red field generates a green afterimage, that viewing a green field generates a red afterimage, and that analogous results occur for blue and yellow, led him to propose that red and green are paired and blue and yellow are paired.

D E M O N S T R A T I O N

Afterimages and Simultaneous Contrast

Cut out a ½-inch square of white paper and place it in the center of the green square in Color Plate 2.4. Cover the other squares with white paper and stare at the center of the white square for about 30 seconds. Then look at a white background and blink to observe the afterimage. What color is the outside area of the afterimage? What color is the small square in the center? Repeat your observations on the red, blue, and yellow squares in Color Plate 2.4.   ●

195   *Perceiving Color*

When you made your observations using the green square, you probably confirmed your previous observation that green and red are paired, since the afterimage corresponding to the green area of the original square is red. But the color of the small square in the center also shows that green and red are paired: Most people see a green square inside the red afterimage. This green afterimage is due to **simultaneous color contrast**, an effect that occurs when surrounding an area with a color changes the appearance of the surrounded area. In this case, the red afterimage surrounds a white area and causes the white area to become green. (See Color Plate 2.5 for another demonstration of simultaneous contrast.) Table 6.2 indicates this result and the results that occur if we repeat this demonstration on the other squares. All of these results show a clear pairing of red and green and of blue and yellow.

This pairing of colors can also be demonstrated by trying to visualize certain colors. Start by visualizing the color red. Attach this color to a specific object such as a fire engine, if that makes your visualizing easier. Now visualize a reddish-yellow and then a reddish-green. Which of these two combinations is easiest to visualize? Now do the same thing for blue. Visualize a pure blue, then a bluish-green and a

Table 6.2

Results of afterimage and simultaneous contrast demonstration

Original Square	Color of Outside Afterimage	Color of Inside Afterimage
Green	Red	Green
Red	Green	Red
Blue	Yellow	Blue
Yellow	Blue	Yellow

bluish-yellow. Again, which of the combinations is easiest to visualize?

Most people find it easy to visualize a bluish-green or a reddish-yellow but find it difficult (or impossible) to visualize a reddish-green or a bluish-yellow. The idea that it is difficult to see blue and yellow or red and green together has also been demonstrated using more quantitative methods. When subjects are asked to state the percentage of blue, green, yellow, and red they perceive at a number of wavelengths across the spectrum, they rarely report seeing blue and yellow or red and green at the same time (Figure 6.13; Abramov and Gordon, 1994; Gordon and Abramov, 1988). You can see that there

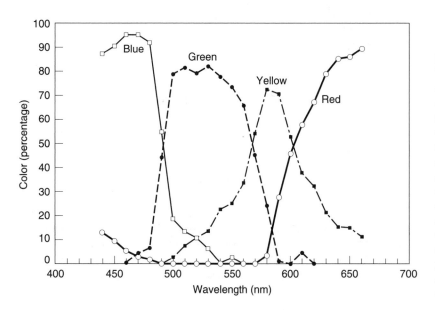

Figure 6.13

The results of a color-scaling experiment. After viewing each stimulus light, the subject rates her or his color sensation by assigning percentages to blue, green, yellow, or red so that they add up to 100 percent. These data, which are averages from a number of subjects, indicate very little overlap between blue and yellow and between red and green. Even this small amount of overlap decreases when we consider the results of individual subjects. (Adapted from Gordon & Abramov, 1988; see also Abramov & Gordon, 1994.)

is very little overlap between the blue and yellow curves and the red and green curves—just as our visualization experiments would predict.[3]

The above observations, plus Hering's observation that people who are color-blind to red are also color-blind to green, and that people who can't see blue also can't see yellow, led to the conclusion that red and green are paired and that blue and yellow are paired. Based on this conclusion, Hering proposed the opponent-process theory of color vision (Hering, 1878, 1905, 1964).

Opponent-Process Theory

The basic idea underlying Hering's theory is shown in Figure 6.14. He proposed three mechanisms, each of which responds in opposite ways to different intensities or wavelengths of light. The Black (−) White (+) mechanism responds positively to white light and negatively to the absence of light. Red (+) Green (−) responds positively to red and negatively to green, and Blue (−) Yellow (+) responds negatively to blue and positively to yellow. Hering thought that these positive and negative responses were caused by the buildup and breakdown of chemicals in the retina, with white, yellow, and red causing a reaction that results in a buildup of the chemicals and black, green, and blue causing a reaction that results in a

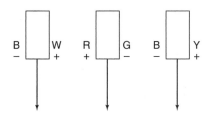

Figure 6.14
The three opponent mechanisms proposed by Hering.

[3] The small overlap between these curves that does exist occurs because the curves represent the judgments of many observers. When we consider the perceptions of individual observers, there is no overlap between red and green and between blue and yellow.

breakdown of the chemicals. Although this part of Hering's theory was not correct, modern physiological research showed that these colors do cause physiologically opposite responses.

The Physiology of Opponent-Process Theory

Although Hering's phenomenological observations supported his theory, opponent-process theory has only recently been taken as seriously as trichromatic theory. One reason for the slow acceptance of opponent-process theory was that people couldn't imagine a physiological process that resulted in opposite responses to different wavelengths. However, with the advent of physiological techniques that made it possible to measure the response of neurons in the retina and lateral geniculate nucleus (LGN), researchers were able to confirm Hering's idea of opposing responses to blue and yellow and to red and green.

Opponent Neurons Evidence for opposing electrical signals began appearing in the 1950s and 60s when researchers began finding **opponent neurons** in the retina and lateral geniculate nucleus that responded with an excitatory response to light from one end of the spectrum and with an inhibitory response to light from the other end (DeValois, 1960; Svaetichin, 1956). For example, Figure 6.15 shows records from four neurons in the lateral geniculate nucleus that respond to light at one end of the spectrum with an increase in nerve firing and to light at the other end of the spectrum with an inhibition of spontaneous activity. For each cell, spontaneous activity is indicated in the top record, and the responses to 450-nm (blue), 510-nm (green), 580-nm (yellow), and 660-nm (red) lights are shown in the other records.

The B+Y− cell responds to the 450-nm light with an increase in firing and to the 580-nm light with an inhibition of spontaneous activity. The G+R− cell increases its firing to the 510-nm light and decreases its firing to the 660-nm light. The Y+B− and R+G− cells also show opponent responses, but they are inhibited by short wavelengths and are excited by long wavelengths (see also DeValois et al., 1966).

Perceiving Color

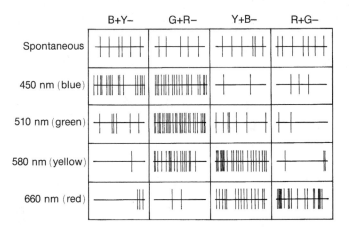

	B+Y−	G+R−	Y+B−	R+G−
Spontaneous				
450 nm (blue)				
510 nm (green)				
580 nm (yellow)				
660 nm (red)				

Figure 6.15

Responses of opponent cells in the monkey's lateral geniculate nucleus. These cells respond in opposite ways to blue and yellow (B+Y− or Y+B−) and to red and green (G+R− or R+G−). (From DeValois & Jacobs, 1968.)

How Opponent Responding Can Be Created by Three Receptors The discovery of opponent neurons provided physiological evidence for opponent-process theory to go with the three different cone pigments of trichromatic theory. When these two theories were first proposed in the 1800s, they were seen as competitors. The idea at that time was that one or the other was correct, but not both. But the discovery of physiological evidence that supported both theories meant that both theories were correct. How could this be? The answer is that the psychophysical findings on which each theory was based were each reflecting physiological activity at different places in the visual system. This is diagrammed in Figure 6.16. The color-matching results, that three wavelengths are needed to match all other wavelengths, come from the cone receptors that are right at the beginning of the visual system, and the perceptual pairing of blue and yellow and red and green that we see in effects like afterimages and simultaneous contrast are created by the opponent neurons that come later in the visual system.

The circuit in Figure 6.17 shows how this works. The L-cone sends excitatory input to a bipolar cell, and the M-cone sends inhibitory input to the cell. This creates an R+G− cell that responds with excitation to the long wavelengths that cause the L-cone to fire and with inhibition to the shorter wavelengths that cause the M-cone to fire. The B+Y− cell also receives inputs from the cones. It receives an excita-

tory input from the S cone and an inhibitory input from cell A, which sums the inputs from the M and L cones. This arrangement makes sense if we remember that we perceive yellow when both the M and the

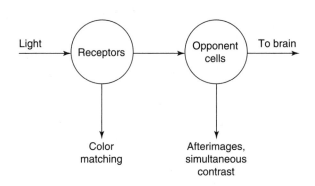

Figure 6.16

Our experience of color vision is shaped by physiological mechanisms both in the receptors and in the opponent neurons. The existence of three different kinds of cone receptors is responsible for the fact that we need a minimum of three wavelengths to match any wavelength in the spectrum. The opponent cells are responsible for perceptual experiences such as afterimages and simultaneous contrast. Note, however, that, although the activity in the receptors and other neurons early in the visual system may shape our perception of color, color perception doesn't actually occur until sometime after the signals from these early neurons reach the brain.

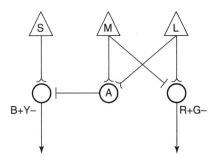

Figure 6.17

Neural circuit showing how the blue-yellow and red-green mechanisms can be created by excitatory and inhibitory inputs from the three types of cone receptors.

L receptors are stimulated. Thus, cell A, which receives inputs from both of these receptors, causes the "yellow" response of the B+Y− mechanism.

Although this diagram is greatly simplified, it illustrates the basic principles of the neural circuitry for color coding in the retina. (See DeValois & DeValois, 1993, for examples of more complex neural circuits that have been proposed to explain opponent responding.) The important thing about this circuit is that its response is determined both by the wavelengths to which the receptors respond best and by the arrangement of inhibitory and excitatory synapses. Processing in this circuit therefore takes place in two stages: First, the receptors respond with different patterns to different wavelengths (trichromatic theory), and then later neurons integrate the inhibitory and excitatory signals from the receptors (opponent-process theory).

What Does the Opponent Response Accomplish?
Our neural circuit shows that wavelengths can be signaled in two ways: (1) by trichromatic signals from the receptors and (2) by opponent signals in later neurons. But why are two different ways of signaling wavelength necessary? Specifically, since the firing pattern of the three types of cone receptors contains enough information to signal which wavelength has been presented, why is this information changed into opponent responses? The answer to this question is that opponent responding provides a way of specify-

ing wavelengths that may be clearer and more efficient than the ratio of the cone receptor responses.

To understand how this works, let's consider how the two receptors in Figure 6.18a respond to two wavelengths, labeled 1 and 2. Figure 6.18b shows that when wavelength 1 is presented, receptor M responds more than receptor L; and, when wavelength 2 is presented, receptor L responds more than receptor M. Although we can tell the difference

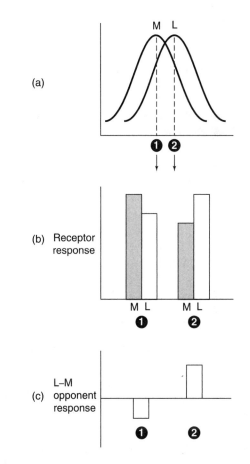

Figure 6.18

(a) Response curves for the M and L receptors. (b) Bar graph indicating the size of the responses generated in the receptors by wavelengths 1 (left pair of bars) and 2 (right pair). (c) Bar graph showing the opponent response of the R+G− cell to wavelengths 1 and 2. The response to 1 is inhibitory, and the response to 2 is excitatory.

Perceiving Color

between the responses to these two wavelengths, the two pairs of bars in Figure 6.18b look fairly similar. But taking the difference between the response of the L cone and the response of the M cone creates an opponent signal that enables us to tell the difference between wavelengths 1 and 2 much more easily (Figure 6.18c). Thus, the information contained in the firing of opponent cells transmits information about wavelength more efficiently than the information contained in the receptor response (Buchsbaum & Gottschalk, 1983), and so the code for color that started with three cones is sent to the brain by opponent neurons.

The physiologist's confirmation of Young, Helmholtz, and Hering's theories of color vision was a triumph for the tactic of using psychophysical observations to predict physiology. With the correspondence between perception and physiology established, researchers began searching for color-opponent cells in the cortex. As it turns out, however, the story for the cortex isn't quite as straightforward as it was for the retina and LGN.

WHAT WE STILL DON'T KNOW ABOUT THE CODE FOR COLOR

How is color represented in the cortex? One answer that was proposed in the 1980s was that there is a specific area in the cortex that is a specialized "color center" that processes information about color (Livingstone & Hubel, 1983; Zeki, 1983 a and b).

One piece of evidence that supports the idea of a color center is the phenomenon of cortical color blindness, like that experienced by Mr. I, the color-blind painter we described at the beginning of this chapter. Mr. I's color blindness was due to an injury to his brain that he suffered in a car accident, and, although this accident deprived him of his color vision, he still had excellent visual acuity and could still see form and movement. This absence of color perception, while other visual functions remained relatively normal, supports the idea that an area specialized for color perception has been damaged.

However, when researchers record from neurons in the cortex, a different picture emerges. Cortical neurons that respond to just some wavelengths in the spectrum, or that have opponent responses, have been found in many areas of the cortex, including the striate cortex (V1) and areas V2 and V4 in the ventral processing stream (see Figure 4.8). But these neurons that respond to color also usually respond to specific forms and orientations (Lennie et al., 1990; Leventhal et al., 1995; Shein & Desimone, 1990). Also, most of the wavelength-selective neurons in area V4, which has been mentioned by many researchers as a center for color processing, also respond to white, making it unlikely that these neurons determine our perception of color (Gordon & Abramov, 2001). Clearly, more research needs to be done to solve the puzzle of how color is coded in the cortex. But for now, it is safe to say that color perception apparently involves a number of different cortical areas, a conclusion that has been supported by recent human fMRI studies (see Brain Scan). See Summary Table 6.1 for an overview of the material we have covered so far.

COLOR DEFICIENCY

WebTUTOR   It has long been known that some people have difficulty perceiving certain colors. A famous early report of **color deficiency**, an inability to perceive some of the colors that people with normal color vision can perceive, was provided by the well-known 18th-century chemist John Dalton (1798/1948), who described his own color perceptions as follows: "All crimsons appear to me to consist chiefly of dark blue: but many of them seem to have a tinge of dark brown. I have seen specimens of crimson, claret, and mud, which were very nearly alike" (p. 102).

Dalton's descriptions of his abnormal color perceptions led to the early use of the term *Daltonism* to describe color deficiency. We now know that there are a number of different types of color deficiency. This has been determined by color vision tests like the ones shown in Color Plate 2.6, which are called **Ishihara plates**. Subjects who are color deficient per-

Brain imaging studies of color vision have typically measured brain activity while a person passively views colored stimuli. These studies have located activity in an area in the ventral processing stream that may correspond to area V4 in the monkey, as well as some other areas, such as V1 and V2, that are earlier in the visual processing stream (Engel, Zhang, & Wandell, 1997; McKeefy and Zeki, 1997; Zeki et al., 1991).

Michael Beauchamp and coworkers (1999) repeated some of the earlier experiments but then went a step farther: In addition to the passive viewing task, they added a task in which subjects were asked to sort a set of colored chips into a sequence so that similar colors were next to each other. Beauchamp and his coworkers found that more than three times

as much of the cortex was activated during this color-sequencing task than when the colors were just viewed passively. Apparently, cognitive activities, such as attention, that are involved in sorting the colors cause this greater cortical activation.

What this result means, according to Beauchamp, is that color processing may be distributed over a wide area in the ventral processing stream rather than in a single color center. This conclusion is supported by the results of experiments that have shown that lesioning just area V4 in monkeys leads to only small impairments in color perception, but that larger lesions cause more severe disturbances of color perception (deWeerd et al., 1996; Heywood et al., 1992, 1995).

SUMMARY TABLE 6.1

Functions of Color

Color serves an important signaling function and helps facilitate perceptual organization. Color perception may have evolved to aid in the detection of food in the forest.

Physical Attributes of Color

Color is closely linked to wavelength. The reflectance curves of achromatic colors are flat—they indicate equal reflection across the spectrum. The reflectance curves for chromatic colors demonstrate selective reflection—some wavelengths are reflected more than others.

Color Experience and the Neural Code

All of the colors we can discriminate can be described by the terms red, yellow, green, blue, and their combinations. Varying the intensity and saturation can create a million or more discriminable colors. The search for the neural code for these colors has focused on determining the code for wavelength.

Trichromatic Theory

The trichromatic theory, which is associated with Young and Helmholtz, states that color vision depends on the activity of three receptor mechanisms. This theory was proposed based on the results of psychophysical color-matching experiments, which showed that by mixing three wavelengths in different proportions we can match any other wavelength in the spectrum.

Physiology of Trichromatic Vision

Trichromatic vision is based on three cone pigments that absorb best in different regions of the spectrum. The code for a particular color is the pattern of firing of the three receptors that contain these three pigments. Two stimuli that are physically different can look the same. These stimuli, which are called metamers, can create the same pattern of firing in the three receptors. Color vision is possible based on two pigments but not on just one. Addition of the third pigment creates more colors than two.

(continued)

Perceiving Color

Summary Table 6.1 (*continued*)

Opponent-Process Theory

The opponent-process theory, which is associated with Hering, states that color vision is caused by opposing responses generated by blue and yellow and by red and green. This theory was based on phenomenological observations involving afterimages, simultaneous contrast, color visualization, and observations of the effect of color blindness.

The Physiology of Opponent-Process Theory

Physiological evidence for opponent-process theory is provided by the existence of opponent neurons. These neurons are created from excitatory and inhibitory inputs from the three types of cone receptors. The conversion from trichromatic to opponent responding creates more efficient information about wavelength than the information contained in the receptor response. It is still unclear how color is represented in the cortex. There is evidence that color perception involves a number of different areas.

ceive either different numbers than does a person with trichromatic vision or no numbers at all, as explained in Color Essay 2. Another way to determine the presence of color deficiency is by using the color-matching procedure to determine the minimum number of wavelengths needed to match any other wavelength in the spectrum. This procedure has revealed the following three types of color deficiency:

1. A **monochromat** can match any wavelength in the spectrum by adjusting the intensity of any other wavelength. Thus, a monochromat needs only one wavelength to match any color in the spectrum (see Figure 6.10).

2. A **dichromat** needs only two wavelengths to match all other wavelengths in the spectrum.

3. An **anomalous trichromat** needs three wavelengths to match any wavelength, just as a normal trichromat does. However, the anomalous trichromat mixes these wavelengths in different proportions from a trichromat, and an anomalous trichromat is not as good at discriminating between wavelengths that are close together.

Once we have determined whether a person's vision is color deficient, we are still left with the question: What colors does a person with color deficiency see? When I pose this question in my class, a few students always suggest that we can answer this question by pointing to objects of various colors and asking a color-deficient person what he sees. (Most color-deficient people are male; see p. 203.) This method does not, however, really tell us what the person perceives, because a color-deficient person may say "red" when we point to a strawberry simply because he has learned that people call strawberries "red." It is, however, quite likely that the color-deficient person's experience of "red" is quite different than the color-normal observer's experience of red. For all we know, he may be having an experience similar to what a person with normal color vision would call "yellow."

To determine what a dichromat perceives, we need to locate a **unilateral dichromat**—a person with trichromatic vision in one eye and dichromatic vision in the other eye. Since both of the unilateral dichromat's eyes are connected to the same brain, this person can look at a color with his dichromatic eye and then determine which color it corresponds to in his trichromatic eye. Although unilateral dichromats are extremely rare, the few who have been tested have helped us determine the nature of a dichromat's color experience (Alpern, Kitahara, & Krantz, 1983; Graham et al., 1961; Sloan & Wollach, 1948). Let's now look at the nature of the color experience of both monochromats and dichromats.

Monochromatism

Monochromatism is a rare form of color blindness that is usually hereditary and occurs in only about 10 people out of 1 million (LeGrand, 1957). Monochromats usually have no functioning cones; therefore, their vision has the characteristics of rod vision in both dim and bright lights. Monochromats see everything in shades of lightness (white, gray, and black) and can therefore be called **color-blind** (as opposed to dichromats, who see some chromatic colors and therefore should be called color deficient). (See Color Plate 2.1b.)

In addition to a loss of color vision, people with hereditary monochromatism have poor visual acuity and are so sensitive to bright lights that they often must protect their eyes with dark glasses during the day. The reason for this sensitivity is that the rod system is not designed to function in bright light and so becomes overloaded in strong illumination, creating a perception of glare.

Dichromatism

Dichromats experience some colors, though a lesser range than trichromats. There are three major forms of dichromatism: protanopia, deuteranopia, and tritanopia. The two most common kinds, protanopia and deuteranopia, are inherited through a gene located on the X chromosome (Nathans et al., 1986). Since males (XY) have only one X chromosome, a defect in the visual pigment gene on this chromosome causes color deficiency. Females (XX), on the other hand, with their two X chromosomes, are less likely to become color deficient, since only one normal gene is required for normal color vision. These forms of color vision are therefore called sex-linked because women can carry the gene for color deficiency without being color-deficient themselves, and they can pass the condition to their male offspring. Thus, many more men than women are dichromats.

- **Protanopia** affects 1 percent of males and 0.02 percent of females and results in the perception of colors across the spectrum indicated in Figure 6.19. A protanope perceives short-wavelength light as blue, and as wavelength is increased, the blue becomes less and less saturated until, at 492 nm, the protanope perceives gray. The wavelength at which the protanope perceives gray is called the **neutral point**. At wavelengths above the neutral point, the protanope perceives yellow, which becomes increasingly saturated as wavelength is

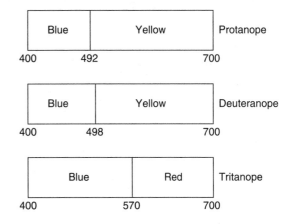

Figure 6.19
The color perceptions of the three kinds of dichromats. The number under the dividing line indicates the wavelength of the neutral point, the wavelength at which gray is perceived.

increased, until at the long-wavelength end of the spectrum the protanope perceives a saturated yellow.

- **Deuteranopia** affects about 1 percent of males and 0.01 percent of females and results in the perception of colors across the spectrum as shown in Figure 6.19. A deuteranope perceives blue at short wavelengths, sees yellow at long wavelengths, and has a neutral point at about 498 nm (Boynton, 1979).

- **Tritanopia** is very rare, affecting only about 0.002 percent of males and 0.001 percent of females. As indicated in Figure 6.19, a tritanope sees blue at short wavelengths, sees red at long wavelengths, and has a neutral point at 570 nm (Alpern et al. 1983).

Physiological Mechanisms of Receptor-Based Color Deficiency

What are the physiological mechanisms of color deficiency? Most monochromats have no color vision because they have just one type of cone or no cones (Review Figure 6.10 to be sure you understand why color vision does not occur if there is just one pigment.) Dichromats are missing one visual pigment, with the protanope missing the long-wavelength pigment and the deuteranope missing the medium-wavelength pigment (Rushton, 1964). Because of the tritanope's rarity and because of the low number of short-wavelength cones, even in normal retinas, it has been difficult to determine which pigment tritanopes are missing, but they are probably missing the short-wavelength pigment.

More recent research has identified differences in the genes that determine visual pigment structure in trichromats and dichromats (Nathans et al., 1986). Based on this gene research, it has also been suggested that anomalous trichromats probably match colors differently from normal trichromats and have more difficulty discriminating between some wavelengths because their M and L pigment spectra have been shifted so they are closer together (Neitz, Neitz, & Jacobs, 1991).

Cortical Color Blindness

So far we have been describing color deficiency caused by receptor problems. But color deficiency can also be caused by problems in the cortex, usually caused by injury or stroke. This condition, in which cone function is normal but color vision is lost due to brain injury, is called **cerebral achromatopsia**. People with this condition typically see a world without color, like Mr. I, who perceived the world as drab and colorless after his automobile accident.

We have already noted that cortical color blindness supports the idea of a color area in the cortex, because the injury often eliminates color vision while leaving other visual functions relatively unaffected (McKeefry and Zeki, 1997; Zeki, 1983 a & b). But perhaps the most interesting thing about cerebral achromatopsia is that it highlights an important principle: Processing information about wavelength is not the same as color perception.

We can differentiate between processing wavelength information and color perception because of patients like M.S., who suffered from achromatopsia due to an illness that left his cone pigments intact but damaged his cortex (Stoerig, 1998). Although he could see no color, he was able to use wavelength information that was being sent to the brain by the cones. For example, he could detect the border between two adjacent fields with different wavelengths even though they both appeared the same shade of gray. This result and others show that wavelength information is being processed by the undamaged area of the brain but that information is not being transformed into the experience of color due to damage to another area. Seeing in color, therefore, involves both determining the wavelengths of a stimulus and further processing of this information to create the experience of color.

CREATING COLOR EXPERIENCE

We know that our experience of color, like all of our sensory experiences, is created by the nervous system. Information about the wavelengths that are reflected from objects is coded in neural impulses, which are then transformed into the experience of color somewhere in the cortex.

But there is something special about the creation of color experience, because unlike some visual qualities like shape, depth, location, and movement, the connection between the central characteristic of the physical stimulus (the wavelength of light) and the experience of color is arbitrary. To understand what this means, let's consider Figure 6.20a, which shows an observer saying that he sees a blue square that is about 4 feet away. We can check the observer's perception of "squareness" by measuring the sides of the object with a ruler; and, when we do this, we confirm that this object is, in fact, a square. We can also check the observer's perception of distance by measuring the actual distance with a tape measure. In this case, we find that the object is actually 3.5 feet away, so the observer's estimate does not exactly match the object's distance.

Although we can check the correctness of the experiences of shape and distance with a physical measuring device like a ruler or tape measure, what about our observer's pronouncement that the object is "blue"? We can measure the object's reflectance curve and find that it reflects a band of short-wavelength light (Figure 6.20b). But is there any reason that we should think that these particular

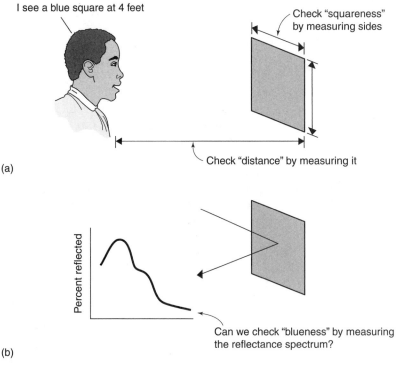

I see a blue square at 4 feet

Check "squareness" by measuring sides

Check "distance" by measuring it

(a)

Percent reflected

Can we check "blueness" by measuring the reflectance spectrum?

(b)

Figure 6.20
(a) We can check perceptions such as shapes and distance with measuring instruments, but (b) we can't check color perception by measuring reflectance. See text for details.

wavelengths should result in "blue," other than the fact that we have learned that short wavelengths are usually associated with "blue"? Isaac Newton didn't think so, as indicated by this statement in his book *Optiks* (1704):

> The Rays to speak properly are not coloured. In them there is nothing else than a certain Power and Disposition to stir up a Sensation of this or that Colour . . . So Colours in the Object are nothing but a Disposition to reflect this or that sort of Rays more copiously than the rest . . .

Newton's idea is that the colors that we see in response to different wavelengths are not contained in the rays of light themselves. Instead, *colors are created by our perceptual system*, and, although specific colors are related to specific wavelengths, the connection between wavelength and the experience we call "color" is an arbitrary one. There is nothing intrinsically "blue" about short wavelengths or "red"

about long wavelengths. In fact, the light rays are simply energy that has no color at all. Looking at it this way, color is not a property of wavelength but is the brain's way of letting us know what wavelengths are present.

We can find similar examples in the other senses. We will see in Chapter 10 that our experience of hearing is caused by pressure changes in the air. But why do we perceive rapid pressure changes as high pitches and slow pressure changes as low pitches? Is there anything intrinsically "high-pitched" about rapid pressure changes? Or consider the sense of smell. We perceive some substances as "sweet" and others as "rancid," but where is the "sweetness" or "rancidity" in the molecular structure of the substances that enter the nose? Again, the answer is that these perceptions are not in the molecular structures. They are created by the action of the molecular structures on our nervous system.

We can better understand the idea that some perceptual qualities—like color, or pitch, or smell—are

Perceiving Color

literally created by our nervous system, by considering animals that can perceive energy that humans can't perceive at all. For example, honeybees are sensitive to light in the ultraviolet region of the spectrum (very short wavelengths) that humans can't see, because one of the honeybee's receptors absorbs maximally at 335 nm (Menzel & Backhaus, 1989; Menzel et al., 1986) (Figure 6.21). What "color" do you think bees perceive at these short wavelengths? You are free to guess, but you really have no way of knowing, since, as Newton stated, "The Rays . . . are not coloured." There is no color in the wavelengths, so the bee's nervous system creates its experience of color. For all we know, the honeybee's experience of color is quite different from ours, even for wavelengths in the middle of the spectrum that both humans and honeybees perceive.

The idea that the experience of color is a creation of the nervous system adds another dimension to the idea that our experience is shaped by physiology. Experience is not only shaped by physiology, but, in cases such as color vision, and hearing, taste, and smell, the very nature of our experience is *created* by physiology.

COLOR CONSTANCY

Our entire discussion so far in this chapter has been based on the idea that our perception of color is linked to the wavelength of light stimulating our receptors. But what about situations in which we first see an object outside, in sunlight, and then see it inside, illuminated by a lightbulb?

We can see why this creates a problem, by looking at the two curves in Figure 6.22, which show the wavelengths that are contained in sunlight and the wavelengths that are contained in light from a lightbulb. The sunlight contains approximately equal amounts of energy at all wavelengths, which is a characteristic of white light. The bulb contains much more energy at long wavelengths. This wavelength distribution is sometimes called "tungsten" light, because it is produced by the tungsten filament inside the lightbulb.

You may notice, when looking at a tungsten bulb, that it looks slightly yellow. That is because of the greater amount of long-wavelength light compared to short-wavelength light that is produced by the bulb. But even though there is a big difference between the wavelength distributions of the lightbulb and sunlight, you may not have noticed much change in how you perceive the colors of objects under these two different light sources. Even though

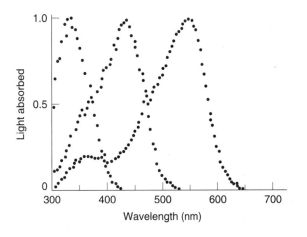

Figure 6.21
Absorption curves of the honeybee's three cone pigments. From these curves we can infer that the honeybee's vision extends into the ultraviolet (very-short-wavelength) region of the spectrum. (Adapted from Menzel et al., 1986.)

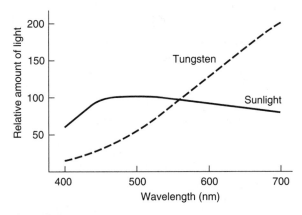

Figure 6.22
The wavelength distribution of sunlight and of light from a tungsten lightbulb. (Based on Judd, MacAdam, & Wyszecki, 1964.)

sunlight has equal amounts of all wavelengths and indoor (tungsten) light is rich in long wavelengths, your white shirt does not turn yellow when you walk from outdoors to indoors (Figure 6.23). This relative stability of color perception under changing illumination is called **color constancy**. Although small shifts of color perception sometimes do occur when the illumination changes (Helson et al., 1956; Hurvich, 1981), our overwhelming experience is that colors remain at least approximately constant under most natural conditions.[4] You can experience the

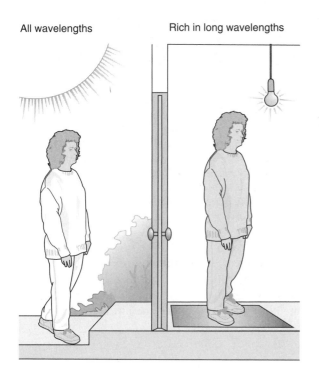

All wavelengths   Rich in long wavelengths

Figure 6.23
If color perception were based only on the wavelengths reaching your retina, then clothes that appeared white in the sunlight (left) would change to a yellowish-red color when illuminated by a lightbulb indoors (right).

[4] In some unnatural conditions, like viewing colors under the sodium vapor lamps that sometimes illuminate highways or parking lots, the true colors of objects can become totally obscured. This occurs because the sodium illumination contains only a narrow band of wavelengths.

effects of color constancy by doing the following demonstration.

DEMONSTRATION

Color Perception Under Changing Illumination

View Color Plates 2.3 and 2.4 so that they are illuminated by natural light by taking them outdoors or illuminating them with light from a window. Then illuminate them with the tungsten lightbulb of your desk lamp. Notice whether the colors change and, if so, how much they change. ●

In this demonstration you may have noticed some change in color as you changed the illumination, but the change was probably much less than we would predict based on the change in the wavelength distribution of the light. Even though the wavelengths reflected from a blue object illuminated by long-wavelength-rich tungsten light can match the wavelengths reflected by a yellow object illuminated by sunlight (Jameson, 1985), our perception of color remains relatively constant with changing illumination. As color-vision researcher Dorthea Jameson puts it, "A blue bird would not be mistaken for a goldfinch if it were brought indoors" (1985, p. 84).

Why does color constancy occur? There are a number of possible reasons.

Chromatic Adaptation

One answer to why color constancy occurs lies in the results of the following demonstration.

DEMONSTRATION

Adapting to Red

Illuminate the red field of Color Plate 2.7 with a bright light from your desk lamp; then, with your left eye near the page and your right eye closed, look at the field with your left eye

Perceiving Color

for about 30 to 45 seconds. At the end of this time, look at various colored objects in your environment, first with your left eye and then with your right. ●

This demonstration shows that color perception can be changed by **chromatic adaptation**—prolonged exposure to chromatic color. Adaptation to the red light selectively bleaches your long-wavelength cone pigment, which decreases your sensitivity to red light and causes you to see the reds and oranges viewed with your left (adapted) eye as less saturated and bright than those viewed with the right eye.

We can understand how chromatic adaptation contributes to color constancy by realizing that, when you walk into a room illuminated with tungsten light, the eye adapts to the long-wavelength-rich tungsten light, which decreases your eye's sensitivity to long wavelengths. This decreased sensitivity causes the long-wavelength light reflected from objects to have less effect than before adaptation, and this compensates for the greater amount of long-wavelength "tungsten" light that is reflected from everything in the room. The result is just a small change in your perception of color.

This idea that chromatic adaptation is responsible for color constancy has been tested in an experiment by Keiji Uchikawa and coworkers (1989), who had subjects view isolated patches of colored paper, as shown in Figure 6.24, under three different conditions: Condition 1, paper and observer illuminated by white light; Condition 2, paper illuminated by red light, observer by white (the illumination of the

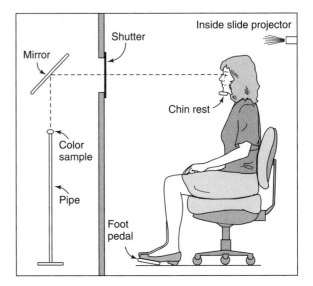

Figure 6.24

The experimental arrangement for Uchikawa et al.'s (1989) experiment. The subject viewed a patch of colored paper (color sample) located on the other side of a partition. The lighting of the color sample was changed by light from a slide projector in the left room (projector not shown). The lighting of the subject's environment was changed by light projected from a slide projector in the right room (inside slide projector).

object is changed but the observer is not chromatically adapted); and Condition 3, both paper and observer illuminated by red light (the illumination of the object is changed, and the observer is chromatically adapted).

Condition	Paper Illumination	Observer Illumination	Perception of Normally Green Paper
1: Baseline	White	White	Green
2: No chromatic adaptation	Red	White	Shifted toward red
3: Chromatic adaptation	Red	Red	Shifted just slightly toward red

Table 6.3

Results of Uchikawa et al.'s (1989) experiment.

The results from these three conditions are shown in Table 6.3. For Condition 1, the baseline condition, a green patch is perceived as green. In Condition 2, where the illumination on the object is changed but the observer experiences no chromatic adaptation, the observer perceives the patches of color as being shifted toward the red. Thus, color constancy did not occur in this condition. But in Condition 3, in which the observer did experience chromatic adaptation, perception was shifted only slightly to the red. Thus, the chromatic adaptation has created **partial color constancy**—the perception of the object is shifted but not as much as when there was no chromatic adaptation. What's happening here is that the eye is adjusting its sensitivity to different wavelengths, in order to keep color perception approximately constant under different illuminations.

The Effect of the Surroundings

An object's perceived color is affected not only by the observer's state of adaptation, but also by the object's surroundings, as shown by the following demonstration.

D E M O N S T R A T I O N

Color and the Surroundings

Illuminate the green quadrant of Color Plate 2.4 with tungsten light. As you illuminate it, then look at the square through a small hole punched in a piece of paper, so that all you see through the hole is part of the green area. Now repeat this observation while illuminating the same area with daylight from your window. ●

When the surroundings are masked, most people perceive the green area to be slightly more yellow under the tungsten light than in daylight. The fact that color constancy works less well when we mask the surroundings has been studied by a number of investigators, who have shown that color constancy works best when an object is surrounded by objects of many different colors, like the display in Color Plate

2.8, which is called a Mondrian display, because of its similarity to works created by the Dutch painter Piet Mondrian (Land, 1983, 1986; Land & McCann, 1971). For some theories about exactly how the presence of the surroundings enhances color constancy, see Brainard and Wandell (1986), Land (1983, 1986), and Pokorny, Shevell, and Smith (1991).

Memory and Color

A small effect, but one worth mentioning, is that past knowledge can have some effect on color perception through the operation of a phenomenon called **memory color**, in which an object's characteristic color influences our perception of its color. Research has shown that since people know the colors of familiar objects, like a red stop sign, or a green tree, they judge these familiar objects as having richer, more saturated colors than unfamiliar objects that reflect the same wavelengths (Jin & Shevell, 1996; Ratner & McCarthy, 1990). Thus, our ability to remember the colors of familiar objects may help us perceive these colors under different illuminations.

Another effect of memory on color perception occurs not because we remember the colors of familiar objects, but because we often don't accurately remember the colors we have seen in the past. Thus, when we see a red stop sign that is illuminated by a street light at night, we may not notice that it appears a slightly different shade of red than when we saw it illuminated by sunlight earlier in the day. Remembering that stop signs are red helps us perceive them as red, but since we don't remember the exact shade of red, we don't notice the slight shifts in our perception that occur under different illuminations (Jin and Shevell, 1996).

LIGHTNESS CONSTANCY

We have seen that color constancy helps keep our perception of chromatic color constant, even as we move from one illumination to another. This is important because it means that we can perceive the actual properties of objects without too much interference from different lighting conditions. It is also important that we perceive achromatic colors of objects accurately, so that we see a Labrador retriever as black both when it is inside and when it is in bright sunlight.

Consider the problem facing the visual system. The Labrador retriever lying on the rug in the living room is illuminated by a 100-watt lightbulb in the overhead light fixture. Some of the light that hits the retriever's black coat is reflected, and we see the coat as black. When the dog goes outside, so its coat is illuminated by bright sunlight, much more light hits its coat, compared to inside, and therefore much more light is also reflected. But the dog still appears black. More light is reflected, but the perception of the shade of achromatic color (white, gray, and black), which we call **lightness**, remains the same. This constancy of achromatic color in the face of changes in the amount of light reflected into the eyes is called **lightness constancy**.

The problem that the visual system must deal with is that the amount of light reaching the eye from an object depends on two things: (1) the illumination, how much light is striking the object's surface; and (2) the object's reflectance, the proportion of this light that the object reflects into our eyes. Under most conditions in which lightness constancy occurs, our perception of lightness is determined not by the illumination but by the reflectance. Objects that look black reflect about 5 percent of the light. Objects that look gray reflect about 10 to 70 percent of the light (depending on the shade of gray); and objects that look white, like the paper in this book, reflect 80 to 90 percent of the light. Thus, our perception of an object's lightness is related not to the *amount* of light that is reflected from the object, which can change depending on the illumination, but on the *percentage* of light reflected from the object, which remains the same no matter what the illumination.

You can appreciate the existence of lightness constancy by imagining a checkerboard illuminated by room light, like the one in Figure 6.25. In this checkerboard, the white squares have a reflectance of 90 percent and the black squares have a reflectance of 5 percent. Since the intensity inside the room is 100 units, the white squares reflect 90 units and the black squares reflect 5 units. Now, we take the checkerboard outside into bright sunlight, where the intensity

is 10,000. In the sunlight, the white squares reflect 9,000 units of light and the black squares reflect 500 units. But even though the black squares now reflect much more light than the white squares did when the checkerboard was inside, they still look black. Your perception is determined by the reflectance, not the amount of light reflected.

What is responsible for lightness constancy? As for color constancy, there are a number of possible causes.

Intensity Relationships: The Ratio Principle

One observation about lightness constancy is that two areas that reflect different amounts of light look the same if the ratios of their intensities to the intensities of the surrounding areas are kept constant (Jacobson & Gilchrist, 1988; Wallach, 1963). Thus, even though the amount of light reflected from our checkerboard is increased by a factor of 100 when we move it outside, the ratios of the amount of light reflected from the white and black squares remains constant at 90 to 5, so our perception of the white and black squares stays the same. This effect, which is called the **ratio principle,** works well for two-dimensional objects like our checkerboard, but things get more complicated for objects in three-dimensional scenes.

Lightness Perception in Three-Dimensional Scenes

If you look around, wherever you are, you will probably notice that the illumination is not even over the entire scene, as was the case for our two-dimensional checkerboard. The illumination in three-dimensional scenes is usually uneven because of shadows cast by one object onto another or because one part of an object faces the light and another part is facing away from the light. (See Figure 5.49 for another example of a three-dimensional scene with uneven illumination.)

The problem for the perceptual system is that it has to somehow take the uneven illumination into account. One way to state this problem is

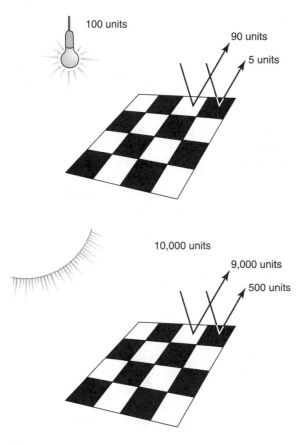

Figure 6.25
A black-and-white checkerboard being illuminated by tungsten light and by sunlight. See text for details.

that the perceptual system needs to distinguish between reflectance edges and illumination edges. A **reflectance edge** is an edge where the reflectance of two surfaces changes. Thus, the borders between the black squares and the white squares of the checkerboard are reflectance edges. An **illumination edge** is an edge where the illumination changes. We can create an illumination edge on our checkerboard by blocking some of the light with our hand (Figure 6.26). The border between the dark shadow and the illuminated checkerboard is an illumination edge. Some explanations for how the visual system distinguishes between these two types of edges have been proposed, but they are too complex to describe here

(see Adelson, 1999; Gilchrist, 1994; and Gilchrist et al., 1999, for details). The basic idea behind these explanations is that the perceptual system uses a number of sources of information to take the illumination into account. Let's look at a few of these sources of information.

The Information in Shadows In order for lightness constancy to work, the visual system needs to be able to take the uneven illumination created by shadows into account. It needs to determine that this change in illumination caused by a shadow is due to an illumination edge and not due to a reflectance edge. Obviously, the visual system usually succeeds in doing this, because although the light intensity is reduced by shadows, you don't usually see shadowed areas as gray or black. For example, in the case of the checkerboard in Figure 6.26, you assume that the shadowed and unshadowed areas are the same checkerboard pattern but that less light falls on some areas than on others.

How does the visual system know that the change in intensity caused by the shadow is an illumination edge and not a reflectance edge? One thing the visual system may take into account is the shadow's meaningful shape. In this particular example, we know that the shadow was cast by a hand, so we know it is the illumination that is changing, not the color of the checkerboard squares. The effect of meaning is also

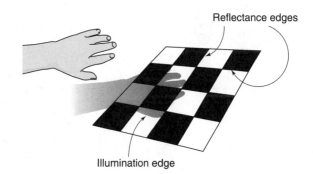

Figure 6.26
A hand casting a shadow on the checkerboard. The edges of the shadow are illumination edges. The edges of the squares on the checkerboard are reflectance edges.

Perceiving Color

illustrated in Figure 6.27, in which it is obvious that the dark area on the wall is the shadow cast by a tree. Another clue that an illumination change is due to a shadow is provided by the nature of the shadow's contour, as illustrated by the following demonstration.

D E M O N S T R A T I O N

The Penumbra and
Lightness Perception

Place an object, such as a cup, on a white piece of paper on your desk. Then illuminate the cup at an angle with your desk lamp and adjust the lamp's position to produce a shadow with a slightly fuzzy border, as in Figure 6.28a. (Generally, moving the lamp closer to the cup makes the border get fuzzier.) The fuzzy border of a shadow is called the shadow's *penumbra*. Now take your marker and draw a thick line, as shown in Figure 6.28b, so you can no longer see the penumbra. What happens to your perception of the shadowed area inside the black line?　●

Covering the penumbra causes most people to perceive a change in the appearance of the shadowed area. Instead of looking like a shadow on a piece of white paper, it looks like a dark spot on the paper. In other words, the shadow and its penumbra are initially perceived as an illumination edge, but masking off the penumbra changes the perception to a reflectance edge.

Taking the Illumination into Account　The next demonstration provides another illustration of the difference between perceiving illumination edges and perceiving reflectance edges in a situation in which an object is unevenly illuminated because part of it is facing the light and part is in shadow.

D E M O N S T R A T I O N

Lightness at a Corner

Stand a folded index card on end so that it resembles the outside corner of a room and illuminate it so that one side is illuminated and the other is in shadow. When you look at the corner, you can easily tell that both sides of the corner are made of the same white material but that the nonilluminated side is shadowed (Figure 6.29a). In other words, you are per-

Figure 6.27
The pattern created by shadows on a surface is usually interpreted as a change in the pattern of illumination, not as a change in the material making up the surface. The fact that we see all of the bricks on this wall as made up of the same material, despite the illumination changes, is an example of lightness constancy.

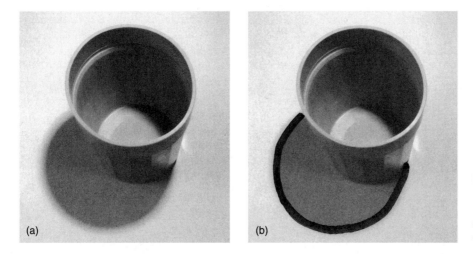

Figure 6.28
(a) A cup and its shadow.
(b) The same cup and shadow with the penumbra covered by a black border.

ceiving the edge between the illuminated and shadowed "walls" as an illumination edge.

Now punch a hole in another card and, with the hole a few inches from the corner of the folded card, view the corner with one eye about a foot from the hole (Figure 6.29b). If, when viewing the corner through the hole, you perceive the corner as a flat surface, your perception of the left and right surfaces will change. ●

Eliminating the perception of depth at the corner eliminates information about the conditions of illumination, so you may perceive the left side as being dark gray or black and the right side as being white. If you perceive it this way, you are perceiving the border between the light and dark surfaces as a reflectance edge.

In both the shadowed checkerboard and the shadowed corner, the perception that results in lightness constancy occurs when information is available to accurately indicate the conditions of illumination. In the case of the checkerboard, the shape of the shadow and the presence of the penumbra provide information that a shadow is present, and our perception of the three-dimensionality of the corner provides information indicating that the illumination is probably different on the two surfaces.

In both of these situations the visual system is making the best guess, given the information avail-

able, as to what the stimulus is. Figure 6.30 provides another example of how lightness perception depends on assumptions about the illumination. If you compare the lightness of the two squares indicated by arrows in Figure 6.30a, you may notice that the top square appears slightly darker than the bottom one. Now compare the two squares indicated by the arrows in Figure 6.30b. Even though the reflectances of these squares are all identical (the two rectangles in Figure 6.30b reflect the same amount of light as

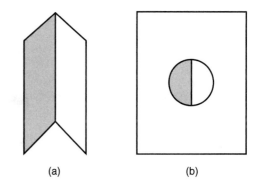

(a)   (b)

Figure 6.29
Viewing a shaded corner. (a) Illuminate the card so one side is illuminated and the other is in shadow; (b) view the card through a small hole so the two sides of the corner are visible, as shown.

Perceiving Color

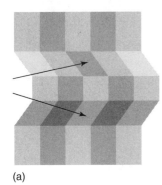

(a)

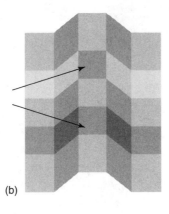

(b)

Figure 6.30
The two areas indicated by arrows in (a) reflect the same amount of light as the two areas indicated in (b). Notice that the lower area in (a) looks lighter. (From Adelson, 1993.)

the squares in Figure 6.30a), the difference in the lightness of the two areas is less in (b) than in (a).

One explanation for this effect is that for the pattern in (b), the two squares appear to be illuminated evenly; but, for the pattern in (a), the bottom rectangle appears to be in shadow, and the top one appears to be in the light. What may be going on here is that the visual system is using a heuristic such as "if two objects reflect the same amount of light and one is in shadow, then the one in shadow must be lighter" (Figure 6.31). Since the bottom square appears to be

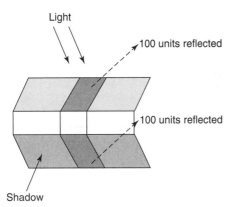

Light

100 units reflected

100 units reflected

Shadow

Figure 6.31
Heuristic for the situation in Figure 6.30a: "If the top and bottom areas both reflect the same amount of light, but the lower area is in shadow, then the bottom area must be reflecting a greater percentage of light and would therefore appear lighter."

in shadow, it appears lighter. (Remember from Chapter 5, page 154, that a heuristic is a "best guess" rule that helps us predict what will happen in a particular situation.)

Finally, consider the following demonstration.

DEMONSTRATION

Surface Curvature and Lightness Perception

Compare the two displays in Figure 6.32. The one at (a) looks like a flat surface, and the one at (b) looks like two curved surfaces. In addition to their difference in surface curvature, they also appear to be shaded differently. The flat surface in (a) appears to be darker on the left than on the right, whereas the curved surfaces in (b) appear more evenly shaded. But now, take two pieces of paper and cover the top and bottom edges of (b) so it has straight edges as in (a). What do you see? ●

Perhaps you were surprised to see that when you turned the curved edges of (b) into straight lines, the left and right sides became much more like those in (a). This is actually not surprising because the intensity distributions of (a) and (b) are, in fact, identical. The visual system is apparently interpreting the border in (a) as a reflectance edge since there is no evidence of uneven illumination; but it interprets the same intensity distribution on the rounded surfaces as

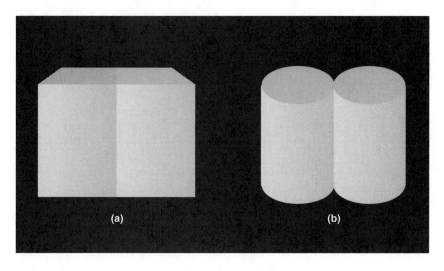

Figure 6.32
The light distribution is identical for (a) and (b), though it appears to be different. See text for further details. (Figure courtesy of David Knill and Daniel Kersten.)

being due to the shadows and highlights that would be expected to occur on a rounded surface.

The overall message here is that lightness perception is determined not by the absolute amount of light or its distribution on the retina but by a combination of information on the retina and information about the three-dimensional configuration and probable illumination.

Perceiving Color

In the examples of neural plasticity that we have discussed in the other chapters, we have described situations in which an animal's environment can shift the tuning of neurons (for Chapter 3 it was orientation; for Chapter 5 faces, or Greebles). This change in tuning occurs during the lifetime of an animal, as the animal is exposed to stimuli in the environment.

But we can also take a longer view of how the environment causes changes in our sensory systems by considering how evolution has caused certain properties to become characteristics of a species because they have proven useful for survival. Color vision provides some evidence for the influence of evolution. In this case, what has evolved is the type of visual pigments in the receptors, which determine the wavelength ranges over which animals are most sensitive.

At the beginning of this chapter we noted that trichromatic vision may have evolved in humans and monkeys in order to enable them to more easily distinguish red and yellow fruits against green leafy backgrounds (Mollon, 1989, 2000). But the idea that color vision evolved to meet requirements in the environment can be demonstrated in other species as well. Consider, for example, birds and insects. Flowers, which are extremely important in their visual worlds, reflect a large proportion of their light between 360 and 520 nm and also reflect long-wavelength light, for flowers that are orange and red.

Looking at the visual systems of birds and insects reveals a tetrachromatic system—they have four different visual pigments, one of which gives them high sensitivity in the short-wavelength ultraviolet range. Their enhanced short-wavelength sensitivity compared to humans and the fact that they have four pigments makes the floral colors that are so important for their survival more distinctive to birds and insects than they are to humans (Kevan & Backhaus, 1998).

In addition to these examples of visual pigments, we can also find evidence for evolutionary adaptations in the design of animals' eyes. For example, the fovea is the area of sharpest vision, both because of the high density of cones and because of the lack of neural convergence. The eagle and the falcon provide examples of foveas with higher cone densities than those in humans; these higher cone densities increase acuity to two to three times that of humans—an asset for detecting small prey from a vantage point high in the sky (Fox, Lehmukuhle, & Westendorf, 1976; Reymond, 1985).

Humans, eagles, and falcons have small pit-shaped foveas, but some other animals have areas of high-detail vision that are spread out over a larger area. The red-eyed turtle provides an example of such an arrangement: It has a horizontal area of high receptor density called the **area centralis** (Brown, 1969) (Figure 6.33). The linear area centralis has a property well suited to the turtle's view of the world since it is lined up with the horizon. This arrangement serves the turtle well, because most of the visual stimuli that are important to the turtle, such as potential predators, appear on the horizon, where the turtle's vision is sharpest. Many other animals that live near to the ground have a linear area centralis, as well as some birds that also depend on the horizon for orientation as they are flying.

Another adaptation is eye placement. Some animals, such as cats and humans, have frontal eyes with overlapping fields of view that provide good depth perception; others, such as rabbits, birds, lizards, and rodents, have lateral eyes (i.e.,

(continued)

The Plasticity of Perception (*continued*)

on the sides of their heads) that provide a more panoramic view of the world, an especially important adaptation for monitoring the environment for the presence of predators (see Figure 7.30). When eyes see different areas of the environment, as in lateral-eyed animals, the eyes sometimes move independently, as in some birds and lizards, so that they can look for the most important objects on the left and the right simultaneously.

In contrast, most frontal-eyed animals use "yoked" or coordinated eye movements to focus on one thing at a time.

What is clear from all of these examples is that while the eyes of most animals all have in common light-sensitive pigments and some kind of device to focus the light, evolution has provided variations that match pigments and eyes to the animals' specific needs (Fernald, 2000).

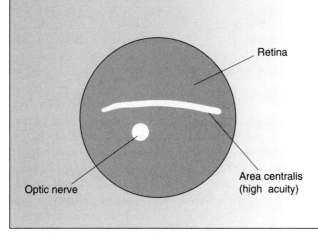

Retina

Optic nerve

Area centralis (high acuity)

Figure 6.33
Looking down on the retina of the red-eyed turtle. The area centralis, which stretches across the retina to form a horizontal line, is the area of highest acuity.

Perceiving Color

HOW COLOR AFFECTS
TASTE AND SMELL

If, when you were younger, you discovered the magic of your mother's food coloring, you may have created, as I once did, such exotic foods as green mashed potatoes or blue applesauce. If you then tried to interest someone in eating your concoctions, you probably found that people are not enthusiastic about trying strangely colored foods. The appearance of food plays an important role in people's attitudes about food, as evidenced by the large sums of money spent to produce appetizing-looking pictures to put on the cans, jars, and boxes that package the food.

There is no question that the appearance of food influences its desirability, and research also indicates that people's ability to identify tastes and smells depends to some degree on color. For example, when Arnold Hyman (1983) asked subjects to identify the taste of samples of white birch beer, he found that subjects correctly identified it 70 percent of the time if the samples were colorless. However, when colored red, accuracy dropped to 25 percent, with various subjects stating that the red-colored birch beer tasted like cherry cough medicine, cherry soda, mint flavor, and dentist's mouthwash.

In Hyman's experiment, the presence of an extraneous color hampered taste identification, but other experiments have shown that when the color matches the taste (for example, red for cherry taste or yellow for lemon taste) people are much better at identifying the taste than if the color doesn't match the taste. Thus, C. N. DuBose and coworkers (1980) found that the taste of cherry, orange, and lime beverages were judged correctly an average of 67 percent of the time if the colors matched their beverages' taste, but were judged correctly only 37

percent of the time if the solutions were colorless or 28 percent if the colors didn't match the taste.

Research on how color affects the identification of odors has obtained essentially similar results—when colors and odors match, subjects are better at identifying the odor (Davis, 1981; Zellner, Bartoli, & Eckard, 1991). A possible explanation for the enhancing effect of color on odor identification is based on the idea that identifying odors appears to involve two processes: First the subject perceives the odor, and then the subject must retrieve the odor's name from his or her memory—something people find very difficult to do. Thus, William Cain (1979, 1980) found that a subject who assigns a correct name to an odor the first time he or she smells it (for example, labeling an orange "orange") will usually identify the object correctly the next time it is presented. If, however, the subject incorrectly labels an object the first time it is smelled (for example, labeling machine oil "cheese"), he or she usually misidentifies it the next time it is presented. Cain concludes that people's difficulty in identifying odors occurs primarily because of their inability to retrieve the odor's name from their memory.

Thus, a color consistent with a substance's odor might aid in identification of that odor because it provides information that signals what the odor is likely to be. Perceiving the color of an orange leads us to expect the smell we associate with an orange, and when we actually smell that odor we can easily identify it. Thus, color provides top-down information that helps us more accurately identify substances based on their smell.

Color Deficiency

People with color deficiency (dichromats) and color blindness (monochromats) need fewer wavelengths than do trichromats to match any wavelength in the spectrum. Anomalous trichromats mix wavelengths in different proportions than trichromats. The color perception of dichromats has been determined by testing a unilateral dichromat. There are more color-deficient males than females because color deficiency is a sex-linked characteristic.

Physiological Mechanisms of Color Deficiency

Receptor-based color deficiency is caused by the absence of one or more cone pigments. Cortical color blindness is due to damage of the cortex. Some patients with cortical color blindness are able to use the information in the wavelengths of the stimulus but are not able to experience color.

Color Experience

Our experience of color is created by the nervous system. Color is the brain's way of letting us know which wavelengths are present, but there is nothing intrinsically blue about short wavelengths or red about long wavelengths.

Color Constancy

Color constancy refers to how our perception of color remains relatively constant even when objects are viewed under different illuminations. This constancy is due to a number of factors including chromatic adaptation, the effect of surrounds, and memory color.

Lightness Constancy

Lightness constancy refers to how our perception of lightness remains relatively constant even when objects are viewed under different intensities of light. Our perception of lightness depends on the percentage of light reflected from an object rather than on the amount of light reflected. Lightness constancy is due to a number of factors, including (1) the way the ratios of light intensities reflected from different areas remain constant under different illuminations and (2) information about the conditions of illumination that helps us differentiate between reflectance edges and illumination edges.

Plasticity:
Color Vision as an Adaptation to the Environment

Evolution adapts the perception of different animals to their environment. Evidence for this adaptation is found in the visual pigments; the characteristics of areas of sharpest vision on the retina, like the fovea and the area centralis; and eye placement.

Across the Senses:
How Color Affects Taste and Smell

The colors of foods and liquids can influence taste judgments, with extraneous colors hampering taste identification. However, when the color matches the taste, people are better at identifying tastes. Similar results have been obtained for odors, and it has been suggested that color provides top-down information that helps us more accurately identify substances based on their smell.

Perceiving Color

STUDY QUESTIONS

1. What happened to Mr. I, the artist, after his accident? (186)

Four Questions About Color

What Are Some Functions of Color Vision?

2. Give an example of the signaling function of color. (186)

3. What is perceptual organization, and how does color perception facilitate it? (186)

4. Why have some researchers proposed that monkey and human color vision evolved for the purpose of detecting fruit in the forest? (187)

What Physical Attributes Are Associated with Color?

5. What is the relationship between wavelength and color perception? (187)

6. What is reflectance? A reflectance curve? (187)

7. How does a leaf's reflectance curve change as the leaf changes color? What does this tell us about the relationship between wavelength and color? (187)

8. What are the achromatic colors? The chromatic colors? (187)

9. What is another term for chromatic color? (187)

10. How does reflectance change across the spectrum for achromatic colors? (188)

11. What is selective reflection? What kinds of colors are associated with selective reflection? (188)

12. Why are parts of some glaciers blue? (188)

Color Experience

13. Which terms are adequate to describe all of the colors we can discriminate? (189)

14. What does the color circle show? How are the colors ordered? (189)

15. How many steps can a person discriminate in the visible spectrum? (189)

16. What two characteristics of color can we change, in addition to wavelength, to create more colors? (189)

17. What is saturation? (189)

18. How many color patches are included in the *Munsell Book of Colors*? (189)

What Is the Neural Code for Color?

19. How has the question "What is the neural code for color?" been restated to enable researchers to deal with this question? (190)

20. Which approach to perception was used in the 1800s to determine the neural code for color? (190)

Trichromatic Theory of Color Vision

21. Which two scientists used color-matching results to propose a theory of color vision? (190)

Color-Matching Experiments

22. What are color-matching experiments? (190)

23. What are the two results of color-matching experiments? (190)

Trichromatic Theory

24. What is another name for trichromatic theory? (191)

25. What does the theory propose? (191)

Physiology of Trichromatic Theory

26. What physiological research involving cone pigments supports the trichromatic theory of color vision? (191)

27. What structural feature is different in the different types of visual pigments? (191)

28. What is the relationship between the absorption spectrum of the visual pigments and the amino acid sequence of the protein opsin? (191)

29. What is the connection between the pattern of cone receptor responding and color perception? (192)

30. Understand how to use the information in 29, above, to predict what colors will result from superimposing colored lights. (192)

31. What is metamerism? What are metamers? (192)

32. What is the physiological basis for metamers? (192)

33. Explain how a mixture of 530-nm and 620-nm wavelengths can result in the same pattern of receptor response as a 580-nm light. (192)

34. Are three different receptor mechanisms necessary for color vision? (193)

35. What is the principle of univariance? (193)

36. Can the responses generated by a single pigment provide the information needed to tell one wavelength from another? (193)

37. Why can't a person with just one pigment see colors? (193)

38. Why is wavelength discrimination and color vision possible if there are two pigments? People whose color vision is based on two pigments are called _____. (194)

39. What does the addition of a third pigment accomplish? (195)

Opponent-Process Theory of Color Vision

40. Who made phenomenological observations that were difficult for trichromatic theory to explain? (195)

41. What does the opponent-process theory state? (195)

The Phenomenological Observations

42. What did Hering conclude about paired colors based on his observations of afterimages? (195)

43. Describe the results of the afterimage and simultaneous contrast demonstration. How do these results show that red and green and blue and yellow are paired? (195)

44. How can the pairing of colors be demonstrated by visualizing colors? (196)

45. What do the results of Figure 6.13 show about blue–yellow and red–green pairing? (196)

Opponent-Process Theory

46. What is the basic idea underlying Hering's theory? (197)

The Physiology of Opponent-Process Theory

47. Describe the response of opponent neurons. (197)

48. Understand how the neural circuit in Figure 6.15 creates opponent cells from signals generated by the three types of cone receptors. (197)

49. What is the advantage of opponent neurons? (Understand the point of Figure 6.18.) (199)

What We Still Don't Know About the Code for Color

50. What idea about how color is represented in the cortex was proposed in the 1980s? (200)

51. How does cortical color blindness support the idea of a color center in the cortex? (200)

52. What did researchers find when they recorded from neurons in the cortex? (200)

53. What are some reasons that it may not be valid to call V4 the "color area"? (200)

54. Does color perception involve mainly one central area or many? (200)

Brain Scan: Distributed Nature of Color Representation in the Human Cortex

55. What areas of the cortex are activated by color stimuli? Describe Beauchamp's experiment in which he used a color sorting test. What does his result mean? (201)

Color Deficiency

56. What is color deficiency? (200)

57. What are two ways to determine color deficiency? (200)

58. What are the three different types of color deficiency? (202)

59. What do we need to do in order to determine what colors are perceived by someone who is color deficient? (202)

Monochromatism and Dichromatism

60. Why do we say that the color deficiency observed in two kinds of dichromats is sex-linked? (203)

61. What colors do monochromats and dichromats perceive? What are the three kinds of dichromats? What is the neutral point? (203)

Physiological Mechanisms of Receptor-Based Color Deficiency

62. What are the receptor-based physiological mechanisms responsible for color deficiency? (203)

Cortical Color Blindness

63. What is cerebral achromatopsia? What can most people with this condition see? (204)

64. How does the case of cerebral achromatopsia described in the text illustrate that processing information about wavelength is not the same as color perception? (204)

Creating Color Experience

65. How does the experience of color differ from perceiving shape or distance in terms of our ability to check experience against a physical measure? (204)

66. Is there a reason that we think that short wavelengths should look "blue"? (204)

67. What did Newton mean when he wrote "the Rays . . . are not coloured"? (205)

68. How are hearing and smell similar to color perception? (205)

69. What does honeybee vision illustrate about the connection between wavelength and experience? (206)

70. What do we mean when we say that color is a creation of the nervous system? (206)

Color Constancy

71. How do the wavelengths contained in sunlight and in the light from a tungsten bulb compare? (206)

72. What is color constancy? Relate the idea of color constancy to how you perceive the color of your shirt outdoors and indoors. (207)

73. Discuss the following explanations of color constancy: chromatic adaptation (understand the Uchikawa et al. experiment) and the effect of the surroundings. (207)

74. What are two ways that memory affects our perception of color? (209)

Lightness Constancy

75. What problem must the visual system solve so that a Labrador retriever will be perceived as black both inside a room and outside in the sunlight? (210)

76. What is lightness? Lightness constancy? (210)

77. What two things determine the amount of light reaching the eye from an object? (210)

78. What is the relationship between lightness constancy and reflectance? (210)

Intensity Relationships: The Ratio Principle

79. What is the ratio principle? (210)

Lightness Perception in Three-Dimensional Scenes

80. Why do three-dimensional scenes pose a problem for our perception of lightness? What does the perceptual system have to take into account? (210)

81. What is a reflectance edge? An illumination edge? (211)

82. Is the edge of a shadow an illumination edge or a reflectance edge? (211)

83. What are two clues that help us identify shadows? (211)

84. What is the penumbra? What happens to our perception of lights when we eliminate it? (212)

85. What does the "lightness at a corner" demonstration illustrate? (212)

86. What do Figures 6.30 and 6.32 illustrate about lightness perception? (214)

87. Why do the left and right sides of Figure 6.32a appear to have different lightnesses? (214)

The Plasticity of Perception: Color Vision as an Adaptation to the Environment

88. What is the evidence to support the idea that the color vision of birds and insects has evolved to match their environment? (216)

89. Describe the following adaptations of the eye: the fovea in the eagle and falcon; the area centralis in turtles; eye placement in animals with frontal eyes and lateral eyes. (216)

Across the Senses: How Color Affects Taste and Smell

90. How does adding extraneous color to a substance affect a person's ability to identify its taste? (218)

91. What is the effect of color on taste if an object's color matches its taste (for example, red for a cherry taste)? If the color does not match its taste? (218)

92. What are the two processes that appear to be involved in identifying odors? (218)

93. Why do people often find it difficult to identify odors? (218)

94. What kind of information does color provide that aids in odor identification? (218)

7

PERCEIVING DEPTH AND SIZE

CHAPTER CONTENTS

SOME QUESTIONS WE WILL CONSIDER

- How can we see far into the distance based on the flat image on the retina? (226)

- Why do we see depth better with two eyes than with one eye? (233)

- Why don't people appear to shrink in size when they walk away? (250)

Y ou can easily tell that this book is about 18 inches away and, when you look up at the scene around you, that other objects are located at distances ranging from the nose on your face (very close!) to across the room, down the street, or even as far as the horizon, depending on where you are. What's amazing about this ability to see the distances of objects in your environment is that these objects, and the scene as a whole, cast a two-dimensional image on your retina.

In this chapter we will describe research on depth perception and also on the perception of the sizes of objects, which asks the following question: What information enables us to perceive the depths and sizes of objects in the environment? We begin by discussing depth perception and will consider the perception of size and illusions of size later in the chapter.

We can begin to appreciate the problem of perceiving depth based on two-dimensional information on the retina by focusing on two points on the retina, N and F, shown in Figure 7.1. These points represent where rays of light been reflected onto the retina from the tree which is near (N) and the house, which is farther away (F). If we look just at these places on the retina, we have no way of knowing how far the light has traveled to reach points N and F. For all we know, the light stimulating either point on the retina could have come from one foot away or from a distant star. Clearly, we need to expand our view beyond single points on the retina to determine where objects are located in space.

When we expand our view from two isolated points to the entire retinal image, we increase the amount of information available to us, because now we can see the images of the house and the tree. However, since this image is two-dimensional, we still need to explain how we get from the flat image on the retina to the three-dimensional perception of the scene. One way researchers have approached this problem is to ask what information is contained in this two-dimensional image that enables us to perceive depth in the scene. This is called the *cue approach* to depth perception.

The **cue approach** to depth perception focuses on identifying information in the retinal image that is correlated with depth in the scene. For example, if one object partially covers another object, as the tree

in the foreground in Figure 7.1 covers part of the house, the object that is partially covered must be at a greater distance than the object that is covering it. This situation, which is called occlusion, is a signal, or cue, that one object is in front of another. According to **cue theory**, we learn the connection between this cue and depth through our previous experience with the environment. After this learning has occurred, the association between particular cues and depth becomes automatic, and, when these **depth cues** are present, we experience the world in three dimensions. A number of different types of cues have been identified that signal depth in the scene. We can divide these cues into three major groups:

1. *Oculomotor.* Cues based on our ability to sense the position of our eyes and the tension in our eye muscles.

2. *Monocular.* Cues that work with one eye.

3. *Binocular.* Cues that depend on two eyes.

OCULOMOTOR CUES

WebTUTOR   The **oculomotor cues** are created by (1) **convergence**, the inward movement of the eyes that occurs when we look at nearby objects, and

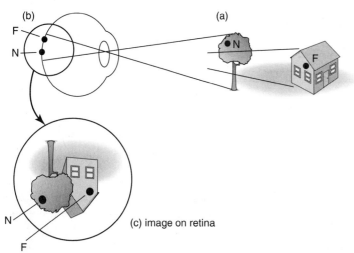

(c) image on retina

Figure 7.1
(a) The house is farther away than the tree, but (b) the images of points F on the house and N on the tree both fall on the two-dimensional surface of the retina, so (c) these two points, considered by themselves, do not tell us the distances of the house and the tree.

(2) **accommodation**, the change in the shape of the lens that occurs when we focus on objects at various distances. The idea behind these cues is that we can *feel* the inward movement of the eyes that occurs when the eyes converge to look at nearby objects, and we feel the tightening of eye muscles that change the shape of the lens to focus on a nearby object. You can experience the feelings in your eyes associated with convergence and accommodation by doing the following demonstration.

 D E M O N S T R A T I O N

Feelings in Your Eyes

Look at your finger as you hold it at arm's length. Then, as you slowly move your finger toward your nose, notice how you feel your eyes looking inward and become aware of the increasing tension inside your eyes.   ●

The feelings you experience as you move your finger closer are caused by (1) the change in **convergence angle** as your eye muscles cause your eyes to look inward, as in Figure 7.2a, and (2) the change in the shape of the lens as the eye accommodates to focus on a near object (see Figure 2.9). If you move your finger farther away, the lens flattens, and your eyes move away from the nose until they are both looking straight ahead, as in Figure 7.2b. Convergence and accommodation indicate when an object is close and are useful up to a distance of about arm's length, with convergence being the more effective of the two (Cutting and Vishton, 1995; Mon-Williams & Tresilian, 1999; Tresilian et al., 1999).

MONOCULAR CUES

Monocular cues work with only one eye. They include accommodation, which we have described under oculomotor cues; pictorial cues, depth information that can be depicted in a two-dimensional picture; and movement-based cues, which are based on depth information created by movement.

Pictorial Cues

Pictorial cues are sources of depth information that can be depicted in a picture, such as the illustrations in this book or the image on the retina (Goldstein, 2001a).

Occlusion   We have already described the depth cue of **occlusion**. When one object hides or partially hides another from view, the object that is hidden is

(a)   (b)

Figure 7.2
(a) Convergence of the eyes occurs when a person looks at something very close. (b) The eyes look straight ahead when the person observes something far away.

Perceiving Depth and Size

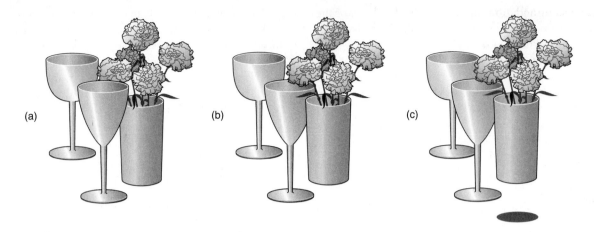

Figure 7.3
(a) Occlusion indicates that the tapered glass is in front of the round glass and vase. (b) Occlusion now indicates that the vase is in front of the tapered glass. However, relative height indicates the opposite. (c) The cast shadow under the vase provides additional information about its position in space, which helps clear up the confusion.

seen as being farther away. Note that occlusion does not provide information about an object's absolute distance; it indicates relative distance—we know that the object that is partially covered is farther away than another object, but we don't know how much farther away it is.

The picture in Figure 7.3a illustrates occlusion. From this picture we can see that the tapered glass is in front of the rounded glass and the vase. It is difficult, however, just from the occlusion information alone, to know exactly how far apart these objects are.

Relative Height In addition to noticing that the objects in Figure 7.3a overlap one another, you can also see that the ones with bases that are higher in the picture appear farther away. This is the cue of **relative height**. Objects with bases that are higher in your field of view are usually seen as being more distant. Based on relative height, we could judge the rounded glass to be farther away than the vase. Similarly, of the three men in Figure 7.4, the ones whose feet are higher appear to be farther away. But notice that the clouds that are lower in Figure 7.4 appear farther away. Thus, objects that are above the horizon appear farther away if they are lower in the field of view.

Figure 7.4
Relative height. Other things being equal, objects below the horizon that appear higher in the field of view are seen as being farther away. Objects above the horizon that appear lower in the field of view are seen as being farther away.

Figure 7.5
We perceive the relative distances of these three tennis balls based on their relative size in the field of view.

Cast Shadows   The shadows cast by objects provide information regarding the locations of these objects. Consider, for example, Figure 7.3b. By changing the occlusion so now the vase occludes the tapered glass, we have created a confusing picture. In Figure 7.3a, both occlusion and relative height indicated that the vase was farther away than the tapered glass, but now occlusion is indicating that it is closer and relative height that it is farther. Perhaps the vase is in front of the glass, but it is floating in the air. Adding the cast shadow in Figure 7.3c indicates that this is, in fact, the case. The shadow indicates where in space the vase is hovering and, in doing this, helps locate the object in depth (Mamassian, Knill, & Kersten, 1998).

Relative Size   If two objects are of equal size, the one that is farther away will take up less of your field of view than the one that is closer. We use the cue of **relative size** to tell that the tennis ball in the lower left of Figure 7.5 is farther away than the other two and that the one in the middle is just slightly closer than the one on the right. This perception is based on our assumption that these three tennis balls are the same size.

Familiar Size   Look at the coins in Figure 7.6. If they were real coins, which would you say is closer? If you are influenced by your knowledge of the actual size of dimes, quarters, and half-dollars, you would probably say that the dime is closer. If you did, the cue of **familiar size** is influencing your judgment of depth. An experiment by William Epstein (1965) shows that, under certain conditions, our knowledge of an object's size influences our perception of that object's distance. The stimuli in Epstein's experiment were equal-sized photographs of a dime, a quarter, and a half-dollar, which were positioned the same

Figure 7.6
Line drawings of the stimuli used in Epstein's (1965) familiar-size experiment. The actual stimuli were photographs that were all the same size as a real quarter.

distance from an observer. By placing these photographs in a darkened room, illuminating them with a spot of light, and having subjects view them with one eye, Epstein created the illusion that these pictures were real coins.

When the observers judged the distance of each of the coin photographs, they estimated that the dime was closest, the quarter was farther than the dime, and the half-dollar was the farthest of them all. The observers' judgments were influenced by their knowledge of the sizes of real dimes, quarters, and half-dollars. This result did not occur, however, when the observers viewed the scene with both eyes, because the use of two eyes provided information indicating the coins were at the same distance. The cue of familiar size is therefore most effective when other information about depth is absent (see also Coltheart, 1970; Schiffman, 1967).

Atmospheric Perspective   **Atmospheric perspective** causes us to see distant objects as less sharp because we observe them by looking through air that contains small particles such as dust, water droplets, and various forms of airborne pollution. The farther away an object is, the more air and particles we have to look through, making objects that are farther away look less sharp than close objects. Figure 7.7 illustrates atmospheric perspective. The hills in the foreground appear much sharper than the hazy hills in the background.

If, instead of viewing these hills, you were standing on the moon, where there is no atmosphere, and hence no atmospheric perspective, far craters would look just as clear as near ones. But on earth, there is atmospheric perspective, with the exact amount depending on the nature of the atmosphere. (Also see Color Plate 3.2.)

Linear Perspective   The term *linear perspective* is used to refer to both a drawing system and to a cue for depth. The **drawing system of linear perspective** was first described in 1435 by Leon Battista Alberti in his book *De Pictura*. Alberti's book describes a geometrical procedure for drawing a picture in linear perspective (see Hagen, 1979, 1986; Kemp, 1989; Kubovy, 1986; White, 1968).

Another technique for creating perspective pictures, which is called **Alberti's window**, makes it pos-

Figure 7.7
This photograph of hills in China is an excellent example of atmospheric perspective, with the mountains becoming less sharp with increasing distance.

sible for anyone to draw in perspective. To create your own Alberti's window, look at a scene through a transparent surface such as a piece of glass or transparent plastic and, while being careful not to move your head, trace the contours of the scene onto the surface. This procedure is being used by the artist in Figure 7.8, but, instead of drawing the picture directly on the window, he is using a grid on the window to transfer the scene to a canvas. This procedure results in a picture drawn in linear perspective that duplicates the pictorial depth cues in the scene, and therefore creates an impression of depth on the canvas. Another way to create a perspective picture is to take a photograph. The optical system of a camera accomplishes essentially the same thing as Alberti's window and records a perspective picture on film.

The **depth cue of linear perspective** is the perceptual convergence of lines that are parallel in the scene as distance increases (Figure 7.9). The greater the distance, the greater the convergence, until, at a distance of infinity (very far away!), these lines meet at a vanishing point. The convergence that we see in perspective pictures also occurs in the environment, as we know from the familiar observation that railway tracks appear to converge as distance increases.

Texture Gradient Another source of depth information is the **texture gradient**: Elements that are equally spaced in a scene appear to be more closely packed as distance increases, such as the square tiles in the floor of Figure 7.9. (Remember that, according to the cue of relative size, more distant objects appear smaller. This is exactly what happens for the far-away elements in the texture gradient.) Texture gradients provide an example of depth information that is located on the "ground," the surface on which objects rest. Research has shown that eliminating the ground decreases our ability to perceive depth. Thus, observers overestimate the distance of an object if they observe it across a gap, but estimate distance accurately if the ground is present (Figure 7.10; Sinai, Ooi, & He, 1998).

Movement-Produced Cues

All of the cues we have described so far work if the observer is stationary. If, however, we decide to take a walk, new cues emerge that further enhance our perception of depth. Hermann von Helmholtz (1866/1911) described the following situation, in which movement enhances depth perception:

Suppose, for instance, that a person is standing still in a thick woods, where it is impossible for him to

Figure 7.8

An artist drawing a picture in perspective using the method of Alberti's window.

Perceiving Depth and Size

Figure 7.9
The Annunciation *(Attributed to Romano). This is an example of a picture drawn in perspective so that lines that are parallel in the actual scene will converge to a vanishing point if extended into the distance.*

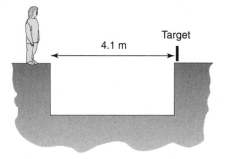

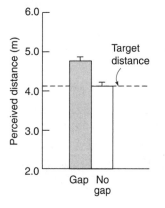

Figure 7.10
Observers underestimate distances viewed across a gap, compared to the same distance viewed across the ground. This may be partially due to loss of information provided by the ground. (Adapted from Sinai et al.,1998.)

distinguish, except vaguely and roughly, in the mass of foliage and branches all around him what belongs to one tree and what to another. But the moment he begins to move forward, everything disentangles itself, and immediately he gets an apperception of the material contents of the woods and their relations to each other in space. (p. 296)

We will describe two different **movement-produced cues**: (1) motion parallax and (2) deletion and accretion.

Motion Parallax   Elaborating further on the effect of movement on depth perception, Helmholtz (1866/1911) described how, as we walk along, nearby objects appear to glide rapidly past us, but more distant objects appear to move more slowly. This effect becomes particularly striking when you look out the side window of a moving car or train. Nearby objects appear to speed by in a blur, while objects on the horizon may appear to be moving only slightly. This difference in the speed of movement for near and far objects is called **motion parallax**, which we can use as a cue to perceive the depths of objects based on how fast they move as we move: Far objects move slowly; near objects move rapidly.

We can understand why motion parallax occurs by looking at the eye in Figure 7.11. This figure

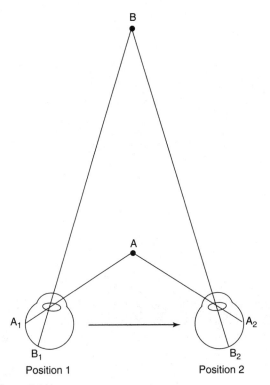

Figure 7.11
One eye, moving from left to right, showing how the images of two objects (A and B) change their position on the retina because of this movement. Notice that the image of the near object, A, moves farther on the retina than the image of the far object, B.

shows what happens to the images of two objects, a near object at A and a far object at B, when the eye moves from position 1 to position 2. When the eye is at position 1, the image of object A is at A_1 on the retina, and when the eye moves to position 2, the image of object A moves all the way across the retina to A_2. The image of object B, on the other hand, moves only from B_1 to B_2 on the retina, What this means for perception is that, as an observer moves from left to right, near objects travel a large distance across the retina and therefore move rapidly across the observer's field of view, but far objects travel a much smaller distance across the retina and therefore move much more slowly across the observer's field of view.

As we will see when we consider how different species perceive depth later in this chapter, motion parallax is one of the most important sources of depth information for many animals. The information provided by motion parallax has also been used to enable human-designed mechanical robots to determine how far they are from obstacles as they navigate through the environment (Srivinisan et al., 1997) and is widely used to create an impression of depth in cartoons and video games.

Deletion and Accretion When two surfaces are located at different distances, as in Figure 7.12a, any sideways movement of the observer causes the surfaces to appear to move relative to one another. The back surface is covered up, or **deleted**, by the one in front when the observer moves in one direction (Figure 7.12b), and the back surface is uncovered, or **accreted**, when the observer moves in the other direction (Figure 7.12c). These cues, which are related both to motion parallax and overlap, since they occur when overlapping surfaces appear to move relative to one another, are especially effective for detecting depth at an edge (Kaplan, 1969).

BINOCULAR DEPTH CUES

web**TUTOR** **Binocular depth cues** depend on both eyes. Convergence of the eyes, which we discussed as an oculomotor cue, can also be classified as a binocular cue since the convergence angle between the eyes specifies depth. Here we will focus on the depth cue of binocular disparity, which is based on the fact that we see two slightly different views of the world because the eyes of the average adult are separated by 6 cm and therefore view the world from different positions.

Binocular Disparity and Stereopsis

The creation of depth perception based on binocular disparity involves two stages. First, **binocular disparity**, the difference in the images on the two eyes, is determined, and then this difference is transformed into the perception of depth. This perception of

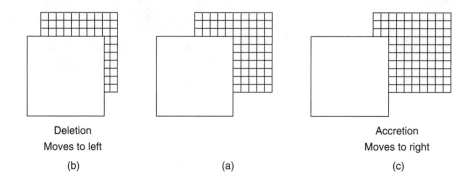

Deletion
Moves to left

(b)

(a)

Accretion
Moves to right

(c)

Figure 7.12

Deletion and accretion occur when an observer moves in a direction not perpendicular to two surfaces that are at different depths. If an observer perceives the two surfaces as in (a) and then moves to the left, deletion occurs so that the front object covers more of the back one, as in (b). If the observer starts at (a) and moves to the right, accretion occurs, so that the front object covers less of the back one, as in (c). Try this with two objects.

depth that results from the information provided by binocular disparity is called **stereopsis** (Figure 7.13). We begin by looking at the first stage of this process, the specification of the differences in the images on the left and right eyes that create disparity. One way to appreciate this difference is through the following demonstration.

◢ **D E M O N S T R A T I O N**

Two Eyes: Two Viewpoints

Hold your two index fingers vertically in front of you, about 6 inches from your face, with about an inch between them. With your right eye closed, position your fingers so that, between them, you can see an object that is a foot or more away (Figure 7.14a). Then close your left eye, open your right eye, and notice how your fingers seem to move to the left, so that the object is no longer visible between them (Figure 7.14b). These two perceptions reflect the different views that are imaged on your left and right retinas (Figures 7.14c and 7.14d). ●

The fact that the two eyes see different views of the world was used by the physicist Charles Wheat-

stone (1802–1875) to create the **stereoscope**, a device that produces a convincing illusion of depth by using two slightly different pictures. This device, extremely popular in the 1800s and reinvented as the View Master in its modern form, presents two photographs that are made with a camera with two lenses separated by the same distance as the eyes. The result is two slightly different views, like those shown in Figure 7.15. The stereoscope presents the left picture to the left eye and the right picture to the right eye so that they combine to result in a convincing three-dimensional perception of the scene.

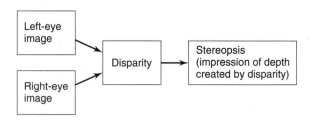

Figure 7.13

Disparity is created by the left-eye and right-eye images, and stereopsis occurs when an impression of depth is created by disparity.

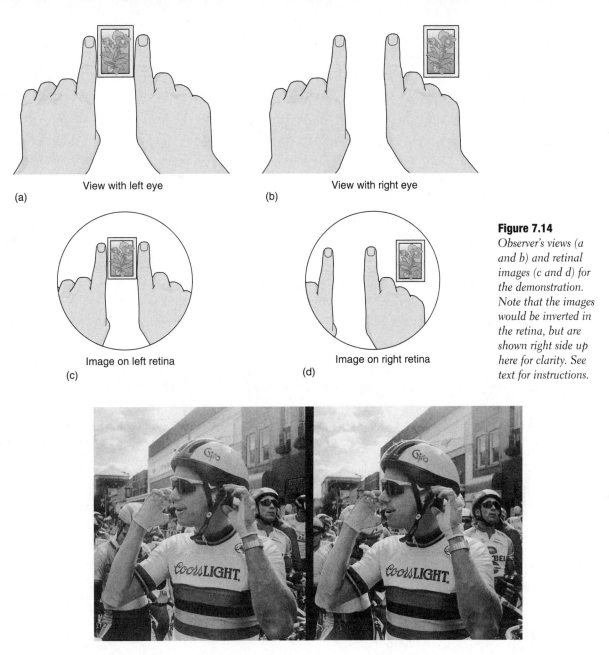

(a) View with left eye

(b) View with right eye

(c) Image on left retina

(d) Image on right retina

Figure 7.14
Observer's views (a and b) and retinal images (c and d) for the demonstration. Note that the images would be inverted in the retina, but are shown right side up here for clarity. See text for instructions.

Figure 7.15
A stereoscopic photograph showing Tour de France winner Greg LeMond at a bicycle race in Ohio in 1989. The picture on the left is the view seen by the left eye, and the picture on the right is the view seen by the right eye. Although the two pictures may at first glance look the same, a closer look reveals differences in the two views. For example, compare the distance between the back of Le Mond's helmet and the man seen over his shoulder in the two views. Differences such as this one result in binocular disparity when a stereoscope presents these two views to each eye separately, and we experience a compelling perception of depth. (Stereogram by Mike Chikiris, Pittsburgh Stereogram Company, Pittsburgh, Pa., 1990.)

Binocular Depth from a Picture, Without a Stereoscope

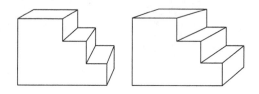

Figure 7.16
See text for instructions on how to view these stairs.

Place a 4 × 6 card vertically, long side up, between the stairs in Figure 7.16, and place your nose against the card so that you are seeing the left-hand drawing with just your left eye and the right-hand drawing with just your right eye. (Blink back and forth to confirm this separation.) Then relax and wait for the two drawings to merge. When the drawings form a single image, you should see the stairs in depth, just as you would if you looked at them through a stereoscope.   ●

The principle behind the stereoscope is also used in 3-D movies. To present different images to the left and right eyes in these movies, the film contains two slightly different images, which are separated into left- and right-eye images when viewed through special glasses (Figure 7.17). The separation of the images can be based on differences in color, in which case the glasses are green for one eye and red for the other, or differences in a property called polarization, in which case the left and right lenses of the glasses admit light that is polarized in different directions.

Figure 7.17
A scene in a movie theater in the 1950s, when three-dimensional movies were first introduced. The glasses create different images in the left and right eyes, and the resulting disparity leads to a convincing impression of depth.

Looking into a stereoscope shows that, when our two eyes receive slightly different images of the same scene, we experience an impression of depth. Wheatstone realized this and coined the term *stereopsis* to describe the impression of depth we experience from the two slightly displaced images on the retina. But what exactly is it about the differences between the images on the two retinas that creates stereopsis? To answer this question, we need to introduce the concept of corresponding retinal points.

Corresponding Retinal Points

For every point on one retina, there is a corresponding point on the other. **Corresponding retinal points** are the places on each retina that connect to the same places in the visual cortex. We can determine approximately where these points are by locating where points on the retinas would overlap if one retina could be slid on top of the other. In Figure 7.18, we see that the two foveas, F and F', fall on corresponding points, and that A and A' and B and B' also fall on corresponding points.

To apply our knowledge of corresponding points to depth perception, assume that the lifeguard in Figure 7.19 is looking directly at Ralph, so his image falls on her foveas (F and F'), which are corresponding points. However, Ralph is not the only person whose image falls on corresponding points.

There is an imaginary circle called the **horopter** that passes through the point of fixation (Figure 7.20). Any object that is on this circle falls on corresponding points on the two retinas. In our example, the

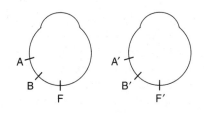

Figure 7.18
Corresponding points on the two retinas. To determine corresponding points, imagine that one eye is slid on top of the other.

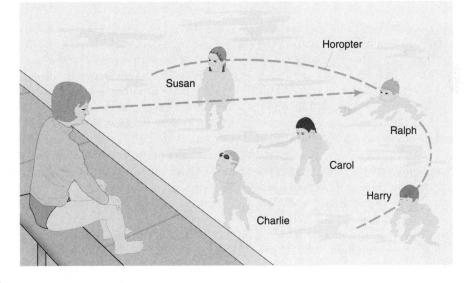

Figure 7.19
When the lifeguard looks at Ralph, the images of Ralph, Susan, and Harry fall on the horopter indicated by the dashed line. Thus, Ralph's, Susan's, and Harry's images fall on corresponding points on the lifeguard's retinas, and the images of all of the other swimmers fall on noncorresponding points.

Perceiving Depth and Size

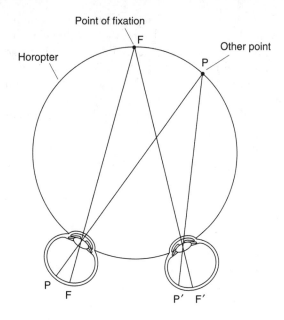

Figure 7.20
The horopter, showing how the images of two points on the horopter, F and P, fall on corresponding points F, F' and P, P', on the retinas. (From Gillam, 1995.)

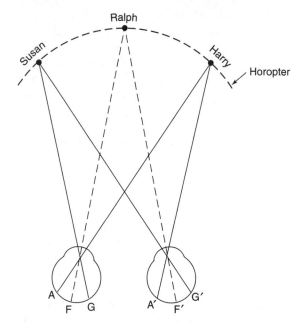

Figure 7.21
What's happening to the images of Susan, Ralph, and Harry inside the lifeguard's eyes? Susan's image falls on corresponding points G and G'; Ralph's image falls on the foveas, F and F' (which are corresponding points); and Harry's image falls on corresponding points A and A'.

horopter not only passes through Ralph's head (the point of fixation) but also through the heads of Harry and Susan. Thus, Harry's and Susan's images fall on corresponding points on the lifeguard's retinas, as shown in Figure 7.21. (The situation we are describing here holds only if the lifeguard is looking at Ralph. If she changes her point of fixation, then a new horopter is created that passes through the new point of fixation.)

What does the horopter have to do with depth perception? To answer this question, let's consider where Carol's and Charlie's images fall on the lifeguard's retinas. Since their heads are not located on the horopter, their images fall on **noncorresponding** (or **disparate**) **points**, as indicated in Figure 7.22. For example, Carol's image falls on noncorresponding points B and G'. (Note that if you slid the retinas on top of each other, points B and G' would not overlap.) The corresponding point to B is, in fact, located at B', far from G'.

The angle between G' and B' is called the **angle of disparity**, and the key to binocular depth perception is that the farther the object is from the horopter, the greater is the angle of disparity. You can understand this by noticing that Charlie's images, which fall on A and H', are more disparate than Carol's images. Thus, the amount of disparity indicates how far Charlie and Carol are from where the lifeguard is looking. Since Charlie's angle of disparity is greater than Carol's, he must be located farther from the horopter and is therefore closer to the lifeguard.

When objects are located in front of the horopter, as Carol and Charlie are, their images move out to the sides of the retinas, and the resulting disparity is called **crossed disparity**. When objects are located beyond the horopter, as in Figure 7.23, their images move inward on the retinas, creating a condition called **uncrossed disparity**. The farther behind the

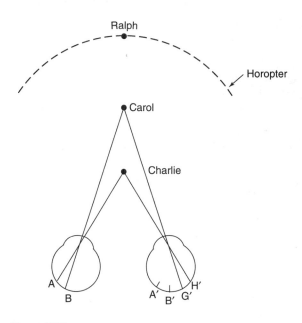

Figure 7.22
What's happening to the images of Carol and Charlie in the lifeguard's eyes? Since Carol and Charlie are not located on the horopter, their images fall on noncorresponding points.

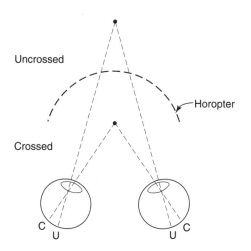

Figure 7.23
Crossed disparity occurs for objects in front of the horopter; uncrossed disparity occurs for objects behind the horopter. Notice how the retinal images move inward, toward the nose, as the object moves farther away.

horopter an object is, the more its images move inward on the retinas, and the greater is its disparity. Thus, crossed disparity indicates that an object is nearer than the horopter, and uncrossed disparity indicates that an object is farther than the horopter. (To remember which disparity is crossed and which is uncrossed, just remember that you have to cross your eyes to fixate on objects as they get nearer. Near objects create crossed disparity.)

We have seen that the disparity information contained in the images on the retinas provides information indicating an object's distance from where we are looking. Thus, when we look in a stereoscope or at a scene in the world, the different views we see with our left and right eyes create disparity, and this disparity generates the impression of depth called stereopsis (Figure 7.13).

Although our conclusion that disparity creates stereopsis may seem reasonable, showing that we perceive depth when two slightly displaced views are presented to the left and the right eyes doesn't prove that disparity is creating the depth we see. We can understand why this is so by realizing that scenes such as the one in Figure 7.15 also contain other depth cues, such as occlusion and relative size, that could be contributing to our perception of depth. How can we tell whether depth perception is caused by disparity, by pictorial cues, or by a combination of both? Bela Julesz answered this question by creating a stimulus that contained no pictorial cues, called the random-dot stereogram.

Random-Dot Stereogram

By creating stereoscopic images of random-dot patterns, Julesz (1971) showed that subjects can perceive depth in displays that contain no depth information other than disparity. Two such random-dot patterns, which constitute a **random-dot stereogram**, are shown in Figure 7.24. These patterns were constructed by first generating two identical random-dot patterns on a computer and then shifting a square-shaped section of the dots to the right, in the pattern on the right. This shift is too subtle to be seen in these dot patterns, but we can understand how it is accomplished by looking at the diagrams

Figure 7.24

Top: A random-dot stereogram.
Bottom: The principle for constructing the stereogram. See text for an explanation.

below the dot patterns. In these diagrams, the black dots are indicated by 0's, A's, and X's and the white dots by 1's, B's, and Y's. The A's and B's indicate the square-shaped section where the shift is made in the pattern. Notice that the A's and B's are shifted one unit to the right in the right-hand pattern. The X's and Y's indicate areas uncovered by the shift that must be filled in with new black dots and white dots to complete the pattern.

The effect of shifting one section of the pattern in this way is to create disparity. When the two patterns are presented to the left and the right eyes in a stereoscope, we perceive a small square floating above the background. Since binocular disparity is the only depth information present in these stereograms, disparity alone must be causing the perception of depth that we perceive.

Psychophysical experiments, particularly those using Julesz's random-dot stereograms, have shown

that retinal disparity gives rise to a perception of depth. But how is this disparity information on the retinas translated into depth information in the brain? A number of researchers have shown that neurons in the visual cortex of the cat and the monkey respond to specific degrees of disparity.

Disparity Information in the Brain

There are cells in the striate cortex (V1) that are called **binocular depth cells** or **disparity detectors** because they respond best to stimuli that fall on points separated by a specific angle of disparity on the two retinas (Barlow, Blakemore, & Pettigrew, 1967; Hubel & Wiesel, 1970). The principle behind these cells is shown in Figure 7.25. Figure 7.25a shows a person's eye as he or she looks at an object at P. Since the person is looking directly at P, the image of object P falls on the foveas of the two eyes and so stimulates corresponding points. The image of object Q falls on the fovea of the left eye but does not fall on the fovea of the right eye. Thus the image of object Q falls on noncorresponding points.

Figure 7.25b and c shows two **binocular depth cells**. Figure 7.25b shows a neuron that responds to simultaneous stimulation of points P and P′. Since P and P′ are corresponding points, there is no disparity between them, and so this neuron responds to **zero disparity**. Figure 7.25c shows a neuron that responds when noncorresponding points Q and Q′ are stimulated. This cell is a **disparity selective neuron**.

Figure 7.26 shows the results of a survey of 272 neurons from areas V1 and V2 of the cat's cortex, which shows that some neurons respond to zero or near-zero disparity and many respond to either crossed (near) or uncrossed (far) disparity (Levay & Voigt, 1988; see also Poggio, 1995). Researchers have also found disparity-selective neurons all along the dorsal ("where" or "how") pathway, in areas V2 and MT (Cumming & Parker, 1999; DeAngelis, Cumming, & Newsome, 2000; Ohzawa, 1998; Ohzawa et al., 1996; Van Essen & DeYoe, 1995); and neurons involved in depth perception are also found in the ventral (or "what") pathway (Tyler, 1990).

Do these disparity-selective neurons cause stereopsis? Showing that these neurons exist does not prove that they have anything to do with perceiving depth. To show that these neurons are actually involved in

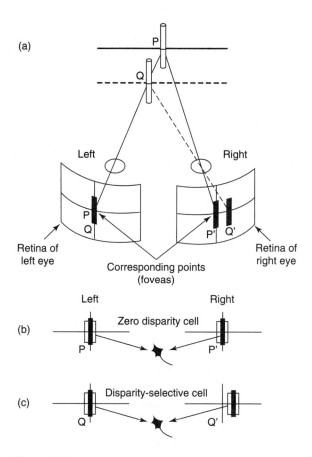

Figure 7.25

(a) The image of P falls on corresponding points since the person is looking at it. The image of Q falls on noncorresponding points. (b) A zero-disparity neuron fires to the images of P, which fall on corresponding points. (c) A disparity-selective neuron responds to the images of Q, on noncorresponding points. This particular neuron is tuned to respond to Q's specific amount of disparity. (From Ohzawa et al., 1996.)

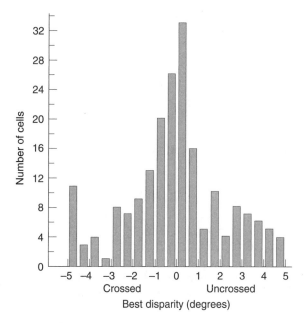

Figure 7.26

Histogram based on 272 neurons, which shows the number of cells that respond best to different angles of disparity. (From LeVay and Voigt, 1988.)

Perceiving Depth and Size

What brain area is activated when stereopsis occurs? Ingrid Kwee and coworkers (1999) answered this question by recording the fMRI response of subjects as they viewed pairs of images of the cerebral circulation. These subjects were neurosurgeons who were trained in stereoscopic vision, so they were able to fuse these images to create a three-dimensional perception of the circulation. This is basically what you were asked to do for the pictures of steps in the Demonstration "Binocular Depth from a Picture, Without a Stereoscope."

The key to this experiment is that two types of pictures were used: (1) A two-dimensional (2-D) set, which created a two-dimensional perception when fused; and (2) a three-dimensional (3-D) set, which created a three-dimensional perception when fused. These images looked almost identical under regular

viewing conditions but looked different when fused, with the 2-D pair appearing two-dimensional and the 3-D pair appearing three-dimensional. Kwee and coworkers used the fMRI subtraction technique (see page 27) to determine the areas of the brain activated by stereopsis. When they subtracted the brain activity caused by fusing the 2-D pair from the activity when fusing the 3-D pair, they found activation in the parietal cortex. This area is in the dorsal ("where" or "how") stream, which makes sense since seeing in depth is important for locating objects and ourselves in space. Also, this area corresponds to the area that contains binocular depth cells in the monkey and that is often damaged in patients who have lost stereoscopic vision due to accidents or stroke (Ptito et al., 1993).

depth perception, we need to do behavioral experiments. Randolph Blake and Helmut Hirsch (1975) did such an experiment, in which they raised cats so that they experienced only monocular vision for the first six months of their lives. Their vision was alternated between the left and right eyes every other day during this period. When Blake and Hirsch recorded from neurons in the cortex, they found that these cats had few binocular neurons, and when they tested them behaviorally they found they were not able to use binocular disparity to perceive depth. Thus, Blake and Hirsch showed that eliminating binocular neurons eliminates stereopsis and confirmed what everyone suspected all along—that disparity-selective neurons are responsible for stereopsis. Thus, if an animal's convergence is fixed (that is, if its eyes are positioned to look at a particular point in space and don't move), the cells that fire best to different disparities will be excited by stimuli lying at different distances

from the animal, and the animal will perceive these stimuli as being at different distances.

Recent research has demonstrated a connection between disparity and depth perception in another way. Gregory DeAngelis, Bruce Cumming, and William Newsome (1998) trained monkeys to indicate the depths of dots that had different depths, indicated by their different disparities. They took advantage of the fact that neurons that are sensitive to the same disparities tend to be organized in clusters in the MT cortex and electrically stimulated one of these clusters. When they did this, they found that the monkey shifted its depth judgments toward the depth favored by the stimulated neurons (Figure 7.27).

The results of this experiment indicate that the firing of these disparity detectors apparently affected the monkey's depth perception. This is an example of an experiment in which both the neural response and perception (relationship C in Figure 1.9) are meas-

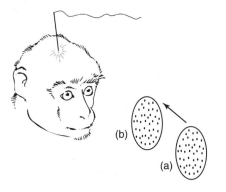

Figure 7.27

DeAngelis and coworkers (1998) stimulated neurons in a monkey's MT cortex that were sensitive to a particular amount of disparity, while the monkey was observing a random-dot stereogram. This stimulation shifted perception of the dots from position (a) to position (b).

ured simultaneously in the same animal. As we mentioned in Chapter 1, simultaneous measurements such as this are difficult to achieve but are the most powerful way to demonstrate connections between physiology and perception.

With the identification of disparity information as an important source of depth information, it may appear that our understanding of binocular depth perception is complete. However, before we conclude our discussion of disparity, we need to consider an important step in the determination of stereopsis that we have so far ignored. To use disparity, the visual system needs to match points on one image with similar points on the other image. This is called the **correspondence problem**.

The Correspondence Problem

To help us understand the correspondence problem, let's return to the stereoscopic images of Figure 7.15. When we view this image in a stereoscope, we see different parts of the image at different depths because of the disparity between images on the left and right retinas. Thus, Greg LeMond and the man on the right appear to be at different distances when viewed through the stereoscope, because they create different amounts of disparity. But in order for the visual sys-

tem to calculate this disparity, it must compare the two images of Greg LeMond on the left and right retinas and the two images of the man on the left and right retinas.

How does the visual system compare the two Greg LeMonds? A possible answer to this question is that the visual system may match LeMond's images on the left and right retinas on the basis of the specific features of the images, matching his face on the left with his face on the right, and so on. Explained in this way, the solution to the correspondence problem seems simple: Since most things in the world are quite discriminable from each other, it is easy to match an image on the left retina with the image of the same thing on the right retina. However, as we have seen many times already in this book, things are often not as simple as they seem. The correspondence problem is a perfect example because it becomes more complex when we consider Julesz's random-dot stereograms.

You can appreciate the problem involved in matching similar parts of a stereogram by trying to match up the points in the left and right images of the stereogram in Figure 7.24. Most people find this to be an extremely difficult task, involving switching their gaze back and forth between the two pictures and comparing small areas of the pictures one after another. Matching similar features on a random-dot stereogram is much more difficult and time consuming than matching features in the real world, yet the visual system somehow matches similar parts of the two stereogram images, calculates their disparities, and creates a perception of depth. A number of proposals, all too complex to describe here, have been put forth to explain how the visual system solves the correspondence problem for random-dot stereograms, but a totally satisfactory answer has yet to be proposed (see Blake & Wilson, 1991; Ohzawa, 1998).

Our discussion of depth perception has revealed that a number of cues contribute to our perception of depth, including the oculomotor cues and the monocular and binocular cues. As shown in Figure 7.28, these cues work over different distances, some working only at close range (convergence and accommodation), some at close and medium ranges (relative height, motion parallax, binocular disparity),

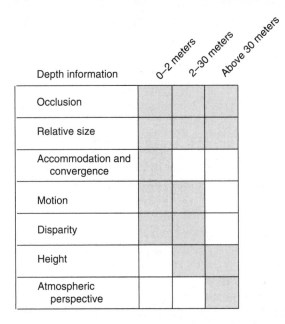

Depth information	0–2 meters	2–30 meters	Above 30 meters
Occlusion	▓	▓	▓
Relative size	▓	▓	▓
Accommodation and convergence	▓		
Motion	▓	▓	
Disparity	▓	▓	
Height		▓	▓
Atmospheric perspective			▓

Figure 7.28

Range of effectiveness of different depth cues. Occlusion and relative size work over the entire range of vision, from close up to very far away. Accommodation is effective only at distances less than 2 meters, and atmospheric perspective provides useful depth information only at distances above 30 meters. (Based on Cutting and Vishton, 1995.)

some at long range (atmospheric perspective), and some at the whole range of depth perception (occlusion and relative size) (Cutting & Vishton, 1995).

No one of these depth cues is crucial to our perception of depth. For example, we can eliminate binocular disparity by closing one eye, yet because of the remaining monocular cues we still see some depth. Depth cues, therefore, provide overlapping information and work together to create our perception of depth (Bruno & Cutting, 1988; Landy et al., 1995; Tittle & Braunstein, 1993).

DEPTH INFORMATION ACROSS SPECIES

Humans make use of a number of different sources of depth information in the environment. But what about other species? Many animals have excellent depth perception. Cats leap on their prey; monkeys swing from one branch to the next; a male housefly follows a flying female, maintaining a constant distance of about 10 cm; and a frog accurately jumps across a chasm (Figure 7.29).

There is no doubt that many animals are able to judge distances in their environment, but what depth information do they use? A survey of mechanisms used by different animals reveals that animals use the

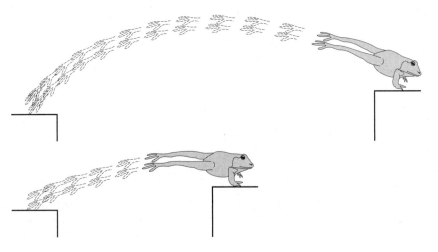

Figure 7.29

These drawings, which are based on photographs of frogs jumping, show that the frog adjusts the angle of its jump based on its perception of the distance across the chasm, with steeper takeoffs being associated with greater distances. (Adapted from Collett & Harkness, 1982.)

entire range of cues described in this chapter, some animals using many cues and others relying on just one or two.

To make use of binocular disparity, an animal must have eyes that have overlapping visual fields. Thus, animals such as cats, monkeys, and humans, that have **frontal eyes** resulting in overlapping fields of view (Figure 7.30a), can use disparity to perceive depth. Animals with **lateral eyes**, such as the rabbit, do not have overlapping visual fields (Figure 7.30b) and therefore cannot use disparity to perceive depth.

The pigeon is an example of an animal with lateral eyes that are placed so the visual fields of the left and right eyes overlap only in a 35-degree area surrounding the pigeon's beak. This overlapping area, however, happens to be exactly where pieces of grain would be located when the pigeon is pecking at them, and psychophysical experiments have shown that pigeons do have a small area of binocular depth perception right in front of their beaks (McFadden, 1987; McFadden & Wild, 1986).

Like humans, many animals use more than one type of depth cue in order to obtain the most accurate depth information possible. For example, frogs and toads use binocular vision to perceive depth; but, if they are able to use only one eye, they can still use accommodation and other cues to judge how far they need to jump to capture prey (Collett & Harkness, 1982).

Many animals use information other than disparity to determine distances. Consider, for example, a rather strange water bug, the back swimmer *Notonecta*, which hangs upside down just below the surface of the water as it lies in wait for prey that may be approaching on the surface above it (Figure 7.31). *Notonecta* initially detects its prey by sensing vibrations and then makes a distance judgment based on the position of the prey's image on its retina. The image of distant prey falls on the part of the retina nearest the surface of the water, and, as the prey approaches, its image moves down on the retina (Collett & Harkness, 1982; Schwind, 1978).

Movement parallax is probably insects' most important method of judging distance, and they use it in a number of different ways (Collett, 1978; Srinivasan et al., 1997). For example, the locust makes a "peering" response—moving its body from side to side to create movement of its head—as it observes potential prey. T. S. Collett (1978) measured a locust's

(a)

(b)

Figure 7.30

(a) Frontal eyes such as those of the cat have overlapping fields of view that provide good depth perception. (b) Lateral eyes such as those of the rabbit provide a panoramic view but poorer depth perception.

Perceiving Depth and Size

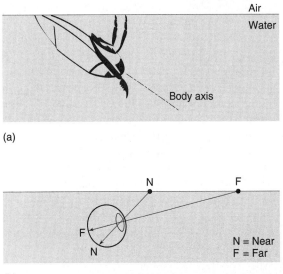

(a)

(b)

N = Near
F = Far

Figure 7.31

The backswimmer Notonecta *awaits beneath the surface of the water. A faraway object located at F on the water creates an image at F on the retina, and, as the object moves toward N on the water, its image moves toward N on the retina. Thus, the backswimmer can detect where its prey is on the surface of the water based on the position of its image on the retina. (From Schwind, 1978.)*

"peering amplitude"—the distance of this side-to-side sway—as it observed prey at different distances and found that the locust swayed more when targets were farther away. Since more distant objects move less across the retina than nearer objects for a particular amount of observer movement (see Figure 7.11), a larger sway would be needed to cause the image of a far object to move the same distance across the retina as the image of a near object. The locust may therefore be judging distance by noting how much sway is needed to cause the image to move a particular distance across its retina (see also Sobel, 1990).

Another example of an animal that uses image movement to detect depth is the honeybee, which uses the information produced by the image movement that occurs as it flies across a field to determine the distances of nearby and faraway flowers (Lehrer et al., 1988; Srinivasan et al., 1997).

All of the above examples show how depth can be determined from different sources of information in light. But bats, who are blind to light, use a form of energy we usually associate with sound to sense depth. Bats sense objects by using a method similar to the sonar system first used in World War II to detect underwater objects such as submarines and mines. Sonar, which stands for **so**und **na**vigation and **ra**nging, works by sending out pulses of sound and using information contained in the echoes of this sound to determine the location of objects. Griffin (1944) coined the term **echolocation** to describe the biological sonar system used by bats to avoid objects in the dark.

Bats emit pulsed sounds that are far above the upper limit of human hearing, and they sense objects' distances by noting the interval between when they send out the pulse and when they receive the echo (Figure 7.32). Since they use sound echoes to sense objects, they can avoid obstacles even when it is totally dark (Suga, 1990). Although we don't have any way of knowing what the bat experiences when these echoes return, we do know that the timing of these echoes provides the information the bat needs to locate objects in its environment. (See also von der Emde et al., 1998, for a description of how electric fish sense depth based on "electrolocation.")

From the examples we have described, we can see that animals use a number of different types of information to determine depth. The type of information used depends on the animal's specific needs and on its anatomy and physiological makeup. *Notonecta*, lying in wait for prey just under the waterline, needs only very rudimentary depth perception and has limited physical capabilities, so it uses a simple system to perceive its potential prey's distance. Humans, monkeys, and pigeons, which must negotiate their way through complex environments, need more precise depth perception that operates over a variety of distances. They therefore make use of a number of different depth cues that enable them to rapidly determine the locations of both nearby and faraway objects. And bats, who have no vision, use a totally different system, involving sound-ranging to locate objects. All of these examples show that there are many different ways to locate objects in space.

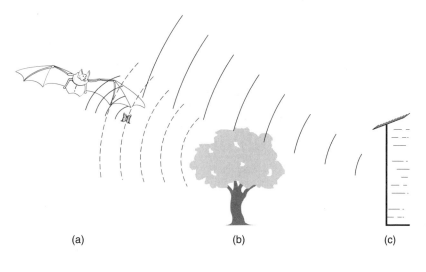

Figure 7.32

When a bat sends out its pulses, it receives echoes from a number of objects in its environment. This figure shows the echoes received by the bat from (a) a moth located about half a meter away; (b) a tree, located about 2 meters away; and (c) a house, located about 4 meters away. The echoes from each object return to the bat at different times, with echoes from more distant objects taking longer to return. The bat locates the positions of objects in the environment by sensing how long it takes the echoes to return.

(a)   (b)   (c)

SUMMARY TABLE 7.1

The Problem of Depth Perception

One of the problems of depth perception is that there is no way to determine the location of a light source based just on individual points of stimulation on the retina. Information in the overall image on the retina needs to be taken into account. One way this has been done is by using the cue approach, which focuses on identifying information in the retinal image that is correlated with depth in the scene.

Oculomotor and Monocular Depth Cues

The oculomotor cues of convergence and accommodation are based on the inward movement of the eyes and the tightening of the eye muscles during focusing. These cues are effective only for nearby objects. The monocular cues, which work with one eye, include the pictorial cues—occlusion, relative height, cast shadows, relative size, familiar size, atmospheric perspective, linear perspective, and texture gradients—and movement-produced cues—motion parallax and deletion and accretion.

Binocular Disparity and Stereopsis

Binocular disparity, the difference in the image on the two eyes, can result in stereopsis, the perception of depth. Disparity, which occurs normally in the environment because the two eyes view a scene from slightly different positions, occurs when some objects are on corresponding retinal points and other objects are on noncorre-

sponding retinal points. The degree of noncorrespondence, which is called disparity, provides information for depth perception.

Random-Dot Stereograms, Physiology, and the Correspondence Problem

By using a random-dot stereogram, it can be demonstrated that disparity alone, without any of the other cues, can result in a perception of depth. There are binocular depth cells in the cortex that are tuned to specific disparities and that are involved in depth perception. Brain imaging experiments indicate that stereopsis activates an area in the parietal cortex. In order for disparity information to be useful, it is necessary to match points on one image in the retina with similar points on the other image. This is called the correspondence problem.

Depth Information Across Species

Different species rely on different types of information to perceive depth. Animals with frontal eyes use disparity, while animals with lateral eyes are unable to use disparity unless there is some overlap in the visual fields of the two eyes, as in the pigeon, which has a small overlap. The water bug *Notonecta* uses relative position on the retina to sense depth, the locust uses movement parallax, and the honeybee also uses movement information. Bats sense depth using sonar.

Perceiving Depth and Size

PERCEIVING SIZE

We discuss size perception next, because our perception of size can be affected by our perception of depth. This link between size perception and depth perception is graphically illustrated by the following example:

> Whiteout—one of the most treacherous weather conditions possible for flying—can arise quickly and unexpectedly. As Frank pilots his helicopter across the Antarctic wastes, blinding light, reflected down from thick cloud cover above and up from the pure white blanket of snow below, makes it difficult to see the horizon, details on the surface of the snow, or even up from down. He is aware of the danger because he has known pilots dealing with similar conditions who had flown at full power directly into the ice. He thinks he can make out a vehicle on the snow far below, and he drops a smoke grenade to check his altitude. To his horror, the grenade falls only three feet before hitting the ground. Realizing that what he thought was a truck was actually a discarded box, Frank pulls back on the controls and soars up, his face drenched in sweat, as he comprehends how close he just came to becoming another whiteout fatality.

The fictional account above is based on actual descriptions of flying conditions at an Antarctic research base. It illustrates that our ability to perceive an object's size can sometimes be drastically affected by our ability to perceive the object's distance. A small box seen close up can, in the absence of accurate information about its distance, be misperceived as a large truck seen from far away (Figure 7.33). The idea that we can misperceive size if accurate depth information is not present was demonstrated in a classic experiment by A. H. Holway and Edwin Boring.

The Holway and Boring Experiment

The setup for Holway and Boring's experiment is shown in Figures 7.34 and 7.35. The observer sits at

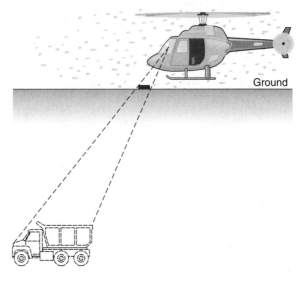

Figure 7.33
When the helicopter pilot loses the ability to perceive distance, due to whiteout, a small box that is close can be mistaken for a truck that is far away.

the intersection of two hallways and sees a luminous test circle when looking down the right hallway and a luminous comparison circle when looking down the left hallway. The comparison circle is always 10 feet from the observer, but the test circles are presented at distances ranging from 10 feet to 120 feet. The observer's task on each trial is to adjust the diameter of the comparison circle to match that of the test circle.

An important feature of the test stimuli is that they all cast exactly the same-sized image on the retina. We can understand how this was accomplished by remembering the concept of visual angle from Chapter 3 (see page 88) and noting that objects with the same visual angle cast the same-sized image on the retina. Each of the test circles has the same visual angle and so creates identical overlapping images on the observer's retina (Figure 7.36).

In the first part of Holway and Boring's experiment, many depth cues were available, so the observer could easily judge the distance of the test circles. The results, indicated by line 1 in Figure 7.37, show that, even though all of the retinal images were the same

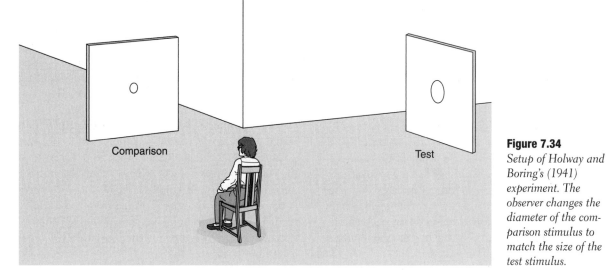

Figure 7.34
Setup of Holway and Boring's (1941) experiment. The observer changes the diameter of the comparison stimulus to match the size of the test stimulus.

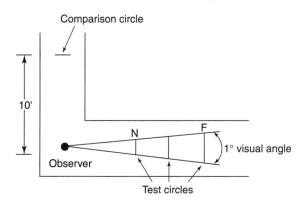

Figure 7.35
Top view of Holway and Boring's experiment. The key feature of this experiment is that the test circles all have the same visual angle and therefore cast the same image on the observer's retinas. (Adapted from Holway & Boring, 1941.)

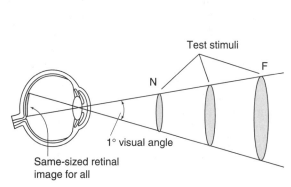

Figure 7.36
All of the test stimuli in the Holway and Boring experiment had the same visual angle. This means that they all cast the same-sized image on the retina.

size, the observers based their judgments on the physical sizes of the circles. When they viewed a large test circle that was located far away (such as F in Figure 7.36), they made the comparison circle large (Point F in Figure 7.37). If, however, they viewed a small test circle that was located nearby (such as N in Figure 7.36), they made the comparison circle small (Point N

in Figure 7.37). The fact that they always adjusted the comparison circle to match the physical size of the test circle means that they were accurately judging the actual sizes of the circles.

Holway and Boring then asked how accurate the subjects' judgments would be if they began eliminating depth information from the hallway. They did this by having the observer view the test circles with one eye (line 2), then by having the observer view the test circles through a peephole (line 3), and finally by adding drapes to the hallway to eliminate reflections

Perceiving Depth and Size

(line 4). The results of these experiments indicate that, as it became harder to determine the distance of the test circles, the observer's perception of the sizes of the circles became very inaccurate. Eliminating depth information makes it more difficult to judge the actual sizes of objects and, when there is little depth information, our perception of size tends to be determined not by the actual sizes of objects but by the size of the objects' retinal images. Since all of the test circles in Holway and Boring's experiment had the same retinal size, they were judged to be the same size once depth information was eliminated. Thus, the results of Holway and Boring's experiment indicate that size estimation is based on the actual sizes of objects when there is good depth information and that size estimation is strongly influenced by the object's visual angle if depth information is eliminated.

Another example of size perception that is determined by visual angle is our perception of the sizes of the sun and the moon, which have the same visual angle. The fact that the sun and the moon have identical visual angles becomes most obvious during an eclipse of the sun. Although we can see the flaming corona of the sun surrounding the moon, as shown in Figure 7.38, the moon's disk almost exactly covers the disk of the sun.

If we calculate the visual angles of the sun and the moon, the result is 0.5 degrees for both. As you can see in Figure 7.38, the moon is small (diameter 2,200 miles) but close (245,000 miles from earth), while the sun is large (diameter 865,400 miles) but far away (93 million miles from earth). Even though these two celestial bodies are vastly different in size, we perceive them to be the same size because, as we are unable to perceive their distance, we base our judgment on their visual angles.

Yet another example of a situation in which visual angle determines our perception of size, because inadequate depth information is available, is the way we perceive objects viewed from a high-flying airplane as being very small. Since we have no way of accurately estimating the distance from the airplane to the ground, we perceive size based on objects' visual angles, which are very small because we are so high up.

Size Constancy

The examples described above all demonstrate a link between our perception of size and our perception of depth, with good depth perception favoring accurate size perception. And even though our perception of size is not always totally accurate (Gilinsky, 1951), it is good enough to cause psychologists to propose the principle of **size constancy**. The principle of size constancy states that our perception of an object's

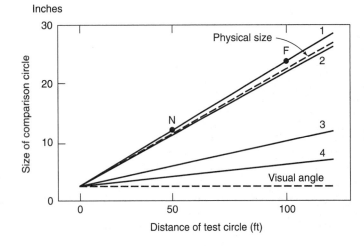

Figure 7.37

Results of Holway and Boring's experiment. The dashed line marked "physical size" is the result that would be expected if the observers adjusted the diameter of the comparison circle to match the actual diameter of the test circle. The line marked "visual angle" is the result that would be expected if the observers adjusted the diameter of the comparison circle to match the visual angle of the test circle. Points N and F correspond to test stimuli N and F in 7.36 for the condition when there was an abundance of depth cues. (Adapted from Holway & Boring, 1941.)

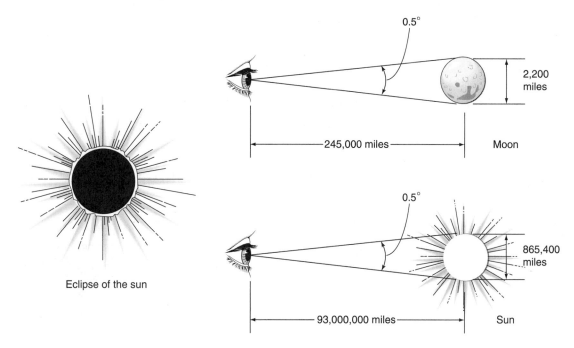

Figure 7.38
The moon's disk almost exactly covers the sun during an eclipse, because the sun and the moon have the same visual angles.

Eclipse of the sun

0.5°

2,200 miles

245,000 miles — Moon

0.5°

865,400 miles

93,000,000 miles — Sun

size remains relatively constant, even when viewing an object from different distances, changing the size of the object's image on the retina.

To introduce the idea of size constancy to my sensation and perception class, I ask for a volunteer from the front row. I stand about 3 feet away and ask the person to estimate my height. They are usually pretty close, guessing around 5 feet 10 inches. I then take one large step back so I am now 6 feet away and ask the person to estimate my height again. It probably doesn't surprise you that their estimate of my height remains about the same, even though I'm twice as far away. The point of this demonstration is that even though the size of my image on the person's retina is halved when I step back to six feet (Figure 7.39), the person senses my size as remaining about the same. This is size constancy. The following demonstration illustrates size constancy in another way.

D E M O N S T R A T I O N

Perceiving Size at a Distance

Hold a quarter between the fingertips of each hand so you can see the faces of both coins. Hold one coin about a foot from you and the other at arm's length. Observe the coins with both of your eyes open and note their sizes. Under these conditions, most people perceive the near and far coins as being approximately the same size. Now close one eye, and holding the coins so they appear side-by-side, notice how your perception of the size of the far coin changes so that it now appears smaller than the near coin. This demonstrates how size constancy is decreased under conditions of poor depth information. ●

The link between size constancy and depth perception has led to the proposal that when depth

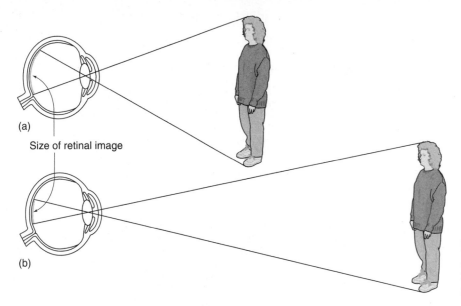

(a)

Size of retinal image

(b)

Figure 7.39
Doubling the distance from the eye halves the size of the image on the retina.

information is available, our perception of size is based on a constancy-scaling mechanism that supplements the information available on the retinas by taking an object's distance into account (Gregory, 1966). This constancy-scaling mechanism, which we will call **size–distance scaling**, operates according to the equation $S = K(R \times D)$, where S is the object's perceived size, K is a constant, R is the size of the retinal image, and D is the perceived distance of the object. Thus, as a person walks away from you, the size of her image on your retina, R, gets smaller, but your perception of her distance, D, gets larger. These two changes balance each other, and the net result is that you perceive her size, S, as remaining constant.

 D E M O N S T R A T I O N

Size–Distance Scaling and Emmert's Law

You can demonstrate size–distance scaling to yourself by looking at the center of the circle in Figure 7.40 for about 60 seconds. Then look at the white space to the side of the circle and blink to see the circle's afterimage. Before the afterimage fades, also look at a wall far across the room. You should see that the size of the afterimage depends on where you look. If you look at a distant surface, such as the far wall of the room, you see a large afterimage that appears to be far away. If you look at a near surface such as the page of this book, you see a small afterimage that appears to be close. ●

Figure 7.41 illustrates the principle underlying the effect you just experienced, which was first described by Emmert in 1881. Staring at the circle in Figure 7.40 bleaches a small circular area of visual pigment on your retina. This bleached area of the retina determines the retinal size of the after-

Figure 7.40
Afterimage stimulus.

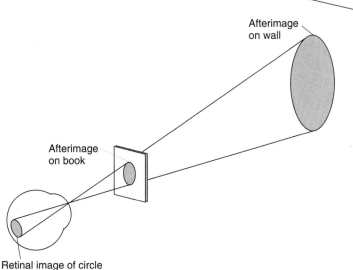

Afterimage on wall

Afterimage on book

Retinal image of circle
(bleached pigment)

Figure 7.41
The principle behind the observation that the size of an afterimage increases as the afterimage is viewed against more distant surfaces.

image and remains constant no matter where you are looking.

The perceived size of the afterimage, as shown in Figure 7.41, is determined by the distance of the surface against which the afterimage is viewed. This relationship between the apparent distance of an afterimage and its perceived size is known as **Emmert's law**: The farther away an afterimage appears, the larger it will seem. This result follows from our size–distance scaling equation, $S = R \times D$. Since the size of the bleached area of pigment on the retina, R, always stays the same, increasing the afterimage's distance, D, increases the magnitude of $R \times D$ so we perceive the size of the afterimage, S, as larger when it is viewed against the far wall.

Although we have been stressing the link between size constancy and depth perception, there are other sources of information in the environment that also help us perceive size accurately. One source of information for size is relative size. We often use the sizes of familiar objects in our environment as a yardstick to judge the size of other objects, as in Figure 7.42. And we can also use the relationship between objects and depth information on the ground to help us judge sizes. Thus, Figure 7.43 shows two cylinders

Figure 7.42
The size of this wheel becomes apparent when it can be compared to an object of known size such as the person. If the wheel were seen in total isolation, it would be difficult to know that it is so large.

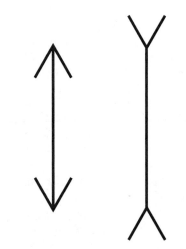

Figure 7.43

A texture gradient with two cylinders. The fact that the bases of both cylinders cover the same number of units on the gradient provides information that the bases of the two cylinders are the same size.

sitting on a texture gradient formed by a cobblestone road. Even if we had trouble perceiving the depth of the near and far cylinders, we can tell that they are the same size, because both cover the same small portion of a paving stone.

VISUAL ILLUSIONS

WebTUTOR Size constancy contributes to our experience of **veridical perception**—perception that matches the actual physical situation. Veridical perception is most likely to occur in well-lit natural environments in which lots of information is available for perception. But if conditions are such that we receive inaccurate information, as did our heli-

copter pilot in whiteout weather conditions, veridical perception breaks down and we experience an **illusion**—a nonveridical perception such as mistaking a small box for a truck.

The size illusion experienced by our helicopter pilot is an example of an illusion occurring in the natural environment. However, most of the illusions that psychologists have studied are ones that they have devised, like the **Müller-Lyer illusion** in Figure 7.44. The goal in constructing these illusions is to do experiments that will uncover the mechanism responsible for the illusion. As we consider some of these illusions, we will see that researchers do not always agree on what causes them.

The Müller-Lyer Illusion

In the Müller-Lyer illusion, the right vertical line appears to be longer than the left vertical line, even though they are both exactly the same length (measure them). The fact that one line appears longer than the other is obvious by just looking at these figures, but you can measure how much longer the right line appears by using the simple matching procedure described in the following demonstration.

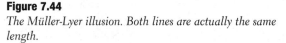

Figure 7.44

The Müller-Lyer illusion. Both lines are actually the same length.

D E M O N S T R A T I O N

Measuring the Müller-Lyer Illusion

The first step in measuring the Müller-Lyer illusion is to create some stimuli. Create a "standard stimulus" by drawing a line 30 millimeters long on an index card and adding outward-going fins, as in the right figure in Figure 7.44. Then, on separate cards, create "comparison stimuli" by drawing lines 28, 30, 32, 34, 36, 38, and 40 millimeters long with inward-going fins, as in the left figure. Then, ask your subject to pick the comparison stimulus that most closely matches the length of the standard stimulus. The difference in length between the standard stimulus and the comparison stimulus chosen by the subject (typically between 10 percent and 30 percent) defines the size of the illusion. Try this procedure on a number of people to see how variable it is. ●

Why does this misperception of size occur? Richard Gregory (1966) explains the Müller-Lyer illusion on the basis of **misapplied size constancy scaling**. He points out that size constancy normally helps us maintain a stable perception of objects, by taking distance into account. Thus, size constancy scaling causes a 6-foot-tall person to appear 6 feet tall, no matter what his distance. Gregory proposes, however, that the very mechanism that helps us maintain stable perceptions in the three-dimensional world sometimes creates illusions when applied to objects drawn on a two-dimensional surface. We can see how this works by comparing the left and right lines in Figure 7.44 to the left and right pictures in Figure 7.45. Gregory suggests that the fins on the right line in Figure 7.45 make this line look like part of an inside corner, and that the fins on the left line make this line look like part of an outside corner. Since the

Figure 7.45
According to Gregory (1973), the Müller-Lyer line on the left corresponds to the outside corner of a building, and the line on the right corresponds to the inside corner of a room.

255   *Perceiving Depth and Size*

inside corner tends to look farther away than the outside corner, we see the right line as being farther away, and our size–distance scaling mechanism causes this line to appear longer. (Remember that $S = R \times D$. The retinal sizes, R, of the two lines are the same, so the perceived size, S, is determined by the perceived distance, D.)

At this point, you may say that, while the Müller-Lyer figures may remind Gregory of the inside corner of a room or the outside corner of a building, they don't look that way to you (or at least they didn't until Gregory told you to see them that way). But according to Gregory, it is not necessary that you be consciously aware that the Müller-Lyer lines can represent three-dimensional structures; your perceptual system unconsciously takes the depth information contained in the Müller-Lyer figures into account, and your size–distance scaling mechanism adjusts the perceived sizes of the lines accordingly.

Gregory's theory of visual illusions has not, however, gone unchallenged. For example, figures like the dumbbell in Figure 7.46, which contain no obvious perspective or depth, still result in an illusion. And Patricia DeLucia and Julian Hochberg (1985, 1986, 1991; Hochberg, 1987) have shown that the Müller-Lyer illusion occurs for a three-dimensional display like the one in Figure 7.47, in which it is obvious that the spaces between the two sets of fins are not at different depths. You can experience this effect for yourself by doing the following demonstration.

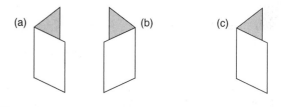

Figure 7.47
A three-dimensional Müller-Lyer illusion. The 2-foot-high wooden "fins" stand on the floor. Although the distances between edges (a) and (b) and between (b) and (c) are the same, the distance between (b) and (c) appears larger, just as in the two-dimensional Müller-Lyer illusion. Gregory's explanation of the illusion in terms of misapplied size constancy does not work in this case, since it is obvious that the spaces between the sets of fins are not at different depths.

DEMONSTRATION

The Müller-Lyer Illusion with Books

Pick three books that are the same size and arrange two of them with their corners making a 90-degree angle and standing in positions A and B, as shown in Figure 7.48. Then, without using a ruler, position the third book at position C, so that distance b appears to be equal to distance a. Check your decision, looking down at the books from the top and from other angles as well. When you are satisfied that distances a and b appear about equal, measure the distances with a ruler. How do they compare?   ●

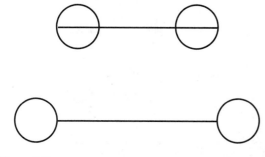

Figure 7.46
The "dumbbell" version of the Müller-Lyer illusion. As in the Müller-Lyer illusion, the two lines are actually the same length.

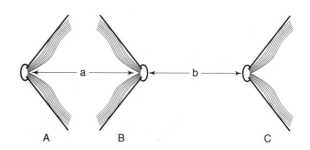

Figure 7.48
Creating a Müller-Lyer illusion with books (seen from the top).

If your perceptions were similar to those of the subjects in DeLucia and Hochberg's (1991) experiment, you set distance b so that it was smaller than distance a. This is exactly the result you would expect from the two-dimensional Müller-Lyer illusion, in which the distance between the outward-going fins appears enlarged compared to the distance between the inward-going fins. You can also duplicate the illusion shown in Figure 7.44 with your books, by using your ruler to make distances a and b equal. Then, notice how the distances actually appear. The fact that we can create the Müller-Lyer illusion by using three-dimensional stimuli such as these, as well as demonstrations like the dumbbell in Figure 7.46, is difficult for Gregory's theory to explain.

Another explanation of the Müller-Lyer illusion has been proposed by R. H. Day (1989, 1990), whose **conflicting cues theory** states that our perception of the length of the lines depends on two cues for length: (1) the actual length of the vertical lines, and (2) the overall length of the figure. According to Day, these two conflicting cues are integrated to form a compromise perception of length. Since the overall length of the right figure in Figure 7.44 is larger because of the outward-oriented fins, this length causes the vertical line to appear larger.

Another version of the Müller-Lyer illusion, shown in Figure 7.49, results in the perception that the space between the dots is greater in the lower figure than in the upper figure, even though the distances are actually the same. According to Day's conflicting cues theory, the space in the lower figure appears greater because the overall extent of the figure is greater. Thus, while Gregory feels that depth information is involved in determining illusions, Day rejects this idea and says that cues for length are what is important. Let's now look at some more examples of illusions and the mechanisms that have been proposed to explain them.

The Ponzo Illusion

In the **Ponzo** (or railroad track) **illusion**, shown in Figure 7.50, both horizontal lines are the same

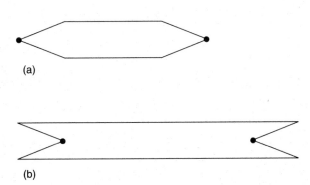

(a)

(b)

Figure 7.49
An alternate version of the Müller-Lyer illusion. It appears that the distance between the dots in A is less than the distance in B, even though the distances are the same. (From Day, 1989)

Figure 7.50
The Ponzo (or railroad track) illusion. The two horizontal rectangles are the same length on the page (measure them), but the far one appears larger.

Perceiving Depth and Size

length and have the same visual angle, but the one on top appears longer. According to Gregory's misapplied scaling explanation, the top line appears longer because of depth information that makes it appear farther away. Thus, just as for the Müller-Lyer illusion, the scaling mechanism corrects for this apparently increased depth (even though there really isn't any, because the illusion is on a flat page) and we perceive the top line to be larger.

The Ames Room

The **Ames room**, which was first constructed by Adelbert Ames, causes two people of equal size to appear very different in size (Ittleson, 1952). In the photograph of the observer's view of an Ames room in Figure 7.51, you can see that the woman on the right looks much taller than the woman on the left. This perception occurs even though both women are actually about the same height. The reason for this erroneous perception of size lies in the construction of the room. Because of the shapes of the wall and the windows at the rear of the room, it looks like a normal rectangular room when viewed from a particular

observation point; however, as shown in the diagram in Figure 7.52, the Ames room is, in fact, shaped so that the left corner of the room is almost twice as far away from the observer as the right corner.

What's happening in the Ames room? Because of the construction of the room, the woman on the left has a much smaller visual angle than the one on the right. We think, however, that we are looking into a normal rectangular room, and, since the two women appear to be at the same distance, we perceive the one with the smaller visual angle as shorter. We can understand why this occurs by returning to our size–distance scaling equation, $S = R \times D$. Since the perceived distance, D, is the same for the two women, but the size of the retinal image, R, is smaller for the woman on the left, her perceived size, S, is smaller.

Another explanation for the Ames room is based not on size–distance scaling, but on relative size. The relative size explanation is that our perception of the size of the two people is based on how they fill the distance between the bottom and top of the room. Since the woman on the right fills the entire space and the woman on the left occupies only a little of it, we perceive the woman on the right as taller (Sedgwick, 2001).

Figure 7.51

The Ames room. The women are actually about the same height, but the shape of the room, which is not obvious from this viewpoint, makes the one on the right appear taller.

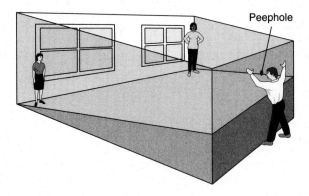

Peephole

Figure 7.52

The Ames room, showing its true shape. The woman on the left is actually almost twice as far away from the observer as the one on the right; however, when the room is viewed through the peephole, this difference in distance is not seen. In order for the room to look normal when viewed through the peephole, it is necessary to enlarge the left side of the room.

The Moon Illusion

You may have noticed that when the moon is on the horizon, it appears much larger than when it is higher in the sky. This enlargement of the horizon moon compared to the elevated moon, shown in Figure 7.53, is called the **moon illusion**. An explanation of the moon illusion that involves depth perception is called the **apparent-distance theory**. This theory is based on the idea that an object on the horizon that is viewed across the filled space of the terrain, which contains depth information, should appear to be farther away than an object that is elevated in the sky and is viewed through empty space, which contains little depth information.

The idea that the horizon is perceived as farther away is supported by the fact that when people estimate the distance to the horizon and the distance to the sky directly overhead, they report that the horizon appears to be farther away. That is, the heavens appear "flattened" (Figure 7.54). The key to the moon illusion, according to apparent-distance theory, is that both the horizon and the elevated moons have the same visual angle, and since the horizon moon

appears farther away, it will appear larger, as shown in Figure 7.54.

The moon illusion is so striking that people often doubt that the horizon and elevated moons have the same visual angle. But since the moon's physical size (2,200 miles in diameter) and distance from the earth (245,000 miles) are constant throughout the night, the moon's visual angle must be constant. If you are still skeptical, photograph the horizon and the elevated moons. You will find that the diameters in the resulting two pictures are identical. Or you can view the moon through a ¼-inch-diameter hole (the size produced by most standard hole punches) held at arm's length. For most people, the moon just fits inside this hole, wherever it is in the sky.

The principle involved in the apparent-distance explanation of the moon illusion is the same one that causes an afterimage to appear larger if it is viewed against a faraway surface. Just as the near and far afterimages created by viewing Figure 7.40 have the same visual angles, so do the horizon and the elevated moons. The afterimage that appears to be on the wall across the room simulates the horizon moon; the circle appears farther away, so your size–distance scaling mechanism makes it appear larger. The afterimage that appears to be on the page of the book simulates

Figure 7.53

An artist's conception of the moon illusion, showing the moon on the horizon and high in the sky simultaneously.

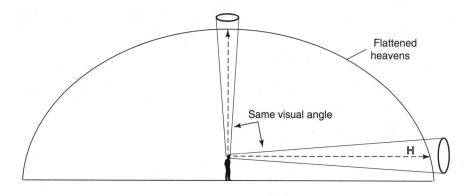

Figure 7.54

If observers are asked to consider that the sky is a surface and are asked to compare the distance to the horizon (H) and the distance to the top of the sky on a clear moonless night, they usually say that the horizon appears farther away. This results in the "flattened heavens" shown here.

the elevated moon; the circle appears closer, so your scaling mechanism makes it appear smaller (King & Gruber, 1962).

Lloyd Kaufman and Irvin Rock have done a number of experiments that support the apparent-distance theory. In one of their experiments, they showed that when the horizon moon was viewed over the terrain, which made it appear farther away, it appeared 1.3 times larger than the elevated moon; however, when the terrain was masked off so that the horizon moon was viewed through a hole in a sheet of cardboard, the illusion vanished (Kaufman and Rock, 1962a, 1962b; Rock & Kaufman, 1962).

Some researchers, however, are skeptical of the apparent-distance theory. For example, they question the idea that the horizon moon appears farther, as shown in the flattened heavens effect in Figure 7.54, because some subjects see the horizon moon as floating in space in front of the sky (Plug & Ross, 1994).

Another theory of the moon illusion, the **angular size-contrast theory**, focuses not on the moon's apparent depth but on the moon's visual angle compared to surrounding objects (Baird, Wagner, & Fuld, 1990).

According to this idea, the moon appears smaller when it is surrounded by larger objects. Thus, when the moon is elevated, the large expanse of sky surrounding it makes it appear smaller. However, when the moon is on the horizon, less sky surrounds it, so it appears larger.

Even though scientists have been proposing theories to explain the moon illusion for hundreds of years, there is still no agreement on an explanation (Hershenson 1989). Apparently a number of factors are involved which, in addition to the ones we have considered here, also include atmospheric perspective (looking through haze on the horizon can increase size perception), color (redness increases perceived size), and oculomotor factors (convergence of the eyes, which tends to occur when we look toward the horizon, can cause an increase in perceived size) (Plug & Ross, 1994). Just as many different sources of depth information work together to create our impression of depth, many different factors may work together to create the moon illusion and perhaps the other illusions as well.

Sensitive Periods in the Development of Binocular Vision

We end this chapter by returning to neurons that respond to binocular disparity. In our discussion of these neurons on page 240, we saw that they are found in abundance in the striate cortex and other areas as well. We also saw that if kittens are raised in an environment in which they never see with both eyes at once they lose their binocular depth cells (Blake & Hirsch, 1975; see page 242). We will now describe evidence that these changes caused by rearing in a deprived environment are most likely to occur if the abnormal conditions occur during a *sensitive period* early in the animal's life.

We will describe research on both animals and humans that has looked at how abnormal visual stimulation early in life affects the functioning of the visual system. One way this abnormal stimulation has been created is through a technique called monocular rearing.

Monocular Rearing of Kittens

One way to deprive an animal of coordinated visual input to both eyes is to use a procedure called **monocular rearing**, in which one eye is sutured shut so the animal has the use of only one eye. The effect of monocular rearing on binocularity is illustrated by **ocular dominance histograms**, such as those in Figure 7.55. These histograms are determined by recording from a large number of cells and then rating each cell's ability to respond to stimulation of both the contralateral eye (the eye on the opposite side of the head from the cell) and the ipsilateral eye (the eye on the same side as the cell). Each cell is placed in one of seven categories according to the degree of ocular dominance, as listed in Table 7.1

Comparing the histograms in Figures 7.55a and 7.55b shows the striking effect of monocular deprivation on the way the kitten's cortical cells responded to stimulation of each eye. Whereas most of the cells in the normal cat respond to both eyes, and therefore fall into categories 2 to 6 of the histogram, all the cells in the deprived kitten responded only to stimulation of the undeprived eye and are placed in category 7 (Hubel & Wiesel, 1970).

Research in which this monocular rearing has been carried out at different times during the

Table 7.1
Categories of binocular response

Category	Description
1	Cell responds only to stimulation of the contralateral eye. Thus, if the cell is in the right hemisphere, it responds only to stimulation of the left eye
2	Cell responds much more to stimulation of the contralateral eye than to stimulation of the ipsilateral eye.
3	Cell responds slightly more to stimulation of the contralateral eye.
4	Cell responds equally to stimulation of each eye.
5	Cell responds slightly more to stimulation of the ipsilateral eye.
6	Cell responds much more to stimulation of the ipsilateral eye.
7	Cell responds only to stimulation of the ipsilateral eye.

(continued)

Perceiving Depth and Size

The Plasticity of Perception (*continued*)

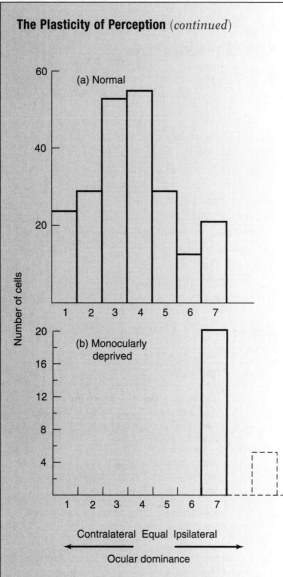

kittens' early development have found that there is a **sensitive period**, early in a kitten's life, during which monocular rearing has a large effect. The sensitive period for kittens extends from birth to about 6 months (Cynader, Timney, & Mitchell, 1980; Jones, Spear, & Tong, 1984; Olson & Freeman, 1980). After that time, monocular rearing has little effect.

"Monocular Rearing" of Children

We've seen that the binocular vision of kittens is disrupted by monocular rearing. Research studying people who, as young children, had one of their eyes patched following an eye operation suggests that similar effects also occur in humans.

Shinobu Awaya and coworkers (1973) investigated the histories of 19 people with a condition called **amblyopia**, in which one eye has poor visual acuity that is not caused by a physical problem in the eye. They found that all of these people had their amblyopic (low visual acuity) eye closed early in life, following an eye operation, and that most of the closures had occurred during the first year after birth.

By having one eye patched early in life, these children were experiencing monocular deprivation similar to that experienced by the cats that had one eye sutured shut. Based on the results of the animal experiments, which showed a decrease

Figure 7.55
(a) An ocular dominance histogram of recordings from 223 neurons in the visual cortex of adult cats. Numbers refer to the categories described in Table 7.1. Note that a large number of cells respond to the stimulation of both eyes. (b) Ocular dominance histogram of 25 cells recorded from the visual cortex of a 2 1/2-month-old kitten that was reared with its right eye occluded until the time of the experiment. The dashed bar on the right indicates that 5 cells did not respond to the stimulation of either eye. The solid bar indicates that all 20 cells that did respond to stimulation responded only in the eye that was opened during rearing. (Wiesel & Hubel, 1963.)

(continued)

The Plasticity of Perception (*continued*)

in response of cortical neurons that respond to stimulation of the deprived eye, we can conclude that perhaps the low visual acuity experienced by the humans in their amblyopic eye is caused by a loss of cortical neurons that respond to stimulation of that eye.

This type of amblyopia has therefore been called **stimulus deprivation amblyopia**, a term that distinguishes it from amblyopia due to other causes (von Noorden & Maumanee, 1968). (See also Aslin & Banks, 1975, for a discussion of how other childhood vision problems can affect the responding of cortical neurons.) The results of these monocular rearing experiments tell us that our ability to use binocular disparity information to perceive depth depends on our binocular neurons receiving appropriate stimulation during a sensitive period early in our lives.

Perceiving Depth and Size

VISUAL AND AUDITORY SPACE

Auditory space extends around your head in all directions, existing wherever there is a sound. The best way to experience auditory space is to close your eyes and notice the sounds around you, paying particular attention to the directions and distances of these sounds. Unless you are in an extremely quiet environment, you will probably get a feeling of objects (a computer humming, for example) and events (people talking, cars driving by) located at various positions in space. When you perceive objects located at different positions based on their sounds, you are experiencing auditory space.

Auditory and visual space are similar in some ways and different in others. One of the most obvious similarities is the parallel between the cue of binocular disparity, for vision, and cues that are based on the left and right ears, for hearing. For vision, the depth cue of binocular disparity depends on differences in the images in the left and right eyes. For hearing, there are cues that depend on differences in the intensity and timing of sounds arriving at the left and right ears. (We will discuss these auditory cues, which are called binaural cues, in more detail in Chapter 11.)

Another similarity between auditory and visual space is that they usually overlap. For example, when an orchestra conductor hears the oboe solo coming from the left side of the orchestra, he also sees the oboe player seated on the left. This overlap between auditory and visual space occurs even when orchestra conductors use a technique called the "inner audition" to practice without their orchestras by imagining a musical score in their minds. When they do this, they imagine not only the sounds of the various instruments but their locations relative to the podium, as well. (See Andersen et al., 1997, for a discussion of multimodal neurons that respond when both visual and auditory stimuli are located at the same positions in space.)

This overlap between where a sound seems to be coming from and where we see the source of this sound is also common in everyday situations far removed from the concert hall. You hear a conversation behind you and turn around to see that two people are, in fact, talking at about the location you would have predicted. But sometimes vision and hearing provide discrepant information, as when the sound is produced at one place but you see the apparent sound source somewhere else. A familiar example of this occurs in movie theaters when an actor's dialogue is produced by a speaker located on the right side of the screen, while the actor who is talking is visually located in the center of the screen, many feet away. When this happens, we hear the sound coming from its seen location (the image at the center of the screen) rather than from where it is actually produced (the speaker to the right of the screen). This effect is called **visual capture** or the **ventriloquism effect**.

Visual and auditory space can differ in the amount of information that they provide. Under conditions of good visibility, visual space is more "filled," extending everywhere we can see (although we do have to turn around to see the visual space behind us). In very noisy environments such as a concert, a sporting event, or a noisy city street, auditory space might be "filled" in this way, but it more usually consists of isolated sounds at specific positions, with spaces between them. However, when visibility is poor, as occurs in the dark, visual space vanishes and auditory space becomes our major source of spatial perception. Blind people deal with this situation all the time, and consequently they pay close attention to what is happening in auditory space. So as people talk or automobiles whiz by, the blind person is taking in not only the meaning of the sounds but also the locations of these sounds in auditory space.

Perceiving Size

The Holway and Boring experiment showed that size perception is influenced by depth perception, with good depth perception resulting in accurate size judgments and poor depth perception resulting in size judgments based on an object's visual angle. Examples of size perception that depends on visual angle are the perception of the sizes of the sun and the moon and the way we perceive the sizes of objects as viewed from an airplane.

Size Constancy

The principle of size constancy states that our perception of an object's size remains relatively constant, even when the object is viewed from different distances, causing changes in the sizes of the object's image on the retina. Size constancy occurs when good depth information is available. The link between size constancy and depth perception has led to the idea of size–distance scaling. Emmert's law, which states that the size of an afterimage depends on the distance at which the afterimage appears, is an example of size–distance scaling.

The Müller-Lyer Illusion

One of the most studied illusions of size is the Müller-Lyer illusion. It has been proposed that this illusion is caused by misapplied size constancy scaling, caused by the appearance that the two lines of the illusion are at different distances. There are a number of demonstrations that question this explanation, and the conflicting cues theory offers an alternative explanation that depends on cues for length rather than on information about depth.

Other Illusions of Size

Other illusions of size include the Ponzo, or railroad track, illusion, the Ames room illusion, and the moon illusion. All three of these have been explained based on misperception of depth. The version of this depth explanation applied to the moon illusion, which is called apparent-distance theory, is based on the idea that the horizon moon (which appears larger than the overhead moon) appears farther away since it is seen over the terrain, which is rich in depth information. Another explanation of the moon illusion is the angular size-contrast theory, which focuses not on the moon's apparent depth, but on the moon's visual angle compared to surrounding objects. No totally satisfactory explanation of the moon illusion has been proposed.

Plasticity: Sensitive Periods for the Development of Binocular Vision

Monocular rearing experiments, in which kittens are reared while being able to see out of only one eye, indicate that experience in binocular vision is necessary during a sensitive period early in the kitten's life if binocular neurons are to develop normally. That sensitive period extends from birth to about six months. A condition called stimulus deprivation amblyopia, which occurs in some adults who had one eye patched when they were children, may be due to a lack of binocular neurons caused by the early deprivation.

Across the Senses: Visual and Auditory Space

Space can be perceived visually and on the basis of sound. Visual depth perception depends at least partially on differences in information received by the two eyes; auditory sound perception depends on differences in information received by the two ears. In addition to this similarity in mechanisms, there are many perceptual similarities between visual and auditory space perception and some differences as well.

Perceiving Depth and Size

STUDY QUESTIONS

1. Can we perceive the distances of objects based on the image at isolated points on the retina? (226)

2. What is the main focus of the cue approach to depth perception? (226)

3. What are the three basic categories of depth cues? (226)

Oculomotor Cues

4. Describe convergence and accommodation. Over what distances are these cues effective for depth perception? (226)

Monocular Cues

Pictorial Cues

5. What are pictorial cues? (227)

6. Describe the following pictorial cues: occlusion, relative height, cast shadows, relative size, familiar size, atmospheric perspective, linear perspective, and texture gradients. (227)

7. Distinguish between the drawing system of linear perspective and the depth cue of linear perspective. What does the drawing system accomplish? (230)

Movement-Produced Cues

8. Describe the two movement-produced cues, motion parallax and deletion and accretion. (231)

9. What is the retinal basis of motion parallax (Figure 7.11)? (231)

Binocular Depth Cues

Binocular Disparity and Stereopsis

10. What are the two stages involved in the creation of depth perception? (233)

11. What is binocular disparity? Stereopsis? (234)

12. What is the principle behind the stereoscope? (234)

Corresponding Retinal Points

13. What are corresponding retinal points? (237)

14. What is the horopter? (237)

15. What are noncorresponding retinal points? (238)

16. What is the angle of disparity, and what information does it provide for depth perception? (238)

17. Define crossed disparity and uncrossed disparity. (238)

18. Does the fact that we perceive depth when disparity is present in two pictures prove that disparity is creating our perception of depth? (239)

Random-Dot Stereogram

19. What is a random-dot stereogram, and what does it tell us about the role of disparity in depth perception? (239)

Disparity Information in the Brain

20. What is a binocular depth cell? A zero-disparity cell? A disparity-selective cell? (240)

21. Which extrastriate pathways contain neurons that are involved in depth perception? (241)

22. Describe Blake and Hirsch's experiment in which they raised cats so they experienced only monocular vision. What do the results of this experiment indicate? (242)

23. Describe the DeAngelis experiment in which disparity-sensitive neurons are stimulated in the monkey. What do the results of this experiment show? (242)

Brain Scan: Stereopsis in the Brain

24. Describe how Kwee and coworkers manipulated stereopsis in their subjects in order to measure the fMRI response to stereopsis. (242)

25. What area of cortex is activated by stereopsis? What stream is it in? (242)

The Correspondence Problem

26. What is the correspondence problem for depth perception? Has it been solved? (243)

27. Over what ranges of distance do the various depth cues provide information for depth perception? (243)

Depth Information Across Species

28. Are frontal eyes or lateral eyes better suited for using binocular disparity for the perception of depth? (245)

29. Describe the pigeon's use of binocular disparity. (245)

30. What kinds of information do the frog and the water bug *Notonecta* use to perceive depth? (245)

31. Describe how it was determined that the locust might use motion parallax to judge depth. (245)

32. What kinds of information does the honeybee use to perceive distances while it is flying? (246)

33. How do bats perceive depth? (246)

Perceiving Size

34. What does the whiteout story illustrate about size perception? (248)

The Holway and Boring Experiment

35. Describe Holway and Boring's experiment, including how the stimuli are arranged, the judgments made by the subjects, and the results. (248)

36. What happens to size perception when depth information is eliminated? (250)

37. Under what conditions is size perception based on the actual sizes of objects? (250)

38. Under what conditions is size perception based on an object's visual angle? (250)

39. What does our perception of the sizes of the sun and the moon demonstrate about size perception? (250)

40. Why do we perceive the sizes of objects viewed from an airplane as being very small? (250)

Size Constancy

41. What is the principle of size constancy? (250)

42. What does the demonstration show in which the author asks a student in the front row to estimate his size and then doubles his distance from the observer? (251)

43. What does the demonstration with the quarters show regarding when size constancy holds? (251)

44. What is size–distance scaling? Know what the terms are in the equation $S = R \times D$ and how to apply it. (252)

45. What is Emmert's law, and how is it related to the equation for size–distance scaling? (252)

Visual Illusions

46. What is veridical perception? When is it most likely to occur? When is it most likely to break down? (254)

The Müller-Lyer Illusion

47. Describe the Müller-Lyer illusion and the misapplied size constancy explanation for this illusion. (254)

48. How do the dumbbell display in Figure 7.46 and the three-dimensional display in Figure 7.47 challenge the misapplied size constancy scaling explanation of the Müller-Lyer illusion? (256)

49. Describe the conflicting cues theory of the Müller-Lyer illusion. (257)

The Ponzo Illusion

50. Describe the Ponzo illusion and how it has been explained in terms of misapplied constancy scaling. (257)

The Ames Room

51. Describe the way people are perceived in the Ames room and how this perception is explained in terms of (a) size–depth scaling and (b) relative size. (258)

The Moon Illusion

52. Describe the moon illusion. (259)

53. What is the apparent-distance explanation for the moon illusion? What are the "flattened heavens"? How does the visual angle of the moon compare when it is on the horizon and high in the sky? (259)

54. Describe the parallel between the apparent-distance explanation of the moon illusion and Emmert's law. (259)

55. What experiment done by Kaufman and Rock supports the apparent-distance explanation? (260)

56. Why are some researchers skeptical of the apparent-distance theory? (260)

57. Describe the angular size-contrast theory of the moon illusion. (260)

58. Which combination of factors is probably responsible for the moon illusion? (260)

The Plasticity of Perception: Sensitive Periods in the Development of Binocular Vision

Monocular Rearing of Kittens

59. What is an ocular dominance histogram? (261)

60. How does monocular rearing affect the binocular responding of cortical neurons as indicated by the ocular dominance histogram? (262)

61. What is the sensitive period for susceptibility to monocular rearing in cats? (262)

62. What is the effect of monocular rearing on adult cats? (262)

"Monocular Rearing" of Children

63. What is amblyopia? (262)

64. What did Awaya find regarding the relationship between early eye patching and amblyopia? (262)

65. How do the results of Awaya's experiment relate to the monocular rearing experiments on kittens? (262)

66. What is stimulus deprivation amblyopia, and what causes it? (263)

Across the Senses: Visual and Auditory Space

67. How are visual space and auditory space similar and different? (264)

68. What happens when there is a discrepancy between visual and auditory space? (264)

69. When do visual stimuli provide more information about space than auditory stimuli? When do auditory stimuli provide more information? (264)

8

PERCEIVING MOVEMENT

CHAPTER CONTENTS

SOME QUESTIONS WE WILL CONSIDER

- Why do some animals freeze in place when they sense danger? (269)

- How do films create movement from still pictures? (273)

- When we scan a room, the image of the room moves across the retina, but we perceive the room and the objects in it as remaining stationary. Why does this occur? (279, 283)

Many animals become totally still when they sense danger. They do this to save their lives, because as long as they remain still they may be unseen by the predator that is stalking them; but, as soon as they move, they become instantly visible. For the predator looking for prey, and the potential prey on the lookout for predators to avoid, the perception of move-

ment is crucial for survival. Although some animals may have poor depth perception or rudimentary color vision, none lacks the ability to perceive motion.

The universality of motion perception is not just because of predator–prey relationships. The ability to perceive movement is such a basic mechanism for interacting with the world that the loss of this ability can become a crippling disability. For example, a 43-year-old woman lost the ability to perceive movement when she suffered a stroke that damaged an area of her cortex that corresponds to the monkey's area MT (which, in Chapter 4, we saw is important for the perception of movement). Her condition, which is called **motion agnosia**, made it difficult for her to pour tea or coffee into a cup, because the liquid appeared to be frozen, so she couldn't perceive the fluid rising in the cup and had trouble knowing when to stop pouring (Figure 8.1)

It was also difficult for her to follow dialogue because she couldn't see movements of a speaker's face and mouth. Perhaps most disturbing, sometimes people seemed to suddenly appear or disappear from rooms, because she couldn't see them walking; and crossing the street presented serious problems, because at first a car might seem far away, but then suddenly, without warning, it would appear very near (Zihl et al., 1983, 1991). This case illustrates how important movement perception is for dealing with everyday activities.

One of the goals of this chapter is to describe some of the mechanisms that are responsible for movement perception. But the purpose of this chapter goes beyond just describing how we perceive movement, because studying movement perception has a lot to teach us about perception in general. As we study the specifics of movement perception, we will also be concerned with the following basic ideas, which hold for perceiving movement and other perceptual qualities as well.

1. Perception is a creation of the nervous system. We perceive motion even when there is no movement, as when our nervous system causes us to perceive motion when stationary lights flash on and off, one after another (Figure 8.2).

2. Visual perception often depends on more than just the image on the retina. We perceive movement when we follow a moving object, even though its image stays at the same place on our retinas (Figure 8.3).

3. Perception often involves an interaction between different perceptual qualities. Our own movements and the movement of objects can help us to more accurately perceive an object's shape and its location in space. This is illustrated in Figure 5.46

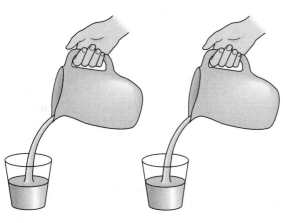

Time 1   Time 2

Figure 8.1
The woman with motion agnosia perceived no change in the level of water being poured into a cup.

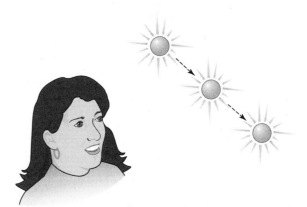

Figure 8.2
When we look at lights that flash on and off one after another, we can perceive movement, indicated by the dashed line, if the timing between the flashes is just right. Since there is no actual movement in the stimulus, our perception of movement must be created by our nervous system.

(page 173), in which the rocks appear to be arranged in a circle when viewed from a particular position but take on a totally different appearance when the observer moves to another position. Or consider Figure 8.4a, which looks like two rectangles, one in front of the other. But moving to a different position reveals the view in Figure 8.4b, which shows that the light object is actually L-shaped and not rectangular. Thus, although our first interpretation of Figure 8.4a was reasonable, our movement shows us that it was incorrect.

4. Perception often depends on heuristics, rules of thumb that provide "best-guess" estimates of what a particular stimulus is, and also on top-down processing based on cognitive factors, such as knowledge an observer brings to a particular situation. We discussed the idea of heuristics when we described Gestalt psychology in Chapter 5 (page 154) and lightness perception in Chapter 6 (page 214). Movement perception provides additional examples of heuristics and top-down processing.

We begin our discussion of movement perception by describing a number of different ways that movement perception can occur. This discussion is relevant to point 1 above, because many of these ways of creating a perception of movement involve illusions of movement that are created by the action of our nervous system.

Figure 8.3

If we follow a flying bird by rotating our head and keeping our eyes fixed on the bird, the bird's image stays on the same place on our retina, yet we still perceive the bird as moving. This means that our perception of movement depends on more than movement of an image across the retina.

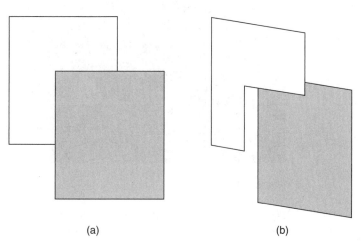

(a) (b)

Figure 8.4

(a) At first this stimulus appears to be two rectangles, (b) but moving to another viewpoint reveals that the white shape is not a rectangle.

Perceiving Movement

FOUR WAYS TO CREATE THE PERCEPTION OF MOVEMENT

WebTUTOR We perceive movement when an object moves across our field of view but also under other conditions as well. We now describe four different ways of creating a perception of movement.

Real Movement

The most straightforward way to create the perception of movement is to simply move an object across an observer's field of view. This situation is called **real movement**, since the object is physically moving. Early researchers studied real movement by measuring basic properties such as the threshold for movement. They found that the threshold for perceiving movement in a homogeneous field is a velocity of about ⅙ to ⅓ of a degree of visual angle per second (Aubert, 1886). This means that you would just barely perceive the movement of the spot in Figure 8.5a if, when you view it from a distance of 1 foot, it takes about 14 seconds to travel from A to B. If, however, we add vertical lines to the space between A and B, as in Figure 8.5b, you would be able to perceive the spot's movement even at velocities as low as 1/60 of a degree of visual angle per second (which translates into a travel time of 280 seconds from A to B when Figure 8.5b is viewed from a distance of 1 foot). These results show that our perception of movement depends both on the velocity of the moving stimulus and on its surroundings.

Apparent Movement

At about the time early researchers were measuring thresholds for the perception of real movement, Exner (1875) demonstrated that a perception of movement can be created even when no movement is actually occurring. He accomplished this by discharging two nearby electrical sparks, one after the other. When he did this, movement appeared to occur across the space between them (Figure 8.6). This perception of movement across empty space, which is called **stroboscopic movement** or **apparent movement**, was put to practical use in the creation of the first motion pictures in the late 1800s (Figure 8.7) and is widely used in signs for advertising and entertainment (Figure 8.8).

Although by the early 1900s the motion picture industry was beginning to flourish, it wasn't until about 1912 that psychologists began to seriously study apparent movement. That was the year Max Wertheimer published his paper on apparent movement, which marked the beginnings of Gestalt psychology. Remember from Chapter 5 that Wertheimer used the existence of the apparent movement that occurs across the empty space between two flashed stimuli to argue against the structuralists' idea that perceptions are created by the addition of sensations (see Figure 5.2). How, argued Wertheimer, can sensations explain a person's perception of something that is happening where there are no actual stimuli?

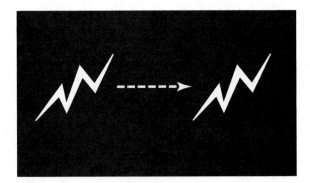

Figure 8.6
When Exner discharged two sparks, one after another, he perceived movement between them. This was one of the earliest scientific demonstrations of apparent movement.

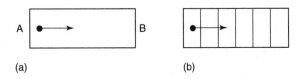

(a)   (b)

Figure 8.5
The context in which movement occurs affects movement perception. It is easier to detect movement in (b) than in (a) because of the structure provided by the vertical lines in (b).

Wertheimer and others began studying apparent movement psychophysically and found that the nature of the movement that occurs between two flashing lights depends on both the timing between the flashes and the distance between them. Figure 8.9 shows how our perception of two flashes of light changes as the time interval between the two flashes, the **interstimulus interval (ISI)**, is increased (Graham, 1965). When the ISI is less than about 30 ms, the lights appear to flash on and off simultaneously. As the interval increases beyond 30 ms, partial movement is perceived between the two lights; at a separation of about 60 ms, the lights appear to move continuously from one to the other. Finally, at time intervals above about 200 to 300 ms, no movement is perceived between the two lights; they appear successively, with first one flashing on and off, and then the other.

The distance between the two lights also affects the perception of apparent movement. As the distance increases, either the time interval between the two flashes or the intensity of the flashes must be increased to maintain the same perception of movement.

DEMONSTRATION

A Demonstration of Apparent Movement

You can demonstrate some of the effects in Figure 8.9 to yourself, as follows: Place a dot on one side of a match as shown in Figure 8.10a and, slightly farther down, place a dot on the other side, as in (b). (This also works with a straw.) Then, with the match between your thumb and forefinger, as shown in (c), slowly begin to roll the match back and forth. Notice that at slow speeds (long ISIs) you see the dots one after another. Then, as you increase the speed, notice when movement occurs. At very high speeds (short ISIs), you will see both dots simultaneously, with no movement between them.

Induced Movement

Apparent movement is an illusion because we perceive movement even though the stimuli are not

Figure 8.7
Eight frames from Edwin S. Porter's 1903 film The Great Train Robbery. *This sequence lasts about 0.4 second when projected. The movement that results is an example of stroboscopic movement.*

Perceiving Movement

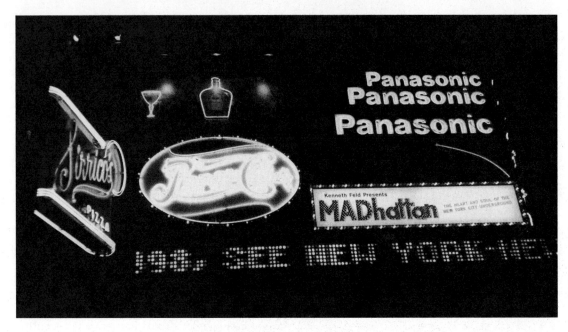

Figure 8.8
We see the message at the bottom of this sign move smoothly to the left, but this perception is created by stationary lights blinking on and off.

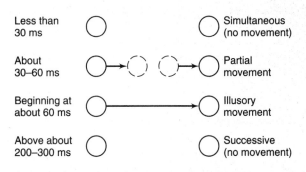

Less than 30 ms	Simultaneous (no movement)
About 30–60 ms	Partial movement
Beginning at about 60 ms	Illusory movement
Above about 200–300 ms	Successive (no movement)

Figure 8.9
The perception of apparent movement depends on the time interval between the flashing of two lights. As the time interval is increased, the observer's perception goes through the stages shown in the figure.

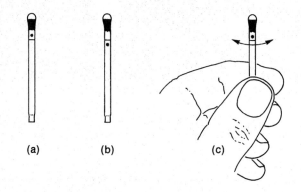

(a)　　　　(b)　　　　(c)

Figure 8.10
You can create apparent movement by drawing a dot on each side of a match (as shown in a and b), and by flipping the match back and forth (as shown in c).

moving. **Induced movement** is an illusion that occurs when movement of one object induces the perception of movement in another object. You've experienced induced movement if you've seen the moon racing through the clouds on a windy night. The moving clouds induce movement in the stationary moon. You can demonstrate induced movement to yourself in the following demonstration.

D E M O N S T R A T I O N

Inducing Movement in a Dot

Stick a small dot of paper on the screen of your television set, as shown in Figure 8.11, and watch a program in which the television camera moves back and forth across a scene or follows a moving person or car (football, basketball, or hockey games are particularly good). These camera movements cause the entire television image to move across the screen, which will induce movement in your dot. ●

Induced movement can also occur in your car. If you've ever jammed on your brakes while sitting at a stop light, to stop your car from drifting backward, only to find out that your car was stopped and the car next to you was drifting forward, you were experiencing a form of induced movement called **vection**, in which you actually feel yourself moving.

Movement Aftereffect

If you look at a waterfall or a flowing stream and then look away, and the ground appears to move in the direction opposite to the movement of the waterfall, you are experiencing a **movement aftereffect** called the **waterfall illusion** (Figure 8.12). Movement aftereffects can also occur when viewing other kinds of motion, such as a spiral that, when rotated, appears to move inward. When you look away after viewing this inward-moving spiral, things appear to expand out. This is the **spiral motion aftereffect.**

Studying Movement Perception

Researchers studying movement perception have investigated all of the types of movement described above and some others that we did not describe. Our purpose, however, is not to understand every type of movement perception but to understand some of the general principles governing movement perception. To do this, we will focus on real movement and apparent movement.

Figure 8.11

As the camera follows these basketball players, the dot stuck to the center of the TV screen appears to move with them, an example of induced movement.

Figure 8.12
Looking at a waterfall, such as this one, can create an after-effect of movement called the waterfall illusion, in which movement is perceived when the observer looks away from the waterfall. (Charles Mauzy/Corbis)

For many years, researchers treated the apparent movement created by flashing lights and the real movement created by actual movement through space as if they were separate phenomena, governed by different mechanisms. However, there is ample evidence that these two types of movement have much in common, including activating the same area of the brain (Stevens et al., 2000), so today's researchers study both types of movement together and concentrate on discovering general mechanisms that apply to both real and apparent movement. In this chapter, we will follow this approach as we look for general mechanisms of movement perception. We begin with a fairly simple situation of a single spot or bar moving across the retina and will show how neural movement detectors

like the ones we described in Chapters 3 and 4 signal the direction in which this stimulus is moving.

NEURAL FEATURE DETECTORS AND MOVEMENT PERCEPTION

One way movement perception has been studied physiologically is by recording from neurons in the cortex, such as Hubel and Weisel's (1959, 1965a) complex and end-stopped cells that respond to specific directions of movement (see Figures 3.11 and 3.12). Figure 8.13 shows a tuning curve that indicates how a complex cell selectively fires to a narrow range of directions.

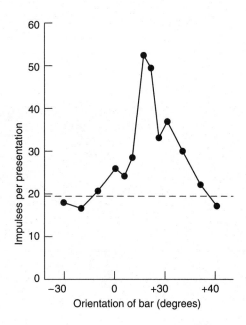

Figure 8.13
A directional tuning curve showing the relationship between the direction a bar is moving and the response of a complex cell in the cat's cortex. The cell responds best when the bar is oriented at about 15 to 20 degrees. The dashed line indicates the rate of spontaneous firing. (Blakemore & Tobin, 1972.)

A Neural Circuit for a Directionally Selective Neuron

How can neural wiring result in a neuron that fires to a specific direction of movement? Werner Reichardt (1961) proposed the simple circuit in Figure 8.14 that results in a neuron that responds to movement in only one direction. To understand how this circuit works, let's look at what happens as a spot of light moves across the retina, stimulating each receptor in turn, beginning with receptor A and moving toward the right (Figure 8.15 a and b). Receptor A synapses with G, so stimulation of A excites G, which then sends an inhibitory signal to H. (The X in Figure 8.15a indicates that H is being inhibited.) While this is occurring, the stimulus moves to receptor B (Figure 8.15b). B fires and sends an excitatory signal to H, but since H has been inhibited by G, it does not fire. Thus, the signals from receptors A and B do not get past H and therefore never reach M, the neuron at the end of the circuit. This process is repeated as the stimulus moves across the remaining receptors. The net result is that M does not respond.

The outcome is different, however, if we begin at receptor F and move the stimulus to the left (Figure 8.15 c and d). Receptor F sends a signal to L, which causes it to fire (Figure 8.15c). The stimulus then moves to receptor E (Figure 8.15d). E fires and causes K to send inhibition to L. This inhibition,

however, arrives too late. L has already fired and has stimulated M (Figure 8.15d). This process is repeated as the stimulus moves across the remaining receptors. The net result is that M fires. Thus, neuron M fires to movement to the left but does not fire to movement to the right.

Neural Firing and Judging the Direction of Movement

Although circuits like the ones described above may be involved in determining the properties of directionally selective neurons in the striate cortex, our perception of movement is probably based on activity of neurons further "upstream" in the visual system. In Chapter 4 we noted that the medial temporal area

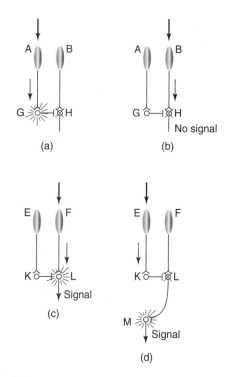

Figure 8.15

What happens as a light moves across the receptors of Figure 8.14. (a and b) Movement of a light from left to right; (c and d) movement from right to left.

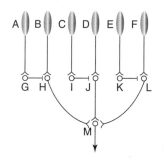

Figure 8.14

A neural circuit in which a neuron (M) responds to the movement of a stimulus across the receptors from right to left. The neuron does not, however, respond to movement from left to right.

Perceiving Movement

(MT) in the dorsal stream is thought to be important for motion perception, because 90 percent of neurons in this area are directionally selective and lesioning this area impairs a monkey's ability to detect the direction of movement. In addition, it has been found that stimulating neurons in MT with very small electrodes (a procedure called microstimulation) causes monkeys to become more sensitive to the directions that the stimulated neuron prefers (Movshon & Newsome, 1992) and that neurons that prefer specific directions are arranged in columns in the MT cortex (Albright, Desimone, & Gross, 1984), just as directionally selective neurons are arranged in columns in the striate cortex (see Figure 3.28) and neurons that respond to similar shapes are arranged in columns in IT cortex (see Figure 4.14).

We will now consider further evidence of a link between MT neurons and movement perception. William Newsome, Kenneth Britten, and Anthony Movshon (1989) demonstrated a connection between the firing of MT neurons and a monkey's ability to judge the direction of movement by presenting a moving-dot display like the one in Figure 8.16 to the receptive field of a neuron in the MT cortex. These displays are like the ones described in Chapter 4 in which the correlation between the dots' directions of movement can be varied from completely random (as in Figure 8.16a) to 100 percent correlated (as in Figure 8.16c).

While the monkey was judging the direction in which the dots were moving, Newsome and coworkers monitored the firing of the MT neuron. They found that as the dots' correlation increased, two things happened: (1) The MT neuron fired more rapidly, and (2) the monkey judged the direction of movement more accurately. In fact, the firing of the MT neuron and the monkey's behavior were so closely related that the researchers could predict one from the other. For example, when the dots' correlation was 0.8 percent, the neuron's response did not differ appreciably from the baseline firing rate on each trial, and the monkey judged the direction of movement with only chance accuracy. But at a correlation of 12.8 percent, the MT neuron always fired faster than its baseline rate, and the monkey judged the direction of movement correctly on virtually every trial.

This result and the results of the experiments we described in Chapter 4 support the idea that MT neurons are responsible for the perception of movement. However, the real significance of these results is that the connection between neural firing and the monkey's behavior is so close that it is possible to predict the monkey's ability to judge the direction of movement by monitoring the firing of only a few MT neurons. Since the firing of only a few neurons contains enough information to accurately signal the direction of movement, we can say that the code for perceiving the direction of movement begins to approach specificity coding at this level of the visual system (Britten et al., 1993; Movshon & Newsome, 1992; Newsome et al., 1995). (See Figure 4.19 to review specificity coding.)

Our analysis of the neural basis of movement perception works well for the straightforward situation in which we perceive movement of a stimulus as

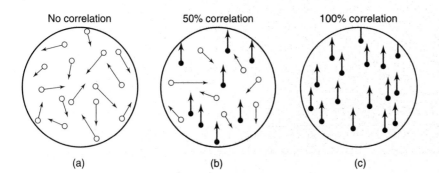

Figure 8.16
Moving-dot displays used by Newsome, Britten, and Movshon. These pictures represent moving-dot displays that were created by a computer. Each dot survives for a brief interval (20 to 30 microseconds), after which it disappears and is replaced by another randomly placed dot. (Newsome & Pare, 1988.)

No correlation

50% correlation

100% correlation

(a)

(b)

(c)

it moves across the retina. But as we stated in point 2 at the beginning of the chapter, one of the things that movement perception teaches us is that perception depends on more than just the image on the retina. As an example of this we noted that we can perceive movement when we track an object, so its image stays on the same place on the retina (usually the fovea, if we are looking right at it) (Figure 8.3b), yet we still perceive movement.

Another situation in which perception doesn't match the image on the retina is shown in Figure 8.17b. This depicts the situation that occurs when we move our eyes to view a stationary scene, such as what happens when we are searching for an object in a room or are looking for a person's face in a crowd. In this case, the movement of the eyes causes the image of stationary objects to move across the retina, but we perceive the objects as stationary. What both of the situations in Figure 8.17 have in common is that the eye is moving, and the question that both of these situations raises is, how do we take this movement of the eyes into account? This question has been addressed physiologically by proposal of a theory called *corollary discharge theory*, which provides a mechanism for taking eye movements into account.

COROLLARY DISCHARGE THEORY: TAKING EYE MOVEMENTS INTO ACCOUNT

WebTUTOR **Corollary discharge theory** proposes that movement perception depends on the following three types of signals that are associated with movement of the eyes or images across the eyes: (1) A **motor signal (MS)**, which is sent to the eye muscles when the observer moves or tries to move her eyes; (2) a **corollary discharge signal (CDS)**, which is a copy of the motor signal; and (3) an **image movement signal (IMS)**, which occurs when an image stimulates the receptors as it moves across the retina (Figure 8.18) (Gyr, 1972; Teuber, 1960; von Holst, 1954).

According to corollary discharge theory, our perception of movement is determined by whether the

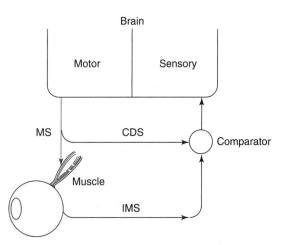

Figure 8.18

Diagram of the corollary discharge model. The motor area sends the motor signal (MS) to move the eyes to the eye muscles and sends the corollary discharge signal (CDS) to a structure called the comparator. Movement of a stimulus across the retina generates an image movement signal (IMS), which also goes to the comparator. The comparator sends its output to the visual cortex. See text for details. (Adapted from Teuber, 1960.)

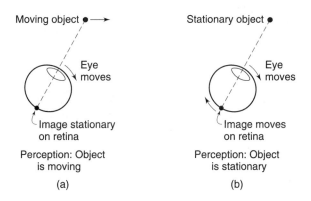

Figure 8.17

Two situations that are difficult to explain based on movement detectors. In (a), a person follows a moving object with her eyes. In (b), a person moves his eyes but the object remains stationary.

corollary discharge signal, the image movement signal, or both reach a structure called the **comparator**, which receives inputs from neurons that carry both of these signals. Movement is perceived when the comparator receives either the image movement signal or the corollary discharge signal separately (Figure 8.19a, b). However, when both signals reach the comparator simultaneously, they cancel each other, and movement is not perceived (Figure 8.19c).

The corollary discharge model has been tested behaviorally by determining whether movement perception does, in fact, occur when only the corollary discharge reaches the comparator. This has been accomplished in the following four ways, three of which you can experience for yourself.

1. By observing an afterimage as you move your eyes in a dark room (Figure 8.20a).

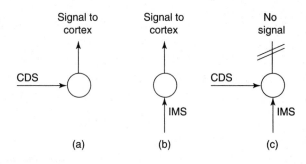

(a)   (b)   (c)

Figure 8.19

How inputs to the comparator (circle) affect movement perception. (a) Receiving the corollary discharge signal alone causes the comparator to send a movement signal to the cortex. (b) Receiving the image movement signal alone also causes the comparator to send a movement signal to the cortex. (c) When both the corollary discharge signal and the image movement signal reach the comparator at the same time, no movement signal is sent to the cortex.

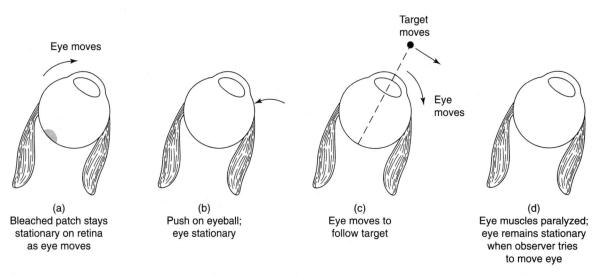

(a)
Bleached patch stays
stationary on retina
as eye moves

(b)
Push on eyeball;
eye stationary

(c)
Eye moves to
follow target

(d)
Eye muscles paralyzed;
eye remains stationary
when observer tries
to move eye

Figure 8.20

Voluntary movement of our eyes usually generates both a corollary discharge (because we send a signal to our eye muscles) and an image movement signal (because movement of the eyes usually causes movement of an image across the retina). There are, however, ways to create a corollary discharge without generating an image movement signal. In all four examples shown in the figure, a signal is sent to the eye muscles, and a corollary discharge is generated. No image movement signal is generated, because (a) staring at a spot for about 30 seconds bleaches a patch of retina, generating an afterimage, and the bleached spot stays at the same place on the retina as the eye moves; (b) when we push on the eyeball, we can send signals to the muscles to hold the eye steady; (c) the eye moves to track a moving object, so the object's image remains stationary on the retina; and (d) the eye is paralyzed so that the signal sent to the muscle cannot cause the eye to move.

DEMONSTRATION

Eliminating the Image Movement Signal with an Afterimage

Illuminate the circle in Figure 7.40 with your desk lamp and look at it for about 60 seconds. Then, go into your closet (or a completely dark room) and observe what happens to the circle's afterimage (blink to make it come back if it fades) as you look around. Notice that the afterimage moves in synchrony with your eye movements.   ●

Why does the afterimage appear to move when you move your eyes? The answer cannot be that an image is moving across your retina, because the circle's image always remains at the same place on the retina. Without movement of the stimulus across the retina, there is no image movement signal. However, a corollary discharge signal accompanies the motor signals sent to your eye muscles. Thus, only the corollary discharge reaches the comparator, and you see the afterimage move. This condition, and the others described below, is summarized in Table 8.1.

2. By pushing on your eyeball while keeping your eye steady (Figure 8.20b).

DEMONSTRATION

Seeing Movement by Pushing on Your Eyeball

While looking steadily at one point, gently push back and forth on the side of your eyelid, as shown in Figure 8.21. As you do this, you will see the scene move.   ●

Figure 8.21
Why is this man smiling? Because every time he pushes on his eyeball he sees the world jiggle.

Table 8.1
Four ways that the corollary discharge can cause the perception of movement when there is no movement on the retina

Condition	Image Movement Signal?	Corollary Discharge Signal?	Perceive Movement?
1. Move eyes while viewing afterimage in the dark (Figure 8.20a).	NO, afterimage always stays on same place on retina.	YES, signal is sent to the eye muscle to move eyes.	YES
2. Push on eyeball while looking at a spot to keep eyes stationary (Figure 8.20b).	NO, the eye remains stationary, since subject is holding fixation on a spot.	YES, signal sent to muscle to keep eye stationary.	YES
3. Move eyes to follow a target (Figure 8.20c).	NO, target stays on fovea at all times.	YES, signal sent to eye muscle to move eye	YES
4. Paralyze eye muscles and try to move eye (Figure 8.20d).	NO, the eye doesn't move because it is paralyzed.	YES, signal sent to eye muscle to attempt to move eye.	YES

Perceiving Movement

Why do you see movement when you push on your eyeball? According to Lawrence Stark and Bruce Bridgeman (1983), when you push on your eyeball while keeping your eye fixed on a particular point, your eyes remain stationary because your eye muscles are pushing against the force of the finger so you can maintain steady fixation on the point. The motor signal sent to the eye muscles to hold the eye in place creates a corollary discharge, which occurs alone, since there is no image movement signal. We therefore see the scene move (also see Bridgeman & Stark, 1991; Ilg, Bridgeman, & Hoffmann, 1989).

3. By following a moving object such as a flying bird with your eyes (Figure 8.20c).

In this situation the eyes move to follow the bird, so the bird's image remains stationary on the observer's retina and there is no image movement signal. But since the eyes are moving, a corollary discharge occurs and the observer perceives the bird's movement.

4. By paralyzing an observer's eye muscles and having the observer try to move his eyes (Figure 8.20d).

In this situation, when the observer tries to move his or her eyes, a motor signal is sent to the eye muscles and causes a corollary discharge. But the paralyzed eye remains stationary, so there is no image movement signal. Since only the corollary discharge reaches the comparator, movement should be perceived. John Stevens (Stevens et al., 1976) showed that this is what occurs by volunteering to be temporarily immobilized by a paralytic drug. When he tried to move his eyes, the scene in front of him appeared to jump to a new position, just as predicted by the corollary discharge model. (See also Matin et al., 1982, for another paralysis experiment.)

These four behavioral demonstrations support the central idea proposed by corollary discharge theory that there is a signal (the corollary discharge) that indicates when the observer moves, or tries to move, his or her eyes. When the theory was first proposed, there was little physiological evidence to support it, but now there is a great deal of research that supports the theory. For example, Claudio Galletti, Paolo Battaglini,

and P. Fattori (1990) found neurons in area V3 of the monkey cortex (in the dorsal stream; see Figure 4.8) that respond strongly when the monkey holds its eyes stationary and a bar is swept across the cell's receptive field. However, this cell does not respond when the bar is held stationary and the monkey moves its eyes so the cell's receptive field sweeps across the bar (Figure 8.22). Galletti called this neuron a **real movement neuron**, because it responds only when the stimulus moves and doesn't respond when the eye moves, even though the stimulus on the retina is the same in both situations. (See also Battaglini, Galletti, & Fattori, 1996; Robinson & Wurtz, 1976.)

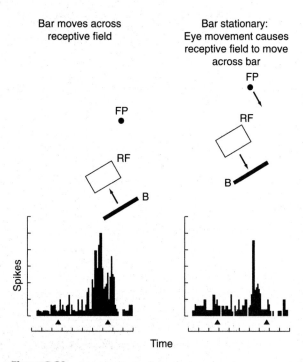

Figure 8.22
(a) When the monkey holds its eyes steady on the fixation point (FP) and the bar stimulus (B) is swept across the receptive field (RF), this neuron responds briskly. (b) When the monkey's eyes follow the moving fixation point (FP), the receptive field sweeps across the bar stimulus. This creates the same effect on the retina as in (a), but the neuron responds poorly. Apparently this neuron is taking the movement of the eyes into account in (b). (Adapted from Galletti, Battaglini, & Fattori, 1990.)

These real movement neurons must be receiving information like the corollary discharge, which tells the neuron when the eye is moving. Corollary discharge theory is a good example of a theory that was originally based on psychophysical results like the ones in Table 8.1 and which later gained physiological support. Although neurons such as the real movement neurons behave in the way corollary discharge theory predicts, researchers have still not discovered the corollary discharge signal itself, where it originates, or where the hypothetical comparator might be.

INFORMATION FOR MOVEMENT IN THE OPTIC ARRAY

All of the examples we have described so far involve signals in the nervous system, either from feature detectors or from a corollary discharge signal. But our perception of movement can be determined not only by signals in the nervous system but also by how things move relative to one another in the environment.

The idea of analyzing movement perception by looking at how things move in the environment was championed by J. J. Gibson (1979), who coined the term **optic array** to refer to the structure created by the surfaces, textures, and contours of the environment. When you look out from where you are right now, all of the surfaces, contours, and textures you see make up the optic array. What is important about the optic array for our consideration of the perception of movement is the way it changes when the observer moves or when something in the environment moves. As we will see, the nature of the changes in the optic array provides information that helps us tell whether the observer is moving or whether objects in the environment are moving.

Local Disturbances in the Optic Array

A local disturbance in the optic array occurs when one object moves relative to the environment, covering and uncovering the stationary background. This cov-

ering and uncovering corresponds to the "deletion" and "accretion" we described in Chapter 7 (see Figure 7.12). This covering and uncovering, which would occur if you were watching a person walk through a scene, as in Figure 8.23, is the local disturbance in the optic array, and it indicates that the man is moving.

This taking into account of the local disturbance in the optic array also works when the observer moves his or her eyes to follow the walking man. Even though the image of the man remains stationary on the observer's retina, the man's image still covers and uncovers the stationary background. Thus, the information provided by the local disturbance leads to the same conclusion ("the man is moving through the scene") if the observer's eyes are stationary or if they are moving.

Global Optical Flow

Global optical flow occurs when all elements of the optic array move, as might occur when the observer

Figure 8.23

Local movement: A person moving from left to right past a stationary observer who is looking at a spot straight ahead. In this situation, the person moves across the observer's field of view, as indicated by the arrows, but the background remains stationary.

Perceiving Movement

walks through the environment (Figure 8.24). This movement of the observer causes movement of the entire optic array, hence the term "global," and this global flow signals that the observer is moving and not the environment.

Gibson's analysis of movement perception in terms of the optic array is important because it illustrates how perception can be analyzed by focusing not on electrical signals in neurons, or on what is happening on the retina, but by considering just what is happening "out there" in the environment. We will have more to say about this approach to perception in Chapter 9.

We will next consider point 3 from the beginning of the chapter, which stated that perception often involves an interaction between different perceptual qualities. We will specifically consider how movement influences perceptual organization and how it helps us more accurately determine the shapes and identities of objects.

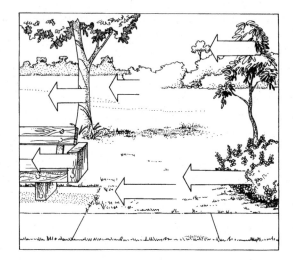

Figure 8.24

Global optical flow: If our observer walks to the right while looking at the scene on the left, the images of the scene flow across the observer's field of view, as indicated by the arrows.

SUMMARY TABLE 8.1

Introduction to Movement Perception

Although some animals may have poor depth perception or rudimentary color vision, none lacks the ability to perceive motion. Losing the ability to perceive movement, as occurs in cases of motion agnosia, poses serious problems for day-to-day living. The study of movement perception provides examples of how perception (1) is a creation of the nervous system; (2) depends on more than the image on the retina; (3) involves interactions between different qualities; and (4) depends on heuristics and cognitive factors. Four types of movement perception are real movement, apparent movement, induced movement, and movement aftereffects.

Neural Feature Detectors

There are neurons in the striate cortex that are tuned to respond to movement in a particular direction. Reichart's neural circuit demonstrates how neural processing could create a neuron that responds to the direction in which a stimulus is moving. The firing of neurons in the MT cortex are so closely linked to the perception of movement that the code for perceiving the direction movement begins to approach specificity for these neurons.

Corollary Discharge Theory

Corollary discharge theory proposes that movement perception depends on three types of signals: the motor signal, the corollary discharge signal, and the image movement signal. A hypothetical structure called the comparator analyzes these signals to determine whether the stimulus information on the retina is due to movement of a stimulus in the environment or to the movement of the observer's eyes. There are neurons called real movement neurons that respond to actual stimulus movement but not to movement of the stimulus on the retina caused by eye or head movements.

Information in the Optic Array

It is possible to analyze movement perception by considering how things move relative to each other in the environment. A local disturbance in the optic array indicates that the object that is causing the disturbance is moving. Global optical flow indicates that the observer is moving through the environment, which is stationary.

PERCEPTUAL ORGANIZATION AND MOVEMENT PERCEPTION

webTUTOR In Chapter 5 we discussed some of the factors that lead to perceptual organization—how elements of a scene are perceptually organized into larger objects. When we discussed the "laws of organization" proposed by the Gestalt psychologists, we saw that some of these laws involved movement. For example, the "law of common fate" stated that elements that are moving in the same direction are seen as being perceptually grouped together. We can illustrate this principle by the following demonstration.

DEMONSTRATION

Perceiving a Camouflaged Bird

For this demonstration, you will need to prepare stimuli by photocopying the bird and the hatched-line pattern in Figure 8.25. Then cut out the bird and the hatched pattern so they are separated. Hold the picture of the bird up against a window during the day. Turn the copy of the hatched pattern over so the pattern is facing out the window (the white side of the paper should be facing you) and place it over the bird. If the window is adequately illuminated by the daylight, you should be able to see the hatched pattern. Notice how the presence of the hatched pattern makes it more difficult to see the bird. Then as you slide the bird back and forth under the pattern notice what happens to your perception of the bird (from Regan, 1986). ●

The stationary bird is difficult to see when covered by the pattern, because the bird and the pattern are made up of similar lines. But as soon as all of the elements of the bird begin moving in the same direction, the bird becomes visible. As we noted at the beginning of the chapter, this is why a mouse freezes when it is being stalked by a cat. It wants to avoid becoming perceptually organized in the cat's mind!

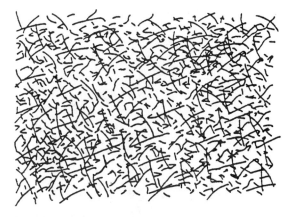

Figure 8.25
The bird becomes camouflaged if a transparency of the random lines is superimposed on a transparency of the bird. When the bird is moved relative to the lines, it becomes visible, an example of how movement enhances the perception of form. (From Regan, 1986.)

We now consider some other ways that movement can lead to perceptual organization.

Movement Creates Perceptual Organization

Movement can contribute to perceptual organization in a number of different ways. We will first consider how movement can cause a number of individual elements to become perceived as a whole object.

The Organization of Dots in Point-Light Walkers
What would you see if you placed small lights on a person's body, as in Figure 8.26, and viewed the lights in a dark room? The answer to this question depends on whether the person is moving or stationary. When the person is stationary, the lights look like a meaningless pattern. However, as soon as the person starts

Perceiving Movement

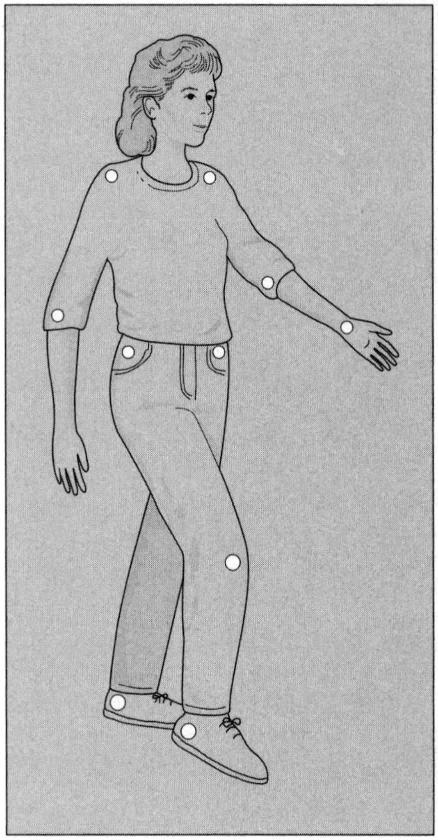

Figure 8.26

A person wearing lights for a biological motion experiment. In the actual experiment, the room is totally dark, and only the lights can be seen.

walking, with arms and legs swinging back and forth and feet moving in flattened arcs, first one leaving the ground and touching down then the other, the lights are immediately perceived as being caused by a walking person. This is the perception of **biological motion** (Johansson, 1975).

Even though the pattern of movement caused by biological motion is extremely complex, observers don't perceive a complex jumble of moving lights. The moving lights create a structure—a person walking—out of what was initially perceived as a random arrangement of dots. This perception of structure is particularly impressive because the movement

of an individual light is not seen as the movement of a person (Figure 8.27). It is only when the dots move together that they become a person.

The perceptual grouping of point-light walker lights has also been studied physiologically, by recording from neurons in an area in the monkey's temporal cortex called the superior temporal area. Some cells in this area respond best to images of people walking. For example, Figure 8.28 shows the response of a neuron that responds best to images of a person walking forward. Some of the neurons that respond to people walking also respond to the movement of point-light walkers. M. W. Oram and David Perrett (1994) recorded from a neuron that responded well to a point-light walker walking backward but responded less well to forward movement or to the random movement of dots (Figure 8.29). This research on the monkey has also been extended to humans by monitoring human brain activity with positron emission tomography (PET). This research has shown that presenting moving point-light walkers causes an increase in activity in the human superior temporal sulcus (Bonda et al., 1996).

Structure from Motion: The Kinetic Depth Effect

The way movement organizes the perception of point-light walkers shows that movement can perceptually organize individual elements into the meaningful form of the human body. Another example of how movement can organize our perception of form is a phenomenon called the **kinetic depth effect**, in

Figure 8.27

The path traced by one of the lights attached to the walking person's ankle. When viewing all of the lights moving together, the observer is unaware of these individual movements and perceives the entire configuration as a walking person.

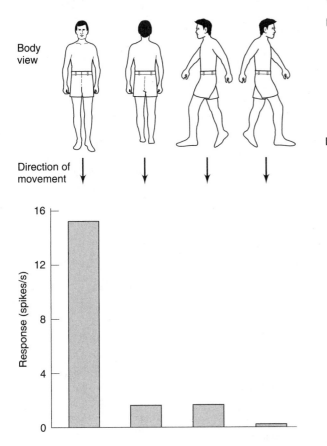

Figure 8.28

The response of a neuron in the macaque monkey's superior temporal sulcus that responded best to a frontal view of a person moving downward. Other views of the body generated little response even though they were moving in the same direction. (Adapted from Perrett et al., 1990.)

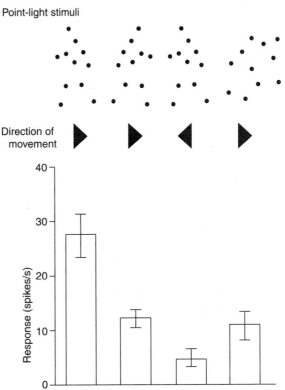

Figure 8.29

Response of a neuron in the superior temporal area of the monkey to point-light walker stimuli (shown at the top) moving in various directions. This cell responds best to backward walking (a) and responds less well to walking forward to the right (b), walking forward to the left (c), and a jumbled motion stimulus moving to the right (d). (Adapted from Oram & Perrett, 1994.)

which movement of an object's two-dimensional shadow can change the perception of the shadow into the perception of a three-dimensional object.

Hans Wallach and D. N. O'Connell (1953) demonstrated this effect by casting a shadow of a cube on a transparent screen (Figure 8.30). When the shadow is stationary it looks flat, but when the cube is rotated, as indicated by the arrow, the shadow takes on a three-dimensional appearance, even though it is seen on a two-dimensional surface. Movement therefore creates the perception of three-dimensional structure on a two-dimensional surface.

D E M O N S T R A T I O N

The Kinetic Depth Effect with Pipe Cleaners

You can demonstrate the kinetic depth effect by bending a pipe cleaner so that it reproduces sides a, b, c, and d of the shape in Figure 8.30. Then, cast a shadow of the pipe cleaner on a piece of paper, as shown in Figure 8.31, and, while viewing the shadow from the other side of the paper, rotate the pipe cleaner. The result should be a perception

Perceiving Movement

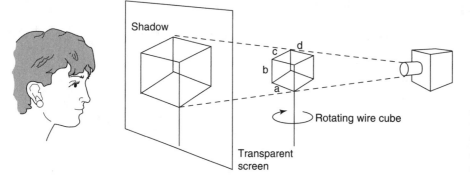

Figure 8.30
Setup similar to the one used by Wallach and O'Connell (1953) to demonstrate the kinetic depth effect.

Shadow

c d
b
a

Rotating wire cube

Transparent screen

Figure 8.31
Shadow-casting by a bent pipe cleaner. To achieve a sharp shadow, position the pipe cleaner about 2 feet from your desk lamp. (If it is too close to the lamp, the shadow will be fuzzy.) To perceive the kinetic depth effect, rotate the pipe cleaner between your fingers while observing the shadow from the other side of the paper.

that is more three-dimensional than when the shadow was stationary. ●

Just as for the point-light walkers, recent research has identified activity in the brain that is associated with perception of the kinetic depth effect. These cells are located in the MT area of the monkey's cortex (Andersen & Bradley, 1998).

Motion Capture Another example of how the movement of elements can create organization is illustrated by the following demonstration.

DEMONSTRATION

TV Dots That
Move Together

To do this demonstration you will need to tune a TV set to a channel that has no station, so you see random "snow." Then make a circle with your fingers, or with a bent paper clip, as shown in Figure 8.32. Close one eye, and view the circle as you move it in front of the screen. As you move the circle, notice what happens to the "snow" inside the circle. ●

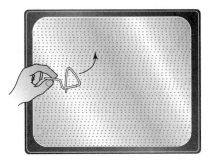

Figure 8.32
How to do the motion capture demonstration: Bend a paper clip as shown and move it around in front of TV "snow." Notice whether the dots appear to move along with the enclosed area of the paper clip.

If it appeared that the dots inside the circle were moving along with the circle, you experienced **motion capture**—small elements that are enclosed within a larger figure appear to move with the figure. For example, when a leopard jumps, we perceive the leopard's body moving, and we also perceive all of the leopard's spots as moving along with it (Figure 8.33). Although it might seem obvious that a leopard's spots would move along with the leopard, this outcome becomes less obvious when we consider a film of a leopard, in which different views of the leopard are flashed, one after another, to create the illusion of movement.

We can appreciate the problem facing the visual system in Figure 8.33 by looking at two film frames showing a simplified 4-spot version of a leopard (Figure 8.34). The rectangle on the left shows the position of the "leopard" in frame 1, and the rectangle on the right shows its new position in frame 2, after the leopard has jumped. The dashed ellipse in frame 2 indicates where the image of the leopard was in frame 1. If we compare the positions of the leopard's spots in the two frames, we see that spot B in Frame 1 is closest to spot A′ in Frame 2 and spot C in Frame 1 is closest to spot D′ in Frame 2. If the dots in Frame 1 moved to the closest dot in Frame 2, we would have a real problem, because B would move to A′ and C would move to D′ and our leopard's spots would fly apart as it moved! Luckily, motion capture comes to the rescue and causes all of the dots to move together, as a unit. Motion capture is, therefore, another example of how movement can cause perceptual organization.

Figure 8.33

Perceiving Movement

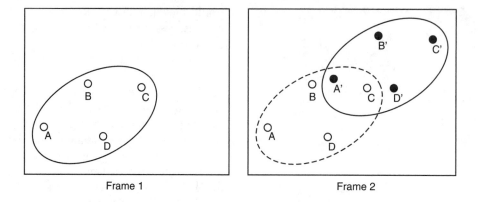

Figure 8.34

The ellipse is a "simplified leopard" that has four spots. Frame 1 shows the position of the leopard's image just before it jumps. Frame 2 shows the position of the leopard's image as it is jumping (solid ellipse and dark spots) and also the position of the leopard's image from frame 1 (dashed ellipse and open spots). The spots do not actually change color, but they are pictured as darker for the jumping leopard to make them easier to distinguish from the other spots, inside the dashed ellipse. See text for further details.

THE INTELLIGENCE OF MOVEMENT PERCEPTION

WebTUTOR   When we considered object perception in Chapter 5, we noted that object perception is "intelligent," because the perceptual system takes characteristics of the environment into account and also uses additional information provided by the observer's knowledge, memories, and expectations. We've already seen some evidence for a similar kind of "intelligence" in movement perception. For example, the reason subjects see human movement when they observe the point-light walkers probably has something to do with the experience they have had in perceiving people walking.

We will now consider some additional examples that lead us to say that movement perception is intelligent. For our first examples, we will return to the idea of perceptual heuristics that we introduced in our discussion of object perception (Chapter 5, page 154; also see lightness perception, Chapter 6, page 214).

Heuristics and Movement Perception

The basic idea behind perceptual heuristics is that the visual stimulus is ambiguous—there are a num-

ber of possible ways we can perceive something—so the perceptual system uses heuristics or "rules of thumb" to choose the perception that is most likely to provide accurate information about the environment. We will now present some examples of how our perception of apparent motion is the outcome of perceptual heuristics.

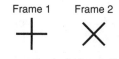

(a) Clockwise or counterclockwise motion

(b) Only clockwise motion

Figure 8.35

(a) Alternating an upright cross and a tilted one creates an ambiguous stimulus in which the rotation can be perceived as either clockwise or counterclockwise. (b) Adding the tilted cross on the left starts a clockwise movement, so that when the third cross is flashed, the movement is perceived as continuing in that direction. Note that the two stimuli in (a) and the final two in (b) are identical.

The "Movement Continues in the Same Direction" Heuristic When the two crosses in Figure 8.35a are presented rapidly, one after the other, subjects perceive either clockwise or counterclockwise rotation. If, however, an initial cross is added to the series, as in Figure 8.35b, subjects perceive clockwise movement (Ramachandran & Anstis, 1986). The heuristic involved here is simply that when an object is rotating in one direction it tends to continue its rotation in that direction. This reflects the way movement usually occurs in the environment, and is similar to the Gestalt principle of good continuation described in Chapter 5 for static stimuli, which states that lines tend to be perceived as following the smoothest path.

The Occlusion Heuristic Consider the display in Figure 8.36a. Vilayanur Ramachandran and Stuart Anstis (1986) presented first the triangle and square on the left together and then the square on the right. Figures 8.36b and c show two possible ways that movement could be perceived. Figure 8.36b shows the triangle and square moving to the right and fusing into a square. Figure 8.36c shows the square moving diagonally to the right and the triangle blinking on and off.

But subjects saw neither of those perceptions. Instead, they saw the lower square move up and to the right and the triangle move to the right and then appear to slide under the square so it was hidden behind it (Figure 8.36d). According to Ramachandran and Anstis, this perception is a reflection of the **occlusion heuristic**, a rule that states that a moving object will cover and uncover the background and that when the background is covered it still exists. Thus, the tri-

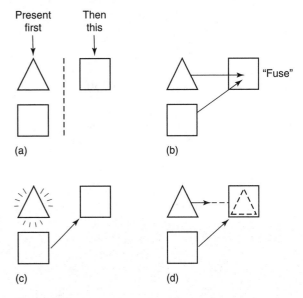

Figure 8.36
(a) Stimulus presentation in the Ramachandran and Anstis experiment. The triangle and lower square are flashed simultaneously, followed by the top square. (b), (c), and (d) are possible perceptions. See text for details.

angle, instead of fusing with the square, slips under it and is covered by it.

In another experiment, Ramachandran and Anstis flashed the two dots on the left in Figure 8.37a, followed by the dot on the right. Subjects perceived this as the two dots moving to the position on the right (Figure 8.37b). But adding a square, as in Figure 8.37c, caused a change in this perception. Now both

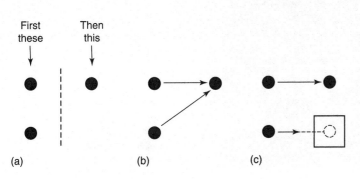

Figure 8.37
(a) Stimulus presentation in the moving dot experiment. (b) Perception that results from the presentation in (a). Both dots move to the position of the dot on the right. (c) Placing an occluder in the position shown changes the perception of the movement of the lower dot, so it moves to the right and under the occluder.

Perceiving Movement

dots moved to the right, with the bottom one hiding behind the square—another example of the occlusion heuristic at work.

Meaning and Movement Perception

Another way to demonstrate the intelligence of movement perception is by examples of how our perception of the meaning of a stimulus can affect how we perceive movement.

An Object's Meaning Influences Movement Perception When subjects first viewed the pictures in Figure 8.38, they often saw a meaningless black-and-white pattern. When these pictures were flashed, one after another, subjects saw random motion, often varying from trial to trial. But, when they realized that these were actually pictures of faces (often after being prompted by the experimenter), they always saw three-dimensional rotation of the face when the images were flashed (Ramachandran et al., 1998). Thus, even though the patterns of light and dark on the retina were the same before and after the subjects saw the patterns as faces, their recognition of the faces caused a drastic change in their perception of motion.

Ramachandran and coworkers drew the following conclusion from this result: Perception of the rotating face must depend on interactions between brain areas concerned with motion, such as MT, and areas involved in recognizing complex objects, such as IT. It is significant that MT is in the dorsal processing stream (where or how) and IT is in the ventral processing stream (what). Thus, even though these two streams are separated, there must be some "crosstalk" between them.

Knowledge About the Human Body Influences Movement Perception We will now describe another experiment, also involving the apparent motion of pictures of people, which also shows that recognition of the meaning of a stimulus can affect motion perception. To set the stage for this experiment, we introduce a principle called the **shortest-path constraint**—movement tends to occur along the shortest path between two stimuli, even though many other paths are also possible (Figure 8.39).

Maggie Shiffrar and Jennifer Freyd (1990, 1993) used pictures like the ones in Figure 8.40 to ask what would happen if observers are shown two meaningful stimuli that would normally violate this constraint.

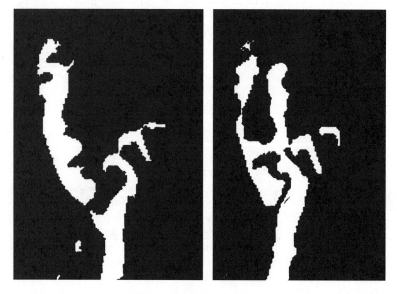

Figure 8.38
Two face stimuli used in the apparent movement experiment described in the text.

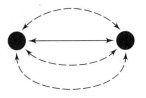

Figure 8.39
According to the shortest-path constraint, the apparent movement between the two rapidly alternating dots should occur along the shortest pathway (solid arrows) even though many other pathways are possible (dashed arrows).

These two pictures are designed to pose the following question: When these pictures are alternated rapidly, will observers perceive the woman's hand as moving through her head (this would follow the shortest-path constraint) or will they perceive her hand as moving around her head (this would violate the shortest path constraint)?

Shiffrar and Freyd found that the answer to this question depends on the length of time between the onset of the first and second pictures, called stimulus onset asynchrony (SOA). At SOAs below about 200 ms, subjects perceive the hand as moving through the head, thereby following the shortest-path constraint.

However, at SOAs longer than 200 ms, the subjects perceived movement along the longer path around the woman's head, which violates the shortest-path constraint. These results are interesting for two reasons: (1) They show that the visual system needs time to process information in order to perceive the movement of complex meaningful stimuli (although 200 ms may seem like a short period of time, it is a long processing time by the nervous system's standards); (2) they suggest that there may be something special about the meaning of the stimulus—in this case, the human body—that influences the way movement is perceived. To test the idea that the human body is special, Shiffrar and coworkers showed that when objects such as boards are used as stimuli instead of humans, movement along the longer path doesn't increase with increasing SOA, as it does for pictures of humans (Chatterjee, Freyd, & Shiffrar, 1996).

What is noteworthy about all of the research we have described on motion perception is the wide range of phenomena it covers, from simple movements like a single dot moving from left to right to complex movements of the human body. And, as we stated at the beginning of the chapter, motion perception illustrates a variety of perceptual principles that also hold for other perceptual qualities as well.

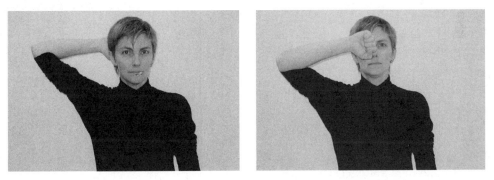

Figure 8.40
Photographs like the ones used to create the stimulus in Shiffrar and Freyd's (1990) apparent movement experiments. When these pictures are alternated rapidly, the hand making a fist appears to move from one position to the other. The hand appears to go through the head at short SOAs and around the head at long SOAs. (Photographs courtesy of Maggie Shiffrar.)

Perceiving Movement

What is happening in the cortex when subjects view apparent motion generated by pictures like the one in Figure 8.40? Jennifer Stevens and coworkers (2000) measured brain activation using the PET scan technique when observers reported seeing movement that went straight through part of the body (impossible movement) and when they reported seeing movement around the body part (possible movement). They found that both types of movement activated areas in the parietal cortex associated with movement, but, when the observers saw the possible movement, the motor cortex was activated as well. Thus, the motor cortex is activated if the perceived movements are humanly possible but isn't activated if the perceived movements are not possible. Stevens and coworkers suggest that the parietal and motor cortex are activated together in response to activities that are within the observer's capabilities. Another possibility is that humans might respond differently to movements they know are possible, whether or not they can carry them out personally. Further research is needed to more precisely define the conditions in which seeing a moving stimulus simultaneously activates both sensory and motor areas of the brain.

THE PLASTICITY OF PERCEPTION
Selective Rearing and Movement Perception

The way mechanisms responsible for movement perception are affected by experience has been demonstrated using the selective rearing procedure that we described for depth perception in Chapter 7. In the depth perception experiments, rearing kittens with one eye shut eliminated binocular neurons, which respond to stimulation of both the left and right eyes. Tatiana Pasternak (1990) did the analogous experiment for movement by rearing kittens in a dark room that was illuminated only by light that constantly flickered eight times per second so that the kittens' vision consisted entirely of still "snapshots" of their environment. Kittens reared in this way became unable to detect the direction of a moving stimulus, even though they were still able to detect the presence of the stimulus. And when Pasternak recorded from neurons in the striate cortex, she found only a few neurons tuned to respond to a particular direction. This contrasts with the normal situation in which most of the cat's neurons are sensitive to a particular direction of movement. Thus, experience with moving stimuli is needed during early development in order for directionally selective neurons to develop normally.

MOVEMENT PERCEPTION
ACROSS THE SENSES

In Chapter 5 we described a number of ways that all of our senses can contribute to object perception. Both seeing an object and manipulating it with our hands provide information for identifying an object, and information for object identification is even provided by the sound an object makes when we tap it and by what it smells like when we sniff it.

Similarly, our perception of movement is not limited to vision. We easily perceive movement of a bug walking across our skin or of a person's hands giving us a back rub. In fact, in laboratory experiments, it has been shown that briefly vibrating one place on the skin, and then vibrating at another location causes subjects to feel movement from one place on the skin to the other (Sherrick & Rogers, 1966). This apparent movement on the skin can't be caused by the spread of vibration into the area between the two places on the skin, because apparent movement can also occur across the space between the two arms. Subjects report that the movement appears to jump into the space between the arms, vanishes for a moment, and then jumps onto the other arm (Figure 8.41) (Sherrick, 1968).

An interesting similarity between visual and tactile apparent movement is shown in Figure 8.42, which plots subject's judgments of the goodness of movement on a scale of 1 to 100 versus the duration of each of the stimulus pulses. As the stimulus duration increases, the "goodness" of the perceived movement increases, both for visual and tactile movement. It is particularly impressive that the data for tactile apparent movement (Kirman, 1974) and visual apparent movement (Kolers, 1964) are almost exactly the same.

Returning to electrophysiological comparisons of vision and touch, a recent study has found that when adjacent areas of skin are stimulated rapidly enough to cause a perception of smooth apparent

movement, neurons in the somatosensory area of the cortex fire smoothly. However, when these same areas of skin are stimulated more slowly, so movement perception is absent (it feels like one point is stimulated and then the other), then these neurons fire in separated bursts (Gardner et al., 1992). Similar studies using visual stimuli have reported the same result: Rapid visual stimulation that results in apparent movement causes continuous firing of neurons in the striate cortex and area MT, but slower visual stimulation that does not cause the perception of apparent movement causes the same kind of firing

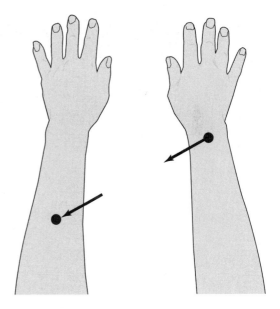

Figure 8.41
Tactile apparent movement that results when a point on the right arm is stimulated and then a point on the left arm is stimulated. The movement appears to jump from one arm to another, as shown.

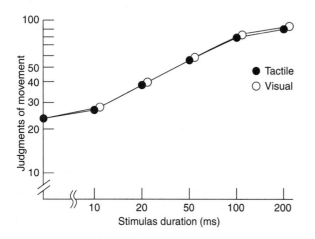

Figure 8.42
Judgments of goodness of movement vs. the duration of the stimuli for tactile apparent movement (filled circles) and visual apparent movement (open circles). (Adapted from Kirman, 1974.)

in bursts that occurs in the somatosensory cortex (Mikami et al., 1986; Newsome et al., 1986). These parallels between movement in vision and touch led Esther Gardner and coworkers (1992) to conclude that "Linkage of successive stimuli appears to be a general property of cortical processing of sensory information" (p. 61).

Of course, our perception of movement is not limited to vision and touch, as evidenced by your ability to stand on a street corner and, with your eyes closed, perceive the movement of passing cars based only by the sound that they make. In Chapter 11 we will describe some of the ways that the auditory system accomplishes this.

Perceptual Organization and Movement Perception

Movement can lead to perceptual organization, so that previously unseen objects, like the camouflaged bird, become visible. The way point-light walkers become visible as soon as the dots begin to move is an example of movement leading to organization, as is the kinetic depth effect, in which movement of an object's two-dimensional shadow can result in perception of the object's three-dimensional structure. Motion capture is another example of movement leading to organization.

Movement Perception and Heuristics

Evidence for the intelligence of motion perception is provided by experiments that show that the system makes use of heuristics in order to determine the perception of apparent movement displays. Two heuristics that operate for apparent movement are one that is based on the observation that movement usually continues in the same direction and another that is based on how perception is influenced by the way objects in the environment occlude each other.

Movement Perception and Meaning

The intelligence of movement perception is also illustrated by how the meaning of a stimulus can influence movement perception.

Examples include how perception of the meanings of high-contrast face stimuli results in movement and how our knowledge of the types of movement possible by the human body influences the path that apparent movement follows. Brain scan experiments have shown that movements that went through parts of the body (impossible movement) and movements that went around the body (possible movement) both activated the parietal cortex, but only the possible movement also activated the motor cortex.

Plasticity: Selective Rearing

When kittens were reared in a dark room illuminated only by flickering lights that prevented the perception of movement, they became unable to detect the direction of a moving stimulus and had few directionally selective neurons in their striate cortex.

Movement Perception Across the Senses

Our perception of movement is not limited to vision. The perception of apparent movement can also be based on stimulation of the skin. There are a number of similarities between visual movement perception and tactile movement perception. Both psychophysical and physiological measurements indicate that both types of movement are affected similarly by the duration of the stimuli.

STUDY QUESTIONS

1. What is motion agnosia? What are its causes and its symptoms? (270)

2. What are the four basic ideas about perception that we are concerned with in this chapter? (270)

Four Ways to Create the Perception of Movement

Real Movement

3. What is real movement? (272)

4. What is the evidence that our perception of movement is affected by the context within which the moving stimulus exists? (272)

Apparent Movement

5. What was Exner's discovery? (272)

6. What was the significance of Wertheimer's work on apparent movement? (272)

7. What is the relationship between the interstimulus interval and the perception of apparent movement? (273)

Induced Movement

8. What is induced movement? Give at least two examples of induced movement. (274)

Movement Aftereffect

9. What is a movement aftereffect? The waterfall illusion? The spiral motion aftereffect? (275)

Studying Movement Perception

10. Do modern researchers see real movement and apparent movement as separate phenomena, involving different mechanisms? (275)

Neural Feature Detectors and Movement Perception

11. Describe the directionally selective neurons in the striate cortex. (276)

A Neural Circuit for a Directionally Selective Neuron

12. Describe Reichart's circuit that responds to movement in one direction. (277)

Neural Firing and Judging the Direction of Movement

13. Which extrastriate area is important for movement perception? (277)

14. How did Newsome and coworkers demonstrate a connection between the firing of MT neurons and movement perception? (278)

15. Why would it be correct to say that the code for the direction of motion approaches specificity coding in MT neurons? (278)

16. What is a situation that is difficult for neural feature detectors to explain because we perceive movement even though there is no movement on the retina? What about the situation in which we perceive no movement even though there is movement on the retina? (279)

Corollary Discharge Theory: Taking Eye Movements into Account

17. What is the basic idea behind corollary discharge theory? (279)

18. Describe what causes the motor signal to occur, the corollary discharge to occur, and the image movement signal to occur. (279)

19. What is the comparator? Which signals in 18, above, are received by the comparator according to corollary discharge theory? (280)

20. What perception occurs when the comparator receives either the image movement signal or the corollary discharge signal separately? What perception occurs when these two signals reach the comparator simultaneously? (280)

21. Explain what happens in the following situations and how these results are explained by corollary discharge theory: (1) You observe an afterimage as you move your eyes in the dark; (2) you push on your eyeball while keeping your eye steady; (3) you follow a moving object with your eyes; (4) an observer with paralyzed eye muscles tries to move his eyes. (280)

22. What is a real movement neuron and how does the way it responds relate to corollary discharge theory? (282)

Information for Movement in the Optic Array

23. What is the optic array, and what is important about it for our consideration of movement perception? (283)

Local Disturbances in the Optic Array

24. When does a local disturbance occur in the optic array? What does it indicate when it occurs? (283)

Global Optical Flow

25. When does global optical flow occur, and what does it indicate? (283)

Perceptual Organization and Movement Perception

26. What does the camouflaged bird demonstration illustrate? (285)

Movement Creates Perceptual Organization

27. What is a point-light walker? What do experiments using point-light walker stimuli tell us about the relationship between movement and perceptual grouping? (285)

28. Describe the response of neurons in the monkey's temporal cortex that respond to images of people walking and to point-light walker stimuli. How has this research been extended to humans? (286)

29. What is the kinetic depth effect? (286)

30. What is motion capture? Why is it possible that a film of a leopard jumping could show the leopard's spots as flying apart? What prevents this from happening? (288)

The Intelligence of Movement Perception

Heuristics and Movement Perception

31. Why are heuristics necessary for perception? (290)

32. Describe how the sequence in which stimuli are presented can influence our perception of apparent movement. (290)

33. What heuristic is involved in 32, above? (291)

34. What heuristic is involved in the movement that occurs in response to the stimuli in Figures 8.36 and 8.37? (291)

Meaning and Movement Perception

35. What do subjects see when the stimuli in Figure 8.38 are flashed to create apparent movement, if they see these stimuli as two-dimensional patterns? If they see the stimuli as three-dimensional faces? (292)

36. What is the shortest-path constraint? (292)

37. What happens if two meaningful stimuli views of a person's body are presented in a way that could violate the shortest-path constraint? (293)

38. Describe two things about the results in 37, above, that make them especially interesting. (293)

Brain Scan: Brain Activity During Apparent Movement of the Human Body

39. What did Stevens and coworkers find when they recorded PET activity as subjects viewed apparent movement stimuli, like the ones in Figure 8.40? (294)

40. According to Stevens, when would the motor cortex be activated in response to a sensory stimulus? What is another possibility? (294)

The Plasticity of Perception:
Selective Rearing and Movement Perception

41. Describe Pasternak's selective rearing experiment. (294)

Across the Senses:
Movement Perception Across the Senses

42. What are some similarities between apparent movement of tactile stimuli and apparent movement on the skin? (295)

43. What happens when points on the two arms are vibrated one after the other? (295)

44. How have electrophysiological experiments illustrated parallels between visual and tactile movement perception? (296)

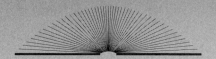

PERCEPTION
AND ACTION

SOME QUESTIONS WE WILL CONSIDER

- How does the way the environment "flows by" outside a moving car help the driver stay on the road? (308)

- How can an outfielder know where to run to get under a fly ball? (314)

- How do the visual system and the system that controls movement of the hand work together to help us pick up a cup? (320)

It is March madness in college basketball, and in a crucial game in the NCAA tournament a player charges toward the basket, stops, twists, takes off on his right foot, and seems to levitate straight up while bringing the ball down through the hoop for a resounding slam dunk. Meanwhile, in spring training, a centerfielder hears the crack of a bat and immediately begins moving toward right field to get under the arcing fly ball. He waves off the right fielder, who is nearby, and makes the catch handily.

These examples of athletic skill are also examples of the close link between perception and action. As we will see in this chapter, just about everything we do involves a close coupling between perception and action. Feats in team sports like basketball and baseball, and in individual sports like gymnastics and figure skating, all involve not only strength and athleticism, but the ability to coordinate movements of various parts of the body relative to each other and movement of the entire body with the rest of the environment. Athletes achieve this coordination by monitoring the relationship between their actions and their perceptions. Thus, the twist added to the basketball player's jump in midair occurs in response to his perception of the position of his own body relative to the basket and to the defender who is attempting to block his shot.

This coordination between perception and action occurs not only when a basketball player is shooting a basket. It also occurs as you walk down the street or negotiate a turn in your car. In fact, perception and action almost always occur together, since most of our perceptions occur as we are moving within the environment or are acting on the environment in some way. As we noted at the beginning of the book, some researchers see action as being the most important outcome of the perceptual process, because of its importance for survival. According to this idea, what is most important about perceiving a car approaching, as we cross the street, is the action we take to get out of the car's way.

In this chapter, we are going to consider a number of different approaches to studying the connection between perception and action. First, we consider some ideas of J. J. Gibson, who was one of the first psychologists to focus on the relationship between perception and movement. We will then describe research that has considered the relationship between perception and movement during everyday tasks such as driving a car, catching a ball, and maintaining an upright posture. Finally, we will take a physiological approach and consider how the firing of neurons in

the brain helps achieve a coordination between perception and movement.

PERCEPTION AND THE MOVING OBSERVER

WebTUTOR   We begin our consideration of the connection between perception and action by describing some of the ideas of J. J. Gibson, a psychologist from Cornell University, who, during a career that spanned 50 years, beginning with his first paper in 1929 and ending with his death just after publication of his third book in 1979, was a pioneer in studying perception of the moving observer (Gibson, 1950, 1966, 1979).

Gibson's Ecological Approach to Perception

Gibson's research and theoretical publications resulted in the founding of the **ecological approach to perception.** The ecological approach focuses on studying perception as it occurs in the natural environment and emphasizes the connection between a person's perceptions and the person's movement through the environment.

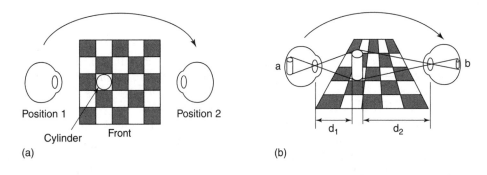

Figure 9.1
Retinal information for the size of a cylinder. (a) An observer looking at a cylinder on a checkerboard from two different positions, indicated by the two eyeballs. (b) Perspective view of the checkerboard. The cylinder's image on the retina is larger when the observer is close (position 1) and becomes smaller when the observer moves to position 2. Arrows d_1 and d_2 indicate the distances between the observer and the cylinder for viewing positions 1 and 2, respectively.

The Beginnings of the Ecological Approach The beginnings of the ecological approach can be traced to Gibson's work during World War II on ways to improve a pilot's ability to land an airplane. Based on this work, Gibson concluded that many of the "textbook" depth cues such as binocular disparity and apparent size, which are ineffective at large distances, could not adequately explain how an airplane pilot judges the distance to the runway during the approach for a landing. Gibson proposed instead that a pilot uses information produced by characteristics of the ground over which the plane is flying and, most important for our purposes, information that is created by the plane's movement.

The Importance of the Moving Observer The idea that perception is most properly studied as it occurs in the natural environment, and as it is experienced by a moving observer, are themes which Gibson developed throughout his career. Gibson felt that traditional laboratory research, in which subjects are often constrained so their heads don't move, is too artificial. He saw this laboratory approach as the study of "snapshot vision," since subjects typically see just one view of a visual stimulus and the stimulus might be just briefly flashed. He considered this laboratory approach as not relevant to understanding perception as it usually occurs in the environment. We will describe Gibson's alternative to this approach by focusing on a few of the major principles of the ecological approach.

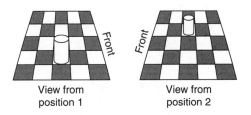

View from position 1   View from position 2

Figure 9.2
Environmental information for the size of a cylinder; what the observer in Figure 9.1 sees from positions 1 and 2. Although moving from position 1 to 2 decreases the size of the cylinder in the field of view, the base of the cylinder always covers one unit of the checkerboard.

Environmental Information and Perception: Ecological Optics

Most of the research we have described in this book has looked to the nervous system and the image on the retina for the information that controls perception, but Gibson focused instead on determining which information in the environment is available for perception. We can appreciate what this means by comparing two possible sources of information for perception: information on the retina and information in the environment.

Information on the Retina vs. Information in the Environment To illustrate the difference between retinal information and environmental information, we will consider the cylinder resting on a checkerboard shown in Figures 9.1 and 9.2. In the top view of the checkerboard in Figure 9.1a, the position of the cylinder is indicated by the circle, and the positions of two different viewpoints taken by an observer are indicated by the two eyes. First the observer views the cylinder from position 1, then moves to position 2. Notice that moving from viewpoint 1 to viewpoint 2 almost doubles the distance between the eye and the cylinder.

Figure 9.1b shows the retinal information for the cylinder as viewed from the two viewing positions. This information, the images a and b on the retina, is different for each viewing position, since the image becomes smaller as the distance between the observer and the cylinder increases. But even though the image becomes smaller as the observer moves from position 1 to 2, the observer perceives the cylinder as remaining the same size. This is the phenomenon of size constancy that we described in Chapter 7: If there is good depth information, we perceive an object's size as remaining constant no matter what its distance.

The explanation for size constancy that we offered in Chapter 7 was that the perceptual system takes the object's distance into account. Thus, even though the retinal image of the cylinder is smaller when the observer is at position 2 than when she or he is at position 1, the perceptual system takes the two distances, d_1 and d_2 into account, and the cylinder is perceived to be the same size from both viewpoints.

Figure 9.2 shows the environmental information for the size of the cylinder as viewed from the two positions. The environmental information is the number of units on the checkerboard covered by the base of the cylinder. Since the base of the cylinder always covers one unit on the checkerboard, no matter what the observer's viewing position, this environmental information indicates that the cylinder's size remains the same without having to take the observer's distance into account, as we did when we

started with the retinal image. This information in the environment was the starting point for Gibson's analysis, and he developed a way of describing it called the ambient optic array.

The Ambient Optic Array Gibson's belief in the importance of environmentally based information for perception led him to develop a way of describing perceptual stimuli that he called ecological optics. **Ecological optics** is the description of stimuli based

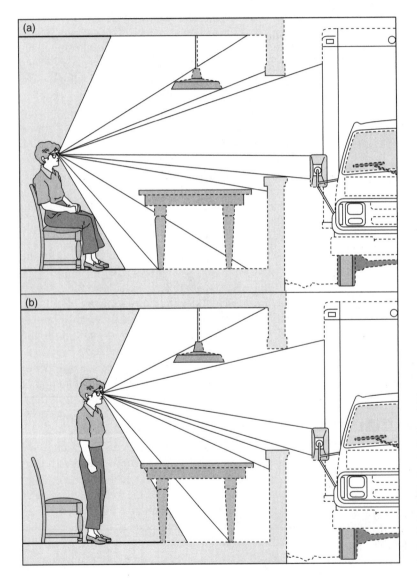

Figure 9.3

The optic array is the structured pattern of light reaching the observer's eye from the environment. Environmental surfaces visible to the observer are indicated by solid lines; invisible surfaces are indicated by dashed lines. Each of the visible surfaces structures the pattern of light entering the observer's eye. (a) The observer is sitting. (b) The observer stands up, which changes the optic array.

on the ambient optic array. The **ambient optic array** (which we will call **optic array**, for short) is the structure of stimulation available at a point in the environment. Figure 9.3a shows a person sitting in a room. The optic array for this person is the structured pattern of light reaching the person's eye. The person perceives the objects, surfaces, and textures in the scene because of the way the light is structured by these objects, surfaces, and textures. From where the observer is sitting, parts of the environment are visible (solid lines) and parts are not (dashed lines).

The Effect of Movement on the Optic Array　In our example of the cylinder on the checkerboard in Figure 9.2, we saw how the optic array created by the checkerboard provided information about the size of the cylinder. The optic array not only provides information to a person observing the checkerboard from one position but also provides information when the person begins moving. Thus, when the person in Figure 9.3a gets up, the optic array changes, as shown in Figure 9.3b, and if the person decides to walk around the room, or outside, the continuous changes that occur in the optic array as the person is moving create **optic flow**—the movement of elements of the environment relative to the observer. We will now see how this optic flow provides valuable information for perception.

Optic Flow: Self-Produced Information for Perception

One way to picture optic flow is to consider what you see when you drive across the bridge in Figure 9.4. You see a **gradient of flow** in which the speed of movement is rapid in the foreground, right next to the car, and becomes slower further down the bridge.

Optic Flow and the Focus of Expansion　According to Gibson, optic flow provides information regarding where the observer is heading. This is illustrated in Figure 9.5, which shows the optic flow experienced by an airplane pilot flying over a runway. The pilot sees a pattern of elements that flow along the ground, as shown. The length of the arrows indicates the speed of flow, which is rapid in the foreground and becomes slower toward the horizon. An important property of the optic flow is that there is a point in the distance where there is no flow. This point, which is marked with a dot in Figure 9.5, is called the **focus of expansion (FOE)**. It is centered on the observer's destination and therefore provides information indicating

Figure 9.4
The flow of the environment as seen from a car speeding across a bridge toward point A. The flow, shown by the arrows, is more rapid closer to the car (as indicated by the increased blur) but occurs everywhere except at A, the focus of expansion, toward which the car is moving.

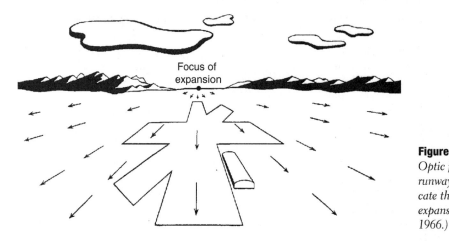

Figure 9.5
Optic flow for an airplane flying over a runway. The length of the arrows indicate the speed of flow. The focus of expansion is at the dot. (From Gibson, 1966.)

where the observer is heading. (Notice that the focus of expansion is at A for the car driving across the bridge in Figure 9.4.)

Figure 9.6 shows what the optic flow would look like for a plane coming in for a landing. The place where the focus of expansion is located on the runway indicates where the plane will touch down. Obviously, for the landing to be successful, the pilot must bring the plane in at the correct angle; otherwise, the focus of expansion indicates where the plane will crash. The pilot determines the angle of approach by using information from the rest of the flow pattern and by also using information provided by the texture gradient on the ground, which, as shown in Figure 9.7, provides information about the angle of the approaching ground.

Invariant Information for Perception Optic flow and texture gradients are important environmental stimuli because they provide information that remains constant even though the observer is moving. Gibson's term for information that remains constant during observer movement is **invariant information**. The fact that the cylinder in Figure 9.2 continues to cover

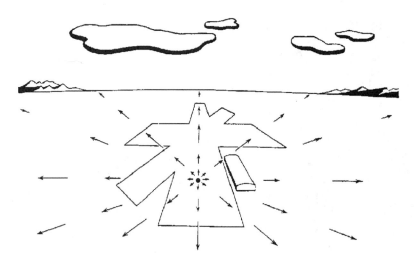

Figure 9.6
Optic flow field for an airplane coming in for a landing. (Gibson, 1966.)

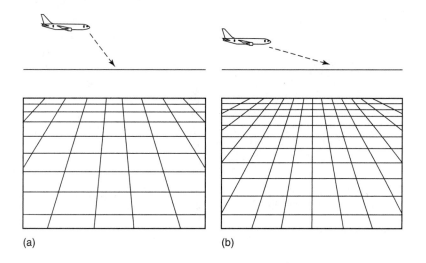

Figure 9.7
Texture gradient on the ground provides information regarding the airplane's angle of approach. The gradient in (a) indicates a steeper approach than is indicated by the gradient in (b).

one unit on the checkerboard, no matter what the observer's viewpoint, is an example of invariant information in a static optic array. The fact that the focus of expansion of the optic flow always remains centered on the observer's destination is an example of invariant information in an optic array that is created by movement.

Optic Flow as Self-Produced Information In addition to invariance, another property of optic flow that is crucial to the moving observer is that it is **self-produced.** Flow is created when the observer moves, and then this flow provides perceptual information that helps the observer carry out further movements. Gibson (1979) described this reciprocal relationship between movement and perception by pointing out that we need to perceive to move but that we also need to move to perceive.

This reciprocal relationship between flow and movement is diagrammed in Figure 9.8. Movement creates flow, which then provides information that guides further movement. The way movement creates information that then helps guide further movement is a basic principle that we will return to again and again as we look at specific examples of how flow and other visual information are used by moving observers.

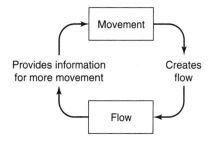

Figure 9.8
The relationship between movement and flow is reciprocal, with movement causing flow and flow guiding movement. This is the basic principle behind much of our interaction with the environment.

VISUAL CONTROL OF ACTION

WebTUTOR A central feature of the ecological approach is how optic flow provides information for movement. We will now describe how researchers have studied the role of optic flow in a number of activities, including helping us reach destinations in our environment, maintaining posture and balance, and determining when we are on a collision course with an object.

Perception and Action

Moving Through the Environment

Gibson's idea that people use optic flow to determine their heading as they move through the environment was based on his observation that flow contains information that indicates the direction in which the observer is moving. But just because flow contains this information doesn't mean that people actually use it. Researchers have, therefore, asked the following two questions:

1. Is the information provided by flow adequate to determine where a moving person is heading?

2. Do people actually use this information?

We will see that the answer to the first question is "yes" and to the second is "Probably, but people use other information, as well."

Is Flow Information Adequate?   Most research on this question has asked subjects to make judgments regarding their heading based on observing computer-generated optic flow stimuli. Two examples of such stimuli are shown in Figure 9.9. Figure 9.9a shows the flow that results from moving straight ahead. Figure 9.9b is the flow resulting from traveling on a curved path.

Subjects in these optic flow experiments are usually asked to judge, based on the flow stimuli, where they are heading relative to the vertical line. The results have generally shown that subjects can do this fairly accurately: They can judge heading to within about 0.5 to 1 degree, under the best conditions (Warren, 1995).

Do People Use Flow Information?   While we know that optic flow provides the information that indicates where a person is heading, it has been difficult to determine how much use they make of this information. Researchers have studied flow and other information that people use while walking and driving. From the results of these studies it appears that observers use both flow and other information to guide them, with the types of information used depending on the task (Wann & Land, 2000).

Drivers use a number of sources of information to keep their cars on the road, especially when navigating through turns. David Lee (1974) points out that keeping the FOE of optical flow centered on the destination won't work for a curved road, because the destination keeps shifting as the car negotiates the curve. He therefore proposes that drivers use optic flow information other than the focus of expansion to help them stay on course. Consider Figure 9.10, which

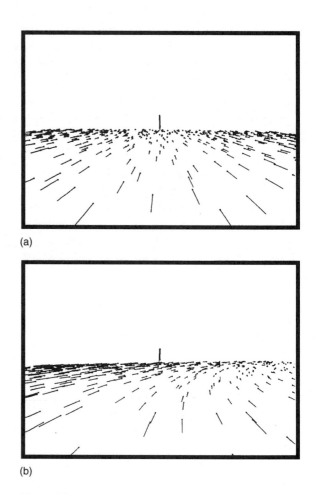

(a)

(b)

Figure 9.9

(a) Optic flow generated by a person moving straight ahead toward the vertical line on the horizon. The lengths of the lines indicate the person's speed, (b) Optic flow generated by a person moving in a curved path that is headed to the right of the vertical line. (From Warren, 1995.)

shows a straight stretch of road and a curve. If the driver is on course on the straight stretch, the optic flow line that passes from view directly below the driver, which Lee calls the **locomotor flow line**, is centered on the road. This line indicates the course that the car will follow if no changes are made in steering.

When the driver is on course, the optic flow lines and the edges of the road coincide (Figure 9.10a). When changes are made in steering, as might occur when negotiating a curve, the optic flow line changes but stays lined up with the road as long as the driver is staying on course (Figure 9.10b). However, if the driver begins going off course, the optic flow line and the road do not match, a situation to avoid if you want to stay on the road (Figure 9.10c). Lee proposes that drivers probably use the locomotor flow line rather than the focus of expansion to help them stay on the road.

In another experiment, Michael Land and Lee (1994) fitted a Jaguar with instruments to record the angle of the steering wheel and the speed and measured the driver's gaze with a video system that displayed the driver's eye position superimposed on the road ahead. Notice, in Figure 9.11a, that when driving straight ahead, the driver looks straight ahead but not directly at the focus of expansion. But the most interesting result is that when negotiating a curve the drivers tend to look at the tangent point of the curve (Figures 9.11b and c). Based on this result, Land and Lee suggested that drivers probably use information in addition to optic flow to determine their heading

(see also Land & Horwood, 1995; Rushton & Salvucci, 2001; Wann & Land, 2000, for more research on the information drivers use to stay on the road).

Researchers studying how we navigate during walking have found evidence that people do use flow information (Warren et al., 2001) but that other information is used as well. For example, there is good evidence that people use landmarks and other information on the ground to navigate while walking, since they tend to follow more accurate paths toward a target when more of this information is present (Harris, 2001; Wood et al., 2000). Apparently, an important strategy used by walkers (and perhaps drivers as well) is the **visual direction strategy** in which observers use the simple strategy of keeping their body pointed toward a target. If they go off course, the target will drift to the left or right, and the walker corrects course to recenter the target (Rushton et al., 1998).

Another indication that flow information is not always necessary for navigation is that we can find our way even when flow information is minimal, such as at night or in a snowstorm (Harris & Rogers, 1999). Also, Jack Loomis and coworkers (Loomis et al., 1992, 1996; Philbeck, Loomis, & Beall, 1997) have used a "blind walking" procedure to show that subjects can locate nearby targets with their eyes closed.

In the blind walking experiments, subjects observe a target object located up to 12 meters away, then walk to the target with their eyes closed. Subjects were able to walk directly toward the target and stop within a fraction of a meter of it. In fact,

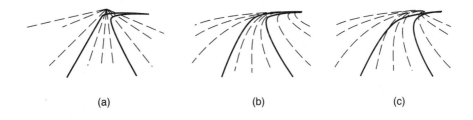

(a)   (b)   (c)

Figure 9.10
Optic flow lines for (a) movement along a straight stretch of road; (b) the correct negotiation of a curved stretch of road; and (c) the incorrect negotiation of a curved stretch of road. In (c) the car will go off the road unless a steering correction is made. (From Lee, 1980.)

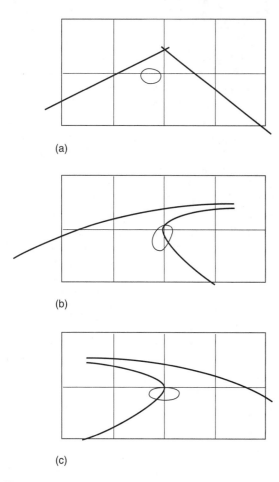

(a)

(b)

(c)

Figure 9.11
Results of Land and Lee's (1994) experiment. The ellipses indicate the place where the drivers were most likely to look while driving down (a) a straight road; (b) a curve to the right; and (c) a curve to the left. The key result is that, when negotiating the curves in (b) and (c), the drivers looked at the place at the edge of the road where the car was heading. This point is called the tangent point of the curve. (Adapted from Land & Lee, 1994.)

was told to turn either at turn point 1 or 2 and walk to a target that was 6.0 meters away. The fact that the subject stopped close to the target shows that we are able to accurately navigate short distances in the absence of any visual stimulation at all.

Posture and Balance

Although it makes sense that flow provides information for heading, especially when the scene is moving rapidly as when you drive down the road, it is not so obvious that flow is involved in an activity, such as standing in one place, that seems to involve little movement at all. But ecological researchers realized that vision is involved in helping us to maintain our balance or posture. You can demonstrate this to yourself by the following demonstration.

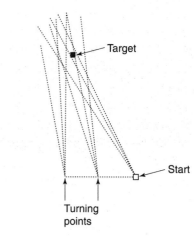

Figure 9.12
The results of a "blind walking" experiment (Philbeck et al., 1997). Subjects looked at the target, which was 6 meters from the starting point, then closed their eyes and walked either (a) toward the target or (b) to the left followed by a turn to the right. Keeping their eyes closed the whole time, they continued walking until they thought they had reached the target. Subjects tended to overshoot the target but walked in the right general direction and stopped near the target. (From Philbeck et al., 1997.)

subjects can do this even if they are asked to walk off to the side first and then make a turn and walk to the target, while keeping their eyes closed. Some records from these "angled" walks are shown in Figure 9.12, which depicts the paths taken when a subject first walked to the left from the "start" position and then

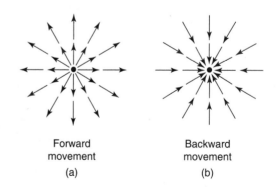

DEMONSTRATION

Keeping Your Balance

Keeping your balance is something you probably take for granted. Stand up. Raise one foot from the ground and stay balanced on the other. Then close your eyes and observe what happens. ●

Did staying balanced become more difficult when you closed your eyes? Vision provides a frame of reference that helps the muscles constantly make adjustments to help maintain balance. Although the

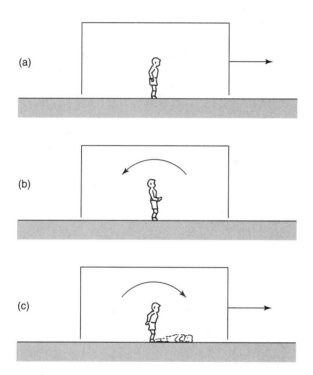

Figure 9.13

Lee and Aronson's swinging room. (a) Moving the room forward creates the optic flow pattern (shown in Figure 9.14b) that occurs when a person sways backward, as in (b). To compensate for this apparent sway, subjects sway forward, as in (c), and often lose their balance and fall down. (Based on Lee & Aronson, 1974.)

vestibular system of the inner ear and the receptors in our muscles and joints, which help us sense the positions of our limbs, are generally considered the major mechanisms of balance, a number of experiments have demonstrated a direct connection between vision and our ability to maintain our balance.

The importance of vision in maintaining balance was demonstrated by David Lee and Eric Aronson (1974). Lee and Aronson placed 13- to 16-month-old toddlers in the "swinging room" in Figure 9.13. In this room, the floor is stationary, but the walls and ceiling of the room can swing forward and backward. The idea behind the swinging room was to duplicate the visual stimulation that normally occurs as our bodies sway forward and backward. Swaying forward and backward creates visual optic flow patterns as we see elements of the environment move relative to us. Swaying forward creates an expanding optic flow pattern (Figure 9.14a), and swaying backward creates a contracting optic flow pattern (Figure 9.14b).

These flow patterns provide information about body sway. Without realizing it, we are constantly using this information to make corrections for this sway so that we can stand upright. Lee and Aronson reasoned that if they created a flow pattern that made people think they were leaning forward or backward, they could cause them to lean in the opposite direction to compensate. They accomplished this by mov-

Forward movement	Backward movement
(a)	(b)

Figure 9.14

Flow patterns that occur (a) when we move forward and (b) when we move backward.

Perception and Action

ing the room either toward or away from the standing children, and the children responded as predicted. When the room moved toward them (creating the flow pattern for swaying forward), they leaned back, and when it moved away (creating the flow pattern for swaying backward), they leaned forward. In fact, many of the children did more than just lean: 26 percent swayed, 23 percent staggered, and 33 percent fell down!

Adults were also affected by the swinging room. If they braced themselves, "oscillating the experimental room through as little as 6 mm caused adult subjects to sway approximately in phase with this movement. The subjects were like puppets visually hooked to their surroundings and were unaware of the real cause of their disturbance" (Lee, 1980, p. 173). Adults who didn't brace themselves could, like the toddlers, be knocked over by their perception of the moving room.

The swinging room experiments show that vision is such a powerful determinant of balance that it can override the traditional sources of balance information provided by the inner ear and the receptors in the muscles and joints (see also Fox, 1990). In a developmental study, Bennett Berthenthal and coworkers (1997) showed that infants as young as 4 months of age sway back and forth in response to movements of a room, and that the coupling between the room's movement and the swaying becomes better with age. (See also Stoffregen et al., 1999, for more evidence that flow information can influence posture while standing still, and Warren et al., 1996, for evidence that flow is involved in maintaining posture while walking.)

Colliding

We generally try to avoid colliding with objects in the environment. As we walk through the environment, we avoid obstacles, and if we see an object that is on a collision course with us, we usually move quickly to get out of the way if the collision would be dangerous.

One type of information that is used by sailors to avoid collision at sea is the perception of the viewing direction, or bearing, of the other boat. If the bearing of the other boat stays the same, this indicates that the boats are on a collision course, and that a course cor-

Figure 9.15
Two boats on a collision course. The fact that the bearing, or angle of view, from one boat to the other remains the same provides a danger signal that a collision will occur if both boats stay on the same course.

rection is therefore necessary (Figure 9.15). Another source of information for collision, which works when an object is approaching head-on, is symmetrical expansion of the image (Figure 9.16).

Once we know that an object is approaching on a collision course, it is also important to know how long it will be before it hits us. One way to do this would be to first estimate the object's distance and then the speed at which it is approaching. A calculation could then be done, based on this data, which

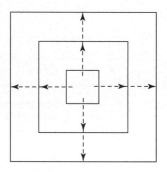

Figure 9.16
Three "snapshots" of a square as it moves directly toward an observer. The dashed arrows indicate that the square appears to be expanding outward as it moves closer.

would indicate when the object will collide. However, a simpler way to determine time to collision was suggested by astrophysicist Sir Fred Hoyle in his science-fiction novel *The Black Cloud* (1957). In this book, Hoyle put forth the idea that a way to determine the time until an approaching asteroid (the black cloud) collides with Earth is to compare two pictures of the asteroid taken two months apart. Hoyle showed that the time to collision can be determined based on the size of the asteroid in the pictures and how fast the size is changing (cited in Proffitt and Kaiser, 1995).

Hoyle's method for determining time to collision anticipated the psychologists' analysis of the optic flow information that is involved in predicting time to collision. This analysis has indicated, as Hoyle suggested, that time to collision can be determined by determining the ratio of the image's size at two different times and dividing this ratio by how fast the object's edges are expanding during that time. David Lee (1976) called this ratio **tau** and did a number of experiments that suggested that observers use the information provided by tau to estimate the time to collision.

A classic experiment on tau was carried out by Lee and P. E. Reddish (1976), who analyzed the behavior of a large bird called the gannet, which catches fish by diving from great heights. The interesting feature of the gannets' behavior, from a perceptual point of view, is that they always retract their wings just before reaching the water (Figure 9.17). Since the gannet always retracts its wings at just the right time, it obviously has a way of estimating when it will be entering the water.

To determine if this estimate might be related to tau, Lee calculated when in the dive the birds would begin retracting their wings if they were using what he called the "tau-strategy" to determine when they would be hitting the water. The calculation indicated that if the birds were following this strategy they should begin retracting their wings sooner if they started their dive from a greater height. When Lee analyzed films of gannets diving he found that this is what they usually do.

Lee's results on plummeting gannets, plus the results of experiments on humans, have led many researchers to conclude that a variable such as tau may be used to judge time to collision (McLeod & Ross, 1983; Regan & Vincent, 1995; Schiff & Detwiller, 1979).

More recent research has shown, however, that the tau-strategy works under some conditions but not others (Tresilean, 1999). For example, Gray and Regan (1998) found that subjects could judge time to collision of an approaching small object accurately when viewing with two eyes but not when viewing with just one eye. Since optic flow information is not affected by closing one eye, it appears that binocular depth information (see Chapter 7, page 233) may be more important than optic flow for judging small-object collisions. In connection with this finding, it is interesting that when 258 Cambridge University undergraduates were placed into "poor" and "good" categories based on their ballplaying skill, the better ballplayers had larger distances between their eyes, a

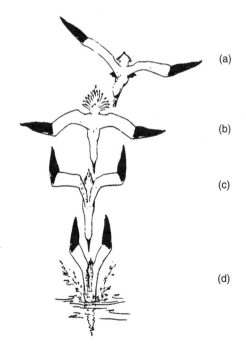

Figure 9.17
Plummeting gannets, showing how they retract their wings just before going into the water (Lee & Reddish, 1976.)

Perception and Action

condition that would result in better depth perception from binocular vision (Bannister & Blackburn, 1931). This doesn't mean that optic flow is not important for judging collisions but just that other information may also be important for certain tasks.

Catching a Fly Ball

A skill that is related to the ability to estimate when an object is on a collision course is the ability to catch a baseball that has been hit into the outfield. An outfielder's ability to do this is amazing, when we consider that although the outfielder may be over 300 feet from home plate, he or she usually starts running almost immediately toward the place where the ball is going to land and then ends up at the landing place, often just before the ball gets there.

When we consider how this might be accomplished, we see similarities to the situation for collisions. We saw that we probably don't determine time to collision by a calculation involving distance and speed but that we use the simpler information of image size and rate of expansion of the sides. The ball-catching problem has been analyzed in the same way.

The outfielder could determine where the ball is going to land by a calculation based on first determining the ball's speed and trajectory and then calculating the parabolic arc that the ball will follow to its destination. The problem with this tactic is not only that it involves a complex calculation but that it would be difficult for an outfielder located 300 feet away from home plate to accurately estimate speed and trajectory.

One proposal for how outfielders actually do position themselves to catch fly balls is diagrammed in Figure 9.18 (McBeath et al., 1995). This diagram proposes a strategy for catching a fly ball called the **linear optical trajectory (LOT) strategy**. The basis of the LOT strategy is that if the ballplayer runs so the ball appears to be following a straight-line path, the ball will always be directly above, so when the ball reaches the ground, the outfielder will be there to catch it.

Although following the LOT strategy would enable an outfielder to arrive at the place where the

ball lands, other researchers have questioned this strategy, based on the fact that outfielders often arrive at the ball's landing spot well before the ball gets there (Chodosh et al., 1995; Jacobs et al., 1996). Apparently ballplayers may take other information into account when catching fly balls, but the important point for our purposes is that whether they use the LOT strategy, another strategy, or a combination of strategies, we can describe the way a ballplayer catches a fly ball as a continuous interaction, like the one diagrammed

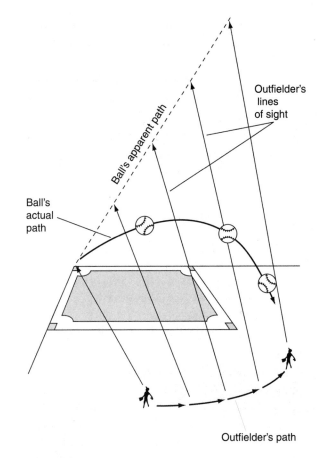

Figure 9.18
A fly ball travels along the path shown by the baseball. The position of an outfielder who runs so the ball appears to follow a straight-line path (dashed line) will eventually intersect with the ball's position. (Adapted from McBeath, Shaffer, & Kaiser, 1995.)

in Figure 9.8, in which the ballplayer's perception guides his or her actions, the actions create a new perception, this new perception guides further action, and so on.

If the connection between perception and action is based on continuous interaction, this means that our actions aren't based on calculations about what will happen in the future, but on movements that are synchronized with the ongoing flow of our perceptions. Think about our discussion of perception and action, so far. Our abilities to move through the environment, to maintain our posture, to avoid collisions, and to catch a fly ball all depend on visual stimuli that are created by the movements involved in each of these actions. If we stand perfectly still, not only does our behavior stop, but the information that we were using to guide this behavior vanishes. Another example of an ongoing interaction between perception and action is provided by somersaulting.

Somersaulting

Gymnastics involves split-second timing and balance. We can appreciate the problem facing a gymnast who wants to execute a backward somersault by realizing that, within 600 ms, the gymnast must execute the somersault and then end in exactly the correct body configuration precisely at the moment that he or she hits the ground (Figure 9.19).

One way this could be accomplished is to learn to run off a predetermined sequence of motions

Figure 9.19
"Snapshots" of a somersault, starting on the left and finishing on the right. (From Bardy and Laurent, 1998.)

within a specific period of time. If this is what is happening, performance should be the same with eyes opened and eyes closed. However, Benoit Bardy and Makel Laurent (1998) found that expert gymnasts performed somersaults more poorly with their eyes closed. Films showed that when their eyes were opened, the gymnasts appeared to be making in-the-air corrections to their trajectory. For example, a gymnast who initiated the extension of his or her body a little too late compensated by performing the rest of the movement more rapidly.

Another interesting result was that closing the eyes did not affect the performance of novice somersaulters as much as it affected the performance of experts. Apparently, experts learn to coordinate their movements with their perceptions, but the novices have not yet learned to do this. Thus, somersaulting, like other forms of actions such as avoiding collisions or catching a fly ball, involves regulation of action during the continuous flow of perceptual information.

Neural Mechanisms for the Visual Control of Action

We have seen that optic flow provides information for controlling action. But how is this information represented in the nervous system? Recent research has revealed neurons that respond to optic flow information. We will describe two examples, one in the pigeon and one in the monkey.

Collision-Sensitive Neurons in the Pigeon Yong-chang Wang and Barrie Frost (1992) recorded from an area in the pigeon's brain called the *nucleus rotundus*, which is located in a pathway that is involved in the perception of space and movement. The pigeon observed images of a sphere covered with a black-and-white pattern like that on some soccer balls. On some trials, the image of the sphere expanded so it appeared to be on a collision course with the pigeon. On other trials, the sphere's expansion appeared to take it to the left or right of the pigeon.

Figure 9.20 shows the response of a neuron to a sphere on a collision course with the pigeon. This neuron starts firing rapidly about 1 second before

Perception and Action

The Ecological Approach to Perception

J.J. Gibson's ecological approach focuses on studying perception as it occurs in the natural environment. It emphasizes the connection between perception and action.

Information for Perception

Environmental information, rather than neural information or information in the retinal image, is the starting point for Gibson's analysis of perception. An important source of environmental information is movement.

The Optic Array

The optic array is the optical structure of the environment at a point. There is information in the static optic array, and additional information becomes available when the observer moves, because movement creates optic flow.

Optic Flow: Theory

Optic flow creates invariant information for perception such as the focus of expansion. Texture gradients also provide examples of invariant information. Optic flow is self-produced, which means that it is created by movement of the observer. Because of this, we can describe the relationship between flow and movement as circular: Movement creates flow, which provides information to guide further movement.

Optic Flow: Practice

Experiments involving optic flow stimuli show that people can potentially use it to determine their heading. It has been suggested that, in driving a car, people use the locomotor flow line rather than the focus of expansion to determine their heading, particularly when negotiating curves. Experiments show that drivers look at the tangent point of a curve while turning. There is evidence that optic flow can be used to guide walking, but other information, such as landmarks and visual direction, can be used as well. In addition, the results of "blind walking" experiments indicate that we can find our way when no optic flow information is available.

Balance and Collision

The swinging room experiments show that keeping your balance is influenced by optic flow information. There is also evidence that flow information, such as that contained in the tau-ratio, helps predict when collisions will occur.

Catching a Ball and Somersaulting

Studies of how visual information is used to help catch a fly ball and to somersault suggest that people probably do not carry out complex calculations to determine their future course of action but instead use self-produced visual information in a way that creates movements that are synchronized with ongoing perceptions.

---

the collision would occur. Notice that the response is the same no matter what the size of the sphere or the velocity of its approach. This neuron is called a **collision-sensitive neuron**, because it responds well when the sphere is on a collision course but responds poorly when the sphere is not on a collision course (Wang & Frost, 1992; see also Rind & Simmons, 1999). Apparently the pigeon is perceiving the difference between collision and noncollision conditions, because its heart rate almost triples for the collision condition but remains unchanged for the noncollision condition (Wang & Frost, 1992).

Optic Flow Neurons in the Monkey Where would we expect to find neurons that respond to optic flow

in the monkey? A logical place to start would be the medial temporal (MT) area in the monkey's dorsal stream, because we know that neurons in this area respond to the direction of movement (see Chapter 4, page 118; Chapter 8, p. 277). As it turns out, neurons in MT do not respond to flow patterns, but neurons in the *medial superior temporal area* (MST), which receives signals from MT (Figure 9.21), do respond to flow patterns.

Figure 9.22 shows the response of neurons in MST that respond best to patterns of dots that are expanding outward (Figure 9.22a) and also neurons that respond best to circular motions (Figure 9.22b). Neurons such as these may provide the physiological mechanism that underlies our perception of environ-

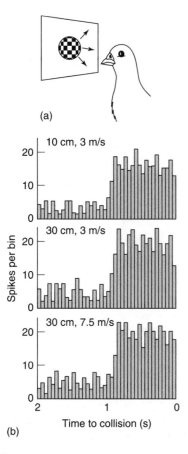

(a)

Spikes per bin

10 cm, 3 m/s

30 cm, 3 m/s

30 cm, 7.5 m/s

Time to collision (s)

(b)

Figure 9.20

(a) The pigeon sees the expanding stimulus (Rind & Simmons, 1999.) (b) Three records for a collision-sensitive neuron, for two sizes of the stimulus (10 cm and 30 cm diameter) and two different approach velocities (3 and 7.5 meters per second). The cell starts firing at about 1 second before a collision would occur in all three conditions. (Wang & Frost, 1992.)

mental stimuli such as optic flow patterns (see also Duffy & Wurtz, 1991; Orban et al., 1992; Regan & Cynader, 1979).

Psychophysics and Optic Flow Neurons in Humans

Is there a link between the responding of the MST optic-flow neurons and perception? Burr and coworkers (1998) have drawn the following parallel between the physiology of MST neurons and people's percep-

tion of flow: (1) MST neurons that respond to flow have large receptive fields—that is, they respond to flow that occurs over a large area of the visual field; and (2) people's perception of flow summates over a large area of the visual field.

We can understand what it means to say that flow *summates* by describing Burr's experiment. Burr presented patterns of moving dots in which a small percentage of the dots were moving together either (a) in circular motions or (b) in contracting or expanding motions. The rest of the dots were moving randomly.

Burr found that subjects could tell whether the dots were moving clockwise or counterclockwise or expanding or contracting, even when only a small percentage of the dots were moving together. But increasing the size of the field of dots made the subjects' task easier, so they could make correct movement judgments when an even smaller percentage of the dots were moving together.

The fact that larger fields made perception easier is an example of **spatial summation**, because perceptual activity is summed over a large area of space. This is exactly what we would expect if neurons with

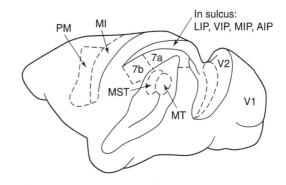

Figure 9.21

Monkey brain, showing key areas for movement perception and visual-motor interaction. MT = medial temporal area; MST = medial superior temporal area. Neurons in MST respond to flow patterns as shown in Figure 9.22. The other areas are important for coordinating activities that involve both vision and action such as grasping. See Figure 9.25 for the names of these areas. The brain is opened to reveal hidden areas. (Adapted from Graziano & Gross, 1998.)

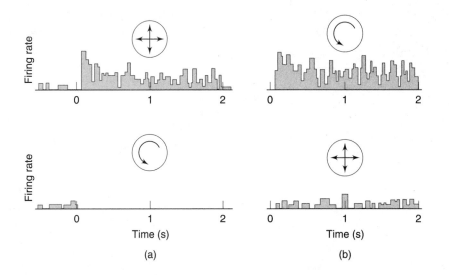

Figure 9.22

(a) Response of a neuron in the monkey's MST that responds with a high rate of firing to an expanding stimulus (top record) but that hardly fires to a stimulus that moves with a circular motion (bottom record) or with other types of motion (not shown). (b) Another neuron that responds best to circular movement (top) but does not respond well to an expanding pattern or other types of movement (bottom). (From Graziano, Andersen, & Snowden, 1994.)

large receptive fields were signaling the flow. (See also Snowden & Milne, 1997, for another example of a psychophysical result that is what we would expect from large receptive fields.)

Judging Slant Based on the Potential for Action

To end this section on perception and the moving observer, we are going to return to some psychophysical experiments that don't involve moving observers but that tell us something important about how a person's perception of the environment may provide information about an action that the person might take in the future. These experiments, which were carried out by Dennis Proffitt and coworkers (1995), measured people's perception of the slant of hills. From the results of these measurements, Proffitt drew some conclusions about the connection between a person's perception of a hill's slant and the person's physical ability to climb the hill.

The stimuli for Proffitt's experiments were hills on the University of Virginia campus, with slopes that ranged from a gentle 2° to an extremely steep 34°. One way to appreciate the steepness of a 34° hill is to realize that 9° is the maximum permissible grade for Virginia roads, some of which traverse the Blue Ridge mountain range.

The experimenters positioned themselves at the bases of these hills near widely traveled routes and asked students to participate in a short psychology experiment. The 300 students who agreed were asked to face the hill and indicate its slant in three ways: (1) verbal—indicate the angle in degrees; (2) visual—set a disc that represented the cross-section of the hill (Figure 9.23a); and (3) haptic—adjust a tilt board to match the hill's slant, without looking at the board or their hand (Figure 9.23b).

The results of the experiment, shown in Figure 9.24, were that subjects greatly overestimated the hills' slants when making verbal or visual judgments. For example, a 5° hill was judged to have a slant of 20°. However, judgments made with the haptic tilt board tended to correspond more closely to the actual slant of the hill. Proffitt suggests that the verbal/visual slant estimate reflects our assessment of how difficult it would be to walk up the hill. He supports this idea by these additional findings (Proffitt et al., 1995; Bhalla & Proffitt, 1999):

- Subjects' slant estimates increased after they had become fatigued by jogging.

- For steep hills, subjects rated the slant as greater when standing on top of the hill looking down than when standing at the bottom looking up. This fits with the observation that it is more difficult to walk down these hills than to walk up

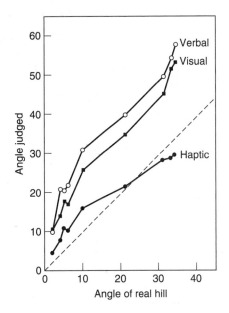

Figure 9.24
Results of Proffit's (1995) experiment. Verbal and visual estimates were much greater than the actual slant of the hill, as indicated by deviation from the dashed line. The haptic estimate corresponded more closely to the actual slant.

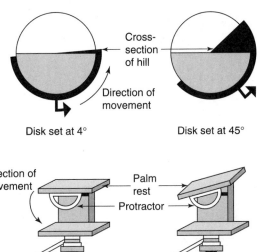

(a)

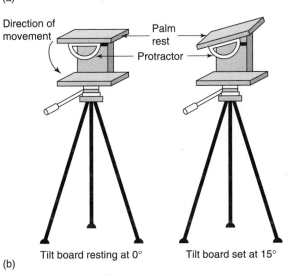

(b)

Figure 9.23
Devices for measuring slant. (a) Subjects set the angle of this disc to indicate their visual estimate of the hill's slant; (b) they adjusted this board with their hand to indicate their haptic estimate of the hill's slant. (Proffitt et al., 1995.)

them. Proffitt reports that while it was possible to walk up a 30° hill, it was too steep to walk down. Thus, a hill that is too steep to walk down is apparently judged to be steeper than a hill that is not too steep to walk up, even if they are the same hill!

- Slant estimates were larger for subjects who were carrying a heavy backpack or were in poor physical condition.

The finding that slant estimates reflect a person's behavioral potential for climbing a hill illustrates how visual perception can be influenced by factors in addition to the visual stimulus. But what about the finding that the visual and verbal judgments were overestimated but that the haptic slant judgments were fairly accurate? Proffitt points out that although we overestimate a hill's slant based on looking at it, we usually have no trouble accurately placing one foot in front of the other if we decide to climb it.

Thus, visual perception, which can result in an overestimation of slant, may be providing information about whether or not we should take action or about how difficult the action might be. However, once we decide to act, mechanisms that control visually controlled actions, like those involved in the haptic judgment in Proffitt's experiments and many of the actions we have been describing throughout this chapter, take over and enable us to act efficiently.

GRASPING OBJECTS: WHERE PERCEPTION MEETS THE MOTOR SYSTEM

We interact with the environment not only by negotiating a curve in a car, or catching a ball, or doing somersaults, but in less dramatic ways as well.

Consider, for example, what will happen as you turn to the next page of this book: You reach for the page, make contact with your fingers, and then turn it. Although this act may seem simple, it involves a precise sequence of arm, hand, and finger movements. You routinely carry out many other actions that, in their seeming simplicity, you probably take for granted. You mark the page with a marker and then perhaps reach for the coffee cup on your desk, grab the handle with your fingers (or maybe the whole cup with your hand), and bring it to your lips. Each of these actions involves the coupling of perception and action that we have been describing in this chapter.

In the next sections we will add another dimension to our knowledge of this coupling between perception and action by describing recent physiological research on how we manipulate and grasp objects. We will see that this research has revealed connections between the perceptual system, which is respon-

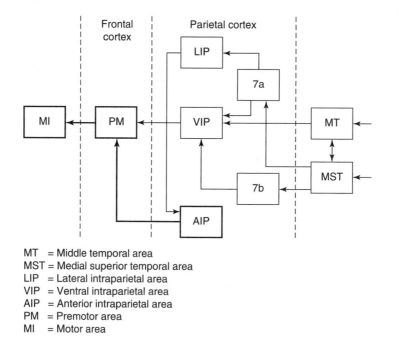

MT = Middle temporal area
MST = Medial superior temporal area
LIP = Lateral intraparietal area
VIP = Ventral intraparietal area
AIP = Anterior intraparietal area
PM = Premotor area
MI = Motor area

Figure 9.25
A simplified diagram showing how neural information flows from areas MT and MST into structures in the parietal and frontal lobes. Note that most of the arrows actually go both ways. See text for details and Figure 9.21 for locations of these structures in the brain. (Adapted from Graziano & Gross, 1998.)

Chapter 9

320

sible for our experiences of vision and touch, and the motor system, which is responsible for creating actions with our muscles.

The Neural Pathway for Perception and Action

How do the perceptual and motor systems work together? The starting point for answering this question is depth perception, since you need to know how far away objects are to accurately reach for them (Jackson & Hausain, 1997). But to get to the heart of the problem, we need to look at the dorsal stream of the extrastriate cortex, which leads from the visual receiving area, V1, to the parietal cortex.

If you turn back to page 114 and look at our picture of the dorsal stream in Figure 4.8, you will notice that this figure pictures signals from MT as flowing into a box labeled "parietal." To understand how you turn a page in a book or pick up your coffee cup, we need to look at what's going on inside this box and then even beyond it, in areas in the frontal lobe and the motor areas of the cortex.

Figure 9.25 diagrams the flow of information from areas MT and MST into the parietal lobe, which consists of a number of separate areas, and from the parietal lobe to the frontal lobe, and then the motor area of the cortex. From Figure 9.21, which indicates where the various structures are in the brain, you can see that the flow of information generally continues toward the premotor area in the front of the brain and then backtracks to end up in the motor cortex.

Although the flow of information diagrammed in Figure 9.25 may seem complex, we have simplified this diagram by omitting many structures and pathways. For example, not all information for coordinating vision and action flows through areas MT and MST, as shown here. But we are now going to simplify even further, by focusing just on the highlighted structures in Figure 9.25.

We begin with the **anterior interparietal area (AIP)**, because it provides a good example of how the visual and motor areas interact in the parietal lobe before passing information to the **premotor area (PM)** and then to the **motor area (M1)**, which sends

instructions to the arm and hand muscles, enabling them to pick up the cup, and to the face, helping bring the lips to the cup.

Mixing Vision and Action in the Parietal Lobe

We are interested in the AIP because it contains a mixture of neurons that respond to vision and to action. Hideo Sakada and coworkers (Sakada et al., 1997; Murata et al., 1996) distinguish three different types of neurons in AIP. **Motor-dominant neurons** respond well to pushing a button in the light and in the dark but don't respond to looking at the button (Figure 9.26a). **Visual-dominant neurons** respond to pushing the button in the light but not in the dark and respond best to just looking at the button (Figure 9.26b). **Visual and motor neurons** respond to pushing the button in the light, but pushing it in the dark or just looking at it results in a smaller response (Figure 9.26c). This mixture of neurons, some that respond best to manipulating objects (motor-dominant), some that respond best to looking at objects (vision-dominant), and some that respond to both manipulation and looking (motor and visual), reflects the fact that the AIP is located between the visual and motor areas. (Other areas in the parietal lobe also contain neurons with similar properties.)

Neurons for Recognizing the Actions of Others

Neurons in area AIP send signals to the premotor cortex in the frontal lobe, where there are neurons that have many of the same properties as those in the parietal cortex (Graziano, Hu, & Gross, 1997). But a type of neuron in the premotor area, which has special properties that are quite remarkable, is a type of neuron called **mirror neurons**. These neurons respond when the monkey grasps an object but also respond when the monkey observes someone else (another monkey or the experimenter) grasping an object. Figure 9.27 shows how a mirror neuron responds. The neuron fires as the monkey watches the experimenter grasp a piece of food on a tray (a) and also as

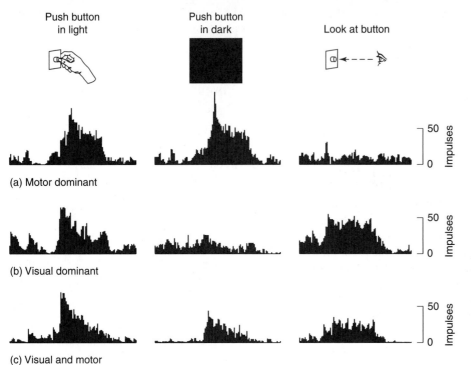

Figure 9.26

Three types of AIP neurons. Note that motor-dominant neurons respond to pushing a button either in the light or in the dark, visual-dominant neurons respond when the button can be seen, and visual and motor neurons respond well only to pushing the button in the light. (Adapted from Sakada et al., 1997.)

the monkey grasps the food (b). Just looking at the food causes no response, and watching the experimenter grasp the food with a pair of pliers, as in (c), causes only a small response (Gallese et al., 1996; Rizzolatti, Forgassi, & Gallese, 2000).

Most mirror neurons are specialized to respond to only one type of action such as grasping or placing an object somewhere. Although you might think that the monkey may have been responding to the anticipation of receiving food, the type of object made little difference. The neurons responded just as well when the monkey observed the experimenter pick up a three-dimensional object that was not food.

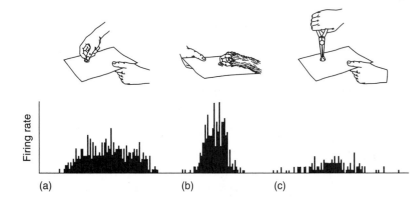

Figure 9.27

Response of a mirror neuron: (a) response to watching the experimenter grasp food on the tray; (b) response when the monkey grasps the food; (c) response to watching the experimenter pick up food with a pair of pliers. (Adapted from Rizzolatti et al., 1996.)

What Are Mirror Neurons For?

Mirror neurons, like other neurons in the parietal and premotor areas, are concerned with action. But mirror neurons are special because they respond both when a monkey performs an action and when the monkey sees another animal perform the same action. Consider what is happening when a mirror neuron fires in response to seeing someone else perform an action. This firing not only indicates what the other person (or monkey) is doing but provides information about the characteristics of the action, since the neuron's response to watching an action is the same as the neuron's response to actually performing the action. This means that one function of the mirror neurons might therefore be to help understand another person's (or monkey's) actions and react appropriately to them (Rizzolatti & Arbib, 1998; Rizzolatti, Fogassi, & Gallese, 2000).

Another function of mirror neurons may be to help imitate the observed action. The idea that there are neurons involved in imitation may even have something to do with an incident involving the golfer Tiger Woods, when he was an infant. The incident, as related by Woods's father, Earl Woods, can be traced to his practice of placing Tiger in a high chair to watch him practice his golf swing by hitting balls into a net in his garage. One day, Tiger, who was still young enough to be an unsteady walker, climbed down from his high chair, picked up a club, and executed a golf swing that was a passable imitation of his father's swing. It was at that point that Earl realized that his son might have a very strong aptitude for golf (Owen, 2000).

Of course, we have no way of knowing what was happening in baby Tiger's brain as he watched his father swing at all of those golf balls, but we can speculate that perhaps he was experiencing his father's swing through the activity of his mirror neurons, and that this experience enabled him to fashion a good imitation of the swing, even though he may never have practiced it. This is not that unlikely a guess, especially since fMRI measurements of brain activity in humans as they are imitating another person's actions show that there may be mirror neurons in the human brain (Fadiga et al., 1995; Hari et al., 1998; Iacobini et al., 1999).

One of the disadvantages of brain imaging methods such as PET or fMRI, which depend on changes in blood flow in the brain, is that they are too slow to provide information about the firing of neurons on a millisecond time scale. However, a technique called **magnetoencephalography (MEG)**, which records rapid magnetic signals that are generated by the responding of neurons, does provide the speed necessary to see rapid brain potentials.

Nishitani and Hari (2000) used the MEG technique to determine how brain activity compares when a person observes an action, imitates an action, or actually carries out the action. They ran the following three groups of subjects:

1. Observation condition: Subjects observed an experimenter pinching a manipulandum (a);

2. Imitation condition: Subjects made finger movements that imitated what the experimenter was doing, but without actually touching the manipulandum; and

3. Execution condition: Subjects reached for and pinched the manipulandum themselves (Hari et al., 2000; Nishitani & Hari, 2000).

One result of this experiment, which took advantage of the fast response of the MEG, was that an area in the frontal lobe suspected of being a human mirror-neuron area responded before the manipulandum was pinched, in all three conditions.

Another result was that neurons in this area responded about twice as strongly to imitation as to execution or observation, as shown in (b).

Results such as these demonstrate properties of a possible mirror-neuron area in the human brain and, most important for our purposes, illustrate how the MEG can be used to measure rapidly occurring responses in the human brain.

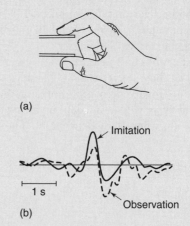

(a)

(b)

(a) Fingers pinching a manipulandum. Subjects either watched someone else do this, imitated the movements, or pinched the manipulandum themselves. (b) MEG response from a possible "mirror neuron" area in the frontal lobe. The response for the imitation condition (solid line) and observation condition (dashed line) are shown. The response for the execution condition was about the same size as the response to observation. (From Nishitani & Hari, 1999.)

ACTION, HEARING, AND VISION

We have focused on links between action and vision in this chapter, but we actually use information from all of our senses as we take action within our environment. Thus, as gymnasts use visual information to help them execute their routines, they also pay attention to sounds as well. This is illustrated by the following description, which was written by Jennifer Steinback, a student in my sensation and perception class:

> As a competitive gymnast I have found hearing to be extremely important. On an apparatus such as the balance beam, I have to do tricks such as jumping forward or backward onto my hands and then back to my feet. Because I'm flipping so fast, it's impossible to always see where I'm landing, but I can hear it. If the time between my takeoff and hearing my hands hit the beam is equal to the time between when my hands hit and when my feet hit, I know that I am going to land the trick OK and stay on the beam. But if I flip onto my hands and then I hear my feet hit the beam too quickly, I know that I'm off balance and am going to fall off. Hearing [sound] is always the first clue that lets me know that I am off balance.

While you may never have done a flip on a balance beam, you have probably been buzzed by a fly or mosquito and been able to take action by swatting at the troublesome intruder with your hands, just on the basis of the information provided by sound alone. Or consider what happens when someone calls your name, or if you hear a loud sound that may indicate danger. Situations such as this often cause you to automatically turn your head in the direction of the sound.

Turning your head in the direction of a sound represents a link between sound and action and also represents a link between sound and vision, since you are turning your head to determine who, or what, is causing the sound. An important link between sound, action, and vision is provided by a group of phenomena called audio-visual speech perception, which refers to how information provided by vision can influence the perception of speech. The best-known of these effects is **speechreading**, in which movements of the lips and face are used by deaf people as an aid to speech perception. These movements are also used by nondeaf people to understand speech in noisy environments (Dodd & Campbell, 1987).

In Chapter 12, we describe another type of audiovisual speech perception called the **McGurk effect**, which works as shown in Figure 9.28. The man is observing a videotape of a woman who is making lip movements for the sound "ga," but the sound coming out of the monitor has been changed

Figure 9.28
The McGurk effect. See text for details.

to "ba." This mismatch between lip movements and sound causes the man to perceive the sound as "da." If, however, the man eliminates his perception of the woman's lips by closing his eyes, he hears the sound "ba" that is actually coming out of the monitor. Thus, the McGurk effect shows that visually perceived action (movement of the lips) and the sound from the monitor are being combined to create a new perception.

The McGurk effect therefore provides an illustration of the link between action, vision, and hearing. Given the interactions that have been observed between vision, action, and hearing, it isn't surprising that researchers have found multimodal neurons that respond to both visual stimuli and sound stimuli that are presented in the same area of space (Graziano, Reiss, & Gross, 1999).

SUMMARY TABLE 9.2

Neural Mechanisms

Collision-sensitive neurons in the pigeon respond to flow stimuli that are on a collision course. There are neurons in the MST of the monkey that respond best to various types of flow stimuli. Psychophysical experiments using flow stimuli show that the perception of flow involves summation over a large area of the visual field. This matches the finding that MST flow neurons have large receptive fields.

Judging Slant Based on the Potential for Action

People tend to overestimate the slant of hills when making visual or verbal judgments, but not when making haptic judgments. The visual and verbal overestimates may reflect a person's judgment of his or her ability to climb the hill. The haptic judgment may be related to the visual-motor coordination that the person uses when climbing the hill.

Neural Pathway for Grasping

Important structures for controlling the coordination between perception and action are located in the parietal cortex. These structures send signals to premotor and motor areas of the cortex.

AIP and Premotor Neurons

There are neurons in the anterior interparietal area (AIP) that are described as motor dominant, visual dominant, and visual and motor. Neurons called mirror neurons respond to grasping an object and to watching another monkey or person grasp an object. These neurons may be involved in understanding the movements of others and in imitation of the movements of others.

Brain Scan: The Magnetoencephalogram

The magnetoencephalogram (MEG) is a technique that makes it possible to record brain responses on a millisecond scale. Research using the MEG shows a strong response to imitation in an area in the frontal lobe.

Across the Senses:
Action Links Between Vision and Hearing

Vision is not the only sense involved in the coordination between perception and action. Hearing can be involved, too, and this involvement can be linked to vision.

STUDY QUESTIONS

1. Why do some researchers see action as the most important outcome of the perceptual process? (302)

Perception and the Moving Observer

Gibson's Ecological Approach to Perception

2. What kind of information did Gibson decide is not useful to a pilot coming in for a landing? What kind of information is useful? (303)

3. What did Gibson think was wrong with traditional laboratory research? (303)

Environmental Information and Perception: Ecological Optics

4. What is the retinal information for the size of the cylinder in Figure 9.1? How is size constancy explained on the basis of this retinal information? (303)

5. What is the environmental information for the size of the cylinder in Figure 9.2? How is size constancy explained on the basis of this environmental information? (304)

6. What is the ambient optic array? What action of the observer creates information in the optic array? (305)

7. What is optic flow? (305)

Optic Flow: Self-Produced Information for Perception

8. What is the gradient of flow? (305)

9. What is the focus of expansion, and what information does it provide for Gibson's airplane pilot in Figure 9.5 or the person driving over the bridge in Figure 9.4? (305)

10. What information do texture gradients on the ground provide for airplane pilots coming in for a landing? (306)

11. What is invariant information? Give an example of invariant information in the static optic array and an example of invariant information in the optic flow pattern. (306)

12. What do we mean when we say that optic flow is self-produced? (307)

13. What is the reciprocal relationship between movement and flow? (307)

Visual Control of Action

Moving Through the Environment

14. Describe the flow fields that result from moving (a) straight ahead and (b) in a curved path. (308)

15. What are subjects in optic flow experiments asked to judge? (308)

16. How accurately can an observer judge heading based on optic flow? (308)

17. What is the locomotor flow line? How is it related to the course a car is following? (309)

18. Where do drivers look when (a) driving straight ahead and (b) negotiating a curve? (309)

19. What did Land and Lee conclude regarding the role of optic flow information in driving? (309)

20. Do we use optic flow information while walking? (309)

21. What is the visual direction strategy? (309)

22. Describe Loomis's "blind walking" experiments. What do the results of this experiment show with regard to the need for optic flow for walking short distances through the environment? (309)

Posture and Balance

23. Describe Lee and Aronson's swinging room experiments. What do the results indicate about the role of optic flow patterns in keeping our balance? (311)

24. What is the youngest age at which it has been shown that movement of a room affects posture? (312)

Colliding

25. How can sailors tell if they are on a collision course with another boat? (312)

26. What is a source of information that indicates that an object is heading straight for us? (312)

27. What procedure would we have to use to determine when an object will collide with us using information about object's distance and speed? (312)

28. What is a simpler way to determine time to collision suggested by Hoyle? Which two aspects of an object need to be taken into account? (313)

29. What is tau? What do the experiments with plummeting gannets indicate about tau? (313)

30. Describe the result of Gray and Regan that indicates that tau is not always used to predict collisions. (313)

Catching a Fly Ball

31. How could we determine where a fly ball is going to land based on the ball's speed and trajectory? Why would this be difficult? (314)

32. What information do people actually use to determine where a fly ball will land, according to the linear optical trajectory strategy? (314)

33. What evidence indicates that the linear optical trajectory strategy may not always be used by ballplayers? (314)

34. Why can we say that the connection between perception and action is based on a continuous interaction? (315)

Somersaulting

35. What is the problem facing the gymnast in executing a somersault? (What two things does he or she need to do?) (315)

36. What is a way that the gymnast could solve the above problem that would not be affected by closing the eyes? (315)

37. How does closing the eyes affect somersaulting performance in expert gymnasts? In novices? What does this indicate about the information used by each group? (315)

38. How is the idea of continuous interaction involved in somersaulting? (315)

Neural Mechanisms for the Visual Control of Action

39. Describe the collision-sensitive neurons in the pigeon. What behavioral evidence supports the idea that the responses of these neurons are correlated with the pigeon's perception of impending collision? (315)

40. Which area in the monkey cortex contains neurons that respond to flow patterns? (316)

41. Are the receptive fields of MST neurons large or small? (316)

42. Describe the psychophysical experiment that supports the idea that neurons with large receptive fields are involved in the human's perception of optic flow. Be sure you understand how the concept of spatial summation was applied in this experiment. (317)

Judging Slant Based on the Potential for Action

43. What did Proffitt find about people's ability to estimate the slant of hills? How well did subjects do using verbal, visual, and haptic methods of measurement? (318)

44. According to Proffitt, what do the verbal and visual estimates of hill slant tell us about the subject's ability to climb or descend a hill? What evidence supports this conclusion? (319)

45. What kinds of mechanisms is the information from the haptic method of measurement associated with, with regard to hill climbing? (319)

Grasping Objects: Where Perception Meets the Motor System

The Neural Pathway for Perception and Action

46. Describe the pathway that information travels from MT into the parietal cortex then through the parietal cortex into the premotor and motor areas. (321)

47. Where is the anterior intraparietal area (AIP)? Where does it receive information from and where does it send it? (321)

Mixing Vision and Action in the Parietal Lobe

48. Describe the following three types of AIP neurons: (a) motor dominant; (b) visual and motor; (c) visual dominant. (321)

Neurons for Recognizing the Actions of Others

49. What do mirror neurons respond to? (321)

What Are Mirror Neurons For?

50. What are two possible functions of mirror neurons? (323)

Brain Scan:
The Magnetoencephalogram (MEG): A Way to Measure Rapid Brain Activity in Humans

51. What kind of brain activity does the magnetoencephalogram reflect? (324)

52. How does the manipulandum experiment show that a possible mirror-neuron area of the human brain responds to observation, imitation, and execution of the manipulandum-pinching action? (324)

Across the Senses:
Action, Hearing, and Vision

53. Describe a few ways that vision and hearing are linked in situations involving action. (325)

10

SOUND, THE AUDITORY SYSTEM, AND PITCH PERCEPTION

SOME QUESTIONS WE WILL CONSIDER

- If a tree falls in the forest and no one is there to hear it, is there a sound? (333)

- What is it that makes sounds high pitched or low pitched? (342)

- How do sound vibrations inside the ear lead to the perception of different pitches? (361)

Hearing has an extremely important function in my life. I was born legally blind, so although I can see, my vision is highly impaired and is not correctable. Even though I am not usually shy or embarrassed, sometimes I do not want to call attention to myself and my disability. . . . There are many methods that I can use to improve my sight in class, like sitting close to the board or copying from a friend, but sometimes these things are impossible. Then I use my hearing to take notes. . . . My hearing is very strong. While I do not need my hearing to identify people who are very close to me, it is definitely necessary when someone is calling my name from a distance. I can recognize their voice, even if I cannot see them.

Jill Robbins

This statement was written by one of my students to illustrate a special effect hearing has had on her life. The next statement illustrates a student's reaction to temporarily losing her ability to hear.

In an experiment I did for my sign language class, I bandaged up my ears so I couldn't hear a sound. I had a signing interpreter with me to translate spoken language. The two hours that I was "deaf" gave me a great appreciation for deaf people and their culture. I found it extremely difficult to communicate, because even though I could read the signing, I couldn't keep up with the pace of the conversation. . . . Also, it was uncomfortable for me to be in that much silence. Knowing what a crowded cafeteria sounds like and not being able to hear the background noise was an uncomfortable feeling. I couldn't hear the buzzing of the fluorescent light, the murmur of the crowd, or the slurping of my friend's Coke (which I usually

object to, but which I missed when I couldn't hear it). I saw a man drop his tray, and I heard nothing. I could handle the signing, but not the silence.

Eileen Lusk

You don't have to bandage up your ears for two hours to appreciate what hearing adds to your life. Just close your eyes for a few minutes, observe the sounds you hear, and notice what they tell you about your environment. What most people experience is that by listening closely they become aware of many events in the environment that without hearing they would not be aware of at all (Figure 10.1). Let's consider this function of hearing, as well as others, in more detail.

THE FUNCTIONS OF HEARING

Our ability to hear events that we can't see serves an important signaling function for both animals and humans. For an animal living in the forest, the rustle of leaves or the snap of a twig may signal the approach of a predator. For humans living in the city, hearing provides signals such as the warning sound of

Figure 10.1
The auditory world of the people sitting on the bench includes a large number of stimuli that are hidden from the visual system but that can be sensed through hearing.

a smoke alarm or an ambulance siren, the distinctive high-pitched cry of a baby who is distressed, or tell-tale noises that signal problems in a car engine that is not running smoothly.

But hearing also has functions in addition to signaling. On the first day of my perception class, I ask my students which sense they would choose to keep if they had to pick between hearing and vision. Two of the strongest arguments for keeping hearing instead of vision are music and speech. Many of my students wouldn't want to give up hearing because of the pleasure they derive from listening to music, and they also realize that speech is important because it facilitates communication between people.

Helen Keller, who was both deaf and blind, stated that she felt being deaf was worse than being blind, because blindness isolated her from things, but deafness isolated her from people. Being unable to hear people talking creates an isolation that makes it difficult to relate to hearing people and sometimes makes it difficult even to know what is going on. To appreciate the importance of hearing for knowing what is going on, try watching a dramatic program on television with the sound turned off. You may be surprised at how little, beyond physical actions and perhaps some intense emotions, you can understand about the story.

Our goal in this chapter is to describe the basic mechanisms responsible for our ability to hear. We will describe the nature of sound and the anatomy of the auditory system and then will focus on the physiological mechanisms for our perception of pitch. In the next chapter, we will ask questions such as: How do we tell where a sound source is located? How do we perceptually organize the sounds in our environment so we can tell one from another? What gives different musical instruments their distinctive tonal qualities? The starting point both for understanding our perception of pitch and for answering these questions is to consider exactly what we mean by the word "sound." One way to do this is to consider the following question:

> If a tree falls in the forest and no one is there to hear it, would there be a sound?

This question is useful because it is based on the fact that we can use the word **sound** in two different ways. Sometimes *sound* refers to a physical stimulus, and sometimes it refers to a perceptual response. The answer to the question about the tree depends on which of the following definitions of sound we use (Figure 10.2):

Figure 10.2

When this tree falls, will there be a sound if no one is there to listen? The answer to this question depends on whether we define sound *as a physical stimulus or as an experience.*

- *Physical definition*: Sound is *pressure changes* in the air or other medium.

  Answer to the question: "Yes," because the falling tree causes pressure changes whether or not someone is there to hear them.

- *Perceptual definition*: Sound is the *experience* we have when we hear.

  Answer to the question: "No," because if no one is in the forest, there would be no experience.

This difference between physical and perceptual is an important one to be aware of as we discuss hearing in this chapter and the next two. Luckily, it is usually easy to tell from the context in which the terms are used whether "sound" refers to the physical stimulus or to the experience of hearing. For example "the sound of the trumpet pierced the air" refers to the experience of sound, but "the sound's level was 10 decibels" refers to sound as a physical stimulus. We will first describe sound as a physical stimulus and will then describe sound as a perceptual experience.

THE SOUND STIMULUS: PRESSURE CHANGES IN THE AIR

webTUTOR A sound stimulus occurs when the movements or vibrations of an object cause pressure changes in air, water, or any other elastic medium that surrounds the object. Let's begin by considering your radio or stereo system's loudspeaker, which is really a device for producing vibrations to be transmitted to the surrounding air.

The Sound Stimulus Produced by a Loudspeaker

People have been known to turn up the volume control on their stereos high enough so vibrations can be felt through a neighbor's wall, but even at lower levels the vibrations are there. You can feel the vibrations produced by your stereo by placing your hand gently on the speaker. (This technique is sometimes used by deaf people to "listen" to music.) Sometimes, if the volume is turned up enough and the music has a lot of percussive bass notes, you can actually feel the pressure changes in the air without even placing your hands on the speaker. Another way to perceive the vibrations at a distance from the speaker is to place your hands on an inflated balloon that is positioned in front of the speaker.

The speaker's vibrations affect the surrounding air, as shown in Figure 10.3. When the diaphragm of the speaker moves out, it pushes the surrounding air molecules together, increasing the density of molecules near the diaphragm. This increased density increases the air pressure. When the speaker diaphragm moves back in, it decreases the density of molecules near the diaphragm, decreasing the air pressure. By repeating this process many hundreds or thousands of times a second, the speaker creates a pattern of alternating high- and low-pressure regions in the air as neighboring air molecules affect each other. This pattern of air pressure changes, which travels through air at 340 meters per second (and through water at 1,500 meters per second), is called a **sound wave**.

The qualities of the sounds we hear, particularly the pitch and loudness of a tone, are related to two properties of sound waves, their frequency and their amplitude. We introduce frequency and amplitude by focusing on a simple kind of sound wave, called a

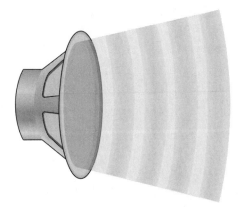

Figure 10.3

The effect of a vibrating speaker diaphragm on the surrounding air. Dark areas represent regions of high air pressure, and light areas represent areas of low air pressure.

pure tone, in which pressure changes occur in a pattern described by a mathematical function called a sine wave, as shown in Figure 10.4. Tones with this pattern of pressure changes are occasionally found in

the environment. A person whistling or the high-pitched notes produced by a flute are close to pure tones. Tuning forks, which are designed to vibrate with a sine-wave motion, also produce pure tones, and pure tones for laboratory studies of hearing are generated by computers, which can cause a speaker diaphragm to vibrate in and out with a sine-wave motion. This vibration can be described by noting its **amplitude**—the distance the diaphragm moves from its rest position (labeled A in Figure 10.4) and its **frequency**—the number of times per second that the speaker diaphragm goes through the cycle of moving out, back in, and then out again.

The diaphragm's sine-wave motion is transferred to the air, creating the pure tone stimulus shown in Figure 10.5. The tone's frequency is indicated in units called **Hertz (Hz)**, where one Hertz is one cycle per second. Thus, a 1,000-Hz tone is a pure tone that goes through 1,000 cycles per second. Humans can hear frequencies between about 20 and 20,000 Hz.

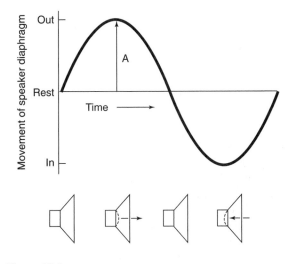

Figure 10.4

In response to a sine-wave stimulus from a computer, a speaker diaphragm moves out and then back in, as shown in the pictures in the figure. The time course of this motion is indicated by the sine-wave curve, which indicates the amount that the diaphragm has moved as a function of time. The amplitude (A) represents the maximum deflection of the speaker diaphragm from its rest position.

Specifying the Amplitude of a Sound Stimulus

One way to specify a sound's amplitude would be to indicate the difference in pressure between the high and low peaks of the sound wave. But this method of specifying amplitude runs into difficulty when we consider the wide range of pressure changes humans can hear. For example, if the pressure change caused

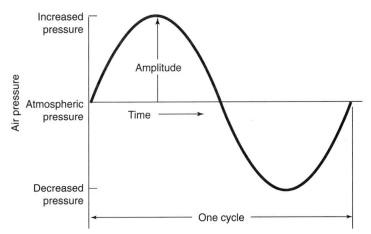

Figure 10.5

The sinusoidal vibration of the speaker diaphragm results in a sinusoidal change in the air pressure, as shown in the figure.

Sound, Auditory System, Pitch Perception

by a near-threshold sound, such as a barely audible whisper, is called 1, then the sound pressure of loud radio music would be about 10,000 and the sound pressure of a jet engine at takeoff would be about 10 million.

To compress this large range into a more manageable scale, auditory researchers use a unit of sound called the **decibel**, which is named after Alexander Graham Bell, the inventor of the telephone. The following equation is used to convert sound pressure into decibels:

$$\text{Number of dB} = 20 \text{ logarithm } \frac{p}{p_0}$$

where dB stands for decibels, p is the sound pressure of the stimulus, and p_0 is a standard sound pressure, which is usually set at 20 micropascals, where a pascal is a unit of pressure and a micropascal is one-millionth of a pascal. This standard pressure is close to the pressure of a 1,000-Hz tone at threshold, measured in a free field, which means that the person is listening to the sound presented by speakers, rather than through earphones. We can use the equation above to calculate the decibels for this 1,000-Hz tone as follows:

If pressure = 20 micropascals,

$$dB = 20 \times \log \frac{p}{p_0}$$

$$= 20 \times \log \frac{20}{20} = 20 \times \log 1.0$$

$$= 20 \times 0 \text{ (the log of } 1.0 = 0)$$

$$= 0 \text{ dB SPL}$$

Adding the notation **SPL**, which stands for **sound pressure level**, indicates that we have used the standard pressure of 20 micropascals as p_0 in our calculation. In referring to the decibels or sound pressure of a sound stimulus, the term **level** or **sound level** is usually used.

Let's now continue our calculation of dB for two higher pressure levels:

If pressure = 200

$$dB = 20 \times \log \frac{200}{20} = 20 \times \log 10$$

$$= 20 \times 1 \text{ (the log of } 10 = 1)$$

$$= 20 \text{ dB SPL}$$

If pressure = 2,000

$$dB = 20 \times \log \frac{2,000}{20} = 20 \times \log 100$$

$$= 20 \times 2 \text{ (the log of } 100 = 2)$$

$$= 40 \text{ dB SPL}$$

Notice that *multiplying* sound pressure by 10 *adds* 20 dB. As you can see from Table 10.1, continuing this process all the way up to a sound pressure of 10 million increases the decibels to only 140. The dB scale is useful, in part, because of the way it compresses the large range of sound pressures. In addition, decibels, which are a physical measure, are related to the psychological experience of loudness, since loudness approximately doubles for every 10 dB increase in sound. This approximate connection between dB and loudness adds to the usefulness of the scale. We will discuss this connection between

Table 10.1
The relation between sound pressure and decibels

Pressure ratio (p/p_0)	dB SPL
1	0
10	20
100	40
1,000	60
10,000	80
100,000	100
1,000,000	120
10,000,000	140

Figure 10.6
Electronic synthesizer. Early synthesizers used the procedure of additive synthesis, in which pure-tone harmonics were added to a fundamental frequency to create musical tones that sounded like different instruments. Advanced models like this one use similar principles plus more advanced procedures involving digital processing of sound sampled from musical instruments.

the physical stimulus and the psychological response further below.

Specifying the Frequencies of Complex Sound Stimuli

A pure tone is, by definition, a single frequency. We have seen that we can specify the frequency of a pure tone stimulus by indicating how many times per second the sine wave repeats itself. Our auditory experience is dominated, however, not by pure tones, but by more complex stimuli such as music, speech, and the various sounds produced by nature and machines. These complex stimuli contain many frequencies.

To understand how complex stimuli are made up of many frequencies, let's consider a technique called **additive synthesis,** which has been used to program electronic synthesizers like the one in Figure 10.6 to produce sounds that resemble various musical instruments. The starting point for creating a complex tone by additive synthesis is a single pure tone, like the one in Figure 10.7a, which is called the **fundamental frequency** of the complex tone. We will assume that the frequency of this fundamental is 440 Hz.

Additional pure tones, called **harmonics,** are then added to this one, each of which has a frequency that is a multiple of the fundamental. For the 440 Hz fundamental, the frequency of the second tone, which is called the second harmonic, is 880 Hz (Figure 10.7b) and the frequency of the third tone, which is called the third harmonic, is 1320 Hz (Figure 10.7c).

The reason for adding these harmonics is that the tones of most musical instruments have many harmonics, with the amounts of the various harmonics giving each instrument its distinctive sound.[1] The pattern of pressure changes for a complex musical tone consists of the sum of these components, as shown in Figure 10.7d. Most musical tones have many more harmonics than this one, so the pattern of

---

[1] Current synthesizer technology uses a technique called sampling in which the sounds produced by actual musical instruments are recorded, digitized, and filtered in various ways to create sounds with different "colorizations" or "timbres." The basic goal is the same as additive synthesis, which is to manipulate the different frequency components of the sound to produce the sounds of different instruments.

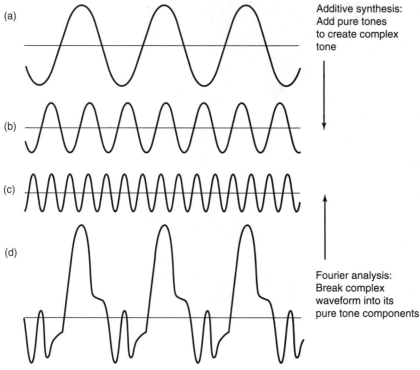

(a)

(b)

(c)

(d)

Additive synthesis:
Add pure tones
to create complex
tone

Fourier analysis:
Break complex
waveform into its
pure tone components

Figure 10.7

Additive synthesis. (a) Pressure changes for a pure tone with frequency of 440 Hz; (b) the second harmonic of (a), with a frequency of 880 Hz; (c) the third harmonic, with a frequency of 1,320 Hz. (d) The sum of the three harmonics above creates the waveform for a complex tone. Working in the other direction, applying Fourier analysis to the complex tone reveals its pure tone components.

pressure changes is even more complex than the one in Figure 10.7d.

We have used the example of additive synthesis to illustrate how a musical tone can be created by adding a number of harmonics. We can also start with a complex tone and work in the opposite direction to break the tone into its harmonics. We can do this by using **Fourier analysis**, the mathematical technique we introduced in Chapter 3 (see page 90), based on a mathematical theorem described by Auguste Fourier, which shows that any complex waveform can be broken down into a series of sine waves. What this means is that we can specify complex sound waves in terms of their harmonics, since each harmonic corresponds to a pure tone sine wave. Thus, application of Fourier analysis to the complex tone in Figure 10.7d reveals the three sine-wave components shown in a, b, and c.

Figure 10.8 shows another way to indicate the components of a musical tone. This plot, a **Fourier frequency spectrum**, indicates each harmonic's frequency by a line's position on the horizontal axis and its amplitude by the height of the line. The line marked F is the fundamental frequency of the tone in Figure 10.7, and the other two lines are the second and third harmonics. Whether represented as sine waves, as in Figure 10.7, or as lines in a Fourier frequency spectrum, as in Figure 10.8, the important point is that most musical tones consist of the sum of a number of pure tones with different frequencies. We will discuss this property of musical tones further in Chapter 11, and we will return to the idea of Fourier analysis later in this chapter, when we discuss how the auditory system breaks complex tones down into their components.

There are many sounds in our environment in addition to pure tones and musical tones. Right now, a cash register drawer has just slammed shut in the coffee shop where I'm writing, two people are having an animated conversation at a table to my right, and cars

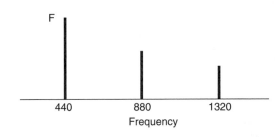

Figure 10.8
The Fourier frequency spectrum for the tone in Figure 10.7. The spectrum indicates that the tone is made up of one component with a frequency of 440 Hz, another with a frequency of 880 Hz, and a third with a frequency of 1,320 Hz. The heights of the lines indicate the amplitude of each frequency.

are driving down the street just outside. The sounds produced by these events are more complex than musical tones, but many of these sound stimuli can also be analyzed into their frequency components. We will describe how we perceive complex environmental stimuli in Chapter 11 and speech stimuli in Chapter 12. We will focus on pure tones and musical tones in this chapter, because these sounds are the ones that have been used in most of the basic research on the operation of the auditory system.

SOUND AS A PERCEPTUAL RESPONSE: THE EXPERIENCE OF HEARING

WebTUTOR We will now consider the relationship between the sound stimulus and perceptual experience.

The Range of Hearing

Just as we can see within only a narrow band of wavelengths called the visible spectrum, we hear within a specific range of frequencies called the range of hearing. For humans, this range extends between about 20 Hz and 20,000 Hz.

Just as we are most sensitive to certain wavelengths within the visible spectrum, we are also most sensitive to certain frequencies within the range of hearing. The curve in Figure 10.9, which is called the **audibility curve**, indicates how the sensitivity changes across the frequencies that we can hear by plotting the threshold for hearing determined by free-field presentation (listening to a loudspeaker) versus frequency. From this curve, we can see that we are most sensitive (the threshold for hearing is lowest) at frequencies between 2,000 and 4,000 Hz, the range of frequencies that is most important for understanding speech.

The area above the audibility curve is called the **auditory response area** because we can hear tones that fall within this area. At intensities below the audibility curve we can't hear a tone. For example, we wouldn't be able to hear a 30-Hz tone at 40 dB SPL (point A). The upper boundary of the auditory response area is the curve marked "threshold for feeling." As we approach this curve, tones become painful and can cause damage to the auditory system. In fact, damage can occur at levels below the threshold for feeling, if the duration of the exposure is long enough. That is why OSHA, which sets government standards for occupational safety, mandates that workers should not be exposed to levels greater than 90 dB for an 8-hour work day.

Although the useful range of hearing for humans extends between about 20 and 20,000 Hz, the audibility curves in Figure 10.10 show that other animals have different "windows" on the auditory world. Elephants can hear stimuli below 20 Hz; the homing pigeon can detect frequencies as low as 0.05 Hz; and dogs, mice, and dolphins are able to hear at frequencies far above the highest frequencies humans can detect. Notice that the frequency scale is logarithmic, so high frequencies are allotted less distance than low frequencies. In general, animals with smaller heads are sensitive to higher frequencies.

Loudness

Loudness is the magnitude of auditory sensation (Plack & Carlyon, 1995). As we have already noted, it is closely associated with the sound pressure of the

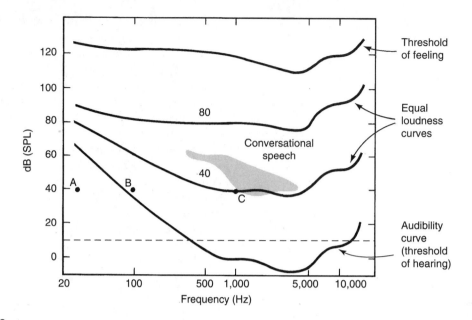

Figure 10.9

The audibility curve and the auditory response area. Hearing occurs between the audibility curve (the threshold for hearing) and the threshold for feeling. Tones with SPLs below the threshold for hearing cannot be heard; tones with SPLs above the threshold of feeling result in pain. SPLs approaching the threshold for feeling can cause damage to the cochlea. The shaded area indicates the frequency and intensity range of conversational speech. The curves marked 40 and 80 are equal loudness curves. The places where the dashed line at 10 dB crosses the audibility function indicate the range of frequencies that can be heard at 10 dB SPL. (From Fletcher & Munson, 1933.)

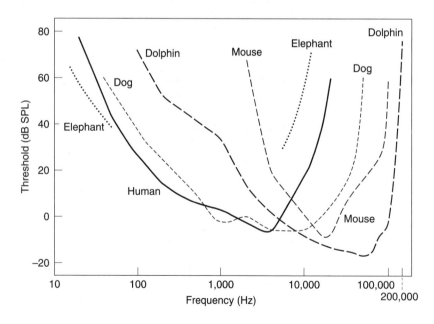

Figure 10.10

Audibility curves for a few animals. Notice that the frequency scale is logarithmic, so high frequencies are allotted less distance than low frequencies. Only the low and high ends of the elephant curve are shown to prevent overlap with the other curves. (Based on data from Au, 1993; Heffner, 1983; Heffner & Heffner, 1980, 1985; Heffner & Masterton, 1980.)

stimulus. Table 10.2 lists some environmental sounds, ranging from ones that aren't very loud, such as a barely audible whisper or leaves rustling, to those that are extremely loud, such as a jet engine at takeoff. From the levels, in decibels, associated with these sound experiences, you can see that increasing the sound pressure of the stimulus increases its loudness.

Figure 10.11 shows the relationship between decibels and loudness for a pure tone, determined by S. S. Stevens's magnitude estimation procedure (see Chapter 1, page 16). Loudness is judged relative to a standard of a 1,000-Hz tone at 40 dB, which is assigned a value of 1. Thus, a tone that sounds 10 time louder than this standard would have a loudness of 10. This curve indicates that increasing the sound level by 10 dB almost (but not quite) doubles the sound's loudness.

The loudness of pure tones depends not only on sound pressure but also on frequency. We can appreciate how loudness depends on frequency by comparing the loudness of two tones that have the same level but different frequencies. For example, point B in Figure 10.9 indicates where a 40-dB SPL 100-Hz tone is located in the response area, and point C indicates where a 40-dB SPL 1000-Hz tone is located. The locations of these two points indicate that these two tones would have very different loudnesses. Since the 100-

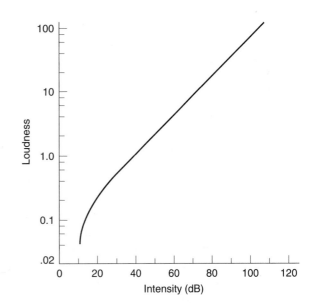

Figure 10.11

Loudness for a 100-Hz tone determined by magnitude estimation, as a function of intensity. (Adapted from Gulick, Gescheider, & Frisina, 1989.) (Listen to WebTutor, Loudness Scaling.)

Hz tone is located just above the audibility curve, it is just above threshold, so would be just barely heard. However, the 1,000-Hz tone is far above threshold, well into the auditory response area, so it would be much louder than the 100-Hz tone. Thus, saying that a pure tone has a level of 40 dB SPL tells us nothing about its loudness unless we know its frequency.

Another way to understand the relationship between loudness and frequency is by looking at the **equal loudness curves** in Figure 10.9. These curves indicate the number of decibels that create the same perception of loudness at different frequencies. We measure an equal loudness curve by designating one tone as a standard and matching the loudness of all other tones to it. For example, the curve marked 40 in Figure 10.9 was determined by matching the loudness of frequencies across the range of hearing to a 1,000-Hz 40-dB SPL tone. Similarly, the curve marked 80 was determined by matching the loudness of different frequencies to a 1,000-Hz 80-dB SPL tone.

Table 10.2

Some common sound pressure levels (in decibels)

Sound	SPL (dB)
Barely audible sound (threshold)	0
Leaves rustling	20
Quiet residential community	40
Average speaking voice	60
Loud music from radio/heavy traffic	80
Express subway train	100
Propeller plane at takeoff	120
Jet engine at takeoff (pain threshold)	140
Spacecraft launch at close range	160

Notice that the audibility curve and the equal loudness curve marked 40 bend up at high and low frequencies, but the equal loudness curve marked 80 is flatter, curving up only at frequencies above about 5,000 Hz. This means that at 80 dB SPL all tones from 30 to 5,000 Hz have about the same loudness. The difference between the relatively flat 80 curve and the upward-bending curves at lower decibel levels explains something that happens as you adjust the volume control on your stereo system. If you are playing music at a fairly high level—say, 80 dB SPL—you should be able to easily hear each of the frequencies in the music because, as the equal loudness curve for 80 indicates, all frequencies between about 20 Hz and 5,000 Hz sound equally loud at this intensity.

However, when you turn the intensity down to 10 dB SPL, all frequencies don't sound equally loud. In fact, from the audibility curve in Figure 10.9 we can see that frequencies below about 400 Hz (the bass notes) and above about 12,000 Hz (the treble notes) are inaudible at 10 dB. (To determine the frequencies below and above which a 10-dB tone is inaudible, notice that the dashed 10-dB line crosses the audibility curve at about 400 Hz and 12,000 Hz. This means that frequencies lower than 400 Hz and higher than 12,000 Hz are not audible at 10 dB.)

Being unable to hear very low and very high frequencies creates a bad situation, because it means that when you play music softly you won't hear the very low or very high frequencies. To compensate for this, most stereo receivers have a button labeled "loudness" that boosts the level of very high and very low frequencies, when the volume control is turned down. This enables you to hear these frequencies, even when you are playing your stereo very softly.

Pitch

Pitch is the quality of a tone that we describe as "high" or "low." The pitch of a pure tone is related to its frequency: Low frequencies cause low pitches, and high frequencies cause high pitches. **Tone height** is the property of increasing pitch that accompanies increases in a tone's frequency. Thus, if we start at the left, or bass, end of a piano keyboard and play a scale

that moves toward the right, or treble, end of the keyboard, the tone height increases.

In addition to the increase in tone height that occurs as we move from the bass to the treble end of the piano keyboard, something else happens: The letters of the notes A, B, C, D, E, F, and G repeat, and we notice that notes with the same letter sound similar. Because of this similarity, we say that notes with the same letter have the same **tone chroma**.

The spiral in Figure 10.12 illustrates the concepts of tone height and tone chroma. Moving upwards on the spiral is equivalent to playing notes

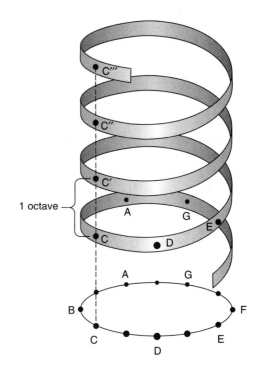

Figure 10.12

Representing the notes of the scale on an ascending spiral graphically depicts the perceptions of tone height and tone chroma. Moving up the spiral increases tone height, with each note sounding higher than the note preceding. The place where the vertical line intersects the spiral indicates the location of notes with the same letter (C in the example shown in the figure) and, therefore, the same tone chroma. These notes are separated by octaves and sound similar to one another. Other vertical lines would intersect other notes with the same tone chroma.

from the left (low) to right (high) on the piano keyboard, so represents increases in tone height. As we move up the spiral, the notes on the scale repeat, and every time we pass the same letter on the spiral we have gone up an interval called an **octave.** Tones separated by octaves have the same tone chroma; a male with a low-pitched voice and a female with a high-pitched voice can be regarded as singing "in unison" even if their voices are separated by an octave or more. This similarity between the same notes in different octaves also makes it possible for a singer on the verge of overreaching his or her voice range to shift the melody down to a lower octave.

Timbre

If two tones have the same loudness, pitch, and duration but sound different, this difference is a difference in **timbre** (pronounced tim´-ber or tam´-bre). For example, a flute and a bassoon playing the same note sound very different. The flute sounds "clear" or "mellow" and the bassoon sounds "nasal" or "reedy." We will see in Chapter 11 that these differences in timbre are caused by a number of factors, including differences in the energy of the harmonics created by different musical instruments. See Summary Table 10.1 for an overview of the material we have covered so far.

AUDITORY SYSTEM: STRUCTURE AND FUNCTION

WebTUTOR The auditory system must accomplish three basic tasks before we can hear. First, it must deliver the sound stimulus to the receptors. Second, it

---

SUMMARY TABLE 10.1

The Functions of Hearing

Hearing enables us to be aware of events we can't see and can also signal environmentally important events, such as signals of danger. It also plays a crucial role in communication.

The Tree in the Forest

The answer to the question, "If a tree falls in the forest and no one is there to hear it, would there be a sound?" depends on the difference between the physical aspect of sound (Answer = Yes) and the perceptual aspect (Answer = No).

The Sound Stimulus

Sound waves, which are pressure changes in the air, can be described in terms of amplitude and frequency. The amplitude of a sound stimulus can be specified in terms of decibels, compressing a large range of pressures into a smaller, more manageable, range.

Complex Sound Stimuli

A complex tone can be created, using additive synthesis, by adding a number of pure tones called harmonics. Conversely, a complex tone can be broken down into a number of sine-wave components by using Fourier analysis.

The Range of Hearing

The audibility curve and auditory response area indicate the range of frequencies we can hear and the thresholds for hearing across the frequency spectrum.

Loudness

Loudness is related to sound pressure level, with higher decibels associated with higher loudness; but loudness is also related to frequency, as can be seen by the audibility curve. Because of the relationship between loudness and frequency, the frequency of a pure tone must be specified in order to know how loud a sound with a given number of decibels will be perceived.

Pitch and Timbre

Pitch is associated with frequency, with high frequencies being associated with high pitches. Tones separated by octaves have a similar sound quality, called tone chroma. Timbre is the difference in the qualities of sounds that have the same loudness, pitch, and duration but sound different.

---

must transduce this stimulus from pressure changes into electrical signals, and third, it must process these electrical signals so they can indicate qualities of the sound source such as pitch, loudness, timbre, and location.

We begin our description of how the auditory system accomplishes these tasks by describing the basic structure of the system. Our first question, "How does energy from the environment reach the receptors?" takes us on a journey through what Diane Ackerman (1990) has described as a device that resembles "a contraption some ingenious plumber has put together from spare parts." We begin our description as the sound stimulus enters the outer ear.

The Outer Ear

When we talk about the "ears" in everyday conversation, we are usually referring to the **pinnae**, the structures that stick out from the sides of the head. While this most obvious part of the ear is of some importance in helping us determine the location of sounds and is of great importance for those who wear eyeglasses, it is the part of the ear we could most easily do without. The major workings of the ear are found inside the head, hidden from view.

Sound waves first pass through the **outer ear**, which consists of the pinna and the **auditory canal** (Figure 10.13). The auditory canal is a tubelike structure about 3 cm long that protects the delicate structures of the middle ear from the hazards of the outside world. The auditory canal's 3-cm recess, along with its wax, which has an unpleasant effect on curious insects (Schubert, 1980), protects the delicate **tympanic membrane**, or **eardrum**, at the end of the canal and helps keep this membrane and the structures in the middle ear at a relatively constant temperature.

In addition to its protective function, the outer ear has another role: to enhance the intensities of some sounds by means of the physical principle of resonance. **Resonance** occurs when sound waves that are reflected back from the closed end of the auditory canal interact with sound waves that are entering the auditory canal. This interaction reinforces some of the sound's frequencies, with the frequency that is reinforced the most being determined by the length of the canal. The frequency reinforced the most is called the **resonant frequency** of the canal.

We can appreciate how the resonant frequency depends on the length of the canal by noting how the tone produced by blowing across the top of a soda bottle changes as we drink more soda. Drinking more soda increases the length of the air path inside the bottle, which decreases the resonant frequency, and this creates a lower-pitched tone. Measurements of the sound pressures inside the ear indicate that the

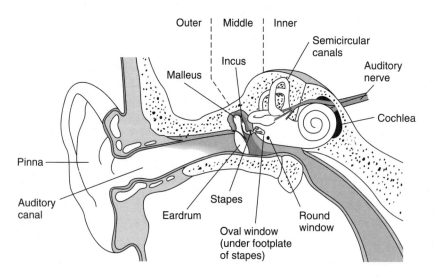

Figure 10.13
The ear, showing its three subdivisions—outer, middle, and inner. (From Lindsay & Norman, 1977.)

resonance that occurs in the auditory canal has a slight amplifying effect on frequencies between about 2,000 and 5,000 Hz.

The Middle Ear

When airborne sound waves reach the tympanic membrane at the end of the auditory canal, they set it into vibration, and this vibration is transmitted to structures in the middle ear, on the other side of the tympanic membrane. The **middle ear** is a small cavity, about 2 cm² in volume, which separates the outer and inner ears (Figure 10.14). This cavity contains the **ossicles**, the three smallest bones in the body. The first of these bones, the **malleus**, is set into vibration by the tympanic membrane, to which it is attached, and transmits its vibrations to the **incus**, which, in turn, transmits its vibrations to the **stapes**. The stapes then transmits its vibrations to the inner ear by pushing on the membrane covering the **oval window**.

Why are the ossicles necessary? We can answer this question by noting that both the outer ear and middle ear are filled with air, but the inner ear contains a watery liquid that is much denser than the air (Figure 10.15). The mismatch between the low density of the air and the high density of this liquid creates a problem: Pressure changes in the air are transmitted poorly to the much denser liquid. If these vibrations had to pass directly from the air to the liquid, only about 3 percent of the vibrations would be transmitted (Durrant & Lovrinic, 1977). The ossicles help solve this problem by amplifying the vibration in two ways: (1) concentrating the vibration of the large tympanic membrane onto the much smaller stapes (Figure 10.16), and (2) being hinged to create a lever action similar to what enables a small weight on the long end of a board balanced on a fulcrum to overcome a larger weight on the short end of the board (Figure 10.17).

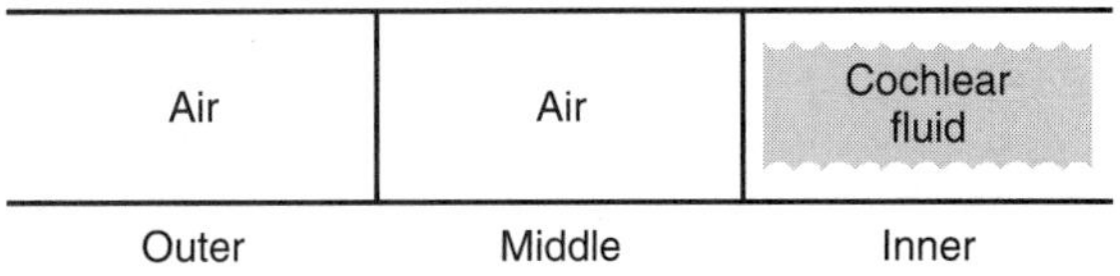

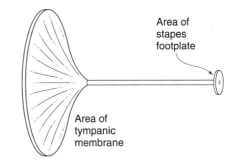

Figure 10.15

Environments inside the outer, middle, and inner ears. The fact that liquid fills the inner ear poses a problem for the transmission of sound vibrations from the air of the middle ear.

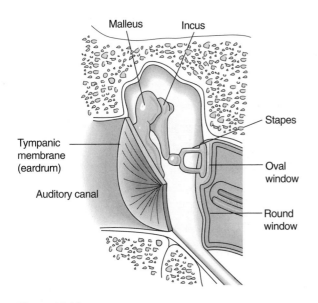

Figure 10.14

The middle ear. The three bones of the middle ear transmit the vibrations of the tympanic membrane to the inner ear.

Figure 10.16

A diagrammatic representation of the tympanic membrane and the stapes, showing the difference in size between the two. (From Schubert, 1980.)

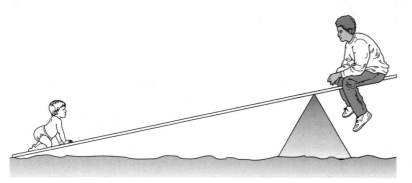

Figure 10.17
The lever principle. The baby on the long end of the board can overcome the weight of the man on the short end. Lever action based on this principle helps the ossicles transmit vibrations from the tympanic membrane to the inner ear.

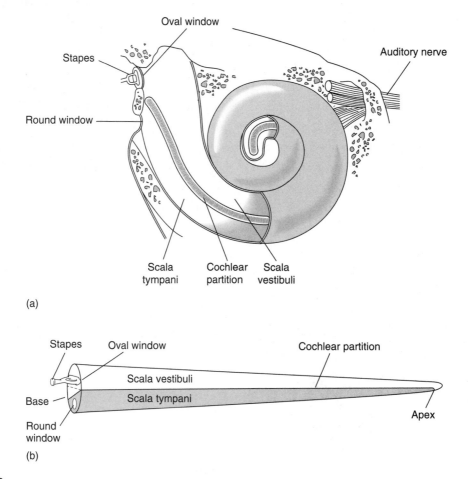

(a)

(b)

Figure 10.18
(a) A partially uncoiled cochlea. (b) A fully uncoiled cochlea. The cochlear partition, which is indicated here by a line, actually contains the basilar membrane and the organ of Corti, which are shown in Figures 10.19 and 10.20.

These two mechanisms amplify the vibrations entering the outer ear enough to set the liquid inside the inner ear into vibration (Durrant & Lovrinic, 1977; Schubert, 1980). We can appreciate the amplifying effect of the ossicles by noting that in patients whose ossicles have been damaged beyond surgical repair, it is necessary to increase the sound by a factor of 10 to 50 to achieve the same hearing as when the ossicles were functioning.

The middle ear also contains the **middle-ear muscles**, the smallest skeletal muscles in the body. These muscles are attached to the ossicles, and at very high sound intensities they contract to dampen the ossicle's vibration, thereby protecting the structures of the inner ear against potentially painful and damaging stimuli.

The Inner Ear

The main structure of the **inner ear** is the liquid-filled **cochlea** (Figure 10.18a). The liquid is set into vibration by the movement of the stapes against the oval window. The cochlea, which is a bony snail-like structure, is difficult to visualize because it is rolled into 2¾ turns. But we can see the structure inside more clearly by imagining how the cochlea would appear if uncoiled to form a long straight tube (Figure 10.18b). The most obvious feature of the uncoiled cochlea is that the upper half, called the scala vestibuli, and the lower half, called the scala tympani, are separated by a structure called the **cochlear partition**, which extends almost the entire length of the cochlea, with the **base** of the cochlear partition located near the stapes and the **apex** at the far end. Note that this diagram is not drawn to scale and so doesn't show the cochlea's true proportions. In reality, the uncoiled cochlea would be a cylinder 2 mm in diameter and 35 mm long.

We can best see the structures within the cochlear partition by looking at the cochlea end-on and in cross section, as in Figure 10.19. When we look at the cochlea in this way, we see that the cochlear partition

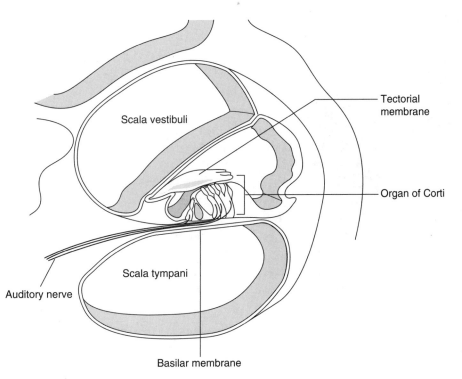

Figure 10.19
A cross section of the cochlea.

Sound, Auditory System, Pitch Perception

contains a large structure called the **organ of Corti**. Details of the organ of Corti are shown in Figure 10.20. From these figures, we can see that (1) the organ of Corti contains the receptors, called **hair cells**; (2) it sits on top of the **basilar membrane**; and (3) it is covered on top by the **tectorial membrane**.

The hair cells are shown in Figure 10.21. There are two types of hair cells, the **inner hair cells** and the **outer hair cells**. The component of these hair cells that gives them their name is the fine **cilia**, which protrude from the tops of the cells.

One of the most important events in the auditory process is the bending of the cilia, because this bending transduces the vibrations caused by the sound stimulus into electrical signals. The cilia bend because the in-and-out movement of the stapes creates pressure changes in the liquid inside the cochlea that sets the cochlear partition into an up-and-down motion.

This up-and-down motion of the cochlear partition causes two effects: (1) The organ of Corti also vibrates with an up-and-down motion, and (2) the tectorial membrane, which covers the organ of Corti,

moves with a back-and-forth motion relative to the cilia of the hair cells (Figure 10.22). These two motions cause the cilia of the inner hair cells to bend because of their movement against the surrounding liquid and the cilia of the outer hair cells to bend because they are embedded in the tectorial membrane (Dallos, 1996).

The bending of the cilia of the inner hair cells generates the electrical signal that is transmitted to fibers in the auditory nerve. (We will describe the function of the outer hair cells later in the chapter.) When the inner hair cells' cilia bend in one direction, the hair cells depolarize (their voltage decreases as does that of the nerve fiber in Figure 1.20), and when the cilia bend in the other direction, the hair cells hyperpolarize (their voltage increases). Each time the cell depolarizes it releases neurotransmitter, and each time it hyperpolarizes the transmitter stops. The result is that the receptor cells release small bursts of transmitter, and this causes bursts of firing that send a neural message along the auditory nerve about the frequency of the sound stimulus (Kelly, 1991).

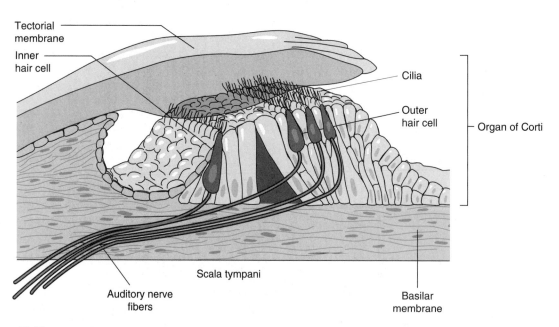

Figure 10.20

A cross section of the organ of Corti, showing how it rests upon the basilar membrane. (Adapted from Denes & Pinson, 1993.)

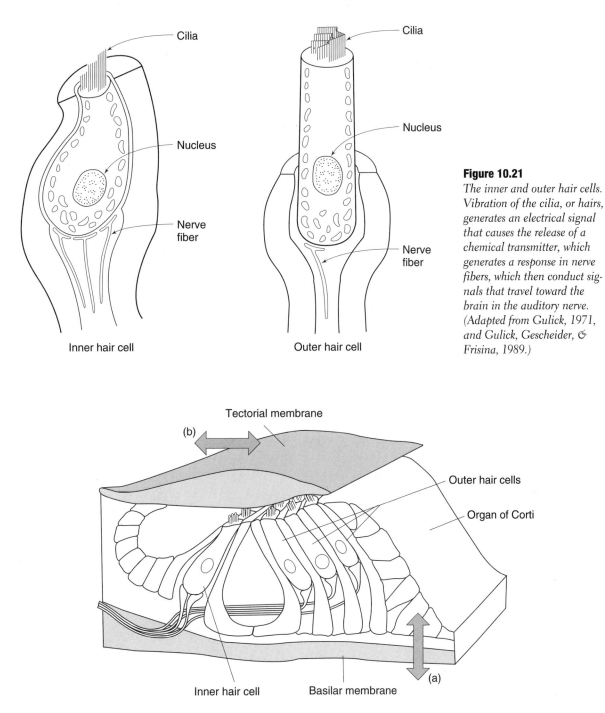

Figure 10.21
The inner and outer hair cells. Vibration of the cilia, or hairs, generates an electrical signal that causes the release of a chemical transmitter, which generates a response in nerve fibers, which then conduct signals that travel toward the brain in the auditory nerve. (Adapted from Gulick, 1971, and Gulick, Gescheider, & Frisina, 1989.)

Figure 10.22
Vibration of the basilar membrane causes (a) the organ of Corti to vibrate up and down and (b) the tectorial membrane to move with a complex back-and-forth motion relative to the hair cells.

The amount the cilia must bend to cause the release of transmitter is extremely small. At the threshold for hearing, cilia movements as small as 100 trillionths of a meter (100 picometers) can generate a response in the hair cell. To give you an idea of just how small a movement this is, consider that if we were to increase the size of a cilium so it was as big as the Eiffel Tower, the movement of the cilia would translate into a movement of the pinnacle of the Eiffel Tower of only 10 mm (Figure 10.23) (Hudspeth, 1983, 1989).

Given the small amount of movement needed to hear a sound, it isn't surprising that the auditory system can detect extremely small pressure changes. In fact, the auditory system can detect pressure changes so small that they cause the eardrum to move only 10^{-11} cm, a dimension that is less than the diameter of a hydrogen atom (Tonndorf & Khanna, 1968), and the auditory system is so sensitive that the air pressure at threshold in the most sensitive range of hearing is only 10 to 15 dB above the air pressure generated by the random movement of air molecules. This means that if our hearing were much more sensitive than it is now, we would hear the background hiss of colliding air molecules!

The Auditory Pathways

The auditory nerve carries the signals generated by the inner hair cells away from the cochlea and toward the auditory receiving area in the cortex. Figure 10.24 shows the pathway the auditory signals follow from the cochlea to the auditory cortex. Auditory nerve fibers from the cochlea synapse in the **cochlear nucleus**. From there, fibers synapse in the **superior olivary nucleus** in the brain stem, the **inferior colliculus** of the midbrain, and the **medial geniculate nucleus** of the thalamus. (Remember that signals from the retina synapse in a nearby area of the thalamus, the lateral geniculate nucleus.)

From the medial geniculate nucleus, fibers go to the primary **auditory receiving area**, in the temporal lobe of the cortex. If you have trouble remembering this sequence of structures, remember the acronym SONIC MG (a very fast sports car), which represents the three structures between the cochlear nucleus

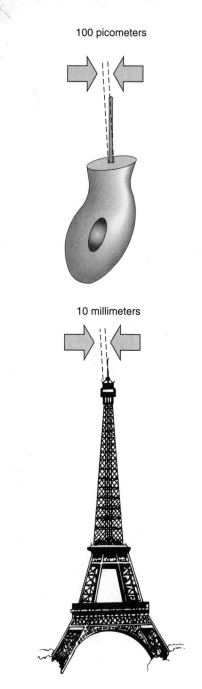

Figure 10.23

The distance the cilia of a hair cell moves at the threshold for hearing is so small that if the volume of an individual cilium is scaled up to that of the Eiffel Tower, the equivalent movement of the Eiffel Tower would be about 10 mm.

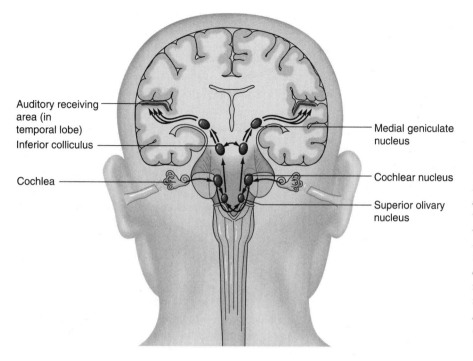

Auditory receiving area (in temporal lobe)

Inferior colliculus

Cochlea

Medial geniculate nucleus

Cochlear nucleus

Superior olivary nucleus

Figure 10.24
Diagram of the auditory pathways. This diagram is greatly simplified, as numerous connections between the structures are not shown. Note that auditory structures are bilateral—they exist on both the left and right sides of the body—and that messages can cross over between the two sides. (Adapted from Wever, 1949.)

and the auditory cortex, as follows: SON = Superior Olivary Nucleus; IC = Inferior Colliculus; MG = Medial Geniculate Nucleus.

The primary auditory receiving area is also called A1, since it is the first place signals are received in the cortex. Just as in the visual system, there are numerous other cortical areas beyond the primary receiving area. We will describe these other areas and what they do later in the chapter. For now we will focus on what's happening in the cochlea and auditory nerve, because it is here that the neural code for sound frequency originates.

FREQUENCY ANALYSIS IN THE COCHLEA AND AUDITORY NERVE

WebTUTOR We will consider two possible ways neurons might signal frequency, by referring to Figure 10.25, which is a schematic view of the cochlear partition, showing the nerve fibers that come from hair

cells all along the length of the partition. Each of these fibers signals the hair cell activity at a particular place along the cochlear partition.

How could sound frequency be represented by the firing of these fibers? Two possibilities are that frequency could be represented (1) by *which* of the fibers are firing or (2) by the *rate* at which these fibers are firing. We will see that the auditory system uses both of these types of information to indicate frequency. We will first describe the research which showed that frequency is coded by *which* fibers are firing. This idea is associated with a series of studies begun by Georg von Békésy in 1928, which culminated in Békésy's being awarded the Nobel Prize in physiology and medicine in 1961.

Békésy's Place Theory of Hearing

Békésy proposed the **place theory of hearing,** which states that the frequency of a sound is indicated by the place along the organ of Corti at which nerve firing is highest. Thus, the place theory states that frequency is indicated by which fibers are firing.

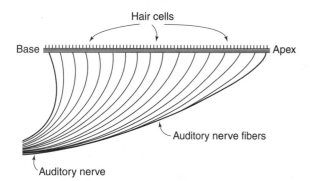

Figure 10.25
A representation of the cochlear partition, showing how nerve fibers receiving signals from hair cells all along the cochlea combine to form the auditory nerve. Note that each hair cell actually contributes one or more fibers to the auditory nerve.

Békésy approached the problem of determining the code for frequency by determining how the basilar membrane vibrated in response to different frequencies. He determined this in two ways: (1) by actually observing the vibration of the basilar membrane and (2) by building a model of the cochlea that took into account the physical properties of the basilar membrane.

Békésy observed the vibration of the basilar membrane by boring a hole in the ear of a human cadaver, stimulating it with sound, and observing the membrane's vibration by using a rapidly flashing light to "freeze" the motion of the membrane and a microscope to enable him to see the tiny movements (Békésy, 1960). He found that the vibrating motion of the basilar membrane is similar to the motion that occurs when one person holds the end of a rope and "snaps" it, sending a wave traveling down the rope.

This **traveling wave** motion of the basilar membrane is shown in Figure 10.26.

Békésy also determined how the basilar membrane vibrates by analyzing its structure. In this analysis he took note of two important facts: (1) The base of the basilar membrane (the end located nearest the stapes) is three or four times narrower than the apex of the basilar membrane (the end of the membrane located at the far end of the cochlea; Figure 10.27), and (2) the base of the membrane is about 100 times stiffer than the apex. Using this information, Békésy constructed models of the cochlea that revealed that the pressure changes in the cochlea cause the basilar membrane to vibrate in a traveling wave.

Figure 10.28 shows the traveling wave at three successive moments in time. The solid horizontal line represents the basilar membrane at rest. Curve 1 shows the position of the basilar membrane at one moment during its vibration, and curves 2 and 3 show the positions of the membrane at two later moments. Since the shape of the traveling wave changes at each point in time, we use the **envelope of the traveling wave** to describe the maximum displacement that the wave causes at each point along the membrane. This maximum displacement, which is indicated by the dashed line, is important because it tells us which hair cells and nerve fibers along the basilar membrane will be affected the most by the membrane's vibration. Since the amount that the cilia move depends on the amount that the basilar membrane is displaced, hair cells located near the place where the basilar membrane vibrates the most will be stimulated the most strongly, and the nerve fibers associated with these hair cells will therefore fire the most strongly.

Békésy's (1960) observations of the basilar membrane's vibrations led him to conclude that the enve-

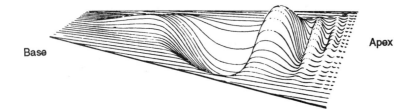

Figure 10.26
A perspective view showing the traveling wave motion of the basilar membrane. This picture shows what the membrane looks like when the vibration is "frozen" with the wave about 2/3 of the way down the membrane. (From Tonndorf, 1960.)

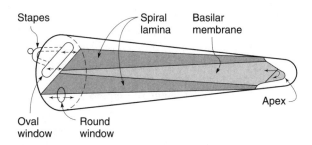

Figure 10.27

A perspective view of an uncoiled cochlea, showing how the basilar membrane gets wider at the apex end of the cochlea. The spiral lamina is a supporting structure that makes up for the basilar membrane's difference in width at the stapes and the apex ends of the cochlea. (From Schubert, 1980.)

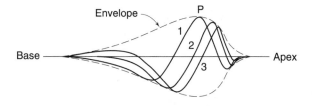

Figure 10.28

Vibration of the basilar membrane, showing the position of the membrane at three instants in time, indicated by the solid lines, and the envelope of the vibration, indicated by the dashed lines. P indicates the peak of the basilar membrane vibration. Hair cells located at this position on the membrane are maximally stimulated by the membrane's vibration. (Adapted from Békésy, 1960.)

lope of the traveling wave of the basilar membrane has two important properties:

1. The envelope is peaked at one point on the basilar membrane. The envelope of Figure 10.28 indicates that point P on the basilar membrane is displaced the most by the traveling wave. Thus, the hair cells near point P will send out stronger signals than those near other parts of the membrane.

2. The position of this peak on the basilar membrane is a function of the frequency of the sound. We can

see in Figure 10.29, which shows the envelopes of vibration for stimuli ranging from 25 to 1,600 Hz, that low frequencies cause maximum vibration near the apex. High frequencies cause less of the membrane to vibrate, and the maximum vibration is near the base. (One way to remember this relationship is to imagine low-frequency waves as being long waves that reach farther.)

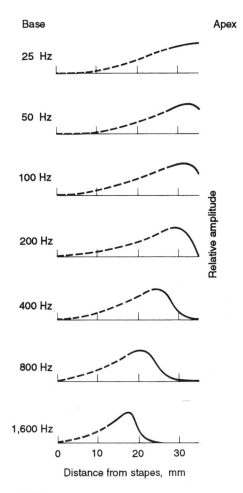

Figure 10.29

The envelope of the basilar membrane's vibration at frequencies ranging from 25 to 1,600 Hz, as measured by Békésy (1960). Note that these envelopes were based on measurements of damaged cochleas. The envelopes are more sharply peaked in healthy cochleas.

These observations of how the vibration of the basilar membrane depends on frequency have been repeated by other researchers using healthier cochleas and techniques more sensitive than the ones available to Békésy. These observations confirmed that the place of maximum basilar membrane vibration depends on frequency and showed that the peak vibration for a particular frequency is even more sharply localized than Békésy had observed (Johnstone & Boyle, 1967; Khanna & Leonard, 1982; Narayan et al., 1998). We will now consider additional physiological evidence for place coding.

Physiological Evidence for Place Coding

Békésy's linking of the place on the cochlea with the frequency of the tone has also been confirmed by measuring the electrical response of the cochlea and of individual hair cells and auditory nerve fibers.

Tonotopic Maps on the Cochlea   Early electrophysiological evidence for place coding was provided by placing disc electrodes at different places along the length of the cochlea and measuring the electrical response to different frequencies. The result is a **tonotopic map**—an orderly map of frequencies along the length of the cochlea (Culler et al., 1943). This result, shown in Figure 10.30, confirms the idea that the apex of the cochlea responds best to low frequencies and the base responds best to high frequencies.

Hair Cell and Auditory Nerve Fiber Tuning   More precise electrophysiological evidence for place coding is provided by microelectrode recording from individual hair cells and auditory nerve fibers. Measuring the level in dB SPL necessary to elicit a small response at each frequency yields a **frequency tuning curve** like the one in Figure 10.31, which is from a single hair cell in the guinea pig's cochlea that is

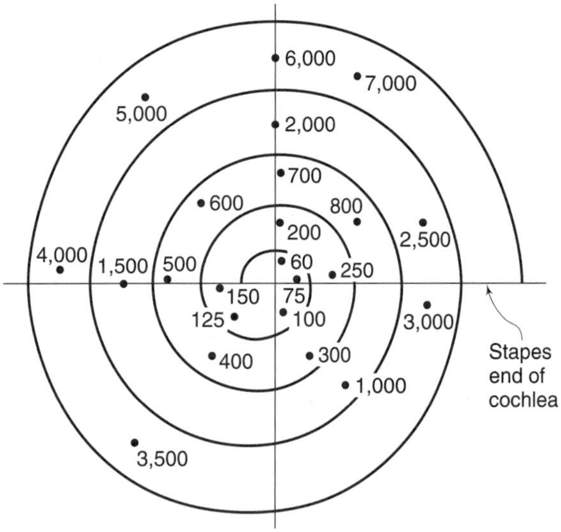

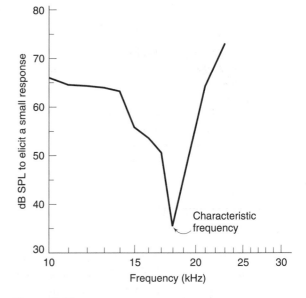

Figure 10.30

Tonotopic map of the cochlea. Numbers indicate the location of the maximum electrical response for each frequency. Low frequencies cause the largest response near the apex end of the spiral, and high frequencies cause the largest response at the base, at the stapes end of the cochlea. (From Culler et al., 1943.)

Figure 10.31

The tuning curve of a single inner hair cell in the guinea pig cochlea. This hair cell is most sensitive at 18,000 Hz and responds well only to a narrow range of frequencies above and below this frequency. (Data from Russell & Sellick, 1977.)

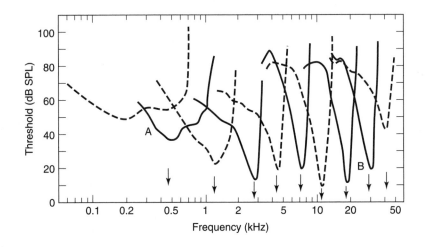

Figure 10.32
Frequency tuning curves of cat auditory nerve fibers. The characteristic frequency of each fiber is indicated by the arrows along the frequency axis. (From Palmer, 1987.)

located near the base of the cochlea and is most sensitive at about 18,000 Hz (Russell & Sellick, 1977). The frequency to which the hair cell is most sensitive is called the **characteristic frequency** of the cell. Figure 10.32 shows that the tuning curves for auditory nerve fibers are similar to hair-cell tuning curves.

It is clear from the physiological evidence that specific frequencies are signaled by basilar membrane vibration at specific places along the cochlea, and this determines which nerve fibers along the cochlea will fire. The idea that frequencies are represented by the firing of fibers located at specific places along the cochlea has been confirmed by the results of psychophysical experiments.

Psychophysical Masking and Place Coding

One confirmation of place theory has been provided by the results of experiments using a psychophysical technique called **auditory masking**. The basic principle behind masking is that one tone, if intense enough, can mask or decrease our perception of another tone that is occurring at the same time.

The procedure for a masking experiment is shown in Figure 10.33. First, the threshold for hearing is determined across a range of frequencies, by determining the lowest intensity at each frequency that can just be heard (Figure 10.33a). Then, a masking stimulus is presented at a particular place along the frequency scale, and, while the masking stimulus

is sounding, the thresholds for all frequencies are redetermined (Figure 10.33b).

We will describe an experiment by J. P. Egan and H. W. Hake (1950) in which they used a masking noise that contained frequencies ranging from 365 to 455 Hz. When Egan and Hake measured the thresholds in the presence of this masking noise, they observed the result shown in Figure 10.34, which indicates how the masking noise increased the original threshold at each frequency. Notice that frequencies near the masking frequencies are affected the most. Also, notice that this curve is not symmetrical.

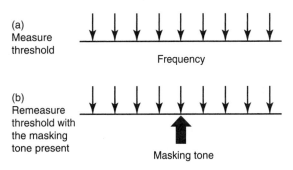

Figure 10.33
The procedure for a masking experiment. (a) Threshold is determined across a range of frequencies. Each arrow indicates a frequency where the threshold is measured. (b) The threshold is redetermined at each frequency (small arrows) in the presence of a masking stimulus (large arrow).

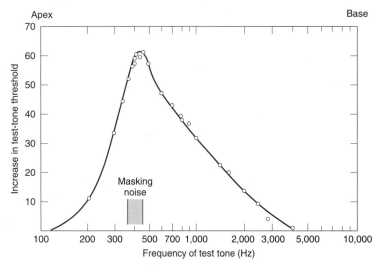

Figure 10.34

Results of Egan and Hake's (1950) masking experiment. The threshold increases the most near the frequencies of the masking noise, and the masking effect spreads more to high frequencies. (Listen to WebTutor, Masking High and Low Frequencies.)

That is, the masking effect spreads more to high frequencies than to low frequencies.

We can relate this asymmetrical effect of the masking tone to the vibration of the basilar membrane, by looking at Figure 10.35, which reproduces the vibration patterns caused by 200- and 800-Hz test tones and a 400-Hz masking tone. We can see how a 400-Hz masking tone would affect the 200- and 800-Hz tones by noting how their vibration patterns overlap. Notice that the pattern for the 400-Hz tone, which is shaded, almost totally overlaps the pattern for the higher-frequency 800-Hz tone, but that it does not overlap the peak vibration of the lower-frequency

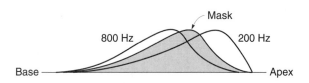

Figure 10.35

Vibration patterns caused by 200- and 800-Hz test tones and the 400-Hz mask, taken from basilar membrane vibration patterns in Figure 10.29. The pattern for a 400-Hz tone is used for the masking pattern (shaded). Since the mask actually contains a band of frequencies, the actual pattern would be wider than is shown here. It would, however, still be asymmetrical and would overlap the 800-Hz vibration more than the 200-Hz vibration.

200-Hz tone. We would therefore expect the masking tone to have a large effect on the 800-Hz tone but a smaller effect on the 200-Hz tone, and this is exactly what happens. Compare the heights of the curve in Figure 10.34 at 200 and 800 Hz. Thus, Békésy's description of the way the basilar membrane vibrates predicts the masking function in Figure 10.34.

The Basilar Membrane as a Frequency Analyzer

We've seen that there is a great deal of evidence to support the idea that a particular frequency causes maximum activity at a specific place along the basilar membrane. Auditory researchers have carried this idea of frequency being represented along the basilar membrane a step farther by proposing that the cochlea operates as if it consists of a bank of filters, each of which processes a limited band of frequencies.

One way to visualize this bank of filters is to look back at the neural tuning curves in Figure 10.32. Each of these curves represents the band of frequencies that causes auditory nerve fibers located at different places along the basilar membrane to fire. For example, Curve A is for a fiber near the apex of the basilar membrane of a cat that responds to frequencies between about 300 and 900 Hz. Curve B is for a fiber near the base of the basilar membrane that responds to frequencies between about 20,000 and 30,000 Hz.

These curves, therefore, represent the shapes of the auditory filters as measured by the responses of auditory nerve fibers. We can also measure the shapes of the filters perceptually by determining a function called the **psychophysical tuning curve**.

The Psychophysical Tuning Curve The procedure for measuring the psychophysical tuning curve is diagrammed in Figure 10.36. First, a low-level 2,000-Hz test tone is presented. Since this test tone has a low level, usually around 10 dB, it causes activity on only a small place on the basilar membrane. To determine which other frequencies also cause activity at this location, we present masking tones with frequencies below, at, and above 2,000 Hz and determine the level of each of these masking tones that eliminates perception of the test tone. The assumption behind this procedure is that if the masking tone eliminates perception of the test tone, it must be causing activity at the location on the basilar membrane that is activated by the test tone.

When we measure the levels of the masking tones needed to eliminate perception of the test tone, we get the psychophysical tuning curve shown in Figure 10.37. This curve shows that the 2,000-Hz test tone is affected by only a narrow band of frequencies above and below 2,000 Hz. This curve provides a picture of the relatively narrow band of frequencies that causes activity at the place stimulated by the 2,000-Hz tone. Repeating this procedure for test tones

across the range of hearing yields a series of tuning curves, as shown in Figure 10.38, along with the audibility curve.

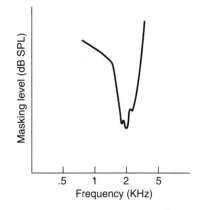

Figure 10.37

Psychophysical tuning curve. This is a plot of the sound levels of masking tone that are needed to mask a 2,000-Hz tone vs. the frequency of the masking tone. The narrow width of the curve indicates that only masking tones with frequencies near 2,000 Hz are capable of masking the 2,000-Hz test tone. This curve indicates the band of frequencies that activate the place on the basilar membrane that is activated by the test tone. (Data from Vogten, 1974.)

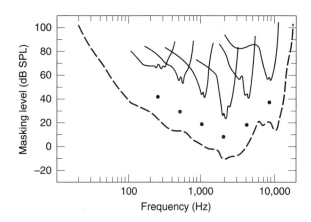

Figure 10.38

Psychophysical tuning curves for a number of test-tone frequencies (dots). Notice how the minimum masking intensities for the curves match the shape of the audibility curve (dashed line). (Based on Vogten, 1974.)

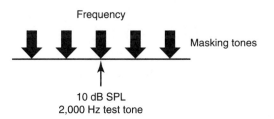

Figure 10.36

The procedure for measuring a psychophysical tuning curve. A 10-dB SPL test tone (small arrow) is presented, and then a series of masking tones (wider arrows) is presented at each frequency. The psychophysical tuning curve is the sound pressures of the masking tones needed to reduce the perception of the test tone to threshold.

Notice that these psychophysical tuning curves, which were determined by measuring *perception*, look very much like the neural curves in Figure 10.32, which were determined by measuring *firing of auditory nerve fibers*. The fact that the neural curves are very similar to the perceptual curves suggests that our perception of frequencies is based largely on information in the firing of these auditory nerve fibers (Moore, 2001).

In addition to suggesting that our perception of frequencies is determined largely from information that is present in auditory nerve fibers, these neural and psychophysical tuning curves also tell us something very important about how the basilar membrane responds to complex tones.

Basilar Membrane's Response to Complex Tones
How does the basilar membrane respond to complex tones like the one in Figure 10.7d? We know that complex tones consist of a number of frequencies and that this particular tone consists of three frequency components, one at 440 Hz, one at 880 Hz, and one at 1,320 Hz (Figure 10.8). Since we know that different places along the basilar membrane respond to narrow bands of frequencies, it seems reasonable to suggest that each of the components of a complex tone might activate a different area of the membrane. Stating this in terms of the idea of filters, we can suggest that each component of a complex tone activates the filter that is tuned to respond to the frequencies of that component.

Research that has measured how the basilar membrane responds to complex tones confirms these ideas. Thus, a complex tone, like the one in Figure 10.7d, will cause the most neural activity in auditory nerve fibers with characteristic frequencies of 440, 880, and 1,320 Hz, as shown in Figure 10.39 (Hudspeth, 1989). We have seen that a complex tone can be separated into its individual frequencies by the technique of Fourier analysis (Figure 10.7). We now see that by responding to the individual components of a complex tone, the basilar membrane is performing its own

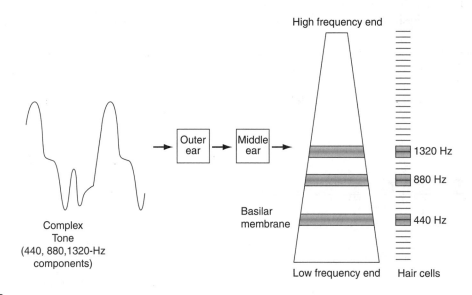

Figure 10.39
The cochlea is called a frequency analyzer because it analyzes incoming sound into its frequency components and translates the components into separated areas of excitation along its length. In this example, the complex tone from Figure 10.7, which consists of frequency components at 440, 880, and 1,320 Hz, enters the outer ear. The shaded areas on the basilar membrane represent places of peak vibration for the tone's three components, and the darkened hair cells represent the hair cells that will be most active in response to this tone.

Fourier analysis on the tone. We can, therefore, think of the cochlea as a frequency analyzer that breaks a complex tone into its harmonics and responds to each harmonic.

Why Are the Tuning Curves So Narrow?

As researchers were measuring the neural tuning curves of Figure 10.32 they were faced with a puzzle: The vibration pattern of the basilar membrane measured in live animals matched these narrow tuning curves, but the vibration patterns of the basilar membrane measured in deceased animals or isolated cochleas were much wider than these tuning curves. Something was causing the narrow pattern of vibration in the live animals, but what was it?

The answer to this question appears to be that in the live animals the outer hair cells respond to sound by moving, and this movement affects the vibration of the basilar membrane. This movement, which is called the **motile response**, is a slight tilting and a change of length. An important property of this motile response is that it is tuned to frequency. Thus, high-frequency sounds cause motile responses in the outer hair cells near the base of the basilar membrane, and low-frequency sounds cause motile responses in outer cells near the apex of the basilar membrane (Brownell et al., 1985; Dallos, 1996; Patuzzi, 1996; Zenner, 1986). Apparently, the motile response causes the outer hair cells to push on the basilar membrane, as shown in Figure 10.40, and this pushing amplifies the motion of the basilar membrane and sharpens its response to specific frequencies.

The idea that outer hair cell movement amplifies the basilar membrane's vibration is supported by the finding that destroying the outer hair cells decreases the response of the inner hair cells (Dallos, 1996; Ryan & Dallos, 1975). Thus, the outer hair cells and the basilar membrane work together to create maximum vibration at a specific place along the cochlea for each frequency, and this vibration is translated into firing of the inner hair cells. Figure 10.41 summarizes the way the inner and outer hair cells and basilar membrane work together to accomplish this.

Another Way to Signal Frequency: The Timing of Nerve Firing

We've seen that the frequency of a sound stimulus is represented by the firing of hair cells that are located at specific places along the basilar membrane. But the frequency of the sound stimulus can also be represented by the timing of neural firing. When we look at how an auditory nerve fiber fires to a particular frequency, we see that the fibers fire in bursts and that the timing of these bursts corresponds to the frequency of the sound stimulus. The way this works is illustrated in Figure 10.42, which shows the pressure changes of a pure tone stimulus and the firing of three auditory nerve fibers.

We can see that each of the fibers fire at or near the peak of the sine-wave stimulus. This property of firing at or near the peak of the stimulus is called **phase locking**, and when large groups of fibers are phase-locked to a stimulus, they create a firing pattern like the one shown in Figure 10.43. The group of fibers fires in bursts separated by silent intervals, with the timing of these bursts depending on the frequency of the stimulus. Thus, the rate of bursting of a

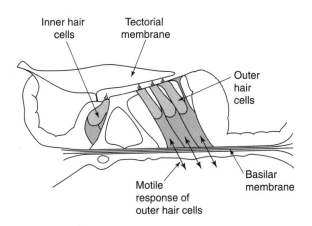

Figure 10.40

A cross section of the organ of Corti, showing the outer hair cells on the right. The arrows at the base of the outer hair cells indicate how movement of the hair cells (the motile response) exerts pressure on the basilar membrane. Since the motile response is tuned to frequency, this pushing on the basilar membrane sharpens the basilar membrane's response to specific frequencies.

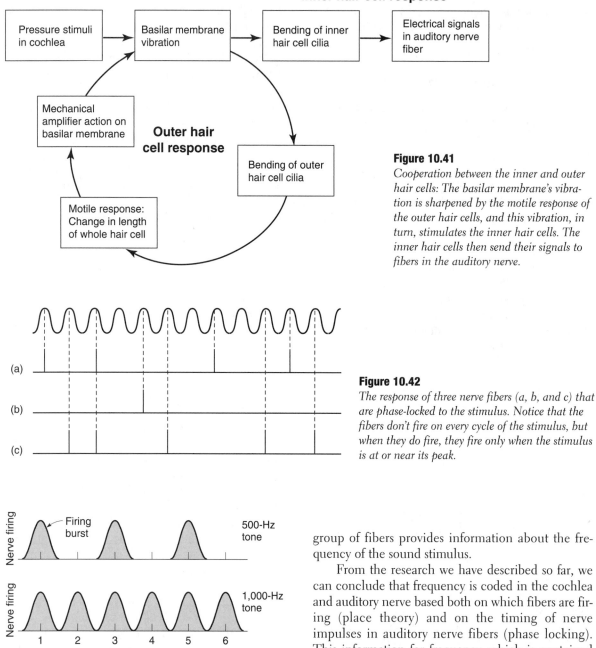

Inner hair cell response

Pressure stimuli in cochlea → Basilar membrane vibration → Bending of inner hair cell cilia → Electrical signals in auditory nerve fiber

Mechanical amplifier action on basilar membrane

Outer hair cell response

Bending of outer hair cell cilia

Motile response: Change in length of whole hair cell

Figure 10.41
Cooperation between the inner and outer hair cells: The basilar membrane's vibration is sharpened by the motile response of the outer hair cells, and this vibration, in turn, stimulates the inner hair cells. The inner hair cells then send their signals to fibers in the auditory nerve.

(a)

(b)

(c)

Figure 10.42
The response of three nerve fibers (a, b, and c) that are phase-locked to the stimulus. Notice that the fibers don't fire on every cycle of the stimulus, but when they do fire, they fire only when the stimulus is at or near its peak.

Firing burst

500-Hz tone

Nerve firing

1,000-Hz tone

Time (1/1,000 s)

Figure 10.43
Phase locking causes large numbers of nerve fibers to fire in bursts with higher frequencies causing faster bursting.

group of fibers provides information about the frequency of the sound stimulus.

From the research we have described so far, we can conclude that frequency is coded in the cochlea and auditory nerve based both on which fibers are firing (place theory) and on the timing of nerve impulses in auditory nerve fibers (phase locking). This information for frequency, which is contained in the auditory nerve fibers, is then transmitted through the series of structures in Figure 10.24 and eventually arrives at the cortex, which is responsible for our perception of the sound.

Auditory System

The auditory system consists of the outer ear, middle ear, and inner ear. The function of the outer and middle ear is to amplify and transmit the sound stimulus to the inner ear. The inner ear contains the organ of Corti, basilar membrane, and hair cells. Pressure changes transmitted to the inner ear bend the hair cells, and this generates electrical signals in the auditory nerve that then begin their journey through the superior olivary nucleus, inferior colliculus, and medial geniculate nucleus in the thalamus to reach the auditory cortex.

Frequency Analysis

The auditory system carries out a frequency analysis of the stimulus by creating maximum vibration of the basilar membrane and therefore maximum hair cell firing at a specific place along the membrane for specific frequencies. Békésy's traveling wave theory describes how the vibration of the basilar membrane depends on frequency.

Physiological Evidence for Place Coding

Tonotopic maps of the cochlea and the narrow tuning curves of hair cells and auditory nerve fibers support Békésy's place coding of frequency.

Psychophysical Masking and Place Coding

Measuring the effect of masking tones on hearing has produced masking functions that are what we would expect based on the place coding of frequency.

The Basilar Membrane as a Frequency Analyzer

The cochlea operates as if it contains a bank of filters, each of which processes a narrow band of frequencies. Neural tuning curves and psychophysical tuning curves indicate the shapes of these filters. The cochlea separates complex sounds into their frequency components, so different components activate different places on the basilar membrane.

Outer Hair Cells Sharpen Basilar Membrane Response

The outer hair cells are the most numerous hair cells but do not send a large electrical response to the auditory nerve. The function of the outer hair cells appears to be to sharpen basilar membrane vibration through a motile response, which pushes and pulls on the basilar membrane.

Timing of Firing

Frequency can also be signaled by the timing of nerve firing, through a mechanism called phase locking.

FREQUENCY ANALYSIS IN THE CORTEX

In Figure 10.24 we followed the auditory signal from the cochlea to the **primary auditory receiving area** in the temporal lobe of the cortex, which is also called A1. After the signals arrive at A1, they travel to a number of other areas in the cortex. This is similar to what happens in the visual system, in which signals arrive at the striate cortex, or V1, in the occipital lobe and then travel to a number of different areas in the extrastriate cortex.

The exact pathways that signals travel from area A1 are still being mapped. Recent research on the monkey describes cortical processing as starting with a **core area**, which includes the primary auditory cortex (A1) and some nearby areas. Signals then travel to an area surrounding the core, called the **secondary auditory cortex**, and then to the **auditory association cortex** (Kaas, Hackett, & Tramo, 1999; Rauschecker, 1997, 1998) (Figure 10.44). For our discussion we will distinguish between the **primary auditory cortex** (core area) and **nonprimary auditory cortex** (secondary and association areas).

Processing Simple Tones

Just as pure tones are arranged in a tonotopic map in the cochlea, with low-frequency tones stimulating the apex of the cochlea and high-frequency tones stimulating the base, the responses to pure tones are also

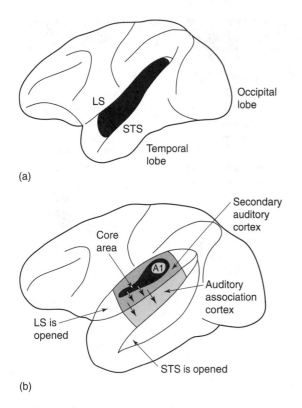

(a)

(b)

Figure 10.44

(a) Monkey brain showing location of the auditory cortex in the temporal lobe, between the lateral sulcus (LS) and the superior temporal sulcus (STS). (b) The lateral sulcus and superior temporal sulcus are opened up to expose the part of the auditory cortex that is not visible from the surface. The three divisions of the auditory cortex are now visible. These divisions are the core area, which contains the primary auditory receiving area A1; the secondary auditory cortex; and the auditory association cortex. Signals are received in the core area and transmitted to the secondary area and then to the association area, as indicated by the arrows. Signals from the secondary and association areas are transmitted to other areas in the temporal and frontal lobes. (Adapted from Kaas, Hackett, & Tramo, 1999.)

In addition to the surface map shown in Figure 10.45, there is also a **columnar arrangement** similar to that observed in the visual system. Neurons recorded along an electrode track that is perpendicular to the surface of the cortex all have the same characteristic frequency (Abeles & Goldstein, 1970). This type of tonotopic map has been found in neurons all along the pathway from the cochlea to the cortex.

Although the tonotopic map persists from the cochlea all the way to the cortex, much of the timing information provided by the phase locking of auditory nerve fibers is lost by the time the signal reaches the cortex. While auditory nerve fibers phase-lock to frequencies up to about 5,000 Hz, neurons in the cortex phase-lock only up to about 500 Hz (Ribaupierre, 1997). Timing information, therefore, plays only a minor role in coding frequency at the cortex, but does provide information about frequency to nuclei earlier in the auditory pathways.

Processing Complex Sound Stimuli

We end the chapter by again considering complex tones. We have seen that the cochlea separates complex musical tones into their harmonics. We will now consider the results of some psychophysical observations that suggest that the cortex probably analyzes these harmonics in order to create our perception of the tone.

Musical Tones: Periodicity Pitch Remember that the pitch of a musical tone is associated with the tone's fundamental frequency. Thus, the tone in Figure 10.46a with a 400-Hz fundamental frequency sounds lower than the tone in Figure 10.46b with an 800-Hz fundamental frequency. From this correspondence between fundamental frequency and pitch, we might conclude that our perception of pitch is determined by the tone's fundamental frequency. This is not the case, however, because when we eliminate the 400-Hz tone's fundamental frequency and leave the 800-, 1,200-, and 1,600-Hz harmonics, as in Figure 10.46c, the tone's timbre changes slightly but its pitch remains the same. The fact that pitch does not change when we remove

arranged in a tonotopic map on the primary auditory cortex, as shown in Figure 10.45. This tonotopic map shows that neurons that respond best to low frequencies are located to the left, and neurons that respond best to higher frequencies are located to the right (Reale & Imig, 1980; Schreiner & Mendelson, 1990).

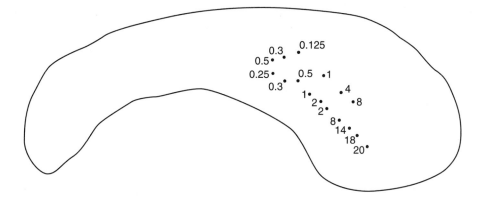

Figure 10.45
The outline of the core area of the monkey auditory cortex, showing the tonotopic map on the primary auditory receiving area, A1, which is located within the core. The numbers represent the characteristic frequencies (CF) of neurons in thousands of Hz. Notice that CFs range from 250 Hz on the left to 20,000 Hz on the right. (Adapted from Kosaki et al., 1997.)

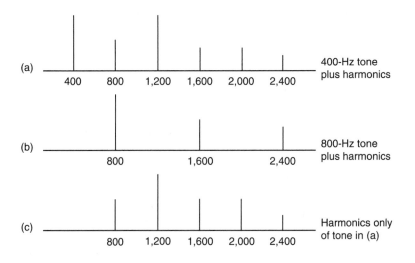

Figure 10.46
Fourier spectra of (a) a 400-Hz tone plus its harmonics, (b) an 800-Hz tone plus its harmonics, and (c) the 400-Hz tone in (a) without its 400-Hz fundamental. (Listen to WebTutor, Periodicity Pitch.)

the fundamental is called the **effect of the missing fundamental**. The pitch that we perceive when we remove the fundamental frequency or some of the harmonics is called **periodicity pitch**.

The phenomenon of periodicity pitch means that the perception of the pitch of complex tones can't be explained by considering only the position of the peak in the vibration pattern caused by the fundamental component of the tone. We say this

because the sound stimuli in Figures 10.46a and 10.46c both have the same pitch, even though they cause different patterns of vibration on the basilar membrane. This means that our perception of pitch must be determined not just by the activity in the cochlea but by the way the brain analyzes the information that originates in the cochlea.

One piece of evidence that pitch perception is determined by processing past the cochlea is the

Sound, Auditory System, Pitch Perception

finding that periodicity pitch is perceived even if two tones are presented to different ears. For example, presenting a 400-Hz tone to the left ear and a 500-Hz tone to the right ear would result in a perception of pitch that corresponds to 100 Hz (see Houtsma & Goldstein, 1972). (Remember that harmonics are always multiples of the fundamental frequency. This means that the difference between two adjacent harmonics corresponds to the fundamental frequency, so in this example, the fundamental frequency associated with these two tones would be 100 Hz.)

The fact that periodicity pitch is perceived when the tones are presented to separate ears means that pitch perception must be determined somewhere in the auditory system where signals from both ears are combined. The first place this occurs is the superior olivary nucleus (see Figure 10.24).

Further evidence that pitch is determined centrally is the finding that patients with damage to a specific area of the auditory cortex in the right hemisphere are not able to hear periodicity pitch (Zatorre, 1988). These results and others have led to the proposal that our perception of the pitch of complex tones is the result of a **central pitch processor**— a central mechanism that analyzes the pattern of harmonics and selects the fundamental frequency that is most likely to have been part of that pattern (see Evans, 1978; Getty & Howard, 1981; Goldstein, 1978; Meddis & Hewitt, 1991; Srulovicz & Goldstein, 1983; and Wightman, 1973, for details of various central processor models).

The phenomenon of periodicity pitch not only gives us some insight into how the auditory system operates but also has a number of practical consequences. Consider, for example, what happens as you listen to music on a cheap radio that can't reproduce frequencies below 300 Hz. If you are listening to music that contains a tone with a fundamental frequency of 100 Hz, your radio can't reproduce the fundamental frequency of the 100-Hz tone or of the 200-Hz second harmonic of that tone. Even though the radio reproduces only the third (300-Hz) and higher (400, 500, 600, and so on) harmonics of this tone, periodicity pitch comes to the rescue and causes you to perceive a pitch equivalent to that produced by a 100-Hz tone. Similarly, even though the telephone

doesn't reproduce the fundamental frequency of the human voice, we are usually able to hear the pitches of people's voices on the phone (Truax, 1984).

Periodicity pitch has also been used to overcome the following problem in the construction of pipe organs: An organ designer wants to produce a pitch corresponding to a 55-Hz tone. However, the longest organ pipe he can use is 1.5 m long, a length that produces a pitch with a 110-Hz fundamental frequency. A longer pipe would be needed to produce the 55-Hz tone. The solution: Use the 1.5-m pipe, with its 110-Hz fundamental, and a 1.0-m pipe, which produces a 165-Hz fundamental. Since 110 Hz and 165 Hz are the second and third harmonics of a 55-Hz tone ($55 \times 2 = 110$; $55 \times 3 = 165$), these two pipes, when sounded together, produce a tone with a pitch corresponding to 55 Hz (Dowling & Harwood, 1986).

Environmental Sounds   Among the most important of the sounds in the environment are those used for communication. This includes speech for humans and various "calls" for monkeys and other animals. These stimuli are very complicated, because they involve a large number of frequencies that occur simultaneously and are also strung together in a particular sequence. Although we are far from understanding the neural processing that is involved in analyzing these complex stimuli, it appears that the processing of complex stimuli occurs in the nonprimary areas of the auditory cortex. For example, neurons have been found in nonprimary auditory cortex that respond poorly to pure tone stimuli but respond vigorously to noise stimuli that contain many frequencies (Rauschecker, Tian, & Hauser, 1995) (Figure 10.47). Some neurons in this area respond best to recordings of rhesus monkey calls. This result is particularly interesting because these *monkey call neurons* are found in an area in the monkey's cortex that is analogous to the human area involved in speech. This suggests that perhaps there are neurons in the human auditory system that respond to specific speech sounds.

Although we don't know whether there are neurons in the human auditory cortex that respond to specific speech sounds, we do know that specific areas in the nonprimary auditory cortex are activated

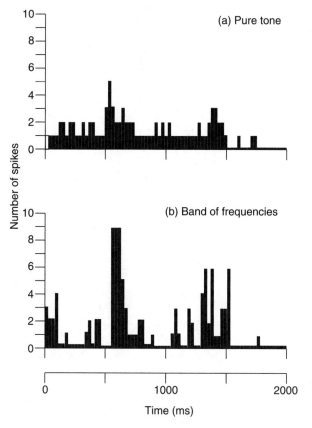

Figure 10.47
Response of a neuron in the monkey cortex that (a) responds poorly to a pure tone but (b) responds well to a noise stimulus that contains many frequencies. (Adapted from Reschecker et al., 1995).

by sequences of tones. Albert Zatorre, Alan Evans, and Ernst Meyer (1994) identified these areas using PET scans to measure brain activity in humans as they listened to simple eight-note melodies played on a synthesizer keyboard. They also found that when people had to decide whether the last tone in the sequence was higher or lower in pitch than the first tone, a number of additional regions were activated.

This task, which involves holding the pitch of the first tone in memory until the last tone is presented, involves higher-level auditory processing. Evidence such as this supports the idea that it is the higher-level processing occuring outside the auditory receiving areas that are responsible for our perception of complex auditory stimuli.

Stimulation Changes the Auditory Cortex

In previous chapters we have seen that there is ample evidence that the types of stimuli to which neurons respond is shaped by the stimuli that the animal experiences. Recent experiments by Rainer Klinke and coworkers (1999) have demonstrated a connection between how much stimulation is received by the cortex and the functioning of the cortex. They used kittens who were deaf because their organ of Corti had degenerated shortly after birth, due to a genetic defect. Because of this degeneration, no nerve impulses reached the auditory cortex in these animals.

The purpose of Klinke's experiments was to see how providing stimulation to the auditory cortex would affect its functioning compared to similar animals whose auditory cortex had received no stimulation. Klinke and coworkers provided this stimulation by implanting a stimulating electrode in the kitten's auditory nerve, which was still intact. This electrode was attached to a microphone that picked up sound stimuli in the environment and caused the electrode to fire and stimulate the auditory nerve.

In the behavioral part of the experiment, Klinke presented a tone to signal the dispensing of food pellets. Within one to three weeks, the kittens responded to the tone by stopping whatever they were doing to get the food pellets. Figure 10.48 shows a video sequence in which a tone was presented while the kitten was eating. Upon hearing the tone, the cat left its food to collect the much more desirable food pellets.

The behavioral experiments showed that the electrode enabled the kittens to hear. But what is particularly significant about this experiment is that, as training progressed, the electrical response of the cat's auditory cortex increased significantly. Not only did long-latency responses develop, indicating high-level processing, but the size of the auditory area expanded, so it became seven times larger than the auditory area of control animals that had been implanted with electrodes that were never activated. The difference between the cortical responding of the experimental and control animals shows that without stimulation, the auditory cortex does not develop, but with stimulation development occurs.

Other experiments, with normal animals, have also shown a connection between cortical stimulation and the response of the cortex. For example, owl monkeys were trained to discriminate between two frequencies near 2,500 Hz. After

(continued)

Figure 10.48
Video sequence showing a cat that has stimulating electrodes implanted in its auditory nerve. It is eating on the left and then responds to a tone, which has activated the stimulating electrode. (From Klinke et al., 1999.)

The Plasticity of Perception (continued)

the training had caused a large improvement in the monkey's ability to tell the difference between frequencies, a tonotopic map of the primary auditory cortex (A1) was determined (Recanzone et al., 1993). The results, shown in Figure 10.49, indicate that, compared to a monkey that had no discrimination training (Figure 10.49a) the trained monkey (Figure 10.49b) had much more

space devoted to neurons that respond best to 2,500 Hz. Thus, the kitten experiments show that stimulation of the auditory cortex causes the size and general responsiveness of the auditory area to increase, and the monkey experiments show that training in a specific task can cause changes in the firing of individual neurons.

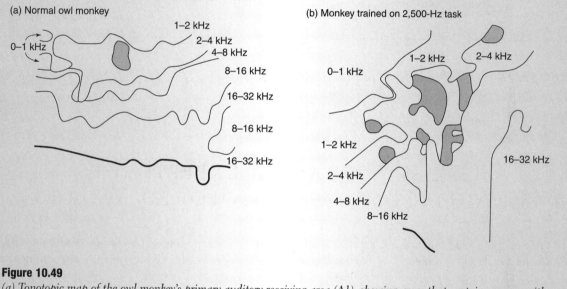

(a) Normal owl monkey

1–2 kHz
2–4 kHz
4–8 kHz
0–1 kHz
8–16 kHz
16–32 kHz
8–16 kHz
16–32 kHz

(b) Monkey trained on 2,500-Hz task

1–2 kHz
2–4 kHz
0–1 kHz
1–2 kHz
16–32 kHz
2–4 kHz
4–8 kHz
8–16 kHz

Figure 10.49
(a) *Tonotopic map of the owl monkey's primary auditory receiving area (A1), showing areas that contain neurons with the characteristic frequencies indicated. The gray area contains neurons with CF = 2,500 Hz. (b) Tonotopic map of an owl monkey that was trained to discriminate between frequencies near 2,500 Hz. The gray areas indicate that there is an expansion of the area that contains neurons with CF = 2,500 Hz.*

Brain imaging has proven to be extremely useful for studying how experience can affect the auditory system. Christo Pantev and coworkers (1998) showed that musical training enlarges the area of auditory cortex that responds to piano tones. They did this by measuring the cortical responses to piano tones of musicians who had been playing their instruments from 12 to 28 years and also measuring the responses in nonmusicians who had never played an instrument. The results indicated that 25 percent more cortex was activated for the musicians compared to the nonmusicians. Other studies have also shown that the cortical area devoted to the fingers of the left hand is enlarged in highly skilled string players, compared to control subjects who did not play string instruments (Elbert et al., 1996).

ACROSS THE SENSES

CROSS-MODALITY EXPERIENCE: BRIGHT TONES AND COLORED WORDS

Presented with a tone pitched at 2,000 cycles per second and having an amplitude of 113 decibels, S said, "It looks something like fireworks tinged with a pink-red hue. The strip of color feels rough and unpleasant and it has an ugly taste—rather like that of a briny pickle." (Luria, 1968, p. 46)

Subject S, whose reaction to a tone is described above, is describing his experience of **synesthesia**—stimulation of one modality that leads to perceptual experience in another. This phenomenon is rare, occurring in less than one percent of people, but has been described in hundreds of published reports since the 18th century (Marks, 1974).

The idea of seeing a colored light in response to a sound stimulus might be viewed as strange and idiosyncratic, but, in surveying many accounts of synesthetic experience, Lawrence Marks (1975) concluded that many of the associations between sound and color are often systematic and constant from one person to another. The strongest associations have been reported between vowel sounds and colors, with the vowel *a* causing sensations of blue and red; *e*, yellow and white; *i*, yellow and white; *o*, yellow, red, and black; and *u*, blue or black.

What is the mechanism responsible for these cross-modality experiences? E. Paulesu and coworkers (1995) approached this question physiologically by measuring brain activity of six women with color-word synesthesia using positron emission tomography (PET). When they presented pure tones to these subjects, they observed activation only in auditory areas, in line with the fact that these subjects did not experience synesthesia to tones. But when words were presented, the subjects experienced visual sensations, and brain activation occurred in the language area and in a number of higher-order visual areas. Based on these results, Paulesu concluded that color-word synesthesias are generated by an interaction between brain areas for language and vision.

If we think about synesthesia in terms of interactions between brain areas, then the phenomenon shares a similarity with many of the perceptions we have described in this book, in which interactions between brain areas are a normal part of the perceptual process. In fact, even people without synesthesia can draw associations between sensations in different modalities. This has been demonstrated using a technique called cross-modality matching in which a subject is presented with a stimulus in one modality and is asked to adjust a stimulus in another modality to match it. When Marks (1974) presented subjects with squares of paper ranging from black to white and asked them to indicate the sound of tone that matched them, he found that the people associated lighter squares with higher pitches (Figure 10.50). Or when subjects were asked to rate the brightness and pitch of color words like "blue" and "red," Marks found that red, white, and yellow are rated brighter and higher in pitch, while black and brown are rated as less bright and lower in pitch (Figure 10.51).

Thus, while people with synesthesia may actually experience colored sounds, people without it can also draw relationships among colors, tones, and brightness. Although the senses are separated in many ways, they also share commonalities of experience.

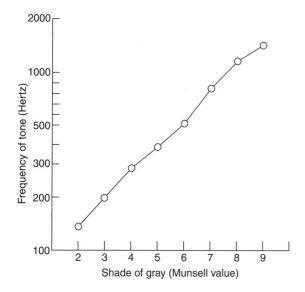

Figure 10.50
Average results for a group of subjects who matched sound frequencies (Hertz) to shades of gray (Munsell value). Higher Munsell values are lighter shades of gray. (From Marks, 1974.)

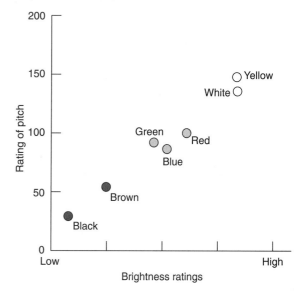

Figure 10.51
Average results for a group of subjects who rated the brightness and pitch of color words. Dark colors such as black and brown were given low pitch and brightness ratings. Light colors such as yellow and white were given high pitch and brightness ratings. (Adapted from Marks, 1974.)

The Auditory Cortex

The auditory cortex consists of a sequence of areas: the core, which contains the primary auditory receiving area (A1); the secondary auditory cortex; and the auditory association cortex. For simplicity, we simply distinguish between the primary auditory cortex (core) and nonprimary auditory cortex (secondary and association).

Frequency Coding in the Auditory Cortex

There is a tonotopic map on the primary auditory cortex, so specific frequencies cause activation of specific places on the cortex. Phase locking information above 500 Hz is lost by the time the auditory signals reach the cortex. The effect of the missing fundamental suggests that the pitch of complex tones is the result of analysis at the level of the cortex.

Plasticity: Stimulation Changes the Cortex

If the cortex of a kitten that has no organ of Corti receives stimulation by presenting shocks to the auditory nerve, the cortical response becomes larger with increased experience. Lack of stimulation results in a poor cortical response. Training monkeys to discriminate between frequencies causes an enlargement of the area of cortex that responds to these frequencies.

Brain Scan: Musicians Have Larger Auditory Areas

The response of the auditory cortex to piano tones is greater in musicians than in nonmusicians.

Across the Senses: Synesthesia

Synesthesia is the situation in which stimulation of one modality (like sound) causes perceptual experience in another modality (like vision). It appears to be caused by excitation of brain areas of the two senses. Cross-modality experience also occurs in people who don't experience synesthesia, so a person might associate the color yellow with a higher pitch than the color green.

STUDY QUESTIONS

The Functions of Hearing

1. Describe the signaling function of hearing. (332)

2. What was Helen Keller's argument in favor of the idea that being deaf was worse than being blind? (333)

3. What are the two answers to the question: If a tree falls in the forest and no one is there to hear it, is there a sound? Explain why each of these answers could be correct by comparing the physical and perceptual definitions of sound. (333)

The Sound Stimulus: Pressure Changes in the Air

4. What is the physical stimulus for the perception of sound? (334)

The Sound Stimulus Produced by a Loudspeaker

5. What generates a sound wave? How do the sound stimuli reach the ear? (334)

6. What is a pure tone? What pure tones are found in the environment? What is amplitude? Frequency? (334)

7. What units are used to measure a tone's frequency? What is the frequency range of human hearing? (335)

Specifying the Amplitude of a Sound Stimulus

8. Describe the decibel scale that is used to specify the amplitude of a tone. How is the zero point of the decibel scale determined? What property of the decibel scale enables it to compress the large range of sound pressures in the environment into a small range of decibels? (335)

9. What do the terms "level" or "sound level" refer to? (336)

10. How does multiplying sound pressure by 10 affect the number of decibels? (336)

11. How does loudness increase when the sound level increases by 10 dB? (336)

Specifying the Frequency of Complex Stimuli

12. How is a complex tone different than a pure tone? (337)

13. What is additive synthesis? How can it be used to create a complex tone from a number of pure tones? (337)

14. What is the fundamental frequency of a tone? What is the first harmonic? Second harmonic? What is the relationship between the various harmonics? (337)

15. What is Fourier analysis? How can it be used to break a complex waveform into its harmonics? (338)

16. What is a Fourier frequency spectrum? (338)

Sound as a Perceptual Response: The Experience of Hearing

The Range of Hearing

17. What is the audibility curve? (339)

18. To which frequencies are humans most sensitive? (339)

19. What is the auditory response area? Know how to determine whether a tone of a particular frequency and sound level will be heard or not. (339)

20. What is the threshold of feeling? (339)

21. At what sound levels can sound cause damage to the auditory system? (339)

22. What animals are sensitive to frequencies below the range of human hearing? above the range of human hearing? (339)

Loudness

23. Define loudness. (339)

24. What is the relationship between sound level and loudness? (341)

25. What do we mean when we say that loudness is based on frequency? (341)

26. Why does saying "the sound level of the pure tone is 40 dB" not really tell us how loud the tone will sound? (341)

27. What is an equal loudness curve? Compare the shapes of equal loudness curves for 40 dB SPL and 80 dB SPL. (341)

28. What happens to your perception of high and low frequencies if you play music on a stereo at a loud level and then turn the intensity down? How does the "loudness" button on a stereo deal with this? (342)

Pitch

29. Define pitch, tone height, and tone chroma. (342)

30. What is the connection between tone chroma and tones separated by an octave? What is the perceptual relationship between tones separated by octaves? (342)

Timbre

31. Define timbre. (343)

Auditory System: Structure and Function

The Outer Ear

32. What are the structures of the outer ear? (344)

33. What is resonance? What effect does it have on the sound stimulus in the outer ear? (344)

The Middle Ear

34. What are the structures of the middle ear? (345)

35. Why are the ossicles necessary? (345)

36. What are two ways that the ossicles increase the strength of the sound stimulus? (345)

37. How does severe damage to the ossicles affect hearing? (347)

38. What is the function of the middle ear muscles? (347)

The Inner Ear

39. What is the main structure of the inner ear? (347)

40. Describe the cochlear partition and the organ of Corti. What are the main structures within the organ of Corti, and what two membranes are closely associated with it? (347)

41. What are the two kinds of hair cells? What structures do they have in common? What causes transduction? (348)

42. What causes the cilia to bend? (348)

43. What happens when the cilia bend first in one direction and then in the other? (348)

44. How much must the hair cells bend in order to generate an electrical signal that results in a sound that is near the threshold for hearing? (350)

45. How does the amplitude of movement of a cilium at threshold compare to the diameter of a hydrogen atom? (350)

The Auditory Pathways

46. Describe the auditory pathway that extends from the auditory nerve to the auditory cortex. (350)

Frequency Analysis in the Cochlea and Auditory Nerve

47. What are two ways that frequency could be represented by the firing of auditory nerve fibers? (351)

Békésy's Place Theory of Hearing

48. What does the place theory state? (351)

49. How did Békésy discover the basilar membrane's traveling wave motion? (352)

50. Describe the traveling wave motion of the basilar membrane that was discovered by Békésy. (352)

51. What is the envelope of the traveling wave, and how does it change as a function of a tone's frequency? (352)

Physiological Evidence for Place Coding

52. Describe the following physiological evidence for place coding: tonotopic maps on the cochlea, the tuning of hair cells, and auditory nerve fibers. (354)

53. What is a frequency tuning curve? (354)

Psychophysical Masking and Place Coding

54. What is auditory masking? Describe Egan and Hake's masking experiment. How can the results of that experiment be related to the vibration of the basilar membrane? (355)

The Basilar Membrane as a Frequency Analyzer

55. What is the procedure for determining a psychophysical tuning curve? What is the assumption behind this procedure? (357)

56. What does a psychophysical tuning curve tell us? What does it tell us about the vibration of the basilar membrane caused by the test tone? (357)

57. Compare the psychophysical tuning curves of Figure 10.38 to the neural tuning curves of Figure 10.32. What does this comparison tell us? (357)

58. How does the basilar membrane respond to a complex tone? (358)

59. What do we mean when we say that (a) the basilar membrane performs a Fourier analysis on a complex tone? (b) The cochlea is a frequency analyzer? (358)

Why Are Tuning Curves So Narrow?

60. What fact about the width of tuning curves puzzled researchers? (359)

61. What is the motile response of the outer hair cells? (359)

62. What do the outer hair cells do to the basilar membrane? (359)

63. What happens to the response of the inner hair cells when the outer hair cells are destroyed? (359)

Another Way to Signal Frequency: The Timing of Nerve Firing

64. What do we mean when we say that the firing of individual nerve fibers is phase-locked to the stimulus? (359)

65. Describe how phase locking of groups of nerve fibers can contain information about the frequency of a tone. (359)

Frequency Analysis in the Cortex

66. What are the three main divisions of the monkey auditory cortex? Which of these divisions contains the primary auditory receiving area (A1)? (361)

67. What is the "primary auditory cortex"? The "nonprimary auditory cortex"? (361)

68. How are signals transmitted from one cortical area to the other? Where do they go from the auditory areas? (361)

Processing Simple Tones

69. Describe the tonotopic map for pure tones in the auditory cortex. (361)

70. Describe the columnar arrangement of the primary auditory cortex. (362)

71. What has happened to timing (phase locking) information by the time signals reach the cortex? (362)

Processing Complex Sound Stimuli

72. What is the effect of the missing fundamental? Periodicity pitch? (362)

73. What is the evidence that periodicity pitch is determined centrally? (363)

74. What is the central pitch processor? What does periodicity pitch suggest about the way the auditory system analyzes the sound stimulus? (364)

75. What are some practical applications of periodicity pitch? (364)

76. Describe the response of neurons in the monkey nonprimary auditory cortex that respond best to complex tones. (364)

77. What have experiments using PET scans told us about the human cortical response to complex tones? (364)

The Plasticity of Perception: Stimulation Changes the Auditory Cortex

78. Describe the experiments in which deaf kittens were stimulated by electrodes implanted in their auditory nerve. (366)

79. How did the brains of the implanted kittens react to the stimulation by the implanted electrodes compared to the control kittens? What does this mean with regard to how stimulation affects the development of the brain? (366)

80. Describe the experiment on the owl monkey that showed that discrimination training can affect the tonotopic map on the cortex. (366)

Brain Scan:
Musicians Have Larger Auditory Areas

81. How does musical training affect the area of cortex that is activated by piano tones? The cortical area devoted to fingers of the left hand in string players? (368)

Across the Senses:
Cross-Modality Experience

82. What is synesthesia? (368)

83. What is the strongest association between sounds and colors? (368)

84. What is the result of PET scan experiments on subjects who experience color-word synesthesia? What does this result tell us about the possible mechanism of synesthesia? (368)

85. What is cross-modality matching? What happens when subjects are asked to match sounds to the shades of paper squares? When they are asked to match the brightness and pitch of color words? (369)

86. What is the significance of the results in 85, above, with regard to synesthesia? (369)

11

AUDITORY LOCALIZATION, SOUND QUALITY, AND THE AUDITORY SCENE

CHAPTER CONTENTS

Auditory Localization:
Locating Single Sounds in Space

BRAIN SCAN:
A Motion Area in the Auditory Cortex

Sound Quality: What a Stimulus Sounds Like

Auditory Scene Analysis: Identifying Sound Sources

ACROSS THE SENSES AND PLASTICITY:
How Vision Can Affect Hearing

SOME QUESTIONS WE WILL CONSIDER

- What makes it possible to tell where a sound is coming from in space? (376)

- Why do saxophones and trumpets sound different, even when they are playing the same note? (391)

- Why does music sound better in some concert halls than in others? (392)

When we studied vision in the early chapters of this book, we saw that visual perception isn't just about seeing light or perceiving an object's color. It's about seeing forms, knowing where they are in space, and being able to separate one object from another in a complex scene. As we study hearing in this chapter, we will see that hearing isn't just about hearing pure tones or musical notes, but it's about identifying sources that create sounds, knowing where the sources are, and

being able to separate different sounds from one another in a sound-filled environment.

In this chapter we first consider auditory localization—how we perceive where single sounds are coming from. We then consider sound quality—what makes a trumpet and an oboe playing the same note sound different and what determines the qualities of other sounds in the environment. And finally, we describe auditory scene perception—how we identify separate sources of sound among many sounds that are occurring at the same time.

AUDITORY LOCALIZATION: LOCATING SINGLE SOUNDS IN SPACE

WebTUTOR   Close your eyes right now and just listen. (Take a moment and try this.) Unless you are in a soundproof room, you heard a number of sounds, and even though you couldn't see the things that were creating these sounds, you could tell approximately where they were coming from. The ability to tell where sounds are coming from is called **auditory localization**. You can measure auditory localization by doing the following demonstration.

DEMONSTRATION

Sound Localization

Have a friend close her eyes. Say that you are going to rattle your keys at various places around her head and that she should point to where the sound is coming from. Do this at locations to the left and right, up and down, and in front and in back of her head. Note how accurate she is for sounds in various locations. After you are through, ask your friend if she found some locations harder to judge than others.   ●

There is substantial variability between different subjects' ability to localize sounds (so you might want to try this on a few people), but when measurements from a number of people are averaged, results like those in Figure 11.1 are obtained. This figure indicates, on an imaginary sphere that surrounds a listener's head, how well listeners can localize sounds that are in different positions in space (Makous & Middlebrooks, 1990; Middlebrooks & Green, 1991). Listeners can localize sounds that are directly in front of them most accurately (localization errors average 2 to 3.5 degrees) and sounds that are off to the side and behind their head least accurately (localization errors are as high as 20 degrees).

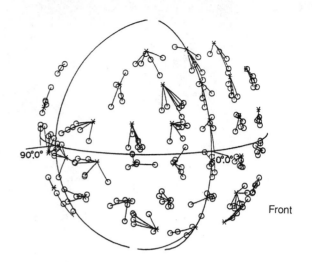

Figure 11.1
Subjects' ability to localize sounds. The asterisks are the actual sound locations, and the circles are the subject's estimates of their location. Longer lines connecting the asterisks and circles indicate less accurate localization. (From Makous & Middlebrooks, 1990.)

Auditory location is commonly described using the following three coordinate systems (Figure 11.2):

1. The **azimuth** (or horizontal) **coordinate** specifies locations that vary from left to right relative to the listener.

2. The **elevation** (or vertical) **coordinate** specifies locations that are up and down relative to the listener.

3. The **distance coordinate** specifies how far the sound source is from the listener.

The problems the auditory system faces in determining locations are formidable. We can appreciate one of the problems by comparing the information available for vision and for hearing in Figure 11.3. Information for the relative locations of the bird and the cat are contained in the image of the bird and the cat on the surface of the retina. However, no such information exists on the receptors of the ear, because information on the auditory receptors has to do with the frequencies of sounds and not with their locations. The auditory system solves this problem by making use of cues for location created by the way

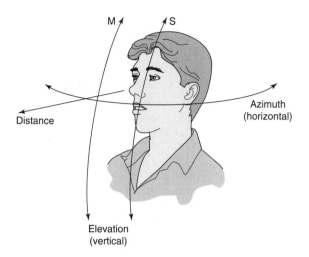

Figure 11.2

Horizontal, vertical, and distance coordinate systems for localization. Two vertical coordinates are shown, one (M) in which the vertical coordinate is positioned on the subject's midline and another vertical coordinate (S) in which vertical position is varied off to the side.

sound interacts with the listener's head and ears. We will describe this information, beginning with how the auditory system determines locations along the azimuth (left–right) coordinate.

Information for Azimuth

The information that the auditory system uses to determine a sound's azimuth is based on **interaural differences**, differences in the stimuli reaching the left and right ears. These interaural differences are called **binaural cues**, since they involve both ears. These cues are analogous to the binocular cues for depth perception, which involve both eyes. The two major interaural cues are *interaural time difference* and *interaural level difference*.

Interaural Time Difference Sounds originating from many locations in space reach one ear before the other. The difference between the times that the sound reaches the left and right ears is called the

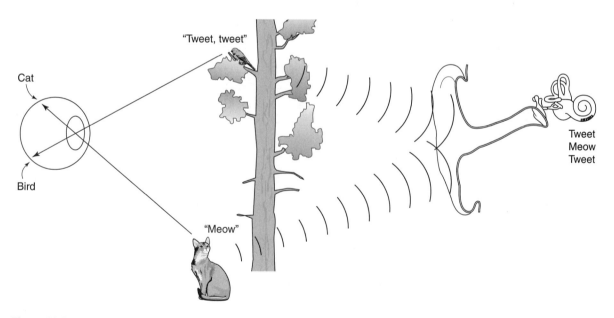

Figure 11.3

Comparing location information for vision and hearing. Vision: The bird and cat are located at different places and are imaged on different places on the retina. Hearing: The frequencies in the sounds from the bird and cat are spread out over the cochlea, with no regard to the locations of the bird and cat.

interaural time difference. The basis for the idea that there is a difference in the time that a sound reaches the left and right ears is illustrated in Figure 11.4. When the source is located directly in front of the listener, at A, the distance to each ear is the same, and the sound reaches the left and right ears simultaneously. However, if a source is located off to the side, at B, the sound reaches the right ear before it reaches the left ear. Since the interaural time difference is larger for sounds that are located more to the side, the magnitude of the interaural time difference can be used as a cue to determine a sound's location.

The way interaural time difference changes with a sound's location has been measured by placing microphones in a person's ears and determining the arrival time of sound stimuli originating from different positions in space. The results of these measurements indicate that the interaural time difference is zero when the source is directly in front of or directly behind the listener. As the source is moved to the side, the delay between the time the sound reaches the near ear and the time it reaches the far ear approaches a maximum of about 600 microseconds ($^6/_{10,000}$ s)

that occurs when the sound is located directly opposite one of the ears, as in B of Figure 11.4 (Feddersen et al., 1957). Although time differences on the order of microseconds are very small, it has been shown psychophysically that we can detect differences in arrival time as short as 10 microseconds (Durlach & Colburn, 1978), and so the delay between the sounds arriving at the two ears can signal the azimuth of a sound source.

Interaural Level Difference The other binaural cue is the **interaural level difference**, the difference in the sound pressure level (or just "level") of the sound reaching the two ears. This interaural level difference occurs because the head creates a barrier that casts an **acoustic shadow** that keeps high-frequency sounds from reaching the far ear (Figure 11.5). We can

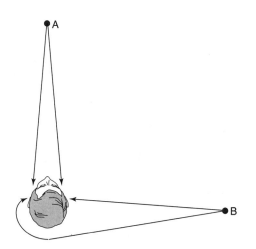

Figure 11.4
The principle behind interaural time difference. The tone directly in front of the listener, at A, reaches the left and the right ears at the same time. However, if the tone is off to the side, at B, it reaches the listener's right ear before it reaches the left ear.

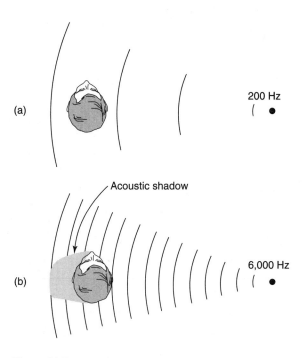

Figure 11.5
The principle behind interaural intensity difference. (a) Low-frequency tones are not affected by the listener's head, so the intensity of the 200-Hz tone is the same at both ears. (b) High-frequency tones are affected by the presence of the listener's head, and the result is an acoustic "shadow" that decreases the intensity of the tone reaching the listener's far ear.

appreciate why only high-frequency sounds are affected by imagining water waves approaching a wooden pole that is protruding from the water (Figure 11.6). Large waves, which have long wavelengths compared to the diameter of the pole, proceed uninterrupted on the other side of the pole (Figure 11.6a). However, small ripples, which have short wavelengths compared to the diameter of the pole, hit the front of the pole and bounce off, so there are fewer small ripples on the other side of the pole (Figure 11.6b). A similar situation occurs for sound waves. Low-frequency (long-wavelength) waves (as in Figure 11.5a) are unaffected by the head, but high-frequency (short-wavelength) waves (as in Figure 11.5b) bounce off of the head, creating the acoustic shadow on the other side of the head.

This effect of frequency on the interaural level difference has been measured by using small microphones to record the intensity of the sound reaching each ear in response to a moveable sound source. The results show that there is little difference in level for frequencies below approximately 1,000 Hz, but that quite sizable differences in level occur for higher frequencies (Figure 11.7).

A Practical Application: Personal Guidance System Based on Binaural Cues Binaural cues for sound localization have been used to design a "Personal Guidance System" to help blind people find their way through the environment (Figure 11.8) (Loomis et al., 1994; Loomis, Hebert, & Cicinelli, 1990). The

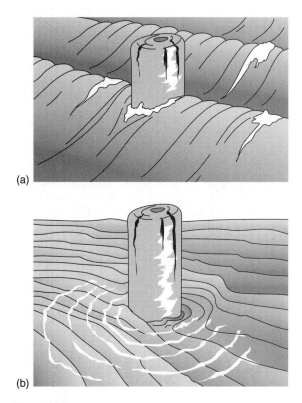

(a)

(b)

Figure 11.6

Top: The low-frequency water waves are hardly affected by the pole, so continue uninterrupted past the pole. Bottom: the high-frequency ripples bounce off of the pole, which changes the motion of the ripples and interrupts the ripples on the other side of the pole. This is similar to the way low- and high-frequency sounds interact with a person's head.

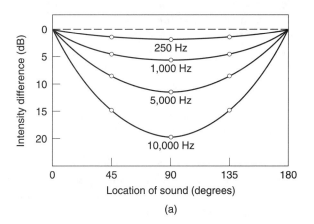

(a)

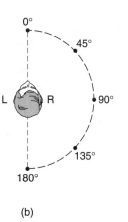

(b)

Figure 11.7

(a) The difference in intensity between the left and right ears for a 70-dB SPL tone of different frequencies located at different places around the head. (From Gulick et al., 1989.) (b) The locations of the tones used for the intensity measurement in the graph in (a). The tones were located 2 m from the center of the head. (From Gulick, Frisina, & Gescheider, 1971.)

Auditory Localization, Quality, Scene

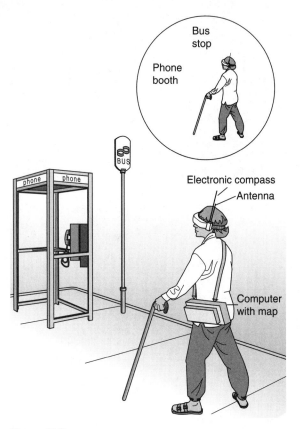

Figure 11.8

A blind person using an electronic navigation system. As the person walks through the environment, her position relative to the objects in the environment is determined by communication with global positioning satellites combined with information provided by the computer, which contains a map of the area within which the person is walking. The circle indicates that the person hears the words bus stop and phone booth, and that these sounds appear to originate from the position in auditory space where these objects are located. The system shown here is a proposed miniaturized version of a larger system that is now being tested. (Adapted from Loomis et al., 1994.)

locations of objects in the scene such as the telephone booth and bus stop.

Based on this information about the locations of objects, the computer generates messages, such as "telephone booth here" or "bus stop 20 feet ahead," which the person hears through earphones. These messages are presented to the earphones so that the level and timing of the sounds reaching the left and right ears corresponds to how the sound would be perceived if the objects themselves were making the sounds. Thus, not only does the person hear "telephone booth here," but the sound appears to come from the location of the telephone booth. The idea behind this is to help the person localize the objects in space (Loomis, Golledge, & Klatzky, 1998). This system has been successfully tested in a prototype that is quite a bit bulkier than the one shown in Figure 11.8.

Any system that is able to signal the positions of objects will work only when an accurate map of the environment can be fed into the computer, so this system can't locate objects, such as cars and people, that are not on the map. Although the availability of actual models of this system is many years away, even the creation of the prototypes that now exist is an impressive demonstration of how basic knowledge about hearing mechanisms can be used for practical applications.

Information for Elevation

Interaural time and level differences provide information about the azimuth of a sound source but are not as well suited for providing information about the elevation of the source, especially when the sounds are located midway between the two ears. We can see why this is so by looking at coordinate M in Figure 11.2. When sounds are located directly in front of a listener, positioning the sound source anywhere along the elevation coordinate results in interaural time or level differences of zero, since the sounds travel the same distance to the left and right ears. Thus, some other information must be involved in judging elevation. The information is provided mainly by **spectral cues** that depend on the way the head and pinnae affect the frequencies in the sound stimulus.

person is fitted with an electronic compass, a computer, and a transmitter and receiver that communicate with global positioning satellites. Signals from these satellites determine the person's location, within 1 meter, relative to a map that has been programmed into the computer. This map indicates the

Spectral Cues Before the sound stimulus enters the auditory canal, it is reflected from the head and back and forth within the various folds of the pinnae. The effect of this interaction with the head and pinnae has been measured by placing small microphones inside a listener's ears and comparing the frequencies picked up by the microphones with the frequencies coming from the sound source. The difference between the sound from the source and the sound actually entering the ears is called the **directional transfer function (DTF)** (Middlebrooks, 1997; Wightman & Kistler, 1993; Yost, 2001). (The DTF is also called the head-related transfer function, or HRTF.)

The DTF provides information for sound localization because the head and pinnae decrease the intensity of some frequencies and enhance others, creating peaks and notches in the distribution of frequencies reaching the ears. Figure 11.9 shows the DTFs for sounds coming from different elevations along the midline. For sound coming from below there are decreases (or notches) in the DTF at around 6,000 Hz, 11,000 Hz and 14,000 Hz; but for sound directly in front, there is a notch at 10,000 Hz and a peak at 13,000 Hz, and, for sound from above, there is a large notch between 8,000 and 10,000 Hz (Middlebrooks, 2000).

The patterns of frequencies that reach the ear from different locations are the spectral cues to localization, and people use this information to localize sounds that are located on the midline elevation coordinate when interaural time and level difference cues are not available. An experiment that demonstrates the role of the pinnae in sound localization was done by Gardner and Gardner (1973), who inserted modeling compound into people's pinnae and measured the people's ability to localize sounds. As the pinnae were made smoother and smoother, the listeners found it more difficult to localize sounds.

You can demonstrate how the pinnae affect localization by placing earphones over your ears that still enable you to hear sounds in the environment. When you do this, pay particular attention to how the earphones affect front–back localization compared to left–right localization. (Front–back should be affected more.) This effect becomes particularly evident when you try to localize sounds with your eyes closed.

Information for Distance

In considering how the auditory system determines how far away a sound is, it is important to distinguish

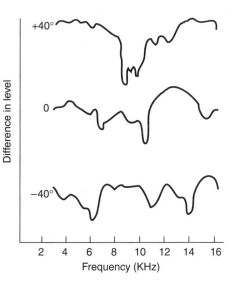

Figure 11.9
Directional transfer functions (DTFs) for sounds located at three elevations along the listener's midline, below the listener (−40 degrees), directly in front (0 degrees), and above the listener (+40 degrees). These functions, which were recorded by a small microphone inside the right ear, indicate how the frequencies of the sound source are affected by interactions of the sound with the head and the pinnae. Notches indicate a decrease in level and peaks an increase. (From Middlebrooks, 1997.)

between judgments of distance for nearby sounds and sounds that are farther away. The distance of sounds that are within arm's length can be estimated quite accurately, because as a sound source comes close to the head the interaural level difference (ILD) becomes very large. For example, the ILD for a 500-Hz tone presented to one side of the head at 90 degrees (see Figure 11.7) is about 4 dB at a distance of a meter and 20 dB at a distance of a few centimeters (Brungart, Durlach, & Rabinowitz, 1999). The distance of sounds that are farther than arm's length is more difficult to determine, with people generally underestimating the distances of faraway sounds (Loomis, Klatzky, & Golledge, 1999; Loomis et al., 1998). There has been very little research on how people make these distance judgments, but a number of cues have been suggested. We will describe four of them.

Sound Level Doubling the distance of a sound source decreases the sound pressure reaching the listener by about 6 dB in an environment such as outside on a grassy field where there are no echoes (Wightman & Jenison, 1995). (The decrease is a little smaller inside a room.) It has, therefore, been suggested that sound pressure provides a cue for distance, with lower pressures indicating greater distance. However, sound level is generally an effective cue for distance only when the sound source is familiar, like the human voice, or for comparing the distance of two identical sources. When Daniel Ashmead and coworkers (1990) presented two identical sound sources at different distances, subjects could judge differences in distance of about 6 percent, based on differences in sound level.

Frequency When we described the visual depth cue of atmospheric perspective, we saw that light is affected by the atmosphere through which it passes on its way from an object to the observer. A similar thing happens to sound, since high frequencies are absorbed by the atmosphere more than low frequencies. This causes sounds that are farther away to sound more dull or muffled than closer sounds.

Movement Parallax This cue parallels the visual depth cue of movement parallax, in which near objects appear to move across the field of view faster than far objects. When we move relative to continuous sounds or when sounds move relative to us, sounds that are nearby will shift their location relative to us faster than sounds that are far away.

Reflection Some sound reaches our ears by being transmitted directly from the sound source to the ear. Other sounds reach our ears after bouncing off surfaces such as walls or the floor or ground. This is illustrated in Figure 11.10, which shows how the nature of the sound reaching your ears depends on the environment in which you hear the sound. If you are sitting outdoors next to someone playing a guitar, some of the sound you hear reaches your ears after being reflected from the ground or objects like trees, but most of the sound travels directly from the sound source to your ears. If, however, you are listening to the same guitar in an enclosed room, then most of the sound bounces off of the room's walls, ceiling, and floor before reaching your ears.

The sound reaching your ears directly, along path a, is called **direct sound**, and the sound reaching your ears later, along paths like b and c, is called **indirect sound**. The amount of sound reflection is one of the cues to distance. At greater distances the amount of reflected sound compared to direct sound increases, and the change in sound quality caused by this higher reflection provides information for distance (Mershon & Bowers, 1979).

Each of these distance cues, plus others we have not mentioned, provides information about a sound's distance. Just as a number of cues for visual depth work together to determine a person's perception of depth, these cues for sound distance also work together to determine a person's perception of a sound's distance.

The Precedence Effect

The fact that sounds reach our ears directly and indirectly also creates a potential problem regarding the perception of the sound's location because a sound that originates from one location in a room reaches the ears directly from that location but also reaches the ears by reflection from other locations.

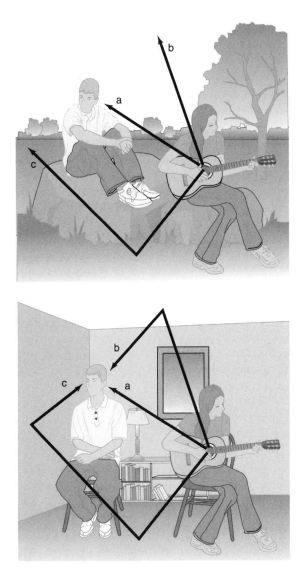

Figure 11.10

Top: When you hear a sound outside, you hear mainly direct sound (path a). Bottom: When you hear a sound inside a room, you hear both direct sound (a) and indirect sound (b and c) that is reflected from the walls, floor, and ceiling of the room.

But even though reflections from surfaces cause our ears to receive a sequence of sounds coming from many directions, we generally perceive the sound as coming from only one location.

Research on the effects of sound reflections on the perception of location has usually simplified the problem by having subjects listen to sounds coming from two speakers separated in space, as shown in Figure 11.11, for an experiment by Ruth Litovsky and coworkers (1997, 1999). The speaker on the right is the *lead speaker*, and the one on the left is the *lag speaker*. When sounds were presented simultaneously in the two speakers, listeners heard one sound centered between the two speakers (Figure 11.11a). This perception of two sounds as one is called **fusion**. When the lead sound was presented first, followed by the lag sound, with a delay of less than 1 millisecond, listeners perceived a single sound located nearer the lead speaker (Figure 11.11b). At delays between about 1 and 5 milliseconds, the sound appeared to be coming from the lead speaker alone (Figure 11.11c). This situation, in which the sound appears to originate from the lead speaker, is called the **precedence effect** because we perceive the sound as coming from the source that reaches our ears first (Wallach, Newman, & Rosenzweig, 1949).

At intervals greater than about 5 milliseconds, Litovsky's listeners began hearing two separate sounds, one after another (Figure 11.11d). The time separation at which the sounds are no longer fused, so two separate sounds are heard, is called the **echo threshold**. The echo threshold is about 5 milliseconds in Litovsky's experiment, in which the stimuli were two identical clicks, but it is longer if the lag sound is at a lower level than the lead sound (as occurs for sound that reaches the ears indirectly after being reflected from surfaces in a room) and also for sounds with long durations, such as speech and music.

The precedence effect governs most of our indoor listening experience. The indirect sounds reflected from the walls have a lower level than the direct sound and reach our ears with delays of about 5 to 10 milliseconds, for small rooms, and with larger delays for larger rooms like concert halls. The operation of the precedence effect means that we generally perceive sound as coming from its source, rather than from many different directions at once. You can demonstrate the precedence effect to yourself by doing the following demonstration.

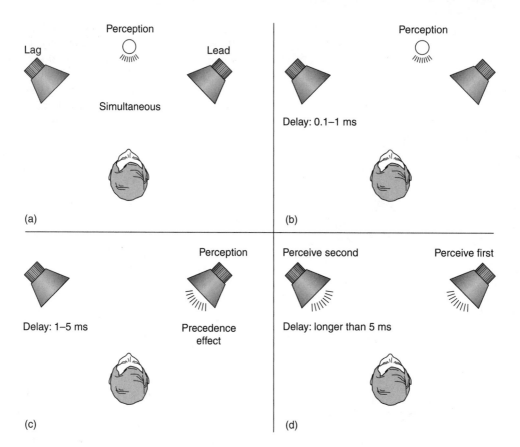

Figure 11.11

Results of an experiment in which sounds are presented by two speakers, one located 45 degrees to the right of a listener (lead speaker), and the other 45 degrees to the left (lag speaker). (a) Sounds from lead and lag speakers presented simultaneously. Perception: Fusion, one sound in between the two speakers. (b) Delay between lead and lag (lead presented first) = 0.1 to 1 ms. Perception: Fusion, one sound nearer lead speaker. (c) Delay = 1 to 5 ms. Perception: Fusion, one sound coming from lead speaker. This is the precedence effect. (d) Delay: longer than 5 ms. Perception: No fusion, first one speaker than the other. (Data from Litovsky et al., 1999.)

 D E M O N S T R A T I O N

Experiencing the Precedence Effect

To demonstrate the precedence effect, turn your stereo system to monaural (or "mixed"), so that both speakers play the same sounds, and position yourself between the speakers, so that you hear the sound coming from a point between both speakers. Then move a small distance to the left or right.

When you do this, does the sound appear to be coming from only the nearer speaker? ●

You perceive the sound as coming from the nearer speaker because the sound from the nearer speaker is reaching your ears first, just as in Figure 11.11c, in which there was a delay between the sounds presented by the two speakers. But even though you hear the sound as coming from the near speaker, this doesn't mean that you aren't hearing the far speaker. The sound from the far speaker changes the quality of the sound, giving it a fuller, more expansive quality (Blauert, 1997; Yost & Guzman, 1996). You can demonstrate this by positioning yourself closer to one speaker and having a friend disconnect the other speaker. When this happens, you will notice a difference in the quality of the sound.

The Physiological Basis for Localization

One thing about the physiological basis of localization is clear: The auditory cortex is extremely important. We will first look at evidence for this and then at research that has investigated how single neurons respond to sound sources that are located at different positions in space.

Role of the Auditory Cortex   The evidence that the auditory cortex is necessary for localization is straightforward: Removal of all or part of the auditory cortex degrades auditory localization. William Jenkins and Michael Merzenich (1984) took advantage of the fact that there is a tonotopic map in the auditory cortex (see Figure 10.45) and placed lesions in parts of a cat's auditory cortex that represented a small band of frequencies. When they tested the cat's ability to localize sounds, they found that its ability to localize was impaired just for the tones with frequencies represented in the band that was lesioned. Other evidence for the importance of the auditory cortex for localization comes from the fact that humans with damage to the auditory cortex due to stroke or injury have difficulty in locating sound position (Klingon & Bontecou, 1966).

Another approach to determining the physiological basis of localization is to work at the level of the single neuron. A number of different types of neurons have been discovered that may signal sound location.

Interaural Time Difference Detectors   Researchers have identified neurons in the monkey's auditory cortex called **interaural time difference detectors** that respond to specific interaural time differences. An example of an interaural time difference detector would be a neuron that responds best when a sound

reaches the left ear first and the right ear 1 millisecond later. Each neuron responds best to a different delay (Brugge & Merzenich, 1973; Litovsky & Lin, 1998). These interaural time difference neurons have been recorded not only from the auditory cortex but also from nuclei as early in the auditory system as the superior olivary nucleus, the first nucleus in the system to receive inputs from both ears (Hall, 1965).

Neurons Tuned to Specific Areas of Space   Although interaural time difference detectors provide information about a sound's location, they don't locate a sound exactly, because a number of different locations can result in the same interaural time difference. Thus, researchers have been searching for neurons that respond to sounds coming from specific locations in space. So far, however, they have found just a few of these neurons (Samson et al., 2000).

The more typical result is shown in Figure 11.12. The darkened area, which is called the **virtual space receptive field,** indicates that this neuron responds when sound is presented over a rather large area (Brugge, Reale, & Hind, 1997).

Panoramic Neurons   Since it has been difficult to find neurons that are sharply tuned to small areas of space, researchers have searched for other ways that

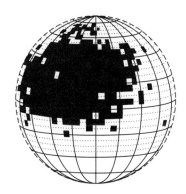

Figure 11.12
Virtual space receptive field of a neuron in the primary auditory cortex. The animal is located inside the sphere. The dark area indicates that the neuron responds when sound is presented within a large area. (From Brugge, 1997.)

Neurons have been discovered in the monkey's auditory cortex that respond to the movement of sound across space (Figure A) (Ahissar et al., 1992). Do humans have such neurons, and is there an area in the human auditory cortex that is specialized to respond to sound movement? Timothy Griffiths and coworkers (1996) studied a patient with damage to the nonprimary auditory cortex in the right hemisphere who had lost his ability to perceive sound movement. Based on this result, they suggested that there is a cortical area in nonprimary auditory cortex that is specialized for the detection of sound motion. Now an fMRI study supports this conclusion. When

Frank Baumgart and coworkers (1997) compared the response of four auditory areas to stationary sound and moving sound, they observed the results shown in Figure B. Although there was little difference between the response to stationary and moving sound in the left hemisphere, or in area A1 in the right hemisphere, there was a large response in an area of nonprimary cortex in the right hemisphere. Therefore, just as there is an area in extrastriate visual cortex that is specialized for perceiving motion, there also appears to be an area in nonprimary auditory cortex that is specialized for perceiving auditory movement.

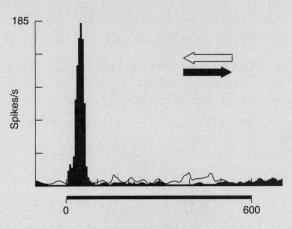

Figure A
Directionally selective neuron. Record from a neuron in the auditory cortex that responds with a large burst of firing to movement of a sound to the right (black record) but doesn't respond to movement of the sound to the left (white record). (From Ahissar et al., 1992.)

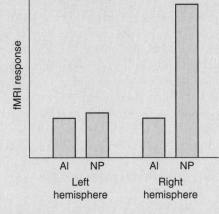

Figure B
How various areas of the human auditory cortex respond to a moving sound, as measured by fMRI. Note that the response at the nonprimary auditory cortex (NP) is small in the left hemisphere but is large in the right hemisphere. The response of the primary auditory cortex (A1) is small in both hemispheres. (From Baumgart et al., 1997.)

Chapter 11

neurons could signal sound location. One possibility is that sound position could be signaled by the timing pattern of the neuron's firing. John Middlebrooks has found neurons in nonprimary auditory cortex of the cat that he calls **panoramic neurons**, which appear to operate in this way (Middlebrooks et al., 1994, 1998).

The way location is signaled by these neurons is illustrated in Figure 11.13, which shows the pattern of firing of one cortical neuron to sounds coming from a number of directions. Notice that the neuron fires to sounds coming from all directions but that the pattern of impulses is different for different directions. That's why this neuron is called a panoramic neuron — it fires to sounds originating from all directions and indicates each location by its pattern of fir-

ing. Since a large number of neurons fire to a particular tone, information from a number of these neurons could help to precisely locate a sound (Barinaga, 1994).

Neurons That Signal Sounds Near the Head   In the "Across the Senses" section at the end of Chapter 4, we described neurons that respond both to touching an area on a monkey's face and to visual stimuli that occur right in front of this area. The same research group that described these neurons has now described neurons in nonprimary auditory cortex that respond to touching the head, to visual stimuli presented near the head, and also to the directions of sounds that are presented within about 30 cm of the head (Figure 11.14) (Graziano, Reiss, & Gross, 1999).

What could be causing neurons to respond just when sounds are near the head? It could be that nearby sounds tend to have high sound levels. But Graziano also found neurons that were unaffected by changes in sound level. Perhaps these neurons use other information, such as reflections or spectral cues

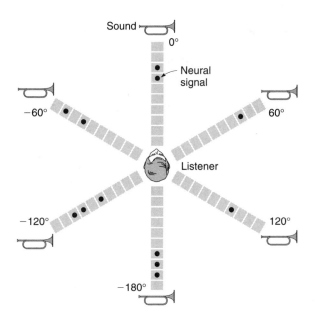

Figure 11.13

Panoramic neuron. How one neuron can indicate the location of a sound based on its pattern of firing. When the sound is directly in front of the listener, at 0 degrees, the nerve fires two impulses in quick succession, as indicated by the dots on the line. However, when the sound is at −60 degrees, there is a slight pause between the two impulses. Other directions cause other patterns of firing. Thus, this neuron has a different timing code for each direction. (Based on data from Middlebrooks et al., 1994.)

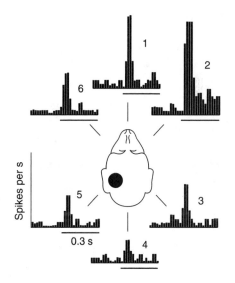

Figure 11.14

Responses of near-head neurons in the nonprimary auditory cortex of the monkey. The neuron responds best at position 2 but fires only if the sound source is within 30 cm of the head. (From Graziano et al., 1999.)

caused by the effects of the head and pinnae on the sound frequencies reaching the ears.

The Barn Owl's Topographic Map of Space We end our discussion of the neural basis of sound location by considering an animal that, unlike the cat or monkey, does have neurons that respond best to sounds coming from small areas of space. Research on the owl has focused on a structure called the mesencephalicus lateralus dorsalis (MLD), which is roughly equivalent to the inferior colliculus of mammals. By presenting stimuli with the apparatus shown in Figure 11.15, Eric Knudsen and Masakazu Konishi (1978a,b) found neurons that respond only when the sound stimulus originated from a small elliptical area in space, the receptive field of the cell. Furthermore, they found that some of these receptive fields have excitatory centers and inhibitory surrounds, so that an excitatory response that was elicited by a sound in the center of the receptive field could be inhibited by another sound presented to the side of or above or below the center. This property of the MLD cells means that center-surround receptive fields exist not only on the retina (Figure 2.36), but also in auditory space.

Knudsen and Konishi not only found cells with receptive fields at particular locations in space but also discovered that these cells are arranged so there is a map of auditory space on the MLD. That is, each cell on the MLD responds to a specific area in space (relative to the position of the head), and adjacent cells respond to adjacent areas of space (Figure 11.16).

We can compare this mapping of space on the MLD to other maps in the nervous system: For example, just as each point on the MLD corresponds to a particular area in space, each point on the retina is represented by a small area on the visual cortex (page 95). Similar point-by-point mapping also occurs in the somatosensory system (see pages 103 and 448).

Although we can see parallels between the point-by-point mapping of space in the owl's MLD and the mapping in the other senses, there is an important difference between them. Consider, for example, the principle behind the map of the retina on the visual cortex. This map occurs because sequences of neurons connect points on the retina to areas on the visual cortex (Figure 11.17a). But where is the connection between points in space and the owl's MLD? Clearly, no connections exist (Figure 11.17b). The

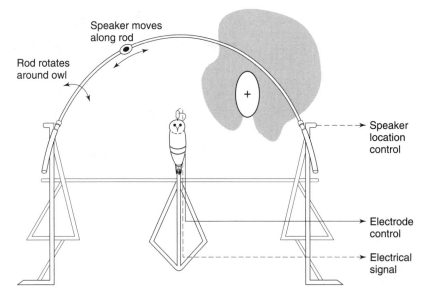

Figure 11.15
The apparatus used by Knudsen and Konishi (1978a,b) to map auditory receptive fields in space. The sound was moved to different positions in space by sliding the speaker along the curved rod and by moving the rod around the owl. The elliptical area marked with a "+" is the excitatory area of a typical receptive field, and the shaded area is the inhibitory area.

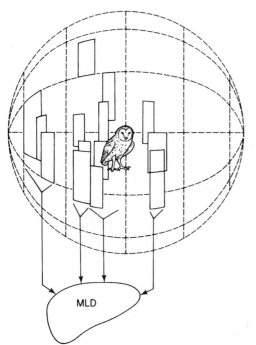

Figure 11.16

The top of this figure shows the owl surrounded by the locations of a number of receptive fields. The receptive fields are indicated by rectangles, although in reality they are shaped more like the one in Figure 11.15. The arrows point to the MLD location from which the bracketed receptive fields were recorded. The three receptive fields to the left of the figure were recorded from the left side of the MLD, whereas the group of receptive fields to the right was recorded from the lower right of the MLD. Thus, there is a map on the MLD that corresponds to the positions of its neurons' receptive fields in space. (Adapted from Knudsen & Konishi, 1978a,b.)

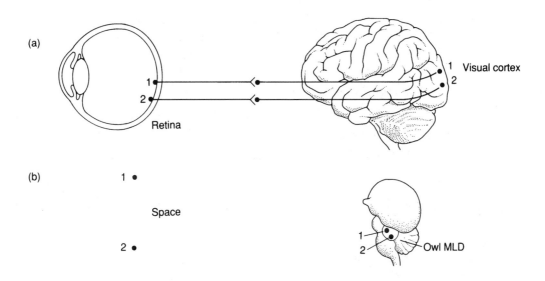

Figure 11.17

(a) The map of retinal locations in the visual cortex (b) and the map of locations in space in the owl's MLD are constructed according to different principles. The retinal map on the visual cortex occurs because there are neural connections linking points on the retina with neurons in the cortex. There is, however, no such anatomical connection between neurons in the owl's MLD and its receptive fields in space. The map in the MLD is constructed from information received by the left and right ears rather than from anatomical connections.

map of space in the MLD is created not by anatomical connections formed by neurons, but by computations made by groups of neurons that receive inputs from both left and right ears.

The fact that the owl's receptive fields in space depend on inputs from both ears is supported by a simple experiment: Plugging one of the owl's ears eliminates the receptive fields in space. And partially plugging one ear, so that it receives less sound than it ordinarily would, shifts the location of the receptive field, so that the sound source must be moved to a new location to cause the neuron to fire (Konishi, 1984).

SUMMARY TABLE 11.1

Localization

Listeners can localize sounds directly in front most accurately and sounds behind the head and off to the side least accurately.

Binaural Cues

Binaural cues for sound localization are interaural time difference and interaural level difference. Interaural level difference is most effective at frequencies above 1,000 Hz. These cues are effective for locating a sound source's azimuth (L–R position).

Personal Guidance System

A practical application of binaural cues is the personal guidance system for the blind, which uses these cues to localize objects in the environment through sounds presented in headphones.

Spectral Cues

Spectral cues are effective for locating a sound's elevation (up–down position) along the midline, where interaural time and level differences are zero. These spectral cues, which are caused by the effect of the head and pinnae on the sound spectrum, are plotted as the directional transfer function (DTF).

Distance Information

Information for perceiving sound distance is sound level, frequency, movement parallax, and reflection.

The Precedence Effect

The precedence effect occurs when our perception of a sound's location is determined by the sound that reaches our ears first. This effect, which occurs for certain delays between direct and indirect sound, causes us to perceive sounds as coming from their original source, even though sound reflected from surfaces in a room reaches our ears from many directions.

Auditory Cortex

The auditory cortex is necessary for accurate localization, since localization decreases if it is removed or damaged.

Single Neuron Responses

Interaural time difference detectors are tuned to respond to specific values of ITD. It has been difficult to find neurons that are tuned to respond to small areas of space, but in nonprimary auditory cortex panoramic neurons respond with different patterns of firing to different distances, and there are neurons that respond best to sounds located in a particular place near the head.

Brain Scan: A Movement Area in the Cortex

There are neurons in the monkey auditory cortex that respond to the direction of sound movement. fMRI research has identified an area in the human cortex that may be specialized for signaling sound movement.

The Owl MLD

The owl is an animal that has neurons that respond best to sounds coming from a specific area of space. There is a map of auditory space on the owl's MLD.

Sound Quality: What a Stimulus Sounds Like

Describing our perception of sounds in terms of pitch (high or low), loudness (loud or soft), duration (long or short), or location (left or right, near or far) does not fully capture the large differences in the qualities of the many sounds that we hear. The difference between a woman's voice and a man's voice isn't just a matter of high frequencies vs. low frequencies. The difference between hearing a radio in a small tiled bathroom and outside isn't just a matter of high sound level vs. low sound level. In this section we will consider some things in addition to frequency and sound level that give sound sources their distinctive characteristics. We will focus on two factors: (1) characteristics of the sound source and (2) characteristics of the environment in which the source is located.

Quality Determined by Characteristics of the Sound Source

As children we learn how to recognize different musical instruments. One particularly delightful way this has been taught is through Prokofief's musical version of *Peter and the Wolf*, which uses the distinctive sounds of each instrument to represent different animals. The flute represents the bird, the French horn represents the wolf, the bassoon represents the grandfather, and the violins and string quartet represent Peter.

One thing that differentiates the sounds of these instruments from one another is their pitch—the flute is high-pitched, and the bassoon is low-pitched. But even when two instruments play the same note with the same loudness, we can still tell them apart, because they differ in timbre (Handel, 1995). We noted in Chapter 10 that when we hear a flute and a bassoon play the same note, we might describe the sound of the flute as *clear* or *mellow* and the sound of the bassoon as *nasal* or *reedy*. These differences in timbre illustrate that sounds can have different qualities in addition to pitch and loudness.

A number of different characteristics of the sound stimulus act together to produce an instru-

ment's timbre. One factor that causes differences in timbre is the relative strengths of the harmonics that occur for all complex musical tones. (Remember from Chapter 10 that complex musical tones contain a fundamental frequency plus harmonics which are multiples of the fundamental frequency.)

Figure 11.18 compares the harmonics of the guitar, the bassoon, and the alto saxophone playing the note G3 with a fundamental frequency of 196 Hz. Both the relative heights of the harmonics and the number of harmonics are different in these instruments. For example, the guitar has more high-frequency harmonics than either the bassoon or the alto saxophone. Although the frequencies of the harmonics are always multiples of the fundamental

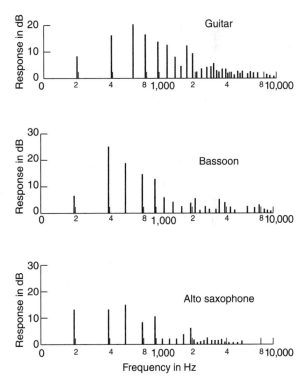

Figure 11.18

Fourier spectra for a guitar, a bassoon, and an alto saxophone playing a tone with a fundamental frequency of 196 Hz. The position of the lines on the horizontal axis indicates the frequencies of the harmonics and their height indicates their intensities. (Olson, 1967.)

frequency, harmonics may be absent, as is true of some of the high-frequency harmonics of the bassoon and the alto saxophone.

The best example of an instrument that produces a tone with few harmonics is the flute. You can see from Figure 11.19 that for a 1,568-Hz tone (G6) the flute has only one harmonic in addition to the fundamental, and this harmonic has very little energy. Because the fundamental contains most of the energy of this tone, the flute has the thinnest and purest tone of all of the musical instruments. At the other extreme, instruments like the guitar and the lower notes on the piano, which have many harmonics, have much fuller, richer tones than the flute.

Timbre also depends on the time course of the tone's **attack** (the buildup of sound at the beginning of the tone) and on the time course of the tone's **decay** (the decrease in sound at the end of the tone). Thus, it is easy to tell the difference between a tape recording of a high note played on the clarinet and a recording of the same note played on the flute if the attack, the decay, and the sustained portion of the tone are heard. It is, however, difficult to distinguish between the same instruments if the tone's attack and decay are eliminated by erasing the first and last one-half second of the recording (Berger, 1964; also see Risset & Mathews, 1969).

Another way to make it difficult to distinguish one instrument from another is to play a tape of an instrument's tone backward. Even though this does not affect the tone's harmonic structure, a piano tone

played backward does not sound like a piano, mainly because the tone's original decay has become the attack and the attack has become the decay (Berger, 1964; Erickson, 1975). Thus, timbre depends both on the tone's steady-state harmonic structure and on the time course of the attack and decay of the tone's harmonics.

Quality Determined by Characteristics of Rooms: Architectural Acoustics

The same sound sources can produce very different perceptions, depending on where they are located. Saying "hello" in a carpeted room and saying "hello" in the depths of a rock-lined cavern will result in very different sounds.

When we studied vision, we saw that our perception of light depends not only on the nature of the light source but also on what happens to the light between the time it leaves its source and the time it enters our eyes. If light passes through haze on its way from an object to our eyes, the object may seem bluer or fuzzier than it would if the haze were not there. Similarly, our perception of sound also depends not only on the sound produced at the source, but also on how much of the sound reaches our ears directly and how much reaches our ears indirectly (Figure 11.10).

Direct Sound, Indirect Sound, and Reverberation Time
The study of direct and indirect sound is a major concern of a field called architectural acoustics, which is largely concerned with how indirect sound changes the quality of the sounds we hear in rooms. The major factor affecting indirect sound is the amount of sound absorbed by the walls, ceiling, and floor of the room. If most of the sound is absorbed, then there are few sound reflections, and we hear little indirect sound. If most of the sound is reflected, then there are many sound reflections, and we hear much indirect sound. Another factor affecting indirect sound is the size and shape of the room. This determines how sound hits surfaces and the directions in which it is reflected.

The amount and duration of indirect sound produced by a room is expressed as **reverberation time**—the time it takes for the sound to decrease to

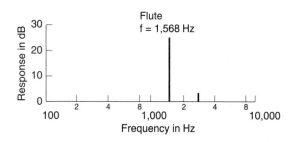

Figure 11.19
Fourier spectrum of a flute playing a tone with a fundamental frequency of 1,568 Hz. (Olson, 1967.)

60 dB less than its original level. If the reverberation time of a room is too long sounds become muddled because the direct and reflected sounds reach the listener with a long delay. In extreme cases, such as cathedrals with stone walls, these delays are perceived as echoes. If the reverberation time is too short, music will sound "dead" and it is difficult to produce sounds of very high intensity.

Because of the relationship between reverberation time and perception, acoustical engineers have tried to design concert halls in which the reverberation time matches the reverberation time of halls that are renowned for their good acoustics, like Symphony Hall in Boston and the Concertgebow in Amsterdam, which have reverberation times of about 2.0 seconds. However, an "ideal" reverberation time does not always predict good acoustics. This is illustrated by the problems associated with the design of New York's Philharmonic Hall. When it opened in 1962, Philharmonic Hall had a reverberation time of close to the ideal of 2.0 seconds. Even so, the hall was criticized for sounding as though it had a short reverberation time, and musicians in the orchestra complained that they could not hear each other. These criticisms resulted in a series of alterations to the hall, made over many years, until eventually, when none of the alterations proved satisfactory, the entire interior of the hall was destroyed and the hall was completely rebuilt and renamed, so it is now called Avery Fisher Hall. The experience with Philharmonic Hall, plus new developments in the field of architectural acoustics, has led architectural engineers to consider factors in addition to reverberation time in designing concert halls.

Beyond Reverberation Time   What other factors, in addition to reverberation time, need to be considered in designing concert halls? The key to answering this question was provided by Leo Beranek (1996), who identified the following physical measures that are associated with how music is perceived in concert halls:

- *Intimacy time*   The time between when sound arrives directly from the stage and when the first reflection arrives.

- *Bass ratio*   The ratio of low frequencies to middle frequencies that are reflected from walls and other surfaces.

- *Spaciousness factor*   The fraction of all of the sound received by a listener that is indirect sound.

To determine the optimal values for these physical measures, acoustical engineers measured them in 20 opera houses and 25 symphony halls in 14 countries. By comparing their measurements with ratings of the halls by conductors and music critics, they confirmed that the best concert halls had reverberation times of about 2 seconds and also found that 1.5 seconds was better for opera houses, with the shorter time being necessary to enable people to clearly hear the singers' voices. They also found that intimacy times of about 20 milliseconds and high bass ratios and spaciousness factors were associated with good acoustics (Glanz, 2000). When these factors have been taken into account in the design of new concert halls, the result has been acoustics rivaling the best halls in the world (Figure 11.20).

The problems facing architects in the design of concert halls emphasizes the complexity of the factors determining sound quality. The sound stimulus that actually reaches a listener is far more complex than single pure tones, or even musical tones, because of the way sounds interact with objects in the environment.

Identifying Environmental Sounds

Our consideration of sound quality has focused on how people hear music inside rooms. But our everyday environment is filled with many sounds in addition to music. Psychologists have just begun studying sounds we hear in our everyday environment. One approach to studying these environmental sounds has been to distinguish between two different ways of describing sounds. William Gaver (1993a,b) distinguishes between **everyday listening**, which focuses on listening to events such as an air conditioner blowing or a chair squeaking, and **musical listening**, which focuses on perceptual qualities such as the sounds' pitch and timbre. People usually describe the

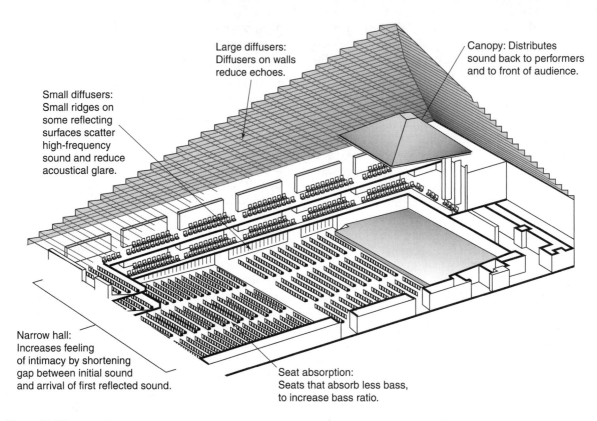

Small diffusers: Small ridges on some reflecting surfaces scatter high-frequency sound and reduce acoustical glare.

Large diffusers: Diffusers on walls reduce echoes.

Canopy: Distributes sound back to performers and to front of audience.

Narrow hall: Increases feeling of intimacy by shortening gap between initial sound and arrival of first reflected sound.

Seat absorption: Seats that absorb less bass, to increase bass ratio.

Figure 11.20

A concert hall designed taking into account the factors discussed in the text, indicating some of the features that contribute to good acoustics.

sounds they hear in terms of everyday listening ("the air conditioner is blowing"), whereas auditory researchers generally describe sound in terms of musical listening ("the sound of the air conditioner is a medium-pitched white-noise sound").

Although everyday listening has to do with our everyday experience, little research has been done on this type of listening. Recently, however, some researchers have taken the first steps toward considering everyday listening. These researchers, who are interested in studying natural sounds as they occur in the environment, are taking an **ecological approach to auditory perception** that is analogous to J. J. Gibson's ecological approach to visual perception, which we discussed in Chapter 9.

The first step in studying everyday listening is to describe the types of sounds in the environment. Gaver distinguishes the following three types of sounds: (1) vibrating solids (sounds like footsteps, a ringing bell, a can opener); (2) aerodynamic events (sounds like the air conditioner or the wind blowing through the trees; and (3) liquid sounds (water pouring or an object being dropped into the water).

Everyday listening has also been studied by determining how well people can identify sounds. When Gaver played taped sounds, he found that subjects could identify whether a person was running up or down stairs, the size of an object dropped into the water, and a cup being filled. Subjects can also tell whether a walker is male or female based on the sounds of the footsteps (Li, Logan, & Pastore, 1991).

How do subjects make these judgments? Some clues can be found in the mistakes they make. For example, subjects often identify the sound made by opening and closing a file drawer as a bowling alley. The reason for this confusion is apparently that both the file drawer and the bowling alley create a rolling sound followed by an impact. Other research has systematically looked at the relationship between physical properties of stimuli and their perceptual effects. For example, Lynn Halpern, Randolph Blake, and James Hillenbrand (1986) wondered what component of a sound that many people find unpleasant, such as the sound made by scraping a garden tool across slate, is responsible for the sound's unpleasant quality. Although they thought that the high-frequency components of the sound would be the culprit, when they presented the low- and high-frequency components of the sound separately, they found that the low frequencies in the sound were responsible for the unpleasantness.

Research like this on everyday sounds represents just the beginnings of attempts to understand how people perceive complex auditory stimuli. The problems involved are difficult, since the stimuli are so complicated, but just as researchers have become more interested in complex visual stimuli like faces and complex forms (see Chapters 4 and 5), they are also becoming more interested in the complexities of everyday auditory stimuli (see Carello et al., 1998).

AUDITORY SCENE ANALYSIS: IDENTIFYING SOUND SOURCES

webTUTOR   We have, up until now, been considering how we perceive sounds produced by a single source. We now consider how we perceive sounds being produced by many sources simultaneously or close together in time.

The Problem of Auditory Scene Analysis

We opened this chapter with the example of a bird chirping in a tree and a cat meowing on the ground below. The point of that example was that we can't tell where the bird and cat are located based on which receptors in the listener's cochlea are stimulated, because these receptors respond to the frequencies in a sound, not to where the sound is located in space.

We now return to our bird and cat to consider a related problem: How does the auditory system tell that there are two sound sources—a bird and a cat? This may seem like a simple problem. After all, the bird and cat make different sounds, which are easy to tell apart. But when we look at the information that these sounds create on the cochlea, we can appreciate that the problem is not so simple.

If the bird and cat are chirping and meowing at exactly the same time, the pressure changes created by each one combine in the ear, as shown in Figure 11.21, and stimulate the receptors in the cochlea. But which hair cells are being stimulated by the cat's cry and which by the bird's song? Since the pressure changes from both sounds are mixed together, there is no way to tell. Just as we can't use place information on the cochlea to determine the locations of the bird and cat, we also can't use this information to determine which sounds are produced by the bird and which are produced by the cat.

Basically, this is the same problem that you face when you are talking to a friend at a noisy party. Even though the sounds produced by your friend's conversation are mixed together on your cochlea with the sounds produced by all of the other people's conversations, plus the music and the sound of the refrigerator door slamming and glasses tinkling, you somehow are able to separate what your friend is saying from all of the other sounds. The array of sound sources in the environment is called the **auditory scene,** and the process by which you separate the stimuli produced by each of the sources in the scene into separate perceptions is called **auditory scene analysis** (Bregman, 1990, 1993; Yost, 2001).

It might seem as if one way to analyze an auditory scene into its separate components would be to use information about where each source is coming from. You can separate your friend's voice and the slamming of the refrigerator door because your friend is standing nearby and the sound of the refrigerator

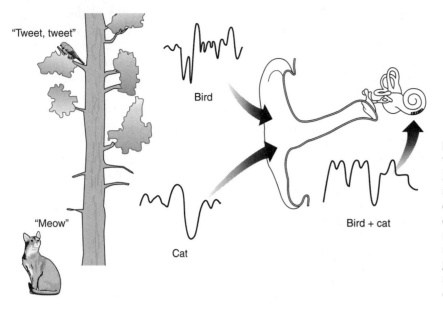

Figure 11.21
The same bird and cat from Figure 11.3, but showing the pattern of pressure changes for each one and the combined signal that enters the ear. The problem in identifying the sounds made by the bird and the cat as coming from the bird and the cat is that they are mixed together on the cochlea.

door is coming from the next room. While the sound sources' positions in space can help you separate the sources from one another, this can't be the whole story, because when you listen to a monaural recording of an orchestra over headphones, you can still hear the separate instruments, even though you have no information about where the instruments are located in space (Yost, 1997). There must, therefore, be other information in addition to spatial location that enables you to analyze an auditory scene into separate sound sources. We can describe this information in terms of principles of auditory grouping

Principles of Auditory Grouping

Just as visual stimuli are perceptually organized so that certain elements of a scene appear to belong together, so are sound stimuli. This perceptual organization occurs according to rules that are based on how sounds originate in the environment. For example, tones that originate from a single source usually come from one point in space. Thus, we have seen that one factor that helps us separate one source from another is their locations. Let's now consider location again, plus some additional principles of auditory

grouping. As we describe them, notice that some are similar to the Gestalt laws we described in Chapter 5 for the grouping of visual stimuli.

Location   Sounds created by a particular source usually come from one position in space or from a slowly changing location. Any time two sounds are separated in space, the cue of location helps us separate them perceptually. In addition, when a source moves, it typically follows a continuous path rather than jumping erratically from one place to another. This continuous movement of sound helps us perceive the sound from a passing car as originating from a single source.

Similarity of Timbre   Sounds that have the same timbre are often produced by the same source. This principle simply means that we tend to group stimuli that sound similar together. We can illustrate this by considering an effect created by David Wessel (1979), who presented listeners with sequences of tones shown in Figure 11.22a. In this figure the filled circles are tones with one timbre, and the open circles are tones with a different timbre. When the tones are played slowly, they sound like three repeated notes that are increasing in pitch and that change in tim-

Chapter 11   **396**

bre, as would occur if a clarinet alternated notes with a trumpet (Figure 11.22b). However, when they are played rapidly, the notes with different timbres are heard as separate descending streams with different timbres, as would occur if the clarinet and trumpet each played separate three-note sequences (Figure 11.22c). This is an example of a phenomenon called **auditory stream segregation**—the separation of the acoustic stimuli entering the ear into different perceptual streams (also see Bregman & Pinker, 1978).

Similarity of Pitch *Sounds with similar frequencies are often produced by the same source.* This principle means that tones that have similar pitches tend to be perceived as belonging together. Composers made use of grouping by similarity of pitch long before psychologists began studying it. Composers in the Baroque period (1600–1750) knew that if a single instrument plays notes that alternate rapidly between high and low tones, the listener perceives two separate melodies, with the high notes perceived as being played by one instrument and the low notes as being played by another. An excerpt from a composition by J. S. Bach that uses this device is shown in Figure 11.23. When this passage is played rapidly, the low notes sound as if they are a melody played by one instrument, and the high notes sound like a different melody played by another instrument. This effect, which has been called *implied polyphony* or *compound melodic line* by musicians, is an example of auditory stream segregation (see Jones & Yee, 1993; Yost & Sheft, 1993).

Albert Bregman and Jeffrey Campbell (1971) demonstrated auditory stream segregation based on pitch by alternating high and low tones, as shown in the sequence in Figure 11.24. When the high-pitched

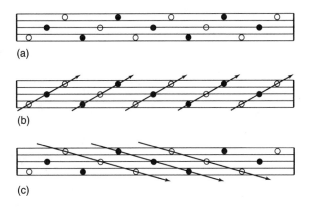

(a)

(b)

(c)

Figure 11.22
(a) The repeating series of three notes presented by Wessel (1979). The open circles stand for a tone with one timbre, and the filled circles for a tone with a different timbre. (b) When the tones are presented slowly, they are perceived as ascending sequences with alternating timbres. (c) When the tones are presented rapidly, they are perceived as descending sequences with the same timbre. This is Wessel's (1979) timbre illusion.

tones were slowly alternated with the low-pitched tones, as in Figure 11.24a, the tones were heard in one stream, one after another: Hi-Lo-Hi-Lo-Hi-Lo, as indicated by the dashed line. But when the tones were alternated very rapidly, the high and low tones became perceptually grouped into two auditory streams so that the listener perceived two separate streams of sound, one high-pitched and one low-pitched, occurring simultaneously (Figure 11.24b) (see Heise & Miller 1951 and Miller & Heise, 1950, for an early demonstration of auditory stream segregation).

This grouping of tones into streams by similarity of pitch is also demonstrated by an experiment done

Figure 11.23
Four measures of a composition by J. S. Bach (Choral Prelude on Jesus Christus unser Heiland, 1739). *When played rapidly, the upper notes become perceptually grouped and the lower notes become perceptually grouped, a phenomenon called* auditory stream segregation.

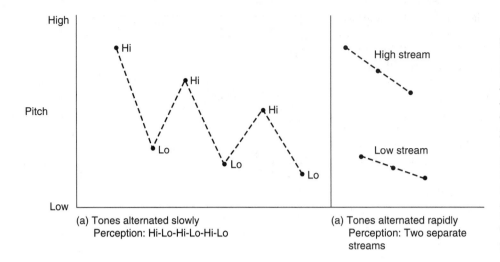

Figure 11.24

(a) When high and low tones are alternated slowly, auditory stream segregation does not occur, so the listener perceives alternating high and low tones. (b) Faster alternation results in segregation into high and low streams. (Listen to WebTutor, Effect of Temporal Proximity on Stream Segregation.*)*

by Bregman and Alexander Rudnicky (1975). The listener is first presented with two standard tones, X and Y (Figure 11.25a). When these tones are presented alone, it is easy to perceive their order (XY or YX). However, when these tones are sandwiched between two distractor (D) tones (Figure 11.25b), it becomes very hard to judge their order. The name *distractor tones* is well taken: They distract the listener, making it difficult to judge the order of tones X and Y.

But the distracting effect of the D tones can be eliminated by adding a series of "captor" tones (C) (Figure 11.25c). Since these captor tones have the

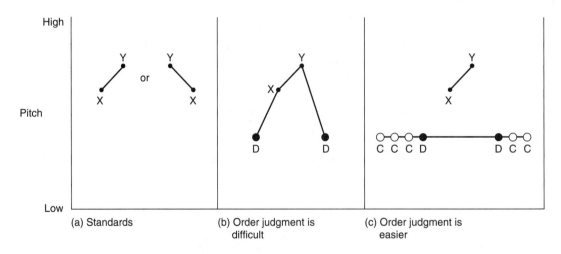

Figure 11.25

Bregman and Rudnicky's (1975) experiment. (a) The standard tones X and Y have different pitches. (b) Test 1: The distractor (D) tones group with X and Y, making it difficult to judge the order of X and Y. (c) Test 2: The addition of captor (C) tones with the same pitch as the distractor tones causes the distractor tones to form a separate stream (law of similarity) and makes it easier to judge the order of tones X and Y. (Based on Bregman & Rudnicky, 1975.) (Listen to WebTutor, Grouping by Similarity of Pitch.*)*

same pitch as the distractors, they capture the distractors and form a stream that separates the distractors from tones X and Y. The result is that X and Y are perceived as belonging to a separate stream, and it is much easier to perceive the order of X and Y.

A final example of how similarity of pitch causes grouping is an effect called the **scale illusion** or **melodic channeling**. Diana Deutsch (1975, 1996) demonstrated this effect by presenting two scales simultaneously, one ascending and one descending (Figure 11.26a). The subjects listened to these scales through earphones that presented successive notes from each scale alternately to the left and right ears (Figure 11.26b). If we focus just on the right ear, the notes alternate from high to low to high. Similarly, if we focus on the left ear, the notes alternate from low to high to low. But this was not what the subjects perceived. They perceived smooth sequences of notes in each ear with the higher notes in the right ear and lower ones in the left ear (Figure 11.26c).

This illusion highlights an important property of perceptual grouping. Most of the time the principles of auditory grouping help us to accurately interpret what is happening in the environment. It is most effective to perceive similar sounds as coming from the same source, because this is what usually happens in the environment. When the perceptual system applies the principle of grouping by similarity to the artificial stimuli presented through earphones, it makes the mistake of assigning similar pitches to the same ear. But most of the time, when psychologists aren't controlling the stimuli, the fact that sounds with similar frequencies often are produced by the same sound source helps the auditory system to correctly determine where sounds are coming from.

Temporal Proximity Sounds that occur in rapid progression tend to be produced by the same source. We can illustrate the importance of timing in stream segregation by returning to our examples of grouping by similarity. Before stream segregation due to similarity of timbre or pitch can occur, tones with similar timbres or frequencies have to occur close together in time. According to the principle of temporal proximity, tones that follow each other rapidly tend to be perceived together. If the tones are too far apart in time, as in Figure 11.24a, segregation will not occur, even if the tones are similar in pitch.

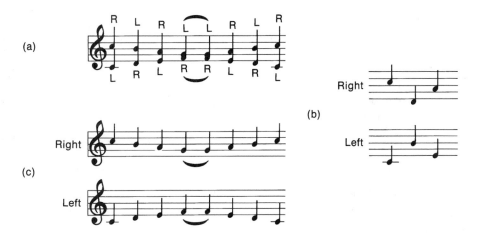

Figure 11.26
(a) These stimuli were presented to the subject's left and right ears in Deutsch's (1975) "scale illusion" experiment. (b) The first three notes presented to the left and right ears in Deutsch's experiment. The notes presented to each ear do not form a scale; they jump up and down. (c) What the subject hears. Although the notes in each ear jump up and down, the subject perceives a smooth sequence of notes in each ear. This effect is called the scale illusion or melodic channeling. (Based on Deutsch, 1975.)

Onset and Offset *Sounds that stop and start at different times tend to be produced by different sources.* If you are listening to one instrument playing and then another one joins in later, you know that two sources are present.

Good Continuation *Sounds that stay constant or that change smoothly are often produced by the same source.* This property of sounds leads to a principle analogous to the principle of good continuation for vision. Sound stimuli with the same frequency or smoothly changing frequencies are perceived as continuous even if they are interrupted by another stimulus.

A musical example of this principle is shown in Figure 11.27a (Deutsch, 1996). This musical excerpt consists of one series of identical repeated notes (top) and another sequence that rises and then falls in pitch (bottom). Even though the pitches of the two musical streams cross (Figure 11.27b), they are perceived as two separate streams.

Richard Warren, C. J. Obuseck, and J. M. Acroff (1972) illustrated good continuation in a different way by presenting the stimuli shown in Figure 11.28. When bursts of tone were interrupted by gaps of silence (Figure 11.28a), listeners perceived the tones as stopping during the silence. If, however, the silent gaps were filled in with noise (Figure 11.28b), the listeners perceived the tone as continuing behind the noise (Figure 11.28c). This demonstration is analogous to the demonstration of visual good continuation in Figure 5.12. Just as the various pipes in this picture are perceived as continuous even though they overlap one another, a tone can be perceived as continuous even though it is interrupted by busts of noise.

Experience An example of how past experience can affect the perceptual grouping of auditory stimuli is provided by W. Jay Dowling (1973), who had his subjects listen to two interleaved melodies by alternating notes of "Three Blind Mice" with notes of "Mary Had a Little Lamb" (Figure 11.29). When the subjects listened to these combined melodies, they reported hearing a meaningless jumble of notes. However, when they were told the names of the

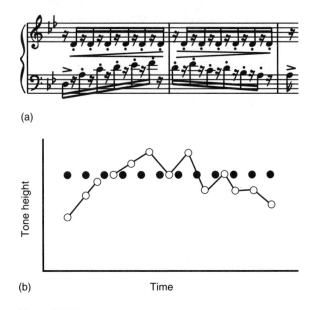

(a)

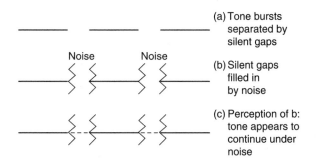

(b)   Time

Figure 11.27
(a) A selection from Leyenda *by Albinez, showing the two musical lines, one of repeating notes and the other a sequence of changing notes. (b) The listeners perceive the repeating notes as one stream (filled circles) and the changing tones as another stream, even though the notes overlap. (Adapted from Deutsch, 1996.)*

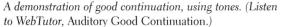

(a) Tone bursts separated by silent gaps

(b) Silent gaps filled in by noise

(c) Perception of b: tone appears to continue under noise

Figure 11.28
A demonstration of good continuation, using tones. (Listen to WebTutor, Auditory Good Continuation.)

songs, they were able to hear the melody to which they were paying attention.

What the listeners were doing, according to Dowling and Dane Harwood (1986), was applying

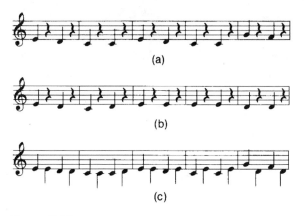

Figure 11.29
*(a) "Three Blind Mice," (b) "Mary Had a Little Lamb,"
and (c) the two melodies interleaved ("Three Blind Mice,"
stems up; "Mary Had a Little Lamb," stems down). (Listen
to WebTutor,* Melody Obscured by Noise.)

a **melody schema** to the interleaved melodies.
A melody schema is a representation of a familiar
melody that is stored in a person's memory. When

people don't know that a melody is present, they have
no access to the schema and therefore have nothing
with which to compare the unknown melody. But if
they are told which melody is present, they compare
what they hear to their stored "Three Blind Mice" or
"Mary Had a Little Lamb" schemas and perceive the
melodies.

Each of the principles of auditory grouping that
we have described provides information about the
number and identity of sources in the auditory environment. But each principle alone is not foolproof,
and basing our perceptions on just one principle can
lead to error, as in the case of the scale illusion,
which is purposely arranged so similarity of pitch
dominates our perception. Thus, in most naturalistic
situations, we base our perceptions on a number of
these cues working together. This is similar to the situation we described for visual perception in which
we saw that our perception of objects depends on a
number of Gestalt laws of organization working
together and our perception of depth depends on a
number of depth cues working together.

How Vision Can Affect Hearing

In this section we combine our description of perceptual plasticity with our description of how perception occurs across the senses. We will first describe a physiological experiment, which shows that depriving an animal of visual stimulation can cause an increase in the size of an area of cortex that is important for auditory localization. We will then describe a psychophysical experiment which shows how visual stimulation can have long-term effects on our ability to locate sound.

The Effect of Visual Deprivation on an Auditory Area

How does depriving an animal of stimulation for one sense affect the operation of another sense? This question was studied by Josef Rauscheker and Martin Korte (1993) by depriving kittens of pattern vision in both eyes, by suturing their eyelids shut at birth. After raising the kittens under these conditions of visual deprivation, Rauschecker and Korte recorded from neurons in the anterior ectosylvian sulcus (AES), which contains an area that is specialized for sound localization and also areas that respond to somatosensory (touch) and visual stimuli (Figure 11.30a).

When they compared this area in the deprived cats to the same area in a control group of sighted cats, they observed an extremely interesting difference: The deprived cats had a smaller visual area and expanded auditory and somatosensory areas. In addition, the neurons in the expanded auditory area were more sharply tuned to detect sound location. As you can see from Figure 11.30b, the auditory and somatosensory areas have taken over some of the space that was once allotted to vision. This is, there-

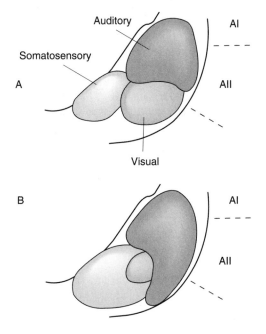

Figure 11.30

The anterior ectosylvian nucleus, which is located near auditory areas AI and AII and which contains auditory, visual, and somatosensory areas. Top: Sizes of the three areas for a normal cat. Bottom: Sizes of the three areas for a cat that had been deprived of pattern vision in both eyes as a kitten. The auditory and somatosensory areas have increased in size at the expense of the visual area. (From Rauschecker & Korte, 1993.)

fore, another example of how the brain is able to change its structure and functioning to adapt to long-term changes in an animal's sensory environment.

The Ventriloquism Aftereffect

For our second example of plasticity involving vision and audition, we will consider a psychophysical effect in humans called the ventriloquism effect, which we described in the "Across the Senses" section in Chapter 7. This effect occurs when a visual stimulus influences our perception of the location of an auditory stimulus. For example, the ventriloquism effect occurs in TV and film when we perceive sound as coming from an actor's mouth, even though it is actually coming from speakers located off to the side.

We now consider an especially interesting aspect of the ventriloquism effect—a shift in the perception of auditory space that persists even after the visual stimulus that caused the ventriloquism effect is no longer present. This persisting ventriloquism effect, which is called the **ventriloquism aftereffect,** was demonstrated by Gregg Recanzone (1998) using the procedure diagrammed in Figure 11.31: First a subject's sound localization was tested using 15 speakers in a dark room. The subjects sat in front of the speakers and when they heard a sound from one of the speakers, they indicated its position by orienting their heads toward the sound (Figure 11.31a). In the training part of the experiment, subjects heard sound from one of the speakers, as before, but this time a light flashed to the right of the speaker that was pro-

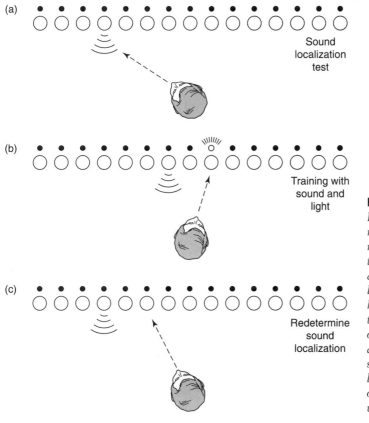

Figure 11.31

Procedure for the ventriloquism effect experiment. (a) People's sound localization is determined by having them turn toward a sound in the dark. (b) The person is trained for 2,500 trials by simultaneously presenting a sound and a light off to the right. The subject turns his or her head to where the sound is perceived, which turns out to be where the light is being flashed, off to the right of the sound. (c) After training, auditory localization is redetermined, using the same procedure as in a, above. The light is no longer present, but subjects' localization is now off to the right of the sound, where the light used to be. (From Recanzone, 1998.)

ducing the sound (Figure 11.31b). To keep the subjects' attention focused on the sound stimulus, they were told to press a button every time a slightly louder tone was presented, which occurred every four or five trials. As you can see from Figure 11.31b, during training the subject perceived the sound as coming from the location indicated by the light.

After 2,500 pairings of the sound and light, the sound localization test was repeated in complete darkness. The subjects' task was the same as before the training: They were to orient their heads toward the sound. However, this time the result was different. They now oriented their heads to the right of the sound, close to where the light had flashed, except now there was no light (Figure 11.31c). Their training with the light had shifted the subjects' perceptions of auditory space.

Recanzone hypothesizes that what must be happening here is that cortical neurons responsible for sound localization were "recalibrated" by the training procedure. If this is true, this means that when the visual stimulus shifts the person's perception of where a sound is coming from, it is causing changes in the person's auditory cortex.

Although the two experiments we have described are very different, they both illustrate how manipulating visual experience can affect auditory functioning. In one case a decrease in visual experience causes increases in the size of an area of the cat's cortex that is important for sound localization. In the other case, adding visual experience causes a change in a person's perception of the location of a tone, which may also be accompanied by changes in the person's auditory cortex.

Sound Quality and the Source

A sound's timbre is determined by the characteristics of the sound source, such as the number and sizes of its harmonics and the attack and decay of a sound.

Sound Quality Determined by Characteristics of Rooms

The environment in which sound is produced determines how much direct sound and indirect sound reaches a listener's ears, and this influences sound quality. The amount of indirect sound and its duration are expressed as a room's reverberation time. The science of architectural acoustics has identified other characteristics of the stimulus, such as intimacy time, bass ratio, and spaciousness factor, that affect sound quality in concert halls.

Environmental Sounds

The ecological approach to auditory perception focuses on analyzing environmental sounds. Everyday listening focuses on listening to common events such as an air conditioner running. Research on everyday listening has described the types of sound in the environment and has determined how well people can identify many types of sounds.

Auditory Scene Analysis

The problem of auditory scene analysis is to separate the different sound sources from all of the simultaneously presented sounds in an auditory scene. The following principles of auditory grouping have been identified that help achieve this analysis: location, similarity of timbre, similarity of pitch, temporal proximity, onset and offset, good continuation, and experience.

Across the Senses and Plasticity: How Vision Can Affect Hearing

Depriving kittens of vision causes an increase in the area of the ectosylvian sulcus that is devoted to auditory localization. The ventriloquism effect is a shift in the heard location of a sound caused by the presence of a visual stimulus. The ventriloquism aftereffect is a persistence of this effect after the visual stimulus is no longer present. This aftereffect may be due to the recalibration of cortical neurons.

STUDY QUESTIONS

Auditory Localization: Locating Single Sounds in Space

1. What is auditory localization? (376)

2. How well can listeners localize sounds? Where is the best and worst localization relative to the head? (376)

3. Describe the three coordinates used to describe auditory localization. (376)

4. What is the problem facing the auditory system in determining locations? How does the information about location available to the auditory system differ from the information for location available to the visual system? (376)

Information for Azimuth

5. What are the two major interaural cues? Why are they called binaural cues? (377)

6. Describe the principle behind interaural time difference. (377)

7. Describe the principle behind interaural level difference. What is the principle behind the acoustic shadow, and why does it occur more for some frequencies than for others? (378)

8. Describe the principle behind the personal guidance system and how it uses binaural cues. (379)

Information for Elevation

9. What are spectral cues? What is the directional transfer function (DTF), and how does it provide information for sound localization? What are the roles of the head and pinnae in determining the DTF? (380)

Information for Distance

10. Describe the following cues for distance: sound level, frequency, movement parallax, reflection. (382)

11. What is direct sound? Indirect sound? (382)

The Precedence Effect

12. How does perception of the location of sounds coming from two speakers separated in space change as the delay between the two speakers increases from zero (simultaneous) to about 10 ms? (383)

13. What is fusion? The echo threshold? The precedence effect? (383)

14. What characteristic of direct sound causes us to hear the sound as coming directly from its source? (384)

15. When we hear direct sound coming from the source, do we hear other sounds that reach our ears with a slight delay? (385)

The Physiological Basis for Localization

16. What is the physiological basis for localization? Describe the role of the auditory cortex, interaural time difference detectors, neurons tuned to specific areas of space, panoramic neurons, and neurons that signal sounds that are occurring near the head. (385)

17. Describe the barn owl's topographic map of space. (388)

18. What are the parallels between the point-by-point mapping of space in the owl's MLD and mapping in the visual cortex? (388)

19. What is a major difference between mapping of space in hearing and in vision? What do we mean when we say that the physiology of sound localization is a computational process? (388)

20. What happens if we plug an owl's ear? if we partially plug the ear? (390)

Brain Scan: A Motion Area in the Auditory Cortex

21. Are there cortical neurons in animals that respond to the direction of sound movement? (386)

22. Describe the experiment that showed that there may be a specialized area in the human cortex for signaling auditory motion. (386)

12

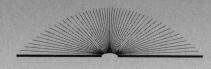

SPEECH PERCEPTION[1]

SOME QUESTIONS WE WILL CONSIDER

- Can computers perceive speech as well as humans? (410)

- Why does an unfamiliar foreign language often sound like a continuous stream of sound, with no breaks between words? (413)

- Does each word that we hear have a characteristic pattern of air pressure changes associated with it? (414)

Speech sounds are, like other sounds, a disturbance of the air. But speech sounds, unlike other sounds, are produced as air is pushed up from the lungs and is shaped into patterns of air pressure changes by actions of the various structures in the vocal tract (Figure 12.1).

Although we perceive speech easily under most conditions, beneath this ease lurks processes as com-

plex as those involved in perceiving the most complicated visual scenes. One way to appreciate this complexity is to consider attempts to use computers to recognize speech. After decades of research into

---

[1] This chapter is dedicated to the memory of Kerry Green, speech researcher and friend.

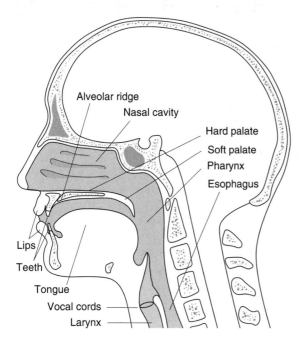

Figure 12.1
The vocal tract includes the nasal and oral cavities and the pharynx, as well as components that move, such as the tongue, lips, and vocal cords.

Alveolar ridge
Nasal cavity
Hard palate
Soft palate
Pharynx
Esophagus
Lips
Teeth
Tongue
Vocal cords
Larynx

computer speech recognition, useful computer speech recognition systems are only now becoming available. The phone company uses computer speech recognition to identify simple messages such as telephone numbers or phrases such as "I want to make a credit card call," and there are software programs that make it possible for personal computers to respond to spoken commands (Markowitz, 1996).

There are dictation machines that can translate speech that is spoken clearly and in a quiet environment into printed text, but these programs must be "trained" to recognize the voices and pronunciations of individual speakers, and even after this training they are still prone to error. For example, the 2000 version of a popular speech recognition program translated "Friends, Romans, countrymen, lend me your ears" into "Friends, Romans, countryman, linear years."

In contrast to computers, humans can perceive speech under a wide variety of conditions, including the presence of various background noises, sloppy pronunciation, speakers with different accents, and the often chaotic give-and-take that routinely occurs when people talk with one another.

This chapter will help you appreciate the complex perceptual problems posed by speech and will describe research that has helped us begin to understand how the human speech perception system has solved some of these problems. We begin by describing the nature of the vibrations produced by our vocal apparatus.

THE SPEECH STIMULUS

Think about what you hear when someone speaks to you. You perceive a series of sounds called syllables, which create words, and these syllables and words appear strung together one after another like beads on a string. For example, we perceive the phrase "perception is easy" as the sequence of units: "per-sep-shon-iz-ee-z." But although our perception of speech may be easy and the sounds we hear may appear to be discrete sounds that are lined up one after another, the actual situation is quite different.

Rather than following each other with one unit of sound ending and then the other beginning, neighboring sounds overlap one another. In addition, the pattern of air pressure changes for a particular word can vary greatly depending on whether the speaker is male or female, is young or old, speaks rapidly or slowly, or has an accent. To understand the way speech sounds overlap and why the same sound can be represented by many different patterns of pressure changes, we need to describe the speech stimulus and how it is produced. We will do this in two ways: (1) in terms of short segments of sound, called phonemes; and (2) in terms of the patterns of frequencies and intensities of the pressure changes in the air, called the acoustic signal.

Phonemes: Sounds and Meanings

Our first task in studying speech perception is to separate speech sounds into manageable units. What are these units? The flow of a sentence? A particular word? A syllable? The sound of a letter? A sentence is too large a unit for easy analysis, and some letters have no sounds at all. Although there are arguments for the idea that the syllable is the basic unit of speech (Mehler, 1981; Segui, 1984), most speech research has been based on a unit called the **phoneme**. The phoneme is the shortest segment of speech that, if changed, changes the meaning of a word. Consider the word *bit*, which contains the phonemes /b/, /i/, and /t/. (Phonemes and other speech sounds are indicated by setting them off with slashes.) We know that /b/, /i/, and /t/ are phonemes, because we can change the meaning of the word by changing each phoneme individually. Thus, *bit* becomes *pit* if /b/ is changed to /p/, it becomes *bat* if /i/ is changed to /a/, and it becomes *bid* if /t/ is changed to /d/.

The phonemes of English, listed in Table 12.1, are represented by phonetic symbols that stand for speech sounds: 13 phonemes have vowel sounds, and 24 phonemes have consonant sounds. Your first reaction to this table may be that there are more vowels than the standard set you learned in grade school (a, e, i, o, and u). The reason is that some vowels can have more than one pronunciation, so there are more vowel sounds than vowel letters. For example, the vowel o sounds different in *boat* and *hot*, and the vowel e sounds different in *head* and *heed*. Phonemes, therefore, refer not to letters but to speech sounds that serve to distinguish meaning.

Because different languages use different sounds, the number of phonemes varies in different languages. While there are only 11 phonemes in Hawaiian, there are 47 in English, and as many as 60 in some African dialects. Thus, phonemes are defined in terms of the sounds that create meaning in a specific language. Each phoneme is produced by the position or the movement of structures within the vocal apparatus, which produce patterns of pressure changes in the air which are called the **acoustic stimulus** or the **acoustic signal**.

Table 12.1

Major consonants and vowels of English and their phonetic symbols

	Consonants				Vowels	
p	*p*ull	s	*s*ip	i	h*ee*d	
b	*b*ull	z	*z*ip	I	h*i*d	
m	*m*an	r	*r*ip	e	b*ai*t	
w	*w*ill	š	*sh*ould	ɛ	h*ea*d	
f	*f*ill	ž	plea*s*ure	æ	h*a*d	
v	*v*et	č	*ch*op	u	wh*o*'d	
θ	*th*igh	ǰ	*g*yp	U	p*u*t	
ǒ	*th*y	y	*y*ip	ʌ	b*u*t	
t	*t*ie	k	*k*ale	o	b*oa*t	
d	*d*ie	g	*g*ale	ɔ	b*ough*t	
n	*n*ear	h	*h*ail	a	h*o*t	
l	*l*ear	ŋ	si*ng*	ə	s*o*fa	
				ɨ	man*y*	

The Acoustic Signal: Patterns of Pressure Changes

The acoustic signal for speech is created by air that is pushed up from the lungs past the vocal cords and into the vocal tract. The sound that is produced depends on the shape of the vocal tract as air is pushed through it. The shape of the vocal tract is altered by moving the **articulators**, which include structures such as the tongue, lips, teeth, jaw, and soft palate (Figure 12.1).

Let's first consider the production of vowels. Vowels are produced by vibration of the vocal cords, and the specific sounds of each vowel are created by changing the overall shape of the vocal tract. This change in shape changes the resonant frequency of the vocal tract and produces peaks of pressure change at a number of different frequencies (Figure 12.2). The frequencies at which these peaks occur are called **formants**.

Each vowel sound has a characteristic series of formants. The first formant has the lowest frequency. The second formant is the next highest, and so on. The formants for the vowel /ae/ are shown on a display called a **sound spectrogram** in Figure 12.3. The sound spectrogram indicates the pattern of

Phoneme symbol	Outline of vocal tract traced from x-ray picture of mouth	Pressure changes

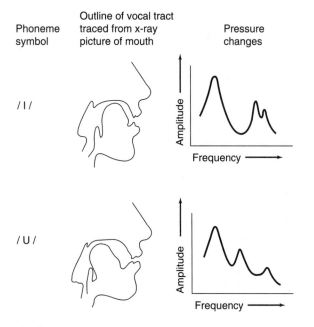

/ I /

/ U /

Figure 12.2

Left: The shape of the vocal tract for the vowels /I/ and /oo/. Right: The amplitude of the pressure changes produced for each vowel. The peaks in the pressure changes are the formants. Each vowel sound has a characteristic pattern of formants which is determined by the shape of the vocal tract for that vowel. (Adapted from Denes & Pinson, 1992.)

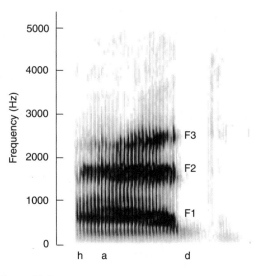

Figure 12.3

Spectrogram of the word had *showing the first (F1), second (F2), and third (F3) formants for the vowel /ae/. (Spectrogram courtesy of Kerry Green.)*

frequencies and intensities over time that make up the acoustic signal. Frequency is indicated on the vertical axis, time on the horizontal axis, and intensity is indicated by the darkness, with more darkness indicating greater intensity. From Figure 12.3 we can see that /ae/ has formants at 500, 1,700, and 2,500 Hz. The vertical lines in the spectrogram are pressure oscillations caused by vibrations of the vocal cord.

Consonants are produced by a constriction or closing of the vocal tract. To illustrate how different consonants are produced, let's focus on the sounds /d/ and /f/. Make these sounds and notice what your tongue, lips, and teeth are doing. As you produce the sound /d/, you place your tongue against the ridge above your upper teeth (the alveolar ridge of Figure 12.1) and then release a slight rush of air as you move your tongue

away from the alveolar ridge (try it). As you produce the sound /f/, you place your bottom lip against your upper front teeth and then push air between the lips and the teeth.

These movements of the tongue, lips, and other articulators create patterns of energy in the acoustic signal that we can observe on the sound spectrogram. For example, the spectrogram for the sentence "Roy read the will" shown in Figure 12.4 shows aspects of the signal associated with vowels and consonants. For example, the three horizontal bands marked F1, F2, and F3 are the three formants associated with the /e/ sound of *read*. Rapid shifts in frequency preceding or following formants are called **formant transitions** and are associated with consonants. For example, T2 and T3 are formant transitions associated with the /r/ of *read*.

Now that we know how speech is produced and how it is represented on a speech spectrogram, we are ready to look at some of the problems that we must solve in order to understand speech perception.

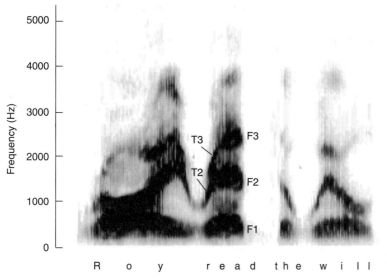

Figure 12.4
Spectgrogram of the sentence "Roy read the will," showing formants such as F1, F2, and F3, and formant transitions such as T2 and T3. (Spectrogram courtesy of Kerry Green.)

PROBLEMS POSED BY THE SPEECH STIMULUS

The main problem facing researchers who are trying to understand speech perception is that the relationships between the acoustic signal and the sounds we hear are extremely complex. One reason for this complexity is that the acoustic signal is not neatly separated into individual words. This lack of separation between the signal for each word creates the **segmentation problem**: How do we perceptually segregate this continuous stream into individual words?

The Segmentation Problem

In Chapter 5 we saw that one task of the visual system is segmentation—separating a visual scene into individual objects. The auditory system faces a similar problem for speech—separating speech stimuli into individual words.

Just as we effortlessly see objects when we look at a visual scene, we usually have little trouble perceiving individual words as we have a conversation with another person. But when we look at the speech spectrogram, we see that the acoustic signal is continuous, with either no physical breaks in the signal or breaks that don't necessarily correspond to the breaks we perceive between words (Figure 12.5). The fact that there are usually no spaces between words becomes obvious when you listen to someone speaking a foreign

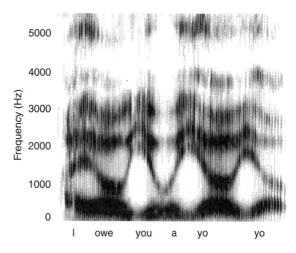

Figure 12.5
Spectrogram of "I owe you a yo-yo." This spectrogram does not contain pauses or breaks that correspond to the words that we hear. The absence of breaks in the acoustic signal creates the segmentation problem. (Spectrogram courtesy of David Pisoni.)

Speech Perception

language. To someone who is unfamiliar with that language, the words seem to speed by in an unbroken string. However, to a speaker of that language, the words seem separated, just as the words of your native language seem separated to you. The solution to the segmentation problem involves determining how we divide the continuous stream of the acoustic signal into a series of individual words.

The Variability Problem

Another problem posed by the speech stimulus is that the acoustic signal is so variable that there is no simple correspondence between the acoustic signal and individual phonemes. This variability comes from the following sources.

Variability from a Phoneme's Context   The acoustic signal associated with a phoneme changes depending on its context. For example, look at Figure 12.6, which shows spectrograms for the sounds /di/ and /du/. These are smoothed hand-drawn spectrograms that show the two most important characteristics of the sounds: the formants and the formant transitions. Since formants are associated with vowels, we know that the formants at 200 and 2,600 Hz are the acoustic signal for the vowel /i/ in /di/ and that the formants at 200 and 600 Hz are the acoustic signal for the vowel /u/ in /du/.

Since the formants are the acoustic signals for the vowels in /di/ and /du/, the formant transitions that precede the formants must be the signal for the consonant /d/. But notice that the formant transitions for the second (higher frequency) formants of /di/ and /du/ are different. For /di/, the formant transition starts at about 2,200 Hz and rises to meet the second formant. For /du/, the second transition starts at about 1,100 Hz and falls to meet the second formant. Thus, even though we perceive the same /d/ sound in /di/ and /du/, the acoustic signals associated with these sounds are different.

This effect of context occurs because of the way speech is produced. The articulators are constantly moving as we talk, so the shape of the vocal tract for a particular phoneme is influenced by the shapes for the phonemes that both precede it and follow it. This overlap between the articulation of neighboring

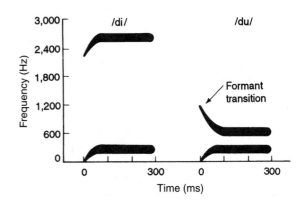

Figure 12.6
Hand-drawn spectrograms for /di/ and /du/. (From Liberman et al., 1967.)

phonemes is called **coarticulation**. You can demonstrate coarticulation to yourself by noting how you produce phonemes in different contexts. For example, say *bat* and *boot*. When you say *bat*, your lips are unrounded, but when you say *boot*, your lips are rounded, even during the initial /b/ sound. Thus, even though the /b/ is the same in both words, you articulate them differently. In this example, the articulation of /oo/ in *boot* overlaps the articulation of /b/, causing the lips to be rounded even before the /oo/ sound is actually produced.

The fact that we perceive the sound of a phoneme as the same, even though the acoustic signal is changed by coarticulation, is an example of perceptual constancy. This term may be familiar to you from our observations of constancy phenomena in the sense of vision, such as color constancy (we perceive an object's chromatic color as constant even when the wavelength distribution of the illumination changes) and size constancy (we perceive an object's size as constant even when the size of its image changes on our retina). Perceptual constancy in speech perception is similar. We perceive the sound of a particular phoneme as constant even when the phoneme appears in different contexts that change its acoustic signal.

Variability from Different Speakers   People say the same words in a variety of different ways. Some people's voices are high pitched, and some are low pitched; people speak with accents; some talk extremely rapidly and others speak e-x-t-r-e-m-e-l-y s-l-o-w-l-y. These wide variations in speech in different speakers mean that for different speakers a particular phoneme or word can have very different acoustic signals.

Speakers also introduce variability by their sloppy pronunciation. For example, say the following sentence at the speed you would use in talking to a friend: "This was a best buy." How did you say "best buy"? Did you pronounce the /t/ of best, or did you say "bes buy"? What about "She is a bad girl"? While saying this rapidly, notice whether your tongue hits the top of your mouth as you say the /d/ in bad.

Many people omit the /d/ and say "ba girl." Finally, what about "Did you go to the store?" Did you say "did you" or "dijoo"? You have your own ways of producing various words and phonemes, and other people have theirs. Analysis of how people actually speak has determined that there are 50 different ways to produce the word "the" (Waldrop, 1988).

That people do not usually articulate each word individually in conversational speech is reflected in the spectrograms in Figure 12.7. The spectrogram in Figure 12.7a is for the question "What are you doing?" spoken slowly and distinctly, whereas the spectrogram in Figure 12.7b is for the same question taken from

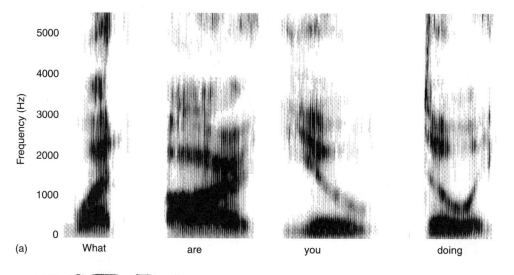

(a) What   are   you   doing   ?

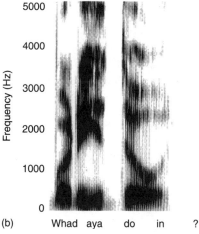

(b) Whad aya do in ?

Figure 12.7

(a) Spectrogram of "What are you doing?" pronounced slowly and distinctly. (b) Spectrogram of "What are you doing?" as pronounced in conversational speech. (Spectrograms courtesy of David Pisoni.)

conversational speech, in which "What are you doing?" becomes "Whad'aya doin'?" This difference shows up clearly in the spectrogram, which indicates that, although the first and last words (*what* and *doing*) create similar patterns in the two spectrograms, the pauses between words are absent or are much less obvious in the spectrogram of Figure 12.7b, and the middle of this spectrogram is completely changed, with a number of speech sounds missing.

The variability in the acoustic signal that is caused by coarticulation, by different speakers, and by sloppy pronunciation creates a problem for the listener: He or she must somehow transform the information contained in this highly variable acoustic signal into familiar words. This variability problem, combined with the segmentation problem, are the reasons that it has been so difficult to design machines that can recognize speech. But humans somehow recognize speech even in the face of what might seem to be extreme difficulties. Although researchers don't yet know exactly how we do it, research conducted over the past 50 years has begun to unravel the mystery of how humans perceive speech. We will describe this research by first considering stimulus dimensions of speech perception and then considering cognitive dimensions of speech perception.

STIMULUS DIMENSIONS OF SPEECH PERCEPTION

WebTUTOR   Our goal in the remainder of this chapter is to highlight our current state of knowledge of the mechanisms involved in speech perception. First, we focus on how speech perception researchers have studied relationships between the acoustic stimulus and the perception of speech.

The Search for Invariant Acoustic Cues: Matching Physical Energy and Phonemes

One of the ongoing projects of speech perception research has been to identify invariant acoustic cues in the acoustic signal. An **invariant acoustic cue** is a feature of the acoustic signal that is associated with a particular phoneme and that remains constant even when phonemes appear in different contexts or are spoken by different speakers. Since invariant acoustic cues are not that obvious from the normal speech spectrogram, researchers searching for these invariant cues have devised new ways of displaying and analyzing the acoustic signal.

One way of displaying the acoustic signal is called the **short-term spectrum**. A short-term spectrum creates a detailed picture of the frequencies that occur within a short segment of time. For example, the short-term spectrum on the left of Figure 12.8 shows the frequencies that occur during the first 26 ms of the sound /ga/ along with the regular spectrogram for /ga/, on the right. The peak in the short-term spectrum labeled a, and the minimum, labeled b, correspond to the dark and light energy bands a and b at the very beginning of the spectrogram. The advantage of the short-term spectrum is that it provides a precise and detailed picture of the acoustic signal. A sequence of short-term spectra can be combined to create a **running spectral display** that shows how the frequencies in the auditory signal change over time (Figure 12.9).

Researchers have identified some invariant acoustic cues in these running spectral displays. The invariance of these cues has been demonstrated by showing that people can identify characteristics of phonemes based on these cues, even in different contexts (Blumstein & Stevens, 1979; Kewley-Port, 1983; Kewley-Port & Luce, 1984; Searle, Jacobson, & Rayment, 1979; Stevens & Blumstein, 1978, 1981). For example, a low-frequency peak that continues in succeeding frames (marked with V in Figure 12.9) indicates that the vocal cords are vibrating. Notice that it occurs for /da/ but not for /pi/. The listener can, therefore, use this information to help differentiate between these two sounds.

Although the search for invariant acoustic cues has yielded some encouraging results, it hasn't been possible to identify invariant cues for all of the speech sounds (Nygaard & Pisoni, 1995). (See also Sussman, Hoemeke, & Ahmed, 1993; Sussman, McCaffrey, & Matthews, 1991, for additional evidence for invariant acoustic cues.) Thus, the search for invariant cues is continuing, but researchers are also looking for other

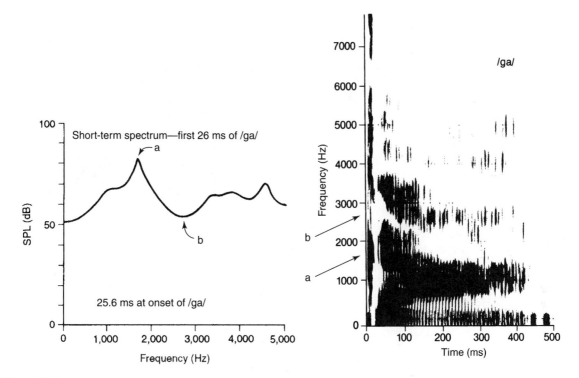

Figure 12.8

Left: A short-term spectrum of the acoustic energy in the first 26 ms of the phoneme /ga/. Right: Sound spectrogram of the same phoneme. The peak in the short-term spectrum marked a corresponds to the dark band of energy marked a in the spectrogram. The minimum in the short-term spectrum marked b corresponds to the light area marked b in the spectrogram. Note that the spectrogram on the right shows the energy for the entire 500-ms duration of the sound, whereas the short-term spectrum only shows the first 26 ms at the beginning of this signal. (Courtesy of James Sawusch.)

connections between the speech signal and speech perception.

Categorical Perception: An Example of Constancy in Speech Perception

In looking for connections between the speech signal and speech perception, researchers have discovered a phenomenon called **categorical perception**, which creates two categories of sounds from a wide range of acoustic signals. We will use a specific example to explain what this means.

The example we will describe involves varying a characteristic of the acoustic signal called **voice onset time (VOT)**. Voice onset time is the time delay between when the sound begins and when the vocal cords begin vibrating. We can illustrate this delay by comparing the spectrograms for the sounds /da/ and /ta/ in Figure 12.10. We can see from these spectrograms that the time between the beginning of the sound /da/ and the beginning of the vocal cord vibrations (indicated by the presence of vertical striations in the spectrogram) is 17 ms for /da/ and 91 ms for /ta/. Thus, /da/ has a short VOT and /ta/ has a long VOT.

By using computers, researchers have created sound stimuli in which the VOT is varied in small steps from short to long. When they vary VOT, using stimuli like the ones in Figure 12.10, and ask subjects to indicate what sound they hear, the subjects report

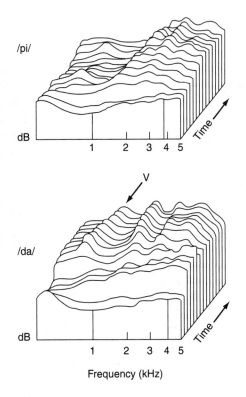

/pi/

dB

1 2 3 4 5

V

/da/

dB

1 2 3 4 5

Frequency (kHz)

Figure 12.9
Running spectral displays for /pi/ and /da/. These displays are made up of a sequence of short-term spectra like the one in Figure 12.8. Each of these spectra is displaced 5 ms on the time axis, so that each step we move along this axis indicates the frequencies present in the next 5 ms. The low-frequency peak (V) in the /da/ display is a cue for vibration of the vocal cords. (From Kewley-Port & Luce, 1984.)

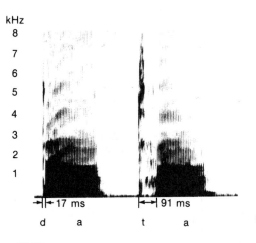

kHz
8
7
6
5
4
3
2
1

17 ms   91 ms

d   a   t   a

Figure 12.10
Spectrograms for /da/ and /ta/. The voice onset time—the time between the beginning of the sound and the onset of vocal cord vibration—is indicated at the beginning of the spectrogram for each sound. (Spectrogram courtesy of Ron Cole.)

hearing only two sounds, /da/ or /ta/, even though a large number of stimuli with different VOTs are presented.

This result is shown in Figure 12.11 (Eimas & Corbit, 1973). At short VOTs, subjects report that they hear /da/, and they continue reporting this even when the VOT is increased. But when the VOT reaches about 35 ms, their perception abruptly changes, so at VOTs above 40 ms, they report hearing /ta/. The VOT when the perception changes from /da/ to /ta/ is called the **phonetic boundary**. The key result of the categorical perception experiment is that, even though the VOT is changed continuously

across a wide range, the listener perceives only two categories: /da/ on one side of the phonetic boundary and /ta/ on the other side.

Once we have demonstrated categorical perception using the procedure above, we can further confirm the existence of just two categories across the range of VOTs by running a discrimination test, in which we present two stimuli with different VOTs and ask the subject whether they sound the same or different. When we present two stimuli that are on the same side of the phonetic boundary, such as 10 and 30 ms VOTs, the listener says they sound the same (Figure 12.12). However, when we present two stimuli that are on opposite sides of the phonetic boundary, such as 30 and 50 ms VOTs, the listener says they sound different. The fact that all stimuli on the same side of the phonetic boundary are perceived as identical is an example of perceptual constancy (Figure 12.13). If this constancy did not exist, we would perceive different sounds every time we changed the VOT. Instead, we experience one sound on each side of the phonetic boundary. This simplifies our perception of phonemes and helps us more easily perceive the wide variety of sounds in our environment.

Chapter 12

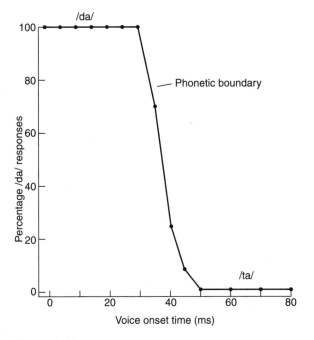

Figure 12.11

The results of a categorical perception experiment indicate that /da/ is perceived for VOTs to the left of the phonetic boundary, and that /ta/ is perceived at VOTs to the right of the phonetic boundary. (From Eimas & Corbit, 1973.) (Listen to WebTutor, Categorical Perception.)

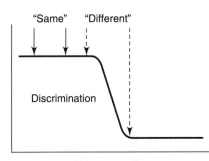

Figure 12.12

In the discrimination part of a categorical perception experiment, two stimuli are presented, and the subject is asked to indicate whether they are the same or different. The typical result is that two stimuli with VOTs on the same side of the phonetic boundary (solid arrows) are judged to be the same, and that two stimuli on different sides of the phonetic boundary (dashed arrows) are judged to be different.

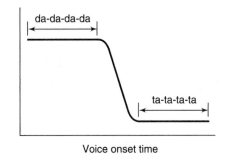

Figure 12.13

Perceptual constancy occurs when all stimuli on one side of the phonetic boundary are perceived to be in the same category even though their VOT is changed over a substantial range. This diagram symbolizes the constancy observed in the Eimas and Corbit (1973) experiment, in which /da/ was heard on one side of the boundary and /ta/ on the other side.

The Multimodal Nature of Speech Perception: Information from Hearing and Vision

Another property of speech perception is that it is **multimodal**. That is, our perception of speech can be influenced by information from a number of different senses. The "Across the Senses" section at the end of the chapter describes how speech can be perceived through touch using a method called Tadoma. Speech perception can also be influenced by visual information, as demonstrated by an effect called the **McGurk effect**, after the man who first described it (McGurk & MacDonald, 1976).

The procedure for achieving the McGurk effect is illustrated in Figure 12.14. A subject observes a videotape showing a person making the lip movements for the sounds /ga-ga/. But as he receives this visual information, he simultaneously receives an auditory sound track, which is the acoustic signal that is usually heard as /ba-ba/. Despite the fact that the subject is receiving the acoustic signal for /ba-ba/, he actually hears the sounds /da-da/. This misperception is a striking perceptual effect in which subjects are convinced that the woman in the videotape is saying /da-da/ even though that stimulus is never actually present. If they close

Speech Perception

Figure 12.14

The McGurk effect. The woman's lips are moving as if she is saying /ga-ga/, but the actual sound being presented is /ba-ba/. The listener, however, reports hearing the sound /da-da/. If the listener closes his eyes, so that he no longer sees the woman's lips, he hears /ba-ba/. Thus, seeing the lips moving influences what the listener hears. (Experience the McGurk effect on WebTutor.)

their eyes, they hear /ba-ba/. If they open them, they hear /da-da/. Thus, although auditory energy is the major source of information for speech perception, visual information can also exert a strong influence on what we hear. This influence of vision on speech perception is called **audiovisual speech perception.** The McGurk effect is one example of audiovisual speech perception. Another example is the way people rou-

---

BRAIN SCAN
Activation of Auditory Cortex During Silent Lipreading

Two examples of interactions between speech perception and visual perception are the McGurk effect (above and pages 325–326) and the fact that speech perception is improved by watching a speaker's lips move, particularly in noisy surroundings (Dodd & Campbell, 1987).

A brain imaging study by Gemma Calvert and coworkers (1997) has investigated which brain areas are activated by this lipreading. In the "silent lipreading" condition, subjects watched a silent videotape of a person saying numbers and silently repeated, in their minds, each number they perceived from the person's mouth movements. In the "static" condition, subjects observed a videotape of a static face

and repeated the number "one" silently to themselves. When the brain activity, recorded by fMRI, was compared from these two conditions, more activity was observed in the silent lipreading condition than in the static condition in areas of visual cortex associated with movement (since the lips of the face in the videotape were moving) and with areas in temporal cortex that are normally activated by actually hearing speech. The fact that visual cues to speech can activate auditory areas, even though no auditory stimuli are present, may be related to the physiological mechanism responsible for our ability to use perceptions of lip movements to help us perceive speech.

Chapter 12

tinely use information provided by the speaker's lip movements to help understand speech in a noisy environment. See Summary Table 12.1 for an overview of the material we have covered so far.

COGNITIVE DIMENSIONS OF SPEECH PERCEPTION

Our discussion so far in this chapter has emphasized the relationship between speech perception and the stimuli we receive. But our perception of speech depends on more than just the energy that reaches our receptors. There is a cognitive dimension to speech perception as well, which depends on information stored in the listener's memory about the nature of language and the voice characteristics of specific speakers. The following demonstration illustrates how our knowledge of the meanings of words

enables us to perceive these words even when the stimulus is incomplete.

DEMONSTRATION

Perceiving Degraded Sentences

Read the following sentences:

(1) M*R* H*D * L*TTL* L*MB I*S FL**C* W*S WH*T* *S SN*W
(2) TH* S*N *S N*T SH*N*NG T*D**
(3) S*M* W**DS *R* EA*I*R T* U*D*R*T*N* T*A* *T*E*S   ●

Your ability to read the sentences, even though up to half of the letters have been eliminated, was aided by your knowledge of English (Denes & Pinson, 1993). This is an example of top-down processing that

---

SUMMARY TABLE 12.1

The Speech Stimulus

Speech is specified in terms of units called phonemes, which are the basic building blocks of words. The stimulus can also be specified in terms of the patterns of pressure changes in sound spectrograms, which display formants associated with vowels and other patterns associated with consonants.

Problems Posed by the Speech Stimulus

The relationship between the speech stimulus and perception is not a simple one. Among the problems the speech system must solve in order to decode the speech stimulus are the segmentation problem, since the speech signal is continuous, and the variability of the speech stimulus, which is caused by coarticulation and across-speaker variability.

Invariant Cues

It has been difficult to find invariant acoustic cues—characteristics of the speech stimulus that are associated with a particular sound and remain constant under a number of different conditions.

Categorical Perception

Categorical perception occurs in speech when a wide range of sound stimuli result in the same perception. This is an example of perceptual constancy.

Multimodal Nature of Speech Perception

Speech perception can be influenced by information from a number of different senses. An example of this is the McGurk effect, in which visual information provided by seeing a speaker's mouth move can change the perception of the sound stimulus.

Brain Scan: Activity in Auditory Cortex During Silent Lipreading

fMRI measurements indicate that watching a person's lips make speech movements activates the auditory areas of the brain even though no sound is present. This provides a physiological mechanism for auditory–visual interactions.

Speech Perception

we have discussed in connection with visual perception (see page 8): Knowledge brought to the situation by the perceiver is used to supplement the bottom-up information provided by stimulation of the receptors (Figure 12.15). One example of the effect of top-down processing in speech perception is provided by the process of segmentation, in which the speaker breaks the continuous acoustic signal into individual words.

Meaning and Segmentation

To help you appreciate the role of meaning in achieving segmentation, do the following demonstration.

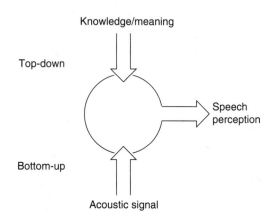

Figure 12.15
Speech perception is the result of top-down processing (based on knowledge and meaning) and bottom-up processing (based on the acoustic signal) working together.

DEMONSTRATION

Segmenting Strings of Sounds

1. Read the following words: Anna Mary Candy Lights Since Imp Pulp Lay Things. Now that you've read the words, what do they mean? If you think that this is a list of unconnected words beginning with the names of two women, Anna and Mary, you're right; but if you read this series of words a little faster, ignoring the spaces between the words on the page, you may hear a connected sentence that does not begin with the names Anna and Mary. (For the answer see the bottom of page 424—but don't peek until you've tried reading the words rapidly.)

2. Read the following phrase fairly rapidly to a few people: "In mud eels are, in clay none are," and ask them to write the phrase. ●

If you succeeded in creating a new sentence from the series of words in the first demonstration, you did so by changing the segmentation, and this change was achieved by your knowledge of the meaning of the sounds. When Raj Reddy (1976) asked subjects to write their perception of "In mud eels are, in clay none are," he obtained responses like "In muddies, sar, in clay nanar"; "In may deals are, en clainanar"; and "In madel sar, in claynanar." In the absence of any context, some of Reddy's listeners had difficulty figuring out what the phrase meant and therefore forced their own interpretation on the sounds they heard. Had the listeners known that the passage was taken from a book about amphibians, their knowledge about possible meanings of the words would have facilitated segmentation and increased probability of their decoding the sentence correctly.

Pairs of words that flow together in speech also exemplify how segmentation results from meaning: "Big girl" can be interpreted as "big Earl," and the interpretation you pick will probably depend on the overall meaning of the sentence in which these words appear. This example is similar to the familiar "I scream, you scream, we all scream for ice cream" that many people learn as children. The acoustic stimuli for "I scream" and "ice cream" are identical, so the different segmentations must be achieved by the meaning of the sentence in which these words appear.

Top-down processing not only helps us to segment the acoustic signal, but also helps us to recognize phonemes and words. We will now describe some experiments that show how meaningful contexts can enhance a listener's ability to recognize phonemes and words.

Meaning and Phoneme Perception

A large amount of research has shown that it is easier to perceive phonemes that appear in a meaningful context. Philip Rubin, M. T. Turvey, and Peter Van Gelder (1976) showed that meaning enhances a listener's ability to recognize phonemes by presenting a series of short words like SIN, BAT, and LEG, or nonwords like JUM, BAF, and TEG, and asking subjects to respond by pressing a key as rapidly as possible whenever they heard a sound that began with /b/. On the average, subjects took 631 milliseconds to respond to the nonwords and 580 ms to respond to the real words. Thus, when a phoneme is at the beginning of a real word, it is identified about 8 percent faster than if it is at the beginning of a meaningless syllable.

The effect of meaning on the perception of phonemes was demonstrated in another way by Richard Warren (1970), who had subjects listen to a recording of the sentence "The state governors met with their respective legislatures convening in the capital city." Warren replaced the first /s/ in "legislatures" with the sound of a cough and told his subjects that they should indicate where in the sentence the cough occurred. No subject identified the correct position of the cough, and, even more significantly, none of the subjects noticed that the /s/ in "legislatures" was missing. This effect, which Warren called the **phonemic restoration effect**, was experienced even by students and staff in the psychology department who knew that the /s/ was missing.

Warren not only demonstrated the phonemic restoration effect but also showed that it can be influenced by the meaning of words following the missing phoneme. For example, the last word of the phrase "There was time to *ave . . ." (where the * indicates the presence of a cough or some other sound) could be shave, save, wave, or rave, but subjects heard the word wave if the remainder of the sentence had to do with saying goodbye to a departing friend.

The phonemic restoration effect was used by Arthur Samuel (1981) to show that speech perception is determined both by a context that produces expectations in the listener (top-down processing) and also by the nature of the acoustic signal (bottom-up pro-

cessing). Samuel demonstrated top-down processing by masking various phonemes in sentences with a white-noise masker, like the sound produced by a television set tuned to a nonbroadcasting channel, and showing that longer words increase the likelihood of the phonemic restoration effect. Apparently, subjects use the additional context provided by the long word to help identify the masked phoneme. Further evidence for the importance of context is Samuel's finding that more restoration occurs for a real word like prOgress (where the capital letter indicates the masked phoneme) than for a similar "pseudoword" like crOgress (Samuel, 1990).

Samuel demonstrated bottom-up processing by showing that restoration is better if the masking sound and the masked phoneme sound similar. Thus, phonemic restoration is more likely to occur for a phoneme such as /s/, which is rich in high-frequency acoustic energy, if the mask also contains a large proportion of high-frequency energy.

What's happening in phonemic restoration, according to Samuel, is that we use the context to develop some expectation of what a sound will be. But before we actually perceive the sound, its presence must be confirmed by the presence of a sound that is similar to it. If the white-noise mask contains frequencies that make it sound similar to the phoneme we are expecting, phonemic restoration occurs, and we are likely to hear the phoneme. If the mask does not sound similar, phonemic restoration is less likely to occur (Samuel, 1990).

Meaning and Word Perception

Meaningfulness also makes it easier to perceive whole words. An early demonstration of this effect by George Miller and Steven Isard (1963) showed that words are more intelligible when heard in the context of a grammatical sentence than when presented as items in a list of unconnected words. They demonstrated this by creating three kinds of stimuli: (1) normal grammatical sentences, such as *Gadgets simplify work around the house*; (2) anomalous sentences, that follow the rules of grammar but make no sense, such as *Gadgets kill passengers from the eyes*;

and (3) ungrammatical strings of words, such as *Between gadgets highways passengers the steal*.

Miller and Isard used a technique called **shadowing**, in which they presented these sentences to subjects through earphones and asked them to repeat aloud what they were hearing. The subjects reported normal sentences with an accuracy of 89 percent, but their accuracy fell to 79 percent for the anomalous sentences, and 56 percent for the ungrammatical strings.

The differences among the three types of stimuli became even greater when the subjects heard the stimuli in the presence of a background noise. For example, at a moderately high level of background noise, accuracy was 63 percent for the normal sentences, 22 percent for the anomalous sentences, and only 3 percent for the ungrammatical strings of words.

This result is telling us that when words are arranged in a meaningful pattern, we can perceive them more easily. But most people don't realize that it is their knowledge of the nature of their language that helps them fill in sounds and words that might be difficult to hear. For example, our knowledge of permissible word structures tells us that ANT, TAN, and NAT are all permissible sequences of letters in English, but that TQN or NQT cannot be English words.

At the level of the sentence, our knowledge of the rules of grammar tells us that *the cat is weird* is a permissible sentence, but *is weird cat the* is not a permissible sentence. Since most of our everyday experience is with meaningful words and grammatically correct sentences, we are continually using our knowledge of what is permissible in our language to help us understand what is being said. This becomes particularly important when listening under less than ideal conditions such as in noisy environments, or if the speaker's voice quality or accent is difficult to understand (see also Salasoo & Pisoni, 1985).

All of these results support the idea that the knowledge a listener brings to a situation helps the listener decode the acoustic signal into phonemes and meaningful words and sentences. In addition, there is also evidence that a listener's experience in listening to specific speakers can enhance his or her ability to perceive what is being said.

Speaker Characteristics

When you're having a conversation, hearing a lecture, or listening to dialogue in a movie, you usually focus on determining the meaning of what is being said. But as you are taking in these messages, you are also, perhaps without realizing it, taking in characteristics of the speaker's voice. These characteristics, which are called **indexical characteristics**, carry information about speakers such as their age, gender, where they are from, their emotional state, and whether they are being sarcastic or serious. Consider, for example, the following joke:

> A linguistics professor was lecturing to his class one day. "In English," he said, "A double negative forms a positive. In some languages, though, such as Russian, a double negative is still a negative. However, there is no language wherein a double positive can form a negative."
>
> A voice from the back of the room piped up, "Yeah, right."

This joke is humorous because "Yeah, right" contains two positive words that, despite the linguistics professor's statement, produce a negative statement that most people who are aware of contemporary English usage would interpret as "I disagree" (or "No way," to use a more colloquial expression.) The point of this example is not just that "Yeah, right" can mean "I disagree," but that the meaning of this phrase is determined by our knowledge of current English usage and also (if we were actually listening to the student's remark) by the speaker's tone of voice, which in this case would be highly sarcastic.

The speaker's tone of voice is one factor that helps listeners determine the meaning of what is being said. But most research on indexical characteristics has focused on how speech perception is influenced by the speaker's identity. Thomas Palmeri,

Answer to question on page 422: "An American delights in simple play things."

Stephen Goldinger, and David Pisoni (1993) demonstrated the effect of speaker identity by having subjects listen to a sequence of words. After each word, the subject indicated whether the word was a new word (this was the first time it appeared) or an old word (it had appeared previously in the sequence). They found that subjects reacted more rapidly and were more accurate when the same speaker said all of the words than if different speakers said the words. This means that the listeners are taking in two levels of information about the word: (1) its meaning and (2) characteristics of the speaker's voice.

In another experiment that demonstrates the importance of the speaker's voice for speech perception, subjects listened to the voices of 10 different speakers. Following this training, the listeners were given a word intelligibility test to determine how well they could identify words spoken by the speakers. When the results of this test were compared to the performance of a control group who were also trained to recognize the same 10 speakers but who heard unfamiliar speakers for the intelligibility test, it was found that those hearing the familiar speakers performed better on the test (Nygaard, Sommers, & Pisoni, 1994).

In order for performance to be better with the familiar speakers, the voice characteristics of these speakers would have to be stored in the listener's long-term memory. When presented with the word intelligibility test, listeners retrieve this information about the familiar speakers from their memory and use it to help them identify the words.

From the results of this experiment and the others we have discussed, we can conclude that speech perception depends both on the bottom-up information provided by the acoustic signal and on the top-down information provided by the meanings of words and sentences, the listener's knowledge of the rules of grammar, and information that the listener has about characteristics of the speaker's voice.

We can appreciate the interdependence of the acoustical and meaningful units of speech when we realize that, although we use the meaning to help us to understand the acoustic signal, the acoustic signal is the starting point for determining the meaning. Look at it this way: There may be enough information in my sloppy handwriting so that a person using bottom-up processing can decipher it solely on the basis of the squiggles on the page, but my handwriting is much easier to decipher if, by using top-down processing, the person takes the meanings of the words into account. And just as previous experience in hearing a particular person's voice makes it easier to understand that person later, previous experience in reading my handwriting would make it easier to read the squiggles on the page. Speech perception apparently works in a similar way. Although most of the information is contained in the acoustic signal, taking meaning and indexical properties into account makes understanding speech much easier.

THE PHYSIOLOGY OF SPEECH PERCEPTION

Researchers have investigated the physiology of speech perception in a number of different ways: (1) by recording neural responses to both natural speech stimuli and stimuli resembling parts of the speech signal; (2) by studying patients who, because of brain damage, have difficulty understanding or producing speech; and (3) by recording the change in blood flow in different parts of the brain during speech perception.

Neural Responses to Speech and Complex Sounds

Most of the research explaining the neural response to speech stimuli has focused on how neurons in the auditory nerve respond to speech sounds. For example, Figure 12.16 shows the short-term spectrum for the sound /da/ and the firing pattern for a representative population of cat auditory nerve fibers with low, medium, and high characteristic frequencies. (Remember from Chapter 10 that the neuron's characteristic frequency is the frequency to which this neuron responds best.) The match between the speech stimulus and the firing of a number of neurons in the auditory nerve indicates that information in the speech stimulus is represented by the pattern

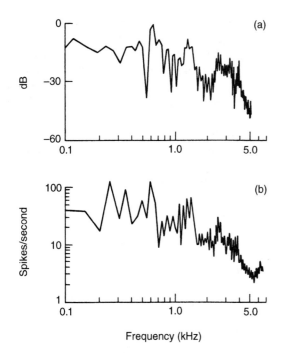

Figure 12.16

(a) Short-term spectrum for /da/. This curve indicates the energy distribution in /da/ between 20 and 40 ms after the beginning of the signal. (b) Nerve firing of a population of cat auditory nerve fibers to the same stimulus. (From Sachs, Young, & Miller, 1981.)

of firing of auditory nerve fibers (also see Delgutte & Kiang, 1984a,b).

Another approach to studying the relation between neural responding and speech perception is to look for neurons that respond to parts of the speech stimulus, such as the formant transitions and formants shown in Figure 12.4. Neurons have been found in a number of animals, including bats, birds, frogs, and cats, that respond best to combinations of tones that, like speech stimuli, have specific timing and frequencies (Fuzessery & Feng, 1983; Margoliash, 1983; Nelson, Erulkar, & Bryan, 1966; Olsen & Suga, 1991a,b). Most significantly, neurons have been found in an area of the monkey cortex that is analogous to human speech areas, which respond to recordings of monkey "calls" (Rauschecker, Tian, & Hauser, 1995). The existence of these neurons in the monkey as well as the other animals opens the possibility that there may be neurons in the human cortex that respond best to complex, speechlike stimuli.

Localization of Function

It has been known for over 150 years that the brain operates according to a principle called **localization of function**—specific functions are localized in specific areas of the brain. One form of localization is lateralization—a particular function is processed more strongly in either the left hemisphere or the right hemisphere. For most people, much of speech is processed in specific areas in the left hemisphere of the brain (Figure 12.17) (although some linguistic information is processed in the right hemisphere; Chairello, 1991).

Damage to **Broca's area**, in the frontal lobe, causes difficulty in speaking, and damage to Wernicke's area, in the temporal lobe, causes difficulty in understanding speech (Geschwind, 1979). These difficulties in speaking and understanding are forms of **aphasia** (Kolb & Whishaw, 1985).

There are numerous forms of aphasia, with the specific symptoms depending on the area and extent of the damage. The form that involves speech perception is called **Wernicke's aphasia**—an inability to

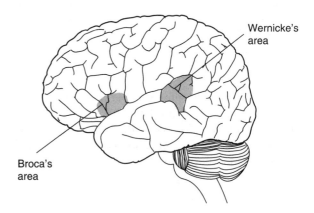

Figure 12.17

Broca's and Wernicke's areas, which are specialized for language production and comprehension, are located in the left hemisphere of the brain in most people.

comprehend words or arrange sounds into coherent speech. Wernicke's aphasia is a form of fluent aphasia, so called because people with this disorder can produce fluent speech, although their production often consists of meaningless strings of words and words in which phonemes are confused, which has been described as "word salad."

We can understand the basis of the problem in Wernicke's aphasia by considering the problem native Japanese speakers have in discriminating between /l/ and /r/. Native Japanese speakers are not able to distinguish /l/ from /r/ when they hear English, because the Japanese they heard spoken when they were infants did not distinguish between the sounds /l/ and /r/. Thus, the necessary templates for these two sounds did not develop in their brains, and as adults they lack the physiological mechanisms to distinguish between these two sounds (see "Plasticity of Perception," page 429). It has been suggested that people with Wernicke's aphasia have a similar problem—because of their brain damage, they cannot isolate phonemes or classify them into known phonemic systems (Kolb & Whishaw, 1985).

Research that used positron emission tomography (PET) on humans to compare brain activation during the perception of pitches to activation during the perception of speech stimuli has shown that pitch stimuli activate areas in the right hemisphere but that speech stimuli activate areas in the left hemisphere (Zatorre et al., 1992). In addition to physiological evidence of the lateralization of speech perception, psychophysical experiments indicate that speech stimuli are more easily processed when presented through earphones to the right ear than when they are presented through earphones to the left ear. Since signals from the right ear are sent preferentially to the left hemisphere, this right-ear preference indicates that most aspects of speech stimuli are processed in the left hemisphere (Kimura, 1961).

IS SPEECH "SPECIAL"?

Some researchers working in the field of speech perception think that there is something special about speech perception that sets it apart from the perception of other auditory stimuli. The idea of a mechanism that is specialized for the perception of speech has its appeal, especially when we remember how the visual system operates. We know that there are nuclei in the visual system that are specialized to process information about different qualities, such as color, depth, and movement (Casagrande, 1994). In addition, there are neurons that are specialized to respond to complex visual stimuli such as faces (Perrett et al., 1992). This evidence from vision, along with the fact that language is processed in specific areas of the cortex, makes it seem reasonable that there could be a specialized mechanism that exists especially to process speech stimuli.

The idea that there is a specialized mechanism for speech is, however, not universally accepted by all speech perception researchers. Some researchers feel that while the speech signal may be extremely complex, the perception of this signal can be explained by regular auditory mechanisms.

The question of whether speech is "special" or if it is served by the same auditory mechanism that serves other auditory stimuli has generated a voluminous amount of research over the more than 30 years since the idea of a special speech mechanism was proposed (Liberman et al., 1967). To illustrate the kinds of evidence that have been presented on both sides of this question, we will consider a phenomenon called duplex perception that was originally introduced to support the idea that speech is special.

Duplex perception is created by splitting the acoustic signal for a sound into two parts and presenting one part to each ear. For example, Figure 12.18a shows the speech spectrogram for the sound /da/, which consists of three formant transitions and their formants. Alvin Liberman and Ignatius Mattingly (1989) created duplex perception by presenting just the transition for the third formant to the left ear (Figure 12.18b), and the rest of the signal, which is called the base, to the right ear (Figure 12.18c). What the listener hears is the speech sound /da/, from the combined acoustic signal from the left and right ears, and a nonspeech "chirp," from the third formant transition from the left ear.

According to proponents of the special speech mechanism, this experiment illustrates that there are

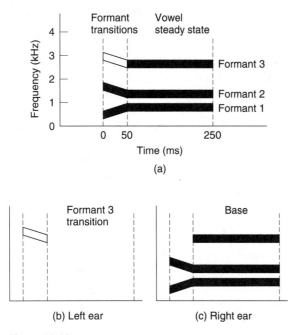

Figure 12.18
(a) The spectrogram for the sound /da/. Duplex perception occurs when the transition for the third formant (b) is presented to the left ear and the rest of the signal, called the base (c), is presented to the right ear. The listener perceives the sound /da/ in the right ear and a "chirp" in the left ear. See text for further details. (From Whalen & Lieberman, 1987.)

two kinds of perception of auditory stimuli: (1) a special speech mode, which combines the formant transition presented to the left ear and the base presented to the right ear to create the speech sound /da/; and (2) the auditory mode, which creates the nonspeech "chirp" sound from the high-frequency formant transition presented to the left ear.

Whalen and Liberman (1987) point out that the third-formant transition has a low intensity; the listener hears only the speech sound. The intensity of the third-formant transition must be increased to a higher level before the listener hears the nonspeech chirp sound as well. They concluded that this result

confirms the special nature of speech, since processing the formant transition as speech (which creates the speech sound) takes priority over processing it as a general auditory signal (which creates the chirp).

However, Carol Fowler and Lawrence Rosenblum (1990) challenged this interpretation of duplex perception by creating an effect similar to duplex perception from the sounds of a door slamming. They split a recording of a metal door closing into two parts, a high-frequency component at the beginning of the sound and a lower-frequency component at the end of the sound. These two components are similar to the formant transition and the base of the speech sound used by Liberman and Mattingly. When Fowler and Rosenblum presented the high-frequency component to the left ear and the low-frequency component to the right ear, subjects heard the sound of a metal door slamming (the combination of the left- and right-ear stimuli) plus a "shaking" sound like the sound made by sand or small pellets being shaken in a cup (the high-frequency left-ear stimulus). According to Fowler and Rosenblum, this demonstration of duplex perception with nonspeech stimuli means that duplex perception can occur for environmental stimuli in general, which includes speech, slamming doors, and other stimuli as well (see Hall & Pastore, 1992, for a musical example).

Which interpretation of duplex perception is correct? Is speech perception served by a mechanism that is specialized for the perception of speech or by a mechanism similar to the ones that help us perceive environmental sounds in general? Is our perception of speech analogous to our perception of faces, which involves a specialized cortical area that may have been shaped by our experience with faces? We don't yet know the answers to these questions, and there are many more experiments in addition to our duplex perception example above that present evidence on either side of this issue (Fowler & Dekle, 1991; Mattingly & Studdert-Kennedy, 1991). This debate, which is still unresolved, is a good example of how researchers have approached the same problem from different perspectives.

A finding that has emerged from studying speech perception in infants in different cultures is that when infants are very young, they can tell the difference between all of the phonemes that are used in the world's languages, but, by the age of one, they have lost the ability to tell the difference between some of these phonemes (Kuhl, 2000).

The classic example of this phenomenon is provided by Japanese children and adults (Strange, 1995). Six-month-old Japanese children can tell the difference between the /r/ and /l/ used in American English just as well as American children. However, by 12 months, the Japanese children can no longer do this, even though, over the same period, the American children have become better at telling the difference between the two sounds (Kuhl et al., 1997). This phenomenon also occurs in early speech production. Infant babbling is basically the same across cultures, but, by the end of the first year, infants have begun to produce just the sounds from the culture in which they were raised.

Iverson and Kuhl (1996) studied speech perception in Japanese and American adults by presenting computer synthesized syllables beginning with /r/ and /l/. The frequencies of the second and third formants of these syllables were set to create a matrix of sounds that differed by equal physical intervals (Figure 12.19a). By having Japanese and American listeners rate all possible pairs of these stimuli for similarity, Iverson and Kuhl produced the "perceptual maps" in Figure 12.19b. These maps clearly show that Americans perceive /r/ and /l/ as two separate groups, while the Japanese do not. The experience of both groups of subjects is "warped" by the language they experienced as infants. Although the physiological research remains to be done, Kuhl (2000) speculates, based on these psychophysical results, that "language input sculpts the brain to create a perceptual system that highlights the contrasts used in language" (p. 103).

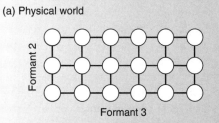

(a) Physical world

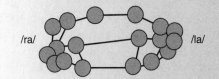

(b) Perceptual world: Americans

/ra/   /la/

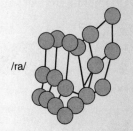

(c) Perceptual world: Japanese

/ra/

Figure 12.19
(a) Sound stimuli related to the sounds /r/ and /l/ were created by varying the frequencies of the second and third formants in equal steps. Each circle represents a sound stimulus. The equal spacing indicates the sounds are equally distant from each other physically.
(b) Perceptual space for these stimuli for American listeners. The sounds on the left were perceived as /ra/ and the ones on the right as /la/. (c) Perceptual space for Japanese listeners. All of the stimuli are perceived as /ra/. (From Kuhl, 2000.)

TADOMA:
"HEARING" WITH TOUCH

How can people who are both deaf and blind know what someone is saying? One way they can accomplish this is to place their hand on the speaker's face and neck and their thumb lightly on the speakers lips. They determine what the speaker is saying by feeling the vibrations and positions of the mouth, lips, and tongue (Figure 12.20). This tactile method of speech perception was introduced in Norway in the 1890s. Later, in the United States, two children, Tad Chapman and Oma Simpson, were taught to use their tactile sense to perceive speech and gave tactile speech perception its name—**Tadoma**.

To appreciate what kind of information can be perceived using the Tadoma method, place your hand on your own face, as shown in Figure 12.20, and, while talking, notice how your fingers can sense the vibrations of the vocal cords on the neck, the shape of the lips, and the air flow through the mouth.

Figure 12.20
The Tadoma method of speech perception. The thumb is placed on the lips and the fingers fan out across the left side of the face. There is also a two-handed version of the Tadoma method.

When you try this, you will see that the information available using this method is incomplete at best, because movements such as the positioning of the tongue in the mouth can't be sensed by this method. Nonetheless, the Tadoma method has proven to be a surprisingly successful way to perceive speech, for the few people who have learned to use it.

One experienced Tadoma user was able to correctly identify 56 percent of consonant–vowel sounds such as *coo, fa,* and *me,* which is an impressive performance since many of these combinations do not form meaningful words (Reed et al., 1982). In fact, when subjects are tested using meaningful speech, their performance increases into the 80 percent range (Norton et al., 1977). Thus, just as for the normal mode of perceiving speech, meaningfulness increases comprehension.

People's ability to perceive speech through the tactile sense adds to the evidence that speech is a multimodal sense. Adding further to this evidence is the results of an experiment in which a tactile version of the McGurk effect (see page 419) has been achieved in hearing subjects (Fowler & Dekle, 1991). Whereas the standard McGurk effect occurs when visual perception of lip movements that don't match the sound changes perception of the sound, the tactile version occurs when tactile perception of lip movements that don't match the sound changes perception of the sound. To achieve the tactile effect, subjects placed their fingers on the lips of a model who was making the movements for /ba/ at the same time they heard a sound that could be perceived as /ba/ or /ga/. The addition of the tactile information for /ba/ made the subjects more likely to identify the sound as /ba/. Thus, speech information can be transmitted through a number of different channels, including not only auditory and visual but tactile as well.

Cognitive Dimensions of Speech Perception

Our perception of speech depends not just on the energy in the speech stimulus but on cognitive factors, such as the meanings of the stimuli and the listener's past experiences. Knowledge of the meanings of the words helps in the segmentation of sentences, as well as other factors, described below.

Meaning and the Perception of Phonemes and Words

Another example of a cognitive effect on speech perception is that it is easier to perceive phonemes and words in a meaningful context. The meaning of a sentence also results in the phonemic restoration effect, in which phonemes that are obscured by noise are still heard.

Speaker Characteristics

Indexical characteristics refer to characteristics of a speaker's voice that carry information about things like the speaker's age, gender, and emotional state. Indexical characteristics help convey meaning and aid the perceptual system in speech recognition.

The Physiology of Speech Perception

Researchers are searching for neural signals that represent speech. Some neurons have been found that respond to complex speechlike stimuli. Broca's and Wernike's areas are specialized for speech perception. People with damage to these areas suffer from aphasia, which is a difficulty in speaking and understanding speech.

Is Speech Special?

Some researchers argue that there is a specialized processing system for speech that sets speech apart from other auditory stimuli. Other researchers feel that speech perception can be explained by regular auditory mechanisms. Research in duplex perception seemed to support the "speech is special" argument, but further research indicates that perhaps it doesn't. The debate between these two approaches to speech perception is continuing.

Plasticity of Perception: Differences Between American and Japanese Listeners

Young infants can perceive and produce all phonemes, but by the time these infants reach one year of age they perceive and produce only sounds characteristic of their own language. This shift in the perception of speech, which has been supported by experiments that show that Japanese and Americans have different "perceptual maps" of sounds, suggests that language input may change the brain during early development.

Across the Senses: Tadoma

Tadoma, "tactile speech," enables people who are blind and deaf to understand speech by sensing the vibrations of a speaker's vocal cords with their hands. A tactile McGurk effect has also been demonstrated in hearing subjects. These are examples of the multimodal nature of speech.

Speech Perception

STUDY QUESTIONS

1. How do the speech recognition capabilities of modern computers compare to the speech recognition ability of humans? (410)

The Speech Stimulus

Phonemes: Sounds and Meanings

2. What unit of analysis is most speech perception research based on? (410)

3. What is the definition of a phoneme? (411)

4. Why are there different numbers of phonemes in different languages? (411)

The Acoustic Signal: Patterns of Pressure Changes

5. What is the acoustic signal, and how is it produced? (411)

6. How are vowels produced, and what causes different vowels to have different frequencies? (411)

7. What is a formant? (411)

8. How is the acoustic stimulus displayed on the sound spectrogram? (411)

9. How are consonants produced? How does this differ from the production of vowels? (412)

10. How come the energy bands for formants aren't always horizontal during natural speech? What is a formant transition? (412)

Problems Posed by the Speech Stimulus

The Segmentation Problem

11. What is the segmentation problem? Why do sounds of an unfamiliar foreign language sometimes appear to be an unbroken string of sound? (413)

The Variability Problem

12. How does variability occur in the acoustic signal because of a phoneme's context? Be sure you understand how the spectrograms in Figure 12.6 show this. (414)

13. What is coarticulation? (414)

14. How does the perception of phonemes provide evidence for perceptual constancy? (414)

15. How does variability occur in the acoustic signal because of different speakers? (414)

16. How is the articulation of conversational speech different than the articulation of individual words? (415)

17. Why has it been so difficult to design machines that can recognize speech? (416)

Stimulus Dimensions of Speech Perception

The Search for Invariant Acoustic Cues

18. What is an invariant acoustic cue? (416)

19. What is a short-term spectrum? A running spectral display? Why are these ways of displaying the acoustic stimulus valuable? (416)

20. Has it been possible to identify invariant acoustic cues for all speech sounds? (416)

Categorical Perception: An Example of Constancy in Speech Perception

21. What is achieved when categorical perception occurs? (416)

22. What is voice onset time? (417)

23. Describe a categorical perception experiment in which voice onset time is varied. (417)

24. What is the phonetic boundary? How do listeners discriminate between sounds that are on the same side of the phonetic boundary? On different sides? (418)

25. What is the relation between categorical perception and constancy for speech sounds? What is the advantage of the existence of constancy? (418)

The Multimodal Nature of Speech Perception: Information from Hearing and Vision

26. What do we mean when we say that speech perception is multimodal? (419)

27. What is the McGurk effect? What does the existence of this effect illustrate? (419)

Brain Scan: Activation of Auditory Cortex During Silent Lipreading

28. Describe the Calvert brain imaging experiment on the effect of silent lipreading on brain activity. (420)

29. What visual–auditory interactions may be partially explained by Calvert's results? (420)

Cognitive Dimensions of Speech Perception

30. What do we mean when we say that there is a cognitive dimension to speech perception? (421)

31. How come you can read sentences in which half of the words are removed? (421)

Meaning and Segmentation

32. Describe Reddy's demonstration in which subjects misperceived speech. What is the point of this demonstration? What is a major factor that helps us to achieve segmentation? (422)

33. How do the acoustic stimuli for "I scream" and "ice cream" compare? What causes us to perceive these words as different from one another? (422)

Meaning and Phoneme Perception

34. Describe Rubin and coworkers' phoneme-identification experiment. What do the results of this experiment demonstrate? (423)

35. What is the phonemic restoration effect? What does it demonstrate about the perception of phonemes? (423)

36. What do Samuel's experiments on the phonemic restoration effect demonstrate? (423)

Meaning and Word Perception

37. Describe Miller and Isard's experiment on the relationship between meaningfulness and the perception of words. (423)

38. Why are words recognized more accurately when they are in a meaningful context? (424)

Speaker Characteristics

39. What are indexical characteristics? What is the point of the joke about the student's response to the linguistics professor? (424)

40. Why are indexical characteristics important? What did Palmeri conclude from the results of his experiment? (425)

41. What was the result of the Nygaard, Sommers, and Pisoni experiment that used familiar and unfamiliar speakers? What was the possible mechanism behind it? (425)

42. What can we conclude from the results of the above experiments with regard to the roles of bottom-up and top-down processing in speech perception? (425)

The Physiology of Speech Perception

Neural Responses to Speech and Complex Sounds

43. What is the relationship between the firing of populations of auditory nerve fibers and the acoustic stimulus for speech? (425)

44. In addition to looking for correspondences between the speech stimulus and neural firing, what other approach has been taken to studying the relationship between neural responding and speech perception? (426)

Localization of Function

45. Define localization of function and lateralization. Speech is lateralized on what side of the brain for most people? (426)

46. What are two areas that are specialized for producing and perceiving speech? (426)

47. What is aphasia? What form of aphasia involves problems in perceiving speech? (426)

48. Describe the basis of the problem people with Wernicke's aphasia have in understanding speech. (427)

49. What does research using PET scans tell us about the lateralization of speech perception? (427)

Is Speech "Special"?

50. Why might it be reasonable to suggest that there is a specialized mechanism for speech perception? (427)

51. What is duplex perception, and how has the existence of duplex perception been interpreted to support the idea that speech is special? (427)

52. Describe Fowler and Rosenblum's duplex perception experiment. How did they interpret their results? (427)

53. Has the debate about whether or not speech is special been resolved? (427)

Plasticity of Perception: Differences Between American and Japanese Listeners

54. Which phonemes can young infants perceive and produce? (429)

55. How does the answer to 54, above, change by the end of the first year of life? Why does this change occur? (429)

56. Describe the Inverson and Kuhl "similarity judgment" experiment on American and Japanese listeners. Why can we say that the results show that neither Japanese listeners or American listeners perceive physical reality? (429)

57. What do the results above tell us about possible brain mechanisms for language perception? (429)

Across the Senses: Tadoma: "Hearing" with Touch

58. Describe how the Tadoma method of tactile speech perception came into being. (430)

59. What is the procedure for Tadoma? What kind of information can it transmit about speech? (430)

60. How well can an experienced Tadoma user identify consonant–vowel sounds? How does performance change for meaningful speech? (430)

61. Describe the experiment that demonstrated a tactile "McGurk effect." (430)

62. What do Tadoma and the tactile McGurk effect tell us about the nature of speech perception? (430)

13

THE CUTANEOUS SENSES

CHAPTER CONTENTS

ACROSS THE SENSES: Parallels Between Touch and Vision

SOME QUESTIONS WE WILL CONSIDER

- Are there specialized receptors in the skin for sensing different tactile qualities? (437)

- What is the most sensitive part of the body? (445)

- Is it possible to reduce pain with your thoughts? (462)

- Do all people experience pain in the same way? (463)

Geerat Vermeij, blind since the age of 4 from a childhood eye disease, had come with his parents from his boyhood home in the Netherlands to live in the United States. After being educated in residential schools for the blind and also the regular school system, he attended Princeton University. During his senior year at Princeton, he applied to a number of graduate schools to study evolutionary biology, with a specialty in mollusks. He was rejected by a number of schools, who said his blindness would make it impossible for him to study biology, but he was granted an interview by Edgar Boell, the director of graduate study in the biology department at Yale. Boell took Vermeij to the museum, introduced him to the curator, and handed him a shell. Here is what happened next, as told by Vermeij (1997):

> "Here's something. Do you know what it is?" Boell asked as he handed me a specimen.

My fingers and mind raced. Widely separated ribs parallel to outer lip; large aperture; low spire; glossy; ribs reflected backward. "It's a Harpa," I replied tentatively. "It must be Harpa major." Right so far.

"How about this one?" inquired Boell, as another fine shell changed hands. Smooth, sleek, channeled suture, narrow opening; could be any olive. "It's an olive. I'm pretty sure it's Oliva sayana, the common one from Florida, but they all look alike."

Both men were momentarily speechless. They had planned this little exercise all along to call my bluff. Now that I had passed, Boell had undergone an instant metamorphosis. Beaming with enthusiasm and warmth, he promised me his full support. (Vermeij, 1997, pp. 79–80)

Vermeij was admitted to graduate study at Yale, graduated with a PhD in evolutionary biology, and is presently Professor of Geology at the University of California at Davis and editor of the scientific journal *Evolution*. He does all of his work with his hands, using his exquisitely trained sense of touch to identify the mollusks he studies. It has, for him, provided a window into the world of shells that has enabled him to surpass many of his sighted colleagues, partially because he, of necessity, ignores visual details that

might be extraneous and focuses on the physical characteristics that he can feel.

Geerat Vermeij's abilities illustrate the amazing capabilities of touch. Another example of the capabilities of touch is provided by braille, the system of raised dots that enables blind people to read with their fingertips (Figure 13.1). A braille character consists of a cell made up of from one to six dots. Different arrangements of dots and blank spaces represent letters of the alphabet, as shown, and, in addition to characters for each letter of the alphabet, there are also characters for numbers, punctuation marks, and common speech sounds and words.

Experienced braille readers can read at a rate of about 100 words per minute, slower than the rate for visual reading, which averages about 250 to 300 words per minute, but impressive nonetheless, when we consider that the sensations experienced as a braille reader's fingertips skim over an array of raised dots are transformed into vast amounts of information that go far beyond simply sensations on the skin.

But the importance of the sense of touch and the other sensations we feel through the skin extends beyond its usefulness as a way to take in information. Imagine how your ability to write might change if your hand were anesthetized. Would you know how firmly to grasp your pen if you had no feeling in your hand? Consider all of the other things you do with

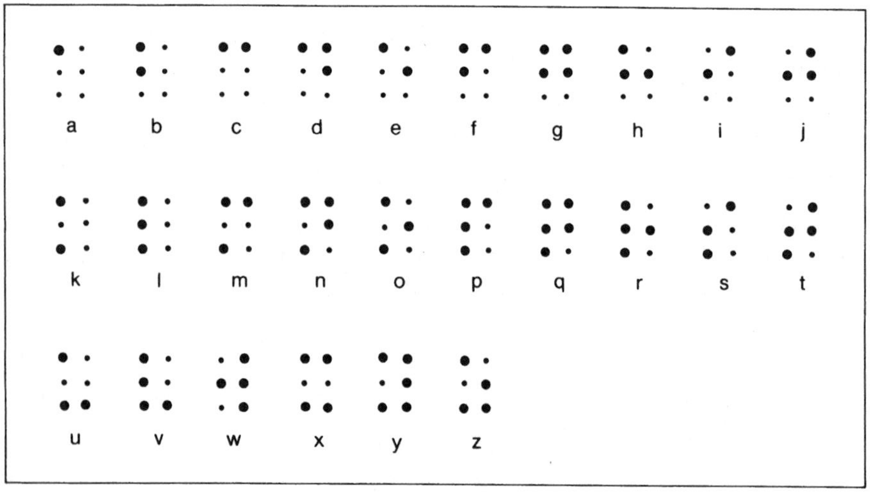

Figure 13.1
The braille alphabet consists of raised dots in a 2 × 3 matrix. The large dots in this alphabet indicate the location of the raised dot for each letter. Blind people read these dots by scanning them with their fingertips.

your hands. How would losing feeling in your hands affect your ability to do these things? We know that a complete loss of our ability to feel with the skin is dangerous, as demonstrated by people who, because they can't feel touch or pain, suffer constant bruises, burns, and broken bones in the absence of the warnings provided by touch and pain (Melzack & Wall, 1983; Rollman, 1991; Wall & Melzack, 1994). And consider for a moment what sex would be like without the sense of touch. Or perhaps a better way to put this is to ask if sex without the sense of touch is something people would be capable of or care about at all.

When we recognize that the perceptions we experience through our skin are crucial for protecting ourselves from injury and for motivating sexual activity, we can see that these perceptions are crucial to our survival and to the survival of our species. We could, in fact, make a good case for the idea that perceptions felt through the skin are more important for survival than those provided by vision and hearing.

In this chapter, we will be considering the **cutaneous sensations**—sensations based on the stimulation of receptors in the skin. The cutaneous sensations are served by the **somatosensory system,** which also includes **proprioception,** the sense of position of the limbs, and **kinesthesis,** the sense of movement of the limbs. In this chapter we will focus our attention primarily on touch and pain. As we look at the anatomy of the somatosensory system by first focusing on the skin, where the receptors for touch and pain are located, we will notice an important parallel with the visual system: The skin, like the retina, contains a number of different kinds of receptors.

THE SKIN AND ITS RECEPTORS

webTUTOR   We begin our discussion of the cutaneous senses by considering the skin, where we feel cutaneous sensations, and the receptors within the skin, which are responsible for these sensations.

The Skin

Comel (1953) called the skin the "monumental facade of the human body" for good reason. It is the heaviest organ in the human body, and, if not the largest (the surface areas of the gastrointestinal tract or of the alveoli of the lungs exceed the surface area of the skin), it is certainly the most obvious, especially in humans, whose skin is not obscured by fur or large amounts of hair (Montagna & Parakkal, 1974).

In addition to its warning function, the skin also prevents body fluids from escaping and at the same time protects us by keeping bacteria, chemical agents, and dirt from penetrating our bodies. Skin maintains the integrity of what's inside and protects us from what's outside, but it also provides us with information about the various stimuli that contact it. The sun's rays heat our skin, and we feel warmth; a pinprick is painful; and, when someone touches us, we experience pressure or other sensations.

Our main experience with the skin is its visible surface, which is actually a layer of tough dead skin cells. (Try sticking a piece of cellophane tape onto your palm and pulling it off. The material that sticks to the tape is dead skin cells). This layer of dead cells is part of the outer layer of skin, which is called the **epidermis.** Below the epidermis is another layer, called the **dermis** (Figure 13.2). It is in these two layers that we find the **mechanoreceptors,** receptors that respond to mechanical stimulation such as pressure, stretching, and vibration.

Mechanoreceptors in the Skin

Many of the tactile perceptions that we feel from stimulation of the skin can be traced to the four types of mechanoreceptors that are located in the epidermis and the dermis (Figures 13.2 and 13.3). We can distinguish between these receptors by their location in the skin and by their distinctive structures.

- The **Merkel receptor** is a disk-shaped receptor located near the border between the epidermis and the dermis.

- The **Meissner corpuscle** is a stack of flattened cells located in the dermis just below the epidermis; a nerve fiber wends its way through these cells.

- The **Ruffini cylinder** is many-branched fibers inside a roughly cylindrical capsule.

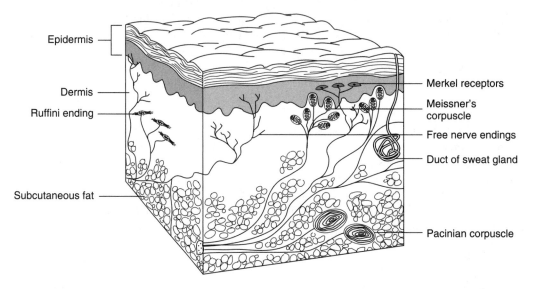

Figure 13.2

A cross section of glabrous (nonhairy) skin, showing the layers of the skin and some of its receptors.

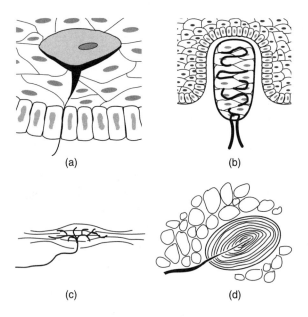

Figure 13.3

The four major receptors for tactile perception: (a) Merkel receptor; (b) Meissner corpuscle; (c) Ruffini cylinder; and (d) Pacinian corpuscle.

• The **Pacinian corpuscle** is a layered, onionlike capsule that surrounds a nerve fiber; located deep in the skin, the Pacinian corpuscle can also be found in many other places, including the intestines and the joints.

The Psychophysics of Mechanoreceptors Psychophysical research by S. J. Bolanowski and coworkers (1988, 1994) has shown that each type of mechanoreceptor responds best to a specific range of frequencies of mechanical stimulation. They isolated the response of each receptor type by using techniques such as cooling the skin (some receptors are sensitive to temperature, and some are not) and presenting masking vibrations that selectively decreased the sensitivity of one receptor type so another one could be studied.

Table 13.1 summarizes the results of their research, which showed that the mechanoreceptors respond to frequencies ranging from 0.3 Hz, which would correspond to someone slowly pushing and releasing your skin about once every three seconds, to over 500 Hz, which corresponds to an extremely

Table 13.1

Properties of mechanoreceptors

Receptors	Frequency Range	Perception
Merkel	0.3–3 Hz (slow pushing)	Pressure
Meissner	3–40 Hz	Flutter
Ruffini	15–400 Hz	Stretching
Pacinian	10–500 Hz (very rapid vibration at the upper range)	Vibration

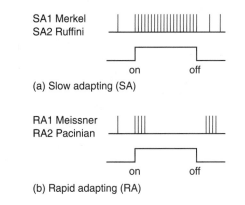

Figure 13.4

Firing patterns of SA and RA fibers. (a) Slowly adapting (SA) fibers continue to fire during a sustained stimulus; (b) rapidly adapting (RA) fibers fire only at the onset and offset of a sustained stimulus.

rapid vibration that might be created by machinery. Bolanowski also determined that each mechanoreceptor is associated with a particular type of tactile perception. For example, the Merkel discs respond to low frequencies and are associated with the perception of pressure, while the Pacinian corpuscles respond to high frequencies and are associated with the perception of vibration.

The Physiology of Mechanoreceptors Most of what we know about the physiology of mechanoreceptors has been determined by recording from nerve fibers in the skin of both animals and humans. This has been accomplished in humans with a technique called **microneurography**, in which a very fine recording electrode is inserted under the skin to record from a single nerve fiber in a person's hand (Vallbo & Hagbarth, 1967).

Mechanoreceptors differ in how they fire to continuous stimulation. The fibers associated with Merkel discs and Ruffini cylinders respond while a stimulus is on, without much decrease in rate, and are therefore called **slowly adapting (SA) fibers** (Figure 13.4a). The fibers associated with Meissner corpuscles and Pacinian corpuscles respond with a burst of firing at the beginning of the stimulus and so are therefore called **rapidly adapting (RA) fibers** (Figure 13.4b). This property of being slow adapting or rapid adapting is considered so important that the mechanoreceptor fibers are generally identified as SA or RA fibers, as indicated in Figure 13.4.

The mechanoreceptors can also be distinguished by the sizes of their receptive fields. The receptive field of a cutaneous neuron is *the area of skin which, when stimulated, influences the firing rate of that neuron.* The SA1 and RA1 fibers have small receptive fields, and the SA2 and RA2 fibers have larger receptive fields. This is indicated in Figure 13.5a, which shows that SA1 fibers have low thresholds over only a small area (Macefield, 1998). This means that these fibers respond well only within this area, so the cell has a small receptive field. RA1 fibers have similar properties.

In contrast, SA2 and RA2 fibers respond over a large area, so they have large receptive fields (Figure 13.5b). Notice that the fibers with small receptive fields (SA1 and RA1) have receptors that are located close to the surface of the skin, and fibers with large receptive fields (SA2 and RA2) have receptors that are located deeper in the skin. The properties of the four receptors are summarized in Figure 13.6.

What Determines Whether a Fiber Adapts Rapidly or Slowly? Why does each type of fiber respond to a different type of stimulation? One thing that determines their response is the type of receptor ending, which can modify the pressure reaching the fiber. This modification of the response by a receptor

The Cutaneous Senses

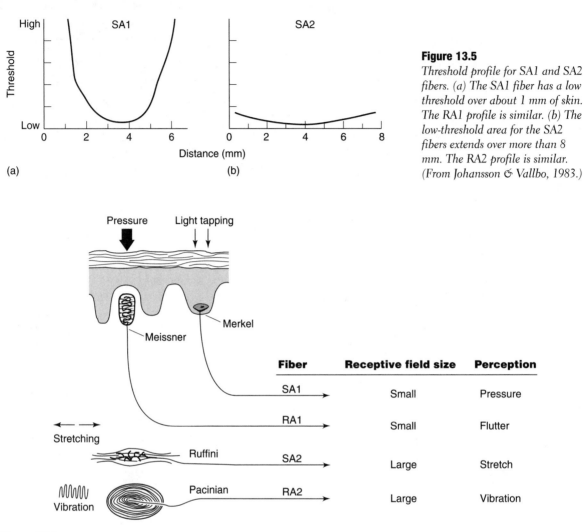

Figure 13.5

Threshold profile for SA1 and SA2 fibers. (a) The SA1 fiber has a low threshold over about 1 mm of skin. The RA1 profile is similar. (b) The low-threshold area for the SA2 fibers extends over more than 8 mm. The RA2 profile is similar. (From Johansson & Vallbo, 1983.)

Fiber	Receptive field size	Perception
SA1	Small	Pressure
RA1	Small	Flutter
SA2	Large	Stretch
RA2	Large	Vibration

Figure 13.6

The four mechanoreceptors, indicating the fiber type, receptive field size, and perception associated with each one. The best stimulus for activating the receptor is indicated near the receptor.

ending has been most thoroughly studied for the Pacinian corpuscle (Figure 13.7), because it is large (about 1 mm long and 0.6 mm thick) and easily accessible (corpuscles can easily be removed from the cat's mesentery, a membrane attached to the intestine).

Werner Loewenstein (1960) describes how the effect of the Pacinian corpuscle receptor structure on the firing of the RA2 fiber was determined by measur-

ing the response of the nerve fiber under two conditions: (1) when the corpuscle was partially dissected away, so that pressure could be applied closer to the nerve fiber, and (2) when the corpuscle remained, so that pressure could be applied to it. When most of the corpuscle was removed, so the stimulus could be presented near the nerve fiber at B (Figure 13.7), the fiber responded when the pressure was first applied, as the pressure continued, and when the pressure was

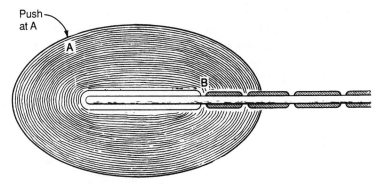

Push at A

A

B

Figure 13.7
A Pacinian corpuscle. (From Loewenstein, 1960.)

removed. However, when the corpuscle was present and the stimulus was presented at A on the intact corpuscle, the fiber responded only when the pressure was first applied and when it was removed. Thus, the Pacinian corpuscle gives its nerve fiber its property of rapid adaptation. It causes the fiber to respond poorly to constant stimulation, such as sustained pressure, but to respond well to changes in stimulation that occur at the beginning and end of a pressure or when stimulation is changing rapidly, as occurs in vibration.

Which Fiber Is Responsible for Our Perception of Detail? While the RA2 fiber is specialized to respond to changes in stimulation, the SA1 fiber is specialized to respond to details. The response of SA1 fibers to details was demonstrated by Kenneth Johnson and Graham Lamb (1981) by recording from fibers in the monkey's finger as raised-dot patterns were presented on a rotating drum (Figure 13.8). By presenting the dots to the receptive field a number of times, and moving the drum down slightly

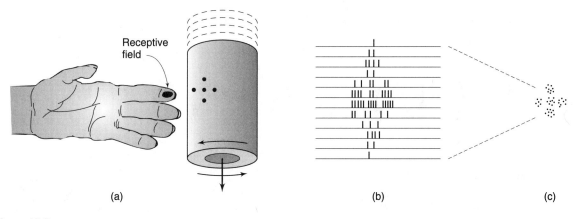

Receptive field

(a)   (b)   (c)

Figure 13.8
(a) Raised-dot stimuli are rolled across the receptive field of a mechanoreceptive fiber on a monkey's fingertip. (b) Sweeping the stimulus across the receptive field generates nerve impulses in the fiber. These nerve impulses are shown on the horizontal lines. Each line represents the impulses generated by one sweep across the receptive field. After each sweep, the drum is moved down slightly, the stimulus is presented again, and a new response is recorded. This process is repeated for a number of positions of the drum. (c) A spatial event plot is created when each nerve impulse is represented by a dot, and the dots are compressed vertically and horizontally so that the pattern of dots has about the same dimensions as the raised-dot stimulus. (Adapted from Martin & Jessell, 1991.)

The Cutaneous Senses

after each scan, Johnson and Lamb were able to create displays called **spatial event plots**, which indicate how well the fibers respond to small details. (See Figure 13.8 for a description of how these spatial event plots are determined.)

Figure 13.9 shows how the spatial event plots for three types of fibers compare to the original raised-dot pattern. The plot for the SA1 fiber looks similar to the dot pattern, whereas the plots for the RA1 and RA2 fibers do not look like the pattern. (SA2 fibers respond poorly to this type of stimulus.) This means that SA1 fibers are good at resolving details.

But just because SA1 fibers respond well to details, does that mean that they are actually used for perception? We can demonstrate a connection between the fiber's response and perception by comparing the fiber's response to what people perceive. Francisco Vega-Bermudez, Kenneth Johnson, and Steven Hsiao (1991) measured perception by determining how well subjects could identify raised letters that were scanned across their fingertips. We can see a connection between their perceptual results and the fiber's physiological response by comparing the letters that are confused perceptually with the spatial event plots shown in Figure 13.10.

People often said C's were O's, and the spatial event plot of C resembles the plot for O. People said

B's were D's, and the plot for B resembles the plot for D. This correspondence between perception and the spatial event plots supports the idea that SA1 fibers are important for identifying details. Other experiments comparing perception and fiber responding

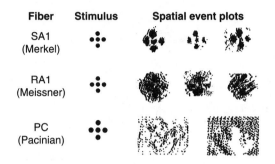

Figure 13.9
Left: Raised-dot stimulus presented as shown in Figure 13.8 to a monkey's fingertip. Right: Some typical spatial event plots generated by this pattern for SA1, RA1, and RA2 fibers that are associated with Merkel receptors, Meissner corpuscles, and Pacinian corpuscles, respectively. The SA2 fiber, which is associated with the Ruffini cylinder, generates only a small response to this type of stimulation. (Adapted from Johnson & Lamb, 1981.)

1 cm

Figure 13.10
Spatial event plots generated by rolling raised letters across the receptive fields of SA1 fibers. (From Vega-Bermudez, Johnson, & Hsiao, 1991.)

have also shown that SA1 fibers are important for sensing the texture of a surface (Blake, Hsiao, & Johnson, 1997; Romo & Salinas, 1999).

Since each mechanoreceptor is specialized to respond to different types of stimulation, stimulating the skin usually activates a number of types of mechanoreceptors, some more strongly than others, depending on the stimulus. Consider, for example, what happens as you grasp a cup, as shown in Figure 13.11. SA1 fibers (Merkel receptors) fire to the raised pattern on the side of the cup and the texture along the rim, SA2 fibers (Ruffini corpuscles) fire to the stretching caused by grasping the cup, RA1 fibers (Meissner receptors) fire when you run your fingers across the ridges along the rim of the cup. Your overall perception of the cup is therefore determined by the pattern of activity of all of these fibers (Roland, 1992). And, in addition to perceiving tactile qualities, we may also perceive the cup as being hot or cold. Our perception of temperature occurs because of thermoreceptors in the skin.

Figure 13.11
Grasping a cup activates a number of different types of mechanoreceptors. Each one creates a particular perception, and, in addition, the overall perception may be determined by a blending of the activity of all of the receptors that are stimulated.

Thermoreceptors: The Neural Response to Temperature

Thermoreceptors respond to specific temperatures and to changes in temperature. There are separate thermoreceptors for warm and cold. Figure 13.12 shows how a **warm fiber** responds to increases in temperature. The response of this neuron illustrates the following properties of a warm fiber: (1) It acts like a thermometer, increasing its response rate as the temperature is increased; (2) it continues to fire as long as the higher temperature continues; (3) it decreases its firing rate when the temperature is decreased; and (4) it does not respond to mechanical stimulation (Duclaux & Kenshalo, 1980; Kenshalo, 1976). **Cold fibers**, on the other hand, increase their firing rate when the temperature is decreased and continue to fire at low temperatures. The different ways that cold and warm fibers respond to steady temperatures are shown in Figure 13.13. Cold fibers respond in the 20°C to 45°C range, with the best response at about 30°. Warm fibers respond in the 30° to 48° range, with the best response at about 44°. (Note that body temperature is 37°C.)

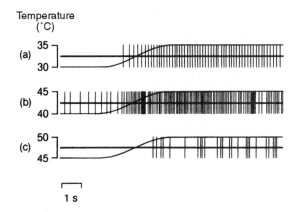

Figure 13.12
The response of a "warm" fiber in the monkey. At the beginning of each record, the firing rate is low because the fiber has been at the same temperature for a while. The fiber fires, however, when the temperature is increased (indicated by the sloping line) and continues to fire for a period of time immediately after the increase. Record (b) indicates that this fiber fires best when the temperature is increased from 40°C to 45°C. (From Duclaux & Kenshalo, 1980.)

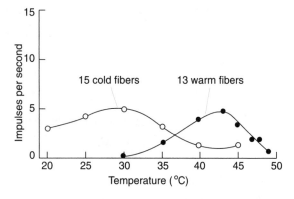

Figure 13.13

Responses of temperature-sensitive fibers in the monkey to constant temperatures. The curve on the left (open circles) shows the average response of a group of 15 "cold" fibers that respond best at about 30°C. The curve on the right (filled circles) shows the average response of a group of 13 "warm" fibers that respond best at about 44°C. (From Kenshalo, 1976.)

NEURAL PROCESSING FOR TOUCH

The receptors in any sense are a powerful influence on perception, because they determine what information gets in. However, we know from our study of vision that perception depends not only on the receptors, but on the neural processing that occurs as the information from the receptors travels toward the brain. In Chapter 2 we saw how the small amount of convergence of the cone receptors compared to the rod receptors results in smaller receptive fields and better acuity, especially in the cone-rich central area of the retina called the fovea, where detail vision is the sharpest (Figure 13.14). We will see that there are close parallels between this visual example and processing in the cutaneous system.

Mechanoreceptors and the Perception of Details

How are signals from the mechanoreceptors processed? One way to answer this question is by show-

ing how people's ability to perceive details on different parts of the body is related to the sizes of the receptive fields of mechanoreceptors serving these parts of the body.

Tactile Acuity on Different Parts of the Body
Tactile acuity is better on some parts of the body, such as the hands and the fingertips, than on others, such as the limbs, the back, and the trunk. This difference in acuity for different parts of the body has been demonstrated by measuring the **two-point threshold**—the smallest separation between two points on the skin that is perceived as two points rather than one. When the two-point threshold is measured on different parts of the body, we find that there are areas on the skin that have higher acuity than others (see also Craig & Johnson, 2000).

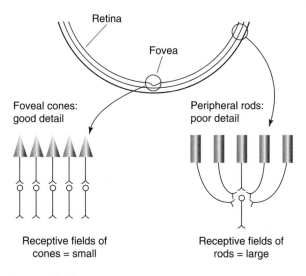

Figure 13.14

In Chapter 2 we saw that the small amount of convergence of the cones is one reason for the high acuity of the cones compared to the rods. In this picture the cones do not converge at all, with each one synapsing on just one neuron. This occurs for many cones in the fovea. Another reason for high cone acuity is that the foveal cones are packed more closely together. Similar principles hold for touch, with areas on the skin that are sensitive to details having small receptive fields.

D E M O N S T R A T I O N

Comparing Two-Point Thresholds

To measure two-point thresholds on different parts of the body, hold two pencils side by side (or better yet, use a drawing compass) so that their points are about 12 mm (0.5 in.) apart; then touch both points simultaneously to the tip of your thumb and determine whether you feel two points. If you feel only one, increase the distance between the pencil points until you feel two; then note the distance between the points. Now move the pencil points to the underside of your forearm. With the points about 12 mm apart (or at the smallest separation you felt as two points on your thumb), touch them to your forearm and note whether you feel one point or two. If you feel only one, how much must you increase the separation before you feel two? ●

If your results from this demonstration match those from the laboratory, you will find that the two-point threshold on your forearm is much larger than the two-point threshold on your thumb. Figure 13.15, which shows how the two-point threshold varies on different parts of the body, indicates that the two-point threshold is over 10 times larger on the forearm than on the thumb. We can relate these acuity differences to physiology by comparing the sizes of the receptive fields on different parts of the body.

Receptive Fields and Tactile Acuity   We would expect that areas with high tactile acuity would have small receptive fields. The reason for this expectation is shown in Figure 13.16a. Figure 13.16 shows the receptive fields of two fibers with large receptive fields and two points stimulating the skin within one of these receptive fields. Since the stimulation falls within only

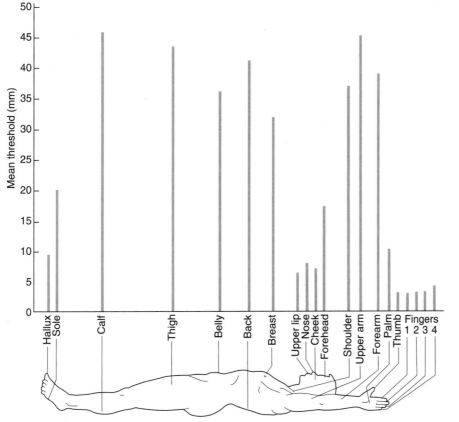

Figure 13.15
Two-point thresholds for males. Two-point thresholds for females follow the same pattern. (From Weinstein, 1968.)

The Cutaneous Senses

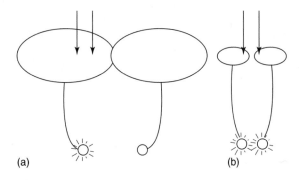

(a)   (b)

Figure 13.16

The reason for the relation between acuity and receptive field size. (a) Two stimuli cause only one neuron to fire when the receptive fields are large. (b) The same two stimuli cause two neurons to fire when the receptive fields are small. The finer-grained analysis provided by the small receptive fields results in smaller two-point thresholds.

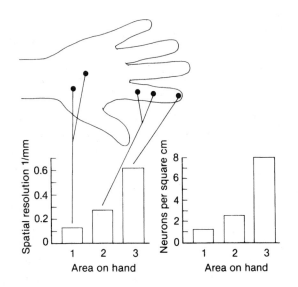

Figure 13.17

Left: The bar graph shows the spatial resolution at one place on the hand and two places on a finger. Spatial resolution, which is determined by taking the inverse of the two-point threshold (so that a small two-point threshold results in high spatial resolution), increases as we move from the hand to the fingertip. Right: The density of small receptive field neurons (RA1 and SA1 fibers) at the same three locations. These data indicate that areas that have high spatial resolution have high densities of small receptive field neurons. (From Vallbo & Johansson, 1978.)

one receptive field, just one neuron fires and we have no information that two points were stimulated.

In Figure 13.16b small receptive fields are stimulated at two points with exactly the same separation as in Figure 13.16a. Since the receptive fields of these neurons are small, the two points stimulate separate neurons, thereby increasing the chances that we would perceive the two stimulations as two separate points. (The same reasoning holds for the better acuity of the cone visual receptors compared to the rods.)

In line with this prediction, Vallbo and Johansson (1978) found that the density of RA1 and SA1 fibers, which have small receptive fields, was higher on the fingertips than on the hand. In fact, Vallbo and Johansson found a direct relationship between the size of the two-point threshold and the density of the small receptive fields of RA1 and SA1 fibers (Figure 13.17). Parts of the body with small two-point thresholds have small receptive fields.

Processing in the Cortex

Processing continues as signals travel from the skin toward the brain.

Anatomy of the Somatosensory System   Modern anatomical studies have identified a web of connec-

tions that transmit signals from the skin to the brain, which appear to rival those of the visual and auditory systems in complexity. We will focus on a few of the basic characteristics of the system.

Nerve fibers from receptors in the skin travel in bundles called peripheral nerves that enter the spinal cord through the dorsal root (Figure 13.18). Once they enter the spinal cord, the nerve fibers go up the spinal cord in two major pathways: the **medial lemniscal pathway** and the **spinothalamic pathway**. Just as parallel pathways in the visual and auditory systems serve different perceptual functions, so it is with the cutaneous system. The lemniscal pathway has large fibers that carry signals related to sensing the positions of the limbs (proprioception) and perceiving touch. The spinothalamic pathway consists of smaller fibers that transmit signals related to temperature and pain.

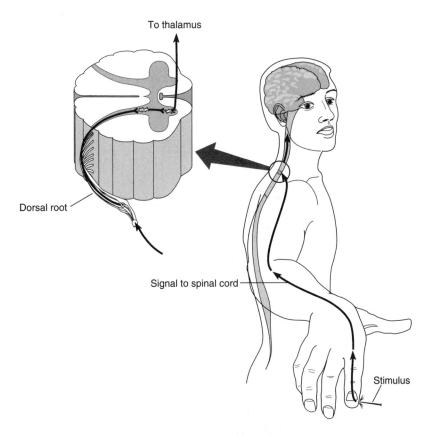

To thalamus

Dorsal root

Signal to spinal cord

Stimulus

Figure 13.18

The pathway from receptors in the skin to the spinal cord. The fiber carrying signals from a receptor in the finger enters the spinal cord through the dorsal root and then travels up the spinal cord toward the thalamus. This picture is greatly simplified, since there are a number of somatosensory pathways traveling up the spinal cord, and some of them cross over to the opposite side at various points along the way.

Fibers from both pathways cross over to the other side of the body during their upward journey to the thalamus. Most of these fibers synapse in the **ventral posterior nucleus** in the thalamus, but some synapse in other thalamic nuclei. (Remember that fibers from the retina and the cochlea also synapse in the thalamus, in the lateral geniculate nucleus for vision and the medial geniculate nucleus for hearing.) Since the signals in the spinal cord have crossed over to the opposite side of the body on their way to the thalamus, signals originating from the left side of the body reach the thalamus in the right hemisphere of the brain, and signals from the right side of the body reach the left hemisphere.

From the thalamus, signals travel to the **somatosensory receiving area (S1)** in the parietal lobe of the cortex and possibly also to the **secondary somatosensory cortex (S2)** (Rowe et al., 1996; Turman et al., 1998) (Figure 13.19). (There is some controversy

regarding whether the thalamus sends signals directly to S2 in monkeys and humans; see Kaas, 1996.) Signals also travel between S1 to S2 and from S1 and S2 to additional somatosensory areas (Figure 13.20).

Research has revealed two important characteristics of the somatosensory cortex: (1) There are maps of the body on the cortex; and (2) There are neurons that fire to specific types of stimuli.

Representation of the Body on the Somatosensory Cortex Just as there is a map of the retina on the visual cortex and a map of sound frequencies on the auditory cortex, there is a map of the body on the somatosensory cortex. Thus, each part of the body is represented on the cortex. This map, shown in Figure 13.21, creates a strangely shaped cortical representation called a **homunculus**, Latin for "little man." The homunculus shows that some areas on the skin are represented by a disproportionately large area of the brain.

The Cutaneous Senses

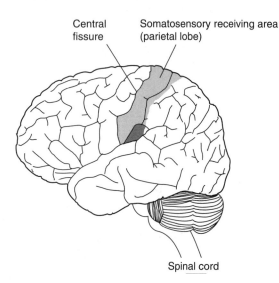

Figure 13.19

The somatosensory cortex in the parietal lobe. The somatosensory system, like the visual and auditory systems, has a number of different areas. The primary somatosensory area, S1 (light shading), receives inputs from the ventral lateral posterior nucleus of the thalamus. The secondary somatosensory area, S2 (dark shading), is partially hidden behind the temporal lobe.

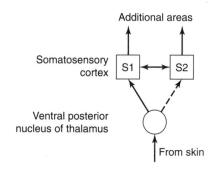

Figure 13.20

Signals that originated in the skin reach the ventral posterior nucleus of the thalamus. From there signals travel to areas S1 and S2 of the somatosensory cortex. The line to S2 is dashed because there is some uncertainty regarding this connection.

The area devoted to the thumb, for example, is as large as the area devoted to the entire forearm.

We can draw a parallel between the large area in the somatosensory cortex devoted to the fingers and the large area in the visual cortex devoted to the fovea of the retina. Remember that the fovea's large representation on the cortex is called the **magnification factor** (see page 95). This large area of visual cortex provides the extra neural processing that is necessary to achieve the good detail vision we experience when we look directly at something.

There is also a magnification factor in the somatosensory cortex, since the fingers and other parts of the body with good detail perception are allotted a large area on the somatosensory cortex. Thus, areas that have good detail perception—the fovea for vision and the fingers for touch—are represented by large areas on the cortex. In general, areas on the skin with small two-point thresholds are represented by large

areas on the cortex. Thus, the map of the body on the brain may look distorted, but the distortions represent the extra neural processing that enables us to accurately sense fine details with our fingers and other parts of the body.

Another way we can appreciate the connection between neural processing in the cortex and the perception of details is to compare the sizes of the receptive fields of neurons located in different parts of the homunculus. Figure 13.22 shows the results of this comparison. Receptive fields are smallest for neurons that serve the fingers, are larger for neurons for the hand, and are even larger for neurons from the arm. Thus, the fingers' excellent detail perception is achieved because the fingers have a large number of neurons in the cortex and because each of these neurons is responsible for only a small area on the finger.

Two additional facts about this map are important. First, the somatosensory cortex is arranged in columns. This means that when an electrode oriented perpendicular to the surface of the cortex is lowered into the cortex, all of the neurons it encounters have receptive fields from the same area of the skin. Thus, like the visual cortex and the auditory cortex, these columns process information from a particular area of the body (Kandel & Jessell, 1991).

Second, there are at least 10 separate maps of the monkey's body in its brain (Kaas & Pons, 1988; Kan-

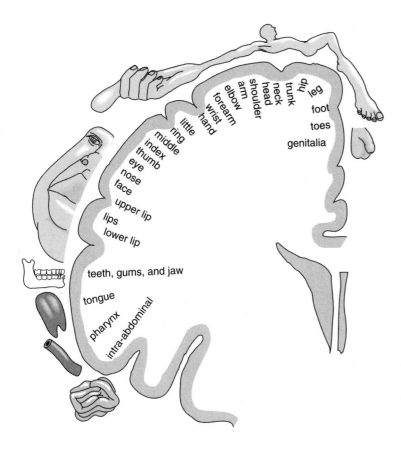

Figure 13.21
The sensory homunculus on the somatosensory cortex. Parts of the body with the highest tactile acuity are represented by larger areas on the cortex. (From Penfield & Rasmussen, 1950.)

del & Jessell, 1991; Nelson et al., 1980). The apparent reason for these multiple representations is that different areas within the somatosensory area have different functions. For example, one area may be specialized for the discrimination of forms and another for the discrimination of textures. Whatever their function, these multiple maps of the body on the brain exhibit the same distortions as our simple homunculus in Figure 13.21: Areas of the body that discriminate fine details are allotted large areas on the cortex.

Tactile Feature Detectors Neural processing in the cutaneous system is reflected not only by the expanded space in the cortex and smaller receptive fields for parts of the body that have good detail perception, but also by changes in the neurons' receptive fields as we move from the mechanoreceptors in the skin toward the cortex. Neurons in the monkey's

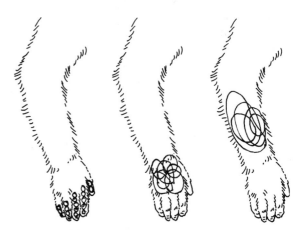

Figure 13.22
Receptive fields of cortical neurons are smallest on the fingers and become larger on the hand and the forearm. (Adapted from Kandel & Jessell, 1991.)

thalamus (the ventral posterior nucleus) have center-surround receptive fields that are similar to the center-surround receptive fields in the visual area of the thalamus (the lateral geniculate nucleus) (Figure 13.23) (Mountcastle & Powell, 1959).

When we move to the cortex, we find some neurons with center-surround receptive fields and also others that respond to more specialized stimulation of the skin. Figures 13.24 and 13.25 show the receptive fields of neurons in the monkey's somatosensory cortex that are quite similar to the receptive fields of simple and complex cells in the visual cortex. The cell in Figure 13.24 responds to an edge oriented horizontally but responds less well to other orientations. Figure 13.25 shows a cell that responds to movement across the skin in a specified direction (Hyvarinin & Poranen, 1978; see also Costanzo & Gardner, 1980; Romo et al., 1998; Warren, Hamalainen, & Gardner, 1986; Whitsel, Roppolo, & Werner, 1972). In Chapter 8, we proposed a neural circuit to explain how visual neurons could respond selectively to movement in one direction (see Figure 8.14). It is likely that a circuit similar to this is behind the directional selectivity of cutaneous neurons like the one in Figure 13.25 (Gardner & Costanzo, 1980).

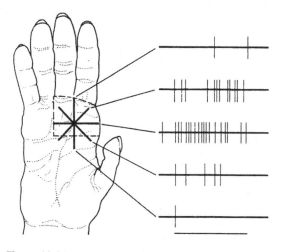

Figure 13.24

The receptive field of a neuron in the monkey's somatosensory cortex that responds when an edge is placed on the hand. This cell responds well when the edge is oriented horizontally but responds less well to other orientations. (From Hyvarinin & Poranen, 1978.)

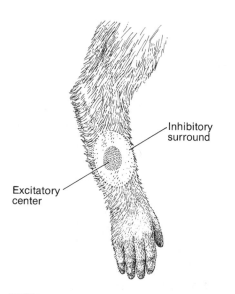

Figure 13.23

An excitatory-center inhibitory-surround receptive field of a neuron in a monkey's thalamus.

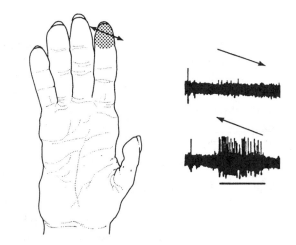

Figure 13.25

The receptive field of a neuron in the monkey's somatosensory cortex that responds to movement across the fingertip from right to left but does not respond to movement from left to right. (From Hyvarinin & Poranen, 1978.)

The Function of Touch

Touch is crucial for carrying out many actions, and serves a protective function by warning of possible tissue damage. This protective function, plus the role of touch in sex, emphasizes its role in survival.

The Skin and Its Receptors

The skin is made up of two layers, the epidermis and dermis. There are four different types of mechanoreceptors in the skin: Merkel receptors, Meissner corpuscles, Ruffini cylinder, and Pacinian corpuscles. Each of these receptors responds to a range of frequencies and results in specific perceptions (see Table 13.1). They are also either slowly adapting (SA) or rapidly adapting (RA) and have either small or large receptive fields.

Receptor Structure and Fiber Response

We know that the Pacinian corpuscle is responsible for the rapid adaptation of the RA2 fibers, because when it is removed, the fibers become slowly adapting. Recording experiments in which spatial event plots are determined indicate that the SA1 fiber (Merkel receptor) responds best to details. SA1 fibers are also important for perceiving texture.

Thermoreceptors

Thermoreceptors—warm fibers and cold fibers—respond best to specific ranges of temperatures.

Tactile Acuity

Tactile acuity varies on different parts of the body. For example, the two-point threshold is much smaller on the fingers than on most other parts of the body. This high acuity of the fingers is associated with smaller receptive fields of RA1 and SA1 fibers, which are densely packed on areas, like the fingers, that have high acuity.

Pathways to the Cortex

There is a complex pathway leading from the skin to the brain. Two of the major pathways in the spinal cord are the medial lemniscal pathway (limb position and touch) and the spinothalamic pathway (temperature and pain). Fibers associated with touch synapse in the ventral posterior nucleus of the thalamus and then go to the primary somatosensory receiving areas, S1 and S2.

Maps on the Cortex

The homunculus is a map of the body on the somatosensory cortex. One of its features is the magnification of the areas representing high-acuity areas of the skin, such as the fingertips. High-acuity areas have a higher density of neurons in the cortex, and these cortical neurons have small receptive fields. There are multiple maps of the body on the cortex and columnar arrangement similar to what is found in the visual system.

Tactile Feature Detectors

There are neurons in the tactile system that have properties similar to neurons in the visual system. Neurons in the thalamus have center-surround receptive fields, and there are neurons in the cortex that respond best to more specialized stimuli, like oriented edges and movement in a particular direction.

TACTILE OBJECT RECOGNITION

So far we've described how a stimulus applied to the skin causes activity in mechanoreceptors, the thalamus, and the cortex, and how neurons in the cortex respond to specific features of this stimulus, such as its orientation or the direction in which it is moving. The research that we've described has usually involved passive subjects who are subjected to whatever stimulus the experimenter has decided to apply to their skin. This kind of stimulation, in which a passive subject receives stimulation from someone else, is called **passive touch**.

Passive Touch and Active Touch

Do we usually sit passively while someone else touches us with separated pencil points or presses dots or raised letters into our fingertips? While there certainly are situations in which we are passive and someone else stimulates our skin, as when someone gives us a backrub, most of the time we play an active role in determining how our skin is stimulated. We run our fingers across the smooth surface of a table, rhythmically hit the keys of our computer, or feel the contours of a pen as we grip it to write. This way of experiencing touch, in which the person controls the touch stimulation, is called **active touch**.

An excellent example of active touch is provided by our description of how Geerat Vermeij used his fingertips to identify different types of shells. His fingers moved across the surfaces of the shells, feeling the textures, tracing the shells' contours, and noticing specific features such as ribs and sutures and the sizes of opening. To appreciate the difference between active touch and passive touch, do the following demonstration.

 D E M O N S T R A T I O N

Comparing Active and Passive Touch

Ask another person to select five or six small objects for you to identify. Close your eyes and have the person place each object in your hand. Your job is to identify the object by touch alone. As you do this, be aware of what you are experiencing: your finger and hand movements, the sensations you are feeling, and what you are thinking. Do this for three objects. Then hold out your hand, keeping it still, with fingers outstretched, and let the person move each of the remaining objects around on your hand, moving their surfaces and contours across your skin. Your task is the same as before: to identify the object and to pay attention to what you are experiencing as the object is moved across your hand. ●

You may have noticed that in the active condition you were much more involved in the process and had more control over what parts of the objects you were exposed to. In the active part of the demonstration you were engaging in **haptic perception**, perception in which three-dimensional objects are explored with the hand.

Identifying Objects by Haptic Exploration

Haptic perception provides a particularly good example of a situation in which a number of different systems are interacting with each other. As you manipulated the objects that you were trying to identify, you were using three distinct systems to arrive at your goal of identifying the objects: (1) the sensory system, which was involved in sensing cutaneous sensations such as touch, temperature, and texture and the movements and positions of your fingers and hands; (2) the motor system, which was involved in moving your fingers and hands; and (3) the cognitive system, which was involved in thinking about the information provided by the sensory and motor systems.

Haptic perception is an extremely complex process because the sensory, motor, and cognitive systems must all be coordinated with one another. For example, the motor system's control of finger and hand movements is guided by cutaneous feelings in the fingers and the hands, by your sense of the positions of the fingers and hands, and by thought processes that determine what information is needed about the object in order to identify it.

The experience created by these processes working together creates an experience of active touch that is quite different than the experience of passive touch. J. J. Gibson (1962), who championed the importance of movement in perception (see Chapter 9), compared the experience of active and passive touch by noting that we tend to relate passive touch to the sensation experienced in the skin, whereas we relate active touch to the object being touched. For example, if someone pushes a pointed object into your skin, you might say, "I feel a pricking sensation on my skin"; if, however, you push on the tip of the pointed object yourself, you might say, "I feel a pointed object" (Kruger, 1970). Thus, for passive touch you experience stimulation of the skin, and for active touch you experience the objects you are touching.

Psychophysical research has shown that people can accurately identify most common objects within one or two seconds (Klatzky, Lederman, & Metzger, 1985). When Susan Lederman and Roberta Klatzky (1987, 1990) observed subjects' hand movements as they made these identifications, they found that people use a number of distinctive movements, which they called **exploratory procedures (EPs)**, and that the types of EPs used depend on the object qualities the subjects are asked to judge.

Four of the EPs observed by Lederman and Klatzky are shown in Figure 13.26, and the frequencies with which they are used to judge different object qualities are shown in Figure 13.27. Subjects tend to use just one or two EPs to determine a particular quality. For example, people use mainly lateral motion and contour following to judge texture, and they use enclosure and contour following to judge exact shape.

The Physiology of Active Touch

What is happening physiologically as we explore an object with our fingers and hands? Researchers have tried to answer this question by recording from mechanoreceptor fibers in the skin, by recording from neurons in areas S1 and S2 of the somatosensory cortex and also from neurons on other areas in the parietal and frontal lobes.

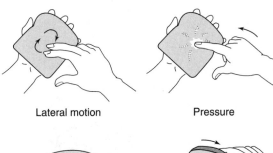
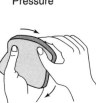

Lateral motion

Pressure

Enclosure

Contour following

Figure 13.26

Some of the exploratory procedures (EPs) observed by Lederman and Klatzky as subjects identified objects. (From Lederman & Klatzky, 1987.)

Mechanoreceptor Response and Object Recognition

In order for the brain to control everyday tasks, such as screwing a lid on a bottle, it needs a lot of information. It needs to know the size and contour of the lid, the amount of force needed to grasp the lid, and other things as well, such as the effect of textures that help achieve a firm grip on the edges of the lid (Figure 13.28a). This information is provided by receptors

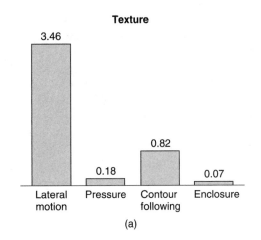

(a)

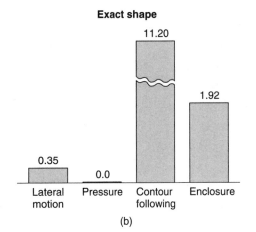

(b)

Figure 13.27

Average duration in seconds that subjects used various exploratory procedures (a) to judge texture and (b) to judge an object's exact shape. Subjects use lateral motion and contour following to judge texture. Contour following is the major exploratory procedure used to judge exact shape. (Based on data in Lederman & Klatzky, 1987.)

The Cutaneous Senses

within the body, which indicate the position of the joints, and by mechanoreceptors in the skin, which indicate the textures and contours of the lid.

The information for indicating the contours of the lid is signaled by the pattern of firing of a large number of mechanoreceptors. This is illustrated by the response profiles in Figures 13.28b and c, which indicate how SA1 fibers in the fingertips respond to contact with two different spheres, one with high curvature relative to the fingertip (13.28b) and one that is more gently curved (13.28c). In both cases, the receptors right at the point where the fingers contact the sphere respond the most, and ones further away fire less, but the *pattern* of response is different in the two cases. It is this overall pattern that provides information to the brain about the curvature of the sphere (Goodwin, 1998).

Remember, however, that the responses in Figure 13.28 represent the pattern of stimulation that occurs at one point in time, and that when you are screwing on a lid, your fingers are constantly moving and creating new patterns of stimulation. This dynamic nature

of tactile object recognition is reflected by the properties of some neurons in the somatosensory cortex, which respond only when the person actively grasps an object.

The Cortical Response to Action and Attention

There are neurons in the monkey's somatosensory cortex that don't respond to passive stimulation of the skin but do respond when the monkey grasps a specific object. Figure 13.29 shows the response of one of these neurons, which responds when the monkey grasps a ruler but does not respond when the monkey grasps a cylinder (also see Iwamura, 1998).

Cortical neurons are affected not only by whether stimulation is active or passive but by whether or not the perceiver is paying attention. Steven Hsiao and coworkers (1993, 1996) recorded the response of neurons in areas S1 and S2 to raised letters that were scanned across a monkey's finger. In the tactile-attention condition the monkey had to do a task that required focusing its attention on the letters being presented to its fingers. In the visual-attention condition,

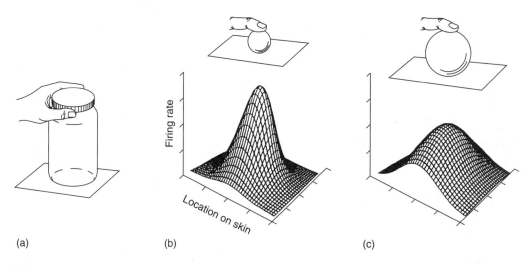

(a)　　　　　　　(b)　　　　　　　(c)

Figure 13.28

(a) Screwing a lid onto a bottle depends on information sent to the brain regarding the positioning and forces exerted by the fingers and the hand. (b) Responses of SA1 fibers in the fingertips to touching a high-curvature stimulus. The height of the profile indicates the firing rate at different places across the fingertip. (c) The profile of firing to touching a stimulus with more gentle curvature. (From Goodwin, 1998.)

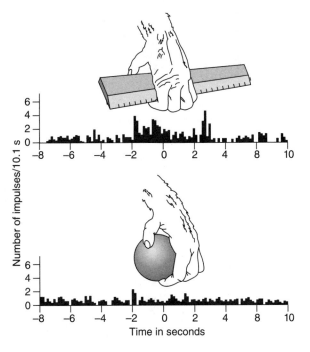

Figure 13.29

The response of a neuron in a monkey's parietal cortex that fires when the monkey grasps a ruler but that does not fire when the monkey grasps a cylinder. The neuron's rate of firing is indicated by the height of the bars. The monkey grasps the objects at time = 0. (From Sakata & Iwamura, 1978.)

the monkey had to focus its attention on an unrelated visual stimulus. The results, shown in Figure 13.30, show that even though the monkey is receiving exactly the same stimulation on its fingertips in both conditions, the response is larger for the tactile-attention condition. Thus, stimulation of the receptors may trigger a response, but the size of the response can then be affected by processes such as attention, thinking,

and other actions of the perceiver (see also Steinmetz et al., 2000).

Cortical Areas Involved in Tactile Object Recognition The picture we have drawn of tactile object recognition just scratches the surface of the processes involved. We have seen that tactile object recognition begins with the mechanoreceptors and then continues in somatosensory cortex (S1 and S2). But, as we saw in Chapter 9, there are neurons in other parietal areas and in the frontal lobe that respond when monkeys grasp objects, and recent brain-imaging studies have revealed that activity also occurs in the visual cortex while a person is identifying objects by touch (Deibert et al., 1999). Of course, since movement of the hands is involved in haptic exploration of objects, the motor cortex is involved as well. (See also Romo & Salinas, 1999.)

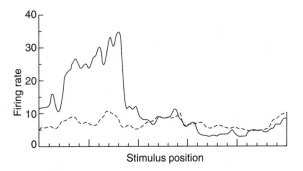

Figure 13.30

Firing rate for a neuron in area S1 of a monkey's cortex that is responding to a raised letter being rolled across the monkey's fingertips. A large response occurs in the tactile-attention condition (solid line), and a small response occurs in the visual-attention condition (dashed line), even though the stimulation on the fingertips was the same in both conditions. (Adapted from Hsiao et al., 1996.)

Plasticity in the Cutaneous System

Brain plasticity—the idea that environmental experience can cause changes in the tuning of cortical neurons and in the organization of cortical areas—has been one of the themes of this book. We've looked at numerous examples of plasticity in the visual and auditory systems, and now we will look at some examples of plasticity in the cutaneous system.

Our discussion of tactile plasticity will include three different examples, because research on the cutaneous system has been at the forefront of plasticity research. Some of the first examples of brain plasticity in adults were demonstrated on the somatosensory cortex (Kaas et al., 1983; Merzenich et al., 1988), with the earliest research showing that the cortical representation of the body can change with experience.

Changes in Cortical Maps Caused by Decreasing or Increasing Stimulation

We've seen from the homunculus (Figure 13.21) that parts of the body that are most sensitive to tactile stimulation have the largest representation on the cortex. Thus, in the cutaneous system, the functioning of the brain is adapted to the organism's needs. Further evidence for this adaptation is provided by experiments that show that the map changes when signals from a particular part of the body are prevented from reaching the cortex. For example, if receptor signals are prevented from reaching the monkey's somatosensory cortex by loss of a finger or by damage to the peripheral nerves conducting impulses from the skin, this reduces the area on the cortex that is devoted to that part of the body (Kaas, 1991; Kaas, Merzenich, & Killackey, 1983; Pettit & Schwark, 1993; Pons et al., 1991).

Maps in the somatosensory cortex can also be changed by increasing the stimulation reaching the cortex. William Jenkins and Michael Merzenich (1987) showed that increasing stimulation of a specific area of the skin causes an expansion of the cortical area receiving signals from that area of skin. They demonstrated this by training monkeys to complete a task that involved the extensive use of a particular location on one fingertip. Comparison of the cortical maps of the fingertip measured just before the training and three months later shows that the area representing the stimulated fingertip was greatly expanded after the training (Figure 13.31). Thus, the cortical area representing part of the fingertip, which is large to begin with, becomes even larger when the area receives a large amount of stimulation.

Research using fMRI has demonstrated an effect of tactile experience in humans by showing that musicians who play stringed instruments have a greater than normal cortical representation for the highly stimulated fingers on their left hand (Elbert et al., 1995). The sensory homunculus is not, therefore, a permanent, static map but can be changed by experience. We will now consider an example of how the cortical area that represents one sense can be changed by loss of another sense.

Plastic Effects of Losing a Sense

When input from one sense is eliminated, then the brain area normally devoted to that sense can be taken over by another sense. Norihiro Sadato and coworkers (1996) demonstrated this by recording brain activity as people who were born blind or who had become blind before the age of seven

(continued)

The Plasticity of Perception (*continued*)

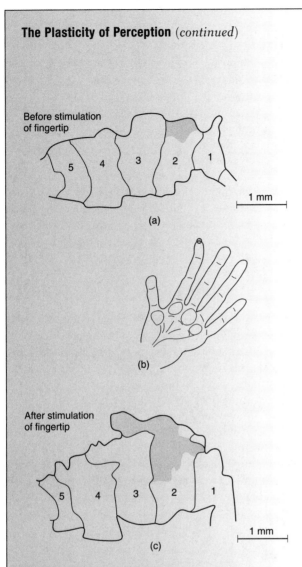

Before stimulation of fingertip

5 4 3 2 1

1 mm

(a)

(b)

After stimulation of fingertip

5 4 3 2 1

1 mm

(c)

Figure 13.31
(a) Each numbered zone represents the area in the somatosensory cortex that represents one of a monkey's five digits. The shaded area on the zone for digit 2 is the part of the cortex that represents the small area on the tip of the digit shown in (b). (c) The shaded region shows how the area representing the fingertip increased in size after this area was heavily stimulated over a two-month period. (From Merzenich et al., 1988.)

scanned braille characters with their fingers. As expected, the somatosensory cortex was activated. However, the visual receiving area in the occipital cortex was activated as well. Apparently, the visual cortex, which receives no stimulation from the visual system in these subjects, becomes reorganized to accept the high levels of tactile information created by reading braille. (Also see page 402 of Chapter 11 for another example of how an area devoted to one sense can be taken over by another.)

Plasticity from Amputation of a Limb

One of the most interesting and mystifying phenomena in perception is the **phantom limb**, in which people who have had a limb amputated continue to experience the limb (Figure 13.32). This perception is so convincing that amputees have been known to try stepping out of a bed onto phantom feet or legs or to attempt lifting a cup with a phantom hand. For many, the limb moves with the body, swinging while walking. For some, the limb is paralyzed so it is fixed in one position, and it is also not uncommon to experience pain in the phantom limb (Jensen & Nikolajssen, 1999; Katz & Gagliese, 1999; Melzak, 1992; Ramachandran & Hirstein, 1998).

Figure 13.32
This person's right arm has been amputated above the elbow. The shaded limb represents the phantom limb that the patient feels.

(*continued*)

The Cutaneous Senses

The Plasticity of Perception (*continued*)

We still don't know exactly what causes perception of the phantom limb, but most researchers agree that the source is in the brain. A number of lines of evidence point to this conclusion. Cutting the nerves that formerly transmited signals from the limb to the brain does not eliminate the phantom. This means that the phantom is not caused by signals that are being sent from the stump that remains after the amputation or from a remaining part of the limb. But perhaps most convincing for a central explanation of phantoms is the fact that people who are born without one or more limbs also experience phantom limbs (Brugger et al., 2000).

This idea that perception of the phantom limb originates in the brain has led to the idea that the experience of the phantom limb is often accompanied by reorganization of the somatosensory cortex. One thing that led to this discovery was research on the somatosensory cortex of a monkey in which the nerves leading from its arm to its brain had been cut. Twelve years after this operation, Tim Pons and coworkers (1991) recorded from neurons in the area in somatosensory cortex that normally would have received signals from the arm. Stimulating the arm had no effect, because no signals were getting through, but stroking the monkey's face caused the neurons to fire. This activation occurred because the cortical representation of the face is located near the cortical representation of the arm (see the homunculus in Figure 13.21), so apparently some nearby face neurons took over the functions of the neurons that had originally served the arm.

If neurons that normally respond to stimulation of the face take over from the nonfunctional arm neurons in this monkey, does the same thing occur for humans who have had their arm amputated? Apparently the answer is yes, because for some patients, light stroking of the face causes them to feel touch sensations in their phantom arm (Figure 13.33) (Ramachandran & Rogers-Ramachandran, 1996). This suggests that the amputation has led to reorganization of the person's brain, with the face taking over some of the neurons from the arm area.

What's important about this result is not just that it provides evidence for plasticity of the brain but also that it illustrates the phenomenon of **referred sensation**, in which stimulating one part of the body (the face, in this case) results in a sensation on another part of the body (the phantom arm, in this case). Thus, even though the face may have taken over some of the cortical neurons that were originally associated with the arm, these cortical neurons are apparently connected both with the face *and* with whatever mechanism causes sensations in the phantom arm (Berlucchi & Agloti, 1997).

This reorganization of the brain that occurs after amputation appears to be the body's way of compensating for the loss of the arm. But unfortunately this reorganization may be having a negative side effect. When H. Flor and coworkers (1995) measured the amount of brain reorganization in amputees using brain imaging and had these people rate the severity of their pain, they found that greater reorganization was associated with more pain (see also Knecht et al., 1996, 1998). Flor suggests that there is something about this brain reorganization that is causing the phantom pain. Exactly what this something is remains to be determined by further research.

One of the things that might help us understand what is causing phantom limb pain would be an understanding of what causes pain that occurs due to damage of actual tissue, such as when you stub your finger or cut yourself. As we consider research on the causes of pain, in the next section, we will see that we still do not completely understand what causes pain even when there is actual tissue damage. We will also see that

(*continued*)

The Plasticity of Perception *(continued)*

there is more to understanding pain perception than just neural impulses triggered at the site of the injury. Pain, as it turns out, is influenced by cogni-

tive factors such as a person's expectations and past experiences.

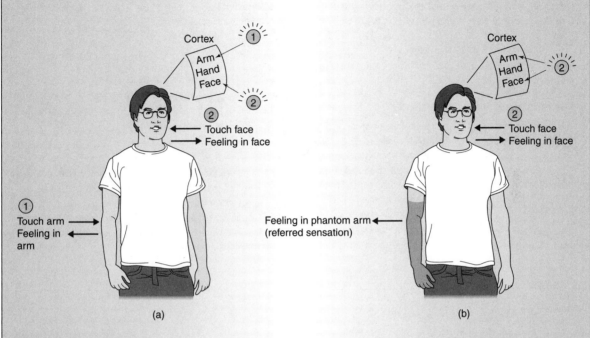

Figure 13.33

(a) Before amputation, touching the arm activates the arm area of the cortex and causes feeling in the arm. Touching the face activates the face area and causes feelings in the face. The strip marked "cortex" represents a portion of the homunculus that normally represents the arm, hand, and face. (b) After amputation, touching the face apparently leads to activation of both the face area and arm area of the cortex and causes feelings in the face and referred sensation in the arm.

The Cutaneous Senses

SUMMARY TABLE 13.2

Tactile Object Recognition

In passive touch, the observer is passive and stimulation is applied by someone else. In active touch, the perceiver controls the stimuli. Active touch involves the sensory, motor, and cognitive systems working together to create a perceptual experience that is different than the experience created by passive touch. Haptic exploration is an aspect of active touch in which a person identifies three-dimensional objects by exploring them with his or her hands using distinctive hand and finger movements called exploratory procedures.

The Physiology of Active Touch

The population of the mechanoreceptor response provides information about features of objects, like their curvature, to the brain. There are cortical neurons that respond only when a monkey grasps a specific object, like a sphere or a straight edge. Tactile object recognition also causes activity in neurons in other parietal areas, in the frontal lobe, and, for neurons involved in grasping objects, the motor cortex. Brain imaging studies on humans also indicate that identification of objects causes activity in the visual cortex, as well.

Plastic Effects of Less or More Stimulation

The map in the somatosensory cortex that represents the body can be changed by experience. Preventing stimulation from reaching the cortex from a specific part of the body causes a decrease in the area devoted to that part of the body. Extra stimulation of a monkey's fingertip increases the area of cortex that represents the finger. The area of human somatosensory cortex devoted to the fingers is larger than normal in musicians who play stringed instruments.

Plastic Effects of Losing a Sense

Braille reading by people who have been blind since birth or who became blind before 7 years of age results in activation of both the somatosensory and visual areas of the cortex.

Plastic Effects of Losing a Limb

Some amputees continue to feel their limbs even after they are amputated. This is called the phantom limb. There is evidence that this perception is mainly centrally determined. There is also evidence that perception of a phantom limb can result in brain reorganization that causes referred sensation and that greater brain reorganization is associated with a higher level of phantom limb pain.

PAIN PERCEPTION: NEURAL FIRING AND COGNITIVE INFLUENCES

WebTUTOR Pain, as we mentioned at the beginning of this chapter, functions to warn us of potentially damaging situations and therefore helps us avoid or deal with cuts, burns, and broken bones. In fact, signaling potential or actual damage is one of the major functions of pain. This function is reflected in the following definition of pain, from the International Association for the Study of Pain: "Pain is an unpleasant sensory and emotional experience associated with actual or potential tissue damage, or described in terms of such damage" (Merskey, 1991).

There are a number of things that are notable about this definition of pain. First, the reference to both sensory *and* emotional experience reflects the **multimodal nature of pain**, which is reflected by how people describe pain. When people describe their pain with words like *throbbing, prickly, hot,* or *dull* they are referring to the sensory component of pain. When they use words like *torturing, annoying, frightful,* or *sickening* they are referring to the emotional component of pain (Melzak, 1999).

Another notable aspect of this definition is its statement that it is associated with actual or *potential* tissue damage. The reference to *potential* tissue damage means that pain can occur even in the absence of actual tissue damage or that the amount of pain may not necessarily correspond to the amount of tissue damage. Pain, as we will see below, is associated not only with tissue damage but with cognitive factors that involve things like the situation in which pain occurs, a person's expectation of the possible consequences of pain, and a person's ability to pay attention to things other than his or her pain.

We will begin our description of pain by looking at the connection between pain and stimulation of pain receptors in the skin, and we will then consider situations in which things in addition to stimulation of the skin influence a person's experience of pain.

The Anatomy and Experience of Pain

Intense pressure, extreme temperature, or burning chemicals stimulate receptors in the skin called **nociceptors**. The relationship between the firing of nociceptors and pain experience is indicated in Figure 13.34, which shows the firing of monkey nociceptors and human psychophysical ratings of pain intensity (Meyer & Campbell, 1981; see also Dong et al., 1994).

Signals from the nociceptors travel up the spinothalamic pathway to the brain, but there are other pathways from receptors to brain as well, and, once we start considering the parts of the brain that are activated by pain, things become complex, because pain is associated with a number of areas of the brain.

Signals associated with pain activate a number of subcortical structures, including the hypothalamus, the limbic system, and the thalamus (Chapman, 1995), and these areas send signals to a number of areas of cortex, including the somatosensory cortex (S1 and S2), the insula, an area deep in the cortex between the parietal and temporal regions, and the anterior cingulate cortex (Derbyshire et al., 1997; Price, 2000; Rainville et al., 1997) (Figure 13.35).

The fact that many areas are involved in pain perception reflects the multimodal nature of pain, which we mentioned above. The sensory component of pain, which is usually associated with the somatosensory areas, S1 and S2, refers to the sensations we usually associate with pain. The emotional component, which refers to the negative emotions usually associated with pain, is associated with the anterior cingulate cortex (ACC), because people with damage to the ACC or who have had frontal lobotomies in which connections to that area are cut report that they feel pain but that it isn't as disturbing as it was before the cortical damage (Rainville et al., 1997).

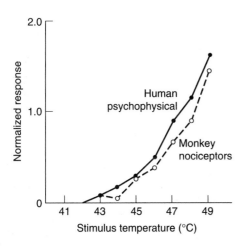

Figure 13.34
How firing of monkey nociceptors and human pain experience increase as temperature on the skin is increased between 43 and 49°C. (From Meyer & Campbell, 1981.)

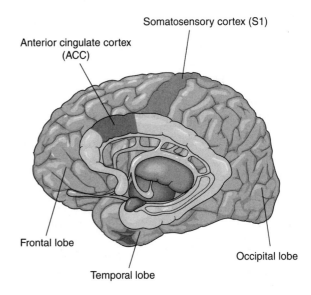

Figure 13.35
Cross section of the brain, showing the location of the somatosensory cortex (S1) and the anterior cingulate cortex, two of the areas involved in processing information about pain.

The Cutaneous Senses

BRAIN SCAN

Where Is the Unpleasantness of Pain Signaled in the Brain?

We know from clinical cases that pain can be divided into sensory and emotional components. One conclusion from these cases has been that the anterior cingulate cortex (ACC) is the area that is involved in the emotional aspect of pain (Figure 13.35). A recent fMRI study by Pierre Rainville and coworkers (1997) has reinforced this conclusion by using hypnosis to manipulate the emotional aspect of the pain experience. The area of cortex activated by pain was determined by comparing brain activity measured when subjects' hands were immersed in neutral (35°C) or painfully hot (47°C) water. The subtraction technique (see page 27) indicated activity in areas S1, S2, the insula, and the ACC, which are usually associated with pain. Repeating the experiment after hypnotizing the subjects caused the same result, so the hypnotism was not affecting brain activity in these areas. But suggesting, under hypnosis, that the pain was more unpleasant or less unpleasant altered activity only in the ACC, with activation being higher in the "high unpleasantness" condition than in the "low unpleasantness" condition. Rainville concludes from this result that the ACC is involved in determining the emotional component of pain.

We are just beginning to understand the connection between neural responding and pain perception, a connection that is made more complicated by the fact that our perception of pain depends not only on stimulation of neurons in the skin but on more central influences as well.

Cognitive and Experiential Aspects of Pain Perception

The fact that pain can't be explained just based on stimulation of the skin is well known to clinicians who, in their attempt to alleviate their patient's pain, have cut nerve fibers that send signals from the skin to the brain, only to find that the pain persists (Tuck & Flor, 1999). Pain is influenced by cognitive factors, as well as a person's experience and physical stimulation that does not involve nociceptors. We will now consider a few examples of the influence of these factors on pain perception.

Expectation   In a hospital study, when surgical patients were told what to expect and were instructed to relax to alleviate their pain, they requested fewer painkillers following surgery and were sent home 2.7 days earlier than patients who were not provided with this information. Studies have also shown that a significant proportion of patients with pathological pain get relief from taking a **placebo**, a pill that they believe contains painkillers but that, in fact, contains no active ingredients (Weisenberg, 1977).

Shifting Attention   In another hospital study, pain reduction has been achieved by using virtual reality techniques. Consider, for example, the case of James Pokorny, who had received third-degree burns over 42 percent of his body when the fuel tank of the car he was repairing exploded. While having his bandages changed at the University of Washington Burn Center, he wore a black plastic helmet with a computer monitor inside, on which he saw a virtual world of multicolored three-dimensional graphics. This world placed him in a virtual kitchen that contained a virtual spider, and he was able to chase the spider into the sink so he could grind it up with a virtual garbage disposal (Robbins, 2000).

The point of this "game" was to reduce Pokorny's pain by shifting his attention from the bandages to the virtual reality world. Pokorny reports that "you're concentrating on different things, rather than your pain. The pain level went down significantly," and studies of other patients indicate that burn patients using this virtual reality technique experienced much greater pain reduction than patients in a control group who were distracted by playing Nintendo (Hoffman et al., 2000).

Content of Emotional Distraction   An experiment by Minet deWied and Marinis Verbaten (2001) shows how the content of distracting materials can influence pain perception. The stimuli were pictures that had been previously rated as being positive (sports pictures and attractive females), neutral (household objects, nature, and people), or negative (burn victims, accidents). Male subjects looked at the pictures as one of their hands was immersed in cold (2°C) water. They were told to keep the hand immersed for as long as possible but to withdraw the hand when it began to hurt.

The results, shown in Figure 13.36, indicate that the length of time the subjects kept their hands in the water depended on the content of the pictures, with longer times associated with more positive pictures.

Since the subjects' ratings of the intensity of their pain, made immediately after removing their hands from the water, was the same for all three groups, deWied and Verbaten concluded that the content of the pictures influenced the time it took to reach the same pain level in the three groups.

Individual Differences   Different people or groups of people may describe the same stimulus differently. Clark and Clark (1980) presented electric shocks to a group of Western subjects and to a group of Nepalese subjects and asked them to indicate the intensities at which they experienced "faint pain" and "extreme pain." Although the Westerners and the Nepalese began detecting the shocks at the same intensity, the Nepalese subjects required much higher stimulus intensities before they said they experienced "faint pain" and "extreme pain" (Figure 13.37).

Analyzing these results by means of a procedure based on signal detection theory (see Appendix) indicated that there was probably no difference in the way

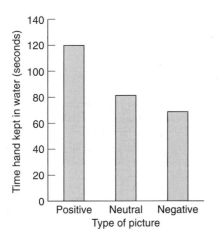

Figure 13.36
The results of the deWied and Verbaten (2001) experiment showing that subjects kept their hands in ice water longer when looking at positive pictures than when looking at neutral or negative pictures.

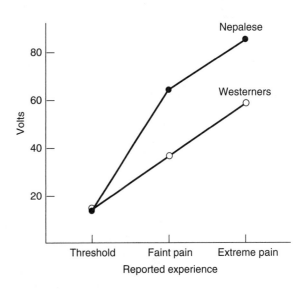

Figure 13.37
Results of the Clark and Clark (1980) experiment, which shows that the threshold for detecting a shock was the same for the Western subjects and the Nepalese subjects, but that the Nepalese subjects took much higher levels of shock before reporting "faint pain" or "extreme pain."

The Cutaneous Senses

both groups of subjects experienced the intensity of the shocks. Apparently the Nepalese subjects withstood higher levels of pain before reaching what they considered faint pain or extreme pain. It may be that Nepalese culture teaches people to withstand pain without complaining.

A similar result was obtained by Evelyn Hall and Simon Davies (1991), who had female varsity track athletes and female nonathletes rate their level of pain in response to immersion of their hands in freezing ice water. Although both groups were exposed to the same stimulus, the athletes rated their pain as less intense (their average rating was 76 on a 150-point pain scale) than the nonathletes (whose average was 130). Perhaps the athletes had learned, during painful training workouts, to withstand higher levels of pain.

The examples above illustrate how pain can be influenced by factors other than stimulation of pain receptors in the skin. The fact that these factors can influence pain perception has been known for many years, but early reports of these kinds of effects were often viewed skeptically, because the accepted explanation for pain was that it was caused by stimulation of receptors in the skin. An important step toward changing this accepted explanation was the introduction of a theory of pain perception called gate control theory in 1965. This theory suggested a way that a person's thoughts and other factors that did not involve the stimulation of nociceptors could have physiological effects that could reduce pain.

Gate Control Theory

Gate control theory was proposed by Ronald Melzack and Patrick Wall (1965, 1988) to explain how pain perception can be affected both by central influences, such as those described above, and by nonpainful tactile stimuli, as when rubbing the skin causes a decrease in the perception of pain.

The gate control system consists of cells in an area of the dorsal horn of the spinal cord called the **substantia gelatinosa** and **transmission cells** (T-cells) located in the dorsal horn near the substantia gelatinosa (Figure 13.38a). The neural circuit containing these cells is shown in Figure 13.38b. The

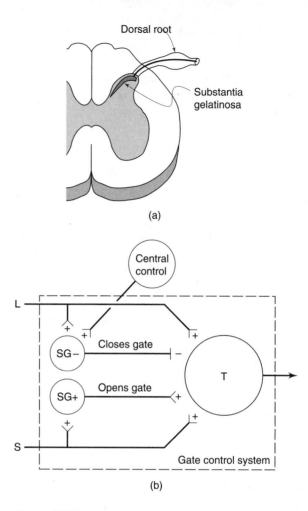

Figure 13.38
(a) Cross section of the spinal cord showing fibers entering through the dorsal root and the substantia gelatinosa (shaded), where some of the cells of Melzack and Wall's (1988) proposed gate control circuit are located. (b) The circuit proposed by Melzack and Wall for their gate control theory of pain perception.

output of the gate control system determines pain perception, with greater activity causing greater pain. This output flows through the T-cells and is controlled by two kinds of substantia gelatinosa cells: one (SG+) that opens the pain gate by sending excitation to the T-cells and one (SG−) that closes the pain gate by sending inhibition to the T-cells.

If only **small-diameter fibers (S-fibers)**, the nociceptors we discussed earlier, are active, then pain occurs, since SG+ cells open the gate. However, when **large-diameter fibers (L-fibers)**, which carry information about nonpainful tactile stimuli, are active, then pain is inhibited, since SG− cells close the gate. Thus, when potentially damaging stimuli cause nociceptors and their S-fibers to fire, the SG+ cells open the gate and pain increases. But when more gentle stimuli, such as massage, rubbing, and gentle vibration, cause activity in L-fibers, the SG− cells close the gate, and pain decreases. Another way to close the gate is by sending signals from the structure labeled "central control," which represents the brain or other higher-order structures that would be activated by the cognitive factors we described above. As indicated in the circuit, signals from central control close the gate by activating SG− cells.

After introduction of gate control theory, an effect called **stimulation-produced analgesia (SPA)** was discovered, which showed that signals from the brain can reduce the perception of pain. SPA occurs when electrical stimulation of an area in a rat's midbrain causes the rat to ignore pinching of its tail or paw that would normally cause a strong withdrawal response. In fact, David Reynolds (1969), who first demonstrated this effect, found that he could even perform abdominal surgery on rats with no anesthesia other than the electrical stimulation.

Although the specific neural circuits that control pain are actually much more complex than what is proposed by gate control theory (Perl & Kruger, 1996), the idea that our perception of pain depends not only on input from nociceptors, but also on input from fibers usually not concerned with pain, and also from central influences, is supported by a large amount of research, and many researchers still consider gate control theory to be a useful way to think, in general terms, about pain mechanisms (Fields & Basbaum, 1999; Turk & Flor, 1999; Weissberg, 1999).

Another important development in our understanding of how central factors influence pain perception is the discovery that the nervous system contains endorphins, chemicals produced by the brain that have properties closely related to those of opiates such as morphine.

Pain Control by Endorphins

A family of substances called **endorphins**, which are endogenous (naturally occurring in the body) morphinelike substances, can have powerful analgesic effects (Mayer, 1979; Watkins & Mayer, 1982). We can link the discovery of endorphins to research on opiate drugs such as opium and heroin, which have been used since the dawn of recorded history to reduce pain and induce feelings of euphoria.

By the 1970s researchers had discovered that the opiate drugs act on receptors in the brain, which respond to stimulation by molecules with specific structures. The importance of the molecule's structure for exciting these "opiate receptors" explains why injecting a drug called **naloxone** into an overdosed heroin addict can almost immediately revive the victim. Since naloxone's structure is similar to heroin's, the naloxone blocks the action of heroin by attaching itself to receptor sites usually occupied by heroin (Figure 13.39a).

Why are there opiate receptor sites in the brain? After all, they most certainly have been present since long before people started taking heroin. Researchers concluded that there must be naturally occurring substances in the body that act on these sites, and in 1975 neurotransmitters were discovered that act on the same receptors that are activated by opium and heroin and that are blocked by naloxone. One group of these transmitters are the pain-reducing endorphins.

Since the discovery of endorphins, researchers have accumulated a large amount of evidence linking endorphins to pain reduction. For example, stimulation-produced analgesia works best when endorphin sites are stimulated, a finding suggesting that SPA works by releasing endorphins into the nervous system (Figure 13.39b).

Further evidence linking endorphins with pain relief is provided by the fact that injection of naloxone decreases the effect of SPA. This decreased effect would occur if naloxone were occupying sites which are normally stimulated by endorphins (Figure 13.39c). This evidence strongly suggests that the brain uses endorphins to control pain.

In addition to decreasing the effect of SPA, naloxone also decreases the analgesic effect of placebos.

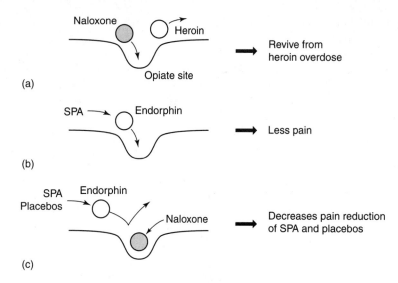

(a)

(b)

(c)

Figure 13.39
(a) Naloxone reduces the effect of heroin by occupying a receptor site normally stimulated by heroin. (b) Stimulation-produced analgesia may work by causing the release of endorphins, which stimulate opiate receptor sites. (c) Injecting naloxone decreases the pain reduction caused by SPA and placebos, since it displaces endorphins (just as it displaced heroin, in part a). This provides evidence that endorphins are released by SPA and placebos.

Since placebos contain no active chemicals, their effects have always been thought to be "psychological." However, the idea that placebos cause the release of endorphins provides a physiological basis for what had previously been described in strictly psychological terms. Thus, the very real and usually negative effects of pain are triggered by nerve firing caused by damage or potential damage to the skin, or receptors within the body associated with conditions such as back pain or cancer. But now we know that these signals can also be influenced by "psychological" effects, which we can link to the firing of descending nerve pathways and to the release of chemicals in the brain.

PARALLELS BETWEEN TOUCH AND VISION

One of the most remarkable things about the material we have covered in this chapter is that, despite the large differences between the experience of touch and the experience of seeing, the two senses that create these experiences share a number of common mechanisms. Table 13.2, which summarizes some of these common mechanisms, shows that there are similarities at the level of the receptors and at the level of the brain, that we can point to examples of plasticity in both senses, and that there are a number of ways in which vision and touch interact.

Table 13.2

Comparing the mechanisms for touch and vision

	Touch	Vision
RECEPTOR SPECIFICITY	Mechanoreceptors respond to specific frequencies and types of stimuli	Rod and cone receptors respond to different areas of the visible spectrum
DETAIL PERCEPTION	SA1 receptors with small receptive fields	Cones with small receptive fields
	More area on somatosensory cortex for fingers and other parts of body with good detail perception	More area on visual cortex for the fovea, which has the best detail perception
RECEPTIVE FIELDS	Center-surround receptive fields early in the system, and feature detectors that respond to specific orientations and directions of movement later in the system	Center-surround receptive fields early in the system, and feature detectors that respond to specific orientations and directions of movement later in the system
PLASTICITY	Stopping signals from part of a monkey's body from reaching S1 causes a decrease in the size of brain area representing that part of the body	Raising kittens so that only one eye is stimulated eliminates neurons that respond to stimulation of both eyes
	Increasing stimulation of a particular body part in monkeys (fingertip stimulation) and humans (string musicians) increases the size of the brain area representing that part of the body	Raising cats in an environment without movement eliminates neurons that respond to the direction of movement
INTERACTIONS BETWEEN TOUCH AND VISION	There are bimodal neurons that respond to both touch and vision. Tactile object recognition causes responding in both somatosensory and visual areas of the cortex.	Reaching out to grasp an object initially involves locating the object visually and then sensing its tactile properties. There are bimodal neurons that respond to both vision and to grasping, and many of these neurons also have connections to the motor cortex. In people who became blind early in life, reading braille activates both the somatosensory and visual areas of the cortex.

The Anatomy and Experience of Pain

Peripherally, pain results from the stimulation of nociceptors. Centrally, a number of different structures are associated with pain, some of which are associated with the sensory component of pain (S1 and S2) and some of which are associated with the affective component of pain (anterior cingulate cortex).

Neural Responding and Pain Perception

A correspondence has been demonstrated between the experience of pain and the firing of nociceptors and the firing of cortical neurons.

Influence of Factors Other Than Skin Stimulation on Pain Perception

There is a great deal of evidence that pain can't be explained just on the basis of stimulation of the skin. Some of this evidence includes the effect of a person's expectations on pain perception; the effect of placebos, attention, and distraction on pain perception; and differences in people's tolerance for pain.

Gate Control Theory

Gate control theory is a circuit that takes into account the contributions of both tissue damage and other things that can affect the perception of pain. Activity in the L-fibers or from central input decreases pain perception by closing the gate. Activity in S-fibers opens the gate and so increases pain perception. The pain reduction that can be achieved by stimulation-produced analgesia and acupuncture can be explained in terms of increased activity in L-fibers.

Endorphins

Naturally occurring opiates called endorphins can cause a reduction in pain. Evidence that endorphins may be involved in pain reduction caused by stimulation-produced analgesia and placebos has been provided by the fact that injection of naloxone, an agent that would block endorphin sites, eliminates the pain reduction associated with these effects.

STUDY QUESTIONS

1. What would be some of the consequences of losing the ability to feel sensations through the skin? (436)

2. What kinds of sensations are served by the somatosensory system? (437)

The Skin and Its Receptors

The Skin

3. What are the main functions of the skin? (437)

4. What is the epidermis? The dermis? What are mechanoreceptors? (437)

Mechanoreceptors in the Skin

5. What are the locations, structures, and functions of the mechanoreceptors? (437)

6. Describe the following properties of the mechanoreceptors: (1) frequency ranges over which they respond; (2) perception associated with each one (Table 13.1). (438)

7. What is microneurography? (439)

8. Which mechanoreceptors are slowly adapting (SA), and which are rapidly adapting (RA)? (439)

9. Which mechanoreceptors have small receptive fields? Which have large receptive fields? How is the size of the receptive field indicated by the relationship between threshold vs. distance across the skin? (439)

10. How does the Pacinian corpuscle determine the type of stimulation to which its fiber responds? The RA2 fiber is specialized to respond to what type of stimulation? (440)

11. The SA1 fiber is specialized to respond to what type of stimulation? Describe the experiments using raised-dot patterns rolled over the fingers that demonstrated this. (441)

12. What is a spatial event plot? What do spatial event plots tell us about why some letters can be identified accurately and others not? (442)

13. Which fibers would fire when we grasp a cup and then run our fingers over ridges in the cup? (443)

Thermoreceptors: The Neural Response to Temperature

14. What is a thermoreceptor? A warm fiber? A cold fiber? (443)

Neural Processing for Touch

15. Describe the connection between convergence and receptive field size and the perception of details in the visual system. (444)

Mechanoreceptors and the Perception of Details

16. What is the two-point threshold? How does it differ on different parts of the body? (444)

17. What is the relationship between the size of the two-point threshold and the size of receptive fields of RA1 and SA1 fibers? The density of RA1 and SA1 fibers? (445)

Processing in the Cortex

18. What are the two pathways that transmit tactile information up the spinal cord? (446)

19. What is the "tactile" nucleus in the thalamus? (447)

20. Where are the somatosensory receiving areas? (447)

21. What is the homunculus? Compare the way the fingers and other parts of the body are represented in the homunculus and the magnification factor in visual perception. (447)

22. What is the relationship between tactile acuity and the size of receptive fields of cortical neurons? (448)

23. Describe the columns and multiple maps that exist in somatosensory cortex. (448)

24. Compare the receptive fields of neurons in the skin to the receptive fields of neurons in the cortex. (449)

25. Compare the receptive fields of neurons in somatosensory cortex to the receptive fields of neurons in the visual cortex. (450)

Tactile Object Recognition

26. What is passive touch? (451)

Passive Touch and Active Touch

27. What is active touch? (452)

Identifying Objects by Haptic Exploration

28. What is haptic perception? What three systems come into play when an object is being identified using haptic perception? (452)

29. How do the experiences of active and passive touch compare, according to J. J. Gibson? (452)

30. What are exploratory procedures, and how do they differ for different object qualities? (453)

The Physiology of Active Touch

31. Is information for tactile object recognition provided by single mechanoreceptors or by populations of mechanoreceptors? (453)

32. How do SA1 fibers in the fingertips respond to spheres with different curvatures? What is it about this response that provides information about curvature to the brain? (454)

33. Describe the neuron that responds when stimulation results from an animal's own actions but does not respond to stimulation by the experimenter. (454)

34. Describe Hsiao's experiment that showed that the response of neurons in the monkey's somatosensory cortex is influenced by the monkey's attentional state. (454)

35. What areas in addition to S1 and S2 are involved in tactile object recognition? (455)

Plasticity in the Cutaneous System

Changes in Cortical Maps Caused by Decreasing or Increasing Stimulation

36. How does (a) reducing stimulation of the skin and (b) increasing stimulation of the skin affect cortical maps? What does this tell us about the plasticity of the sensory homunculus? (456)

37. What does fMRI research indicate about the cortical representation for the fingers of musicians who play string instruments? (456)

Plastic Effects of Losing a Sense

38. What areas of cortex are activated by braille reading in people who have become blind before the age of 7? (456)

Plasticity from Amputation of a Limb

39. What is a phantom limb? Describe some of the sensations experienced by people with phantom limbs. (457)

40. What is the evidence for a central explanation for phantom limbs? (458)

41. What is the evidence that phantom limbs are associated with reorganization of the cortex? What is referred sensation? (458)

42. What is the evidence that brain reorganization is associated with phantom limb pain? (458)

Pain Perception: Neural Firing and Cognitive Influences

43. What is the definition of pain? Is tissue damage always involved, according to this definition? (460)

44. Which two types of experience are associated with pain? Why do we say pain is multimodal? (460)

The Anatomy and Experience of Pain

45. What is a nociceptor? (461)

46. What areas of the brain are activated by presentation of pain stimuli? (461)

47. What area of the cortex is associated with the emotional component of pain? (461)

Cognitive and Experiential Aspects of Pain Perception

48. What are some examples of situations in which the perception of pain is determined by factors in addition to stimulation of receptors in the skin? Consider examples associated with expectation, shifting attention, content of emotional distraction, and individual differences. (462)

Gate Control Theory

49. Describe gate control theory. Which types of fibers are responsible for opening the gate? For closing the gate? What stimuli are responsible for opening and closing the gate? (464)

50. What is stimulation-produced analgesia (SPA), and why is it important? (465)

Pain Control by Endorphins

51. What are endorphins? How was naloxone used to demonstrate a link between endorphins and heroin? (465)

52. What is the effect of naloxone on SPA and placebos? What does this result mean? (465)

Across the Senses: Parallels Between Touch and Vision

53. What are the parallels between touch and vision (Table 3.2)? (467)

14

THE CHEMICAL SENSES

CHAPTER CONTENTS

SOME QUESTIONS WE WILL CONSIDER

- Why is a dog's sense of smell so much better than a human's? (476)

- Why does a cold inhibit the ability to taste? (496)

- How do neurons in the cortex combine smell and taste? (499)

...We have five senses, but only two that go beyond the boundaries of ourselves. When you look at someone, it's just bouncing light, or when you hear them, it's just sound waves, vibrating air, or touch is just nerve endings tingling. Know what smell is?... It's made up of the molecules of what you're smelling.

Angels in America, p. 17

The character speaking the lines above in the play *Angels in America* probably did not take a course in sensation and perception and so leaves out the fact that vision and hearing are "just nerve endings tingling" as well. But the point he is making—that smell involves taking molecules of the thing you are smelling into your body—is one of the properties of the chemical senses that distinguishes them from the

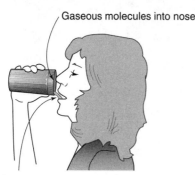

Gaseous molecules into nose

Liquid onto tongue

Figure 14.1
As this woman drinks coffee, molecules of coffee in gaseous form enter her nose, and molecules in liquid form enter her mouth. Olfaction and taste are unique among the senses in that the stimuli become incorporated into the receptors and, in the case of taste, enter the digestive system.

other senses. Thus, as the person in Figure 14.1 drinks her coffee, she smells it because molecules of the coffee in gas form are entering her nose, and she tastes it because molecules of coffee in liquid form are stimulating her tongue. Smell and taste have been called molecule detectors because they endow these gas and liquid molecules with distinctive smells and tastes (Cain, 1988; Kauer, 1987).[1]

Since the stimuli responsible for tasting and smelling are on the verge of being assimilated into the body, these senses are often seen as "gatekeepers," which function (1) to identify things that the body needs for survival and that should therefore be consumed and (2) to detect things that would be bad for the body and that should therefore be rejected. This role as a detector of dangerous solutions is demonstrated by the fact that rats tend to avoid chemicals that are highly toxic (Scott & Giza, 2000) (Figure 14.2).

[1] In addition to creating experiences associated with tasting and smelling, molecules entering the nose and mouth can also cause experiences such as the irritation of breathing ammonia or the burning sensation from eating chili peppers. This component of chemical sensitivity, which is called **chemesthesis**, is related to the cutaneous senses we discussed in Chapter 13 (Doty, 1995; Silver & Finger, 1991).

The gatekeeper function of taste and smell is aided by a large affective, or emotional, component, since things that are bad for us often taste or smell unpleasant, and things that are good for us generally taste or smell good. In addition to assigning "good" and "bad" affect, smelling an odor associated with a past place or event can trigger memories, which in turn may create emotional reactions.

Because the receptors that serve taste and smell are constantly exposed not only to the chemicals that they are designed to sense but also to irritants such as bacteria and dirt, they undergo a cycle of birth, development, and death over a 5- to 7-week period (Figure 14.3). This constant renewal of the receptors, which is called **neurogenesis**, is unique to these senses. In vision, hearing, and the cutaneous senses, the receptors are safely protected inside structures such as the eye, the inner ear, and under the skin; however, the receptors for taste and smell are relatively unprotected and therefore need a mechanism for renewal.

We consider olfaction first and then taste. Although we will be considering olfaction and taste separately, we will see that they often interact. Thus, as you savor the "taste" of something you are eating,

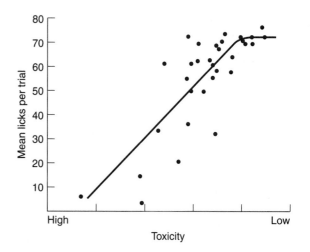

Figure 14.2
The relationship between how much of a substance a rat will drink versus the toxicity of the substance. In general, rats avoid highly toxic substances and seek out substances that are not toxic. (Adapted from Scott & Giza, 2000.)

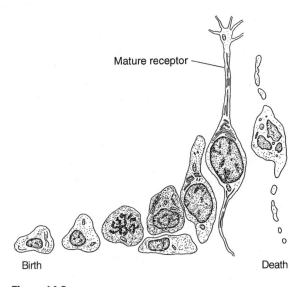

Figure 14.3

Neurogenesis of an olfactory receptor. A unique feature of smell and taste, compared to the other senses, is the way the receptors for smell and taste develop and then die over a 5- to 7-week period. The mature receptor develops from the cell on the left and then dies, as shown on the right. (From Graziadei, 1976.)

you probably, in fact, are experiencing a combination of taste and smell. We will have more to say about this combined experience, which is called flavor, when we consider the perception of food at the end of the chapter.

OLFACTION: USES AND FACTS

Olfaction is extremely important in the lives of many species, since it is often their primary window to the environment (Ache, 1991). One important contrast between humans and other species is that many animals are **macrosmatic** (having a keen sense of smell that is important to their survival), whereas humans are **microsmatic** (having a less keen sense of smell that is not crucial to their survival). The survival value of olfaction for many animals lies in their use of olfaction to provide cues to orient themselves in space, to mark territory, and to guide them to specific places, other animals, and food sources (Holley,

1991). Olfaction is also extremely important in sexual reproduction, since it triggers mating behavior in many species (Doty, 1976; Pfeiffer & Johnston, 1994).

Although smell may not be crucial to the survival of humans, the vast sums of money spent yearly on perfumes and deodorants (Rossiter, 1996), as well as the emergence of a new billion-dollar-a-year industry called environmental fragrancing, which offers products to add pleasing scents to the air in both homes and businesses, attests to the fact that the role of smell in our daily lives is not inconsequential.

But perhaps the most convincing argument for the importance of smell to humans comes from those who suffer from **anosmia**, the loss of the ability to smell due to injury or infection. People suffering from anosmia describe the great void created by their inability to taste many foods because of the close connection between smell and flavor. One woman who suffered from anosmia and then briefly regained her sense of smell stated, "I always thought I would sacrifice smell to taste if I had to choose between the two, but I suddenly realized how much I had missed. We take it for granted and are unaware that everything smells: people, the air, my house, my skin" (Birnberg, 1988; quoted in Ackerman, 1990, p. 42). Olfaction is more important in our lives than most of us realize, and, while it may not be essential to our survival, life is often enhanced by our ability to smell and becomes a little more dangerous if we lose the olfactory warning system that alerts us to spoiled food, leaking gas, or smoke from a fire.

The powers of the human olfactory system have often been underrated, especially when human olfactory capabilities are compared to the olfactory powers of other animals. Let's consider some facts that put our olfactory abilities into perspective:

- *Fact 1: Although humans are less sensitive than many other animals to odors, our olfactory receptors are exquisitely sensitive.* Rats are 8 to 50 times more sensitive to odors than humans, and dogs are from 300 to 10,000 times more sensitive, depending on the odorant (Laing, Doty, & Breipohl, 1991). But even though other animals can detect odors of which humans are unaware, the human's

The Chemical Senses

individual olfactory receptors are as sensitive as any animal's. H. deVries and M. Stuiver (1961) demonstrated this by showing that human olfactory receptors can be excited by the action of just one molecule of odorant. Nothing can be more sensitive than one molecule per receptor, so the human's lower sensitivity to odors compared to that of other animals must be due to something else. That something else is the number of receptors: only about 10 million in humans compared to about 1 billion in dogs (Dodd & Squirrell, 1980; Moulton, 1977).

- *Fact 2: Humans are capable of detecting small differences in odor intensity.* The ability to detect differences in intensity is indicated by the difference threshold—the smallest difference in intensity between two stimuli that can just be detected (see Chapter 1). In the past, olfaction has been reputed to have the largest difference threshold of all the senses, with typical values ranging from about 25 to 33 percent (Gamble, 1898; Stone & Bosley, 1965). That is, the concentration of an odorant must be increased by 25 to 33 percent before a person can detect an increase in odor intensity.

  When William Cain (1977) carefully measured the difference threshold by placing two odorants of different concentrations on absorbent cotton balls and asking subjects to judge which was more intense, his results were better than those of most other studies, with an average difference threshold of 19 percent and a relatively low difference threshold of 7 percent for *n*-butyl alcohol. But Cain didn't stop with these measurements, because an average difference threshold of 19 percent still seemed high to him. He next analyzed the stimuli he had presented to his human subjects using a gas chromatograph, a device that accurately measures the concentration of the vapor emitted by each stimulus. Cain found what he had suspected: Stimuli that were supposed to have the same concentration actually varied considerably, apparently because of differences in the airflow pattern through the cotton in different samples.

  By eliminating this variability in stimulus concentration, Cain was able to demonstrate that the difference threshold was smaller than had been previously measured. When he presented stimuli to subjects by using an **olfactometer**, a device that presents olfactory stimuli with much greater precision than cotton balls, Cain found an average difference threshold of 11 percent, with *n*-butyl alcohol having an impressively low threshold of only 5 percent. These figures, which begin to approach the difference thresholds for vision and hearing, show that our ability to detect differences in smell intensity is, in fact, not that poor compared to the other senses.

- *Fact 3: Although it is often difficult to recognize some odors, the ability to do this improves with training.* Although humans can tell the difference between approximately 10,000 different odors (Axel, 1995), early research on odor identification seemed to indicate that our ability to name specific odors is poor, because when asked to identify odors people were typically successful only about half the time (Engen & Pfaffmann, 1960). However, later experiments showed that, under the right conditions, our ability to identify odors is actually quite a bit better than that. For example, J. A. Desor and Gary K. Beauchamp (1974) found that subjects could identify only about half of the smells of familiar substances like coffee, bananas, and motor oil. But when Desor and Beauchamp named the substances when they were first presented and then reminded their subjects of the correct names when they failed to respond correctly on subsequent trials, the subjects could, after some practice, correctly identify 98 percent of the substances.

  According to Cain (1979, 1980), the key to the good performance in Desor and Beauchamp's experiment is that their subjects were provided with the correct names, or labels, at the beginning of the experiment. In his own experiments, Cain showed that when subjects assign a correct label to a familiar object the first time they smell it (for example, labeling an orange "orange"), or when the experimenter provides the correct labels, the subjects usually identify the object correctly the next time it is presented. When, however, subjects assign an incorrect label to an object the first time they smell it (for example, labeling machine oil as "cheese"), they usually misidentify it the next time it is presented. Thus, according to Cain, when we have trouble identifying odors, this trouble results not from a deficiency in our olfactory system, but from an inability to retrieve the odor's name from our memory.

The amazing thing about the role that memory plays in odor identification is that knowing the correct label for the odor actually seems to transform our perception into that odor. Cain (1980) gives the example of an object initially identified by the subject as "fishy-goaty-oily." When the experimenter tells the subject that the fishy-goaty-oily smell actually comes from leather, the smell is then transformed into that of leather. I recently had a similar experience when a friend gave me a bottle of Aquavit, a Danish drink with a very interesting smell. As I was sampling this drink with some friends, we tried to identify its smell. Many odors were proposed ("anise," "orange," "lemon"), but it wasn't until someone turned the bottle around and read the label on the back that the truth became known: "Aquavit (Water of Life) is the Danish national drink—a delicious, crystal-clear spirit distilled from grain, with a slight taste of caraway." When we heard the word *caraway*, the previous hypotheses of anise, orange, and lemon were instantly transformed into caraway. Thus, the olfactory system has the information needed to identify specific odors but needs assistance from memory to apply that information to the actual naming of these odors.

DEMONSTRATION

Naming and Odor Identification

To demonstrate the effect of naming substances on odor identification, have a friend collect a number of familiar objects for you and, without looking, try to identify the odors. You will find that you can identify some but not others, and when your friend tells you the correct answer for the ones you identified incorrectly, you will wonder how you could have failed to identify such a familiar smell. But don't blame your mistakes on your nose; blame them on your memory. ●

- *Fact 4: Human olfaction has the potential to provide information about other people.* Many animals use their sense of smell to recognize other animals. As McKenzie (1923) remarked about the dog, "He can recognize his master by sight, no doubt, yet, as we know, he is never perfectly satisfied until he has taken stock also of the scent, the more precisely to do so bringing his snout into actual contact with the person he is examining. It is as if his eyes might deceive him, but never his nose." Humans, however, are socially constrained from behaving like dogs. Except in the most intimate situations, it is considered poor form to smell other people at close range. However, what if we lived in a society that condoned this kind of behavior? Could we identify other people based on their smell? A recent experiment suggests that the answer to this question may be "yes."

Michael Russell (1976) had subjects wear undershirts for 24 hours, without showering or using deodorant or perfume. The undershirts were then sealed in a bag and given to the experimenter, who, in turn, presented each subject with three undershirts to smell: One was the subject's own shirt, one was a male's, and one was a female's. About three-quarters of the subjects succeeded in identifying their own undershirt, based on its odor, and also correctly identified which of the other shirts had been worn by males or females (see also McBurney, Levine, & Cavanaugh, 1977). Similar results have also been reported for breath odors, which subjects can identify as being produced by a male or a female (Doty et al., 1982). It has also been shown that young infants can identify the smell of their mother's breast or armpits (Cernoch & Porter, 1985; Macfarlane, 1975). These results don't suggest that people can identify other people solely by their smell, but they do show that our ability to use smell in such situations may be underrated.

The Chemical Senses

The phenomenon of **menstrual synchrony** also suggests a role for smell in interpersonal relations. Martha McClintock (1971) noted that women who live or work together often report that their menstrual periods begin at about the same time. For example, one group of seven female lifeguards had widely scattered menstrual periods at the beginning of the summer, but by the end of the summer, all were beginning their periods within four days of each other. To investigate this phenomenon, McClintock asked 135 females, aged 17 to 22, living in a college dormitory, to indicate when their periods began throughout the school year. She found that women who saw each other often (roommates or close friends) tended to have synchronous periods by the end of the school year. After eliminating other explanations such as awareness of the other person's period, McClintock concluded that "there is some interpersonal physiological process which affects the menstrual cycle" (p. 246).

What might this physiological process be? Michael Russell, G. M. Switz, and K. Thompson (1980) conducted an experiment that suggests that smell has something to do with this process. He had a "donor" woman wear cotton pads in her armpits for 24 hours, three times a week. The sweat extracted from these pads was then rubbed onto the upper lip of a woman in the experimental group. A control group of women received the same treatment, but without the sweat. The results for the experimental group showed that before the experiment there had been an average of 9.3 days between the onset of the donor's and the subject's periods; but, after five months, the average time between onsets was reduced to 3.4 days. The control group showed no such synchrony. Since the donors and the subjects in the experimental group never saw each other, Russell concluded that odor must be the factor that causes menstrual synchrony (see also Preti et al., 1986).

From these facts about olfaction, it is clear that the human olfactory system has capacities that are more impressive than often believed. We will now describe some of the physiological properties of olfaction.

THE OLFACTORY SYSTEM

webTUTOR   To introduce the olfactory system, we will describe the anatomy of the receptors that generate electrical signals from olfactory stimuli and the central destination of these signals.

The Olfactory Mucosa

The picture in Figure 14.4 is not an underwater coral reef or vegetation on the forest floor. It is a picture of the surface of the **olfactory mucosa**, the dime-sized region located high in the nasal cavity that contains the receptors for olfaction and is therefore where transduction occurs. Figure 14.5a shows the location of the

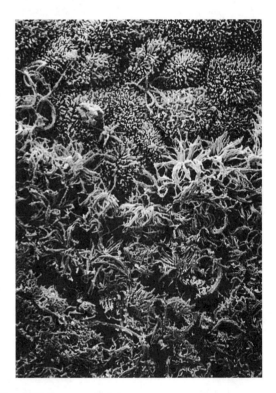

Figure 14.4

A scanning electron micrograph of the surface of the olfactory mucosa. The region in the foreground is densely covered with the cilia of olfactory receptors. (From Morrison & Moran, 1995.)

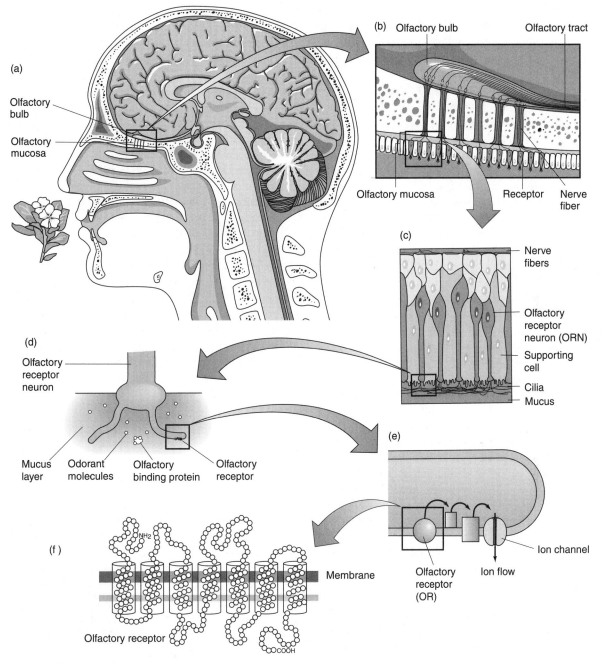

Figure 14.5

(a) The olfactory mucosa, with the olfactory bulb just above (Amoore, Johnston, & Rubin, 1964); (b) & (c) olfactory receptor nerons (ORN) have cilia that protrude into the mucosa; (d) olfactory receptors (OR) on the cilia are where transduction occurs; (e) stimulation of an OR triggers a series of reactions that result in ion flow across the membrane of the cilium; (f) the OR is part of the membrane, crossing it seven times.

The Chemical Senses

mucosa, on the roof of the nasal cavity and just below the olfactory bulb, which is actually an outcropping of the brain (Figures 14.5a and b). We will now zoom in on the mucosa to the place where transduction occurs.

Olfactory Receptor Neurons and Olfactory Receptors The **olfactory receptor neuron (ORN)** is where transduction—the transformation from chemicals into electrical signals—occurs (Figure 14.5c and d). The exact site of this transformation is the **olfactory receptor (OR)**. Olfactory receptors are found on cilia located at the ends of ORNs. Figure 14.5d shows a close-up of two of the many cilia on an ORN, and Figure 14.5e shows that the OR is part of the wall of the cilium.

A close-up of an OR is shown in Figure 14.5f. The OR is a protein molecule consisting of strings of amino acids (circles) that cross the membrane of the ORN seven times. There are many different types of ORs, each made up of different sequences of amino acids. You may remember that the visual pigment molecule in the visual receptors also crosses the membrane seven times (see Figure 2.17). Olfaction and vision both have active molecules in their receptors that come from the same molecular family (Buck & Axel, 1991; Shepherd, 1994).

Using new genetic techniques that make use of the fact that ORs are created from instructions coded in genes, researchers have recently been able to show that there are about 1,000 different kinds of ORs, each of which responds to the same group of odorants (Axel, 1995). Another important property of ORs is that the ORs on a particular ORN are all the same. Thus, the response of an ORN reflects the properties of the types of receptors that dot its cilia (see Table 14.1).

Activation of Olfactory Receptors The first step in the process of olfaction is the stimulation of the ORs by the odorants. Odorants must contact the ORs in order to stimulate them. This can occur in two ways: (1) Odorants can flow to the receptors directly in the stream of inhaled air; or (2) odorants can become attached to molecules called **olfactory binding proteins**, which transport odorants through the mucosa to the receptors (Figure 14.5d) (Pelosi, 1996; Pevsner et al., 1985, 1990).

When odorants reach ORs they trigger a series of reactions that lead to the opening of ion channels in the membrane. This process is shown schematically in Figure 14.5e. When the ion channels open, ion flow occurs across the membrane, and the flow of ions across the membrane causes an electrical signal in the cilium (Firestein, 1992; Lancet, 1992; Reed et al., 1992; Shepherd, 1992a, 1992b). This signal is transmitted to the rest of the ORN and into its axon, which, as part of the olfactory nerve, transmits the signal toward the olfactory bulb of the brain.

Organization of the ORNs on the Olfactory Mucosa There are about 1,000 different kinds of ORNs, with about 10,000 of each type (see Table 14.2). The olfactory mucosa is divided into four zones. A particular type of ORN is found in only one of these zones, although there are many different types of ORNs randomly scattered throughout a zone. Although we still don't know the function of these zones, we do know that when the ORNs send their axons out of the mucosa in the olfactory nerve, all of the axons from one area of the mucosa go to the same area of the olfactory bulb (Figure 14.6).

Table 14.1

The olfactory mucosa and associated structures

Structures	Description
Olfactory mucosa	A sheet of neurons located at the top of the nasal cavity, it includes olfactory receptor neurons and supporting cells.
Olfactory receptor neurons (ORN)	Neurons in the mucosa, which have cilia at the end. There are about 10 million ORNs.
Olfactory receptors (OR)	Seven stranded proteins located on the cilia of the ORN. There are about 1,000 different kinds of ORs, but only one kind is found on a particular ORN.

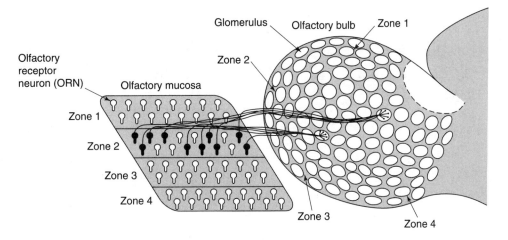

Figure 14.6

Organization of the olfactory mucosa. The olfactory mucosa, on the left, is divided into four zones. Each zone contains a mixture of different kinds of olfactory receptor neurons, as indicated by the black-and-white neurons in Zone 1. However, a particular kind of olfactory receptor neuron is found only in one zone. The olfactory bulb, on the right, is also divided into zones. Each type of olfactory receptor neuron in the olfactory mucosa sends its axons to just one or two glomeruli in the olfactory bulb. (Adapted from Mori et al., 1999.)

Table 14.2

Numbers and types of olfactory receptor neurons and glomeruli in the olfactory system

Types of ORNs (Each type has a particular type of OR.)	1,000 (Comparison to vision: There are 3 types of cone receptors and 1 type of rod receptor.)
Number of ORNs	10 million (Comparison to vision: There are 6 million cone receptors and 120 million rod receptors in each retina.)
Number of each type of ORN	10,000
Glomeruli in olfactory bulb (Each glomerulus receives signals mainly from one type of ORN.)	1,000–2,000

The Brain

The 10 million axons of the ORNs stream out of the mucosa in the olfactory nerve and immediately reach the **olfactory bulb**, the first destination of olfactory signals in the brain.

The Olfactory Bulb The ORNs' short trip to the brain is remarkable when we compare it to the situation in the other senses. For example, the signals from the rods and cones in the retina must pass through many synapses before reaching the brain. Olfactory signals, in contrast, reach the brain with no intervening synapses. When the ORN axons reach the olfactory bulb, they fan out to synapse in small round structures called **glomeruli**, which are indicated by the circles on the olfactory bulb in Figure 14.6.

The 10 million ORN axons reaching the olfactory bulb synapse in about 1,000 to 2,000 glomeruli. This means that each glomerulus receives about 5,000 to 10,000 ORN fibers. The important feature of this input to the glomeruli is that a particular glomerulus receives signals mainly from one type of ORN. Another way to describe this is to say that a given type of ORN sends most of its axons to just one or two glomeruli. Since each glomerulus collects information from receptor neurons that all respond to the same odorants, the glomeruli have been compared to columns in the visual cortex that respond best to similar forms and to similar orientations

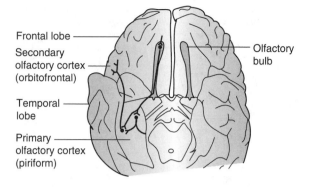

Figure 14.7
The underside of the brain, showing the neural pathways for olfaction. On the left side, the temporal lobe has been deflected to expose the olfactory cortex. (From Frank & Rabin, 1989.)

(Shepherd, 1994). It is clear that one of the main functions of the glomeruli is to collect information about small groups of odorants.

Central Destinations Olfactory signals are transmitted from the glomeruli to a few different places in the cerebral cortex. One designation is the **primary olfactory cortex**, or **piriform cortex**, a small area under the temporal lobe, and another is the **secondary olfactory cortex**, or **orbitofrontal cortex**, located in the frontal lobe, near the eyes (Figure 14.7) (Cinelli, 1993; Dodd & Castellucci, 1991; Frank & Rabin, 1989; McLean & Shipley, 1992; Price et al., 1991; Rolls, 2000; Takagi, 1980). Olfactory signals also reach the **amygdala,** a structure deep in the cortex that is involved in emotional responding. We will return to these central destinations shortly, but first we will consider how information about odor is processed in the mucosa and olfactory bulb.

THE NEURAL CODE
FOR ODOR MOLECULES

How does the brain know what odorant molecules are entering the nose? This is the problem of neural coding for olfaction. One problem facing olfactory researchers is that while we know that odor quality is affected by physical and chemical properties, such as chemical reactivity, the electrical charge of the elements in a molecule, and the structure of a molecule, it has been difficult to determine a simple relationship between these physical and chemical properties and the odor qualities we perceive. For example, some molecules that are similar can smell very different (Figure 14.8a), and molecules that are different can smell similar (Figure 14.8b). Because of the difficulty in linking molecular properties with smells, researchers have focused on determining not which *smells* cause neurons to fire, but on which *chemical odorants* cause them to fire.

The Response of ORNs

Individual ORNs usually respond to a number of different chemicals (Bozza & Kauer, 1998; Duchamp-Viret et al., 1999; Malnic et al., 1999; Sicard & Holley, 1984). For example, Figure 14.9 shows that olfactory receptor neurons in the frog respond to a number of different odorants. By reading across this

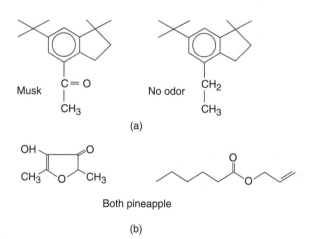

Figure 14.8
(a) Two molecules that have the same structures, but one smells like musk and the other is odorless; (b) two molecules with different structures but similar odors.

figure from left to right, we can see that some of the receptors respond to just a few of the odorants, and others respond to a larger group of odorants. Sometimes a particular receptor responds mainly to odorants that have similar physical properties, but other receptors respond to seemingly unrelated odorants. Figure 14.10 shows the response of an ORN in the rat that responds to a wide range of odorants.

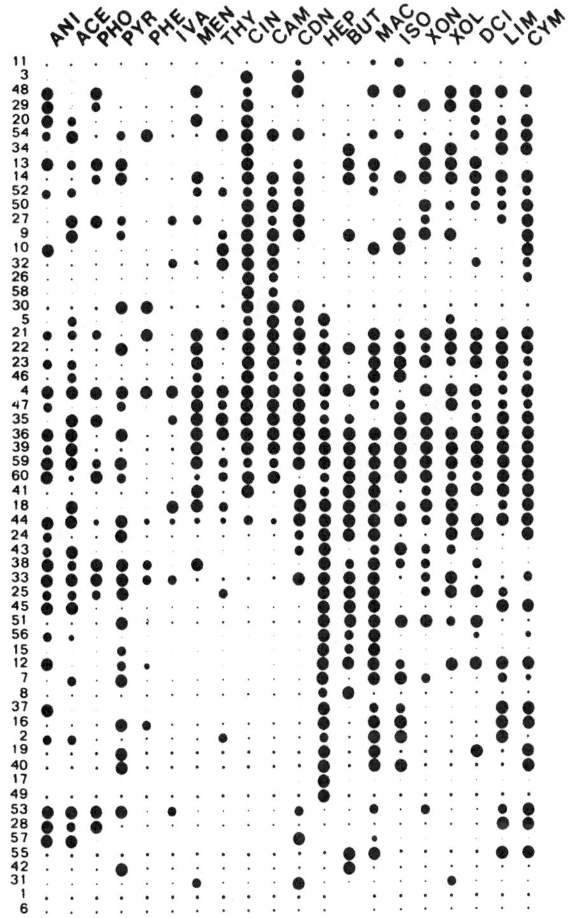

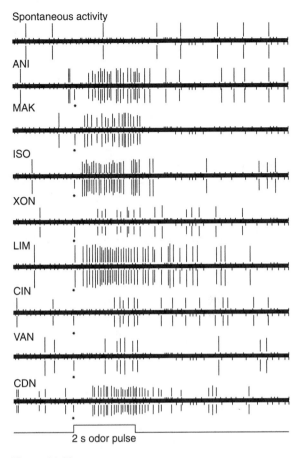

Figure 14.10
Response of a rat olfactory receptor neuron to a number of different compounds. This neuron responds well to all of the compounds except vanilla (VAN). (From Duchamp-Viret et al., 1999.)

The Response of Glomeruli

A similar picture emerges when we move up to the olfactory bulb. This isn't surprising, since ORNs with similar properties send their axons to the same glomeruli. Thus, a particular glomerulus typically responds to a number of different odorants (Rubin & Katz, 1999).

However, there are also glomeruli that appear to be specialized to respond to molecules with specific structures. For example, Figure 14.11 shows the response of a neuron in the rabbit that responds to

Figure 14.9
Responses of frog olfactory receptors (numbers on the left) to different compounds (letters along the top). The sizes of the spots are roughly proportional to the sizes of the responses. See text for further details. (From Sicard & Holley, 1984.)

The Chemical Senses

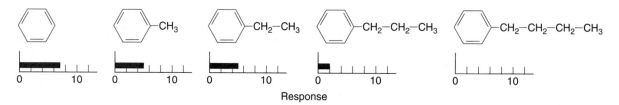

Figure 14.11

Response of a cell in the glomerulus of the rabbit. The response is indicated by the length of the black bar below each compound. Benzene, the ring structure with no side chains, is on the left. As a side chain is added and then lengthened, the response of the neuron decreases until there is no response for the compound with the long side chain on the right. (Adapted from Katoh et al., 1993.)

benzene molecules (the ring structure) with short side chains but does not respond when the length of the side chain is increased (Katoh et al., 1993). Kensaku Mori and coworkers (Mori & Yoshihara, 1995; Mori, Nagao, & Yoshihara, 1999) have coined the term **odotope** to indicate a group of odorants that share a specific chemical feature, such as the length of the side chain, that determines neural firing. According to this idea, neurons in the glomeruli are tuned to specific molecular features of odorants.

The Olfactory Code Is a Pattern

Although there is some controversy among olfactory researchers regarding how specialized olfactory neurons are, one thing is clear from all of the research: A particular odorant is indicated by the pattern of responding of a number of ORNs and of a number of glomeruli (Cowart & Rawson, 2001).

The patterned olfactory code is shown schematically in Figure 14.12, which indicates that chemical #1 will cause a number of ORNs to fire and chemical #2 will cause a different pattern of ORNs to fire. Notice that although the patterns are different, there are some ORNs that respond to both chemicals. Since different patterns of ORNs are activated by different chemicals, and similar ORNs connect to the same glomerulus, a similar situation occurs for glomeruli in the olfactory bulb.

These different patterns for different odorants have been demonstrated using the 2-deoxyglucose (2-DG) technique that was used in research investigating the visual system. When we first described this

technique on page 97, we saw that 2-deoxyglucose has three important properties: (1) Since its structure is similar to glucose, a primary source of energy for neurons, it is taken up by neurons as though it were glucose—the more active the neuron, the more 2-DG is taken up by the neuron; (2) when 2-DG is taken up by a neuron, it accumulates inside the neuron; and (3) 2-DG can be labeled with a radioactive isotope, carbon 14. By measuring the amount of radioactivity in the various parts of a structure, we can determine which neurons are most active.

Rats injected with radioactively labeled 2-DG were exposed to different chemicals, and the resulting pattern of radioactivity in the glomeruli of the olfactory bulb was measured. The results, shown in

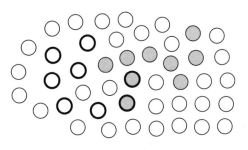

Figure 14.12

Each circle represents an olfactory receptor neuron (ORN) in the olfactory mucosa. Chemical #1 causes the ORNs indicated by the darkened circles to fire, and chemical #2 causes the ORNs indicated by the dots to fire. Thus, each chemical causes a different pattern of activation of ORNs. Notice that two of the ORNs respond to both chemicals.

Figure 14.13, indicate that different chemicals activate glomeruli that are located in different areas (Shepherd & Firestein, 1991). Thus, odor stimuli are mapped into spatial patterns in the glomeruli in the olfactory bulb (Shepard, 1991, 1995).

Central Processing of Olfactory Information

How is information about odorants coded in the cortex? Although the piriform cortex is the primary cortical receiving area for olfaction, little is known about how information about different odorants is processed in this area (Wilson, 1998). However, research on the secondary olfactory area in the orbital frontal cortex (OFC) has shown that neurons in this area respond to a number of chemicals but respond more strongly to some than to others (Figure 14.14). Notice that one of the cells in Figure 14.14 responds well to a number of odorants and the other responds strongly to one and weakly to the others.

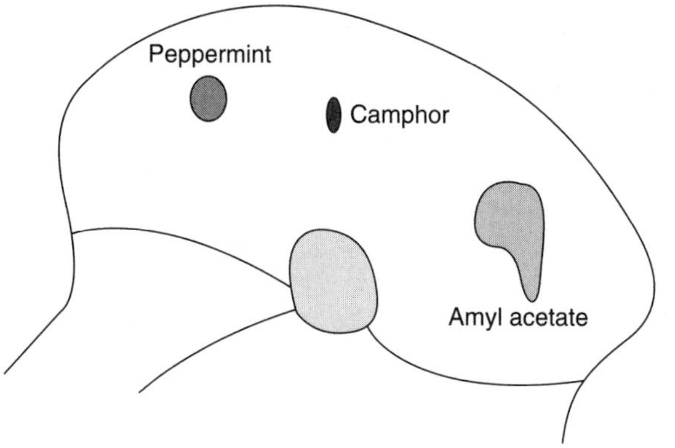

Figure 14.13

A portion of the olfactory bulb showing sites where peppermint, camphor, and amyl acetate caused buildups of radioactivity in different glomeruli. This shows that specific chemicals activate glomeruli that are located in different areas of the olfactory bulb. The result is a map of odorants on the olfactory bulb. (Adapted from Shepherd & Firestein, 1991.)

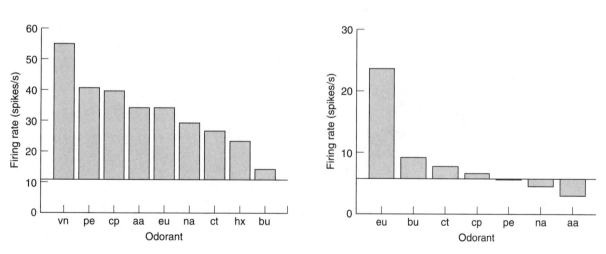

Figure 14.14

Firing of two neurons in the monkey's orbital frontal cortex (OFC) to a number of different odorants. The neuron on the left responds best to vanillin (va) (perceived as vanilla) but also responds well to a number of other chemicals. The neuron on the right responds best to eugenol (eu) (perceived as cloves) but does not respond well to the rest of the chemicals tested. Note that the chemicals for the two neurons are not in the same order in the two graphs, and that vanillin and hexylamine (hx) were not presented to the neuron on the right. (From Rolls, Critchley, & Treves, 1996.)

The Chemical Senses

Recently, Noam Sobel and coworkers (1998, 2000) have used fMRI in humans to show that the primary olfactory cortex (piriform) responds not only to presentation of odors but to the sniffing that accompanies smelling. When they compared the brain's response to sniffing air without any odor to the response to not sniffing, they found that sniffing causes a response in the primary olfactory cortex and that the timing of the cortical response was the same as the timing of the sniffs (left figure). To determine what aspect of the sniffing was causing the brain's response, they determined that the cortex responded when air was puffed into the nostrils but didn't respond when the nose was anesthetized so that the person couldn't feel the air entering the nose. What this means is that the brain's activity is related to the sensation of air flowing into the nostrils.

Sobel suggests that the function of the brain activity generated by sniffing is to provide a warning that an olfactory signal is about to arrive. This "sniff-detector" system could also help explain the fact that people's perception of the strength of an odor doesn't depend on how hard they sniff. This result is shown in the figure on the right, which shows that subjects' ratings of the strength of the chemical butanol is the same whether they use strong sniffs (filled circles) or weak sniffs (open circles). The subjects must be taking sniff intensity into account, because the odor ratings are the same even though the strong sniff delivers more odorant to the receptors than the weak sniff. This taking sniff into account has practical consequences, because it means that if a person sniffs strongly to detect weak odorants and sniffs weakly to sense strong, possibly toxic, odorants, they can still tell that one odorant is weak and the other is strong.

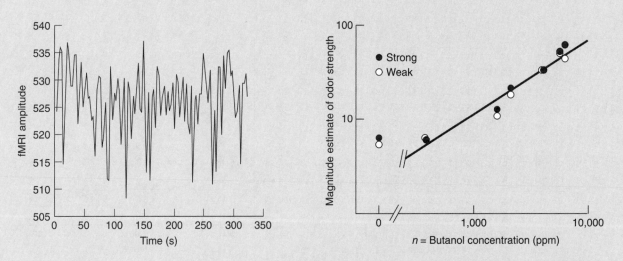

Left: *The fMRI response of the human piriform cortex to sniffing. The timing of the up-and-down oscillations of the response matches the rate of sniffing. (From Sobel et al., 2000.)* Right: *Magnitude estimates of odor strength for butanol. Odor strength increases at higher butanol concentrations, but is the same for strong sniffs (filled circles) and weak sniffs (open circles). (Adapted from Teghtsoonian et al., 1978.)*

We will see at the end of this chapter, when we consider the role of these neurons in the perception of food, that the firing of these neurons can be affected by the pairing of odorants with specific tastes.

See Summary Table 14.1 for an overview of the material we have covered so far.

THE TASTE SYSTEM

To introduce the taste system, we will first describe the anatomy of the tongue and the process of transduction that generates electrical signals from taste stimuli. We will then describe the central destinations of these signals.

The Tongue and Transduction

The process of tasting begins with the tongue (Figure 14.15a and Table 14.3), when receptors are stimulated by taste stimuli. The surface of the tongue contains many ridges and valleys due to the presence of structures called **papillae**, of which there are four kinds: (1) filiform papillae, which are shaped like cones and are found over the entire surface of the tongue, giving it its rough appearance; (2) fungiform papillae, which are shaped like mushrooms and are found at the tip and sides of the tongue; (3) foliate papillae, which are a series of folds along the sides of the tongue; and (4) circumvallate papillae, which are shaped like flat mounds surrounded by a trench and are found at the back of the tongue (see also Figure 14.16).

SUMMARY TABLE 14.1

The Special Nature of the Chemical Senses

Two special things about the chemical senses are that molecules are taken into the body and that the receptors are renewed.

Olfaction: Uses and Facts

While olfaction isn't as important for humans as it is for some animals, (1) human olfactory receptors can respond to the action of just one molecule of odorant; (2) humans can detect differences in intensity of 5 to 10 percent; (3) with training, people can identify almost 100 percent of common substances based on their odors; (4) humans can distinguish between males and females based on their odors, and babies can identify the smell of their mother's breast; and (5) the phenomenon of menstrual synchrony suggests a role for olfaction in interpersonal relations.

The Olfactory System

The olfactory mucosa contains olfactory receptor neurons (ORNs), each of which is dotted with identical olfactory receptors (ORs). When odorants contact ORs, transduction occurs and activates the ORN. ORNs with the same kind of ORs are located in one of four zones in the mucosa. Signals from the ORNs in a particular zone on the mucosa reach glomeruli in the corresponding zone of the olfac-

tory bulb. Since each glomerulus receives signals mostly from the same type of ORN, they collect information from small groups of odorants. They send their signals to the primary olfactory cortex (piriform cortex), and signals also reach the secondary olfactory cortex (orbital frontal cortex).

The Neural Code for Odor Molecules

It has been difficult to link molecular structures with smells, so researchers focus on how chemical odorants are represented in the olfactory system. Individual ORNs and their glomeruli usually respond to a group of chemicals. Some glomeruli may respond specifically to odorants that share a chemical feature, called an odotope, but it appears that odorants are generally represented by the pattern of response of a number of glomeruli. Individual neurons in the OFC also respond to a number of different odorants.

Sniff Detection

Neurons in the primary olfactory (piriform) cortex respond not only to the presence of odorants but to the sensation of air flowing through the nostrils. This provides a signal that informs the brain of the strength of the sniff.

The Chemical Senses

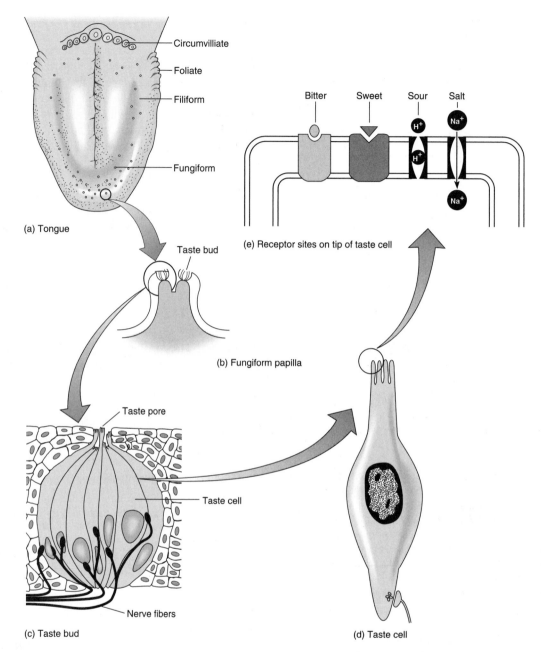

Figure 14.15

(a) The tongue, showing the four different types of papillae. (b) A fungiform papilla on the tongue; each papilla contains a number of taste buds. (c) Cross section of a taste bud showing the taste pore where the taste stimulus enters. (d) The taste cell; the tip of the taste cell is positioned just under the pore. (e) Close-up of the membrane at the tip of the taste cell, showing the receptor sites for bitter, sour, salty, and sweet substances. Stimulation of these receptor sites, as described in the text, triggers a number of different reactions within the cell (not shown) that lead to movement of charged molecules across the membrane, which creates an electrical signal in the receptor.

Table 14.3

The tongue and associated structures

Structures	Description
Tongue	The receptor sheet for taste. Contains papillae and all of the other structures described below.
Papillae	The structures that give the tongue its rough appearance. There are four kinds, each with a different shape.
Taste buds	Contained on the papillae. There are about 10,000 taste buds.
Taste cells	Cells that make up a taste bud. There are a number of cells for each bud, and the tip of each one sticks out into a taste pore. One or more nerve fibers are associated with each cell.
Receptor sites	Sites located on the tips of the taste cells. There are different types of sites for different chemicals. Chemicals contacting the sites cause transduction by affecting ion flow across the membrane of the taste cell.

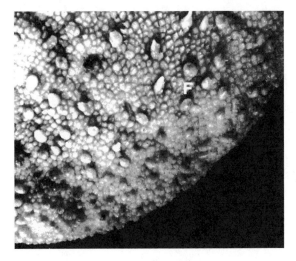

Figure 14.16

The surface of the tongue, showing fungiform (F) papillae. (From Miller, 1995.)

All of the papillae except the filiform papillae contain **taste buds** (Figure 14.15b & c), and the whole tongue contains about 10,000 taste buds (Bartoshuk, 1971). Since the filiform papillae contain no taste buds, stimulation of the central part of the tongue, which contains only these papillae, causes no taste sensations. However, stimulation of the back or perimeter of the tongue results in a broad range of taste sensations.

A taste bud (Figure 14.15c) contains a number of **taste cells**, which have tips that protrude into the **taste pore** (Figure 14.15d). Transduction occurs when chemicals contact **receptor sites** located on the tips of these taste cells (Figure 14.15e). The details of this transduction process involve complex chemical events within the taste cell (Hoon et al., 1999; Kinnamon, 1988; Ye, Heck, & DeSimone, 1991).

Transduction occurs when taste substances affect ion flow across the membrane of the taste cell. Different types of substances affect the membrane in different ways. As shown in Figure 14.15e, molecules of bitter and sweet substances bind to receptor sites, which release other substances into the cell, whereas sour substances contain H^+ ions that block channels in the membrane, and the sodium in salty substances becomes sodium ions (Na^+) in solution that flow through membrane channels directly into the cell. Each of these mechanisms affects the cell's electrical charge by affecting the flow of ions into the cell.

Central Destinations of Taste Signals

Electrical signals generated in the taste cells are transmitted from the tongue in two pathways: the **chorda tympani nerve**, which conducts signals from the front and sides of the tongue, and the **glossopharyngeal nerve**, which conducts signals from the back of the tongue. Signals from taste receptors in the mouth and the larynx are transmitted in the **vagus nerve**. The fibers in these three nerves make connections in the brain stem in the **nucleus of the solitary tract (NST)**, and from there, signals travel to the thalamus and then to two areas in the frontal lobe—the **insula** and the **frontal operculum cortex**—that are partially hidden behind the temporal lobe (Figure 14.17) (Finger, 1987; Frank & Rabin, 1989). In addition, fibers serving the taste system also reach the orbital frontal cortex (OFC), which also receives olfactory signals (Rolls, 2000; see Figure 14.5).

The Chemical Senses

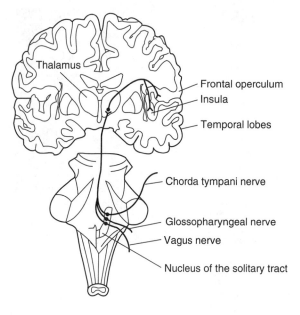

Figure 14.17
The central pathway for taste signals, showing the nucleus of the solitary tract (NST), where nerve fibers from the tongue and the mouth synapse in the medulla at the base of the brain. From the NST, these fibers synapse in the thalamus and the frontal lobe of the brain. (From Frank & Rabin, 1989.)

TASTE QUALITY

When considering taste quality, we are in a much better position than we were for olfaction. Although we have not been able to fit the many olfactory sensations into a small number of categories or qualities, taste researchers generally describe taste quality in terms of four basic taste sensations: salty, sour, sweet, and bitter. (Although not all researchers agree; see Halpern, 1997, and Schiffman & Erickson, 1993.) It has also been suggested that there is a fifth basic taste called *umami*, which has been described as meaty, brothy, or savory, and is often associated with the flavor-enhancing properties of the chemical monosodium glutamate (MSG) (Nagodawithana, 1995; Scott, 1987). We will focus on salty, sour, bitter, and sweet since most research has used these four qualities.

The Four Basic Taste Qualities

People can describe most of their taste experiences on the basis of the four basic taste qualities. For example, Donald McBurney (1969) presented taste solutions to subjects and asked them to give magnitude estimates of the intensity of each of the four taste qualities. He found that some substances have a predominant taste and that other substances result in combinations of the four tastes. For example, sodium chloride (salty), hydrochloric acid (sour), sucrose (sweet), and quinine (bitter) are compounds that come the closest to having only one of the four basic tastes, but the compound potassium chloride (KCl) has substantial salty and bitter components (Figure 14.18). Similarly, sodium nitrate ($NaNO_3$) results in a taste consisting of a combination of salty, sour, and bitter. Subjects, therefore, can describe their taste sensations based on these four qualities. Thus, salty, sour, sweet, and bitter have been generally used by researchers to describe our taste experiences.

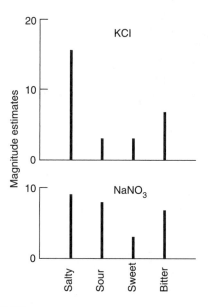

Figure 14.18
The contribution of each of the four basic tastes to the tastes of KCl and $NaNO_3$, determined by the method of magnitude estimation. The height of the line indicates the size of the magnitude estimate for each basic taste. (McBurney, 1969.)

The Genetics of Taste Experience

Although most people describe their taste preferences in terms of four basic qualities, there are differences among people, based on genetics, that affect people's ability to sense the taste of certain substances. One of the best-documented genetic effects in taste involves people's ability to taste the bitter substance phenylthiocarbamide (PTC). Linda Bartoshuk (1980) describes the discovery of this PTC effect:

> The different reactions to PTC were discovered accidentally in 1932 by Arthur L. Fox, a chemist working at the E. I. DuPont deNemours Company in Wilmington, Delaware. Fox had prepared some PTC, and when he poured the compound into a bottle, some of the dust escaped into the air. One of his colleagues complained about the bitter taste of the dust, but Fox, much closer to the material, noticed nothing. Albert F. Blakeslee, an eminent geneticist of the era, was quick to pursue this observation. At a meeting of the American Association for the Advancement of Science (AAAS) in 1934, Blakeslee prepared an exhibit that dispensed PTC crystals to 2,500 of the conferees. The results: 28 percent of them described it as tasteless, 66 percent as bitter, and 6 percent as having some other taste. (p. 55)

People who can taste PTC are described as tasters, and those who cannot are called **nontasters** (or **taste-blind** to PTC). Molly Hall and coworkers (1975) have found that most people who can taste PTC also perceive a bitter taste in caffeine at much lower concentrations of caffeine than do nontasters, and Bartoshuk (1979) reported a similar result for the artificial sweetener saccharin. That some people are much more sensitive to the bitter tastes of caffeine and saccharin than others is particularly interesting, since caffeine is found in many common foods, and saccharin used to be a popular sugar substitute in foods and is still used in many fountain drinks. Caffeine makes coffee taste bitter to tasters but has little effect on nontasters, and saccharin, in the concentrations that were added to soft drinks before it was replaced by other artificial sweeteners, tastes more bitter to tasters than to nontasters.

Recently, additional experiments have been done with a substance called 6-*n*-propylthiouracil, or PROP, that has properties similar to those of PTC (Lawless, 1980, 2001). Researchers have found that about one-third of people report that PROP is tasteless and that two-thirds can taste it. The people who can taste PROP (tasters) also report more bitterness in caffeine, Swiss cheese, and cheddar cheese than nontasters. This result, which is similar to that found for PTC, becomes more interesting when combined with anatomical measurements using a new technique called **video microscopy**, which by combining video technology and microscopy enables researchers to count the taste buds on people's tongues that contain the receptors for tasting.

The key result of these studies is that people who could taste the PROP had higher densities of taste buds than those who couldn't taste it (Figure 14.19) (Bartoshuk & Beauchamp, 1994). Thus, the next time you disagree with someone else about the taste of a particular food, don't automatically assume that your disagreement is simply a reflection of the fact that you prefer different tastes. It may reflect not a difference in preference (you like sweet things more than John does) but a difference in taste experience (you experience more intense sweet tastes than John does) that could be caused by differences in the number of taste receptors on your tongues.

This connection between the density of taste buds on the tongue and whether a person is a taster or a nontaster is an example of how receptors can affect perception. But perception also depends on the processing that occurs after the signals leave the receptors. We now consider how this processing may create a neural code for taste quality.

THE NEURAL CODE FOR TASTE QUALITY

What is the neural code for taste quality? In Chapter 3, when we introduced the idea of sensory coding, we distinguished between specificity coding, the idea that quality is signaled by the activity in neurons that are tuned to respond to specific qualities, and distributed

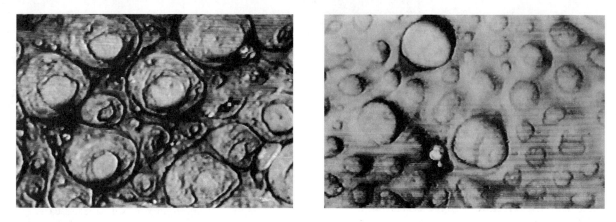

Figure 14.19
Left: Videomicrograph of the tongue showing the fungiform papillae of a "supertaster"—a person who is very sensitive to the taste of PROP. Right: Papillae of a "nontaster," who cannot taste PROP. The supertaster has both more papillae and more taste buds than the nontaster. (Photographs courtesy of Linda Bartoshuk.)

coding, the idea that quality is signaled by the pattern of activity distributed across many fibers. In that discussion, and in others throughout the book, we have generally favored distributed coding. The situation for taste, however, is not clear-cut, and there are arguments in favor of both specificity and distributed coding.

Distributed Coding

Let's consider some evidence for distributed coding. Robert Erickson (1963) conducted one of the first experiments that demonstrated this type of coding by presenting a number of different taste stimuli to a rat's tongue and recording the response of the chorda tympani nerve. Figure 14.20 shows how 13 nerve fibers responded to ammonium chloride (NH_4Cl), potassium chloride (KCl), and sodium chloride (NaCl). Erickson called these patterns the **across-fiber patterns**, which is another name for distributed coding. The solid and dashed lines show that the across-fiber patterns for ammonium chloride and potassium chloride are similar to each other but are different from the pattern for sodium chloride, indicated by the open circles.

Erickson reasoned that if the rat's perception of taste quality depends on the across-fiber pattern, then two substances with similar patterns should taste similar. Thus, the electrophysiological results would

predict that ammonium chloride and potassium chloride should taste similar and that both should taste different from sodium chloride. To test this hypothesis, Erickson shocked rats while they were drinking potas-

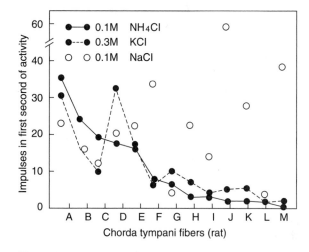

Figure 14.20
Across-fiber patterns of the response of fibers in the rat's chorda tympani nerve to three salts. Each letter on the horizontal axis indicates a different single fiber. (From Erickson, 1963.)

sium chloride and then gave them a choice between ammonium chloride and sodium chloride. If potassium chloride and ammonium chloride taste similar, the rats should avoid the ammonium chloride when given a choice. This is exactly what they did. And when the rats were shocked for drinking ammonium chloride, they subsequently avoided the potassium chloride, as predicted by the electrophysiological results.

But what about the perception of taste in humans? When Susan Schiffman and Robert Erickson (1971) asked humans to make similarity judgments between a number of different solutions, they found that substances that were perceived to be similar were related to patterns of firing for these same substances in the rat. Solutions judged more similar psychophysically had similar patterns of firing, as distributed coding would predict.

Specificity Coding

Evidence that taste quality is coded by the activity in single neurons comes from experiments that show that there are four different types of fibers in the monkey's chorda tympani nerve (Sato, Ogawa, & Yamashita, 1994). Figure 14.21 shows how 66 fibers in the monkey's chorda tympani responded to four substances, each representing one of the basic tastes: sucrose (sweet); salt (NaCl, salty); hydrogen chloride (HCl, sour); and quinine (bitter). We can see that some fibers responded well to sucrose but poorly to almost all other compounds. For example, look at how fiber 5 responded to each substance by noticing the responses where the dashed line crosses the record for each substance. Fibers 1 to 16 are called sucrose-best since they respond best to sucrose. Figure 14.22 shows an example of the response of one of the sucrose-best fibers (Sato, Ogawa, & Yamashita, 1975). A similar situation exists for the quinine-best fibers (numbers 56–66), most of which respond only to quinine. The NaCl- and HCl-best fibers fire predominantly to one solution, but some fire to both NaCl and HCl (also see Frank, Bieber, & Smith, 1988, for similar results in the hamster).

Another test for the operation of specificity coding was conducted by Kimberle Jacobs, Gregory Mark, and Thomas Scott (1988) who recorded from NST neurons in the rat's medulla (Figure 14.23) before and after depriving the rats of sodium. Before sodium deprivation, about 60 percent of the neurons in this area responded vigorously to sodium. However, after deprivation, these formerly sodium-active neurons fell silent. Apparently, the lack of stimulation caused by the sodium deprivation caused these neurons to become insensitive to sodium. These results are in line with specificity coding, since sodium deprivation causes only sodium-best neurons to decrease their sensitivity.

Another finding in line with specificity theory is the recently discovered transduction mechanisms, which indicate that salty, sweet, sour, and bitter substances each use different mechanisms to change the taste cell's membrane properties. Thus, the presentation of a substance called **amiloride**, which blocks the flow of sodium into taste receptors, causes a decrease in the responding of rat NST neurons that respond best to salt (Figure 14.22a) but has little effect on neurons that respond best to a combination of salty and bitter tastes (Figure 14.22b) (Scott & Giza, 1990). As we would expect from these results, applying amiloride to a human's tongue eliminates the perception of saltiness (McCutcheon, 1992; Scott & Giza, 2000; but see Smith et al., 2000).

Is Coding Distributed or Specific?

What does all of this evidence mean? Some experiments support distributed coding, and others support specificity coding. It is difficult to choose between the two because both can explain most of the data (Scott & Plata-Salaman, 1991). For example, David Smith and coworkers (1983) point out that, while similar-tasting compounds have highly similar across-fiber patterns, these patterns are dominated by activity in neurons that respond best to specific compounds. Thus, sweet-tasting compounds produce highly similar across-fiber patterns in the hamster, primarily because of the high firing rates contributed by the sucrose-best neurons.

But Smith et al. (2000) also point out that even if salt-best neurons make the main contribution to the across-fiber pattern for salt, this doesn't mean that salt is signaled by just this type of neuron. We can

The Chemical Senses

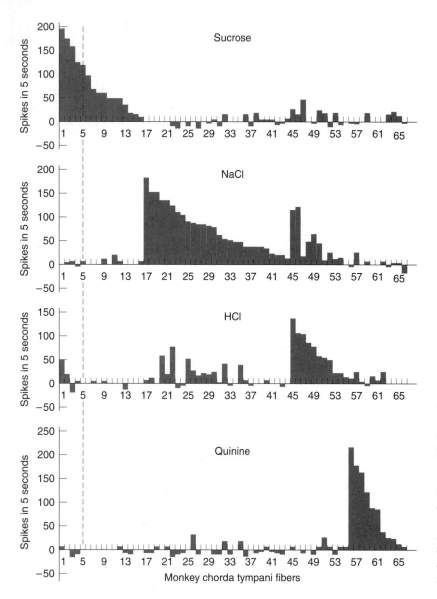

Figure 14.21

Responses of 66 different fibers in the monkey's chorda tympani nerve, showing how they responded to four types of stimuli: sucrose (sweet); sodium chloride (salty); hydrogen chloride (sour); and quinine (bitter). To determine the response of a particular fiber, pick its number and note the height of the bars for each compound. For example, fiber 5 (dashed line) fired well to sucrose but didn't fire to each of the other compounds. Fiber 5 is therefore called a sucrose-best *fiber. (From Sato & Ogawa, 1994.)*

appreciate why this is so by remembering how color vision works. Even though presenting a long-wavelength light that appears red may cause the highest activation in the long-wavelength cone pigment (Figure 6.7), our perception of red still depends on the combined response of both the long- and medium-wavelength pigments. Similarly, salt stimuli may cause high firing in salt-best neurons, but other neurons are probably also involved in creating saltiness, as well.

The need for taking into account more than one type of neuron is most apparent when we look at the way fibers in Figure 14.21 fire to NaCl (salty) and HCl (sour). Look at neuron 25. The firing rate of this neuron is about 100 spikes to NaCl and about 50 spikes to HCl. But increasing the concentration of

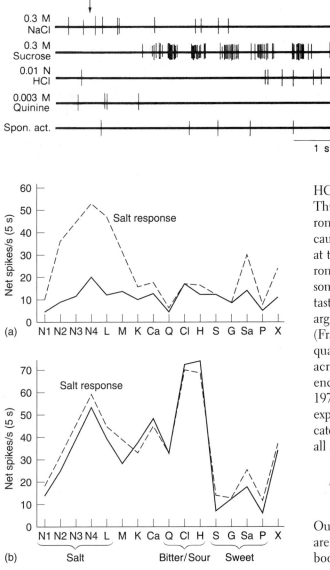

Figure 14.22

Response of a single fiber in the monkey's chorda tympani nerve to salt, sucrose, hydrochloric acid, and quinine. The bottom record indicates the rate of spontaneous activity. The arrow above the record for NaCl indicates the time of application of the stimuli. (Sato, Ogawa, & Yamashita, 1975.)

Figure 14.23

The dashed lines show how two neurons in the rat NST respond to a number of different taste stimuli (along the horizontal axis). The neuron in (a) responds strongly to compounds associated with salty tastes. The neuron in (b) responds to a wide range of compounds. The solid lines show how these two neurons fire after the sodium-blocker amiloride is applied to the tongue. This compound inhibits the responses to salt of neuron (a) but has little effect on neuron (b). (From Scott & Giza, 1990.)

HCl can increase this neuron's firing to 100 spikes. Thus, if we record a firing of 100 spikes from this neuron, there is no way to tell whether the response is caused by NaCl or HCl. The only way to tell is to look at the pattern of responding across a number of neurons. Because of this, some researchers believe that some type of distributed coding must be involved in taste (Scott & Giza, 2000), but it is still possible to argue for a specificity code, especially for sweetness (Frank, 2000). Another possibility is that basic taste quality is determined by a specific code and that across-fiber patterns could determine subtle differences between tastes within a category (Pfaffmann, 1974; Scott & Plata-Salaman, 1991). This would help explain the fact that not all substances in a particular category have the same taste. For example, the taste of all sweet substances is not identical (Lawless, 2001).

THE PERCEPTION OF FLAVOR

Our society is obsessed with the taste of food. There are cooking shows on TV, shelves of cookbooks at the bookstore, and restaurants whose reputations are made or broken based on the taste of the food they serve. Most people look forward to eating not because it is necessary for survival but because of the pleasure it brings. Consider, for example, how Ruth Reichl (1994), then the *New York Times* food critic and currently editor of *Gourmet* magazine, describes her experience at a four-star restaurant:

> It is a surprise to dip your spoon into this mild-mannered soup and experience an explosion of

flavor. Mushroom is at the base of the taste sensation, but it is haunted by citric tones—lemongrass, lime perhaps—and high at the top, a resonant note of sweetness. What is it? No single flavor ever dominates a dish. At first you find yourself searching for flavors in this complex tapestry, fascinated by the way they are woven together. In the end, you just give in and allow yourself to be seduced. Each meal is a roller coaster of sensations.

Reichl's description captures not only her enjoyment but also the complexity of some of the aspects of perceiving the flavors of food. Notice that she opens the review by commenting on the food's "flavor." What most people refer to as "taste" when describing their experience of food ("that tastes good, Mom") is usually a combination of taste, from stimulation of the receptors in the tongue, and smell, from stimulation of the receptors in the olfactory mucosa. This combination of taste and smell, as we will see below, is called flavor.

Another thing Reichl captures in her review is the complexity of the perceptions created by foods. We are usually dealing with not just one or two different flavors, but many, and, as Reichl points out, the flavors often are contained within a "complex tapestry."

The fact that we are able to pick a particular flavor out of a complex tapestry of flavors becomes even more amazing when we consider the complexity of the chemical stimuli that create these flavors. For example, consider a situation that occurs when you wake up to the smells of coffee, bacon, and toast that are coming from the kitchen. The fact that you can identify these different smells may not seem particularly surprising until we recognize that the smell of coffee can arise from more than 100 different chemical constituents and that the toast and bacon smells are also the result of a large number of different molecules that have been released into the air. Somehow, your olfactory system takes this vast array of airborne chemicals, with their various physical qualities, and groups them into the three classifications: coffee, toast, and bacon (Bartoshuk, Cain, & Pfaffmann, 1985).

This creation of the perception of coffee, toast, and bacon that occurs when hundreds of chemicals enter the nose is an amazing feat of perceptual organization that also occurs for flavor. This process of perceptual organization rivals the processes that occur when we separate a complex visual scene into individual objects or the sounds of a symphony orchestra into individual instruments. We are, however, far from being able to understand how we accomplish this feat for flavor. Most of the basic research on flavor has focused on showing how taste and smell interact and on factors that influence our perception of flavor. Let's first consider evidence that flavor is the combination of taste and smell.

Flavor = Taste + Olfaction

Flavor is the overall impression that we experience from the combination of nasal and oral stimulation (Lawless, 2001). You can demonstrate how smell affects flavor with the following demonstration.

DEMONSTRATION

"Tasting" with and Without the Nose

While holding your nostrils shut, drink a beverage with a distinctive taste, such as grape juice, cranberry juice, or coffee. Notice both the quality and the intensity of the taste as you are drinking it. (Take just one or two swallows, as swallowing with your nostrils closed can cause a buildup of pressure in your ears.) After one of the swallows, open your nostrils and notice whether you perceive a flavor. Finally, just drink the beverage normally with nostrils open and notice the flavor. You can also do this demonstration with fruits or cooked foods. ●

During this demonstration you probably noticed that, when your nostrils were closed, it was difficult to identify the substance you were drinking or eating, but as soon as you opened your nostrils, the flavor became obvious. This occurred because odor stimuli from the food reached the olfactory mucosa by following the **retronasal route**, from the mouth through the **nasal pharynx**, the passage that connects the oral and nasal cavities (Figure 14.24). Although pinching the nostrils shut does not close the nasal pharynx, it prevents vapors from reaching the olfactory receptors by eliminating the circulation of air through this channel (Murphy & Cain, 1980).

The importance of olfaction in the sensing of flavor has been demonstrated experimentally by using both chemical solutions and typical foods. For example, when Maxwell Mozell and coworkers (1969) asked subjects to identify common foods with the nostrils opened or with the nostrils pinched shut, every substance they tested was easier to identify in the nostrils-open condition (Figure 14.25). In a more recent experiment, Thomas Hettinger, Walter Myers, and Marion Frank (1990) had subjects rate the strength of various qualities experienced when solutions were applied to the tongue with the nostrils either open or clamped shut. The results for two of the chemicals, sodium oleate and ferrous sulfate (Figure 14.26a and b), show that the oleate had a strong soapy flavor when the nostrils were open but was judged tasteless when they were closed. Similarly, the ferrous sulfate normally has a metallic flavor but was judged predominantly tasteless when the nostrils were closed. Some compounds are not influenced by olfaction. For example, monosodium glutamate (MSG) had about the same flavor whether or not the nose was clamped (Figure 14.26c). Thus, in this case, the sense of taste predominated.

The results of these experiments indicate that many of the sensations that we call taste, and that we assume are caused only by stimulation of the tongue, are greatly influenced by stimulation of the olfactory receptors. Apparently, we often mislocate the source

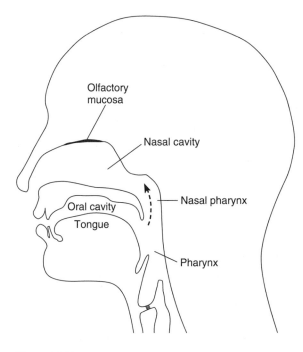

Figure 14.24
Odorant molecules released by food in the oral cavity and pharynx can travel through the nasal pharynx (dashed arrow) to the olfactory mucosa in the nasal cavity. This is the retronasal route to the olfactory receptors.

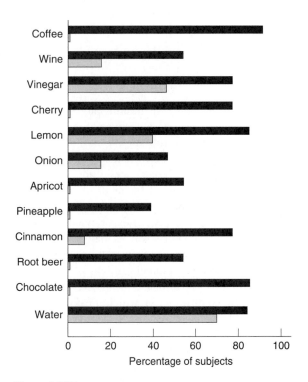

Figure 14.25
Percentage of subjects correctly identifying each flavor listed on the left, with nostrils open (solid bars) and nostrils pinched shut (shaded bars). (Adapted from Mozell et al., 1969.)

The Chemical Senses

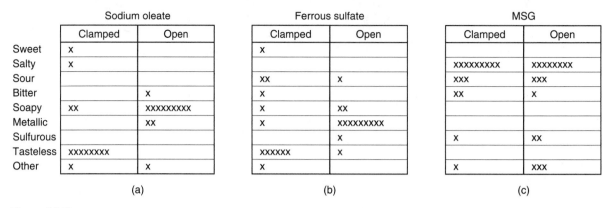

Figure 14.26
How subjects described the flavors of three different compounds when they tasted them with nostrils clamped shut and with nostrils open. Each X represents the judgment of one subject. (From Hettinger, Myers, & Frank, 1990.)

of our sensations as being in the mouth, partially because the stimuli physically enter the mouth and partially because we experience the tactile sensations associated with chewing and swallowing (Murphy & Cain, 1980; Rozin, 1982).

Changes in Flavor During a Meal

Just as the painfulness of a stimulus presented to the skin can be decreased by factors in addition to the primary stimulus, such as rubbing the skin (page 464), the pleasantness of a food's flavor can change from consuming more food. The general finding for flavor is that the pleasantness of flavor or of smell often decreases as food is consumed. So as you begin eating a piece of banana cream pie (or whatever *your* favorite desert is) the first few bites may taste rich and creamy, but, as you are finishing it, the taste may not seem quite as good as it did at first.

One mechanism associated with decreased pleasantness is called **alliesthesia**, which means "changed sensation." Cananac (1971, 1979) demonstrated alliesthesia by having subjects rate the pleasantness of a sugar solution when they first drank it and then after they had consumed a quantity of the solution. Eventually, the originally pleasant sugar solution became unpleasant, and the subjects refused to drink any more. According to Cabanac, this experiment and many others with similar results illustrate that

a given stimulus can be pleasant or unpleasant, depending on signals from inside the body.

The basis of alliesthesia is central. That is, the decrease in pleasantness of a sugar solution after drinking a large amount of it is caused by the effect of the solution on the stomach. One result that supports this idea is that the alliesthesia effect takes time to develop, as the person consumes food. Another result supporting a central mechanism is that alliesthesia occurs when a solution of glucose is tubed directly into the stomach (Cabanac & Fantino, 1977).

In addition to the slow-acting central effect of alliesthesia, the pleasantness of food can also be changed by a faster-acting mechanism called **sensory-specific satiety** (Rolls et al., 1981). Figure 14.27 shows a demonstration of this effect. Subjects first rated the pleasantness of the smell of various foods, then ate one of the foods until full (satiated), and then rated the pleasantness again. One characteristic of this effect is that it is specific: Eating bananas decreased the pleasantness of the smell of bananas but didn't affect the pleasantness of the other smells. Similarly, eating chicken decreased the pleasantness of the smell of chicken but not of banana or the smells of most of the other substances (there was a slight decrease in pleasantness for fish) (Rolls & Rolls, 1997).

You might think that this is the same as alliesthesia, since the subjects ate until they felt full. However,

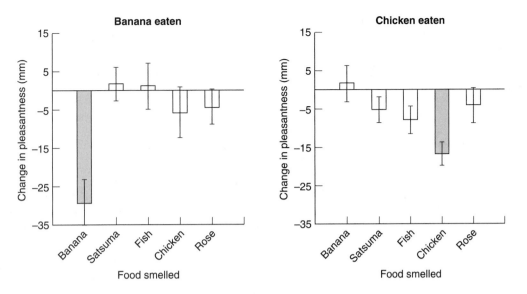

Figure 14.27
The change in the pleasantness of the smell of five different foods after eating banana (left) or chicken (right) until full. Notice that pleasantness decreases for the food that was eaten (shaded bars). Similar results also occur if the foods are smelled or chewed but not swallowed. (From Rolls & Rolls, 1997.)

the decrease in pleasantness occurred within minutes after eating and also occurred if the substances were just chewed, without swallowing, or just smelled (although the effects were smaller than for the "chewing and swallowing" condition). Similar results also occurred when subjects rated the pleasantness of the food's flavor (they did not, however, taste the rose water!). Thus, whereas alliesthesia is due to activation of receptors in the stomach, sensory-specific satiety is due to activation of the receptors in the nose and mouth. We will see below that sensory-specific satiety has also been observed in the firing of cortical neurons.

The Physiology of Flavor Perception

A number of cortical areas that serve both taste and olfaction are probably involved in the perception of the flavor of food. Presently, however, most of the work on the cortical response to food has focused not on the primary olfactory cortex, but on the orbital frontal cortex (OFC), because it is here that responses from taste and smell are first combined.

Multimodal Nature of the Orbital Frontal Cortex
The OFC receives inputs from the primary cortical areas for taste and olfaction, plus from the primary somatosensory cortex and from the inferotemporal cortex in the visual "what" pathway (Rolls, 2000) (Figure 14.28). Because of this convergence of neurons from different senses, the OFC contains many bimodal neurons that respond to more than one sense. Figure 14.29 shows a neuron that responds to both taste and smell (Figure 14.29a) and one that responds to taste and vision (Figure 14.29b).

An important property of these bimodal neurons is that they often respond to similar qualities. Thus, a cell that responds to the taste of sweet fruits would also respond to the smell of these fruits. Because of these properties, and the fact that the OFC is the first place where taste and smell information is combined, it has been suggested that the OFC is a cortical center for detecting flavor and for the perceptual representation of foods (Rolls & Baylis, 1994).

But there is also another reason to think that the OFC is important for flavor perception: Unlike neurons in the primary taste area, which are not affected

The Chemical Senses

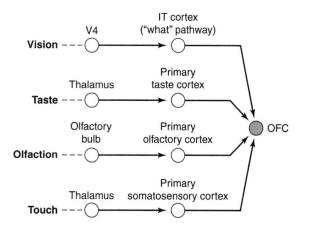

Figure 14.28

The orbital frontal cortex (OFC) receives inputs from vision, taste, olfaction, and touch, as shown. It is the first area where signals from the taste and smell systems meet. (Adapted from Rolls, 2000.)

by hunger, the firing of neurons in the OFC is influenced by an animal's hunger for a specific food.

Hunger Influences the Responding of OFC Neurons
We've seen that eating bananas or chicken can decrease the pleasantness of both the tastes and odors of these foods. A similar effect for a neuron in the monkey's OFC is shown in Figure 14.30. The top graph shows that this neuron fires at about 10 spikes per second to the odor of dairy cream, and that the response had decreased to 3 spikes per second (the level of spontaneous activity) after 50 ml of the cream had been presented. The bottom graph shows the monkey's behavioral reaction to presentation of the cream. At the beginning of the experiment, the monkey enthusiastically licked the feeding tube to receive the solution, but at the end it rejected the solution and tried to push it away. Thus, as the monkey's hunger for

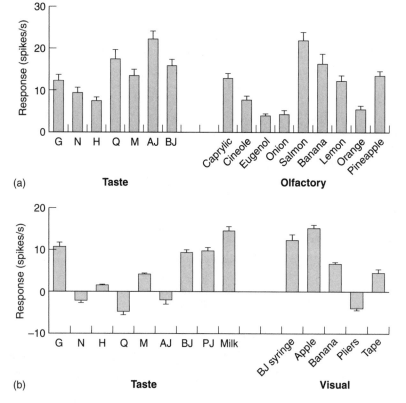

Figure 14.29

How two bimodal cells in the monkey OFC respond to a number of different substances. The neuron in (a) responds to taste and smell. The taste substances are glucose (G), sodium chloride (N), hydrochloric acid (H), quinine (Q), MSG (M), apple juice (AJ), and black currant juice (BJ). The neuron in (b) responds to presentation of taste stimuli on the tongue and when the monkey saw the stimulus (a piece of banana, for example). (From Rolls & Baylis, 1994.)

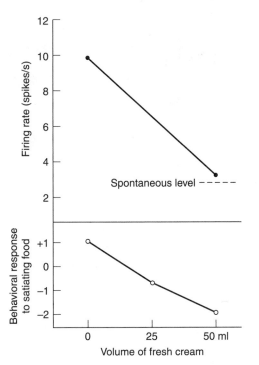

Figure 14.30

How consuming dairy cream affects the firing rate of neurons in the monkey's OFC (top panel), and the monkey's response to the cream (bottom panel). Consuming the cream causes a decrease in the neuron's response to the cream, but not to other substances (not shown). It also causes the monkey to become less interested in drinking the cream, and eventually, by the time 50 ml have been offered to the monkey, to actively reject it. (Adapted from Critchley & Rolls, 1996.)

the cream decreased, the firing of the cell to the cream's odor decreased as well. Just as was the case for sensory-specific satiety, the behavioral and neural response was specific to the food being ingested. Thus, while the response to cream decreased, the response to the odor of apples or bananas increased slightly (Critchley & Rolls, 1996). Similar results also occur for tastes (Rolls et al., 1989).

In addition to being affected by hunger, the response of OFC neurons can also be affected by learned associations between smell and taste. Rolls and coworkers (1996b) did an experiment that demonstrated this, by presenting a number of odorants to monkeys for 1 second each, with some odorants signaling that licking on a tube would result in a sugar reward (the S+ condition), and other odorants indicating that licking the tube would result in an unpleasant salt solution (the S− condition).

Rolls and coworkers found that some neurons were influenced by this pairing, as shown in Figure 14.31. In the initial training, the smell of cineole was paired with the sweet taste, and the smell of amyl acetate was paired with the unpleasant salt solution. The result was a large response to the cineole and a smaller response to the amyl acetate. Then the reward was switched, so the smell of cineole was now associated with the salt and the amyl acetate with the sugar. By about 20 to 40 trials after the switch, the monkey's behavior had switched, so the amyl acetate now caused licking to get the sugar, and the cineole caused avoidance of the salt. The reversal in the neural response, as shown on the right of Figure 14.31, occurs over a longer period of time, taking 80 to 100 trials. The result of this experiment shows how the response of an olfactory neuron can be affected by the reward-meaning of an odor rather than the quality of the odor.

Rolls and coworkers suggest that some of the properties of bimodal neurons that respond to both taste and smell may be caused by the kind of learning shown in Figure 14.31. Remember that some of these bimodal neurons responded similarly to the smell and taste of the same substances, so a neuron that responded well to the taste of sweet fruits also responded well to the smell of these fruits. Since these tastes and smells are always paired when these fruits are being consumed, it is likely that the neurons may have "learned" that these tastes and smells go together. Note, however, that not all neurons show this correspondence between taste and smell and also that not all neurons show the learning effect. Some neurons just keep responding in the same way to odors, no matter what taste they are paired with. Thus, some neurons are plastic, and others are not.

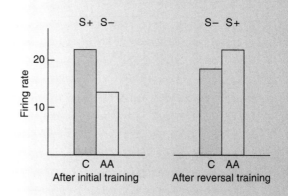

Figure 14.31
The effect of smell–taste associations on firing of neurons in the monkey's OFC. In the initial training the smell of cineole (C) was paired with the sweet taste (S+) and the smell of amyl acetate (AA) was paired with the salty taste (S−). Then the pairings were reversed so C was paired with salty and AA was paired with sweet. When this happens, the response to C decreased and the response to AA increased. The data in this graph represents the firing rates after 60 trials of initial training and 120 trials of training after the reversal. (Based on data in Rolls et al., 1996b.)

SEEING A SMELL:
A COLOROMETRIC ELECTRONIC NOSE

We've seen that smell and taste provide excellent examples of an "across the senses" effect, since flavor is determined by the combination of smell and taste, and bimodal neurons in the OFC respond to both smell and taste and in some cases to vision and touch as well.

We will now describe a completely different example of an across the senses effect by considering devices called **electronic noses**, which a number of researchers and companies have designed to detect and identify chemicals in the air. These devices are designed for practical applications such as odor quality control and sensing hazardous chemicals, but they are interesting to us for the following two reasons:

1. They mimic the way the human olfactory system probably recognizes complex odors, because these electronic noses detect chemicals by using a number of sensors that each respond to a number of chemicals. Thus, a particular chemical is indicated by the pattern of response across many sensors.

2. Some electronic noses provide an output in the form of different colored pictures for different chemicals that we can distinguish visually.

Neil Rakow and Kenneth Sushick (2000) designed an electronic nose that consists of a sensor array like the one in Figure 14.32. Each circle is the end of a fiber optic bundle coated with a polymer–dye combination that reacts to gas mixtures by changing color. Each of these sensors uses different polymer–dye combinations, and so they have different sensitivities to various chemicals. The different polymer–dye combinations also cause each sensor to respond with a distinctive color change when activated. Because this device creates a different array of colors for each chemical, it is called a *colorometric electronic nose* (Lindstrom, 2000).

Many electronic nose devices use sensors that create electrical responses that feed into computers that analyze the electronic pattern using powerful pattern-recognition software. The beauty of the colorometric

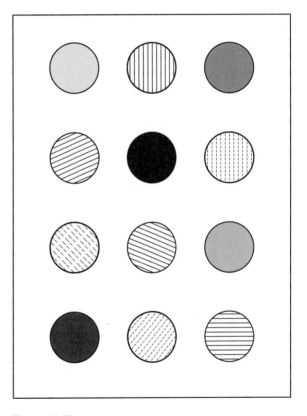

Figure 14.32
Display panel for Rakow and Sushick's (2000) electronic nose. In the actual device, the display is in color, with different substances resulting in different "color fingerprints." In this illustration, the different colors are symbolized by different shadings and symbols inside each element of the sensor array.

device designed by Rakow and Sushick is that it doesn't need a computer because it uses the most powerful pattern-recognition system of all: the human eye–brain system. Thus, a particular chemical creates a "color fingerprint" on the sensor array, and a person observing this array can easily tell the difference between the fingerprints for different chemicals.

The ease with which we can identify different smells "by eye" may be telling us something about natural odor perception: A wide range of odors can be differentiated based on sensors that each respond to a range of chemicals, just like the ORNs and glomeruli that create the "neural fingerprint" of odors in biological olfactory systems. It is important to note, however, that electronic noses are no match for our biological olfactory system, because these electronic devices are specialized to identify the presence of just a few dozen specific chemicals, whereas our nose–brain system can detect thousands of different odors.

The Taste System

The tongue contains papillae, which contain taste buds that are made up of taste cells. These taste cells are dotted with receptor sites that are specialized to respond to different types of chemicals. Transduction occurs when taste solutions activate the receptor sites. The signal generated in the taste cells travels to the nucleus of the solitary tract in the brainstem and then to the insula and frontal operculum cortex in the brain.

Taste Quality

Taste sensations can be described in terms of four basic tastes—salty, sour, sweet, and bitter—and perhaps a fifth, umami. People differ in their ability to detect some qualities, such as the bitterness of caffeine, because they have different densities of taste buds.

The Neural Code for Taste Quality

There is some uncertainty regarding whether the neural code for taste quality is distributed or specific. Evidence for distributed coding includes neurons that respond to many substances, substances that have the same across-fiber pattern taste similar, and the fact that it is sometimes not possible to tell what substance is present based on the firing of only one type of neuron. Evidence for specific coding includes the existence of narrowly tuned neurons, the four transduction mechanisms that are specialized for specific molecular characteristics, the selective effects of deprivation on sodium-active neurons, and the selective effects of amelioride on salty taste. Coding could be a combination of specific coding to indicate a quality and distributed to indicate differences in tastes within a quality.

Flavor Perception

Flavor is a combination of taste and smell. The olfactory receptors are stimulated through the retronasal pathway as we eat. There is evidence that flavors can change in pleasantness as we become satiated, through the slow central process of alliesthesia and the more rapid process of sensory-specific satiety.

Physiology of Flavor Perception

The orbital frontal cortex (OFC) appears to be a control center for detecting flavor, because it is the first place where taste and smell signals meet, and it contains many bimodal neurons. Decreases in hunger that occur due to eating are associated with decreases in the responding of some OFC neurons.

Plasticity: Learning Smell–Taste Associations

By using smells as a signal for the presence of positive or negative tastes, it has been possible to show that the tuning of neurons in OFC to specific odorants can be shaped by the tastes they are paired with.

Across the Senses: Colorometric Electronic Nose

Devices called electronic noses can detect chemicals in the air. One version of this device uses an array of sensors that turn different colors to create different color fingerprints for different chemicals. This pattern of colors can be discriminated by the visual pattern-recognition system.

STUDY QUESTIONS

1. What are some unique properties of taste and smell compared to other senses? (473)

2. What is the relation between ingestion of a substance and its toxicity? (474)

3. What is neurogenesis, and why is it necessary? (474)

Olfaction: Uses and Facts

4. Define *microsmatic*, *macrosmatic*, and *anosmia*. (475)

5. How does the sensitivity of human olfactory receptors compare to the sensitivity of dog and cat olfactory receptors? How does the sensitivity of humans to odors compare to the sensitivity of dogs and cats to odors? Why is there a difference between human sensitivity and dog and cat sensitivity? (475)

6. Why were early measurements of the olfactory difference threshold too high? How did Cain determine that the threshold was smaller than originally reported? (476)

7. About what percentage of odors of familiar substances can humans identify? How can this percentage be improved? What is the role of memory in odor identification? (476)

8. Describe the undershirt experiment and the menstrual synchrony experiments. What is the possible mechanism for menstrual synchrony? (477)

The Olfactory System

The Olfactory Mucosa

9. Where is the olfactory mucosa located? (478)

10. Describe the olfactory receptor neurons (ORNs). (480)

11. Where does transduction occur? (480)

12. Where are the olfactory receptors (ORs) located? (480)

13. How are olfactory receptors similar to the visual pigment molecule? (480)

14. About how many different kinds of ORs are there? (480)

15. How do the ORs on a particular ORN compare to one another? (480)

16. What are two ways that odorant molecules can reach active sites on the receptor neuron? (480)

17. What happens when odorants reach ORs? (480)

18. How many different kinds of ORN are there? (480)

19. How is the olfactory mucosa divided into zones? (480)

20. What do these zones tell us about how signals are sent from the mucosa to the olfactory bulb? (480)

The Brain

21. Why is the axons of the ORNs short trip to the olfactory bulb "remarkable?" (481)

22. What structures do the ORN axons reach? (481)

23. What signals do the glomeruli receive? What is one of the main functions of glomeruli? (481)

24. What are the two major cortical areas for olfaction? Which subcortical structure is involved in emotional responding? (482)

The Neural Code for Odor Molecules

25. What is the relationship between physical and chemical properties of chemicals and their odors? (482)

The Response of ORNs

26. Do individual ORNs respond to just one or two chemicals or to many? (482)

The Response of Glomeruli

27. Do individual glomeruli respond to just one or two chemicals or to many? (483)

28. Describe the glomeruli that appear to be specialized to respond to molecules with specific structures. What is an odotope? (484)

The Olfactory Code Is a Pattern

29. What does the response to a particular odorant look like across a number of ORNs? (484)

30. How was the 2-deoxyglucose technique used to determine how areas in the olfactory bulb respond to specific odorants? (484)

Central Processing of Olfactory Information

31. How do neurons in the orbital frontal cortex (OFC) respond to different odorants? (485)

Brain Scan:
Sniff Responses in the Human Brain

32. What did Sobel's research show about how the piriform cortex responds to sniffing? What is a practical outcome of having information available about sniffing? (486)

The Taste System

The Tongue and Transduction

33. Describe the structure of the tongue as depicted in Figure 14.15. (487)

34. What is the difference between a taste bud, a taste cell, and a taste pore? (489)

35. When does transduction occur? How does transduction differ for different chemicals? (489)

Central Destinations of Taste Signals

36. Which nerves conduct signals from the tongue toward the brain? (489)

37. What are some of the central structures that receive signals from the tongue? (489)

Taste Quality

The Four Basic Taste Qualities

38. What are the four basic taste qualities and a possible fifth one? (490)

The Genetics of Taste Experience

39. What is the relationship between genetics and taste experience? What is a taster? A nontaster? (491)

40. What is the relationship between being a taster or a nontaster and the taste receptors? (491)

The Neural Code for Taste Quality

Distributed Coding

41. Describe Erickson's experiment that supports the idea of distributed coding. (492)

42. What is the evidence that distributed coding for taste might work for humans? (493)

Specificity Coding

43. What is the evidence for specificity coding in the taste system? (493)

Is Coding Distributed or Specific?

44. What is an argument in favor of at least some form of distributed coding being involved in taste perception? (493)

45. Is it possible that some coding is specific, as well? (495)

The Perception of Flavor

46. What is flavor? (496)

47. Why would it be correct to say that sensing the smells and tastes of different foods is a feat of perceptual organization? (496)

Flavor = Taste + Olfaction

48. What is the retronasal route for odor stimuli? (496)

49. What is the evidence that odor influences "taste"? (497)

50. Why do we mislocate the source of flavor sensations in the mouth? (498)

Changes in Flavor During a Meal

51. What is alliesthesia? What is the evidence that it is a central effect? (498)

52. What is sensory-specific satiety? What do we mean when we say it is specific? (498)

53. What is the evidence that sensory-specific satiety is sensory as opposed to central? (498)

The Physiology of Flavor Perception

54. What is the basis of the multimodal nature of the OFC? (499)

55. What is an important property of how bimodal cells in the OFC respond to the taste and smell of the same substance? (499)

56. Why has it been suggested that the OFC is the control center for detecting flavor? (499)

57. Describe the experiments that show that the response of OFC neurons can be affected by hunger. (500)

Plasticity of Perception: Learning Smell–Taste Associations

58. Describe the experiments that show that the response of OFC neurons to odors can be influenced by the taste the odor is paired with. (502)

59. How does the result above explain how some bimodal neurons in the OFC respond similarly to the odor and taste of a particular food? (502)

Across the Senses: Seeing a Smell: A Colorometric Electronic Nose

60. What is an "electronic nose," and what is its purpose? (503)

61. What are two reasons, in addition to their practical value, that these electronic noses are interesting to us? (503)

62. What is a colorometric electronic nose? How is it different than electronic noses that use computers to analyze their response to chemicals? (503)

63. What pattern-recognition device is used by the colorometric electronic nose? (503)

15

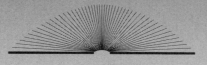

PERCEPTUAL DEVELOPMENT

Our senses endow us with truly amazing capacities. We can see fine details and keep them in focus when an object moves from close to far away. We see something move and can follow the moving object with our eyes, keeping its image on our foveas so we can see the object clearly. We can perceive the location of a sound, transform pressure changes in the air into meaningful sentences, and create myriad tastes and smells from our molecular environment.

As adults, we can do all these things and more. But were we born with these abilities? Most 19th-century psychologists would have answered this question by saying that newborns and young infants experience a totally confusing perceptual world, in which they either perceive nothing or can make little sense of the stimulation to which they are exposed.

One of the things we will do in this chapter is to deal directly with this idea by asking what perceptual capacities are present in the newborn and very young infant. We will see that while newborns have great perceptual deficiencies compared to older children or adults, they can perceive quite a bit more than the 19th-century psychologists believed.

But our goal in this chapter goes beyond simply establishing what newborns and young infants can perceive. We will be looking at a number of the questions asked by psychologists and physiologists who are interested in perceptual development. The following are some of these questions, along with brief previews of the answers that we will expand upon in the chapter.

1. *How do perceptual capacities present in the newborn develop with age?*
   Most capacities develop rapidly during the first year of life.

2. *When do new perceptual capacities emerge?*
   Some capacities that aren't present at birth emerge during the first few months of life.

3. *What aspects of stimuli are important to newborns and young infants?*
   Movement is an example of an aspect of stimulation that helps infants perceive shapes as separated from one another.

4. *What are the mechanisms that underlie perceptual development?*
   Development is governed by an interaction between biological programming and the infant's perceptual experience.

Determining the answers to these questions depends on our ability to determine what an infant is perceiving. This is one of the great challenges of the study of perceptual development, and one of the accomplishments of modern perceptual research has been the discovery of ways to uncover some of the characteristics of the infant's perceptual world.

MEASURING INFANT PERCEPTION

Why did the early psychologists think that the newborn's perceptual world was either nonexistent or very confusing, whereas present-day psychologists think that newborns have some perceptual abilities? Did infants learn to see and hear better between the 19th century and now? Obviously not. What did happen is that psychologists learned how to measure infants' perceptual abilities that were there all along.

Problems in Measuring Infant Perception

The following statement, by a well-known researcher who studies perceptual development in 3- to 5-month-old infants, captures some of the difficulties involved in doing research on human newborns:

> I admit I've never had the courage to run a full-blown experiment with human newborns. For those who may not be aware of the difficulties involved, running such an experiment can be a formidable task: convincing hospital administrators and personnel in the neonatal nursery that the research is worthwhile; setting up elaborate equipment often in cramped, temporary quarters; obtaining permission from mothers who are still recovering from their deliveries; waiting, sometimes for hours, until the infant to be tested is in a quiet, alert state; coping with the infant's inevitable changes in state after testing has begun; and interpreting the infant's responses that at one moment may seem to be nothing more than a blank stare and at another moment active involvement with the stimulus. (Cohen, 1991, p. 1)

Not only do newborns and young infants exhibit behaviors such as crying, sleeping, and not paying attention while the experimenter is trying to test them, but the fact that they can't understand or respond to verbal instructions presents a special challenge. Even if the infant is cooperating by being quiet and paying attention, the researcher is still faced with the problem of devising methods that will make it possible to determine what the infant is perceiving.

The key to measuring infant perception is to pose the correct question. To understand what we mean by this, let's consider two questions we can ask to determine visual acuity, the ability to see details. One question we can ask is "What do you see?" This is the question that you're answering when you read the letters on an eye chart like the one in Figure 15.1. Acuity is determined using this technique by noting the smallest letters a person can accurately identify. This technique is obviously, however, not suitable for infants. To test infant acuity, we have to ask another question and use another procedure.

D S R K N	20/400
C K Z O H	20/300
O N R K D	20/250
K Z V D C	20/200
V S H Z O	20/150
H D K C R	20/125
C S R H N	20/100
S V Z D K	20/80
N C V O Z	20/60
R H S D V	20/50
S N R O H	20/40
K K E N	20/30
	20/25
	20/20

Figure 15.1

An eye chart for measuring visual acuity. This works well for older children and adults who can answer the question "What do you see?" but does not work for infants. To measure their acuity, we need to ask a different question and use a different stimulus.

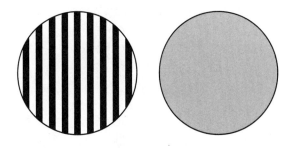

Figure 15.2

A grating stimulus and gray field of the same average intensity. This stimulus is better suited for measuring infant acuity, because the infants can answer the question "Can you tell me the difference between these two fields?" They answer this question by where they look, and this enables us to measure their acuity. See text for further details.

A question that works for infants is "Can you tell the difference between the stimulus on the left and the one on the right?" Infants answer this question not by responding verbally but by moving their eyes.

Preferential Looking

The way infants look at stimuli in their environment provides a way to determine whether they can tell the difference between two stimuli. In the **preferential looking (PL) technique** two stimuli like the ones in Figure 15.2 are presented to the infant, and the experimenter watches the infant's eyes to determine where the infant is looking. If the infant looks at one stimulus more than the other, the experimenter concludes that he or she can tell the difference between them.

The reason preferential looking works is that infants have *spontaneous looking preferences*; that is, they prefer to look at certain types of stimuli. For example, to measure visual acuity, we can use the fact that infants choose to look at objects with contours

over one that is homogeneous (Fantz, Ordy, & Udelf, 1962). When we present a grating with large bars and a homogeneous field that reflects the same amount of light that the grating would reflect if the bars were spread evenly over the whole area, the infant can easily see the bars and therefore looks at the side with the bars more than the side with the gray field (the grating and homogeneous field are switched randomly from side to side on each trial). By preferentially looking at the side with the bars the infant is telling us, "I see the grating" (Figure 15.3).

As we decrease the size of the bars, it becomes more difficult for the infant to tell the difference between the grating and gray stimuli, until, when they become indiscriminable, the infant looks equally at each display. We determine the infant's acuity by determining the narrowest stripe width that results in looking more to one side.

Habituation

Use of the preferential looking technique to measure acuity is based on the existence of the infant's spontaneous looking preference for contours. But to measure other perceptual capacities, we often want to know whether the infant perceives a difference between two stimuli that the infant normally looks at equally. Researchers have solved this problem by

Perceptual Development

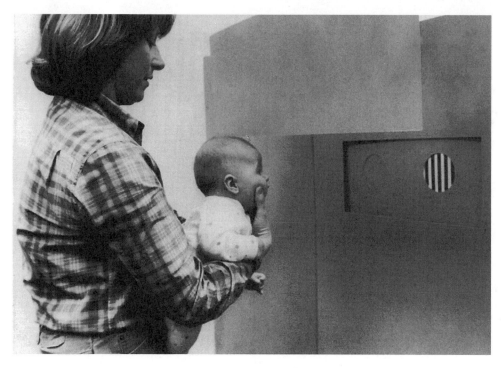

Figure 15.3
An infant being tested by the preferential looking procedure. The mother holds the infant in front of the display: a grating on the right and a homogeneous gray field on the left with the same average intensity as the grating. An experimenter, who does not know which side the grating is on in any given trial, looks through a small peephole located between the grating and the gray field and judges whether the infant is looking to the left or to the right. (Photograph courtesy of Velma Dobson.)

using the following fact about infant looking behavior: When given a choice between a familiar stimulus and a novel one, an infant is more likely to look at the novel one (Fagan, 1976; Slater, Morison, & Rose, 1984).

Since infants are more likely to look at a novel stimulus, we can create a preference for one stimulus over another one by familiarizing the infant with one stimulus but not with the other. For this technique, which is called **habituation**, one stimulus is presented to the infant repeatedly, and the infant's looking time is measured on each presentation (Figure 15.4). As the infant becomes more familiar with the stimulus, he or she habituates to it, looking less and less on each trial.

Once the infant has habituated to this stimulus, we now determine whether the infant can tell the dif-

ference between it and another stimulus by replacing it with a new stimulus. In Figure 15.4, the new stimulus is presented on the eighth trial. If the infant can tell the difference between the habituation stimulus and the new stimulus he or she will exhibit **dishabituation**, an increase in looking time when the stimulus is changed, as shown by the open circles in Figure 15.4. If, however, the infant cannot tell the difference between the two stimuli he or she will continue to habituate to the new stimulus (since it will not be perceived as novel), as shown by the open squares in Figure 15.4.

When we report the results of habituation experiments in this chapter, we will usually use the format shown in Figure 15.5. The stimulus to which the infant is habituated will appear on the left, and stimuli that are presented after habituation has occurred

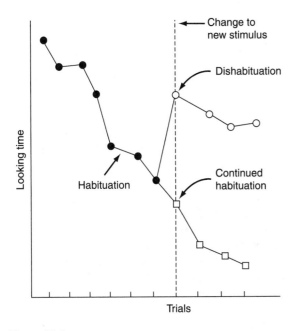

Change to
new stimulus

Dishabituation

Looking time

Habituation

Continued
habituation

Trials

Figure 15.4
Possible results of a habituation experiment. See text for details.

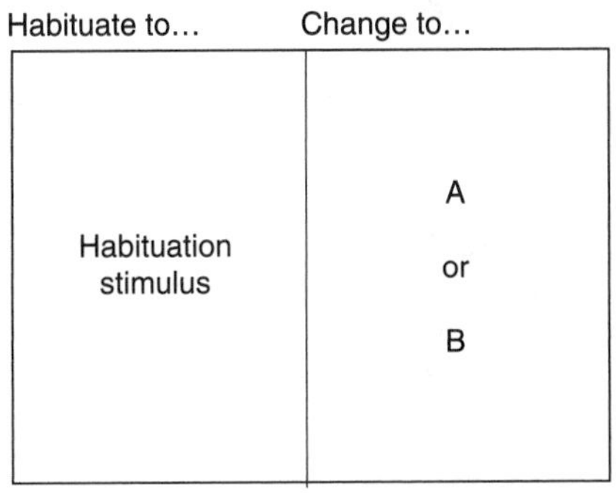

Habituate to...	Change to...
Habituation stimulus	A or B

Figure 15.5
Standard format for presenting habituation results. The habituation stimulus will appear on the left, and the new stimuli will appear on the right. The new stimulus that causes dishabituation is always placed on top.

will appear on the right. The stimulus that causes dishabituation is placed on top. Thus, in this example, changing to stimulus A causes dishabituation,

but changing to B does not. Remember that the occurrence of dishabituation means that the second stimulus (the one on the top right of the figure) appears different to the infant than the habituation stimulus (the one on the left).

INFANT PERCEPTUAL CAPACITIES: VISION

Now that we have described the procedures used to measure infant perception, we are ready to describe the perceptual capacities that have been discovered using these procedures. We begin by considering a number of visual capacities (see also Gwiazda & Birch, 2001; Teller, 1997).

Acuity and Contrast

One of the most basic questions we can ask about infant perception is how well infants can perceive details and contrast.

Perceiving Details Visual acuity is poorly developed at birth (about 20/400 to 20/600 at 1 month),[1] and then rapidly increases over the first six months to just below the adult level of 20/20 (Banks & Salapatek, 1978; Dobson & Teller, 1978; Harris, Atkinson, & Braddick, 1976; Salapatek, Bechtold, & Bushnell, 1976). Acuity has been measured using the preferential looking technique (comparing gratings and homogeneous fields) and by measuring an electrical response called the **visual evoked potential (VEP)**, which is recorded by disc electrodes placed on the back of the infant's head, over the visual cortex. The VEP is the pooled response of thousands of neurons that are near the electrode.

When a researcher is using the VEP to measure acuity, the infant looks at a gray field, which is briefly replaced by either a grating or a checkerboard pattern.

---

[1] The expression 20/400 means that the infant must view a stimulus from 20 feet to see the same thing that a normal adult observer can see from 400 feet. (see Chapter 16.)

Perceptual Development

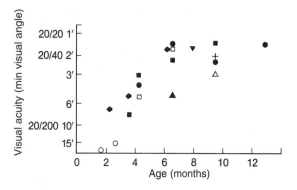

Figure 15.6
The improvement of acuity over the first year of life, as measured by the VEP technique. The numbers on the vertical axis indicate the smallest stripe width that results in a detectable evoked response. Snellen acuity values (see Chapter 16) are also indicated on this axis. The different symbols represent measurements of different subjects. (Pirchio et al., 1978.)

If the stripes or checks are large enough to be detected by the visual system, the visual cortex generates a visual evoked potential. If, however, the pattern cannot be resolved, no response is generated. Thus, the VEP provides an objective measure of the ability of the visual system to detect details. Figure 15.6 shows the acuities of a number of subjects measured using this technique. The rapid improvement of acuity until the sixth month is followed by a leveling-off period, and full adult acuity is not reached until sometime after 1 year of age.

Acuity is one of the few perceptual capacities for which we can demonstrate parallels between psychophysically measured development and physiological development. Thus, although our survey of visual capabilities will be focusing on psychophysical measurements, let's consider, for acuity, the nature of this parallel between perceptual development and physiology.

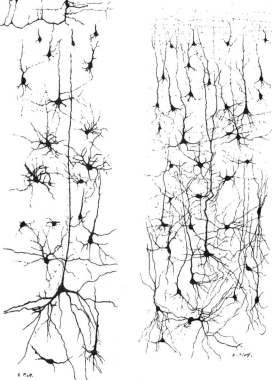

(a) Newborn (b) 3-month-old (c) 6-month-old

Figure 15.7
Drawings of neurons in the visual cortex of the newborn, the 3-month-old, and the 6-month-old human infant. (Conel, 1939, 1947, 1951.)

The parallel between perception and physiology becomes obvious when we look at the state of the retina and cortex at birth. One reason for the infant's low acuity is that the infant's visual cortex is not fully developed. Figure 15.7 shows the state of cortical development at birth, at 3 months, and at 6 months (Conel, 1939, 1947, 1951). These pictures indicate that the visual cortex is only partially developed at birth and becomes more developed at 3 and 6 months, the time when significant improvements in visual acuity are occurring. However, the state of the cortex is not the whole explanation for the infant's low visual acuity. If we look at the newborn's retina, we find that, although the rod-dominated peripheral retina appears adultlike in the newborn, the all-cone fovea contains widely spaced and very poorly developed cone receptors (Abramov et al., 1982).

Figure 15.8 compares the shapes of newborn and adult foveal cones. The newborn's cones have fat inner segments and very small outer segments, whereas the adult's inner and outer segments are larger and are about the same diameter (Banks & Bennett, 1988; Yuodelis & Hendrickson, 1986). These differences in shape and size have a number of consequences. The small size of the outer segment means that the newborn's cones contain less visual pigment and therefore do not absorb light as effectively as adult cones. In addition, the fat inner segment creates the coarse receptor lattice shown in Figure 15.9a, with large spaces between the outer segments. In contrast, the thin adult cones are closely packed, as in Figure

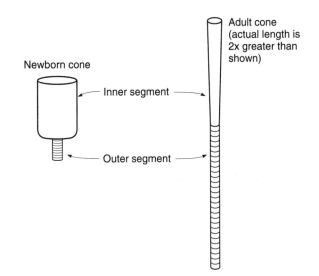

Figure 15.8
Idealized shapes of newborn and adult foveal cones. (Real cones are not so perfectly straight and cylindrical.) Foveal cones are much narrower and longer than the cones elsewhere in the retina, so these look different from the ones shown in Figures 2.10 and 2.11. The adult cone is actually twice as long as shown here. See text for details. (From Banks & Bennett, 1988.)

15.9b, creating a fine lattice that is well suited to detecting fine details. Martin Banks and Patrick Bennett (1988) calculated that the cone receptors' outer segments effectively cover 68 percent of the adult fovea but only 2 percent of the newborn fovea.

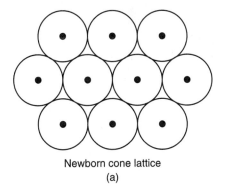

Newborn cone lattice
(a)

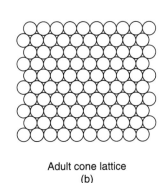

Adult cone lattice
(b)

Figure 15.9
Receptor lattices for (a) newborn and (b) adult foveal cones. The newborn cone outer segments, indicated by the dark circles, are widely spaced because of the fat inner segments. In contrast, the adult cones, with their slender inner segments, are packed closely together. (Adapted from Banks & Bennett, 1988.)

Perceptual Development

This means that most of the light entering the newborn's fovea is lost in the spaces between the cones and is therefore not useful for vision.

Acuity is an example of a capacity we can measure at or near birth and then follow as it improves with time. We can also do this for contrast sensitivity, which provides information that goes beyond what measurements of acuity tell us. Visual acuity indicates the visual system's capacity to resolve fine details under optimum conditions. Acuity tells us little, however, about how well we can see under lower contrasts and how well we can see forms that are larger than fine details. We can determine the visual system's ability to see at a wide range of contrasts, by measuring the contrast sensitivity function (CSF). (Review Chapter 3 for a description of the CSF.)

Perceiving Contrast The contrast sensitivity functions for 1-, 2-, and 3-month-old infants and for adults, shown in Figure 15.10, indicate that (1) the infant's ability to perceive contrast is restricted to low frequencies; (2) at these low frequencies the infant's contrast

sensitivity is lower than the adult's by a factor of 20 to 100; and (3) the infant can see little or nothing at frequencies above about 2 to 3 cycles/degree, the frequencies to which adults are most sensitive (Banks, 1982; Banks & Salapatek, 1978, 1981; Salapatek & Banks, 1978).

What does the young infant's depressed CSF tell us about its visual world? Clearly, infants are sensitive to only a small fraction of the pattern information available to the adult. At 1 month, infants can see no fine details and can see only relatively large objects with high contrast. The vision of infants at this age is slightly worse than adult night vision (Fiorentini & Maffei, 1973; Pirchio et al., 1978), a finding consistent with the fact that the undeveloped state of the infant's fovea forces it to see primarily with the rod-dominated peripheral retina.

We should not conclude from the young infant's poor vision, however, that it can see nothing at all. At very close distances, a young infant can detect some gross features, as indicated in Figure 15.11, which simulates how 1-, 2-, and 3-month-old infants perceive a woman's face from a distance of about 50 cm. At 1 month the contrast is so low that it is difficult to recognize facial expressions, but it is possible to see very high-contrast areas, such as the contour between the woman's hairline and forehead. By 3 months, however, the infant's contrast perception has improved so that the perception of facial expressions is possible, and behavioral tests indicate that, by 3 to 4 months, infants can tell the difference between a face that looks happy and faces that show surprise or anger or are neutral (LaBarbera et al., 1976; Young-Browne, Rosenfield, & Horowitz, 1977).

Infants have a very different "window on the world" from that of adults; infants see the world as if they are looking through a frosted glass that filters out the high frequencies that would enable them to see fine details but leaves some ability to detect larger, low-frequency forms.

Perceiving Objects

The newborn's ability to use visual information exceeds what we might expect based simply on measurements of acuity or contrast sensitivity. For example,

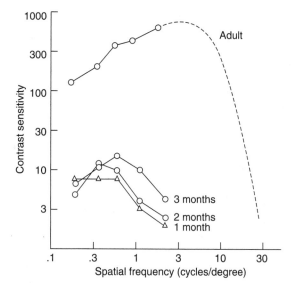

Figure 15.10

Contrast sensitivity functions for an adult and for infants tested at 1, 2, and 3 months of age.

1 month

2 months

3 months

Adult

Figure 15.11
Simulations of what 1-, 2-, and 3-month old infants see when they look at a woman's face from a distance of about 50 cm. These pictures were obtained by using a mathematical procedure that applies infant CSFs to the photograph on the right, which depicts what an adult perceives. (From Ginsberg, 1983.)

in spite of its poor acuity and contrast sensitivity, a 2- to 3-day-old infant can recognize its mother's face.

Recognizing the Mother's Face   Research on the infant's ability to recognize faces provides an example of how research in perceptual development often progresses. First, an infant's ability to perceive a particular stimulus is demonstrated. Then, the result is confirmed by replicating it, perhaps also using improved procedures to rule out possible sources of bias. Finally, experiments are done to determine the information the infant is using to achieve its perception.

Using preferential looking in which 2-day-old infants were given a choice between their mother's face and a stranger's face, Bushnell, Sai, and Mullin (1989) found that infants looked at the mother about 63 percent of the time. Since this result is above the 50 percent chance level, Bushnell concluded that the 2-day-olds could recognize their mother's face. It is

possible, however, that this result could have occurred because the mother was doing something to attract the infant's attention. Or perhaps the infant could detect the mother's familiar smell. Bushnell did take precautions to guard against these potential sources of bias, but, just to be sure that the result was valid, Gail Walton and coworkers (1992) showed that infants still respond to the mother more than strangers when their mothers' faces are presented on videotape.

To determine what information the infants might be using to recognize the mother's face, Olivier Pascalis and coworkers (1995) showed that when the mother and stranger wore pink scarves that covered their hairline, the preference for the mother disappeared. The high-contrast border between the mother's dark hairline and light forehead apparently provides important information about the mother's physical characteristics that the infant uses to recognize its mother.

Distinguishing Figure from Ground We have considered the newborn's ability to detect the presence of visual stimuli. But detecting stimuli is just the first step in perception. To perceive objects in the environment, stimuli that are detected must become perceptually organized. This organization is often described in terms of figure–ground segregation—the separation of a display into a figure that is seen in front of the ground (see page 156 for more details on the differences between figure and ground).

Researchers have asked whether infants are capable of figure–ground segregation and, if they are, which aspects of the visual environment they use to achieve this separation of figure and ground. One conclusion from this research is that motion is an important source of information for infant perception.

Lincoln Craton and Albert Yonas (1990) used motion as a way to achieve figure–ground segregation in 5-month-old infants by using the stimulus shown in Figure 15.12. The two areas were filled with a computer-generated pattern of moving dots that created the perception that one area was covering the other area. In the example we will describe, adults saw the area on the left as the figure and the area on the right as the ground.

After the infants habituated to this stimulus, they saw either stimulus A or stimulus B. Since dishabituation occurred to stimulus A, this means that the infant perceived the left side of the habituation stimulus as figure, just as adults did. (Remember that dishabituation occurs when a stimulus looks different from the habituation stimulus.) Thus, 5-month-old infants can separate areas into figure and ground based on movement.

Grouping by Lightness Similarity To determine whether infants can perceptually group elements based on their lightness (see the Gestalt law of similarity in Chapter 7), Paul Quinn, S. Burke, and A. Rush (1993) habituated 3-month-old infants to the pattern on the left in Figure 15.13 and then presented either horizontal bars (A) or vertical bars (B). Dishabituation occurred to the horizontal bars, indicating that the infants perceptually organized the squares into vertical columns.

Perceiving an Object as Continuing Behind an Occluder We will now describe a series of experiments that are interesting (1) because they consider a basic perceptual ability—the ability to perceive one stimulus as continuing behind an occluding stimulus—

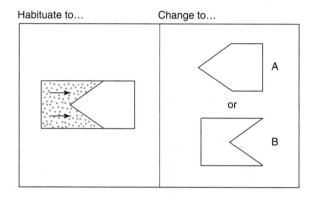

Figure 15.12
The Craton (1989) experiment. Infants are habituated to the stimulus on the left. Dishabituation occurs to new stimulus A but not to B. See text for details.

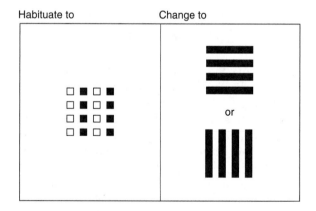

Figure 15.13
The Quinn, Burke, and Rush (1993) experiment. Infants habituated to the stimulus on the left show dishabituation to the horizontal bars. The experiment was also repeated with a habituation stimulus in which squares in horizontal rows were the same color. In that case, habituation occurred to the vertical bars.

and (2) because they illustrate how researchers have zeroed in on the age at which a capacity first appears.

When adults look at the person in Figure 15.14, they perceive the man's body as continuing behind the fence. But does a young infant perceive the parts of the person that are visible as separate objects or as a single object that continues behind the fence? Philip Kellman and Elizabeth Spelke (1983) showed that movement helps infants perceive objects as continuing behind an occluding object, by habituating 4-month-old infants to a rod moving back and forth behind a block (left stimulus in Figure 15.15) and then presenting either two separated rods or a single longer rod (right stimuli in Figure 15.15).

Since dishabituation occurred to the two separated rods, Kellman and Spelke concluded that 4-month-old infants perceive the partly occluded mov-

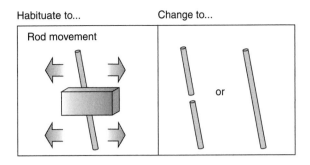

Figure 15.15
The Kellman and Spelke (1983) experiment. See text.

ing rod as continuing behind the block. This result does not, however, occur when the infant is habituated to a stationary rod and block display. Thus, movement provides information that a 4-month-old infant uses to infer that one object extends behind another. It appears that the 4-month-olds are making the following inference: If the top and bottom units are moving together, then they must be part of the same object.

If 4-month-olds perceive a moving object as continuing behind an occluding stimulus, can younger infants do this as well? When Alan Slater and coworkers (1990) repeated Kellman and Spelke's experiment for newborns, they found that when the newborns saw the moving rod during habituation, they looked more at the single rod during dishabituation. This suggests that they saw the moving rods as two separate units and not as a single rod extending behind the occluder. Apparently newborns do not make the inference that 4-month-olds make about the moving display.

Thus, the capacity demonstrated at 4 months does not exist (or can't be measured using this particular procedure) at birth. But when does it appear? Scott Johnson and Richard Aslin (1995) helped determine the answer to this question when they tested 2-month-olds and obtained results similar to what had previously been observed for the 4-month-olds. Apparently, the ability to use movement as a way to organize the perceptual world develops rapidly over the first few months of life.

We have described some experiments that have looked at the infant's ability to perceive a number of different kinds of objects. Within a few days after

Figure 15.14
An occluded person.

Perceptual Development

birth, the infant can recognize its mother, apparently based on the ability to distinguish the mother's distinctive high-contrast hairline. Within the first few months of age infants can begin to perceptually organize stimuli, distinguish figure from ground, and infer the existence of stimuli that continue behind an occluder. We will now consider some experiments that used older infants as subjects. These experiments make two important points: (1) they confirm the importance of movement for organizing the perception of objects, and (2) they show that at 10 months of age the infant's ability to perceive objects is still developing.

Perceiving Adjacent Objects as Separate What characteristics of stimuli enable infants to tell that two objects that share a border are two separate objects? F. Xu and Susan Carey (1994) showed that for 10-month-old infants differences in shape or color may not be enough to signal that two objects are separate but that movement information does help them reach this conclusion.

They habituated 10-month-old infants to a yellow toy duck sitting on top of a red toy truck (left stimulus in Figure 15.16). They then showed the infant either a hand lifting the duck away from the truck (A) or a hand lifting the duck and truck together as if they were one object (B). Dishabituation occurred when the duck was lifted away from the truck (A). This result suggests that they perceived the habituation display as one object.

However, when the duck was moving back and forth on top of the truck during habituation (left stimulus in Figure 15.17), the infants looked longer when the duck and truck were lifted together (top right stimulus) suggesting that they saw the duck and truck as two separate objects. Thus, when the duck was stationary relative to the truck it did not appear separated from the truck, even though it had a different shape and color. However, when it was moving it appeared to be a separate object (Spelke, Gutheil, & Van de Walle, 1995). Apparently, 10-month-olds still lack some of the ability to differentiate adjacent objects from one another that older children have but are able to distinguish between objects when one is moving and the other is not.

Habituate to...   Change to...

or

Figure 15.16

The Xu and Carey experiment in which the duck on top of the truck is stationary. See text for details.

Our conclusion from all of these experiments is that during the early months of life infants gain the ability to perceptually organize objects in their environment. Movement is a particularly important source of information, but other information such as differences in lightness can be used as well.

By 3 to 4 months of age, infants can not only segregate some objects from one another but are able to make discriminations between different categories of objects. For example, Peter Eimas and Paul Quinn (1994) showed that 3- to 4-month-old infants can tell the difference between pictures of dogs and pictures of cats. Although infants this age do not yet possess the concepts of "cat" and "dog," their ability to perceptually discriminate between them is the beginning of the process that culminates in the ability to under-

| Habituate to... | Change to... |

Figure 15.17
The Xu and Carey experiment in which the duck is moving on top of a stationary truck. See text for details.

stand categories and to use these categories to think and reason about the world.

Perceiving Color

We know that our perception of color is determined by the action of three different types of cone receptors. Since the cones are poorly developed at birth, we can guess that the newborn would not have good color vision. However, research has shown that color vision develops early and that appreciable color vision is present within the first few months of life.

One of the challenges in determining whether infants have color vision is created by the fact that a light stimulus can vary on at least two dimensions: (1) its chromatic color and (2) its brightness. Thus, if we presented the red patch located at 12 o'clock on the color circle of Color Plate 2.3 and the yellow patch located at 3 o'clock to a totally color-blind person and asked him if he could tell the difference between them, he would say yes, because the yellow patch is brighter than the red one.

A way to do this experiment, if you don't have access to a color-blind person, is to use a "color-blind" black-and-white photocopier as your "subject." The picture you obtain by photocopying the color circle will tell you that even though the machine can't "see" in color, it can tell that there are differences between the two patches, based on the difference in the amount of light reflected by the two patches. This means that the stimuli used in testing for the presence of color vision should differ in wavelength but should be the same brightness. The experiments we will now describe have done this.

Perceiving Color Categories Marc Bornstein, William Kessen, and Sally Weiskopf (1976) assessed the color vision of 4-month-old infants by asking whether they perceive the same color categories in the spectrum as adults. People with normal trichromatic vision see the spectrum as a sequence of color categories, starting with blue at the short-wavelength end and followed by green, yellow, orange, and red, with fairly abrupt transitions between one color and the next (see spectrum of Color Plate 1.1).

Bornstein and his coworkers first habituated the infants to a 510-nm light—a wavelength that appears green to a trichromat—and then presented either a 480-nm light, which looks blue to a trichromat, or a 540-nm light, which is on the other side of the blue–green border and therefore appears green to a trichromat (Figure 15.18a). Since dishabituation occurred to the 480-nm light but not to the 540-nm light (Figure 15.18b), the 480-nm light apparently looks different than the 510-nm light, and the 540-nm light looks similar to it. From this result and the results of other experiments, Bornstein concluded that 4-month-old infants categorize colors the same way adult trichromats do.

Bornstein and coworkers dealt with the problem of equating brightness by setting the intensity at each wavelength so each stimulus looked equally bright to adults. This is not an ideal procedure, since infants

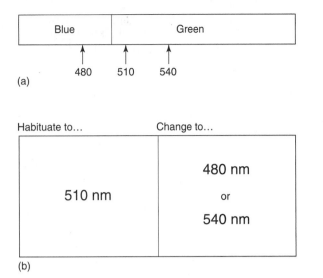

(a)

Habituate to...	Change to...
510 nm	480 nm or 540 nm

(b)

Figure 15.18

(a) The three wavelengths used in the Bornstein, Kessen, and Weiskopf (1976) experiment. The 510- and 480-nm lights are in different perceptual categories (one appears green, the other blue to adults), but the 510- and 540-nm lights are in the same perceptual category (both appear green to adults). (b) The habituation procedure and results. See text for details.

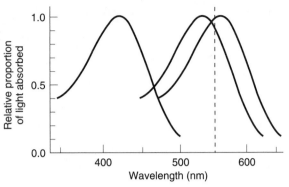

Figure 15.19

Cone absorption spectra. Notice that above the vertical line at 550 nm, only the medium- and long-wavelength pigments absorb light. (From Dartnall, Bowmaker, & Mollon, 1983.)

may perceive brightness differently than adults. However, as it turns out, Bornstein's result appears to be correct, since later research has shown that even younger infants have color vision.

Discriminating Between Long-Wavelength Lights
We will now describe a psychophysical experiment that was designed to answer the question, "At what age do both medium- and long-wavelength cone pigments become operational?" We can understand why it is possible to use psychophysics to answer this question by looking at the cone pigment absorption spectra in Figure 15.19. Notice that only the medium- and long-wavelength pigments absorb light above 550 nm. Thus, when one of these pigments is missing, the person is left with only one kind of pigment in this part of the spectrum and, without the minimum of two kinds of pigments required for color vision (see Chapter 5), will perceive the world as a monochromat would—all

wavelengths would appear gray or the same chromatic color and would differ only in brightness.

To determine whether 1-, 2-, and 3-month-old infants can discriminate between a green (550 nm) and a yellow (589 nm) with the same brightness, Russell Hamer, Kenneth Alexander, and Davida Teller (1982) used the preferential looking technique and the display in Figure 15.20. This display contains a green test square that was presented either on the left or the right side of the yellow background. If infants can differentiate the green square from its background, they will direct their eyes to the green square.

Hamer and coworkers knew that in order to draw any conclusion about the infant's color vision they had to be sure the green square and the yellow background had the same brightness. They accomplished this by presenting the green square at a wide range of intensities, so for at least one of the intensities the green square would have the same brightness as the yellow background. They reasoned that if the infant can discriminate between green and yellow based on chromatic color, they should be able to tell the difference between the green square and the yellow square at all intensities—both the ones where the brightness would be different than the yellow background and the one where it would be the same.

Hamer and coworkers found that about one-half of the 1-month-old infants could discriminate be-

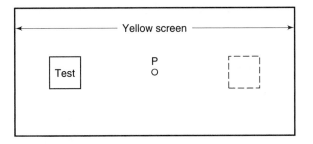

Figure 15.20

The stimulus used by Hamer, Alexander, and Teller (1982) to determine whether infants can tell the difference between two wavelengths above 550 nm that have the same brightness. A test square that appears green to an adult is presented either on the left or on the right side of a yellow screen. The infant's looking behavior is monitored by an observer who views the infant through the peephole, P.

tween green and yellow at all of the intensities and that by 3 months almost all of the infants could make this discrimination (Figure 15.21). Based on this result, Hamer et al. concluded that some 1-month-old infants, most 2-month-old infants, and all 3-month-old infants have operational medium- and long-wavelength cone receptors.

Researchers have also asked whether infants have short-wavelength receptors. Using a procedure similar to Hamer's, D. Varner and coworkers (1985) tested infants' ability to see short-wavelength light and found that, by 2 months of age, infants have functioning short-wavelength cones. Our conclusion from the Hamer and Varner experiments is that all three types of cones are present by at least 2 to 3 months of age and that some infants show evidence of three-cone vision even earlier. This infant trichromatic vision may not be identical to normal adult color vision, but it does seem likely that infants as young as 2 or 3 months old experience a wide range of colors.

Perceiving Depth

When infants are born, they have poor visual acuity and little or no depth perception. At what age are infants able to use different kinds of depth information? The answer to this question is that different types of information become operative at different times. Binocular disparity becomes functional early, and pictorial depth cues become functional later.

Using Binocular Disparity One requirement for the operation of binocular disparity is that the eyes must be able to **binocularly fixate** so that the two foveas are directed to exactly the same place. Newborns have only a rudimentary ability to fixate binocularly, so their binocular fixation is imprecise,

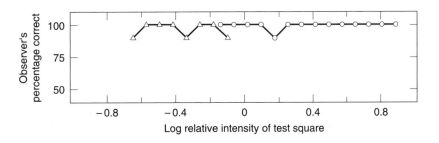

Figure 15.21

Results of the Hamer, Alexander, and Teller experiment for a 4-week-old infant. The infant's ability to detect the green test square was measured at a range of intensities of the test square, indicated along the horizontal axis. The intensity marked 0 represents the intensity at which the green and the yellow have the same brightness for an adult. Since the infant's performance ranged from 80% to 100% correct at all intensities, we can infer that she was, in fact, able to distinguish the green square from the yellow background on the basis of color alone.

especially on objects that are changing in depth (Slater & Findlay, 1975).

Richard Aslin (1977) determined when binocular fixation develops by making some simple observations. He filmed infants' eyes while moving a target back and forth between 12 cm and 57 cm from the infant. If the infant is directing both eyes at a target, the eyes should diverge (rotate outward) as the target moves away and should converge (rotate inward) as the target moves closer (Figure 15.22). Aslin's films indicate that while some divergence and convergence does occur in 1- and 2-month-old infants, these eye movements do not reliably direct both eyes toward the target until about 3 months of age.

Although binocular fixation may be present by 3 months of age, this does not guarantee that the infant can use the resulting disparity information to perceive depth. To determine when infants can use this information to perceive depth, Robert Fox and coworkers (1980) presented random-dot stereograms to infants ranging in age from 2 to 6 months.

The beauty of random-dot stereograms is that the binocular disparity information in the stereograms results in stereopsis (the perception of depth due to binocular disparity) only (1) if the stereogram is observed with a device that presents one picture to the left eye and the other picture to the right eye and (2) if

the observer's visual system can convert this disparity information into the perception of depth. Thus, if we present a random-dot stereogram to an infant whose visual system cannot yet use disparity information, all he or she will see is a random collection of dots.

In Fox's experiment, a child wearing special viewing glasses was seated in his or her mother's lap in front of a television screen (Figure 15.23). The child viewed a random-dot stereogram that appeared, to an observer sensitive to disparity information, as a rectangle-in-depth, moving either to the left or to the right. Fox's premise was that an infant sensitive to disparity will move his or her eyes to follow the moving rectangle. He found that infants younger than about 3 months of age would not follow the rectangle, but that infants between 3 and 6 months of age would follow it. He therefore concluded that the ability to use disparity information to perceive depth emerges sometime between 3 1/2 and 6 months of age.

Richard Held, Eileen Birch, and Jane Gwiazda (1980) showed that infants develop the ability to use disparity information by about 3 1/2 months of age by measuring infants' **stereoacuity**, the smallest amount of disparity that results in the perception of depth. They measured the infants' stereoacuity by having them view the display shown in Figure 15.24. One stimulus in this display was a flat picture of three black

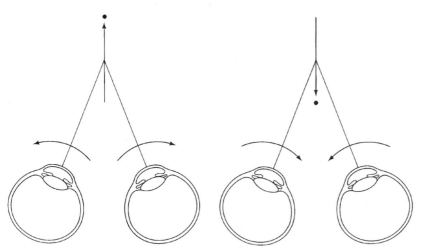

(a) Object moves away: eyes diverge   (b) Object moves closer: eyes converge

Figure 15.22

If an infant is fixating on an object that is moving, its eyes (a) diverge (rotate outward) as they follow an object that is moving away and (b) converge (rotate inward) as they follow an object that is moving closer.

Figure 15.23
*The setup used by Fox and coworkers (1980) to test infants'
ability to use binocular disparity information. An infant
who can use disparity information to see depth sees a rectangle moving back and forth in front of the screen.*

The development of the ability to use disparity to
detect depth beginning just after 3 months of age is
probably due to development of the physiological
mechanisms involved in maintaining good binocular
fixation and on the development of the neural connections necessary to create disparity-selective neurons (see page 240).

Another type of depth information, which we
also discussed in Chapter 8, is the pictorial cues.
These cues develop later than disparity, presumably
because they depend on experience with the environment and the development of cognitive capabilities. In general, infants begin to use pictorial cues
such as overlap, familiar size, relative size, shading,
linear perspective, and texture gradients sometime
between about 5 and 7 months of age (Granrud &
Yonas, 1984; Granrud, Haake, & Yonas, 1985; Granrud, Yonas, & Opland, 1985; Yonas et al., 1986; Yonas,
Pettersen, & Granrud, 1982). We will describe research on two of these cues—overlap and familiar size.

bars, and the other was a stereogram that, when
viewed through special glasses, appeared to be three-
dimensional to adults. This type of stereogram can
create smaller differences in disparity than the random-
dot stereogram and therefore provides a more sensitive
measure of infants' abilities.

Using the preferential looking technique, Held
determined that, by about $3^{1}/2$ months of age, infants
preferentially look at the three-dimensional stimulus.
By showing the infants stereograms with a number of
different disparities, Held was able to trace the development of the ability to use disparity. At $3^{1}/2$ months,
infants are able to detect disparities of about 1 degree
of visual angle, and, by $4^{1}/2$ months, stereoacuity
has inceased to less than 1 minute of visual angle
(1 minute of visual angle = $1/60$ degree). Thus, Held
showed that once the ability to detect disparity
appears, infants show a rapid increase in stereoacuity
to fairly good levels by between 4 and 5 months of age.

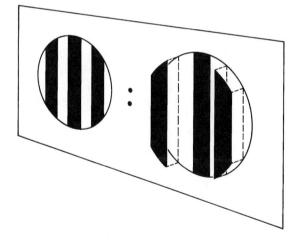

Figure 15.24
*Stimuli used by Held, Birch, and Gwiazda (1980) to test
stereoacuity. The pattern on the left is a two-dimensional
grating. The one on the right is a stereogram that looks
three-dimensional when viewed through special glasses. This
three-dimensional perception occurs, however, only if the
subject can perceive depth based on disparity.*

Depth from Overlap To test infants' ability to perceive depth from overlap, Carl Granrud and Albert Yonas (1984) showed them two-dimensional cardboard cutouts of the displays depicted in Figure 15.25. The infants viewed the cutouts with just one eye, because binocular viewing would reveal that the displays were flat and could lower the chances that the infants would respond to the pictorially induced depth. Display (a) includes the depth cue of overlap, whereas displays (b) and (c) do not. Since infants tend to reach for objects they perceive as being nearer, they will reach more for (a) than for (b) or (c) if they are sensitive to overlap. This was the result for 7-month-olds but not for 5-month-olds. Thus, the ability to perceive depth based on overlap appears sometime between 5 and 7 months.

Depth from Familiar Size Granrud, Haake, and Yonas (1985) conducted a two-part experiment to see if infants can use their knowledge of the sizes of objects to help them perceive depth. In the familiarization period, 7-month-old infants played with a pair of wooden objects for 10 minutes. One of these objects was large (Figure 15.26a) and one was small (Figure 15.26b). In the test period, objects (c) and (d) were presented at the same distance from the infant. The prediction was that infants sensitive to familiar size would perceive object c to be closer if they remembered, from the familiarization period, that this shape was smaller than the other one.

When tested monocularly, the 7-month-olds did reach for object c. The 5-month-olds, however, did not reach for object c, a result indicating that these infants did not use familiar size as information for depth. Thus, just as for overlap, the ability to use

familiar size to perceive depth appears to develop sometime between 5 and 7 months.

This experiment is interesting not only because it indicates when the ability to use familiar size develops, but also because the infant's response in the test phase depends on a cognitive ability—the ability to remember the sizes of the objects that he or she played with in the familiarization phase. The 7-month-old infant's depth response in this situation is therefore based both on what is perceived and what is remembered.

Perceiving Movement

Human infants come into the world specially adapted to perceive motion, and this ability is apparent shortly after birth (Nelson & Horowitz, 1987).

Perception of a Moving Object One of the best ways to attract a young infant's attention is to move something across his or her visual field. Newborns direct their eyes at moving stimuli and follow them with a combination of head and eye movements (Haith, 1983; Kremenitzer et al., 1979). When presented with a choice between a moving stimulus and a complex three-dimensional form, the infant prefers the moving stimulus (Fantz & Nevis, 1967), and, when presented with two stimuli that are identical in all respects except movement, infants as young as 2 weeks old will look at the moving stimulus (Nelson & Horowitz, 1987).

It isn't surprising that infants begin perceiving movement at an early age. After all, movement is everywhere in an infant's environment, and it provides the infant with rich information about various

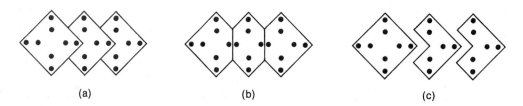

(a)   (b)   (c)

Figure 15.25
Stimuli for Granrud and Yonas's (1984) interposition experiment. See text for details.

characteristics of its world. But although infants perceive movement at an early age, this doesn't mean that they perceive movement in the same way as adults. For example, although infants can follow moving objects with their eyes, their eyes initially move in a series of short, jerky movements, called saccades. It isn't until about 10 to 12 weeks that infants can make smooth eye movements to follow a moving stimulus (Aslin, 1981a).

One of the characteristics of movement that we discussed in Chapter 8 and earlier in this chapter is that it can create perceptual organization. Two objects that are moving in the same direction at the same speed appear to belong together. One of the most interesting examples of movement creating perceptual organization is biological movement. We saw in Chapter 8 that we can create a stimulus called a point-light walker by placing a number of lights on a person's body (see Figure 8.26).

A subject who views the point-light walker in the dark will see the lights as individual unrelated dots when the person is stationary. However, as soon as the point-light walker begins moving, the pattern of lights is suddenly perceived as a moving person. Perceiving the moving lights as a person involves perceptually organizing the individual lights into a single unit, something that infants begin doing at around 4 months of age.

Perceiving Biological Motion Robert Fox and Cynthia McDaniel (1982) used the preferential looking technique to determine whether infants are capable of recognizing biological motion. A videotape of the lights attached to a running person was shown on one screen, and another videotape of randomly moving lights was shown on the other screen. When placed in front of the two screens, 2-month-old infants showed no preference, looking at both screens equally. But 4- and 6-month-old infants looked at the biological motion tape about 70 percent of the time. Thus, by age 4 months, infants can tell the difference between these two types of motion and prefer the biological motion.

The fact that infants are sensitive to biological motion by 4 months of age fits our earlier results, which showed that infants were capable of perceptu-

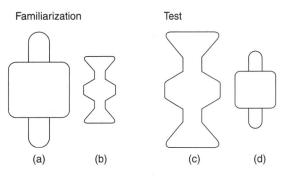

Figure 15.26
Stimuli for Granrud, Haake, and Yonas's (1985) familiar-size experiment. See text for details.

ally organizing visual stimuli by about 4 months of age. But does the fact that infants can discriminate between biological motion and other types of motion mean that infants perceive biological motion in the same way as adults? The results of an experiment by Bertenthal and coworkers (1985) suggest that the answer to this question may be *no*. In this experiment, Bertenthal and coworkers tested infants to determine whether they were sensitive to a property of point-light walkers that is obvious to adults—as the walker moves, certain lights are occluded from view by movement of the walker's limbs relative to other parts of the body. For example, notice in Figure 8.26 that the light on the walker's left knee is blocked from view by her right leg. As she walks, this light will become visible, then it will become occluded again, and so on.

The occlusion of some of the lights during the walker's movement is one of the properties that helps make moving point-light walker stimuli appear three-dimensional to adults. They easily recognize displays with occlusion as a walking person, but they rarely perceive a walking person when they are shown displays in which occlusion has been eliminated so that all of the lights are always visible. When Bertenthal and coworkers presented occluded and nonoccluded displays to infants, they found that 8-month-old infants were able to discriminate the occluded from the nonoccluded displays, but 5-month-old infants were not.

The results of this experiment suggest that although 5-month-olds can discriminate between the

Perceptual Development

biological motion of point-light walkers and other types of point-light movement, they may not perceive the biological motion as a three-dimensional walking person, as adults do. Before they can achieve this perception, they need to become sensitive to occlusion, which occurs at about 8 months of age. Of course, we don't really know what 8-month-old infants perceive. All we can safely say is that their perception of point-light walkers is probably more adultlike than the 5-month-olds' perception.

See Summary Table 15.1 for an overview of the material we have covered so far.

INFANT PERCEPTUAL CAPACITIES: HEARING AND THE CHEMICAL SENSES

In addition to the large body of research that has uncovered the newborn's visual abilities and their development, a great deal of research has been done on development of the hearing, the chemical senses and touch, as well (Werner & Bernstein, 2001). We will now describe the development of hearing and the chemical senses.

SUMMARY TABLE 15.1

Measuring Infant Perception

The first step in measuring infant perception is to ask the infant a question he or she can answer, such as "Can you tell the difference between these two stimuli?" This can be accomplished by measuring which stimulus an infant looks at or how long the infant looks at a particular stimulus. The two main techniques that accomplish this are the preferential looking technique and habituation.

Acuity and Contrast

Visual acuity, measured both by preferential looking and the visual evoked potential, is poor at birth but increases rapidly to just below the adult level by 6 months of age. One reason for the newborn's low acuity is the poor development of both the cortex and foveal receptors at birth. Contrast sensitivity is also poor at birth, but infants can see gross features and can recognize facial expressions by 3 or 4 months.

Perceiving Objects

Newborns can tell the difference between their mother's face and the face of a stranger, probably by using information provided by the mother's hairline. Five-month-old infants can distinguish figure from ground, 3-month-olds can perceptually group elements based on lightness, and 2-month-olds can tell that one stimulus continues behind an occluding stimulus based on movement of the stimulus. Movement is also used by 10-month-olds to tell that two adjacent objects are separate.

Perceiving Color

Habituation has shown that 4-month-olds categorize colors in the same way as adult trichromats. Preferential looking and a procedure that takes into account the fact that different wavelengths can differ in brightness, as well as in color, has shown that infants around 2 months of age have operational medium- and long-wavelength cone receptors. All three types of cones appear to be present by 2 or 3 months of age.

Perceiving Depth

Infants can binocularly fixate by 3 months of age, as measured by the way their eyes move in response to near and far targets. An experiment using random-dot stereograms showed that the ability to use disparity information emerges sometime between $3^1/2$ and 6 months of age. Once the ability to detect disparity appears, infants show a rapid rise in stereoacuity to fairly good levels by 4 or 5 months of age. Pictorial depth cues, such as overlap, familiar size, and texture gradients, become important later, sometime between 5 to 7 months.

Perceiving Movement

Infants can perceive movement shortly after birth. Preferential looking has shown that 5-month-olds can tell the difference between the biological motion of point-light walkers and other types of point-light movement, but that they may not yet perceive biological motion in the same way as adults do, because they don't become sensitive to occlusion until about 8 months of age.

Hearing

What do newborn infants hear, and how does their hearing change over time? Although some early psychologists felt that newborns were functionally deaf, recent research has shown that newborns do have some auditory capacities and that this capacity improves as the child gets older (Werner & Bargones, 1992).

Recognizing the Mother's Voice   One approach to determining the newborn's ability to hear is to show that they can identify sounds they have heard before. Anthony DeCasper and William Fifer (1980) demonstrated this capacity in newborns by showing that 2-day-old infants will modify their sucking on a nipple in order to hear the sound of their mother's voice. They first observed that infants usually suck on a nipple in bursts separated by pauses. They fitted infants with earphones and let the length of the pause in the infant's sucking determine whether the infant heard a recording of its mother's voice or a recording of a stranger's voice (Figure 15.27). For half of the infants, long pauses activated the tape of the mother's voice, and short pauses activated the tape of the stranger's voice. For the other half, these conditions were reversed.

DeCasper and Fifer found that the babies regulated the pauses in their sucking so that they heard their mother's voice more than the stranger's voice. This is a remarkable accomplishment for a 2-day-old, especially since most of them had been with their mothers for only a few hours between the time they were born and the time they were tested.

Why did the newborns prefer their mother's voice? DeCasper and Fifer suggested that newborns recognize their mother's voice because they heard the mother talking while they were developing in the mother's womb. This suggestion is supported by the results of another experiment, in which DeCasper and M. J. Spence (1986) had one group of pregnant women read from Dr. Seuss's book *The Cat in the Hat* and another group read the same story with the words *cat* and *hat* replaced with *dog* and *fog*. When the children were born, they regulated their sucking pattern to hear the version of the story their mother

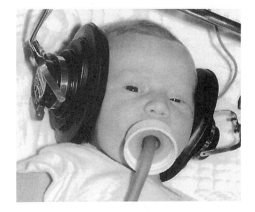

Figure 15.27
This baby, a subject in DeCasper and Fifer's (1980) study, could control whether she heard a recording of her mother's voice or a stranger's voice by the way she sucked on the nipple. (© Anthony DeCasper.)

had read when they were in the womb. In another experiment, 2-day-old infants regulated their sucking to hear a recording of their native language rather than of a foreign language (Moon, Cooper, & Fifer, 1993). Apparently, even when in the womb, the fetus becomes familiar with the intonation and rhythm of the mother's voice and also with the sounds of specific words. (See also DeCasper et al., 1994.)

Thresholds for Hearing a Tone   A simple way to determine whether infants can hear is to determine if they will orient toward the source of a sound. Darwin Muir and Jeffry Field (1979) presented newborn infants with a loud (80-dB) rattle sound 20 cm from either their right or their left ear and found that the infants usually turned toward the sound (Figure 15.28). Newborns can therefore hear and are capable of at least crude sound localization.

More precise measurements of infants' capacities have been achieved with older infants, who have a wider repertoire of responses to sound. Lynne Werner Olsho and coworkers (1988) used the following procedure to determine infants' audibility curves: An infant is fitted with earphones and sits on the parent's lap. An observer, sitting out of view of the infant, watches the infant through a window. A light blinks

Perceptual Development

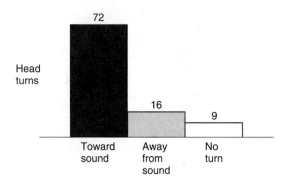

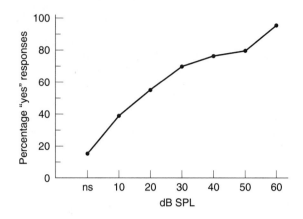

Figure 15.28

Number of head turns made by newborns in response to an 80-dB SPL sound. Most of the turns were toward the sound, a response indicating that the infants could localize the sound. (Based on data from Muir & Field, 1979.)

Figure 15.29

The percentage of trials on which a 3-month-old infant responded to a 2000-Hz tone presented at different intensities. NS indicates no sound. The threshold for hearing the tone is determined from this curve. (From Olsho et al., 1988.)

on, indicating that a trial has begun, and the infant is either presented with a tone or is not. The observer's task is to decide whether or not the infant heard the tone (Olsho et al., 1987).

How can observers tell whether the infant has heard a tone? They decide by looking for responses such as eye movements, changes in facial expression, a wide-eyed look, a turn of the head, or changes in activity level. Although this determination is not an easy task for observers, we can see from the data in Figure 15.29 that it works (Olsho et al., 1988). Observers only occasionally indicated that the

3-month-old infants heard a 2,000-Hz tone that was presented at low intensities or not at all. But as the tone's intensity was increased, the observers were more likely to say that the infant had heard the tone. The infant's threshold at 2,000 Hz was determined from this curve, and the results from a number of frequencies were combined to create audibility curves, such as those in Figure 15.30. This figure, which shows curves for 3- and 6-month-olds and adults, indi-

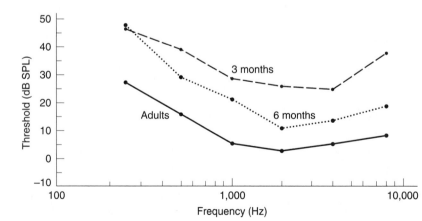

Figure 15.30

Audibility curves for 3- and 6-month-old infants. The curve for 12-month-olds is similar to the curve for 6-month-olds. The adult curve is shown for comparison. (Adapted from Olsho, 1988.)

cates that infant and adult audibility functions look similar and that, by 6 months of age, the infant's threshold is within about 10 to 15 dB of the adult threshold.

Localizing Sounds   Using a procedure similar to the one used to measure thresholds described above, Barbara Morrongiello (1988; Morrongiello, Fenwick, & Chance, 1990) measured infants' ability to locate sounds presented to their left or right. She measured the **minimum audible angle**—the angle between two sounds that the infant could perceive—and found that at 8 weeks of age the minimum audible angle is 27 degrees, but by the time the child is a year and a half old, it has decreased to about 5 degrees (Figure 15.31). The minimum audible angle for adults is about 1 degree (see also Ashmead et al., 1991).

Speech Perception

Research on speech perception in adults has demonstrated a phenomenon called *categorical perception.* We can illustrate categorical perception by reviewing an experiment we described in Chapter 12. A subject

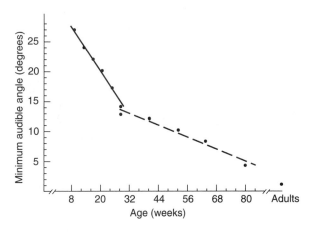

Figure 15.31

The minimum audible angle as a function of age. The infants' ability to localize sounds improves to almost adult levels over the first year and a half. (From Morrongiello, Fenwick, & Chance, 1990.)

is presented with a sound stimulus that sounds like "ba." A characteristic of this stimulus, called *voice onset time* (VOT), which is the time delay between the beginning of a sound and when the vocal cords start vibrating, is then systematically changed, using a computer, and the subject reports what he or she hears. (See page 417 for a more detailed description of voice onset time and categorical perception experiments.)

The main result of an experiment such as this one is that even when VOT is changed over a wide range, subjects tend to hear only two categories of sound. At short voice onset times they hear the sound "ba," and at long voice onset times they hear the sound "pa." There is a place between these two extremes where changing the VOT just a little causes the person's perception to change from "ba" to "pa." This place is called the *phonetic boundary*.

The fact that subjects perceive only "ba" and "pa" over a wide range of VOTs is categorical perception—we perceive speech sounds as being in a limited number of categories. Categorical perception was first reported for adults in 1967 (Liberman et al., 1967). In 1971, Peter Eimas and coworkers began the modern era of research on infant speech perception by showing that young infants perceive speech in categories, just as adults do.

Perceiving Speech Sounds in Categories   Eimas used a habituation procedure to show that infants as young as 1 month old perform similarly to adults in categorical perception experiments. The basis of these experiments was the observation that an infant will suck on a nipple in order to hear a series of brief speech sounds, but, when the same speech sounds are repeated, the infant's sucking eventually habituates to a low level. By presenting a new stimulus after the rate of sucking has decreased, Eimas determined whether the infant perceived the new stimulus as sounding the same as or different from the old one.

The results of Eimas and coworkers' experiment are shown in Figure 15.32. The number of sucking responses when no sound was presented is indicated by the point at B. When a sound with voice onset time (VOT) = 20 ms (sounds like "ba" to an adult) is presented when the infant sucks, the sucking increases to a high level and then begins to decrease. When the

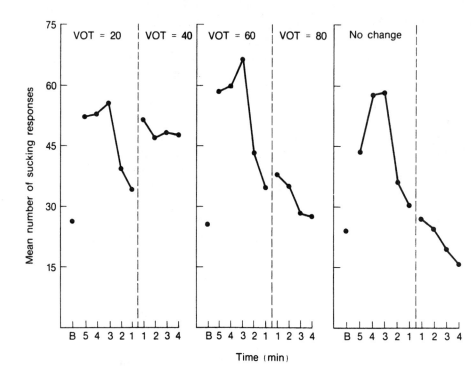

Figure 15.32
Results of a categorical perception experiment on infants, using the habituation procedure. In the left panel, VOT is changed from 20 to 40 ms (across the phonetic boundary). In the center panel, VOT is changed from 60 to 80 ms (not across the phonetic boundary). In the right panel, the VOT was not changed. See text for details. (Eimas et al., 1971.)

VOT is changed to 40 ms (sounds like "pa" to an adult), sucking increases, as indicated by the points to the right of the dashed line. This result means that the infant perceives a difference between sounds with VOTs of 20 and 40 ms. The center graph, however, shows that changing the VOT from 60 to 80 ms (both sound like "pa" to an adult) has only a small effect on sucking, indicating that the infants perceive little, if any, difference between the two sounds. Finally, the results for a control group (the right graph) show that, when the sound is not changed, the number of sucking responses decreases throughout the experiment.

These results show that, when the VOT is shifted across the phonetic boundary (left graph), the infants perceive a change in the sound, and when the VOT is shifted on the same side of the phonetic boundary (center graph), the infants perceive little or no change in the sound. That infants as young as 1 month old are capable of categorical perception is particularly impressive, especially since these infants have had virtually no experience in producing speech sounds and only limited experience in hearing them.

Perceiving Vowels Made by Different Speakers as Being in the Same Class Another parallel between infant and adult speech perception is Patricia Kuhl's (1983, 1989) finding that infants have an ability called **equivalence classification**—the ability to classify vowel sounds as belonging to a class, even when the speakers are different. Adults have this ability, so they can classify an /a/ sound as the vowel a whether it is spoken by a male or a female. By using a conditioning procedure (Figure 15.33), Patricia Kuhl (1983, 1989) showed that 6-month-old infants are capable of equivalence classification. The infant sat on a parent's lap and heard a speech sound such as /a/ repeated over and over. At some point, the sound changed from /a/ to /i/, and when this change happened, a bear playing a drum was activated, and the child looked toward the bear.[2] After this procedure was repeated a number of

[2] The symbols /a/ and /i/ stand for the sounds "ah" (hot) and "ee" (heed), respectively.

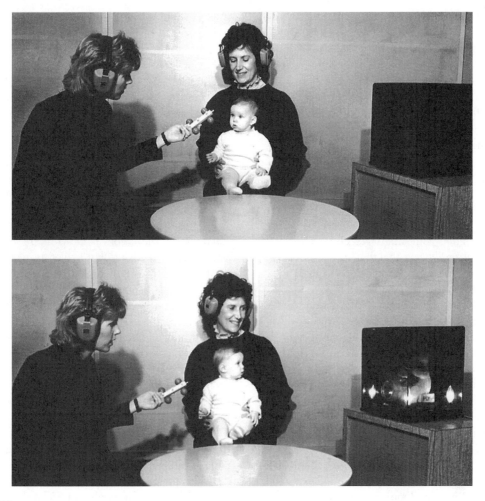

Figure 15.33
In the conditioning procedure used by Kuhl (1983, 1989), infants are trained to turn their heads toward the toy bear on their left when they hear a change from one speech category to another.

times, the child learned to look toward the bear anytime the sound changed from /a/ to /i/. The experimenter was therefore able to tell when the infant perceived a change by noting when the infant looked toward the bear.

Kuhl then asked whether the infant perceived all /a/ sounds as belonging to the same category, even when other characteristics of the sound were changed. She answered this question by presenting a male voice saying /a/ and then changing it to a female voice saying /a/. Even though the voice changed, no head turn occurred. However, when the stimulus was changed from a male voice saying /a/, to either a male's voice, a female's voice, or a child's voice saying /i/, head turning did occur, a result indicating that the child reacted in the same way to the /i/ stimulus no matter which voice was saying it.

From these results, Kuhl concluded that infants do achieve classification: They classify all /a/ sounds as the same and all /i/ sounds as the same, no matter what the quality of the voice saying them. (See also Marean, Werner, & Kuhl, 1992, for similar results for 2-month-olds.) Equivalence classification is important to infants because, when they eventually begin imitating adult speech, their imitations will be much higher pitched than the speech sounds made by most of the adults in their environment. They need to know that their production is equivalent to the adults' even though the pitch is different.

How Experience Affects Speech Perception We have seen that mechanisms for speech perception are in place at a very early age. However, this early speech perception ability can be affected by the child's experience with language. One example of the effects of experience is that there are some speech stimuli that infants can distinguish from each other but that adults cannot distinguish. Thus, a Japanese infant might respond differently to /r/ and /l/, two sounds that Japanese adults have difficulty distinguishing, since they are in the same category in the Japanese language. However, by the time the children are a year old, they are no longer able to make distinctions between all pairs of sounds. Their experience in listening to other people speak has changed their speech perception so that they are sensitive only to distinctions between sounds that are important in their native language (Kuhl et al., 1992; Werker, 1991; Werker & Tees, 1984). Apparently, infants possess mechanisms for perceiving all speech sounds fairly early in their development, and during the first year of life these mechanisms become tuned to the language that the child experiences. (This difference between American and Japanese speech perception is also discussed on page 429 of Chapter 12.)

Olfaction and Taste

Discriminating Between Different Smells Do newborn infants perceive odors and tastes? Early researchers, noting that a number of olfactory stimuli elicited responses such as body movements and facial expressions from newborns, concluded that newborns can smell (Kroner, 1881; Peterson & Rainey, 1911). However, some of the stimuli used by these early researchers may have irritated the membranes of the

infant's nose, so the infants may have been responding to irritation rather than to smell (Beauchamp, Cowart, & Schmidt, 1991; Doty, 1991). Modern studies using nonirritating stimuli have, however, provided evidence that newborns can smell and can discriminate between different olfactory stimuli. J. E. Steiner (1974, 1979) used nonirritating stimuli to show that infants respond to banana extract or vanilla extract with sucking and facial expressions that are similar to smiles, and that they respond to concentrated shrimp odor and an odor resembling rotten eggs with rejection or disgust responses (Figure 15.34).

Recognizing the Odor of the Mother's Breast It is perhaps not surprising that newborns would respond to strong odors such as rotten eggs. But recent research has also shown that infants can differentiate between subtle qualities in olfactory stimuli. These studies have shown that nursing infants can differentiate the odor of their mother's breast from the odor from the breast of another mother who is also nursing her infant. A. Macfarlane (1975) demonstrated this preference for the mother's breast odor by presenting breast pads from the mother and the other lactating female to infants in their cribs and by noting that the infants spent significantly more time turning toward their mother's pads than toward the other woman's pad (Figure 15.35).

This preference for the mother's odor is probably learned. Jennifer Cernoch and Richard Porter (1985) demonstrated that 2-week-old breast-fed infants turn toward a pad containing their mother's axillary (armpit) odors in preference to the axillary odors of either unfamiliar lactating or nonlactating women or their father. However, bottle-fed infants did not prefer their mother's odor. Cernoch and Porter concluded that the basis for the breast-fed infants' recognition was that they had learned to recognize their mother's unique olfactory signature while feeding (see also Porter et al., 1992).

Further evidence that learning is important comes from an experiment by Rene Balogh and Richard Porter (1986), in which they exposed 1-day-old infants to either an artificial cherry odor or an artificial ginger odor in their bassinets for two days. After

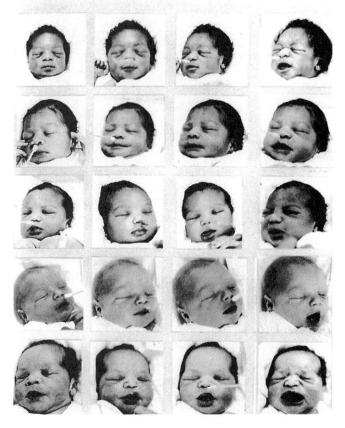

Figure 15.34

The facial expressions of 3- to 8-hour-old infants in response to some food-related odors. In each of the horizontal rows, the reactions of the same infant can be seen to the following stimulation: C = control, odorless cotton swab; BA/VA = artificial solution of banana or vanilla; FI = artificial fish or shrimp odor; R.E. = artificial rotten egg odor. The infants were tested prior to the first breast- or bottle-feeding. (Photographs courtesy of J. E. Steiner, The Hebrew University, Jerusalem.)

Figure 15.35

Device used to test infants' response to odorized pads. (From Porter & Schaal, 1995.)

Perceptual Development

this exposure, the infants were tested by the presentation of two pads, one with cherry odor and the other with ginger odor, on either side of the head for two minutes. The results indicated that female infants preferentially turned toward the odor to which they had previously been exposed. This result supports the idea that infants can perceive odors and that they can develop preferences for odors through learning.

Discriminating Between Different Tastes   Research investigating infants' reactions to taste has included numerous studies showing that newborns can discriminate sweet, sour, and bitter stimuli (Beauchamp et al., 1991). For example, newborns react with different facial expressions to sweet, sour, and bitter stimuli but show little or no response to salty stimuli (Figure 15.36) (Ganchrow, 1995; Ganchrow, Steiner, & Daher, 1983; Rosenstein & Oster, 1988).

Although responses to taste and olfaction do show some changes as the infant grows into childhood (for example, young infants are indifferent to the taste of salt but develop a response to salty stimuli as they get older; Beauchamp, Bertino, & Engelman, 1991; Beauchamp, Cowart, & Moran, 1986), we could argue that taste and olfaction are the most highly developed of all of the senses at birth.

The research we have surveyed in this chapter clearly indicates that although newborn perception is

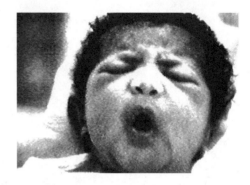

Figure 15.36
The facial expression of an infant who is less than 10 hours old to a sour taste. Specific facial expressions are also associated with bitter and sweet tastes. (From Rosenstein & Oster, 1988.)

not as developed as adult perception, the newborn's perceptual abilities far surpass anything imagined by the early psychologists. Newborns can recognize some of their mother's facial features and the sound of her voice, can differentiate tastes and smells, and are capable of intermodal perception (see Across the Senses on page 540). These capacities, as well as others that develop over the first year of life, are summarized in Table 15.1.

Table 15.1

Milestones in perceptual development. The ages indicated in this table are the youngest ages at which a particular capacity has been observed. Note that (1) these ages are subject to change, based on future research, usually in the direction of younger ages for a particular capacity, and (2) just because a capacity is listed doesn't mean it is fully developed. For example, although 3-month-old infants can perceive facial expression, their perception of facial expressions is still rudimentary compared to adults.

Age	Capacity
Newborn	Recognize mother's face
	Discriminate sound of mother's voice
	Differentiate smell and test stimuli
	Intermodal matching
2 weeks	Looks at moving stimuli
1 month	Visual acuity = 20/600. Vision slightly worse than adult night vision. Sees large objects with high contrast.
	Categorical perception of speech stimuli
2 months	Use motion information to see rod continuing behind occluder
	Short-wavelength cone present
	Minimum audible angle = 27° (Adult = 1°) (Decreases to 5 degrees by 18 months)
3 months	Grouping by lightness similarity
	Perception of facial expressions
	All three types of cones present
	Binocular fixation
	Follow moving stimuli with smooth eye movement
4 months	Categorize colors like adults
	Discriminate between different categories of objects
	Perceive biological movement
	Spontaneous reaching for nearer object
	Binocular disparity (3.5–5 months)
5 months	Pictoral depth cues (5–7 months)
6 months	Visual acuity is close to adult (doesn't reach adult until after 1 year)
	Hearing thresholds are within 10–15 dB of adult
	Equivalence classification for speech
8 months	Sensitive to occlusion in biological motion
1 year	Speech perception narrows so infant is only sensitive to differences in sounds used in own language

Perceptual Development

Myopia, or nearsightedness, affects about 25 percent of the adults in the United States (Sperduto et al., 1983), and it has been estimated that Americans with myopia spend 4.6 billion dollars annually for eye examinations, glasses, and contact lenses (Mutti et al., 1996). In this section, as we discuss research on the causes of myopia, we will see that both genetics and the environment appear to be involved.

Focusing Light on the Retina

To understand myopia, we have to understand how light is focused onto the retina by the lens and cornea. For normal vision the power of the eye's focusing system matches the length of the eyeball so that light is focused on the retina (Figure 15.37a). This normal focusing results in **emmetropic vision** or **emmetropia**. However, if the power of the focusing system does not match the length of the eyeball, then two conditions can result:

1. The cornea and lens bend the light too much, or the eyeball is too long, so the retinal image is blurred because the focus point for light is in front of the retina (Figure 15.37b). This results in **myopic vision** or **myopia.**

2. The eyeball is too short, so the retinal image is blurred because the focus point for light is behind the retina (Figure 15.37c). This results in **hyperopic vision** or **hyperopia.**

Young infants are often either myopic or hyperopic, with only a small percent having emmetropic vision (Gwiazda & Birch, 2001). However, if development is normal, a process of **emmetropization** occurs, with the visual system adjusting its power so light is focused sharply on the retina. But, in people who develop myopia, emmetropization does not fully occur. This failure of emmetropization has been linked to both genetics and the environment.

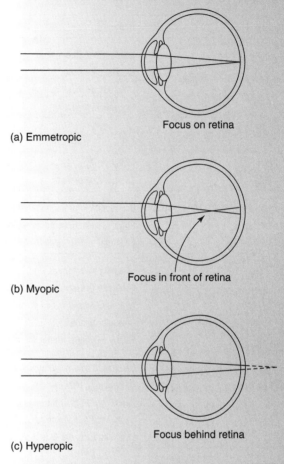

(a) Emmetropic — Focus on retina

(b) Myopic — Focus in front of retina

(c) Hyperopic — Focus behind retina

Figure 15.37
(a) normal eye ; (b) myopic eye; (c) hyperopic eye. See text for details.

Genetic Links to Myopia

Myopia runs in families. The degree of myopia is more closely related in identical twins than in nonidentical (fraternal) twins, and there is a clear

(*continued*)

relationship between parents' myopia and children's myopia. Thirty to forty percent of children with two myopic parents have myopia, 20 to 25 percent with one myopic parent have myopia, and only 10 percent with no myopic parents have myopia (Gwiazda et al., 1993).

A particularly interesting finding about children who are at risk for myopia because they have two myopic parents is that even before they become myopic, their eyes are longer than the eyes of children with no myopic parents (Zadnick et al., 1994). This observation that children at risk for myopia have longer eyeballs has led to the suggestion that "the 'seeds' of myopia may be sown early in life" (Mutti et al., 1996).

Environmental Links to Myopia

There is also evidence that the environment can affect the likelihood of myopia. Myopia is more likely in groups that experience more education or who do more near work. For example, myopia became much more common in Eskimo children after the introduction of Western education (Mutti et al., 1996); the prevalence of myopia is as high as 70 percent in Asian children, who are subjected to a stringent educational system and high near-work demands (Au Eong, Tay, & Lum, 1993; Lin, Chen, & Hung, 1986), and myopia is more prevalent in male orthodox Jewish teenagers, who study up to 16 hours a day, compared to orthodox Jewish females, who study 8 or 9 hours a day (Zylbermann, Landau, & Berson, 1993).

The role of the environment has also been demonstrated in animal research by manipulating the animal's visual environment. Torsten Wiesel and Elio Raviola (1977) found that depriving monkeys of form vision when they are young causes them to develop myopia because their eyes become too long. Also, when just-hatched chicks are fitted with lenses that push the focus point back (so they are more hyperopic, as in Figure 15.37c),

the chick's eyes grow longer to compensate (Irving, Sivak, & Callender, 1992). Similarly, if the chicks are fitted with lenses that move the focus point forward, their eyes grow shorter to compensate. These links between near work and myopia in children and environmental stimulation and eye length in animals have led to the proposal of the visual feedback model of emmetropization.

The Visual Feedback Model

According to the **visual feedback model** of emmetropization, the growth of the eyeball that usually occurs during emmetropization is controlled by errors in the focusing of light on the retina. Thus, if there is an error in focusing, the eye grows to eliminate that error. If this process proceeds normally, the eyeball grows just the right amount to eliminate the out-of-focus condition that exists at birth. If, however, information about focus is not available, as when an animal is deprived of form vision, no image is present to indicate when the appropriate length has been reached, and elongation of the eyeball occurs. Or, if incorrect information about the eye's natural focusing power is created by fitting an animal with lenses, the length of the eyeball becomes too long or too short, as it strives to bring the lens-altered image into focus.

Although there is good evidence that visual feedback helps create emmetropic vision in humans, we still don't know what goes wrong in people who develop myopia. We have seen that there is some evidence that myopia is inherited and also that, in people who are susceptible to it, more visual experience is associated with greater myopia. Thus, we can describe myopia as being caused by a biological mechanism (biologically programmed visual feedback) that is affected by the environmental input it receives. Researchers are now working to understand how the visual feedback mechanism of people with myopic vision differs from the visual feedback mechanism of people with normal vision.

INTERMODAL PERCEPTION
IN INFANTS

An adult who first feels a baseball and then sees the baseball plus a number of other objects can easily choose the baseball as the shape he or she was feeling. This ability to match shapes presented in two different modalities is called **intermodal matching**. One idea about how intermodal matching ability develops is that it is based on people's experience in simultaneously seeing and feeling a variety of shapes. Another idea is that it is an inborn ability. Andrew Meltzoff and Richard Borton (1979) investigated the question of whether intermodal abilities are learned or inborn by first having 1-month-old infants suck on one of the two pacifiers shown in Figure 15.38 and then presenting the two shapes visually.

Of the 32 infants tested, 24 looked longer at the shape they had experienced when they had sucked on the pacifier. Meltzoff and Burton concluded that infants do not need to learn about correspondences between touch and vision but that they are able to sense and store abstract information (for example, "bumpy surface" or "smooth surface") and generalize this information across senses.

Recently, another experiment, again using pacifiers as the tactual stimulus but a different method of measurement, showed that 1-day-old newborns are capable of matching a shape they feel to a shape they can see. Kelly Kaye and T. G. R. Bower (1994) placed one of two pacifiers in the infant's mouth. When the infant began sucking, a large image of the end of one of the pacifiers appeared on a computer monitor located directly in front of the newborn (Figure 15.39). As long as the infant continued sucking, the image remained on the screen. But pausing for longer than 1 second caused the image of the other, differently shaped, pacifier to appear on the screen. Thus, the infant could determine which image appears on the screen by the way he or she sucked on the pacifier.

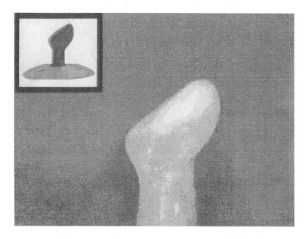

Figure 15.39
Large image: Picture of the end of the pacifier as seen by infants who were looking at a TV monitor. Insert: Actual pacifier on which the infant was sucking. See text for details. (From Kay & Bower, 1994.)

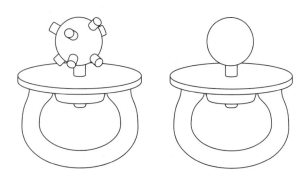

Figure 15.38
Pacifiers used by Meltzoff and Borton (1979).

The results of this experiment showed that infants controlled their sucking so that in their initial exposures to the images of the pacifiers, 11 of the 12 infants caused the image of the pacifier on which they were sucking to appear on the screen longer than the image of the other pacifier. This means that newborns are capable of sensing the shape of a pacifier in their mouths and can generalize this perception from the tactual to the visual mode.

How does the newborn achieve this feat? Clearly, it can't be due to learning, because the infant is only 1 day old. Because the effect happened as soon as the infant began sucking on the pacifier, Kaye and Bower (1994) suggest that it doesn't seem likely that the infants create a tactual image of the pacifier that they compare to the visual image on the screen. Instead, they propose that the information in both tactile and visual form creates an **amodal representation**—a description that holds across more than one modality. For example, an amodal description of the pacifier in Figure 15.39 would be: "A smooth elongated object, with a rounded side and a flat side." Since this description is valid for both the visual and tactual presentations, it is amodal.

Whether or not this is the actual mechanism involved, it is clear that infants are capable of matching felt shapes and visual images from a very young age. Other experiments have demonstrated similar abilities in 11-month-old infants who are old enough to explore three-dimensional objects with their hands (Bushnell & Weinberger, 1987).

Hearing

Two-day old infants will modify their sucking to hear the sound of their mother's voice. This ability can be traced to the fact that infants hear their mother's voices while they are in the womb. Thresholds for hearing can be measured by noting whether an infant reacts to a tone. By using this procedure it has been determined that infant audibility curves become close to adult levels by around 6 months. The ability to localize sounds improves over the first years of life.

Speech Perception

Using the habituation procedure to determine the infant's ability to tell the difference between two sounds with different voice onset times has shown that infants as young as 1 month old are capable of categorical perception. By training infants to look at a toy bear in response to changes in vowel sounds, it has been determined that 6-month-olds can classify vowel sounds as belonging to a particular class, such as /a/ or /i/. The role of experience in the development of speech perception is illustrated by the way infants can perceive all speech sounds at an early age, but during the first year they become able to perceive only the sounds of the language they experience while growing up.

Olfaction and Taste

By measuring infants' reactions to odors, it has been determined that newborns can tell the difference between some odors and that infants probably learn to prefer their mother's odor by a few weeks of age. Newborns can also discriminate between different taste stimuli.

Development of Myopia

The development of myopia appears to be influenced by both genetic and environmental factors. The visual feedback model states that the growth of the eyeball during development is controlled by errors in the focusing of light on the retina. This mechanism appears to be involved in developing emmetropic vision and may also be involved in the development of myopia.

Intermodal Perception in Infants

Experiments in which infants have to use information from one sense to respond to information presented in another sense indicate that very young infants can match a shape they can feel to a shape they can see. It has been suggested that tactile and visual forms create representations for infants that hold across modalities.

STUDY QUESTIONS

Measuring Infant Perception

1. What are two questions we can ask to determine visual acuity and how would we answer each of them? Which one works for infants? (510)

Preferential Looking

2. Describe the preferential looking technique. Why does the preferential looking technique work? How would we use it to measure acuity? (511)

Habituation

3. Describe the habituation technique. When would it be used instead of preferential looking? What fact about infant looking behavior is it based on? (511)

Infant Perceptual Capacities: Vision

Acuity and Contrast

4. What is a newborn's visual acuity and how does it increase over the first months of life? How is the visual evoked potential used to measure visual acuity? (513)

5. What are the physiological reasons for the newborn's poor visual acuity? Consider the state of both the cortex and the foveal cones in your answer. (515)

6. How does the contrast sensitivity function of infants compare to the contrast sensitivity function of adults? What does this mean about how the infant perceives the visual world? (516)

Perceiving Objects

7. What kinds of things can young infants detect at close distances? (517)

8. Describe the research that has shown that newborns can recognize their mother's face. What is the experiment that indicates what information the newborn may be using to make this judgment? (517)

9. Describe Craton's experiment in which it was determined that infants can distinguish figure from ground. Be sure you understand how habituation was used to determine this. (518)

10. Describe Quinn's experiment that showed that infants can perceptually group elements by lightness similarity. (518)

11. At what age can an infant infer the existence of an object extending behind an occluder? Describe the series of three experiments that led to this conclusion. What information do infants use to make this inference? (519)

12. How did Xu and Carey use habituation to show that infants use movement to help them distinguish between two objects that are adjacent to one another? (520)

Perceiving Color

13. What is a special challenge facing anyone who wants to test for the presence of color vision? (521)

14. Describe Bornstein's experiment on color categorization. Understand how habituation was used and the principle of color categories that Bornstein used in the design of his experiment. (521)

15. What is the principle that allows us to use a psychophysical procedure to determine whether an infant has both its medium- and long-wavelength cones? (522)

16. Describe Hamer's experiment and its conclusions. How did he deal with the "special challenge" mentioned in 13, above? (522)

17. At what age do infants probably have some form of trichromatic vision? (523)

Perceiving Depth

18. What is one requirement that must be met before binocular disparity can be effective? (523)

19. How did Aslin determine when infants can binocularly fixate? (524)

20. How were random-dot stereograms used to determine when infants can use binocular disparity to perceive depth? At what age are infants able to do this? (524)

21. How were stereograms used to determine infant stereoacuity? At what age is stereoacuity first measurable? How rapidly does stereoacuity develop once it appears? (524)

22. Describe the procedures that were used to determine when infants can use the depth cues of overlap and familiar size. At what age are infants first able to use this information? (526)

23. How come infants need to be older to use pictorial depth cues than to use binocular disparity? (526)

Perceiving Movement

24. At what age can infants first perceive movement? How do infant eye movements compare to adults'? When are they similar to adult eye movements? (526)

25. What technique was used to determine whether infants can see biological movement? At what age can infants discriminate between the biological movement of point-light walkers and random movement? (527)

26. Does the fact that infants can discriminate between the biological movement and random movement mean that they see biological movement in the same way as adults? Explain your answer and the experiment that was done to investigate this question. (527)

Infant Perceptual Capacities: Hearing and the Chemical Senses

Hearing

27. How did DeCasper and Fifer show that newborns can recognize their mother's voice? (529)

28. What does newborn head turning behavior tell us about their ability to hear a tone? (529)

29. How is the infant's threshold for hearing a tone determined? What do the audibility curves determined using this procedure tell us about how infant hearing compares to adult hearing? (529)

30. What is the minimum audible angle? Has it decreased to adult levels by a year and a half of age? (531)

Speech Perception

31. What is categorical perception in speech? How did Eimas show that infants are capable of categorical perception? (531)

32. How did Kuhl show that infants can tell that a vowel, like /a/, is the same sound even when it is spoken by different speakers? What is equivalence classification? (532)

33. How does an infant's experience with speech affect its ability to perceive speech sounds? Why can we say that infants lose the ability to differentiate sounds as they gain the ability to perceive speech? (534)

Olfaction and Taste

34. What is the evidence that newborns can discriminate between different smells? (534)

35. What is the evidence that newborns can recognize the odor of the mother's breast? What is the evidence that learning is involved in the infant's ability to recognize odors? (534)

36. What is the evidence that newborns can discriminate between different taste stimuli? (536)

The Plasticity of Perception: Development of Myopia

37. Describe the process of emmetropization. (538)

38. What are some examples of genetic links to myopia? (539)

39. What are some examples of environmental links to myopia? (539)

40. What evidence led to the proposal of the visual feedback model of emmetropization? (539)

Across the Senses: Intermodal Perception in Infants

41. What is intermodal matching? (540)

42. Describe the Melzoff and Burton experiment on intermodal perception involving sucking on a pacifier and seeing the pacifier. (540)

43. Describe Kaye and Bower's experiment that showed that one-day-old newborns are capable of matching a shape they feel to a shape they can see. (540)

44. How does the newborn accomplish the matching of shape and vision, according to Kaye and Bower? What is an amodal representation? (541)

16

CLINICAL ASPECTS OF VISION AND HEARING

SOME QUESTIONS WE WILL CONSIDER

- What are the major causes of impaired vision and hearing? (546, 564)

- Can a person be legally blind but have 20/20 vision? (551)

- How can diseases of the ear and eye be treated? (552, 567)

Although it is obvious that the man in Figure 16.1 is examining the woman's eye, most people do not understand exactly what he is seeing or what he is looking for. Even though most Americans have had their eyes and ears examined because of problems with either vision or hearing or just as part of a routine physical examination, few people understand exactly what is going on during these examinations. One of the purposes of this chapter is to demystify what goes on during examinations of the eye and the ear.

Before we can understand what eye and ear specialists look for during an examination, we must understand the major problems that can cause impairments in vision and hearing. We therefore begin this

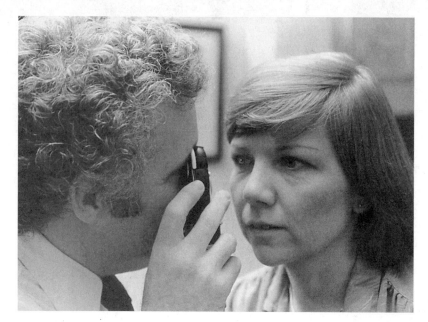

Figure 16.1
Ophthalmologist examining patient.

chapter by describing a number of the most common visual problems and how they are treated to improve or restore vision. After we understand the nature of the most common causes of visual problems, we will describe how a routine eye examination detects these problems. Following our discussion of vision, we take the same approach for hearing.

VISUAL IMPAIRMENT

HOW CAN VISION BECOME IMPAIRED?

Four major types of problems can cause poor vision (Figure 16.2):

1. Light is not focused clearly on the retina. Problems in focusing light can occur because the eyeball is too short or too long or because the cornea or the lens does not function properly. We will describe the following specific problems: myopia (nearsightedness), hyperopia (farsightedness), presbyopia ("old eye"), and astigmatism.

2. Light is blurred as it enters the eye. Scarring of the cornea or clouding of the lens blurs light as it enters the eye. Specific problems: corneal injury or disease, cataract.

3. There is damage to the retina. The retina can be damaged by disruption of the vessels that supply it with blood, by its separation from the blood supply,

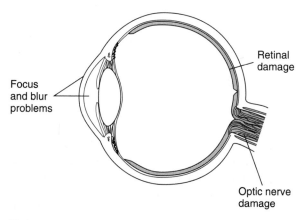

Figure 16.2
Places in the eye where visual problems can occur.

and by diseases that attack its receptors. Specific problems we will discuss include macular degeneration, diabetic retinopathy, detached retina, and hereditary retinal degeneration.

4. There is damage to the optic nerve. The optic nerve can degenerate. When this degeneration is due to a pressure buildup inside the eyeball, the cause is glaucoma. In addition, degeneration can be caused by poor circulation, toxic substances, or the presence of a tumor. We will focus on glaucoma in our discussion.

We begin by considering a problem that affects more people than all the others combined: an inability to adequately focus incoming light onto the retina.

FOCUSING PROBLEMS

In Chapter 2, we described the optical system of the eye—the cornea and the lens—which, if everything is working properly, brings light entering the eye to a sharp focus on the retina. We also described the process of accommodation, which adjusts the focusing power of the eye to bring both near and far objects into focus.

We will now consider the conditions myopia, hyperopia, presbyopia, and astigmatism, four problems that affect a person's ability to focus an image on the retina.

Myopia

Myopia, or nearsightedness, is an inability to see distant objects clearly. The reason for this difficulty, which affects over 70 million Americans, is illustrated in Figure 16.3a: In the myopic eye, parallel rays of light are brought to a focus in front of the retina so that the image reaching the retina is blurred. This problem can be caused by either of two factors: (1) **refractive myopia**, in which the cornea and/or the lens bends the light too much, or (2) **axial myopia**, in which the eyeball is too long. Either way, light comes to a focus in front of the retina, so that the image on the retina is out of focus, and far objects look blurred. (See Chapter 15 for a discussion of how myopia develops.)

How can we deal with this problem? One way to create a focused image on the retina is to move the stimulus closer. This pushes the focus point further back (see Figure 2.10), and if we move the stimulus close enough, we can push the focus point onto the retina (Figure 16.3b). The distance at which the spot of light becomes focused on the retina is called the **far point**, and when our spot of light is at the far

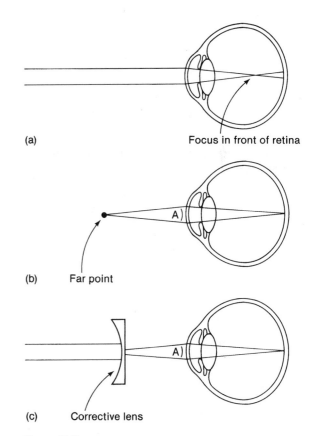

(a)   Focus in front of retina

(b)   Far point

(c)   Corrective lens

Figure 16.3
Focusing of light by the myopic (nearsighted) eye. (a) Parallel rays from a distant spot of light are brought to a focus in front of the retina, so distant objects appear blurred. (b) As the spot of light is moved closer to the eye, the focus point is pushed back until, at the far point, the rays are focused on the retina, and vision becomes clear. Vision is blurred beyond the far point. (c) A corrective lens, which bends light so that it enters the eye at the same angle as light coming from the far point, brings light to a focus on the retina. Angle A is the same in (b) and (c).

point, a myope can see it clearly. Although a person with myopia can see nearby objects clearly (which is why a myopic person is called nearsighted), objects beyond the far point are still out of focus (see the left column of Table 16.1). The solution to this problem is well known to anyone with myopia: corrective eyeglasses or contact lenses. These corrective lenses bend incoming light so that it is focused as if it were at the far point (Figure 16.3c). Notice that the lens placed in front of the eye causes the light to enter the eye at exactly the same angle as light coming from the far point in Figure 16.3b.

Table 16.1

Comparisons of focusing problems associated with the far point and the near point

Far Point (Farthest Distance for Clear Vision)	Near Point (Closest Distance for Clear Vision)
Problem: In myopia, the far point is close to the eye, and vision is blurred beyond the far point.	Problem: In presbyopia, the near point moves away from the eye, and vision is blurred closer than the near point.

Before leaving our discussion of myopia, let's consider the following question: How strong must a corrective lens be to give the myope clear far vision? To answer this question, we have to keep in mind what is required of a corrective lens: It must bend parallel rays so that light enters the eye at the same angle as a spot of light positioned at the far point. Figure 16.4 shows what this means for two different locations of the far point. When the far point is close, as in Figure 16.4a, we need a powerful corrective lens to bend the light in the large angle shown in Figure 16.4b. However, when the far point is distant, as in Figure 16.4c, we need only a weak corrective lens to bend the light in the small angle shown in Figure 16.4d. Thus, the strength of the corrective lens depends on the location of the far point: A powerful lens is needed to correct vision when the far point is close, and a weak lens is needed to correct vision when the far point is distant.

When ophthalmologists or optometrists write a prescription for corrective lenses, they specify the strength of the lens in **diopters**, using the following relationship: number of diopters = 1/far point in meters. Thus, a slightly myopic person with a far

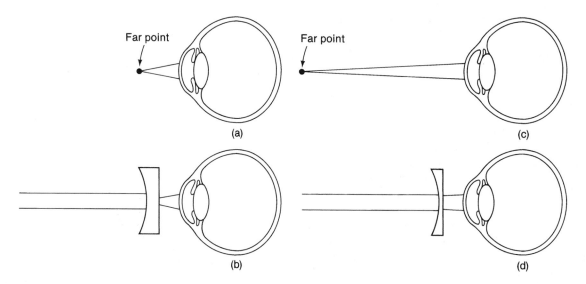

Figure 16.4

The strength of a lens required to correct myopic vision depends on the location of the far point. (a) A close far point requiring (b) a strong corrective lens. (c) A distant far point requiring (d) a weak corrective lens.

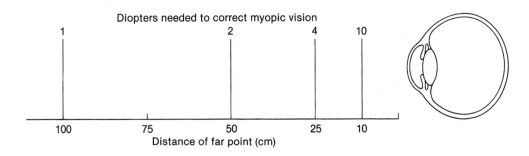

Figure 16.5

The number of diopters of lens power needed to correct myopic vision for different far points. Without a corrective lens, vision is blurred at distances greater than the far point. A far point of 10 cm represents severe myopia, and a far point of 100 cm represents mild myopia.

point at 1 meter (100 cm) requires a 1-diopter correction (diopters = 1/1 = 1.0). However, a very myopic person with a far point at 2/10 of a meter (20 cm) requires a 5-diopter correction (diopters = 1/0.2 = 5.0). This relationship between the distance of the far point and the required number of diopters of correction is shown in Figure 16.5.

Although glasses or contact lenses are the major route to clear vision for the myope, surgical procedures in which lasers are used to change the shape of the cornea have been introduced that enable people to experience good vision without corrective lenses. The first widely used laser procedure, **photorefractive keratotomy (PRK)**, was introduced in the United States around 1980. In this procedure, a type of laser called an excimer laser, which does not heat tissue, sculpts the cornea to give it either less power (for myopia; Figure 16.6a) or more power (for hyperopia; Figure 16.6b). This procedure appears to be most effective for myopia.

Recently, PRK has been largely replaced with another laser procedure, **laser-assisted in situ keratomileusis (LASIK)**. This procedure also involves sculpting the cornea with an excimer laser, but before the cornea is sculpted, a small flap, less than the thickness of a human hair, is cut into the surface of the cornea. The flap is folded out of the way, the cornea is sculpted by the laser, and the flap is then folded back into place. This procedure results in faster healing and less discomfort than the PRK procedures.

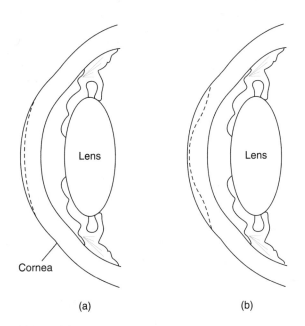

Figure 16.6

In the laser photorefractive keratotomy operation, an excimer laser is used to reshape the cornea, as shown by the dashed lines. (a) Reducing the curvature of the cornea on the myopic eye reduces the focusing power of the cornea so that the focus point moves back. (b) Increasing the curvature of the cornea in the hyperopic eye increases the focusing power of the cornea so that the focus point moves forward.

Hyperopia

A person with hyperopia, or **farsightedness**, can see distant objects clearly but has trouble seeing nearby objects (Figure 16.7a). In the hyperopic eye, the focus point for parallel rays of light is located behind the retina, usually because the eyeball is too short. By accommodating to bring the focus point back to the retina, people with hyperopia are able to see distant objects clearly.

Nearby objects, however, are more difficult for the hyperope to deal with, because moving an object closer pushes the focus point farther back. The hyperope's focus point, which is behind the retina for far objects, is pushed even farther back for nearby objects, so the hyperope must exert a great deal of accommodation to return the focus point to the retina. The hyperope's constant need to accommodate when looking at nearby objects (as in reading or doing close-up work) results in eyestrain and, in older people, headaches. Headaches do not usually occur in young people since they can accommodate easily, but older people, who have more difficulty accommodating because of a condition called presbyopia, which we will describe next, are more likely to experience headaches and may therefore require a corrective lens that brings the focus point forward onto the retina (Figure 16.7b).

Presbyopia

A decrease in the ability to accommodate due to old age is called presbyopia, or "old eye." This decrease in accommodation affects the location of the near point, the closest distance at which a person can still see an object in focus (see the right column of Table 16.1). As a person ages, the near point moves farther and farther away, as shown in Figure 16.8. The near point for most 20-year-olds is at about 10 cm, but it increases to 14 cm by age 30, 22 cm at 40, and 100 cm at 60. This loss in the ability to accommodate occurs because the lens hardens with age, and the ciliary muscles, which control accommodation, become weaker. These changes make it more difficult for the lens to change its shape for vision at close range. Though this gradual decrease in accommodative ability poses little prob-

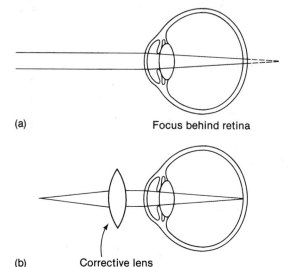

(a)   **Focus behind retina**

(b)   **Corrective lens**

Figure 16.7

Focusing of light by the hyperopic (farsighted) eye. (a) Parallel rays from a distant spot of light are brought to a focus behind the retina, so that, without accommodation, far objects are blurred. Hyperopes can, however, achieve clear vision of distant objects by accommodating. (b) If hyperopia is severe, the constant accommodation needed for clear vision may cause eyestrain, and a corrective lens is required.

lem for most people before the age of 45, at around that age the ability to accommodate begins to decrease rapidly, and the near point moves beyond a comfortable reading distance. This is the reason you may have observed older people holding their reading material at arm's length. But the real solution to this problem is a corrective lens that provides the necessary focusing power to bring light to a focus on the retina.

Astigmatism

Imagine what it would be like to see everything through a pane of old-fashioned wavy glass, which causes some things to be in focus and others to be blurred. This describes the experience of a person with a severe astigmatism; a person with an astigmatism sees through a misshapen cornea, which correctly focuses some of the light reaching the retina

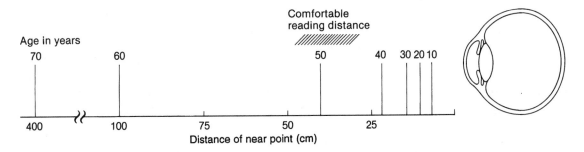

Figure 16.8

The near point as a function of age. The distance of the near point in centimeters is indicated on the scale at the bottom, and various ages are indicated by the vertical lines. Objects closer than the near point cannot be brought into focus by accommodation. Thus, as age increases, the ability to focus on nearby objects becomes poorer and poorer; eventually, past the age of about 50, reading becomes impossible without corrective lenses.

but distorts other light. The normal cornea is spherical, curved like a round kitchen bowl, but an astigmatic cornea is somewhat elliptical, curved like the inside of a teaspoon. Because of this elliptical curvature, a person with astigmatism will see the astigmatic fan in Figure 16.9 partially in focus and partially out of focus. As in hyperopia, eyestrain is a symptom of astigmatism, because no matter how much the person accommodates to try to achieve clear vision, something is always out of focus. Fortunately, astigmatism can be corrected with the appropriate lens.

DECREASED TRANSMISSION OF LIGHT

The focusing problems described above are the most prevalent visual problems, as evidenced by the large number of people who wear glasses or contact lenses. Because these problems can usually be corrected, most people with focusing problems see normally or suffer only mild losses of vision. We will now consider situations in which disease or physical damage causes severe visual losses or, in some cases, blindness. But before we begin to discuss these problems, we will define what we mean by blindness.

What Is Blindness?

It is a common conception that a person who is blind lives in a world of total darkness or formless diffuse light. While this description is true for some blind people, many people who are classified as legally blind do have some vision, and many can read with the aid of a strong magnifying glass. According to the definition of **blindness** accepted in most states, a person is considered legally blind if, after correction with glasses or contact lenses, he or she has a visual acuity of 20/200 or less in the better eye. A visual acuity of 20/20 means that a person can see at 20 feet what a

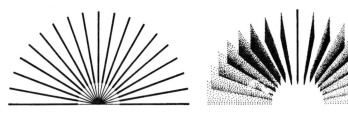

Figure 16.9

Left: Astigmatic fan chart used to test for astigmatism. Right: An astigmatic patient will perceive the lines in one orientation (in this case vertical) as sharp and the lines in the other orientation as blurred. (From Trevor-Roper, 1970.)

person with normal vision can see at 20 feet. However, a person with an acuity of 20/200 needs to be at a distance of 20 feet to see what a person with normal vision can see from a distance of 200 feet.

When we define blindness in terms of visual acuity, we are evaluating a person's ability to see with his or her fovea (which, as we saw in Chapter 2, is the cone-rich area of the retina that is responsible for detail vision). While poor foveal vision is the most common reason for legal blindness, a person with good foveal vision but little peripheral vision may also be considered legally blind. Thus, a person with normal (20/20) foveal vision but little or no peripheral vision may be legally blind. This situation, which is called **tunnel vision**, results from diseases that affect the retina, such as advanced glaucoma or retinitis pigmentosa (a form of retinal degeneration), which affect peripheral vision but leave the foveal cones unharmed until the final stages, when central vision can also be affected.

We begin our discussion of problems caused by disease or injury by considering some conditions that affect both peripheral and central vision because they affect the perception of light at the beginning of the visual process, as light enters the eye through the cornea and the lens.

Corneal Disease and Injury

The cornea, which is responsible for about 70 percent of the eye's focusing power (Lerman, 1966), is the window to vision because light first passes through this structure on its way to the retina. In order for a sharp image to be formed on the retina, the cornea must be transparent, but this transparency is occasionally lost when injury, infection, or allergic reactions cause the formation of scar tissue on the cornea. This scar tissue decreases visual acuity and sometimes makes lights appear to be surrounded by a halo, which looks like a shimmering rainbow. In addition, **corneal disease and injury** can also cause pain. Drugs, which often bring the cornea back to its transparent state, are the first treatment for corneal problems. If drugs fail, however, clear vision can often be restored by a **corneal transplant** operation.

The basic principle underlying a corneal transplant operation is shown in Figure 16.10. The scarred area of the cornea, usually a disk about 6 to 8 mm in diameter, is removed and replaced by a piece of cornea taken from a donor. For best results, this donor should be a young adult who died of an acute disease or of an injury that left the corneal tissue in good condition. In the past, a major problem with this operation was the necessity of transplanting the donor cornea within a few hours after the donor's death. Now, however, donor corneas are preserved by low-temperature storage in a specially formulated solution.

Of the over 10,000 corneal transplants performed every year, about 85 percent are successful. Remember, however, that a corneal transplant operation involves only a small piece of the eye—there is no such thing as an eye transplant. Indeed, the problems involved in transplanting a whole eye are overwhelming. For one thing, the optic nerve and the retina are sensitive to lack of oxygen, so that, once the circulation is cut off, irreversible damage occurs within minutes, just as is the case for the brain. Thus, keeping the donor's eye alive presents a serious problem. And even if it were possible to keep an eye alive, there is the problem of connecting the 1 million optic nerve fibers of the donor's eye to the corresponding nerve fibers of the patient's optic nerve. At this point, whole eye transplants are purely science fiction.

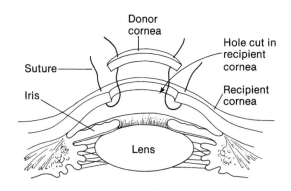

Figure 16.10

Corneal transplant operation. The scarred part of the cornea has been removed, and the donor cornea is about to be sutured in place.

Clouding of the Lens (Cataract)

Like the cornea, the lens is transparent and is important for focusing a sharp image on the retina. Clouding of the lens, which is called a **cataract**, is sometimes present at birth (**congenital cataract**), may be caused by an eye disease (**secondary cataract**), or may be caused by injury (**traumatic cataract**), but the most common cause of cataract is old age (**senile cataract**). Cataracts develop, for reasons as yet unknown, in 75 percent of people over 65 and in 95 percent of people over 85.

Although millions of people have cataracts, in only about 15 percent of the cases does the cataract interfere with a person's normal activities, and only 5 percent of cataracts are serious enough to require surgery—the only treatment. The basic principle underlying a cataract operation is illustrated in Figure 16.11a. A small opening is made in the eye, and the surgeon removes the lens while leaving in place the capsule, the tissue that forms a baglike structure that helps support the lens. A method for removing the lens that has the advantage of requiring only a small incision in the eye is **phacoemulsification** (Figure 16.11b). In this procedure, a hollow tubelike instrument that emits ultrasound vibrations of up to 40,000 cycles per second is inserted through a small incision in the cornea. The vibrations break up the lens, and the resulting pieces are sucked out of the eye through the tube.

Removal of the clouded lens clears a path so that light can reach the retina unobstructed, but, in removing the lens, the surgeon has also removed some of the eye's focusing power. (Remember that the cornea accounts for 70 percent of the eye's focusing power; the lens is responsible for the remaining 30 percent.) Although the patient can be fitted with glasses, these create problems of their own, because glasses enlarge the image falling on the retina by as much as 20 to 35 percent. If one eye receives this enlarged image and the other receives a normal image, the brain cannot combine the two images to form a single, clear perception. The **intraocular lens**, a plastic lens which is placed inside the eye where the original lens used to be, is the solution to this problem.

The idea of implanting a lens inside the eye goes back 200 years, but the first workable design for an

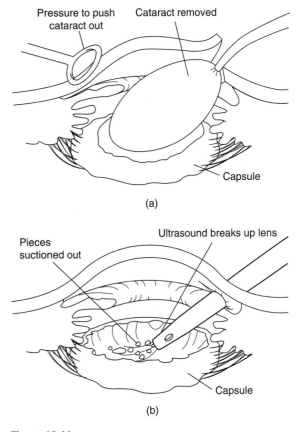

Figure 16.11
A cataract operation. (a) The cataract (the clouded lens) is removed through an incision in the cornea. (b) The phacoemulsification procedure for removing the cataract. High-frequency sound vibrations break up the lens, and the pieces are sucked into the tube. After the lens is removed, an intraocular lens is inserted.

intraocular lens was not proposed until 1949. Although lenses introduced in the 1950s were not very successful, recent developments in plastics have resulted in small ultralightweight lenses, like the one shown in Figure 16.12, and installing an intraocular lens is now a routine part of most cataract operations. Notice that the lens is placed in the same location as the clouded lens that was removed, just above the capsule, which the surgeon was careful to leave in place when removing the cataract. The presence of the capsule helps hold the intraocular lens in place.

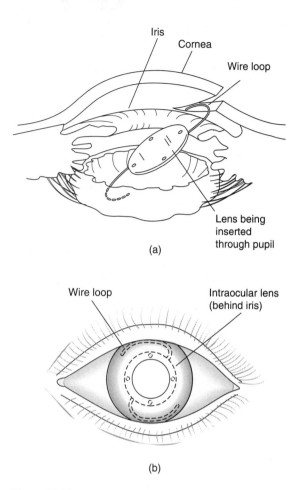

Figure 16.12

Installing an intraocular lens in the eye after the cataract has been removed. (a) The lens is inserted through an incision in the cornea. Notice that it is being inserted through the pupil so that it will be positioned where the original lens was, behind the iris and just above the capsule.
(b) Frontal view, showing the lens in place behind the iris. The small wire loops hold the lens in place.

DAMAGE TO THE RETINA

The retina receives nourishment from the retinal circulation and from the pigment epithelium on which it rests. All four conditions described below cause a loss of vision because of their effects on the retinal cir-

culation and on the relationship between the retina and the pigment epithelium.

Diabetic Retinopathy

Before the isolation of insulin in 1922, most people with severe **diabetes**, a condition in which the body doesn't produce enough insulin, had a life expectancy of less than 20 years. The synthesis of insulin (which won the 1923 Nobel Prize for its discoverers) greatly increased the life expectancy of diabetics, but one result of this greater life expectancy has been a great increase in an eye problem called **diabetic retinopathy**. Of the 10 million diabetics in the United States, about 4 million show some signs of this problem.

Figure 16.13 shows what happens as the disease progresses. At first, the capillaries swell, and although most cases of diabetic retinopathy stop here, a large number of diabetics suffer vision losses even when the disease stops at this point. The disease's further progression, which occurs in a small percentage of patients, involves a process called **neovascularization**. Abnormal new blood vessels are formed (Figure 16.13b), which do not supply the retina with adequate oxygen and which are fragile and so bleed into the **vitreous humor** (the jellylike substance that fills the eyeball); this bleeding interferes with the passage of light to the retina. Neovascularization can also cause scarring of the retina and retinal detachment (see below).

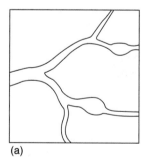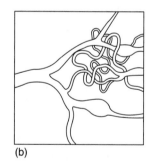

Figure 16.13

Blood vessels in diabetic retinopathy. (a) In early stages of the disease, the blood vessels swell and leak slightly. (b) In later stages, in a process called neovascularization, abnormal new blood vessels grow on the surface of the retina.

One technique for stopping neovascularization is called **laser photocoagulation**, in which a laser beam of high-energy light is aimed at leaking blood vessels. The laser "photocoagulates," or seals off, these vessels and stops the bleeding. A procedure called **panretinal photocoagulation** has been used with considerable success. In this technique, the laser scatters 2,000 or more tiny burns on the retina, as shown in Figure 16.14. The burns do not directly hit the leaking blood vessels, but, by destroying part of the retina, they decrease the retina's need for oxygen, so that the leaking blood vessels dry up and go away.

If laser photocoagulation is not successful in stopping neovascularization, a procedure called a **vitrectomy,** shown in Figure 16.15, is used to eliminate the blood inside the eye. In this operation, which is done only as a last resort, a hollow tube containing a guillotine-like cutter takes in the vitreous humor and chops it into pieces small enough to be sucked out of the eye through the tube. When the vitreous humor and blood are removed, they are replaced with a salt solution. This procedure removes the blood inside the eye and often prevents further bleeding.

Macular Degeneration

Imagine your frustration if you could see everywhere except where you were looking, so that every time you looked at something you lost sight of it. That is exactly what happens if a region of the retina called the macula is damaged. The **macula** is an area about 5 mm in diameter that surrounds and includes the cone-rich fovea (itself only slightly larger than one of the periods on this page). If the macula degenerates, blindness results in the center of vision (Figure 16.16). This condition is extremely debilitating because, although peripheral vision remains intact, the elimination of central vision makes reading impossible.

There are a number of forms of **macular degeneration**, but the most common is called **age-related macular degeneration** because it occurs, without obvious reason, in older people. In its mild form, there is a slight thinning of the cone receptors and the formation of small white or yellow lumps on the retina. This form of macular degeneration usually progresses slowly and may not cause serious visual

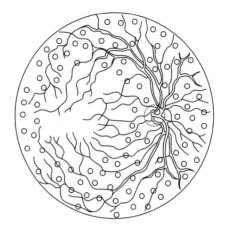

Figure 16.14

Laser photocoagulation in the treatment of diabetic retinopathy. The picture illustrates the technique of panretinal photocoagulation. Each dot represents a small laser burn on the retina.

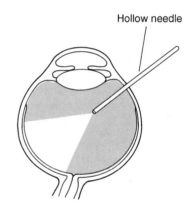

Figure 16.15

Vitrectomy. The hollow needle inserted into the eyeball first sucks out the liquid inside the eye and then fills the eyeball with a salt solution.

problems. In 5 to 20 percent of the cases, however, small new blood vessels, similar to those in diabetic retinopathy, grow underneath the macular area of the retina. These new blood vessels form very rapidly—over a period of only one or two months—and leak fluid into the macula, killing the cone receptors.

Figure 16.16
Macular degeneration causes a loss of central vision.

Until recently, there was no treatment for age-related macular degeneration. However, a study by the National Eye Institute indicates that, if the problem can be caught at an early stage in some patients with the more severe form of the disease, laser photocoagulation can stop or greatly reduce leakage of the newly formed vessels.

Detached Retina

Detached retina, a condition in which the retina becomes separated from the underlying pigment epithelium (Figure 16.17), has occurred in a number of athletes because of traumatic injuries to the eye or the head. Sugar Ray Leonard, the former welterweight boxing champion, retired temporarily from boxing because of a detached retina. He returned to boxing a number of years later amid much discussion about whether returning to the ring was worth the risk of losing his sight in one eye. As it turned out, Leonard won both the fight and the gamble with his sight, apparently escaping without further damaging his eye.

A detached retina affects vision for two reasons: (1) For good image formation, the retina must lie smoothly on top of the pigment epithelium, and (2) when the retina loses contact with the pigment epithelium, the visual pigments in the detached area are separated from enzymes in the epithelium necessary for pigment regeneration. When the visual pigment can no longer regenerate, that area of the retina becomes blind.

The treatment for a detached retina is an operation to reattach it. The basic idea behind this operation is to cause the formation of scar tissue inside the eye that will attach itself to the retina and anchor it in place. This process is accomplished by applying either a cooling or a heating probe to exactly the right place on the outside of the eyeball. Figure 16.17b shows the procedure used to determine where to apply the probe. While looking into the eye with a special viewing device, the surgeon presses on the outside of the eyeball, which causes an indentation that can be seen inside the eye. The surgeon presses at a number of points, until the indentation inside the eyeball matches the location of the tear or hole in the retina, where the detachment originated.

Once the point where the detachment has occurred is located, it is marked on the outside of the eyeball, and that point is cooled or heated to create an

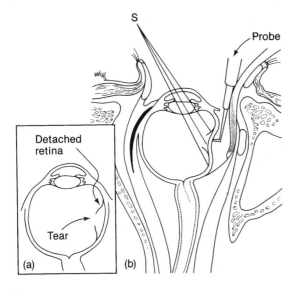

Figure 16.17
(a) A detached retina. (b) Procedure for reattaching the retina. To locate the site of detachment, a probe pushes the eyeball from outside while the surgeon, at S, looks into the eye. Once the site of the detachment is located, the outside of the eye is marked, and a cooling or heating probe is applied at the marked point.

inflammatory response. The retina must then be pushed flush with the wall of the eyeball. This is accomplished by placing a band around the outside of the eyeball that creates a dumbbell-shaped eye. Then, with the retina pressed against the wall of the eye, the inflammation causes scarring that "welds" the retina back onto the pigment epithelium. If the area of detached retina is not too big, there is a 70 to 80 percent chance that this procedure will work. In most cases, it restores vision, although vision is sometimes not restored even though the retina is successfully reattached. The larger the detached area, the less likely it is that this operation (or others, which we will not describe here) will work. Sometimes, if a retinal tear can be caught at an early stage, before fluid has gotten through it and caused the retina to detach, it is possible to prevent detachment by surrounding the tear with laser burns. This is a quick procedure that can be carried out in the ophthalmologist's office and requires no surgery.

Hereditary Retinal Degeneration

The most common form of hereditary retinal degeneration is a disease called **retinitis pigmentosa**, a degeneration of the retina that is passed from one generation to the next (although not always affecting everyone in a family). We know little about what actually causes the disease, although one hypothesis is that it is caused by a problem in the pigment epithelium.

A person with retinitis pigmentosa usually shows no signs of the disease until reaching adolescence. At this time, the person may begin to notice some difficulty in seeing at night, since the disease first attacks the rod receptors. As the person gets older, the disease slowly progresses, causing further losses of vision in the peripheral retina. Then, in its final stages, which may occur as early as a person's 30s or as late as the 50s or 60s (depending on the strain of the disease), retinitis pigmentosa also attacks the cones, and the result is complete blindness.

OPTIC NERVE DAMAGE: GLAUCOMA

A leading cause of blindness in the United States is **glaucoma,** which causes nerve fibers in the optic nerve to degenerate and therefore prevents the nerve impulses generated by the retina from being transmitted to the brain.

Although the end result of glaucoma is damage to the optic nerve, the source of the problem is at the front of the eye. We can understand how damage to the front of the eye affects the optic nerve by looking at the cross section of the eye in Figure 16.18a. Under normal conditions, the aqueous humor (the liquid found in the space between the cornea and the lens), which is continuously produced at A, passes between the iris and the lens following the path indicated by the arrows; it then drains from the eye at B. In glaucoma, the drainage of aqueous humor is partially blocked. **Closed-angle glaucoma** is a rare form of glaucoma in which a **pupillary block** (Figure 16.18b) constricts the opening between the iris and the lens and causes a pressure buildup that pushes the iris up, thereby closing the angle between the

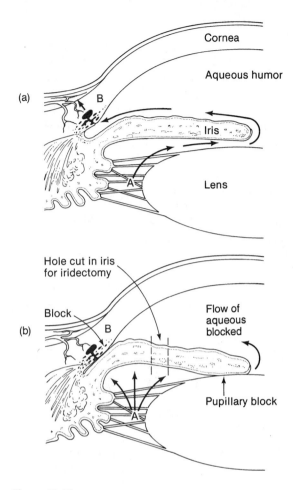

Cornea

Aqueous humor

(a)

B

Iris

Lens

A

Hole cut in iris
for iridectomy

Block

(b)

B

Flow of
aqueous
blocked

A

Pupillary block

Figure 16.18

(a) Arrows indicate the flow of aqueous humor in the normal eye. The aqueous humor is produced at A and leaves the eye at B. In open-angle glaucoma, the aqueous humor cannot leave the eye because of a blockage at B. (b) In closed-angle glaucoma, the raised iris hinders the flow of aqueous humor from the eye. An iridectomy—cutting a hole in the iris—can provide a way for the aqueous humor to reach B.

humor to leave the eye. The blocks that occur in both closed- and open-angle glaucoma result in a large resistance to the outflow of aqueous humor, and since the aqueous humor continues to be produced inside the eye, the **intraocular pressure**—the pressure inside the eyeball—rises. This increase in intraocular pressure presses on the head of the optic nerve at the back of the eye. This pressure cuts off circulation to the head of the optic nerve, which results in the degeneration of the optic nerve fibers that causes blindness.

The increase in pressure that occurs in closed-angle glaucoma usually happens very rapidly and is accompanied by pain. The treatment for this type of glaucoma is an operation called an **iridectomy**, in which a small hole is created in the iris with a laser (Figure 16.18b). This hole opens a channel through which the aqueous humor can flow and releases the pressure on the iris. With the pressure gone, the iris flattens out and uncovers the area at B so that aqueous humor can flow out of the eye.

Intraocular pressure increases more slowly in open-angle glaucoma, so the patient may be unaware of any symptoms. In many cases, visual loss is so gradual that much of the patient's peripheral vision is gone before its loss is noticed. For that reason, ophthalmologists strongly recommend that people over 40 have their eyes checked regularly for glaucoma, since early detection greatly enhances the chances of effective treatment by medication. In 5 to 10 percent of the cases of open-angle glaucoma, medications do not decrease the pressure, and an operation becomes necessary. The goal of this operation is to cut an opening in the wall of the eyeball that creates a new route for fluid to leave the eye.

THE EYE EXAMINATION

So far, we have described some of the things that can go wrong with the eye and how these problems are treated. In this part of the chapter, we will describe the procedures used to uncover some of these problems. Before describing the eye examination, we will consider who examines the eyes.

cornea and the iris and blocking the area at B where the aqueous humor leaves the eye.

In **open-angle glaucoma**, which is the most common form of the disease, the eye looks normal (Figure 16.18a), but the drainage area at B is partially blocked, so that it is more difficult for the aqueous

Who Examines Eyes?

Three types of professionals are involved in eye care: ophthalmologists, optometrists, and opticians.

1. An **ophthalmologist** is an M.D. who has completed undergraduate school and four years of medical school, which provide general medical training. In order to become an ophthalmologist, a person needs four or more years of training after graduation from medical school to learn how to treat eye problems medically and surgically. Some ophthalmologists receive even further training and then specialize in specific areas, such as pediatric ophthalmology (practice limited to children), diseases of the cornea, retinal diseases, or glaucoma. Most ophthalmologists, however, treat all eye problems, as well as prescribing glasses and fitting contact lenses.

2. An **optometrist** has completed undergraduate school and, after four years of additional study, has received a doctor of optometry (O.D.) degree. Optometrists can examine eyes and fit and prescribe glasses or contact lenses. In some states, optometrists have won the right to include medical treatment using drugs for some eye conditions. Surgery, however, is still done exclusively by ophthalmologists.

3. An **optician** is trained to fabricate and fit glasses and, in some states, contact lenses, on the prescription of an ophthalmologist or an optometrist.

What Happens During an Eye Exam?

The basic aims of an eye exam are (1) to determine how well the patient can see, (2) to correct vision if it is defective, (3) to determine the causes of defective vision by examining the optics of the eye and checking for eye diseases, and (4) to diagnose diseases that the patient may not even be aware of. To accomplish these aims, an examination by an eye specialist usually includes the following.

Medical History   The first step in an eye exam is to take a medical history. This history focuses on any eye problems that the patient may have had in the past, on any current eye problems, and on any general medical problems that may be related to the patient's vision.

Visual Acuity   This is the familiar part of the eye exam, in which you are asked to read letters on an eye chart like the one in Figure 15.1. The old version of the eye chart, which most people are familiar with, had a large E at the top. This new version results in more accurate measurements of acuity because there are the same number of letters on each line and the spacing between the letters is proportional to the sizes of the letters. The top row of letters is the 20/400 line. This means that a person with normal vision should be able to see these letters from a distance of 400 feet. Since the eye chart is usually viewed from about 20 feet, people with normal vision see these letters easily. When asked to read the smallest line he or she can see, the patient usually picks a line that is easily read. With a little encouragement, however, most patients find that they can see lines smaller than the one they originally picked, and the examiner has the patient read smaller and smaller lines until letters are missed. The smallest line a person can read indicates his or her visual acuity, with normal vision defined as an acuity of 20/20. A person with worse than normal acuity—say, 20/40—must view a display from a distance of 20 feet to see what a person with normal acuity can see at 40 feet. A person with better than normal acuity—say, 20/10—can see from a distance of 20 feet what a person with normal vision can see only at 10 feet.

The visual acuity test described above tests only foveal vision, since the patient looks directly at each letter, so the image of that letter falls on the fovea. Thus, as mentioned earlier, a person who scores 20/20 on a visual acuity test may still be classified as legally blind if he or she has little or no peripheral vision. Testing peripheral vision is usually not part of a routine eye exam, but when peripheral vision problems are suspected, a technique called **perimetry** is used, in which the patient is asked to indicate the location of small spots of light presented at different locations in the periphery. This test locates blind spots (called scotomas) that may be caused by retinal degeneration, detachment of the retina, or diseases such as glaucoma.

In addition to using the eye chart to test far vision, it is also customary to test near vision, especially in older patients who may be experiencing the effects of presbyopia. This testing is done by determining the smallest line of a card like the one in Figure 16.19 that the patient can see from a comfortable reading distance.

Refraction   A score of 20/60 on a visual acuity test indicates worse than normal acuity but does not indicate what is causing this loss of acuity. Acuity could be decreased by one of the diseases described earlier or by a problem in focusing: myopia, hyperopia, presbyopia, or astigmatism. If the problem lies in the focusing mechanism of the eye, it is usually easily corrected by glasses or contact lenses. **Refraction** is the procedure used to determine the power of the corrective lenses needed to achieve clear vision.

The first step in refraction is a **retinoscopy exam**, an examination of the eye with a device called a *retinoscope*. This device projects a streak of light into the eye that is reflected into the eye of the examiner. The examiner moves the retinoscope back and forth and up and down across the eye, noticing what the reflected light looks like. If the patient's eye is focusing the light correctly, the examiner sees the whole pupil filled with light, and no correction is necessary (in this case, the patient will usually have tested at 20/20 or better in the visual acuity test). If, however, the patient's eye is not focusing the light correctly, the examiner sees a streak of light move back and forth across the pupil as the streak of light from the retinoscope is moved across the eye.

To determine the correction needed to bring the patient's eye to 20/20 vision, the examiner places corrective lenses in front of the eye while still moving the streak of light from the retinoscope back and forth. One way of placing these lenses in front of the eye is to use a device like the one shown in Figure

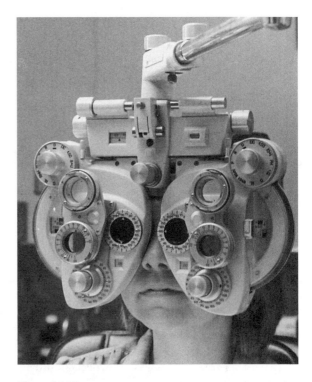

Figure 16.20
A device for placing different corrective lenses in front of the patient's eyes. Different lenses are placed in front of the eye during the retinoscopy exam and again as the patient looks at the eye chart.

No. 1
In short-sighted persons the eye-ball is too long, and the light rays come to a focus in front of the retina,
No. 2
while in far-sighted persons the eye-ball is too short, and the focal point, therefore, falls be-
No. 3
hind the retina. In either case a blurred image is received upon the retina. In order
No. 4
to overcome this blurring, and thus correct the optical defect, the eye un-
No. 6
consciously makes an effort by which the ciliary muscle acts on
No. 8
the lens. This effort explains why eye-strain may cause
No. 10
pain and discomfort. An optical correction for
No. 12
the refractive error is found in specta-

Figure 16.19
A card for testing close vision. The patient's close vision is determined by the smallest line that he or she can read from a comfortable reading distance.

16.20. This device contains a variety of lenses that can be changed by turning a dial. The examiner's goal is to find the lens that causes the whole pupil to fill up with light when the retinoscope is moved back and forth. This lens brings light to a focus on the retina and is usually close to the one that will be prescribed to achieve 20/20 vision.

The retinoscopy exam results in a good first approximation of the correct lens to prescribe for a patient, but the ultimate test is what the patient sees. To determine this, the examiner has the patient look at the eye chart and places lenses in front of the patient's eyes to determine which one results in the clearest vision. When the examiner determines which lens results in 20/20 vision, he or she writes a prescription for glasses or contact lenses. To fit contact lenses after determining the prescription, the examiner must match the shape of the contact lens to the shape of the patient's cornea.

Refraction is used to determine the correction needed to achieve clear far vision. Using a procedure we will not describe here, the examiner also determines whether a correction is needed to achieve clear near vision. This determination is particularly important for patients over 45 years old, who may experience reading difficulties due to presbyopia.

External Eye Exam In an **external eye exam**, the examiner uses a variety of tests to check the condition of the external eye. The examiner checks pupillary reaction by shining light into the eye, to see if the pupil responds by closing when the light is presented and by opening when the light is removed. The examiner also checks the color of the eye and the surrounding tissues. "Red eye" may indicate that an inflammation is present. The movement of the eyes is checked by having the patient follow a moving target, and the alignment of the eyes is checked by having the patient look at a target. If the eyes are aligned correctly, both eyes will look directly at the target, but, if the eyes are misaligned, one eye will look at the target, and the other will veer off to one side.

Slit-Lamp Examination The **slit-lamp examination** checks the condition of the cornea and the lens. The slit lamp, shown in Figure 16.21, projects a narrow slit of light into the patient's eye. This light can be precisely focused at different places inside the eye, and the examiner views this sharply focused slit of light through a binocular magnifier. This slit of light is like the sharp edge of a knife that cuts through the eye.

What does the examiner see when looking at the "cutting edge" of light from the slit lamp? By focusing

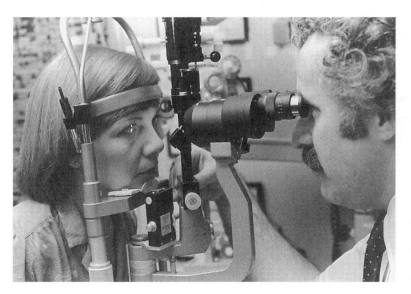

Figure 16.21
A patient being examined with a slit lamp. The examiner is checking the condition of the lens and the cornea by viewing the slit of light through a binocular magnifier.

Clinical Aspects of Vision and Hearing

the light at different levels inside the cornea and lens, the examiner can detect small imperfections—places where the cornea or the lens is not completely transparent—that cannot be seen by any other method. These imperfections may indicate corneal disease or injury or the formation of a cataract.

Tonometry **Tonometry** measures intraocular pressure, the pressure inside the eye, and is therefore the test for glaucoma. Nowadays, an instrument called a **tonometer** is used to measure intraocular pressure, but before the development of this device, it was known that large increases of intraocular pressure, which accompany severe cases of glaucoma, cause the eye to become so hard that this hardness could be detected by pushing on the eyeball with a finger.

There are several types of tonometers, which measure the intraocular pressure by pushing on the cornea. The Schiotz tonometer is a hand-held device that consists of a small plunger attached to a calibrated weight. The weight pushes the plunger and indents the cornea. If the intraocular pressure is high, the plunger causes a smaller indentation than if the intraocular pressure is normal. Thus, intraocular pressure is determined by measuring the indentation of the cornea. (Though this procedure may sound rather painful, it is not, because the examiner applies a few

drops of anesthetic to the cornea before applying the tonometer.)

The applanation tonometer, shown being applied to a patient's cornea in Figure 16.22, is a more sophisticated and accurate instrument than the Schiotz tonometer. After a few drops of anesthetic are applied to the cornea, the flat end of a cylindrical rod, called an **applanator**, is slowly moved against the cornea by the examiner, who watches the applanator's progress through the same magnifiers used for the slit-lamp exam (Figure 16.22). The examiner pushes the end of the applanator against the cornea until enough pressure is exerted to flatten a small area on the cornea's curved surface. The greater the force that must be exerted to flatten the cornea, the greater the intraocular pressure.

Ophthalmoscopy So far, we have looked at the outside of the eye (external eye exam), examined the lens and cornea (slit-lamp exam), and measured the intraocular pressure (tonometry), but we have yet to look at perhaps the most important structure of all: the retina. Since there is a hole (the pupil) in the front of the eye, it should be simple to see the retina; we only have to look into the hole. Unfortunately, it's not that simple; if you've ever looked into a person's pupil, you realize that it's dark in there. In order to

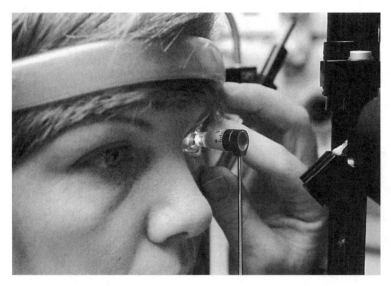

Figure 16.22
An applanation tonometer being applied to a patient's cornea.

see the retina, we must find some way to light up the inside of the eye. This is accomplished by the **ophthalmoscope**, which was first developed by Hermann von Helmholtz, of the Young-Helmholtz theory of color vision, in 1850.

The principle underlying Helmholtz's ophthalmoscope is shown in Figure 16.23. A light off to the side is directed into the patient's eye with a half-silvered mirror. The half-silvered mirror reflects some of the light and transmits the rest, so that an examiner positioned as shown in Figure 16.23 can see through the mirror and into the patient's eye. Actual ophthalmoscopes are much more complicated than the one diagrammed here, since they include numerous lenses, mirrors, and filters, but the basic principle remains the same as that of the original ophthalmoscope designed by Helmholtz in 1850.

Figure 16.24 is a patient's-eye view of an examination with an ophthalmoscope, although the examiner is actually very close, as shown in Figure 16.1. Figure 16.25 shows a close-up of what the ophthalmologist

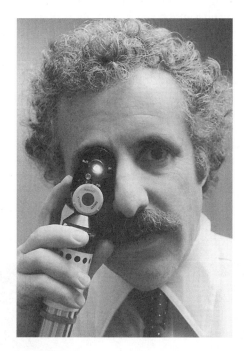

Figure 16.24
Patient's-eye view of an ophthalmoscopic exam.

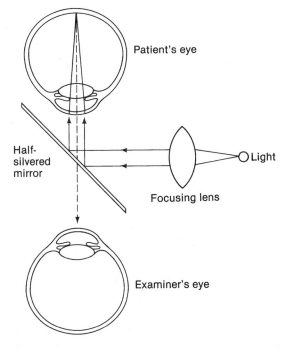

Figure 16.23
The principle behind the ophthalmoscope. Light is reflected into the patient's eye by the half-silvered mirror. Some of this light is then reflected into the examiner's eye (along the dashed line), allowing the examiner to see the inside of the patient's eye.

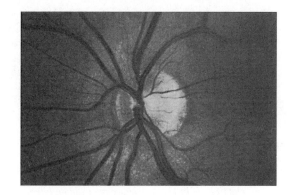

Figure 16.25
Close-up view of the head of the optic nerve and the retinal circulation as seen through an ophthalmoscope.

sees if the patient has a normal retina. The most prominent features of this view of the retina are the optic disk, the place where the ganglion cell fibers leave the eye to form the optic nerve, and the arteries and veins of the retina. In this examination, the ophthalmologist focuses on these features, noting any abnormalities in the appearance of the optic disk and the retinal circulation. For example, the ophthalmologist may detect the presence of diabetic retinopathy by noticing a number of very small blood vessels (neovascularization). In fact, all the retinal injuries and diseases described above cause some change in the appearance of the retina, which can be detected by looking at the retina with an ophthalmoscope.

Our description of an eye examination has covered most of the tests included in a routine exam. The examiner may decide to carry out other tests if a problem is suggested by the routine tests. For example, a technique called **fluorescein angiography** is used to

examine more closely the retinal circulation in patients with diabetic retinopathy. A fluorescent dye is injected intravenously into the arm, and when this dye reaches the retina, it sharply outlines the retinal arteries and veins, as shown in Figure 16.26. Only by this technique can we observe the leakage of fluid that occurs in the abnormal neovascularized blood vessels that accompany diabetic retinopathy. Determining the location of the leakage identifies areas that are to be treated with photocoagulation.

Other tests, which we will not describe here, include the electroretinogram, which measures the electrical response of the rod and cone receptors and is therefore useful in diagnosing such retinal degeneration as retinitis pigmentosa, and the cortical evoked potential, which measures the electrical response of the visual cortex and is useful for diagnosing vision problems caused by head injuries or tumors.

See Summary Table 16.1 for an overview of the material we have discussed so far.

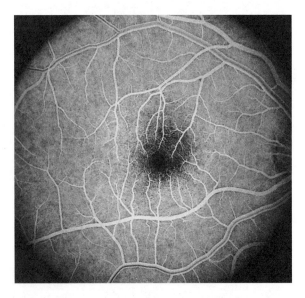

Figure 16.26
Fluorescein angiograph of a normal eye. In this view, the head of the optic nerve is on the far right, just outside the picture. The fovea is in the dark space near the middle of the picture. In the normal eye, the blood vessels stand out in sharp contrast to the background. (Photograph courtesy of Eye and Ear Hospital of Pittsburgh.)

In our consideration of the clinical aspects of vision, we saw that visual functioning can be impaired because of problems in delivering the stimulus to the receptors, because of damage to the receptors, and because of damage to the system that transmits signals from the receptors toward the brain. An analogous situation exists in hearing, as we will see by considering the various causes of hearing impairment.

HOW CAN HEARING BECOME IMPAIRED?

In considering the question "How can hearing become impaired?" it is important to distinguish between impairments in the auditory system and what effects these impairments have on a person's hearing. A **hearing impairment** is a deviation or change for the worse in either the structure or the functioning of the auditory system. A **hearing handicap** is the disadvantage that a hearing impairment causes in a person's ability

Focusing Problems

Focusing problems connected with incorrect bending of the light by the cornea and lens or an eyeball that is too long or short include myopia and hyperopia. The power of a lens needed to correct myopia is expressed in diopters, which is 1 divided by the far point. PRK and LASIK are two laser surgery techniques that can be used to reduce or eliminate myopia or hyperopia. Other focusing problems are presbyopia, decreased ability to accommodate that occurs when a person gets older, and astigmatism, blurring of stimuli in some orientations due to a misshapen cornea.

What Is Blindness?

Blindness is legally defined in terms of either reduced acuity or reduced visual fields.

Decreased Transmission of Light

Conditions that decrease the amount of light that is transmitted to the retina include corneal disease or injury and cataracts. Problems that cause clouding or scarring of the cornea can be treated with drugs or corrected with a corneal transplant operation. Cataract, a clouding of the lens, can be treated by removal of the lens and replacement with an intraocular lens.

Damage to the Retina

Diabetic retinopathy and macular degeneration cause a loss of vision because of their effects on the retinal circulation. Diabetic retinopathy is a swelling of the capillaries and, in more extreme cases, neovascularization. One treatment is laser photocoagulation. Macular degeneration is a degeneration of the area around the fovea. It is related to old age and can sometimes be treated with laser photocoagulation. Detached retina causes problems because the retina becomes detached from the enzyme-rich pigment epithelium. It can be reattached through surgery. Hereditary retinal degenerations like retinitis pigmentosa attack the receptors.

Optic Nerve Damage

Glaucoma, a leading cause of blindness in the United States, is usually connected with a blockage of drainage of the aqueous humor out the front of the eye. This blockage results in increased intraocular pressure, which can led to blindness by pushing on the circulation that enters the eye at the optic nerve. Treatments include drugs and surgery to restore the flow by eliminating the blockage.

The Eye Examination

Ophthalmologists, optometrists, and opticians are all professionals involved in eye care. In general, ophthalmologists and optometrists are trained to both fit glasses and also detect abnormalities of the eye. The eye exam consists of the following components: medical history, visual acuity test (far and near), refraction, external eye exam, slit-lamp examination, tonometry, ophthalmoscopy, and sometimes techniques such as fluorescein angiography.

---

to communicate or in the person's daily living. The distinction between an impairment and a handicap means that a hearing impairment does not always cause a large hearing handicap. For example, although a person who has lost the ability to hear all sounds above 6,000 Hz has lost a substantial portion of his or her range of hearing, this particular hearing loss has little effect on the person's ability to hear and understand speech. We can appreciate this when we realize that, even though telephones transmit frequencies only between about 500 and 3,000 Hz, most people have no trouble using the telephone for communication. Such a hearing impairment would, however, change a person's perception of music, which often contains frequencies above 6,000 Hz, and would therefore have some impact on the person's quality of life.

Problems can develop in the auditory system for the following reasons: (1) problems in delivering the sound stimulus to the receptors, (2) damage to the receptors, (3) damage to the transmission system, and (4) damage to the auditory cortex (Figure 16.27). The following is a list of the types of things that can go wrong in the auditory system within each of these categories:

1. Sound is not properly transmitted to the receptors. Problems in delivering sound to the receptors can occur because of problems such as blockage of the

Clinical Aspects of Vision and Hearing

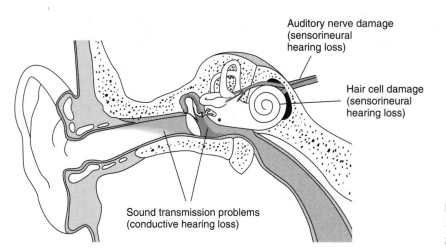

Auditory nerve damage
(sensorineural
hearing loss)

Hair cell damage
(sensorineural
hearing loss)

Sound transmission problems
(conductive hearing loss)

Figure 16.27

Places in the ear where hearing problems can occur.

outer ear or damage to the system that transmits vibrations through the middle ear. These types of problems result in *conductive hearing losses*.

2. The hair cells are damaged, so they can't generate electrical signals. This problem and the one below result in *sensorineural hearing losses*.

3. There is damage to the auditory nerve or the brainstem that keeps signals that are generated from being transmitted to the auditory area of the brain. Damage at the brainstem level can interfere with the listener's ability to integrate the signals coming from the left and right ears.

4. There is damage at the auditory cortex, so when the signal reaches the cortex, it is not processed properly.

We will describe some of the major ways in which these problems occur in the auditory system, focusing on the first two categories above: conductive hearing loss and sensorineural hearing loss.

CONDUCTIVE HEARING LOSS

A **conductive hearing loss** is one in which the vibrations that would normally be caused by a sound stimulus are not conducted from the outer ear into the cochlea. This kind of loss can occur in either the outer ear or the middle ear.

Outer-Ear Disorders

Sound can be blocked at the ear canal by the buildup of excessive cerumen (ear wax) or by the insertion of objects, as might occur when children decide it would be fun to put beans or wads of paper into their ears. A more serious problem occurs in children who are born with outer- or middle-ear malformations that prevent sound from traveling down the outer-ear canal and through the middle ear. Blockage may also occur because of a swelling of the canal caused by infection by microorganisms, a situation that often occurs in swimmers when water is trapped in the ear, hence the name "swimmer's ear."

Another problem occurs if the tympanic membrane at the end of the outer ear is ruptured either by a very loud noise such as an explosion or by the insertion of a sharp object too far into the ear. Such a rupture may allow microorganisms into the middle ear that may cause infection. Also, once the tympanic membrane is ruptured, it does not efficiently set the ossicles into vibration, which may cause hearing loss. Problems of the outer ear are generally treated with medication or surgery. Normal hearing is often restored after these treatments.

Middle-Ear Disorders

Most people have experienced **otitis media**, middle-ear infection, at some time. Middle-ear infections are caused by bacteria that cause swelling of the eustachian tube, the passageway that leads from the middle ear to the pharynx, which normally opens when a person swallows. This natural opening allows the pressure in the middle ear space to equalize with the pressure in the environment. However, if the eustachian tube is blocked, the pressure in the middle ear starts to decrease. With the eustachian tube closed, the bacteria have a nice, warm place to grow inside the middle ear space, and this growth eventually produces fluid in the middle ear, which prevents the tympanic membrane and the ossicles from vibrating properly.

Repeated exposure to middle-ear infections may cause a tissue buildup in the middle ear called a *cholesteatoma*. This growth interferes with the vibrations of the tympanic membrane and the ossicles and must be surgically removed. If a person does not seek treatment for a middle-ear infection, the fluid may build up until the tympanic membrane ruptures in order to release the pressure. An infection that is left untreated also may diffuse through the porous mastoid bone, which creates the middle-ear cavity. This is a very serious condition and must be treated immediately before the infection is allowed to spread to the brain. Luckily, diffusion through the mastoid bone rarely occurs if middle-ear infections are promptly treated by antibiotics.

Otosclerosis is a hereditary condition in which there is a growth of bone in the middle ear. Usually, the stapes becomes fixed in place, so it can't transmit vibrations to the inner ear. This was the condition that caused Beethoven to become so deaf that, late in his career, he was unable to hear his own music. Today, this condition can be successfully treated by a surgical procedure called stapedectomy, in which the stapes is replaced with an artificial strut.

SENSORINEURAL HEARING LOSS

Sensorineural hearing loss is caused by a number of factors that have in common their site of action in the inner ear.

Presbycusis

The most common form of sensorineural hearing loss is called **presbycusis**, which means "old hearing" (remember that the equivalent term for vision is *presbyopia*, for "old eye"). This loss of sensitivity, which is greatest at higher frequencies, accompanies aging and affects males more severely than females. Figure 16.28 shows the progression of loss as a function of age. The most common complaint of people with presbycusis is that they have difficulty hearing people talking when there is noise or when other people are talking at the same time. Presbycusis is treated by the amplification provided by hearing aids and by teaching people more effective communication strategies.

Unlike the visual problem of presbyopia, which is an inevitable consequence of aging, presbycusis is apparently caused by factors in addition to aging, since people in preindustrial cultures, who have not been exposed to the noises that accompany industrialization or to drugs that could damage the ear, often do not experience a decrease in high-frequency hearing in old age. This may be why males, who are exposed to more workplace noise than females, as well as to noises associated with hunting and wartime, experience a greater presbycusis effect. Because of its link to environmental conditions, presbycusis is also called sociocusis.

Noise-Induced Hearing Loss

Noise-induced hearing loss occurs when loud noises cause degeneration of the hair cells. This degeneration has been observed in examinations of the cochleas of people who have worked in noisy environments and have willed their ear structures to medical research. Damage to the organ of Corti is often observed in these cases. For example, examination of the cochlea of a man who worked in a steel mill indicated that his organ of Corti had collapsed and no receptor cells remained (Miller, 1974). Apparently, this kind of damage also occurs in people who have exposed themselves to loud music for extended periods of time. Because of this exposure to loud music, rock musicians such as Steven Stills and Peter Townsend have become partially deaf and have urged

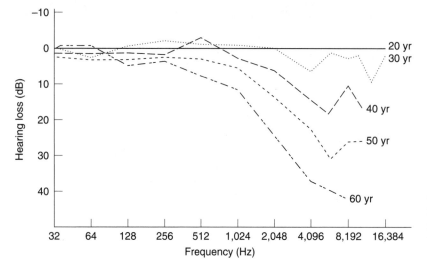

Figure 16.28

Hearing loss in presbycusis as a function of age. All of the curves are plotted relative to the 20-year curve, which is taken as the standard. (Adapted from Bunch, 1929.)

musicians and concertgoers to wear earplugs (Ackerman, 1995). In fact, members of many symphony orchestras, including the Chicago Symphony, wear ear protection to preserve their hearing.

Acoustic trauma caused by implosive noises, such as explosions or machines that create a loud impact, also can result in sensorineural hearing loss. An example is a 21-year-old college student who was in the process of raiding a rival fraternity house when a firecracker exploded in his hand, 15 inches from his right ear. The result was a hearing loss of over 50 dB at frequencies above 3,000 Hz. In addition, the student also experienced a ringing sensation in his ear that was still present two years after the accident (Ward & Glorig, 1961).

Tinnitus

Ringing in the ears, which is known as **tinnitus** (ti-NYE-tus or TIN-ni-tus, from the Latin for "tinkling"), affects more than 36 million Americans, nearly 8 million of them severely. The most common cause of tinnitus is exposure to loud sounds, although this condition also can be caused by certain drugs, ear infections, or food allergies.

Whatever causes tinnitus, it is an extremely debilitating condition. According to Jack Vernon,

director of the Kresge Hearing Research Laboratory at the University of Oregon, tinnitus is the third worst thing that can happen to a person, ranking only below intractable severe pain and intractable severe dizziness. In its most serious form, the constant noise of tinnitus is totally incapacitating, making it impossible for people to maintain their concentration long enough to complete a task and, in some cases, even driving people to suicide.

Is there a cure for tinnitus? Unfortunately, for most people the answer to this question is no. Some people, however, can gain relief by using a device called a **tinnitus masker**. The masker, which is worn in the ear like a hearing aid, produces noise that sounds like a waterfall. This externally produced noise masks the internal noise of tinnitus, making life bearable for some tinnitus sufferers. Also, tinnitus sufferers who use a hearing aid to compensate for a loss of hearing sometimes find that they are unaware of the tinnitus while using the hearing aid and for several hours after taking the hearing aid off.

Meniere's Disease

Another cause of sensorineural hearing loss is **Meniere's disease**, a debilitating condition that is caused by an excessive buildup of the liquid that fills the cochlea and the semicircular canals. The symptoms of the disease include fluctuating hearing loss, tinnitus, and severe vertigo (dizziness) that is often accompanied by nausea and vomiting. By the end of the disease, the vertigo subsides, but some people are left with a sensorineural hearing loss. Physicians attempt a variety of treatments to relieve the symptoms and to treat the increase in fluid, but no one treatment is effective for all patients. The fluctuating hearing loss can be helped by a flexible hearing aid that can be reprogrammed as the hearing loss changes.

Neural Hearing Loss

All of the conditions described above have their effects primarily in the inner ear and on the hair cells. A type of sensorineural hearing loss called neural hearing loss may be caused by tumors on the auditory nerve along the auditory pathways in the brainstem. These tumors generally grow slowly and are benign. However, when they are surgically removed, the patient is often left with some hearing loss. In addition, neural hearing loss also can be caused by tumors or damage further along the auditory pathway.

THE EAR EXAMINATION AND HEARING EVALUATION

We begin our description of the ear examination and hearing evaluation by considering the types of professionals involved in the care of the ear and in helping people maintain their hearing.

Who Examines Ears and Evaluates Hearing?

A number of types of professionals examine the ear and test hearing. The two main categories are otorhinolaryngologists and audiologists.

1. An **otorhinolaryngologist** is an M.D. who has specialized in the treatment of diseases and disorders affecting the ear, nose, and throat, and so the name of this specialty is often abbreviated ENT,

for "ear, nose, and throat." ENT specialists carry out physical examinations of the ear, nose, and throat and provide treatment through drugs and surgery. Some physicians with ENT training specialize in one area. For example, an otologist is an otorhinolaryngologist whose practice is limited to problems involving the auditory and vestibular (balance) system.

2. An **audiologist** is a professional with a master's or doctoral degree who measures the hearing ability of children and adults and identifies the presence and severity of any hearing problems. If a hearing loss is identified, the audiologist can fit the person with a hearing aid to make sound audible and also may work with the person on a long-term basis to teach communication strategies such as speech reading (also called *lipreading*) and other techniques for more effective communication. The audiologist may also recommend assistive devices such as telephone amplifiers and alerting systems. When hearing loss is found in children, the audiologist works with other professionals to make sure that the child develops a communication system (speech or sign language) and has access to appropriate schooling.

ENT specialists and audiologists often work together in dealing with hearing problems and the ear. For example, sometimes a person has a problem that needs medical treatment by a physician and at the same time sees an audiologist who helps the person deal with the hearing loss.

What Happens During an Ear Examination and Hearing Evaluation?

The basic aims of the ear examination and hearing evaluation are to assess hearing and to determine the cause of defective hearing so it can be treated. The basic components of the examination are the following.

Medical History The medical history focuses on hearing problems that the patient now has or may have had in the past, on general medical problems that could affect the person's hearing, on medications that may be responsible for a hearing loss, and on noisy work environments or hobbies, such as hunting, that could affect hearing.

Otoscopy The purpose of otoscopy is to examine the tympanic membrane. To do this, the physician looks into the ear using an **otoscope**, which, much in the manner of the ophthalmoscope used to see the inside of the eye, illuminates the ear and makes it possible to view the illuminated area. The physician inspects the ear canal for foreign objects and signs of disease, notes the color of the tympanic membrane, and inspects it for evidence of tears.

Hearing Evaluation A person's hearing is typically measured in two ways: (1) by *pure-tone audiometry*, which determines an audiogram, the function relating hearing loss to frequency and (2) by *speech audiometry*, which determines a person's ability to recognize words as a function of the intensity of the speech stimulus.

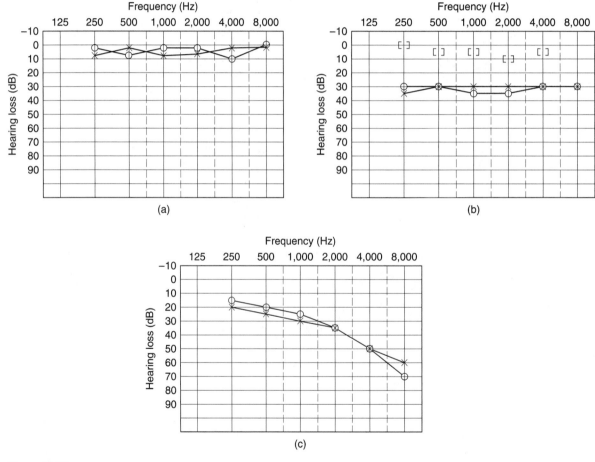

Figure 16.29
Audiograms for people with (a) normal hearing, (b) conductive hearing loss, and (c) sensorineural hearing loss. Symbols: O = right ear; X = left ear; [and] indicate bone conduction for the left and right ears for (b). The bone conduction results for (c) are not shown but followed the same function as the regular audiogram. See text for details.

Pure-tone audiometry is typically measured by a device called an audiometer, which can present pure tone stimuli at different frequencies and intensities. The audiologist varies the intensity of the test tone and instructs the patient to indicate when he or she hears it. When the person's threshold has been determined at a number of frequencies, the audiometer creates an audiogram, a plot of degree of hearing loss (compared to normal) versus frequency. Figure 16.29a shows the audiogram of a patient with normal hearing, and the audiograms in Figures 16.29b and 16.29c are of a patient with about a 30-dB loss of hearing at all frequencies and a patient with high-frequency loss, respectively. Audiograms are plotted so the curve for a person with normal hearing falls between the zero line and 15-dB hearing loss for all frequencies, and any hearing loss is indicated by symbols below the 15-dB hearing loss line.

The pattern of hearing loss sometimes provides information regarding the nature of the patient's problem. For example, the audiogram in Figure 16.29b, in which the hearing loss is approximately the same across the range of hearing, is typical of a patient with a conductive hearing loss. The record in Figure 16.29c, in which hearing becomes progressively worse at high frequencies, is typical of sensorineural hearing loss. Hearing loss due to exposure to noise typically shows a maximum loss at about 4,000 Hz.

The way to differentiate between sensorineural and conductive hearing losses is to compare a person's hearing when the stimulation is presented through the air, as when sound is heard from a loudspeaker or through earphones, and when it is presented by vibrating the mastoid bone, which is located just in back of the ear. Bone conduction is measured by means of an audiometer connected to an electronic vibrator that presents vibrations of different frequencies to the mastoid. The person responds to the bone-vibrated signal in the same way as to air-conducted signals, and thresholds for bone conduction hearing are plotted on the audiogram. If air-conduction hearing is worse than bone-conduction hearing, this result indicates that something must be blocking sound in the outer or middle ear. If the bone conduction and air conduction results are the same, the problem must be beyond the outer and middle ear. The bracket symbols ([and

]) in Figure 16.29b indicate normal bone conduction in the patient with conductive hearing loss.

Another way to measure hearing, which is particularly important in people with sensorineural loss, is to measure their word recognition ability. To do this, the audiologist presents a series of tape-recorded words at different intensities, and the patient is asked to identify the words that are spoken. The result is an articulation function like the one in Figure 16.30, which plots the percentage of words identified correctly versus the intensity of the sound. Patients with conductive losses tend to have articulation functions that are shifted to higher intensities, but, if the intensity is high enough, they can understand the words. Patients with sensorineural loss have functions that are also shifted to higher intensities, but they often fail to reach 100 percent performance. Thus, in sensorineural hearing loss, many words cannot be consistently identified, no matter what their intensity.

Other diagnostic techniques, which we will not describe here, include tympanometry, in which a

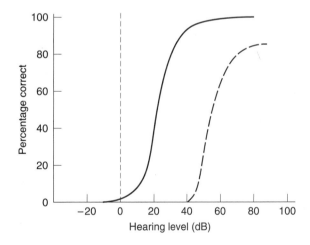

Figure 16.30
Articulation functions for a patient with conductive hearing loss (solid line) and a patient with sensorineural hearing loss (dashed line). Both curves are shifted to the right compared to normal, indicating that the patient requires greater than normal intensity to recognize the words. Also, notice that the curve for sensorineural hearing loss never reaches 100 percent, no matter what the intensity.

device called a **tympanometer** is used to measure how well the tympanic membrane and the middle-ear bones are responding to sound vibrations, and measurement of the acoustic reflex threshold. The **acoustic reflex** is the activation of the middle-ear muscles in response to high-intensity sounds. This activation stiffens the chain of ossicles and dampens their vibration, perhaps to protect the inner ear from being overstimulated. The acoustic reflex can be measured with the tympanometer.

In addition to these diagnostic techniques that access hearing and the functioning of structures in the ear, there are also tests that measure the electrical responses of the auditory nerve and the auditory cortex, which are important if there is a hearing loss even though the structures of the ear seem to be operating normally. These electrophysiological measures can therefore be useful in determining the location of sensorineural hearing loss.

MANAGING HEARING LOSS

Hearing loss covers a very large continuum, from the individual with mild hearing loss to someone who is totally deaf and cannot make use of sound for the purpose of communication (Figure 16.31). Different individuals need different types of technology and strategies in order to communicate effectively.

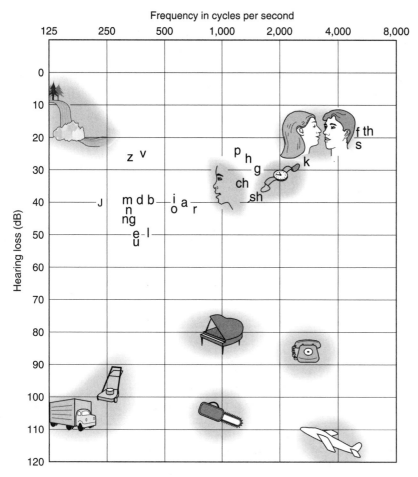

Figure 16.31

Audiogram showing the frequencies and degree of hearing loss that cause difficulties in the perception of various environmental sounds. The letters represent spoken sounds. For example, a person with a hearing loss of 100 dB around 250 Hz will not be able to hear the lawn mower. (From Northern & Downs, 1978.)

The majority of individuals with conductive hearing loss receive medical treatment for their condition, and the hearing loss is eliminated as soon as the disease process is eliminated. Patients who cannot or do not choose to take advantage of surgical or medical procedures may use an amplification system such as a hearing aid to help them hear. As we noted when describing word recognition tests, as long as the sound is loud enough, these patients can hear quite well.

Individuals with sensorineural hearing loss generally use some kind of amplification. Hearing aids have changed drastically since the beginning of the 1990s, with the development of smaller hearing aids that can be automatically programmed to work effectively in different listening situations. Almost all individuals with sensorineural hearing loss can benefit from a hearing aid, which is fitted by an audiologist.

Hearing-impaired individuals also may receive training in speech reading (often called lipreading) and communication strategies. This type of training is often called **aural rehabilitation** and is conducted by an audiologist. Some individuals have so much hearing loss that they cannot benefit from amplification. Many of these individuals consider themselves part of the deaf culture and are happy to communicate using sign language. However, most people who lose their hearing after being able to hear for the majority of their lives wish to continue to be connected to the hearing world. For these people, a new technology called the cochlear implant is available.

A **cochlear implant** is a device in which electrodes are inserted in the cochlea to create hearing by electrically stimulating the auditory nerve fibers. This device offers the hope of regaining some hearing to some people who have lost their hearing because of damaged hair cells, so that hearing aids, which can amplify sound but can't cause that sound to be translated into electrical signals in the hair cells, are ineffective.

The cochlear implant bypasses the damaged hair cells and stimulates auditory nerve fibers directly. The following are the basic components of a cochlear implant (Figure 16.32):

- The microphone (1), which is worn behind the person's ear, receives the speech signal, transforms it into electrical signals, and sends these signals to the speech processor.

- The speech processor (2), which looks like a small transistor radio, shapes the signal generated by the microphone to emphasize the information needed for the perception of speech by splitting the range of frequencies received by the microphone into a number of frequency bands. These signals are sent, in the form of an electrical code, from the processor to the transmitter. Newer versions of cochlear implants now package the entire speech processor in what looks like a behind-the-ear hearing aid.

- The transmitter (3), mounted on the mastoid bone, just behind the ear, transmits the coded signals received from the processor through the skin to the receiver.

- The receiver (4) is surgically mounted on the mastoid bone, beneath the skin. It picks up the coded signals from the transmitter and converts the code into signals that are sent to electrodes implanted inside the cochlea (5).

The implant makes use of Békésy's observation, which we described in Chapter 10, that there is a tonotopic map of frequencies on the cochlea, high frequencies being represented by activity near the base of the cochlea and low frequencies being represented by activity at the apex of the cochlea. The most widely used implants therefore have a multichannel design, which uses a number of electrodes to stimulate the cochlea at different places along its length, depending on the frequencies in the stimuli received by the microphone. This electrical stimulation of the cochlea then causes signals to be sent to the auditory area of the cortex, and hearing results.

What does a person using this system hear? The answer to this question depends on the person. Most patients are able to recognize a few everyday sounds, such as horns honking, doors closing, and water running. In addition, many patients are able to perceive speech. In the best cases, patients can perceive speech on the telephone, but it is more common for cochlear-implant patients to use the sounds perceived from their implant in conjunction with speech reading. In one test, 24 patients scored 54 percent on a

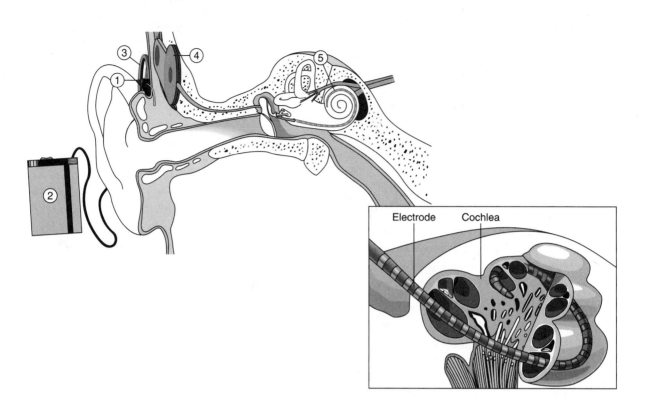

Figure 16.32
Cochlear implant device. See text for details.

Electrode   Cochlea

test of speech reading alone and 83 percent when speech reading was combined with sound from the implant. In addition, the implant enabled patients to track speech much more rapidly—16 words per minute using speech reading alone, and 44 words per minute with speech reading plus the implant (Brown, Dowell, & Clark, 1987; Owens, 1989). In another test it was found that deaf children who received a cochlear implant before the age of 5 years were able to learn to produce speech more easily than children who received the implant when they were older (Tye-Murray, Spencer, & Woodworth, 1995).

As of 1995, over 10,000 people had received cochlear implants. The best results occur for postlingually deaf individuals—people who were able to perceive speech before they became deaf. These people are most likely to be able to understand speech with the aid of the implant because they already know how

to connect the sounds of speech with specific meanings. Thus, these people's ability to perceive speech often improves with time, as they again learn to link sounds with meanings.

To place a more human face on the effects of the cochlear implant operation, we will end by relating the story of Gil McDougald, the standout New York Yankee infielder who played in eight World Series in the 1950s. McDougald, who in 1995 was 66 years old, had gradually gone deaf in both ears after an accident in which he was hit by a line drive during batting practice in 1955. He was almost completely deaf for about 20 years, being able to make out some sounds but no intelligible words. His deafness cut him off from other people. He could no longer talk on the telephone, and he stopped attending "oldtimers'" functions with ex-teammates like Yogi Berra and Mickey Mantle because he was unable to communicate with them. At family functions, he would leave the table because of his frustration at not being able to hear what was going on.

McDougald heard about the implant operation and, in 1995, called implant specialist Noel Cohen at New York University Medical Center. After testing had determined that he was a good candidate for an implant, he underwent the operation. Six weeks after the operation, he went to see Betsy Bromberg, an audiologist, to have the apparatus programmed and activated (Figure 16.33). The following is an excerpt from a newspaper account of what transpired in her office (Berkow, 1995):

> In the office, McDougald sat at a desk with a computer on it. Bromberg sat across from him. His wife, Lucille, and daughter, Denise, sat within arm's length.
>
> A small microphone was set behind his ear, and a transmitter with a magnet was placed over the site of the implant. A cable was extended from the microphone to a speech processor the size of a hand calculator that can be worn on a belt or placed in a breast pocket.
>
> Then Bromberg began the test that would determine how much McDougald's hearing had improved.

Bromberg covered her mouth with a sheet of paper so he could not lip read.

> "Tell me," she said, "what you hear."
>
> She said, "aah." He hesitated. "Aah," he answered. She went, "eeeh." He said, "eeeh."
>
> "Hello," she said. "Hello," he said. "I'm going to count to five," she said. "Do you hear me?"
>
> "Oh yeah!" he said. "Wow! This is exciting!"
>
> His wife and daughter stared, hardly moving.
>
> Bromberg wrote down four words on a pad of paper and said them: "football," "sidewalk," "cowboy," and "outside." "Now Gil," she said, "I'm going to mix up the word order and cover my mouth and you tell me the word I say."
>
> "Cowboy," she said. "Cowboy," he said. "Outside," she said. "Outside," he said. And then he began to flush. Tears welled in his eyes.
>
> "This is the first time in . . ." Lucille said and then choked up, unable to finish her sentence. "It's unbelievable."
>
> "It's a miracle," said Denise.
>
> Both began crying.
>
> Bromberg said, "It's O.K. Everybody cries at times like this." And then mother and daughter embraced. And they hugged Gil. And they hugged Bromberg, and hugged the director of the unit, Susan Waltzman, who had been observing. . . .

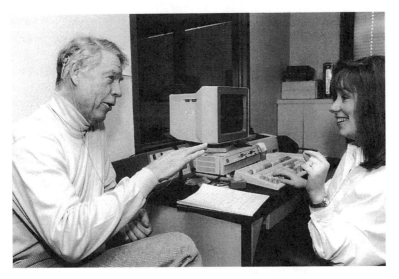

Figure 16.33
Gil McDougald trying out his cochlear implant for the first time, with audiologist Betsy Bromberg. In the office, McDougald sat at a desk with a computer on it. Bromberg sat across from him. His wife, Lucille, and daughter, Denise, sat within arm's length.

Last night, the McDougald household was bursting with children and grandchildren. "Everyone," said Lucille McDougald, "has come to watch grandpa hear." (p. B8)

Cochlear implantation is an impressive demonstration of how basic research yields practical benefits. Advances such as this, which have proven to be effective in bringing deaf adults and children into the world of hearing (Kiefer et al., 1998; Tye-Murray et al., 1995), are the end result of discoveries that began in perception or physiology laboratories many years earlier. In this case, it was George von Békésy's research on how the vibration of the basilar membrane depends on the frequency of the sound that provided the knowledge about the operation of the ear that made implants possible. Systems also have been proposed for restoring vision to people who are blind, by stimulating their visual cortex (Dobelle, 1977; Dobelle, Mladejovsky, & Girvin, 1974; Dobelle et al., 1976), and for guiding blind people through the environment by applying the principles of auditory localization to the design of a "personal guidance system" (see Chapter 11, page 379).

It is clear that the study of both the psychophysics and the physiology of perception has yielded not only knowledge about how our senses operate but also ways to apply this knowledge to create new perceptual worlds for people like Gil McDougald and countless others.

Decrease in Cortical Function Due to Aging

As people age they experience decreases in visual acuity, contrast sensitivity, motion sensitivity, and wavelength sensitivity. We've seen that some of these decreases can be attributed to problems at the "front end" of the visual system, such as cataracts, the clouding of the lens that causes blurred vision. Another problem that occurs in the eye is presbyopia, the loss of the ability to accommodate. Both of these problems involve a disruption of the processes that normally focus light as it enters the eye. However, these problems cannot totally explain the degree of decline in acuity and other functions that occurs with aging. To understand the overall effect of the aging process in vision, we need to consider how aging affects the brain.

Matthew Schmolesky and coworkers (2000) investigated cortical changes due to aging, by recording from neurons in area V1 of the monkey and determining how the neurons' tuning for orientation changes with age. They found that the fairly narrow orientation tuning observed in most of the neurons of the young monkeys was less common in the older monkeys.

Figure 16.34 shows the orientation tuning for two neurons recorded from old monkeys. Curve (a) is a narrowly tuned neuron and curve (b) is a broadly tuned neuron. Only 42 percent of the neurons in the older monkeys were narrowly tuned, compared to 90 percent in young monkeys. Schmolesky and coworkers suggest that as monkeys age they lose the inhibitory connections between neurons that are needed to create orientation tuning.

What might be going on for the old monkeys may be similar to what happens when kittens or young monkeys are raised in environments that contain just one orientation (see page 100). In these selective rearing experiments, neurons that normally respond to the orientations that are absent lose their ability to respond to those orientations. A similar thing may be occurring in aging, except that the properties that change rapidly when young animals are visually deprived or reared in selective environments change slowly, over a much longer period of time, during aging.

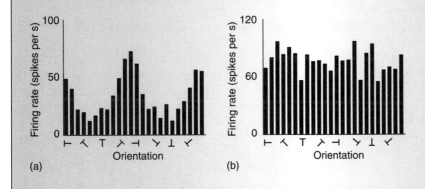

Figure 16.34
Orientation tuning of neurons in area V1 of an older monkey: (a) a tuned neuron that responds better to some orientations than others and (b) a nonselective neuron that has broad tuning, responding almost equally well to all orientations. (From Schmolesky et al., 2000.)

DEAFNESS AND VISUAL ATTENTION

There is evidence supporting the idea that the senses are linked to each other during development (Smith & Katz, 1996). According to this idea, both seeing and hearing develop in tandem with one another, so that if one sense becomes deficient during development, it is possible that the other will be deficient as well. Alexandra Quittner and her coworkers (1994) tested the idea that loss of hearing causes a change in the capacity for visual attention by testing three groups of children, a deaf group, a deaf group who had received cochlear implants, and a group without hearing impairment. Subjects in each of these groups were shown a sequence of numbers presented visually, one after another, and were told to push a button every time they saw a 9 after a 1. This task, which requires that the subject pay close attention to the numbers at all times, is used to identify children with serious attentional deficits.

The results of this experiment, shown in Figure 16.35, supported the idea of a link between vision and hearing. The deaf subjects had the poorest performance, those with the cochlear implant did better, and the hearing subjects performed best of all. Thus, the better the subjects could hear, the better they performed on a task that was purely visual.

Quittner checked this result in another way by testing the visual attention of subjects after they had been using a cochlear implant for 10 months and then testing them again at 18 months. When they compared their performance to a group of deaf subjects who were tested at the same time intervals, they found that there was no difference at 10 months but that by 18 months the cochlear implant group was less likely to commit "false alarms"—that is they were less likely to say the target (the 9) was there when it actually wasn't.

Why should deaf children be more likely to be distracted from a visual attention task than are chil-

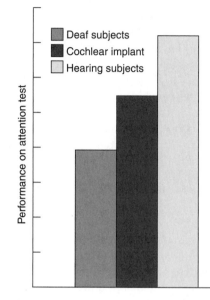

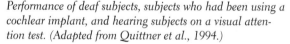

Figure 16.35
Performance of deaf subjects, subjects who had been using a cochlear implant, and hearing subjects on a visual attention test. (Adapted from Quittner et al., 1994.)

dren with normal hearing or children who have some hearing, because of a cochlear implant? Although we don't know the answer to this question, we can guess that it may have something to do with how the ability to hear might affect attention in general. A person hears a sound and turns his head toward it. A person in a crowded room that is pulsating with many conversations directs her attention to the one person with whom she is talking. A person sitting in a coffee house alive with conversation and music has learned to focus his attention on the book he is reading. Each of these examples involves both the focusing of attention and hearing. Because deaf people do not have any of these experiences, they are missing opportunities that might help them become better at focusing their attention. Thus, the loss of ability in one sense might in an indirect way cause a decrease in a person's ability in another sense.

SUMMARY TABLE 16.2

Conductive Hearing Loss

Conductive hearing loss is associated with reduced transmission of sound stimuli into the cochlea. Outer-ear disorders include damage due to putting objects in the ear, infection, and rupturing of the tympanic membrane. Middle-ear disorders include the infection otitis media, a condition in which tissue builds up called cholesteatoma, and otosclerosis, a hereditary condition in which there is a growth of bone in the middle ear.

Sensorineural Hearing Loss

Sensorineural hearing loss is associated with damage to the inner ear. Presbycusis is a loss of high-frequency sensitivity that is connected with aging. Noise-induced hearing loss occurs when loud noises cause degeneration of the hair cells. This can occur due to long-term exposure or implosive noises such as explosions. Tinnitus is a ringing in the ears that can be extremely debilitating. Meniere's disease is caused by excessive buildup of the liquid that fills the cochlea. All of the sensorineural conditions described above affect the inner ear and the hair cells. Neural hearing loss describes conditions caused by damage to the auditory nerve or other auditory system structures.

The Ear Examination and Hearing Evaluation

Ear examinations are carried out by otorhinolaryngologists (ear, nose, and throat specialists) and audiologists. The ear examination and hearing evaluation consist of the following components: medical history; otoscopy, to check the integrity of the tympanic membrane; hearing evaluation, measured by pure-tone audiometry or word recognition tests; and tympanometry, to check the response of the tympanic membrane.

Managing Hearing Loss

Hearing loss can be managed by using hearing aids and training in speech reading. For people whose hair cells are damaged, installation of a cochlear implant is an option for partially restoring hearing.

Plasticity: Decrease in Cortical Function Due to Aging

A number of visual functions decrease as a consequence of aging. The cause of this decrease can be traced to problems with the eye and also to changes in the visual cortex. Research on monkeys shows that many of the neurons in area V1 of older monkeys have lost their orientation tuning.

Across the Senses: Deafness and Visual Attention

In a test of visual attention, deaf subjects had the poorest performance, those with cochlear implants did better, and hearing subjects performed best of all. The reason for this may be that in hearing subjects sound often helps orient visual attention.

STUDY QUESTIONS

How Can Vision Become Impaired?

1. What are the four major types of problems that can cause poor vision? (546)

Focusing Problems

Myopia

2. What is myopia? How are parallel rays of light brought to a focus in the myopic eye? What are the two possible causes for this incorrect focusing? (547)

3. How can we cause the point of focus to fall on the retina of a myopic eye without using corrective lenses? (547)

4. What is the far point? Where does the focus point fall if an object is farther from the eye than the far point? At the far point? Closer to the eye than the far point? Can a myope bring faraway objects into focus by accommodation? (548)

5. How must a corrective lens bend light so that a myope can see clearly? (548)

6. What is a diopter? Be able to calculate the correction in diopters if you are given the distance of the far point. (548)

7. What are two surgical procedures involving lasers that can correct myopic vision? (549)

Hyperopia

8. What is hyperopia? How are parallel rays of light brought to a focus in the hyperopic eye? How is this condition corrected? (550)

Presbyopia

9. What is presbyopia? What is the near point? What happens to the near point as a person ages? (550)

Astigmatism

10. What is astigmatism? What causes it? How is this condition corrected? (550)

Decreased Transmission of Light

What Is Blindness?

11. What is the legal definition of blindness? Can a person who is legally blind have 20/20 vision? Explain your answer. (551)

Corneal Disease and Injury

12. The cornea is responsible for about _____ percent of the eye's focusing power. (552)

13. What can cause corneal diseases or injury? What is the first treatment for corneal disease or injury? If this treatment fails, what is the next alternative? (552)

14. Describe a corneal transplant operation. Exactly what is transplanted? What is the success rate of corneal transplants? (552)

Clouding of the Lens (Cataract)

15. What is a cataract? What is the most common kind of cataract, and what percentage of people over the age of 65 have cataracts? What percentage of cataracts are serious enough to interfere with a person's normal activities? What percentage require surgery? (553)

16. Describe a cataract operation. (553)

17. When we remove the lens in a cataract operation, we decrease the focusing power of the eye. Why are glasses an unacceptable solution to this problem? What is the solution to this problem? (553)

Damage to the Retina

Diabetic Retinopathy

18. What is the tissue upon which the retina rests? (554)

19. Describe what happens to the retinal circulation in mild and severe cases of diabetic retinopathy. (554)

20. Describe a procedure that has been used to stop neovascularization. (555)

21. What is a vitrectomy operation? What does it accomplish? (555)

Macular Degeneration

22. Describe the mild and severe types of macular degeneration. What is a treatment that can be successfully used in some patients? (555)

Detached Retina

23. What is a detached retina? What are two reasons that a detached retina can affect vision? (556)

24. Describe the procedure used to reattach a detached retina. (556)

Hereditary Retinal Degeneration

25. What is retinitis pigmentosa? (557)

Optic Nerve Damage: Glaucoma

26. Describe the two forms of glaucoma. How are these two types treated? (557)

The Eye Examination

Who Examines Eyes?

27. Describe the training and capabilities of ophthalmologists, optometrists, and opticians. (558)

What Happens During an Eye Exam?

28. What are the four basic aims of an eye examination? (559)

29. How is visual acuity determined? What does it mean to say that a person has 20/200 vision? (559)

30. What is visual perimetry? (560)

31. What is the purpose of the refraction part of the eye examination? What are the two steps in the refraction exam? (561)

32. What is the purpose of the external eye examination? (561)

33. What is the purpose of the slit-lamp examination? (561)

34. What does the tonometry exam measure? For what disease does it test? What is the basic principle behind the tonometry exam? (561)

35. What is the basic principle behind an ophthalmoscope? Be able to draw a diagram of an ophthalmoscope. (563)

36. What does the examiner look for in an ophthalmoscopic exam? (563)

37. What is fluorescein angiography, and what does it accomplish? (564)

How Can Hearing Become Impaired?

38. What is the difference between a hearing impairment and a hearing handicap? (564)

39. What are the four types of things that can go wrong in the auditory system? (565)

Conductive Hearing Loss

40. What is conductive hearing loss? (566)

41. Describe outer-ear disorders and middle-ear disorders. (566)

Sensorineural Hearing Loss

42. What is sensorineural hearing loss? (567)

43. What is the most common form of sensorineural hearing loss? Describe the role of aging and environmental exposure in causing this condition. (567)

44. Where is the main damage in noise-induced hearing loss? (567)

45. What is tinnitus? How can it be treated? (568)

46. Describe Meniere's disease. (568)

47. What is neural hearing loss? (569)

The Ear Examination and Hearing Evaluation

Who Examines Ears and Evaluates Hearing?

48. Describe the training and capabilities of otorhinolaryngologists and audiologists. (569)

What Happens During an Ear Examination and Hearing Evaluation?

49. What is the purpose of otoscopy, and how is it conducted? (570)

50. Describe pure-tone audiometry. What is an audiogram? Describe how the pattern of hearing loss can provide information regarding the nature of a patient's problem. (570)

51. Describe how vibration of the mastoid bone can be used to differentiate between sensorineural hearing loss and conductive hearing loss. (571)

52. What is the articulation function? (571)

53. Describe tympanometry and the acoustic reflex. (571)

Managing Hearing Loss

54. What types of treatment are used for conductive hearing loss and sensorineural hearing loss? (572)

55. What is aural rehabilitation? (573)

56. Describe how a cochlear implant operates. How successful have cochlear implants been in restoring hearing? (573)

The Plasticity of Perception: Decrease in Cortical Function Due to Aging

57. What kinds of decreases in vision occur due to aging? (577)

58. How do problems in the eye contribute to these visual decreases? (577)

59. What is the evidence from monkey recording experiments that aging affects neurons in area V1? (577)

Across the Senses: Deafness and Visual Attention

60. Describe the experiment of Quittner and coworkers that tested the idea that a loss of hearing causes a change in the capacity for visual attention. (578)

61. Describe Quittner's other experiment in which she used subjects who had been using a cochlear implant. (578)

62. What is a possible explanation for the fact that deaf children are more easily distracted from a visual attention task than children with normal hearing or children with a cochlear implant? (578)

APPENDIX A

SIGNAL DETECTION: PROCEDURE AND THEORY

In Chapter 1, we surveyed various psychophysical methods that can be used to determine an observer's absolute threshold. For example, using the method of constant stimuli to randomly present tones of different intensities, we can determine the intensity to which the subject reports "I hear it" 50 percent of the time. But can the experimenter be confident that this intensity truly represents the subject's sensory threshold? There are reasons to question the idea of an absolute measure of sensitivity, called the threshold, which can be measured by the classic psychophysical methods. We will first discuss why the idea of an absolute threshold has been questioned and will then describe a way of thinking about measuring sensitivity, called signal detection theory, that takes into account both the characteristics of the sensory system and the characteristics of the observer.

IS THERE AN ABSOLUTE THRESHOLD?

To understand why there might be reason to question the idea of an absolute threshold, let's consider a hypothetical experiment. In this experiment, we use the method of constant stimuli to measure two subjects' thresholds for hearing a tone. We pick five different tone intensities, present them in random order, and ask our subjects to say "yes" if they hear the tone and "no" if they don't hear it. Our first subject, Laurie, thinks about these instructions and decides that she wants to appear supersensitive to the tones; since she knows that tones are being presented on every trial, she will answer "yes" if there is even the slightest possibility that she hears the tone. We could call Laurie a liberal responder: She is more willing to say "Yes, I hear the tone" than to report that no tone was present. Our second subject, Chris, is given the same instructions, but Chris is different from Laurie; she doesn't care about being supersensitive. In fact, Chris wants to be totally sure that she hears the tone before saying "yes." We could call Chris a conservative responder: She is not willing to report that she hears the tone unless it is very strong.

The results of this hypothetical experiment are shown in Figure A.1. Laurie gives many more "yes" responses than Chris and therefore ends up with a lower threshold. But given what we know about Laurie and Chris, should we conclude that Laurie is more sensitive to the tones than Chris? It could be that their actual sensitivity to the tones is exactly the

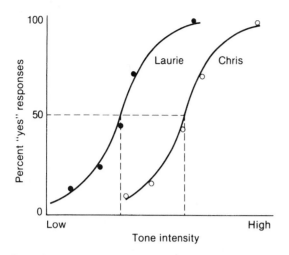

Figure A.1

Data from experiments in which the threshold for hearing a tone is determined for Laurie and Chris by means of the method of constant stimuli. These data indicate that Laurie's threshold is lower than Chris's. But is Laurie really more sensitive to the tone than Chris, or does she just appear to be more sensitive because she is a more liberal responder? Signal detection theory helps provide an answer to this question.

same, but Laurie's apparently lower threshold is simply due to her being more willing than Chris to report that she heard a tone. A way to describe this difference between the two subjects is that each has a different **response criterion**. Laurie's response criterion is low (she says "yes" if there is the slightest chance there is a tone present), whereas Chris's response criterion is high (she says "yes" only when she is sure that she heard the tone). That factors other than the subject's sensitivity to the signal may influence the results of a psychophysical experiment has caused many researchers to doubt the validity of the absolute threshold, as determined by these psychophysical experiments, and to create new procedures based on a theory called **signal detection theory (SDT)**.

In the next section, we will describe the basic procedure of a signal detection experiment and will show how we can tell whether Chris and Laurie are, in fact, equally sensitive to the tone even though their response criteria are very different. After describing the signal detection experiment, we will look at the theory on which the experiment is based.

A Signal Detection Experiment

Remember that, in a psychophysical procedure such as the method of constant stimuli, at least five different tone intensities are presented and that a stimulus is presented on every trial. In a signal detection experiment we use only a single low-intensity tone that is difficult to hear, and we present this tone on some of the trials and present no tone at all on the rest of the trials. Thus, a signal detection experiment differs from a classical psychophysical experiment in two ways: In a signal detection experiment (1) only one stimulus intensity is presented and (2) on some of the trials, no stimulus is presented. Let's consider the results of such an experiment, using Laurie as our subject. We present the tone for 100 trials and no tone for 100 trials, mixing the tone and no-tone trials at random. Laurie's results are as follows:

When the tone is presented, Laurie

- Says "yes" on 90 trials. This correct response—saying "yes" when a stimulus is present—is called a **hit** in signal detection terminology.

- Says "no" on 10 trials. This incorrect response—saying "no" when a stimulus is present—is called a **miss.**

When no tone is presented, Laurie

- Says "yes" on 40 trials. This incorrect response—saying "yes" when there is no stimulus—is called a **false alarm.**

- Says "no" on 60 trials. This correct response—saying "no" when there is no stimulus—is called a **correct rejection.**

These results are not very surprising, given that we know Laurie has a low criterion and likes to say "yes" a lot. This gives her a high hit rate of 90 percent but also causes her to say "yes" on many trials when no tone is present at all, so her 90 percent hit rate is accompanied by a 40 percent false-alarm rate. If we do a similar experiment on Chris, who has a higher criterion and therefore says "yes" much less often, we find that she has a lower hit rate (say, 60 percent) but also a lower false-alarm rate (say, 10 percent). Note that, although Laurie and Chris say "yes" on numerous trials on which no stimulus is presented, that result would not be predicted by classical threshold theory. Classical theory would say "no stimulus, no response," but that is clearly not the case here.

By adding a new wrinkle to our signal detection experiment, we can obtain another result that would not be predicted by classical threshold theory. Without changing the tone's intensity at all, we can cause Laurie and Chris to change their percentages of hits and false alarms. We do this by manipulating each subject's motivation by means of **payoffs.** Let's look at how payoffs might influence Chris's responding. Remember that Chris is a conservative responder who is hesitant to say "yes." But being clever experimenters, we can make Chris say "yes'" more frequently by adding some financial inducements to the experiment. "Chris," we say, "we are going to reward you for making correct responses and are going to penalize you for making incorrect responses by using the following payoff scale:

Hit:	Win $100
Correct rejection:	Win $10
False alarm:	Lose $10
Miss:	Lose $10

What would you do if you were in Chris's position? Being smart, you analyze the payoffs and realize that the way to make money is to say "yes" more. You can lose $10 if a "yes" response results in a false alarm, but this small loss is more than counterbalanced by the $100 you can win for a hit. While you don't decide to say "yes" on every trial—after all, you want to be honest with the experimenter about whether or not you heard the tone—you do decide to stop being so conservative. *You decide to change your criterion for saying "yes."* The results of this experiment are interesting. Chris becomes a more liberal

responder and says "yes" a lot more, responding with 98 percent hits and 90 percent false alarms.

This result is plotted as data point L (for "liberal" response) in Figure A.2, a plot of the percentage of hits versus the percentage of false alarms. The solid curve going through point L is called a **receiver operating characteristic (ROC) curve.** We will see why the ROC curve is important in a moment, but first let's see how we determine the other points on the curve. Determining the other points on the ROC curve is simple: All we have to do is to change the payoffs. We can make Chris raise her criterion and therefore respond more conservatively by means of the following payoffs:

Hit:	Win $10
Correct rejection:	Win $100
False alarm:	Lose $10
Miss:	Lose $10

This schedule of payoffs offers a great inducement to respond conservatively, since there is a big reward for saying "no" when no tone is presented. Chris's criterion is therefore shifted to a much higher

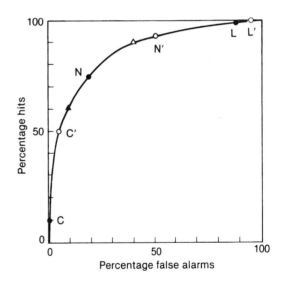

Figure A.2

A receiver operating characteristic (ROC curve). The fact that Chris's and Laurie's data points all fall on this curve means that they have the same sensitivity to the tone.

level, so Chris now returns to her conservative ways and says "yes" only if she is quite certain that a tone is presented; otherwise she says "no." The result of this newfound conservatism is a hit rate of only 10 percent and a minuscule false-alarm rate of 1 percent, indicated by point C (for "conservative" response) on the ROC curve. We should note that, although Chris hits on only 10 percent of the trials in which a tone is presented, she scores a phenomenal 99 percent correct rejections on trials in which a tone is not presented. (This result follows from the fact that, if there are 100 trials in which no tone is presented, then correct rejections + false alarms = 100. Since there was one false alarm, there must be 99 correct rejections.)

Chris, by this time, is rich and decides to put a down payment on the Miata she's been dreaming about. (So far she's won $8,980 in the first experiment and $9,090 in the second experiment, for a total of $18,070! To be sure you understand how the payoff system works, check this calculation yourself. Remember that the signal was presented on 100 trials and was not presented on 100 trials.) However, we point out that she may need a little extra cash to have a CD player installed in her car, so she agrees to stick around for one more experiment. We now use the following neutral schedule of payoffs:

Hit:	Win $10
Correct rejection:	Win $10
False alarm:	Lose $10
Miss:	Lose $10

and obtain point N on the ROC curve: 75 percent hits and 20 percent false alarms. Chris wins $1,100 more and becomes the proud owner of a Miata with a CD player, and we are the proud owners of the world's most expensive ROC curve. (Do not, at this point, go to the psychology department in search of the nearest signal detection experiment. In real life, the payoffs are quite a bit less than in our hypothetical example.)

Chris's ROC curve shows that factors other than sensitivity to the stimulus determine the subject's response. Remember that in all of our experiments the intensity of the tone has remained constant. The only thing we have changed is the subject's criterion.

However, in doing this, we have succeeded in drastically changing the subject's responses.

What does the ROC curve tell us in addition to demonstrating that subjects will change how they respond to an unchanging stimulus? Remember, at the beginning of this discussion, we said that a signal detection experiment can tell us whether or not Chris and Laurie are equally sensitive to the tone. The beauty of signal detection theory is that the subject's sensitivity is indicated by the shape of the ROC curve, so if experiments on two subjects result in identical ROC curves, their sensitivities must be equal. (This conclusion is not obvious from our discussion so far. We will explain below why the shape of the ROC curve is related to the subject's sensitivity.) If we repeat the above experiments on Laurie, we get the following results (data points L', N' and C' in Figure A.2):

Liberal payoff:
Hits = 99 percent
False alarms = 95 percent

Neutral payoff:
Hits =92 percent
False alarms = 50 percent

Conservative payoff:
Hits = 50 percent
False alarms = 6 percent

The data points for Laurie's results are shown by the open circles in Figure A.2. Note that although these points are different from Chris's, they fall on the same ROC curve as do Chris's. We have also plotted the data points for the first experiments we did on Laurie (open triangle) and Chris (filled triangle) before we introduced payoffs. These points also fall on the ROC curve.

That Chris's and Laurie's data both fall on the same ROC curve indicates their equal sensitivity to the tones, thus confirming our suspicion that the method of constant stimuli misled us into thinking that Laurie is more sensitive, when the real reason for her apparently greater sensitivity is her lower criterion for saying "yes."

Before we leave our signal detection experiment, it is important to note that signal detection procedures can be used without the elaborate payoffs that we described for Chris and Laurie. Much briefer procedures, which we will describe below, can be used to determine whether differences in the responses of different subjects are due to differences in threshold or to differences in the subjects' response criteria.

What does signal detection theory tell us about functions such as the spectral sensitivity curves (Figure 2.23) and the audibility function (Figure 10.9), which are usually determined using one of the classical psychophysical methods? When the classical methods are used to determine functions such as the spectral sensitivity curve and the audibility function, it is usually assumed that the subject's criterion remains constant throughout the experiment, so that the function measured is due not to changes in the subject's criterion but to changes in the wavelength or some other physical property of the stimulus. This is a good assumption, since changing the wavelength of the stimulus probably has little or no effect on factors such as motivation, which would shift the subject's criterion. Furthermore, experiments such as the one for determining the spectral sensitivity curve usually use highly practiced subjects who are trained to give stable results. Thus, even though the idea of an "absolute threshold" may not be strictly correct, classical psychophysical experiments run under well-controlled conditions have remained an important tool for measuring the relationship between stimuli and perception.

SIGNAL DETECTION THEORY

We will now discuss the theoretical basis for the signal detection experiments we have just described. Our purpose is to explain the theoretical bases underlying two ideas: (1) The percentage of hits and false alarms depends on the subject's criterion and (2) a subject's sensitivity to a stimulus is indicated by the shape of the subject's ROC curve. We will begin by describing two of the key concepts of signal detection theory (SDT): signal and noise. (See Swets, 1964.)

Signal and Noise

The **signal** is the stimulus presented to the subject. Thus, in the signal detection experiment we described above, the signal is the tone. The **noise** is all the other stimuli in the environment, and since the signal is usually very faint, noise can sometimes be mistaken for the signal. Seeing what appears to be a flicker of light in a completely dark room is an example of visual noise. Seeing light when there is none is what we have been calling a false alarm, according to signal detection theory. False alarms are caused by the noise. In the experiment we described above, hearing a tone on a trial in which no tone was presented is an example of auditory noise.

Let's now consider a typical signal detection experiment, in which a signal is presented on some trials and no signal is presented on the other trials. Signal detection theory describes this procedure not in terms of presenting a signal or no signal, but in terms of presenting signal plus noise (S + N) or noise (N). That is, the noise is always present, and on some trials, we add a signal. Either condition can result in the perceptual effect of hearing a tone. A false alarm occurs if the subject says "yes" on a noise trial, and a hit occurs if the subject says "yes" on a signal-plus-noise trial. Now that we have defined signal and noise, we introduce the idea of probability distributions for noise and signal plus noise.

Probability Distributions

Figure A.3 shows two probability distributions. The probability distribution on the left represents the probability that a given perceptual effect will be caused by noise (N), and the one on the right represents the probability that a given perceptual effect will be caused by signal plus noise (S + N). The key to understanding these distributions is to realize that the value labeled "Perceptual effect" on the horizontal axis is what the subject experiences on each trial. Thus, in an experiment in which the subject is asked to indicate whether or not a tone is present, the perceptual effect is the perceived loudness of the tone. Remember that in an SDT experiment the tone always has the same intensity. The loudness of the

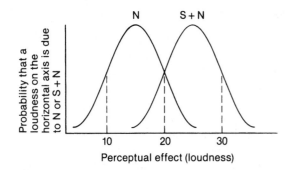

Figure A.3
Probability distributions for noise alone (N), on the left, and for signal plus noise (S + N), on the right. The probability that any given perceptual effect is caused by the noise (no signal is presented) or by the signal plus noise (signal is presented) can be determined by finding the value of the perceptual effect on the horizontal axis and extending a vertical line up from that value. The place where that line intersects the (N) and (S + N) distributions indicates the probability that the perceptual effect was caused by (N) or by (S + N).

tone, however, can vary from trial to trial. The subject perceives different loudnesses on different trials, because of either trial-to-trial changes in attention or changes in the state of the subject's auditory system.

The probability distributions tell us what the chances are that a given loudness of tone is due to (N) or to (S + N). For example, let's assume that a subject hears a tone with a loudness of 10 on one of the trials of a signal detection experiment. By extending a vertical dashed line up from 10 on the "Perceptual effect" axis in Figure A.3, we see that the probability that a loudness of 10 is due to (S + N) is extremely low, since the distribution for (S + N) is essentially zero at this loudness. There is, however, a fairly high probability that a loudness of 10 is due to (N), since the (N) distribution is fairly high at this point.

Let's now assume that, on another trial, the subject perceives a loudness of 20. The probability distributions indicate that, when the tone's loudness is 20, it is equally probable that this loudness is due to (N) or to (S + N). We can also see from Figure A.3 that a tone with a perceived loudness of 30 would have a high probability of being caused by (S + N) and only a small probability of being caused by (N).

Now that we understand the curves of Figure A.3, we can appreciate the problem confronting the subject. On each trial, she has to decide whether no tone (N) was present or whether a tone (S + N) was present. However, the overlap in the probability distributions for (N) and (S + N) means that for some perceptual effects this judgment will be difficult. As we saw above, it is equally probable that a tone with a loudness of 20 is due to (N) or to (S + N). So, on a trial in which the subject hears a tone with a loudness of 20, how does she decide whether or not the signal was presented? According to signal detection theory, the subject's decision depends on the location of her criterion.

The Criterion

We can see how the criterion affects the subject's response by looking at Figure A.4. In this figure, we have labeled three different criteria: liberal (L), neutral (N), and conservative (C). Remember that we can cause subjects to adopt these different criteria by means of different payoffs. According to signal detection theory, once the subject adopts a criterion, he or she uses the following rule to decide how to respond on a given trial: If the perceptual effect is greater than (to the right of) the criterion, say, "Yes, the tone was

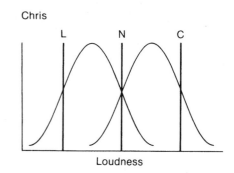

Figure A.4
The same probability distributions from Figure A.3, showing three criteria: liberal (L), neutral (N), and conservative (C). When a subject adopts a criterion, he or she uses the following decision rule: Respond "yes" ("I detect the stimulus") if the perceptual effect is greater than the criterion and respond "no" ("I do not detect the stimulus") if the perceptual effect is less than the criterion.

present"; if the perceptual effect is less than (to the left of) the criterion, say, "No, the tone was not present." Let's consider how different criteria influence the subject's hits and false alarms.

Liberal Criterion   To determine how criterion L will affect the subject's hits and false alarms, let's consider what happens when we present (N) and when we present (S + N):

1. *Present (N):* Since most of the probability distribution for (N) falls to the right of the criterion, the chances are good that presenting (N) will result in a loudness to the right of the criterion. This means that the probability of saying "yes" when (N) is presented is high; therefore, the probability of a false alarm is high.

2. *Present (S + N):* Since the entire probability distribution for (S + N) falls to the right of the criterion, the chances are excellent that presenting (S + N) will result in a loudness to the right of the criterion. Thus, the probability of saying "yes" when the signal is presented is high; therefore, the probability of a hit is high. Since criterion L results in high false alarms and high hits, adopting that criterion will result in point L on the ROC curve in Figure A.5.

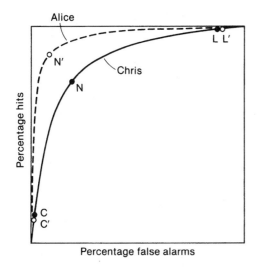

Figure A.5
ROC curves for Chris (solid) and Alice (dashed).

Neutral Criterion

1. *Present (N):* The subject will answer "yes" only rarely when (N) is presented, since only a small portion of the (N) distribution falls to the right of the criterion. The false-alarm rate, therefore, will be fairly low.

2. *Present (S + N):* The subject will answer "yes" frequently when (S + N) is presented, since most of the (S + N) distribution falls to the right of the criterion. The hit rate, therefore, will be fairly high (but not as high as for the L criterion). Criterion N results in point N on the ROC curve in Figure A.5.

Conservative Criterion

1. *Present (N):* False alarms will be very low, since none of the (N) curve falls to the right of the criterion.

2. *Present (S + N):* Hits will also be low, since only a small portion of the (S + N) curve falls to the right of the criterion. Criterion C results in point C on the ROC curve in Figure A.5.

You can see that applying different criteria to the probability distributions generates the solid ROC curve in Figure A.5. But why are these probability distributions necessary? After all, when we described the experiment with Chris and Laurie, we determined the ROC curve simply by plotting the results of the experiment. The reason the (N) and (S + N) distributions are important is that, according to signal detection theory, the subject's sensitivity to a stimulus is indicated by the distance (d') between the peaks of the (N) and (S + N) distributions, and this distance affects the shape of the ROC curve. We will now consider how the subject's sensitivity to a stimulus affects the shape of the ROC curve.

The Effect of Sensitivity on the ROC Curve

We can understand how the subject's sensitivity to a stimulus affects the shape of the ROC curve by considering what the probability distributions would look like for Alice, a subject with supersensitive hearing.

Alice's hearing is so good that a tone barely audible to Chris sounds very loud to Alice. If presenting (S + N) causes Alice to hear a loud tone, this means that Alice's (S + N) distribution should be far to the right, as shown in Figure A.6. In signal detection terms, we would say that Alice's high sensitivity is indicated by the large separation (d') between the (N) and the (S + N) probability distributions. To see how this greater separation between the probability distributions will affect Alice's ROC curve, let's see how she would respond when adopting liberal, neutral, and conservative criteria.

Liberal Criterion

1. *Present (N):* high false alarms.

2. *Present (S + N):* high hits.

The liberal criterion, therefore, results in point L′ on the ROC curve of Figure A.5.

Neutral Criterion

1. *Present (N):* low false alarms. It is important to note that Alice's false alarms for the neutral criterion will be lower than Chris's false alarms for the neutral criterion, because only a small portion of Alice's (N) distribution falls to the right of the crite-

rion, whereas some of Chris's (N) distribution falls to the right of the neutral criterion (Figure A.4).

2. *Present (S + N):* high hits. In this case Alice's hits will be higher than Chris's, because all of Alice's (S + N) distribution falls to the right of the neutral criterion, whereas not all of Chris's does (Figure A.4). The neutral criterion, therefore, results in point N′ on the ROC curve in Figure A.5.

Conservative Criterion

1. *Present (N):* low false alarms.

2. *Present (S + N):* low hits. The conservative criterion, therefore, results in point C′ on the ROC curve.

The difference between the two ROC curves in Figure A.5 is obvious, since Alice's curve is more "bowed." But before you conclude that the difference between these two ROC curves has anything to do with where we positioned Alice's L, N, and C criteria, see if you can get an ROC curve like Alice's from the two probability distributions of Figure A.4. You will find that, no matter where you position the criteria, there is no way that you can get a point like point N′(with very high hits and very low false alarms) from the curves of Figure A.4. In order to achieve very high hits and very low false alarms, the two probability distributions must be spaced far apart, as in Figure A.6.

Thus, increasing the distance (d') between the (N) and the (S + N) probability distributions changes the shape of the ROC curve. When the subject's sensitivity (d') is high, the ROC curve is more bowed. In practice, d' can be determined by comparing the experimentally determined ROC curve to standard ROC curves (see Gescheider, 1976), or d' can be calculated from the proportions of hits and false alarms that occur in an experiment, by means of a mathematical procedure we will not discuss here. This mathematical procedure for calculating d' enables us to determine a subject's sensitivity by determining only one data point on an ROC curve. Thus, this mathematical procedure makes it possible to use the signal detection procedure without running a large number of trials.

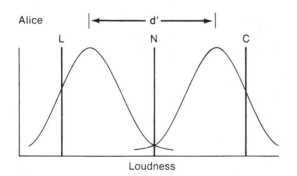

Figure A.6
Probability distributions for Alice, a subject who is extremely sensitive to the signal. The noise distribution remains the same, but the (S + N) distribution is shifted to the right.

APPENDIX B

DETERMINING SPATIAL FREQUENCIES USING FOURIER ANALYSIS

In Chapter 3 we saw that one way to determine the spatial frequency of a grating is to measure how many cycles of the grating (one pair of black and white bars) are contained within one degree of visual angle. We used the square-wave grating of Figure 3.14 to illustrate how to measure the grating's contrast and mentioned that spatial frequency is a useful measure of the grain of visual stimuli, because we can determine the spatial frequency not only of gratings but also of real world scenes.

In this appendix we will describe the mathematical technique of Fourier analysis, which is used to determine the spatial frequency components of visual scenes and can also be used to break complex auditory stimuli into their frequency components (see Chapter 10). To describe Fourier analysis, we need to introduce another kind of grating, the sine-wave grating shown on the right of Figure B.1. The intensity distribution of this grating is a sine wave, so the transitions between the black and white bars is gradual rather than abrupt, as in the square-wave grating on the left.

Fourier analysis is a mathematical procedure that enables us to analyze any pattern of intensities into sine-wave components. Figure B.2 shows the result of this mathematical procedure as applied to a square wave like the one on the left of Figure B.1. The intensity distribution of the square wave, shown on top, is broken into the following sine-wave components:

- A sine wave with amplitude and frequency equal to that of the square wave. This is called the fundamental (Figure B.2b).

- A sine wave with amplitude equal to one-third of the square wave and frequency three times greater (Figure B.2c). This is called the third harmonic.

- A sine wave with amplitude equal to one-fifth of the square wave and frequency five times greater (Figure B.2d). This is called the fifth harmonic.

When we add these sine waves together, we get the curve in Figure B.2e, which looks something like a square wave. By adding the seventh and ninth harmonics and additional odd-numbered harmonics (according to Fourier's equations a square wave consists of only odd-numbered harmonics), the result gets closer and closer to our square wave. This shows that the square wave is, in fact, made up of a number of sine waves with different spatial frequencies.

We can understand why the square wave contains the harmonics by remembering that we defined spatial frequency as how rapidly a stimulus changes across space. For the square-wave grating, there are

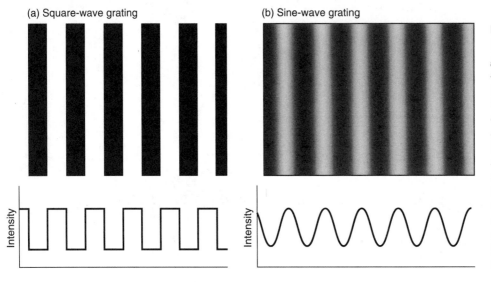

(a) Square-wave grating

(b) Sine-wave grating

Intensity

Intensity

Figure B.1

(a) A square-wave grating and its intensity distribution. (b) A sine-wave grating and its intensity distribution. The abrupt changes in intensity of the square-wave gratings are seen as sharp contours, whereas the more gradual changes in intensity of the sine-wave grating are seen as fuzzy contours.

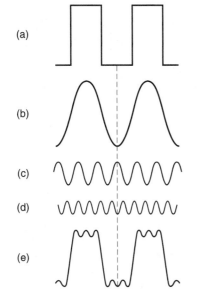

(a)

(b)

(c)

(d)

(e)

Figure B.2

The sine-wave components for the square-wave grating at the top of the figure, determined by Fourier analysis. When Fourier analysis is applied to the square-wave grating with the intensity distribution shown in (a), the sine waves shown in (b), (c), and (d) result. Adding curves (b), (c), and (d) together results in the intensity distribution in (e). The dashed line is included to emphasize that the sine waves must be lined up correctly. See text for details.

two things that cause changes in the stimulus across space: (1) the repetition of the black and white bars and (2) the abrupt intensity changes that occur at the borders of these bars (Figure B.3a). The fundamental frequency of the Fourier analysis (Figure B.2b) indicates the spatial frequency determined by the way the grating repeats, and the harmonics (B.2c; B.2d) indicate the frequencies that occur because of the abrupt intensity change that occurs between the black and white bars of the grating.

What if the grating in Figure B.2 was a sine-wave grating? Since the intensity changes gradually between

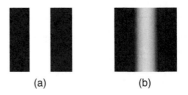

(a)   (b)

Figure B.3

Close-ups of the borders between light and dark bars of (a) a square-wave grating and (b) a sine-wave grating. The sharp change in intensity at the borders between the dark and light bars in (a) is a source of high spatial frequencies. These high spatial frequencies do not occur for the sine-wave grating because the intensity changes gradually at the borders.

Appendix B   592

the bars of a sine-wave grating (Figure B.3b), we would expect that a sine-wave grating wouldn't contain the additional higher spatial frequencies that we observed in the square wave. To convince ourselves of this, we carry out a Fourier analysis on the sine wave. Remember that the Fourier procedure analyzes any pattern into its sine-wave components. Since our grating is already a sine wave, our Fourier analysis results in just one sine wave, identical to the original one and without any higher-frequency components.

GLOSSARY

The number in parentheses after each item indicates the chapter in which the term is introduced. When more than one chapter is indicated, this means that the term is also discussed at length in the second chapter.

Absolute threshold. See Threshold, absolute. (1)

Absorption spectrum. A plot of the amount of light absorbed by a visual pigment versus the wavelength of light. (2)

Accommodation (depth cue). A depth cue. Muscular sensations that occur when the eye accommodates to bring objects at different distances into focus may provide information regarding the distance of that object. (7)

Accommodation (focus). The eye's ability to bring objects located at different distances into focus by changing the shape of the lens. (2)

Accretion. The uncovering of the farther of two surfaces due to observer movement. (7)

Achromatic color. Colors without hue; white, black, and all the grays between these two extremes are achromatic colors. (6)

Acoustic reflex. Activation of the middle ear muscles in response to high-intensity sounds. (16)

Acoustic shadow. Shadow created by the head that blocks high-frequency sounds from getting to the opposite side of the head. (11)

Acoustic signal. The pattern of frequencies and intensities of the sound stimulus. (12)

Acoustic stimulus. Physical pressure changes in the air that potentially can cause the perception of sound. (12)

Acoustic trauma. Damage to the inner ear caused by implosive noises such as those created by explosions or machines. (16)

Across-fiber patterns. The pattern of firing that a stimulus causes across a number of neurons. This is the same thing as distributed coding. (14)

Action. Motor activities such as moving the head or eyes and locomoting through the environment. (1)

Action pathway. See Dorsal pathway. (4)

Action potential. Rapid increase in positive charge in a nerve fiber that is propagated down the fiber. Also called a nerve impulse. (1)

Active touch. Touch in which the observer plays an active role in touching and exploring an object, usually with his or her hands. (13)

Additive color mixture. See Color mixture, additive. (Color essay)

Additive synthesis. In hearing, the process of building a complex tone by starting with the fundamental frequency and adding pure tone harmonics. (11)

Adjustment, method of. A psychophysical method in which the experimenter or the observer slowly changes the stimulus until the observer detects the stimulus. (1)

Aerial perspective. See Atmospheric perspective. (7)

Afterimage. An image that is perceived after the original source of stimulation is removed. A visual afterimage usually occurs after one views a high-contrast stimulus for 30 to 60 seconds. (6)

Age-related macular degeneration. Degeneration of the macular area of the retina associated with old age. (16)

Alberti's window. A transparent surface on which an artist traces the scene viewed through the surface in order to draw a picture in linear perspective. (7)

Algorithm. A procedure that is guaranteed to result in the solution to a problem. For example, the procedures we learn for addition, subtraction, and long division are algorithms. (5)

Alliesthesia. "Changed sensation." The change in reaction to a stimulus, which may be positive when we first experience it but, after repeated presentations, becomes more negative. (14)

Alphanumeric category effect. Letters "pop out" when seen with digits, so they are identified faster when surrounded with digits than when surrounded by other letters. (5)

Amacrine cell. A neuron that transmits signals laterally in the retina. Amacrine cells synapse with bipolar cells and ganglion cells. (2)

Ambient optic array. See Optic array. (9)

Amblyopia. A large reduction in the acuity in one eye. (7)

Ames room. A distorted room, first built by Adelbert Ames, that creates an erroneous perception of the sizes of people in the room. The room is constructed so that two people at the far wall of the room appear to stand at the same distance from an observer. In actuality, one of the people is much farther away than the other. (7)

Amiloride. A substance that blocks the flow of sodium into taste receptors. (14)

Amodal representation. An internal description of a stimulus that holds across more than one modality. (15)

Amplitude. In the case of a repeating sound wave, such as the sine wave of a pure tone, amplitude represents the pressure difference between atmospheric pressure and the maximum pressure of the wave. (10)

Amygdala. A subcortical structure that is involved in emotional responding and in processing olfactory signals. (14)

Angle of disparity. The visual angle between the images of an object on the two retinas. If the images of an object fall on corresponding points, the angle of disparity is zero. If the images fall on noncorresponding points, the angle of disparity indicates the degree of noncorrespondence. (7)

Angular size-contrast theory. An explanation of the moon illusion that states that the perceived size of the moon is determined by the sizes of the objects that surround it. According to this idea, the moon appears small when it is surrounded by large objects, such as the expanse of the sky when the moon is overhead. (7)

Anomalous trichromat. A person who needs to mix a minimum of three wavelengths to match any other wavelength in the spectrum but mixes these wavelengths in different proportions from a trichromat. (6)

Anosmia. Loss of the ability to smell due to injury or infection. (14)

Anterior interparietal area (AIP). An area in the parietal lobe that is important for the coordination of visual and motor information. (9)

Apex (of the basilar membrane). The end of the basilar membrane farthest from the middle ear. (10)

Aphasia. Difficulties in speaking or understanding speech due to brain damage. (12)

Apparent-distance theory. An explanation of the moon illusion that is based on the idea that the horizon moon, which is viewed across the filled space of the terrain, should appear farther away than the zenith moon, which is viewed through the empty space of the sky. This theory states that, since the horizon and zenith moons have the same visual angle, the farther-appearing horizon moon should appear larger. (7)

Apparent movement (or stroboscopic movement). An illusion of movement that occurs between two objects separated in space when the objects are flashed rapidly on and off, one after another, separated by a brief time interval. (5, 8)

Applanator. The part of an applanation tonometer that is pushed against the patient's cornea to determine the intraocular pressure. (16)

Area centralis. The horizontal area of high receptor density found in some animals, such as the turtle. (6)

Articulation function. A plot of the percentage of words identified correctly versus the intensity of the words. (16)

Articulators. Structures involved in speech production, such as the tongue, lips, teeth, jaw, and soft palate. (12)

Astigmatism. A condition in which vision is blurred in some orientations because of a misshapen cornea. (3)

Atmospheric perspective. A depth cue. Objects that are farther away look more blurred and bluer than objects that are closer, because we must look through more air and particles to see them. (7)

Attack. The buildup of sound at the beginning of a tone. (11)

Attention. The process of seeking out and focusing on stimuli that are of interest. (4)

Attentional blink. The inability to see a second target stimulus that is presented as one of a string of briefly presented stimuli within about half a second after the first target stimulus. (4)

Audibility curve. A curve that indicates the sound pressure level (SPL) at threshold for frequencies across the audible spectrum. (10)

Audiogram. A plot of the threshold for hearing pure tones versus the frequencies of the tones. Threshold in an audiogram is plotted relative to "normal threshold," which is set at 0. Thus, normal hearing would be a horizontal line at 0 threshold. (16)

Audiologist. A professional with a master's or doctoral degree who measures the hearing ability of children and adults to identify the presence and severity of any hearing problems. Audiologists also fit hearing-impaired people with hearing aids and teach them strategies for more effective communication. (16)

Audiometer. A device for measuring an audiogram. (16)

Audio-visual speech perception. A perception of speech that is affected by both auditory and visual stimulation, as when a person sees a tape of someone saying /ga/ with the sound /ba/ substituted and perceives /da/. (12)

Auditory association cortex. Area in the temporal lobe that receives signals from the secondary auditory cortex. It is sometimes classified as the nonprimary auditory cortex, along with the secondary auditory cortex. (10)

Auditory canal. The canal through which air vibrations travel from the environment to the tympanic membrane. (10)

Auditory localization. The perception of the location of a sound source. (11)

Auditory masking. A psychophysical technique in which one sound is presented that decreases (masks) a person's ability to hear another sound. (10)

Auditory receiving area. The area of the cortex, located in the temporal lobe, that is the primary receiving area for hearing. (10)

Auditory response area. The psychophysically measured area that defines the frequencies and sound pressure levels over which hearing functions. This area extends between the audibility curve and the curve for the threshold of feeling. (10)

Auditory scene. The sound environment, which includes the locations and qualities of individual sound sources. (11)

Auditory scene analysis. The process by which listeners sort superimposed vibrations into separate sounds. (11)

Auditory stream segregation. The effect that occurs when a series of tones that differ in pitch are played so that the high- and low-pitched tones alternate so rapidly that the high and low pitches become perceptually separated into simultaneously occurring independent streams of sound. (11)

Aural rehabilitation. Training for hearing-impaired people that consists of training in speech reading and other communication strategies. (16)

Axial myopia. See Myopia, axial. (16)

Axon. The part of the neuron that conducts nerve impulses over distances. Also called the nerve fiber. (1)

Azimuth coordinate. In hearing, specifies locations that vary from left to right relative to the listener. (11)

Base (of the basilar membrane). The part of the basilar membrane nearest the middle ear. (10)

Basilar membrane. A membrane that stretches the length of the cochlea and controls the vibration of the cochlear partition. (10)

Belongingness. The hypothesis that an area's appearance is influenced by which part of the surroundings that the area appears to belong to. This principle has been used to explain the perception of lightness in the Benary cross and White's illusion. (2)

Benary Cross. A display in which two gray wavelengths associated with a black cross look different even though they are physically the same. It is perceptually significant because the two areas that appear different both receive the same amount of lateral inhibition. (2)

Bimodal neurons. Neurons that responds to stimulation of two senses; for example, a neuron that responds to both visual and tactile stimulation. (4)

Binaural cues. Sound localization cues that involve both ears. (11)

Binding problem. The problem of how neural activity in many separated areas in the brain is combined to create a perception of a coherent object. (4)

Binocular depth cell. A neuron in the visual cortex that responds best to stimuli that fall on points separated by a specific degree of disparity on the two retinas. (7)

Binocular depth cue. A depth cue that requires the participation of both eyes. Binocular disparity is the major binocular depth cue. (7)

Binocular disparity. The result when the retinal images of an object fall on disparate points on the two retinas. (7)

Binocular fixation. Simultaneous direction of the foveas of both eyes at an object. (15)

Binocular rivalry. The situation that occurs when two different images are presented to the left and right eyes and perception alternates back and forth between the two images. (4)

Binocularly fixate. Directing both eyes to a visual target, so the image of the target falls on corresponding points on the retina. (15)

Biological movement. Motion produced by biological organisms. Most of the experiments on biological motion have used walking humans with lights attached to their joints and limbs as stimuli. (8)

Bipolar cell. A neuron that is stimulated by the visual receptors and sends electrical signals to the retinal ganglion cells. (2)

Blind spot. The small area where the optic nerve leaves the back of the eye; there are no visual receptors in this area so small images falling directly on the blind spot can't be seen. (2)

Blindness. A visual acuity of 20/200 or less after correction or little peripheral vision (the legal definition of blindness). (16)

Body-centered neuron. Neuron that has a visual receptive field that responds when a visual stimulus is presented near a particular part of the body. (4)

Bottom-up processing. Processing in which a person constructs a perception by first analyzing small units such as primitives. Treisman's preattentive stage of processing, in which a stimulus is analyzed into parts, is an example of bottom-up processing. (1)

Broca's area. An area in the frontal lobe that is important for language perception and production. One effect of damage is difficulty in speaking. (12)

Cataract. A lens that is clouded. (16)

Cataract, congenital. A cataract present at birth. (16)

Cataract, secondary. A cataract caused by another eye disease. (16)

Cataract, senile. A cataract due to old age. This is the most common form of cataract. (16)

Cataract, traumatic. A cataract caused by injury. (16)

Categorical perception. In speech perception, perceiving one sound at short voice onset times and another sound at longer voice onset times. The listener perceives only two categories across the whole range of voice onset times. (12)

Cell assembly. A group of neurons that fire together in response to a particular stimulus. (3)

Cell body. The part of a neuron that contains the neuron's metabolic machinery and that receives stimulation from other neurons. (1)

Center-surround antagonism. The competition between the center and surround regions of a center-surround receptive field. (2)

Center-surround receptive field. A receptive field that consists of a roughly circular excitatory area surrounded by an inhibitory area, or a circular inhibitory center surrounded by an excitatory surround. (2)

Central pitch processor. A hypothetical central mechanism that analyzes the pattern of a tone's harmonics and selects the fundamental frequency that is most likely to have been part of that pattern. (10)

Cerebral achromatopsia. A loss of color vision caused by brain injury. (6)

Cerebral cortex. Thin layer of neurons that covers the surface of the brain, which is responsible for higher functions such as perception and thinking. (1)

Characteristic frequency. The frequency at which a neuron in the auditory system has its lowest threshold. (10)

Chemesthesis. The sense responsible for detecting chemical substances that are irritating or that have a tactile component. Also called the common chemical sense. (14)

Chorda tympani nerve. A nerve that transmits signals from receptors on the front and sides of the tongue. (14)

Chromatic adaptation. The adaptation of the eye to chromatic light. Chromatic adaptation is selective adaptation to wavelengths in a particular region of the visible spectrum. (6)

Chromatic color. Colors with hue, such as blue, yellow, red, and green. (6)

Cilia. Fine hairs that protrude from the inner and outer hair cells of the auditory system. Bending the cilia of the inner hair cells leads to transduction. (10)

Classical psychophysical methods. The methods of limits, adjustment, and constant stimuli, described by Fechner for measuring thresholds. (1)

Closed-angle glaucoma. See Glaucoma, closed angle. (16)

Coarticulation. The overlapping articulation of different phonemes. (12)

Cochlea. The snail-shaped, liquid-filled structure that contains the structures of the inner ear, the most important of which are the basilar membrane, the tectorial membrane, and the hair cells. (10)

Cochlear implant. A device in which electrodes are inserted into the cochlea to create hearing by electrically stimulating the auditory nerve fibers. This device is used to restore hearing in people who have lost their hearing because of damaged hair cells. (16)

Cochlear nucleus. The nucleus where nerve fibers from the cochlea first synapse. (10)

Cochlear partition. A partition in the cochlea, extending almost its full length, that separates the scala tympani and the scala vestibuli. (10)

Cognitive influences on perception. How the knowledge, memories, and expectations that a person brings to the situation influence his or her perception. (1)

Cold fiber. A nerve fiber that responds to decreases in temperature or to steady low temperatures. (13)

Collision-sensitive neuron. A neuron in the pigeon that responds well when an object is on a collision course, but responds poorly when an object is not on a collision course. (9)

Color, achromatic. See Achromatic color. (5)

Color-blind. A condition in which a person perceives no chromatic color. This can be caused by absent or malfunctioning cone receptors or by cortical damage. (6)

Color, chromatic. See Chromatic color. (5)

Color constancy. The effect in which the perception of an object's hue remains constant even when the wavelength distribution of the illumination is changed. Approximate color constancy means that our perception of hue usually changes a little when the illumination changes, though not as much as we might expect from the change in the wavelengths of light reaching the eye. (6)

Color deficiency. People with color deficiency (sometimes incorrectly called color blindness) see fewer colors than people with normal color vision and need to mix fewer wavelengths to match any other wavelength in the spectrum. (6)

Color-matching experiment. A procedure in which observers are asked to match the color in one field by mixing two or more lights in another field. (6)

Color mixing. Combining two or more different colors to create a new color (see Color mixture, additive, and Color mixture, subtractive). (Color essay 3)

Color mixture, additive. The result when lights of different colors are superimposed. (Color essay 3)

Color mixture, subtractive. The result when paints of different colors are mixed together. (Color essay 3)

Columnar arrangement. The arrangement of neurons with similar properties in columns perpendicular to the surface of the cortex. For example, there are location, orientation, and ocular dominance columns in the visual system and frequency columns in the auditory system. (10)

Common chemical sense. See Chemesthesis. (14)

Common fate, law of. Gestalt law: Things that are moving in the same direction appear to be grouped together. (5)

Common region, principle of. A modern Gestalt principle that states that elements that are within the same region of space appear to be grouped together. (5)

Comparator. A structure hypothesized by the corollary discharge theory of movement perception. The corollary discharge signal and the sensory movement signal meet at the comparator. (8)

Complex cell. A neuron in the visual cortex that responds best to moving bars with a particular orientation. (3)

Componential recovery, principle of. A principle stating that, if an object's geons can be identified, then the object can be rapidly and correctly recognized. (5)

Computational approach. An approach to explaining object perception that treats perception as the end result of a mathematical analysis of the retinal image. (5)

Conductive hearing loss. Hearing loss that occurs when the vibrations of a sound stimulus are not conducted normally from the outer ear into the cochlea. (16)

Cones. Cone-shaped receptors in the retina that are primarily responsible for vision in high levels of illumination and for color vision and detail vision. (2)

Conflicting cues theory. A theory of visual illusions proposed by R. H. Day, which states that our perception of the length of lines depends on an integration of the actual length of lines and the overall length of the figure. (7)

Congenital cataract. See Cataract, congenital. (16)

Constant stimuli, method of. A psychophysical method in which a number of stimuli with different intensities are presented repeatedly in a random order. (1)

Contextual modulation. When the response to a stimulus is influenced by the context within which the stimulus occurs. This term has been used to refer to the situation in which a neuron's response is influenced by stimulation of an area outside its receptive field. (4)

Contralateral eye. The eye on the opposite side of the head from a particular structure. (3)

Contrast. The difference in light intensity between two areas. For a visual grating stimulus, the contrast is the amplitude of the grating divided by its mean intensity. (3)

Contrast sensitivity. Sensitivity to the difference in the light intensities in two adjacent areas. Contrast sensitivity is usually measured by taking the reciprocal of the minimum intensity difference between two bars of a grating necessary to see the bars. (3)

Contrast sensitivity function (CSF). A plot of contrast sensitivity versus the spatial frequency of a grating stimulus. (3)

Contrast threshold. The intensity difference that can just barely be seen between two areas. This is often measured using gratings with alternating light and dark bars. (3)

Convergence (depth cue). A depth cue. Muscular sensations that occur when the eyes move inward (convergence) or outward (divergence) to view objects at different distances may provide information regarding the depth of that object. (7)

Convergence (neural). The process of many neurons synapsing onto fewer neurons. (2)

Convergence angle. The angle between the two eyes as they fixate on an object. (7)

Co-occurance hypothesis. Stimuli that occur together will tend to be represented by activity in the same, or nearby, areas of the cortex. (5)

Core area. The area in the temporal lobe that includes the primary auditory cortex (A1) and some nearby areas. Signals from the core area are transmitted to the secondary auditory cortex. (10)

Cornea. The transparent focusing element of the eye that is the first structure through which light passes as it enters the eye and that is the eye's major focusing element. (2)

Corneal disease and injury. Any disease or injury that damages the cornea, causing a loss of transparency. (16)

Corneal transplant. The replacement of a damaged piece of cornea with a piece of healthy cornea taken from a donor. (16)

Corollary discharge signal (CDS). A copy of the signal sent from the motor area of the brain to the eye muscles. The corollary discharge signal is sent not to the eye muscles, but to the hypothetical comparator of corollary discharge theory. (8)

Corollary discharge theory. According to the corollary discharge theory of motion perception, the corollary discharge signal is sent to a structure called the comparator, where the information in the corollary discharge is compared to the sensory movement signal. If the corollary discharge signal and the sensory movement signal do not cancel each other, movement is perceived. (8)

Correct rejection. In a signal detection experiment, saying, "No, I don't detect a stimulus" on a trial in which the stimulus is not presented (a correct response). (Appendix)

Correspondence problem. The visual system's matching of points on one image with similar points on the other image in order to determine binocular disparity. (7)

Corresponding retinal points. The points on each retina that would overlap if one retina were slid on top of the other. Receptors at corresponding points send their signals to the same location in the brain. (7)

Cortical magnification factor. See Magnification factor. (3)

Cross-correlograms. Plots that indicate whether neurons are firing in synchrony with each other. (4)

Crossed disparity. Binocular disparity in which objects are located in front of the horopter (see Uncrossed disparity). (7)

Cue approach. In depth perception, this approach focuses on identifying information in the retinal image that is correlated with depth in the scene.

Cue theory. The approach to depth perception that focuses on identifying information in the retinal image that is correlated with depth in the world. (7)

Cutaneous sensations. Sensations based on the stimulation of receptors in the skin. (13)

Dark adaptation. Visual adaptation that occurs in the dark, during which the sensitivity to light increases. (2)

Dark adaptation curve. The function that traces the time course of the increase in visual sensitivity that occurs during dark adaptation. (2)

Dark-adapted sensitivity.   The sensitivity of the eye after it has completely adapted to the dark. (2)

Decay.   The decrease in sound at the end of a tone. (11)

Decibel (dB).   A unit that indicates the presence of a tone relative to a reference pressure: dB = 20 log (p/p_o) where p is the pressure of the tone and p_o is the reference pressure. (10)

Deletion.   The covering of the farther of two surfaces due to observer movement. This provides information for depth. (7)

Dendrites.   Nerve processes on the cell body that receive stimulation from other neurons. (1)

2-Deoxyglucose technique.   An anatomical technique that makes it possible to see which neurons in a structure have been activated. For example, this technique was used to visualize the orientation columns in the visual cortex. (3)

Depth cue.   Two-dimensional information on the retina that is correlated with depth in the scene. (7)

Dermis.   The inner layer of skin that contains nerve endings and receptors. (13)

Desaturated.   Low saturation in chromatic colors as would occur when white is added to a color. For example, pink is not as saturated as red. (6)

Detached retina.   A condition in which the retina is detached from the back of the eye. (16)

Deuteranopia.   A form of red–green color dichromatism caused by lack of the middle-wavelength cone pigment. (6)

Diabetes.   A condition in which the body doesn't produce enough insulin. One side effect of diabetes is a loss of vision due to diabetic retinopathy. (16)

Diabetic retinopathy.   Damage to the retina that is a side effect of diabetes. This condition causes neovascularization—the formation of abnormal blood vessels that do not supply the retina with adequate oxygen and that bleed into the vitreous humor. (16)

Dichromat.   A person who has a form of color deficiency. Dichromats can match any wavelength in the spectrum by mixing two other wavelengths. Deuteranopes, protanopes, and tritanopes are all dichromats. (6)

Difference threshold.   See Threshold, difference. (1)

Diopter.   The strength of a lens. Diopters = 1/far point in meters. (16)

Direct sound.   Sound that is transmitted to the ears directly from a sound source. (11)

Directional transfer function (DTF).   The difference between the sound from a source and the sound actually entering the ears. This difference provides a cue for auditory localization. (11)

Dishabituation.   An increase in looking time that occurs when a stimulus is changed. This response is used in testing infants to see if they can differentiate two stimuli. (15)

Disparate points.   See Noncorresponding points. (7)

Disparity detectors.   Neurons that respond best to stimuli that fall on retinal points separated by a specific angle of disparity. Also called binocular depth cells. (7)

Dissociation.   A situation that occurs as a result of brain damage when one function is present and another is absent. See also Double dissociation, Single dissociation. (4)

Distance coordinate.   In hearing, this coordinate specifies how far the sound source is from the listener. (11)

Distributed coding.   Type of neural code in which different perceptions are signaled by the pattern of activity that is distributed across many neurons (see Specificity coding). (4)

Doctrine of specific nerve energies.   A principle stating that the brain receives environmental information from sensory nerves and that the brain distinguishes between the different senses by monitoring the activity in these sensory nerves. (1)

Dorsal pathway.   Pathway that conducts signals from the striate cortex to the parietal lobe. This has also been called the "where," the "how," and the "action" pathway to indicate its function. (4)

Double dissociation.   In brain damage, when function A is present and function B is absent, and, in another person, when function A is absent and function B is present. Presence of a double dissociation means that the two functions involve different mechanisms and operate independently of one another. (4)

Duplex perception.   The result when one stimulus causes a person to hear both speech and nonspeech sounds simultaneously. (12)

Eardrum.   Another term for the tympanic membrane, the membrane located at the end of the auditory canal that vibrates in response to sound. (10)

Echo threshold.   The time separation at which two sounds presented at different locations are no longer fused, so two separate sounds are heard. At separations shorter than the echo threshold, the two sound sources are heard as one. (11)

Echolocation. Locating objects by sending out high-frequency pulses and sensing the echo created when these pulses are reflected from objects in the environment. Echolocation is used by bats and dolphins. (7)

Ecological approach. The approach to perception that emphasizes studying perception as it occurs in natural settings, particularly emphasizing the role of observer movement. (9, 11)

Ecological optics. The description of stimuli based on the optic array. (9)

Effect of the missing fundamental. See Periodicity pitch. (10)

Elaborate cells. Neurons in the IT cortex that respond best to complex stimuli such as specific shapes or shapes combined with a color or texture (see Primary cells). (4)

Electromagnetic spectrum. Continuum of electromagnetic energy that extends from very-short-wavelength gamma rays to long-wavelength radio waves. Visible light is a narrow band within this spectrum. (2)

Electronic noses. Electronic devices that can differentiate between a number of different odorants. They are designed primarily for practical applications such as odor quality control and sensing hazardous materials. (14)

Elevation coordinate. In hearing, sound locations that are up and down relative to the listener. (11)

Emmert's law. A law stating that the size of an afterimage depends on the distance of the surface against which the afterimage is viewed. The farther away the surface against which an afterimage is viewed, the larger the afterimage appears. (7)

Emmetropia. The condition in which the eye brings the images of objects into accurate focus on the retina. (15)

Emmetropization. The developmental process by which the length of the eyeball and focusing power of the eye's optical system become adjusted so light is focused sharply on the retina. (15)

Endorphins. Chemicals that are naturally produced in the brain and that cause analgesia. (13)

End-stopped cell. A cortical neuron that responds best to lines of a specific length that are moving in a particular direction. (3)

Envelope of the traveling wave. A curve that indicates the maximum displacement at each point along the basilar membrane caused by a traveling wave. (10)

Enzyme cascade. Sequence of reactions triggered by an activated visual pigment molecule that results in transduction. (2)

Epidermis. The outer layers of the skin, including a layer of dead skin cells. (13)

Equal loudness curve. A curve that indicates the sound pressure levels that result in a perception of the same loudness at frequencies across the audible spectrum. (10)

Equivalence classification. In speech perception, the ability to classify vowel sounds as belonging to the same class, even if the speakers are different. (15)

Everyday listening. Listening that focuses on events such as an air conditioner blowing or a chair squeaking (see Musical listening). (11)

Evoked potential. See Visual evoked potential. (1)

Excitation. A condition that facilitates the generation of nerve impulses. (1)

Excitatory-center-inhibitory-surround receptive field. A center-surround receptive field in which stimulation of the center area causes an excitatory response and stimulation of the surround causes an inhibitory response. (2)

Excitatory response. The response of a nerve fiber in which the firing rate increases. (2)

Exploratory procedures (EPs). People's movements of their hands and fingers while they are identifying three-dimensional objects by touch. (13)

External eye exam. Examination of the condition of the outer eye. This exam includes, among other things, examination of the reaction of the pupil to light, the color of the eye, and the alignment of the eyes. (16)

Extrastriate cortex. Areas in the cerebral cortex outside the striate cortex. (2, 4)

Eye. The eyeball and its contents, which include focusing elements, the retina, and supporting structures. (2)

False alarm. In a signal detection experiment, saying, "Yes, I detect the stimulus" on a trial in which the stimulus is not presented (an incorrect response). (Appendix)

Familiar size. A depth cue. Our knowledge of an object's actual size sometimes influences our perception of an object's distance. (7)

Familiarity, law of. Gestalt law: Things are more likely to form groups if the groups appear familiar or meaningful. (5)

Far point. The distance at which the rays from a spot of light are focused on the retina of the unaccommodated eye. For a person with normal vision, the far point is at infinity. For a person with myopic vision, the spot must be moved closer to the eye to bring the rays to a focus on the retina. (16)

Farsightedness.   See Hyperopia. (16)

Feature detector.   A neuron that responds selectively to a specific feature of the stimulus. (3)

Feature integration theory.   A sequence of steps proposed by Treisman to explain how objects are broken down into primitives and how these primitives are recombined to result in a perception of the object. (5)

Figure–ground segregation.   In object perception, the perceptual separation of an area from its background. (5)

Flavor.   The perception that occurs from the combination of taste and olfaction. (14)

Flow.   See Gradient of flow; Optic flow. (9)

Fluorescein angiography.   A technique in which a fluorescent dye is injected into a person's circulation. The outline of the retinal arteries and veins produced by this dye gives information about the condition of the retinal circulation. (16)

Focus of expansion (FOE).   The point in the flow pattern caused by observer movement in which there is no expansion. According to Gibson, the focus of expansion always remains centered on the observer's destination. (9)

Focused-attention stage of processing.   The stage of processing in which the primitives are combined. This stage requires conscious attention. (5)

Focusing power.   The degree to which a structure such as the lens or the cornea bends light. The greater the focusing power, the more the light passing through the structure is bent. (2)

Formant.   Horizontal band of energy in the speech spectrogram associated with vowels. (12)

Formant transitions.   In the speech stimulus, the rapid shifts in frequency that precede formants. (12)

Fourier analysis.   A mathematical technique that analyzes complex periodic waveforms into a number of sine-wave components. (3, 10)

Fourier spectrum.   The sine-wave components that make up a periodic waveform. Fourier spectra are usually depicted by a line for each sine-wave frequency, the height of the line indicating the amount of energy at that frequency. (10)

Fovea.   A small area in the human retina that contains only cone receptors. The fovea is located on the line of sight, so that when a person looks at an object, its image falls on the fovea. (2)

Frequency.   In the case of a sound wave that repeats itself like the sine wave of a pure tone, frequency is the number of times per second that the wave repeats itself. (10)

Frequency tuning curve.   Curve relating the threshold intensity for stimulating an auditory neuron and frequency. (10)

Frontal eyes.   Eyes located in front of the head, so the views of the two eyes overlap. (7)

Frontal operculum cortex.   An area in the frontal lobe of the cortex that receives signals from the taste system. (14)

Functional magnetic resonance imaging (fMRI).   A brain imaging technique that indicates brain activity in awake behaving humans, in response to perceptual stimuli. (1)

Fundamental frequency.   Usually the lowest frequency in the Fourier spectrum of a complex tone. The tone's other components, called harmonics, have frequencies that are multiples of the fundamental frequency. (11)

Fusiform face area (FFA).   An area in the human IT cortex that contains neurons that are specialized to respond to faces. (4)

Fusion.   In hearing, when sounds that are presented simultaneously at two different locations are perceived as one sound coming from a single location. (11)

Ganglion cell.   A neuron in the retina that receives inputs from bipolar and amacrine cells. The axons of the ganglion cells are the fibers that travel toward the lateral geniculate nucleus of the thalamus in the optic nerve. (2)

Gate control theory.   Melzak and Wall's idea that our perception of pain is controlled by a neural circuit that takes into account the relative amount of activity in large (L) fibers and small (S) fibers. (13)

Geon.   "Geometric ion"; volumetric features of Biederman's Recognition-By-Components theory. (5)

Gestalt psychology.   A school of psychology that has focused on developing principles of perceptual organization, proposing that "the whole is different from the sum of its parts." (7)

Glaucoma.   A disease of the eye that usually results in an increase in intraocular pressure. (16)

Glaucoma, closed-angle.   A rare form of glaucoma in which the iris is pushed up so that it closes the angle between the iris and the cornea and blocks the area through which the aqueous humor normally drains out of the eye. (16)

Glaucoma, open-angle. A form of glaucoma in which the area through which the aqueous humor normally drains out of the eye is blocked. In this form of glaucoma, the iris remains in its normal position so that the angle between the iris and the cornea remains open. (16)

Global optical flow. Information for movement that occurs when all elements in a scene move. (8)

Glomeruli. Small structures in the olfactory bulb that receive signals from similar olfactory receptor neurons. One function of each glomerulus is to collect information about a small group of odorants. (14)

Glossopharyngeal nerve. A nerve that transmits signals from receptors located at the back of the tongue. (14)

Good continuation, law of. Gestalt law: Points that, when connected, result in straight or smoothly curving lines are seen as belonging together, and lines tend to be seen in such a way as to follow the smoothest path. (5)

Good figure, law of. Gestalt law: Every stimulus pattern is seen so that the resulting structure is as simple as possible. (5)

Gradient of flow. In a flow pattern, a gradient is created by movement of an observer through the environment. The speed of movement is rapid in the foreground and becomes slower as distance from the observer increases. (9)

Grating. A stimulus pattern consisting of alternating bars with different lightnesses or colors. (3)

Ground. In object perception, the background is called the ground.

Habituation. The result when the same stimulus is presented repeatedly. For example, infants look at a stimulus less and less on each succeeding trial. (15)

Hair cells. Neurons in the cochlea that contain small hairs, or cilia, that are displaced by vibration of the basilar membrane and fluids inside the inner ear. There are two kinds of hair cells: inner and outer. (10)

Hair cells, inner. Auditory receptor cells in the inner ear that are primarily responsible for auditory transduction and the perception of pitch. (10)

Hair cells, outer. Auditory receptor cells in the inner ear that amplify the responce of the inner hair cells (see Motile response). (10)

Haptic perception. The perception of three-dimensional objects by touch. (13)

Harmonics. Fourier components of a complex tone with frequencies that are multiples of the fundamental frequency. (10)

Hearing handicap. The disadvantage that a hearing impairment causes in a person's ability to communicate or in the person's daily living. (16)

Hearing impairment. A deviation or change for the worse in either the structure or the functioning of the auditory system (see Hearing handicap). (16)

Hereditary retinal degeneration. A degeneration of the retina that is inherited. Retinitis pigmentosa is an example of a hereditary retinal degeneration. (16)

Hermann grid. A geometrical display that results in the illusion of dark areas at the intersection of two white "corridors." This perception can be explained by lateral inhibition. (2)

Hertz (Hz). The unit for designating the frequency of a tone. One Hertz equals one cycle per second. (10)

Heuristics. In perception, heuristics are rules of thumb that provide "best guess" estimates of the identity of a particular stimulus. (5)

Hit. In a signal detection experiment, saying, "Yes, I detect astimulus" on a trial in which the stimulus is present (a correct response). (Appendix)

Homunculus. "Little man," a term referring to the map of the body in the somatosensory cortex. (13)

Horizontal cell. A neuron that transmits signals laterally across the retina. Horizontal cells synapse with receptors and bipolar cells. (2)

Horopter. An imaginary surface that passes through the point of fixation. Objects falling on this surface result in images that fall on corresponding points on the two retinas. (7)

How pathway. See Dorsal pathway. (4)

Hue. The experience of a chromatic color such as red, green, yellow, or blue or combinations of these colors. (6)

Hypercolumn. A column of cortex about 1 mm on a side that contains a location column for a particular area of the retina, left and right ocular dominance columns, and a complete set of orientation columns. A hypercolumn can be thought of as a processing module for a particular location on the retina. (3)

Hyperopia (farsightedness). The inability to see near objects clearly because the focus point for parallel rays of light is behind the retina. (15)

Hyperopic vision. See Hyperopia. (15)

Illumination edge. The border between two areas with different light intensities. (6)

Illusion. A situation in which an observer's perception of a stimulus does not correspond to the physical properties of the stimulus. For example, in the Müller-Lyer illusion, two lines of equal length are perceived to be of different lengths. (7)

Illusory conjunctions. Illusory combinations of primitives that are perceived when stimuli containing a number of primitives are presented briefly. (5)

Illusory contours. Contours that are perceived even though they are not present in the physical stimulus. (5)

Image movement signal (IMS). In corollary discharge theory, the signal that occurs when an image stimulates the receptors by moving across them. (8)

Inattentional blindness. A situation in which a stimulus that is not attended is not perceived, even though a person is looking directly at it. (4)

Incus. The second of the three ossicles of the middle ear. It transmits vibrations from the malleus to the stapes. (10)

Indexical characteristics. Characteristics of the speech stimulus that indicate information about things such as the speaker's age, gender, and emotional state. (12)

Indirect sound. Sound that reaches the ears after being reflected from a surface such as a room's walls. (11)

Induced movement. The illusory movement of one object that is caused by the movement of another object that is nearby. (8)

Inferior colliculus. A nucleus in the hearing system along the pathway from the cochlea to the auditory cortex. The inferior colliculus receives inputs from the superior olivary nucleus. (10)

Inhibition. A condition that decreases the likelihood that nerve impulses will be generated. (1)

Inhibitory-center-excitatory-surround receptive field. A center-surround receptive field in which stimulation of the center causes an inhibitory response and stimulation of the surround causes an excitatory response. (2)

Inhibitory response. The response of a nerve fiber in which the firing rate decreases due to inhibition from another neuron. (2)

Inner ear. The innermost division of the ear, containing the cochlea and the receptors for hearing. (10)

Inner hair cells. See Hair cells, inner. (10)

Insula. An area in the frontal lobe of the cortex that receives signals from the taste system. (14)

Interaural differences. Differences in the stimuli reaching the left and right ears, especially the level and frequency of the stimuli. (11)

Interaural level difference. The greater level of a sound at the closer ear when a sound source is positioned closer to one ear than to the other. This effect is most pronounced for high-frequency tones. (11)

Interaural time difference. When a sound is positioned closer to one ear than to the other, the sound reached the close ear slightly before reaching the far ear, so there is a difference in the time of arrival at the two ears. (11)

Interaural time difference detector. A neuron that fires only when a stimulus is presented first to one ear and then to the other, with a specific delay between the stimulation of the two ears. (11)

Intermodal matching. Ability to match shapes presented in two different modalities. (15)

Interstimulus interval (ISI). The time interval between two flashes of light in an apparent movement display. (8)

Intraocular lens. A plastic or silicone lens that is inserted into the eye after the removal of a cataract. This lens partially compensates for the loss of focusing power caused by removal of the patient's lens. (16)

Intraocular pressure. Pressure inside the eyeball. (16)

Invariant acoustic cues. In speech perception, aspects of an auditory signal that remain constant even in different contexts. (12)

Invariant information. Environmental properties that do not change as the observer moves. For example, the spacing, or texture, of the elements in a texture gradient does not change as the observer moves on the gradient. The texture of the gradient therefore supplies invariant information for depth perception. (9)

Inverse projection problem. A particular image on the retina could have been caused by an infinite number of different objects. Thus, the retinal image does not unambiguously specify a stimulus. (5)

Ions. Charged molecules found floating in the liquid that surrounds nerve fibers. (1)

Ipsilateral eye. The eye on the same side of the head of the structure to which the eye sends inputs. (3)

Iridectomy. A procedure used to treat closed-angle glaucoma, in which a small hole is cut in the iris. This hole opens a channel through which aqueous humor can flow out of the eye. (16)

Ishihara plate. A display made up of colored dots used to test for the presence of color deficiency. The dots are colored so that people with normal (trichromatic) color vision can perceive numbers in the plate, but people with color deficiency cannot perceive these numbers or perceive different numbers than someone with trichromatic vision. (6)

Isomerization. Change in shape of the retinal part of the visual pigment molecule that occurs when the molecule absorbs a quantum of light. (2)

K-cell. A third kind of ganglion cell (along with M- and P-cells), in which the K stands for kinocellular. Its function is unclear. (3)

Kinesthesis. The sense that enables us to feel the motions and positions of the limbs and body. (13)

Kinetic depth effect. Occurs when a stimulus's three-dimensional structure becomes apparent from viewing a two-dimensional image of the stimulus as it rotates. (8)

Large-diameter fiber (L-fiber). According to gate control theory, activity in L-fibers closes the gate control mechanism and therefore decreases the perception of pain. (13)

Laser-assisted in situ keratomileusis (LASIK). A procedure for correcting vision by cutting a small flap in front of the cornea and then modifying the shape of the cornea with an excimer laser. (16)

Laser photocoagulation. A procedure in which a laser beam is aimed at blood vessels that are leaking because of neovascularization. This laser beam photocoagulates—seals off—the blood vessels and stops the leaking. (16)

Lateral eyes. Eyes located on opposite sides of an animal's head, so the views of the two eyes do not overlap or overlap only slightly, as in the pigeon and rabbit. (7)

Lateral geniculate nucleus (LGN). The nucleus in the thalamus that receives inputs from the optic nerve and sends fibers to the cortical receiving area for vision. (2)

Lateral inhibition. Inhibition that is spread laterally across a nerve circuit. In the retina, lateral inhibition is spread by the horizontal and amacrine cells. (2)

Lateral plexus. A structure that transmits nerve impulses laterally in the limulus eye. (2)

Laws of perceptual organization. See Perceptual organization, laws of. (5)

Lens. The transparent focusing element of the eye through which light passes after passing through the cornea and the aqueous humor. The lens's change in shape to focus at different distances is called accommodation. (2)

Level of analysis. The idea that we can observer processes at different scales. Perception can be studied at the psychophysical and physiological levels of analysis. (1)

Light-adapted sensitivity. The sensitivity of the light-adapted eye. (2)

Light-from-above heuristic. The assumption that light is usually coming from above, which influences our perception of form in some situations. (5)

Lightness. Perception of reflectance. The perception of lightness is usually associated with the achromatic colors: white, gray, and black. (6)

Lightness constancy. The constancy of our perception of an object's lightness under different intensities of illumination. (6)

Limits, method of. A psychophysical method for measuring threshold in which the experimenter presents stimuli in alternating ascending and descending series. (1)

Linear circuit. A type of neural circuit in which there is no convergence so that the signal generated by each neuron travels straight to the next neuron, with no other neurons being involved. (2)

Linear optical trajectory (LOT) strategy. A strategy for catching a fly ball based on the idea that if the ballplayer runs so the ball appears to be following a straight-line path, the ball will always be directly above, so when the ball reaches the ground, the outfielder will be there to catch it. (9)

Linear perspective (depth cue). The visual effect that parallel lines (like railroad tracks) converge as they get farther away. This convergence of parallel lines is a depth cue, with greater convergence indicating greater distance. (7)

Linear perspective (drawing system). A method of representing three-dimensional space on a two-dimensional surface. (7)

Localization of function. The principle that specific areas of the brain serve specific functions. (12)

Location column. A column in the visual cortex that contains neurons with the same receptive field locations on the retina. (3)

Location-invariant neurons. Neurons that respond to a stimulus over large areas of the retina. (4)

Location-specific neuron. Neurons in the inferior temporal area that respond only to an object when it is in a specific location. (4)

Locomotor flow line. The flow line that passes directly under a moving observer. (9)

Long-wavelength pigment. A cone visual pigment that absorbs light maximally at the long-wavelength end of the spectrum. In humans, this pigment absorbs maximally at 558 nm. (2)

Loudness. The quality of sound that ranges from soft to loud. For a tone of a particular frequency, loudness usually increases with increasing decibels. (10)

Mach bands. A perceptual effect that causes a thin dark band on the dark side of a light–dark border and a thin light band on the light side of the border even though corresponding intensity changes do not exist. (2)

Macrosmatic. Having a keen sense of smell that is important to an animal's survival. (14)

Macula. An area about 5 mm in diameter that surrounds and includes the fovea. (16)

Macular degeneration. A degeneration of the macula area of the retina. See also Age-related macular degeneration. (16)

Magnetoencephalograpgy (MEG). A technique in which magnetic signals generated by the brain are used to measure rapid potentials associated with perception. (9)

Magnification factor. The apportioning of proportionally more space on the cortex to the representation of specific areas of sensory receptors. For example, a small area on the retina in or near the fovea receives more space on the cortex than the same area of peripheral retina. Similarly, the fingertips receive more space on the somatosensory cortex than the forearm or leg. (3, 13)

Magnitude estimation. A psychophysical method in which the subject assigns numbers to a stimulus that are proportional to the subjective magnitude of the stimulus. (1)

Magnocellular (or magno) layer. Layers 1 and 2 of the lateral geniculate nucleus that receive inputs from the M ganglion cells. (3)

Malleus. The first of the ossicles of the middle ear. Receives vibrations from the tympanic membrane and transmits these vibrations to the incus. (10)

M-cells. Retinal ganglion cells that have large cell bodies and that fire in brief bursts. M-cells synapse in the magnocellular layer of the LGN. (3)

McGurk effect. See Audio-visual speech perception. (9, 12)

Mechanoreceptor fibers. Fibers that respond to mechanical displacements of the skin. There are two types of mechanoreceptive fibers, rapidly adapting fibers (the two main kinds being RA1 and PC) and slowly adapting fibers (the two main kinds being SAI and SAII). (13)

Medial geniculate nucleus. A nucleus in the auditory system along the pathway from the cochlea to the auditory cortex. The medial geniculate nucleus receives inputs from the inferior colliculus. (10)

Medial lemniscal pathway. A pathway in the spinal cord that transmits signals from the skin toward the thalamus. (13)

Medium-wavelength pigment. A cone visual pigment that absorbs light maximally in the middle of the spectrum. In humans, this pigment absorbs maximally at 531 nm. (2)

Meissner corpuscle. A receptor in the skin, associated with RA I mechanoreceptors, that responds best to taps on the skin. (13)

Melodic channeling. See Scale illusion. (11)

Melody schema. A representation of a familiar melody that is stored in a person's memory. (11)

Memory color. The idea that an object's characteristic color influences our perception of that object's color. (6)

Meniere's disease. A form of sensorineural hearing loss caused by an excessive buildup of the liquid that fills the cochlea and the semicircular canals. (16)

Menstrual synchrony. Women who live together experience menstrual periods that begin at approximately the same time. (14)

Meridional amblyopia. A condition in which a person has an astigmatism that cannot be optically corrected. (3)

Merkel receptor. A disk-shaped receptor in the skin associated with slowly adapting fibers, small receptive fields, and the perception of pressure. (13)

Metamerism. The situation in which two physically different stimuli are perceptually identical. In color vision, this refers to two lights with different wavelength distributions that appear identical. (6)

Metamers. Two lights that have different wavelength distributions but are perceptually identical. (6)

Method of adjustment. See Adjustment, method of. (1)

Method of constant stimuli. See Constant stimuli, method of. (1)

Method of limits. See Limits, method of. (1)

Microelectrode. A thin piece of wire or glass that is small enough to record electrical signals from single nerve fibers. (1)

Microneurography. A procedure for recording the activity of single neurons in the skin of awake humans. (13)

Microsmatic. Having a weak sense of smell that is not crucial to an animal's survival. (14)

Middle ear. The small air-filled space between the auditory canal and the cochlea that contains the ossicles. (10)

Middle-ear muscles. Muscles attached to the ossicles in the middle ear. The smallest skeletal muscles in the body, they contract in response to very intense sounds and dampen the vibration of the ossicles. (10)

Minimum audible angle. The smallest angle between two sound sources that results in the perception of two separate sounds. (15)

Mirror neurons. Neurons in the premotor area of the monkey's cortex that respond when the monkey grasps an object and also when the monkey observes someone else (another monkey or the experimenter) grasping the object. (9)

Misapplied size constancy. A principle, proposed by Gregory, that when mechanisms that help maintain size constancy in the three-dimensional world are applied to two-dimensional pictures, an illusion of size sometimes results. (7)

Miss. In a signal detection experiment, saying, "No, I don't detect a stimulus" on a trial in which the stimulus is present (an incorrect response). (Appendix)

Missing fundamental, effect of. See Periodicity pitch. (11)

Modular organization. The organization of specific functions into specific brain structures. (1)

Modularity. Specialization of the brain in which specific cortical areas processes information about specific perceptual qualities. (4)

Module. A structure that processes information about a specific behavior or perceptual quality. Often identified as a structure that contains a large proportion of neurons that respond selectively to a particular quality. (4)

Monochromat. A person who is completely color-blind and therefore sees everything as black, white, or shades of gray. A monochromat can match any wavelength in the spectrum by adjusting the intensity of any other wavelength. (6)

Monochromatic light. Light that contains only a single wavelength. (2)

Monocular depth cues. Depth cues, such as overlap, relative size, relative height, familiar size, linear perspective, movement parallax, and accommodation that work if we use only one eye. (7)

Monocular rearing. Rearing an animal so it has use of only one eye. When begun at a young age, this rearing affects development of binocular neurons in the cortex. (7)

Moon illusion. An illusion in which the moon appears to be larger when it is on or near the horizon than when it is high in the sky. (7)

Motile response. A response to sound of the outer hair cells in which the cells move. The cells tilt and get slightly longer, which amplifies basilar membrane vibration and therefore amplifies the response of the inner hair cells. (10)

Motion agnosia. An effect of brain damage in which the ability to perceive motion is disrupted. (8)

Motion capture. A situation in which small elements that are enclosed within a larger figure appear to move with the figure. (8)

Motion parallax. A depth cue. As an observer moves, nearby objects appear to move rapidly whereas far objects appear to move slowly. (7)

Motor area (M1). The area at the rear of the frontal lobe that plays an important role in controlling motor activity. (9)

Motor-dominant neurons. Neurons in the anterior intraparietal cortex (AIP) of the monkey that respond well when a monkey carries out a motor action like pushing a button but don't respond well when the monkey looks at the button. (9)

Motor signal (MS). In corollary discharge theory, the signal that is sent to the eye muscles when the observer moves or tries to move his or her eyes. (8)

Movement aftereffect. An illusion of movement that occurs after a person views an inducing stimulus such as a waterfall. (8)

Movement-produced cues. Cues that create the impression of depth from movement. The movement-produced cues are motion parallax and deletion and accretion. (7)

Müller-Lyer illusion. An illusion consisting of two lines of equal length that appear to be different lengths because of the addition of "fins" to the ends of the lines. (7)

Multimodal. The involvement of a number of different senses in determining perception. For example, speech perception can be influenced by information from a number of different senses, including audition, vision, and touch. See Multimodal neurons. (12)

Multimodal nature of pain. The fact that the experience of pain has both sensory and emotional components. (13)

Multimodal neurons. Neurons that respond to stimulation of two or more senses. (4)

Musical listening. Listening that focuses on the perceptual qualities of a sound—things such as a sound's pitch or timbre (see Everyday listening). (11)

Myopia (nearsightedness). The inability to see distant objects clearly because parallel rays of light are brought to a focus in front of the retina. (15)

Myopia, axial. Myopia caused by an elongated eyeball. (16)

Myopia, refractive. Myopia that occurs when the cornea and the lens bend light too much (they have too much focusing power). (16)

Myopic vision. See Myopia. (15)

Naloxone. A substance that inhibits the activity of opiates. It is hypothesized that naloxone also inhibits the activity of endorphins. (13)

Nasal pharynx. A passageway that connects the mouth cavity and the nasal cavity. (14)

Natural constraints. Basic properties of the environment, such as the fact that intensity usually changes gradually at the borders of shadows. According to some theories of object perception, our perceptual system takes these properties into account as part of the process of object perception. (5)

Near point. The distance at which the lens can no longer accommodate enough to bring close objects into focus. Objects nearer than the near point can be brought into focus only by corrective lenses. (2)

Neovascularization. The formation of abnormal small blood vessels that occurs in patients with diabetic retinopathy. (16)

Nerve. A group of nerve fibers traveling together. (1)

Nerve fiber. In most sensory neurons, the long part of the neuron that transmits electrical impulses from one point to another. Also called the axon. (1)

Neural circuit. A number of neurons that are connected by synapses. (2)

Neural plasticity. The fact that the anatomy and functionality of the nervous system can change in response to experience. Examples are how early visual experience can change the proportion of binocular neurons in the visual cortex and how tactile experience can change the sizes of areas in the cortex that represent different parts of the body. (14)

Neural processing. Operations that transform electrical signals within a network of neurons or that transform the response of individual neurons. (1)

Neurogenesis. The cycle of birth, development, and death of a neuron. This process occurs for the receptors for olfaction and taste. (14)

Neuroimaging. Techniques such as PET and fMRI that have enabled researchers to visualize activity in the human brain in response to both perceptual and other types of stimuli. (1)

Neuron. A cell in the nervous system that generates and transmits electrical impulses. (1)

Neuropsychology. The study of how brain damage affects a person's behavior. (1, 4)

Neurotransmitter. A chemical stored in synaptic vesicles that is released in response to a nerve impulse and has an excitatory or inhibitory effect on another neuron. (1)

Neutral point. The wavelength at which a dichromat perceives gray. (6)

Nociceptor. A fiber that responds to stimuli that are damaging to the skin. (13)

Noise. All stimuli in the environment other than the signal. Noise can also be generated within a person's nervous system. The subject's perception of noise in a signal detection experiment sometimes causes the subject to think mistakenly that a signal has been presented. (Appendix)

Noise-induced hearing loss. A form of sensorineural hearing loss that occurs when loud noises cause degeneration of the hair cells. (16)

Noncorresponding (disparate) points. Two points, one on each retina, that would not overlap if the retinas were slid onto each other. (7)

Nonprimary auditory cortex. Part of the cortex in the temporal lobe that consists of the secondary auditory cortex and the auditory association area. (10)

Nontasters. People who cannot taste the compound phenylthiocarbamide (PTC). (14)

Nucleus of the solitary tract (NST). The nucleus in the brain stem that receives signals from the tongue, the mouth, and the larynx transmitted by the chorda tympani, glossopharyngeal, and vagus nerves. (14)

Oblique effect. The enhanced sensitivity to vertically and horizontally oriented visual stimuli. (3)

Occipital lobe. A lobe at the back of the cortex that is the site of the cortical receiving area for vision. (1)

Occlusion. Depth cue in which one object hides or partially hides another object from view, causing the hidden object to be perceived as being farther away. (7)

Occlusion heuristic. The assumption that a moving object will cover and uncover the background and that when the background is covered it still exists. Thus, when a large object is occluded by a smaller one, we see the larger one as continuing behind the occluder. (5, 8)

Octave. Tones that have frequencies that are binary multiples of each other (×2, ×4, etc.). For example, an 800-Hz tone is one octave above a 400-Hz tone. (10)

Ocular dominance. The degree to which a neuron is influenced by stimulation of each eye. A neuron has a large amount of ocular dominance if it responds only to stimulation of one eye. There is no ocular dominance if the neuron responds equally to stimulation of both eyes. (3)

Ocular dominance column. A column in the visual cortex that contains neurons with the same ocular dominance. (3)

Ocular dominance histogram. A histogram that indicates the degree of ocular dominance of a large population of neurons. (7)

Oculomotor cues. Depth cues that depend on our ability to sense the position of our eyes and the tension in our eye muscles. Accommodation and convergence are oculomotor cues. (7)

Odotope. A group of odorants that share a specific chemical feature that determines neural firing. (14)

Off response. A burst of firing when a stimulus is turned off. (2)

Olfactometer. A device that presents olfactory stimuli with great precision. (14)

Olfactory binding proteins. Proteins contained in the olfactory mucosa that are secreted into the nasal cavity, bind to olfactory stimuli, and transport them to active sites on the olfactory receptors. (14)

Olfactory bulb. The structure that receives signals directly from the olfactory receptors. (14)

Olfactory mucosa. The region inside the nose that contains the receptors for the sense of smell. (14)

Olfactory receptor neurons (ORN). Neurons in the olfactory mucosa that contain the olfactory receptor proteins that respond to odor stimuli. (14)

Ommatidium. A structure in the eye of the *Limulus* that contains a small lens, located directly over a visual receptor. The Limulus eye is made up of hundreds of these ommatidia. (2)

On response. The response of a nerve fiber in which there is an increase in the firing rate when the stimulus is turned on; the same as an excitatory response. (2)

Open-angle glaucoma. See Glaucoma, open-angle. (16)

Ophthalmologist. A person who has specialized in the medical treatment of the eye by completing four or more years of training after receiving the M.D. degree. (16)

Ophthalmoscope. A device that enables an examiner to see the retina and the retinal circulation inside the eye. (16)

Opponent neuron. A neuron that has an excitatory response to wavelengths in one part of the spectrum and an inhibitory response to wavelengths in the other part of the spectrum. (6)

Opponent-process theory of color vision. A theory stating that our perception of color is determined by the activity of two opponent mechanisms: a blue–yellow mechanism and a red–green mechanism. The responses to the two colors in each mechanism oppose each other, one being an excitatory response and the other an inhibitory response. (This theory also includes a black–white mechanism, which is concerned with the perception of brightness.) (6)

Opsin. The protein part of the visual pigment molecule, to which the light-sensitive retinal molecule is attached. (2)

Optic array. The way the light of the environment is structured by the presence of objects, surfaces, and textures. (8)

Optic flow. The flow that occurs when an observer moves relative to the environment. Forward movement causes an expanding optic flow, whereas backward movement causes a contracting optic flow. The term *optic flow field* is used by some researchers to refer to this flow. (9)

Optic nerve. Bundle of nerve fibers that carry impulses from the retina to the lateral geniculate nucleus and other structures. Each optic nerve contains about 1 million ganglion cell fibers. (2)

Optician. A person who is trained to fit glasses and, in some cases, contact lenses. (16)

Optometrist. A person who has received the doctor of optometry (O.D.) degree by completing four years of postgraduate study in optometry school. (16)

Orbitofrontal cortex (OFC). An area in the frontal lobe, near the eyes, that receives signals originating in the olfactory receptors. (14)

Organ of Corti. The major structure of the cochlear partition, containing the basilar membrane, the tectorial membrane, and the receptors for hearing. (10)

Organization, laws of. See Perceptual organization, laws of. (5)

Orientation. The angle of a stimulus relative to vertical. (3)

Orientation column. A column in the visual cortex that contains neurons with the same orientation preference. (3)

Orientation tuning curve. A function relating the firing rate of a neuron to the orientation of the stimulus. (3)

Ossicles. Three small bones in the middle ear that transmit vibrations from the outer to the inner ear. (10)

Otitis media. An infection of the middle ear. (16)

Otorhinolaryngologist. A medical doctor who has specialized in the treatment of diseases and disorders affecting the ear, nose, and throat. More commonly known as an ENT (ear, nose, and throat) specialist. (16)

Otosclerosis. A hereditary condition in which there is a growth of bone in the middle ear. (16)

Otoscope. A device used to see the tympanic membrane. (16)

Outer ear. The pinna and the external auditory meatus. (10)

Outer hair cells. See Hair cells, outer. (10)

Oval window. A small membrane-covered hole in the cochlea that receives vibrations from the stapes. (10)

Pacinian corpuscle. A receptor with a distinctive elliptical shape associated with RA II mechanoreceptors. It transmits pressure to the nerve fiber inside it only at the beginning or end of a pressure stimulus. (13)

Panoramic neuron. A neuron in the auditory system that fires to sounds originating in any direction and that indicates each location by its temporal pattern of firing. (11)

Panretinal photocoagulation. A procedure in which a laser is used to create many small burns on the retina.

This procedure has been successful in treating the neovascularization associated with diabetic retinopathy. (16)

Papillae. Ridges and valleys on the tongue, some of which contain taste buds. There are four types of papillae: filiform, fungiform, foliate, and circumvallate. (14)

Parietal lobe. A lobe at the top of the cortex that is the site of the cortical receiving area for touch. (1)

Partial color constancy. When the perception of an object's color is shifted by a change in illumination, but not as much as would be expected based on the change in the wavelengths reflected from the object. (6)

Parvocellular (or parvo) layers. Layers 3, 4, 5, and 6 of the lateral geniculate nucleus. These neurons receive inputs from the P ganglion cells. (3)

Passive touch. The situation in which a passive subject receives tactile stimulation that is presented by someone else. (13)

Payoffs. A system of rewards and punishments used to influence a subject's motivation in a signal detection experiment. (Appendix)

P-cells. Retinal ganglion cells that have smaller cell bodies than the M-cells and that respond with sustained firing. P-cells synapse in the parvocellular area of the LGN. (3)

Penumbra. The fuzzy border at the edge of a shadow. (6)

Perception. Conscious sensory experience. (1)

Perceptual organization. The process by which small elements become perceptually grouped into larger objects. (5)

Perceptual organization, laws of. Series of rules proposed by the Gestalt psychologists that specify how we organize small parts into wholes. (5)

Perceptual process. A sequence of steps leading from the environment to perception of a stimulus, recognition of the stimulus, and action with regard to the stimulus. (1)

Perceptual segregation. Perceptual organization in which one object is seen as separate from other objects. (5)

Perimetry. A technique in which a small spot of light is presented to different areas of the visual field, to determine areas in which subjects can and cannot perceive the spot. Used to determine the location and extent of scotomas. (16)

Periodicity pitch. The effect in which a complex tone's pitch remains the same even if we eliminate the fundamental frequency. This is also called the effect of the missing fundamental. (10)

Peripheral retina. All of the retina except the fovea and a small area surrounding the fovea. (2)

Permeability. A property of a membrane that refers to the ability of molecules to pass through the membrane. If the permeability to a molecule is high, the molecule can easily pass through the membrane. (1)

Phacoemulsification. A technique for removing a cataract by breaking up the lens with ultrasonic vibrations and then sucking the pieces of lens out of the eye through a hollow needle. (16)

Phantom limb. A person's continued perception of a limb, such as an arm or a leg, even though that limb has been amputated. (13)

Phase locking. Auditory neurons' firing in synchrony with the phase of an auditory stimulus. (10)

Phenomenological method. Method of determining the relationship between stimuli and perception in which the experimenter asks the subject to describe what he or she perceives. (1)

Phoneme. The shortest segment of speech that, if changed, would change the meaning of a word. (12)

Phonemic restoration effect. An effect that occurs in speech perception when listeners perceive a phoneme in a word even though the acoustic signal of that phoneme is obscured by another sound, such as white noise or a cough. (12)

Phonetic boundary. The voice onset time when perception changes from one speech category to another in a categorical perception experiment. (12)

Photorefractive keratotomy (PRK). The first widely used laser procedure for correcting vision. It uses an excimer laser to correct the focusing power of the cornea by modifying its shape (see Laser assisted in situ keratomileusis). (16)

Physiological level of analysis. Analyzing perception by determining how a person's perception is related to physiological processes that are occurring within the person. This approach focuses on determining the relationship between stimuli and physiological responding and between physiological responding and perception. (1)

Pictorial cues. Depth cues, such as overlap, relative height, and relative size, that can be depicted in pictures. (7)

Pigment bleaching. The process that begins when a visual pigment molecule absorbs light. The molecule changes shape, and the color of the rod visual pigment changes from red to transparent. Sometimes, early in this process, visual transduction takes place. (2)

Pigment epithelium. A layer of cells that lines the inside of the eyeball under the retina. (2)

Pigment regeneration. The reconstruction of the visual pigment molecule from its bleached state to its original unbleached state. (2)

Pinna. The part of the ear that is visible on the outside of the head. (10)

Piriform cortex. The primary olfactory cortex, which is located under the temporal lobe. (14)

Pitch. The quality of sound, ranging from low to high, that is most closely associated with the frequency of a tone. (10)

Place theory of hearing. The proposal that the frequency of a sound is indicated by the place along the Organ of Corti at which nerve firing is highest. Modern place theory is based on Békésy's traveling wave theory of hearing. (10)

Placebo. A substance that a person believes will relieve symptoms such as pain but that contains no chemicals that actually act on these symptoms. (13)

Ponzo illusion. An illusion of size in which two rectangles of equal length that are drawn between two converging lines appear to be different in length. Also called the railroad track illusion. (7)

Pop-out. When a stimulus in a perceptual display is immediately evident without search. (5)

Pop-out boundaries. Boundaries between areas in a display that are seen almost immediately because they "pop out." (5)

Positron emission tomography (PET). A technique that can be used in aware human subjects to determine which brain areas are activated by various tasks. (1)

Power function. A mathematical function of the form $P = KS^n$, where P is perceived magnitude, K is a constant, S is the stimulus intensity, and n is an exponent. (1)

Pragnanz, law of. A Gestalt law that is also called the law of good figure or the law of simplicity. It states that every stimulus pattern is seen in such a way that the resulting structure is as simple as possible. (5)

Preattentive stage of processing. An automatic and rapid stage of processing, during which a stimulus is decomposed into small units called primitives. (5)

Precedence effect. The effect that occurs when two identical or very similar sounds reach a listener's ears separated by a time interval of less than about 50 to 100 ms, and the listener hears the sound that reaches his or her ears first. (11)

Preferential looking (PL) technique. A technique used to measure perception in infants. Two stimuli are presented, and the infant's looking behavior is monitored for the amount of time the infant spends viewing each stimulus. (15)

Premotor area. An area in the frontal lobe adjacent to the motor cortex, which transmits signals to the motor cortex. (9)

Presbycusis. A form of sensorineural hearing loss that occurs as a function of age and is usually associated with a decrease in the ability to hear high frequencies. Since this loss also appears to be related to exposure to environmental sounds, it is also called sociocusis. (16)

Presbyopia ("old eye"). The inability of the eye to accommodate due to the hardening of the lens and a weakening of the ciliary muscles. It occurs as people get older. (2)

Primary auditory cortex. Area A1 that is contained in the core area of the monkey auditory cortex in the temporal lobe. (10)

Primary auditory receiving area. See Primary auditory cortex. (10)

Primary cells. Neurons in the IT cortex that respond best to simple stimuli like slits, spots, ellipses, and squares. (See Elaborate cells). (4)

Primary olfactory cortex. The piriform cortex, a small area under the temporal lobe, that receives signals from glomeruli in the olfactory bulb. (14)

Primary receiving area. The area of the cerebral cortex that first receives most of the signals initiated by a sense's receptors. (1)

Principle of componential recovery. Biederman's principle stating that we can identify an object if we can perceive its individual geons. (7)

Principle of univariance. Absorption of a photon by a visual pigment molecule causes the same effect no matter what the wavelength. (6)

Propagated response. A response, such as a nerve impulse, that travels all the way down the nerve fiber without decreasing in amplitude. (1)

Proprioception. The sensing of the position of the limbs. (13)

Prosopagnosia. A form of visual agnosia in which the person can't recognize faces. (4)

Protanopia. A form of red–green dichromatism caused by a lack of the long-wavelength cone pigment. (6)

Proximity, law of. Gestalt law: Things that are near to each other appear to be grouped together. Also called the law of nearness. (5)

Psychophysical level of analysis. Analyzing perception by determining how a person's perception is related to stimulation of environment. This approach focuses on determining the relationship between stimuli in the environment and perceptual responding. (1)

Psychophysical tuning curve. A function that indicates the intensity of masking tones of different frequencies that cause a low-intensity pure tone to become just barely detectable. (10)

Psychophysics. Methods for quantitatively measuring the relationship between properties of the stimulus and the subject's experience. (1)

Pupillary block. A blockage that constricts the opening between the iris and the lens of the eye, making it difficult for aqueous humor to leave the eye. It is caused by the pushed-up iris characteristic of closed-angle glaucoma. (16)

Pure tone. A tone with pressure changes that can be described by a single sine wave. (10)

Pure-tone audiometry. Measurement of the threshold for hearing as a function of the frequency of a pure tone. (16)

Purkinje shift. The shift from cone spectral sensitivity to rod spectral sensitivity that takes place during dark adaptation. (2)

Random-dot stereogram. A stereogram in which the stimuli are pictures of random dots. If one section of this pattern is shifted slightly in one direction, the resulting disparity causes the perception of depth when the patterns are viewed in a stereoscope. (7)

Rapid serial visual presentation (RSVP). The procedure used for determining the attentional blink, in which 10 to 20 stimuli are rapidly presented one after another. (4)

Rapidly adapting (RA) fiber. A mechanoreceptive fiber that adapts rapidly to continuous stimulation of the skin. Rapidly adapting fibers are associated with Meissner corpuscle and Pacinian corpuscle receptors. (13)

Ratio principle. A principle stating that two areas that reflect different amounts of light will look the same if the ratios of their intensities to the intensities of their surrounds are the same. (6)

Rat–man demonstration. The demonstration in which presentation of a "ratlike" or "manlike" picture influences an observer's perception of a second picture, which can be interpreted either as a rat or as a man. (1)

Raw primal sketch. In Marr's computational approach to object perception, a rough sketch of the object that basically overlaps the light and dark areas of an image and that consists of an object's primitives and its edges. The raw primal sketch occurs at an early stage of image processing and is not available to consciousness. (5)

Rayleigh scattering. The scattering of sunlight by small particles in the earth's atmosphere, the amount of scatter being inversely proportional to the fourth power of the light's wavelength. This means that short-wavelength light is scattered more than long-wavelength light and is why we see the sky as blue. (Color essay 3)

Real movement. The physical movement of a stimulus. (8)

Real movement neuron. Neuron in area V3 of the monkey cortex that responds when the stimulus moves but not when movement across the retina is caused by movement of the eyes.

Receiver-operating-characteristic (ROC) curve. A graph in which the results of a signal detection experiment are plotted as the proportion of hits versus the proportion of false alarms for a number of different response criteria. (Appendix)

Receptive field. A neuron's receptive field is the area on the receptor surface (the retina, for vision; the skin, for touch) that, when stimulated, affects the firing of that neuron. There are some exceptions, however, such as receptive fields for auditory space perception in the owl (Chapter 11). In this case, the receptive fields are locations in space rather than areas on the receptor surface. Also, for body-centered visual neurons (Chapter 4), the receptive field is referenced to the body rather than to the retina. (2)

Receptor. A sensory receptor is a neuron sensitive to environmental energy that changes this energy into electrical signals in the nervous system. (1)

Receptor sites. Small areas on the postsynaptic neuron that are sensitive to specific neurotransmitters. (1)

Recognition. The ability to place an object in a category that gives it meaning; for example, recognizing a particular red object as a tomato. (1)

Recognition by components (RBC). A mechanism of object perception proposed by Biederman, in which we recognize objects by decomposing them into volumetric primitives called geons. (5)

Referred sensation. Situation that occurs when stimulating one part of the body results in a sensation in another part of the body. This happens in amputees when stimulating the face causes a sensation in the person's phantom limb (13)

Reflectance. The percentage of light reflected from a surface. (6)

Reflectance curve. A plot showing the percentage of light reflected from an object versus wavelength. (6)

Refraction. A procedure used to determine the power of the corrective lenses needed to achieve clear vision. (16)

Refractive myopia. See Myopia, refractive. (16)

Refractory period. The time period of about 1/1,000 second that a nerve fiber needs to recover from conducting a nerve impulse. No new nerve impulses can be generated in the fiber until the refractory period is over. (1)

Relative height. A depth cue. Objects that have bases below the horizon appear to be farther away if they are higher in the field of view. If the object's bases are above the horizon, they appear to be farther away if they are lower in the field of view. (7)

Relative size. A cue for depth perception. If two objects are of equal size, the one that is farther away will take up less of the field of view. (7)

Repetition discrimination task. Subjects look at a series of objects and respond as quickly as possible when they perceive two identical shapes next to each other. Responding is faster if the shapes form a perceptual group. (5)

Resonance. A mechanism that enhances the intensity of certain frequencies because of the reflection of sound waves in a closed tube. Resonance occurs in the auditory canal. (10)

Resonant frequency. The frequency that is most strongly enhanced by resonance. The resonance frequency of a closed tube is determined by the length of the tube. (10)

Response compression. The result when doubling the physical intensity of a stimulus less than doubles the subjective magnitude of the stimulus. (1)

Response criterion. In a signal detection experiment, the subjective magnitude of a stimulus above which the subject will indicate that the stimulus is present. (Appendix)

Response expansion.   The result when doubling the physical intensity of a stimulus more than doubles the subjective magnitude of the stimulus. (1)

Resting potential.   The difference in charge between the inside and the outside of the nerve fiber when the fiber is not conducting electrical signals. (1)

Retina.   A complex network of cells that covers the inside back of the eye. These cells include the receptors, which generate an electrical signal in response to light, as well as the horizontal, bipolar, amacrine, and ganglion cells. (2)

Retinal.   The light-sensitive part of the visual pigment molecule. (2)

Retinitis pigmentosa.   A retinal disease that causes a gradual loss of vision. (16)

Retinoscopy exam.   Examination with a device called a retinoscope that indicates the power of the corrective lenses needed to achieve normal vision. (16)

Retinotopic map.   A map on a structure in the visual system, such as the lateral geniculate nucleus or the cortex, that indicates locations on the structure that correspond to locations on the retina. In retinotopic maps, locations adjacent to each other on the retina are usually represented by locations that are adjacent to each other on the structure. (3)

Retronasal route.   The opening from the oral cavity, through the nasal pharynx, and into the nasal cavity. This route is the basis for the way smell combines with taste to create flavor. (14)

Reverberation time.   The time it takes for a sound produced in an enclosed space to decrease to 1/1,000 of its original pressure. (11)

Reversible figure–ground.   A figure–ground pattern that perceptually reverses as it is viewed, so that the figure becomes the ground and the ground becomes the figure. (5)

Rod.   Rod-shaped receptor in the retina primarily responsible for vision at low levels of illumination. The rod system is extremely sensitive in the dark but cannot resolve fine details. (2)

Rod–cone break.   The point on the dark adaptation curve at which vision shifts from cone vision to rod vision. (2)

Rod monochromat.   A person who has a retina in which the only functioning receptors are rods. (2)

Ruffini cylinder.   A receptor structure in the skin associated with slowly adapting fibers, large receptive fields, and the perception of "buzzing," stretching of the skin, and limb movements. (13)

Running spectral display.   A way of representing the speech stimulus in which a number of short-term spectra are arranged to show how the frequencies in the speech stimulus change as time progresses. (12)

Salience.   The degree to which an object stands out from a display. (4)

Saturation (color).   The relative amount of whiteness in a chromatic color. The less whiteness a color contains, the more saturated it is. (6)

Scale illusion.   An illusion that occurs when successive notes of a scale are presented alternately to the left and the right ears. Even though each ear receives notes that jump up and down in frequency, smoothly ascending or descending scales are heard in each ear. (11)

Secondary auditory cortex.   Auditory area A2, located next to the primary auditory area (A1). (10)

Secondary cataract.   See Cataract, secondary. (16)

Secondary somatosensory receiving area (S2).   The area in the parietal lobe next to the primary somatosensory area (S1) that processes neural signals related to touch, temperature, and pain. (13)

Segmentation problem.   The problem of perceptually segmenting the continuous speech stimulus into individual words. (12)

Selective adaptation.   A procedure in which a person or animal is selectively exposed to one stimulus and then the effect of this exposure is assessed by testing with a wide range of stimuli. Exposing a person to vertical bars and then testing a person's sensitivity to bars of all orientations is an example of selective adaptation to orientation. Selective adaptation can also be carried out for spatial frequency, wavelength, and speech sounds. (3)

Selective rearing.   A technique in which animals are reared in special environments, usually during their sensitive period. (3)

Selective reflection.   When an object reflects some wavelengths of the spectrum more than others. (6)

Self-produced.   A property of optic flow, which refers to the fact that the moving observer produces this flow by his or her own movement. (9)

Senile cataract.   See Cataract, senile. (16)

Sensations. Elementary elements, which, according to the structuralists, combined to create perceptions. (5)

Sensitive period. A period of time, usually early in an organism's life, during which changes in the environment have a large effect on the organism's physiology or behavior. (7)

Sensitivity. 1.0 divided by the threshold for detecting a stimulus. Thus, lower thresholds correspond to higher sensitivities. (2)

Sensorineural hearing loss. Hearing loss caused by damage within the inner ear. (16)

Sensory code. The information contained in the firing of neurons, which represents what we perceive. (4)

Sensory-specific satiety. The decrease in the pleasantness of food that occurs during eating or smelling the food, caused by stimulation of sensory receptors in the mouth or nose. (14)

Sensory substitution. Substituting one sense for the function served by another, as when touch is substituted for vision. (5)

Shadowing. Subjects' repetition aloud of what they hear as they are hearing it. (12)

Shortest-path constraint. The principle that apparent movement occurs along the shortest path between two stimuli that cause apparent movement when flashed on and off with the appropriate timing. (8)

Short-term spectrum. A plot that indicates the frequencies in a sound stimulus during a short period, usually at the beginning of the stimulus. (12)

Short-wavelength pigment. The cone visual pigment that absorbs maximally at short wavelengths. In the human, this pigment absorbs maximally at about 419 nm. (2)

Signal. The stimulus presented to a subject. A concept in signal detection theory. (Appendix)

Signal detection theory (SDT). A theory stating that the detection of a stimulus depends both on the subject's sensitivity to the stimulus and on the subject's response criterion. (Appendix)

Similarity, law of. A Gestalt law stating that similar things appear to be grouped together. (5)

Simple cortical cell. A neuron in the visual cortex that responds best to bars of a particular orientation. (3)

Simplicity, law of. See Good figure, law of. (5)

Simultaneous color contrast. The change in the perception of a color that occurs when a colored field is surrounded by a differently colored background. (6)

Simultaneous contrast. The effect that occurs when surrounding one color with another changes the appearance of the surrounded color. (2)

Simultaneous lightness contrast. Effect that occurs when one area is surrounded by another area that is either lighter or darker. The surrounding area changes the lightness of the area that is surrounded. (2)

Single dissociation. When, as a result of brain damage, one function is present and another is absent. Existence of a single dissociation indicates that the two functions involve different mechanisms but may not be totally independent of one another. (4)

Size constancy. The constancy of the perception of the size of a stimulus that is maintained even when the object is viewed from different distances. (7)

Size-distance scaling. A hypothesized mechanism that helps maintain size constancy by taking an object's distance into account. (7)

Size-invariant neurons. Neurons that respond equally well to stimuli of various sizes. (4)

Size-specific neuron. Neurons in the IT cortex that respond only to objects with a specific size. (4)

Slit-lamp examination. An examination that checks the condition of the cornea and lens. (16)

Slowly adapting (SA) fiber. A mechanoreceptive fiber in the skin that adapts slowly to continuous stimulation of the skin. Slowly adapting fibers are associated with Merkel receptors and Ruffini cylinders. (13)

Small-diameter fiber (S-fiber). According to gate control theory, activity in S-fibers opens the gate control mechanism and therefore increases the perception of pain. (13)

Somatosensory receiving area (S1). An area in the parietal lobe of the cortex that receives inputs from the skin and the viscera that are associated with somatic senses such as touch, temperature, and pain (see Secondary somatosensory receiving area). (13)

Somatosensory system. The system that includes the cutaneous senses (senses involving the skin), proprioception (the sense of position of the limbs), and kinesthesis (sense of movement of the limbs). (13)

Somatotopic map. A map created on the somatosensory area of the brain by the arrangement of neurons so that neurons that respond to adjacent parts of the body are found next to each other on the brain. (3)

Sound. The experience of hearing. Sound also refers to the physical stimulus for hearing. To avoid confusion, the term acoustic stimulus or sound stimulus can be used to denote the physical sound stimulus. (10)

Sound level. In hearing, short for sound pressure level, which indicates that we have used the standard pressure of 20 micropascals as the standard pressure in determining the decibel level of a stimulus. (10)

Sound pressure level (SPL). A designation used to indicate that the reference pressure used for calculating a tone's decibel rating is set at 2×10^{-5} micropascals, near the threshold in the most sensitive frequency range for hearing. (10)

Sound spectrogram. A plot showing the pattern of intensities and frequencies of a speech stimulus. (12)

Sound waves. Pressure changes in a medium. Most of the sounds we hear are due to pressure changes in the air. (10)

Spatial event plots. Plots showing the pattern of response generated by a neuron to a touch stimulus. (13)

Spatial frequency. For a grating stimulus, spatial frequency refers to the frequency with which the grating repeats itself per degree of visual angle. For more natural stimuli, high spatial frequencies are associated with fine details, and low spatial frequencies are associated with grosser features. (3)

Spatial frequency analyzers. Neurons in the striate cortex that are tuned to respond best to specific spatial frequencies. (3)

Spatial summation. The summation, or accumulation, of the effect of stimulation over a large area. (2, 9)

Specificity coding. Type of neural code in which different perceptions are signaled by activity in specific neurons (see Distributed coding). (4)

Spectral cues. In hearing, the distribution of frequencies reaching the ear that are associated with specific locations of a sound (see Directional transfer function). (11)

Spectral sensitivity. The sensitivity of visual receptors to different parts of the visible spectrum (see Spectral sensitivity curve). (2)

Spectral sensitivity curve. The function relating a subject's sensitivity to light to the wavelength of the light. (2)

Speech reading. The technique of using movement of a speaker's lips and face as an aid to speech perception. (9)

Spinothalamic pathway. One of the nerve pathways in the spinal cord that conducts nerve impulses from the skin to the somatosensory area of the thalamus. (13)

Spontaneous activity. Nerve firing that occurs in the absence of environmental stimulation. (1)

Stapes. The last of the three ossicles in the middle ear. It receives vibrations from the incus and transmits these vibrations to the oval window of the inner ear. (10)

Stereoacuity. The ability to resolve small differences in disparity. (15)

Stereopsis. The impression of depth that results from differences in the images on the retinas of the two eyes. (7)

Stereoscope. A device that presents pictures to the left and the right eyes so that the binocular disparity a person would experience when viewing an actual scene is duplicated. The result is a convincing illusion of depth. (7)

Stevens's power law. A law concerning the relationship between the physical intensity of a stimulus and the perception of the subjective magnitude of the stimulus. The law states that $P = KS^n$, where P is perceived magnitude, K is a constant, S is the stimulus intensity, and n is an exponent. (1)

Stimulation-produced analgesia (SPA). Brain stimulation that eliminates or strongly decreases the perception of pain. (13)

Stimulus deprivation amblyopia. Amblyopia due to early closure of one eye. (7)

Striate cortex. The visual receiving area of the cortex, located in the occipital lobe. (2)

Stroboscopic movement. See Apparent movement. (8)

Structuralism. The approach to psychology, prominent in the late 19th and early 20th centuries, that postulated that perceptions result from the summation of many elementary sensations. (5)

Substantia gelatinosa. A nucleus in the spinal cord that, according to gate control theory, receives inputs from S-fibers and L-fibers and sends inhibition to the T-cell. (13)

Subtraction technique. A technique used to analyze the results of neuroimaging experiments, in which brain activity elicited by a control condition is subtracted from the activity elicited by an experimental condition in order to determine the activity that can be attributed to the experimental condition alone. (1)

Subtractive color mixture. See Color mixture, subtractive. (Color Essay 3)

Superior olivary nucleus. A nucleus along the auditory pathway from the cochlea to the auditory cortex. The superior olivary nucleus receives inputs from the cochlear nucleus. (10)

Synapse. A small space between the end of one neuron and the cell body of another neuron. (1)

Synaptic vesicles. Small compartments at the end of the presynaptic neuron that contain neurotransmitter. (1)

Synchrony, principle of. A modern principle of organization that states that visual events that occur at the same time will be perceived as belonging together. (5)

Synesthesia. Occurs when stimulation of one modality leads to perceptual experience in another modality, as when hearing sounds results in the perception of colors. (10)

Tadoma. A method of tactile speech perception in which a person identifies speech sounds by feeling the vibrations of a speaker's vocal cords. (12)

Taste-blind. A person who is taste-blind cannot taste phenylthiocarbamide (PTC) and also tends to be less sensitive to certain other tastes than someone who is not taste-blind. (14)

Taste bud. A structure located within papillae on the tongue that contains the taste cells. (14)

Taste cells. Cells located in taste buds that cause the transduction of chemical to electrical energy when chemicals contact receptor sites or channels located at the tips of these cells. (14)

Taste pore. An opening in the taste bud through which the tips of taste cells protrude. When chemicals enter a taste pore, they stimulate the taste cells and result in transduction. (14)

Tau. The ratio of an approaching object's image size at two different times divided by how fast the object's edges are expanding. Tau may play a role in determining time to collision. (9)

Tectorial membrane. A membrane that stretches the length of the cochlea and is located directly over the hair cells. Vibrations of the cochlear partition cause the tectorial membrane to stimulate the hair cells by rubbing against them. (10)

Temporal lobe. A lobe on the side of the cortex that is the site of the cortical receiving area for hearing. (1)

Texture gradient. The pattern formed by a regularly textured surface that extends away from the observer. The elements in a texture gradient appear smaller as distance from the observer increases. (7)

Texture segregation. The perceptual separation of fields with different textures. (7)

Thalamus. A nucleus in the brain where neurons from all of the senses, except smell, synapse on their way to their cortical receiving areas. (2)

Thermoreceptor. Receptors in the skin that respond to specific temperatures or changes in temperature. (13)

Threshold, absolute. The minimum stimulus energy necessary for an observer to detect a stimulus. (1)

Threshold, difference. The minimal detectable difference between two stimuli. (1)

Timbre. The quality of a tone. Different musical instruments have different timbres, so when we play the same note on different instruments, the notes have the same pitch but sound different. (10, 11)

Tinnitus. A condition caused by damage in the inner ear in which a person experiences ringing in the ears. (16)

Tinnitus masker. A unit that generates white noise to mask the ringing in the ears associated with tinnitus. (16)

Tone chroma. The perceptual similarity of notes separated by one or more octaves. (10)

Tone height. The increase in pitch that occurs as frequency is increased. (10)

Tonometer. A device for measuring the eye's intraocular pressure. (16)

Tonometry. An examination that determines the pressure inside the eye. (16)

Tonotopic map. The frequency map that is formed on an auditory structure when neurons with the same characteristic frequency are grouped together and neurons with nearby characteristic frequencies are found near each other. (3, 10)

Top-down processing. Processing that starts with the analysis of high-level information, such as the context in which a stimulus is seen. (1)

Transduction. In the senses, the transformation of environmental energy into electrical energy. For example, the retinal receptors transduce light energy into electrical energy. (1)

Transmission cell (T-cell). According to gate control theory, the cell that receives input from the L- and S-fibers. Activity in the T-cell determines the perception of pain. (13)

Traumatic cataract. See Cataract, traumatic. (16)

Traveling wave. In the auditory system, vibration of the basilar membrane in which the peak of the vibration travels from the base of the membrane to its apex. (10)

Trichromat. A person with normal color vision. Trichromats can match any wavelength in the spectrum by mixing three other wavelengths in various proportions. (5)

Trichromatic theory of color vision. A theory postulating that our perception of color is determined by the ratio of activity in three cone receptor mechanisms with different spectral sensitivities. (6)

Tritanopia. A form of dichromatism thought to be caused by a lack of the short-wavelength cone pigment. (6)

Tuning curve, frequency. See Frequency tuning curve. (10)

Tuning curve, orientation. See Orientation tuning curve. (3)

Tunnel vision. Vision that results when there is little peripheral vision. (16)

$2^1/_2$-D sketch. The second stage of Marr's computational process. This stage is the result of processing the primitives. The resulting $2^1/_2$-D sketch is then transformed into the 3-D representation. (5)

Two-point threshold. The smallest separation between two points on the skin that is perceived as two points; a measure of acuity on the skin. (13)

Tympanic membrane (eardrum). A membrane at the end of the auditory canal that vibrates in response to vibrations of the air and transmits these vibrations to the ossicles in the middle ear. (10)

Tympanometer. A device for measuring how well the tympanic membrane and the middle-ear bones respond to sound vibrations. (16)

Tympanometry. Procedure for measuring how well the tympanic membrane and middle ear bones are responding to sound vibrations. (16)

Uncrossed disparity. Binocular disparity that occurs when objects are located beyond the horopter (see Crossed disparity). (7)

Unilateral dichromat. A person who has dichromatic vision in one eye and trichromatic vision in the other eye. (6)

Vagus nerve. A nerve that conducts signals from taste receptors in the mouth and larynx. (14)

Ventral pathway. Pathway that conducts signals from the striate cortex to the temporal lobe. This has also been called the "what" pathway to indicate its function. (4)

Ventral posterior nucleus. A nucleus in the thalamus that receives inputs from the somatosensory system, primarily from the spinothalamic and lemniscal pathways. (13)

Ventriloquism aftereffect. A ventriloquism effect that continues even after the visual stimulus that caused the original ventriloquism effect is no longer present. (11)

Ventriloquism effect. See Visual capture. (7)

Veridical perception. Perception that matches the actual physical situation. (7)

Video microscopy. A technique that has been used to take pictures of papillae and taste buds on the tongue. (14)

View invariant. Shapes that have properties that don't change when viewed from different angles. The geons in the RBC theory of object perception are view invariant. (5)

View-invariant neurons. Neurons that respond equally well to different views of an object. View-invariant neurons for faces have been found in IT cortex (see View-specific neurons). (4)

View-specific neurons. Neurons that respond best to specific views of a stimulus. View-specific neurons that respond best to specific views of faces have been found in IT cortex (see View-invariant neurons). (4)

Virtual space receptive field. The locations in space to which a cortical neuron responds to auditory stimuli. (11)

Visible light. Band of electromagnetic energy that can be perceived with the visual system. For humans, visible light has wavelengths between 400 and 700 nanometers. (2)

Visual acuity. The ability to resolve small details. (2)

Visual and motor neurons. Neurons in the monkey's anterior intraparietal cortex that respond to both pushing a button and looking at it. (9)

Visual angle. The angle between two lines that extend from the observer's eye, one line extending to one end of an object and the second to the other end of the object. An object's visual angle is always determined relative to an observer; therefore, an object's visual angle changes as the distance between the object and the observer changes. (3)

Visual capture. When sound is heard coming from its seen location, even though it is actually originating somewhere else. Also called the ventriloquism effect. (7)

Visual direction strategy. A strategy used by moving observers to reach a destination by keeping their body oriented toward the target. (9)

Visual-dominant neurons. Neurons in the monkey's anterior intraparietal cortex that respond to pushing a button in the light, but not in the dark, and respond best to just looking at the button. (9)

Visual evoked potential (VEP). An electrical response to visual stimulation recorded by the placement of disk electrodes on the back of the head. This potential reflects the activity of a large population of neurons in the visual cortex. (1, 15)

Visual feedback model. Explanation for the development of emmetropia that states that the growth of the eyeball that occurs during this development is controlled by errors in the focusing of light on the retina. Thus, if there is an error in focusing, the eye grows to eliminate this error. (15)

Visual form agnosia. A condition in which a person can see clearly but has difficulty recognizing what he or she sees. This condition, which is often caused by brain injuries, makes it difficult for people to synthesize parts of an object into an integrated whole. (1, 4)

Visual pigment. A light-sensitive molecule contained in the rod and cone outer segments. The reaction of this molecule to light results in the generation of an electrical response in the receptors. (2)

Visual receiving area (or visual cortex). The area in the occipital lobe, also called the striate cortex, that receives inputs from the lateral geniculate nucleus. (2)

Visual search. A procedure in which a subject's task is to find a particular element in a display that contains a number of elements. (5)

Visual transduction. Transformation of light energy into electrical energy that occurs in the rod and cone receptors in the retina. (2)

Vitrectomy. A procedure in which a needle placed inside the eye removes vitreous humor and replaces it with a salt solution. This procedure is used if the vitreous humor is filled with blood, usually because of neovascularization. (16)

Vitreous humor. The jellylike substance that fills the eyeball. (16)

Voice onset time (VOT). In speech production, the time delay between the beginning of a sound and the beginning of the vibration of the vocal chords. (12)

Volumetric primitives. Primitives proposed in the recognition-by-components theory of recognition that are three-dimensional shapes roughly corresponding to an object's parts. (5)

Warm fiber. A nerve fiber that responds to increases in temperature or to steady high temperatures. (13)

Waterfall illusion. An aftereffect of movement that occurs after viewing a stimulus moving in one direction, such as a waterfall. Viewing the waterfall creates other objects to appear to move in the opposite direction. (8)

Wavelength. For light energy, the distance between one peak of a light wave and the next peak. (2)

Weber's law. A law stating that the difference threshold (DL) equals a constant (K), called the Weber fraction, times the size of the stimulus (S). This law is usually expressed in the form $K = JND/S$. (1)

Wernike's aphasia. An inability to comprehend words or arrange sounds into coherent speech. (12)

What pathway. See Ventral pathway. (4)

Where pathway. See Dorsal pathway. (4)

White's illusion. A display in which two rectangles are perceived as differing in lightness even though they both reflect the same amount of light and even though the rectangle that is perceived as lighter receives more lateral inhibition than the one perceived as darker. (2)

Young-Helmholtz theory of color vision. See Trichromatic theory of color vision. (6)

Zero disparity cell. A neuron in the visual cortex that responds best when the images of an object fall on corresponding points in each eye. (7)

References

Abbott, L. F., Rolls, E. T., & Tovee, M. J. (1996). Representational capacity of face coding in monkeys. *Cerebral Cortex, 6,* 498–505.

Abeles, M., & Goldstein, M. H. (1970). Functional architecture in cat primary auditory cortex: Columnar organization and organization according to depth. *Journal of Neurophysiology, 33,* 172–187.

Abramov, I., & Gordon, J. (1994). Color appearance: On seeing red, or yellow, or green, or blue. *Annual Review of Psychology, 45,* 451–485.

Abramov, I., Gordon, J., Hendrickson, A., Hainline, L., Dobson, V., & LaBossiere, E. (1982). The retina of the newborn human infant. *Science, 217,* 265–267.

Ache, B. W. (1991). Phylogeny of smell and taste. In T. V. Getchell, R. L. Doty, L. M. Bartoshuk, & J. B. Snow (Eds.), *Smell and taste in health and disease* (pp. 3–18). New York: Raven Press.

Ackerman, D. (1990). *A natural history of the senses.* New York: Vintage Books.

Ackerman, D. (1995). *Mystery of the senses: Taste.* Boston: WGBH-TV and Washington, DC: WETA-TV.

Adelson, E. H. (1999). Light perception and lightness illusions. In M. Gazzaniga (Ed.), *The new cognitive neurosciences.* Cambridge, MA: MIT Press, pp. 339–351.

Adelson, E. H. (1993). Perceptual organization and the judgment of brightness. *Science, 262,* 2042–2044.

Adrian, E. D. (1928). *The basis of sensation.* New York: Norton.

Adrian, E. D. (1932). *The mechanism of nervous action.* Philadelphia: University of Pennsylvania Press.

Ahissar, M., Ahissar, E., Bergman, H., & Vaadia, E. (1992). Encoding of sound-source location and movement: Activity of single neurons and interactions between adjacent neurons in the monkey auditory cortex. *Journal of Neurophysiology, 67,* 203–215.

Albrecht, D. G., DeValois, R. L., & Thorell, L. G. (1980). Visual cortical neurons: Are bars or gratings the optimal stimuli? *Science, 207,* 88–90.

Albright, T. (1994). Why do things look as they do? *Trends in Neurosciences, 17,* 175–177.

Albright, T. D., Desimone, R., & Gross, C. A. (1984). Columnar organization of directionally selective cells in visual area MT of the macaque. *Journal of Neurophysiology, 51,* 16–31.

Alpern, M., Kitahara, K., & Krantz, D. H. (1983). Perception of color in unilateral tritanopia. *Journal of Physiology, 335,* 683–697.

Andersen, R. A., Snyder, L. H., Bradley, D. C., & Xing, J. (1997). Multimodal representation of space in the posterior parietal cortex and its use in planning movements. *Annual Review of Neuroscience, 20,* 303–330.

Anderson, R. A., & Bradley, D. C. (1998). Perception of three-dimensional structure from motion. *Trends in Cognitive Sciences, 2,* 222–228.

Arnheim, R. (1974). *Art and visual perception* (2nd ed.). Berkeley: University of California Press.

Ashmead, D. H., Davis, D. L., Whalen, T., & Odom, R. (1991). Sound localization and sensitivity to interaural time differences in human infants. *Child Development, 62,* 1211–1226.

Ashmead, D. H., DeFord, L., & Odom, R. D. (1990). Perception of relative distances of nearby sound sources. *Perception and Psychophysics, 47,* 326–331.

Aslin, R. N. (1977). Development of binocular fixation in human infants. *Journal of Experimental Child Psychology, 23,* 133–150.

Aslin, R. N. (1981). Development of smooth pursuit in infants. In D. F. Fisher, R. A. Monty, & J. W. Senders (Eds.), *Eye movements: Cognition and visual perception.* Hillsdale, NJ: Erlbaum.

Aubert, H. (1886). Die Bewegungsempfindung. *Archiv für die gesamte Physiologie des Menschen und der Tiere, 39,* 347–370.

Au, W. W. L. (1993). *The sonar of dolphins.* New York: Academic Press.

Au Eong, K. G., Tay, T. H., & Lim, M. K. (1993). Race, culture and myopia in 110,236 young Singaporean males. *Singapore Medical Journal, 34,* 29–32.

Awaya, S., Miyake, Y., Imayuni, Y., Shiose, Y., Kanda, T., & Komuro, K. (1973). Amblyopia in man, suggestive of stimulus deprivation amblyopia. *Japanese Journal of Ophthalmology, 17,* 69–82.

Axel, R. (1995, April). The molecular logic of smell. *Scientific American 273,* 154–159.

Azzopardi, P., & Cowey, A. (1993). Preferential representation of the fovea in the primary visual cortex. *Nature, 361,* 719–721.

Bach-y-Rita, P. (1972). *Brain mechanisms in sensory substitution.* New York: Academic Press.

Bach-y-Rita, P., Collins, C. C., Saunders, F., White, B., & Scadden, L. (1969). Vision substitution by tactile image projection. *Nature, 221,* 963–964.

Bach-y-Rita, P., Collins, C. C., Scadden, C., Holmlund, G. W., & Hart, B. K. (1970). Display techniques in a tactile vision substitution system. *Medical and Biological Illustration, 20,* 6–12.

Backhaus, W. G. K. (1998). Physiological and psychophysical simulations of color vision in humans and animals. In W. G. K. Backhaus, R. Kliegl, & J. S. Werner (Eds.), *Color vision: Perspectives from different disciplines.* New York: Walter de Gruyter, pp. 45–77.

Backus, J. (1977). *The acoustical foundations of music* (2nd ed.). New York: Norton.

Baird, J. C., Wagner, M., & Fuld, K. (1990). A simple but powerful theory of the moon illusion. *Journal of Experimental Psychology: Human Perception and Performance, 16,* 675–677.

Balogh, R. D., & Porter, R. H. (1986). Olfactory preferences resulting from mere exposure in human neonates. *Infant Behavior and Development, 9,* 395–401.

Banks, M. S. (1982). The development of spatial and temporal contrast sensitivity. *Current Eye Research, 2,* 191–198.

Banks, M. S., & Bennett, P. J. (1988). Optical and photoreceptor immaturities limit the spatial and chromatic vision of human neonates. *Journal of the Optical Society of America, A5,* 2059–2079.

Banks, M. S., & Salapatek, P. (1978). Acuity and contrast sensitivity in 1-, 2-, and 3-month-old human infants. *Investigative Ophthalmology and Visual Science, 17,* 361–365.

Banks, M. S., & Salapatek, P. (1981). Infant pattern vision: A new approach based on the contrast sensitivity function. *Journal of Experimental Child Psychology, 31,* 1–45.

Bannister, H., & Blackburn, J. M. (1931). An eye factor affecting proficiency at ball games. *British Journal of Psychology, 21,* 382–384.

Bardy, B. G., & Laurent, M. (1998). How is body orientation controlled during somersaulting? *Journal of Experimental Psychology: Human Perception and Performance, 24,* 963–977.

Barinaga, M. (1994). Neurons tap out a code that may help locate sounds. *Science, 264,* 775.

Barlow, H. B., Blakemore, C., & Pettigrew, J. D. (1967). The neural mechanism of binocular depth discrimination. *Journal of Physiology, 193,* 327–342.

Barlow, H. B., & Mollon, J. D. (Eds.). (1982). *The senses.* Cambridge, England: University of Cambridge Press.

Barrow, H. G., & Tannenbaum, J. M. (1986). Computational approaches to vision. In K. R. Boff, L. Kaufman, & J. P. Thomas (Eds.), *Handbook of perception and human performance* (Chapter 35). New York: Wiley.

Bartoshuk, L. M. (1971). The chemical senses: I. Taste. In J. W. Kling & L. A. Riggs (Eds.), *Experimental psychology* (3rd ed.). New York: Holt, Rinehart and Winston.

Bartoshuk, L. M. (1979). Bitter taste of saccharin: Related to the genetic ability to taste the bitter substance propylthioural (PROP). *Science, 205,* 934–935.

Bartoshuk, L. M. (1980, September). Separate worlds of taste. *Psychology Today, 243,* 48–56.

Bartoshuk, L. M., & Beauchamp, G. K. (1994). Chemical senses. *Annual Review of Psychology, 45,* 419–449.

Bartoshuk, L. M., Cain, W. S., & Pfaffmann, C. (1985). Taste and olfaction. In G. A. Kimble & K. Schlesinger (Eds.), *Topics in the history of psychology* (Vol. 1, pp. 221–260). Hillsdale, NJ: Erlbaum.

Battaglini, P. P., Galletti, C., & Fattori, P. (1996). Cortical mechanisms for visual perception of object motion and position in space. *Behavioural Brain Research, 76,* 143–154.

Baumgart, F., Gaschler-Markefski, B., Woldorff, M. G., Heinze, H-J., Scheich, H. (1997). A movement-sensitive area in auditory cortex. *Nature, 400,* 724–726.

Baylis, G. C., & Driver, J. (1995). One-sided edge assignment in vision: 1. Figure–ground segmentation and attention to objects. *Current Directions in Psychological Science, 4,* 140–146.

Baylor, D. (1992). Transduction in retinal photoreceptor cells. In P. Corey & S. D. Roper (Eds.), *Sensory transduction* (pp. 151–174). New York: Rockefeller University Press.

Beauchamp, G. K., Bertino, M., & Engelman, K. (1991). Human salt appetite. In M. I. Friedman, M. G. Tordoff, & M. R. Kare (Eds.), *Chemical senses* (Vol. 4, pp. 85–108). New York: Marcel Dekker.

Beauchamp, G. K., Cowart, B. J., & Moran, M. (1986). Developmental changes in salt acceptability in human infants. *Developmental Psychobiology, 19,* 17–25.

Beauchamp, G. K., Cowart, B. J., & Schmidt, H. J. (1991). Development of chemosensory sensitivity and preference. In T. V. Getchell, R. L. Doty, L. M. Bartoshuk, & J. B. Snow (Eds.), *Smell and taste in health and disease* (pp. 405–416). New York: Raven Press.

Beauchamp, M. S., Hazby, J. V., Jennings, J. E., & DeYoe, E. A. (1999). An fMRI version of the Farnsworth-Munsell 100-hue test reveals multiple color-selective areas in human ventral occipitotemporal cortex. *Cerebral Cortex, 9,* 257–263.

Beck, J. (1982). Textural segmentation. In J. Beck (Ed.), *Organization and representation in perception.* Hillsdale, NJ: Erlbaum.

Beck, J., Hope, B., & Rosenfeld, A. (Eds.). (1983). *Human and machine vision.* New York: Academic Press.

Békésy, G. von (1960). *Experiments in hearing.* New York: McGraw-Hill.

Benary, W. (1924). Beobachtungen zu einem. Experiment uber Helligkeitz-kontrast (Observations concerning an experiment on brightness contrast). *Psychologische Forschung, 5,* 131–142.

Beranek, L. L. (1996). *Concert and opera halls: How they sound.* Woodbury, NY : Acoustical Society of America.

Berger, K. W. (1964). Some factors in the recognition of timbre. *Journal of the Acoustical Society of America, 36,* 1881–1891.

Berkow, I. (1995, January 5). The sweetest sound of all. *New York Times,* p. B8.

Berlucchi, G., & Agloti, S. (1997). The body in the brain: neural bases of corporeal awareness. *Trends in Neurosciences, 20,* 560–564.

Bertenthal, B. I., Proffitt, D. R., Spetner, N. B., & Thomas, M. A. (1985). The development of infant sensitivity to biomechanical motions. *Child Development, 56,* 531–543.

Berthenthal, B. I., Rose, J. L., & Bai, D. L. (1997). Perception-action coupling in the development of visual control of posture. *Journal of Experimental Psychology: Human Perception and Performance, 23,* 1631–1643.

Bhalla, M., & Proffitt, D. R. (1999). Visual-motor recalibration in geographical slant perception. *Journal of Experimental Psychology: Human Perception and Performance, 25,* 1076–1096.

Biederman, I. (1987). Recognition-by-components: A theory of human image understanding. *Psychological Review, 94,* 115–147.

Biederman, I., & Cooper, E. E. (1991). Priming contour-deleted images: Evidence for intermediate representations in visual object recognition. *Cognitive Psychology, 23,* 393–419.

Biederman, I., Cooper, E. E., Hummel, J. E., & Fiser, J. (1993). Geon theory as an account of shape recognition in mind, brain, and machine. In J. Illingworth (Ed.), *Proceedings of the Fourth British Machine Vision Conference* (pp. 175–186). Guildford, Surrey, U.K.: BMVA Press.

Birnberg, J. R. (1988). My turn. *Newsweek,* March 21.

Blake, R., & Hirsch, H. V. B. (1975). Deficits in binocular depth perception in cats after alternating monocular deprivation. *Science, 190,* 1114–1116.

Blake, R., & Wilson, H. R. (1991). Neural models of stereoscopic vision. *Trends in Neuroscience, 14,* 445–452.

Blakemore, C., & Cooper, G. G. (1970). Development of the brain depends on the visual environment. *Nature, 228,* 477–478.

Blakemore, C., & Tobin, E. A. (1972). Lateral inhibition between orientation detectors in the cat's visual cortex. *Experimental Brain Research, 15,* 439–440.

Blauert, J. (1997). *Spatial hearing: The psychophysics of human sound localization, Revised edition.* Cambridge, MA: MIT Press.

References

Bloom, F., Lazerson, A., & Hofstadter, L. (1985). *Brain, mind, and behavior*. New York: Freeman.

Blumstein, S. E., & Stevens, K. N. (1979). Acoustic invariance in speech production: Evidence from measurements of the spectral characteristics of stop consonants. *Journal of the Acoustical Society of America, 66*, 1001–1007.

Bolanowski, S. J., Gescheider, G. A., & Verrillo, R. T. (1994). Hairy skin: Psychophysical channels and their physiological substrates. *Somatosensory and Motor Research, 11*, 279–290.

Bolanowski, S. J., Gescheider, G. A., Verrillo, R. T., & Checkosky, C. M. (1988). Four channels mediate the mechanical aspects of touch. *Journal of the Acoustical Society of America, 84*, 1680–1694.

Bonda, E., Petrides, M., Ostry, D., & Evans, A. (1996). Specific involvement of human parietal systems and the amygdala in the perception of biological motion. *Journal of Neuroscience, 161*, 3737–3744.

Boring, E. G. (1942). *Sensation and perception in the history of experimental psychology*. New York: Appleton-Century-Crofts.

Bornstein, M. H., Kessen, W., & Weiskopf, S. (1976). Color vision and hue categorization in young human infants. *Journal of Experimental Psychology: Human Perception and Performance, 2*, 115–119.

Boussourd, D., Ungerleider, L. G., & Desimone, R. (1990). Pathways for motion analysis: Cortical connections of the medial superior temporal and fundus of the superior temporal visual areas in the macaque. *Journal of Comparative Neurology, 296*, 462–495.

Bowmaker, J. K., & Dartnall, H. J. A. (1980). Visual pigments of rods and cones in a human retina. *Journal of Physiology, 298*, 501–511.

Boynton, R. M. (1979). *Human color vision*. New York: Holt, Rinehart and Winston.

Bozza, T. C. & Kauer, J. S. (1998). Odorant response properties of convergent olfactory receptor neurons. *Journal of Neuroscience, 18*, 4560–4569.

Bradley, D. R., & Petry, H. M. (1977). Organizational determinants of subjective contour: The subjective Necker cube. *American Journal of Psychology, 90*, 253–262.

Brainard, D. H., & Wandell, B. A. (1986). Analysis of the retinex theory of color vision. *Journal of the Optical Society of America, A3*, 1651–1661.

Bregman, A. (1981). Asking the "what for" question in auditory perception. In M. Kubovy & J. R. Pomerantz (Eds.), *Perceptual organization*. Hillsdale, NJ: Erlbaum, pp. 99–119.

Bregman, A. S. (1990). *Auditory scene analysis*. Cambridge: MIT Press.

Bregman, A. S. (1993). Auditory scene analysis: Hearing in complex environments. In S. McAdams & E. Bigand (Eds.), *Thinking in sound: The cognitive psychology of human audition* (pp. 10–36). Oxford, England: Oxford University Press.

Bregman, A. S., & Campbell, J. (1971). Primary auditory stream segregation and perception of order in rapid sequence of tones. *Journal of Experimental Psychology, 89*, 244–249.

Bregman, A. S., & Pinker, S. (1978). Auditory streaming and the building of timbre. *Canadian Journal of Psychology, 32*, 19–31.

Bregman, A. S., & Rudnicky, A. I. (1975). Auditory segregation: Stream or streams? *Journal of Experimental Psychology: Human Perception and Performance, 1*, 263–267.

Bridgeman, B., & Stark, L. (1991). Ocular proprioception and efference copy in registering visual direction. *Vision Research, 31*, 1903–1913.

Britten, K. H., Shadlen, M. N., Newsome, W. T., & Movshon, J. A. (1993). Responses of neurons in macaque MT to stochastic motion signals. *Visual Neuroscience, 10*, 1157–1169.

Brosch, M., Bauer, R., & Eckhorn, R. (1997). Stimulus-dependent modulations of correlated high-frequency oscillations in cat visual cortex. *Cerebral Cortex, 7*, 70–76.

Brown, A. A., Dowell, R. C., & Clark, G. M. (1987). Clinical results for postlingually deaf patients implanted with multichannel cochlear prosthetics. *Annals of Otology, Rhinology, and Laryngology, 96*(Suppl. 128), 127–128.

Brown, C. M. (1984). Computer vision and natural constraints. *Science, 224*, 1299–1305.

Brown, K. T. (1969). A linear *area centralis* extending across the turtle retina and stabilized to the horizon by nonvisual cues. *Vision Research, 9*, 1053–1062.

Brown, P. K., & Wald, G. (1964). Visual pigments in single rods and cones of the human retina. *Science, 144*, 45–52.

Brownell, W. E., Bader, C. R., Bertrand, D., & Ribaupierre, Y. D. (1985). Evoked mechanical responses of isolated cochlear outer hair cells. *Science, 227*, 194–196.

Bruce, C., Desimone, R., & Gross, C. G. (1981). Visual properties of neurons in a polysensory area in the superior temporal sulcus of the macaque. *Journal of Neurophysiology, 46*, 369–384.

Brugge, J. F., & Merzenich, M. M. (1973). Responses of neurons in auditory cortex of the macaque monkey to monaural and binaural stimulation. *Journal of Neurophysiology, 36,* 1138–1158.

Brugge, J. F., Reale, R. A., & Hind, J. E. (1997). Auditory cortex and spatial hearing. In R. H. Kilkey & T. R. Anderson. (Eds.) *Binaural and spatial hearing in real and virtual environments.* Hillsdale, NJ: Erlbaum pp. 447–473.

Brugger, P., Kollias, S. S., Muri, R. M., Crelier, G., Hepp-Reymond, M-C., & Regard, M. (2000). Beyond remembering: Phantom sensations of congenitally absent limbs. *Proceedings of the National Academy of Sciences, 97,* 6167–6172.

Brungart, D. S., Durlach, N. I., & Rabinowitz, W. M. (1999). Auditory localization of nearby sound sources II: Localization of a broadband source. *Journal of the Acoustical Society of America, 106,* 1956–1968.

Bruno, N., & Cutting, J. E. (1988). Minimodularity and the perception of layout. *Journal of Experimental Psychology: General, 117,* 161–170.

Buchsbaum, G., & Gottschalk, A. (1983). Trichromacy, opponent colours coding and optimum colour information transmission in the retina. *Proceedings of the Royal Society of London, B220,* 89–110.

Buck, L., & Axel, R. (1991). A novel multigene family may encode odorant receptors: A molecular basis for odor recognition. *Cell, 65,* 175–187.

Bugelski, B. R., & Alampay, D. A. (1961). The role of frequency in developing perceptual sets. *Canadian Journal of Psychology, 15,* 205–211.

Bunch, C. C. (1929). Age variations in auditory acuity. *Archives of Otolaryngology, 9,* 625–626.

Burr, D. C., Morrone, M. C., & Vaina, L. M. (1998). Large receptive fields for optic flow detection in humans. *Vision Research, 38,* 1731–1743.

Burton, A. M., Young, A. W., Bruce, V., Johnston, R. A., & Ellis, A. W. (1991). Understanding covert recognition. *Cognition, 39,* 129–166.

Bushnell, E. W., & Weinberger, N. (1987). Infants' detection of visual–tactual discrepancies: Asymmetries that indicate a directive role of visual information. *Journal of Experimental Psychology: Human Perception and Performance, 13,* 601–608.

Bushnell, I. W. R., Sai, F., & Mullin, J. T. (1989). Neonatal recognition of the mother's face. *British Journal of Developmental Psychology, 7,* 3–15.

Cabanac, M. (1971). Physiological role of pleasure. *Science, 173,* 1103–1107.

Cabanac, M. (1979). Sensory pleasure. *Quarterly Review of Biology, 54,* 1–29.

Cabanac, M., & Fantino, M. (1977). Origin of olfacto-gustatory alliesthesia: Intestinal sensitivity to carbohydrate concentration? *Physiology & Behavior, 18,* 1039–1045.

Cain, W. S. (1977). Differential sensitivity for smell: "Noise" at the nose. *Science, 195,* 796–798.

Cain, W. S. (1979). To know with the nose: Keys to odor identification. *Science, 203,* 467–470.

Cain, W. S. (1980). *Sensory attributes of cigarette smoking* (Branbury Report: 3. A safe cigarette?, pp. 239–249). Cold Spring Harbor, NY: Cold Spring Harbor Laboratory.

Cain, W. S. (1988). Olfaction. In R. A. Atkinson, R. J. Herrnstein, G. Lindzey, & R. D. Luce (Eds.), *Stevens' handbook of experimental psychology: Vol. 1. Perception and motivation* (Rev. ed., pp. 409–459). New York: Wiley.

Calvert, G. A., Bullmore, E. T., Brammer, M. J., Campbell, R., Williams, S. C. R., McGuire, P. K., Woodruff, P. W. R., Iversen, S. D., & David, A. S. (1997). Acitvation of auditory cortex during silent lipreading. *Science, 276,* 593–595.

Campbell, F. W., Kulikowski, J. J., & Levinson, J. (1966). The effect of orientation on the visual resolution of gratings. *Journal of Physiology (Lond.), 187,* 427–436.

Campbell, F. W., & Robson, J. G. (1968). Application of Fourier analysis to the visibility of gratings. *Journal of Physiology, 197,* 551–566.

Carello, C., Anderson, K. L., & Kunkler-Peck, A. J. (1998). Perception of object length by sound. *Psychological Science, 9,* 211–214.

Casagrande, V. A. (1994). A third parallel visual pathway to primate area V1. *Trends in Neuroscience, 17,* 305–310.

Casagrande, V. A., & Norton, T. T. (1991). Lateral geniculate nucleus: A review of its physiology and function. In J. R. Coonley-Dillon (Vol. Ed.) & A. G. Leventhal (Ed.), *Vision and visual dysfunction: The neural basis of visual function* (Vol. 4, pp. 41–84). London: Macmillan.

Cernoch, J. M., & Porter, R. H. (1985). Recognition of maternal axillary odors by infants. *Child Development, 56,* 1593–1598.

Chairello, C. (1991). Interpretation of word meanings by the cerebral hemispheres: One is not enough. In P. J. Schwanenflugel (Ed.). *The psychology of word meanings.* Hillsdale, NJ: Erlbaum, pp. 251–276.

References

Chapman, C. R., (1995). The affective dimension of pain: A model. In B. Bromm & J. Desmedt (Eds.), *Pain and the brain: From nociception to cognition: Advances in pain research and therapy, Volume 22.* New York: Raven, pp. 283–301.

Chatterjee, S. H., Freyd, J. J., & Shiffrar, M. (1996). Configural processing in the perception of apparent biological meotion. *Journal of Experimental Psychology: Human Perception and Performance, 22,* 916–929.

Chino, Y., Smith, E., Hatta, S., & Cheng, H. (1997). Postnatal development of binocular disparity sensitivity in neurons of the primate visual cortex. *Journal of Neuroscience, 17,* 296–307.

Chodosh, L. A., Lifson, L. E., & Tabin, C. (1995). Play ball! *Science, 268,* 1682–1683.

Churchland, P. S., & Ramachandran, V. S. (1996). Filling in: Why Dennett is wrong. In K. Atkins (Ed.), *Perception.* Oxford, England: Oxford University Press.

Cinelli, A. R. (1993). Review of "Science of olfaction." *Trends in Neurosciences, 16,* 123–124.

Clark, V. P., Keil, K., Maisog, J. M., Courtney, S. M., Ungerleider, L. G., & Haxby, J. V. (1996). Functional magnetic resonance imaging of human visual corex during face matching: A comparison with positron emission tomography. *NeuroImage, 4,* 1–15.

Clark, W. C., & Clark, S. B. (1980). Pain responses in Nepalese porter. *Science, 209,* 410–412.

Clulow, F. W. (1972). *Color: Its principles and their applications.* New York: Morgan & Morgan.

Cohen, L. B. (1991). Infant attention: An information processing approach. In M. J. Weiss & P. R. Zelazo (Eds.), *Newborn attention: Biological constraints and the influence of experience* (pp. 1–21). Norwood, NJ: ABLEX.

Colby, C. L., Duhamel, J.-R, & Goldberg, M. E. (1995). Oculocentric spatial representation in parietal cortex. *Cerebral Cortex, 5,* 470–481.

Collett, T. S. (1978). Peering—A locust behavior pattern for obtaining motion parallax information. *Journal of Experimental Biology, 76,* 237–241.

Collett, T. S., & Harkness, L. I. K. (1982). Depth vision in animals. In D. J. Ingle, M. A. Goodale, & R. J. W. Mansfield (Eds.), *Analysis of visual behavior* (pp. 111–176). Cambridge, MA: MIT Press.

Coltheart, M. (1970). The effect of verbal size information upon visual judgments of absolute distance. *Perception and Psychophysics, 9,* 222–223.

Comel, M. (1953). *Fisiologia normale e patologica della cute umana.* Milan: Fratelli Treves Editori.

Cometto-Muniz, J. E., & Cain, W. S. (1984). Temporal integration of pungency. *Chemical Senses, 8,* 315–327.

Conel, J. L. (1939). *The postnatal development of the cerebral cortex* (Vol. 1). Cambridge: Harvard University Press.

Conel, J. L. (1947). *The postnatal development of the cerebral cortex* (Vol. 2). Cambridge: Harvard University Press.

Conel, J. L. (1951). *The postnatal development of the cerebral cortex* (Vol. 3). Cambridge: Harvard University Press.

Connolly, M., & Van Essen, D. (1984). The representation of the visual field in parvocellular and magnocellular layers of the lateral geniculate nucleus in the macaque monkey. *Journal of Comparative Neurology, 226,* 544–565.

Coppola, D. M., White, L. E., Fitzpatrick, D., & Purves, D. (1998). Unequal distribution of cardinal and oblique contours in ferret visual cortex. *Proceedings of the National Academy of Sciences, 95,* 2621–2623.

Costanzo, R. M., & Gardner, E. B. (1980). A quantitative analysis of responses of direction-sensitive neurons in somatosensory cortex of awake monkeys. *Journal of Neurophysiology, 43,* 1319–1341.

Cowart, B. J., & Rawson, N. E. (2001). Olfaction. In E. B. Goldstein (Ed.) *Blackwell handbook of perception.* Oxford, UK: Blackwell, pp. 567–600.

Cowey, A., & Heywood, C. A. (1995). There's more to color than meets the eye. *Behavioral and Brain Research, 71,* 89–100.

Craig, J. C., & Johnson, K. O. (2000). The two-point threshold: Not a measure of tactile spatial resolution. *Current Directions in Psychological Science, 9,* 29–32.

Craton, L. G., & Yonas, A. (1990). The role of motion in infants' perception of occlusion. In J. T. Enns (Ed.), *The development of attention: Research and theory* (pp. 21–46). London: Elsevier.

Critchley, H. D., & Rolls, E. T. (1996a). Olfactory neuronal responses in the primate orbitofrontal cortex: Analysis in an olfactory discrimination task. *Journal of Neurophysiology, 75,* 1659–1672.

Critchley, H. D., & Rolls, E. T. (1996b). Hunger and satiety modify the responses of olfactory and visual neurons in the primate orbitofrontal cortex. *Journal of Neurophysiology, 75,* 1673–1686.

Culler, E. A., Coakley, J. D., Lowy, K., & Gross, N. (1943). A revised frequency-map of the guinea-pig cochlea. *American Journal of Psychology, 56,* 475–500.

Cumming, B. G., & Parker, A. J. (1999). Binocular neurons in V1 of awake monkeys are selective for absolute, not relative, disparity. *Journal of Neuroscience, 19,* 5602–5618.

Cutting, J. E., & Vishton, P. M. (1995). Perceiving layout and knowing distances: The integration, relative potency, and contextual use of different information about depth. In W. Epstein & S. Rogers (Eds.), *Handbook of perception and cognition: Perception of space and motion* (pp. 69–117). New York: Academic Press.

Cynader, M., Timney, B. N., & Mitchell, D. E. (1980). Period of susceptibility of kitten visual cortex to the effects of monocular deprivation extends beyond six months of age. *Brain Research, 191,* 545–550.

Dallos, P. (1996). Overview: Cochlear neurobiology. In P. Dallos, A. N. Popper, & R. R. Fay (Eds.), *The cochlea* (pp. 1–43). New York: Springer.

Dalton, J. (1948). Extraordinary facts relating to the vision of colour: With observations. In W. Dennis (Ed.), *Readings in the history of psychology* (pp. 102–111). New York: Appleton-Century-Crofts. (Original work published 1798)

Dartnall, H. J. A., Bowmaker, J. K., & Mollon, J. D. (1983). Human visual pigments: Microspectrophotometric results from the eyes of seven persons. *Proceedings of the Royal Society of London, 220B,* 115–130.

Davis, R. G. (1981). The role of nonolfactory context cues in odor identification. *Perception and Psychophysics, 30,* 83–89.

Day, R. H. (1989). Natural and artificial cues, perceptual compromise and the basis of veridical and illusory perception. In D. Vickers & P. L. Smith (Eds.), *Human information processing: Measures and mechanisms* (pp. 107–129). North Holland, The Netherlands: Elsevier Science.

Day, R. H. (1990). The Bourdon illusion in haptic space. *Perception and Psychophysics, 47,* 400–404.

DeAngelis, G. C., Cumming, B. G., & Newsome, W. T. (2000). A new role for cortical area MT: The perception of stereoscopic depth. In M. Gazzaniga (Ed.), *The new cognitive neurosciences.* Cambridge, MA: MIT Press, pp. 305–314.

DeCasper, A. J., & Fifer, W. P. (1980). Of human bonding: Newborns prefer their mothers' voices. *Science, 208,* 1174–1176.

DeCasper, A. J., Lecanuet, J.-P., Busnel, M.-C., Deferre-Granier, C., & Maugeais, R. (1994). Fetal reactions to recurrent maternal speech. *Infant Behavior and Development, 17,* 159–164.

DeCasper, A. J., & Spence, M. J. (1986). Prenatal maternal speech influences newborn's perception of speech sounds. *Infant Behavior and Development, 9,* 133–150.

Deibert, E., Kraut, M., Kremen, S., & Hart, J. Jr. (1999). Neural pathways in tactile object recognition. *Neurology, 52,* 1413–1417.

Delgutte, B., & Kiang, N. Y. S. (1984a). Speech coding in the auditory nerve: 1. Vowel-like sounds. *Journal of the Acoustical Society of America, 75,* 887–896.

Delgutte, B., & Kiang, N. Y. S. (1984b). Speech coding in the auditory nerve: 3. Voiceless fricative consonants. *Journal of the Acoustical Society of America, 75,* 887–896.

DeLucia, P., & Hochberg, J. (1985). Illusions in the real world and in the mind's eye [Abstract]. *Proceedings of the Eastern Psychological Association, 56,* 38.

DeLucia, P., & Hochberg, J. (1986). Real-world geometrical illusions: Theoretical and practical implications [Abstract]. *Proceedings of the Eastern Psychological Association, 57,* 62.

DeLucia, P., & Hochberg, J. (1991). Geometrical illusions in solid objects under ordinary viewing conditions. *Perception and Psychophysics, 50,* 547–554.

Denes, P. B., & Pinson, E. N. (1993). *The speech chain* (2nd ed.). New York: Freeman.

Derbyshire, S. W. G., Jones, A. K. P., Gyulia, F., Clark, S., Townsend, D., & Firestone, L. L. (1997). Pain processing during three levels of noxious stimulation produces differential patterns of central activity. *Pain, 73,* 431–445.

Desor, J. A., & Beauchamp, G. K. (1974). The human capacity to transmit olfactory information. *Perception and Psychophysics, 13,* 271–275.

Deutsch, D. (1975). Two-channel listening to musical scales. *Journal of the Acoustical Society of America, 57,* 1156–1160.

Deutsch, D. (1996). The perception of auditory patterns. In W. Prinz & B. Bridgeman (Eds.), *Handbook of perception and action* (Vol. 1, pp. 253–296). San Diego, CA: Academic Press.

DeValois, K. K., DeValois, R. L., & Yund, E. W. (1979). Responses of striate cortex cells to gratings and checkerboard patterns. *Journal of Physiology, 291,* 483–505.

DeValois, R. L. (1960). Color vision mechanisms in monkey. *Journal of General Physiology, 43,* 115–128.

DeValois, R. L., Abramov, I., & Jacobs, G. H. (1966). Analysis of response of LGN cells. *Journal of the Optical Society of America, 56,* 966–977.

DeValois, R. L., & DeValois, K. K. (1993). A multistage color model. *Vision Research, 33,* 1053–1065.

DeValois, R. L., & Jacobs, G. H. (1968). Primate color vision. *Science, 162,* 533–540.

DeValois, R. L., Yund, E. W., & Hepler, N., (1982). The orientation and direction selectivity of cells in macaque visual cortex. *Vision Research, 22,* 531–544.

deVries, H., & Stuiver, M. (1961). The absolute sensitivity of the human sense of smell. In W. A. Rosenblith (Ed.), *Sensory communication.* Cambridge, MA: MIT Press.

deWeid, M. & Verbaten, M. N. (2001). Affective pictures processing, attention, and pain tolerance. *Pain, 90,* 163–172.

Dobelle, W. H. (1977). Current status of research on providing sight to the blind by electrical stimulation of the brain. *Journal of Visual Impairment and Blindness, 71,* 290–297.

Dobelle, W. H., Mladejovsky, M. G., Evans, J. R., Roberts, T. S., & Girvin, J. P. (1976). "Braille" reading by a blind volunteer by visual cortex stimulation. *Nature, 259,* 111–112.

Dobelle, W. H., Mladejovsky, M. G., & Girvin, J. P. (1974). Artificial vision for the blind: Electrical stimulation of visual cortex offers hope for a functional prosthesis. *Science, 183,* 440–444.

Dobson, V., & Teller, D. (1978). Visual acuity in human infants: Review and comparison of behavioral and electrophysiological studies. *Vision Research, 18,* 1469–1483.

Dodd, B., & Campbell, R. (Eds.) (1987). *Hearing by eye: The psychology of lip-reading.* Hillsdale, NJ: Erlbaum.

Dodd, G. G., & Squirrell, D. J. (1980). Structure and mechanism in the mammalian olfactory system. *Symposium of the Zoology Society of London, 45,* 35–56.

Dodd, J., & Castellucci, V. F. (1991). Smell and taste: The chemical senses. In E. R. Kandel, J. H. Schwartz, & T. M. Jessell (Eds.), *Principles of neural science* (3rd ed., pp. 512–529). New York: Elsevier.

Dong, W. K., Chudler, E. H., Sugiyama, K., Roberts, V. J., & Hayashi, T. (1994). Somatosensory, multisensory, and task-related neurons in cortical area 7b (PF) of unanesthetized monkeys. *Journal of Neurophysiology, 72,* 542–564.

Doty, R. L. (Ed.). (1976). *Mammalian olfaction, reproductive processes and behavior.* New York: Academic Press.

Doty, R. L. (1991). Olfactory system. In T. V. Getchell, R. L. Doty, L. M. Bartoshuk, & J. B. Snow (Eds.), *Smell and taste in health and disease* (pp. 175–203). New York: Raven Press.

Doty, R. L. (1995). Intranasal trigeminal chemoreception. In R. L. Doty (Ed.), *Handbook of olfaction and gustation* (pp. 821–833). New York: Marcel Dekker.

Doty, R. L., Green, P. A., Ram, C., & Yankell, S. L. (1982). Communication of gender from human breath odors: Relationship to perceived intensity and pleasantness. *Hormones and Behavior, 16,* 13–22.

Dowling, J. E., & Boycott, B. B. (1966). Organization of the primate retina. *Proceedings of the Royal Society of London, 166B,* 80–111.

Dowling, W. J. (1973). The perception of interleaved melodies. *Cognitive Psychology, 5,* 322–337.

Dowling, W. J., & Harwood, D. L. (1986). *Music cognition.* New York: Academic Press.

DuBose, C. N., Cardello, A. V., & Maller, O. (1980). Effects of colorants and flavorants on identification, perceived flavor intensity, and hedonic quality of fruit-flavored beverages and cake. *Journal of Food Science, 45,* 1393–1400.

Duchamp-Viret, P., Chaput, M. A., & Duchamp, A. (1999). Odor response properties of rat olfactory receptor neurons. *Science, 284,* 2171–2174.

Duclaux, R., & Kenshalo, D. R. (1980). Response characteristics of cutaneous warm fibers in the monkey. *Journal of Neurophysiology, 43,* 1–15.

Duffy, C. J., & Wurtz, R. H. (1991). Sensitivity of MST neurons to optic flow stimuli: 2. Mechanisms of response selectivity revealed by small-field stimuli. *Journal of Neurophysiology, 65,* 1346–1359.

Durlach, N. I., & Colburn, H. S. (1978). Binaural phenomena. In E. C. Carterette & M. P. Friedman (Eds.), *Handbook of perception* (Vol. 4, pp. 365–466). New York: Academic Press.

Durrant, J., & Lovrinic, J. (1977). *Bases of hearing science.* Baltimore: Williams & Wilkins.

Egan, J. P., & Hake, H. W. (1950). On the masking pattern of a simple auditory stimulus. *Journal of the Acoustical Society of America, 22,* 622–630.

Eimas, P. D., & Corbit, J. D. (1973). Selective adaptation of linguistic feature detectors. *Cognitive Psychology, 4,* 99–109.

Eimas, P. D., & Quinn, P. C. (1994). Studies on the formation of perceptually based basic-level categories in young infants. *Child Development, 65,* 903–917.

Eimas, P. D., Siqueland, E. R., Jusczyk, P., & Vigorito, J. (1971). Speech perception in infants. *Science, 171,* 303–306.

Eisenberg, A. (2000). What's next: computer controls? Save your breath. *New York Times, November 2. (Circuits).*

Elbert, T., Pantev, C., Wienbruch, C., Rockstroh, B., & Taub, E. (1995). Increased cortical representation of the fingers of the left hand in string players. *Science, 270,* 305–307.

Emmert, E. (1881). Grossenverhaltnisse der Nachbilder. *Klinische Monatsblaetter fuer Augenheilkunde, 19,* 443–450.

Engel, A. K., Konig, P., Kreiter, A. K., Schillen, T. B., & Singer, W. (1992). Temporal coding in the visual cortex: New vistas on integration in the nervous system. *Trends in Neurosciences, 15,* 218–226.

Engel, A. K., Konig, P., Kreiter, A. K., & Singer, W. (1991). Interhemispheric synchronization of oscillatory neuronal responses in cat visual cortex. *Science, 252,* 1177–1179.

Engel, A. K., Konig, P., & Singer, W. (1991). Direct physiological evidence for scene segmentation by temporal coding. *Proceedings of the National Academy of Sciences, 88,* 9136–9140.

Engel, S., Zhang, X., & Wandell, B. (1997). Colour tuning in human visual cortex measured with functional magnetic resonance imaging. *Nature, 388,* 68–71.

Engen, T. (1972). Psychophysics. In J. W. Kling & L. A. Riggs (Eds.), *Experimental psychology* (3rd ed., pp. 1–46). New York: Holt, Rinehart and Winston.

Engen, T., & Pfaffmann, C. (1960). Absolute judgments of odor quality. *Journal of Experimental Psychology, 59,* 214–219.

Epstein, W. (1965). Nonrelational judgments of size and distance. *American Journal of Psychology, 78,* 120–123.

Epstein, W. (1977). What are the prospects for a higher-order stimulus theory of perception? *Scandinavian Journal of Psychology, 18,* 164–171.

Erickson, R. (1975). *Sound structure in music.* Berkeley: University of California Press.

Erickson, R. P. (1963). Sensory neural patterns and gustation. In Y. Zotterman (Ed.), *Olfaction and taste* (Vol. 1, pp. 205–213). Oxford, England: Pergamon Press.

Evans, E. F. (1978). Place and time coding of frequency in the peripheral auditory system: Some physiological pros and cons. *Audiology, 17,* 369–420.

Exner, S. (1875). Uber das Sehen von Bewegung und die Theorie des zasammengestzten Auges. *Sitzber. Akad. Wiss. Wien, 72,* 156–190.

Fadiga, L., Fogassi, L., Pavesi, G., & Rizzolatti, G. (1995). Motor facilitation during action observation: A magnetic stimulation study. *Journal of Neurophysiology, 73,* 2608–2611.

Fagan, J. F. (1976). Infant's recognition of invariant features of faces. *Child Development, 47,* 627–638.

Fantz, R. L., & Nevis, S. (1967). Pattern preferences and perceptual-cognitive development in early infancy. *Merrill-Palmer Quarterly, 13,* 77–108.

Fantz, R. L., Ordy, J. M., & Udelf, M. S. (1962). Maturation of pattern vision in infants during the first six months. *Journal of Comparative and Physiological Psychology, 55,* 907–917.

Feddersen, W. E., Sandel, T. T., Teas, D. C., & Jeffress, L. A. (1957). Localization of high frequency tones. *Journal of the Acoustical Society of America, 5,* 82–108.

Felleman, D. J., & Van Essen, D. C. (1991). Distributed hierarchical processing in the primate cerebral cortex. *Cerebral Cortex, 1,* 1–47.

Fernald, R. D. (2000). Evolution of eyes. *Current Opinion in Neurobiology, 10,* 444–450.

Fields, H. L., & Basbaum, A. I. (1999). Central nervous system mechanisms of pain modulation. In P. D. Wall & R. Melzak (Eds.) *Textbook of pain.* New York: Churchill Livingstone, pp. 309–328.

Finger, T. E. (1987). Gustatory nuclei and pathways in the central nervous system. In T. E. Finger & W. L. Silver (Eds.), *Neurobiology of taste and smell* (pp. 331–353). New York: Wiley.

Fiorentini, A., & Maffei, L. (1973). Contrast in night vision. *Vision Research, 13,* 73–80.

Firestein, S. (1992). Physiology of transduction in the single olfactory sensory neuron. In D. P. Corey & S. D. Roper (Eds.), *Sensory transduction* (pp. 61–71). New York: Rockefeller University Press.

Fletcher, H., & Munson, W. A. (1933). Loudness: Its definition, measurement, and calculation. *Journal of the Acoustical Society of America, 5,* 82–108.

Flor, H., Elbert, T., Knecht, S., Weinbruch, C., Pantev, C., Birbaumer, N., Larbig, W., & Taub, E. (1995). Phantom-limb pain as a perceptual correlate of cortical reorganization following arm amputation. *Nature, 375,* 482–484.

Fodor, J. A. (1984). *The modularity of mind.* Cambridge, MA: MIT Press.

Fowler, C. A., & Dekle, D. J. (1991). Listening with eye and hand: Cross-modal contributions to speech perception. *Journal of Experimental Psychology: Human Perception and Performance, 17,* 816–828.

Fowler, C. A., & Rosenblum, L. D. (1990). Duplex perception: A comparison of monosyllables and slamming doors. *Journal of Experimental Psychology: Human Perception and Performance, 16,* 742–754.

Fox, C. R. (1990). Some visual influences on human postural equilibrium: Binocular versus monocular fixation. *Perception and Psychophysics, 47,* 409–422.

Fox, R., Aslin, R. N., Shea, S. L., & Dumais, S. T. (1980). Stereopsis in human infants. *Science, 207,* 323–324.

Fox, R., Lehmukuhle, S. W., & Westendorf, D. H. (1976). Falcon visual acuity. *Science, 192,* 263–265.

Fox, R., & McDaniel, C. (1982). The perception of biological motion by human infants. *Science, 218,* 486–487.

Frank, M. E. (2000). Neuron types, receptors, behavior, and taste quality. *Physiology and Behavior, 69,* 53–62.

Frank, M. E., Bieber, S. L., & Smith, D. V. (1988). The organization of taste sensibilities in hamster chorda tympani nerve fibers. *Journal of General Physiology, 91,* 861–896.

Frank, M. E., & Rabin, M. D. (1989). Chemosensory neuroanatomy and physiology. *Ear, Nose and Throat Journal, 68,* 291–292, 295–296.

Freeman, R. D., & Pettigrew, J. D. (1973). Alterations of visual cortex from environmental asymmetries. *Nature, 246,* 359–360.

Fujita, I., Tanaka, K., Ito, M., & Cheng, K. (1992). Columns for visual features of objects in monkey inferotemporal cortex. *Nature, 360,* 343–346.

Fuld, K., Wooten, B. R., & Whalen, J. J. (1981). Elemental hues of short-wave and spectral lights. *Perception and Psychophysics, 29,* 317–322.

Furmanski, C. S., & Engel, S. A. (2000). An oblique effect in human primary visual cortex. *Nature Neuroscience, 3,* 535–536.

Fuzessery, Z. M., & Feng, A. S. (1983). Mating call selectivity in the thalamus and midbrain of the leopard frog (*Rana p. pipiens*): Single and multiunit analyses. *Journal of Comparative Physiology, 150A,* 333–344.

Galletti, C., Battaglini, P. P., & Fattori, P. (1990). "Real-motion" cells in area V3A of macaque visual cortex. *Experimental Brain Research, 82,* 67–76.

Gallese, V., Fadiga, L., Fogassi, L., & Rizzolatti, G. (1996). Action recognition in the premotor cortex. *Brain, 119,* 593–609.

Gamble, A. E. McC. (1898). The applicability of Weber's law to smell. *American Journal of Psychology, 10,* 82–142.

Ganchrow, J. R. (1995). Ontogeny of human taste perception. In R. L. Doty (Ed.), *Handbook of olfaction and gustation* (pp. 715–729). New York: Marcel Dekker.

Ganchrow, J. R., Steiner, J. E., & Daher, M. (1983). Neonatal facial expressions in response to different qualities and intensities of gustatory stimuli. *Infant Behavior and Development, 6,* 473–484.

Gardner, E. P., & Costanzo, R. M. (1980). Neuronal mechanisms underlying direction sensitivity of somatosensory cortical neurons in awake monkeys. *Journal of Neurophysiology, 43,* 1342–1354.

Gardner, E. P., Palmer, C. I., Hamalainen, H. A., & Warren, S. (1992). Simulation of motion on the skin: V. Effect of stimulus temporal frequency on the representation of moving bar patterns in primary somatosensory cortex of monkeys. *Journal of Neurophysiology, 67,* 37–63.

Gardner, M. B., & Gardner, R. S. (1973). Problem of localization in the median plane: Effect of pinnae cavity occlusion. *Journal of the Acoustical Society of America, 53,* 400–408.

Gauthier, I. (1999). What constrains the organization of the ventral temporal cortex? *Proceedings of the National Academy of Sciences, 96,* 9379–9384.

Gauthier, I., Skudlarski, P., Gore, J. C., & Anderson, A. W. (2000). Expertise for cars and birds recruits brain areas involved in face recognition. *Nature Neuroscience, 3,* 191–197.

Gauthier, I., Tarr, M. J., Anderson, A. W., Skudlarski, P., & Gore, J. C. (1999). Activation of the middle fusiform "face area" increases with expertise in recognizing novel objects. *Nature Neuroscience, 2,* 568–573.

Gaver, W. W. (1993a). How do we hear in the world?: Explorations in ecological acoustics. *Ecological Psychology, 5,* 285–313.

Gaver, W. W. (1993b). What in the world do we hear? An ecological approach to auditory event perception. *Ecological Psychology, 5,* 1–29.

Gescheider, G. A. (1976). *Psychophysics: Method and theory.* Hillsdale, NJ: Erlbaum.

Geschwind, N. (1979, September). Specializations of the human brain. *Scientific American, 241,* 108–119.

Getty, D. J., & Howard, J. H. (Eds.). (1981). *Auditory and visual pattern recognition.* Hillsdale, NJ: Erlbaum.

Gibson, J. J. (1950). *The perception of the visual world.* Boston: Houghton Mifflin.

Gibson, J. J. (1962). Observations on active touch. *Psychological Review, 69,* 477–491.

Gibson, J. J. (1966). *The senses considered as perceptual systems.* Boston: Houghton Mifflin.

Gibson, J. J. (1979). *The ecological approach to visual perception.* Boston: Houghton Mifflin.

Gilbert, C. D., & Wiesel, T. N. (1989). Columnar specificity of intrinsic horizontal and corticocortical connections in cat visual cortex. *Journal of Neuroscience, 9,* 2432–2442.

Gilchrist, A., Kossyfidis, C., Agostini, T., Li, Xiaojun, Bonato, F., Cataliotti, J., Spehar, B., Annan, V., & Economou, E. (1999). An anchoring theory of lightness perception. *Psychologicl Review, 106,* 795–834.

Gilchrist, A. L. (Ed.) (1994). *Lightness, brightness, and transparency.* Hillsdale, NJ: Erlbaum.

Gilinsky, A. S. (1951). Perceived size and distance in visual space. *Psychological Review, 58,* 460–482.

Gillam, B. (1995). The perception of spatial layout from static optical information. In W. Epstein & S. Rogers (Eds.), *Handbook of perception and cognition: Perception of space and motion* (pp. 23–67). New York: Academic Press.

Ginsburg, A. (1983). *Contrast perception in the human infant.* Unpublished manuscript.

Glanz, J. (2000). Art + physics = beautiful music. *New York Times,* April 18, 2000. D1–D4.

Glickstein, M. (1988, September). The discovery of the visual cortex. *Scientific American, 259,* 118–127.

Goldstein, E. B. (2001a). Cross-talk between psychophysics and physiology in the study of perception. In E. B. Goldstein (Ed.), *Blackwell handbook of perception.* Oxford, UK: Blackwell, pp. 1–23.

Goldstein, E. B. (2001b). Pictorial perception and art. In E. B. Goldstein (Ed.), *Blackwell handbook of perception.* Oxford, UK: Blackwell, pp. 344–378.

Goldstein, J. L. (1978). Mechanisms of signal analysis and pattern perception in periodicity pitch. *Audiology, 17,* 421–445.

Goodale, M. A., & Humphrey, G. K. (2001). Separate visual systems for action and perception. In E. B. Goldstein (Ed.), *Blackwell handbook of perception.* Oxford, UK: Blackwell, pp. 311–343.

Goodwin, A. W. (1998). Extracting the shape of an object from the responses of peripheral nerve fibers. In J. W. Morley (Ed.). *Neural aspects of tactile sensation.* New York: Elsevier Science, pp. 55–87.

Gordon, J., & Abramov, I. (1988). Scaling procedures for specifying color appearance. *Color Research Applications, 13,* 146–152.

Gordon, J., & Abramov, I. (2001). Color vision. In E. B. Goldstein (Ed.), *Blackwell Handbook of Perception.* Oxford: Blackwell Publishers, pp. 92–127.

Gouras, P. (1991). Color vision. In E. R. Kandel, J. H. Schwartz, & T. M. Jessell (Eds.), *Principles of neural science* (3rd ed., pp. 467–480). New York: Elsevier.

Graham, C. H. (1965). Perception of movement. In C. Graham (Ed.), *Vision and visual perception* (pp. 575–588). New York: Wiley.

Graham, C. H., Sperling, H. G., Hsia, Y., & Coulson, A. H. (1961). The determination of some visual functions of a unilaterally color-blind subject: Methods and results. *Journal of Psychology, 51,* 3–32.

Granrud, C. E., Haake, R. J., & Yonas, A. (1985). Infants' sensitivity to familiar size: The effect of memory on spatial perception. *Perception and Psychophysics, 37,* 459–466.

Granrud, C. E., & Yonas, A. (1984). Infants' perception of pictorially specified interposition. *Journal of Experimental Child Psychology, 37,* 500–511.

Granrud, C. E., Yonas, A., & Opland, E. A. (1985). Infants' sensitivity to the depth cue of shading. *Perception and Psychophysics, 37,* 415–419.

Gray, C. M., & Singer, W. (1989). Stimulus specific neuronal oscillations in orientation columns of cat visual cortex. *Proceedings of the National Academy of Sciences, 86,* 1698–1702.

Gray, R., & Regan, D. (1998). Accuracy of estimating time to collision using binocular and monocular information. *Vision Research, 38,* 499–512.

Graziadei, P. P. C. (1976). Functional anatomy of the mammalian chemoreceptor system. In D. Muller-Schearze & M. Mozell (Eds.), *Chemical signals in vertebrates* (pp. 435–454). New York: Plenum Press.

Graziano, M. S. A., Andersen, R. A., & Snowden, R. J. (1994). Tuning of MST neurons to spiral motions. *Journal of Neuroscience, 14,* 54–67.

Graziano, M. S. A., & Gross, C. G. (1995). The representation of extrapersonal space: A possible role for bimodal, visual-tactile neurons. In M. S. Gazzaniga (Ed.), *The cognitive neurosciences* (pp. 1021–1034). Cambridge, MA: MIT Press.

Graziano, M. S. A., & Gross, C. G. (1998). Spatial maps for the control of movement. *Current Opinion in Neurobiology, 8,* 195–201.

Graziano, M. S. A., Hu, X. T., & Gross, C. G. (1997). Coding the locations of objects in the dark. *Science, 277,* 239–241.

Graziano, M. S. A., Reiss, L. A., J., & Gross, C. G. (1999). A neuronal representation of the location of nearby sounds. *Nature, 397,* 428–430.

Gregory, R. L. (1966). *Eye and brain.* New York: McGraw-Hill.

Griffin, D. R. (1944). Echolocation by blind men and bats. *Science, 100,* 589–590.

Griffiths, T. D., Rees, A., Witton, C., Shakir, R. A., Henning, G. B., & Green, G. G. R. (1996). Evidence for a sound movement area in the human cerebral cortex. *Nature, 383,* 425–427.

Grimes, J. (1996). On the failure to detect changes in scenes across saccades. In K. Akins (Ed.), *Perception* (pp. 89–110). New York: Oxford University Press.

Gross, C. G. (1992). Representation of visual stimuli in inferior temporal cortex. *Transactions of the Royal Society of London, B335,* 3–10.

Gross, C. G. (1994). How inferior temporal cortex became a visual area. *Cerebral Cortex, 5,* 455–469.

Gross, C. G., Bender, D. B., & Rocha-Miranda, C. E. (1969). Visual receptive fields of neurons in inferotemporal cortex of the monkey. *Science, 166,* 1303–1306.

Gross, C. G., Rocha-Miranda, C. E., & Bender, D. B. (1972). Visual properties of neurons in inferotemporal cortex of the macaque. *Journal of Neurophysiology, 35,* 96–111.

Gulick, W. L. (1971). *Hearing.* New York: Oxford University Press.

Gulick, W. L., Gescheider, G. A., & Frisina, R. D. (1989). *Hearing.* New York: Oxford University Press.

Gwiazda, J., & Birch, E. E. (2001). Perceptual development: Vision. In E. B. Goldstein (Ed.), *Blackwell handbook of perception.* Oxford, UK: Blackwell, pp. 636–668.

Gwiazda, J., Thorn, F., Bauer, J., & Held, R. (1993). Emmetropization and the progression of manifest refraction in children followed from infancy to puberty. *Clinical Visual Science, 8,* 337–344.

Gyr, J. W. (1972). Is a theory of direct perception adequate? *Psychological Bulletin, 77,* 246–261.

Hagen, M. A. (Ed.). (1979). *The perception of pictures* (Vols. 1, 2). New York: Academic Press.

Hagen, M. A. (1986). *Varieties of realism.* Cambridge, England: Cambridge University Press.

Haith, M. M. (1983). Spatially determined visual activity in early infancy. In A. Hein & M. Jeannerod (Eds.), *Spatially oriented behavior.* New York: Springer.

Hall, E. G., & Davies, S. (1991). Gender differences in perceived intensity and affect of pain between athletes and nonathletes. *Perceptual and Motor Skills, 73,* 779–786.

Hall, J. L. (1965). Binaural interaction in the accessory superior-olivary nucleus of the cat. *Journal of the Acoustical Society of America, 37,* 814–823.

Hall, M. D., & Pastore, R. E. (1992). Musical duplex perception: Perception of figurally good chords with subliminal distinguishing tones. *Journal of Experimental Psychology: Human Perception and Performance, 18,* 752–762.

Hall, M. J., Bartoshuk, L. M., Cain, W. S., & Stevens, J. C. (1975). PTC taste blindness and the taste of caffeine. *Nature, 253,* 442–443.

Halpern, B. (1997). Psychophysics of taste. In G. K. Beauchamp & L. Bartoshuck (Eds.), *Tasting and smelling. Handbook of perception and cognition, 2nd ed.* San Diego, CA: Academic Press, pp. 72–123.

Halpern, D. L., Blake, R., & Hillenbrand, J. (1986). Psychoacoustics of a chilling sound. *Perception and Psychophysics, 39,* 77–80.

Hamer, R. D., Alexander, K. R., & Teller, D. Y. (1982). Rayleigh discriminations in young human infants. *Vision Research, 22,* 575–587.

Handel, S. (1995). Timbre perception and auditory object identification. In B. C. J. Moore (Ed.), *Hearing* (pp. 425–461). San Diego, CA: Academic Press.

Hari, R., Forss, N., Avikainen, S., Kirveskari, E., Salenious, S., & Rizzolatti, G. (1998). Activation of human primary motor cortex during action observation: A neuromagnetic study. *Proceedings of the National Academy of Sciences USA, 95,* 15061–15065.

Hari, R., Levanen, S., & Raij, T. (2000). Timing of human cortical functions during cognition: Role of MEG. *Trends in Cognitive Sciences, 4,* 455–462.

Harris, J. M. (2001). The future of flow? *Trends in Cognitive Sciences, 5,* 7.

Harris, J. M., & Rogers, B. J. (1999). Going against the flow. *Trends in Cognitive Sciences, 3,* 449–450.

Harris, L., Atkinson, J., & Braddick, O. (1976). Visual contrast sensitivity of a 6-month-old infant measured by the evoked potential. *Nature, 246,* 570–571.

Hartline, H. K., Wagner, H. G., & Ratliff, F. (1956). Inhibition in the eye of *Limulus. Journal of General Physiology, 39,* 651–673.

Haxby, J. V., Horwitz, B., Ungerleider, L. G., Maisog, J. M., Pietrini, P., & Grady, C. L. (1994). The functional organization of human extrastriate cortex: A PET-rCBF study of selective attention to faces and locations. *Journal of Neuroscience, 14,* 6336–6353.

Hebb, D. O. (1949). *The organization of behavior.* New York: Wiley.

Hecaen, H., & Angelerques, R. (1962). Agnosia for faces (prosopagnosia). *Archives of Neurology, 7,* 92–100.

Hecht, S., Shlaer, S., & Pirenne, M. H. (1942). Energy, quanta, and vision. *Journal of General Physiology, 25,* 819–840.

Heffner, H. E. (1983). Hearing in large and small dogs. Absolute thresholds and size of the tympanic membrane. *Behavioral Neuroscience, 97,* 310–318.

Heffner, H. E., & Masterton, R. B. (1980). Hering in glires: Domestic rabbit, cotton rat, feral house mouse, and kangaroo rat. *Journal of the Acoustical Society of America, 68,* 1584–1599.

Heffner, R. S., & Heffner, H. E. (1980). Hearing in the elephant (Elephas maximus). *Science, 208,* 518–520.

Heffner, R. S., & Heffner, H. E. (1985). Hearing in mammals: The least weasel. *Journal of Mammalogy, 66,* 745–755.

Heise, G. A., & Miller, G. A. (1951). An experimental study of auditory patterns. *American Journal of Psychology, 57,* 243–249.

Held, R., Birch, E. E., & Gwiazda, J. (1980). Stereoacuity of human infants. *Proceedings of the National Academy of Sciences, 77,* 5572–5574.

Helmholtz, H. von (1852). On the theory of compound colors. *Philosophical Magazine, 4,* 519– 534.

Helmholtz, H. von (1911). *Treatise on physiological optics* (J. P. Southall, Ed. & Trans.) (3rd ed., Vols. 2 & 3). Rochester, NY: Optical Society of America. (Original work published 1866)

Helson, H. (1933). The fundamental propositions of Gestalt psychology. *Psychological Review, 40,* 13–32.

Helson, H., Judd, D. B., & Wilson, M. (1956). Color rendition with fluorescent sources of illumination. *Illuminating Engineering, 51,* 329–346.

Hering, E. (1878). *Zur Lehre vom Lichtsinn.* Vienna: Gerold.

Hering, E. (1905). Grundzuge der Lehre vom Lichtsinn. In *Handbuch der gesamter Augenheilkunde* (Vol. 3, Chap. 13). Berlin.

Hering, E. (1964). *Outlines of a theory of the light sense* (L. M. Hurvich & D. Jameson, Trans.). Cambridge, MA: Harvard University Press.

Hershenson, M. (Ed.). (1989). *The moon illusion.* Hillsdale, NJ: Erlbaum.

Hettinger, T. P., Myers, W. E., & Frank, M. E. (1990). Role of olfaction in perception of nontraditional "taste" stimuli. *Chemical Senses, 15,* 755–760.

Heywood, C. A., Cowey, A., & Newcombe, F. (1991). Chromatic discrimination in a cortically colour blind observer. *European Journal of Neuroscience, 3,* 802–812.

Heywood, C. A., Gadotti, A., & Cowey, A. (1992). Cortical area V4 and its role in the perception of color. *Journal of Neuroscience, 12,* 4056–4065.

Hochberg, J. E. (1971). Perception. In J. W. Kling & L. A. Riggs (Eds.), *Experimental psychology* (3rd ed., pp. 396–550). New York: Holt, Rinehart and Winston.

Hochberg, J. E. (1987). Machines should not see as people do, but must know how people see. *Computer Vision, Graphics and Image Processing, 39,* 221–237.

Hoffman, E. J., Phelps, M. E., Mullani, N. A., Higgins, C. S., & Ter-Pogossian, M. M. (1976). Design and performance characteristics of a whole-body positron tranxial tomograph. *Journal of Nuclear Medicine, 17,* 493–502.

Hoffman, H. G., Doctor, J. N., Patterson, D. R., Carrougher, G. J., & Furness, T. A. III (2000). Virtual reality as an adjunctive pain control during burn wound care in adolescent patients. *Pain, 85,* 305–309.

Holley, A. (1991). Neural coding of olfactory information. In T. V. Getchell, R. L. Doty, L. M. Bartoshuk, & J. B. Snow (Eds.), *Smell and taste in health and disease* (pp. 329–343). New York: Raven Press.

Holway, A. H., & Boring, E. G. (1941). Determinants of apparent visual size with distance variant. *American Journal of Psychology, 54,* 21–37.

Hoon, M. A., Adler, E., Lindemeier, J., Battey, J. F., Ryba, N. J. P., & Zuker, C. S. (1999). Putative mammalian taste receptors: A class of taste-specific GPCRs with distinct topographic selectivity. *Cell, 96,* 541–551.

Houtsma, A. J. M., & Goldstein, J. L. (1972). Perception of musical intervals: Evidence for the central origin of the pitch of complex tones. *Journal of the Optical Society of America, 51,* 520–529.

Hoyle, F. (1957). *The black cloud.* New York: The New American Library.

Hsiao, S. S., Johnson, K. O., Twombly, A., & DiCarlo, J. (1996). Form processing and attention effects in the somatosensory system. In O. Franzen, R. Johannson, & L. Terenius (Eds.), *Somesthesis and the neurobiology of the somatosensory cortex* (pp. 229–247). Basel: Biorkhauser Verlag.

Hsiao, S. S., O'Shaughnessy, D. M., & Johnson, K. O. (1993). Effects of selective attention on spatial form processing in monkey primary and secondary somatosensory cortex. *Journal of Neurophysiology, 70,* 444–447.

Hubel, D. H. (1982). Exploration of the primary visual cortex, 1955–1978. *Nature, 299,* 515–524.

Hubel, D. H., & Wiesel, T. N. (1959). Receptive fields of single neurons in the cat's striate cortex. *Journal of Physiology, 148,* 574–591.

Hubel, D. H., & Wiesel, T. N. (1961). Integrative action in the cat's lateral geniculate body. *Journal of Physiology, 155,* 385–398.

Hubel, D. H., & Wiesel, T. N. (1963). Receptive fields of cells in striate cortex of very young, visually inexperienced kittens. *Journal of Neurophysiology, 26,* 994–1002.

Hubel, D. H., & Wiesel, T. N. (1965). Receptive fields and functional architecture in two non-striate visual areas (18 and 19) of the cat. *Journal of Neurophysiology, 28*, 229–289.

Hubel, D. H., & Wiesel, T. N. (1970). Cells sensitive to binocular depth in area 18 of the macaque monkey cortex. *Nature, 225*, 41–42.

Hubel, D. H., & Wiesel, T. N. (1977). Functional architecture of macaque monkey cortex. *Proceedings of the Royal Society of London, 198*, 1–59.

Hubel, D. H., Wiesel, T. N., & Stryker, M. P. (1978). Anatomical demonstration of orientation columns in macaque monkey. *Journal of Comparative Neurology, 177*, 361–379.

Hudspeth, A. J. (1983). The hair cells of the inner ear. *Scientific American, 248*(1), 54–64.

Hudspeth, A. J. (1989). How the ear's works work. *Nature, 341*, 397–404.

Humphrey, A. L., & Saul, A. B. (1994). The temporal transformation of retinal signals in the lateral geniculate nucleus of the cat: Implications for cortical function. In D. Minciacchi, M. Molinari, G. Macchi, & E. G. Jones (Eds.), *Thalamic networks for relay and modulation* (pp. 81–89). New York: Pergamon Press.

Hurvich, L. (1981). *Color vision*. Sunderland, MA: Sinauer Associates.

Hyman, A. (1983). The influence of color on the taste perception of carbonated water preparations. *Bulletin of the Psychonomic Society, 21*, 145–148.

Hyvarinin, J., & Poranen, A. (1978). Movement-sensitive and direction and orientation-selective cutaneous receptive fields in the hand area of the postcentral gyrus in monkeys. *Journal of Physiology, 283*, 523–537.

Iacobini, M., Woods, R. P., Brass, M., Bekkering, H., Mazziotta, J. C., & Rizzolatti, G. (1999). Cortical mechanism of human imitation. *Science, 286*, 2526–2528.

Ilg, U. J., Bridgeman, B., & Hoffmann, K. P. (1989). Influence of mechanical disturbance on oculomotor behavior. *Vision Research, 29*, 545–551.

Irving, E. L., Sivak, J. G., & Callender, M. G. (1992). Refractive plasticity of the developing chick eye. *Ophthalmology and Physiological Optics, 12*, 448–456.

Ito, M., Tamura, H., Fujita, I., & Tanaka, K. (1995). Size and position invariance of neuronal responses in monkey inferotemporal cortex. *Journal of Neurophysiology, 73*, 218–226.

Ittleson, W. H. (1952). *The Ames demonstrations in perception*. Princeton, NJ: Princeton University Press.

Iverson, P., & Kuhl, P. K. (1996). Influences of phonetic identification and category goodness on American listeners' perception of /r/ and /l/. *Journal of the Acoustical Society of America, 99*, 1130–1140.

Iwamura, Y. (1998). Representation of tactile functions in the somatosensory cortex. In J. W. Morley (Ed.). *Neural aspects of tactile sensation*. New York: Elsevier Science, pp. 195–238.

Jackson, S. R., & Hausain, M. (1997). Visual control of hand action. *Trends in Cognitive Sciences, 1*, 310–317.

Jacobs, K. M., Mark, G. P., & Scott, T. R. (1988). Taste responses in the nucleus tractus solitarius of sodium-deprived rats. *Journal of Physiology, 406*, 393–410.

Jacobs, T. M., Lawrence, M. D., Hong, K., Giordano, N., Jr., Giordano, N., Sr. (1996). On catching fly balls. *Science, 273*, 257–258.

Jacobson, A., & Gilchrist, A. (1988). The ratio principle holds over a million-to-one range of illumination. *Perception and Psychophysics, 43*, 1–6.

James, W. (1890/1981). *The principles of psychology* (Rev. ed.). Cambridge, MA: Harvard University Press. (Original work published 1890)

Jameson, D. (1985). Opponent-colors theory in light of physiological findings. In D. Ottoson & S. Zeki (Eds.), *Central and peripheral mechanisms of color vision* (pp. 8–102). New York: Macmillan.

Jenkins, W. M., & Merzenich, M. M. (1984). Role of cat primary auditory cortex for sound-localization behavior. *Journal of Neurophysiology, 52*, 819–847.

Jenkins, W. M., & Merzenich, M. M. (1987). Reorganization of neocortical representations after brain injury: A neurophysiological model of the bases of recovery from stroke. *Progress in Brain Research, 71*, 249–266.

Jensen, T. S., & Nikolajsen, L. (1999). Phantom pain and other phenomena after amputation. In P. D. Wall & R. Melzak (Eds.), *Textbook of pain*. New York: Churchill Livingstone, pp. 799–814.

Jessell, T. M., & Kelly, D. D. (1991). Pain and analgesia. In E. R. Kandel, J. H. Schwartz, & T. M. Jessell (Eds.), *Principles of neural science* (3rd ed., pp. 385–399). New York: Elsevier.

Jin, E. W., & Shevell, S. K. (1996). Color memory and color constancy. *Journal of the Optical Society of America, A, 13*, 1981–1991.

Johansson, G. (1975). Visual motion perception. *Scientific American, 232*, 76–89.

Johansson, R. S., & Vallbo, A. B. (1983). Tactile sensory coding in the glabrous skin of the human hand. *Trends in Neuroscience, 6*, 27–31.

Johnson, K. O., & Lamb, G. D. (1981). Neural mechanisms of spatial tactile discrimination: Neural patterns evoked by braille-like dot patterns in the monkey. *Journal of Physiology, 310,* 117–144.

Johnson, S. P., & Aslin, R. N. (1995). Perception of object unity in 2-month-old infants. *Developmental Psychology, 31,* 739–745.

Johnstone, B. M. & Boyle, A. J. F. (1967): Basilar membrane vibrations examined with the Mossbauer technique. *Science, 158,* 390–391.

Jones, K. R., Spear, P., & Tong, L. (1984). Critical periods for effects of monocular deprivation differences between striate and extrastriate cortex. *Journal of Neuroscience, 4,* 2543–2552.

Jones, M. R., & Yee, W. (1993). Attending to auditory events: The role of temporal organization. In S. McAdams & E. Bigand (Eds.), *Thinking in sound: The cognitive psychology of human audition* (pp. 69–112). Oxford, England: Oxford University Press.

Judd, D. B., MacAdam, D. L., & Wyszecki, G. (1964). Spectral distribution of typical daylight as a function of correlated color temperature. *Journal of the Optical Society of America, 54,* 1031–1040.

Julesz, B. (1971). *Foundations of cyclopean perception.* Chicago: University of Chicago Press.

Julesz, B. (1981). Textons, the elements of texture perception, and their interactions. *Nature, 290,* 91–97.

Julesz, B. (1984). A brief outline of the texton theory of human vision. *Trends in Neuroscience, 7,* 41–45.

Kaas, J. H. (1991). Plasticity of sensory and motor maps in adult mammals. *Annual Review of Neuroscience, 14,* 137–167.

Kaas, J. H., Hackett, T. A., & Tramo, M. J. (1999). Auditory processing in primate cerebral cortex. *Current Opinion in Neurobiology, 9,* 164–170.

Kaas, J. H., Merzenich, M. J., & Killackey, H. P. (1983). The reorganization of somatosensory cortex following peripheral nerve damage in adult and developing mammals. *Annual Review of Neuroscience, 6,* 325–356.

Kaas, J. H., & Pons, T. P. (1988). The somatosensory system of primates. In H. D. Steklis & J. Erwin (Eds.), *Comparative primate biology* (Vol. 4, pp. 421–468). New York: Liss.

Kalat, J. W. (2001). *Biological psychology, 7th edition.* Belmont, CA: Wadsworth.

Kandel, E. R., & Jessell, T. M. (1991). Touch. In E. R. Kandel, J. H. Schwartz, & T. M. Jessell (Eds.), *Principles of neural science* (3rd ed., pp. 367–384). New York: Elsevier.

Kanwisher, N., McDermott, J., Chun, M. M. (1997). The fusiform face area: A module in human extrastriate cortex specialized for face perception. *Journal of Neuroscience, 17,* 4302–4311.

Kapadia, M. K., Ito, M., Gilbert, C. D., & Westheimer, G. (1995). Improvement in visual sensitivity by changes in local context: Parallel studies in human observers and in V1 of alert monkeys. *Neuron, 15,* 843–856.

Kaplan, E., Mukherjee, P., & Shapley, R. (1993). Information filtering in the lateral geniculate nucleus. In R. Shapley & D. Man-Kit Lam (Eds.), *Contrast sensitivity* (Vol. 5). Cambridge, MA: MIT Press.

Kaplan, G. (1969). Kinetic disruption of optical texture: The perception of depth at an edge. *Perception and Psychophysics, 6,* 193–198.

Katoh, K., Koshimoto, H., Tani, A., & Mori, K. (1993). Coding of odor molecules by mitral/tufted cells in rabbit olfactory bulb. II. Aromatic compounds. *Journal of Neurophysiology, 70,* 2161–2175.

Katz, J. & Gagliese, L. (1999). Phantom limb pain: A continuing puzzle. In R. J. Gatchel & D. C. Turk (Eds.) *Psychosocial factors in pain.* New York: Guilford, pp. 284–300.

Kauer, J. S. (1987). Coding in the olfactory system. In T. E. Finger & W. C. Silver (Eds.), *Neurobiology of taste and smell* (pp. 205–231). New York: Wiley.

Kaufman, L., & Rock, I. (1962a). The moon illusion. *Science, 136,* 953–961.

Kaufman, L., & Rock, I. (1962b). The moon illusion. *Scientific American, 207,* 120–132.

Kawase, T., Delgutte, B., & Liberman, M. C. (1993). Antimasking effects of the olivocochlear reflex: II. Enhancement of auditory-nerve response to masked tones. *Journal of Neurophysiology, 70,* 2533–2549.

Kaye, K. L., & Bower, T. G. R. (1994). Learning and intermodal transfer of information in newborns. *Psychological Science, 5,* 286–288.

Kellman, P., & Spelke, E. (1983). Perception of partly occluded objects in infancy. *Cognitive Psychology, 15,* 483–524.

Kelly, J. P. (1991). Hearing. In E. R. Kandel, J. H. Schwartz, & T. M. Jessell (Eds.), *Principles of neural science* (3rd ed., pp. 481–499). New York: Elsevier.

Kemp, M. (1989). *The science of art.* New Haven, CT: Yale University Press.

Kenshalo, D. R. (1976). Correlations of temperature sensitivity in man and monkey, a first approximation. In Y. Zotterman (Ed.), *Sensory functions of the skin in primates, with special reference to man* (pp. 305–330). New York: Pergamon Press.

Kevan, P. G., & Backhaus, W. G. K. (1998). Color vision: ecology and evolution in making the best of the photic environment. In W. G. K. Backhaus, R. Kliegl, & J. S. Werner (Eds.) *Color vision: Perspectives from different disciplines*. New York: Walter de Gruyter, pp. 163–183.

Kewley-Port, D. (1983). Time-varying features as correlates of place of articulation in stop consonants. *Journal of the Acoustical Society of America, 73*, 322–335.

Kewley-Port, D., & Luce, P. A. (1984). Time-varying features of initial stop consonants in auditory running spectra: A first report. *Perception and Psychophysics, 35*, 353–360.

Khanna, S. M., & Leonard, D. G. B. (1982). Basilar membrane tuning in the cat cochlea. *Science, 215*, 305–306.

Kiang, N. Y. S. (1975). Stimulus representation in the discharge patterns of auditory neurons. In E. L. Eagles (Ed.), *The nervous system*, Vol. 3. New York: Raven, pp. 81–96.

Kiefer, J, von Ilberg, C., Reimer, B., Knecht, R., Gall, V., Diller, G., Sturzebecher, E., Pfenningdorff, T., & Spelsberg, A. (1996). Results of cochlear implantation in patients with severe to profound hearing loss: Implications for the indications. *Audiology, 37*, 382–395.

Kimura, D. (1961). Cerebral dominance and the perception of verbal stimuli. *Canadian Journal of Psychology, 15*, 166–171.

King, W. L., & Gruber, H. E. (1962). Moon illusion and Emmert's law. *Science, 135*, 1125–1126.

Kinnamon, S. C. (1988). Taste treanduction: A diversity of mechanisms. *Trends in Neurosciences, 11*, 491–496.

Kirman, J. H. (1974). Tactile apparent movement: The effects of interstimulus onset interval and stimulus duration. *Perception and Psychophysics, 15*, 1–6.

Klatzky, R. L., Lederman, S. J., & Metzger, V. A. (1985). Identifying objects by touch: An "expert system." *Perception and Psychophysics, 37*, 299–302.

Kleffner, D. A., & Ramachandran, V. S. (1992). On the perception of shape from shading. *Perception and Psychophysics, 52*, 18–36.

Klingon, G. H., & Bontecou, D. C. (1966). Localization in auditory space. *Neurology, 16*, 879–886.

Klinke, R., Kral, A., Heid, S., Tillein, J., & Hartmann, R. (1999). Recruitment of the auditory cortex in congenitally deaf cats by long-term cochlear electrostimulation. *Science, 285*, 1729–1733.

Knecht, S., Henningsen, H., Elbert, T., Flor, H., Hohling, C., Pantev, C., & Taub, E. (1996). Reorganizational and perceptual changes after amputation. *Brain, 119*, 1213–1219.

Knecht, S., Henningsen, H., Hohling, C., Elbert, T., Flor, H., Pantev, C., & Taub, E. (1998). Plasticity of plasticity? Changes in the pattern of perceptual correlates of reorganization after amputation. *Brain, 121*, 717–724.

Knill, D. C., & Kersten, D. (1991). Apparent surface curvature affects lightness perception. *Nature, 351*, 228–230.

Knudsen, E. I., & Konishi, M. (1978a). Center-surround organization of auditory receptive fields in the owl. *Science, 202*, 778–780.

Knudsen, E. I., & Konishi, M. (1978b). A neural map of auditory space in the owl. *Science, 200*, 795–797.

Kobatake, E., & Tanaka, K. (1994). Neuronal selectivities to complex object features in the ventral visual pathway of the macaque cerebral cortex. *Journal of Neurophysiology, 71*, 856–867.

Kobatake, E., Wang, G., & Tanaka, K. (1998). Effects of shape-discrimination training on the selectivity of inferotemporal cells in adult monkeys. *Journal of Neurophysiology, 80*, 324–330.

Kolb, B., & Whishaw, I. Q. (1985). *Fundamentals of human neuropsychology* (2nd ed.). New York: Freeman.

Kolers, P. S. (1964). The illusion of movement. *Scientific American, 211*, 98–106.

Konishi, M. (1984). Spatial receptive fields in the auditory system. In L. Bolis, R. D. Keynes, & S. H. Maddrell (Eds.), *Comparative physiology of sensory systems* (pp. 103–113). Cambridge, England: Cambridge University Press.

Kosaki, H., Hashikawa, T., He, J., & Jones, E. G. (1997). Tonotopic organization of auditory cortical fields delineated by parvalbumin immunoreactivity in Macaque monkeys. *Journal of Comparative Neurology, 386*, 304–316.

Kosslyn, S. M. (1994). *Image and brain: The resolution of the imagery debate*. Cambridge, MA: MIT Press.

Kreithen, M. L., & Quine, D. B. (1979). Infrasound detection by the homing pigeon: A behavioral audiogram. *Journal of Comparative Physiology, 129*, 1–4.

Kremenitzer, J. P., Vaughn, H. G., Kurtzberg, D., & Dowling, K. (1979). Smooth-pursuit eye movements in the newborn infant. *Child Development, 50*, 442–448.

Kroner, T. (1881). Über die Sinnesempfindungen der Neugeborenen. *Breslauer aerzliche Zeitschrift*. (Cited in Peterson, F., & Rainey, L. H. (1910–1911). The beginnings of mind in the newborn. *Bulletin of the Lying-In Hospital, 7*, 99–122.

Kruger, L. E. (1970). David Katz: Der Aufbau der Tastwelt [The world of touch: A synopsis]. *Perception and Psychophysics, 7*, 337–341.

Kubovy, M. (1986). *The psychology of perspective and Renaissance art.* Cambridge, England: Cambridge University Press.

Kuffler, S. W. (1953). Discharge patterns and functional organization of mammalian retina. *Journal of Neurophysiology, 16,* 37–68.

Kuhl, P. K. (1983). Perception of auditory equivalence classes for speech in early infancy. *Infant Behavior and Development, 6,* 263–285.

Kuhl, P. K. (1989). On babies, birds, modules, and mechanisms: A comparative approach to the acquisition of vocal communication. In R. J. Dooling & S. H. Hulse (Eds.), *Comparative psychology of audition* (pp. 379–419). Hillsdale, NJ: Erlbaum.

Kuhl, P. K. (2000). Language, mind and brain: Experience alters perception. In M. Gazzaniga (Ed.), *The new cognitive neurosciences.* Cambridge, MA: MIT Press, pp. 99–115.

Kuhl, P. K., Kirtani, S., Deguchi, T., Hayashi, A., Stevens, E. B., Dugger, C. D., & Iverson, P. (1997). Effects of language experience on speech perception: American and Japanese infants' perception of /ra/ and /la/. *Journal of the Acoustical Society of America, 102,* 3125.

Kuhl, P. K., Williams, K. A., Lacerda, F., Stevens, K. N., & Lindblom, B. (1992). Linguistic experience alters phonetic perception in infants by 6 months of age. *Science, 255,* 606–608.

Kunnapas, T. (1957). Experiments on figural dominance. *Journal of Experimental Psychology, 53,* 31–39.

Kwee, I., Fujii, Y., Matsuzawa, H., & Nakada, T. (1999). Perceptual processing of stereopsis in humans: GH High-field (3.0 tesla) functional MRI study. *Neurology, 53,* 1599–1601.

LaBarbera, J. D., Izard, C. E., Vietze, P., & Parisi, S. A. (1976). Four- and six-month-old infants' visual responses to joy, anger, and neutral expressions. *Child Development, 47,* 535–538.

Laing, D. D., Doty, R. L., & Breipohl, W. (Eds.). (1991). *The human sense of smell.* New York: Springer.

Lamme, V. A. F., & Roelfsema,, P. R. (2000). The distinct modes of vision offered by feedforward and recurrent processing. *Trends in Neurosciences, 23,* 571–579.

Lancet, D. (1992). Olfactory reception: From transduction to human genetics. In D. P. Corey & S. D. Roper (Eds.), *Sensory transduction* (pp. 73–91). New York: Rockefeller University Press.

Land, E. H. (1983). Recent advances in retinex theory and some implications for cortical computations: Color vision and the natural image. *Proceedings of the National Academy of Sciences, USA, 80,* 5163–5169.

Land, E. H. (1986). Recent advances in retinex theory. *Vision Research, 26,* 7–21.

Land, E. H., & McCann, J. J. (1971). Lightness and retinex theory. *Journal of the Optical Society of America, 61,* 1–11.

Land, M., & Horwood, J. (1995). Which parts of the road guide steering? *Nature, 377,* 339–340.

Land, M. F., & Lee, D. N. (1994). Where we look when we steer. *Nature, 369,* 742–744.

Landy, M. S., Maloney, L. T., Johnston, E. B., & Young, M. (1995). Measurement and modeling of depth cue combination: In defense of weak fusion. *Vision Research, 35,* 389–412.

Lawless, H. (1980). A comparison of different methods for assessing sensitivity to the taste of phenylthiocarbamide PTC. *Chemical Senses, 5,* 247–256.

Lawless, H. (2001). Taste. In E. B. Goldstein (Ed.), *Blackwell handbook of perception.* Oxford, UK: Blackwell, pp. 601–635.

Lederman, S. J., & Klatzky, R. L. (1987). Hand movements: A window into haptic object recognition. *Cognitive Psychology, 19,* 342–368.

Lederman, S. J., & Klatzky, R. L. (1990). Haptic classification of common objects: Knowledge-driven exploration. *Cognitive Psychology, 22,* 421–459.

Lee, D. N. (1974). Visual information during locomotion. In R. B. MacLeod & H. L. Pick, Jr. (Eds.), *Perception: Essays in honor of J. J. Gibson* (pp. 250–267). Ithaca, NY: Cornell University Press.

Lee, D. N. (1976). A theory of visual control of braking based on information about time to collision. *Perception, 5,* 437–459.

Lee, D. N. (1980). The optic flow field: The foundation of vision. *Transactions of the Royal Society, 290B,* 169–179.

Lee, D. N., & Aronson, E. (1974). Visual proprioceptive control of standing in human infants. *Perception and Psychophysics, 15,* 529–532.

Lee, D. N. & Reddish, P. E. (1976). Plummeting gannets: A paradigm of ecological optics. *Nature, 293,* 293–294.

LeGrand, Y. (1957). *Light, color and vision.* London: Chapman & Hall.

Lehrer, M., Srinivasan, M. V., Zhang, S. W., & Horridge, G. A. (1988). Motion cues provide the bee's visual world with a third dimension. *Nature, 332,* 356–357.

Lennie, P., Krauskopf, J., & Sclar, G. (1990). Chromatic mechanisms in striate cortex of macaque. *Journal of Neuroscience,* 649–669.

Lerman, S. (1966). *Basic ophthalmology.* New York: McGraw-Hill.

LeVay, S., & Voigt, T. (1988). Ocular dominance and disparity coding in cat visual cortex. *Visual Neuroscience, 1, 395–414.*

Leventhal A. G., Thompson, K. G., Liu, D., Zhou, Y., & Ault, S. J. (1995). Concomitant sensitivity to orientation, direction, and color of cells in layers 2, 3, and 4 of monkey striate cortex. *Journal of Neuroscience, 15, 1808–1818.*

Levin, D. & Simons, D. (1997). Failure to detect changes in attended objects in motion pictures. *Psychonomic Bulletin and Review, 4, 501–506.*

Lewis, E. R., Zeevi, Y. Y., & Werblin, F. S. (1969). Scanning electron microscopy of vertebrate visual receptors. *Brain Research, 15, 559–562.*

Li, S., Logan, R., & Pastore, R. (1991). Perception of acoustic source characteristics: Walking sounds. *Journal of the Acoustical Society of America, 90, 3036–3049.*

Liberman, A. M., Cooper, F. S., Shankweiler, D. P., & Studdert-Kennedy, M. (1967). Perception of the speech code. *Psychological Review, 74, 431–461.*

Liberman, A. M., & Mattingly, I. G. (1989). A specialization for speech perception. *Science, 243, 489–494.*

Lin, L. L., Chen, C. J., Hung, P. T., & Ko, L. S. (1988). Nation-wide survey of myopia among school-children in Taiwan. *Acta Ophthalmol, 185(Suppl.), 29–33.*

Lindsay, P. H., & Norman, D. A. (1977). *Human information processing* (2nd ed.). New York: Academic Press.

Litovsky, R. Y., Colburn, H. S., Yost, W. A., & Guzman, S. J. (1999). The precedence effect. *Journal of the Acoustical Society of America, 106, 1633–1654.*

Litovsky, R. Y., Rakerd, B., Yin, T. C. T., & Hartmann, W. M. (1997). Psychophysical and physiological evidence for a precedence effect in the median saggital plane. *Journal of Neurophysiology, 77, 2223–2226.*

Litovsky, R. Y., & Yin, T. C. T. (1998). Physiological studies of the precedence effect in the inferior colliculus of the cat. *Journal of Neurophysiology, 80, 1302–1316.*

Livingstone, M., & Hubel, D. (1988). Segregation of form, color, movement, and depth: Anatomy physiology and perception. *Science, 240, 740–749.*

Livingstone, M. S., & Hubel, D. H. (1988). Segregation of form, color, movement, and depth: Anatomy, physiology, and perception. *Science, 240, 740–749.*

Logothetis, N. K., & Pauls, J. (1995). Psychophysical and physiological evidence for viewer-centered object representations in the primate. *Cerebral Cortex, 5, 270–288.*

Logothetis, N. K., Pauls, J., Bulthoff, H. H., & Poggio, T. (1994). View-dependent object recognition by monkeys. *Current Biology, 4, 401–414.*

Logothetis, N. K., Pauls, J., & Poggio, T. (1995). Shape representation in the inferior temporal cortex of monkeys. *Current Biology, 5, 552–563.*

Loomis, J. M., DaSilva, J. A., Fujita, N., & Fulusima, S. S. (1992). Visual space perception and visually directed action. *Journal of Experimental Psychology: Human Perception and Performance, 18, 906–921.*

Loomis, J. M., DaSilva, J. A., Philbeck, J. W., & Fukusima, S. S. (1996). Visual perception of location and distance. *Current Directions in Psychological Science, 5, 72–77.*

Loomis, J. M., Golledge, R. G., Klatzky, R. L., Speigle, J. M., & Tietz, J. (1994). *Personal guidance system for the visually impaired.* Proceedings of the First Annual International ACM/SIGCAPH Conference on Assistive Technologies, Marina del Rey, CA.

Loomis, J. M., Hebert, C., & Cicinelli, J. G. (1990). Active localization of virtual sounds. *Journal of the Acoustical Society of America, 88, 1757–1764.*

Loomis, J. M., Klatzky, R. L., & Golledge, R. G. (1999). Auditory distance perception in real, virtual, and mixed environments. In Y. Hota & H. Tamura (Eds.). *Mixed reality: merging real and virtual worlds.* Tokyo: Ohmsha, pp. 201–214.

Loomis, J. M., Klatzky, R. L., Philbeck, J. W., & Golledge, R. G. (1998). Assessing auditory distance perception using perceptually directed action. *Perception & Psychophysics, 60, 966–980.*

Lowenstein, W. R. (1960). Biological transducers. *Scientific American, 203, 98–108.*

Lumer, E. D., Friston, K. J., & Rees, G. (1998). Neural correlates of perceptual rivalry in the human brain. *Science, 280, 1930–1934.*

Lundstrom, I. (2000). Picture the smell. *Nature, 406, 682–683.*

Luria, A. R. (1968). *The mind of a mnemonist.* New York: Basic Books.

Macefield, V. G. (1998). The signaling of touch, finger movements and manipulation forces by mechanoreceptors in human skin. In J. W. Morley (Ed.), *Neural aspects of tactile sensation.* New York: Elsevier Science, pp. 89–130.

Macfarlane, A. (1975). Olfaction in the development of social preferences in the human neonate. In A. Macfarlane (Ed.), *Ciba Foundation Symposium, 33, 103–117.*

Mack, A., & Rock, I. (1998). *Inattentional blindness.* Cambridge, MA: MIT Press.

Maffei, L., & Fiorentini, A. (1973). The visual cortex as a spatial frequency analyzer. *Vision Research, 13, 1255–1267.*

Makous, J. C., & Middlebrooks, J. C. (1990). Two-dimensional sound localization by human listeners. *Journal of the Acoustical Society of America*, 87, 2188–2200.

Malnic, B., Hirono, J., Sata, T., & Buck, L. B. (1999). Combinatorial receptor codes for odors. *Cell*, 96, 713–723.

Mamassian, P., Knill, D., & Kersten, D. (1998). The perception of cast shadows. *Trends in Cognitive Sciences*, 2, 288–295.

Marean, G. C., Werner, L. A., & Kuhl, P. K. (1992). Vowel categorization by very young infants. *Developmental Psychology*, 28, 396–405.

Margoliash, D. (1983). Acoustic parameters underlying the responses of song-specific neurons in the white-crowned sparrow. *Journal of Neuroscience*, 3, 1029–1057.

Markowtiz, J. A. (1996). *Using speech recognition*. Upper Saddle River, NJ: Prentice-Hall.

Marks, L. E. (1974). On associations of light and sound: The mediation of brightness, pitch, and loudness. *American Journal of Psychology*, 87, 173–188.

Marks, L. E. (1975). On colored-hearing synesthesia: Cross-modal translations of sensory dimensions. *Psychological Bulletin*, 82, 303–331.

Marr, D. (1976). Early processing of visual information. *Transactions of the Royal Society of London*, 275B, 483–524.

Marr, D. (1982). *Vision*. San Francisco: Freeman.

Marr, D., & Hildreth, E. (1980). Theory of edge detection. *Proceedings of the Royal Society of London*, 207B, 187–207.

Marr, D., & Nishihara, H. K. (1978). Representation and recognition of the spatial organization of three-dimensional shapes. *Proceedings of the Royal Society of London*, 200B, 269–294.

Martin, J. H., & Jessell, T. M. (1991). Modality coding in the somatic sensory system. In E. R. Kandel, J. H. Schwartz, & T. M. Jessell (Eds.), *Principles of neural science* (3rd ed., pp. 339–352). Norwalk, CT: Appleton & Lange.

Masland, R. H. (1988). Amacrine cells. *Trends in Neuroscience*, 9, 405–410.

Matin, L., Picoult, E., Stevens, J., Edwards, M., & MacArthur, R. (1982). Oculoparalytic illusion: Visual-field dependent spatial mislocations by humans partially paralyzed with curare. *Science*, 216, 198–201.

Mattingly, I., & Studdert-Kennedy, M. (Eds.). (1991). *Modularity and the motor theory of speech perception*. Hillsdale, NJ: Erlbaum.

Maunsell, J. H. R., & McAdams, C. J. (2000). Effects of attention on neuronal reponse properties in visual cerebral cortex. In M. Gazzaniga (Ed.). *The new cognitive neurosciences*. Cambridge, MA: MIT Press, pp. 315–324.

Maunsell, J. H. R., Nealey, T. A., & DePriest, D. D. (1990). Magnocellular and parvocellular contributions to responses in the middle temporal visual area (MT) of the macaque monkey. *Journal of Neuroscience*, 10, 363–401.

Mayer, D. J. (1979). Endogenous analgesia systems: Neural and behavioral mechanisms. In J. J. Bonica (Ed.), *Advances in pain research and therapy* (Vol. 3, pp. 385–410). New York: Raven Press.

McArthur, D. J. (1982). Computer vision and perceptual psychology. *Psychological Bulletin*, 92, 283–309.

McBeath, M. K., Shaffer, D. M., & Kaiser, M. K. (1995). How baseball outfielders determine where to run to catch fly balls. *Science*, 268, 569–573.

McBurney, D. H. (1969). Effects of adaptation on human taste function. In C. Pfaffmann (Ed.), *Olfaction and taste* (pp. 407–419). New York: Rockefeller University Press.

McBurney, D. H., Levine, J. M., & Cavanaugh, P. H. (1977). Psychophysical and social ratings of human body odor. *Personality and Social Psychology Bulletin*, 3, 135–138.

McClintock, M. K. (1971). Menstrual synchrony and suppression. *Nature*, 229, 244–245.

McCutcheon, N. B. (1992). Human psychophysical studies of saltiness suppression by amiloride. *Physiology and Behavior*, 51, 1069–1074.

McFadden, S. A. (1987). The binocular depth stereoacuity of the pigeon and its relation to the anatomical resolving power of the eye. *Vision Research*, 27, 1967–1980.

McFadden, S. A., & Wild, J. M. (1986). Binocular depth perception in the pigeon. *Journal of the Experimental Analysis of Behavior*, 45, 149–160.

McGurk, H., & MacDonald, T. (1976). Hearing lips and seeing voices. *Nature*, 264, 746–748.

McKeefry, D. J., & Zeki, S. (1997). The position and topography of the human colour centre as revealed by functional magnetic resonance imaging. *Brain*, 120, 2229–2242.

McKenzie, D. (1923). *Aromatics and the soul: A study of smells*. New York: Hoeber.

McLean, J. H., & Shipley, M. T. (1992). Neuroanatomical substrates of olfaction. In M. J. Serby & K. L. Chobor (Eds.), *Science of olfaction* (pp. 126–171). New York: Springer-Verlag.

McLeod, R. W., & Ross, H. E. (1983). Optic-flow and cognitive factors in time-to-collision estimates. *Perception*, 12, 417–423.

Meddis, R., & Hewitt, M. J. (1991). Virtual pitch and phase sensitivity of a computer model of the auditory periphery: I. Pitch identification. *Journal of the Acoustical Society of America*, 89, 2866–2882.

Mehler, J. (1981). The role of syllables in speech processing: Infant and adult data. *Transactions of the Royal Society of London*, B295, 333–352.

Meltzoff, A. N., & Borton, R. W. (1979). Intermodal matching by human neonates. *Nature*, 282, 403–404.

Melzack, R. (1992). Phantom limbs. *Scientific American*, 266, 121–126.

Melzack, R. (1999). From the gate to the neuromatrix. *Pain*, Suppl. 6, S121–S126.

Melzack, R., & Wall, P. D. (1965). Pain mechanisms: A new theory. *Science*, 150, 971–979.

Melzack, R., & Wall, P. D. (1983). *The challenge of pain*. New York: Basic Books.

Melzack, R., & Wall, P. D. (1988). *The challenge of pain* (Rev. ed.). New York: Penguin Books.

Menzel, R., & Backhaus, W. (1989). Color vision in honey bees: Phenomena and physiological mechanisms. In D. G. Stavenga & R. C. Hardie (Eds.), *Facets of vision* (pp. 281–297). Berlin: Springer-Verlag.

Menzel, R., Ventura, D. F., Hertel, H., deSouza, J., & Greggers, U. (1986). Spectral sensitivity of photoreceptors in insect compound eyes: Comparison of species and methods. *Journal of Comparative Physiology*, 158A, 165–177.

Merigan, W. H., & Maunsell, J. H. R. (1993). How parallel are the primate visual pathways? *Annual Review of Neuroscience*, 16, 369–402.

Mershon, D. H., & Bowers, J. N. (1979). Absolute and relative cues for the auditory perception of egocentric distance. *Perception*, 8, 311–322.

Merskey, H. (1991). The definition of pain. *European Journal of Psychiatry*, 6, 153–159.

Merzenich, M. M., Recanzone, G., Jenkins, W. M., Allard, T. T., & Nudo, R. J. (1988). Cortical representational plasticity. In P. Rakic & W. Singer (Eds.), *Neurobiology of neocortex* (pp. 42–67). Berlin: Wiley.

Merzlyak, M. N., Gitelson, A. A., Chivkunova, O. B., & Raktin, V. Y. (1999). Non-destructive optical detection of pigment changes during leaf senescence and fruit ripening. *Physiologia Plantarum*, 106, 135–141.

Meyer, R. A., & Campbell, J. N. (1981). Myelinated nociceptive afferents account for the hyperalgesia that follows a burn to the hand. *Science*, 213, 1527–1529.

Middlebrooks, J. C. (1997). Spectral shape cues for sound localization. In R. H. Gilkey and T. R. Anderson (Eds.) Hillsdale, NJ: Erlbaum, pp. 77–97.

Middlebrooks, J. C. (2000). Cortical representations of auditory space. In M. Gazzaniga (Ed.). *The new cognitive neurosciences*. Cambridge, MA: MIT Press, pp. 425–436.

Middlebrooks, J. C., Clock, A. E., Xu, L., & Green, D. M. (1994). A panoramic code for sound location by cortical neurons. *Science*, 264, 842–844.

Middlebrooks, J. C., & Green, D. M. (1991). Sound localization by human listeners. *Annual Review of Psychology*, 42, 135–159.

Middlebrooks, J . C., Xu, L., Eddins, C., & Green, D. M. (1998). Codes for sound-source location in nontonotopic auditory cortex. *Journal of Neurophysiology*, 80, 863–881.

Mikami, A., Newsome, W. T., & Wurtz, R. H. (1986). Motion selectivity in macaque visual cortex: I. Mechanisms of direction and speed selectivity in extrastriate area MT. *Journal of Neurophysiology*, 55, 1308–1327.

Miller, G. A., & Heise, G. A. (1950). The trill threshold. *Journal of the Acoustical Society of America*, 22, 637–683.

Miller, G. A., & Isard, S. (1963). Some perceptual consequences of linguistic rules. *Journal of Verbal Learning and Verbal Behavior*, 2, 212–228.

Miller, I. J. (1995). Anatomy of the peripheral taste system. In R. L. Doty (Ed.), *Handbook of olfaction and gustation* (pp. 521–548). New York: Marcel Dekker.

Milner, A. D., & Goodale, M. A. (1995). *The visual brain in action*. New York: Oxford University Press.

Mishkin, M. (1986, January 24). *Two visual systems*. Talk presented at Western Psychiatric Institute and Clinic, Pittsburgh.

Mishkin, M., Ungerleider, L. G., & Macko, K. A. (1983). Object vision and spatial vision: Two central pathways. *Trends in Neuroscience*, 6, 414–417.

Mitchell, D. E., & Timney, B. (1984). Postnatal development of function in the mammalian visual system. In J. M. Brookhart & V. B. Mountcastle (Eds.), *Handbook of physiology: The nervous system III* (pp. 507–555). Bethesda, MD: American Physiological Society.

Mitchell, D. E., & Wilkinson, F. (1974). The effect of early astigmatism on the visual resolution of gratings. *Journal of Physiology*, 243, 739–756.

Mollon, J. D. (1989). "Tho' she kneel'd in that place where they grew..." *Journal of Experimental Biology*, 146, 21–38.

Mollon, J. D. (1990). The club-sandwich mystery. *Nature*, 343, 16–17.

Mollon, J. D. (1993). Mixing genes and mixing colours. *Current Biology*, 3, 82–85.

Mollon, J. D. (1997). "Tho she kneel'd in that place where they grew..." The uses and origins of primate colour visual information. In A. Byrne & D. R. Hilbert (Eds.), *Readings on color, vol. 2: The science of color*. Cambridge, MA: MIT Press, pp. 379–396.

Montagna, W., & Parakkal, P. F. (1974). *The structure and function of skin* (3rd ed.). New York: Academic Press.

Mon-Williams, M., & Tresilian, J. R. (1999). Some recent studies on the extraretinal contribution to distance perception. *Perception*, 28, 167–181.

Moon, C., Cooper, R. P., & Fifer, W. P. (1993). Two-day-olds prefer their native language. *Infant Behavior and Development*, 16, 495–500.

Moore, B. C. J. (2001). Loudness, pitch and timbre. In E. B. Goldstein (Ed.), *Blackwell handbook of perception*. Oxford, UK: Blackwell, pp. 408–436.

Moore, C., & Engel, S. A. (1999). Neural response to 2D and 3D objects measured with fMRI. *Investigative Ophthalmology and Visual Science*, 40, S351.

Moran, J., & Desimone, R. (1985). Selective attention gates visual processing in the extrastriate cortex. *Science*, 229, 782–784.

Mori, K., Nagao, H., & Yoshihara, Y. (1999). The olfactory bulb: Coding and processing of odor molecule information. *Science*, 286, 711–715.

Mori, K., & Yoshihara, Y. (1995). Molecular recognition and olfactory processing in the mammalian olfactory system. *Progress in Neurobiology*, 45, 585–619.

Morrison, E. E., & Moran, D. T. (1995). Anatomy and ultrastructure of the human olfactory neuroepithelium. In R. L. Doty (Ed.), *Handbook of olfaction and gustation* (pp. 75–101). New York: Marcel Dekker.

Morrongiello, B. A. (1988). Infants' localization of sounds along the horizontal axis: Estimates of minimum audible angle. *Developmental Psychology*, 24, 8–13.

Morrongiello, B. A., Fenwick, K. D., & Chance, G. (1990). Sound localization acuity in very young infants: An observer-based testing procedure. *Developmental Psychology*, 26, 75–84.

Moulton, D. G. (1977). Minimum odorant concentrations detectable by the dog and their implications for olfactory receptor sensitivity. In D. Miller-Schwarze & M. M. Mozell (Eds.), *Chemical signals in vertebrates* (pp. 455–464). New York: Plenum Press.

Mountcastle, V. B., & Powell, T. P. S. (1959). Neural mechanisms subserving cutaneous sensibility, with special reference to the role of afferent inhibition in sensory perception and discrimination. *Bulletin of the Johns Hopkins Hospital*, 105, 201–232.

Movshon, J. A., & Newsome, W. T. (1992). Neural foundations of visual motion perception. *Current Directions in Psychological Science*, 1, 35–39.

Mozell, M. M., Smith, B. P., Smith, P. E., Sullivan, R. L., & Swender, P. (1969). Nasal chemoreception in flavor identification. *Archives of Otolaryngology*, 90, 131–137.

Muir, D., & Field, J. (1979). Newborn infants orient to sounds. *Child Development*, 50, 431–436.

Murata, A., Gallese, V., Kaseda, M., & Sakata, H. (1996). Parietal neurons related to memory-guided hand manipulation. *Journal of Neurophysiology*, 75, 2180–2186.

Murphy, C., & Cain, W. S. (1980). Taste and olfaction: Independence vs. interaction. *Physiology and Behavior*, 24, 601–606.

Murphy, K. J., Racicot, C. I., & Goodale, M. A. (1996). The use of visuomotor cues as a strategy for making perceptual judgements in a patient with visual form agnosia. *Neuropsychology*, 10, 396–401.

Mutti, D. O., Zadnik, K., & Adams, A. J. (1996). Myopia: The nature versus nurture debate goes on. *Investigative Ophthalmology and Visual Science*, 37, 952–957.

Nagodawithana, T. W. (1995). *Sensory flavors*. Milwaukee, WI: Esteekay Associates.

Nakamura, H., Gattass, R., Desimone, R., & Ungerleider, L. G. (1993). The modular organization of projections from areas V1 and V2 to areas V4 and TEO in macaques. *Journal of Neuroscience*, 13, 3681–3691.

Narayan, S. S., Temchin, A. N., Recio, A., & Ruggero, M. A. (1998). Frequency tuning of basilar membrane and auditory nerve fibers in the same cochleae. *Science*, 282, 1882–1884.

Nathans, J., Thomas, D., & Hogness, D. S. (1986). Molecular genetics of human color vision: The genes encoding blue, green, and red pigments. *Science*, 232, 193–202.

Neitz, M., Neitz, J., & Jacobs, G. H. (1991). Spectral tuning of pigments underlying red–green color vision. *Science*, 252, 971–974.

Nelson, C. A., & Horowitz, F. D. (1987). Visual motion perception in infancy: A review and synthesis. In P. Salapatek & L. Cohen (Eds.), *Handbook of infant perception* (Vol. 2, pp. 123–153). New York: Academic Press.

Nelson, M. E., & Bower, J. M. (1990). Brain maps and parallel computers. *Trends in Neuroscience*, 13, 403–408.

Nelson, P. G., Erulkar, S. D., & Bryan, S. S. (1966). Responses of units of the inferior colliculus to time-varying acoustic stimuli. *Journal of Neurophysiology, 29*, 834–860.

Nelson, R. J., Sur, M., Felleman, D. J., & Kaas, J. H. (1980). Representations of the body surface in postcentral parietal cortex of *Macaca fasicularis. Journal of Comparative Neurology, 192*, 611–643.

Neuenschwander, S., & Singer, W. (1996). Long-range synchronization of oscillatory light responses in the cat retina and lateral geniculate nucleus. *Nature, 379*, 728–733.

Newsome, W. T., Britten, K. H., & Movshon, J. A. (1989). Neuronal correlates of a perceptual decision. *Nature, 341*, 52–54.

Newsome, W. T., Mikami, A., & Wurtz, R. H. (1986). Motion selectivity in macaque visual cortex: III. Psychophysics and physiology of apparent motion. *Journal of Neurophysiology, 55*, 1340–1351.

Newsome, W. T., & Paré, E. B. (1988). A selective impairment of motion perception following lesions of the middle temporal visual area (MT). *Journal of Neuroscience, 8*, 2201–2211.

Newsome, W. T., Shadlen, M. N., Zohary, E., Britten, K. H., & Movshon, J. A. (1995). Visual motion: Linking neuronal activity to psychophysical performance. In M. S. Gazzaniga (Ed.), *The cognitive neurosciences* (pp. 401–414). Cambridge, MA: MIT Press.

Newton, I. (1704). *Optiks.* London: Smith and Walford.

Nishitani, N., & Hari, R. (2000). Temporal dynamics of cortical representation for action. *Proceedings of the National Academy of Sciences USA, 97*, 913–918.

Nordby, K. (1990). Vision in a complete achromat: A personal account. In R. F. Hess, L. T. Sharpe, & K. Nordby (Eds.), *Night vision* (pp. 290–315). Cambridge, England: Cambridge University Press.

Northern, J., & Downs, M. (1978). *Hearing in children* (2nd ed.). Baltimore, MA: Williams & Wilkins.

Norton, S. J., Schultz, M. C., Reed, C. M., Briada, L. D., Durlach, N. L., & Rabinowitz, W. M. (1977). Analytic study of the Tadoma method: Background and preliminary results. *Journal of Speech and Hearing Research, 20*, 574–595.

Nothdurft, H. C. (1990). Texton segregation by associated differences in global and local luminance distribution. *Proceedings of the Royal Society of London, B239*, 295–320.

Nygaard, L. C., & Pisoni, D. B. (1995). Speech perception: New directions in research and theory. In J. L. Miller & P. D. Eimas (Eds.), *Speech, language, and communication* (pp. 63–97). San Diego, CA: Academic Press.

Nygaard, L. C., Sommers, M. S., & Pisoni, D. B. (1994). Speech perception as a talker-contingent process. *Psychological Science, 5*, 42–46.

Ohzawa, I. (1998). Mechanisms of stereoscopic vision: The disparity energy model. *Current Opinion in Neurobiology, 8*, 509–515.

Ohzawa, I., DeAngelis, G. C., & Freeman, R. D. (1996). Encoding of binocular disparity by simple cells in the cat's visual cortex. *Journal of Neurophysiology, 75*, 1779–1805.

Olsen, J. F., & Suga, N. (1991a). Combination sensory neurons in the medial geniculate body of the mustache bat: Encoding of relative velocity information. *Journal of Neurophysiology, 65*, 1254–1273.

Olsen, J. F., & Suga, N. (1991b). Combination sensory neurons in the medial geniculate body of the mustache bat: Encoding of target range information. *Journal of Neurophysiology, 65*, 1275–1296.

Olsho, L. W., Koch, E. G., Carter, E. A., Halpin, C. F., & Spetner, N. B. (1988). Pure-tone sensitivity of human infants. *Journal of the Acoustical Society of America, 84*, 1316–1324.

Olsho, L. W., Koch, E. G., Halpin, C. F., & Carter, E. A. (1987). An observer-based psychoacoustic procedure for use with young infants. *Developmental Psychology, 23*, 627–640.

Olson, C. R., & Freeman, R. D. (1980). Profile of the sensitive period for monocular deprivation in kittens. *Experimental Brain Research, 39*, 17–21.

Olson, H. (1967). *Music, physics, and engineering* (2nd ed.). New York: Dover.

Oram, M. W., & Perrett, D. I. (1994). Responses of anterior superior temporal polysensory (STPa) neurons to "biological motion" stimuli. *Journal of Cognitive Neuroscience, 6*, 99–116.

Orban, G. A., Lagae, L., Verri, A., Raiguel, S., Xiao, D., Maes, H., & Torre, V. (1992). First-order analysis of optical flow in monkey brain. *Proceedings of the National Academy of Sciences, 89*, 2595–2599.

Orban, G. A., Vandenbussche, E., & Vogels, R. (1984). Human orientation discrimination tested with long stimuli. *Vision Research, 24*, 121–128.

O'Shea, R. P. (1991). Thumb's rule tested: Visual angle of thumb's width is about 2 deg. *Perception, 20*, 415–418.

Owen, D. (2000). The chosen one. *The New Yorker*, August 21 & 28, 106–119.

Owens, E. (1989). Present status of adults with cochlear implants. In E. Owens & D. K. Kessler (Eds.), *Cochlear implants in young deaf children* (pp. 25–52). Boston: Little, Brown.

Oxford American Dictionary. (1980). New York: Oxford University Press.

Oyama, T. (1960). Figure-ground dominance as a function of sector angle, brightness, hue, and orientation. *Journal of Experimental Psychology, 60,* 299–305.

Palmer, S. E. (1975). The effects of contextual scenes on the identification of objects. *Memory and Cognition, 3,* 519–526.

Palmer, S. E. (1999). *Vision science.* Cambridge, MA: MIT Press.

Palmeri, T. J., Goldinger, S. D., & Pisoni, D. B. (1993). Episodic encoding of voice attributes and recognition memory for spoken words. *Journal of Experimental Psychology: Learning Memory and Cognition, 19,* 309–328.

Pantev, C., Oostenveld, R., Engelien, A., Ross, B., Roberts, L. E., & Hoke, M. (1998). Increased auditory cortical representation in musicians. *Nature, 392,* 811–814.

Parkin, A. J. (1996). *Explorations in cognitive neuropsychology.* Oxford, England: Blackwell.

Pascalis, O., deSchonen, S., Morton, J., Deruelle, C., & Fabre-Grenet, M. (1995). Mother's face recognition by neonates: A replication and an extension. *Infant Behavior and Development, 18,* 79–85.

Pascual-Leone, A., & Torres, F. (1993). Plasticity of sensorimotor cortex reprsentation of the reading finger in Braille readers. *Brain, 116,* 39–52.

Pasternak, T. (1990). Vision following loss of cortical directional selectivity. In M. A. Berkley & W. C. Stebbins (Eds.), *Comparative perception* (Vol. 1, pp. 407–428). New York: Wiley.

Pasternak, T., & Merigan, E. H. (1994). Motion perception following lesions of the superior temporal sulcus in the monkey. *Cerebral Cortex, 4,* 247–259.

Patuzzi, R. (1996). Cochlear micromechanics and macromechanics. In P. Dallos, A. N. Popper, & R. R. Fay (Eds.), *The cochlea* (pp. 186–257). New York: Springer.

Paulesu, E., Harrison, J., Baron-Cohen, S., Watson, J. D. G., Goldstein, L., Heather, J., Frackowiak, R. S. J., & Frith, C. D. (1995). The physiology of colored hearing. *Brain, 118,* 661–676.

Pelosi, P. (1996). Odorant-binding proteins. *Current Reviews in Biochemistry and Molecular Biology, 29,* 199–228.

Penfield, W., & Rasmussen, T. (1950). *The cerebral cortex of man.* New York: Macmillan.

Perl, E. R., & Kruger, L. (1996). In L. Kruger (Ed.), *Pain and touch* (pp. 179–221). San Diego, CA: Academic Press.

Perrett, D. I., Harries, M. H., Benson, P. J., Chitty, A. J., & Mistlin, A. J. (1990). Retrieval of structure from rigid and biological motion: An analysis of the visual responses of neurones in the macaque temporal cortex. In A. Blake & T. Troscianko (Eds.), *AI and the eye* (pp. 181–200). New York: Wiley.

Perrett, D. I., Hietanen, J. K., Oram, M. W., & Benson, P. J. (1992). Organization and function of cells responsive to faces in the temporal cortex. *Transactions of the Royal Society of London, B225,* 23–30.

Perrett, D. I., & Oram, M. W. (1993). Neurophysiology of shape processing. *Image and visual computing, 11,* 317–333.

Peterson, F., & Rainey, L. H. (1911). The beginnings of mind in the newborn. *Bulletin of the Lying-In Hospital, 7,* 99–122.

Peterson, M. A. (1994). Object recognition processes can and do operate before figure-ground organization. *Current Directions in Psychological Science, 3,* 105–111.

Pettit, M. J., & Schwark, H. D. (1993). Receptive field reorganization in dorsal column nuclei during temporary denervation. *Science, 262,* 2054–2056.

Pevsner, J., Hou, V., Snowman, A. M., & Snyder, S. H. (1990). Odorant-binding protein: Characterization of ligand binding. *Journal of Biological Chemistry, 265,* 6118–6125.

Pevsner, J., Trifletti, R. R., Strittmatter, S. M., & Snyder, S. H. (1985). Isolation and characterization of an olfactory protein for odorant pyrazines. *Proceedings of the National Academy of Sciences, 82,* 3050–3054.

Pfaffmann, C. (1974). Specificity of the sweet receptors of the squirrel monkey. *Chemical Senses, 1,* 61–67.

Pfeiffer, C. A., & Johnston, R. E. (1994). Hormonal and behavioral responses of male hamsters to females and female odors: Roles of olfaction, the vemeronasal system, and sexual experience. *Physiology and Behavior, 55,* 129–138.

Philbeck, J. W., Loomis, J. M., & Beall, A. C. (1997). Visually perceived location is an invariant in the control of action. *Perception & Psychophysics, 59,* 601–612.

Pirchio, M., Spinelli, D., Fiorentini, A., & Maffei, L. (1978). Infant contrast sensitivity evaluated by evoked potentials. *Brain Research, 141,* 179–184.

Plack, C. J., & Carlyon, R. P. (1995). Loudness perception and intensity coding. In B. C. J. Moore (Ed.), *Hearing* (pp. 123–160). San Diego: Academic Press.

Plug, C., & Ross, H. E. (1994). The natural moon illusion: A multifactor account. *Perception, 23,* 321–333.

Poggio, G. F. (1990). Cortical neural mechanisms of stereopsis studied with dynamic random-dot stereograms. *Cold Spring Harbor Symposia on Quantitative Biology, 55*, 749–758.

Poggio, G. F. (1995). Mechanisms of stereopsis in monkey visual cortex. *Cerebral Cortex, 5*, 193–204.

Poggio, T. (1984, April). Vision by man and machine. *Scientific American*, 106–116.

Pokorny, J., Shevell, S. K., & Smith, V. C. (1991). Color appearance and color constancy. In P. Gouras (Ed.), *The perception of color: Vol. 6. Vision and visual dysfunction* (pp. 43–61). Boca Raton, FL: CRC Press.

Polk, T. A., & Farah, M. J. (1998). The neural development and organization of letter recognition: Evidence from functional neuroimaging, computational modeling, and behavioral studies. *Proceedings of the National Academy of Sciences USA, 95*, 847–852.

Pons, T. P., Garraghty, P. E., Ommaya, A. K., Kaas, J. H., Taub, E., & Mishkin, M. (1991). Massive cortical reorganization after sensory deafferentation in adult macaques. *Science, 252*, 1857–1860.

Porter, R. H., Makin, J. W., Davis, L. B., & Christensen, K. M. (1992). Breast-fed infants respond to olfactory cues from their own mother and unfamiliar lactating females. *Infant Behavior and Development, 15*, 85–93.

Porter, R. H., & Schaal, B. (1995). Olfaction and development of social preferences in neonatal organisms. In R. L. Doty (Ed.), *Handbook of olfaction and gustation* (pp. 299–321). New York: Marcel Dekker.

Preti, G., Cutler, W. B., Garcia, C. R., Huggins, G. R., & Lawley, H. J. (1986). Human axillary secretions influence women's menstrual cycles: The role of donor extract from females. *Hormones and Behavior, 20*, 474–482.

Price, D. D. (2000). Psychological and neural mechanisms of the affective dimension of pain. *Science, 288*, 1769–1772.

Price, J. L., Carmichael, S. T., Carnes, K. M., Clugnet, M. C., Kuroda, M., & Ray, J. P. (1991). Olfactory output to the prefrontal cortex. In J. L. Davis & H. Eichenbaum (Eds.), *Olfaction: A model system for computational neuroscience* (pp. 101–120). Cambridge, MA: MIT Press.

Proffitt, D. R., Bhalla, M., Gossweiler, R., & Midgett, J. (1995). Perceiving geographical slant. *Psychonomic Bulletin & Review, 2*, 409–428.

Proffitt, D. R., & Kaiser, M. K. (1995). Perceiving events. In W. Epstein & S. Rogers (Eds.), *Perception of space and motion* (pp. 227–261). San Diego, CA: Academic Press.

Ptito, A., Zatorre, R. J., Petrides, M., Frey, S., Salivisatos, B., & Evans, A. C. (1993). Localization and lateralization of stereoscopic processing in the human brain. *Neuroreport, 4*, 1155–1158.

Puce, A., Allison, T., Asgari, M., Gore, J. C., & McCarthy, G. (1995). Face-sensitive regiions in extrastriate cortex studied by functional MRI. *Journal of Neurophysiology, 74*, 1192–1199.

Puce, A., Allison, T., Asgari, M., Gore, J. C., & McCarthy, G. (1996). Differential sensitivity of human visual cortex to faces, letterstrings, and textures: A functional magnetic resonsnce imaging study. *Journal of Neuroscience, 16*, 5205–5215.

Quinn, P. C., Burke, S., & Rush, A. (1993). Part–whole perception in early infancy: Evidence for perceptual grouping produced by lightness similarity. *Infant Behavior and Development, 16*, 19–42.

Quinn, P. C., Rosano, J. L., & Wooten, B. R. (1988). Evidence that brown is not an elemental color. *Perception and Psychophysics, 43*, 156–164.

Quittner, A. L., Smith, L. B., Osberger, M. J., Mitchell, T. V., & Katz, D. B. (1994). The impact of audition on the development of visual attention. *Psychological Science, 5*, 347–353.

Rainville , P., Duncan, G. H., Price, D. D., Carrier, B., & Bushnell, C. (1997). Pain affect encoded in human anterior cingulate but not somatosensory cortex. *Science, 277*, 968–971.

Rakow, N. A., & Suslick, K. S. (2000). A colorimetric sensory array for odour visualization. *Nature, 406*, 710–713.

Ramachandran, V. S. (1992, May). Blind spots. *Scientific American*, 86–91.

Ramachandran, V. S., & Anstis, S. M. (1986, May). The perception of apparent motion. *Scientific American*, 102–109.

Ramachandran, V. S., Armel, C., Foster, C., & Stoddard, R. (1998). Object recognition can drive motion perception. *Nvature, 395*, 852–853.

Ramachandran, V. S., & Hirstein, W. (1998). The perception of phantom limbs. *Brain, 121*, 1603–1630.

Ramachandran, V. S., & Rogers-Ramachandran, D. (1996). Synaesthesia in phantom limbs induced with mirrors. *Proceedings of the Royal Society of London. B., 263*, 377–386.

Ranganathan, R., Harris, W. A., & Zuker, C. S. (1991). The molecular genetics of invertebrate phototransduction. *Trends in Neurosciences, 14*, 486–493.

Ratliff, F. (1965). *Mach bands: Quantitative studies on neural networks in the retina.* New York: Holden-Day.

Ratner, C., & McCarthy, J. (1990). Ecologically relevant stimuli and color memory. *Journal of General Psychology, 117*, 369–377.

Rauschecker, J. P. (1997). Processing of complex sounds in the auditory cortex of cat, monkey, and man. *Acta Otolaryngol, Suppl 532*, 34–38.

Rauschecker, J. P. (1998). Cortical processing of complex sounds. *Current Opinion in Neurobiology, 8*, 516–521.

Rauschecker, J. P., & Korte, M. (1993). Auditory compensation for early blindness in cat cerebral cortex. *Journal of Neuroscience, 13*, 4538–4548.

Rauschecker, J. P., Tian, B., & Hauser, M. (1995). Processing of complex sounds in the macaque nonprimary auditory cortex. *Science, 268*, 111–114.

Reale, R. A., & Imig, T. J. (1980). Tonotopic organization in auditory cortex of the cat. *Journal of Comparative Neurology, 192*, 265–291.

Recanzone, G. H. (1998). Rapidly induced auditory plasticity: The ventriloquism aftereffect. *Proceedings of the National Academy of Sciences USA, 95*, 869–875.

Recanzone, G. H., Schreiner, C. E., & Merzenich, M. M. (1993). Plasticity in the frequency representation of primary auditory cortex following discrimination training in adult owl monkeys. *Journal of Neuroscience, 13*, 87–103.

Reddy, D. R. (1976). Speech recognition by machine: A review. *Proceedings of the Institute of Electrical and Electronic Engineers, 64*, 501–531.

Reed, C. M., Durlach, N. I., Braida, L. D., & Schultz, M. C. (1982). Analytic study of the Tadoma method: Identification of consonants and vowels by an experienced Tadoma user. *Journal of Speech and Hearing Research, 25*, 108–116.

Reed, R. R., Bakalyar, H. A., Cunningham, A. M., & Levy, N. S. (1992). The molecular basis of signal transduction in olfactory sensory neurons. In D. P. Corey & S. D. Roper (Eds.), *Sensory transduction* (pp. 53–60). New York: Rockefeller University Press.

Regan, D. (1986). Luminance contrast: Vernier discrimination. *Spatial Vision, 1*, 305–318.

Regan, D., & Cynader, M. (1979). Neurons in area 18 of cat visual cortex selectively sensitive to changing size: Nonlinear interactions between responses to two edges. *Vision Research, 19*, 699–711.

Regan, D., & Vincent, A. (1995). Visual processing of looming and time to contact throughout the visual field. *Vision Research, 35*, 1845–1857.

Reichardt, W. (1961). Autocorrelation, a principle for the evaluation of sensory information by the central nervous system. In W. A. Rosenblith (Ed.), *Sensory communication* (pp. 303–318). New York: Wiley.

Reichl, R. (1994, March 11). Dining in New York. *New York Times.*

Rensink, R. A., O'Regan, J. K., & Clark, J. J. (1995). Image flicker is as good as saccades in making large scene changes invisible. *Perception, 24*(Suppl.), 26–27.

Rensick, R. A., O'Regan, J. K., & Clark, J. J. (1996). To see or not to see: The need for attention to perceive changes in scenes. *Investigative Opthalmology and Visual Science, 37*, S215.

Reymond, L. (1985). Spatial visual acuity of the eagle *Aquila audax*: A behavioral, optical and anatomical investigation. *Vision Research, 25*, 1477–1491.

Reynolds, D. V. (1969). Surgery in the rat during electrical analgesia induced by focal brain stimulation. *Science, 164*, 444–445

Rhoorda, A., & Williams, D. R. (1999). The arrangement of the three cone classes in the living human eye. *Nature, 397*, 520–522.

Ribaupierre, F. de. (1997). Acoustical information processing in the auditory thalamus and cerebral cortex. In G. Ehret & R. Romand (Eds.), *The central auditory system* (pp. 317–398). New York: Oxford University Press.

Riggs, L. A. (1965). Visual acuity. In C. Graham (Ed.), *Vision and visual perception.* New York: Wiley.

Rind, F. C., & Simmons, P. J. (1999). Seeing what is coming: Building collision-sensitive neurones. *Trends in Neurosciences, 22*, 215–220.

Risset, J. C., & Mathews, M. W. (1969). Analysis of musical instrument tones. *Physics Today, 22*, 23–30.

Rizzolatti, G., Forgassi, L., & Gallese, V. (2000). Cortical mechanisms subserving object grasping and action recognition: A new view on the cortical motor functions. In M. Gazzaniga (Ed.), *The new cognitive neurosciences.* Cambridge, MA: MIT Press, pp. 539–552.

Robbins, J. (2000). Virtual reality finds a real place. *New York Times,* July 4.

Robinson, D. L., & Wurtz, R. (1976). Use of an extra-retinal signal by monkey superior colliculus neurons to distinguish real from self-induced stimulus movement. *Journal of Neurophysiology, 39*, 852–870.

Robson, J. G., Tolhurst, D. J., Freeman, R. D., & Ohzawa, I. (1988). Simple cells in the visual cortex of the cat can be narrowly tuned for spatial frequency. *Visual Neuroscience, 1*, 415–419.

Rock, I., & Kaufman, L. (1962). The moon illusion: Part 2. *Science, 136*, 1023–1031.

Roland, P. (1992). Cortical representation of pain. *Trends in Neuroscience, 15*, 3–5.

Rollman, G. B. (1991). Pain responsiveness. In M. A. Heller & W. Schiff (Eds.), *The psychology of touch* (pp. 91–114). Hillsdale, NJ: Erlbaum.

Rolls, B. J., Rolls, E. T., Rowe, E. A., & Sweeney, K. (1981). Sensory specific satiety in man. *Physiology and Behavior, 27,* 137–142.

Rolls, E. D. (1996). The orbitofrontal cortex. *Philosophical Transactions of the Royal Society of London, 351,* 1433–1444.

Rolls, E. T. (1992). Neurophysiological mechanisms underlying face processing within and beyond the temporal cortical visual areas. *Transactions of the Royal Society of London, B335,* 11–21.

Rolls, E. T. (2000). The orbitofrontal cortex and reward. *Cerebral Cortex, 10,* 284–294.

Rolls, E. T., and Baylis, L. L. (1994). Gustatory, olfactory, and visual convergence within the primate orbitofrontal cortex. *Journal of Neuroscience, 14,* 5437–5452.

Rolls, E. T., Critchley, H. D., Mason, R., & Wakeman, E. A. (1996b). Orbitofrontal cortex neurons: Role in olfactory and visual association learning. *Journal of Neurophysiology, 75,* 1970–1981.

Rolls, E. T., Critchley, H. D., & Treves, A. (1996a). Representation of olfactory information in the primate orbitofrontal cortex. *Journal of Neurophysiology, 75,* 1982–1996.

Rolls, E. T., & Rolls, J. H. (1997). Olfactory sensory-specific satiety in humans. *Physiology & Behavior, 61,* 461–473.

Rolls, E. T., Sienkiewicz, Z. J., & Yaxley, S. (1989). Hunger modulates the responses to gustatory stimuli of single neurons in the caudolateral orbitofrontal cortex of the macaque monkey. *European Journal of Neuroscience, 1,* 53–60.

Rolls, E. T., & Tovee, M. J. (1995). Sparseness of the neuronal representation of stimuli in the primate temporal visual cortex. *Journal of Neurophysiology, 73,* 713–726.

Romo, R., Hernandez, A., Zainos, A., & Salinas, E. (1998). Somatosensory discrimination based on cortical microstimulation. *Nature, 392,* 387–390.

Romo, R., & Salinas, E. (1999). Sensing and deciding in the somatosensory system. *Current Opinion in Neurobiology, 9,* 487–493.

Rosenstein, D., & Oster, H. (1988). Differential facial responses to four basic tastes in newborns. *Child Development, 59,* 1555–1568.

Rosenthal, E. (1992, December 29). Chronic pain fells many yet lacks clear cause. *New York Times,* pp. B5, B6.

Roskies, A. L. (1999). The binding problem. *Neuron, 24,* 7–9.

Rosowski, J. J. (1996). Models of external–and middle-ear function. In H. Hawkins, T. A. McMullen, A. N. Popper, & R. R. Fay (Eds.), *Auditory computation* (pp. 15–61). New York: Springer-Verlag.

Rossiter, K. J. (1996). Structure–odor relationships. *Chemical Reviews, 96,* 3201–3240.

Rouiller, E. M. (1997). Functional organization of the auditory pathways. In G. Ehret & R. Romand (Eds.), *The central auditory system* (pp. 3–96). Oxford, England: Oxford University Press.

Rowe, M. J., Turman, A. A., Murray, G. M., & Zhang, H. Q. (1996). Parallel processing in somatosensory areas I and II of the cerebral cortex. In O. Franzen, R. Johansson, & L. Terenius (Eds.), *Somesthesis and the neurobiology of the somatosensory cortex.* Basel: Birkhauser Verlag, pp. 197–212.

Royden, C. S., Banks, M. S., & Crowell, J. A. (1992). The perception of heading during eye movements. *Nature, 360,* 583–585.

Rozin, P. (1976). The selection of foods by rats, humans, and other animals. In J. S. Rosenblatt, R. A. Hinde, & C. Beer (Eds.), *Advances in the study of behavior.* New York: Academic Press.

Rozin, P. (1982). "Taste–smell confusions" and the duality of the olfactory sense. *Perception and Psychophysics, 31,* 397–401.

Rozin, P. (1990). Development in the food domain. *Developmental Psychology, 26,* 555–562.

Rubin, B. D., & Katz, L. C. (1999). Optical imaging of odorant representations in the mammalian olfactory bulb. *Neuron, 23,* 499–511.

Rubin, E. (1915). *Synoplevde Figurer.* Copenhagen: Gyldendalske.

Rubin, P., Turvey, M. T., & Van Gelder, P. (1976). Initial phoneme are detected faster in spoken words than in spoken nonwords. *Perception and Psychophysics, 19,* 394–398.

Rushton, S. K., Harris, J. M., Jloyd, M. R., & Wann, J. P. (1998). Guidance of locomotion on foot uses perceived target location rather than optic flow. *Current Biology, 8,* 1191–1194.

Rushton, S. K., & Salvucci, D. D. (2001). An egocentric account of the visual guidane of locomotion. *Trends in Cognitive Sciences, 5,* 6–7.

Rushton, W. A. H. (1961). Rhodopsin measurement and dark adaptation in a subject deficient in cone vision. *Journal of Physiology, 156,* 193–205.

Rushton, W. A. H. (1964). Color blindness and cone pigments. *American Journal of Optometry and Archives of the American Academy of Optometry, 41,* 265–282.

Russell, I. J., & Sellick, P. M. (1977). Tuning properties of cochlear hair cells. *Nature, 267,* 858–860.

Russell, M. J. (1976). Human olfactory communication. *Nature, 260,* 520–522.

Russell, M. J., Switz, G. M., & Thompson, K. (1980). Olfactory influence on the human menstrual cycle. *Pharmacology, Biochemistry and Behavior, 13,* 737–738.

Ryan, A., & Dallos, P. (1975). Absence of cochlear outer hair cells: Effect on behavioral auditory threshold. *Nature, 253,* 44–46.

Sachs, M. B., Young, E. D., & Miller, M. I. (1981). Encoding of speech features in the auditory nerve. In R. Carson & B. Grandstrom (Eds.), *The representation of speech in the peripheral auditory system* (pp. 115–139). New York: Elsevier.

Sackett, B. (1972). Counting every quantum. *Journal of Physiology, 223,* 131–150.

Sacks, O. (1985). *The man who mistook his wife for a hat.* London: Duckworth.

Sadato, N., Pascual-Leone, A., Grafman, J., Ibanez, V., Deiber, M-P., Dold, G., & Hallett, M. (1996). Activation of the primary visual cortex by Braille reading in blind subjects. *Nature, 380,* 526–528.

Sakada, H., Taira, M., Kusunoki, M., Murata, A., & Tanaka. (1997). The parietal association cortex in depth perception and visual control of hand action. *Trends in Neurosciences, 20,* 350–357.

Sakata, H., & Iwamura, Y. (1978). Cortical processing of tactile information in the first somatosensory and parietal association areas in the monkey. In G. Gordon (Ed.), *Active touch* (pp. 55–72). Elmsford, NY: Pergamon Press.

Sakata, H., Taira, M., Mine, S., & Murata, A. (1992). Hand-movement-related neurons of the posterior parietal cortex of the monkey: Their role in visual guidance of hand movements. In R. Caminiti, P. B. Johnson, & Y. Burnod (Eds.), *Control of arm movement in space: Neurophysiological and computational approaches* (pp. 185–198). Berlin: Springer-Verlag.

Salapatek, P., & Banks, M. S. (1978). Infant sensory assessment: Vision. In F. D. Minifie & L. L. Lloyd (Eds.), *Communicative and cognitive abilities: Early behavioral assessment* (pp. 61–106). Baltimore: University Park Press.

Salapatek, P., Bechtold, A. G., & Bushnell, E. W. (1976). Infant visual acuity as a function of viewing distance. *Child Development, 47,* 860–863.

Salasoo, A., & Pisoni, D. B. (1985). Interaction of knowledge sources in spoken word identification. *Journal of Memory and Language 24,* 210–231.

Samson, F. K., Barone, P., Irons, W. A., Clarey, J. C., Poirier, P., & Imig, T. J. (2000). Directionality derived from differential sensitivity to monaural and binaural cues in the cat's medial geniculate body. *Journal of Neurophysiology, 84,* 1330–1345.

Samuel, A. G. (1981). Phonemic restoration: Insights from a new methodology. *Journal of Experimental Psychology: General, 110,* 474–494.

Samuel, A. G. (1990). Using perceptual-restoration effects to explore the architecture of perception. In G. T. M. Altmann (Ed.), *Cognitive models of speech processing* (pp. 295–314). Cambridge, MA: MIT Press.

Sato, M., & Ogawa, H. (1994). Neural coding of taste in macaque monkeys. In K. Kurihara, N. Suzuki, & H. Ogawa (Eds.), *Olfaction and taste* (Vol. 11, pp. 388–392). Tokyo: Springer-Verlag.

Sato, M., Ogawa, H., & Yamashita, S. (1994). Gustatory responsiveness of chorda tympani fibers in the cynomolgus monkey. *Chemical Senses, 19,* 381–400.

Schacter, D. L., Reiman, E., Uecker, A., Polster, M. R., Yun, L. S., & Cooper, L. A. (1995). Brain regions associated with retrieval of structurally coherent visual information. *Nature, 376,* 587–590.

Schiff, W., & Detwiler, M. L. (1979). Information used in judging impending collision. *Perception, 8,* 647–658.

Schiffman, H. R. (1967). Size-estimation of familiar objects under informative and reduced conditions of viewing. *American Journal of Psychology, 80,* 229–235.

Schiffman, S. S., & Erickson, R. P. (1971). A psychophysical model for gustatory quality. *Physiology and Behavior, 7,* 617–633.

Schiffman, S. S., & Erickson, R. P. (1993). Psychophysics: Insights into transduction mechanisms and neural coding. In S. A. Simon & S. D. Roper (Eds.), *Mechanisms of taste transduction* (pp. 395–424). Boca Raton, FL: CRC Press.

Schiller, P. H. (1992). The on and off channels of the visual system. *Trends in Neurosciences, 15,* 86–92.

Schiller, P. H., Logothetis, N. K., & Charles, E. R. (1990). Functions of the colour-opponent and broad-band channels of the visual system. *Nature, 343,* 68–70.

Schmolesky, M. T., Wang, Youngchange, Pu, Mingliang, & Leventhal, A. G. (2000). Degradation of stimulus selectivity of visual cortical cells in senescent rhesus monkeys. *Nature Neuroscience, 3,* 384–390.

Schnapf, J. L., Kraft, T. W., & Baylor, D. A. (1987). Spectral sensitivity of human cone photoreceptors. *Nature, 325,* 439–441.

Schreiner, C. H., & Mendelson, J. R. (1990). Functional topography of cat primary auditory cortex: Distribution of integrated excitation. *Journal of Neurophysiology, 64,* 1442–1459.

Schubert, E. D. (1980). *Hearing: Its function and dysfunction.* Wien: Springer-Verlag.

Schwind, R. (1978). Visual system of Notonecta glaucia: A neuron sensitive to movement in the binocular visual field. *Journal of Comparative Physiology, 123,* 315–328.

Scott, T. R. (1987). Coding in the gustatory system. In T. E. Finger & W. L. Silver (Eds.), *Neurobiology of taste and smell* (pp. 355–378). New York: Wiley.

Scott, T. R., & Giza, B. K. (1990). Coding channels in the taste system of the rat. *Science, 249,* 1585–1587.

Scott, T. R., & Giza, B. K. (2000). Issues of gustatory neural coding: Where they stand today. *Physiology and Behavior, 69,* 65–76.

Scott, T. R., & Plata-Salaman, C. R. (1991). Coding of taste quality. In T. V. Getchell, R. L. Doty, L. M. Bartoshuk, & J. B. Snow (Eds.), *Smell and taste in health and disease* (pp. 345–368). New York: Raven Press.

Searle, C. L., Jacobson, J. Z., & Rayment, S. G. (1979). Stop consonant discrimination based on human audition. *Journal of the Acoustical Society of America, 65,* 799–809.

Sedgwick, H. (2001). Visual space perception. In E. B. Goldstein (Ed.), *Blackwell Handbook of Perception.* Oxford: Blackwell Publishers, pp. 128–167.

Segui, J. (1984). The syllable: A basic perceptual unit in speech processing? In H. Bouma & D. G. Gouwhuis (Eds.), *Attention and performance X* (pp. 165–181). Hillsdale, NJ: Erlbaum.

Shapiro, K. L., Arnell, K. M., & Raymond, J. E. (1997). The attentional blink: A view on attention and glimpse on consciousness. *Trends in Cognitive Science, 1,* 291–296.

Shapley, R., & Ringach, D. (2000). Dynamics of responses in visual cortex In M. Gazzaniga (Ed.), *The new cognitive neurosciences.* Cambridge, MA: MIT Press, pp. 253–261.

Shein, S. J., & DeSimone, R. (1990). Spectral properties of V4 neurons in the Macaque. *Journal of Neuroscience, 10,* 3369–3389.

Sheinberg, D. L., & Logothetis, N. K. (1997). The role of temporal cortical areas in perceptual organization. *Proceedings of the National Academy of Sciences, 94,* 3408–3413.

Shepherd, G. M. (1991). Sensory transduction: Entering the mainstream of membrane signaling. *Cell, 67,* 845–851.

Shepherd, G. M. (1992a). Modules for molecules. *Nature, 358,* 457–458.

Shepherd, G. M. (1992b). Toward a consensus working model for olfactory transduction. In D. P. Corey & S. D. Roper (Eds.), *Sensory transduction* (pp. 19–37). New York: Rockefeller University Press.

Shepherd, G. M. (1994). Discrimination of molecular signals by the olfactory receptor neuron. *Neuron, 13,* 771–790.

Shepherd, G. M. (1995). Toward a molecular basis for sensory perception. In M. S. Gazzaniga (Ed.), *The cognitive neurosciences* (pp. 105–118). Cambridge, MA: MIT Press.

Shepherd, G. M., & Firestein, S. (1991). Making scents of olfactory transduction. *Current Biology, 1,* 204–206.

Sherk, H., & Stryker, M. P. (1976). Quantitative study of cortical orientation selectivity in visually inexperienced kittens. *Journal of Neurophysiology, 39,* 63–70.

Sherman, S. M., & Koch, C. (1986). The control of retinogeniculate transmission in the mammalian lateral geniculate nucleus. *Experimental Brain Research, 63,* 1–20.

Sherrick, C. E. (1968). Bilateral apparent haptic movement. *Perception and Psychophysics, 4,* 159–160.

Sherrick, C. E., & Rogers, R. (1966). Apparent haptic movement. *Perception and Psychophysics, 1,* 175–180.

Shiffrar, M. (1994). When what meets where. *Current Directions in Psychological Science, 3,* 96– 100.

Shiffrar, M., & Freyd, J. J. (1990). Apparent motion of the human body. *Psychological Science, 1,* 257–264.

Shiffrar, M., & Freyd, J. J. (1993). Timing and apparent motion path choice with human body photographs. *Psychological Science, 4,* 379–384.

Sicard, G., & Holley, A. (1984). Receptor cell responses to odorants: Similarities and differences among odorants. *Brain Research, 292,* 283–296.

Silver, W. L., & Finger, T. E. (1991). The trigeminal system. In T. V. Getchell, R. L. Doty, L. M. Bartoshuk, & J. B. Snow (Eds.), *Smell and taste in health and disease* (pp. 97–108). New York: Raven Press.

Sinai, M. J., Ooi, T. L., & He, Z. J. (1998). Terrain influences the accurate judgement of distance. *Nature, 395,* 497–500.

Singer, W., Artola, A., Engel, A. K., Konig, P., Kreiter, A. K., Lowel, S., & Schillen, T. B. (1993). Neuronal representations and temporal codes. In T. A. Poggio & D. A. Glaser (Eds.), *Exploring brain functions: Models in neuroscience* (pp. 179–194). New York: Wiley.

Slater, A. M., & Findlay, J. M. (1975). Binocular fixation in the newborn baby. *Journal of Experimental Child Psychology, 20,* 248–273.

Slater, A. M., Morison, V., & Rose, D. (1984). Habituation in the newborn. *Infant Behavior and Development, 7,* 183–200.

Slater, A. M., Morison, V., Somers, M., Mattock, A., Brown, E., & Taylor, D. (1990). Newborn and older infants' perception of partly occluded objects. *Infant Behavior and Development, 13,* 33–49.

Sloan, L. L., & Wollach, L. (1948). A case of unilateral deuteranopia. *Journal of the Optical Society of America, 38,* 502–509.

Smith, D., Van Buskirk, R. L., Travers, J. B., & Bieber, S. L. (1983). Coding of taste stimuli by hamster brain stem neurons. *Journal of Neurophysiology, 50,* 541–558.

Smith, D. V., St. John, S. J., & Boughter, J. D. Jr. (2000). Neuronal cell types and taste quality coding. *Physiology & Behavior, 69,* 77–85.

Smith, L. B., & Katz, D. B. (1996). Activity-dependent processes in perceptual and cognitive development. In R. Gelman (Ed.), *Perceptual and cognitive development* (pp. 413–445). San Diego, CA: Academic Press.

Snowden, R. J., & Milne, A. B. (1997). Phantom motion aftereffects—Evidence of detectors for the analysis of optic flow. *Current Biology, 7,* 717–722.

Sobel, E. C. (1990). The locust's use of motion parallax to measure distance. *Journal of Comparative Physiology, 167,* 579–588

Sobel, N., Prabhakaran, V., Desmond, J. E., Glover, G. H., Goode, R. L., Sullivan, E. V. and Gabrieli, D. E. (1998). Sniffing and smelling: Separate subsystems in the human olfactory cortex. *Nature, 392,* 282–286.

Sobel, N., Prabhakaran, V., Zhao, Z., Desmond, J. E., Glover, G. H., Sullivan, E. V., & Gabrieli, J. D. E. (2000). Time course of odorant-induced activation in the human primary olfactory cortex. *Journal of Neurophysiology, 83,* 537–551.

Spear, P. D., Kim, C. B-Y., Ahmad, A., & Tom, B. W. (1996). Relationship between numbers of retinal ganglion cells and lateral geniculate neurons in the rhesus monkey. *Visual Neuroscience, 13,* 199–203.

Spelke, E. S., Gutheil, G., & Van de Walle, G. (1995). The development of object perception. In S. M. Kosslyn & D. N. Osherson (Eds.), *Visual cognition* (pp. 297–330). Cambridge, MA: MIT Press.

Sperduto, R. D., Siegel, D., Roberts, J., & Rowland, M. (1983). Prevalence of myopia in the United States. *Archives of Ophthalmology, 101,* 405–407.

Srivinisan, M V., Chahl, J. S., Nagle, M. G., & Zhang, S. W. (1997). Embodying natural vision into machines. In M. V. Srinivasan & S. Ventatesh (Eds.) *From living eyes to seeing machines.* New York: Oxford.

Srinivasan, M. V., & Ventatesh, S. (Eds.) (1997). *From living eyes to seeing machines.* New York: Oxford.

Srulovicz, P., & Goldstein, J. L. (1983). A central spectrum model: A synthesis of auditory-nerve timing and place cues in monaural communication of frequency spectrum. *Journal of the Acoustical Society of America, 73,* 1266–1276.

Stark, L., & Bridgeman, B. (1983). Role of corollary discharge in space constancy. *Perception and Psychophysics, 34,* 371–380.

Steiner, J. E. (1974). Innate, discriminative human facial expressions to taste and smell stimulation. *Annals of the New York Academy of Sciences, 237,* 229–233.

Steiner, J. E. (1979). Human facial expressions in response to taste and smell stimulation. *Advances in Child Development and Behavior, 13,* 257–295.

Steinmetz, P. N., Roy, A., Fitzgerald, P. J., Hsiao, S. S., Johnson, K. O., & Niebur, E. (2000). Attention modulates synchronized neuronal firing in primate somatosensory cortex. *Nature, 404,* 187–189.

Stevens, J. A., Fonlupt, P., Shiffrar, M., & Decety, J. (2000). New aspects of motion perception: Selective neural encoding of apparent human movements. *NeuroReport, 11,* 109–115.

Stevens, J. K., Emerson, R. C., Gerstein, G. L., Kallos, T., Neufeld, G. R., Nichols, C. W., & Rosenquist, A. C. (1976). Paralysis of the awake human: Visual perceptions. *Vision Research, 16,* 93–98.

Stevens, K. N., & Blumstein, S. (1978). Invariant cues for place of articulation in stop consonants. *Journal of the Acoustical Society of America, 64,* 1358–1368.

Stevens, K. N., & Blumstein, S. (1981). The search for invariant acoustic correlates of phonetic features. In P. D. Eimas & L. L. Miller (Eds.), *Perspectives on the study of speech.* Hillsdale, NJ: Erlbaum.

Stevens, S. S. (1957). On the psychophysical law. *Psychological Review, 64,* 153–181.

Stevens, S. S. (1961). To honor Fechner and repeal his law. *Science, 133,* 80–86.

Stevens, S. S. (1962). The surprising simplicity of sensory metrics. *American Psychologist, 17,* 29–39.

Stiles, W. S. (1953). Further studies of visual mechanisms by the two-color threshold method. Coloquio sobre problemas opticos de la vision. Madrid: *Union Internationale de Physique Pure et Appliqué, 1,* 65.

Stoerig, P. (1998). Wavelength information processing versus color perception: Evidence from blindsight and color-blind sight. In W. G. K. Backhaus, R. Kliegl, &

J. S. Werner (Eds.) *Color vision: perspectives from different disciplines*. New York: Walter de Gruyter, pp. 131–147.

Stoffregen, T. A., Smart, J. L., Bardy, B. G., & Pagulayan, R. J. (1999). Postural stabilization of looking. *Journal of Experimental Psychology: Human Perception and Performance, 25*, 1641–1658.

Stone, H., & Bosley, J. J. (1965). Olfactory discrimination and Weber's law. *Perceptual and Motor Skills, 20*, 657–665.

Stone, J. (1965). A quantitative analysis of the distribution of ganglion cells in the cat's retina. *Journal of Comparative Neurology, 124*, 277–352.

Strange, W. (Ed.)(1995). *Speech perception and linguistic experience: Issues in cross-language research*. Timonium, MD: York.

Stryer, L. (1986). Cyclic GMP cascade of vision. *Annual Review of Neuroscience, 9*, 87–119.

Stryker, M. P. (1989). Is grandmother an oscillation? *Nature, 338*, 297–298.

Suga, N. (1990, June). Biosonar and neural computation in bats. *Scientific American*, 60–68.

Sussman, H. M., Hoemeke, K. A., & Ahmed, F. S. (1993). A cross-linguistic investigation of locus equations as a phonetic descriptor for place of articulation. *Journal of the Acoustical Society of America, 94*, 1256–1268.

Sussman, H. M., McCaffrey, H. A., & Matthews, S. A. (1991). An investigation of locus equations as a source of relational variance for stop place categorization. *Journal of the Acoustical Society of America, 90*, 1309–1325.

Svaetichin, G. (1956). Spectral response curves from single cones. *Acta Physiologica Scandinavica Supplementum, 134*, 17–46.

Swets, J. A. (1964). *Signal detection and recognition by human observers*. New York: Wiley.

Taira, M., Mine, S., Georgopoulos, A. P., Murata, A., & Sakata, H. (1990). Parietal cortex neurons of the monkey related to the visual guidance of hand movement. *Experimental Brain Research, 83*, 29–36.

Takagi, S. F. (1980). Dual nervous systems for olfactory functions in mammals. In H. Van der Starre (Ed.), *Olfaction and taste* (Vol. 7, pp. 275–278). London: IRC Press.

Tanaka, K. (1993). Neuronal mechanisms of object recognition. *Science, 262*, 684–688.

Tanaka, K., Siato, H.-A., Fukada, Y., & Moriya, M. (1991). Coding visual images of objects in inferotemporal cortex of the Macaque monkey. *Journal of Neurophysiology, 66*, 170–189.

Tarr, M. J. (1994). Visual representation. In V. Ramachandran (Ed.), *Encyclopedia of human behavior* (Vol. 4, pp. 503–512). New York: Academic Press.

Teghtsoonian, R., Teghtsoonian, M., Berglund, B., & Berglund, U. (1978). Invariance of odor strength with sniff vigor: An olfactory analogue to size constancy. *Journal of Experimental Psychology: Human Perception and Performance, 4*, 144–152.

Teller, D. Y. (1990). The domain of visual science. In L. Spellman & J. S. Werner (Eds.), *Visual perception: The neurophysiological foundations* (pp. 11–21). San Diego, CA: Academic Press.

Teller, D. Y. (1997). First glances: The vision of infants. *Investigative Ophthalmology and Visual Science, 38*, 2183–2199.

Ter-Pogossian, M. M., Phelps, M. E., Hoffman, E. J., & Mullani, N. A. (1975). A positron-emission tomograph for nuclear imaging (PET). *Radiology, 114*, 89–98.

Terwogt, M. M., & Hoeksma, J. B. (1994). Colors and emotions: Preferences and combinations. *Journal of General Psychology, 122*, 5–17.

Tessier-Lavigne, M. (1991). Phototransduction and information processing in the retina. In E. R. Kandel, J. H. Schwartz, & T. M. Jessell (Eds.), *Principles of neural science* (3rd ed., pp. 400–417). New York: Elsevier.

Teuber, H. L. (1960). Perception. In J. Field, H. W. Magoun, & V. E. Hall (Eds.), *Handbook of physiology* (Sect. 1, Vol. 3). Washington, DC: American Physiological Society.

Tittle, J. S., & Braunstein, M. L. (1993). Recovery of depth from binocular disparity and structure from motion. *Perception and Psychophysics, 54*, 509–523.

Tonndorf, J. (1960). Shearing motion in scala media of cochlear models. *Journal of the Acoustical Society of America, 44*, 1546–1554.

Tonndorf, J., & Khanna, S. M. (1968). Submicroscopic displacement amplitudes of the tympanic membrane (cat) measured by laser interferometer. *Journal of the Acoustical Society of America, 44*, 1546–1554.

Treisman, A. (1986). Features and objects in visual processing. *Scientific American, 255*, 114B–125B.

Treisman, A. (1987). Properties, parts, and objects. In K. R. Boff, L. Kaufman, & F. P. Thomas (Eds.), *Handbook of perception and human performance* (Chapter 35). New York: Wiley.

Treisman, A. (1992). Perceiving and re-perceiving objects. *American Psychologist, 47*, 862–875.

Treisman, A. (1993). The perception of features and objects. In A. Baddeley & L. Weiskrantz (Eds.), *Attention: Selection, awareness, and control* (pp. 5–34). Oxford, England: Clarendon Press.

Treisman, A. (1998). The perception of features and objects. In R. D. Wright (Ed.), *Visual attention.* New York: Oxford University Press, pp. 26–54.

Treisman, A. (1999). Solutions to the binding problem: Progress through controversy and convergence. *Neuron, 24,* 105–110.

Tresilean, J. R. (1999). Visual timed action: Time-out for "tau"? *Trends in Cognitive Sciences, 3,* 301–309.

Tresilian, J., R., Mon-Williams, M., & Kelly, B. (1999). Increasing confidence in vergence as a cue to distance. *Proceedings of the Royal Society of London, 266B,* 39–44.

Trevor-Roper, P. (1970). *The world through blunted sight.* Indianapolis, IN: Bobbs-Merrill.

Truax, B. (1984). *Acoustic communication.* Norwood, NJ: ABLEX.

Turk, D. C., & Flor, H. (1999). Chronic pain: a biobehavioral perspective. In R. J. Gatchel & D. C. Turk (Eds.) *Psychosocial factors in pain.* New York: Guilford, pp. 18–34.

Turman, A. B., Morley, J. W., & Rowe, M. J. (1998). Functional organization of the somatosensory cortex in the primate. In J. W. Morley (Ed.). *Neural aspects of tactile sensation.* New York: Elsevier Science, pp. 167–193.

Tye-Murray, N., Spencer, L., & Woodworth, G. G. (1995). Acquisition of speech by children who have prolonged cochlear implant experience. *Journal of Speech and Hearing Research, 38,* 327–337.

Tyler, C. W. (1990). A stereoscopic view of visual processing streams. *Vision Research, 30,* 1877–1895.

Tyler, C. W. (1997a). Analysis of human receptor density. In V. Lakshminarayanan (Ed.), *Basic and clinical applications of vision science* (pp. 63–71). Norwell, MA: Kluwer Academic.

Tyler, C. W. (1997b). *Human cone densities: Do you know where all your cones are?* Unpublished manuscript.

Uchikawa, K., Uchikawa, H., & Boynton, R. M. (1989). Partial color constancy of isolated surface colors examined by a color-naming method. *Perception, 18,* 83–91.

Ungerleider, L. G., & Haxby, J. V. (1994). "What" and "where" in the human brain. *Current Opinion in Neurobiology, 4,* 157–165.

Ungerleider, L. G., & Mishkin, M. (1982). Two cortical visual systems. In D. J. Ingle, M. A. Goodale, & R. J. Mansfield (Eds.), *Analysis of visual behavior* (pp. 549–580). Cambridge, MA: MIT Press.

Valdez, P., & Mehribian, A. (1994). Effect of color on emotions. *Journal of Experimental Psychology: General, 123,* 394–409.

Vallbo, A. B., & Hagbarth, K. E. (1967). Impulses recorded with microelectrodes in human muscle nerves during stimulation of mechano-receptors and voluntary contractions. *Electroencephalography and Clinical Neurophysiology, 23,* 392.

Vallbo, A. B., & Johansson, R. S. (1978). The tactile sensory innervation of the glabrous skin of the human hand. In G. Gordon (Ed.), *Active touch* (pp. 29–54). New York: Oxford University Press.

Van Essen, D. C., & Anderson, C. H. (1995). Information processing strategies and psthways in the primate visual system. S. F. Zornetzer, J. L. Davis, & C. Lau *(Eds), An introduction to neural and electronic networks, 2nd edition.* San Diego: Academic Press, pp. 45–75.

Van Essen, D. C., & DeYoe, E. A. (1995). Concurrent processing in the primary visual cortex. In M. S. Gazzaniga (Ed.), *The cognitive neurosciences.* Cambridge, MA: MIT Press, pp. 383–400.

Varner, D., Cook, J. E., Schneck, M. E., McDonald, M., & Teller, D. Y. (1985). Tritan discriminations by 1- and 2-month-old human infants. *Vision Research, 25,* 821–831.

Vecera, S. P., & O'Reilly, R. C. (2000). Graded effects in hierarchical figure-ground organization: Reply to Patterson (1999). *Journal of Experimental Psychology: Human Perception and Performance, 26,* 1221–1231.

Vega-Bermudez, F., Johnson, K. O., & Hsiao, S. S. (1991). Human tactile pattern recognition: Active versus passive touch, velocity effects, and patterns of confusion. *Journal of Neurophysiology, 65,* 531–546.

Vermeij, G. (1997). *Privileged hands: A scientific life.* New York: Freeman.

Vogten, L. L. M. (1974). Pure-tone masking: A new result from a new method. In E. Zwicker & E. Terhardt (Eds.), *Facts and models in hearing.* Berlin: Springer-Verlag, pp. 142-155.

Von der Emde, G., Schwarz, S., Gomez, L., Budelli, R., & Grant, K. (1998). Electric fish measure distance in the dark. *Nature, 395,* 890–894.

von Holst, E. (1954). Relations between the central nervous system and the peripheral organs. *British Journal of Animal Behaviour, 2,* 89–94.

von Noorden, G. K., & Maumanee, A. E. (1968). Clinical observations on stimulus deprivation amblyopia (amblyopia ex anopsia). *American Journal of Ophthalmology, 65,* 220–224.

Wachmuth, E., Oram, M. W., & Perrett, D. I. (1994). Recognition of objects and their component parts: Responses of single units in the temporal cortex of the macaque. *Cerebral Cortex, 4*, 509–522.

Wald, G. (1964). The receptors of human color vision. *Science, 145*, 1007–1017.

Wald, G., & Brown, P. K. (1958). Human rhodopsin. *Science, 127*, 222–226.

Waldrop, M. M. (1988). A landmark in speech recognition. *Science, 240*, 1615.

Wall, P. D., & Melzack, R. (Eds.). (1994). *Textbook of pain* (3rd ed.). Edinburgh, UK: Churchill Livingstone.

Wallace, M. A. (1994). Implicit perception in visual neglect: Implications for theories of attention. In M. J. Farah & G. Ratcliff (Eds.), *Neuropsychology of high level vision* (pp. 359–370). Hillsdale, NJ: Erlbaum.

Wallach, H. (1963). The perception of neutral colors. *Scientific American, 208*(1), 107–116.

Wallach, H., Newman, E. B., & Rosenzweig, M. R. (1949). The precedence effect in sound localization. *American Journal of Psychology, 62*, 315–336.

Wallach, H., & O'Connell, D. N. (1953). The kinetic depth effect. *Journal of Experimental Psychology, 45*, 205–217.

Walls, G. L. (1942). *The vertebrate eye.* New York: Hafner. (Reprinted in 1967)

Walls, G. L. (1953). *The lateral geniculate nucleus and visual histophysiology.* Berkeley: University of California Press.

Walton, G. E., Bower, N. J. A., & Power, T. G. R. (1992). Recognition of familiar faces by newborns. *Infant Behavior and Development, 15*, 265–269.

Wang, Y., & Frost, B. J. (1992). Time to collision is signalled by neurons in the nucleus rotundus of pigeons. *Nature, 356*, 236–238.

Wann, J., & Land, M. (2000). Steering with or without the flow: Is the retrieval of heading necessary? *Trends in Cognitive Science, 4*, 319–324.

Ward, W. D., & Glorig, A. (1961). A case of firecracker-induced hearing loss. *Laryngoscope, 71*, 1590–1596.

Warren, R. M. (1970). Perceptual restoration of missing speech sounds. *Science, 167*, 392–393.

Warren, R. M., Kay, B. A., Zosh, W. D., Duchon, A. P., & Suhac, S. (2001). Optic flow is used to control human walking. *Nature Neuroscience, 4*, 213–216.

Warren, R. M., Obuseck, C. J., & Acroff, J. M. (1972). Auditory induction of absent sounds. *Science, 176*, 1149.

Warren, S., Hamalainen, H., & Gardner, E. P. (1986). Objective classification of motion- and direction-sensitive neurons in primary somatosensory cortex of awake monkeys. *Journal of Neurophysiology, 56*, 598–622.

Warren, W. H. (1995). Self-motion: Visual perception and visual control. In W. Epstein & S. Rogers (Eds.), *Handbook of perception and cognition: Perception of space and motion* (pp. 263–323). New York: Academic Press.

Warren, W. H., Kay, B. A., Yilmaz, E. H. (1996). Visual control of posture during walking: Functional specificity. *Journal of Experimental Psychology: Human Perception and Performance, 22*, 818–838.

Wassle, H., Grunert, U., Rohrenbeck, J., & Boycott, B. B. (1990). Retinal ganglion cell density and cortical magnification factor in the primate. *Vision Research, 30*, 1897–1911.

Watkins, C. R., & Mayer, D. J. (1982). Organization of endogenous opiate and nonopiate pain control system. *Science, 176*, 1149.

Webster's new collegiate dictionary. (1956). Springfield, MA: Merriam.

Weinstein, S. (1968). Intensive and extensive aspects of tactile sensitivity as a function of body part, sex, and laterality. In D. R. Kenshalo (Ed.), *The skin senses* (pp. 195–218). Springfield, IL: Thomas.

Weisenberg, M. (1977). Pain and pain control. *Psychological Bulletin, 84*, 1008–1044.

Weissberg, M. (1999). Cognitive aspects of pain. In P. D. Wall and R. Melzak (Eds). *Textbook of pain, 4th edition.* New York: Churchill Livingstone, pp. 345–358.

Werker, J. (1991). The ontogeny of speech perception. In I. G. Mattingly & M. Studdert-Kennedy (Eds.), *Modularity and the motor theory of speech perception* (pp. 91–109). Hillsdale, NJ: Erlbaum.

Werker, J. F., & Tees, R. C. (1984). Cross-language speech perception: Evidence for perceptual reorganization during the first year of life. *Infant Behavior and Development, 7*, 49–63.

Werner, L. A., & Bargones, J. Y. (1992). Psychoacoustic development of human infants. In C. Rovee-Collier & L. Lipsett (Eds.), *Advances in infancy research* (Vol. 7, pp. 103–145). Norwood, NJ: ABLEX.

Werner, L. A., & Bernstein, I. L. (2001). Development of the auditory, gustatory, olfactory, and somatosensory systems. In E. B. Goldstein (Ed.), *Blackwell handbook of perception.* Oxford, UK: Blackwell, pp. 669–708.

Wertheimer, M. (1912). Experimentelle Stuidien uber das Sehen von Beuegung. *Zeitchrift fuer Psychologie, 61*, 161–265.

Wessel, D. L. (1979). Timbre space as a musical control structure. *Computer Music Journal*, 3, 45–52.

Wever, E. G. (1949). *Theory of hearing*. New York: Wiley.

Whalen, D. H., & Liberman, A. M. (1987). Speech perception takes precedence over non-speech perception. *Science*, 237, 169–171.

White, J. (1968). *The birth and rebirth of pictorial space* (2nd ed.). London: Faber & Faber.

White, M. (1981). The effect of the nature of the surround on the perceived lightness of grey bars within square-wave test gratings. *Perception*, 10, 215–230.

Whitsel, B. L., Roppolo, J. R., & Werner, G. (1972). Cortical information processing of stimulus motion on primate skin. *Journal of Neurophysiology*, 35, 691–717.

Wiesel, T. N., & Hubel, D. H. (1963). Single cell responses in striate cortex of kittens deprived of vision in one eye. *Journal of Neurophysiology*, 26, 1003–1017.

Wiesel, T. N., & Raviola, E. (1977). Myopia and eye enlargement after neonatal lid fusion in monkeys. *Nature*, 266, 66–68.

Wightman, F. L. (1973). Pitch and stimulus fine structure. *Journal of the Acoustical Society of America*, 54, 397–406.

Wightman, F. L., & Jenison, R. (1995). Auditory spatial layout. In W. Epstein & S. Rogers (Eds.), *Perception of space and motion* (pp. 365–400). San Diego, CA: Academic Press.

Wightman, F. L., & Kistler, D. J. (1993). Sound localization. In W. Yost, R. R. Fay, & A. N. Popper (Eds.), *Human psychophysics* (pp. 155–192) New York: Springer-Verlag.

Wildsoet, C. F. (1997). Active emmetropization–evidence for its existence and ramifications for clinical practice. *Ophthalmology and Physiological Optics*, 17, 279–290.

Williams, S. M., McCoy, A. N., & Purves, D. (1998). The influence of depicted illumination on brightness. *Proceedings of the National Academy of Sciences USA*, 95, 13296–13300.

Wilson, D. A. (1998). Synaptic correlates of odor habituation in the rat anterior piriform cortex. *Journal of Neurophysiology*, 80, 998–1001.

Wilson, J. R., Friedlander, M. J., & Sherman, M. S. (1984). Ultrastructural morphology of identified X- and Y-cells in the cat's lateral geniculate nucleus. *Proceedings of the Royal Society*, B211, 411–436.

Wolfe, J. M. (1997). Inattentional amnesia. In V. Goltheart (Ed.), *Fleeting memories*. Cambridge, MA: MIT Press.

Wood, R. M., Harvey, M. A., Young, C. E., Beedie, A., & Wilson, T. (2000). Weighting to go with the flow. *Current Biology*, 10, 545R–546R.

Wysecki, G., & Stiles, W. S. (1965). *Color science: Concepts and methods, quantitative data and formulae*. New York: Wiley.

Xu, F., & Carey, S. (1994, June). *Infants' ability to individuate and trace the identity of objects*. Paper presented at the International Conference on Infant Studies, Paris.

Ye, Q., Heck, G., & DeSimone, J. A. (1991). The anion paradox in sodium taste reception: Resolution by voltage-clamp studies. *Science*, 254, 724–726.

Yonas, A., Granrud, C. E., Arterberry, M. E., & Hanson, B. L. (1986). Infant's distance from linear perspective and texture gradients. *Infant Behavior and Development*, 9, 247–256.

Yonas, A., Pettersen, L., & Granrud, C. E. (1982). Infant's sensitivity to familiar size as information for distance. *Child Development*, 53, 1285–1290.

Yost, W. A. (1997). The cocktail party problem: Forty years later. In R. H. Kilkey & T. R. Anderson. (Eds.) *Binaural and spatial hearing in real and virtual environments*. Hillsdale, NJ: Erlbaum, pp. 329–347.

Yost, W. A. (2001). Auditory localization and scene perception. In E. B. Goldstein (Ed.), *Blackwell handbook of perception*. Oxford, UK: Blackwell, pp. 437–468.

Yost, W. A., & Guzman, S. J. (1996). Auditory processing of sound sources: Is there an echo in here? *Current Directions in Psychological Science*, 5, 125–131.

Yost, W. A., & Sheft, S. (1993). Auditory processing. In W. A. Yost, A. N. Popper, & R. R. Fay (Eds.), *Handbook of auditory research* (Vol. 3). New York: Springer-Verlag.

Young, M. P. (1995). Open questions about the neural mechanisms of visual pattern recognition. In M. S. Gazzaniga (Ed.), *The cognitive neurosciences* (pp. 463–474). Cambridge, MA: MIT Press.

Young, R. S. L., Fishman, G. A., & Chen, F. (1980). Traumatically acquired color vision defect. *Investigative Ophthalmology and Visual Science*, 19, 545–549.

Young, T. (1802). On the theory of light and colours. *Transactions of the Royal Society of London*, 92, 12–48.

Young-Browne, G., Rosenfield, H. M., & Horowitz, F. D. (1977). Infant discrimination of facial expression. *Child Development*, 48, 555–562.

Yuodelis, C., & Hendrickson, A. (1986). A qualitative and quantitative analysis of the human fovea during development. *Vision Research*, 26, 847–855.

Zadnik, K., Satariano, W. A., Mutti, D. O., Sholtz, R. I., & Adama, A. J. (1994). The effect of parental history of myopia on children's eye size. *Journal of the American Medical Association*, 271, 1323–1327.

Zapadia, M. K., Ito, M., Gilbert, C. G., & Westheimer, G. (1995). Improvement in visual sensitivity by changes in local context: Parallel studies in human observers and in V1 of alert monkeys. *Neuron, 15,* 843–856.

Zatorre, A. J. (1988). Pitch perception of complex tones and human temporal-lobe function. *Journal of the Acoustical Society of America, 84,* 566–572.

Zatorre, A. J., Evans, A. C., & Meyer, E. (1994). Neural mechanisms underlying melodic perception and memory for pitch. *Journal of Neuroscience, 14,* 1908–1919.

Zatorre, A. J., Evans, A. C., Meyer, E., & Gjedde, A. (1992). Lateralization of phonetic and pitch discrimination in speech processing. *Science, 256,* 846–849.

Zeki, S. (1990). A century of cerebral achromatopsia. *Brain, 113,* 1721–1777.

Zeki, S., Watson, J. D. G., Lueck, C. J., Friston, K. J., Kennard, C., & Frackowiak, R. S. J. (1991). A direct demonstration of functional specialization in human visual cortex. *Journal of Neuroscience, 11,* 641–649.

Zellner, D. A., Bartoli, A. M., & Eckard, R. (1991). Influence of color on odor identification and liking ratings. *American Journal of Psychology, 104,* 547–561.

Zenner, H. P. (1986). Motile responses in outer hair cells. *Hearing Research, 22,* 83–90.

Zihl, J., von Cramon, D., & Mai, N. (1983). Selective disturbance of movement vision after bilateral brain damage. *Brain, 106,* 313–340.

Zihl, J., von Cramon, D., Mai, N., & Schmid, C. (1991). Disturbance of movement vision after bilateral posterior brain damage. *Brain, 114,* 2235–2252.

Zipser, K., Lamme, V. A. F., & Schiller, P. H. (1996). Contextual modulation in primary visual cortex. *Journal of Neuroscience, 15,* 7376–7389.

Zohary, E., Celebrini, S., Britten, K. H., Newsome, W. T. (1994). Neuronal plasticity that underlies improvement in perceptual performance. *Science, 263,* 1289–1292.

Zylbermann, R., Landau, D., & Berson, D. (1993). The influence of study habits on myopia in Jewish teenagers. *Journal of Pediatric Ophthalmology and Strabismus, 30,* 319–322.

Author Index

Abbott, L. F., 125
Abeles, M., 362
Abramov, I., 189, 196, 200, 515
Ache, B. W., 475
Ackerman, D., 344, 475, 568
Acroff, J. M., 400
Adelson, E. H., 70, 211, 214
Adrian, E. D., 20
Agloti, S., 458
Ahissar, E., 386
Ahissar, M., 386
Ahmed, F. S., 416
Alampay, D. A., 8, 10, 12
Alberti, L. B., 230
Albrecht, D. G., 91
Albright, T. D., 69, 278
Alexander, K. R., 522, 523
Alpern, M., 202, 203
Ames, A., 258
Andersen, R. A., 264, 288, 318
Anderson, C. H., 95
Angelerques, R., 123
Anstis, S. M., 291
Aristotle, 18
Arnell, K. M., 131
Arnheim, R., 148
Aronson, E., 311
Ashmead, D. H., 382, 531
Aslin, R. N., 263, 519, 524, 527
Atkinson, J., 513
Au, W. W. L., 340
Aubert, H., 272
Au Eong, K. G., 539
Awaya, S., 262
Axel, R., 476, 480
Azzopardi, P., 96

Bach, J. S., 397

Bach-y-Rita, P., 179
Backhaus, W. G. K., 189, 206, 216
Baird, J. C., 260
Balogh, R. D., 534
Banks, M. S., 513, 515, 516
Bannister, H., 314
Bardy, B. G., 315
Bargones, J. Y., 529
Barinaga, M., 387
Barlow, H. B., 56, 240
Barrow, H. G., 174
Bartoli, A. M., 218
Bartoshuk, L. M., 489, 491, 496
Basbaum, A. I., 465
Battaglini, P., 282
Bauer, R., 136
Baumgart, F., 386
Baylis, L. L., 499, 500
Bayliss, G. C., 159
Baylor, D. A., 48, 56, 191
Beall, A. C., 309
Beauchamp, G. K., 476, 491, 534, 536
Beauchamp, M. S., 201
Bechtold, A. G., 513
Beck, J., 155, 165, 174
Békésy, G. von, 351, 352, 353, 576
Bell, A. G., 336
Benary, W., 69
Bennett, P. J., 515
Beranek, L., 393
Berger, K. W., 392
Bergman, H., 386
Berkow, I., 575
Berlucchi, G., 458
Bernstein, I. L., 528
Berson, D., 539
Bertenthal, B. I., 312, 527

Bertino, M., 536
Bhalla, M., 319
Bieber, S. L., 493
Biederman, I., 168, 169, 170, 171
Birch, E. E., 513, 524, 525, 538
Birnberg, J. R., 475
Blackburn, J. M., 314
Blake, R., 242, 243, 261, 395
Blakemore, C., 100, 101, 240, 276
Blakeslee, A. F., 491
Blauert, J., 385
Bloom, F., 18
Blumstein, S. E., 416
Boell, E., 435
Bolanowski, S. J., 438
Bonda, E., 286
Bontecou, D. C., 385
Boring, E. G., 147, 248, 249, 250
Bornstein, M. H., 521, 522
Borton, R., 540
Bosley, J. J., 476
Boussourd, D., 114
Bower, J. M., 18
Bower, T. G. R., 540, 541
Bowers, J. N., 382
Bowmaker, J. K., 54, 522
Boycott, B. B., 41
Boyle, A. J. F., 354
Boynton, R. M., 203
Bozza, T. C., 482
Braddick, O., 513
Bradley, D. C., 288
Bradley, D. R., 147
Brainard, D. H., 209
Braunstein, M. L., 244
Bregman, A. S., 175, 395, 397, 398
Breipohl, W., 475
Bridgeman, B., 282

Britten, K., 278
Bromberg, B., 575
Brosch, M., 136
Brown, A. A., 574
Brown, C. M., 175
Brown, K. T., 216
Brown, P. K., 53, 54, 191
Brownell, W. E., 359
Bruce, C., 120
Brugge, J. F., 385
Brugger, P., 458
Brungart, D. S., 382
Bruno, N., 244
Bryan, S. S., 426
Buchsbaum, G., 200
Buck, L., 480
Bugelski, B. R., 8, 10, 12
Bunch, C. C., 568
Burke, S., 518
Burr, D. C., 317
Burton, A. M., 123
Bushnell, E. W., 513, 541
Bushnell, I. W. R., 517

Cabanac, M., 498
Cain, W. S., 218, 474, 476, 477, 496, 497, 498
Callender, M. G., 539
Calvert, G. A., 420
Campbell, F. W., 89, 92
Campbell, J., 397
Campbell, J. N., 461
Campbell, R., 325, 420
Carello, C., 395
Carey, S., 520, 521
Carlyon, R. P., 339
Casagrande, V. A., 78, 81, 427
Castellucci, V. F., 482
Cavanaugh, P. H., 477
Cernoch, J. M., 477, 534
Chairello, C., 426
Chance, G., 531
Chapman, T., 430
Charles, E. R., 81
Chatterjee, S. H., 293
Chen, C. J., 539
Chen, F., 186
Chikiris, M., 235
Chino, Y., 127
Chodosh, L. A., 314

Churchland, P. S., 45
Cicinelli, J. G., 379
Cinelli, A. R., 482
Clark, G. M., 574
Clark, J. J., 133
Clark, S. B., 463
Clark, V. P., 123
Clark, W. C., 463
Clulow, F. W., 188
Cohen, L. B., 510
Cohen, N., 575
Colburn, H. S., 378
Colby, C., 133, 134
Cole, R., 418
Collett, T. S., 244, 245
Coltheart, M., 230
Comel, M., 437
Conel, J. L., 514, 515
Connolly, M., 81
Cooper, E. E., 170
Cooper, G. G., 100, 101
Cooper, R. P., 529
Coppola, D. M., 89
Corbit, J. D., 418, 419
Costanzo, R. M., 450
Cowart, B. J., 484, 534, 536
Cowey, A., 96, 186
Craig, J. C., 444
Cramon, D., 271
Craton, L., 518
Critchley, H. D., 485, 501
Culler, E. A., 354
Cumming, B. G., 241, 242
Cutting, J. E., 227, 244
Cynader, M., 262, 317

Daher, M., 536
Dallos, P., 348, 359
Dalton, J., 200
Dartnall, H. J. A., 54, 191, 522
Davies, S., 464
Davis, R. G., 218
Day, R. H., 257
DeAngelis, G. C., 241, 242, 243
DeCasper, A., 529
Deibert, E., 455
Dekle, D. J., 428, 430
Delgutte, B., 426
DeLucia, P., 256, 257
Denes, P. B., 348, 412, 421

DePriest, D. D., 114
Derbyshire, S. W. G., 461
Descartes, R., 18
DeSimone, J. A., 489
Desimone, R., 114, 120, 133, 200, 278
Desor, J. A., 476
Detwiler, M. L., 313
Deutsch, D., 399, 400
DeValois, K. K., 91, 199
DeValois, R. L., 89, 91, 197, 198, 199
deVries, H., 476
deWeid, M., 463
DeYoe, E. A., 241
Dobelle, W. H., 576
Dobson, V., 512, 513
Dodd, B., 325, 420
Dodd, G. G., 476
Dodd, J., 482
Dong, W. K., 461
Doolittle, B., 152, 153
Doty, R. L., 474n, 475, 477, 534
Dowell, R. C., 574
Dowling, J. E., 41
Dowling, W. J., 364, 400
Downs, M., 572
Driver, J., 159
DuBose, C. N., 218
Duchamp-Viret, P., 482, 483
Duclaux, R., 443
Duffy, C. J., 317
Durlach, N. I., 378, 382
Durrant, J., 345, 347

Eckard, R., 218
Eckhorn, R., 136
Egan, J. P., 355, 356
Eimas, P. D., 418, 419, 520, 531, 532
Elbert, T., 368, 456
Emmert, E., 252
Engel, A. K., 135, 136
Engel, S., 201
Engel, S. A., 71, 89
Engelman, K., 536
Engen, T., 16, 476
Epstein, W., 229
Erickson, R., 392
Erickson, R. P., 490, 492, 493

Turk, D. C., 462, 465
Turman, A. A., 447
Turvey, M. T., 423
Tye-Murray, N., 574, 576
Tyler, C. W., 44, 241

Uchikawa, K., 208
Udelf, M. S., 511
Ungerleider, L. G., 112, 113, 114

Vaadia, E., 386
Valdez, P., 185
Vallbo, A. B., 439, 440, 446
Van de Walle, G., 520
Van Essen, D. C., 82, 95, 118, 241
Van Gelder, P., 423
Varner, D., 523
Vecera, S. P., 159
Vega-Bermudez, F., 442
Ventatesh, S., 175
Verbaten, M. N., 463
Vermeij, G., 179, 435–436
Vernon, J., 568
Vincent, A., 313
Vishton, P. M., 227, 244
Vogten, L. L. M., 357
Voigt, T., 241
Von der Emde, G., 246
Von Holst, E., 279
Von Noorden, G. K., 263

Wachsmuth, E., 120, 121
Wagner, H., 63
Wagner, M., 260
Wald, G., 53, 54, 191
Waldrop, M. M., 415
Wall, P. D., 437, 464
Wallace, M. A., 130
Wallach, H., 210, 287, 288, 383
Walls, G. L., 80, 187
Walton, G., 517

Wandell, B. A., 201, 209
Wang, Y., 315, 316, 317
Wann, J., 308, 309
Ward, W. D., 568
Warren, R. M., 400, 423
Warren, S., 450
Warren, W. H., 308, 309, 312
Wassle, H., 95
Watkins, C. R., 465
Weber, E., 15
Weinberger, N., 541
Weinstein, S., 445
Weisenberg, M., 462
Weiskopf, S., 521, 522
Weissberg, M., 465
Werblin, F. S., 43
Werker, J. F., 534
Werner, G., 450
Werner, L. A., 528, 529, 534
Wertheimer, M., 147, 171, 272
Wessel, D. L., 396, 397
Westendorf, D. H., 216
Wever, E. G., 351
Whalen, D. H., 428
Whalen, J. J., 189
Wheatstone, C., 234
Whishaw, I. Q., 426, 427
White, J., 230
White, M., 69
Whitsel, B. L., 450
Wiesel, T. N., 62, 82, 83, 84, 85, 97, 98, 100, 135, 171, 240, 261, 262, 276, 539
Wightman, F. L., 364, 381, 382
Wild, J. M., 245
Wilkinson, F., 102
Williams, R., 186n
Williams, S. M., 70
Wilson, D. A., 485
Wilson, H. R., 243
Wilson, J. R., 79
Wolfe, J. M., 133

Wollach, L., 202
Wood, R. M., 309
Woods, E., 323
Woods, T., 323
Woodworth, G. G., 574
Wooten, B. R., 189
Wundt, W., 146
Wurtz, R., 282
Wurtz, R. H., 317
Wyszecki, G., 189, 206

Xu, F., 520, 521

Yamashita, S., 493
Ye, Q., 489
Yee, W., 397
Yin, T. C. T., 385
Yonas, A., 518, 525, 526, 527
Yoshihara, Y., 484
Yost, W. A., 381, 385, 395, 396, 397
Young, E. D., 426
Young, M. P., 120
Young, R. S. L., 186
Young, T., 190–191
Young-Brown, G., 516
Yund, E. W., 91
Yuodelis, C., 515

Zadnik, K., 539
Zapadia, M. K., 110, 172
Zatorre, A. J., 364, 365, 427
Zeevi, Y. Y., 43
Zeki, S., 186, 200, 201, 204
Zellner, D. A., 218
Zenner, H. P., 359
Zhang, X., 201
Zihl, J., 270
Zipser, K., 111, 112
Zohary, E., 137
Zuker, C. S., 48
Zylbermann, R., 539

Subject Index

Absolute threshold, 13–15
Absorption spectra, 53–54
Accommodation, 42, 227
Accretion, 233, 234
Achromatic colors, 187
Acoustic reflex, 572
Acoustics, 392–393, 394
Acoustic shadow, 378–379
Acoustic signal, 411–412
Acoustic stimulus, 411
Acoustic trauma, 568
Across-fiber patterns, 492
Action, 6, 13, 28, 301–329
    brain scans of, 324
    hearing and vision linked with, 325–326
    motor system and, 320–323
    moving observer and, 302–307
    study questions on, 327–329
    visual control of, 307–320
Action pathway, 117
Action potential, 21, 22–23, 30
Active touch, 452, 453–455, 460
Acuity. *See* Visual acuity
Adaptation
    color vision as, 216–217
    dark, 49–52
    selective, 85–87
    spatial frequency, 92–94
Additive synthesis, 337–338
Adjustment, method of, 13–14
Afterimages
    color vision and, 195–196
    movement perception and, 275, 276, 280–281
    size perception and, 252–253
Age-related macular degeneration, 555–556

Aging
    cortical function and, 577
    hearing impairments and, 567, 568
    visual impairments and, 43, 550, 551, 555–556
Alberti's window, 230–231
Algorithms, 154
Alliesthesia, 498–499
Alphanumeric category effect, 178
Amacrine cells, 40
Ambient optic array, 304–305
Amblyopia, 262–263
Ames room, 258–259
Amiloride, 493
Amodal representation, 541
Amplitude, 335–337
Amputation, 457–459
Amygdala, 482
Angle of disparity, 238
Angular size-contrast theory, 260
Animals
    color vision in, 216–217
    depth perception in, 244–247
    hearing in, 340
    monocular rearing of, 261–262
    olfaction in, 475
    research studies using, 9n
    selective rearing for orientation in, 100–101
Anomalous trichromatism, 202
Anosmia, 475
Anterior cingulate cortex (ACC), 461, 462
Anterior ectosylvian sulcus (AES), 402
Anterior interparietal area (AIP), 321, 322, 326

Apex of cochlear partition, 347
Aphasia, 426
Apparent-distance theory, 259–260
Apparent movement, 12, 147, 272–273, 274
    brain activity during, 294
    shortest-path constraint and, 292–293
    study questions on, 298
    tactile, 295
Applanator, 562
Aqueous humor, 558
Architectural acoustics, 392–393, 394
Area centralis, 216
Articulation functions, 571
Articulators, 411
Astigmatism, 101–102, 550–551
Atmospheric perspective, 230
Attack, tone, 392
Attended stimulus, 4
Attention, 130
    focused, 167–168
    hearing impairments and, 578–579
    neural responding and, 133–134
    pain perception and, 462–463
    selectivity of, 130–131
    study questions on, 142–143
    touch perception and, 454–455
    visual processing and, 131–133, 140
Attentional blink, 131
Audibility curve, 339, 340
Audiograms, 570–571, 572
Audiologist, 569
Audiometer, 571
Audiovisual speech perception, 420

Computational approach, 160–163, 171, 181

Computers
object perception and, 172–175, 181
speech recognition and, 410

Conductive hearing loss, 566–567, 579

Cones, 40
color perception and, 191–195, 198–199, 203–204
dark adaptation of, 49–52
deficiency of, 203–204
development of, 515–516
signal convergence and, 54–58
spectral sensitivity of, 52–54
stimulation of, 43–45
See also Rods

Conflicting cues theory, 257

Congenital cataracts, 553

Conservative criterion, 589, 590

Constancy
color, 206–209, 219
lightness, 209–215, 219
size, 250–252, 265
speech perception, 417–419

Constant stimuli, method of, 14

Context
color perception and, 209
movement perception and, 272
size perception and, 253–254
speech perception and, 414, 423–424

Contextual modulation, 111

Contours, and figure-ground segregation, 158–159

Contralateral eye, 79

Contrast, 87
gratings illustrating, 86
infant perception of, 516
simultaneous, 68–70, 195, 196

Contrast sensitivity, 87

Contrast sensitivity function (CSF), 92, 516

Contrast threshold, 87

Convergence, 54–58, 73, 226–227

Convergence angle, 227

Co-occurrence hypothesis, 178, 181

Core area, 361

Cornea, 40

Corneal disease and injury, 552

Corneal transplants, 552

Corollary discharge signal (CDS), 279

Corollary discharge theory, 279–283, 284

Correct rejection, signal detection, 584

Correspondence problem, 243–244, 247

Corresponding retinal points, 237–239

Cortex
age-related changes, 577
extrastriate, 110
inferotemporal, 118–123
middle temporal, 118
olfactory, 482
primary auditory, 361
secondary auditory, 361
somatosensory, 447–449
striate, 39, 81–99

Cortical magnification factor, 95–96

Criterion, signal detection, 588–589, 590

Cross-correlograms, 136

Crossed disparity, 238–239

Cross-modality experience, 368–369

Cue approach to depth perception, 226–244
binocular cues and, 233–244
monocular cues and, 227–233
oculomotor cues and, 226–227

Cue theory, 226

Cutaneous sensations, 437

Cutaneous senses, 435–471
neural processing for, 444–450
object recognition with, 451–455
pain perception and, 460–466
plasticity of, 456–459
skin receptors and, 437–444
study questions on, 469–471
See also Touch perception

Daltonism, 200

Dark adaptation, 49–52

Dark-adaptation curve, 49–50, 51

Dark-adapted sensitivity, 50

Deafness, 578–579

Decay, tone, 392

Decibels, 336, 341–342

Deletion, 233, 234

Dendrites, 19

2–deoxyglucose (2–DG) technique, 97, 98, 484

Depth cues, 226
atmospheric perspective, 230
auditory, 264
binocular, 233–244, 264, 523–525
disparity information, 240–243
height, 228
linear perspective, 230–231
monocular, 227–233
movement-produced, 231–233
occlusion, 227–228
oculomotor, 226–227
overlapping, 526
pictorial, 227
range of effectiveness of, 244
size, 229–230, 526
texture gradient, 231

Depth perception, 225–247
animals and, 244–247
binocular cues and, 233–244
cue theory and, 226
development of, 523–526
infants and, 523–526
monocular cues and, 227–233
oculomotor cues and, 226–227
problem of, 225–226, 247
sensitive periods in development of, 261–263, 265
size perception and, 248–254, 526
study questions on, 266–267
visual and auditory space in, 264

Dermis, 437

Desaturated color, 189

Description, 12

Detached retina, 556–557

Detail perception
development of, 513–516
touch and, 441–443, 444–446, 448
vision and, 57–58, 444, 513–516

Detection
signal, 583–590
stimulus, 12–16, 30

Detectors
feature, 84
molecule, 474

movement, 118, 119
orientation, 85–87
Deuteranopia, 203
Development of perception. *See*
  Perceptual development
Diabetes, 554
Diabetic retinopathy, 554
Dichromatism, 202, 203
Difference threshold (DL), 15–16
Diopters, 548–549
Directionally-selective neurons, 277,
  386
Directional transfer function (DTF),
  381
Direct sound, 382, 383, 392
Discriminability, 169
Dishabituation, 512–513
Disparity
  angle of, 238
  cells for detecting, 240–243
  correspondence problem and, 243
  crossed vs. uncrossed, 238–239
  zero, 241
Disparity detectors, 240–243
Disparity-selective neurons, 241
Dissociations, 115
Distance coordinate, 376
Distance cues, 381–382
Distractor tones, 398
Distributed coding, 124–126, 140
  for taste, 492–493, 495
  for vision, 124–126
Doctrine of specific nerve energies,
  19
Dorsal pathway, 112–114
Double dissociation, 115, 116
Drawing system of linear
  perspective, 230
Duplex perception, 427–428

Eardrum, 344
Ears
  auditory pathways and, 350–351
  examinations of, 569–572, 579
  inner, 347–350
  middle, 345–347
  outer, 344–345
  structure of, 343–351
  See also Auditory system
Echolocation, 246

Echo threshold, 383
Ecological approach, 302–307, 316
  auditory perception and, 394
  beginnings of, 303
  environmental information and,
    303–305
  self-produced information and,
    305–307
Ecological optics, 304–305
Effective stimulus, 130
Effect of the missing fundamental,
  363
Elaborate cells, 119
Electricity, and visual transduction,
  46–48
Electromagnetic spectrum, 37, 38
Electronic noses, 503–504
Electroretinogram, 564
Element connectedness, principle
  of, 155
Elements of Psychophysics (Fechner),
  12
Elevation coordinate, 376
Elevation cues, 380–381
Emmert's law, 252–253
Emmetropia, 538
Emmetropization, 538
Emotions
  detected by infants, 516
  pain perception and, 461, 462,
    463
Endorphins, 465–466, 468
End-stopped cells, 84–85
ENT (ear, nose, and throat)
  specialists, 569
Envelope of the traveling wave,
  352–353
Environment
  color vision as adaptation to,
    216–217
  myopia linked to, 539
Environmental information
  collision avoidance and, 312–314
  ecological optics and, 304–305
  movement through the
    environment and, 308–310
  posture and balance and, 310–312
  retinal information vs., 303–304
  study questions on, 327
Environmental sounds

cortical processing of, 364–365
  identifying, 393–395
Environmental stimulus, 4
Enzyme cascade, 48
Epidermis, 437
Equal loudness curves, 341–342
Equivalence classification, 532
Everyday listening, 393–395
Evoked potentials, 26
Evolution
  color perception and, 187, 216
  neural selectivity and, 127
  visual system and, 127, 187, 216
Excitation, 24, 25, 73
Excitatory-center-inhibitory-
  surround receptive fields, 62
Excitatory response, 61–62
Expectation
  pain perception and, 462
  perception influenced by, 8
Experience
  auditory grouping and, 400–401
  neural selectivity and, 127–129
  speech perception and, 534
Exploratory procedures (EPs), 453
External eye exam, 561
Extrastriate cortex, 39, 110, 112–123
  modularity in, 117–123
  processing streams in, 112–117,
    124
  study questions on, 141–142
Eyes, 39
  blind spot of, 45
  dark adaptation of, 49–52
  examinations of, 558–564, 565
  focusing power of, 40, 41, 42–43
  frontal vs. lateral, 216–217, 245
  ipsilateral and contralateral, 79–80
  movement perception and,
    279–283
  spectral sensitivity of, 52–54
  structure of, 40, 41
  types of problems with, 546–547
  visual receptors of, 43–45
  See also Visual system

Faces
  brain area for responding to, 123
  infant recognition of, 517
  neural response to, 121–123

age-related, 567, 568, 577
conductive hearing loss, 566–567
cortical function and, 577
exams for detecting, 569–572
managing, 572–576, 579
sensorineural hearing loss, 567–569
study questions on, 581–582
types of, 564–566
visual attention and, 578–579
Heredity. *See* Genetics
Hermann grid, 64–66
Hertz (Hz), 335
Heuristics, 154
algorithms compared to, 154
Gestalt principles as, 154
light-from-above, 176–177
movement perception and, 290–292, 297
object perception and, 153–155, 175–177, 181
occlusion, 175–176, 291–292
origin of, 155
study questions on, 182, 184
Hidden objects, 174
Hits, signal detection, 584
Homunculus, 447–449
Honeybees, 206, 246
Horizontal cells, 40
Horopter, 237–238
How pathway, 117
Hue, 187*n*
Hypercolumns, 98–99
Hyperopia, 538, 550

Illumination
color constancy and, 206–207
lightness constancy and, 209–215
Illumination edge, 211
Illusions
of movement, 147, 275, 276
of size, 254–260, 265
See also Visual illusions
Illusory conjunctions, 166
Illusory contours, 147–148
Image movement signal (IMS), 279
Imitation, 323
Implied polyphony, 397
Inattentional blindness, 131
Incus, 345

Indexical characteristics, 424–425
Indirectness of perception, 72, 73
Indirect sound, 382, 383, 392–393
Induced movement, 273–275
Ineffective stimulus, 130
Infants
color perception in, 521–523
depth perception in, 523–526
hearing perception in, 529–534
intermodal perception in, 540–541
measuring perception in, 510–513
milestones in perceptual development of, 537
movement perception in, 526–528
object perception in, 516–521
olfactory perception in, 534–535
study questions on perception in, 543–544
taste perception in, 536
visual perception in, 513–528
See also Children
Inferior colliculus, 350
Inferotemporal cortex, 118–123
Information
disparity, 240–243
environmental, 303–305
invariant, 306–307
problem of combining, 134–136
self-produced, 307
Inhibition, 24, 25, 73
Inhibitory-center-excitatory-surround receptive fields, 62
Inhibitory response, 62
Inner ear, 347–350
Inner hair cells, 348, 349
Insects, 245–246
Insula, 489
Intensity relationships, 210
Interaural differences, 377
Interaural level difference (ILD), 378–379, 382
Interaural time difference, 377–378, 385
Interaural time difference detectors, 385
Intermodal matching, 540
Intermodal perception, 540–541
Interstimulus interval (ISI), 273

Intimacy time, 393
Intraocular lens, 553, 554
Intraocular pressure, 558
Invariant acoustic cues, 416–417, 421
Invariant information, 306–307
Invariant neurons, 125–126
Inverse projection problem, 173
Ions, 20
Ipsilateral eye, 79
Iridectomy, 558
Ishihara plates, 200
Isomerization, 46

K-cells, 81
Kinesthesis, 437
Kinetic depth effect, 286–288
Kittens
monocular rearing of, 261–262
selective rearing for orientation in, 100–101
Knowledge, 7–8, 10
See also Cognition

Landolt rings, 57
Large-diameter fibers (L-fibers), 465
Laser-assisted in situ keratomileusis (LASIK), 549
Laser photocoagulation, 555
Lateral eyes, 245
Lateral geniculate nucleus (LGN), 39, 78–81
information flow in, 78–79, 94
organization in, 79–81, 94
receptive fields in, 85
study questions on, 105
Lateral inhibition, 63, 64, 73
Hermann grid and, 64–66
Mach bands and, 66–68
simultaneous contrast and, 68–70
Lateralization, 426
Lateral sulcus (LS), 362
Laws
of common fate, 151–152
of familiarity, 152
of good continuation, 150, 151, 400
of good figure, 148–149
of perceptual organization, 148–153, 161

pictorial cues and, 227–231
Monocular rearing, 261–262
Moon illusion, 259–260
Motile response, 359, 360
Motion
    aftereffects, 275, 276
    biological, 286, 527–528
    sound, 386
Motion agnosia, 270
Motion capture, 288–289, 290
Motion parallax, 232–233, 245, 382
Motor area (M1), 321
Motor-dominant neurons, 321, 322
Motor signal (MS), 279
Motor system, 320–323
Movement
    apparent, 12, 147, 272–273, 274
    depth cues produced by, 231–233
    detecting, 118, 119
    induced, 273–275
    judging direction of, 277–279
    module for processing, 118, 119,
        124
    optic flow information and,
        308–310
    posture and balance in, 310–312
    real, 272
Movement perception, 269–300
    aftereffects of, 275, 276
    basic principles of, 270–271
    corollary discharge theory and,
        279–283
    creating, 272–276
    development of, 526–528
    eye movement and, 280–282
    heuristics and, 290–292, 297
    infants and, 526–528
    intelligence of, 290–293
    loss of, 269–270
    meaning and, 292, 297
    neural feature detectors and,
        276–279, 284
    optic array and, 283–284
    perceptual organization and,
        285–290, 297
    selective rearing and, 294, 297
    studying, 275–276
    study questions on, 298–300
    tactile stimulation and, 295–296
Moving observer, 302–303

MRI scans. *See* Functional magnetic
    resonance imaging
Müller-Lyer illusion, 254–257, 265
Multimodal nature
    of flavor perception, 499–500
    of pain perception, 460
    of speech perception, 419–420,
        421, 430
Multimodal neurons, 138, 264
Munsell Book of Colors, 189
Musical instruments, 391–392
Musical listening, 393
Musical tones, 362–364, 391–392
Musicians, 368
Myopia, 538–539, 542, 547–549

Naloxone, 465, 466
Nasal pharynx, 496–497
Natural constraints, 161
Near-head neurons, 387–388
Nearness, law of, 151
Near point, 43
Nearsightedness, 538–539, 542,
    547–549
Neovascularization, 554–555
Nerve fibers, 19
Nerve impulses, 20
Nerves, 19
Neural circuits, 58–60
Neural code
    color perception and, 189–190,
        200, 201
    movement perception and,
        276–279
    olfaction and, 482–485
    taste and, 491–495, 505
    See also Sensory code
Neural hearing loss, 569
Neural plasticity. *See* Plasticity of
    perception
Neural processing, 5–6
    convergence and, 54–58, 73
    distributed coding and, 124–126
    excitation and inhibition in,
        58–64
    perception and, 64–70, 129–130
    specificity coding and, 124, 126
    touch perception and, 444–450
Neural response
    attention and, 133–134

effects of experience on, 127–129
faces and, 121–123
plasticity of perception and, 137
speech and, 425–426
Neural selectivity, 127–129
    evolution and, 127
    experience and, 127–129
    study questions on, 142
Neurogenesis, 474
Neuroimaging, 26
Neurons
    action potentials and, 22–23
    bimodal, 138–139, 140, 499
    body-centered, 139
    collision-sensitive, 315–316, 317
    directionally-selective, 277, 386
    disparity-selective, 241
    electrical signals in, 20–22, 30
    invariant, 125–126
    mirror, 321–323, 324
    motor-dominant, 321, 322
    multimodal, 138, 264
    olfactory, 479, 480–481, 482–485
    opponent, 197–198
    panoramic, 385, 387
    real movement, 282–283
    specialization of, 127–129, 140
    structure of, 19–20
    synaptic transmission between,
        23–24
    terminology used for, 62
    visual and motor, 321, 322
    visual-dominant, 321, 322
Neuropsychology, 25, 115, 124
Neurotransmitters, 24
Neutral criterion, 589, 590
Neutral point, 203
Newborns. *See* Infants
Nociceptors, 461
Noise, 587
Noise-induced hearing loss, 567–568
Noncorresponding (disparate) points,
    238
Nonprimary auditory cortex, 361
Nontasters, 491
Notonecta, 245, 246
Nucleus of the solitary tract (NST),
    489, 490

Object perception, 145–184

Panretinal photocoagulation, 555
Pantone Matching System, 189
Papillae, 487–489
Parallel rays, 42
Parietal lobe, 25, 448
Partial color constancy, 209
Parvocellular (or parvo) layers, 81
Passive touch, 451–452
Payoffs, signal detection, 585
Penumbra, 212
Perception
    action and, 301–329
    categorical, 417–419, 421,
        531–532
    cognitive influences on, 9–11, 13
    complexity of, 2
    cross-modality, 368–369
    definition of, 6
    development of, 509–544
    ecological approach to, 302–307,
        316
    environmental information and,
        303–305, 316
    importance of, 2–3
    indirectness of, 72, 73
    levels of analysis in studying, 8–9,
        10
    motor system and, 320–323
    neural processing and, 64–70,
        129–130
    physiological approach to, 18–28
    plasticity of, 28
    process of, 4–8
    psychophysical approach to,
        11–18, 30
    study of, 8–11, 28
Perceptual constancy, 418, 419
Perceptual development, 509–544
    color perception and, 521–523
    depth perception and, 523–526
    hearing and, 529–534
    measuring in infants, 510–513
    milestones in, 537
    movement perception and,
        526–528
    object perception and, 516–521
    olfaction and, 534–536
    speech perception and, 531–534
    study questions on, 543–544
    taste and, 536

vision and, 513–528, 538–539
Perceptual organization, 148
    laws and principles of, 148–155
    movement perception and,
        285–290, 297
Perceptual plasticity. See Plasticity of
    perception
Perceptual process
    demonstration of, 7–8
    description of, 4–8
    study of, 8–11
    summary of, 13
Perceptual segregation, 156–160,
    174
Periodicity pitch, 363–364
Peripheral retina, 44
Peripheral vision, 57
Permeability, 21–22
Personal guidance system, 379–380
PET scans. See Positron emission
    tomography
Phacoemulsification, 553
Phantom limb, 457–459
Phase locking, 359–360
Phenomenological method, 12, 30
Phenylthiocarbamide (PTC), 491
Phonemes, 410–411
    meaning and perception of, 423,
        431
    variability problem and, 414
Phonemic restoration effect, 423
Phonetic boundary, 418, 531
Photorefractive keratotomy (PRK),
    549
Physiological approach to
    perception, 18–28
    study questions on, 32–33
    summary definition of, 30
Physiological level of analysis, 9, 10
Pictorial cues, 227–231, 525
Pigment absorption spectra, 53–54
Pigment bleaching, 52
Pigment epithelium, 45
Pigment regeneration, 52
Pinnae, 344
Piriform cortex, 482
Pitch, 342–343
    auditory grouping and, 397–399
    central pitch processor, 364
    periodicity, 363–364

Placebos, 462, 465–466
Place coding
    description of, 351–354
    physiological evidence for,
        354–355, 361
    psychophysical masking and,
        355–356, 361
Place theory of hearing, 351–354
Plasticity of perception, 28, 100
    age-related cortical changes, 577
    auditory cortex stimulation,
        366–367
    binocular vision development,
        261–263
    color vision and adaptation,
        216–217
    co-occurrence effect, 178, 181
    cutaneous system, 456–459
    development of myopia, 538–539
    effect of vision on hearing,
        402–404
    Greeble experiments, 128–129
    learning taste-smell associations,
        502
    movement perception, 294
    neural responding and perception,
        137
    neural selectivity, 127–128
    phantom limb phenomenon,
        457–459
    selective rearing for orientation,
        100–102, 104
    speech perception, 429
Point-light walkers, 285–286, 287,
    527–528
Ponzo illusion, 257–258
Pop-out boundary method, 164
Pop-out effect, 165
Positron emission tomography
    (PET), 26–27
    See also Brain imaging
Postsynaptic neuron, 24
Posture, 310–312
Potassium ions, 20–22
Power functions, 17
Pragnanz, law of, 148–149
Preattentive stage, 163, 166–167, 181
Precedence effect, 382–385, 390
Preferential looking (PL) technique,
    511, 512

Premotor area (PM), 321
Presbycusis, 567, 568
Presbyopia, 43, 550
Presynaptic neuron, 24
Primary auditory cortex, 361
Primary auditory receiving area, 361, 363
Primary cells, 119
Primary olfactory cortex, 482
Primary receiving areas, 25, 26
Principles
    of belongingness, 70
    of common region, 155
    of componential recovery, 169–170
    of element connectedness, 155
    of perceptual organization, 155, 161
    of synchrony, 155
    of univariance, 193
    See also Laws
Probability distributions, 587–588, 590
Processing streams, 112–117
Propagated response, 22
Proprioception, 437
Prosopagnosia, 123
Protanopia, 203
Proximity, law of, 151
Psychophysical approach to perception, 11–18
    study questions on, 32
    summary definition of, 30
Psychophysical level of analysis, 9, 10
Psychophysical tuning curve, 357–358
Psychophysics, 9
Pupillary block, 557
Pure-tone audiometry, 570–571
Pure tones, 335, 337
Purkinje shift, 53

Raised-dot stimulus, 441–442
Random-dot stereogram, 239–240, 247
Rapidly adapting (RA) fibers, 439
Rapid serial visual presentation (RSVP), 131
Rat-man demonstration, 8

Raw primal sketch, 161–162
Real movement, 272
Real movement neurons, 282–283
Receiver operating characteristic (ROC) curve, 585–586
    effect of sensitivity on, 589–590
Receptive fields, 60–63, 73
    auditory, 388–390
    center-surround, 62
    ganglion cell, 60–61, 85
    striate cortex, 82–85, 94
    tactile, 445–446, 450
    virtual space, 385
Receptors, 20
    skin, 437–444
    smell, 474, 475
    stimulus on, 4–5
    taste, 474, 475
    visual, 43–45
Receptor sites, 24, 489
Recognition, 6, 13, 30
    figure-ground segregation and, 159
    infant perception and, 517, 529, 534, 536
    movement perception and, 292
    odor perception and, 534–536
    procedure for measuring, 12
Recognition-by-components (RBC) approach, 168–171, 181
Red-eyed turtle, 216, 217
Referred sensation, 458
Reflectance, 187
Reflectance curve, 187–188
Reflectance edge, 211
Reflection
    light, 187–188
    selective, 188
    sound, 382
Refraction, 560–561
Refractive myopia, 547
Refractory period, 23
Relative height, 228
Relative size, 229
Repetition discrimination task, 156
Resistance to visual noise, 169
Resonance, 344
Resonant frequency, 344
Response compression, 17
Response criterion, 584

Response expansion, 17
Resting potential, 20
Retina, 41, 44–45
    binocular depth cues and, 237–239
    conditions causing damage to, 554–557, 565
    detached, 556–557
    examination of, 562–564
    focusing of light on, 538, 547–551
    hereditary degeneration of, 557
Retinal, 46
Retinitis pigmentosa, 557
Retinoscopy exam, 560–561
Retinotopic map, 103
    on cortex, 95–96
    on LGN, 80
Retronasal route, 496
Reverberation time, 392–393
Reversible figure-ground, 156–157
Rod-cone break, 51
Rod monochromat, 50
Rods, 40
    dark adaptation of, 49–52
    signal convergence and, 54–58
    spectral sensitivity of, 52–54
    stimulation of, 43–45
    See also Cones
Ruffini cylinder, 437, 438, 439, 440, 442
Running spectral display, 416, 418

Salience, 111
Saturation, 189
Scale illusion, 399
Searching, 18, 30
Secondary auditory cortex, 361
Secondary cataracts, 553
Secondary olfactory cortex, 482
Secondary somatosensory cortex, 447
Segmentation problem, 413–414
Segregation, perceptual, 156–160
Selective adaptation, 85–87
    experiment on, 86–87
    rationale behind, 85–86
    spatial frequencies and, 93
    stimulus for measuring, 86–87
Selective rearing
    movement perception and, 294, 297

for orientation, 100–102, 104
Selective reflection, 188
Self-produced information, 307
Senile cataracts, 553
Sensations, 146–147
    cutaneous, 437
    referred, 458
Senses
    considering perception across, 28
    plastic effects of losing, 456–457
    primary receiving areas for, 25, 26
Sensitive period, for binocular
        vision, 261–263
Sensitivity, 52, 589–590
    contrast, 87
    olfactory, 475–476
    ROC curves and, 589–590
    spectral, 52–54
    visual, 55–57
Sensorineural hearing loss, 567–569,
        579
Sensory code, 123–126, 140
    color perception and, 189–190,
        200
    distributed coding and, 124–126
    specificity coding and, 124, 125
    study questions on, 142
    See also Neural code
Sensory-specific satiety, 498
Sensory substitution system, 179
Shadowing technique, 424
Shadows
    acoustic, 378–379
    depth cues and, 229
    lightness constancy and, 211–214
    Mach bands and, 66, 67
Shortest-path constraint, 292–293
Short-term spectrum, 416, 417, 426
Short-wavelength pigment, 54, 523
Sight. See Vision
Signal, 587
Signal detection theory (SDT),
        583–590
Silent lipreading, 420
Similarity, law of, 149–150
Simple cortical cells, 83–84, 85
Simplicity, law of, 148–149
Simultaneous color contrast, 196
Simultaneous contrast, 68–70, 195,
        196

Simultaneous lightness contrast,
        68–69
Sine-wave components, 591–593
Sine-wave grating, 592–593
Sine-wave motion, 335
Single dissociation, 115, 117
Size constancy, 250–252, 265
    misapplied scaling and, 255
    size-distance scaling and, 252–254
    veridical perception and, 254
Size-distance scaling, 252–254
Size-invariant neurons, 125, 126
Size perception, 248–260, 265
    depth perception and, 248–254,
        526
    illusions of, 254–260, 265
    size constancy and, 250–252
    size-distance scaling and, 252–254
    study questions on, 267
    visual angles and, 248–250, 251
Size-specific neurons, 126
Skin, 437–444, 451
    layers of, 437
    mechanoreceptors in, 437–443
    study questions on, 469
    thermoreceptors in, 443–444
Slant, judging, 318–320, 326
Slit-lamp examination, 561–562
Slowly adapting (SA) fibers, 439
Small-diameter fibers (S-fibers), 465
Smell. See Olfaction
Snellen letters, 57
Sniff responses, 486, 487
Sodium ions, 20–22
Sodium-potassium pump, 22n
Somatosensory cortex
    effect of attention on, 454–455
    important characteristics of, 447
    map of the body in, 447–449, 456
    pain perception and, 461
    study questions on, 469
    tactile object recognition and, 455
Somatosensory receiving area, 447
Somatosensory system, 437
    anatomy of, 446–447
    brain map of, 447–449
    tactile feature detectors in,
        449–450
    visual system and, 467
    See also Touch perception

Somatotopic map, 103, 447–449
Somersaults, 315, 316
Sound
    air pressure changes and, 334–339
    amplitude of, 335–337
    color associated with, 368–369
    definitions of, 333–334
    direct vs. indirect, 382, 383,
        392–393
    environmental, 364–365
    frequency of, 335, 337–339
    infant perception of, 529–534
    localizing, 376–390
    loudspeakers and, 334–335
    movement perception and, 296
    musical, 362–364
    object perception and, 180
    perceptual experience and,
        339–343
    reflected, 382
    speech, 409–434, 531–534
Sound level, 336, 382
Sound pressure level (SPL), 336
Sound quality, 391–395, 405
    architectural acoustics and,
        392–393
    environmental sound
        identification and, 393–395
    sound source characteristics and,
        391–392
    study questions on, 407
Sound spectrogram, 411–412, 413
Sound waves, 334–335, 379
Space
    topographic map of, 388–390
    visual and auditory, 264, 265
Spaciousness factor, 393
Spatial frequency, 88–95
    adaptation to, 93
    explained, 88
    Fourier analysis and, 90–91,
        591–593
    study questions on, 106
    visual angle and, 88–90
Spatial frequency analyzers
    physiology of, 91
    psychophysics of, 92–95
Spatial plot events, 442
Spatial resolution, 446
Spatial summation, 57, 317–318

learning olfactory associations with, 502
neural code for, 491–495
overview of, 473–475
qualities of, 490
study questions on, 507–508
system of, 487–490
Taste-blindness, 491
Taste buds, 489
Taste cells, 489
Taste pores, 489
Tau ratio, 313
Tectorial membrane, 348, 349
Temperature perception, 443–444
Temporal lobe, 25
Temporal proximity, 399
Texture gradient, 231
Thermoreceptors, 443–444, 451
Three-dimensional images
brain representation of, 170, 181
depth perception and, 236
lightness perception and, 210–214
Müller-Lyer illusion and, 256–257
Thresholds
absolute, 13–15
contrast, 87
difference, 15–16
echo, 383
two-point, 444–445
Thumb method, 90
Timbre, 343, 392, 396–397
Tinnitus, 568
Tinnitus masker, 568
Tone chroma, 342–343
Tone height, 342–343
Tongue, 487–489
Tonometer, 562
Tonometry, 562
Tonotopic map, 104, 354, 361–362, 363
Top-down processing, 8, 13
object perception and, 177–178, 181
speech perception and, 422
Touch perception, 435–471
active touch and, 452, 453–455
bimodal neurons and, 138–139
blind people and, 435–436
detail perception and, 441–443, 444–446, 448

feature detectors and, 449–450
hearing and, 430
importance of, 436–437
mechanoreceptors and, 437–443
movement perception and, 295–296
neural processing for, 444–450
object perception and, 179, 451–455
pain perception and, 460–466
passive touch and, 451–452
plasticity of, 456–459
skin receptors and, 437–443
somatotopic map and, 103
study questions on, 469–471
thermoreceptors and, 443–444
vision perception and, 467, 540–541
See also Somatosensory system
Transduction, 5
auditory, 348–350
olfactory, 478–481
taste, 487–489
visual, 46–48
Transmission cells (T-cells), 464
Traumatic cataracts, 553
Traveling wave, 352
Trichromatic theory of color vision, 190–195, 201
color-matching experiments and, 190, 191
description of, 190–191
physiology of, 191–195, 201
study questions on, 220–221
Tritanopia, 203
Tuning curves
frequency, 354–355, 359
orientation, 83–84, 577
psychophysical, 357–358
Tuning forks, 335
Tunnel vision, 552
$2^1/_2$ -D sketch, 162
Two-point threshold, 444–445
Tympanic membrane, 344, 345, 346
Tympanometer, 572
Tympanometry, 571–572

Uncrossed disparity, 238
Unilateral dichromatism, 202
Univariance, principle of, 193

Vagus nerve, 489
Variability problem, 414–416
Vection, 275
Ventral pathway, 112–114
Ventral posterior nucleus, 447
Ventriloquism effect, 264, 403–404
Veridical perception, 254
Video microscopy, 491, 492
View invariance, 168–169
View-invariant neurons, 125–126
View-specific neurons, 126
Virtual space receptive field, 385
Visible light, 37, 38, 39
Vision
action and, 301–329
attention and, 131–133, 140
binocular rivalry and, 129–130
clinical aspects of, 546–564
color perception and, 185–223
dark adaptation and, 49–52
depth perception and, 225–247
detail and, 57–58, 444
development of, 513–528
examinations of, 558–564
focusing power and, 40, 41, 42–43
hearing related to, 264, 402–404, 578–579
impairments of, 546–564
infant perception and, 513–528
location information for, 377
movement perception and, 269–300
myopia and, 538–539
object perception and, 145–184
olfaction and, 503–504
size perception and, 248–260
spectral sensitivity and, 52–54
stimulus for, 37–39
touch perception and, 467, 540–541
See also Visual system
Visual acuity, 57–58
development of, 513–516
test of, 559–560
Visual and motor neurons, 321, 322
Visual angle
size perception and, 248–250, 251
spatial frequency and, 88–90
Visual capture, 264

Subject Index

Visual direction strategy, 309
Visual-dominant neurons, 321, 322
Visual evoked potential (VEP),
513–514
Visual feedback model, 539
Visual form agnosia, 6, 115
Visual illusions, 254–260
    Ames room, 258–259
    moon illusion, 259–260
    Müller-Lyer illusion, 254–257
    Ponzo illusion, 257–258
    study questions on, 267–268
    waterfall illusion, 275, 276
Visual impairments, 546–564
    age-related, 43, 550, 551,
        555–556, 577
    blindness, 551–552
    cataracts, 553–554
    color blindness, 186, 200,
        202–204
    corneal disease and injury, 552
    cortical function and, 577
    decreased light transmission,
        551–554
    detached retina, 556–557
    diabetic retinopathy, 554–555
    exams for detecting, 558–564
    focusing problems, 547–551
    glaucoma, 557–558
    heredity retinal degeneration, 557
    macular degeneration, 555–556
    retinal damage, 554–557
    study questions on, 580–581
    types of, 546–547
Visual pigments, 48–54

color perception and, 191,
    203–204
dark adaptation and, 49–52
regeneration of, 52
spectral sensitivity and, 52–54
Visual receiving area, 39
Visual search procedure, 164
Visual space, 264, 265
Visual system
    attention and, 130–134, 140
    bimodal neurons and, 138–139
    binding problem and, 134–136
    color perception and, 191–195,
        197–200, 205
    convergence in, 54–58
    development of, 513–528
    examinations of, 558–564
    excitation and inhibition in,
        58–64
    higher-level processing in,
        109–143
    impairments of, 546–564
    lateral geniculate nucleus and,
        78–81
    localization components in,
        385–390
    myopia and, 538–539
    neural processing in, 58–70
    plasticity of, 137, 178, 181,
        216–217
    processing streams of, 112–117
    receptors in, 43–45
    retinotopic maps and, 80, 95–96,
        103
    sensory coding in, 123–126

somatosensory system and, 467
striate cortex and, 81–99
structure of, 38, 39–40, 41
study questions on, 74–76,
    105–107, 141–143
synesthesia and, 368–369
transduction process in, 46–48
See also Eyes; Vision
Visual transduction, 46–48
Vitrectomy, 555
Vitreous humor, 554
Vocal characteristics, 424–425
Vocal tract, 409, 410, 411–412
Voice onset time (VOT), 417–419,
    531
Volumetric primitives, 168

Warm fibers, 443
Waterfall illusion, 275, 276
Wavelength, 37
Weber fraction, 16
Weber's law, 16
WebTutor site, 18
Wernicke's aphasia, 426–427
What pathway, 114
Where pathway, 114
Whiteout, 248
White's illusion, 69–70
Word perception, 423–424

Young-Helmholtz theory of color
    vision, 191

Zero disparity, 241

CREDITS

This page constitutes an extension of the copyright page. We have made every effort to trace the ownership of all copyrighted material and to secure permission from copyright holders. In the event of any question arising as to the use of any material, we will be pleased to make the necessary corrections in future printings. Thanks are due to the following authors, publishers, and agents for permission to use the material indicated.

Photos

About the Author: Christopher Baker. **Color essays. Plate 1.3:** Courtesy of Mitchell Glickstein. **Plate 1.4a,b:** F. De Monasterio et al., 1981. **Plate 2.1a,b:** © James P. Blair/CORBIS. **Plate 2.2a,b:** Ruth Dixon/Stock, Boston. **Plate 3.8:** *Place des Lices, Saint Tropez*, by Paul Signac (1893), Carnegie Museum of Art, Pittsburgh; Acquired through the generosity of the Sarah Mellon Scaife family, 66.24.2. **Chapter 1. 3:** © George Hall/CORBIS. **27:** © Leif Skoogfors/CORBIS. **Chapter 2. 43:** From "Scanning Electron Microscopy of Vertebrate Visual Receptors," by E. R. Lewis, Y. Y. Zeevi, & F. S. Werblin, 1969, *Brain Research*, 15, 559–562. Copyright © 1969 Elsevier Science Publishers, B. B. Reprinted by permission. **67:** From *Mach Bands: Quantitative Studies on Neural Networks in the Retina*, by F. Ratcliff, 1965, figure 3.25, p. 107. Copyright © 1965 Holden-Day, Inc. Reprinted by permission. **Chapter 3. 79:** From "Segregation of Form, Color, Movement and Depth: Anatomy, Physiology and Perception," by M. Livingston and D. H. Hubel, 1988, *Science*, 240, 740–749. Copyright © 1988 by the American Association for the Advancement of Science. Reprinted by permission of M. Livingston. **82:** From "Functional Architecture of Macaque Monkey Cortex," by D. H. Hubel and T. N. Wiesel, 1977, *Proceedings of the Royal Society of London*, 198, 1–59. Copyright © 1977 by the Royal Society. Reprinted by permission of D. H. Hubel. **88:** © Dave G. Houser/CORBIS. **91:** *Seeing—Illusion, Brain and Mind*, © John P. Frisby, 1979 by permission of Oxford University Press. **98:** From Hubel, Wiesel, & Stryker, 1978. **Chapter 4. 122:** From "Sparseness of the Neuronal Representation of Stimuli in the Primate Temporal Visual Cortex," by E. T. Rolls and M. J. Tovee, 1995, *Journal of Neurophysiology*, 73, 713–726. Copyright © 1995 by The American Physiological Society. Reprinted by permission. **123:** Courtesy of Dr. Dana Copeland. **129:** Figure 1a, p. 569, from Gauthier, I., Tarr, M. J., Anderson, A. W., Skudlarski, P. L., & Gore, J. C. (1999). Activation of the middle fusiform "face area" increases with experience in recognizing novel objects. *Nature Neuroscience*, 2, 568–573. **132:** From "Failure to Detect Changes in Attended Objects in Motion Pictures," by D. Levin and D. Simons, 1997, *Psychonomic Bulletin and Review*, 209, Courtesy of Telesensory Corporation. **Chapter 5. 149:** R. C. James **150:** Courtesy of the Pittsburgh Ballet Theater/Randy Choura. **151:** Energy Issues Master Collection CD/CORBIS. **152 top:** © Julie Lemberger/CORBIS. **152 bottom:** *The Forest Has Eyes* by Bev Doolittle (1985). **153:** *Pintos* by Bev Doolittle, 1979. **173:** Courtesy of Thomas Macaulay. **174:** © Mary Ann McDonald/CORBIS. **176:** Richard Hamilton/CORBIS. **Chapter 7. 229:** © Randy Faris/CORBIS. **230:** © Keren Su/CORBIS. **232:** *The Annunciation*. Attributed to Antoniazzo Romano © Burstein Collection/CORBIS. **235:** Mike Chikiris/Pittsburgh Stereogram Company, Pittsburgh, PA, 1990. **236:** © Bettmann/CORBIS. **240 top:** From *Foundations of Cyclopean Perception*, by B. Julesz, 1971, figures 2.4-1 and 2.4-3. Copyright © 1971 University of Chicago Press. Reprinted by permission. **245 right:** © Niall Benvie/CORBIS **258:** © Phil Schermeister/CORBIS. **Chapter 8. 273:** From Edwin S. Porter's *The Great Train Robbery*, 1903. **276:** © Galen Rowell/CORBIS. **292:** "Object recognition can drive motive perception" by V.S. Ramachandran, C. Armel, C. Foster, and R. Stoddard. *Nature*, 1998, 395:852–853." **293:** Courtesy of Maggie Shiffrar. **Chapter 10. 337:** © Henry Diltz/CORBIS. **366:** From Klinke et al., 1999. **Chapter 12. 412:** Courtesy of Kerry Green. **413 top:** Courtesy of Kerry Green. **413 bottom:** Courtesy of David Pisoni. **415:** Courtesy of David Pisoni. **417 right:** Courtesy of James Sawusch. **418 right:** Courtesy of Ron Cole. **Chapter 14. 478:** From Morrison, E.E., & Moran, D.T. (1995). Anatomy and ultrastructure of the human olfactory neuroepithelium. In R. L. Doty (Ed.), *Handbook of Olfaction and Gustation* (pp. 75–101). New York: Marcel Dekker. **489:** From Miller, I. J. (1995). Anatomy of the peripheral taste system. In R. L. Doty (Ed.), *Handbook of Olfaction and Gustation* (pp. 521–548). New York: Marcel Dekker. **492:** Courtesy of Linda Bartoshuk. **Chapter 15. 512:** Courtesy of Velma Dobson. **517:** From Ginsburg, A. (1983). Contrast perception in the human infant. Unpublished manuscript. **529:** Walter Salinger/Photo property of Anthony DeCasper. DeCasper, A. J., & Fifer, W. P. (1980). Of human bonding: Newborns prefer their mothers' voices. *Science*, 208, 1174–1176.) **533 a,b:** Kuhl, P. K. (1989). On babies, birds, modules, and mechanisms: A comparative approach to the acquisition of vocal communication. In R. J. Dooling & S. H. Hulse (Eds.), *Comparative psychology of audition* (pp. 379–419). Hillsdale, NJ: Erlbaum. **535:** Courtesy of J. E. Steiner, The Hebrew University, Jerusalem. **535:** Photographs courtesy of J. E. Steiner, The Hebrew University, Jerusalem. **536:** Rosenstein, D., & Oster, H. (1988). Differential facial responses to four basic tastes in newborns. *Child Development*, 59, 1555–1568. **536:** Photographs courtesy of J. E. Steiner, The Hebrew University, Jerusalem. **540:** From "Learning and Intermodal Transfer of Information in Newborns," by K. L. Kaye and T. G. R. Bower, 1994, *Psychological Science*, 5, 286–288. **Chapter 16. 564:** Courtesy of Eye and Ear Hospital of Pittsburgh. **575:** Chester Higgins Jr./NYT Pictures. **Right front endpaper: top left,** © Dave G. Houser/CORBIS. **bottom left,** Paul J. Sutton/© Duomo/CORBIS. **top right,** © Phil Schermeister/CORBIS. **bottom right,** Courtesy of Noam Sobel.

Photographs not credited are courtesy of the author, E. Bruce Goldstein.

Text and illustrations

Chapter 1. 8: Adapted from "The Role of Frequency in Developing Perceptual Sets," by B. R. Bugelski and D. A. Alampay, 1961, *Canadian Journal of Psychology*, 15, 205–211. Copyright ©1961 by the Canadian Psychological

Association. Reprinted with permission. **10:** Adapted from "The Role of Frequency in Developing Perceptual Sets," by B. R. Bugelski and D. A. Alampay, 1961, *Canadian Journal of Psychology, 15,* 205–211. Copyright © 1961 by the Canadian Psychological Association. Reprinted with permission. **12:** Adapted from "The Role of Frequency in Developing Perceptual Sets," by B. R. Bugelski and D. A. Alampay, 1961, *Canadian Journal of Psychology, 15,* 205–211. Copyright ©1961 by the Canadian Psychological Association. Reprinted with permission. **16:** Adapted from "The Surprising Simplicity of Sensory Metrics" by S. S. Stevens, 1962, *American Psychologist, 17,* p. 29–39. Copyright © 1962 by the American Psychological Association. **17:** Adapted from "The Surprising Simplicity of Sensory Metrics" by S. S. Stevens, 1962, *American Psychologist, 17,* p. 29–39. Copyright © 1962 by the American Psychological Association. **Chapter 2. 38:** Adapted from *Human Information Processing,* by P. Lindsay and D. A. Norman, 1977, 2nd ed., p. 216. Copyright ©1977 Academic Press, Inc. Adapted by permission. **41:** Adapted from "Organization of the Primate Retina," by J. E. Dowling and B. B. Boycott, 1966. *Proceedings of the Royal Society of London, 16,* Series B., 80–111. Copyright ©1966 by The Royal Society. Adapted by permission. **43:** From "Scanning Electron Microscopy of Vertebrate Visual Receptors," by E. R. Lewis, Y. Y. Zeevi, & F. S. Werblin, 1969, *Brain Research, 15,* 559–562. Copyright ©1969 Elsevier Science Publishers, B. V. Reprinted with permission. **44:** Adapted from *Human Information Processing,* by P. Lindsay and D. A. Norman, 1977, 2nd ed., p. 126. Copyright ©1977 Academic Press, Inc. Adapted with permission. **46:** From a figure by Johnny Johnson on page 88 of "Blind Spots," by Vilaynaur S. Ramachandran, *Scientific American,* May 1992. Reprinted with permission. Copyright ©1992 by Scientific American, Inc. All rights reserved. **51:** Partial data from "Rhodopsin Measurement and Dark Adaptation in a Subject Deficient in Cone Vision," by W. A. H. Ruston, 1961, *Journal of Psychology, 156,* 193–205. Copyright ©1961 by the Psychological Society, Cambridge University Press. **53:** Adapted from "The Receptors of Human Color Vision," by E. Wald, 1964, *Science, 145,* pp. 1009 and 1011. Copyright ©1964 by the American Association for the Advancement of Science. Adapted with permission. **53:** From "Human Rhodopsin," by G. Wald and P. K. Brown, 1958, *Science, 127,* p. 222–226, figure 6, and "The Receptors of Human Color Vision," by E. Wald, 1964, *Science, 145,* p. 1007–1017. Copyright ©1964 by the American Association for the Advancement of Science. Adapted with permission. **56:** From "Amacrine Cells," by R. H. Masland, 1988, *Trends in Neuroscience, 11*(9), 405–410, figure 2. Copyright ©1988 by Elsevier Science Ltd. Reprinted by permission. **57:** From "Visual Acuity," by L. A. Riggs, 1965. In C. Graham, Ed., *Vision and Visual Perception,* figure 11.4, p. 324. Copyright ©1965 by John Wiley & Sons, Inc. Reprinted by permission of John Wiley & Sons. **62:** From "Integrative Action in the Cat's Lateral Geniculate Body," by D. H. Hubel and T. N. Wiesel, 1961, *Journal of Physiology, 155,* 385–398, figure 1. Copyright ©1961 by The Physiological Society, Cambridge University Press. Reprinted by permission. **64:** From *Mach Bands: Quantitative Studies on Neural Networks in the Retina,* by F. Ratliff, 1965, figure 3.25, p. 107. Copyright ©1965 Holden-Day, Inc. Reprinted with permission. **70:** From *Perception,* 1981, 10, p. 215–230, fig 1a, p. 216. Reprinted with permission from Pion, Ltd., London. **Chapter 3. 79:** From Livingstone & Hubel, 1988. **81:** Reprinted with permission from *Nature,* "Functions of the Colour-Opponents and Broad Channels of the Visual System," by P. H. Schiller, N. K. Logthetis & E. R. Charles, 1990, 343, p. 68, figure 1a & b. Copyright ©1990 by Macmillan Magazine, Ltd. **82:** From Hubel & Wiesel, 1977. **83:** From "Receptive Fields of Single Neurons in the Cat's Striate Cortex," by D. H. Hubel and T. N. Wiesel, 1959, *Journal of Physiology, 148,* 574–591, figure 2. Copyright © 1959 by The Physiological Society, Cambridge University Press. Reprinted by permission. **84:** From "Receptive Fields of Single Neurons in the Cat's Striate Cortex," by D. H. Hubel and T. N. Wiesel, 1959, *Journal of Physiology, 148,* 574–591, figure 2. Copyright © 1959 by The Physiological Society, Cambridge University Press. Reprinted by permission. **85:** From "Receptive

Fields of Single Neurons in the Cat's Striate Cortex," by D. H. Hubel and T. N. Wiesel, 1959, *Journal of Physiology, 148,* 574–591, figure 8. Copyright © 1959 by The Physiological Society, Cambridge University Press. Reprinted by permission. **88:** From "Size Adaptation: A New Aftereffect," by C. Blakemore and P. Sutton, 1969, *Science, 166,* 245–247, figure 1. Copyright © 1969 by the American Association for the Advancement of Science. Reprinted by permission. **89:** From C. S. Furmanski and S. A. Engel (2000). An oblique effect in human primary visual cortex. *Nature Neuroscience, 3,* 535–536. Reprinted by permission. **91:** From "The Visual Cortex as a Spatial Frequency Analyzer," by L. Maffei and A. Fiorentini, 1973, *Vision Research, 13,* 1255–1267, figure 3. Copyright © 1973 with kind permission from Elsevier Science Ltd., The Boulevard, Langford Land, Kidlington 0X5 1GB, UK. **92:** From "Application of Fourier Analysis to the Visibility of Gratings," by F. W. Campbell and J. G. Robson, 1968, *Journal of Physiology, 197,* 551–556, figure 2. Copyright © 1968 Physiological Society, Cambridge University Press. Reprinted by permission. **98:** From Hubel, Wiesel, & Stryker, 1978. **Chapter 4. 111:** Reprinted with permission from *Neuron, 15,* M. K. Zapadia et al., "Improvement in visual sensitivity by changes in local cortex: Parallel studies in human observers and in V1 of alert monkey," pp. 843–856. Copyright © 1995 Elsevier Science. **112:** From K. Zipser et al., "Contextual modulation in primary visual context," *Journal of Neuroscience, 15,* pp. 7376–7389. Copyright © 1996 by the Society for Neuroscience. Reprinted by permission. **112:** From "Object Vision and Spatial Vision: Two Central Pathways," by M. Mishkin, L. G. Ungerleider & K. A. Makco, 1983, *Trends in Neuroscience, 6,* 414–417, figure 1. Copyright © 1983 Elsevier Science Publishers B.V. Reprinted by permission. **113:** From "Object Vision and Spatial Vision: Two Central Pathways," by M. Mishkin, L. G. Ungerleider & K. A. Makco, 1983, *Trends in Neuroscience, 6,* 414–417, figure 2. Copyright © 1983 Elsevier Science Publishers B.V. Reprinted by permission. **116:** From *The Visual Brain in Action* by A. D. Milner and M. A. Goodale. Copyright © 1995 by Oxford University Press. Reprinted by permission. **117:** From *The Visual Brain in Action* by A. D. Milner and M. A. Goodale. Copyright © 1995 by Oxford University Press. Reprinted by permission. **118:** Adapted from "How Parallel Are the Primate Visual Pathways," by W. H. Merigan and J. H. R. Maunsell [from data from Felleman & Van Essen, 1987], 1992, *Annual Review of Neuroscience, 16,* 369–402, figure 3. Annual Reviews, Inc. **119:** From "A Selective Impairment of Motion Perception Following Lesions of the Middle Temporal Visual Area (MT)," by W. T. Newsome and E. B. Pare, 1988, *Journal of Neuroscience, 8* (6), 2201–2211, figure 1. Copyright © 1988 by Society for Neuroscience. Reprinted by permission of Oxford University Press. **119:** From "Coding Visual Images of Objects in Inferotemporal Cortex of the Macaque Monkey," by K. Tanaka, H-A. Siato, Y. Fukada, and M. Moriya, 1991, *Journal of Neurophysiology, 66,* 170–189. Copyright © 1981 by The American Physiological Society. Reprinted by permission. **120:** From "Open Questions about the Neural Mechanisms of Visual Pattern Recognition," by M. P. Young in *The Cognitive Neurosciences,* edited by M. S. Gazzaniga. Copyright © 1995 by MIT Press. Reprinted by permission. **120:** From "Visual Properties of Neurons in a Polysensory Area in the Superior Temporal Sulcus of the Macaque," by C. Bruce, R. Desimone & C. G. Gross, 1981, *Journal of Neurophysiology, 46,* 369–384, figure 7. Copyright © 1981 by The American Physiological Society. Reprinted by permission. **120:** From "Recognition of Objects and Their Component Parts: Responses of Single Units in the Temporal Cortex of the Macaque," by E. Washmuth, M. W. Oram, and D. I. Perrett, 1994, *Cerebral Cortex, 4,* Copyright © 1994 by Oxford University Press. **121:** From "Sparseness of the Neuronal Representation of Stimuli in the Primate Temporal Visual Cortex," by E. T. Rolls and M. J. Tovee, 1995, *Journal of Neurophysiology, 73,* 713–726. Copyright © 1995 by The American Physiological Society. Reprinted by permission. **126:** From "Coding Visual Images of Objects in Inferotemporal Cortex of the Macaque Monkey," by K. Tanaka, H-A. Siato, Y. Fukada, and M. Moriya, 1991, *Journal of Neurophysiology, 66,* 170–189. Copyright © 1981 by The American Physiological Society. Reprinted by permission. **127:** From "Psychophysical and Physiological Evidence for Viewer-Centered Object Representations in the Primate," by N. K. Logothetis and J. Pauls, 1995, *Cerebral Cortex, 5.* Copyright © 1995 by Oxford University Press. **128:** From "Psychophysical and Physiological Evidence for Viewer-Centered Object Representations in the Primate," by N. K. Logothetis and J. Pauls, 1995, *Cerebral Cortex, 5.* Copyright © 1995 by Oxford University Press. **133:** Adapted from "Selective Attention Gates Visual Processing in the Extrastriate Cortex," by J. Moran and R. Desimone, 1985, *Science,* 229, 782–784. Copyright © 1985 by the American Association for the Advancement of Science. **134:** From "Oculocentric Spatial Representation in Parietal Cortex," by C. L. Colby, J-R. Duhamel, and M. E. Goldberg, 1995, *Cerebral Cortex, 5.* Copyright © 1995 by Oxford University Press. Reprinted by permission. **135:** Adapted from "Temporal Coding in the Visual Cortex: New Vistas on Integration in the Nervous System," by A. K. Engel, P. Konig, A. K. Kreiter, T. B. Schillen & W. Singer, 1992, *Trends in Neuroscience,* 15, 218–226, figure 1. Copyright © 1992 by Elsevier Science Ltd. Adapted by permission. **138:** From "The Representation of Extrapersonal Space: A Possible Role for Bimodal, Visual-Tactile Neurons," by M. S. A. Graziano and C. G. Gross in *The Cognitive Neurosciences,* edited by M. S. Gazzaniga. Copyright © 1995 by MIT Press. Reprinted by permission. **139:** From "The Representation of Extrapersonal Space: A Possible Role for Bimodal, Visual-Tactile Neurons," by M. S. A. Graziano and C. G. Gross in *The Cognitive Neurosciences,* edited by M. S. Gazzaniga. Copyright © 1995 by MIT Press. Reprinted by permission. **Chapter 5. 147:** Based on "Organizational Determinants of Subjective Contour: The Subjective Necker Cube," by D. R. Bradley and H. M. Petry, 1977, *American Journal of Psychology,* 90, 253–262, American Psychological Association. **148:** From *Art and Visual Perception,* by R. Arnheim, 1974, p 27. Copyright © 1974 University of California Press, Berkeley. Reprinted by permission. **150:** Ishihara Color Blind Test, courtesy of Graham-Fields, Inc. **158:** From "Perception," by Julian Hochberg: Figure from Woodworth & Schlosberg's *Experimental Psychology,* Third Edition by J. W. Kling and Lorrin A. Riggs, Copyright © 1971 by Holt, Rinehart & Winston. Reproduced by permission of the publisher. **160:** From "Object Recognition Processes Can and Do Operate Before Figure–Ground Orientation," by M. A. Peterson, 1994, *Current Directions in Psychological Science 3,* 105–111. Copyright © 1994 by Cambridge University Press. **164:** From "Texton Segregation by Associated Differences in Global and Local Luminance Distribution," by H. C. Nothdurft, 1990, *Proceedings of the Royal Society of London, B239,* 296–320. Reprinted by permission of The Royal Society. **169:** From "Recognition-by-Components: A Theory of Human Image Understanding," by I. Biederman, 1985, *Computer Vision, Graphics and Image Processing,* 32, 29–73. Copyright © 1985 Academic Press. Reprinted by permission. **170:** D. L. Schacter, E. Reiman, A. Uecker, M. R. Polster, L. S. Yun, & L. A. Cooper (1995). Brain regions associated with retrieval of structurally coherent visual information. *Nature,* 376, pp. 587–590. Reprinted with permission from *Nature.* Copyright © 1995 Macmillan Magazines Limited. **172:** Reprinted with permission from *Neuron,* 15, M. K. Zapadia et al., "Improvement in visual sensitivity by changes in local cortex: Parallel studies in human observers and in V1 of alert monkey," pp. 843–856. Copyright © 1995 Elsevier Science. **175:** A. Bregman (1981). Asking the "what for" question in auditory perception. In M. Kubovy & J. R. Pomerantz (Eds.), *Perceptual Organization.* Hillsdale, NJ: Erlbaum, pp. 99–119. **Chapter 6. 187:** Adapted with permission from Mark Merzylak et al. Nondestructive optical detection of pigment changes during leaf senescence and fruit ripening. *Physiologia Platarum,* 106, pp. 135–141, Fig. 1. **188:** Adapted from *Color: Its Principles and Their Applications,* by F. W. Clulow, 1972, Morgan and Morgan. Copyright © 1972 by F. W. Clulow. Used by permission of the author. **189:** From *Color Vision,* by Leo M. Hurvich, 1981. Reprinted by permission of Dr. Leo M. Hurvich. **196:** From "Color Appearance: On Seeing Red—or Yellow, or Green, or Blue," by I. Abramov and J. Gordon, 1994. Reproduced ,with permission, from *Annual Review of*

Psychology, 45, 451–485, figure 1a. Copyright © 1994 by Annual Reviews, Inc. **198:** From "Primate Color Vision," by R. L. DeValois and G. H. Jacobs, 1968, *Science,* 162, 533–540, figure 5. Copyright © 1968 by the American Association for the Advancement of Science. Reprinted by permission. **206:** From "Color Vision Honey Bees: Phenomena and Physiological Mechanisms," by R. Menzel and W. Backhaus, 1989. In Stavenga and Hardie (Eds.) *Facets of Vision,* p. 283. Copyright © 1989 Springer-Verlag BV, Berlin. Reprinted by permission. **206:** Based on data from "Spectral Distribution of Typical Daylight as a Function of Correlated Color Temperature," by D. B. Judd, D. L. MacAdam & G. Wyszecki, 1964, *Journal of the Optical Society of America,* 54, 1031–1040. **208:** From "Partial Color Constancy of Isolated Surface Colors Examined by a Color-Naming Method," by K. Uchikawa, H. Uchikara, and R. M. Boynton, 1989, *Perception,* 18, 83–91. Copyright © 1989 by Pion Ltd., London. Reprinted by permission. **Chapter 7. 232:** From M. Sinai, T. Ooi Leng, and Z. He (1998), "Terrain Influences the Accurate Judgment of Distance," *Nature,* 395, pp. 497–500. Adapted by permission of Macmillan Magazines Limited. **238:** From "The Perception of Spatial Layout from Static Optical Information," by B. Gilliam in *Handbook of Perception and Cognition: Perception of Space and Motion,* edited by W. Epstein and Rogers, pp. 23–67. Copyright © 1995 by Academic Press. Reprinted by permission. **240:** Figure from *Foundations of Cyclopean Perception,* by B. Julesz, 1971, figures 2.4-1 and 2.4-3. Copyright © 1971 University of Chicago Press. Reprinted by permission. **241:** I. Ohzaw (1998). Mechanisms of stereoscopic visions: The disparity energy model. *Current Opinion in Neurobiology,* 8, pp. 509–515. **241:** Adapted from "Ocular Dominance and Disparity Coding in Cat Visual Cortex," by S. LeVay and T. Voigt, 1988, *Visual Neuroscience,* 1, 395–414, figure 5 b. Cambridge University Press. **249:** From "Determinants of Apparent Visual Size with Distance Variant," by A. H. Holway and E. G. Boring, 1941, *American Journal of Psychology,* 54, 21–34, figure 2. University of Illinois Press. **250:** From "Determinants of Apparent Visual Size with Distance Variant," by A. H. Holway and E. G. Boring, 1941, *American Journal of Psychology,* 54, 21–34, figure 2. University of Illinois Press. **262:** From "Single Cell Responses in Striate Cortex of Kittens Deprived of Vision in One Eye," by T. N. Wisel and D. H. Hubel, 1963, *Journal of Neurophysiology,* 26, 1002–1017, figures 1 and 3. Copyright © 1963 by The American Physiological Society. Reprinted by permission. **Chapter 8. 276:** From "Lateral Inhibition Between Orientation Detectors in the Cat's Visual Cortex," by C. Blakemore and E. A. Tobin, 1972, *Experimental Brain Research,* 15, 439–440, figure 1. Copyright © 1972 Springer-Verlag Publishers. Reprinted by permission. **278:** From "A Selective Impairment of Motion Perception Following Lesions of the Middle Temporal Visual Area (MT)," by W. T. Newsome and E. B. Pare, 1988, *Journal of Neuroscience,* 8(6), 2201–2211, figure 1. Copyright © 1988 by Society for Neuroscience. Reprinted by permission of Oxford University Press. **279:** From "Perception," by H. L. Teuber, 1960. In J. Field, H. W. Magoun & V. E. Hall (Eds.) *Handbook of Physiology,* Section 1, *Neurophysiology,* Vol. 3, pp. 1595–1668, figure 31. Copyright © 1960 by the American Physiological Society. Reprinted by permission. **282:** From "'Real Motion' Cells in Area V3A of Macaque Visual Cortex," by C. Galletti, P. P. Battaglini, and P. Fattori, 1990, *Experimental Brain Research,* 82, 67–76, figure 1. Copyright © 1990 Springer-Verlag Publishers. Reprinted by permission. **285:** From *Form in Motion Parallax* and from "Luminance Contrast: Vernier Discrimination," *Spatial Vision,* 1, 305–318. Reprinted by permission of David Regan. **287:** From "Retrieval of Structure from Rigid and Biological Motion: An Analysis of the Visual Responses of Neurons in the Macaque Temporal Cortex" by D. I. Perrett, M. H. Harries, P. J. Bensen, A. J. Chitty, & A. J. Mistlin, 1990. In A. Blake and T. Troscianko, *AI and the Eye,* 181–200, figure 2. Copyright © 1990 by John Wiley & Sons Ltd. Reprinted by permission of D. I. Perrett and John Wiley & Sons, Ltd. **287:** Adapted from "Responses of Anterior Superior Temporal Polysensory (STPa) Neurons to 'Biological Motion' Stimuli," by M. W. Oram and D. I. Perrett, 1994, *Journal of Cognitive Neuroscience,* 6, 99–116.

Credits

Denes and E. N. Pinson. Copyright © 1993 by W. H. Freeman and Company. Reprinted by permission. **414:** From "Perception of the Speech Code," by A. M. Liberman, 1967, *Psychological Review*, 74, 431–461, figure 1. Copyright © 1967 by the American Psychological Association. Reprinted by permission of the author. **418:** From "Time-Varying Features of Initial Stop Consonants in Auditory Running Spectra: A First Report," by D. Kewley-Port and P. A. Luce, 1984, *Perception and Psychophysics*, 35, 353–360, figure 1. Copyright © 1984 by Psychonomic Society Publications. Reprinted by permission. **419:** From "Selective Adaptation of Linguistic Feature Detectors," by P. Eimas and J. D.Corbit, 1973, *Cognitive Psychology*, 4, 99–109, figure 2. Copyright © Academic Press, Inc. Reprinted by permission. **426:** From "Encoding of Speech Features in the Auditory Nerve," by M. B. Sachs, E. D. Young & M. I. Miller, 1981. In R. Carlson and B. Granstrom (Eds.) *The Representation of Speech in the Peripheral Auditory System*. pp. 115–130. Copyright © 1981 by Elsevier Science Publishing, New York. Reprinted by permission. **428:** Adapted from "Speech Perception Takes Precedence Over Nonspeech Perception," by D. H. Whalen and A. M. Liberman, 1987, *Science* ,237, 169–171, 10 July 1987, figure 1. Copyright © 1987 by the American Association for the Advancement of Science. Adapted by permission . **429:** From M. Gazzanaga, *The New Cognitive Neurosciences*, Second Edition, © 2000 MIT Press, Fig. 8.3. Reprinted with permission. **Chapter 13. 440:** From R. S. Johansson and A. B. Vallbo. Tactile sensory coding in the glabrous skin of the human hand. *Trends in Neuroscience*, 6, 27–31. Copyright © 1983 Elsevier Science. Reprinted by permission. **441:** From "Biological Transducers," by W. R. Lowenstein, 1960, p. 103. Copyright © 1960 by Scientific American, Inc. All rights reserved. **441:** From "Modality Coding in the Somatic Sensory System," by J. H. Martin and T. M. Jessell, 1991. In E. R. Kandel, J. H. Schwartz & T. M. Jessell (Eds.) *Principles of Neural Science*, 3rd ed. ,figure 24.10. Copyright © 1991 by Appleton & Lange, Norwalk, CT. Reprinted by permission of McGraw-Hill Companies. **442:** Adapted from "Neural Mechanisms of Spatial Tactile Discrimination: Neural Patterns Evoked by Braille-Like Dot Patterns in the Monkey," by K. O. Johnson and G. D. Lamb, 1981, *Journal of Physiology*, 310, 117–144. Copyright © 1981 by The Physiological Society, Oxford. Adapted by permission. **442:** From "Human Tactile Pattern Recognition: Active Versus Passive Touch, Velocity Effects, and Patterns of Confusion," by F. Vega-Bermudez, K. O. Johnson & S. S. Hsiao, 1991, *Journal of Neurophysiology*, 65, 531–546, fig. 12. Copyright © 1991 by The American Physiological Society. Reprinted by permission. **443:** From "Response Characteristics of Cutaneous Warm Fibers in the Monkey," by R. Duclaux and D. R. Kenshalo, 1980, *Journal of Neurophysiology*, 43, 1–15, figure 3. Copyright © 1980 by The American Physiological Society. Reprinted by permission. **444:** From "Correlations of Temperature Sensitivity in Man and Monkey, A First Approximation," by D. R. Kenshalo, 1976. In Y. Zotterman (Ed.), *Sensory Functions in the Skin of Primates*, p. 309. Copyright © 1976 by Plenum Publishing Group. Reprinted by permission. **445:** From "Intensive and Extensive Aspects of Tactile Sensitivity as a Function of Body Part, Sex, and Laterality," by S. Weinstein, 1968. In D. R. Kenshalo (Ed.), *The Skin Senses*, pp. 206, 207. Copyright © 1968 by Charles C. Thomas. Courtesy of Charles C. Thomas, Publishers, Springfield, IL. **446:** From "The Tactile Sensory Innervation of the Glabrous Skin of the Human Hand," by A. B. Ballbo and R. S. Johansson, 1978. In G. Gordon (Ed.), *Active Touch*, figure 1, p. 45. Copyright © 1978 by Pergamon Press, Ltd. Reprinted by permission. **449:** Reprinted with permission of the Gale Group, from *The Cerebral Cortex of Man*, by Wilder Penfield and Theodore Rasmussen, 1950, p. 214. Copyright © 1950 by Macmillan Publishing Co., renewed 1978 by Theodore Rasmussen. **449:** From "Touch," by E. R. Kandel and T. M. Jessell, 1991. In E. R. Kandel, J. H. Schwartz & T. M. Jessell (Eds.) *Principle of Neural Science*, 3rd ed., figure 26-8 a. Copyright © 1991 Appleton & Lange, Norwalk, CT. Reprinted with permission of McGraw-Hill Companies. **450:** From "Movement-Sensitive and Direction and Orientation Selective Cutaneous Receptive Fields in the Hand Area of the Postcentral Gyrus in Monkeys," by L. Hyvarinen and A. Poranen, 1978, *Journal of Physiology*, 283, 523–537, figure 3. Copyright © 1978 by The Physiological Society, UK. Reprinted by permission. **453:** From "Hand Movements: A Window into Haptic Object Recognition," by S. J. Lederman and R. L. Klatzky, 1987, *Cognitive Psychology*, 19, 342–368, figure 1. Academic Press, Inc. **454:** From A. W. Goodwin (1998). Extracting the shape of an object from the responses of peripheral nerve fibers. In J. W. Morely (Ed.), *Neural aspects of tactile sensation*. Elsevier Science, pp. 55–87, Fig. 12a, b. Used with permission. **455:** From "Cortical Processing of Tactile Information in the First Somatosensory and Parietal Association Areas in the Monkey," by H. Sakata and Y. Iwamura, 1978. In G. Gordon (Ed.), *Active Touch*, p. 61. Copyright © 1978 by Pergamon Press, Ltd. Reprinted by permission. **455:** From "Effects of Selective Attention on Spatial Form Processing in Monkey Primary and Secondary Somatosensory Cortex," by S. S. Hsiao, D. M. O'Shaughnessy, and K. O. Johnson, 1993, *Journal of Neurophysiology*, 70, 444–447. Copyright © 1993 by The American Physiological Society. Reprinted by permission. **457:** From "Cortical Representational Plasticity," by M. M. Merzenich, G. Reconzone, W. M. Jenkins, T. T. Allard, & R. J. Nudo, 1988. In P. Rakic and W. Singer (Eds.) *Neurobiology of Neocortex*, pp. 42–67, figure 1. Copyright © 1988 John Wiley & Sons. Reproduced by permission of M. M. Merzenich. **459:** Adapted from R. A. Meyer & J. N. Campbell (1981). Peripheral neural coding of pain sensation. *Johns Hopkins APL Technical Digest*, 2, pp. 164–171. Used with permission from the publisher and the author. **459:** Adapted from M. deWeid and M. N. Verbaten (2001). Affective pictures processing, attention, and pain tolerance. *Pain*, 90, 163–172. **Chapter 14. 474:** From T. R. Scott and B. K. Giza (2000). Issues of gustatory neural coding: Where they stand today. *Physiology & Behavior*, 69, 65–76, Fig 1. **479:** Adapted from "The Stereochemical Theory of Odor," by J. E. Amoore, J. W. Johnston, Jr., & M. Rubin, from figures on pp. 43a and 44–45, *Scientific American*, 210, Feb. Copyright © 1964 by Scientific American, Inc. All rights reserved. **481:** Adapted from K. Mori, H. Nagao, & Y. Yoshihara (1999). The olfactory bulb: Coding and processing of odor molecule information. *Science*, 286, 711–715, Fig 2. Reprinted with permission. **482:** Adapted from "Chemosensory Neuroanatomy and Physiology," by M. E. Frank and M. D. Rabin, 1989, *Ear, Nose and Throat Journal*, 68. **483:** From "Receptor Cell Responses to Odorants: Similarities and Differences Among Odorants," by G. Sicard and A. Holley, 1984, *Brain Research*, 292, 283–296, figure 4. Copyright © 1984 by Elsevier Science Publishing. Reprinted by permission. **483:** From P. Duchamp-Viret, M. A. Chaput, & A. Duchamp (1999). Odor response properties of a rat olfactory receptor neurons. *Science*, 284, 2171–2174, Fig. 1. Reprinted with permission. **484:** From K. Katoh, H. Koshimoto, A. Tani, & K. Mori (1993). Coding of odor molecules by mitral/tufted cells in rabbit olfactory bulb. II. Aromatic compounds. *Journal of Neurophysiology*, 70, 2161–2175, Fig. 6a. Reprinted with permission of American Physiological Society. **485:** From "Discrimination of Molecular Signals by the Olfactory Receptor Neuron," by G. M. Shepherd, 1994, *Neuron*, 13, 771–790. Copyright © 1994 by Cell Press. **485:** From E. T. Rolls, H. D. Critchley, and A. Treves (1996). Representation of olfactory information in the primate orbitofrontal cortex. *Journal of Neurophysiology*, 75, 1982–1996, Figs. 3a, 6a. Reprinted with permission of American Physiological Society. **486:** Left figure from N. Sobel, V. Prabhakaran, J. E. Desmond, G. H. Glover, E. V. Sullivan, & D. E. Gabrieli (2000). Time course of odorant-induced activation in the human primary olfactory cortex. *Journal of Neurophysiology*, 83, 537–551. Reprinted with permission of American Physiological Society. **492:** From "Sensory Neural Patterns and Gustation," by R. Erickson, 1963. In Y. Zotterman (Ed.), *Olfaction and Taste*, Vol. 1, pp. 205–213, figure 4. Copyright © 1963 by Pergamon Press, Ltd. Reprinted by permission. **494:** Adapted from "Neural Coding of Taste in Macaque Monkeys," by M. Sato and H. Ogawa, 1993. In K. Kurihara, N. Suzuki, & H. Ogawa (Eds.), *Olfaction and Taste XI*, p. 398. Copyright © 1993 by Springer-Verlag. Adapted by permission. **495:** Reproduced from

Credits

"Response Properties of Macaque Monkey Chorda Tympani Fibers," by M. Sato, H. Ogawa, & S. Yamashita, 1975, *The Journal of General Physiology*, 66, 781–810, figure 4, Copyright © 1975 by permission of The Rockefeller University Press. **495:** Adapted from "Coding Channels in the Taste System of the Rat," by T. R. Scott and B. K. Giza, 1990, *Science*, 249, 1585–1587, figure 1. Copyright © 1990 by the American Association for the Advancement of Science. Adapted by permission. **497:** Adapted from *Nasal Chemoreception in Flavor Identification*, by M. M. Mozell, B. P. Smith, P. E. Smith, R. L. Sullivan & P. Swender, 1969, *Archives of Otolaryngology*, 90, 367–373, figure 3. Copyright © 1969 by the American Medical Association. Adapted by permission of M. M. Mozell. **498:** Adapted from "Role of Olfaction in Perception of Non-Traditional 'Taste' Stimuli," by T. P. Hettinger, W. E. Myers & M. E. Frank, 1990, *Chemical Senses*, 15, 755–760, fig. 2. Copyright © 1990 by Oxford University Press. Adapted by permission of Oxford University Press, UK. **499:** From E. T. Rolls & J. H. Rolls (1997), Olfactory sensory-specific satiety in humans. *Physiology and Behavior*, 61, 461–473, Fig. 1. **500:** Adapted from E. T. Rolls (2000). The orbitofrontal cortex and reward. *Cerebral Cortex*, 10, 284–294, Fig. 2. Reprinted with permission from Oxford University Press. **500:** From E. T. Rolls & L. L. Baylis (1994). Gustatory, olfactory, and visual convergence within the primate obitofrontal cortex. *Journal of Neuroscience*, 14, 5437–5452, Figs. 5 & 8. Reprinted by permission. **501:** Adapted from E. T. Rolls & L. L. Baylis (1994). Gustatory, olfactory, and visual convergence within the primate obitofrontal cortex. *Journal of Neuroscience*, 14, 5437–5452, Fig. 15. Reprinted by permission of the American Physiological Society. **Chapter 15. 514:** From "Infant Contrast Sensitivity Evaluated by Evoked Potentials," by M. Pirchio, D. Spinelli, A. Fiorentini & L. Maffei, 1978, *Brain Research*, 141, 179–184, figure 3C. Copyright © 1978 Elsevier Biomedical Press B.V. Reprinted by permission. **514:** From *The Postnatal Development of the Cerebral Cortex*, Vol. 1, 1939, and Vol. 3, 1947, and *The Postnatal Development of the Human Cerebral Cortex*, Vol. 4, 1951, by J. L. Conel, plates LVIII, LXIV, and LXIV. Copyright © 1939, 1947, 1951 by Harvard University Press. Reprinted by permission of the publisher. **518:** From "Part–Whole Perception in Early Infancy: Evidence for Perceptual Grouping Produced by Lightness Similarity," by P. C. Quinn, S. Burke, and A. Rush, 1993, *Infant Behavior and Development*, 16, 19–42. Copyright © 1993 by Ablex Publishing Corporation. Reprinted by permission of the author. **519:** From "Perception of Partly Occluded Objects in Infancy," by P. J. Kellman and E. S. Spelke, 1983, *Cognitive Psychology*, 15, 483–524, figure 3. Copyright © 1983 by Academic Press. Reprinted by permission. **523:** Reprinted from *Vision Research*, 22, 575–587, "Rayleigh Discriminations in Young Human Infants," by R. D. Hamer, K. R. Alexander & D. Y. Teller, 1982. Copyright © 1982 with kind permission from Elsevier Science Ltd. The Boulevard, Langford Lane, Kidlington 0X5 1GB, UK. **525:** From "Assessment of Stereopsis in Human Infants," by S. L. Shea, R. Fox, R. Aslin, & S. T. Dumais, 1980, *Investigative Ophthalmology*

and Visual Science, 19, 1440–1404, figure 1. Copyright © 1980 C. V. Mosby Company, St. Louis, MO. Reprinted by permission. **525:** From "Stereoacuity of Human Infants," by R. Held, E. E. Birch, & J. Gwiazda, 1980, *Proceedings of the National Academy of Sciences*, 77, 5572–5574, figure 1. Copyright © 1980 by R. Held, E. E. Birch & J. Gwiazda. Reprinted by permission. **526:** From "Infants' Perception of Pictorially Specified Interposition," by C. E. Granrud and A. Yonas, 1984, *Journal of Experimental Child Psychology*, 27, 500–511, figure 1 b and d. Copyright © 1984 Academic Press, Inc. Reprinted by permission. **527:** From "Infants' Sensitivity to Familiar Size: The Effect of Memory on Spatial Perception," by C. E. Granrud, R. J. Haake & A. Yonas, 1985, *Perception and Psychophysics*, 37, 459–466. Copyright © 1985 by Psychonomic Society Publications. Reprinted by permission. **529:** © Anthony DeCasper. **530:** Data from "Newborn Infants Orient to Sounds," by D. Muir and J. Field, 1979, *Child Development*, 50, 431–436. Society for Research in Child Development. **530:** Adapted from "Pure-Tone Sensitivity of Human Infants," by L. W. Olsho, E. G. Koch, E. A. Carter, C. F. Halpin & N. B. Spetner, 1988, *Journal of the Acoustical Society of America*, 84, 1316–1324. American Institute of Physics. **531:** From "Sound Localization Acuity in Very Young Infants: An Observer-Based Testing Procedure," by B. A. Morrongiello, K. D. Fenwick, and G. Chance, 1990, *Developmental Psychology*, 26, 75–84. Copyright © 1990 by the American Psychological Association, Inc. **532:** From "Speech Perception in Infants," by P. Eimas, E. P. Siqueland, P. Jusczyk, J. Vigorito, 1971, *Science*, 171, 303–306, figure 2. Copyright © 1971 by the American Association for the Advancement of Science. Reprinted by permission. **535:** From "Olfaction and Development of Social Preferences in Neonatal Organisms," by R. H. Porter and B. Schaal, 1995. In R. L. Doty, (Ed.), *Handbook of Olfaction and Gustation*, pp. 299–321, figure 1. Copyright © Marcel Dekker, Inc. Reprinted by permission. **540:** From "Intermodal Matching by Human Neonates," by A. N. Meltzoff and R. W. Borton, 1979, *Nature*, 282, 403–404. Copyright © 1979 by Macmillan Journals, Ltd. Reprinted by permission. **Chapter 16. 551:** From *The World Through Blunted Sight*, by P. Trevor-Roper, 1970, p. 39. Copyright © 1970 by Bobbs Merrill Company . Reprinted by permission. **566:** Adapted from *Human Information Processing*, 2nd ed., by Peter Lindsay and Donald Norman, 1977. Copyright © Academic Press, Inc. Adapted by permission. **568:** Adapted from "Age Variations in Auditory Acuity," by C. C. Bunch, 1929, *Archives of Otolaryngology*, 9, 625–636. Copyright © 1929 by the American Medical Association. Adapted by permission. **572:** Based on a figure in *Hearing in Children*, 2nd ed., by J. Northern and M. Downs, 1978. Williams & Wilkins. **577:** From Schmolesky et al. (2000). *Nature Neuroscience*, 3, pp. 384–390. **578:** From "The Impact of Audition on the Development of Visual Attention," by A. L. Quittner, L. B. Smith, M. J. Osberger, T. V. Mitchell, and D. B. Katz, 1994, *Psychological Science*, 5, 347–353. Copyright © 1994 by the American Psychological Society. Reprinted by permission.

TO THE OWNER OF THIS BOOK:

We hope that you have found *Sensation and Perception, 6th Edition,* useful. So that this book can be improved in a future edition, would you take the time to complete this sheet and return it? Thank you.

School and address: _____

Department: _____

Instructor's name: _____

1. What I like most about this book is: _____

_____

_____

2. What I like least about this book is: _____

_____

_____

3. My general reaction to this book is: _____

_____

4. The name of the course in which I used this book is: _____

_____

5. Were all of the chapters of the book assigned for you to read? _____

   If not, which ones weren't? _____

6. In the space below, or on a separate sheet of paper, please write specific suggestions for improving this book and anything else you'd care to share about your experience in using the book.

_____

_____

_____

_____

_____

Optional:

Your name: _____ Date: _____

May Wadsworth quote you, either in promotion for *Sensation and Perception* or in future publishing ventures?

Yes: _____ No: _____

Sincerely,

Bruce Goldstein